Y0-ELJ-513

American Casebook Series
Hornbook Series and Basic Legal Texts
Black Letter Series and Nutshell Series

of

WEST PUBLISHING
P.O. Box 64526
St. Paul, Minnesota 55164–0526

Accounting

FARIS' ACCOUNTING AND LAW IN A NUTSHELL, 377 pages, 1984. Softcover. (Text)

FIFLIS' ACCOUNTING ISSUES FOR LAWYERS, TEACHING MATERIALS, Fourth Edition, 706 pages, 1991. Teacher's Manual available. (Casebook)

SIEGEL AND SIEGEL'S ACCOUNTING AND FINANCIAL DISCLOSURE: A GUIDE TO BASIC CONCEPTS, 259 pages, 1983. Softcover. (Text)

Administrative Law

AMAN AND MAYTON'S HORNBOOK ON ADMINISTRATIVE LAW, 917 pages, 1993. (Text)

BONFIELD AND ASIMOW'S STATE AND FEDERAL ADMINISTRATIVE LAW, 826 pages, 1989. Teacher's Manual available. (Casebook) 1993 Supplement.

GELLHORN AND LEVIN'S ADMINISTRATIVE LAW AND PROCESS IN A NUTSHELL, Third Edition, 479 pages, 1990. Softcover. (Text)

MASHAW, MERRILL, AND SHANE'S CASES AND MATERIALS ON ADMINISTRATIVE LAW—THE AMERICAN PUBLIC LAW SYSTEM, Third Edition, 1187 pages, 1992. Teacher's Manual available. (Casebook)

ROBINSON, GELLHORN AND BRUFF'S THE ADMINISTRATIVE PROCESS, Fourth Edition, approximately 1000 pages, 1993. (Casebook)

Admiralty

HEALY AND SHARPE'S CASES AND MATERIALS ON ADMIRALTY, Second Edition, 876 pages, 1986. (Casebook)

MARAIST'S ADMIRALTY IN A NUTSHELL, Second Edition, 379 pages, 1988. Softcover. (Text)

SCHOENBAUM'S HORNBOOK ON ADMIRALTY AND MARITIME LAW, Student Edition, 692 pages, 1987 with 1992 pocket part. (Text)

Agency—Partnership

DEMOTT'S FIDUCIARY OBLIGATION, AGENCY AND PARTNERSHIP: DUTIES IN ONGOING BUSINESS RELATIONSHIPS, 740 pages, 1991. Teacher's Manual available. (Casebook)

FESSLER'S ALTERNATIVES TO INCORPORATION FOR PERSONS IN QUEST OF PROFIT, Third Edition, 339 pages, 1991. Softcover. (Casebook)

HENN'S CASES AND MATERIALS ON AGENCY, PARTNERSHIP AND OTHER UNINCORPORATED BUSINESS ENTERPRISES, Second Edition, 733 pages, 1985. Teacher's Manual available. (Casebook)

REUSCHLEIN AND GREGORY'S HORNBOOK ON THE LAW OF AGENCY AND PARTNERSHIP, Second Edition, 683 pages, 1990. (Text)

SELECTED CORPORATION AND PARTNERSHIP STATUTES, RULES AND FORMS. 1993 Edition, approximately 975 pages. Softcover.

STEFFEN AND KERR'S CASES ON AGENCY-PARTNERSHIP, Fourth Edition, 859 pages, 1980. (Casebook)

STEFFEN'S AGENCY–PARTNERSHIP IN A NUTSHELL, 364 pages, 1977. Softcover. (Text)

Alternative Dispute Resolution

NOLAN–HALEY'S ALTERNATIVE DISPUTE RESOLUTION IN A NUTSHELL, 298 pages, 1992.

List current as of July, 1993

Alternative Dispute Resolution—Cont'd

Softcover. (Text)

RISKIN AND WESTBROOK'S DISPUTE RESOLUTION AND LAWYERS, 468 pages, 1987. Teacher's Manual available. (Casebook) 1993 Supplement.

RISKIN AND WESTBROOK'S DISPUTE RESOLUTION AND LAWYERS. Abridged Edition, 223 pages, 1987. Softcover. Teacher's Manual available. (Casebook) 1993 Supplement.

RISKIN'S DISPUTE RESOLUTION FOR LAWYERS VIDEO TAPES, 1992. (Available for purchase by schools and libraries.)

American Indian Law

CANBY'S AMERICAN INDIAN LAW IN A NUTSHELL, Second Edition, 336 pages, 1988. Softcover. (Text)

GETCHES, WILKINSON AND WILLIAMS' CASES AND MATERIALS ON FEDERAL INDIAN LAW, Third Edition, approximately 900 pages, 1993. Teacher's Manual expected. (Casebook)

Antitrust—see also Regulated Industries, Trade Regulation

BARNES AND STOUT'S ECONOMIC FOUNDATIONS OF REGULATION AND ANTITRUST LAW, 102 pages, 1992. Softcover. Teacher's Manual available. (Casebook)

FOX AND SULLIVAN'S CASES AND MATERIALS ON ANTITRUST, 935 pages, 1989. Teacher's Manual available. (Casebook) 1993 Supplement.

GELLHORN AND KOVACIC'S ANTITRUST LAW AND ECONOMICS IN A NUTSHELL, Fourth Edition, approximately 475 pages, 1993. Softcover. (Text)

HOVENKAMP'S BLACK LETTER ON ANTITRUST, Second Edition, 347 pages, 1993. Softcover. (Review)

HOVENKAMP'S HORNBOOK ON ECONOMICS AND FEDERAL ANTITRUST LAW, Student Edition, 414 pages, 1985. (Text)

POSNER AND EASTERBROOK'S CASES AND ECONOMIC NOTES ON ANTITRUST, Second Edition, 1077 pages, 1981. (Casebook) 1984–85 Supplement.

SULLIVAN'S HORNBOOK OF THE LAW OF ANTITRUST, 886 pages, 1977. (Text)

Appellate Advocacy—see Trial and Appellate Advocacy

Architecture and Engineering Law

SWEET'S LEGAL ASPECTS OF ARCHITECTURE, ENGINEERING AND THE CONSTRUCTION PROCESS, Fourth Edition, 889 pages, 1989. Teacher's Manual available. (Casebook)

Art Law

DUBOFF'S ART LAW IN A NUTSHELL, Second Edition, 350 pages, 1993. Softcover. (Text)

Banking Law

BANKING LAW: SELECTED STATUTES AND REGULATIONS. Softcover. 263 pages, 1991.

LOVETT'S BANKING AND FINANCIAL INSTITUTIONS LAW IN A NUTSHELL, Third Edition, 470 pages, 1992. Softcover. (Text)

SYMONS AND WHITE'S BANKING LAW: TEACHING MATERIALS, Third Edition, 818 pages, 1991. Teacher's Manual available. (Casebook)

Statutory Supplement. *See Banking Law: Selected Statutes*

Bankruptcy—see Creditors' Rights

Business Planning—see also Corporate Finance

PAINTER'S PROBLEMS AND MATERIALS IN BUSINESS PLANNING, Second Edition, 1008 pages, 1984. (Casebook) 1990 Supplement.

Statutory Supplement. *See Selected Corporation and Partnership*

Civil Procedure—see also Federal Jurisdiction and Procedure

AMERICAN BAR ASSOCIATION SECTION OF LITIGATION—READINGS ON ADVERSARIAL JUSTICE: THE AMERICAN APPROACH TO ADJUDICATION, 217 pages, 1988. Softcover. (Coursebook)

CLERMONT'S BLACK LETTER ON CIVIL PROCEDURE, Third Edition, 318 pages, 1993. Softcover. (Review)

COUND, FRIEDENTHAL, MILLER AND SEXTON'S CASES AND MATERIALS ON CIVIL PROCEDURE, Sixth Edition, approximately 1300 pages, 1993. Teacher's Manual available. (Casebook)

COUND, FRIEDENTHAL, MILLER AND SEXTON'S

Civil Procedure—Cont'd

CIVIL PROCEDURE SUPPLEMENT. Approximately 475 pages, 1993. Softcover. (Casebook Supplement)

FEDERAL RULES OF CIVIL PROCEDURE—1993–94 EDUCATIONAL EDITION. Softcover. Approximately 1200 pages, 1993.

FRIEDENTHAL, KANE AND MILLER'S HORNBOOK ON CIVIL PROCEDURE, Second Edition, approximately 1000 pages, 1993. (Text)

KANE AND LEVINE'S CIVIL PROCEDURE IN CALIFORNIA: STATE AND FEDERAL 1992 Edition, 551 pages. Softcover. (Casebook Supplement)

KANE'S CIVIL PROCEDURE IN A NUTSHELL, Third Edition, 303 pages, 1991. Softcover. (Text)

LEVINE, SLOMANSON AND WINGATE'S CALIFORNIA CIVIL PROCEDURE, CASES AND MATERIALS, 546 pages, 1991. Teacher's Manual available. (Casebook)

MARCUS, REDISH AND SHERMAN'S CIVIL PROCEDURE: A MODERN APPROACH, 1027 pages, 1989. Teacher's Manual available. (Casebook) 1991 Supplement.

MARCUS AND SHERMAN'S COMPLEX LITIGATION–CASES AND MATERIALS ON ADVANCED CIVIL PROCEDURE, Second Edition, 1035 pages, 1992. Teacher's Manual available. (Casebook)

PARK AND MCFARLAND'S COMPUTER-AIDED EXERCISES ON CIVIL PROCEDURE, Third Edition, 210 pages, 1991. Softcover. (Coursebook)

SIEGEL'S HORNBOOK ON NEW YORK PRACTICE, Second Edition, Student Edition, 1068 pages, 1991. Softcover. (Text) 1993–94 Supplement.

SLOMANSON AND WINGATE'S CALIFORNIA CIVIL PROCEDURE IN A NUTSHELL, 230 pages, 1992. Softcover. (Text)

Commercial Law

ALCES AND BENFIELD'S PAYMENT SYSTEMS: CASES, MATERIALS, AND PROBLEMS, 569 pages, 1993. Teacher's Manual available. (Casebook)

BAILEY AND HAGEDORN'S SECURED TRANSACTIONS IN A NUTSHELL, Third Edition, 390 pages, 1988. Softcover. (Text)

EPSTEIN, MARTIN, HENNING AND NICKLES' BASIC UNIFORM COMMERCIAL CODE TEACHING MATERIALS, Third Edition, 704 pages, 1988. Teacher's Manual available. (Casebook)

HENSON'S HORNBOOK ON SECURED TRANSACTIONS UNDER THE U.C.C., Second Edition, 504 pages, 1979, with 1979 pocket part. (Text)

MEYER AND SPEIDEL'S BLACK LETTER ON SALES AND LEASES OF GOODS, 317 pages, 1993. Softcover. (Review)

MURRAY AND FLECHTNER'S SALES AND LEASES: PROBLEMS AND MATERIALS ON NATIONAL AND INTERNATIONAL TRANSACTIONS, Approximately 650 pages, September, 1993 pub. Teacher's Manual available. (Casebook)

NICKLES' BLACK LETTER ON NEGOTIABLE INSTRUMENTS (AND OTHER RELATED COMMERCIAL PAPER), Second Edition, 574 pages, 1993. Softcover. (Review)

NICKLES, MATHESON AND DOLAN'S MATERIALS FOR UNDERSTANDING CREDIT AND PAYMENT SYSTEMS, 923 pages, 1987. Teacher's Manual available. (Casebook)

NORDSTROM, MURRAY AND CLOVIS' PROBLEMS AND MATERIALS ON SALES, 515 pages, 1982. (Casebook)

RUBIN AND COOTER'S THE PAYMENT SYSTEM: CASES, MATERIALS AND ISSUES, 885 pages, 1989. Teacher's Manual Available. (Casebook)

SELECTED COMMERCIAL STATUTES. Softcover. Approximately 1900 pages, 1993.

SPEIDEL AND NICKLES' NEGOTIABLE INSTRUMENTS AND CHECK COLLECTION IN A NUTSHELL, Fourth Edition, 544 pages, 1993. Softcover. (Text)

SPEIDEL, SUMMERS AND WHITE'S PAYMENT SYSTEMS: TEACHING MATERIALS, Fifth Edition, approximately 575 pages, 1993. Softcover. Teacher's Manual available. (Casebook)

SPEIDEL, SUMMERS AND WHITE'S SALES AND SECURED TRANSACTIONS: TEACHING MATERIALS, Fifth Edition, approximately 1150 pages, 1993. Teacher's Manual available. (Casebook)

SPEIDEL, SUMMERS AND WHITE'S SECURED TRANSACTIONS: TEACHING MATERIALS, Fifth

Commercial Law—Cont'd

Edition, approximately 500 pages, October, 1993 pub. Reprint from Speidel et al., Sales and Secured Transactions, Fifth Edition. Softcover. Teacher's Manual available. (Casebook)

STOCKTON AND MILLER'S SALES AND LEASES OF GOODS IN A NUTSHELL, Third Edition, 441 pages, 1992. Softcover. (Text)

STONE'S UNIFORM COMMERCIAL CODE IN A NUTSHELL, Third Edition, 580 pages, 1989. Softcover. (Text)

WHITE AND SUMMERS' HORNBOOK ON THE UNIFORM COMMERCIAL CODE, Third Edition, Student Edition, 1386 pages, 1988 with 1993 pocket part (covering Rev. Arts. 3, 4, new 2A, 4A). (Text)

Community Property

MENNELL AND BOYKOFF'S COMMUNITY PROPERTY IN A NUTSHELL, Second Edition, 432 pages, 1988. Softcover. (Text)

VERRALL AND BIRD'S CASES AND MATERIALS ON CALIFORNIA COMMUNITY PROPERTY, Fifth Edition, 604 pages, 1988. (Casebook)

Comparative Law

BARTON, GIBBS, LI AND MERRYMAN'S LAW IN RADICALLY DIFFERENT CULTURES, 960 pages, 1983. (Casebook)

GLENDON, GORDON AND OSAKWE'S COMPARATIVE LEGAL TRADITIONS: TEXT, MATERIALS AND CASES ON THE CIVIL LAW, COMMON LAW AND SOCIALIST LAW TRADITIONS, 1091 pages, 1985. (Casebook)

GLENDON, GORDON AND OSAKWE'S COMPARATIVE LEGAL TRADITIONS IN A NUTSHELL. 402 pages, 1982. Softcover. (Text)

Computers and Law

MAGGS, SOMA AND SPROWL'S COMPUTER LAW—CASES, COMMENTS, AND QUESTIONS, 731 pages, 1992. Teacher's Manual available. (Casebook)

MASON'S USING COMPUTERS IN THE LAW: AN INTRODUCTION AND PRACTICAL GUIDE, Second Edition, 288 pages, 1988. Softcover. (Coursebook)

Conflict of Laws

CRAMTON, CURRIE, KAY AND KRAMER'S CASES—COMMENTS—QUESTIONS ON CONFLICT OF LAWS, Fifth Edition, approximately 750 pages, 1993. (Casebook)

HAY'S BLACK LETTER ON CONFLICT OF LAWS, 330 pages, 1989. Softcover. (Review)

SCOLES AND HAY'S HORNBOOK ON CONFLICT OF LAWS, Student Edition, 1160 pages, 1992. (Text)

SIEGEL'S CONFLICTS IN A NUTSHELL, 470 pages, 1982. Softcover. (Text)

Constitutional Law—Civil Rights—see also First Amendment and Foreign Relations and National Security Law

ABERNATHY'S CIVIL RIGHTS AND CONSTITUTIONAL LITIGATION, CASES AND MATERIALS, Second Edition, 753 pages, 1992. (Casebook)

BARNES AND STOUT'S THE ECONOMICS OF CONSTITUTIONAL LAW AND PUBLIC CHOICE, 127 pages, 1992. Softcover. Teacher's Manual available. (Casebook)

BARRON AND DIENES' BLACK LETTER ON CONSTITUTIONAL LAW, Third Edition, 440 pages, 1991. Softcover. (Review)

BARRON AND DIENES' CONSTITUTIONAL LAW IN A NUTSHELL, Second Edition, 483 pages, 1991. Softcover. (Text)

ENGDAHL'S CONSTITUTIONAL FEDERALISM IN A NUTSHELL, Second Edition, 411 pages, 1987. Softcover. (Text)

FARBER, ESKRIDGE AND FRICKEY'S CONSTITUTIONAL LAW: THEMES FOR THE CONSTITUTION'S THIRD CENTURY, 1127 pages, 1993. Teacher's Manual available. (Casebook) 1993 Supplement.

FARBER AND SHERRY'S HISTORY OF THE AMERICAN CONSTITUTION, 458 pages, 1990. Softcover. Teacher's Manual available. (Text)

FISHER AND DEVINS' POLITICAL DYNAMICS OF CONSTITUTIONAL LAW, 333 pages, 1992. Softcover. (Casebook Supplement)

GARVEY AND ALEINIKOFF'S MODERN CONSTITUTIONAL THEORY: A READER, Second Edition, 559 pages, 1991. Softcover. (Reader)

LOCKHART, KAMISAR, CHOPER AND SHIFFRIN'S CONSTITUTIONAL LAW: CASES—COMMENTS—QUESTIONS, Seventh Edition, 1643 pages, 1991. (Casebook) 1993 Supplement.

LOCKHART, KAMISAR, CHOPER AND SHIFFRIN'S

Constitutional Law—Civil Rights—Cont'd

THE AMERICAN CONSTITUTION: CASES AND MATERIALS, Seventh Edition, 1255 pages, 1991. Abridged version of Lockhart, et al., Constitutional Law: Cases–Comments–Questions, Seventh Edition. (Casebook) 1993 Supplement.

LOCKHART, KAMISAR, CHOPER AND SHIFFRIN'S CONSTITUTIONAL RIGHTS AND LIBERTIES: CASES AND MATERIALS, Seventh Edition, 1333 pages, 1991. Reprint from Lockhart, et al., Constitutional Law: Cases–Comments–Questions, Seventh Edition. (Casebook) 1993 Supplement.

MARKS AND COOPER'S STATE CONSTITUTIONAL LAW IN A NUTSHELL, 329 pages, 1988. Softcover. (Text)

NOWAK AND ROTUNDA'S HORNBOOK ON CONSTITUTIONAL LAW, Fourth Edition, 1357 pages, 1991. (Text)

ROTUNDA'S MODERN CONSTITUTIONAL LAW: CASES AND NOTES, Fourth Edition, 1137 pages, 1993. (Casebook) 1993 Supplement.

VIEIRA'S CONSTITUTIONAL CIVIL RIGHTS IN A NUTSHELL, Second Edition, 322 pages, 1990. Softcover. (Text)

WILLIAMS' CONSTITUTIONAL ANALYSIS IN A NUTSHELL, 388 pages, 1979. Softcover. (Text)

Consumer Law—see also Commercial Law

EPSTEIN AND NICKLES' CONSUMER LAW IN A NUTSHELL, Second Edition, 418 pages, 1981. Softcover. (Text)

SELECTED COMMERCIAL STATUTES. Softcover. Approximately 1900 pages, 1993.

SPANOGLE, ROHNER, PRIDGEN AND RASOR'S CASES AND MATERIALS ON CONSUMER LAW, Second Edition, 916 pages, 1991. Teacher's Manual available. (Casebook)

Contracts

BARNES AND STOUT'S THE ECONOMICS OF CONTRACT LAW, 127 pages, 1992. Softcover. Teacher's Manual available. (Casebook)

CALAMARI AND PERILLO'S BLACK LETTER ON CONTRACTS, Second Edition, 462 pages, 1990. Softcover. (Review)

CALAMARI AND PERILLO'S HORNBOOK ON CONTRACTS, Third Edition, 1049 pages, 1987. (Text)

CALAMARI, PERILLO AND BENDER'S CASES AND PROBLEMS ON CONTRACTS, Second Edition, 905 pages, 1989. Teacher's Manual Available. (Casebook)

CORBIN'S TEXT ON CONTRACTS, One Volume Student Edition, 1224 pages, 1952. (Text)

FRIEDMAN'S CONTRACT REMEDIES IN A NUTSHELL, 323 pages, 1981. Softcover. (Text)

FULLER AND EISENBERG'S CASES ON BASIC CONTRACT LAW, Fifth Edition, 1037 pages, 1990. (Casebook)

HAMILTON, RAU AND WEINTRAUB'S CASES AND MATERIALS ON CONTRACTS, Second Edition, 916 pages, 1992. Teacher's Manual available. (Casebook)

KEYES' GOVERNMENT CONTRACTS IN A NUTSHELL, Second Edition, 557 pages, 1990. Softcover. (Text)

SCHABER AND ROHWER'S CONTRACTS IN A NUTSHELL, Third Edition, 457 pages, 1990. Softcover. (Text)

SUMMERS AND HILLMAN'S CONTRACT AND RELATED OBLIGATION: THEORY, DOCTRINE AND PRACTICE, Second Edition, 1037 pages, 1992. Teacher's Manual available. (Casebook)

Copyright—see Intellectual Property

Corporate Finance—see also Business Planning

HAMILTON'S CASES AND MATERIALS ON CORPORATION FINANCE, Second Edition, 1221 pages, 1989. (Casebook)

OESTERLE'S THE LAW OF MERGERS, ACQUISITIONS AND REORGANIZATIONS, 1096 pages, 1991. (Casebook) 1992 Supplement.

Corporations

HAMILTON'S BLACK LETTER ON CORPORATIONS, Third Edition, 732 pages, 1992. Softcover. (Review)

HAMILTON'S CASES AND MATERIALS ON CORPORATIONS—INCLUDING PARTNERSHIPS AND LIMITED PARTNERSHIPS, Fourth Edition, 1248 pages, 1990. Teacher's Manual available. (Casebook) 1990 Statutory Supplement.

HAMILTON'S THE LAW OF CORPORATIONS IN A NUTSHELL, Third Edition, 518 pages, 1991. Softcover. (Text)

Corporations—Cont'd

HENN AND ALEXANDER'S HORNBOOK ON LAWS OF CORPORATIONS, Third Edition, Student Edition, 1371 pages, 1983, with 1986 pocket part. (Text)

SELECTED CORPORATION AND PARTNERSHIP STATUTES, RULES AND FORMS. 1993 Edition, approximately 975 pages. Softcover.

SOLOMON, SCHWARTZ AND BAUMAN'S MATERIALS AND PROBLEMS ON CORPORATIONS: LAW AND POLICY, Second Edition, 1391 pages, 1988. Teacher's Manual available. (Casebook) 1992 Supplement.

Statutory Supplement. *See Selected Corporation and Partnership*

Corrections

KRANTZ' THE LAW OF CORRECTIONS AND PRISONERS' RIGHTS IN A NUTSHELL, Third Edition, 407 pages, 1988. Softcover. (Text)

KRANTZ AND BRANHAM'S CASES AND MATERIALS ON THE LAW OF SENTENCING, CORRECTIONS AND PRISONERS' RIGHTS, Fourth Edition, 619 pages, 1991. Teacher's Manual available. (Casebook) 1993 Supplement.

Creditors' Rights

BANKRUPTCY CODE, RULES AND OFFICIAL FORMS, LAW SCHOOL EDITION. Approximately 925 pages, 1993. Softcover.

EPSTEIN'S DEBTOR-CREDITOR LAW IN A NUTSHELL, Fourth Edition, 401 pages, 1991. Softcover. (Text)

EPSTEIN, LANDERS AND NICKLES' CASES AND MATERIALS ON DEBTORS AND CREDITORS, Third Edition, 1059 pages, 1987. Teacher's Manual available. (Casebook)

EPSTEIN, NICKLES AND WHITE'S HORNBOOK ON BANKRUPTCY, 1077 pages, 1992. (Text)

LOPUCKI'S PLAYER'S MANUAL FOR THE DEBTOR-CREDITOR GAME, 123 pages, 1985. Softcover. (Coursebook)

NICKLES AND EPSTEIN'S BLACK LETTER ON CREDITORS' RIGHTS AND BANKRUPTCY, 576 pages, 1989. (Review)

RIESENFELD'S CASES AND MATERIALS ON CREDITORS' REMEDIES AND DEBTORS' PROTECTION, Fourth Edition, 914 pages, 1987. (Casebook) 1990 Supplement.

WHITE AND NIMMER'S CASES AND MATERIALS ON BANKRUPTCY, Second Edition, 764 pages, 1992. Teacher's Manual available. (Casebook)

Criminal Law and Criminal Procedure—see also Corrections, Juvenile Justice

ABRAMS AND BEALE'S FEDERAL CRIMINAL LAW AND ITS ENFORCEMENT, Second Edition, approximately 990 pages, 1993. (Casebook)

BUCY'S WHITE COLLAR CRIME, CASES AND MATERIALS, 688 pages, 1992. Teacher's Manual available. (Casebook)

DIX AND SHARLOT'S CASES AND MATERIALS ON CRIMINAL LAW, Third Edition, 846 pages, 1987. (Casebook)

GRANO'S PROBLEMS IN CRIMINAL PROCEDURE, Second Edition, 176 pages, 1981. Teacher's Manual available. Softcover. (Coursebook)

HEYMANN AND KENETY'S THE MURDER TRIAL OF WILBUR JACKSON: A HOMICIDE IN THE FAMILY, Second Edition, 347 pages, 1985. (Coursebook)

ISRAEL, KAMISAR AND LAFAVE'S CRIMINAL PROCEDURE AND THE CONSTITUTION: LEADING SUPREME COURT CASES AND INTRODUCTORY TEXT. Approximately 825 pages, 1993 Edition. Softcover. (Casebook)

ISRAEL AND LAFAVE'S CRIMINAL PROCEDURE—CONSTITUTIONAL LIMITATIONS IN A NUTSHELL, Fifth Edition, 475 pages, 1993. Softcover. (Text)

JOHNSON'S CASES, MATERIALS AND TEXT ON CRIMINAL LAW, Fourth Edition, 759 pages, 1990. Teacher's Manual available. (Casebook)

JOHNSON'S CASES AND MATERIALS ON CRIMINAL PROCEDURE, 859 pages, 1988. (Casebook) 1993 Supplement.

KAMISAR, LAFAVE AND ISRAEL'S MODERN CRIMINAL PROCEDURE: CASES, COMMENTS AND QUESTIONS, Seventh Edition, 1593 pages, 1990. (Casebook) 1993 Supplement.

KAMISAR, LAFAVE AND ISRAEL'S BASIC CRIMINAL PROCEDURE: CASES, COMMENTS AND QUESTIONS, Seventh Edition, 792 pages, 1990. Softcover reprint from Kamisar, et al., Modern Criminal Procedure: Cases, Comments and Questions, Seventh Edition. (Casebook) 1993 Supplement.

Criminal Law and Criminal Procedure—Cont'd

LaFave's Modern Criminal Law: Cases, Comments and Questions, Second Edition, 903 pages, 1988. (Casebook)

LaFave and Israel's Hornbook on Criminal Procedure, Second Edition, 1309 pages, 1992 with 1992 pocket part. (Text)

LaFave and Scott's Hornbook on Criminal Law, Second Edition, 918 pages, 1986 with 1993 pocket part. (Text)

Loewy's Criminal Law in a Nutshell, Second Edition, 321 pages, 1987. Softcover. (Text)

Low's Black Letter on Criminal Law, Revised First Edition, 443 pages, 1990. Softcover. (Review)

Podgor's White Collar Crime in a Nutshell, Approximately 300 pages, 1993. Softcover. (Text)

Saltzburg and Capra's Cases and Commentary on American Criminal Procedure, Fourth Edition, 1341 pages, 1992. Teacher's Manual available. (Casebook) 1993 Supplement.

Subin, Mirsky and Weinstein's The Criminal Process: Prosecution and Defense Functions, 470 pages, 1993. Softcover. Teacher's Manual available. (Text)

Vorenberg's Cases on Criminal Law and Procedure, Second Edition, 1088 pages, 1981. Teacher's Manual available. (Casebook) 1993 Supplement.

Domestic Relations

Clark's Hornbook on Domestic Relations, Second Edition, Student Edition, 1050 pages, 1988. (Text)

Clark and Glowinsky's Cases and Problems on Domestic Relations, Fourth Edition. 1150 pages, 1990. Teacher's Manual available. (Casebook) 1992 Supplement.

Krause's Black Letter on Family Law, 314 pages, 1988. Softcover. (Review)

Krause's Cases, Comments and Questions on Family Law, Third Edition, 1433 pages, 1990. (Casebook) 1993 Supplement.

Krause's Family Law in a Nutshell, Second Edition, 444 pages, 1986. Softcover. (Text)

Economics, Law and—see also Antitrust, Regulated Industries

Barnes and Stout's Cases and Materials on Law and Economics, 538 pages, 1992. Teacher's Manual available. (Casebook)

Malloy's Law and Economics: A Comparative Approach to Theory and Practice, 166 pages, 1990. Softcover. (Text)

Education Law

Alexander and Alexander's The Law of Schools, Students and Teachers in a Nutshell, 409 pages, 1984. Softcover. (Text)

Yudof, Kirp and Levin's Educational Policy and the Law, Third Edition, 860 pages, 1992. (Casebook)

Employment Discrimination—see also Gender Discrimination

Estreicher and Harper's Cases and Materials on the Law Governing the Employment Relationship, Second Edition, 966 pages, 1992. (Casebook) 1992 Statutory Supplement.

Jones, Murphy and Belton's Cases and Materials on Discrimination in Employment, (The Labor Law Group). Fifth Edition, 1116 pages, 1987. (Casebook) 1990 Supplement.

Player's Federal Law of Employment Discrimination in a Nutshell, Third Edition, 338 pages, 1992. Softcover. (Text)

Player's Hornbook on Employment Discrimination Law, Student Edition, 708 pages, 1988. (Text)

Player, Shoben and Lieberwitz' Cases and Materials on Employment Discrimination Law, 827 pages, 1990. Teacher's Manual available. (Casebook) 1992 Supplement.

Energy and Natural Resources Law—see also Oil and Gas

Laitos' Cases and Materials on Natural Resources Law, 938 pages, 1985. Teacher's Manual available. (Casebook)

Laitos and Tomain's Energy and Natural Resources Law in a Nutshell, 554 pages, 1992. Softcover. (Text)

Selected Environmental Law Statutes—1993–94 Educational Edition. Softcover. Approximately 1300 pages, 1993.

Environmental Law—see also Energy and Natural Resources Law; Sea, Law of

CAMPBELL-MOHN, BREEN AND FUTRELL'S ENVIRONMENTAL LAW: FROM RESOURCES TO RECOVERY, (Environmental Law Institute) Approximately 975 pages, 1993. (Text)

BONINE AND MCGARITY'S THE LAW OF ENVIRONMENTAL PROTECTION: CASES—LEGISLATION—POLICIES, Second Edition, 1042 pages, 1992. (Casebook)

FINDLEY AND FARBER'S CASES AND MATERIALS ON ENVIRONMENTAL LAW, Third Edition, 763 pages, 1991. Teacher's Manual available. (Casebook) 1993 Supplement.

FINDLEY AND FARBER'S ENVIRONMENTAL LAW IN A NUTSHELL, Third Edition, 355 pages, 1992. Softcover. (Text)

PLATER, ABRAMS AND GOLDFARB'S ENVIRONMENTAL LAW AND POLICY: NATURE, LAW AND SOCIETY, 1039 pages, 1992. Teacher's Manual available. (Casebook)

RODGERS' HORNBOOK ON ENVIRONMENTAL LAW, 956 pages, 1977, with 1984 pocket part. (Text)

SELECTED ENVIRONMENTAL LAW STATUTES—1993–94 EDUCATIONAL EDITION. Softcover. Approximately 1300 pages, 1993.

Equity—see Remedies

Estate Planning—see also Trusts and Estates; Taxation—Estate and Gift

LYNN'S INTRODUCTION TO ESTATE PLANNING IN A NUTSHELL, Fourth Edition, 352 pages, 1992. Softcover. (Text)

Evidence

BERGMAN'S TRANSCRIPT EXERCISES FOR LEARNING EVIDENCE, 273 pages, 1992. Softcover. Teacher's Manual available. (Coursebook)

BROUN AND BLAKEY'S BLACK LETTER ON EVIDENCE, 269 pages, 1984. Softcover. (Review)

BROUN, MEISENHOLDER, STRONG AND MOSTELLER'S PROBLEMS IN EVIDENCE, Third Edition, 238 pages, 1988. Softcover. Teacher's Manual available. (Coursebook)

CLEARY, STRONG, BROUN AND MOSTELLER'S CASES AND MATERIALS ON EVIDENCE, Fourth Edition, 1060 pages, 1988. (Casebook)

FEDERAL RULES OF EVIDENCE FOR UNITED STATES COURTS. Softcover. Approximately 575 pages, 1993.

FRIEDMAN'S THE ELEMENTS OF EVIDENCE, 315 pages, 1991. Teacher's Manual available. (Coursebook)

GRAHAM'S FEDERAL RULES OF EVIDENCE IN A NUTSHELL, Third Edition, 486 pages, 1992. Softcover. (Text)

LEMPERT AND SALTZBURG'S A MODERN APPROACH TO EVIDENCE: TEXT, PROBLEMS, TRANSCRIPTS AND CASES, Second Edition, 1232 pages, 1983. Teacher's Manual available. (Casebook)

LILLY'S AN INTRODUCTION TO THE LAW OF EVIDENCE, Second Edition, 585 pages, 1987. (Text)

MCCORMICK, SUTTON AND WELLBORN'S CASES AND MATERIALS ON EVIDENCE, Seventh Edition, 932 pages, 1992. Teacher's Manual available. (Casebook)

MCCORMICK'S HORNBOOK ON EVIDENCE, Fourth Edition, Student Edition, 672 pages, 1992. (Text)

ROTHSTEIN'S EVIDENCE IN A NUTSHELL: STATE AND FEDERAL RULES, Second Edition, 514 pages, 1981. Softcover. (Text)

Federal Jurisdiction and Procedure

CURRIE'S CASES AND MATERIALS ON FEDERAL COURTS, Fourth Edition, 783 pages, 1990. (Casebook)

CURRIE'S FEDERAL JURISDICTION IN A NUTSHELL, Third Edition, 242 pages, 1990. Softcover. (Text)

FEDERAL RULES OF CIVIL PROCEDURE—1993–94 EDUCATIONAL EDITION. Softcover. Approximately 775 pages, 1993.

REDISH'S BLACK LETTER ON FEDERAL JURISDICTION, Second Edition, 234 pages, 1991. Softcover. (Review)

REDISH'S CASES, COMMENTS AND QUESTIONS ON FEDERAL COURTS, Second Edition, 1122 pages, 1989. (Casebook) 1992 Supplement.

WRIGHT'S HORNBOOK ON FEDERAL COURTS, Fourth Edition, Student Edition, 870 pages, 1983. (Text)

First Amendment

BARRON AND DIENES' FIRST AMENDMENT LAW IN A NUTSHELL, Approximately 450

First Amendment—Cont'd

pages, September, 1993 pub. Softcover. (Text)

GARVEY AND SCHAUER'S THE FIRST AMENDMENT: A READER, 527 pages, 1992. Softcover. (Reader)

SHIFFRIN AND CHOPER'S FIRST AMENDMENT, CASES—COMMENTS—QUESTIONS, 759 pages, 1991. Softcover. (Casebook) 1993 Supplement.

Foreign Relations and National Security Law

FRANCK AND GLENNON'S FOREIGN RELATIONS AND NATIONAL SECURITY LAW, Second Edition, approximately 1150 pages, 1993. (Casebook)

Future Interests—see Trusts and Estates

Gender Discrimination—see also Employment Discrimination

KAY'S TEXT, CASES AND MATERIALS ON SEX-BASED DISCRIMINATION, Third Edition, 1001 pages, 1988. (Casebook) 1992 Supplement.

THOMAS' SEX DISCRIMINATION IN A NUTSHELL, Second Edition, 395 pages, 1991. Softcover. (Text)

Health Law—see Medicine, Law and

Human Rights—see International Law

Immigration Law

ALEINIKOFF AND MARTIN'S IMMIGRATION: PROCESS AND POLICY, Second Edition, 1056 pages, 1991. (Casebook)

Statutory Supplement. *See Immigration and Nationality Laws*

IMMIGRATION AND NATIONALITY LAWS OF THE UNITED STATES: SELECTED STATUTES, REGULATIONS AND FORMS. Softcover. 519 pages, 1992.

WEISSBRODT'S IMMIGRATION LAW AND PROCEDURE IN A NUTSHELL, Third Edition, 497 pages, 1992. Softcover. (Text)

Indian Law—see American Indian Law

Insurance Law

DEVINE AND TERRY'S PROBLEMS IN INSURANCE LAW, 240 pages, 1989. Softcover. Teacher's Manual available. (Coursebook)

DOBBYN'S INSURANCE LAW IN A NUTSHELL, Second Edition, 316 pages, 1989. Softcover. (Text)

KEETON'S COMPUTER-AIDED AND WORKBOOK EXERCISES ON INSURANCE LAW, 255 pages, 1990. Softcover. (Coursebook)

KEETON AND WIDISS' INSURANCE LAW, Student Edition, 1359 pages, 1988. (Text)

WIDISS AND KEETON'S COURSE SUPPLEMENT TO KEETON AND WIDISS' INSURANCE LAW, 502 pages, 1988. Softcover. Teacher's Manual available. (Casebook)

WIDISS' INSURANCE: MATERIALS ON FUNDAMENTAL PRINCIPLES, LEGAL DOCTRINES AND REGULATORY ACTS, 1186 pages, 1989. Teacher's Manual available. (Casebook)

YORK AND WHELAN'S CASES, MATERIALS AND PROBLEMS ON GENERAL PRACTICE INSURANCE LAW, Second Edition, 787 pages, 1988. Teacher's Manual available. (Casebook)

Intellectual Property Law—see also Trade Regulation

CHOATE, FRANCIS AND COLLINS' CASES AND MATERIALS ON PATENT LAW, INCLUDING TRADE SECRETS, COPYRIGHTS, TRADEMARKS, Third Edition, 1009 pages, 1987. (Casebook)

HALPERN, SHIPLEY AND ABRAMS' CASES AND MATERIALS ON COPYRIGHT, 663 pages, 1992. (Casebook)

MILLER AND DAVIS' INTELLECTUAL PROPERTY—PATENTS, TRADEMARKS AND COPYRIGHT IN A NUTSHELL, Second Edition, 437 pages, 1990. Softcover. (Text)

NIMMER, MARCUS, MYERS AND NIMMER'S CASES AND MATERIALS ON COPYRIGHT AND OTHER ASPECTS OF ENTERTAINMENT LITIGATION—INCLUDING UNFAIR COMPETITION, DEFAMATION, PRIVACY, ILLUSTRATED, Fourth Edition, 1177 pages, 1991. (Casebook) Statutory Supplement. See *Selected Intellectual Property Statutes*

SELECTED INTELLECTUAL PROPERTY AND UNFAIR COMPETITION STATUTES, REGULATIONS AND TREATIES. Softcover.

International Law—see also Sea, Law of

BERMANN, DAVEY, FOX AND GOEBEL'S CASES AND MATERIALS ON EUROPEAN COMMUNITY LAW, 1218 pages, 1993. (Casebook) Statutory Supplement. *See European Economic Community: Selected Documents*

International Law—Cont'd

BUERGENTHAL'S INTERNATIONAL HUMAN RIGHTS IN A NUTSHELL, 283 pages, 1988. Softcover. (Text)

BUERGENTHAL AND MAIER'S PUBLIC INTERNATIONAL LAW IN A NUTSHELL, Second Edition, 275 pages, 1990. Softcover. (Text)

EUROPEAN COMMUNITY LAW: SELECTED DOCUMENTS. 687 pages, 1993. Softcover

FOLSOM'S EUROPEAN COMMUNITY LAW IN A NUTSHELL, 423 pages, 1992. Softcover. (Text)

FOLSOM, GORDON AND SPANOGLE'S INTERNATIONAL BUSINESS TRANSACTIONS—A PROBLEM-ORIENTED COURSEBOOK, Second Edition, 1237 pages, 1991. Teacher's Manual available. (Casebook) 1991 Documents Supplement.

FOLSOM, GORDON AND SPANOGLE'S INTERNATIONAL BUSINESS TRANSACTIONS IN A NUTSHELL, Fourth Edition, 548 pages, 1992. Softcover. (Text)

HENKIN, PUGH, SCHACHTER AND SMIT'S CASES AND MATERIALS ON INTERNATIONAL LAW, Third Edition, approximately 1500 pages, 1993. (Casebook) 1993 Documents Supplement.

INTERNATIONAL LITIGATION AND ARBITRATION: SELECTED TREATIES, STATUTES AND RULES. 277 pages, 1993. Softcover

INTERNATIONAL ORGANIZATIONS IN THEIR LEGAL SETTING: SELECTED DOCUMENTS. 371 pages, 1993. Softcover

JACKSON AND DAVEY'S CASES, MATERIALS AND TEXT ON LEGAL PROBLEMS OF INTERNATIONAL ECONOMIC RELATIONS, Second Edition, 1269 pages, 1986. (Casebook) 1989 Documents Supplement.

KIRGIS' INTERNATIONAL ORGANIZATIONS IN THEIR LEGAL SETTING, Second Edition, 1119 pages, 1993. Teacher's Manual available. (Casebook) Statutory Supplement.

LOWENFELD'S INTERNATIONAL LITIGATION AND ARBITRATION, 869 pages, 1993. Teacher's Manual available. (Casebook) Statutory Supplement. *See International Litigation: Selected Documents*

WESTON, FALK AND D'AMATO'S INTERNATIONAL LAW AND WORLD ORDER—A PROBLEM-ORIENTED COURSEBOOK, Second Edition, 1335 pages, 1990. Teacher's Manual available. (Casebook) 1990 Documents Supplement.

Interviewing and Counseling

BINDER AND PRICE'S LEGAL INTERVIEWING AND COUNSELING, 232 pages, 1977. Softcover. Teacher's Manual available. (Coursebook)

BINDER, BERGMAN AND PRICE'S LAWYERS AS COUNSELORS: A CLIENT-CENTERED APPROACH, 427 pages, 1991. Softcover. (Coursebook)

SHAFFER AND ELKINS' LEGAL INTERVIEWING AND COUNSELING IN A NUTSHELL, Second Edition, 487 pages, 1987. Softcover. (Text)

Introduction to Law—see Legal Method and Legal System

Introduction to Law Study

HEGLAND'S INTRODUCTION TO THE STUDY AND PRACTICE OF LAW IN A NUTSHELL, 418 pages, 1983. Softcover. (Text)

KINYON'S INTRODUCTION TO LAW STUDY AND LAW EXAMINATIONS IN A NUTSHELL, 389 pages, 1971. Softcover. (Text)

Judicial Process—see Legal Method and Legal System

Jurisprudence

CHRISTIE'S JURISPRUDENCE—TEXT AND READINGS ON THE PHILOSOPHY OF LAW, 1056 pages, 1973. (Casebook)

SINHA'S JURISPRUDENCE (LEGAL PHILOSOPHY) IN A NUTSHELL. 379 pages, 1993. Softcover. (Text)

Juvenile Justice

FOX'S JUVENILE COURTS IN A NUTSHELL, Third Edition, 291 pages, 1984. Softcover. (Text)

Labor and Employment Law—see also Employment Discrimination, Workers' Compensation

CONISON'S EMPLOYEE BENEFIT PLANS IN A NUTSHELL, Approximately 465 pages, 1993. Softcover. (Text)

FINKIN, GOLDMAN AND SUMMERS' LEGAL PROTECTION OF INDIVIDUAL EMPLOYEES, (The Labor Law Group). 1164 pages, 1989. (Case-

Labor and Employment Law—Cont'd

book)

GORMAN'S BASIC TEXT ON LABOR LAW—UNIONIZATION AND COLLECTIVE BARGAINING, 914 pages, 1976. (Text)

LESLIE'S LABOR LAW IN A NUTSHELL, Third Edition, 388 pages, 1992. Softcover. (Text)

NOLAN'S LABOR ARBITRATION LAW AND PRACTICE IN A NUTSHELL, 358 pages, 1979. Softcover. (Text)

OBERER, HANSLOWE, ANDERSEN AND HEINSZ' CASES AND MATERIALS ON LABOR LAW—COLLECTIVE BARGAINING IN A FREE SOCIETY, Third Edition, 1163 pages, 1986. Teacher's Manual available. (Casebook) 1986 Statutory Supplement. 1991 Case Supplement.

RABIN, SILVERSTEIN AND SCHATZKI'S LABOR AND EMPLOYMENT LAW: PROBLEMS, CASES AND MATERIALS IN THE LAW OF WORK, (The Labor Law Group). 1014 pages, 1988. Teacher's Manual available. (Casebook) 1988 Statutory Supplement.

WOLLETT, GRODIN AND WEISBERGER'S COLLECTIVE BARGAINING IN PUBLIC EMPLOYMENT, (The Labor Law Group). Fourth Edition, approximately 425 pages, 1993. (Casebook)

Land Finance—Property Security—see Real Estate Transactions

Land Use

CALLIES AND FREILICH'S CASES AND MATERIALS ON LAND USE, 1233 pages, 1986. (Casebook) 1991 Supplement.

HAGMAN AND JUERGENSMEYER'S HORNBOOK ON URBAN PLANNING AND LAND DEVELOPMENT CONTROL LAW, Second Edition, Student Edition, 680 pages, 1986. (Text)

WRIGHT AND GITELMAN'S CASES AND MATERIALS ON LAND USE, Fourth Edition, 1255 pages, 1991. Teacher's Manual available. (Casebook)

WRIGHT AND WRIGHT'S LAND USE IN A NUTSHELL, Second Edition, 356 pages, 1985. Softcover. (Text)

Legal History—see also Legal Method and Legal System

PRESSER AND ZAINALDIN'S CASES AND MATERIALS ON LAW AND JURISPRUDENCE IN AMERICAN HISTORY, Second Edition, 1092 pages, 1989. Teacher's Manual available. (Casebook)

Legal Method and Legal System—see also Legal Research, Legal Writing

BERCH, BERCH AND SPRITZER'S INTRODUCTION TO LEGAL METHOD AND PROCESS, Second Edition, 585 pages, 1992. Teacher's Manual available. (Casebook)

BODENHEIMER, OAKLEY AND LOVE'S READINGS AND CASES ON AN INTRODUCTION TO THE ANGLO-AMERICAN LEGAL SYSTEM, Second Edition, 166 pages, 1988. Softcover. (Casebook)

KEETON'S JUDGING, 842 pages, 1990. Softcover. (Coursebook)

KELSO AND KELSO'S STUDYING LAW: AN INTRODUCTION, 587 pages, 1984. (Coursebook)

KEMPIN'S HISTORICAL INTRODUCTION TO ANGLO-AMERICAN LAW IN A NUTSHELL, Third Edition, 323 pages, 1990. Softcover. (Text)

MEADOR'S AMERICAN COURTS, 113 pages, 1991. Softcover. (Text)

REYNOLDS' JUDICIAL PROCESS IN A NUTSHELL, Second Edition, 308 pages, 1991. Softcover. (Text)

Legal Research

COHEN AND OLSON'S LEGAL RESEARCH IN A NUTSHELL, Fifth Edition, 370 pages, 1992. Softcover. (Text)

COHEN, BERRING AND OLSON'S HORNBOOK ON HOW TO FIND THE LAW, Ninth Edition, 716 pages, 1989. (Text)

COHEN, BERRING AND OLSON'S FINDING THE LAW, 570 pages, 1989. Softcover reprint from Cohen, Berring and Olson's How to Find the Law, Ninth Edition. (Coursebook)

Legal Research Exercises, 4th Ed., for use with Cohen, Berring and Olson, 253 pages, 1992. Teacher's Manual available.

HAZELTON'S COMPUTER–ASSISTED LEGAL RESEARCH: THE BASICS, Approximately 70 pages, 1993. Softcover. (Coursebook)

ROMBAUER'S LEGAL PROBLEM SOLVING—ANALYSIS, RESEARCH AND WRITING, Fifth

Legal Research—Cont'd

Edition, 524 pages, 1991. Softcover. Teacher's Manual with problems available. (Coursebook)

TEPLY'S LEGAL RESEARCH AND CITATION, Fourth Edition, 436 pages, 1992. Softcover. (Coursebook)

Student Library Exercises, Fourth Edition, 276 pages, 1992. Answer Key available.

Legal Writing and Drafting

CHILD'S DRAFTING LEGAL DOCUMENTS: PRINCIPLES AND PRACTICES, Second Edition, 425 pages, 1992. Softcover. Teacher's Manual available. (Coursebook)

FELSENFELD AND SIEGEL'S WRITING CONTRACTS IN PLAIN ENGLISH, 290 pages, 1981. Softcover. (Text)

MARTINEAU'S DRAFTING LEGISLATION AND RULES IN PLAIN ENGLISH, 155 pages, 1991. Softcover. Teacher's Manual available. (Text)

MELLINKOFF'S DICTIONARY OF AMERICAN LEGAL USAGE, 703 pages, 1992. Softcover. (Text)

MELLINKOFF'S LEGAL WRITING—SENSE AND NONSENSE, 242 pages, 1982. Softcover. Teacher's Manual available. (Text)

PRATT'S LEGAL WRITING: A SYSTEMATIC APPROACH, Second Edition, 426 pages, 1993. Teacher's Manual available. (Coursebook)

RAY AND COX'S BEYOND THE BASICS: A TEXT FOR ADVANCED LEGAL WRITING, 427 pages, 1991. Softcover. Teacher's Manual available. (Text)

RAY AND RAMSFIELD'S LEGAL WRITING: GETTING IT RIGHT AND GETTING IT WRITTEN, Second Edition, approximately 350 pages, 1993. Softcover. (Text)

SQUIRES AND ROMBAUER'S LEGAL WRITING IN A NUTSHELL, 294 pages, 1982. Softcover. (Text)

STATSKY AND WERNET'S CASE ANALYSIS AND FUNDAMENTALS OF LEGAL WRITING, Third Edition, 424 pages, 1989. Teacher's Manual available. (Text)

TEPLY'S LEGAL WRITING, ANALYSIS AND ORAL ARGUMENT, 576 pages, 1990. Softcover. Teacher's Manual available. (Coursebook)

WEIHOFEN'S LEGAL WRITING STYLE, Second Edition, 332 pages, 1980. (Text)

Legislation—see also Legal Writing and Drafting

DAVIES' LEGISLATIVE LAW AND PROCESS IN A NUTSHELL, Second Edition, 346 pages, 1986. Softcover. (Text)

ESKRIDGE AND FRICKEY'S CASES AND MATERIALS ON LEGISLATION: STATUTES AND THE CREATION OF PUBLIC POLICY, 937 pages, 1988. Teacher's Manual available. (Casebook) 1992 Supplement.

STATSKY'S LEGISLATIVE ANALYSIS AND DRAFTING, Second Edition, 217 pages, 1984. Teacher's Manual available. (Text)

Local Government

FRUG'S CASES AND MATERIALS ON LOCAL GOVERNMENT LAW, 1005 pages, 1988. (Casebook) 1991 Supplement.

MCCARTHY'S LOCAL GOVERNMENT LAW IN A NUTSHELL, Third Edition, 435 pages, 1990. Softcover. (Text)

REYNOLDS' HORNBOOK ON LOCAL GOVERNMENT LAW, 860 pages, 1982 with 1993 pocket part. (Text)

VALENTE AND MCCARTHY'S CASES AND MATERIALS ON LOCAL GOVERNMENT LAW, Fourth Edition, 1158 pages, 1992. Teacher's Manual available. (Casebook)

Mass Communication Law

GILLMOR, BARRON, SIMON AND TERRY'S CASES AND COMMENT ON MASS COMMUNICATION LAW, Fifth Edition, 947 pages, 1990. (Casebook)

GINSBURG, BOTEIN AND DIRECTOR'S REGULATION OF THE ELECTRONIC MASS MEDIA: LAW AND POLICY FOR RADIO, TELEVISION, CABLE AND THE NEW VIDEO TECHNOLOGIES, Second Edition, 657 pages, 1991. (Casebook) 1991 Statutory Supplement.

ZUCKMAN, GAYNES, CARTER AND DEE'S MASS COMMUNICATIONS LAW IN A NUTSHELL, Third Edition, 538 pages, 1988. Softcover. (Text)

Medicine, Law and

FISCINA, BOUMIL, SHARPE AND HEAD'S MEDICAL LIABILITY, 487 pages, 1991. Teacher's

Medicine, Law and—Cont'd

Manual available. (Casebook)

FURROW, JOHNSON, JOST AND SCHWARTZ' HEALTH LAW: CASES, MATERIALS AND PROBLEMS, Second Edition, 1236 pages, 1991. Teacher's Manual available. (Casebook)

FURROW, JOHNSON, JOST AND SCHWARTZ' BIOETHICS: HEALTH CARE LAW AND ETHICS, Reprint from Furrow et al., Health Law, Second Edition. Softcover. Teacher's Manual available. (Casebook)

FURROW, JOHNSON, JOST AND SCHWARTZ' THE LAW OF HEALTH CARE ORGANIZATION AND FINANCE, Reprint from Furrow et al., Health Law, Second Edition. Softcover. Teacher's Manual available.

FURROW, JOHNSON, JOST AND SCHWARTZ' LIABILITY AND QUALITY ISSUES IN HEALTH CARE, Reprint from Furrow et al., Health Law, Second Edition. Softcover. Teacher's Manual available. (Casebook)

HALL AND ELLMAN'S HEALTH CARE LAW AND ETHICS IN A NUTSHELL, 401 pages, 1990. Softcover (Text)

JARVIS, CLOSEN, HERMANN AND LEONARD'S AIDS LAW IN A NUTSHELL, 349 pages, 1991. Softcover. (Text)

KING'S THE LAW OF MEDICAL MALPRACTICE IN A NUTSHELL, Second Edition, 342 pages, 1986. Softcover. (Text)

SHAPIRO AND SPECE'S CASES, MATERIALS AND PROBLEMS ON BIOETHICS AND LAW, 892 pages, 1981. (Casebook) 1991 Supplement.

Mining Law—see Energy and Natural Resources Law

Mortgages—see Real Estate Transactions

Natural Resources Law—see Energy and Natural Resources Law, Environmental Law

Negotiation

GIFFORD'S LEGAL NEGOTIATION: THEORY AND APPLICATIONS, 225 pages, 1989. Softcover. (Text)

TEPLY'S LEGAL NEGOTIATION IN A NUTSHELL, 282 pages, 1992. Softcover. (Text)

WILLIAMS' LEGAL NEGOTIATION AND SETTLEMENT, 207 pages, 1983. Softcover. Teacher's Manual available. (Coursebook)

Office Practice—see also Computers and Law, Interviewing and Counseling, Negotiation

MUNNEKE'S LAW PRACTICE MANAGEMENT: MATERIALS AND CASES, 634 pages, 1991. Teacher's Manual available. (Casebook)

Oil and Gas—see also Energy and Natural Resources Law

HEMINGWAY'S HORNBOOK ON THE LAW OF OIL AND GAS, Third Edition, Student Edition, 711 pages, 1992. (Text)

KUNTZ, LOWE, ANDERSON AND SMITH'S CASES AND MATERIALS ON OIL AND GAS LAW, Second Edition, approximately 1000 pages, 1993. (Casebook) 1993 Forms Manual.

LOWE'S OIL AND GAS LAW IN A NUTSHELL, Second Edition, 465 pages, 1988. Softcover. (Text)

Patents—see Intellectual Property

Partnership—see Agency—Partnership

Products Liability

FISCHER AND POWERS' CASES AND MATERIALS ON PRODUCTS LIABILITY, 685 pages, 1988. Teacher's Manual available. (Casebook)

PHILLIPS' PRODUCTS LIABILITY IN A NUTSHELL, Fourth Edition, approximately 325 pages, 1993. Softcover. (Text)

Professional Responsibility

ARONSON, DEVINE AND FISCH'S PROBLEMS, CASES AND MATERIALS IN PROFESSIONAL RESPONSIBILITY, 745 pages, 1985. Teacher's Manual available. (Casebook)

ARONSON AND WECKSTEIN'S PROFESSIONAL RESPONSIBILITY IN A NUTSHELL, Second Edition, 514 pages, 1991. Softcover. (Text)

DVORKIN, HIMMELSTEIN AND LESNICK'S BECOMING A LAWYER: A HUMANISTIC PERSPECTIVE ON LEGAL EDUCATION AND PROFESSIONALISM, 211 pages, 1981. Softcover. (Text)

LESNICK'S BEING A LAWYER: INDIVIDUAL CHOICE AND RESPONSIBILITY IN THE PRACTICE OF LAW, 422 pages, 1992. Softcover. Teacher's Manual available. (Coursebook)

MELLINKOFF'S THE CONSCIENCE OF A LAWYER, 304 pages, 1973. (Text)

MOLITERNO AND LEVY'S ETHICS OF THE LAWYER'S WORK, 305 pages, 1993. Softcover.

Professional Responsibility—Cont'd

Teacher's Manual available. (Coursebook)

PIRSIG AND KIRWIN'S CASES AND MATERIALS ON PROFESSIONAL RESPONSIBILITY, Fourth Edition, 603 pages, 1984. Teacher's Manual available. (Casebook)

ROTUNDA'S BLACK LETTER ON PROFESSIONAL RESPONSIBILITY, Third Edition, 492 pages, 1992. Softcover. (Review)

SCHWARTZ, WYDICK AND PERSCHBACHER'S PROBLEMS IN LEGAL ETHICS, Third Edition, 402 pages, 1993. (Coursebook)

SELECTED STATUTES, RULES AND STANDARDS ON THE LEGAL PROFESSION. Softcover. Approximately 950 pages, 1993.

SMITH AND MALLEN'S PREVENTING LEGAL MALPRACTICE, 264 pages, 1989. Reprint from Mallen and Smith's Legal Malpractice, Third Edition. (Text)

SUTTON AND DZIENKOWSKI'S CASES AND MATERIALS ON PROFESSIONAL RESPONSIBILITY FOR LAWYERS, 839 pages, 1989. Teacher's Manual available. (Casebook)

WOLFRAM'S HORNBOOK ON MODERN LEGAL ETHICS, Student Edition, 1120 pages, 1986. (Text)

WYDICK AND PERSCHBACHER'S CALIFORNIA LEGAL ETHICS, 439 pages, 1992. Softcover. (Coursebook)

Property—see also Real Estate Transactions, Land Use, Trusts and Estates

BARNES AND STOUT'S THE ECONOMICS OF PROPERTY RIGHTS AND NUISANCE LAW, 87 pages, 1992. Softcover. Teacher's Manual available. (Casebook)

BERNHARDT'S BLACK LETTER ON PROPERTY, Second Edition, 388 pages, 1991. Softcover. (Review)

BERNHARDT'S REAL PROPERTY IN A NUTSHELL, Third Edition, 475 pages, 1993. Softcover. (Text)

BOYER, HOVENKAMP AND KURTZ' THE LAW OF PROPERTY, AN INTRODUCTORY SURVEY, Fourth Edition, 696 pages, 1991. (Text)

BROWDER, CUNNINGHAM, NELSON, STOEBUCK AND WHITMAN'S CASES ON BASIC PROPERTY LAW, Fifth Edition, 1386 pages, 1989. Teacher's Manual available. (Casebook)

BRUCE, ELY AND BOSTICK'S CASES AND MATERIALS ON MODERN PROPERTY LAW, Second Edition, 953 pages, 1989. Teacher's Manual available. (Casebook)

BURKE'S PERSONAL PROPERTY IN A NUTSHELL, Second Edition, 399 pages, 1993. Softcover. (Text)

CUNNINGHAM, STOEBUCK AND WHITMAN'S HORNBOOK ON THE LAW OF PROPERTY, Second Edition, approximately 900 pages, 1993. (Text)

DONAHUE, KAUPER AND MARTIN'S CASES AND MATERIALS ON PROPERTY, AN INTRODUCTION TO THE CONCEPT AND THE INSTITUTION, Third Edition, 1189 pages, 1993. Teacher's Manual available. (Casebook)

HILL'S LANDLORD AND TENANT LAW IN A NUTSHELL, Second Edition, 311 pages, 1986. Softcover. (Text)

JOHNSON, JOST, SALSICH AND SHAFFER'S PROPERTY LAW, CASES, MATERIALS AND PROBLEMS, 908 pages, 1992. Teacher's Manual available. (Casebook)

KURTZ AND HOVENKAMP'S CASES AND MATERIALS ON AMERICAN PROPERTY LAW, Second Edition, 1232 pages, 1993. Teacher's Manual available. (Casebook)

MOYNIHAN'S INTRODUCTION TO REAL PROPERTY, Second Edition, 239 pages, 1988. (Text)

Psychiatry, Law and

REISNER AND SLOBOGIN'S LAW AND THE MENTAL HEALTH SYSTEM, CIVIL AND CRIMINAL ASPECTS, Second Edition, 1117 pages, 1990. Teacher's Manual available. (Casebook) 1992 Supplement.

Real Estate Transactions

BRUCE'S REAL ESTATE FINANCE IN A NUTSHELL, Third Edition, 287 pages, 1991. Softcover. (Text)

MAXWELL, RIESENFELD, HETLAND AND WARREN'S CASES ON CALIFORNIA SECURITY TRANSACTIONS IN LAND, Fourth Edition, 778 pages, 1992. Teacher's Manual available. (Casebook)

NELSON AND WHITMAN'S BLACK LETTER ON LAND TRANSACTIONS AND FINANCE, Second Edition, 466 pages, 1988. Softcover. (Review)

NELSON AND WHITMAN'S CASES AND MATERI-

Real Estate Transactions—Cont'd

ALS ON REAL ESTATE TRANSFER, FINANCE AND DEVELOPMENT, Fourth Edition, 1346 pages, 1992. (Casebook)

NELSON AND WHITMAN'S HORNBOOK ON REAL ESTATE FINANCE LAW, Second Edition, 941 pages, 1985 with 1989 pocket part. (Text)

Regulated Industries—see also Mass Communication Law, Banking Law

GELLHORN AND PIERCE'S REGULATED INDUSTRIES IN A NUTSHELL, Second Edition, 389 pages, 1987. Softcover. (Text)

MORGAN, HARRISON AND VERKUIL'S CASES AND MATERIALS ON ECONOMIC REGULATION OF BUSINESS, Second Edition, 666 pages, 1985. (Casebook)

Remedies

DOBBS' HORNBOOK ON REMEDIES, Second Edition, approximately 900 pages, 1993. (Text)

DOBBS AND KAVANAGH'S PROBLEMS IN REMEDIES, Second Edition, 218 pages, 1993. Softcover. Teacher's Manual available. (Coursebook)

DOBBYN'S INJUNCTIONS IN A NUTSHELL, 264 pages, 1974. Softcover. (Text)

FRIEDMAN'S CONTRACT REMEDIES IN A NUTSHELL, 323 pages, 1981. Softcover. (Text)

LEAVELL, LOVE AND NELSON'S CASES AND MATERIALS ON EQUITABLE REMEDIES, RESTITUTION AND DAMAGES, Fourth Edition, 1111 pages, 1986. Teacher's Manual available. (Casebook)

O'CONNELL'S REMEDIES IN A NUTSHELL, Second Edition, 320 pages, 1985. Softcover. (Text)

SCHOENBROD, MACBETH, LEVINE AND JUNG'S CASES AND MATERIALS ON REMEDIES: PUBLIC AND PRIVATE, 848 pages, 1990. Teacher's Manual available. (Casebook) 1992 Supplement.

YORK, BAUMAN AND RENDLEMAN'S CASES AND MATERIALS ON REMEDIES, Fifth Edition, 1270 pages, 1992. Teacher's Manual available. (Casebook)

Sea, Law of

SOHN AND GUSTAFSON'S THE LAW OF THE SEA IN A NUTSHELL, 264 pages, 1984. Softcover. (Text)

Securities Regulation

HAZEN'S HORNBOOK ON THE LAW OF SECURITIES REGULATION, Second Edition, Student Edition, 1082 pages, 1990. (Text)

RATNER'S SECURITIES REGULATION IN A NUTSHELL, Fourth Edition, 320 pages, 1992. Softcover. (Text)

RATNER AND HAZEN'S SECURITIES REGULATION: CASES AND MATERIALS, Fourth Edition, 1062 pages, 1991. Teacher's Manual available. (Casebook) 1991 Problems and Sample Documents Supplement.

Statutory Supplement. *See Securities Regulation, Selected Statutes*

SECURITIES REGULATION, SELECTED STATUTES, RULES, AND FORMS. Softcover. Approximately 1375 pages, 1993.

Sports Law

CHAMPION'S SPORTS LAW IN A NUTSHELL. 325 pages, 1993. Softcover. (Text)

SCHUBERT, SMITH AND TRENTADUE'S SPORTS LAW, 395 pages, 1986. (Text)

WEILER AND ROBERTS' CASES, MATERIALS, AND PROBLEMS ON THE LAW OF SPORTS, Approximately 765 pages, 1993. (Casebook) 1993 Statutory and Document Supplement.

Tax Policy

DODGE'S THE LOGIC OF TAX, 343 pages, 1989. Softcover. (Text)

UTZ' TAX POLICY: AN INTRODUCTION AND SURVEY OF THE PRINCIPAL DEBATES, 260 pages, 1993. Softcover. Teacher's Manual available. (Coursebook)

Tax Practice and Procedure

GARBIS, RUBIN AND MORGAN'S CASES AND MATERIALS ON TAX PROCEDURE AND TAX FRAUD, Third Edition, 921 pages, 1992. (Casebook)

MORGAN'S TAX PROCEDURE AND TAX FRAUD IN A NUTSHELL, 400 pages, 1990. Softcover. (Text)

Taxation—Corporate

KAHN AND GANN'S CORPORATE TAXATION, Third Edition, 980 pages, 1989. Teacher's Manual available. (Casebook) 1991 Supplement.

SCHWARZ AND LATHROPE'S BLACK LETTER ON

Taxation—Corporate—Cont'd

CORPORATE AND PARTNERSHIP TAXATION, 537 pages, 1991. Softcover. (Review)

WEIDENBRUCH AND BURKE'S FEDERAL INCOME TAXATION OF CORPORATIONS AND STOCKHOLDERS IN A NUTSHELL, Third Edition, 309 pages, 1989. Softcover. (Text)

Taxation—Estate & Gift—see also Estate Planning, Trusts and Estates

MCNULTY'S FEDERAL ESTATE AND GIFT TAXATION IN A NUTSHELL, Fourth Edition, 496 pages, 1989. Softcover. (Text)

PEAT AND WILLBANKS' FEDERAL ESTATE AND GIFT TAXATION: AN ANALYSIS AND CRITIQUE, 265 pages, 1991. Softcover. (Text)

PENNELL'S CASES AND MATERIALS ON INCOME TAXATION OF TRUSTS, ESTATES, GRANTORS AND BENEFICIARIES, 460 pages, 1987. Teacher's Manual available. (Casebook)

Taxation—Individual

GUNN AND WARD'S CASES, TEXT AND PROBLEMS ON FEDERAL INCOME TAXATION, Third Edition, 817 pages, 1992. Teacher's Manual available. (Casebook)

HUDSON AND LIND'S BLACK LETTER ON FEDERAL INCOME TAXATION, Fourth Edition, 410 pages, 1992. Softcover. (Review)

MCNULTY'S FEDERAL INCOME TAXATION OF INDIVIDUALS IN A NUTSHELL, Fourth Edition, 503 pages, 1988. Softcover. (Text)

POSIN'S FEDERAL INCOME TAXATION, Second Edition, approximately 550 pages, 1993. Softcover. (Text)

ROSE AND CHOMMIE'S HORNBOOK ON FEDERAL INCOME TAXATION, Third Edition, 923 pages, 1988, with 1991 pocket part. (Text)

SELECTED FEDERAL TAXATION STATUTES AND REGULATIONS. Softcover. Approximately 1700 pages, 1994.

Taxation—International

DOERNBERG'S INTERNATIONAL TAXATION IN A NUTSHELL, Second Edition, approximately 375 pages, 1993. Softcover. (Text)

KAPLAN'S FEDERAL TAXATION OF INTERNATIONAL TRANSACTIONS: PRINCIPLES, PLANNING AND POLICY, 635 pages, 1988. (Casebook)

Taxation—Partnership

BERGER AND WIEDENBECK'S CASES AND MATERIALS ON PARTNERSHIP TAXATION, 788 pages, 1989. Teacher's Manual available. (Casebook) 1991 Supplement.

BISHOP AND BROOKS' FEDERAL PARTNERSHIP TAXATION: A GUIDE TO THE LEADING CASES, STATUTES, AND REGULATIONS, 545 pages, 1990. Softcover. (Text)

BURKE'S FEDERAL INCOME TAXATION OF PARTNERSHIPS IN A NUTSHELL, 356 pages, 1992. Softcover. (Text)

SCHWARZ AND LATHROPE'S BLACK LETTER ON CORPORATE AND PARTNERSHIP TAXATION, 537 pages, 1991. Softcover. (Review)

Taxation—State & Local

GELFAND AND SALSICH'S STATE AND LOCAL TAXATION AND FINANCE IN A NUTSHELL, 309 pages, 1986. Softcover. (Text)

HELLERSTEIN AND HELLERSTEIN'S CASES AND MATERIALS ON STATE AND LOCAL TAXATION, Fifth Edition, 1071 pages, 1988. (Casebook)

Torts—see also Products Liability

BARNES AND STOUT'S THE ECONOMIC ANALYSIS OF TORT LAW, 161 pages, 1992. Softcover. Teacher's Manual available. (Casebook)

CHRISTIE AND MEEKS' CASES AND MATERIALS ON THE LAW OF TORTS, Second Edition, 1264 pages, 1990. (Casebook)

DOBBS' TORTS AND COMPENSATION—PERSONAL ACCOUNTABILITY AND SOCIAL RESPONSIBILITY FOR INJURY, Second Edition, approximately 1050 pages, 1993. Teacher's Manual available. (Casebook)

KEETON, KEETON, SARGENTICH AND STEINER'S CASES AND MATERIALS ON TORT AND ACCIDENT LAW, Second Edition, 1318 pages, 1989. (Casebook)

KIONKA'S BLACK LETTER ON TORTS, Second Edition, approximately 350 pages, 1993. Softcover. (Review)

KIONKA'S TORTS IN A NUTSHELL, Second Edition, 449 pages, 1992. Softcover. (Text)

PROSSER AND KEETON'S HORNBOOK ON TORTS, Fifth Edition, Student Edition, 1286 pages, 1984 with 1988 pocket part. (Text)

ROBERTSON, POWERS AND ANDERSON'S CASES

Torts—Cont'd

AND MATERIALS ON TORTS, 932 pages, 1989. Teacher's Manual available. (Casebook)

Trade Regulation—see also Antitrust, Regulated Industries

MCMANIS' UNFAIR TRADE PRACTICES IN A NUTSHELL, Third Edition, 471 pages, 1993. Softcover. (Text)

SCHECHTER'S BLACK LETTER ON UNFAIR TRADE PRACTICES AND INTELLECTUAL PROPERTY, Second Edition, approximately 300 pages, 1993. Softcover. (Review)

WESTON, MAGGS AND SCHECHTER'S UNFAIR TRADE PRACTICES AND CONSUMER PROTECTION, CASES AND COMMENTS, Fifth Edition, 957 pages, 1992. Teacher's Manual available. (Casebook)

Trial and Appellate Advocacy—see also Civil Procedure

APPELLATE ADVOCACY, HANDBOOK OF, Third Edition, 101 pages, 1993. Softcover. (Text)

BERGMAN'S TRIAL ADVOCACY IN A NUTSHELL, Second Edition, 354 pages, 1989. Softcover. (Text)

BINDER AND BERGMAN'S FACT INVESTIGATION: FROM HYPOTHESIS TO PROOF, 354 pages, 1984. Teacher's Manual available. (Coursebook)

CARLSON'S ADJUDICATION OF CRIMINAL JUSTICE: PROBLEMS AND REFERENCES, 130 pages, 1986. Softcover. (Casebook)

CARLSON AND IMWINKELRIED'S DYNAMICS OF TRIAL PRACTICE: PROBLEMS AND MATERIALS, 414 pages, 1989. Teacher's Manual available. (Coursebook) 1990 Supplement.

CLARY'S PRIMER ON THE ANALYSIS AND PRESENTATION OF LEGAL ARGUMENT, 106 pages, 1992. Softcover. (Text)

DESSEM'S PRETRIAL LITIGATION IN A NUTSHELL, 382 pages, 1992. Softcover. (Text)

DESSEM'S PRETRIAL LITIGATION: LAW, POLICY AND PRACTICE, 608 pages, 1991. Softcover. Teacher's Manual available. (Coursebook)

DEVINE'S NON-JURY CASE FILES FOR TRIAL ADVOCACY, 258 pages, 1991. (Coursebook)

GOLDBERG'S THE FIRST TRIAL (WHERE DO I SIT? WHAT DO I SAY?) IN A NUTSHELL, 396 pages, 1982. Softcover. (Text)

HAYDOCK, HERR, AND STEMPEL'S FUNDAMENTALS OF PRE-TRIAL LITIGATION, Second Edition, 786 pages, 1992. Softcover. Teacher's Manual available. (Coursebook)

HAYDOCK AND SONSTENG'S TRIAL: THEORIES, TACTICS, TECHNIQUES, 711 pages, 1991. Softcover. (Text)

HEGLAND'S TRIAL AND PRACTICE SKILLS IN A NUTSHELL, 346 pages, 1978. Softcover. (Text)

HORNSTEIN'S APPELLATE ADVOCACY IN A NUTSHELL, 325 pages, 1984. Softcover. (Text)

JEANS' TRIAL ADVOCACY, Second Edition, approximately 575 pages, 1993. Softcover. (Text)

LISNEK AND KAUFMAN'S DEPOSITIONS: PROCEDURE, STRATEGY AND TECHNIQUE, Law School and CLE Edition. 250 pages, 1990. Softcover. (Text)

MARTINEAU'S CASES AND MATERIALS ON APPELLATE PRACTICE AND PROCEDURE, 565 pages, 1987. (Casebook)

SONSTENG, HAYDOCK AND BOYD'S THE TRIALBOOK: A TOTAL SYSTEM FOR PREPARATION AND PRESENTATION OF A CASE, 404 pages, 1984. Softcover. (Coursebook)

WHARTON, HAYDOCK AND SONSTENG'S CALIFORNIA CIVIL TRIALBOOK, Law School and CLE Edition. 148 pages, 1990. Softcover. (Text)

Trusts and Estates

ATKINSON'S HORNBOOK ON WILLS, Second Edition, 975 pages, 1953. (Text)

AVERILL'S UNIFORM PROBATE CODE IN A NUTSHELL, Third Edition, approximately 450 pages, 1993. Softcover. (Text)

BOGERT'S HORNBOOK ON TRUSTS, Sixth Edition, Student Edition, 794 pages, 1987. (Text)

CLARK, LUSKY AND MURPHY'S CASES AND MATERIALS ON GRATUITOUS TRANSFERS, Third Edition, 970 pages, 1985. (Casebook)

DODGE'S WILLS, TRUSTS AND ESTATE PLANNING–LAW AND TAXATION, CASES AND MATERIALS, 665 pages, 1988. (Casebook)

MCGOVERN, KURTZ AND REIN'S HORNBOOK ON WILLS, TRUSTS AND ESTATES–INCLUDING

Trusts and Estates—Cont'd

TAXATION AND FUTURE INTERESTS, 996 pages, 1988. (Text)

MENNELL'S WILLS AND TRUSTS IN A NUTSHELL, 392 pages, 1979. Softcover. (Text)

SIMES' HORNBOOK ON FUTURE INTERESTS, Second Edition, 355 pages, 1966. (Text)

TURANO AND RADIGAN'S HORNBOOK ON NEW YORK ESTATE ADMINISTRATION, 676 pages, 1986 with 1991 pocket part. (Text)

UNIFORM PROBATE CODE, OFFICIAL TEXT WITH COMMENTS. 863 pages, 1991. Softcover.

WAGGONER'S FUTURE INTERESTS IN A NUTSHELL, 361 pages, 1981. Softcover. (Text)

Water Law—see also Energy and Natural Resources Law, Environmental Law

GETCHES' WATER LAW IN A NUTSHELL, Second Edition, 459 pages, 1990. Softcover. (Text)

SAX, ABRAMS AND THOMPSON'S LEGAL CONTROL OF WATER RESOURCES: CASES AND MATERIALS, Second Edition, 987 pages, 1991. Teacher's Manual available. (Casebook)

TRELEASE AND GOULD'S CASES AND MATERIALS ON WATER LAW, Fourth Edition, 816 pages, 1986. (Casebook) 1993 Supplement.

Wills—see Trusts and Estates

Workers' Compensation

HOOD, HARDY AND LEWIS' WORKERS' COMPENSATION AND EMPLOYEE PROTECTION LAWS IN A NUTSHELL, Second Edition, 361 pages, 1990. Softcover. (Text)

LITTLE, EATON AND SMITH'S CASES AND MATERIALS ON WORKERS' COMPENSATION, 537 pages, 1992. Teacher's Manual available. (Casebook)

WEST'S LAW SCHOOL ADVISORY BOARD

---

*

SALES AND SECURED TRANSACTIONS

TEACHING MATERIALS

Fifth Edition

By

Richard E. Speidel
Beatrice Kuhn Professor of Law
Northwestern University School of Law

Robert S. Summers
McRoberts Research Professor of Law
Cornell University School of Law

James J. White
Robert A. Sullivan Professor of Law
University of Michigan School of Law

AMERICAN CASEBOOK SERIES®

WEST PUBLISHING CO.
ST. PAUL, MINN., 1993

610 Opperman Drive
P.O. Box 64526
St. Paul, MN 55164–0526
1–800–328–9352

Printed in the United States of America

ISBN 0–314–02344–5

(S., S. & W.) Sales & Sec.Trans., 5th Ed. ACB

PRINTED ON 10% POST CONSUMER RECYCLED PAPER

Preface

This book, R. Speidel, R. Summers and J. White, SALES AND SECURED TRANSACTIONS—TEACHING MATERIALS (West 1993) contains comprehensive materials on Sales and Leases of Goods and Secured Transactions. There is a companion volume by the same editors called PAYMENT SYSTEMS—TEACHING MATERIALS (West 1993).

This fifth edition includes a number of new cases, problems, and textual notes, including problems and notes on some of the proposed revisions of Article Two now under study. The edition also takes account of developments under Article Nine, including recent cases and the new definition of security interest in section 1–201(37). There are also entirely new materials on Article 2A on leases of goods.

R.E.S.
R.S.S.
J.J.W.

*

Acknowledgments

Professor Speidel wishes to thank his secretary, Ms. Shirley Scott, and his research assistant, Mr. Mike Willisch, Northwestern Law School Class of 1994 for assistance on this edition.

Professor Summers wishes to thank his secretary, Mrs. Sandra Markham, and his research assistants, Mr. Tim Fraelich and Mr. Christian Mammen, Cornell Law School Class of 1993.

Professor White wishes to record his gratitude to his secretary, Mrs. Kathy West, and to his research assistants, Mr. Jack Baughman, U. of Michigan Law School Class of 1993, Mr. Robert Fogler and Mr. Aaron Ahola, U. of Michigan Law School Class of 1994.

We acknowledge and thank the many publishers and authors who graciously consented to the reprinting herein of extracts from copyrighted materials.

R.E.S.
R.S.S.
J.J.W.

*

Summary of Contents

Table of Contents

PART FIVE. THE RECEIPT-INSPECTION STAGE

Table of Cases

The principal cases are in bold type. Cases cited or discussed in the text are roman type. References are to pages. Cases cited in principal cases and within other quoted materials are not included.

*

Table of Statutes

UNIFORM COMMERCIAL CODE

UNIFORM COMMERCIAL CODE

UNIFORM COMMERCIAL CODE

UNIFORM COMMERCIAL CODE

UNIFORM COMMERCIAL CODE

UNIFORM COMMERCIAL CODE

UNIFORM COMMERCIAL CODE

UNIFORM COMMERCIAL CODE

UNIFORM COMMERCIAL CODE

UNIFORM COMMERCIAL CODE

UNIFORM COMMERCIAL CODE

UNIFORM COMMERCIAL CODE

UNIFORM COMMERCIAL CODE

UNIFORM COMMERCIAL CODE

UNIFORM COMMERCIAL CODE

UNIFORM COMMERCIAL CODE

UNIFORM COMMERCIAL CODE

UNIFORM COMMERCIAL CODE

UNIFORM COMMERCIAL CODE

UNIFORM COMMERCIAL CODE

UNIFORM COMMERCIAL CODE

UNIFORM COMMERCIAL CODE

UNIFORM COMMERCIAL CODE

UNIFORM COMMERCIAL CODE

UNIFORM COMMERCIAL CODE

UNIFORM COMMERCIAL CODE

UNITED STATES

UNITED STATES CONSTITUTION

UNITED STATES CODE ANNOTATED

7 U.S.C.A.—Agriculture

9 U.S.C.A.—Arbitration

11 U.S.C.A.—Bankruptcy

UNITED STATES CODE ANNOTATED

11 U.S.C.A.—Bankruptcy

UNITED STATES CODE ANNOTATED

11 U.S.C.A.—Bankruptcy

UNITED STATES CODE ANNOTATED

11 U.S.C.A.—Bankruptcy

12 U.S.C.A.—Banks and Banking

15 U.S.C.A.—Commerce and Trade

18 U.S.C.A.—Crimes and Criminal Procedure

21 U.S.C.A.—Food and Drugs

26 U.S.C.A.—Internal Revenue Code

UNITED STATES CODE ANNOTATED

28 U.S.C.A.—Judiciary and Judicial Procedure

42 U.S.C.A.—The Public Health and Welfare

46 U.S.C.A.—Shipping

49 U.S.C.A.—Transportation

STATUTES AT LARGE

POPULAR NAME ACTS

BANKRUPTCY ACT

FEDERAL ARBITRATION ACT

FEDERAL BILLS OF LADING ACT

INTERSTATE COMMERCE ACT

PERISHABLE AGRICULTURAL COMMODITIES ACT

UNIFORM ARBITRATION ACT

UNIFORM SALES ACT

ARKANSAS STATUTES

ILLINOIS REVISED STATUTES

KANSAS STATUTES ANNOTATED

MASSACHUSETTS UNIFORM COMMERCIAL CODE

MINNESOTA STATUTES ANNOTATED

CODE OF FEDERAL REGULATIONS

SALES AND SECURED TRANSACTIONS

TEACHING MATERIALS

Fifth Edition

*

CHAPTER ONE

THE NATURE AND SOURCES OF COMMERCIAL LAW

SECTION 1. A BRIEF CURRICULAR NOTE TO THE STUDENT

A glance back at the table of contents will show that these materials are divided into two "books," one on security, and one on sales. But the student must not think of these as wholly separate subjects. They are closely related, functionally, analytically, and historically, and we have sought to integrate them here. Instructors differ, however, on modes of integration and we have arranged the materials to facilitate varied approaches.

The materials have this in common, too: They may be viewed, in part, as a kind of advanced course in contracts. Contract necessarily undergirds nearly the whole of the law school curriculum; we do not apologize for its reappearance here. Indeed, our own classroom experience tells us that a great many students would profit from an exact repetition of their first year contracts course! (And two of us teach first year contracts regularly.) But the materials we offer here will duplicate few of your first year experiences. These materials will treat a few contracts topics to which you were exposed in your first year, but generally in greater depth or from a quite different angle. Further, we will take you into new and distinctive areas of advanced contracts including security, credit, documents of title, and commercial paper. In addition, here you will encounter far more regulatory law than is true in first year contracts courses. As we shall see, in some branches of our subject, freedom of contract is dramatically waning and regulatory law is rapidly supplanting it. Finally, and perhaps most important of all, the materials that follow afford students opportunities to develop skills in working with complex statutory schemes far beyond anything possible in the first year contracts course. We are now in the Age of the Statute.

SECTION 2. ORIGINS OF NEEDS FOR COMMERCIAL LAW

Millions of "deals" occur each day in the United States. Many are between businessmen and many are between businessmen and consumers. These deals and their performance are the stuff of commercial and consumer life to which these materials will be addressed.

The deals involved vary greatly. Many involve sales of goods or intangibles, and the like. Many consist of leasing arrangements. Many involve loans or extensions of credit, with or without "security interests" (interests that give a creditor priority rights in a specific asset of the debtor). Many involve the rendition of services by insurers, carriers, storers and the like. Many involve the use of notes, checks and other "negotiable instruments." The overwhelming majority of these deals go through without incident. But when something does go wrong, there may be occasion to resort to law and to legal processes. What kinds of law? What kinds of processes? The answers to these questions turn on the nature of the real world problems which generate the needs for laws and legal processes in the first place.

Suppose, for example, that one party to an alleged deal simply denies that a deal was ever made. He, in effect, says that under the law no binding relationship came into being. To determine whether he is correct, resort to what might be called *rules of validation* is required. These rules specify the requisites of a valid contract of sale, or of a valid security interest, and so on. The legal need is for *such rules,* and for them to be clear, definite, accessible, and ascertainable, in advance of deals. Rules specifying *how* to "make it legal" are fundamental. Without them, private ordering under law could not exist. One of the primary functions of bodies of commercial and consumer law is to facilitate and sanction private ordering and private autonomy. In our system there is, we think, positive value in affording individuals extensive power to give their deals the force of law. *How* they must do this is the province of rules of validation.

Parties to a transaction may have sought, in writing, to specify their wants and expectations in Durer-like detail, only to find, at a later point, that they disagree over the interpretation or construction of some part of their agreement. Here the specific legal need is for rational and just *rules of interpretation and construction.* Such rules guide courts; they facilitate counseling; they may also lead parties to settle their differences without resort to courts.

Assume the parties have not planned out their deal in detail. At some later stage, something goes wrong or some question arises on which their written agreement or their general understanding, as the case may be, is wholly silent. For example, goods contracted for are destroyed by fire while in transit. Or a pledgee of goods pledged to secure a loan decides he would like to repledge these same goods to a third party. Or a borrower wants to know if he has the right to pay back a loan without penalty. Here the legal need is for substantive *suppletive rules,* rules which presuppose and supplement the incomplete private transaction with specific "terms." To be generally fair and just, such rules should be based upon the likely commercial or consumer understanding of such matters. For, insofar as there is a standard understanding, it is not unreasonable to feed it into the skeletal deal.

A variation on the immediately preceding problem is this: The reality of many deals is that parties typically do not specify their expected performances in detail. Here the legal need is for rationally conceived suppletive rules which specify the substance of the deal. In modern law, "implied warranties" are perhaps the best example. In many simple sales nothing is ever said at the time of the deal about the standard to which the goods must conform. Such warranty or warranties are left to be supplied by law. The very existence of such suppletive law gives rise to a further distinctive kind of legal need: the need for *rules of disclaimer,* rules which specify *how* the parties can modify or exclude altogether what the suppletive law would otherwise supply. That such rules should generally be clear, definite, and ascertainable in advance requires no argument.

People being what they are, and society being what it is, some parties will try to take advantage of others and some sometimes will not know what is in their own best interest. For example, a consumer may enter an entirely lopsided and unfair deal. The "real" world thus generates the problem of whether or not the terms of such deals are to be enforced. And the law must then face another specific kind of legal need—a need for what might be called *regulatory policing rules.* It has been suggested that the "core task" of commercial and consumer law is "to determine the relatively few rules which are not subject to change by agreement, the rules which are designed to stake out the necessary minimum area of protection for parties whose bargaining power is inferior." See Schlesinger, *The Uniform Commercial Code in the Light of Comparative Law,* 1 Inter-Am.L.Rev. 11, 33 (1959). Extensive needs for policing rules to regulate exchanges have only recently been recognized in our system. Such rules plainly invade the province of private autonomy and limit freedom of contract. That, so far as possible, parties should know in advance what they cannot enforceably agree to seems obvious.

Akin to regulatory policing rules are rules which may be designated as *third party protection rules.* Many consumer and commercial transactions, occurrences, and events impinge directly or indirectly on the interests of third parties not privy to the transaction at hand. Some occur fraudulently, as where a seller of goods in his possession sells these same goods successively to two different parties and then absconds. But other such transactions are not necessarily dishonest, as where a creditor establishes a preferred position *vis a vis* other creditors of the same debtor. Here the specific legal need is for rules which protect, as far as possible, the interests of all concerned. For example, in the creditor situation, the law might require that any creditor seeking such a preferred position must in some way give public notice of this fact so that interested third parties may act accordingly. Like policing rules, third party protection rules limit freedom of contract, for to be effective they must not be subject to variation by agreement of the parties.

Within the world of commerce, the activities of selling and buying and of lending and borrowing are ubiquitous. And they are often intertwined. Buyer-debtors are actually more common than general debtors. Seldom is a debtor a debtor of only one person. Moreover, in a typical year, a significant minority of debtors fall into financial difficulty. Assuming that such a debtor does not have enough assets to pay all of his debts, which creditors are to receive what? The specific legal need generated by such problems is for *rules of priority,* rules which, in circumstances of scarcity, determine who gets what. Prospective lenders, as well as sellers selling on credit, would often want to know in advance the bearing such rules could have on their situations.

Failure to pay a debt when due is but one kind and perhaps the simplest kind of failure of promised performance known to the law. Among others are non-delivery or nonconforming delivery of, goods; failure of a carrier or a bank to obey agreed instructions from the seller or the buyer; misconduct of a warehouseman, and so forth. Here, the specific legal need is for *suppletive remedial rules and procedures.* Of course, the parties themselves might agree in advance on remedies and on the steps to be taken to perfect rights to such remedies. But in most transactions, remedies and remedial procedures are left to be supplied by the law. "Remedies" is used here in an appropriately broad sense to include all of the permissible responses to breach of a deal: abandonment, specific relief, and damages. "Procedures" is used here to include the various hoops to be jumped through in order to perfect rights to particular remedies. Thus the law might, with reason, require a disgruntled buyer to notify his seller immediately of any specific defects in goods he wishes to reject for nonconformity. Similarly, the law might specify a whole series of steps that a creditor should take in order to walk off with some asset of a debtor against the protests of other similarly unpaid creditors. The law must provide remedial rules and procedures if "making a deal legal" is to have any meaning at all in that vast majority of transactions in which the parties, assuming business will go forward as usual, say nothing of such matters in their agreement. To be fair, and in order to further one of the fundamental purposes of our law, such rules and procedures must, over the mine-run of conflict situations, provide remedies that protect the general expectations of parties similarly situated in deals of that kind. What such expectations are is a fact to be approximated, if not ascertained, and then embodied in the relevant legal doctrines.

Rules of validation, rules of interpretation and construction, substantive suppletive rules, rules of disclaimer, policing rules, third party protection rules, priority rules, and remedial suppletive rules and procedures: these, and others, are the kinds of rules that a legal system must introduce, through code law or case law, to meet legal needs arising out of commercial and consumer activities. One or more of these kinds of rules, in turn, furthers one or more of the varied general aims of such law, whether it be statutory or judge-made: to minimize the occasions for disputes in the course of commercial and consumer dealings; to facilitate *private* ordering of human relations; to protect justified expectations; to protect individuals from various forms of over-reaching and from their own improvidence; to safeguard the interests of third parties; and more.

There is one further type of legal need that the stuff of consumer and commercial life generates, one which cuts across most of the others identified here. This is the need for rules, principles, and processes capable of accommodating and governing the *ever changing varieties* of transaction patterns that occur in the real world of commerce and business. Change and variety are now, have been, and certainly will continue to be distinctively dominant themes in this field.

SECTION 3. THE UNIFORM COMMERCIAL CODE AND ITS ANTECEDENTS—CODIFICATION OF COMMERCIAL LAW

The foremost champion of codification in the entire history of the Common Law was the 19th Century British jurist Jeremy Bentham. His pupil, John Austin, favored codification, but was cautious about it.

AUSTIN, 2 LECTURES ON JURISPRUDENCE 132–133 (Campbell ed. 1869).

"Whoever has considered the difficulty of making a good statute, will not think lightly of the difficulty of making a code. To conceive distinctly the general purpose of a statute, and the subordinate provisions through which that must be accomplished, and to express both in adequate and unambiguous language, is a task of extreme delicacy and difficulty. It is far easier to conceive justly what would be useful law, than so to construct that same law that it may accomplish the design of the lawgiver. Accordingly, statutes made with great deliberation, and by learned and judicious lawyers, have been expressed so obscurely, or constructed so unaptly, that decisions interpreting or supplementing their provisions, have been of necessity heaped upon them by the Courts of Justice. Such is notably the case with the celebrated Statute of Frauds.

"It follows that the question of Codification is a question of time and place. Speaking in abstract, or without reference to the circumstances of a given community, there can be no doubt that a complete code is better than a body of judiciary law; or is better than a body of law partly consisting of judiciary law, and partly of statute law stuck patchwise on a body of judiciary.

"But taking the question in concrete, or with a view to the expediency of codification in this or that community, a doubt may arise. For here we must contrast the existing law—not with the beau idéal of possible codes, but—with that particular code which an attempt to codify would then and there engender. And that particular and practical question, as Herr von Savigny has rightly judged, will turn mainly on the answer that must be given to another: namely, Are there men, then and there, competent to the difficult task of successful codification? of producing a code, which, on the whole, would more than compensate the evil that must necessarily attend the change?

"The vast difficulty of successful codification, no rational advocate of codification will deny or doubt. Its impossibility none of its rational opponents will venture to affirm."

Bentham, had he heard them, might have been offended by these remarks, for he considered himself competent to codify any law, anywhere, any time. Bentham died in 1832 without having much impact on the codification of English law during his lifetime. But partly as a result of his posthumous influence, a codification movement in England and in America began within fifty years of his death. Interestingly enough, some of these early efforts at codification were in fields of commercial law. The British Bills of Exchange Act of 1882 was the first successful attempt to codify a major branch of English commercial law. This Act was followed in 1893 by the British Sale of Goods Act. M.D. Chalmers, the principal draftsman of these two Codes, was invited to address the convention of the American Bar Association in 1902 on the desirability of codifying commercial law. He closed his speech with these remarks:

CHALMERS, CODIFICATION OF MERCANTILE LAW, 19 L.Q.Rev. 10, 17–18 (1903).

"In the United States, the case for codifying mercantile law is stronger than in England. I am told that an American lawyer who wishes to keep abreast of the current of judicial decision has to take in some fifty-eight volumes of Law Reports every year. In America, there is no choice between common law on the one hand and statute law on the other. Each state is independent in matters of legislation and judicature. The American lawyer, therefore, has to deal not with one but with forty streams of common law, each of which is liable to be disturbed by the action of an independent

Legislature. But Commerce knows nothing of State boundaries, and it seems intolerable that if a man in Chicago makes a contract with a man in New York, his rights and duties cannot be determined without an elaborate investigation into the conflict of laws. The only possible remedy that I can see for this state of affairs is codification."

At the time Chalmers spoke, the movement to codify particular branches of commercial law in the United States was already underway. In the 1890's the National Conference of Commissioners on Uniform State Laws had been formed, with representatives from each state many of whom were dedicated to the cause of uniform codification. In 1896, the Conference promulgated the Negotiable Instruments Law, a Code governing the rights and liabilities of parties to checks, promissory notes, and other kinds of commercial paper. Ultimately, the "NIL" was adopted by all state legislatures. In 1906, the Conference presented the Uniform Sales Act for adoption and more than two-thirds of the states enacted it. With this Act, American law professors entered the codification arena, and have been central figures there ever since. Professor Samuel Williston of the Harvard Law School drafted the Uniform Sales Act on behalf of the Conference, and also the Uniform Warehouse Receipts Act, promulgated in 1906, and the Uniform Bills of Lading Act promulgated in 1909 both of which became law in all states. Later, Professor Karl Llewellyn of the Columbia Law School drafted the Uniform Trust Receipts Act, which the Conference promulgated in 1933. Thirty-two states adopted it. Another uniform commercial act, dealing with "conditional" sales, was drafted by Professor Bogert, but it met with success in only ten state legislatures.

In 1940, the idea of a single comprehensive commercial code covering all the foregoing branches of commercial law was conceived and proposed to the Conference of Commissioners on Uniform State Laws. The foregoing uniform acts had become outdated in two ways: changes had occurred in the patterns of commercial activity extant when these laws were enacted, and wholly new patterns had emerged giving rise to new kinds of legal needs. Moreover, even with the Uniform Acts most widely enacted, uniformity no longer existed, for the various state legislatures and judiciaries had added their own distinctive amendments and glosses.

The American Law Institute joined with the National Conference of Commissioners to co-sponsor the "Uniform Commercial Code" project. Professor Karl Llewellyn, then still at Columbia Law School, became chief architect, and his wife, Ms. Soia Mentschikoff, his principal assistant (designated, respectively, "Chief Reporter" and "Associate Chief Reporter"). Ms. Mentschikoff described the drafting process, in Mentschikoff, *The Uniform Commercial Code: An Experiment in Democracy in Drafting,* 36 A.B.A.J. 419 (1950). The drafting process is also discussed extensively in a recent symposium to which five drafters contributed. See *Symposium, Origins and Evolution: Drafters Reflect Upon the Uniform Commercial Code,* 43 Ohio St.L.J. 537–642 (1982).

In 1951, the sponsors promulgated the Uniform Commercial Code, and, with minor revisions, it was enacted in Pennsylvania in 1953, effective July 1, 1954. Between 1953 and 1955, the New York Law Revision Commission dropped all other work and made a thorough study of the Code, recommending many changes in the official text. During the hearings there were, from time to time, rather sharp conflicts between academicians defending the Code and practitioners attacking it.

In 1956, the Editorial Board of the Code made recommendations for revision of the 1952 Official Text, many of which were based on criticisms made at the New York Law Revision Commission Hearings. In 1957 a revised Official Text was promulgated incorporating recommended changes. Further Official Texts, with minor changes, were promulgated in 1958 and 1962.

By 1968, the Uniform Commercial Code had been enacted by all but one state in the United States. A "Permanent Editorial Board" was established by the sponsoring organizations primarily to consider the wisdom of proposed amendments to the Code. (The idea for such a Board was set forth in Schlesinger, *The Uniform Commercial Code in the Light of Comparative Law,* 1 N.Y.Law Revision Commission 87 (1955). This Board has made various reports and prepared careful commentaries on disputed questions.

The Code's sponsors, the American Law Institute and the National Conference of Commissioners on Uniform State Laws (NCCUSL) have not left it alone. In 1972, the new "1972" Official Text of the Code was promulgated. That text left nearly all of the 1962 Official Text intact, except for secured transactions governed by Article 9. Article 9 was overhauled without altering its basic theory, structure and scope and, as of July, 1992, the revision was law in every state except Vermont. Next came the 1978 Official Text, which made major changes in Article 8, Investment Securities. Forty-six states have enacted revised Article 8.

Although there was a transition Official Text in 1987 and 1988, the 1990 Official Text contains the structure that will carry the Code into the twenty-first century. First, there is a new Article 2A, dealing with leases of goods. Second, Article 3, Negotiable Instruments, and Article 4, Bank Deposits and Collections, have been revised. Third, there is a new Article 4A, dealing with commercial funds transfers. Finally, NCCUSL has recommended that Article 6, Bulk Sales, be repealed and either not replaced or replaced with a revised Article 6. Moreover, every other Article is either under study or in the process of revision. In the next five years, *every* Article of the Code will have undergone a major revision since the 1962 Text. See Miller, *The Uniform Commercial Code: Will the Experiment Continue?,* 43 Mercer L.Rev. 799 (1992).

In addition to Article 1, General Provisions, the 1990 Official Text contains ten Articles dealing with substantive commercial law. Some brief remarks on each article are in order.

Article 2: Sales

Article 2, which replaced the Uniform Sales Act, deals primarily with the formation, adjustment, construction, performance and enforcement of contracts for the sale of goods. Article 2 rejects the concept of title as a problem solving device, but does define when title passes in contracts for the sale of goods. This definition is still important in disputes over when a seller can pass better title to a buyer than it has, see UCC 2–403, and in disputes outside of Article 2, such as the scope of insurance policies and the incidence of state and local personal property taxation.

A Drafting Committee has been appointed by NCCUSL to make appropriate revisions in Article 2, with a target completion date of August, 1995. One of your co-authors is Reporter for this project. A reprint and appraisal of the Preliminary Report on the revision of Article 2 is printed in 16 Delaware J. of Corp. Law 981–1325 (1991).

Article 2A: Leases

Article 2A covers all leases of goods, but is primarily concerned with equipment and finance leasing. The organization, similar to Article 2, contains five parts: General Provisions, Formation and Construction, Effect of Lease Contract, Performance, and Default. The differences from Article 2 arise where special principles are needed to deal with the transfer of a property interest for a limited period of time (the lease) as opposed to the transfer of ownership from a seller to a buyer (the sale). Note that a "true" lease, as defined in UCC 1–201(37), is neither a secured transaction nor a sale.

Article 3: Commercial Paper

Revised Article 3, as did its predecessor, deals with the negotiability, negotiation, rights and liabilities of the parties to, and the enforcement and discharge of commercial paper, including drafts, checks, certificates of deposit and notes. It does not apply to documents of title, Article 7, or investment securities, Article 8, even though they may be negotiable and negotiated for value. When issued, a negotiable note or check becomes the tangible and legal embodiment of the underlying obligation of the parties. Article 3 is designed to maximize the certainty and minimize the costs when that instrument is transferred.

Article 4: Bank Deposits and Collection

Revised Article 4 deals with checks and other demand instruments that are drawn on a bank and collected through the banking system. Covered are the contractual relationship between the drawer and the Payor Bank, the relationship between the payee and the Depositary Bank, and the relationship among the banks in the collection process, including the responsibilities of the Payor Bank when a check is presented for payment. Article 4 governs Article 3 to the extent that there are conflicts, but in many cases Article 3 supplements Article 4.

Article 4's viability as state law is open to question. For example, Federal Reserve Regulation J rather than Article 4 governs check collection relationships among federal reserve banks. Similarly, the Federal Expedited Funds Availability Act preempts Article 4 on questions of when deposited funds are available for withdrawal as a matter of right and Federal Reserve Regulation CC, subpart C, preempts most of Article 4 after a check presented for payment has been dishonored.

Article 4A: Funds Transfers

New Article 4A, first promulgated in the 1988 Official Text, governs commercial payment orders directing the transfer of funds from one bank account to another. It does not cover electronic transfers where consumers are involved. The transfer is initiated by a payment order issued by a customer to its bank and concluded when the beneficiary's bank accepts the payment order for the benefit of the beneficiary. The payment order is usually communicated over the Federal Reserve wire transfer network (Fedwire) or, in international transfers, the New York Clearing House Interbank Payments Systems (CHIPS). Money, however, is not transferred by wire. Once a payment order is accepted, bank accounts are adjusted and settlements are made under Federal Reserve regulations or other applicable agreements.

Article 5: Letters of Credit

In a typical letter of credit transaction, a bank, at the buyer's request, issues a "letter" to the seller, providing that the bank will, under certain conditions, honor drafts drawn by the seller on the buyer for payment of the purchase price. Article 5 governs this transaction and others, such as "standby" letters of credit, where a bank has agreed to pay if specified conditions are satisfied.

Article 5 is under revision. Once again, one of your co-authors is Reporter for that project.

Article 6: Bulk Sales

Article 6 deals with bulk transfers by a seller and, as such, emphasizes protection of the transferor's unsecured creditors. In light of strong criticism, NCCUSL has recommended that Article 6 be repealed and replaced, if at all, by a revised Article 6.

Article 7: Documents of Title

Article 7 applies both to warehouse receipts and bills of lading, two types of documents of title. These documents were formerly governed by the Uniform Warehouse Receipts Act and the Uniform Bills of Lading Act.

Article 8: Investment Securities

Article 8, often called the "negotiable instruments" law for investment securities, endows certain bonds, stocks and other securities with attributes of negotiability and defines the rights and liabilities of issuers, transferors, and transferees. It also controls the creation and perfection of security interests in investment securities. Article 8, however, does not supersede state or federal regulatory laws governing the issuance of securities.

The 1978 Official Text revised Article 8 to cover more explicitly uncertificated investment securities. It attempted to keep abreast of the new technology. A drafting committee is again at work on Article 8.

Article 9: Secured Transactions

Article 9 deals with the creation, perfection, priority and enforcement of security interests in personal property. It is the most innovative Article, in that it substitutes a unitary security device for the plethora of security devices previously in use. Terms such as "mortgagee," "pledgee," "conditional sale," and "trust receipt" do not appear in Article 9. Instead, its unitary security device is formulated in terms of four basic concepts: "secured party," "debtor," "collateral," and "security interest."

Article 9 was revised for the 1972 Official Text and the Permanent Editorial Board for the Uniform Commercial Code has issued a Report which has resulted in the appointment of another NCCUSL committee to revise Article 9. See Report, PEB Study Group, Uniform Commercial Code, Article 9 (Dec. 1, 1992).

The foregoing, then, represents the general structure of the Code and demonstrates that its scope is broad. Chronologically, the Code applies to transactions "entered into" after its effective date. See UCC 10–102(2). In terms of territorial application, it applies to transactions "bearing an appropriate relation" to the enacting state. In terms of subject-matter, it applies to a wide-range of transactions. There is not, in the Code, a single "scope" provision which defines the *subject-matter* to which the *entire* Code applies. Instead, the Code is divided into twelve "articles," ten of which purport to govern aspects of basic types of commercial transactions. The precise scope of each such article must usually be determined by examining not merely a specific "scope" provision within the article (if there be one) but other provisions as well, some of which are definitional in nature. The student should, at this point, become familiar with the basic "scope" provisions of Articles 9, 2, and 3.

There is no general "de-minimus" limitation on the Code's application. Thus, for example, Article 2 could apply to the sale of a fifteen-cent hamburger. See UCC 2–314.

While many of the articles of the Code can, in relation to some kinds of transactions, apply separately and alone, frequently provisions from more than one article will be applicable to the transaction at hand.

The Code recognizes the possibilities of conflict between Articles, and includes provisions governing such possibilities. See, e.g., UCC 2–102, 9–113, 3–102, 4–102(a), 8–102(1)(c), and 9–102.

SECTION 4. WHAT KIND OF A CODE IS THE UNIFORM COMMERCIAL CODE?

One of the Code drafters had this to say:

GILMORE, ARTICLE 9: WHAT IT DOES FOR THE PAST, 26 La.L.Rev. 285, 286 (1966).

"Surely the principal function of a Code is to abolish the past. At least a common lawyer assumes that that was the theory on which the great civil law codes were based. From the date of the Code's enactment, the pre-Code law is no longer available as a source of law. The gaps, the ambiguities, the unforeseen situations cannot be referred for decision to the accumulated wisdom of the past. There is a fresh start, a new universe of legal discourse, in which the only permissible way of solving a problem is to find (or pretend to find) the answer in the undefiled, the unconstrued, the uncontaminated text of the Code itself. How well the theory worked in practice, or whether it worked at all, you, as civilians, are much better equipped to say than I.

"The Uniform Commercial Code, so-called, is not that sort of Code—even in theory. It derives from the common law, not the civil law, tradition. We shall do better to think of it as a big statute—or a collection of statutes bound together in the same book—which goes as far as it goes and no further. It assumes the continuing existence of a large body of pre-Code and non-Code law on which it rests for support, which it displaces to the least possible extent, and without which it could not survive. The solid stuff of pre-Code law will furnish the rationale of decision quite as often as the Code's own gossamer substance."

A useful general discussion of the jurisprudence of the Uniform Commercial Code, primarily Article 2, appears in Danzig, *A Comment on the Jurisprudence of the Uniform Commercial Code,* 27 Stan.L.Rev. 621 (1975).

SECTION 5. THE SPECIAL PITFALLS IN USING THE UNIFORM COMMERCIAL CODE (AND SIMILAR CODES)

These pitfalls are numerous. First, the Code includes more than the usual quota of definitions. Consider, for example, the first *line* of UCC 2–205. How many of the fourteen words in that line are defined in other provisions of the Code? Where is "offer" defined? How is the researcher to know what words are defined and what ones are not? Are the "Definitional Cross References" in the Comments always exhaustive? They purport to be, but, as will be seen, they are not.

Once all defined terms have been looked up, it is still not possible to be sure that the Code answer has been found. It is essential that the researcher also check the bearing of any related provisions in the Code. The Code is an "integrated" and "interrelated" body of law. This poses a special pitfall, for it means that it often compels research beyond what seems on the surface to be the controlling provision. Check, for example, the bearing of UCC 2–508 and 2–609 on 2–601. How is one to know of such related provisions? There are "Cross References" in the Comments, but it should not be assumed that they are exhaustive.

The "legislative history" relevant to interpreting the Code is of several kinds, each posing its own special problems. The four types of such history are: (1) Official Comments, (2) Prior versions of the Code, (3) Legislative hearings and reports made prior to enactment in specific states, and (4) Books and articles by Code draftsmen. See generally, Braucher, *Legislative History of the Uniform Commercial Code,* 58 Colum.L.Rev. 798 (1958). An extensive treatment of the major research sources on the Uniform Commercial Code is Kavass, *Uniform Commercial Code Research: A Brief Guide to the Sources,* 88 Commercial L.J. 547 (1983). See also, Kelly, *Uniform Commercial Code Drafts* (1984), Vols. I & II.

As promulgated by the American Law Institute and the Conference of Commissioners on Uniform State Laws, the Official Text of the Code appears with comments on each section. As enacted by state legislators, however, only the Official Text (with whatever amendments were made) appears on the statute books. In many states the Code with comments (and local annotations) is available to the bar through private publishing houses. A lawyer must, however, bear in mind that the Official Comments are not authoritative and further that they do not cover a state's changes in the Official Text.

The Comment to each section usually contains five parts. In the first, entitled "Prior Uniform Statutory Provisions," there appears a list of references to provisions of prior Uniform Acts displaced by the section. In the second part, designated "Changes," the difference, if any, between the superseded law and the Official Text are indicated in a general way. In the third part of the Comments, called "Purposes of Changes" or "Purposes of Changes and New Matter," the purposes of the particular Official Text Code section are explained, and, in some instances, illustrated. In the fourth part, "Cross References," there is a list of related Code provisions. In the last part there appears a list of definitional cross references.

It should not be assumed that for purposes of interpretation and construction, the Official Comments stand in the same relation to the Official Text as true legislative history typically stands to the language of ordinary statutes. The Comments, or some of them, differ from such history in several ways. They were not always laid before the enacting legislators at the time of Code adoption. Some of the present Comments were not even in existence when the sections commented on were enacted into law in some states. Some of the existing Comments appear to have been addressed to earlier drafts of sections of the Code different from the later sections enacted into law. In some important parts of the Code, the draftsman of the Comments was not the draftsman of the section commented on. See generally Skilton, *Some Comments on the Comments to the Uniform Commercial Code,* 1966 Wis.L.Rev. 597.

Still, the Comments have influenced many judicial decisions and will certainly continue to do so. That they are not entitled to exactly the same weight as true legislative history may, therefore, be unimportant. But it is important to appreciate the special hazards and pitfalls in the use of the Comments. A detailed appreciation of these must await immersion in the processes of problem solving that lie ahead in this book. For now, a general survey of the most common hazards and pitfalls must do.

Perhaps the principal hazard in using the Comments (apart from the inexhaustiveness of their cross references) is that they not uncommonly add to or vary the Code language. Some insight into why this is so is revealed in the following passage from a speech made by the chief draftsman of the Code, Karl N. Llewellyn:

LLEWELLYN, WHY A COMMERCIAL CODE? 22 Tenn.L.Rev. 779, 784, 794, 782 (1953).

"I am ashamed of it in some ways; there are so many places that I could make a little better, there are so many beautiful ideas I tried to get in that would have been good for the law, but I was voted down * * * when we weren't allowed to put in where we wanted to go * * *, we at least got the thing set up so that we are allowed to state in accompanying comments where the particular sections are trying to go."

The Comments are both expansive and restrictive in nature. Their expansiveness frequently takes the form of explicit rejection of negative implications from the text of the section. In view of such Comments, the maxim *expressio unius exclusio alterius est* (the expression of one thing is the exclusion of the other) loses some of its force. (See, for an example, the Comments to UCC 2–318.) On the restrictiveness of Comments, it has been remarked that, "it would not be difficult to cite examples where the draftsman has wisely left a breathing space, so to say, in the text to allow a free case-law development and then come back to the comment to nail the coffin lid down tightly." Gilmore, *On the Difficulties of Codifying Commercial Law,* 57 Yale L.J. 1341, 1355 (1948). Of course, if the Comments are not *law* then perhaps the lid is not so tight as all that.

It has been said that the definitional and sectional "cross references" in the Comments cannot be relied on as exhaustive. As an example, note that the definitional cross references to UCC 2–316 fail to mention the crucial fact that "conspicuous" is defined in UCC 1–201(10). And there are still other sources of frustration. Comments often blithely assume that the reader is familiar with the details of prior law. Some Comments deal with sections other than the one they are addressed to. (See, e.g., Comment 2 to UCC 2–312 dealing with UCC 2–607). Comments vary greatly in quality. Some are overly long, others not long enough. Some offer insight. Some confuse.

We turn, now, to earlier versions of the Code as a distinctive source of guidance and misguidance in resolving problems of interpretation and construction. The lawyer should know of the existence of such earlier drafts. The main prior drafts are:

1945 Drafts and Redrafts of Parts of the Proposed Code (Unpublished).
1949 Proposed Draft with Comments.
1950 Proposed Final Draft with Comments.
1951 Final Text with Comments.
Amendments in May, 1951.
Amendments in September, 1951.
1952 Official Text with Comments.
1953 Changes Recommended by a Meeting of the Enlarged Editorial Board. Part A, Part B.
1956 Recommendations of the Editorial Board.
1957 Official Text with Comments.
Supplement to the 1957 Official Edition of the Code.
1958 Official Text with Comments.
1962 Amendments to the Uniform Commercial Code, Permanent Editorial Board for the U.C.C., Report 1.
1962 Official Text with Comments.
1965 Report No. 2 of the Permanent Editorial Board for the Uniform Commercial Code.
1966 Report No. 3 of the Permanent Editorial Board for the Uniform Commercial Code.
1971 Review Committee for Article Nine, Final Report.
1972 Official Text with Comments.
1978 Official Text with Comments.
1987 Official Text with Comments.
1988 Official Text with Comments.
1990 Official Text with Comments.

Inferences based on changes in the language of successive revisions of Code sections are inherently unreliable. They are all the more unreliable because "frequently matters have been omitted as being implicit without statement and language has been changed or added solely for clarity." This quote comes from the comment to a section in the 1952 text of the Code which read: "Prior drafts of text and comments may not be used to ascertain legislative intent." This section itself was eventually deleted from the Official Text of the Code. It should have been left in. It will have to be left to the Supreme Court of the United States to rule out the use of prior versions of sections and comments as an unconstitutional form of cruel and inhuman punishment of fellow lawyers. Or perhaps the decisive argument will be that because of their scarcity (only a few libraries have them) their use denies equal protection of the laws.

Another basic type of material that is of relevance in resolving problems of Code interpretation and construction consists of legislative hearings and official reports made by agencies of enacting states. These form the more immediate background of Code enactment. Their status is somewhat uncertain in regard to the Code, for it includes its own "legislative" history in the form of comments. In the face of conflict, which is to control? And there are other problems.

A further type of material that has figured in Code interpretation and construction consists of books and articles and memoranda written by persons who participated in the drafting of the Code. The outstanding instance to appear to date is a two volume treatise: Gilmore, Security Interests in Personal Property (1965). In a footnote at p. 289 of the first volume of this treatise, Professor Gilmore confesses that he had a large hand in the drafting of Article 9 of the Code. And his treatise has been justly acclaimed in reviews.

John Locke might have said that Professor Gilmore's treatise has a natural and inalienable right to be quoted and cited on any and all Article 9 problems. Actually such is not without parallel. After the Uniform Sales Act, promulgated in 1906, was widely enacted, its draftsman, Professor Samuel Williston, published a treatise, *Williston on Sales,* which explained what the Act was all about. It would startle no one to find that Williston's treatise influenced the law. Similarly, Gilmore's has influenced the law.

An exceptionally fine article on methods of interpreting the Uniform Commercial Code is: McDonnell, *Purposive Interpretation of the Uniform Commercial Code: Some Implications for Jurisprudence,* 126 U.Pa.L.Rev. 795 (1978). See also, Gedid, *U.C.C. Methodology: Taking a Realistic Look at the Code,* 29 Wm. & Mary L.Rev. 341 (1988). Modesty forbids two of us from calling undue attention to another book that lawyers and judges regularly resort to: J. White and R. Summers, The Uniform Commercial Code (3d ed. 1988). In moments of levity we will refer to it as the "Crutch." Otherwise, it is known as "White and Summers."

SECTION 6. COMMERCIAL LAW NOT IN THE UNIFORM COMMERCIAL CODE

Despite its seemingly wide sweep, the Code is far from comprehensive. There are some transactions it does not govern at all, and there are many aspects of many transactions to which its provisions might apply but will not, for various reasons.

First and at the fore, the parties can generally make their own "law." As one authority has put it, "We are within that area of law where—to use an old-fashioned, pre-positivistic phrase—businessmen are free to make their own law. They do so expressly through contract, implicitly through a course of dealing, collectively through custom and resultant business understanding." By their own agreement, then, the parties to a commercial deal can vary most of the provisions of the Code.

Second, the Code itself, by its own terms, does not purport to control many important types of transactions that can fairly be called commercial. For example, it does not apply to sales of commercial realty nor to security interests therein. It does not apply to the formation, performance, and enforcement of insurance contracts. It does not apply to suretyship transactions (except where a surety is a party to a negotiable instrument). It does not encompass the law of bankruptcy. It does not govern legal tender.

Third, the Code does not even purport to govern exhaustively all aspects of all transactions to which its provisions do apply. Many of its provisions obviously can come into play only by virtue of some key event, e.g., "default," which may be defined by the terms of the agreement between the parties. See, e.g., UCC 9–501(1). Furthermore, resort to supplemental principles of law outside the Code will often be necessary. See generally, UCC 1–103. Consider the following three examples. To apply the provisions on authorized and unauthorized signatures in Article 3 (UCC 3–402 and 3–403), local agency principles must be considered. To determine what title a "transferor" has under UCC 2–403, it is essential to refer to non-Code law. The "grounds" of impossibility and frustration as a defense to the breach of a contract of sale are not exhaustively stated in the Code. See UCC 2–613, 2–614, and 2–615. Presumably additional grounds recognized in "general contract law" can be invoked. In addition, the Code has its own "gaps"—situations arising within the framework of the Code on specific aspects of which the Code is altogether silent.

Fourth, there are state statutes, most of which are regulatory in nature, which either supplement or supersede Code provisions altogether. See, e.g., UCC 2–102, 9–201, and 9–203(4) for references to the possible existence of such statutes. Usury laws and so-called "Retail Installment Sales Acts" are outstanding examples. It is appropriate at this point to emphasize that the Code does *not,* in terms, concern itself with the general problems of the *consumer* as consumer.

Fifth, the Uniform Commercial Code is *state* law. This means that any valid and conflicting federal commercial law supersedes it. Thus, for example, there are the Federal Consumer Protection Act and the Magnuson-Moss Warranty Act. The Federal Bills of Lading Act (sometimes called the Pomerene Act) 49 U.S.C.A. §§ 81–124, rather than Article 7 of the Code, applies to all interstate bills of lading transactions. In addition, one must consider the preemptive effect of the Convention on the International Sale of Goods (CISG), effective in the United States on January 1, 1988, and the Expedited Funds Availability Act, 12 U.S.C.A. §§ 4001–4010 implementing Federal Regulation CC.

Sixth, there is a growing body of federal regulatory law that supplements commercial law at many points. For example, the federal Food and Drug Act imposes controls on the quality of goods sold and on the ways they are marketed. The Robinson-Patman Act operates to regulate the price of some goods. Federal statutes govern the creation of security interests in some types of collateral. See, e.g., the Ship Mortgage Act, 1920, referred to in UCC 9–104 Comment 1.

Seventh, this survey of non-Code sources of commercial law would not be complete without some reference to procedural law. Generally, commercial claims are litigated in accordance with the procedures applicable in any ordinary case. There are, however, a few procedural doctrines that have a distinctively commercial flavor. Some of these are incorporated in the Code, although it generally does not purport to cover procedural law. See, e.g., the "vouching in" provisions of UCC 2–607(5).

Finally, there are practices and attitudes of legal officials and of men of commerce which cannot really be captured in the language of any Code but which, nonetheless, have an inevitable impact on legal evolution. Professor Edwin W. Patterson has said of these that they seem "to be a part of the societal matrix, a kind of semantic and narrative substratum of law and other articulate forms of social control." 1 N.Y. Law Revision Commission Report 56 (1955) (footnote omitted).

SECTION 7. THE SCOPE OF ARTICLE 1: AN EXERCISE IN CODE METHODOLOGY

Prior to the 1990 Official Text, there was a genuine controversy over the scope and effect of UCC 1–207, a provision in Article 1. The issue concerned the extent to which UCC 1–207 displaced the common law doctrine of accord and satisfaction. Also involved was the scope of Article 1 in general and the methodology necessary to achieve a sound interpretation.

We have reprinted edited versions of two courts in disagreement on the issues and some relevant commentary by Professor Bruce Frier. After you have read this material, please consult UCC 1–207 and UCC 3–311 in the 1990 Official Text to see how the issue was resolved.

HORN WATERPROOFING CORP. v. BUSHWICK IRON & STEEL CO.

Court of Appeals of New York, 1985.
66 N.Y.2d 321, 497 N.Y.S.2d 310, 488 N.E.2d 56.

JASEN, JUDGE.

This appeal presents an issue of first impression: whether the common-law doctrine of accord and satisfaction has been superseded by operation of Uniform Commercial Code § 1–207 in situations involving the tender of a negotiable instrument as full payment of a disputed claim.

The relevant facts are uncomplicated. The parties entered into an oral agreement whereby plaintiff was to repair the leaking roof on defendant's building. After two days work, plaintiff concluded that a new roof was needed and submitted a bill for work already done. Defendant disputed the amount charged and plaintiff revised the bill downward from $1,241 to $1,080. Defendant remained unsatisfied with the charges and sent plaintiff a check for only $500. The check bore the following notation affixed on the reverse side: "This check is accepted in full payment, settlement, satisfaction, release and discharge of any and all claims and/or demands of whatsoever kind and nature." Directly thereunder, plaintiff printed the words "Under Protest", indorsed the check with its stamp, and deposited the $500 into its account.

Plaintiff then commenced this action in Civil Court seeking $580 as the balance due on its revised bill. Defendant moved for summary judgment on the ground that plaintiff's acceptance and negotiation of the check constituted an accord and satisfaction. The motion was denied and the Appellate Term affirmed. The court held that the Uniform Commercial Code (the Code) was applicable to the type of commercial transaction in which the parties were involved and that, under the provisions of section 1–207, plaintiff was entitled to reserve its right to demand the balance due.

On appeal by leave of the Appellate Term, the Appellate Division, 105 A.D.2d 684, 481 N.Y.S.2d 125, reversed, granted defendant's motion, and dismissed the complaint. The majority of that court held that the parties' agreement, being a contract for the performance of services, fell outside the scope of the Code. It was, therefore, concluded that the common law applied and that the doctrine of accord and satisfaction precluded plaintiff's recovery. In dissent, Justice Weinstein argued that application of the common-law doctrine to the facts of this case is inequitable and needlessly constricts the modernizing effect of the Code. We now reverse and hold that, under section 1–207 of the Code, a creditor may preserve his right to the balance of a disputed claim, by explicit reservation in his indorsement of a check tendered by the debtor as full payment.

The effect of Code § 1–207 upon the common-law doctrine of accord and satisfaction has been much debated.[1] Indeed, the courts that have addressed the issue in this State have rendered conflicting decisions,[2] and our sister

1. Among the commentaries which have taken an unequivocal position on the issue, *see, e.g.,* 1 Anderson, Uniform Commercial Code § 1-207:7; 4 Anderson §§ 3-408:54—3-408:57 (3d ed.) (the majority and sounder rule is that it does not apply to the full payment check); Calamari and Perillo, Contracts §§ 4–12, 5–16 (the debtor may now accept the check under protest and reserve his rights); 6 Corbin, Contracts § 1279 (2d ed., 1984 Supp.) (the common-law doctrine is not affected); Restatement (Second) of Contracts § 281 comment d (§ 1–207 "need not be read as changing" the common law); White and Summers, Uniform Commercial Code § 13–21 (2d ed.) (§ 1–207 permits a debtor to accept with explicit protest and still claim the balance due him). See also the discussions in the following: Hawkland, *The Effect of UCC § 1–207 on the Doctrine of Accord and Satisfaction by Conditional Check,* 74 Comm.L.J. 329; Rosenthal, *Discord and Dissatisfaction: Section 1–207 of the Uniform Commercial Code,* 78 Colum.L.Rev. 48; Caraballo, *The Tender Trap: UCC § 1–207,* 11 Seton Hall L.Rev. 445; Grosse and Goggin, Accord and Satisfaction and the 1–207 Dilemma, 89 Comm.L.J. 537; Comment, *UCC Section 1–207 and the Full Payment Check,* 7 U.Dayton L.Rev. 421; Comment, *Section 1–207,* 1 Mem.St.U.L.Rev. 425; Comment, *Accord and Satisfaction: Conditional Tender by Check Under the Uniform Commercial Code,* 18 Buffalo L.Rev. 539; Note, *Does UCC Section 1–207 Apply to the Doctrine of Accord and Satisfaction by Conditional Check?,* 11 Creighton L.Rev. 515.

2. In the following, the courts of this State held that section 1–207 has superseded the common-law doctrine of accord and satisfaction in the "full payment" or "conditional" check situation: *Braun v. C.E.P.C. Distribs.,* 77 A.D.2d 358, 433 N.Y.S.2d 447 (1st Dept.); *Continental Information Sys. v. Mutual Life Ins. Co.,* 77 A.D.2d 316, 432 N.Y.S.2d 952 (4th Dept.); *Ayer v. Sky Club,*

state courts are likewise divided.[3] In our view, applying section 1–207 to a "full payment" check situation, to permit a creditor to reserve his rights and, thereby, preclude an accord and satisfaction, more nearly comports with the content and context of the statutory provision and with the legislative history and underlying purposes of the Code as well, and is a fairer policy in debtor-creditor transactions.

It has long been the general rule in this State that "if a debt or claim be disputed or contingent at the time of payment, the payment, when accepted, of a part of the whole debt is a good satisfaction and it matters not that there was no solid foundation for the dispute. The test in such cases is, Was the dispute honest or fraudulent? If honest, it affords the basis for an accord between the parties, which the law favors, the execution of which is the satisfaction." (*Simons v. American Legion of Honor,* 178 N.Y. 263, 265, 70 N.E. 776; *see also, Nassoiy v. Tomlinson,* 148 N.Y. 326, 42 N.E. 715.)

The theory underlying this common-law rule of accord and satisfaction is that the parties have thus entered into a new contract displacing all or part of their original one. (*Merrill Lynch Realty v. Skinner,* 63 N.Y.2d 590, 596, 483 N.Y.S.2d 979, 473 N.E.2d 229.) Although the creditor might have been confronted with an "embarrassing * * * choice" upon the debtor's presentment to him of partial payment (*Hudson v. Yonkers Fruit Co.,* 258 N.Y. 168, 172, 179 N.E. 373), such as in the case of a "full payment" or "conditional" check, nevertheless, the rule of accord and satisfaction has generally been accepted as a legitimate and expeditious means of settling contract disputes. (*See, Merrill Lynch Realty v. Skinner, supra; Post v. Thomas,* 212 N.Y. 264, 106 N.E. 69; 6 Corbin, Contracts § 1276 *et seq.* [2d ed.]; Restatement [Second] of Contracts § 281.) As this court stated more

70 A.D.2d 863, 418 N.Y.S.2d 57 (1st Dept.), *appeal dismissed* 48 N.Y.2d 705, 422 N.Y.S.2d 68, 397 N.E.2d 758; *Kroulee Corp. v. Klein & Co.,* 103 Misc.2d 441, 426 N.Y.S.2d 206; *Lange–Finn Constr. Co. v. Albany Steel & Iron Supply Co.,* 94 Misc.2d 15, 403 N.Y.S.2d 1012; *Cohen v. Ricci,* 120 Misc.2d 712, 466 N.Y.S.2d 121; *Hanna v. Perkins* (2 UCC Rep.Serv. 1044). Some courts in this State have ruled otherwise: *Geelan Mechanical Corp. v. Dember Constr. Corp.,* 97 A.D.2d 810, 468 N.Y.S.2d 680 (2d Dept.); *Schenectady Steel Co. v. Trimpoli Gen. Constr. Co.,* 43 A.D.2d 234, 350 N.Y.S.2d 920 (3d Dept.), *affd. on other grounds* 34 N.Y.2d 939, 359 N.Y.S.2d 560, 316 N.E.2d 875; *Channave v. Kraal,* 120 Misc.2d 859, 466 N.Y.S.2d 916; *Blottner, Derrico, Weiss & Hoffman v. Fier,* 101 Misc.2d 371, 420 N.Y.S.2d 999.

3. In the following cases, the courts adopted the view that section 1–207 has altered the doctrine of accord and satisfaction by permitting the creditor to reserve his rights: *United States v. Consolidated Edison Co.,* 590 F.Supp. 266 (S.D.N.Y.); *Majestic Bldg. Material Corp. v. Gateway Plumbing,* 694 S.W.2d 762 (Mo.Ct.App.); *Bivens v. White Dairy,* 378 So.2d 1122 (Ala.Civ.App.); *Miller v. Jung,* 361 So.2d 788 (Fla.Ct.App.); *Kilander v. Blickle Co.,* 280 Or. 425, 571 P.2d 503; *Scholl v. Tallman,* 247 N.W.2d 490 (S.D.); *Baillie Lbr. Co. v. Kincaid Carolina Corp.,* 4 N.C.App. 342, 167 S.E.2d 85).

On the other hand, an admittedly greater number of jurisdictions have held that the common-law rule is not affected: *Milgram Food Stores v. Gelco Corp.,* 550 F.Supp. 992 (W.D.Mo.); *Stultz Elec. Works v. Marine Hydraulic Eng. Co.,* 484 A.2d 1008 (Me.); *Flambeau Prods. Corp. v. Honeywell Information Sys.,* 116 Wis.2d 95, 341 N.W.2d 655; *Air Van Lines v. Buster,* 673 P.2d 774 (Alaska); *Schwab Tire Centers v. Ivory Ranch,* 63 Or. App. 364, 664 P.2d 419 (distinguishing *Kilander v. Blickle Co., supra*); *Connecticut Printers v. Gus Kroesen,* 134 Cal.App.3d 54, 184 Cal.Rptr. 436; *Eder v. Gervey Interiors,* 407 So.2d 312 (Fla.Ct.App.) (noting a conflict with *Miller v. Jung, supra*); *American Food Purveyors v. Lindsay Meats,* 153 Ga.App. 383, 265 S.E.2d 325; *Chancellor, Inc. v. Hamilton Appliance Co.,* 175 N.J.Super. 345, 418 A.2d 1326; *Sharpe v. Nationwide Mut. Fire Ins. Co.,* 62 N.C.App. 564, 302 S.E.2d 893; *Brown v. Coastal Truckways,* 44 N.C.App. 454, 261 S.E.2d 266 (distinguishing *Baillie Lbr. Co. v. Kinkaid Carolina Corp., supra*); *State Dept. of Fisheries v. J–Z Sales Corp.,* 25 Wash.App. 671, 610 P.2d 390; *Jahn v. Burns,* 593 P.2d 828 (Wyo.).

than 70 years ago: "The law wisely favors settlements, and where there is a real and genuine contest between the parties and a settlement is had without fraud or misrepresentation for an amount determined upon as a compromise between the conflicting claims such settlement should be upheld, although such amount is materially less than the amount claimed by the person to whom it is paid." (*Post v. Thomas, supra,* at pp. 273, 274, 106 N.E. 264.)

Still, where the creditor is presented with partial payment as satisfaction in full, but, nevertheless, wishes to preserve his claim to the balance left unpaid, it cannot be gainsaid that conflicting considerations of policy and fairness are implicated. This is particularly so in the case of a full payment check. On the one hand, the debtor, as the master of his offer, has reason to expect that his offer will either be accepted or his check returned. At the same time, however, the creditor has good cause to believe that he is fully entitled to retain the partial payment that is rightfully his and presently in his possession, without having to forfeit entitlement to whatever else is his due.

In dismissing these latter considerations with specific regard to the applicability of Code § 1–207 to a check tendered as "full payment", one commentary argued that: "Besides operating as an unnecessary destruction of a valuable common law doctrine, the expansive interpretation of U.C.C. § 1–207 * * * conflicts with another basic principle of the Uniform Commercial Code, the duty of good faith imposed by § 1–203, certainly the more fundamental concept * * * It is unfair to the party who writes the check thinking that he will be spending his money only if the whole dispute will be over, to allow the other party, knowing of that reasonable expectation, to weasel around the deal by putting his own markings on the other person's checks. There is no reason why § 1–207 should be interpreted as being an exception to the basic duty of good faith, when it is possible to interpret the two sections consistently. The academic writers who support this result offer no analysis, to the current knowledge of this treatise, which would justify licensing the recipient of the check to so deceive the drawer." (Corbin, Contracts § 1279, at 473 [Kaufman Supp., 1984].)

However, an entirely different conclusion is reached in another commentary which explains that:

"Offering a check for less than the contract amount, but 'in full settlement' inflicts an exquisite form of commercial torture on the payee. If the offer is reasonable it creates a marvelous anxiety in some recipients: 'Shall I risk the loss of $9,000 for the additional $1,000 that the bloke really owes me?' In general the law has authorized such drawer behavior by regarding such a check as an offer of accord and satisfaction which the payee accepts if he cashes the check. Traditionally the payee could write all manner of disclaimers over his indorsement without avail; by cashing the check he was held to have accepted the offer on the drawer's terms. Even if he scratched out the drawer's notation or indorsed it under protest he was deemed to have accepted subject to the conditions under which the drawer offered it.

* * *

"However, we believe * * * that 1–207 authorizes the payee to indorse under protest and accept the amount of the check without entering an accord and satisfaction or otherwise forsaking his claim to any additional sum allegedly due him." (White and Summers, Uniform Commercial Code § 13–21, at 544–547 [2d ed.].)

We concur with the latter view. Indeed, the common-law doctrine of accord and satisfaction creates a cruel dilemma for the good-faith creditor in possession of a full payment check. Under that rule, the creditor would have no other choice but to surrender the partial payment or forfeit his right to the remainder. (*See generally,* Note, *Role of the Check in Accord and Satisfaction: Weapon of the Overreaching Debtor,* 97 U.Pa.L.Rev. 99.) We are persuaded, however, that the common law was changed with the adoption of section 1–207 pursuant to which a fairer rule now prevails.

Section 1–207 provides: "A party who with explicit reservation of rights performs or promises performance or assents to performance in a manner demanded or offered by the other party does not thereby prejudice the rights reserved. Such words as 'without prejudice', 'under protest' or the like are sufficient." The plain language of the provision, "without much stretching",[4] would seem applicable to a full payment check.[5] A fortiori, if liberally construed, as the Code's provisions are explicitly intended to be,[6] it seems clear that the reach of section 1–207 is sufficiently extensive to alter the doctrine of accord and satisfaction by permitting a creditor to reserve his rights though accepting the debtor's check.

The Comment prepared by the National Conference of Commissioners on Uniform State Laws and the American Law Institute is fairly subject to a variety of interpretations as to the purpose of section 1–207. It simply does not, however, specifically address the law of accord and satisfaction and how it might have been altered.[7] By contrast, the Report of the State of New

4. Rosenthal, *supra,* n. 1, at 49.

5. *See, id.,* at 49, 64; Hawkland, *supra,* n. 1, at 329, 332. Despite the view shared by Rosenthal and Hawkland that section 1–207 was not intended by the drafters to alter the common-law doctrine in a full payment check situation, they each acknowledge that, if literally construed, the provision does permit such a result. *See also,* Calamari and Perillo, *supra,* n. 1 § 5–16, at 197; White and Summers, *supra,* n. 1 § 13–21, at 547.

6. U.C.C. § 1–102 provides in part:

"(1) This Act shall be liberally construed and applied to promote its underlying purposes and policies.

"(2) Underlying purposes and policies of this Act are

"(a) to simplify, clarify and modernize the law governing commercial transactions;

"(b) to permit the continued expansion of commercial practices through custom, usage and agreement of the parties;

"(c) to make uniform the law among the various jurisdictions."

See also, A.M. Knitwear Corp. v. All Am. Export–Import Corp., 41 N.Y.2d 14, 390 N.Y.S.2d 832, 359 N.E.2d 342; *Agar v. Orda,* 264 N.Y. 248, 190 N.E. 479; Comment to UCC 1–102, McKinney's Cons Laws of N.Y., Book 62½, p. 5; New York Anns. to UCC 1–102, McKinney's Cons Laws of N.Y., Book 62½, p. 7; McDonnel, *Purposive Interpretation of the Uniform Commercial Code: Some Implications for Jurisprudence,* 126 U.Pa. L.Rev. 795, 824–828.

7. The Official Comment to section 1–207 states in pertinent part: "This section provides machinery for the continuation of performance along the lines contemplated by the contract despite a pending dispute, by adopting the mercantile device of going ahead with delivery, acceptance, or payment 'without prejudice', 'under protest', 'under reserve', 'with reservation of all our rights', and the like. All of these phrases completely reserve all rights within the meaning of this section. The section therefore contemplates that limited as well as general reservations and acceptance by a party may be made 'subject to satisfaction of our purchaser', 'subject to acceptance by our customers',

York Commission on Uniform State Laws quite clearly took the position that the common-law doctrine would be changed. With specific reference to section 1–207, the report stated:

"This section permits a party involved in a Code-covered transaction to accept whatever he can get by way of payment, performance, etc., without losing his rights to demand the remainder of the goods, to set-off a failure of quality, or to sue for the balance of the payment, so long as he explicitly reserves his rights.

"* * * In *Nassoiy v. Tomlinson,* 148 N.Y. 326, 42 N.E. 715 (1896), the debtor paid no more than the exact amount he claimed was due. The court held that the conditional payment was payment of an unliquidated claim if any part was disputed, and that the acceptance of the payment discharged the entire debt. [Citations omitted.] The Code rule would permit, in Code-covered transactions, the acceptance of a part performance or payment tendered in full settlement without requiring the acceptor to gamble with his legal right to demand the balance of the performance or payment." (Report of Commn. on Uniform State Laws to Legislature, at 19–20 [1961].)[8]

This interpretive analysis, which was submitted to the Legislature together with the Commission's recommendation for enactment of the Code, unmistakably addresses the common-law doctrine and notes that the section permits a reservation of rights upon acceptance of partial payment where an accord and satisfaction might otherwise have resulted. Particularly significant is the reference to *Nassoiy v. Tomlinson,* 148 N.Y. 326, 42 N.E. 715, *supra,* a seminal decision in this State applying the doctrine of accord and satisfaction under facts involving a full payment check. This commentary clearly apprised the Legislature that section 1–207 would change the rule upheld in that case. Moreover, it is notable that the analysis explicitly speaks of the acceptance of part "*payment* tendered in full settlement." The section was clearly not deemed restricted to situations involving the acceptance of goods or such other "performance" in part.[9]

or the like." (As quoted in Official Comment, U.C.C. 1-207, McKinney's Cons. Laws of N.Y., Book 62½, p. 64 [1964].) Hawkland suggests that section 1-207 permits a party to proceed with the "contemplated performance of the original contract" without fear of a waiver. (Hawkland, *supra,* n. 1, at 331.) Rosenthal takes issue with Hawkland and contends that the provision was only intended to apply where one party's acquiescence in the other's performance or demand might, *"by operation of law",* effectuate a waiver or other prejudicing of his rights. (Rosenthal, *supra,* n. 1, at 63; *see also,* Corbin, *supra,* n. 1.)

8. This comment, together with all the section by section comments prepared by Professors William E. Hogan and Norman Penney, was submitted to the Legislature as part of the Commission's Report, prepared pursuant to Executive Law § 165, and subsequently has served as part of the "New York Annotations" to the Consolidated Laws of New York. (*See,* New York Anns, McKinney's Cons. Laws of N.Y., Book 62½, U.C.C. 1-207, p. 65 [1964].)

9. The commentators and the courts of other jurisdictions agree that the New York Annotations are quite expansive and do deal with the full payment check situation. (*See, e.g.,* Hawkland, *supra,* n. 1, at 332; Rosenthal, *supra,* n. 1, at 61–62; *Flambeau Prods. v. Honeywell Information Sys.,* 116 Wis.2d 95, 341 N.W.2d 655, 661–662; *Chancellor, Inc. v. Hamilton Appliance Co.,* 175 N.J.Super. 345, 418 A.2d 1326, 1328.) Moreover, as noted by Rosenthal, "[i]n view of the importance of New York's adoption of the Code to the national decision to do so, as well as the especially intensive study of the Code by that state's Law Revision Commission before enactment, interpretative clues derived from the New York experience may be of particularly great weight." (Rosenthal, *supra,* n. 1, at 62; *see also, Flambeau Prods. v. Honeywell Information Sys., supra,* 341 N.W.2d at p. 662.)

This view derives further support from the very context of section 1–207 within the Code. The provision is set forth in the introductory article 1, among the general provisions of the Code dealing with such matters as its title, underlying purposes, general definitions, and principles of interpretation. Presumably, section 1–207, as with other provisions in the introductory article, is to apply to any commercial transaction within the reach of one of the substantive articles—i.e., to any "Code-covered" transaction, as denominated in the New York Annotations. There is simply no language in section 1–207 expressing or intimating a more restrictive intention to limit its application to specific kinds of transactions particular to one of the articles, or sections, of the Code such as the purchase and acceptance of goods (art. 2), investment securities (art. 8) or chattel paper (art. 9). Rather, the nonlimiting language of section 1–207 and its placement in the Code with the other generally applicable provisions of article 1 is persuasive that the section is, indeed, applicable to all commercial transactions fairly considered to be "Code-covered".

Hence, the payment of a contract debt by check or other commercial paper and its acceptance by the creditor fall within the reach of section 1–207. Whether the underlying contract between the parties be for the purchase of goods, chattel paper or personal services, the use of a negotiable instrument for the purpose of payment or attempted satisfaction of a contract debt is explicitly and specifically regulated by the provisions of article 3 and, therefore, undeniably a Code-covered transaction. Consequently, a debtor's tender of a full payment check is an article 3 transaction which is governed by section 1–207, regardless of the nature of the contract underlying the parties' commercial relationship.

Indeed, Dean Rosenthal, who otherwise contended that section 1–207 was not originally intended by the drafters to alter the doctrine of accord and satisfaction by full payment checks, observed that:

"Article three ('Commercial Paper'), however, is a special case. Does the fact that a check is used as the device to effect a settlement in itself bring the transaction within the Code (and therefore make section 1–207 arguably applicable) even if the underlying transaction was one not otherwise covered by the Code? Article three contains no scope provision analogous to the 'transactions in goods' language in [article 2].

* * *

"[I]t seems fairly clear that if such a check is tendered in settlement, the transaction must be regarded as being within article three, and if section 1–207 is otherwise relevant its application cannot be avoided by showing either that article one was not meant to be applied to non-Code transactions or that the underlying obligation did not arise out of one of the other substantive articles of the Code." (Rosenthal, *Discord and Dissatisfaction: Section 1–207 of the Uniform Commercial Code,* 78 Colum.L.Rev. 48, 70.) [10]

10. With regard to article 3, it is also notable that a proposed subdivision three to section 3–802, specifically giving accord and satisfaction effect to a negotiated full payment check, was ultimately deleted from the Code prior to its adoption. The proposed provision in the May 1949 Official Draft stated: "Where an instrument by its terms provides that it is taken in full satisfaction of an obligation the payee by obtaining payment of the instrument or by negotiating it discharges the obligation unless he establish-

Finally, as Justice Weinstein noted below, such a reading of section 1–207 would seem to promote the underlying policies and purposes of the Code. (*See,* Code § 1–102, *supra,* n. 6.) By construing the section to permit a reservation of rights wherever a negotiable instrument is used to make payment on an existing debt, regardless of the nature of the underlying obligation between the parties, the commercial law of negotiable instruments is rendered more simple, clear and uniform. Moreover, the policy embodied in section 1–207, to favor a preservation of rights despite acceptance of partial satisfaction of the underlying obligation, is thus extended to reach all commercial transactions in which the Code is implicated by reason of payment by an article 3 instrument. As a consequence, such a reading of section 1–207 serves to liberalize, or "de-technicalize", that important branch of commercial law governing the full payment check. (*See,* White and Summers, Uniform Commercial Code § 4, at 14–18 [2d ed.]; *Cohen v. Ricci,* 120 Misc.2d 712, 715, 466 N.Y.S.2d 121.) [11]

Application of the foregoing to the facts of this case is evident. Defendant presented a "full payment" check for $500 in satisfaction of a debt in the amount of $1,080. Plaintiff indorsed the check below its notation, "Under Protest", thereby indicating its intent to preserve all rights to the $580 balance. Such an explicit reservation of rights, falling squarely within section 1–207 as we construe that provision today, was an effective means of precluding an accord and satisfaction or any other prejudice to the rights thus reserved. Regardless of whether the underlying transaction between the parties was a contract for the performance of services rather than for the sale of goods, defendant's tender of a check to plaintiff brought the attempted full payment or satisfaction of the underlying obligation within the scope of article 3, thereby rendering it a "Code-covered" transaction to which the provisions of section 1–207 are applicable.

Accordingly, the order of the Appellate Division should be reversed, with costs, and defendant's motion to dismiss denied.

es that unconscionable advantage has been taken by the obligor, or unless the drawer initiates the collection of the instrument on behalf of the payee."

In the 1952 Official Draft, it was somewhat modified: "Where a check or similar payment instrument provides that it is in full satisfaction of an obligation the payee discharges the underlying obligation by obtaining payment of the instrument unless he establishes that the original obligor has taken unconscionable advantage in the circumstances."

The Official Comments explained the intended effect of this codification of the law of accord and satisfaction. In part, it was noted: "Checks are frequently given with a term providing that they are 'in full payment of all claims', or similar language. The holder who obtains payment of such a check takes its benefits subject to the drawer's stipulation that he releases the original obligation. Even where the obligation is for an undisputed and liquidated debt there is no unfairness in the tender and acceptance of an accord and satisfaction; and in this respect subsection (3) changes the law in a number of states."

Ultimately, the provision was dropped in the 1956 Official Draft. Its withdrawal had been recommended by the sponsors, who stated: "Reason: The change consists in the deletion of (3); that subsection had provided that a check reciting full satisfaction of an obligation discharges the obligation, *but this provision evoked criticism on the ground that it would work hardship, and was open to abuse.*" (Emphasis added; *see generally,* discussion in Rosenthal, *supra,* n. 1, at 58–61.)

11. If the further purpose stated in Code § 1–102(2)(c) "to make uniform the law among the various jurisdictions" is to be achieved, the National Conference of Commissioners should give serious thought to a clarifying revision. Until such revision is forthcoming and until or unless it is adopted by the Legislature, the foregoing analysis represents our view of the meaning of Code § 1–207.

WACHTLER, C.J., and MEYER, SIMONS, KAYE, ALEXANDER and TITONE, JJ., concur.

Order reversed, etc.

COUNTY FIRE DOOR CORP. v. C.F. WOODING CO.

Supreme Court of Connecticut, 1987.
202 Conn. 277, 520 A.2d 1028.

PETERS, CHIEF JUSTICE.

The principal issue in this appeal is whether the Uniform Commercial Code modifies the common law of accord and satisfaction so that a creditor can now effectively reserve his rights against a debtor while cashing a check that the debtor has explicitly tendered in full satisfaction of an unliquidated debt. The plaintiff, County Fire Door Corporation, brought an action in two counts against the defendant, C.F. Wooding Company, to recover moneys allegedly owed for goods sold and delivered. Before trial, the plaintiff withdrew the first count, a suit on a default judgment obtained in New York. On the second count, the trial court found the issues for the plaintiff and awarded it damages of $2100. The defendant has appealed from the trial court's subsequent denial of its motion to set aside the judgment against it. We find error.

The trial court's articulation and the exhibits at trial establish the following facts. On November 17, 1981, the defendant ordered a number of metal doors and door frames from the plaintiff. The plaintiff undertook responsibility for delivery of the goods to the worksite. Alleging that the plaintiff's delay in delivery of the doors and frames had caused additional installation expenses, the defendant back charged the plaintiff an amount of $2180. The defendant informed the plaintiff that, on the basis of this back charge, and other payments and credits not at issue, the remaining balance due the plaintiff was $416.88. The plaintiff responded by denying the validity of this back charge. According to the plaintiff, the balance due on its account was $2618.88. The defendant immediately replied, in writing, that it would stand by its position on the validity of the back charge and the accuracy of its calculation of the amount owed to the plaintiff.

The defendant thereafter, on January 10, 1983, sent the plaintiff the check that is at the heart of the present controversy. The check was in the amount of $416.88. It bore two legends. On its face was the notation:

"Final payment
Upjohn Project
Purchase Order # 3302 dated 11/17/81."

On the reverse side, the check stated: "By its endorsement, the payee accepts this check in full satisfaction of all claims against the C.F. Wooding Co. arising out of or relating to the Upjohn Project under Purchase Order # 3302, dated 11/17/81." The plaintiff did not advise the defendant directly that it planned to cash this check under protest. Instead, the plaintiff crossed out the conditional language on the reverse side of the check and added the following: "This check is accepted under protest and with full reservation of rights to collect the unpaid balance for which this check is offered in settlement." The plaintiff then indorsed and deposited the check in its account.

The defendant made no further payments to the plaintiff and the plaintiff brought the present action to recover the remaining amount to which it claimed it was entitled. The trial court rendered judgment for the plaintiff on two grounds. The court agreed with the plaintiff that the enactment of General Statutes § 42a–1–207 [1] had deprived debtors generally of the power unilaterally to enforce the terms of a conditional tender of a check to their creditors. Furthermore, in the specific circumstances of this case, the court concluded that the plaintiff could rightfully treat the defendant's offer of an accord as if it had been a payment on account, because the amount of the tender had been no more than the amount the defendant itself had calculated to be due and owing to the plaintiff. For these reasons, the court awarded the plaintiff $2100 as the unpaid balance of the account.

The defendant's appeal does not contest the monetary calculation used by the court in arriving at the amount of the judgment against the defendant, but maintains instead that the trial court erred because the plaintiff's cause of action was foreclosed as a matter of law. The defendant maintains that, when the plaintiff knowingly cashed a check explicitly tendered in full satisfaction of an unliquidated debt, the plaintiff became bound by the terms of settlement that the check contained. The defendant's argument takes issue with both aspects of the contrary ruling of the trial court. First, the defendant claims that the plaintiff's action of cashing this check constituted an acceptance of its offer, including its terms of settlement, despite the plaintiff's reliance on § 42a–1–207 for authority to substitute words of protest for words of satisfaction. Second, the defendant claims that the amount that it tendered the plaintiff constituted a valid offer of an accord and satisfaction because the underlying debt was unliquidated in amount. We agree with both of the defendant's claims. We will, however, take them up in reverse order, because we would not reach the statutory issue if the defendant had failed to establish its common law defense to the plaintiff's cause of action.

I

When there is a good faith dispute about the existence of a debt or about the amount that is owed, the common law authorizes the debtor and the creditor to negotiate a contract of accord to settle the outstanding claim. Such a contract is often initiated by the debtor, who offers an accord by tendering a check as "payment in full" or "in full satisfaction." If the creditor knowingly cashes such a check, or otherwise exercises full dominion over it, the creditor is deemed to have assented to the offer of accord. Upon acceptance of the offer of accord, the creditor's receipt of the promised payment discharges the underlying debt and bars any further claim relating thereto, if the contract of accord is supported by consideration.[2] *Kelly v.*

1. General Statutes § 42a–1–207 provides: "A party who with explicit reservation of rights performs or promises performance or assents to performance in a manner demanded or offered by the other party does not thereby prejudice the rights reserved. Such words as 'without prejudice,' 'under protest' or the like are sufficient."

2. It may well be that an accord is enforceable, even in the absence of consideration, if it is supported by a debtor's reasonable and foreseeable reliance on a promise

Kowalsky, 186 Conn. 618, 621, 442 A.2d 1355 (1982); *W.H. McCune, Inc. v. Revzon,* 151 Conn. 107, 109, 193 A.2d 601 (1963); *Bull v. Bull,* 43 Conn. 455, 462 (1876); 2 Restatement (Second), Contracts (1981) § 281; E.A. Farnsworth, Contracts (1982) § 4.23, esp. p. 282.

A contract of accord and satisfaction is sufficiently supported by consideration if it settles a monetary claim that is unliquidated in amount. This court has had numerous occasions to decide whether, in the context of accord and satisfaction, a claim is unliquidated when the debtor tenders payment in an amount that does not exceed that to which the creditor is concededly entitled. "Where it is admitted that one of two specific sums is due, but there is a dispute as to which is the proper amount, the demand is regarded as unliquidated, within the meaning of that term as applied to the subject of accord and satisfaction * * *. Where the claim is unliquidated any sum, given and received in settlement of the dispute, is a sufficient consideration." *Hanley Co. v. American Cement Co.,* 108 Conn. 469, 473, 143 A. 566 (1928); *W.H. McCune, Inc. v. Revzon,* supra; *Crowder v. Zion Baptist Church, Inc.,* 143 Conn. 90, 98–99, 119 A.2d 736 (1956); *Perryman Burns Coal Co. v. Seaboard Coal Co.,* 128 Conn. 70, 73, 20 A.2d 404 (1941); *Bull v. Bull,* supra [3]; see also 1 Restatement (Second), Contracts (1981) § 74, esp. illustration 4; E.A. Farnsworth, supra, § 4.23 p. 281.

Application of these settled principles to the facts of this case establishes, as the defendant maintains, that the parties entered into a valid contract of accord and satisfaction. The defendant offered in good faith to settle an unliquidated debt by tendering, in full satisfaction, the payment of an amount less than that demanded by the plaintiff.[4] Under the common law, the plaintiff could not simultaneously cash such a check and disown the condition on which it had been tendered. *Kelly v. Kowalsky,* supra, and authorities therein cited. Having received the promised payment, the plaintiff discharged the defendant from any further obligation on this account, unless the enactment of § 42a–1–207 of the Uniform Commercial Code has changed this result.

II

The principal dispute between the parties is what meaning to ascribe to § 42a–1–207 when it states that "[a] party who with explicit reservation of rights * * * assents to performance in a manner * * * offered by the other party does not thereby prejudice the rights reserved. Such words as 'without prejudice,' 'under protest' or the like are sufficient." The plaintiff contends, as the trial court concluded, that this section gave the plaintiff the authority to cash the defendant's check "under protest" while reserving the

by a creditor to forgive the remainder of an outstanding debt. See *D'Ulisse–Cupo v. Board of Directors,* 202 Conn. 206, 218, 520 A.2d 217 (1987); *Finley v. Aetna Life & Casualty Co.,* 202 Conn. 190, 205, 520 A.2d 208 (1987); 2 Restatement (Second), Contracts (1981) § 281, comment d and § 290.

3. "It would be too technical a use of the doctrine of consideration to release a well-counselled debtor who tenders a nominal amount beyond his admitted debt but to trap one less sophisticated who is induced to pay the undisputed amount in return for his creditor's illusory promise to forgive the rest." *Kilander v. Blickle Co.,* 280 Or. 425, 429, 571 P.2d 503 (1977).

4. When the parties in this case asked the trial court for an articulation of its rulings in favor of the plaintiff, the plaintiff sought a finding that the defendant's tender had been in bad faith. The trial court made no such finding.

right to pursue the remainder of its underlying claim against the defendant at a later time. The defendant maintains that the statutory reference to "performance" contemplates something other than the part payment of an unliquidated debt. We noted in *Kelly v. Kowalsky,* supra, 186 Conn. at 622 and n. 3, 442 A.2d 1355, that there was considerable disagreement in the cases and the scholarly commentaries about the scope of the transactions governed by § 42a–1–207, but did not then undertake to resolve this disagreement. We now decide that § 42a–1–207 does not displace the common law of accord and satisfaction and that the trial court erred in so concluding.

Because § 42a–1–207 is part of the Uniform Commercial Code, it is important to reconcile its provisions with those found in other articles of the code. See *Barco Auto Leasing Corporation v. House,* 202 Conn. 106, 115, 520 A.2d 162 (1987); *Galvin v. Freedom of Information Commission,* 201 Conn. 448, 456, 518 A.2d 64 (1986); W. Grosse & E. Goggin, "Accord and Satisfaction and the 1–207 Dilemma," 89 Com.L.J. 537, 544 (1984). Two likely candidates for such a reconciliation are the provisions of article 3, dealing generally with the law of negotiable instruments, including checks; General Statutes §§ 42a–3–101 through 42a–3–305; and the provisions of article 2, dealing generally with contracts for the sale of goods. General Statutes §§ 42a–2–101 through 42a–2–725.

Article 3 provides little support for reading § 42a–1–207 to permit a creditor unilaterally to change the terms of a check tendered in full satisfaction of an unliquidated debt. As the parties have noted, § 42a–3–112(1)(f) preserves the negotiability of a check that includes "a term * * * providing that the payee by indorsing or cashing it acknowledges full satisfaction of an obligation of the drawer." [5] There is no such validation, anywhere in article 3, for a term on a check that negates a condition that a drawer has incorporated in a negotiable instrument.[6] On the contrary, General Statutes § 42a–3–407 takes a dim view of the unauthorized alteration of an instrument. Under § 42a–3–407(1) "[*a*]*ny* alteration of an instrument is material which changes the contract of *any* party thereto in *any* respect * * *." (Emphasis added.) The effect of the material alteration of a completed instrument is either to discharge the liability, on the instrument, of "any party whose contract is thereby changed," or to continue the enforceability of the instrument "according to its original tenor." General Statutes § 42a–3–407(2) and (3). According to this section, the plaintiff's conduct in substituting words of protest for words of satisfaction would have put the plaintiff at risk of discharging the defendant entirely, if such conduct were deemed to

5. A check is a draft drawn on a bank and payable on demand. General Statutes § 42a–3–104(2)(b).

6. General Statutes § 42a–3–407 provides: "(1) Any alteration of an instrument is material which changes the contract of any party thereto in any respect, including any such change in (a) the number or relations of the parties; or (b) an incomplete instrument, by completing it otherwise than as authorized; or (c) the writing as signed, by adding to it or by removing any part of it.

"(2) As against any person other than a subsequent holder in due course (a) alteration by the holder which is both fraudulent and material discharges any party whose contract is thereby changed unless that party assents or is precluded from asserting the defense; (b) no other alteration discharges any party and the instrument may be enforced according to its original tenor, or as to incomplete instruments according to the authority given.

"(3) A subsequent holder in due course may in all cases enforce the instrument according to its original tenor, and when an incomplete instrument has been completed, he may enforce it as completed."

have been fraudulent. General Statutes § 42a–3–407(2)(a). Even without a finding of fraud, however, the most for which the plaintiff could hope, under article 3, was to enforce the instrument "in full satisfaction," because that was "its original tenor." This result is supported by § 42a–3–802(1)(b), which provides that, presumptively, the taking of a negotiable instrument suspends the underlying obligation "until the instrument is due," and that "discharge of the underlying obligor on the instrument also discharges him on the obligation." [7] Under General Statutes § 42a–3–603(1), a drawer is discharged from liability on an instrument "to the extent of his payment or satisfaction." [8]

The impact of these various article 3 rules is clear. Because the check tendered by the defendant was only enforceable "according to its original tenor," the plaintiff, by receiving "payment or satisfaction," discharged the defendant not only on the instrument but also on the underlying obligation. See J. White & R. Summers, Uniform Commercial Code (2d Ed.1980) pp. 603–604 n. 57. To read § 42a–1–207 to validate the plaintiff's conduct in this case would, therefore, fly in the face of the relevant provisions of article 3, which signal the continued vitality of the common law principles of accord and satisfaction.[9]

Although § 42a–1–207 does not fit easily within the principles of article 3 that govern checks, the section has a close and harmonious connection

7. General Statutes § 42a–3–802 provides: "(1) Unless otherwise agreed where an instrument is taken for an underlying obligation (a) the obligation is pro tanto discharged if a bank is drawer, maker or acceptor of the instrument and there is no recourse on the instrument against the underlying obligor; and (b) in any other case the obligation is suspended pro tanto until the instrument is due or if it is payable on demand until its presentment. If the instrument is dishonored action may be maintained on either the instrument or the obligation; discharge of the underlying obligor on the instrument also discharges him on the obligation.

"(2) The taking in good faith of a check which is not post-dated does not of itself so extend the time on the original obligation as to discharge a surety."

8. General Statutes § 42a–3–603(1) provides: "The liability of any party is discharged to the extent of his payment or satisfaction to the holder even though it is made with knowledge of a claim of another person to the instrument unless prior to such payment or satisfaction the person making the claim either supplies indemnity deemed adequate by the party seeking the discharge or enjoins payment or satisfaction by order of a court of competent jurisdiction in an action in which the adverse claimant and the holder are parties. This subsection does not, however, result in the discharge of the liability (a) of a party who in bad faith pays or satisfies a holder who acquired the instrument by theft or who, unless having the rights of a holder in due course, holds through one who so acquired it; or (b) of a party, other than an intermediary bank or a payor bank which is not a depositary bank, who pays or satisfies the holder of an instrument which has been restrictively endorsed in a manner not consistent with the terms of such restrictive endorsement."

9. An earlier version of the Uniform Commercial Code, prior to its enactment in this state, contained a provision, § 3–802(3), that would have permitted a check tendered in full satisfaction of an obligation to discharge an underlying obligation even when that obligation was undisputed and liquidated. Section 3–802(3) read as follows: "Where a check or similar payment instrument provides that it is in full satisfaction of an obligation the payee discharges the underlying obligation by obtaining payment of the instrument unless he establishes that the original obligor has taken unconscionable advantage in the circumstances." It was deleted in 1952 "on the ground that it would work hardship and was open to abuse." Uniform Commercial Code, 1952 Official Draft (Sup. No. 1) p. 25. None of the legislative history surrounding this section indicates that the draftsmen of article 3 contemplated that § 1–207 would affect § 3–802(3). This conclusion is further buttressed by the fact that these two sections were never cross-referenced in the relevant Official Comments. See A.J. Rosenthal, "Discord and Dissatisfaction: Section 1–207 of the Uniform Commercial Code," 78 Colum.L.Rev. 48, 58–61 (1978).

with article 2. Article 2 regulates ongoing conduct relating to performance of contracts for the sale of goods. That article recurrently draws inferences from acquiescence in, or objection to, the performance tendered by one of the contracting parties. A course of performance "accepted or acquiesced in without objection" is relevant to a determination of the meaning of a contract of sale. General Statutes § 42a–2–208(1).[10] Between merchants, proposals for additional terms will be added to a contract of sale unless there is a timely "notification of objection." General Statutes § 42a–2–207(2)(c); see W. Grosse & E. Goggin, supra, 551.[11] A buyer who is confronted by a defective tender of goods must make a seasonable objection or lose his right of rejection. General Statutes §§ 42a–2–602(1), 42a–2–605, 42a–2–606(1), 42a–2–607(2);[12] *Plateq Corporation v. Machlett Laboratories, Inc.*, 189 Conn. 433, 441–42, 456 A.2d 786 (1983); *Bead Chain Mfg. Co. v. Sexton Products, Inc.*, 183 Conn. 266, 270–72, 439 A.2d 314 (1981). In an instalment sale, a party aggrieved by nonconformity or default that substantially impairs the value of the contract as a whole will nonetheless have reinstated the contract "if he accepts a nonconforming instalment without seasonably notifying of cancellation * * *." General Statutes § 42a–2–612(3).[13] A contract whose performance has become impracticable requires the buyer, after notification by the seller, to offer reasonable alternatives for the

10. General Statutes § 42a–2–208(1) provides: "Where the contract for sale involves repeated occasions for performance by either party with knowledge of the nature of the performance and opportunity for objection to it by the other, any course of performance accepted or acquiesced in without objection shall be relevant to determine the meaning of the agreement."

11. General Statutes § 42a–2–207(2) provides: "The additional terms are to be construed as proposals for addition to the contract. Between merchants such terms become part of the contract unless: (a) The offer expressly limits acceptance to the terms of the offer; (b) they materially alter it; or (c) notification of objection to them has already been given or is given within a reasonable time after notice of them is received."

12. General Statutes § 42a–2–602(1) provides: "Rejection of goods must be within a reasonable time after their delivery or tender. It is ineffective unless the buyer seasonably notifies the seller."

General Statutes § 42a–2–605 provides: "(1) The buyer's failure to state in connection with rejection a particular defect which is ascertainable by reasonable inspection precludes him from relying on the unstated defect to justify rejection or to establish breach (a) where the seller could have cured it if stated seasonably; or (b) between merchants when the seller has after rejection made a request in writing for a full and final written statement of all defects on which the buyer proposes to rely.

"(2) Payment against documents made without reservation of rights precludes recovery of the payment for defects apparent on the face of the documents."

General Statutes § 42a–2–606(1) provides: "Acceptance of goods occurs when the buyer (a) after a reasonable opportunity to inspect the goods signifies to the seller that the goods are conforming or that he will take or retain them in spite of their nonconformity; or (b) fails to make an effective rejection as provided by subsection (1) of section 42a–2–602, but such acceptance does not occur until the buyer has had a reasonable opportunity to inspect them; or (c) does any act inconsistent with the seller's ownership; but if such act is wrongful as against the seller it is an acceptance only if ratified by him."

General Statutes § 42a–2–607(2) provides: "Acceptance of goods by the buyer precludes rejection of the goods accepted and if made with knowledge of a nonconformity cannot be revoked because of it unless the acceptance was on the reasonable assumption that the nonconformity would be seasonably cured but acceptance does not of itself impair any other remedy provided by this article for nonconformity."

13. General Statutes § 42a–2–612(3) provides: "Whenever nonconformity or default with respect to one or more instalments substantially impairs the value of the whole contract there is a breach of the whole. But the aggrieved party reinstates the contract if he accepts a nonconforming instalment without seasonably notifying of cancellation or if he brings an action with respect only to past instalments or demands performance as to future instalments."

modification or the termination of the affected contract; the buyer's failure to respond, within a reasonable period of time, causes the sales contract to lapse. General Statutes § 42a–2–616(1) and (2).[14] In these and other related circumstances, article 2 urges the contracting parties to engage in a continuing dialogue about what will constitute acceptable performance of their sales contract. See generally J. White & R. Summers, supra, §§ 3–1 through 3–9. It is entirely consistent with this article 2 policy to provide, as does § 42a–1–207, a statutory methodology for the effective communication of objections. See J. McDonnell, "Purposive Interpretation of the Uniform Commercial Code: Some Implications for Jurisprudence," 126 U.Pa.L.Rev. 795, 828 (1978).

From the vantage point of article 2, it is apparent that § 42a–1–207 contemplates a reservation of rights about some aspect of a possibly nonconforming tender of goods or services or payment in a situation where the aggrieved party may prefer not to terminate the underlying contract as a whole. See, e.g., *Cherwell–Ralli, Inc. v. Rytman Grain Co.,* 180 Conn. 714, 718, 433 A.2d 984 (1980); W. Grosse & E. Goggin, supra, 551; A. Rosenthal, "Discord and Satisfaction: Section 1–207 of the Uniform Commercial Code," 78 Colum.L.Rev. 48, 63 (1978). Indeed, the Official Comment to § 42a–1–207 itself explains that the section supports ongoing contractual relations by providing "machinery for the continuation of performance along the lines contemplated by the contract despite a pending dispute." See W.D. Hawkland, "The Effect of U.C.C. § 1–207 on the Doctrine of Accord and Satisfaction by Conditional Check," 74 Com.L.J. 329, 331 (1969). It is significant, furthermore, that the text of § 42a–1–207 recurrently refers to "performance," for "performance" is a central aspect of the sales transactions governed by article 2. By contrast, article 3 instruments, which promise or order the payment of money, are not characteristically described as being performed by anyone. The contracts encapsulated in various forms of negotiable instruments instead envisage conduct of negotiation or transfer, indorsement or guaranty, payment or acceptance, and honor or dishonor. See, e.g., §§ 42a–3–201, 42a–3–413, 42a–3–414, 42a–3–416, 42a–3–418; see generally J. White & R. Summers, supra, §§ 13–6 through 13–10, 13–12. We conclude, therefore, that, in circumstances like the present, when performance of a sales contract has come to an end, § 42a–1–207 was not intended to empower a seller, as payee of a negotiable instrument, to alter that instrument by adding words of protest to a check tendered by a buyer on condition that it be accepted in full satisfaction of an unliquidated debt.

Our conclusion is supported by the emerging majority of cases in other jurisdictions. While the case law was divided five years ago, when we postponed resolution of the controversy about the meaning of § 42a–1–207;

14. General Statutes § 42a–2–616(1) and (2) provide: "(1) Where the buyer receives notification of a material or indefinite delay or an allocation justified under the preceding section he may by written notification to the seller as to any delivery concerned, and where the prospective deficiency substantially impairs the value of the whole contract under the provisions of section 42a–2–612 relating to breach of instalment contracts then also as to the whole, (a) terminate and thereby discharge any unexecuted portion of the contract; or (b) modify the contract by agreeing to take his available quota in substitution.

"(2) If after receipt of such notification from the seller the buyer fails so to modify the contract within a reasonable time not exceeding thirty days the contract lapses with respect to any deliveries affected."

Kelly v. Kowalsky, supra, 186 Conn. at 621–22, 442 A.2d 1355; it is now the view of the substantial majority of courts that have addressed the issue that § 42a–1–207 does not overrule the common law of accord and satisfaction * * * * The majority finds support as well in much of the recent scholarly commentary. See 2 Restatement (Second), Contracts (1981) § 281, comment d; R. Anderson, Uniform Commercial Code (1984) § 3–408–56; W. Grosse & E. Goggin, supra, 546; W.D. Hawkland, supra, 331; J. McDonnell, supra, 824–28; A. Rosenthal, supra, 61; contra, J. Calamari & J. Perillo, Contracts (2d Ed.1977) § 5–16; J. White & R. Summers, supra, § 18–21.

Both under prevailing common law principles, and under the Uniform Commercial Code, the parties in this case negotiated a contract of accord whose satisfaction discharged the defendant from any further monetary obligation to the plaintiff. The plaintiff might have avoided this result by returning the defendant's check uncashed, but could not simultaneously disregard the condition on which the check was tendered and deposit its proceeds in the plaintiff's bank account.

There is error, the judgment is set aside and the case is remanded with direction to render judgment for the defendant.

In this opinion the other Justices concurred.

BRUCE W. FRIER, INTERPRETING CODES

89 Mich.L.Rev. 2201.
2201–2205, 2209–2214 (1991).

On December 1, 1944, the National Conference of Commissioners on Uniform State Laws and the American Law Institute formally agreed to cosponsor the creation of a Uniform Commercial Code (UCC), with Professor Karl Llewellyn serving as its Chief Reporter and Soia Mentschikoff as Associate Chief Reporter.[1] Two years later, as the earliest drafts of the UCC were circulating, Dean Roscoe Pound published a general article on the character of modern law.[2] In this article he surveyed the modern codification movement, as well as the objections to it. He concluded:

> The most serious objection to a code in a common-law jurisdiction is that we have no well developed common-law technique of developing legislative texts. Our technique of statutory interpretation is not adequate to the application of a code.[3]

If correct, Pound's objection is a serious one. Of course, it can be argued that the UCC is not a code at all, but rather "a big statute or a collection of statutes bound together in the same book";[4] and certainly the UCC is at some remove from traditional civil law codes. The UCC does not strive for completeness even within the commercial sphere, nor is it nearly so closely

1. For a historical reconstruction, see W. Twining, Karl Llewellyn and the Realist Movement 270–301 (1973).

2. Pound, *Sources and Forms of Law,* 22 Notre Dame Law. 1, 46–80 (1946).

3. *Id.* at 76.

4. Gilmore, *Article 9: What It Does for the Past,* 26 La.L.Rev. 285, 286 (1966). Gilmore believed that the UCC would not substantially displace "[t]he solid stuff of pre-Code law." *Id.* at 286. But it is doubtful that pre-Code law has much current influence in interpreting the UCC.

drafted as the traditional codes of European civil law.[5] More important is the UCC's status not as a national law, but as state law within numerous distinct jurisdictions; this has meant not only appreciable variations in enacted wording and in judicial interpretation, but also a complex and shifting interaction with both federal and state laws and regulations.[6]

Still, because of its nearly universal adoption in a form and wording that approximate the model, the UCC can at least be described as "code-like"—something more, in any case, than an ordinary statute.[7] In this brief article, rather than tackling the exceptionally difficult question of how the UCC is (or ought to be) interpreted as a code,[8] I want only to point to some features of European experience in interpreting codes, and to argue that these features are not inconsistent with, and may even to some extent prefigure, emerging patterns in the interpretation of the UCC. Since these shared interpretive patterns have arisen independently, they suggest that the form of legal materials can exert considerable influence on the formation of legal cultures.

The Salience of General Clauses. Like the UCC, European codes contain norms that vary widely in the breadth of their formulation and in the level of their abstraction. An example is the German Civil Code (the BGB), whose articles range from the extreme specificity of section 961 ("If a swarm of bees moves out, it becomes ownerless if the owner does not immediately pursue it or if the owner gives up the pursuit")[9] to the sweeping breadth of section 138(1) ("A legal transaction which is against public policy is void").[10] "General clauses" (*General-klauseln, principes géneraux*) of the latter type, with a vague but undeniable ethical content, appear in all European civil codes.

In the present century, European judges have seized upon such general clauses as a legislative derogation to them of a general "moral" authority and supervision in administering the codes; the general clauses have accordingly become a standard vehicle for achieving what is now almost universally recognized (at least in academic circles) as judicial legislation.[11] An outstanding example is BGB section 242, providing that: "The debtor is bound to effect performance according to the requirements of good faith,

5. For a short description of the major European codes, see A. Watson, The Making of the Civil Law 99–130 (1981)....

6. J. White & R. Summers, Uniform Commercial Code § 3, at 6–9 (3d ed. 1988) (student edition).

7. On the nature of codification, see Bergel, *Principal Features and Methods of Codification,* 48 La.L.Rev. 1073 (1988). Bergal distinguishes two types: "substantive or true codification," the goal of which is "to achieve a material and systematic structure of the law," and "formal codification," aiming "only to succeed in regrouping and classifying existing texts." *Id.* at 1097. The UCC is a clear example of the former. *Id.* at 1076, 1092.

8. *See, e.g.,* Hawkland, *Uniform Commercial "Code" Methodology,* 1962 U.Ill.L.F. 291 (arguing that the UCC should be interpreted as a "true code"); *see also* McDonnell, *Purposive Interpretation of the Uniform Commercial Code: Some Implications for Jurisprudence,* 126 U.Pa.L.Rev. 795 (1978).

9. The German Civil Code § 961 (I. Forrester, S. Goren & H. Ilgen trans. 1975) (English translation of Burgerliches Gesetzbuch, commonly known as BGB).

10. The German Civil Code, *supra* note 9, § 138(1).

11. R. David, French Law: Its Structures, Sources, and Methodology 194–207 (M. Kindred trans. 1972) ("Supereminent Principles"); *see also* O. Kahn–Freund, C. Levy & B. Rudden, Source–Book on French Law 176–98 (2d ed. 1979) (a thorough discussion with some excellent illustrations); *cf.* K. Larenz, Methodenlehre der Rechtswissenschaft 276–81 (5th ed. 1983).

giving consideration to common usage."[12] Although this section was originally "confined to regulating the manner and method of the duty to perform," it has been judicially transformed into "a 'super control norm' for the whole BGB, and indeed for large parts of German law outside it.... a 'principle of legal ethics,' which dominates the entire legal system."[13] A recent exhaustive commentary on section 242 alone runs to some 1553 pages.[14]

In a thoughtful article, the late John Dawson tried to assess the significance of such general clauses in the development of modern German law.[15] On the one hand, he accepted the logic that had converted such clauses into "super control norms": "By including these clauses the draftsmen of the Code and legislature acknowledged both that the Code was incomplete and that it needed to be supplemented, primarily through judicial action, from sources outside the Code."[16] On the other hand, he admitted the dangers of the temptation they provided as "express licenses to judges to go out hunting anywhere and bring back their trophies, to be hung then in the living room."[17]

The UCC, of course, also contains general clauses of wide breadth, such as section 2–302 (on unconscionable contracts or contract clauses),[18] or section 1–203, providing that: "Every contract or duty within this Act imposes an obligation of good faith in its performance or enforcement."[19] But as yet it can hardly be said that either section has emerged as a "super control norm."[20] Of course, American judges do not necessarily require legislative authorization for the equitable expansion of law.

12. The German Civil Code, *supra* note 9, § 242.

13. N. Horn, H. Kötz & H. Leser, German Private and Commercial Law: An Introduction 135 (T. Weir trans. 1982) (footnote omitted) (quoting I Protokolle zum BGB 303); *cf. id.* at 135–45 ("The Principle of Good Faith: § 242 BGB;" "its function is to justify the value-judgments of the judge").

14. 2 W. Weber, J. von Staudingers Kommentar zum Bürgerlichen Gessetzbuch, Teil 1b: § 242 (11th ed. 1961), *cited in* 1 E. Cohen, Manual of German Law 101 (1968).

15. Dawson, *The General Clauses, Viewed from a Distance,* 41 Rabels Zeitschrift 441 (1977).

16. *Id.* at 444. In fact, this "acknowledgement" is usually a legal action.

17. *Id.* at 445. On the German "flight into the general clauses" during the troubled 1920s and 1930s, see J. Dawson, The Oracles of the Law 461–79 (1968). The phrase is from J. Hedemann, Die Flucht in die Generalklauseln (1933).

18. U.C.C. § 2–302 (1987).

19. U.C.C. § 1–203 (1987).

20. For a discussion of § 2–302 as a "supereminent provision," see Hawkland, *supra* note 8, at 305–07. It is doubtful, however, that the section has yet been used by courts more generally as a key to understanding the UCC in its entirety. On unconscionability in German and American law, see Dawson, *Unconscionable Coercion: The German Version,* 89 Harv.L.Rev. 1041, 1042–44 (1976) (stressing the narrowness of the American doctrine). This fine article raises many of the themes I am touching on.

The good faith required under the UCC is generally conceptualized fairly narrowly, as an "excluder" aimed at specific types of undesirable conduct. *See* Summers, *"Good Faith" in General Contract Law and the Sales Provisions of the Uniform Commercial Code,* 54 Va.L.Rev. 195 (1968); *see also* Summers, *The General Duty of Good Faith—Its Recognition and Conceptualization,* 67 Cornell L.Rev. 810 (1982) (arguing that the concept of good faith in the Restatement (Second) of Contracts § 205, is broader than that in the U.C.C. § 1–203).

But see also the related issue of whether U.C.C. § 1–203 generates claims based upon a duty of good faith alone, apart from duties imposed by other UCC clauses: *compare* Chandler v. Hunter, 340 So.2d 818, (Ala.App. 1976) (no) *with* Reid v. Key Bank of S. Maine, Inc., 821 F.2d 9 (1st Cir.1987) (yes, through reference to U.C.C. § 1–106).

More significant, perhaps, has been the fate of less grandiose general clauses such as UCC section 1–106(1), which provides for the "liberal administration" of UCC remedies with the stated goal of placing "the aggrieved party ... in as good a position as if the other party had fully performed." [21] This clause has frequently been used to solve knotty problems arising out of the draftsmanship of UCC remedy clauses,[22] for example, in the case of defaulting sellers, the vexed issue of the interrelationship of cover with market-difference damages under sections 2–712 and 713; [23] or, in the case of defaulting buyers, the awkward language of section 2–708 in determining whether to award market-difference damages or lost profits.[24] Reasonable solutions have been located virtually in the teeth of the UCC's express wording.[25]

The success of section 1–106 has largely depended on the dexterity of commentators and judges in bringing it to bear on clear and specific problems, with the aim "to scale down the apparently unlimited mandate of the general clause, to restructure it into distinct subordinate norms that become intelligible and manageable through their narrowed scope and function." [26] The fate of still broader sections, such as section 1–203 or section 2–302, is likely to depend on whether this interpretive process can be replicated for them.[27]

* * *

Expanded Concepts of Interpretation. The salience of general clauses, coupled with the existence of a larger and more intricate interpretive community, fosters the emergence of interpretive concepts that are more venturesome than those courts traditionally apply to statutes. To be sure, European legal theory normally does not draw sharp methodological distinctions between interpreting codes and statutes.[54] But the comprehensive character of codes, and also their intricacy and long-term stability, have tended to encourage greater breadth of interpretation.[55]

Traditional European theory distinguishes four types of interpretation: (1) grammatical or literal interpretation of what a given text means or may

21. U.C.C. § 1–106(1).

22. 1 J. White & R. Summers, Uniform Commercial Code 17 n. 86 (3d ed. 1988) (practitioner edition) (cases cited).

23. The leading case is Allied Canners & Packers, Inc. v. Victor Packing Co., 162 Cal. App.3d 905, 209 Cal.Rptr. 60, 39 U.C.C. 1567 (1984). *See generally* J. White & R. Summers, *supra* note 6, § 6–4, at 263–65.

24. J. White & R. Summers, *supra* note 6, §§ 7-11—7-12, at 318–24. A major case is Nobs Chemical, USA v. Koppers Co., 616 F.2d 212 (5th Cir.1980) (restricting buyer to lost profit under § 2–708(2), and not allowing a claim for market-based damages, despite the clear statutory language against such restriction); *see also* White, *The Decline of the Contract Market Damage Model*, 11 U.Ark. Little Rock L.J. 1 (1988–89).

25. By contrast, U.C.C. §§ 1–102(1) and (2), setting out the Code's general purposes and principles of construction, has had more limited effect. *See* J. White & R. Summers, *supra* note 6, § 4, at 14–18.

26. Dawson, *supra* note 20, at 1044.

27. Dawson seems pessimistic: "We have much to learn from German law and should be willing to admire the German achievement. It does not follow that we have the means to emulate it." *Id.* at 1126.

54. R. David & J. Brierly, Major Legal Systems in the World Today: An Introduction to the Comparative Study of Law 104 (2d ed. 1978) ("When interpreted by [European] jurists, codes and statutes are treated on exactly the same basis.").

55. R. David, *supra* note 11, at 159–60 (noting a tendency of French courts "to consider new statutes as abnormal appendages to the French legal system, to restrict their scope, applicability and effects," until these statutes become fully integrated into the legal system).

mean; (2) logical interpretation of the text in the context of all other rules of positive law; (3) historical interpretation based upon evidence of the legislator's actual intent or purpose; and (4) teleological interpretation construing a text in the way that best represents or promotes a contemporary view of social welfare and justice.[56] In practice, arguments from these four types of interpretation are flexibly combined within a single, continuous interpretive process, the various types played off against one another as the exigencies of a situation demand. But it is usually conceded that, *ceteris paribus,* this list of types is hierarchical, in the sense that a clearly convincing grammatical or logical interpretation will ordinarily defeat one based on legislative intent or on a contemporary construction of purpose.[57]

Despite the difference in wording, much of this apparatus has its fairly clear counterpart in traditional Anglo–American statutory interpretation. Although various commentators have recommended interpreting the UCC largely or solely on the basis of legislative purpose or a "rationale-oriented" approach,[58] it is unclear, at least to me, that traditional modes of interpretation are much disturbed by the existence of the UCC; both scholarly and judicial arguments still usually begin from the apparent meaning of the UCC's provisions, and move on to other types of interpretation only when no satisfactory answer is obtained. What has changed, of course, is the willingness of interpreters to be satisfied with quick answers based on "plain meaning." The intricacy of the UCC has encouraged judges to hold themselves open to a deeper probe of its meaning.

Nonetheless, the existence of codes, with more or less stable and therefore predictable texts,[59] has eventually brought about a changed attitude toward more fundamental issues of interpretation. This changed attitude is clearly illustrated in an influential passage from the German jurist Rudolph Sohm:

> A rule of law may be worked out either by developing the consequences which it involves, or by developing the wider principles which it presupposes.... The more important of these two methods of procedure is the second, *i.e.* the method by which, from given rules of law, we ascertain the major premises which they presuppose. For having ascertained such major premises, we shall find that they involve, in their logical consequences, a series of other legal rules not directly contained in the sources from which we obtained our rule.[60]

In relationship to codes, the inductive process that Sohm recommends is expansive in two senses: first, it aims to solve problems arising *under* a code through reference to broader principles that the code may be held to

56. *See id.* at 157–60; K. Larenz, *supra* note 11, at 305–25.

57. R. David, *supra* note 11, at 164–67.

58. *See* J. White & R. Summers, *supra* note 6, § 4, at 18 ("rationale-oriented" approach); McDonnell, *supra* note 8, at 829–55 (legislative purpose). The authors of the UCC clearly favored such approaches. "This Act shall be liberally construed and applied to promote its underlying purposes and policies." U.C.C. § 1–102(1); *see also* U.C.C. § 1–102(1) official comment 1.

59. In the case of the UCC, however, textual stability is a problem in itself. J. White & R. Summers, *supra* note 6, §§ 3, 7, at 7–9, 21 ("the continuing stream of 'official' amendments alone accounts for much of today's lack of uniformity in the text").

60. R. Sohm, The Institutes: A Textbook of the History and System of Roman Private Law 30 (J. Ledlie trans. 3d ed. 1907 & reprint 1970).

embody; second, it aims to solve problems arising *outside* a code through extension of these same principles, by the application of analogy.[61] The general clauses of a code take on particular force in the context of such inductive reasoning.

As to analogy, the drafters of the UCC expressly favored its use,[62] and academic commentators swiftly adopted a similar line.[63] In a steadily growing number of decisions, courts have been willing to extend the UCC by analogy, thereby abandoning older doctrine on narrow construction of statutes.[64]

More intricate is the process of solving interpretive problems that arise under the UCC. An example is UCC section 1–207, which provides that: "A party who with explicit reservation of rights performs or promises performance or assents to performance in a manner demanded or offered by the other party does not thereby prejudice the rights reserved. Such words as 'without prejudice,' 'under protest' or the like are sufficient." [65] If a debtor offers a check for less than the full amount claimed by the creditor but in "full satisfaction," and the creditor then cashes the check after writing "under protest" on it, does this section have the effect of reserving the creditor's right to then claim the balance due? Does section 1–207 therefore replace earlier common law rules on accord and satisfaction?

This vexed problem has deeply divided both commentators and courts.[66] The issue is very close, and reasonable persons are bound to differ. The broad language of section 1–207 fairly clearly favors its application to "full satisfaction" checks, as does the section's placement among the "General Provisions" of article 1. On the other hand, both the Official Comments to the section and its legislative history seem to argue against application, though they are not decisive. Nor do the equities of the situation seem completely clear. Final resolution of the debate will doubtless require altering the UCC; [67] in the meantime, however, it is appalling, and entirely

61. On analogy, see the good discussion by K. Larenz, *supra* note 11, at 365–75. Larenz stresses the difference between the "isolated analogy" (*Einzelanalogie:* direct extension of a rule governing *A* to a similar but unregulated *B*) and "general analogy" (*Gesamtanalogie:* recognition of a broader principle above the rule governing *A,* followed by the principle's extension to similar situations). The latter method, which is especially common in constitutional law, uses induction.

62. *E.g.,* U.C.C. § 1–102 official comment 1 ("This Act is drawn to provide flexibility so that, since it is intended to be a semi-permanent piece of legislation, it will provide its own machinery for the expansion of commercial practices."). Note how the Comment relates semi-permanence to the use of analogy.

63. *See* Note, *The Uniform Commercial Code as a Premise for Judicial Reasoning,* 65 Colum.L.Rev. 880 (1965). For a later example, see Rapson, *A "Home Run" Application of Established Principles of Statutory Construction: UCC Analogies,* 5 Cardozo L.Rev. 441 (1984).

64. Some examples are listed in J. White & R. Summers, *supra* note 6, at 18, n. 88.

65. U.C.C. § 1–207.

66. As to commentators, compare, for example, J. White & R. Summers, *supra* note 6, § 13–24, at 607–10 (for applying § 1–207) with Rosenthal, *Discord and Dissatisfaction: Section 1–207 of the Uniform Commercial Code,* 78 Colum.L.Rev. 48 (1978) (against). As to courts, compare Horn Waterproofing Corp. v. Brunswick Iron & Steel Co., 66 N.Y.2d 321, 497 N.Y.S.2d 310, 488 N.E.2d 56 (1985) (for application) with County Fire Door Corp. v. C.F. Wooding Co., 202 Conn. 277, 520 A.2d 1028 (1987) (against). Both are exceptionally well-reasoned cases.

67. An officially proposed amendment to § 1–207 has eliminated the section's applicability to accord and satisfaction, in conformance with the added § 3–311 ("Accord and Satisfaction by Use of Instrument"). U.C.C. Foll. § 3–605, 2 U.L.A. official comment 3, at 500–01 (West 1991).

contrary to the UCC's spirit, that different laws prevail, in jurisdictions so closely commercially linked as New York State and Connecticut, on such a common device as a "full satisfaction" check.

In the 1987 *Country Fire Door* decision,[68] Chief Justice Ellen Peters of Connecticut articulates what is now the majority position against applying section 1–207 to "full satisfaction" checks. She argues for the importance of reconciling this provision with those found in other articles of the UCC, including both article 3 on commercial paper including checks, and article 2 on the sale of goods. While "Article 3 provides little support for reading [section 1–207] to permit a creditor unilaterally to change the terms of a check tendered in full satisfaction of an unliquidated debt," section 1–207 "has a close and harmonious connection with article 2." [69] As she reasons:

> Article 2 regulates ongoing conduct in the performance of contracts for the sale of goods. That article recurrently draws inferences from acquiescence in, or objection to, the performance tendered by one of the contracting parties. A course of performance "accepted or acquiesced in without objection" is relevant to a determination of the meaning of a contract of sale. [U.C.C. § 2–208.] ... A buyer who is confronted by a defective tender of goods must make a seasonable objection or lose his right of rejection. [U.C.C. §§ 2–602(1), 2–605, 2–606(1), 2–607(2).] ... In an installment sale, a party aggrieved by nonconformity or default that substantially impairs the value of the contract as a whole will nonetheless have reinstated the contract "if he accepts a non-conforming installment without seasonably notifying of cancellation...." [U.C.C. § 2–612.] ... A contract whose performance has become impracticable requires the buyer, after notification by the seller, to offer reasonable alternatives for the modification or the termination of the affected contract; the buyer's failure to respond, within a reasonable period of time, causes the sales contract to lapse. [U.C.C. § 2–616(1) and (2).] ... In these and other related circumstances, article 2 urges the contracting parties to engage in a continuing dialogue about what will constitute acceptable performance of their sales contract.... It is entirely consistent with this article 2 policy to provide, as does [§ 1–207], a statutory methodology for the effective communication of objections....
>
> From the vantage point of article 2, it is apparent that [§ 1–207] contemplates a reservation of rights about some aspect of a possibly nonconforming tender of goods or services or payment in a situation where the aggrieved party may prefer not to terminate the underlying contract as a whole.... We conclude, therefore, that in circumstances like the present, when performance of a sales contract has come to an end, [§ 1–207] was not intended to empower a seller, as payee of a negotiable instrument, to alter that instrument by adding words of protest to a check tendered by a buyer on condition that it be accepted in full satisfaction of an unliquidated debt.[70]

68. County Fire Door Corp. v. C.F. Wooding Co., 202 Conn. 277, 520 A.2d 1028 (1987).

69. 202 Conn. at 285, 287, 520 A.2d at 1032–33.

70. 202 Conn. at 287–90, 520 A.2d at 1033–35 (footnotes omitted).

Whether or not this argument convinces, its importance lies in its form. Justice Peters rests her case neither on the apparent meaning nor on the legislative purpose and "rationale" of section 1–207; both forms of interpretation have proved to be inconclusive.[71] Although her argument might be described as logical interpretation in that it implicates the context of articles 2 and 3, in reality the "logic" is gossamer thin; there is no necessary reason that a possible "close and harmonious connection with article 2" should matter much in interpreting section 1–207, which is in a different article and could as easily stand on its own legs.

Yet the numerous particular provisions that Justice Peters cites from article 2 do have the effect of establishing, through induction, one of the larger commercial principles of the UCC, that "the contracting parties [should] engage in a continuing dialogue about what will constitute acceptable performance of their sales contract." [72] This is an important principle, which would indeed be somewhat displaced by allowing a creditor unilaterally to convert a debtor's offer of compromise into a partial payment of a disputed debt. There is nothing improper about allowing such a principle to control interpretation of section 1–207, although other principles may conceivably point in a different direction.[73]

But it is the principles themselves that are potent in developing future commercial law. Their number need not be large, but they must be realized in order to be effective. For example, it bears considering whether the various article 2 provisions favoring timely dialogue between the parties to a sale are subsumed within the more general requirement of good faith in performance under section 1–203. If so, then this section should also be dispositive of the issue in section 1–207; surely a creditor cannot, in good faith, unilaterally turn to his own advantage a debtor's offer of compromise.[74]

What I have been suggesting is that large, systematically codified bodies of law, such as the European codes or the UCC, gradually effect, or at least encourage, a different kind of legal culture, in which, as such codes are integrated within a national legal heritage, general clauses and principles become more salient within an expanded interpretive community. Because of the open texture of their rules, codes foster an altered legal posture; ancient judicial vigilance against the intrusive legislation may give way to a new ethos of cooperation in the development of law. To be sure, it remains uncertain whether the resulting law will be, in fact, "better," or even more uniform.[75] In the case of the UCC, a major American experiment in codification is only a generation old. The consequence of this experiment is still unfolding. [Reprinted by permission of the author and the Michigan Law Review Association.]

71. Contrast the more mundane approach of Flambeau Prod. Corp. v. Honeywell Information Sys., Inc. 116 Wis.2d 95, 341 N.W.2d 655 (1984) (reaching the same result). On Justice Peter's approach to commercial law, see Note, *Ellen Ash Peters and the Uniform Commercial Code,* 21 Conn. L.Rev. 753 (1989).

72. 202 Conn. at 289, 520 A.2d at 1034.

73. *See* Horn Waterproofing Corp. v. Brunswick Iron & Steel Co., 66 N.Y.2d 321, 331, 497 N.Y.S.2d 310, 316, 488 N.E.2d 56, 62 (1985) (emphasizing simplicity, clarity, and liberalization of commercial law).

74. *Contra* J. White & R. Summers, *supra* note 6, § 13–24, at 609. This seems to be the real issue, and not whether "the offeror is 'master of his offer.' "

75. For contrasting views of the UCC, see J. White & R. Summers, *supra* note 6, at 20–22.

BOOK ONE

SECURITY INTERESTS IN PERSONALTY

CHAPTER TWO

AN INTRODUCTION TO PERSONAL PROPERTY SECURITY

SECTION 1. WHAT IS A SECURITY INTEREST AND WHY DOES IT MATTER?

According to section 1–201(37) "Security interest means an interest in personal property or fixtures which secures payment or performance of an obligation." The section goes on to embellish the definition in various ways not relevant for our introductory purposes. The following examples illustrate common types of security interests:

(1) Edgar Jarvis bought a dump truck from Hellas Trucking Company pursuant to an agreement whereby Edgar paid $5,000 down and agreed to pay $500 a month for five years. Edgar signed a promissory note for the unpaid balance, naming the trucking company as payee. Edgar also signed a piece of paper headed "security agreement." This piece of paper included a clause whereby the Trucking Company retained a "security interest" in the truck sold to Edgar as security for the unpaid balance.

(2) Irene Watson owned a bookstore. She sold large batches of books to public schools in the area on open account pursuant to arrangements whereby she was paid by the public school system involved once every sixty days. Irene wished to enlarge her store. She borrowed $20,000 from Ready Bank, signed a promissory note in that amount and a security agreement giving the Bank a "security interest" in her book inventory and in her accounts receivable as security for the repayment of the $20,000 (in $1,000 monthly installments).

(3) Fred Wirtz was a tomato grower. Canwell Company was a major tomato canning company in the area, and usually bought Fred's tomatoes. To finance Fred's planting, cultivating, and harvesting, for the upcoming crop, Canwell lent Fred $50,000 pursuant to a promissory note and a security agreement which gave Canwell a "security interest" in the growing crops and provided in effect that Wirtz was obligated to sell his tomato crop to Canwell.

In all three of these transactions, the parties entered into a *contract* that provided for a "security interest." The legal consequences of so agreeing to a "security interest" are crucial, and we turn to these in the next paragraph. Although many persons (especially consumers) who agree to a "security interest" probably do not fully understand these consequences, they are nonetheless taken to have *agreed* thereto. The theory and much of the reality is that security interests under Article 9 are consensual. This does not mean there are no limits on freedom of contract here. We will see that there are some major ones. The security interest in each of the above cases was in some species of *personal property:* a truck, books, accounts receivable, and crops. The security interest in each instance also secured the *repayment or performance of an obligation.* For now, read UCC 1–201(3) and (11), 9–203(1), 9–105(1)(*l*).

What if the debtor in the above examples failed to repay or perform? That is, what if the debtor defaulted? In that event, the secured creditor would be entitled under Article 9, Part 5, of the Code to have the collateral sold and the proceeds applied on the debt, or, in some cases, to take the collateral in satisfaction of the debt. These rights are called rights to "foreclose." Thus, the idea of a *conditional property right* is the conceptual key to understanding what a security interest is. A creditor can fall back on this right and exercise it *if* his debtor fails to pay (or perform) as promised. An extensive set of Article 9 rules governs how a security interest is created, how it may be made as effective as possible against third parties (often debtors deal with other creditors and still other third parties who will have their just claims as well), who has priority in the property subject to the creditor's security interest when two or more parties claim it, what rights the creditor has against the property on default, and so on.

Some creditors take security interests not in "personal property or fixtures" to which Article 9 applies, but in real estate. These interests are governed by a vast, ancient and complex body of law dealing with mortgages, land sale contracts, and the like, a body of law studied in other courses, but on which we will draw from time to time by way of historical background and analogy.

A great many creditors are unsecured. That is, they do not take security interests in personalty or in realty, even though they lend money or extend credit. They therefore do not have the conditional property rights that secured creditors do. This frequently puts them at a real disadvantage. If the debtor defaults, they cannot simply take specific property of the debtor and dispose of it to pay off their claims. They have no right of foreclosure against particular assets of the debtor (as above). They must first file a law suit, reduce their claims to judgment, and proceed from there. Also, certain other creditors (and many purchasers) who do have security interests in the debtor's property will usually take *priority* over the claims of unsecured creditors.

It is easy to see, then, why creditors take security interests when they lend or extend credit. This gives them a right to foreclose and certain priority rights against third persons, in the event the debtor defaults. But why would anyone who lends or extends credit *not* take security? Another basic question is this: Is the legal recognition and enforcement of security interests a good thing for society on the whole? Some scholars have recently expressed doubt. An example is Schwartz, *Security Interests and Bankruptcy Priorities: A Review of Current Theories,* 10 J. Legal Stud. 1 (1981). A more recent analysis of the competing theories can be found in Scott, *A Relational Theory of Secured Financing,* 86 Colum.L.Rev. 901 (1986). We will return to this question in due course.

Of course the debtor who defaults may also be a debtor who "files for bankruptcy." We will shortly see that bankruptcy can operate to eliminate or to limit drastically the advantage that the secured creditor has over the unsecured creditor.

Problem 2–1

Sam Seller sells a used car to Ben Buyer for $2500 with Ben paying $500 down and signing a promissory note for the balance, which is to be repaid monthly. One month later, unknown to Sam, Ben borrows $2000 from Ace Finance Company pursuant to a valid security agreement duly created and perfected (by a notation on the certificate of title). The agreement gives Ace a security interest in Ben's car. Ben defaults on his obligation to Sam. He also defaults on his debt to Ace. Sam goes to Ben's house where he sees the car parked in the street (Ben having gone on vacation). Can Sam lawfully drive it off (assuming he has a key)? Can Ace, who arrives at the same time? See UCC 9–503. If Sam takes the car, will he be liable for the tort of conversion? Can Ace sell the car and apply the proceeds to its loan? See UCC 9–504. Suppose both Sam and Ace claim the proceeds of the foreclosure sale ($1000), who wins? See UCC 9–201.

SECTION 2. PRE–ARTICLE 9 LAW ON PERSONAL PROPERTY SECURITY INTERESTS: SOME HISTORY AND SOME FUNDAMENTALS OF THEORY

In the next section, we provide a detailed roadmap and introduction to Article 9 of the Uniform Commercial Code on secured transactions. Article 9 is a single integrated body of rules governing the creation and effect of consensual security interests in personal property (of nearly all kinds). This body of law was drafted in the late 1940's and early 1950's. It is widely heralded as one of the great statutory advances in modern times. You are not yet fully in a position to understand why this is so, but here we will identify the main explanations so that you can bear them in mind as we proceed.

First, Article 9 gathered up not only some statutory but also the vast case law on personal property security, modernized it, and put all of its essential elements into statutory form. Since the law of security interests is largely planner's law, the more accessible and certain statutory form represents a major improvement. Second, in place of the plethora of pre-Code personal property security devices to which we will turn immediately, i.e., the pledge, the chattel mortgage, the conditional sale, the trust receipt, the factor's lien (and more), Article 9 substituted *one* basic security device and one body of law. This represents the most significant single unification effort in the history of modern American private law. At one fell swoop, the Many became the One, with corresponding elimination of excess concepts, needless boundary disputes, and much else. Third, Article 9 extended and rationalized beyond any body of law before it one of the most basic policies in the field, namely, that in general a party with a security interest in personal property should not prevail over most competing claimants unless that party has in effect given the world notice or potential notice of that interest either by taking possession of the collateral or by making a public filing of the interest in a publicly accessible filing office where third parties can go to learn of it or of its possible existence.

Before the magnitude of all these changes can be grasped, it is essential to consider some historical background. We will also see that this background can be useful in still other important ways.

The document (called a "security agreement" in the Uniform Commercial Code) that creates a security interest then is both a contract and a conveyance which finds its roots not only in contract but also in property. As we will see below, the typical commercial security agreement will run to tens of (and perhaps many more) pages. It will be full of promises, mostly made by the debtor, but also some by the creditor. Of course, the most basic promise of the debtor will simply be a promise to pay off the indebtedness owed the secured party. Unlike the typical deed, the agreement is not necessarily formal; as long as it contains a few fundamental terms, it can contain most others that the parties might wish. Typically the creditor agrees to lend money and the debtor promises to pay it back according to explicit terms, perhaps to operate his business in a specific way, to make reports to the creditors and to limit his behavior in other ways.

Invariably the document is also a conveyance of some property interest of the debtor to the creditor. This is the creditor's "security interest." Such an interest is a conditional property right—the right to repossess an asset of the debtor on default, and (within limits) to take an asset ahead of others.

Absent overreaching or some other unusual and egregious event, the agreement controls the rights of the debtor and the secured creditor. That is not necessarily true of the rights of the secured creditor versus third parties who have also dealt with the debtor such as purchasers, secured and unsecured creditors, and the debtor's trustee in bankruptcy (if there be one). The presence of such persons presents different questions. Recall the real property recording statutes that you have studied in your first-year property course. For example, those statutes modify what would otherwise be legal rights of various parties to lend based on conventional common law doctrines such as *nemo dat quod non habaet* (he who hath not cannot give.) If A transfers his real estate to B, presumably A has no title left and cannot transfer anything to C, yet that is not the outcome if B fails to record. Here if B fails to record C may take ahead of B if C is a bona fide purchaser. You learned that real property recording statutes in effect undo our conventional views about conveyance of property and in some cases grant title to a party later in time (C above) who, according to conventional common law doctrine, would be thought to have received no title, since the seller had already conveyed it to another.

The very same idea has also emerged in the field of personal property security. In the early days, the courts faced essentially the same problems in personal property security as they faced in structuring fair and appropriate rules with respect to real estate conveyances. The basic question is: To what extent should a court be allowed to disregard the rights contractually established between the parties when those rights are challenged by a third person? In pre-industrial society the possessor of personal property was generally expected to be the owner or his agent. Indeed it was thought to be fraudulent and misleading to keep possession of that very property while at the same time creating a security interest in it in favor of a creditor. In fact, giving such a creditor possession was generally deemed to put others on notice of the creditor's interest. But suppose the debtor retains possession of his personalty while giving a security interest in it. Or suppose the debtor buys property on credit, takes possession of it, yet grants the seller a security interest. In such cases, should the courts recognize the secured creditor's interest ahead of claims by other creditors? Should not these other creditors prevail on the ground that they were misled by the debtor's possession and "ostensible ownership"? See, generally, Baird, *Notice Filing and the Problem of Ostensible Ownership,* 12 J. Legal Studies 53 (1983).

Consider the cases that follow with the foregoing questions in mind. Here we see earlier courts wrestling with such questions. The cases involve pre-Uniform Commercial Code security arrangements called "conditional sales contracts" under which, in the jurisdictions at hand, title remained with the seller of goods until the condition was met, namely payment of the full price. If that condition was not met, title never went to the buyer; it follows, too, that on conventional property analysis the buyer did not have the power to convey it to, or to create a security interest in it on behalf of, third parties. Of course, this was contrary to the principle of ostensible ownership according to which the possessor has such rights. Moreover, there was no recording statute in the jurisdiction providing that the secured creditor could file notice of a security interest and thus give public notice that the possessor-debtor was not the sole owner. The student should also keep these cases in mind when reading the materials that follow on the history of personal property in the United States. Of course, today, Article 9 of the UCC generally requires that the secured creditor either take possession or file to maximize rights against third parties. The notion that a creditor-seller of goods could effectively provide by agreement for the retention of "good title" (until payment) against third parties to goods that had been sold and delivered to a debtor-buyer under a conditional sale contract without public notice to such third parties now seems laughable. The modern student of Article 9 would cut quickly through the language and would recognize this agreement, in conditional sale terms, to be no more than an "unperfected security interest," and would decide against the secured creditor. Earlier, the problem was not so easy.

McINTOSH & BEGAN v. HILL

Supreme Court of Arkansas, 1886.
47 Ark. 363, 1 S.W. 680.

COCKRILL, C.J. This is replevin for the possession of a mule. The facts, as taken from the abstract, are as follows: "In March, 1884, S.S. Wann contracted to sell to one Overton the mule in controversy, for $90, due in the fall. Until the purchase money was paid the mule was to be and remain the property of Wann, and, upon failure to pay in the fall, Overton was to deliver the mule to Wann, and pay for its *use.* Soon after the purchase, Overton mortgaged the mule, with the crop to be raised by him, to the appellants, for supplies for the year 1884; and at the time told the appellants that he had bought the mule on a credit. Overton died soon after the mortgage. The mule was used to make the crop, a part of which was paid on the mortgage. The parties, not being able to pay for the mule in the fall, returned it to Wann, and settled for the use of it. Wann then sold the mule to the appellee, from whom it was replevied by the appellants under their mortgage. The value of the mule was fifty or sixty dollars. The mortgage was duly acknowledged and recorded while the mule was in Overton's possession, and the sum of about $40 was still due on it." The judgment of the court was against the right of the mortgagees.

The question presented, put in the best light for them, is whether the title of a vendor parting with the possession of a chattel, upon the condition that the title shall not pass until the purchase money is paid, shall prevail against a *bona fide* purchaser for value from the vendee in possession, before the condition is complied with, without notice of the original seller's claim of ownership, or of the condition upon which the delivery was made.

In *Carroll v. Wiggins,* 30 Ark. 402, it was decided that a sale and delivery of personal property, on condition that the title is not to pass until payment of the purchase price, does not vest the title in the vendee until the condition is performed, and the rule was enforced against a purchaser from the vendee with notice of the condition.

In *Andrews v. Cox,* 42 Ark. 473, the question as to the attitude of a purchaser, without notice from a vendee holding subject to a like condition, was discussed by the court in considering a kindred question, and, though this question is not expressly ruled, the intimation is very strong that the title of the original vendor must prevail.

The hardship that is sometimes discovered when the condition is to be enforced against a *bona fide* purchaser has induced some of the courts to come to the conclusion that, as against him, possession is *per se* a badge of fraud; and that the doctrine that, where one of two innocent parties must suffer, the loss should fall on the one who caused the dilemma, protects the *bona fide* purchaser. But possession alone gives no right to transfer title, and one who has no title (and the conditional vendee before performance of the condition has none, according to *Carroll v. Wiggins, supra*) can confer none. Possession of personal property is only *prima facie* evidence of title, and the doctrine of *caveat emptor* prevails, notwithstanding the possession. The *prima facie* title must yield to the actual title, when it is asserted, and the buyer who trusts to appearances must suffer the loss, if they prove delusive. If the vendor is estopped from reclaiming his property from an innocent purchaser, there is no principle, as was said in *Andrews v. Cox,* upon which we could stop short of holding that one who had borrowed or hired any personal property might divest the true owner of his title simply by assuming the power to sell. We think that reason and the overwhelming weight of authority pronounce in favor of the right of the original vendor. The leading case on the subject is that of *Coggill v. Hartford, etc., R.R.,* 3 Gray, 545. See, too, *Ketchum v. Brennan,* 53 Miss. 596; *Fairbanks v. Eureka*

Co., 67 Ala. 109; *Blackwell v. Walker,* 5 Fed.Rep. 419; cases cited in note to *Stadtfield v. Huntsman,* 37 Amer.Rep. 661, 662; Schouler, Pers. Prop. § 300.

Affirmed.

IN RE CRAIG LUMBER CO.

Circuit Court of Appeals, Ninth Circuit, 1921.
269 Fed. 755.

[In the court below, in a bankruptcy proceeding, the appellees filed their petition to reclaim certain machinery and fittings which they had placed in the bankrupt's sawmill in accordance with a contract performed before the bankruptcy. The court below upon the pleadings and the evidence found the facts to be substantially as follows:

That on October 31, 1917, the appellees and the bankrupt entered into a contract whereby the appellees agreed to furnish all machinery, fittings, etc., necessary to equip the bankrupt's sawmill at Craig, Alaska, in accordance with specifications, and agreed to install said machinery and erect necessary buildings therefor. The contract provided that the cost of the sawmill complete should not exceed the estimate of $32,125. It contained a provision that the title to the "apparatus and material herein agreed to be sold" should not pass from the appellees until fully paid for in cash, that upon defaults in payments the appellees might retake the property "agreed to be sold," and in that event it was agreed that the money theretofore paid to the appellees on the contract should be presumed to be the amount of their liquidated damages to be retained by them for breach of the agreement; that the contract further bound the bankrupt to pay the appellees the actual cost of labor and machinery, equipment, and building material, cost of insurance charges, of material and men from Seattle, Wash., to Craig, Alaska, plus 10 per cent., and the bankrupt agreed to pay the appellees in installments, the last of which to be due 30 days from completion of contract; that the appellees fulfilled their contract on or about May 1, 1918; that there remained due them the sum of $12,980.36 on the contract; that before the trial of the cause the trustee in bankruptcy and the Bank of Alaska entered into a stipulation with the appellees whereby the bank took possession of the property described in the contract, and stipulated with the appellees that, if the court should find the contract to be a conditional sale contract, it should make a further finding as to the amount due the appellees under the contract, which sum, if so found, the bank undertook to pay; that the sawmill is constructed on piles on tidelands in a forest reservation, title to which is in the government, and that all the machinery, etc., were so attached to the building as to be easily removable therefrom without damaging the same; that the Bank of Alaska, a party to the suit, holds a mortgage upon the mill and the machinery, but at the time of the execution of said mortgage the bank had notice of the conditional sale contract, and that the appellees had not been fully paid for the machinery; that the material, etc., furnished under the contract by the appellees, together with the work performed thereunder, and the percentages agreed upon in the contract, amount to the sum of $32,539.74, and that in addition thereto the appellees also furnished and delivered to the bankrupt other material, machinery, etc., not included in the contract, amounting to $5,958.79; that after allowing the total credits for payments made there remained a balance due the appellees under the contract of $9,827.39, and the court entered judgment for the appellees for that sum.]

Before GILBERT, ROSS, and HUNT, CIRCUIT JUDGES.

GILBERT, CIRCUIT JUDGE (after stating the facts as above). The appellants contend that it was error to hold that the contract was an agreement for a conditional sale, and they argue that at the time when it was made the appellees had nothing to sell, that the lumber company was merely employing them to build and equip their mill according to plans and specifications at a cost not to exceed a specified sum, that in buying the machinery and fulfilling the contract the appellees were merely agents or employés, and that in paying for the same out of their own funds they but advanced the purchase money as agents for their principal. It has been held that conditional contracts of sale are not favored in the law, and where it is doubtful upon the face of the instrument whether the contract is a conditional sale or a mortgage, it should generally be treated as a mortgage. But here the terms of the instrument leave no room to doubt that a conditional sale was provided for. The appellees were to buy and pay for the machinery and to take title thereto in the first instance in their own name. The purchase price therefor was to be paid by them, not with funds advanced by the lumber company, but with their own money. There is nothing in the instrument to give color to the suggestion that they were agents for the lumber company. On the contrary, it appears that they were contractors, who bound themselves to furnish machinery which the contract provided was thereafter to be sold to the lumber company. There is nothing in the instrument to rebut the intention, expressed in clear terms, that the sale is conditional and that—

"Title to the apparatus and material herein agreed to be sold shall not pass from the company until all payments hereinunder shall have been fully paid in cash. Upon default in any such payments, the company may retake the property agreed to be sold."

It is not rebutted by the fact that the contract provided that the title should not pass until the payment of, not only the cost of the machinery and material, but also the expense of erecting buildings and installing the machinery. All of these sums were reckoned together as constituting the cost of that which was agreed to be conditionally sold. But whether or not the appellees could retain title to the machinery until all these sums were paid is immaterial here.

Under the appropriation of payments which the court below made, the unpaid balance is solely for the purchase price of the machinery and apparatus. In Harkness v. Russell, 118 U.S. 663, 7 Sup.Ct. 51, 30 L.Ed. 285, Mr. Justice Bradley said:

"Such contracts are well known in the law and often recognized, and when free from any fraudulent intent are not repugnant to any principle of justice or equity, even though possession of the property be given to the proposed purchaser."

* * *

We find no merit in the contention that the trustee is, as to the mill and the machinery, in the position of an attaching creditor with rights superior to those of the appellees. Under the amendment of 1910 (section 47a of the Bankruptcy Act [Comp.St. § 9631]), the trustee may attack the validity of any lien or other claims against the bankrupt's property which a creditor holding a lien by legal or equitable proceedings might have attacked. * * * But it does not appear that creditors holding such liens could have successfully attacked the appellees' title.

The appellants cite Washburn v. Inter-Mountain Min. Co., 56 Or. 578, 109 Pac. 382, Ann.Cas. 1912C, 357, a case in which a stamp mill, title to which was reserved by the seller, was with his consent permanently affixed to the freehold; the conditional agreement not being recorded. The court affirmed the rule that an agreement for the conditional sale of a chattel is valid, as well against third parties as against parties to the transaction, but held that the rule relates to parties dealing for the property as a chattel, and does not apply to third parties without notice of the condition, where the character of the property has been changed to realty by being affixed to the soil. In the present case there is no realty and no freehold estate, and the machinery never became a fixture. * * *

"If a person owns a building, and has no property in the land, and may remove the structure when and where he pleases, it is a chattel." 11 R.C.L. 1081; Curry v. Commonwealth Ins. Co., 10 Pick. (Mass.) 535, 20 Am.Dec. 547.

The sawmill was constructed on piles on the tideland, within a forest reservation, to which no one had any title, except the government of the United States.

The decree is affirmed.

Notes

1 This case is a classic priority case. One competitor is the appellee, seller of the goods, who claims to have title because he sold goods under a conditional sales contract whose condition was never met. A second potential competitor was the Bank of Alaska who had a mortgage on the real estate and on the goods but who apparently conceded that it was subordinate to the seller's claim because, according to the court, it had "notice of the conditional sale contract." The third competitor is the trustee in bankruptcy who then, as today, asserts the rights of a hypothetical lien creditor (the rights that would have been those of a creditor under state law had he procured a lien on the date the bankruptcy petition was filed). Today, the trustee prevails under UCC 9–301(1)(b) and section 544(a) of the Bankruptcy Code. But to a lawyer steeped in the logic of real property conveyancing who views the world from the perspective of 1920 and before, the court's logic is unassailable: "Because the debtor never complied with the condition he never received the title and therefore his successors could do no better than he. Therefore appellee (conditional seller) must prevail over mortgagee and trustee."

In using the court's logic, would you come to a different conclusion if the appellee's document was not a conditional sale contract but a mortgage?

The case demonstrates the inevitable conflict between recognition of conveyancing ideas and the policy that one should not be entitled to priority unless he has given publicity to his interest sufficient to put third parties on notice of it.

The fact that the outcome might be different if the lawyer had used a mortgage form instead of a conditional sale form and even though the underlying commercial transaction was the same, should also make one question the holding. Rights of third parties, those by definition not party to the contract, should vary according to commercial realities, not according to the boilerplate used by the lawyer, not so? Put more bluntly, if public policy demands public notice to third parties for one to have priority, the law should not allow lawyers to escape that policy by choice of a different form to which the aggrieved party is not a signatory.

2. In Chapter Seven we will discover that we should not be so confident of our superiority over the early courts. Even under the Uniform Commercial Code we will find difficulty in deciding who should take goods allegedly belonging to one that are in the possession of another under a form titled a "lease" or a "consignment" or a "contract for processing." Do you suppose that the answers to those questions that now trouble American courts will be as obvious to our successors as the answers to *Craig Lumber* are to us? That is a terrible thought.

SECTION 3. PRE–CODE PERSONAL PROPERTY SECURITY LAW IN THE UNITED STATES

The Pledge

Security in some form has existed at least since the time of Hammurabi. In primitive society, and even in rather well developed ancient societies, personal property security typically took the form of the pledge. We will see the modern version of the pledge in UCC 9–305. Its identifying characteristic is that the creditor takes possession of the debtor's personal property. This not only prevents the debtor from squandering the property, but also puts all others on notice of the creditor's interest. The mortgage on real property is also a time honored security device. The mortgage is the transfer of a conditional interest in the debtor's realty to the creditor to secure the debt. In some settings this transfer took the form of an absolute conveyance with the understanding, oral or written, that the creditor will reconvey the real estate upon the debtor's payment. In its modern form there is no such absolute deed but rather a document variously described as a mortgage, a deed of trust, or something of the kind that can be recorded in the real estate records and that discloses certain of the terms of the agreement between the parties. In effect it clouds the debtor's title and precludes him from conveying good title to a third party.

For several quite obvious reasons the pledge cannot be widely used as a security device in a modern society. In the first place, certain intangible rights are not "pledgeable." That is, there is no talisman that identifies the right that can be passed from hand to hand and will put others on notice. Thus, it would be impossible to do an effective "pledge" of an account receivable or of a right to a royalty. Equally important, most debtors need to enjoy the use of their personal property in their business or personal life and are unwilling to part with possession while paying the debt. While pledges of certain passive assets such as stock certificates or bonds still take place, pledges are obviously unsuitable with respect to industrial equipment, inventory, or even a consumer's car.

The Chattel Mortgage

With the coming of industrial society in the nineteenth century and the increase in wealth represented by personal property in the form of goods and intangibles, creditors and debtors sought alternatives to the pledge and to the real estate mortgage. A first and most obvious step was to apply real estate mortgage rules to personal property; so in the 1820's the "chattel mortgage," in which the debtor retained possession of the property, came into being. This child of the real estate mortgage inhabiting the household of the pledge suffered from grossly debilitating genetic difficulties. The courts had become accustomed to the pledge as the exclusive type of personal property security. The courts were also influenced by early cases such as *Twyne's case*, 76 Eng.Rep. 809, 3 Cone 80 (Star Ch. 1601) in which it was held that allowing a debtor possession of collateral was in and of itself a form of fraud. It is therefore hardly surprising that the courts at first were most hostile to the chattel mortgage. Although the chattel mortgage was usually authorized by statute, some courts found it still to be a jury question whether allowing the debtor's possession of the collateral was itself fraudulent. They conceded to the legislature only the fact that such possession was no longer fraudulent as a matter of law and allowed the creditor to get to the jury because of the statute that apparently authorized the chattel mortgage. That judicial response to the chattel mortgage statute shows how deeply entrenched was the idea that possession was critical to an effective security interest in personal property.

The chattel mortgage also suffered from its real estate mortgage lineage. The real estate cases brought with them a nearly fanatical insistence upon accurate description of the collateral and slavish attention to detail in the execution of the instrument and in compliance with the statutory requirements. Thus many chattel mortgages were struck down as invalid because they described property plainly known to all as subject to the chattel mortgage in a way that was insignificantly deviant from an accurate description, as for example, the transposition of two numbers in a thirteen digit motor number in an automobile.

When the parties attempted to apply the chattel mortgage to inventory, they met yet further obstacles. For example, some courts held that the idea of a creditor's security interest in a debtor's inventory was fundamentally inconsistent with the idea that the debtor could convey good title to that inventory to third-party ordinary course purchasers. Furthermore the courts were unwilling to accept the proposition that a chattel mortgage could attach to after-acquired property. Again, real estate conveyance ideas were influential: The courts decided that one could not make a valid present transfer of property to be acquired in the future. Finally, the chattel mortgage did not cover intangibles. Here the courts were doubtless correct in concluding that certain intangibles such as negotiable notes should not and could not be property covered by a chattel mortgage statute without seriously interfering with the free transferability of such assets or with the expectations of those who took them expecting to get good title by possession.

Because the chattel mortgage statutes, again following real estate law, required that a chattel mortgage be executed with respect to each particular piece of property and that the mortgage itself be recorded, the taking of such mortgages in property that was likely to depreciate or be exchanged for other property was exceedingly expensive and cumbersome. Moreover, the courts' incorporation of real estate foreclosure procedures, procedures with a long and tedious history designed to protect debtors, imposed heavy burdens on a creditor who sought to repossess and resell.

Thus—because retention of possession by the debtor had traditionally been thought to be a sign of fraud, because of the excessively formal rules for creating security, because of the difficulties of adaptation to a changing body of goods such as inventory, and because of inapplicability to intangibles—the chattel mortgage was only marginally better than the pledge.

Professor Gilmore has described the process of escaping from the idea that debtors' possession is equivalent to fraud as follows: "That process, however, took the best part of a century, during which the law of personal property security transactions came to resemble the obscure wood in which Dante once discovered the gates of hell." [1 Gilmore, *Security Interests in Personal Property,* 27 (1965).] Professor Gilmore describes the courts' reaction to the chattel mortgage statutes as follows:

> "Anyone could give a chattel mortgage on any of his property (except his stock in trade) to anyone to secure any sort of obligation. However, chattel mortgage law more than made up for the relative simplicity of its theoretical structure by a fastidious, cranky, at times almost insane insistence on documentary formalities * * * The description requirement was sometimes treated as a sort of statute of frauds, so that failure to describe the mortgaged property in terms which suited the court's arbitrary whim voided the mortgage and could not be cured even by uncontroverted and uncontrovertible proof of what was covered by the mortgage. A typical case of this sort would set aside a mortgage of machinery, described in the mortgage in such a way that there could be no possible doubt what machinery was meant, because the serial numbers of the machines were missing."
>
> Id. at 52–53.
>
> "Nineteenth century cases of this sort can be explained on the grounds that the real estate mortgage analogy was more compelling seventy-five years ago than it is today and that the period was one of generalized judicial hostility to all chattel security transactions with the borrower remaining in possession. If it is assumed that the only good mortgage is a dead mortgage, it must be a laudable act to do a mortgage to death with any weapon that comes to hand (footnotes omitted)."

Of course, today Article Nine allows the creation of perfected non-possessory security interests. See UCC 9–303(1).

The Conditional Sale

A third personal property security device, one with attributes superior not only to the pledge but also to the chattel mortgage is the "conditional sales contract." In the eighteenth century a clever English lawyer proposed and Lord Mansfield adopted at common law the idea that a seller of goods could make passage of title to his buyer "conditional" on payment. In this transaction the seller would provide that he would retain title until all paid off. If the buyer failed to make the payments, the seller who had retained title had a right to the goods. Because the buyer had breached the contract, typically he had no right to the return of the payments that he had made. In certain obvious respects this device was far superior to the chattel mortgage. In the first place, it found its roots in the law governing sale of goods. That law did not encourage the judges to require that the parties execute any documents, let alone execute them with great formality and obsessive attention to detail. Thus, a clerical error in the preparation of the document did not mean instant death to the security interest. If the debtor was willing to give up the goods upon his default, no judicial or other foreclosure proceeding was necessary because title had always remained with the seller and nothing was necessary to return it to him. Presumably, even if the debtor was unwilling, the procedure in sales for the return of property owned by the seller was quicker and less cumbersome than the comparable procedure might have been had it been the foreclosure of a chattel mortgage. Finally, the conditional sale did not necessarily require any recording of a document. Thus, one possibility for error was omitted at least until statutes were passed that required recording.

Nevertheless the conditional sale contract had its limitations. It applied only to sellers of goods. Banks or other financing agencies wishing to finance a debtor's personal property could not invoke the device. The device contemplated the sale of individual goods and their use by the buyer and retention of title by the seller. Thus, it was not adaptable to inventory which by definition would be passed on to third parties. Of course, the device also did not apply to intangibles, accounts receivable, and such. Thus, the conditional sale contract found its principal use in the sale by sellers of industrial equipment for use in plants and of consumer hard goods. Even today one will find occasional reference in the cases to the "conditional sale" of a television to a consumer. In Article 9 itself, particularly in the area of purchase money security interests in consumer goods, UCC 9–302(1)(d), one sees the residue of the classical conditional sale contract, the purchase money security interest perfected without filing.

The Trust Receipt

A fourth security device, developed early in the twentieth century, was the trust receipt. This device originated initially with the grain trade and was developed to finance buyer's purchase of imported goods. In the classical common-law trust receipt, an east coast bank would finance a buyer's purchase of goods from Europe. The bank would take possession of the bill of lading or other document, pay the seller of the goods, and retain a claim against the goods in the hands of the buyer until paid. The buyer was thought to be a "trustee" holding the goods in trust for the bank. At common law the bank's claim was held to be superior to the claims of the other creditors of the "trustee" and that was so despite the fact that when the trust receipt first developed, the bank was not required to give any public notice.

For a time after 1930 it looked as though the trust receipt would become the dominant form of personal property security at least in the commercial context. The Uniform Trust Receipts Act was widely adopted and that act validated and elaborated upon the common law trust receipt transaction. It found its most common use in domestic transactions in bank financing of the purchase of autos by dealers. In that setting the bank would pay the price of the automobile to the manufacturer. It would give possession of the automobile to the car dealer who was the trustee. The debtor-dealer would make out a trust receipt with respect to the automobile and the bank gave notice of its interest by filing a general and singular public notice. Note that this was the first deviation from the idea of *recording* of the operative document. Unlike the chattel mortgage where the document itself had to be recorded, here the secured creditor merely filed a notice that dealt with all of the transactions to be undertaken with the debtor.

The Uniform Trust Receipts Act was thus a large step beyond the chattel mortgage law, for it did not require the same fanatical insistence upon detail; it did not require a recording of each document. Moreover it allowed the automatic transfer of the secured creditor's claim from the automobile to the proceeds upon its sale.

Yet this act too had its limitations. First, it was designed for, and largely limited to, purchase money loans against goods. It was doubtful whether it could be adapted to securing an existing unsecured debt against existing collateral or to serving as a loan against existing and presently owned collateral that would not be purchased with the loan proceeds. Moreover, it was apparently limited to lenders and did not apply to sellers in most circumstances. It did not provide for a continuing or "floating" lien that would float over all of the debtor's assets without respect to individual trust receipts on a particular asset. Nor did it permit a general loan against intangibles. While it apparently worked well on import transactions and with purchase money security interests in large-item collateral such as automobiles, it was not readily adaptable to inventory lending as a general matter.

So it was with tangible personal property on the eve of the UCC's birth. The nineteenth and twentieth centuries saw a similar haphazard common law and legislative development of a body of law to permit secured lending against intangibles. Of course to the extent an intangible was pledgeable, as was a note, there had always been a mode of financing against an intangible. But many intangibles such as accounts receivable, were thought not to be pledgeable and did not fit under any of the other obvious security devices.

The Factor's Lien

One device, originally specific to the textile trade (a large part of its history) is the factor's lien. Originally factors were persons who took the output of textile mills on commission, had a common law lien with respect to the goods in their possession, and sold them to third parties for a commission. If that sale was on credit, the payment was presumably to be made directly to the factor and served as security for any amount owed him by the textile manufacturer. In time the factor ceased selling the goods and became nothing more or less than a lender to the textile manufacturer. The factor would claim a lien on the inventory of the mill owner to whom he had made a loan. Since the factor was not in possession of the inventory, there was no public notice of his interest, and that raised a serious question about the validity of this lien. The principal value of the collateral was the receivables produced on sale of the inventory. The factor became a "buyer" of these accounts. That is to say, the factor took the credit risk inherent in the account and if the account debtor failed to pay, it was his loss, not the loss of the textile manufacturer. Moreover, typically the factor gave notice of the sale of the account to the account debtor and required that the account debtor make payments directly to him, not to the debtor (textile manufacturer). Often the term "factor" is used in this sense today, but not invariably so. Usually one who refers to a "factor" today refers to a party who buys accounts, i.e., who takes them and assumes the credit risk, not one who lends against them with full recourse against his assignor-debtor.

Ultimately factoring was blessed by section 45 of the Personal Property Law, enacted in 1911 in New York. This section was applied many times by the courts, was amended, and ultimately copied in other states. Whether the factor's lien could be used as a device for a long-term loan secured by a "floating lien" on the revolving inventory and accounts was unclear—that was not the normal mode of financing and apparently the issue was not tested. Likewise, section 45 was not designed and apparently not used for a loan secured only by accounts receivable without regard to inventory and there were questions whether it authorized non-notification financing (taking security in accounts without notifying the account debtor). In any event the factors' lien laws did not constitute a wholesale indorsement of accounts receivable lending. Even in the later stages, factoring acts lending was limited mostly to the textile industry and expanded only in a hesitating way under the newly enacted statutes to other areas. It was doubtful under most of the factors lien acts whether one could engage in what would now be regarded as traditional, non-notification accounts receivable financing not accompanied by a prior security interest in the inventory.

The Assignments of Accounts

At common law there was a development parallel to the New York factor's lien law that permitted accounts receivable financing. This was to treat an assignment of an account receivable for the purpose of security like any other assignment and to grant priority to the assignee over other parties claiming the account either on the basis of the time of assignment or on the basis of the time of notification to the account debtor. If one analyzed the problem merely as a question of "assignment" and "ownership," there was no requirement of a public filing nor any doubt about the superior ownership of the first assignee.

The decision in Corn Exchange National Bank and Trust Co. v. Klauder, 318 U.S. 434, 63 S.Ct. 679, 87 L.Ed. 884 (1943), disrupted the comfortable relationship of the bank and others, who being first assignees, were thought to be true owners. It held that, at least in a jurisdiction where priority dated from the time of notification to the account debtor, a creditor who had taken an assignment was subordinate to the debtor's bankruptcy trustee unless the notification had been given more than four months before the debtor's bankruptcy. That decision called into question the lender's claim in accounts in states that followed the notification rules at least where there had not been notification. Following in its wake, most states passed accounts receivable statutes that validated lenders' interests. Some of these did not require notification as a condition of perfection, but ultimately most of them were amended to require public notification. Many of the statutes covered all assignments of accounts and so included in their scope many assignments that were not intended for security. Moreover they wrestled with the question how to define an account, whether it was to include rights represented by negotiable instruments or certain non-negotiable instruments (such as security agreements). Some of the Article 9 distinctions among different forms of Article 9 collateral, "chattel paper," "accounts," "instruments" and "general intangibles," grow out of the learning under the accounts receivable statutes.

The Field Warehouse

The field warehouse is a final pre-Code personal property security device that merits a word. This was a device under which the debtor put his goods out of his possession and into the hands of a "field warehouse." It was said to be a "field" warehouse because the warehouse was located on the debtor's own premises. Typically such a warehouse would be set off from the debtor's own inventory by a chicken wire or other fence, or consisted of a locked room to which the debtor theoretically did not have access. A person in the employ of the warehouse company (but often a former employee of the debtor) was assigned to oversee the goods, to issue receipts to the lender covering them, and to deliver them only upon direction from the holder of the warehouse receipt, the lender. By limiting the debtor's physical possession and use of the asset and by holding the warehouseman's net worth available for claim in case the warehouse was not properly run, this device protected not only against the claims of third party creditors and trustees in bankruptcy, but also against certain fraudulent behavior of the debtor himself. With the passage of the Uniform Commercial Code and the appearance of an easy method of perfecting a security interest in a shifting mass of inventory, the field warehouse has doubtless declined in importance. Yet even today it persists. Although it is more expensive than a conventional inventory loan, it protects against serious risks (i.e., the debtor's own fraud) that a conventional security interest does not touch.

Although we will not return to the history of personal property security as such, the student should not dismiss it as unimportant. A knowledge of this history will help the student both to understand some of the provisions of Article 9 of the Uniform Commercial Code and to appreciate the significance of some decisions under the Code. The roots of personal property security in real estate mortgage law explain the nineteenth century judicial insistence that secured creditors dot their i's and cross their t's. The occasional recurrence of such cases, despite Article 9's instruction that the courts should interpret the filing and notice requirements in a less formal way may, too, be the product of a real estate mentality. Conceivably historic skepticism about the propriety of non-possessory security in personal property also stems from this mentality. We believe that such skepticism forms the basis for an occasional modern decision in which the court strikes down a secured creditor's claim on grounds that seem inappropriate under Article 9.

Our review of the varied forms of pre-Code personal property security suggests how radical, even heretical, was the idea that a single statute could embody a single form of security device that would cover all personal property security. The entire pre-Code history of American personal property law reveals a crazy quilt evolution of various security devices designed to solve particular problems. The very idea of a single, unitary security device to cover all of these must have seemed bizarre in the extreme when it was first proposed after World War II.

The study of Article 9 will reveal, however, some residual traces of various pre-Code personal property security devices. A security interest in certain collateral can be perfected only by possession (see UCC 9–304(1)): a security interest in other forms of collateral can be perfected only by acts excluding possession (see UCC 9–302). Here we can detect pre-Code notions of what could be pledged and what not. The Code recognizes automatic perfection without either possession by the creditor or the filing of a financing statement in some situations. These are the natural descendents of the conditional sale contract (and to a lesser extent of the common law accounts receivable lien). Thus to say we today have but one security device is not to say there is only one mode of perfection or to say that all of the legal rules apply to every transaction irrespective of the type of collateral.

Finally, history should tell us something of the future, at least if we read it with care. In the nineteenth century we saw how a major personal property security device, the chattel mortgage, grew out of real estate mortgage law and carried with it the burdens of that law. Later we saw clever lawyers and judges adapting and developing ideas from sales law, such as the conditional sale, and from trust law, such as the trust receipt. Like the chattel mortgage, these devices have the genetic imprint of their predecessors and not surprisingly courts respond to that imprint. On the other hand, the drafters of Article 9 forgot to insulate that body of law from "outside" influence. For example, they recognized that the rules that might be appropriate and fair for a two-party sales contract ought not necessarily be carried over to a security transaction where the interests of third-party creditors were often at stake. But as we will see, the drafters were not completely successful in stifling the imaginations of lawyers and judges. Some of the most interesting questions under Article 9 have to do with the scope and coverage of present day transactions designed to function as security but also to escape some of the Article 9 requirements. For example, the courts have been faced with the recurring question: Is this document a lease to be analyzed under the common law of bailments or is it a security agreement to be governed by Article 9 of the Uniform Commercial Code? They have struggled at length with the question whether one taking an interest in a real estate mortgagee's right was governed by Article 9 or by some other law. We will deal with these and other scope questions in Chapter Seven, and they may fairly be regarded as reminiscent of earlier developments that brought us the conditional sale contract, the trust receipt and other security devices. Time and experience foretell that the drafters' attempt to bring all conceivable personal property security devices and quasi security devices entirely under Article 9's tent was doomed from the start. No drafter's pen can be equal to the ingenuity and imagination of creditors and their lawyers.

SECTION 4. STRUCTURE OF ARTICLE 9, A ROADMAP

A. Scope

In Chapter Seven we will deal with some subtle and difficult scope problems. For the time being, however, the student should understand what kinds of transactions in general are covered and what are excluded. The basic scope provision is UCC 9–102; that provision is supplemented by UCC 9–104, titled "Transactions Excluded from Article." Consistent with the idea that there is but a single security interest and security agreement, that substance is everything, and that form is very little, section 9–102(1) provides that the article applies "to any transaction (regardless of its form) which is intended to create a security interest in personal property * * *." Thus, Article 9 would cover transactions that were formerly chattel mortgages, conditional sales, liens on accounts receivable under statute or at common law, and uniform trust receipt lending. Section 9–102(2) contains a laundry list making it clear that a security agreement "regardless of its form" is to be included. Section 9–102(1)(b) includes certain "sales" and 9–102(3) extends it to security in security interests outside the article, e.g., security interests in notes and mortgages.

Section 9–104 has 12 exclusions from Article 9. Most of those apply to transactions that either are only marginally related to financing and already have a separate body of statutory or common law that govern them or that are almost completely unrelated to commercial financing. An example of the former would be UCC 9–104(i) excluding from Article 9 coverage "any right of set-off." An example of the latter would be 9–104(k) that excludes from Article 9 the transfer of an interest in a tort claim. Despite the breadth of 9–102 and the specificity of 9–104, Chapter Seven reveals that there remain many complicated scope issues, issues that will dog the courts and scholars as long as Article 9 survives.

The student should appreciate that there are several basic types of scope questions. For example, there is the question of the *geographic scope* of Article 9 as it is enacted in any particular state. Put in its most common form: Does A perfect a security interest by filing in State Y or State Z? Section 9–103 answers that question in most circumstances.

There is also a scope *conflict with federal law.* The most common such conflict arises between Article 9 and the federal Bankruptcy Code, but there is a variety of other arguably relevant federal laws such as those dealing with copyrights, patents, filing of liens on aircraft, ship mortgages, etc. There is also the federal common law that applies to the United States government in its capacity as a lender and there is the potential for conflict with other state statutory law. For example every state has a statute that confers liens, sometimes referred to as mechanics liens, on those who do certain work on real or personal property and improve its value. For the most part, the rights of such claimants and their priority are governed by these specialized statutes and are entirely outside of Article 9. Ironically, therefore, one of the most interesting and difficult lawyer questions has nothing whatever to do with the substance of Article 9 but with the question: does Article 9 govern this transaction at all?

Problem 2–2

Alfredo is a contractor who builds houses and small buildings. Typically he sells the building at the end of its construction to the owner and takes back a land-sale contract or a mortgage and note. The bank asks you if it must comply with Article 9 if it wishes to enjoy the economic value in the mortgagee's interest in the note or the vendor's interest in the land-sale contract. These are the intangible assets that the contractor Alfredo has offered to transfer to the bank. See UCC 9–102 and 9–104.

Problem 2–3

Edgar has a savings account with First Bank. If he wishes to borrow from the University Credit Union, giving a security interest in his account, will it be sufficient for the Credit Union to comply with Article 9 rules on the creation and perfection of the security interest?

Problem 2–4

Irene bought a heavy plastic swimming pool from Ajax Co. on credit. She plans to have a large hole dug in her back yard, where she will install the pool. She also plans to construct firm wooden walkways around the edge of the pool. If Ajax wants to perfect a security interest in the pool, does Article 9 apply?

B. Creation of the Security Interest

At the outset we have seen that Article 9 visualizes a security interest that arises when the events under UCC 9–203 have occurred. Section 9–203, like UCC 9–102, contemplates a single document called a security agreement as the typical means of creating a security interest. While a security agreement to give a security interest in accounts receivable might be quite unlike a security agreement giving a security interest in an automobile, each would be titled "Security Agreement" and each would be tested by the same rules under UCC 9–203. Under that provision a security interest arises and becomes enforceable between the parties and third parties when there is an appropriate writing (or when the creditor has possession pursuant to agreement) and has given value (usually making the loan), see UCC 1–201(44), and when the debtor has "rights in the collateral" (usually title). Note the absence of any formal requirement other than a signature. There is no requirement of notarization or of witnesses to the signature; there is no requirement that the description of the collateral be specific and, indeed, UCC 9–110 provides that it need only be such as would "reasonably identify" what is described. There is no particular form; it may be written on the back of an envelope or on a plain sheet of paper.

As we have indicated above, section 9–203 rejects the formalism of much pre-Code law. In each of the following cases a security interest would be enforceable and "attached," would it not?

(1) Johnny, a close friend of Robert in a northern Alabama hill town, has agreed to lend Robert $3,000 for one year. In return Robert has agreed to give Johnny a lien on his 1983 F–100 pickup. Robert writes out the following statement on the back of an envelope and gives it to Johnny:

> I give Johnny title to my pickup until I pay him off. Robert.

Johnny gives the $3,000 to Robert and later when Robert fails to repay it, Johnny has a valid and enforceable security interest against Robert's pickup. Certainly value has been given (the loan). The debtor has rights in the collateral (presumably Robert had title to the pickup). Is the document they signed a "security agreement" which contains a "description of the collateral"? We would argue that it is, and we would argue that the description is adequate. What do you think?

(2) In a more formal way Robert might choose to borrow $9,000 to purchase his pickup from his local credit union. As a part of that transaction he is likely to sign a document similar to the following. It too would be an adequate security agreement and the credit union, like Johnny, would have a valid and enforceable agreement once the loan had been made and the document had been signed.

DATE

SECURITY AGREEMENT

CREDIT UNION COPY

(hereinafter called "Debtor"; said term "Debtor" to be read as if in the plural where more than one debtor is a party hereto), for valuable consideration, receipt whereof is hereby acknowledged, hereby grants to

THE UNIVERSITY OF MICHIGAN CREDIT UNION
333 WILLIAM STREET • ANN ARBOR, MICHIGAN 48107
(Hereinafter called secured party)

ACCOUNT NUMBER

a security interest in the property described below, in any accessions thereto, in proceeds of such property or accessions, and, if farm crops, in the products thereof growing, or to be grown, on the premises indicated below (hereinafter called the "Collateral").

COLLATERAL

TITLED PROPERTY ▶	MAKE	YEAR	MODEL	BODY STYLE	IDENTIFICATION NUMBER

All Household Goods, Furniture, and Appliances of Debtor(s) now located in or about the residence of the first named Debtor including, but not limited to, the items described in Schedule B attached hereto and made a part hereof. (APPLICABLE ONLY WHEN CHECKED)

I/We, the undersigned, hereby jointly and severally pledge all paid shares and deposits and payments on shares and deposits which I/we now have or hereafter may have in this credit union, except shares or deposits which may be held pursuant to any "Individual Retirement Trust" or "Keogh Plan" or as an All-Savers Certificate, as security for (1) principal and interest of the loan evidenced by the Note of even date herewith and of any refinancing of all or any part thereof and (2) any other sums which may become due under the Security Agreement and/or real estate mortgage securing such obligations. Shares, deposits and payments thereon are only pledged to an amount equal to the unpaid balance of such indebtedness. I/We hereby authorize the credit union in the event of default to apply any or all such paid shares and deposits and payments on same to the repayment of any such indebtedness.

However, Borrower may withdraw shares or deposits in excess of $ ____ if loan payments are up to date.

as security for (1) principal and interest of the loan evidenced by the Note of even date herewith and of any refinancing of all or any part thereof and (2) any other sums which may become due under any real estate mortgage securing said Note or under this Security Agreement.

Any Debtor who has joined herein solely for the purpose of supplying Collateral, and is not a party of the Note, shall not be liable for the debt, or for any deficiency after resale of the Collateral.

Authority is hereby given the Secured Party to complete this Security Agreement in any necessary respect in the event that it is executed while still incomplete.

DEBTOR HEREBY WARRANTS AND COVENANTS THAT:

(A) The collateral is bought or used primarily for

☐ Personal, family, or household purposes ☐ Farming operations use ☐ Business use and, if checked here ▶ ☐ is being acquired with the proceeds of the note or notes, the check for which secured party may make payable to the debtor and seller, or may disburse directly to the seller of the collateral.

(B) The Collateral will be kept at the address shown at the beginning of this Security Agreement or at any other place in the State of Michigan if Debtor notifies Secured Party of such location. Debtor shall not remove such Collateral from the State of Michigan without the consent of Secured Party.

(C) If the collateral is bought or used primarily for business use, debtor's principal place of business in said state (if any) is that shown at the beginning of this agreement; and all other places of business in said state outside of the town or city mentioned in the previous clause are located as follows:

→

→

(D) The following is the legal description of real estate on which farm crops are growing or to be grown, or to which collateral is to be attached.

→

→

and the name and address of the record owner is

→

(E) Debtor represents that Debtor's residence (place of business) is that shown opposite Debtor's name above, and agrees that all notices required to be sent or received shall be sent to or received at said address or any subsequent address of which Debtor gives written notice to Secured Party.

This Security Agreement is subject to and includes the additional provisions set forth on the reverse side hereof, the same being incorporated herein by reference. The word "herein" shall refer to and include the provisions of both sides hereof.

Debtor hereby acknowledges receipt of a duplicate original of this Security Agreement

DEBTOR ✕	DEBTOR ✕
DEBTOR ✕	DEBTOR ✕
DEBTOR ✕	DEBTOR ✕

(Where the Collateral is Household Goods, Furniture, and Appliances, the instrument must be signed by both husband and wife)

[E1224]

ADDITIONAL PROVISIONS

FURTHER WARRANTIES AND COVENANTS OF DEBTOR. Debtor hereby warrants, covenants and agrees that:

1. (a) Except for the security interest granted hereby, Debtor is the owner of the Collateral free from any adverse lien, security interest or encumbrance; and Debtor will defend the Collateral against all claims and demands of all persons at any time claiming the same or any interest therein.
   (b) There is no unpaid balance of principal or interest owing on the purchase price of the Collateral or for money loaned for the acquisition of the Collateral or any unpaid charges in connection therewith.
   (c) No financing statement covering any of the Collateral is on file in any public office other than contemplated by this Security Agreement.
2. (a) Debtor will join with the Secured Party in executing one or more financing statements in form satisfactory to the Secured Party.
   (b) Debtor will join with the Secured Party in executing one or more amendments to the financing statement when same may be necessary to correct any errors in the financing statement.
3. Debtor will not sell or otherwise transfer any part or all of the Collateral or any interest therein without the written consent of Secured Party.
4. (a) Debtor shall maintain in force at Debtor's expense at all times theft, fire and extended coverage and, for motor vehicle collateral, physical damage insurance on all of the Collateral now or hereafter subject to the terms of this Security Agreement in such amounts as approved by the Secured Party. Such insurance shall be payable to Secured Party and Debtor as their interests shall appear, and shall require not less than 10 days written notice of cancellation to the Secured Party.
   (b) If the Debtor does not maintain the insurance as required, the Secured Party may procure same and pay the premiums thereon. The amount of premiums so paid shall be due and payable forthwith by the Debtor to the Secured Party and shall be secured by the Collateral hereunder pursuant to the terms of this Security Agreement. Such action by the Secured Party shall not constitute a waiver of the Debtor's default.
5. Debtor shall at all times keep the Collateral:
   (a) Free from any adverse liens, encumbrances or other security interests.
   (b) In good order and repair and in as good condition as the Collateral now is, reasonable wear and tear excepted.
   (c) Available for examination and inspection by the Secured Party at the address of the Debtor.
   (d) If the Debtor does not comply with "5(a)" above, the Secured Party may discharge the liens, security interests or encumbrances. If the Debtor does not maintain the Collateral as required by "5(b)" above, the Secured Party may procure and pay for the maintenance or repair. In such events the amounts paid by the Secured Party shall be due and payable forthwith by the Debtor to the Secured Party and shall be secured by the Collateral hereunder pursuant to the terms of this Security Agreement. Such action by the Secured Party shall not constitute a waiver of the Debtor's default.
6. Debtor shall not use the Collateral in violation of any statute or ordinance.
7. (a) Debtor shall pay when due all taxes and assessments upon the Collateral or in connection with its use or operation or upon this Security Agreement or upon any Note or Notes secured by this Security Agreement.
   (b) Upon failure to make such payments when due, same may be made by Secured Party. Amounts so paid by the Secured Party shall be due and payable forthwith by the Debtor to the Secured Party and shall be secured by the Collateral hereunder pursuant to the terms of this Security Agreement. Such payment by the Secured Party shall not constitute a waiver of Debtor's default.

DEBTOR: READ CAREFULLY

8. Debtor shall forthwith cause the security interest of the Secured Party in the Collateral to be noted or endorsed upon a certificate of title, or application therefor, where required to perfect that interest.

MUTUAL COVENANTS. The parties hereto agree that:

9. This Security Agreement, any financing statement or amendments thereof, any continuation statement, termination statement, statement of release of collateral, and statement of assignment may be produced in as many counterparts through carbon impression or imprintation or other methods, ~~and may be executed through signature of the top document and through carbon or other simultaneous~~ impressions or imprintation of the succeeding duplicates thereof. Each of such documents so prepared and executed shall be deemed fully executed duplicate originals.

10. From time to time additional or substituted collateral may be made subject to the terms of this Security Agreement by the execution of an amendment to the financing statement setting forth such additional collateral. This Security Agreement shall be deemed so amended upon the execution of such amended financing statement or statements.
11. Secured Party shall have authority to complete any financing statement or amendment thereof in any necessary respect in the event same shall be executed while still incomplete.
12. If Debtor does not reimburse Secured Party for any amount advanced by Secured Party pursuant to paragraphs 4(b), 5(d) or 7(b) hereof, Secured Party may add the unreimbursed amounts to the principal balance of the loan secured by this Security Agreement.

EVENTS OF DEFAULT. The Debtor shall be in default under the terms of this Security Agreement:
13. Upon default in whole or in part of any payment or payments due under any Note or indebtedness secured by the terms of this Security Agreement.
14. If any warranty, representation or statement made or furnished to Secured Party by or on behalf of the Debtor proves to have been false in any material respect when made or furnished.
15. Upon the loss, theft, substantial damage, destruction, sale or encumbrance to or of any of the Collateral, or the making of any levy, seizure or attachment thereof or thereon.
16. Upon the insolvency of the Debtor, or the appointment of a receiver over any of Debtor's property, or upon the institution of any proceeding for the liquidation of the debts of the Debtor in any State or Federal Court.
17. Upon removal of the Collateral by Debtor from the place of keeping herein designated, except as permitted by paragraph (B) on the reverse hereof.
18. In the event of the falsity or upon the breach of any of the warranties or covenants set forth in paragraphs one through eight inclusive above.
19. When funds are loaned for the acquisition of specified Collateral, failure of the Debtor to acquire the specified Collateral with the loan proceeds.

REMEDIES.
20. In the event of a default listed in paragraphs 13 through 19 above and at any time thereafter Secured Party may declare all obligations secured hereby immediately due and payable and Secured Party shall have the right to take possession of the Collateral wherever located without judicial process if such taking can be made without breach of the peace but otherwise by use of judicial process. In the event of such taking possession, the parties hereto shall have the rights and duties with respect to such Collateral, and otherwise, as prescribed by law.
21. Secured Party may require Debtor to assemble the Collateral and make it available to Secured Party at a place to be designated by Secured Party which is reasonably convenient to both parties.
22. Unless the Collateral is perishable or threatens to decline speedily in value or is of a type customarily sold on a recognized market, Secured Party will give Debtor reasonable notice of the time and place of any public sale thereof or of the time after which any private sale or any other intended disposition thereof is to be made. The requirements of reasonable notice shall be met if such notice is mailed, postage prepaid, to the address of Debtor specified in paragraph (E) on the reverse hereof at least five days before the time of the sale or disposition.
23. Expenses of retaking, holding, preparing for sale, selling or the like shall include such reasonable attorney fees and expenses as may be legally permitted, and if paid by Secured Party shall be secured by the Collateral hereunder pursuant to the terms of this Security Agreement.
24. Debtor agrees that Secured Party or its agents in taking possession of any vehicle after default may also take possession of any personal property therein. If during said repossession, personal property within the vehicle is seized, such property shall be held by the Secured Party or its agents for a period of 5 days after such seizure and if the Debtor does not within that time deliver to the Secured Party a written request for said property, same shall be deemed abandoned by the Debtor.

GENERAL.
25. No waiver by Secured Party of any other default shall operate as a waiver of any other default or of the same default on a future occasion.
26. All rights of Secured Party hereunder shall inure to the benefit of its successors and assigns; and all obligations of Debtor shall bind Debtor's heirs, executors, administrators, successors or assigns.
27. if there be more than one Debtor, their obligations hereunder shall be joint and several.

[E1225]

(3) In large commercial transactions the security agreement is likely to look quite different from the document set out above. In that transaction lawyers on both sides will have been involved and while some of the terms will be boilerplate, others may be specifically drawn for the particular transaction. For an example of such a security agreement, see p. 126 (Chapter Three).

In Chapter Three we will deal with some of the more intricate questions involved in UCC 9–203 and with the law's application to the imperfect attempts by creditors and debtors to comply with UCC 9–203. Occasionally, for example, a creditor is embarrassed to find that he has no security agreement at all because it was lost or never signed even though the parties agreed on security and executed many other documents that indicate they intended such. All of these complications together with questions involving subsequent advances, after-acquired property, and various description issues, we will confront in the next chapter.

Problem 2–5

Fritz owned a racehorse which was kept by Richard at his farm. Fritz sold the horse on January 1 to Jean for $7,500, Jean to pay $1,500 down on January 10 and the balance on March 1. Fritz told Jean: "I'll keep title until you pay me" and Jean said: "O.K." Does Fritz have an enforceable security interest?

C. Perfection of the Security Interest

(1) Is Filing Required?

Section 9–203 describes "attachment and enforceability." To say that a security agreement is valid between the creditor and the debtor is important, but a question of equal or greater importance deals with its enforceability against third parties. When a third party gets a lien on the asset or the debtor grants a security interest to a third party, is that person's claim superior to or subordinate to the secured creditor's claim? When the debtor goes into bankruptcy, can the secured creditor take the asset in preference to the trustee? These questions relate to "priority," which typically depends upon "perfection." See UCC 9–303(1). To say that a security interest is "perfected" is to say that the secured creditor has complied with UCC 9–302 and, usually, that his interest will therefore be superior to others whose claims against the property arise later. Attachment produces enforceability against the debtor; perfection gives rise to enforceability against third parties. (As we will see, in some situations, attachment constitutes perfection.)

An unperfected security interest is not worthless, but section 9–301 tells us that it may be nearly so. That section, 9–301(1)(b), says that an unperfected security interest is subordinated to the interests of a lien creditor. Technically, a lien creditor is a party who has acquired a lien on the debtor's property by attachment, levy, or the like. But the archetype lien creditor is the trustee in bankruptcy. The combination of UCC 9–301(1)(b) and section 544(a) of the Bankruptcy Code (giving the trustee the rights of a lien creditor) means that the trustee will be entitled to assets in which there is a secured but unperfected interest. Generally the opposite will be true if the interest has been perfected prior to bankruptcy. Thus, one may assume that no secured creditor in his right mind intentionally remains unperfected. He finds himself so because he has failed to file in the proper place or failed to file at all or because he has stumbled in some other way along the road to perfection. Rarely, if ever, will he have consciously adopted the position of an unperfected secured creditor.

Section 9–302 may be read as an inventory of the ways in which one becomes perfected. It is important to read part 3 of Article 9 together with the definitional sections, 9–105, 9–106, 9–107, and 9–109. Those sections distinguish accounts from general intangibles and from chattel paper. They identify which goods are consumer goods, which are equipment and which are farm products, and they add some other definitions as well. The definitions find their principal use in instructing the lawyer which mode of perfection is permitted and which may be necessary. For example, UCC 9–302(1)(a) defines possession as provided in 9–305 as a mode of perfection. However, reading UCC 9–305, one discovers that only certain assets "may be perfected" by the creditor's possession. These of course include goods. They also include certain intangibles appropriately represented, e.g., a negotiable instrument. The comments to 9–305 make it clear that they exclude things such as general intangibles and accounts receivable for which there is no such representative embodiment.

If we have followed a single strand through UCC 9–102 and 9–203, it now breaks into individual threads in 9–302 and to some extent leads along individual paths through the remainder of Article 9. The student who has read the history above can now see the reappearance of some of the threads that come from that history. For example, 9–302(1)(d) provides for the automatic perfection (i.e., without filing or taking possession or any other act) of a "purchase money security interest in consumer goods." Here we encounter descendants of the conditional sale.

Return now to UCC 9–302(1). In a kind of back-handed way it states the general proposition of Article 9: "A financing statement must be filed to perfect all security interests except the following." Thus, filing is the normal mode of perfection under Article 9. Putting aside for the moment the consumer goods exception, filing must outstrip all other modes of perfection by a factor of thousands to one.

By now it should be obvious that the usual function of "perfection" is to provide a notice or a warning to later creditors that tells them of the earlier creditor's interest. The penalty for not giving notice to such third parties in the prescribed form is usually to be subordinated to them whether they be the trustee in bankruptcy or a later secured creditor. The student should read through Part 3 of Article 9, and bear in mind that filing is the norm and that the events described in UCC 9–304 and 9–305 deal with a small minority of all the transactions. Most of the learning about perfection as to proceeds of collateral can wait, but it is not too soon to look at 9–306, a provision that both authorizes a security interest in "identifiable" proceeds (e.g., a check which is received on the sale of inventory collateral), and also specifies in 9–306(3) the rules for perfecting a security interest in proceeds.

The bank's security interest in our last example above would be perfected by filing a document like those set out below, would it not?

Financing Statement—Form UCC–1—Central Filing—1972 Illinois Article 9

STATE OF ILLINOIS

UNIFORM COMMERCIAL CODE—FINANCING STATEMENT—FORM UCC-1

INSTRUCTIONS:
1. PLEASE TYPE this form. Fold only along perforation for mailing.
2. Remove Secured Party and Debtor copies and send other 3 copies with interleaved carbon paper to the filing officer. Enclose filing fee.
3. If the space provided for any item(s) on the form is inadequate the item(s) should be continued on additional sheets, preferably 5" x 8" or 8" x 10". Only one copy of such additional sheets need be presented to the filing officer with a set of three copies of the financing statement. Long schedules of collateral, indentures, etc., may be on any size paper that is convenient for the secured party.

This STATEMENT is presented to a filing officer for filing pursuant to the Uniform Commercial Code.

Debtor(s) (Last Name First) and address(es)	Secured Party(ies) and address(es)	For Filing Officer (Date, Time, Number, and Filing Office)

1. This financing statement covers the following types (or items) of property:

ASSIGNEE OF SECURED PARTY

2. ☐ Products of Collateral are also covered.

______ Additional sheets presented.
______ Filed with Office of Secretary of State of Illinois.
______ Debtor is a transmitting utility as defined in UCC §9-105.

By:____________________
Signature of (Debtor)
(Secured Party)*

*Signature of Debtor Required in Most Cases:
Signature of Secured Party in Cases Covered By UCC §9-402 (2)

(1) Filing Officer Copy - Alphabetical

This form of financing statement is approved by the Secretary of State.

STANDARD FORM UNIFORM COMMERCIAL CODE - FORM UCC-1 - REV. 2-74

[B1132]

Financing Statement—Form UCC–2—Local Filing—1972 Illinois Article 9

STATE OF ILLINOIS

UNIFORM COMMERCIAL CODE—FINANCING STATEMENT—FORM UCC-2

INSTRUCTIONS:
1. PLEASE TYPE this form. Fold only along perforation for mailing.
2. Remove Secured Party and Debtor copies and send other 3 copies with interleaved carbon paper to the filing officer. Enclose filing fee.
3. If the space provided for any item(s) on the form is inadequate the item(s) should be continued on additional sheets, preferably 5" x 8" or 8" x 10". Only one copy of such additional sheets need be presented to the filing officer with a set of three copies of the financing statement. Long schedules of collateral, indentures, etc., may be on any size paper that is convenient for the secured party.

This STATEMENT is presented to a filing officer for filing pursuant to the Uniform Commercial Code.

Debtor(s) (Last Name First) and address(es)	Secured Party(ies) and address(es)	For Filing Officer (Date, Time, Number, and Filing Office)

1. This financing statement covers the following types (or items) of property:

ASSIGNEE OF SECURED PARTY

2. (If collateral is crops) The above described crops are growing or are to be grown on:
(Describe Real Estate)

3. (If applicable) The above goods are to become fixtures on (The above timber is standing on . . .) (The above minerals or the like (including oil and gas) or accounts will be financed at the wellhead or minehead of the well or mine located on . . .) (Strike what is inapplicable) (Describe Real Estate)

and this financing statement is to be filed in the real estate records. (If the debtor does not have an interest of record)
The name of a record owner is

4. ☐ Products of Collateral are also covered.

______ Additional sheets presented.
______ Filed with Recorder's Office of ________________ County, Illinois.

By:____________________
Signature of (Debtor)
(Secured Party)*

*Signature of Debtor Required in Most Cases
Signature of Secured Party in Cases Covered By UCC §9-402 (2)

(1) Filing Officer Copy - Alphabetical

This form of financing statement is approved by the Secretary of State.

STANDARD FORM UNIFORM COMMERCIAL CODE FORM UCC-2 REV. 4-73

[B1137]

Statements of Continuation, Partial Release, Assignment, Termination or Amendment—Form UCC–3—1972 Illinois Article 9

STATE OF ILLINOIS
UNIFORM COMMERCIAL CODE
STATEMENTS OF CONTINUATION, PARTIAL RELEASE, ASSIGNMENT, ETC.—FORM UCC-3

INSTRUCTIONS:
1. PLEASE TYPE this form. Fold only along perforation for mailing.
2. Remove Secured Party and Debtor copies and send other 3 copies with interleaved carbon paper to the filing officer.
3. Enclose filing fee.
4. If the space provided for any item(s) on the form is inadequate the item(s) should be continued on additional sheets, preferably 5" x 8" or 8" x 10". Only one copy of such additional sheets need be presented to the filing officer with a set of three copies of Form UCC-3. Long schedules of collateral, etc., may be on any size paper that is convenient for the secured party.
5. At the time of filing, filing officer will return third copy as an acknowledgement.

This STATEMENT is presented to THE FILING OFFICER for filing pursuant to the Uniform Commercial Code:

Debtor(s) (Last Name First) and address(es)	Secured Party(ies) and address(es)	For Filing Officer (Date, Time, Number, and Filing Office)

This Statement refers to original Financing Statement No. ____________

Date filed: ____________, 19____ Filed with ____________

A. ☐ CONTINUATION..... The original financing statement between the foregoing Debtor and Secured Party, bearing the file number shown above, is still effective.

B. ☐ PARTIAL RELEASE.. From the collateral described in the financing statement bearing the file number shown above, the Secured Party releases the property indicated below.

C. ☐ ASSIGNMENT.......... The Secured Party certifies that the Secured Party has assigned to the Assignee whose name and address is shown below, Secured Party's rights under the financing statement bearing the file number shown above in the property indicated below.

D. ☐ TERMINATION........ The Secured Party certifies that the Secured Party no longer claims a security interest under the financing statement bearing the file number shown above.

E. ☐ AMENDMENT.......... The financing statement bearing the above file number is amended.
☐ To show the Secured Party's new address as indicated below.
☐ To show the Debtor's new address as indicated below.
☐ As set forth below:

____________ (Debtor)
(Signature of Debtor, if required)

____________ (Secured Party)

Dated ____________, 19____

By ____________
(Signature of Secured Party)

(1) Filing Officer Copy - Alphabetical

This form of Financing Statement is approved by the Secretary of State.

STANDARD FORM - UNIFORM COMMERCIAL CODE FORM UCC-3 REV. 4-73 (B1142)

Financing Statement/Fixtures—Form UCC–1A—1972 Michigan Article 9

FORM UCC-1A
(4-79)

STATE OF MICHIGAN
UNIFORM COMMERCIAL CODE FINANCING STATEMENT/FIXTURES (to be Recorded with register of deeds)
(Approved by the Secretary of State and Michigan Association of Registers of Deeds)

INSTRUCTIONS:

1. Use this Form instead of Form UCC-1 where the goods are of the types described in Item 4a, b, c, d, or e.
2. Submit this Form to the register of deeds where the land is located. If land is located in two areas, separate Forms should be filed in each locality.
3. TYPE OR PRINT all the information required on this Form.
4. Send WHITE copies to Secretary of State, YELLOW copies to the register of deeds. Appropriate fees should accompany the filing.
5. Retain PINK copies for files of the secured party and debtor.
6. IF ADDITIONAL SPACE IS NEEDED for any items on this Form, continue the items on separate sheets of paper (5" x 8"). One copy of these additional sheets should accompany the Yellow Forms. USE PAPER CLIPS to attach these sheets to the Form (DO NOT USE STAPLES, GLUE, TAPE, ETC.) and indicate in Item 1 the number of additonal sheets attached.
7. At the time of filing, the filing officer will return acknowledgement.
8. Filing Officer copies (register of deeds and Secretary of State) must have original signatures. Only the debtor must sign the financing statement, and the signature of the secured party is not necessary, except that the secured party alone may sign the financing statement in the following four (4) instances: Please specify action in Item 5 below.
   (1) Where the collateral which is subject to the security interest in another state is brought into Michigan or the location of the deptor is changed to Michigan.
   (2) "For proceeds if the security interest in the original collateral was perfected."
   (3) The previous filing has lapsed.
   (4) For collateral acquired after a change of debtor name, and a filing is required under MCLA 440.9402 (2) and (7); MSA 19.9402 (2) and (7).

- -

1. No. of additional sheets	Liber	Page	For Filing Officer (Date, Time, Number, and Filing Office)
2. Debtor(s) (Last Name First) and address(es)	3. Secured Party(ies) and address(es)		

4. This financing statement covers the following types (or items) of property: (Describe) ______

a. The goods are to become fixtures on ☐
b. The above described timber is standing on ☐
c. The goods are crops growing or to be grown on ☐
d. The above described minerals or the like (including oil and gas) are to be extracted from the wellhead or minehead of the well or mine located on ☐
e. The above described accounts include accounts resulting from the sale of minerals or the like (including oil and gas) to be extracted from the well head or minehead of the well or mine located on ☐

(Describe real estate): ______

NAME AND ADDRESS OF ASSIGNEE

And this financing statement is to be recorded in the real estate records, if 1 of the above boxes is checked (if the debtor does not have an interest of record) the name of the record owner is ______

5. | Check if covered: ☐ Products of collateral

______ SIGNATURE OF DEBTOR

______ SIGNATURE OF DEBTOR by: ______ SIGNATURE OF SECURED PARTY OR ASSIGNEE OF RECORD

Filing Officer Copy (C207)

Compare the UCC–1 form set out above with the requirements specified in 9–402. Think for a moment about the ways in which Murphy's Law could apply to the preparation of a UCC–1. For example, the signature might not correspond to the name of the debtor. The debtor's name might be abbreviated in a variety of ways and, of course, it is always possible that the description of the collateral will be found to be too broad to be meaningful or will be so narrow that it excludes some of the assets. In the chapter that follows we will deal with the question whether the financing statement need describe after-acquired property or proceeds.

Problem 2–6

Bank will lend against debtor's inventory and accounts receivable. Assume in turn that the debtor and the debtor's assets are located in a state that has UCC 9–401 alternative 1, alternative 2 and alternative 3. In each case a filing at the Secretary of State's office would be necessary. Would it be sufficient in all cases?

Return now to the transactions involving Johnny and Robert, described on pp. 57–58. How should the secured parties perfect?

The credit union would be perfected without filing anything. That would be because of UCC 9–302(1)(d). Can you see why we tolerate perfection without filing in the 9–302(1)(d) case and why that non-filing rule is *not* extended to purchase money security interest in motor vehicles? Note that the credit union can be a purchase money lender under UCC 9–107(b) even though it is not the seller of the commodity.

Johnny would perfect his security interest in Robert's pickup truck neither automatically nor by filing a UCC–1 form. To see why that is so, read UCC 9–302(3). The interrelationship between the certificate of title legislation and Article 9 is one that we will explore again. In almost all states today the effect of UCC 9–302(3) is to defer to the perfection rules laid down in certificate of title legislation. For some transactions in a few states, a certificate of title listing may still be an optional, rather than a required, mode of perfection.

(2) Where to File the Financing Statement

Section 9–302 and its allies are interesting and perhaps even fun to play with but part 4 of Article 9 is where the battles are fought—where the secured creditor is vanquished, or where he defeats the trustee and subsequent parties. More frequent than any other Article 9 claim is the allegation on behalf of a trustee in bankruptcy (or occasionally a subsequent creditor) that our classical secured creditor has not filed the right document, has not filed it in the right place, or has omitted some relevant information. Finding that the creditor has not complied with part 4 of Article 9 typically leaves him unperfected under UCC 9–302 and naked to the priority attack of most third parties, including the trustee under § 544 of the Bankruptcy Code and UCC 9–301(1)(b). Thus, the legal issues in such a law suit have not to do with UCC 9–302 or 9–301, or even with any provision of the Bankruptcy Code. They are all fought out on the battleground of UCC 9–401, 9–402 and, to a lesser extent, the remaining sections of part 4 in Article 9.

Section 9–401(1) defines the "where" of intrastate filing. Note the three alternatives and bear in mind that when one is practicing law, it is not enough to look merely at the uniform version of the UCC. Lawyers must examine their own state's law to see which of these variants has been adopted. Each requires marginally different filing; the first alternative has the most central filing, the third alternative requires more local filing than the others.

Problem 2–7

Assume that debtor is located in Lansing, Michigan, or alternatively, in Syracuse, New York. Michigan has the second alternative of UCC 9–401; New York has the third. If secured creditor were going to perfect a security interest by filing on a piece of industrial equipment in the possession of debtor in Lansing or Syracuse, where would he file? Michigan would not require a local filing, would it? New York might require a local filing. From the facts given, can one be sure?

One should read UCC 9–401 together with 9–103, the provision which directs one to a particular state or another in the case of collateral with actual or possible multi-state contacts. A filing in Albany is no good if New York's version of 9–103 directs one to file in Columbia, South Carolina, because that is the debtor's residence. Why did the drafters suggest three alternatives? Would it not have been simpler to have had a single filing place for all financing statements in the world located at The Hague or, if one wished to think less globally, in St. Louis (where the Cardinals are)? Why, in this day of rapid data transmission and of instantaneous computer conversation, should we require a Dallas creditor to file in Amarillo?

Part 4 of Article 9 contains more mysteries than may be apparent to the unstudied eye. If, for example, the county recorder of deeds has separate indices for personal property and for real property, should a financing statement be filed in one or in the other with respect to fixtures? What if a financing statement is passed across the counter, the fee paid, but it is then left in a shoe box for a month and other later-presented documents are ultimately filed before it? Recorders and their employees are fallible, and a student dealing with 9–401 should appreciate that.

Even more than UCC 9–401, section 9–402 is the battleground between trustees and secured creditors. Note that it provides for a financing statement that "indicates the types or describes the items of collateral." Because it provides that the financing statement need only indicate "the types," it is clear that this is the kind of filing that was contemplated, for example, by the Uniform Trust Receipts Act, not the kind contemplated by the chattel mortgage statutes. It is not the operative document, the security agreement (the big, fat agreement in a commercial transaction) that is filed. Rather, it is a single-page document describing the collateral in quite general terms, in many cases (all automobiles and other inventory of debtor). On reading the financing statement, one finds little more than whom to pursue for more information. The required public filing will not reveal the amount of the debt or even if there is one. It will not indicate whether there is one or many cars subject to the security agreement, what the interest rate or the term of the loan is or any of the other provisions. Section 9–402 adopts the "notice" filing rule and rejects the idea that the operative document should be "recorded."

Section 9–402(8) is an explicit direction to courts to abandon the kind of fanatical insistence upon detail that characterized judicial behavior with respect to chattel mortgages, at least in the nineteenth century. Even though a financing statement contains "minor errors which are not seriously misleading," it is a valid financing statement. Thus, transposition of motor numbers, description of a blue car as a red one, mistakes in the debtor's or creditor's address, possibly even in the debtor's name, all may be overlooked if they are not seriously misleading.

What do you suppose is the most important thing on the financing statement that is described in UCC 9–402(1) and (3)? The debtor's name or the debtor's address? Is the address of the secured party more important than that of the debtor? Undoubtedly the debtor's name is the single most important factor on the financing statement. Do you see why? The remainder of part 4 of Article 9 contains a series of relatively straightforward and infrequently used provisions. Read them; someday they may be important to you.

Problem 2–8

Assume that the bank had decided to go ahead and make the loan to Alfredo in Problem 2–2. The Bank is going to take security in his interest in the note and mortgage, and in his interest in the land-sale contract. If you decide that the transaction will be governed by Article 9, how would you suggest the bank create a security interest? Perfect it? Note that perfection in this case turns on the definition of the type of collateral. The note is surely an instrument. What if it were not negotiable? What about the vendor's interest in the land-sale contract? Is it critical for the purpose of perfection to determine the identity and classification of the collateral?

D. Priority of the Security Interest

In addition to Sections 9–201 and 9–301, and commencing with UCC 9–306(5), the remaining sections in part 3 of Article 9 are priority sections. They neither describe the mode of attachment nor the mode of perfection but in general establish the relative status of a perfected secured creditor, vis a vis another party, whether that party be a purchaser, a subsequent secured creditor, or a lien holder.

It is not too soon to understand that even a perfected security interest is not perfect. Section 9–307(1) tells us that a retail purchaser takes free of a perfected security interest in the retailer's inventory. When one buys a washing machine from the local department store, he does not expect to have to search the files and to make arrangements to get it free from the department store's bank; the law does not expect one to do that either. Even if the security agreement provides otherwise, the buyer in the ordinary course of business takes free under 9–307(1). Less important are the priority provisions in UCC 9–308, 9–309 and 9–310.

The most basic priority provisions are UCC 9–201 and 9–312. Read both. Section 9–312 is unhappily complex. The student should focus particularly on 9–312(5) under which most cases are resolved.

Every first-year student encounters the priority rules in real estate recording statutes. These typically provide "first in time, first in right," but that statement itself, as we shall see, is wildly ambiguous. The common real estate statute is a "notice-race" statute. It gives priority to a transferee of the debtor who is second in time only if this transferee takes without notice (no "notice") and files first (wins the "race" to the courthouse filing). Actually, such statutes might better be called "no notice-race winner" statutes. Section 9–312 is *not* such a statute. It is a "pure race" statute; knowledge of another's security interest does not subordinate the claim to that interest. (Recall how the Bank of Alaska, in *In Re Craig Lumber Co.*, supra at p. 45, apparently conceded that it was inferior to the conditional seller's rights because of its notice of the conditional sale. Under UCC 9–312 the bank's knowledge of the security interest would not have subordinated it; it presumably would have pursued its rights more vigorously.) Read UCC 9–312 carefully and see if you can extract that conclusion. The section is complicated and is filled with references that resolve some of the problems of the nineteenth century discussed earlier. For example, 9–312 explicitly addresses priority questions with respect to future advances, after-acquired property, and the rights of a purchase-money lender who comes second in time but who provides financing for specific assets.

Section 9–313 on fixtures is also unhappily complex, and we will deal with it at length. Sections 9–314 and 9–315 are at least superficially easy to understand. Section 9–318 is an old friend from the contracts course that has some, but limited, relevance to security interests.

Again, to conclude that a security interest is perfected is not necessarily to say that it has "priority." That should be obvious, first of all, because two parties presumably could have perfected security interests in the same collateral, yet one would enjoy priority over the other under UCC 9–312(5), for example. A large share of all Article 9 lawsuits ultimately involve the relative priority of competing third parties, and many of these involve two secured creditors. Few lawsuits are between the debtor and the creditor.

If one assumes that one competitor is a secured creditor under Article 9, the initial question to be asked in determining relative priority is the identity of the other competitor. If the other competitor is a lien creditor, the proper rule of priority is to be found in UCC 9–201 and 9–301. If the other competitor is a perfected secured creditor, the rule normally is to be found in UCC 9–312 or, with respect to fixtures, UCC 9–313, or occasionally with respect to proceeds in UCC 9–306. If the competitor is a buyer of goods, one should look to UCC 9–301, 9–306(2), and 9–307. If the competitor is a purchaser of notes or chattel paper, or the like, UCC 9–308 and 9–309 contain the rules of priority. So initially the question should be: Who is the competitor, unsecured creditor, secured creditor, purchaser, assignee, trustee, lien creditor?

An examination of the sections cited above that deal with priority tells one that the most commonly applicable priority rule in Article 9 is first in time, first in right. Now we come to the ambiguities in this seemingly simple principle. First what? One could give priority to the person who takes the "first conveyance" from the debtor. Alternatively one might look to the first public notice or to the first public notice by one who is himself without knowledge of any prior transfer, or possibly to the time when the first loan was made irrespective of when the conveyance occurred or of when the financing statement was filed. In the history of American commercial law and, indeed, in current commercial law, one can find precedents for each of the proposed first-in-time rules—conveyance, public notification, public notification by one ignorant of prior conveyances, or the time the loan is made.

Moreover, a first-in-time rule may be subject to significant exceptions. For example, the purchase money loan provisions of UCC 9–312(3) and (4) give priority to a party second in time. The same is true of certain provisions protecting the interest of the buyer in ordinary course under UCC 9–307.

Of course the basic and most commonly applicable rule, that embodied in UCC 9–312(5) is that the person who first files (or in case of other forms of perfection, perfects) has priority over later parties irrespective of the time of signing the security agreement, the time the first loan is made, or the time the debtor acquires rights in the collateral. As we have indicated above, this is a "pure race," not a "notice race" statute. Consider Example 1 from Comment 5 to UCC 9–312:

> "A files against X (debtor) on February 1. B files against X on March 1. B makes a non-purchase money advance against certain collateral on April 1. A makes an advance against the same collateral on May 1. A has priority even though B's advance was made earlier and was perfected when made. It makes no difference whether or not A knew of B's interest when he made his advance."

Note, however, that Article 9 makes a minor bow to notice in UCC 9–401(2) (seeing an improperly filed financing statement will likely subordinate one).

The student should start giving some thought to the question why the drafters of the Article 9 priority rules picked any one particular event as opposed to another for determining priority: for example, filing first regardless of notice vs. filing first without notice of a prior interest? Similarly, why do some parties who are second in time, such as buyers in the ordinary course under 9–307 and purchase money lenders under UCC 9–312(3) and (4), enjoy priority even over prior perfected security interests? Surely the general answer to the former question is that the law here should favor certainty even at the cost of fairness. Here the legislature is really enacting traffic rules among relatively sophisticated commercial parties. Better to let the first filer with notice prevail and thus the ignorant second filer suffer than to take up the court's time determining whether or not a particular party's knowledge of specific facts was knowledge of the security agreement which subordinated him. It seems equally obvious why 9–307 should protect the second in time interest at least of the consumer buyer over the bank with an inventory security interest who buys out of the retailer's inventory. Here the law is doing no more than recognizing common expectations, expectations that the law has little power to change. It would be unfair to allow the secured creditor to repossess the refrigerator that Mr. Jones had purchased from the floor of his local appliance dealer. Less obvious are the reasons for recognizing purchase money security interests as superior to prior perfected security interests. We will deal with that question later.

It is not too early to note two areas where there are additional complexities in the priority rules. The first is with respect to fixtures where 9–313 contemplates separate rules of priority with respect to real property claimants and to personal property claimants. Some filings may protect against both, some only as to one but not the other. (Recall in the *Craig* case at p. 45 the court was careful to state that the equipment at issue had not been affixed to the realty in such a way as to become a fixture. Had that happened, the bank with the mortgage on the realty might well have prevailed over the conditional seller. Who is to prevail when one properly files in the real estate records and another properly files in the personal property records as to an item which was once goods, but which has now become quasi real estate in the form of a fixture? Section 9–313 answers most of those questions.) More important is the priority between the secured creditor, on the one hand, and the trustee in bankruptcy on the other. Most such priority disputes are resolved under 9–301, but we will see that the trustee in bankruptcy has a series of rights conferred by federal law, namely the Bankruptcy Code. In Chapter Eight we will give special attention to the trustee in bankruptcy.

Problem 2–9

Edith bought a boat from George, a retail boat dealer. George had bought the boat from Ajax, a wholesale boat dealer. Ajax had granted a security interest in the boat to TIA Finance Company, which TIA perfected by filing. Ajax has not paid TIA, which now seeks to repossess the boat from Edith. Who wins?

Problem 2–10

Jean wanted to borrow $10,000 from Ready Bank. At the start of the negotiations, July 2, Ready Bank filed a financing statement naming Jean as debtor and describing the collateral as "equipment." Meanwhile, Jean, on July 20, borrowed $5,000 from Ideal Finance Company, giving Ideal a security interest in her equipment, which was perfected by filing on the same day. On July 30, Ready Bank lent Jean $10,000 under an enforceable security agreement. Jean defaulted on both loans and both Ready Bank and Ideal claim the equipment. Who wins?

Problem 2–11

Credit Union had a perfected security interest in furniture owned by Tenant. Tenant was in default on the loan to Credit Union and three months in arrears on the rent. Both Credit Union and Landlord claim the furniture. Who wins?

SECTION 5. TRUSTEE IN BANKRUPTCY

By far the most important type of priority conflict in the life of the typical secured creditor is that with the trustee in bankruptcy. While one may be captivated by the intricacies of UCC 9–312, 9–308, and 9–313 on relative priorities among creditors, one must not assume that these conflicts are the most common daily fare. For every competing secured creditor or actual creditor with a judicial lien, there are hundreds, perhaps thousands, of bankruptcies and bankruptcy trustees. For that reason alone, the rights of the trustee—some derived from Article 9 and some from the bankruptcy law—are of much greater practical significance than the rights, for example, of a mechanics' lienor or of another secured creditor or even of a buyer. It has been said many times and correctly that survival despite bankruptcy is the acid test of a security interest.

There are several kinds of bankruptcy proceedings. For our purposes it is sufficient if the student knows Chapter 11 and Chapter 7. Chapter 7 of the Bankruptcy Code provides for the liquidation of the debtor's assets. Typically in a Chapter 7 proceeding, a trustee is appointed who will collect and liquidate the debtor's property. This independent party can be expected to challenge defective security interests in order to bring that property into the estate for distribution to the unsecured creditors. Note, incidentally, most increases in the value of the estate increase the trustee's fee. In Chapter 11 the trustee's role is played by, and powers are held by, a person called the "debtor-in-possession." The debtor-in-possession is in fact the same person who was the debtor the day before the petition was filed. Chapter 11 contemplates continuation of the business during its reorganization. Invariably in Chapter 11 the business continues for a time although it often winds up in liquidation. One reading a Chapter 11 opinion will find the court speaking of the "debtor-in-possession" sometimes shortened to DIP. For our purposes, the trustee encompasses both the trustee in Chapter 7 and the debtor-in-possession in Chapter 11.

In theory a perfected security interest prevails over the trustee in bankruptcy. In theory, the perfected secured creditor has a right to his collateral or its value and, if he is fully secured, cannot lose anything by his debtor's bankruptcy. In general, this theory does not conform to reality, and this is one of the worst kept secrets of modern commercial law. In the first place, when the debtor goes bankrupt, the trustee is treated as though he has a lien on all of the debtor's assets acquired by judicial process. Section 544 of the Bankruptcy Act gives the trustee that right and section 9–301 of Article 9 specifically recognizes the trustee as a lien creditor.

The upshot of this unequivocal grant of lien creditor status to the trustee in bankruptcy is that there are no complex or interesting legal issues associated with that power. The interesting questions in the cases in which the trustee is asserting his 544 right have to do with the perfection or not of the security interest. In those cases one encounters the complicated perfection questions under Article 9 of the UCC. The other side of the 544(a) coin is that the trustee can never invoke this section to defeat a security interest that is perfected before the bankruptcy petition is filed. Like others, the trustee is subordinated to the perfected security interest (to the extent he is a lien creditor) by 9–201 and by the negative implication from 9–301(1)(b).

Problem 2–12

Assume that our bank in Problem 2–2 filed a financing statement covering all "notes, mortgages, land-sale contracts, and other accounts receivable" of Alfredo. Because these are real estate transactions the bank filed its financing statement with the local register of deeds office in a state with the second alternative to 9–401. You have been employed as the lawyer for the trustee in bankruptcy in Alfredo's Chapter 11.

1. Can you attack the bank's security interest, and if so, how?

2. Be careful to articulate the trustee's argument in detail.

3. If *In re Craig Lumber* now arose (see p. 45), and you represented the trustee in bankruptcy in that case, explain how you would defeat the "conditional seller's" interest.

One should not assume, however, that the trustee is without weapons against even a perfected secured creditor. Section 547 on voidable preferences can sometimes be used to require the creditor to disgorge payments that have been made to him and in other cases to overturn a security interest that was perfected within 90 days, or in some instances within one year of the filing of the petition. Section 547 is designed to prohibit "secret liens" and thus, in effect, it allows the trustee to set aside virtually every security interest where there is a gap between the making of the loan, on the one hand, and/or the giving of the security interest and its perfection where the perfection occurs within 90 days of the bankruptcy, on the other. Thus, if a secured creditor takes a security interest in 1983 but fails to perfect it until the eve of bankruptcy, the "transfer" will be deemed to have occurred within 90 days of the bankruptcy and the trustee will be able to upset it under section 547. In that context the section is designed to prohibit collusion between the debtor and a particularly friendly creditor to enable the former to mislead other creditors by keeping the security interest secret. The rules under section 547 are complex and important; we will devote substantial time to them in Chapter 8.

Other sections from 548 through 553 give the trustee the power to challenge secured creditors, sometimes perfected secured creditors, and we will deal in passing with many of those. They are much less significant than section 544, on the trustee's rights as a lien creditor, and section 547, on the trustee's power to invalidate preferential transfers by the debtor to others. For the time being, the student should proceed with the assumption that a security interest perfected within 10 days of making a loan, or perfected before 90 days prior to the petition is valid against the trustee in bankruptcy.

The theory of the supremacy of the perfected security interest falls not only to direct attack via section 547 on preferences or the other avoidance powers of the trustee under the Bankruptcy Code that allow for explicit and complete subordination of the perfected secured creditor; that theory falls also in the light of the more subtle provisions of the Bankruptcy Code: the "automatic stay" under section 362 and the "cramdown" rules of Chapters 11 and 13 of the Bankruptcy Act. To lose to the trustee under section 547 is to be struck dead by lightning. To lose to the trustee because of section 362 (the automatic stay) and attendant provisions, or because of the cramdown rules is to suffer a lingering illness which may, nonetheless, prove fatal. Section 362 simply says that the status quo is preserved upon filing of the petition. This is the section that stops the creditor lawsuits and Article 9 foreclosure proceedings the moment the debtor files bankruptcy; this is the section that prohibits a secured creditor from repossessing when the debtor files bankruptcy; this is the section that prohibits an unsecured creditor from engaging in any self help collection activity. In general, the "cramdown" rules in Chapters 11 and 13 and the rules having to do with lifting the stay and adequate protection under section 362 and section 361 give the trustee the right to keep the collateral, perhaps indefinitely, if he can convince the court that he can give the secured creditor assurances that are roughly equivalent to it. Equivalence in the mind of the bankruptcy judge may differ substantially from equivalence in the mind of the secured creditor.

Inevitably therefore the filing of a bankruptcy petition burdens the secured creditor. Almost without exception it means the secured creditor will suffer a loss of interest on the money lent for a time and perhaps suffer certain other opportunity costs, and at least in some cases it means that he will be crammed down, i.e., that he will be made to take something which he does not regard as equivalent to his collateral, but which the court finds to be so. The operation of section 362 and of the general cramdown provisions are to a considerable extent hidden in the mists of the bankruptcy court and in the negotiations that surround a classic Chapter 11 case. For those reasons they are more subtle, harder to see, and more difficult to grasp. Yet, they are often no less significant than the more obvious and crude powers under sections 544 and 547.

The trustee in bankruptcy may thus be regarded as a particularly powerful and important competitor to the secured creditor. The student should now read sections 544 through 553. We will return to all of these and to sections 361 and 362 in Chapter 8.

SECTION 6. DEFAULT, REPOSSESSION AND FORECLOSURE

Part 5 of Article 9 deals with default. When the debtor who owes $1,000,000 and who has granted a security interest in his grain in a grain elevator defaults on the loan, the grain is not turned into money instantaneously. Part 5 of Article 9 governs the process by which the creditor himself or through others transforms the collateral in the debtor's hands into cash in his own. We use foreclosure here as a generic word to refer to the process by which a secured creditor ultimately liquidates collateral, whether that collateral be an automobile, a farm, or an account receivable.

The foreclosure laws, as they deal with real estate (to which Article 9 does not apply), have been a major scene of battles between creditors and debtors throughout the history of the United States. We will pause now to explore some of these battles, as general background. In times of economic stress, debtors have frequently turned to the state legislatures and to the Congress for help. There debtors argue that foreclosure proceedings invariably fail to bring fair prices for collateral sold and fail to give the honest debtor a fair opportunity to get back on his feet once he has stumbled. With respect to farmland, the debtors occasionally make another argument, namely that the creditors are about to destroy an important part of the American heritage by driving the small farmer off his land and replacing him with a corporation or worse, a foreigner.

The creditors respond to such an argument by pointing out that they must comply with a specific set of foreclosure laws and by arguing that these laws necessarily do not bring the highest price because they inevitably conclude in a forced auction. Moreover, the creditors will suggest that the very failure of the debtor is evidence that the collateral cannot produce the kind of income that would support the high price that the debtor assigns to it. The creditors will argue that adding additional burdens to the foreclosure process will merely reduce the ranks of creditors willing to lend and will therefore increase the cost of borrowing to the detriment of all.

In one way or another nearly every legislature has, at one or more times, responded to the debtor's argument and, one suspects, thousands of different courts have responded in individual cases to those arguments. In the real estate arena the legislative response has taken several forms. The first and almost universal response is to enact a rigid, lengthy and formal procedure which the creditor must follow in order to sell the land and realize on his collateral. Typically such statutes will require publication over a long period in a local newspaper, demand that the sale be at a specified place and conducted in a specified way. Some states have other and more novel ways of encouraging that the largest possible amount be bid in at the sale. For example, some states have "upset" prices under which the sale is upset unless a price equal to a specified percentage of the fair market value of the land (as found by a third party) is bid in at the sale. All of these devices are designed to protect the debtor's interest by realizing the fair value of the collateral on sale. One perceives that most of them are not effective to achieve the debtor's desire. In many cases that is because the debtor's desire is unattainable. In fact the property does not have as high a value as the debtor would assign to it.

Many states also add a "redemption" period. During the redemption period the debtor and certain junior creditors have the right to repurchase the property sold at foreclosure for the amount bid at the time of the sale. Typically the debtor also has the right to continued possession of the land during the redemption period which may be six months or a year.

We now turn to Article 9. A quick reading of the basic foreclosure provision of Article 9, section 9–504, will show that the drafters were skeptical of the capacity of formal devices to produce the highest prices. The core of the foreclosure rules in part 5 of Article 9 is found in section 9–504(3) which provides that "disposition of the collateral may be by public or private proceedings and may be made by way of one or more contracts. Sale or other disposition may be as a unit or in parcels or at any time and place and on any terms, but every aspect of the disposition, including the method, manner, time, place, and terms must be commercially reasonable." Not only does the section reject a formal approach, it encourages the use of any method, however informal, that will produce the best price. It explicitly authorizes private sale and is careful to include not just sales, but also "other dispositions." Comment 1 to UCC 9–504 makes the point as follows:

> "Although public sale is recognized, it is hoped that private sale will be encouraged where, as is frequently the case, private sale through commercial channels will result in higher realization on collateral for the benefit of all parties. The only restriction placed on the secured party's method of disposition is that it must be commercially reasonable."

In effect, section 9–504 may be read as inviting the creditor to deal with the goods as though they were his own. Mr. Banker if this were your car, how would you dispose of it? If at a private sale, then presumably the private sale is appropriate. If at a dealer auction, then presumably a dealer auction is appropriate. Note, too, that there is no post-sale redemption period (UCC 9–505), that the creditor need not go to court for a court order to seize the property (if he can get it without breach of the peace, UCC 9–503), nor to authorize or approve the sale (UCC 9–504). The entire process often is carried out without any party ever setting foot in court.

That is not to say there are no legal issues associated with part 5 of Article 9. Exactly what constitutes a breach of the peace is a much litigated issue under UCC 9–503. What is and is not commercially reasonable is often disputed under UCC 9–504. Harking back to the earlier times, debtors often beseech the court to read the procedural requirements of notice under UCC 9–504(3) narrowly and to find that the creditor failed to comply with them.

Part 5 of Article 9 does not articulate all of the debtor's remedies for the creditor's violation of that part. Certain rights are explicitly granted under UCC 9–507, including the right to punitive damages under certain circumstances, but the courts have not found UCC 9–507 to be exclusive. Many courts have held that one who does not comply with UCC 9–504 loses his right to a deficiency judgment (a deficiency in this case is equal to the amount of the debt less the amount realized on sale of the collateral). Other courts have found creditors guilty of conversion or of other torts in the process of repossessing. Of course, section 9–507 invites the court to grant the debtor actual damages suffered from a violation of that part.

In general, however, the legal issues in part 5 of Article 9 are not as difficult and complex as in other parts of Article 9.

SECTION 7. NON-UNIFORMITY IN A UNIFORM STATUTE

A principal aim of the Uniform Commercial Code was that of having commercial law that would be uniform throughout the United States. Of course, it was obvious from the outset that perfect uniformity could not be achieved and one sees many optional, and necessarily non-uniform, provisions sprinkled throughout the Code. Some of these were initially inserted to meet the concerns of those who would otherwise have been powerful opponents of the Code. In other cases these were inserted in recognition that differing conditions called for different outcomes.

The principal non-uniformity in the Code, however, came not from these optional provisions. Rather, in Article 9 it came from the fact that the drafters themselves found many faults with the Code as originally enacted in most states, and proposed a set of uniform amendments in 1972. Not all states immediately adopted these 1972 amendments. Thus when one refers to the uniform version of Article 9, typically one is referring to the 1972 version. Nevertheless, one should be aware that until recently a few states still had the 1962 version and that almost all UCC states had it for a time, and that many cases were decided thereunder. In some circumstances a case decided under the 1962 version is not good precedent under the 1972 version.

A second substantial source of non-uniformity arises within the states themselves. For example, many states have chafed at the rule embodied in 9–307 that allows a perfected security interest to carry over against a bona fide purchaser of farm products. As we will see, the courts have restricted that rule by a variety of forms of judicial manipulation. More recently the legislatures have also come to the aid of buyers and have modified 9–307 to allow many buyers to take free of perfected security interests even in farm products. For example, Tennessee now has an extensive non-uniform version of 9–307; California never adopted the farm products limitation in 9–307. Furthermore, with the Food Security Act of 1985, Congress enacted legislation which grants purchasers of farm products federal protection. Farm products legislation is further discussed in Chapter 5.

The supreme nonconformist jurisdiction in Article 9 matters, California, adopted a large set of non-uniform provisions when it passed the Code originally, and this non-uniformity has grown with time. Doubtless the drafters will have to confront this piecemeal enactment of non-uniform versions. For the time being, the student should understand that while the Uniform Commercial Code is highly uniform, it has never been completely so, and it is becoming less so with the passage of time.

SECTION 8. THE UNDERLYING OBLIGATION OF THE DEBTOR AND THE SPECIAL BODIES OF LAW DEALING WITH THE NEGOTIABLE NOTE

It is easy to be misled by the intense and detailed study which we will devote to the security interest, to all of its intricacies and legal attributes, for the security is not the all important thing. The debt owed by the debtor to the creditor is the all important thing. The collateral, the security interest, and all of the attendant trappings are no more than parasites that have found a home in the debt transaction. In the final chapters of this book we will deal at length with Articles 3 and 4 of the Uniform Commercial Code. Those articles govern commercial paper and set out rules for the presentation and collection of debts evidenced by checks and other commercial paper. For now, however, it is important for the student to understand how the underlying obligation arises and to appreciate some of the attributes of the negotiable note embodying this obligation, an instrument often also signed by the debtor at the time the loan transaction takes place.

Our review in Section 2 of the history of personal property security in the United States provides the student with some taste of the variety of transactions in which security interests arise. Among them is the conventional contract obligation found under Article 2 of the UCC in which a buyer agrees to pay a certain amount "on time" to the seller for the purchase of goods. Another is a loan from either the seller or the bank to purchase a piece of equipment. Another is an outright loan of a specified amount from the bank secured by assets already owned.

The standard debt might involve a single transaction in which the entire amount is advanced by the creditor either in the form of money or in the form of goods sold in which the debtor makes periodic payment or in some cases a single repayment. A form of debt frequently found in modern transactions is one with no fixed amount. An example would be a bank granting a line of credit to a debtor with the expectation that the debtor would make periodic draws and periodic payments but that the amount of debt would fluctuate and would not be paid to zero for an indefinite period. Such arrangements are familiar to the consumer in the form of credit card advances and checking account overdraft protection. These are merely consumer lines of credit, and they contemplate a wide variety of uses to which the credit may be put.

The nature of the liability secured presents only a few problems. Most of those we will deal with in the next chapter. One recurring issue is whether a provision in a security agreement that purports to cover "all indebtedness of the debtor" in fact is intended to cover not only debts of the kind incurred at the time the agreement was made but also debts that might arise out of another business or even out of a consumer transaction by the business debtor.

The other issues relate to the negotiable note. One is more likely to find a negotiable note in the single-shot transaction described above than in a line of credit. In the standard deal, the debtor signs a note at the time he signs the mortgage or security agreement. Thereafter, he makes either a single payment or periodic repayments on the note. In Chapter 24, Section 2, we will deal extensively with the requirements of negotiability and with the intricacies of Article 3 that relate to negotiability. For now the student should understand some of the rules and some of the consequences of negotiability. The idea of negotiability is defended principally as a mode of enabling one creditor to sell his debt to another and thus to allow money to flow from places where there is excess to places where there is too little. Thus, for example, a local bank in Osage, Iowa might make a loan to farmer for the purchase of a $100,000 combine. The farmer may sign a negotiable note for $100,000 plus interest, and sign a security agreement. Wishing further money to lend to others, Osage then might assign that note to a New York bank who might pay face value. It would be uneconomical for the New York bank to lend directly to the farmer in Osage. It might not be uneconomical for it to buy a negotiable note from the Osage bank, particularly if the Osage bank agreed to repurchase it on default, and that is more likely true if the note is negotiable.

By saying that the note is negotiable, a lawyer typically means that one who takes it for value and in good faith takes it free of the defenses that the farmer in Osage might be able to raise on the underlying contract against the seller of the combine (should it, for example, be defective) or under the note itself against the Osage bank. By being a "holder in due course" (roughly, a "bona fide purchaser") of the negotiable note, the New York bank limits its risk to the credit risk; it becomes merely a lender who can insist upon its money irrespective of hanky panky in the underlying transaction, of disputes between the underlying parties, or of setoffs the parties may have arising out of other transactions. These rights are summarized in two very basic provisions of Article 3—sections 3–305 and 3–306; the student should read these sections now.

Fifty years ago the importance of negotiability would have gone unquestioned. Whether it is critical in today's credit market is subject to much dispute. In the area of consumer paper, the Federal Trade Commission has effectively wiped out holder in due course status. There the doctrine of negotiability disappeared without a measurable impact upon that market. Whether the same would be true in the non-consumer market is uncertain.

It is clear that every commercial lawyer needs to know something about negotiability and that it will often be in the interest of a plaintiff to be able to maintain that he is a holder in due course. To that end let us paint the requirements of negotiability with a relatively broad brush through Article 3 of the UCC. We have already started with the operative provision which allows a holder in due course to take free of most defenses of the underlying maker. Proceeding backwards from UCC 3–305, one sees the definition of a holder in due course in UCC 3–302 as a person who takes (1) an instrument, (2) for value, (3) in good faith, (4) without notice that it is overdue, has been dishonored, or of a claim or defense. Section 3–303 defines taking for value and, to the surprise of some, includes one who takes an instrument in payment of or as security for an antecedent debt. Section 3–305 tells us who is to be regarded as having notice of a claim or defense and who has not. Under section 3–304(a)(2), a check taken more than 90 days after its date is treated overdue; accordingly, one taking a check after that time cannot be a holder in due course.

A more troublesome and subtle requirement for the holder in due course status, is that the holder be a holder of a negotiable instrument. Note that in Article 3 the word "instrument" means "negotiable instrument" (see UCC 3–104(b)). Section 3–104 defines the form of negotiable instruments; note how restrictive the definition is. Note particularly that section 3–104(a) requires an "unconditional promise or order to pay a fixed amount of money." Under subsection (a)(3), a negotiable instrument must not "state any other undertaking or instruction . . . to do any act in addition to the payment of money. . . ." Thus, the typical sales contract which surely includes a promise to pay cannot be a negotiable instrument, at least because it will include many other promises. By the same token, a promise that is construed to be "conditional" cannot be a negotiable instrument, nor can one that is to be payable to a specific person, as opposed to "order or bearer," or is payable at an uncertain time. What is the purpose of these rigid rules? Why does the Code, an enlightened and modern document, take a position that seems so formal, and thus so inconsistent with the looseness of Article 2 and Article 9? Part of the answer is to put those on notice who deal with negotiable instruments. Presumably not only the maker but also the payee and most of all the indorsee or assignee wish to be certain that they are dealing with a negotiable instrument when that is so. Conceivably some of the limitations have been imposed by the powerful buyers of these instruments to free them from the need to examine closely maverick instruments to decide whether the conditions are important or not, and to minimize the transaction costs of the transfer of such documents.

One authority has explained the rationale for each of these requisites in the following terms:

HAWKLAND, COMMERCIAL PAPER 5, 11, 14, 19 (1959).

"* * * The Promise or Order Must be Unconditional—3–105.

"One function of negotiable instruments is to supplement the supply of currency. Another function is to represent the future payment of money. These currency and credit functions would be defeated by conditional promises, for costly and time-consuming investigations would be made necessary by such promises, and circulation, therefore, would be impeded. Risks would be great and discount rates high. Substitutes for money must be capable of rapid circulation at minimum risks, and credit documents are feasible only when low discounting prevails. Obviously, then, negotiable instruments must be unconditional to serve the purposes for which they were created. * * *

"The Instrument Must Be Payable in Money and the Sum of Money Must Be Certain—3–106 and 3–107.

"In order for an instrument to be negotiable at common law and under the N.I.L. [Uniform Negotiable Instruments Law] it is essential that it be payable in money and that its sum be certain. These formal requisites of negotiability are designed to promote certainty in ascertaining the present value of the instrument, and they have been long regarded as indispensible to the concept of negotiability. Consequently, it is not surprising to note that these requisites have been retained, with little change, by sections 3–106 and 3–107 of the Commercial Code. A few changes have been made by these Code sections in the interests of clarification and completeness. * * *

"The Instrument Must Be Payable at a Time Certain—3–108 and 3–109.

"The N.I.L. requires that a negotiable instrument either be payable on demand or at a fixed or determinable time. This requirement, like the other formal requisites of negotiability, is designed to promote certainty in ascertaining the present value of a negotiable instrument. In determining the value of an instrument, it is necessary to know when the obligor can be compelled to pay, when the obligations of secondary parties will arise, and when the statute of limitations will start to run. Without this information, interest and discount rates, which vary according to the duration of the obligation, cannot be fixed. Nor can credit risks be properly assessed. In short, the present value of the instrument cannot be rationally determined.

"Because 'time certain' is important to the concept of negotiability, it has been retained by the Commercial Code. * * *

"The Instrument Must Contain Words of Negotiability—3–104(1)(d).

"The formal requisites of negotiability were formulated to bring about certainty, and the use in instruments of words of negotiability is one of the most clear indications that the parties have intended the paper to be negotiable. The N.I.L., accordingly, requires negotiable instruments to contain words of negotiability. The Code (3–104(1)(d)) continues this requirement with little or no change. * * *"

The rigidity of section UCC 3–104 is alleviated somewhat by UCC 3–105, 3–112, and by some of the other provisions in part 1 of Article 3. The student should read those sections and should note, for example, that UCC 3–112(1)(b) would permit a statement on the note that collateral has been given to secure it.

Problem 2–13

Do you think the note set out below is negotiable?

DATE OF NOTE ▶		ACCOUNT NUMBER

NOTE

For value received, I/WE, jointly and severally promise to pay to the order of

THE UNIVERSITY OF MICHIGAN CREDIT UNION, A MICHIGAN CORPORATION AT 333 WILLIAM STREET, ANN ARBOR, MICHIGAN, the sum of

.... dollars and .... cents $...............

WITH INTEREST ON UNPAID BALANCES AT THE RATE OF per cent per year	PAYABLE IN	INSTALLMENTS OF $ (inclusive of Principal and Interest)	THE FIRST PAYMENT TO BE MADE ON	AND A LIKE AMOUNT	PLUS AN IRREGULAR OR FINAL PAYMENT OF .... DUE ON ....

COLLATERAL

TITLED PROPERTY ▶	MAKE	YEAR	MODEL	BODY STYLE	IDENTIFICATION NUMBER

(APPLICABLE ONLY WHEN CHECKED) HOUSEHOLD GOODS, FURNITURE, AND APPLIANCES AS DESCRIBED IN SECURITY AGREEMENT

I/We, the undersigned, hereby jointly and severally pledge all paid shares and deposits and payments on shares and deposits which I/we now have or hereafter may have in this credit union, except shares or deposits which may be held pursuant to any "Individual Retirement Trust" or "Keogh Plan" or as an All-Savers Certificate, as security for (1) principal and interest of the loan evidenced by this Note and of any refinancing of all or any part thereof and (2) any other sums which may become due under the Security Agreement and/or real estate mortgage securing such obligations. Shares, deposits and payments thereon are only pledged to an amount equal to the unpaid balance of such indebtedness. I/We hereby authorize the credit union in the event of default to apply any or all such paid shares and deposits and payments on same to the repayment of any such indebtedness. However, Borrower may withdraw shares or deposits in excess of $ if loan payments are up to date.

INSURANCE ADVANCES

The Credit Union hereby agrees to loan the Borrower(s) an amount equal to the Total Premium indicated below, plus any increase thereof resulting from Borrower(s) not making payments on time, in a series of monthly advances for the term of this loan or until the Borrower's insurance is terminated. Borrower(s) hereby agree(s) to the monthly addition of such insurance premiums to the outstanding principal balance owing hereunder. Credit Union shall not be obligated to extend credit for premiums that cause the outstanding principal balance to exceed legal limits. The amount of the insurance premium to be added to the loan is based on the rates now in use by the insurance company as determined by the original term of the loan as applied on the same day of each month to the outstanding principal balance.

INSURANCE PREMIUMS (CHECK IF APPLICABLE) ▶	☐ GROUP CREDIT LIFE	$

Credit Union wavies any and all security for the indebtedness evidenced by this Note or for any refinancing of all or any part thereof or for any other sums which may become due under the Security Agreement and/or real estate mortgage securing such obligations other than security granted by such Security Agreement and/or real estate mortgage by the foregoing pledge of shares and/or deposits, or provided by statute. Fines or charges may be imposed for late payments as provided in the Credit Union's bylaws. In the event any payment on this loan account is not made when due, or if an "event of default" occurs under any Security Agreement given by the member(s), then the entire unpaid balance of this loan account plus accrued interest shall become immediately due and payable without notice at the option of the Credit Union. The undersigned further agrees to pay all usual and customary costs of collection including reasonable attorney fees and all taxable court costs permitted by law. Each party to this Note, whether as maker, comaker, indorser or guarantor, severally wavies presentment for payment, demand, protest or notice of protest and dishonor of same.

Authority is hereby given the Credit Union to complete this Note in any necessary respect in the event it is executed while still incomplete. This Note is secured by a Security Agreement and/or real estate mortgage of even date herewith.

SIGNATURE OF MAKER	SIGNATURE OF COMAKER
✕ (SEAL)	✕ (SEAL)
SIGNATURE OF MAKER	SIGNATURE OF COMAKER
✕ (SEAL)	✕ (SEAL)

CHAPTER THREE

CREATION OF THE SECURITY INTEREST

SECTION 1. INTRODUCTION

In Chapter Two we outlined the history of personal property security in the United States. There we noted a frequent insistence on or fanatical attention to detail in the documents creating a security interest. For example, judges struck down chattel mortgages because of very minor errors in the description of the collateral. This formalistic attitude derived partly from a similar approach to real estate mortgages; indeed one still encounters it in the formalities required for the execution of deeds and other such documents (e.g., witnessing, notarization, affidavits, etc.).

An examination of UCC 9–203, the principal section that governs the creation of an enforceable Article 9 security interest, reveals none of this. Moreover, UCC 9–203 purports to cover all personal property security transactions regardless of form and rejects pre-Code rules requiring one to label certain documents "conditional sales contracts", others "chattel mortgages," and still others, "factor's liens."

The student should now examine UCC 9–203, 9–204 and the comments to each section. Although we have labeled this chapter the "creation" of a security interest, the Code in the title to UCC 9–203 and the cases sometimes refer to "attachment." Under the 1972 version of Article 9, the terms are interchangeable: Both refer to the enforceability of the security interest. Both of these terms, however, are to be distinguished from perfection, an event considered in the next chapter. Note that UCC 9–204 deals explicitly with after-acquired property and future advances, including "optional" advances.

The general thrust of UCC 9–203 and UCC 9–204 is to make the granting of security easy and inexpensive. Presumably this reflects the drafters' belief that no rigid formalities are necessary here to impress the debtor with the importance of the transaction or to attempt to protect against ignorant or fraudulent behavior. That thrust is strengthened by UCC 9–110 which instructs the courts to adopt a liberal rule for the description of property covered by the security agreement.

Despite the simplicity of the requirements of UCC 9–203 and 9–204 and the ease with which one may acquire a security agreement, there remain a variety of ways to go wrong. For example, a debtor (1) might forget to sign the security agreement, or (2) might materially misdescribe the collateral, or (3) a series of loans might be made at different times and the debtor might argue that some were intended to be covered and others not, or (4) a dispute might arise over the debtor's rights in the underlying collateral and thus about the capacity of the debtor to pass those rights on to the secured creditor. We will deal with all these problems.

Note that UCC 9–203 (1)(a) does not require a writing if "the collateral is in the possession of the secured party pursuant to agreement * * *". Presumably possession by the secured creditor sufficiently meets the statute of frauds concern about the likely existence of an agreement. Otherwise why would the secured creditor have possession of the debtor's assets? Possession—the pledge—is now an uncommon means of creating and perfecting a security interest. We will discuss some of the problems with it in the next chapter. Presently it is largely limited to pawn shop loans, loans against certificated securities and some other relatively uncommon and unusual transactions.

SECTION 2. THE REQUIREMENTS OF UCC 9–203

A. *Rights in the Collateral*

Recall that under pre-Code law, it was often the case that some security interests could not be created in property acquired by the debtor after the loan was made, and could secure only the debt that existed at the time the agreement was signed and not future advances. The Code blesses both after acquired property and future advance clauses. See UCC 9–204. Some serious issues remain.

IN RE SAMUELS & CO.

United States Court of Appeals, Fifth Circuit, 1976.
526 F.2d 1238, *cert. denied* 429 U.S. 834, 97 S.Ct. 98, 50 L.Ed.2d 99.

[Owners of cattle sold them to Samuels, a packing house. Samuels had previously given a perfected security interest in its inventory (pursuant to an after-acquired property clause) and in other property to CIT. Samuels had paid the sellers for the cattle by checks that ultimately were dishonored. Samuels in turn sold the carcasses to third parties. Both the sellers and CIT, the secured creditor, claimed the proceeds of the sale when Samuels defaulted and went bankrupt. One issue was whether and to what extent CIT's security interest had attached to the cattle when they became a part of Samuels' inventory. The sellers' principal arguments were based on various provisions of Article 2, which give the seller a limited right to reclaim the goods from a buyer. In one way or another all of the sellers' Article 2 arguments sought to undermine the secured creditors' claim that the debtor had adequate "rights in the collateral" pursuant to UCC 9–203(1)(c).

[The Referee in Bankruptcy held for the unpaid sellers over C.I.T. The district court reversed, holding for the secured party. The Court of Appeals reversed the district court and held for the unpaid sellers, Judge Godbold dissenting. The gist of the decision was that the sellers had priority under the Packers and Stockyard Act. 483 F.2d 557 (5th Cir.1973). The Supreme Court reversed, holding that the Packers and Stockyards Act did not determine priorities between the competing parties and remanded the case for that determination under state law. Mahon v. Stowers, 416 U.S. 100, 94 S.Ct. 1626, 40 L.Ed.2d 79 (1974). On remand, the court of appeals held that the Texas Uniform Commercial Code dictated that the sellers prevail. 510

F.2d 139 (5th Cir.1975). Judge Godbold again dissented. The decision of the panel was then reversed *per curiam* by the court en banc, the judgment of the district court was affirmed and the dissent of Judge Godbold, reprinted in part below, was adopted by the majority. Five judges dissented from the majority opinion.]

* * *

GODBOLD, CIRCUIT JUDGE.

This case raises one primary question: under the Uniform Commercial Code as adopted in Texas, is the interest of an unpaid cash seller in goods already delivered to a buyer superior or subordinate to the interest of a holder of a perfected security interest in those same goods? In my opinion, under Article Nine, the perfected security interest is unquestionably superior to the interest of the seller. Moreover, the perfected lender is protected from the seller's claims by two independent and theoretically distinct Article Two provisions. My result is not the product of revealed truth, but rather of a meticulous and dispassionate reading of Articles Two and Nine and an understanding that the Code is an integrated statute whose Articles and Sections overlap and flow into one another in an effort to encourage specific types of commercial behavior. The Code's overall plan, which typically favors good faith purchasers, and which encourages notice filing of nonpossessory security interests in personalty through the imposition of stringent penalties for nonfiling, compels a finding that the perfected secured party here should prevail.

My brothers have not concealed that their orientation in the case before us is to somehow reach a result in favor of the sellers of cattle, assumed by them to be "little fellows," and against a large corporate lender, because it seems the "fair" thing to do. We do not sit as federal chancellors confecting ways to escape the state law of commercial transactions when that law produces a result not to our tastes. Doing what seems fair is heady stuff. But the next seller may be a tremendous corporate conglomerate engaged in the cattle feeding business, and the next lender a small town Texas bank. Today's heady draught may give the majority a euphoric feeling, but it can produce tomorrow's hangover.

I. RIGHTS UNDER § 2.403

My analysis begins with an examination of the relative rights of seller and secured party under § 2.403(a).

Section 2.403 gives certain transferors power to pass greater title than they can themselves claim. Section 2.403(a) gives good faith purchasers of even fraudulent buyers-transferors greater rights than the defrauded seller can assert. This harsh rule is designed to promote the greatest range of freedom possible to commercial vendors and purchasers.

The provision anticipates a situation where (1) a cash seller has delivered goods to a buyer who has paid by a check which is subsequently dishonored, § 2.403(a)(2), (3), and where (2) the defaulting buyer transfers title to a Code-defined "good faith purchaser." The interest of the good faith purchaser is protected pro tanto against the claims of the aggrieved seller. §§ 2.403(a); 2.403, Comment 1. The Code expressly recognizes the power of the defaulting buyer to transfer good title to such a purchaser even though the transfer is wrongful as against the seller. The buyer is granted the *power* to transfer good title despite the fact that under § 2.507 he lacks the *right* to do so.

The Code definition of "purchaser" is broad, and includes not only one taking by sale but also covers persons taking by gift or by voluntary mortgage, pledge or lien. § 1.201(32), (33). It is therefore broad enough to include an Article Nine secured party. §§ 1.201(37); 9.101, Comment; 9.102(a), (b). Thus, if C.I.T. holds a valid Article Nine security interest, it is by virtue of that status *also* a purchaser under § 2.403(a) * * *.

While I shall discuss in detail infra, the implications of C.I.T.'s security interest under Article Nine and under other Article Two provisions, I here note that C.I.T. is the holder of a perfected Article Nine interest which extends to the goods claimed by the seller Stowers.

Attachment of an Article Nine interest takes place when (1) there is agreement that the interest attach to the collateral; (2) the secured party has given value; and (3) the debtor has rights in the collateral sufficient to permit attachment. § 9.204(a).

(1) The agreement: In 1963, Samuels initially authorized C.I.T.'s lien in its after-acquired inventory. The agreement between these parties remained in effect throughout the period of delivery of Stowers' cattle to Samuels.

(2) Value: At the time of Stowers' delivery, Samuels' indebtedness to C.I.T. exceeded $1.8 million. This pre-existing indebtedness to the lender constituted "value" under the Code. § 1.201(44).

(3) Rights in the collateral: Finally, upon delivery, Samuels acquired rights in the cattle sufficient to allow attachment of C.I.T.'s lien. The fact that the holder of a voluntary lien—including an Article Nine interest—is a "purchaser" under the Code is of great significance to a proper understanding and resolution of this case under Article Two and Article Nine. The Code establishes that purchasers can take from a defaulting cash buyer, § 2.403(a). Lien creditors are included in the definition of purchasers, § 1.201(32), (33). A lien is an Article Nine interest, §§ 9.101, Comment; 9.102(b); 9.102, Comment. The existence of an Article Nine interest presupposes the debtor's having rights in the collateral sufficient to permit attachment, § 9.204(a). Therefore, since a defaulting cash buyer has the power to transfer a security interest to a lien creditor, including an Article Nine secured party, the buyer's rights in the property, however marginal, must be sufficient to allow attachment of a lien. And this is true even if, arguendo, I were to agree that the cash seller is granted reclamation rights under Article Two * * *.

If the Article Nine secured party acted in good faith, it is prior under § 2.403(a) to an aggrieved seller. Under the facts before us, I think that C.I.T. acted in good faith. The Code good faith provision requires "honesty in fact", § 1.201(19), which, for Article Two purposes, is "expressly defined as * * * reasonable commercial standards of fair dealing." §§ 1.201, Comment 19; 2.103(a)(2). There is no evidence that C.I.T. acted in bad faith in its dealings with Samuels, or that Stowers' loss resulted from any breach of obligation by C.I.T. There is no claim that the 1963 security agreement was the product of bad faith. The lender's interest had been perfected and was of record for six years when Stowers' delivery to Samuels occurred. There is no suggestion that the $1.8 million debt owing from Samuels to C.I.T. was the result of bad faith or of a desire to defeat Stowers' $50,000 claim. There is no claim that C.I.T. exercised or was able to exercise control over Samuels' business operations. There is no evidence that C.I.T. authorized or ordered or suggested that Samuels dishonor Stowers' check. There is no contention that C.I.T.'s refusal to extend credit on May 23, the date Samuels filed a voluntary petition on bankruptcy at a time when it owed C.I.T. more than $1.8 million, was violative of an obligatory future advances clause. The Code's good faith provision requires "honesty in fact", § 1.201(19); it hardly requires a secured party to continue financing a doomed business enterprise.

The majority deny that C.I.T. acted in good faith because, they claim, the lender had "intimate" knowledge of Samuels' business operations. The majority's source of information on the scope of C.I.T.'s knowledge is a little puzzling. The Referee in Bankruptcy found only that "C.I.T. knew or should have known of the manner by which the bankrupt bought livestock * * * on a grade and yield basis." In the Matter of Samuels & Co., Inc., No. BK 3–1314 (N.D.Tex., order of Jan. 19, 1972). This factual finding was affirmed by the District Court which reversed the Referee and upheld C.I.T.'s priority over Stowers. Id., orders of Nov. 24, 1972, and Jan. 16, 1973. Neither the Referee nor the District Court found, nor have the parties alleged, that C.I.T.'s knowledge of Samuels' business extended to knowledge of the debtor's obligations to third party creditors.

However, even if evidence had established that C.I.T. knew of Samuels' nonpayment and of Stowers' claim, C.I.T.'s status as an Article Two good faith purchaser would be unaffected. Lack of knowledge of outstanding claims is necessary to the common law BFP, and is similarly expressly required in many Code BFP and priority provisions. See e.g., §§ 3.302; 6.110; 8.301, 8.302; 9.301(a)(2). But the Code's definition of an Article Two good faith purchaser does not expressly or impliedly include lack of knowledge of third-party claims as an element. The detailed definition of the Article's counterpart of the common law BFP requires only honesty in fact, reasonable commercial behavior, fair dealing. And this describes precisely C.I.T.'s dealings with Samuels: during the period May 13–22—the time when the bulk of Stowers' cattle were delivered and the time of the issuance of the NSF checks—C.I.T.'s advances to Samuels totalled $1 million. The advances were curtailed on May 23 because of Samuels' taking voluntary bankruptcy at a time when its indebtedness to C.I.T. was enormous. The decision to terminate further funding was clearly reasonable. It was also fair, and honest, and, as the majority have failed to grasp, was not the cause of Stowers' suffering. As I note infra in my analysis of rights under Article Nine, the sellers' loss was avoidable through perfection of their security interests in the cattle. If they had perfected, they would not only have been prior to C.I.T. as an Article Nine lender, § 9.312, but also protected against C.I.T. as an Article Two purchaser, § 9.201. As it happens, Stowers did not perfect. I believe the sellers cannot now be permitted to force an innocent, if prosperous, secured creditor to shoulder their loss for them.

II. Rights Under § 2.507

The majority opinion devotes much of its concentration and energy to an analysis of the sellers' "reclamation right" under § 2.507 and § 2.702. Relying on an expansive reading of these Sections, the opinion concludes that a cash seller whose right to payment is frustrated through a check ultimately dishonored can "reclaim" proceeds of goods delivered to the buyer despite an interim third-party interest, and despite a year-long delay in seeking reclamation. I am unable to accept this reading of Code policy and requirements.

Although the Code expressly grants a credit seller the right and power to reclaim goods from a breaching buyer, the right is triggered only by specific and limited circumstances; it can be asserted only if an exacting procedure is followed; and the right can never be asserted to defeat the interests of certain third parties who have dealt with the defaulting buyer. § 2.702(b), (c). There is no Code Section expressly granting a similar reclamation right to a cash seller.

The seller's remedies upon breach are enumerated in § 2.703. These provisions do not include or suggest a right or power in a cash seller to recover goods already delivered to a breaching buyer. Nevertheless the courts have read a reclamation right into the Code. It is this judicially-confected right to reclaim goods in which the majority's reclamation analysis is grounded. However, the majority take the reclamation right beyond anything intimated by the Code or heretofore permitted by courts recognizing a cash seller's reclamation right.

The cash seller's right to reclaim has been drawn from the language of § 2.507(b) and § 2.507, Comment 3. I note, first, that the remedy granted by § 2.507(b) is one of seller against buyer, see In re Helms Veneer Corp., 287 F.Supp. 840 (W.D.Va., 1968). It does not concern rights of seller against third parties. Section 2.507, Comment 3 explains that the seller's rights under § 2.507 must "conform with the policy set forth in the bona fide purchase section of this Article," i.e., with § 2.403. As I have noted above, under this provision the rights of an aggrieved cash seller are subordinated to those of the buyer's good-faith purchasers, including Article Nine lenders such as C.I.T. Thus, the Code provisions supporting a cash seller's reclamation right expressly precluded recovery by Stowers as against C.I.T. See §§ 2.507(b); 2.507, Comment 3; 2.702(b), (c) * * *.

Moreover, those courts which have permitted reclamation under § 2.507 have invariably adhered to § 2.507, Comment 3's express requirement that demand for return be made within ten days after receipt by the buyer or else be lost.

* * *

In the instant case, demand was not made within ten days or ten weeks; it came a full year after delivery to Samuels. The majority excuse this gross noncompliance by finding that the sellers' failure was the product of innocent error, and, in any event, was not required since the "purpose" of the demand rule—protection of purchasers of the delivered goods—was served through C.I.T.'s alleged intimate knowledge of Samuels' business operations.

The Code's ten-day provision is an absolute requirement. There is no exception in the Code Sections or Comments, express or implied, to the statutory period. I would be hesitant to read any extension into a statute of limitations clear and unambiguous on its face, and particularly unwilling to allow an extension some 36 times greater than the statutory maximum. My reluctance is all the greater where the right at issue is not granted by the Code but is rather the product of judicial interpretation of a Comment which, whatever grant of power it may suggest, expressly limits that right to a ten-day life.

The spirit in which the rule was broken seems to me irrelevant. Even conceding that Stowers' noncompliance occurred in absolute good faith, it was nonetheless noncompliance. Mistake of law does not constitute excuse of mistake.

C.I.T.'s apocryphal intimate knowledge of Samuels' business operations is, I believe, also irrelevant to a determination of the validity of Stowers' claim. The majority find the purpose of the ten-day rule to be one of notice to third parties that a claim exists. I have somewhat greater difficulty than my brothers in pinpointing the purpose of the ten-day rule. But I am convinced that the goal is not one of protection or notice to third-party purchasers, for their rights are secure under the Code as against the aggrieved seller even if demand is timely made. §§ 2.507, Comment 3; 2.702(c). The Code does not condition the purchasers' rights on a lack of knowledge of the seller's interest. With or without knowledge, the purchaser rests secure. I am therefore forced to conclude that the ten-day rule serves some function other than notifying third-party takers, and, consequently, that even if C.I.T. knew of Stowers' claim, the sellers' obligation under the ten-day rule would not have been excused. And even if knowledge by the purchaser suspended the sellers' duty to make a timely demand, the record in this case is devoid of any hint that C.I.T. knew of Samuels' breach and Stowers' reclamation right.

Moreover, § 2.507 and § 2.702 speak of a right to reclaim goods. Neither provision grants a right to go after proceeds of those goods. Where a right or interest in proceeds is recognized by the Code it is recognized expressly. See e.g., § 9.306. The right granted by § 2.507 is narrowly defined. I am unwilling to imply an extension to such a short-lived and precisely drawn remedy.

Finally, even if there were a right to reclaim proceeds, even if the right had been timely exercised, and even if it could have been exercised despite the transfer of interest to C.I.T., Stowers would have taken subject to C.I.T.'s perfected Article Nine interest. See §§ 9.201, 9.301, 9.306, 9.312. See also my discussion of C.I.T.'s rights and interest under Article Nine, infra.

III. Rights Under § 2.511

The majority opinion states that C.I.T.'s interest cannot be found superior to Stowers' because such a finding would violate § 2.511's prohibition on penalizing a seller for accepting as payment a check which is ultimately dishonored. I believe the majority have misconstrued the scope and significance of § 2.511.

Like § 2.507, § 2.511 concerns claims of the seller as against the buyer. See § 2.511(c), § 2.511, Comment 4. On its face it does not affect the rights of third parties taking from the defaulting buyer. Moreover, and more important, the seller is not here "penalized" for taking an N.S.F. check. Such loss as Stowers suffered is the direct result of his failure to comply with Code provisions which, once followed—and regardless of Stowers' acceptance of Samuels' check—would have made his interest invulnerable to claims by C.I.T. See, e.g., §§ 9.107; 9.201; 9.312(c), (d).

IV. RIGHTS UNDER ARTICLE NINE

I am also unable to agree with the majority's conclusion that, under the Code, Stowers' interest is different from and greater than a security interest. Similarly, I disagree with the theory that by virtue of Stowers' power under Article Two, C.I.T.'s security interest is subject to defeat since it (1) could not attach because the debtor's rights in the collateral were too slight to permit attachment and (2) was subject to defeat even if it attached because a security interest collapses if the debtor's right to the property is extinguished. The majority's result is achieved only by ignoring or circumventing the plain meaning of Article Nine and Article Two.

Prior to the enactment of the Uniform Commercial Code, seller and buyer could agree that, despite buyer's possession, title to goods sold was to remain in the seller until he was paid. Such a reservation of title under the "cash sale" doctrine would defeat not only a claim to the goods by the defaulting buyer, but also the claims of lien creditors of the buyer, for the buyer's naked possession could give rise to no interest to which a lien could attach.

However, the UCC specifically limits the seller's ability to reserve title once he has voluntarily surrendered possession to the buyer: "Any retention or reservation by the seller of the title (property) in goods shipped or delivered to the buyer is limited in effect to a reservation of a security interest." § 2.401(a). See also § 1.201(37). The drafters noted the theory behind this provision: "Article [Two] deals with the issues between seller and buyer in terms of step by step performance or non-performance under the contract for sale and not in terms of whether or not 'title' to the goods has passed." § 2.401, Comment 1.

The majority opinion interprets § 2.401(a) as applying only to "credit" sales, and of no effect where the parties have contracted a "cash" sale. However, the Code provision speaks of "any reservation of title." It does not on its face apply solely to credit sales. There is no authority under the Code for the majority's restrictive interpretation. Numerous courts have, in fact, applied § 2.401 to cash sales.

* * * I have been unable to find even one case suggesting that § 2.401 applies only to credit sales.

If the majority were correct, the section would be merely definitional, for a credit sale is but a sales transaction in which the seller reserves a security interest. However, § 2.401 is not definitional. It is operational and concerns the effect of transfer of possession under a sales contract upon any reservation of title. Neither law nor logic leads me to believe that § 2.401 is correctly interpreted to exclude cash sales.

The majority also suggest that Stowers' interest cannot be characterized as a security interest subject to Article Nine requirements and priorities since, the majority conclude, such interests must be "consensual". While it is true that many interests governed by Article Nine are consensual, §§ 9.102; 9.102, Comment, the Code clearly subjects Article Two security interests arising not by consent but by operation of law to Article Nine. See §§ 2.401(a); 9.113; 9.113, Comment 2. See also §§ 2.326; 9.114; 9.102, Comment 1.

Since Stowers' interest upon delivery of the cattle to Samuels was limited to a security interest subject to Article Nine, §§ 2.401(a); 9.113, the validity of C.I.T.'s Article Nine interest becomes crucial. If C.I.T. is the holder of a perfected Article Nine interest in the collateral claimed by Stowers through its unperfected § 2.401 interest, C.I.T.'s interest will prevail over Stowers, § 9.312(e).

The majority assert that C.I.T. cannot claim an interest in the cattle because Samuels' interest was too slight to permit attachment. See § 9.204(a). As I noted in my discussion of rights under § 2.403, this argument ignores the significance of § 2.403(a) and § 1.201(32), (33). The Code anticipates a situation where the interest of an unpaid cash seller who has delivered goods to a breaching buyer is subordinated to the interest of "purchasers" of the buyer. Lien creditors are included in the definition of "purchasers"; in order that there *be* lien creditors, the buyer's interest must be great enough to allow attachment. Therefore, however Samuels' interest upon delivery of the cattle is defined, and however slight or tenuous or marginal it was, it was necessarily great enough to permit attachment of a lien, including C.I.T.'s Article Nine interest.

The majority find that even if attachment occurred, C.I.T.'s interest would be defeated by Stowers' reclamation. The theory behind this argument is that the rights of the Article Nine secured party are at best coextensive with the rights of the debtor; if the debtor loses his rights, the security interest too is lost.

Upon nonpayment Samuels lost the right to retain or dispose of the property, but the Code recognizes that the breaching buyer had the power to encumber, despite nonpayment, so long as he retained possession. §§ 2.403(a); 1.201(32), (33). In the instant case, this power arose as a result of Stowers' delivery, and it did not terminate while the goods remained in Samuels' hands. The whole point of Article Nine is the continuity of perfected security interests *once they have properly attached,* despite subsequent loss of control or possession of the collateral by the debtor. § 9.201. Article Nine does not except an unpaid cash seller from this overall plan. In fact it specifically provides a means for him to perfect and become prior to previous perfected security interests. § 9.312(c), (d).

To hold that a reclaiming seller is given the power to sweep away a security interest which was able to attach only as a direct and Code-approved result of his voluntary act of delivery to the buyer would require ignoring the meaning and interplay of Article Two and Article Nine. Article Two recognizes the continuous vitality and priority of an Article Nine interest over the rights of an aggrieved seller. See §§ 2.403(a); 2.507, Comment 3; 2.702(c). It would be error to believe that a proper analysis of Article Nine could require the extinction of an identical Article Nine interest in the very circumstances specified by Article Two as triggering the priority of lienor over seller. See §§ 2.403(a); 2.507(b); 2.507, Comment 3; 2.702(b), (c); 9.102; 9.107(1); 9.312(c), (d).

Any seeming unfairness to Stowers resulting from the Code's operation is illusory, for the sellers could have protected their interests, even as against C.I.T.'s prior perfected interest, if they had merely complied with the UCC's purchase-money provisions. §§ 9.107, 9.312(c), (d). The Code favors purchase-money financing, and encourages it by granting to a seller of goods the power to defeat prior liens. The seller at most need only (1) file a financing statement and (2) notify the prior secured party of its interest before delivery of the new inventory. The procedure is not unduly complex or cumbersome. But whether cumbersome or not, a lender who chooses to ignore its provisions takes a calculated risk that a loss will result.

In the instant case Stowers did not utilize § 9.312's purchase-money provision. The sellers never perfected. Thus, in a competition with a perfected secured party they are subordinated, and, in this case, lose the whole of their interests. See §§ 9.201, 9.301, 9.312(e). * * *

Note: "Rights in the Collateral"

One of the principal issues in the *Samuels* case concerns the nature of "rights in the collateral" held by Samuels, the debtor. Presumably the seller's theory was that CIT, the secured creditor, derived its title—here a security interest—from the title held by Samuels. If Samuels did not get title or sufficient title from the sellers of the cattle it would be incapable of passing title or greater rights on to a third party, namely, the secured creditor. This is the basic property rule *nemo dat quod non habet.* (He who hath not cannot give.) In *Samuels* that argument failed and essentially the court found that title had passed from the sellers to Samuels, the debtor, and that C.I.T.'s interest attached free of the claimed reclamation rights. Note that initially the question of the title of the debtor is to be determined by Article 2 and the common law. As a general rule one can start with the proposition that the debtor cannot convey greater rights to a secured creditor than he himself has, but as we saw in Chapter Two, clearly such a rule cannot govern all transactions. See UCC 2–401(1).

If we were to say that a debtor can never convey greater rights in collateral than he himself has, we would be reverting to rules of the kind we encountered in *In re Craig Lumber,* supra at p. 45, rules of the nineteenth century. Under such rules the owner of property could put the property in the hands of a third party under a conditional sale contract, for example, and retain a completely secret and private interest. Article 9 in many respects rejects such outcomes and at least in some cases establishes rules of substantive law that allow a third party to achieve greater rights than the debtor himself had. See, e.g., UCC 9–307(1). The starting point in each case, however, should be to examine the debtor's title under non-Article 9 law. Does the debtor have good title under Article 2? Does the debtor have good title under rules of common law dealing with leases, bailments, and other relevant areas? If the secured creditor who has been granted a security interest or a third party who has a claim against the debtor's property now asserts *greater* rights than have been conveyed to the debtor himself, that person must find a rule of substantive law somewhere that endows him with those rights. In *Samuels* ultimately the court finds that the debtor procured title to the carcasses from the seller despite the fact that the sellers were unpaid. Thus CIT was not claiming greater rights than Samuels had acquired. But in some settings the relevant substantive law will give greater title to those buyers because they are in effect bona fide purchasers. That can be the outcome under UCC 2–702(3), the section also applied in *Samuels.* Suppose that Samuels had defrauded the sellers and the sellers had a good claim *against Samuels* under UCC 2–702(2). CIT would still prevail under UCC 2–702(3), thereby taking greater rights than the sellers had conveyed to Samuels.

Note

The *Samuels* case demonstrates a complex interrelationship between certain of the sections of Article 2 and Article 9. It would have been a wonderful thing if Article 9 could have been put together with impermeable membranes so that all security questions were answered within its boundaries, none migrated in and out, and none had to be answered elsewhere. But this was not to be. As the case shows, sometimes it will be in the secured creditor's interest to argue that *it* was a bonafide claimant under Article 2 (it is a purchaser under 1–201) who cut off other people's prior rights under 2–702(3) or section 2–403. In other cases title holders that precede the debtor may claim that the provisions of Article 2 and provisions of other law allow them to retain their interests. They may claim (as the sellers in *Samuels* did) that the debtor has received only a limited interest from them and therefore that the security interest attached only to that limited interest. As *Samuels* shows, both the provisions of Article 2 and those of Article 9 have diminished the efficacy of that argument, but they have not wiped it out. Let the case stand as a vivid reminder of the fact that the lawyer for the secured creditor must often resort to Article 2, sometimes to protect its own interest and sometimes to respond to arguments of others who wage war from Article 2 as their base.

If the secured creditor cannot find a rule of law outside of Article 9 that grants him greater rights than his debtor had, we believe that the rule of *nemo dat* should be applied and that he should be limited to the rights of his debtor. For that reason, in problem 3–1 we would decide that the lessor gets the Electra without paying any part of the fixed base operator's bill.

Problem 3–1

Lessor was the owner of a Lockheed Electra for which it no longer had any use. Lessor entered into a ten-year lease for a specified payment with an air freight service, Freight Service, that was located in Sacramento, California. Freight Service granted a security interest in the aircraft to a local fixed-base operator for $100,000 worth of unpaid work done on the aircraft. The Operator perfected its security interest on the aircraft by an appropriate filing under the federal law. If Freight Service defaults on its lease obligation to Lessor, must the Lessor pay off the entire $100,000 debt to Operator to get the Electra or is the airplane to be returned to the Lessor simply because the Freight Service is in default? Clearly the lessee had some possessory "rights in the collateral" and thus was capable of granting a security interest. Is it equally clear that UCC 9–203 states that Operator has greater rights than Lessor? If not, Operator could achieve priority over the Lessor only if the court made a mistake (as the court in fact did in a similar case) or if the secured creditor could find some rule of common law dealing with bailment that would say that those who lease items of this kind lose their rights to bona fide purchasers. This, however, would not be a rule found in Article 9. See, e.g., UCC 2–403(2). Could Operator go outside of Article 9, via UCC 1–103 for such a rule?

For states that have adopted Article 2A, the rule governing Problem 3–1 is stated in 2A–307(1). What policy supports 2A–307(2)(a)?

The fixed-based operator may have been wiser to have asserted a mechanic's lien under California law. To see how that might have given the fixed-based operator priority over the lessor, read 2A–306.

Problem 3–2

Debtor One has given a perfected security interest in a large and expensive piece of industrial machinery to Bank One. Debtor One then sold the machine to Debtor Two whose bill of sale explicitly provided that Debtor Two took subject to Bank One's security interest. Debtor Two then went to Bank Two, represented that he (Debtor Two) owned the machine free and clear and procured a $200,000 loan against it. Bank Two checked the files under Debtor Two's name and, finding nothing, perfected its security interest by a filing. When the scheme was discovered, both Bank One and Bank Two claimed the asset. Assume that there was a defect in Bank One's financing statement that caused it to be unperfected. Bank Two argues that it is a perfected secured creditor and as such has priority over Bank One's interest because of UCC 9–201 and UCC 9–312.

Can you see an argument that you would make on behalf of Bank One? Who prevails?

B. Scope of the Security Agreement

As secured transactions have become more complex, collateral more diverse, and the Code has expanded the capacity of the parties to cover not only existing loans but new loans and not only existing collateral but subsequently acquired collateral, courts have had to deal with a variety of new circumstances. Repeatedly courts are asked to determine whether security agreement covers a *new loan* or a loan made after the original one in an apparently unrelated transaction. Even more frequently, with poorly drafted clauses, courts are asked to decide whether the security agreement covers *after-acquired collateral* of the same type as the original collateral. In general the Code treats these matters as simply matters of contract between the debtor and creditor. If the security agreement is carefully drafted, seldom will a problem arise. However, an examination of the cases shows that many security agreements are not carefully drafted or, when so drafted, are later distorted by the interpretation of one party or another. Only UCC 9–110 deals with this question at all. It requires only that a description of the property "reasonably identify" the collateral or other property.

Two questions must be separated. The first question is whether the security agreement covers this loan and this collateral. If not, the security interest is not enforceable. The second is whether the financing statement that was filed is adequate to perfect a security interest in this collateral or as to this loan. As to the second question, section 9–402(8) says that "minor errors that are not seriously misleading" do not invalidate the perfection. There is no comparable provision with respect to the security agreement. Our focus in this chapter is on the first question. The second is taken up in the next chapter.

In some cases one may be able to infer from the general description of the property such as "inventory" or "accounts receivable" that the parties intend to cover not only existing but after-acquired accounts. Otherwise, given that the collateral "turns over," the creditor would soon be entirely unsecured. In other cases, such as where a security agreement covers "all indebtedness of debtor now or hereafter incurred," the issue of interpretation is much more problematic. Here, the court may find that the agreement does not reach certain debt, as for example, when the original indebtedness was a $1,000,000 business debt and one later sought to be included was a $5,000 debt for the purchase of a personal car. To the extent that these questions deal with the creation of a security interest and depend upon private documents not subject to public scrutiny, namely the security agreement, these are presumably contract interpretation questions. To the extent that they affect third parties who lend or act in reliance upon the public record, a rather different question arises. With this background consider *Idaho Bank and Trust v. Cargill.* It deals at length with just these questions.

IDAHO BANK & TRUST CO. v. CARGILL, INC.

Court of Appeals, Idaho, 1983.
105 Idaho 83, 665 P.2d 1093.

SWANSTROM, J. Idaho Bank & Trust Co. made a series of loans to Floyd Idle, a grain dealer at Rupert, Idaho. Some of the loans had not been repaid when Idle declared bankruptcy in 1977. The bank sought payment of the unpaid loans from Cargill, Inc., under the theory that Cargill was an "account debtor" who had wrongfully made several payments to Idle on grain contracts, the proceeds of which Idle had assigned to the bank as security. When Cargill refused to accept liability for the bank's losses, the bank brought this suit. Following trial, the district court held that the bank did not have a security interest in the disputed contracts and entered judgment for Cargill. We affirm.

Broadly phrased, the issue is whether Cargill, having paid Idle on certain grain contracts, should be compelled to pay again—this time to the bank—for failing to honor the assignment. The answer to this question depends on whether Cargill was an "account debtor" with respect to the disputed contracts. To decide this question, we must address two legal issues. Did Idle and the bank have a written security agreement meeting the minimum requirements of IC § 28–9–203? Did the parties' security agreement apply to "future advances" and "after-acquired collateral"?

* * * Idle's business consisted of purchasing grain from farmers and reselling it to large, west coast grain concerns, such as Cargill, Inc. Early in

1974, Idle had obtained a $50,000 line of credit with the bank. His line of credit was unsecured, and the bank was unwilling to increase the credit limits without collateral for the loans.

The bank agreed to loan Idle 80% of the face value of the grain contracts he made with Cargill in exchange for an assignment of contract proceeds, as security for the loans. The only document the bank and Idle used to evidence this arrangement was entitled an "Assignment" prepared by the bank and signed by Idle. It reads as follows:

> KNOW ALL MEN BY THESE PRESENTS: That I, Floyd Idle dba Idle Warehouse the undersigned, of Minidoka County, Idaho, for value received, do hereby set over, assign and transfer all monies now due or to become due under certain Grain Contracts held in your Warehouse. All checks are to be made payable to Idle Warehouse and Idaho Bank & Trust Company. Mail all checks to Box 604, Rupert, Idaho, 83350.
>
> Floyd E. Idle
>
> Floyd E. Idle dba Idle Warehouse

In November of 1974, the bank sent a copy of the assignment to Cargill. Accompanying the document was a letter giving notice that Idle had assigned to the bank "all funds due him from the sale of grain to your Corporation" and requesting that the bank be listed as a joint payee on all future checks. On December 2 Cargill acknowledged receipt and acceptance of the assignment. This was the last communication between the bank and Cargill until the end of April, 1977.

At Idle's direction Cargill placed the bank's name and Idle's name on each grain contract that Idle made with Cargill. Idle would bring these contracts to the bank and obtain advances from the bank of up to 80% of the cash value of each contract, by executing a promissory note for the amount of each advance. In all, the bank made short term loans on approximately two hundred contracts. When paying the contracts on which the bank's name appeared Cargill placed the bank's name as a joint payee on the checks. Cargill mailed these checks to Idle who took them to the bank. The bank routinely endorsed the checks for deposit to Idle's account and computed the amount of any loan then due. Idle wrote his check to the bank for the amount then due on his loans.

* * * Trouble began in early 1977 when the bank cut off Idle's line of credit. In response, Idle temporarily stopped performing the contracts on which he had received advances from the bank. Instead, he entered into a new series of grain contracts with Cargill. Idle directed Cargill not to put the bank's name on these contracts and Idle did not use them to obtain loans. In payment of these contracts, Cargill issued checks to Idle in his name alone. After performing seven of these contracts, Idle resumed performance of the contracts on which the bank had loaned money. However, he directed Cargill to scratch the bank's name off these remaining contracts and to issue checks without the bank's name as a co-payee. In all, Cargill issued checks to Idle for $77,667.34 on which the bank's name did not appear. These checks were issued in payment of five grain contracts on which the bank had loaned money to Idle in 1977.

In the spring of 1977, Idle went bankrupt. Idle defaulted in repayment of five promissory notes leaving him approximately $56,000 in debt to the bank. The bank sued Cargill on the theory that Cargill was an "account debtor" as that term is used in the Uniform Commercial Code. The bank contends that as an account debtor Cargill should be held liable for the losses the bank sustained when Cargill, in disregard of the notice sent by the bank, paid the proceeds of the grain contracts to Idle. The bank claimed that if Cargill had obeyed the assignment the bank would have received sufficient funds to cover Idle's $56,000 debt. This likewise is the theory of liability the bank advances on appeal.

It is obvious the bank intended Idle's assignment would provide security for loans the bank made to Idle. Accordingly, IC § 28–9–102(1)(a) provides that Chapter 9—"Secured Transactions" of our Uniform Commercial Code—shall apply. * * *

The basic premise on which the bank stakes its claim against Cargill is * * * as follows:

> "Section 9–318(3) [of the UCC] clearly delineates the legal relationship between the account debtor and the assignee once the account debtor receives adequate notification of an assignment. The account debtor, upon receipt of said notification, is duty-bound to pay the assignee and not the assignor. Payment to an assignor, after notification of assignment, does not relieve the account debtor of his obligation to pay the assignee unless the assignee consents to such a collection process. (See official comment # 3, 9–318.) The account debtor's failure to pay the assignee after receiving due notification gives rise to an assignee's claim for wrongful payment."

The dispute in this case focuses upon whether Cargill was an account debtor in respect to certain contracts coming into existence after the assignment was given. The district court determined that the assignment contained neither a "future advances" clause nor an "after-acquired property" clause. The court concluded as a matter of law that the assignment did not contain a description of the collateral sufficient to create a security interest in the proceeds of contracts which did not come into existence until 1977. The court also held the assignment did not protect the bank with respect to advances made by the bank in 1977.

Underlying the court's reasoning is the assumption that the relationship of assignee to account debtor does not come into existence unless the assignee has a security interest in the subject of the assignment. In other words, where, as here, the assignment is used as a security device, the mere fact of assignment, even coupled with notice, does not suffice to create the relationship of assignee to account debtor. There must be an underlying security interest. This conclusion of the trial court is supported by the language of the code.

Former IC § 28–9–105(1)(a) defined "Account debtor" as "the person who is obligated on an account, chattel paper, contract right or general intangible." Official Comment No. 2 to that section stated in part: "Where the *collateral* is an account, contract right, chattel paper or general intangible the original obligor is called the 'account debtor' * * *." [Emphasis added.] "Collateral" was defined in former IC § 28–9–105(1)(c) as "the property subject to a *security interest,* and includes accounts, contract rights and chattel paper which have been sold." [Emphasis added.] It is implicit from these definitions and comments that an obligor's legal status as an "account debtor" comes into being only when the assigned "contract rights" are collateral subject to a security interest. The Code extends no protection to an assignee if a security interest has not attached to the assigned contract rights.

* * * What concerns us here is whether the assignment given by Idle to the bank met the code's requirement for a written security agreement. We must also determine whether the language in the assignment was adequate to secure future advances with after-acquired collateral.

Courts have often repeated that no magic words are necessary to create a security interest and that the agreement itself need not even contain the term "security interest." This is in keeping with the policy of the Code that form should not prevail over substance and that, whenever possible, effect should be given to the parties' intent. For example, former § 28–9–102 provided in part as follows:

> "[T]his chapter applies * * * to any transaction (regardless of its form) which is intended to create a security interest in personal property or fixtures including ... contract rights; * * *
>
> "This chapter applies to security interests created by contract including pledge, assignment * * * or consignment intended as security * * *."

One court noted "there must be language * * * in the instrument which when read and construed leads to the logical conclusion that it was the intention of the parties that a security interest be created." * * *

We conclude that the document satisfied the requirement of IC § 28–9–203(1) that there be a written security agreement.

Former IC § 28–9–203(1)(b) also required that the security agreement contain a description of the collateral. To satisfy this requirement, "any description of personal property * * * is sufficient whether or not it is specific if it reasonably identifies what is described. * * * " IC § 28–9–110. The Official Comment to this section makes it clear that the policy of the Code with regard to this provision is quite liberal. The Comment urges courts to reject the view contained in older chattel mortgage cases that descriptions of collateral are "insufficient unless they are of the most exact and detailed nature." In this case the assignment describes the collateral as "all monies now due or to become due under certain Grain Contracts held in your Warehouse." We believe that this description minimally meets the requirements of IC § 28–9–110 as to any grain contracts existing between Idle and Cargill at the time Cargill received notice of the assignment. As the Comment to that section notes, "the test of sufficiency of a description laid down by this section is that the description do the job assigned to it—that it make possible the identification of the thing described."

The question remains, does the assignment give the bank a security interest in "after-acquired collateral," that is, proceeds of contracts entered into by Idle and Cargill subsequent to the assignment? Under former IC § 28–9–106 the collateral, which the bank claims in this case, was defined as a "Contract right," meaning "any right to payment under a contract not yet earned by performance and not evidenced by an instrument or chattel paper." Former IC § 28–9–204(3) stated that "a security agreement may provide that collateral, whenever acquired, shall secure all obligations covered by the security agreement." [2] The comments to this section make it clear that a security interest arising by virtue of an after-acquired property clause is no longer a disfavored arrangement. As specified in this section a security interest will attach in such collateral when value has been given and when the contract has been made. * * *

Section 28–9–110 of the code provides in part: "For the purposes of this chapter any description of personal property * * * is sufficient whether or not it is specific if it reasonably identifies what is described. * * *" The Official Comment to this section notes:

> "The test of sufficiency of a description laid down by this section is that the description do the job assigned to it—that it make possible the identification of the thing described. Under this rule courts should refuse to follow the holdings, often found in the older chattel mortgage cases, that descriptions are insufficient unless they are of the most exact and detailed nature, the so-called 'serial number' test. * * *"

In the present case the bank argues that the language used in the assignment gave the bank a security interest in the proceeds of all contracts on which it loaned money to Idle during the course of their two-year relationship. Moreover, the bank contends that provisions of the assignment, coupled with the course of dealing between Idle and the bank, make it obvious that the assignment was also intended to apply to future as well as present loans made by the bank.

We are not persuaded by the bank's argument. Whatever the parties may have intended, their intent is not clearly expressed by the assignment. The phrase "all monies now due or to become due under certain Grain Contracts held in your Warehouse" hardly encompasses the collateral to which the bank lays claim—the proceeds of five contracts entered into by Cargill and Idle in early 1977. The quoted language could reasonably be construed to mean monies due and coming due on *existing* contracts, at the time of the assignment in 1974. Moreover, this construction of the language is consistent with provisions of the UCC as it existed at the time of these transactions. An example of this is the comment to the official text under former § 9–106. It states that " 'Contract right' is a right to be earned by future performance under an *existing contract.*" [Emphasis added.] See also Comment No. 2 to § 28–9–318. We agree with the trial court that the assignment did not reasonably identify or describe the after-acquired collateral, that is, Idle-Cargill contracts not then in existence. But compare Valley National Bank of Arizona v. Flagstaff Dairy, 570 P.2d 200 (Ariz.App. 1977) ("all monies due or to become due debtor from the sale of milk" held sufficient to include accounts receivable earned after the date of the security agreement).

2. Former § 28–9–204 was repealed in 1980, and was replaced by a new section. Now, § 28–9–204(1) provides: "Except as provided in subsection (2), a security agreement may provide that any or all obligations covered by the security agreement are to be secured by after-acquired collateral."

The assignment was similarly inadequate in providing security for future advances. There is absolutely no mention in the assignment of future advances. Under former IC § 28–9–204(5) "obligations covered by a security agreement may include future advances." Official Comment No. 8 to this section stated that in pre-code law there was a "vaguely articulated prejudice against future advance agreements." The comment goes on to observe, however, that § 9–204 "validates the future advance interest, *provided only that the obligation be covered by the security agreement.*" [Emphasis added.] This comment has been interpreted to mean that "to cover future advances, the security agreement must clearly specify that the security interest in the collateral is meant to secure future advances." Texas Kenworth Co. v. First National Bank of Bethany, 564 P.2d 222, 225 (Okla.1977). We agree with this interpretation. Absent a clause in the security agreement which clearly covers future advances, such advances do not fall within the scope of the agreement. * * *

The bank argues that the "course of dealing" and "course of performance" of the parties should be considered in construing the scope and meaning of the assignment. Indeed, the Code provides that a course of dealing between parties may "give particular meaning to and supplement or qualify terms of an agreement." IC § 28–1–205(3). Likewise, § 28–2–208(1) provides that where a "contract for sale involves repeated occasions for performances by either party with knowledge of the nature of the performance and opportunity for objection to it by the other, any course of performance accepted or acquiesced in without objection shall be relevant to determine the meaning of the agreement." See also IC § 28–1–201(3).

We have already related the course of conduct which occurred during the two years after notice of the assignment was given. There was no communication between the bank and Cargill. Idle alone dealt with Cargill and all of Cargill's checks were mailed to Idle.

As mentioned earlier, in late 1976 the bank suspended its loan commitment, while it pondered whether a renewed commitment would be made. At the bank's request Idle reduced his loan balance to zero around December 1. The bank nevertheless made several additional loans to Idle upon contracts that Idle brought to the bank between December 6, 1976, and February 16, 1977. On February 16 Idle learned the bank would make no more loans. Idle then stopped having Cargill place the bank's name on his contracts. Idle even instructed Cargill to strike the bank's name from some contracts previously entered into, but which neither Idle nor Cargill had then performed. When Idle did deliver grain on these contracts, Cargill made payment to Idle. These are the payments the bank seeks to recover from Cargill.

The bank argues that, by reason of Cargill's conduct in providing joint payment checks over a long period of time, we should construe the assignment to cover future advances and we should hold that Cargill had notice of the true nature of the security agreement between Idle and the bank. However, Cargill was not a party to the assignment and played no part in selecting the language employed by the bank to create its security interest in the Idle-Cargill contracts. Idaho Code § 8–9–201 provides in part that "except as otherwise provided in this act, a security agreement is effective according to its terms between the parties, against purchasers of the collateral and against creditors." In addition, subsection (3) of § 9–318 provided:

> "The account debtor is authorized to pay the assignor until the account debtor receives notification that the account has been assigned and that payment is to be made to the assignee. A notification which does not reasonably identify the rights assigned is ineffective. If requested by the account debtor, the assignee must seasonably furnish reasonable proof that the assignment has been made and unless he does so the account debtor may pay the assignor."

Cargill, as much as anyone, had a right to rely on the assignment language, in determining whether it could safely follow Idle's request to discontinue issuing joint payment checks after the bank terminated Idle's former line of credit. Nothing in the 1974 assignment indicated it was to cover future advances made by the bank. We are therefore not persuaded that any legal or equitable principles require us to construe the assignment so as to cover loans made by the bank after the date of the assignment. To do so would not, in our view, be consistent with the stated policies of the UCC "to simplify, clarify and modernize the law governing commercial transactions." IC § 28–1–102. * * *

In summary, we hold that the assignment was adequate to create a security interest in existing contracts. However, after-acquired collateral was not reasonably identified or described. The assignment created no security interest in the after-acquired collateral and it did not cover future advances. An examination of the course of performance by the parties does not reveal legal or equitable reasons to construe the language against Cargill. We conclude that Cargill was not an account debtor with respect to the proceeds in question. Thus, Cargill cannot be held liable to the bank under IC § 28–9–318(3) for breaching the assignment by paying the proceeds of these contracts to Idle rather than to the bank. * * *

WALTERS, C.J., concurs.

Problem 3–3

The bank could have cured its problem by a modest change in its security agreement. Draft the change.

To see how a clever lawyer might attempt to solve this problem, consider the security agreement set out above at p. 126.

Problem 3–4

Assume that the granting clause in the security agreement contains the following language:

1. Debtor hereby grants a security interest to creditor in its inventory.
2. Debtor hereby grants a security interest to creditor in its machinery.
3. Debtor hereby grants a security interest to creditor in its crops.

Do any of the grants include after-acquired property? How might one justifiably distinguish among them? Do any of the grants include proceeds?

We will return to questions of the proper description in our consideration of perfection by filing under Article 9 in the next chapter. For now the student should ask whether the policy should be different with respect to the security agreement description on the one hand and the financing statement description on the other. Compare UCC 9–110 with UCC 9–402(1).

C. *Value*

We have given little consideration to the requirement of value, because that is seldom at issue. Section 1–201(44) contains an expansive definition of value. Under it, for example, a creditor who agreed to make a loan, would have given value even before the money was advanced. In most cases the making of the loan itself, the advance of the money, will be value; thus there will be no issue about that.

D. *Requirement of a Signed Writing*

A common defect "in" the security agreement is its nonexistence. In a surprising number of cases the parties prepare all the necessary documents, but when trouble strikes, the creditor has no security agreement in the file or the one in the file has never been signed. It then falls to the creditor to argue that the note, the financing statement, and any other scraps of paper that may have been signed by the debtor can be pasted together to constitute a security agreement. Courts approaching this question as a "statute of frauds" issue have sometimes concluded that UCC 9–203 can be satisfied by other documents if the parties intended a security agreement although it was never signed. Other courts, more deeply influenced by the relatively formalistic history of real and personal property security, have taken the position that the creditor is in control and is required to cross his t's and dot his i's. The latter conclude that the absence of a "granting" clause or the presence of a defect in the description of the collateral renders the secured creditor unsecured. The case that follows is among the former group. Is its reasoning persuasive?

IN RE BOLLINGER

United States Court of Appeals, Third Circuit, 1980.
614 F.2d 924.

ROSENN, CIRCUIT JUDGE. This appeal from a district court review of an order in bankruptcy presents a question that has troubled courts since the enactment of Article Nine of the Uniform Commercial Code (UCC) governing secured transactions. Can a creditor assert a secured claim against the debtor when no formal security agreement was ever signed, but where various documents executed in connection with a loan evince an intent to create a security interest? The district court answered this question in the affirmative and permitted the creditor, Zimmerman & Jansen, to assert a secured claim against the debtor, bankrupt Bollinger Corporation, in the amount of $150,000. We affirm.

I.

Industrial Credit Corporation (ICC) made a loan to Bollinger Corporation (Bollinger) on January 13, 1972, in the amount of $150,000. As evidence of

the loan, Bollinger executed a promissory note in the sum of $150,000 and signed a security agreement with ICC giving it a security interest in certain machinery and equipment. ICC in due course perfected its security interest in the collateral by filing a financing statement. * * *

Bollinger faithfully met its obligations under the note and by December 4, 1974, had repaid $85,000 of the loan, leaving $65,000 in unpaid principal. Bollinger, however, required additional capital and on December 5, 1974, entered into a loan agreement with Zimmerman & Jansen, Inc. (Z & J), by which Z & J agreed to lend Bollinger $150,000. Z & J undertook as part of this transaction to pay off the $65,000 still owed to ICC in return for an assignment by ICC to Z & J of the original note and security agreement between Bollinger and ICC. Bollinger executed a promissory note to Z & J, evidencing the agreement containing the following provision:

> "Security. This promissory note is secured by security interests in a certain security agreement between Bollinger and Industrial Credit Company * * * and in a financing statement filed by [ICC] * * *, and is further secured by security interests in certain security agreement to be delivered by Bollinger to Z and J with this promissory note covering the identical machinery and equipment as identified in the ICC security agreement and with identical schedule attached in the principal amount of Eighty-Five Thousand Dollars ($85,000)."

No formal security agreement was ever executed between Bollinger and Z & J. Z & J did, however, in connection with the promissory note, record a new financing statement signed by Bollinger containing a detailed list of the machinery and equipment originally taken as collateral by ICC for its loan to Bollinger.

Bollinger filed a petition for an arrangement under Chapter XI of the Bankruptcy Act in March, 1975 and was adjudicated bankrupt one year later. In administrating the bankrupt's estate, the receiver sold some of Bollinger's equipment but agreed that Z & J would receive a $10,000 credit on its secured claim.

Z & J asserted a secured claim against the bankrupt in the amount of $150,000, arguing that although it never signed a security agreement with Bollinger, the parties had intended that a security interest in the sum of $150,000 be created to protect the loan. The trustee in bankruptcy conceded that the assignment to Z & J of ICC's original security agreement with Bollinger gave Z & J a secured claim in the amount of $65,000, the balance owed by Bollinger to ICC at the time of the assignment. The trustee, however, refused to recognize Z & J's asserted claim of an additional secured claim of $85,000 because of the absence of a security agreement between Bollinger and Z & J. The bankruptcy court agreed and entered judgment for Z & J in the amount of $55,000, representing a secured claim in the amount of $65,000 less $10,000 credit received by Z & J.

Z & J appealed to the United States District Court for the Western District of Pennsylvania, which reversed the bankruptcy court and entered judgment for Z & J in the full amount of the asserted $150,000 secured claim. The trustee in bankruptcy appeals.

II.

* * * The requirements of § 9–203(1)(b) further two basic policies. First, an evidentiary function is served by requiring a signed security agreement and second, a written agreement also obviates any Statute of Frauds problems with the debtor-creditor relationship. Id. Comments 3, 5.

* * * The financing statement serves the purpose of giving public notice to other creditors that a security interest is claimed in the debtor's collateral.

Despite the minimal formal requirements set forth in § 9–203 for the creation of a security agreement, the commercial world has frequently neglected to comply with this simple Code provision. Soon after Article Nine's enactment, creditors who had failed to obtain formal security agreements, but who nevertheless had obtained and filed financing statements, sought to enforce secured claims. Under § 9–402, a security agreement may serve as a financing statement if it is signed by both parties. The question arises whether the converse is true: Can a signed financing statement operate as a security agreement? The earliest case to consider this question was American Card Company v. H.M.H. Co., 196 A.2d 150, 152 (R.I. 1963) which held that a financing statement could *not* operate as a security agreement because there was no language *granting* a security interest to a creditor. Although § 9–203(1)(b) makes no mention of such a grant language requirement, the court in American Card thought that implicit in the definition of "security agreement" under § 9–105(1)(h) was such a requirement; some grant language was necessary to "create or provide security." * * *

The Ninth Circuit in In Re Amex-Protein Development Corporation, 504 F.2d 1056 (9th Cir.1975), echoed criticism by commentators of the American Card rule. The court wrote: "There is no support in legislative history or grammatical logic for the substitution of the word grant for the phrase creates or provides for." Id. at 1059. It concluded that as long as the financing statement contains a description of the collateral signed by the debtor, the financing statement may serve as the security agreement and the formal requirements of § 9–203(1)(b) are met. The tack pursued by the Ninth Circuit is supported by legal commentary on the issue. See G. Gilmore, Security Interests in Personal Property, § 11.4 at 347–48 (1965).

Some courts have declined to follow the Ninth Circuit's liberal rule allowing the financing statement alone to stand as the security agreement, but have permitted the financing statement, when read in conjunction with other documents executed by the parties, to satisfy the requirements of § 9–203(1)(b). The court in In re Numeric Corp., 485 F.2d 1328 (1st Cir.1973) held that a financing statement coupled with a board of directors' resolution revealing an intent to create a security interest were sufficient to act as a security agreement. The court concluded from its reading of the Code that there appears no need to insist upon a separate document entitled "security agreement" as a prerequisite for an otherwise valid security interest.

> "A writing or writings, regardless of label, which adequately describes the collateral, carries the signature of the debtor, and establishes that in fact a security interest was agreed upon, would satisfy both the formal requirements of the statute and the policies behind it."

Id. at 1331. The court went on to hold that "although a standard form financing statement by itself cannot be considered a security agreement, an adequate agreement can be found when a financing statement is considered together with other documents." Id. at 1332.

More recently, the Supreme Court of Maine in Casco Bank & Trust Co. v. Cloutier, 398 A.2d 1224, 1231–32 (Me.1979) considered the question of whether composite documents were sufficient to create a security interest within the terms of the Code. Writing for the court, Justice Wernick allowed a financing statement to be joined with a promissory note for purposes of determining whether the note contained an adequate description of the collateral to create a security agreement. The court indicated that the evidentiary and Statute of Frauds policies behind § 9–203(1)(b) were satisfied by reading the note and financing statement together as the security agreement.

In the case before us, the district court went a step further and held that the promissory note executed by Bollinger in favor of Z & J, standing alone, was sufficient to act as the security agreement between the parties. In so doing, the court implicitly rejected the American Card rule requiring grant language before a security agreement arises under § 9–203(1)(b). But although we agree that no formal grant of a security interest need exist before a security agreement arises, we do not think that the promissory note standing alone would be sufficient under Pennsylvania law to act as the security agreement. We believe, however, that the promissory note, read in conjunction with the financing statement duly filed and supported, as it is here, by correspondence during the course of the transaction between the parties, would be sufficient under Pennsylvania law to establish a valid security agreement.

III.

When the parties have neglected to sign a separate security agreement, it would appear that the better and more practical view is to look at the transaction as a whole in order to determine if there is a writing, or writings, signed by the debtor describing the collateral which demonstrates an intent to create a security interest in the collateral. In connection with Z & J's loan of $150,000 to Bollinger, the relevant writings to be considered are: (1) the promissory note; (2) the financing statement; (3) a group of letters constituting the course of dealing between the parties. The district court focused solely on the promissory note finding it sufficient to constitute the security agreement. Reference, however, to the language in the note reveals that the note standing alone cannot serve as the security agreement. The note recites that along with the assigned 1972 security agreement between Bollinger and ICC, the Z & J loan is "further secured by security interests in a certain Security Agreement *to be delivered* by Bollinger to Z & J with this Promissory Note, * * *" (Emphasis added.) The bankruptcy judge correctly reasoned that "[t]he intention to create a separate security agreement negates any inference that the debtor intended that the promissory note constitute the security agreement." At best, the note is some evidence that a security agreement was contemplated by the parties, but by its own terms, plainly indicates that it is not the security agreement.

Looking beyond the promissory note, Z & J did file a financing statement signed by Bollinger containing a detailed list of all the collateral intended to secure the $150,000 loan to Bollinger. The financing statement alone meets the basic § 9–203(1)(b) requirements of a writing, signed by the debtor, describing the collateral. However, the financing statement provides only an inferential basis for concluding that the parties intended a security agreement. There would be little reason to file such a detailed financing statement unless the parties intended to create a security interest. The intention of the parties to create a security interest may be gleaned from the expression of future intent to create one in the promissory note and the intention of the parties as expressed in letters constituting their course of dealing.

The promissory note was executed by Bollinger in favor of Z & J in December 1974. Prior to the consummation of the loan, Z & J sent a letter to Bollinger on May 30, 1974, indicating that the loan would be made "provided" Bollinger secured the loan by a mortgage on its machinery and equipment. Bollinger sent a letter to Z & J on September 19, 1974, indicating:

> "With your [Z & J's] stated desire to obtain security for material and funds advanced, it would appear that the use of the note would answer both our problems. Since the draft forwarded to you offers full collateralization for the funds to be advanced under it and bears normal interest during its term, it should offer you maximum security."

Subsequent to the execution of the promissory note, Bollinger sent to Z & J a list of the equipment and machinery intended as collateral under the security agreement which was to be, but never was, delivered to Z & J. In November 1975, the parties exchanged letters clarifying whether Bollinger could substitute or replace equipment in the ordinary course of business without Z & J's consent. Such a clarification would not have been necessary had a security interest not been intended by the parties. Finally, a letter of November 18, 1975, from Bollinger to Z & J indicated that "any attempted impairment of the collateral would constitute an event of default."

From the course of dealing between Z & J and Bollinger, we conclude there is sufficient evidence that the parties intended a security agreement to be created separate from the assigned ICC agreement with Bollinger. All the evidence points towards the intended creation of such an agreement and since the financing statement contains a detailed list of the collateral, signed by Bollinger, we hold that a valid Article Nine security agreement existed under Pennsylvania law between the parties which secured Z & J in the full amount of the loan to Bollinger.

* * *

Affirmed. [Footnotes omitted.]

Notes

As we have seen, UCC 9–203(1)(a) is said to be in the nature of a statute of frauds. *In re Bollinger* and other cases like it show how critical the framing of the issue can be. The statute of frauds is a much despised statute that has fallen into disrepute in the United States, is the laughing stock of Article 2, and has been repealed in England. Section 2–201 of Article 2 is so full of holes today that only a lawyer totally devoid of imagination will fail to find some plausible argument to sustain an oral contract of sale. There are the standard exceptions such as part performance, special manufacture and such. Also, arguments have been upheld that there is fraud, that the contract was admitted by the defendant, and on and on. Moreover, it is today thought to be "good" to strike down barriers to recognition of true intent and to enforce oral contracts notwithstanding the absence of a writing.

On the other hand, one finds a long history of judicial hostility to secured creditors, and an insistence that they comply with the law in exacting detail. This, too, is said to be a "good" thing, for many believe that secured creditors are oppressors, that they manipulate the legislatures and thus that they should be required to toe the line before getting what the law allows.

With the two opposing general attitudes, then if the lawyer can get the court to adopt one as opposed to the other, one suspects that the case itself is over. In cases such as *Bollinger* there is rarely any doubt that the debtor and the creditor intended a security interest, intended that the debt be paid off with specific interest and on a particular schedule. There has been performance and there is evidence in the form of cancelled checks, a financing statement, letters or other documents, usually undenied by the debtor, that show the intention to create a security interest. These are not merely statute of frauds cases; they are easy statute of frauds cases.

If, on the other hand, one approaches the case with a deep suspicion of secured creditors, and harbors true concern about their overreaching, it is equally easy to conclude that they should be made to comply strictly with the laws that so obviously favor them. Having so concluded, it is easy to throw out a security interest that does not comply with the simple rules of UCC 9–203.

Among the various actors, who is most likely to be injured by a law that diminishes the amount of proof necessary to establish a valid security interest? Consider the possibilities.

1. The debtor? Of course if the debtor is in bankruptcy, the debtor often has no interest in this question since few if any of the assets will be returned to the debtor; they will go to other creditors.

2. Unsecured creditors? These surely will share in the assets if there is bankruptcy and if a security interest is struck down by any means.

3. Courts? A greater requirement of and respect for formality might ease the courts' work.

4. Lawyers and trustees in bankruptcy? In theory the lawyers and the trustee are merely representatives of the secured and unsecured creditors and of the debtor. In reality they have an independent and selfish interest.

Problem 3–5

Because it is usually a form and usually properly completed, it is easy to overlook the lowly security agreement. In the great majority of cases the lender will be using a form drafted by its lawyer, or perhaps, purchased from a commercial seller of documents. When the security agreement is properly drafted with knowledge of the underlying transaction and when the loan officer uses the proper form for the transaction, there are seldom difficulties, but think for a moment how Murphy's Law could intervene. First, the lawyer who drafts the document might be ignorant of the underlying transaction. The drafter might visualize a conventional inventory loan when the collateral is accounts receivable or equipment. Or, the lawyer might not appreciate that the client intends to use the form for a purchase money loan and needs to enjoy priority as a purchase money lender over prior lenders. Yet more likely is the possibility that the form drafted properly and according to the lender's instructions to apply to an inventory loan will be used by a hurried loan officer for an equipment loan, or the document drafted for pigs will be used for airplanes. When that happens, all kinds of mischief can occur and inevitable interpretive difficulties will confront a judge and lawyers who must now apply a security agreement to a Boeing 747 that was designed for Chester Whites.

There are other problems too. For example, the lawyer drafting the document may have used great care not only to state the kind of collateral in the body of the security agreement, but also to provide for blocks to be checked off or for exhibits to be attached. When a loan officer is hurried, ignorant, or careless, the officer may fail to check blocks, or may check the wrong blocks, or may entirely forget the exhibit so carefully provided for by the lawyer.

In addition, there will be deviant cases, not recognized as such by the loan officer, such as cases in which one party (a spouse or a subsidiary) arranges for the loan that is in fact to be made to another. When, in those cases, the "nondebtor" signs the security agreement, there will be trouble.

Through all of this the student should remember that the security agreement is both a contract and a conveyance. Unless the security agreement is properly executed (or there is an estoppel or the like) no property interest will be conveyed to the lender and thus the lender will not be a holder of an interest in the debtor's assets. Some courts' conception of the security agreement as a conveyance has led them to insist on a "granting clause" for a valid security agreement.

But the security agreement is much more than a conveyance; it is also a contract between the debtor and creditor—one having to do mainly with the latter's rights and the former's obligations. As a contract it is subject to all of the rules and problems of interpretation applicable to other contracts. Because the typical security agreement is a form drafted by one party (usually a skilled lawyer), completed by another (usually a skilled layman), potential for ambiguity and error abound. The four problems that follow are taken from actual cases and illustrate the difficulties that recur in the execution and interpretation of security agreements.

Assume that you represent the trustee in bankruptcy in each of the following cases. How would you challenge the security agreement? Do you think you would be successful?

A. Joseph Corsi bought an automobile for his wife Mary. He gave the car to her and she procured a certificate of title listing herself as the owner and Ford Motor Credit as the first lien holder. Joseph signed a security agreement that granted a security interest to Stewart who assigned it to Ford Motor Credit. Mary's name did not appear on the security agreement. When Mary went into bankruptcy both the trustee and Ford Motor Credit claimed the car. Would it matter whether Joseph signed the security agreement before or after he made the gift to Mary?

In discussing the rights of the secured creditors here, the court held as follows:

"The fallacy with Stewart's position is that it concludes that the application for a certificate of title containing the name and address of the lienholder perfects a security interest in a vehicle. Stewart presumes the existence of such a security interest when in fact none exists. A security agreement was in fact executed on November 28, 1975 between Stewart and Joseph D. Corsi, husband of Mary W. Corsi, to whom he made a gift of the vehicle. The certificate of title issued by the Vermont Department of Motor Vehicles shows the owner as Mary W. Corsi and Ford Motor Cr. Co. as first lienholder. There was never any security agreement by and between the owner of the vehicle, Mary W. Corsi, and Stewart or Ford Motor Credit Co., its purported assignee.

"Under the UCC as adopted in Vermont a security interest cannot attach until there is agreement that it attach and value is given and the debtor has rights in the collateral. It attaches as soon as all of the events in the preceding sentence have taken place unless explicit agreement postpones the time of attaching. 9A VSA sec. 9–204(1).

"In the instant case, there was no agreement between the owner of the vehicle, Mary W. Corsi, and Stewart at the time that the application for a certificate of title was made by her showing Ford Motor Credit Co. as lienholder."

The case is wrong if the security agreement was granted prior to the making of the gift. True? The court quotes from a Connecticut case involving a similar matter in which the court made the following statement:

"[A] bank listed as first lienor on a certificate of title issued in the name of a wife acquired no security interest in two vehicles since the wife never signed the retail installment contracts covering them and purchased by the husband and wife. Nor did the bank acquire an enforceable security interest in the vehicles through the husband who had signed the security agreements since the husband had not acquired title to the automobiles and had no rights in them to which a security interest could attach."

If the husband had signed a security agreement (as he may have) prior to the purchase of the automobile and had then made a gift of that automobile (before he bought it) to his wife, the title would still pass through his hands, would it not? If that is true, the security would have attached, like a barnacle to the hull of a ship, as the car passed through the husband's hands. Only the "debtor's equity" would pass on to the wife by gift, not so? Ford Motor Credit was not that lucky. As the quote from the case suggests, the courts do not often look for ways to protect secured creditors who failed to protect themselves.

B. On his bankruptcy, debtor owned a 1980 and a 1981 Yamaha motorcycle, a 1980 Jeep Wagoneer, and three cash registers that he used in his business. The Jeep was worth more than $6,000 and the remaining balance on the debt originally incurred to Bank for the Jeep was under $2,000. The value of the other collateral was in each case less than the amount of the outstanding debt. Bank claimed the right to realize the debt existing on the other three items out of the proceeds of sale of the Wagoneer.

On page one of the Bank's Security Agreement form, "1980 Jeep Wagoneer SN# JOE15NN048763" was typed in the space for collateral. In small typed letters the form stated:

"To secure payment of the indebtedness evidenced by *a* certain promissory note of even date herewith, in the amount of *$7494.84*

( ) and any other indebtedness, present or future, of the debtor, payable to the secured party or order.

(x) payable to the Secured Party, or order, repayable as follows: $209 monthly for 36 months."

The first box is *not* checked.

On page two of the security agreement the following appeared:

"In addition, I give the Bank a security interest in my *1980 Jeep Wagoneer SN# JOE15NN048763* and have executed a security agreement on this date that fully describes this property. The security agreement secures not only this, but any other debt which I owe the Bank, including future debts, and covers property (subject to the limitation of the UCC) which I might not now have, but may acquire in the future."

Can the bank use the proceeds from sale of the Wagoneer to satisfy the other debts (a) if it checks the first block; (b) if it does not check the first block? See UCC 9–203, 9–204 & 9–306.

Here we see the loan officer and the lawyer-drafter tripping over one another's feet. The lawyer has conveniently given the loan officer a block to check in order to include "other indebtedness." Being careful and compulsive, the loan officer has gone the lawyer one better and has drafted a specific agreement that covers other debts and other collateral. But because the loan officer has failed to check the "other indebtedness" block, the debtor (or possibly the trustee in bankruptcy) is now free to argue that the agreement is ambiguous and that the other loans are not secured by the Jeep Wagoneer. This is nothing more than a contract ambiguity, and a small one at that. In any other contract we would surely overlook the fact that the debtor failed to check the "other indebtedness" block and would give effect to the specific statement included in the last paragraph. Presumably if the debtor admits the security agreement covers other loans, the matter is closed, not so? After all this is a contract and if both the debtor and secured creditor agree on its meaning, no other party should be able to complain.

But what of the case in which the debtor denies knowledge of the last paragraph or even asserts that the loan officer assured him that only the debt on the Wagoneer was covered? Then there are problems, and in that case it is quite possible that the secured creditor should lose.

C. Assume that both the security agreement and the financing statement filed in the register of deeds office contains the following description:

"Crops growing or to be grown on the following real estate:

Farm(s) or Other Real Estate Owner	Appx. No. of Acres	County & State	Appx. Distance and Direction From a Named Town or Other Description
Faye McMannis	160	Pratt	From Iuka: 2 N 2¼ W
McMannis Heirs	1100	Pratt	4¼ W
Helena Thompson	80	Pratt	4 W ½ N
Orvalene Becker	160	Pratt	½ N

Would the security agreement cover a herd of sheep maintained on the same McMannis land?

No farmer would describe sheep as crops. There is no definition of crops in Article 9, but 9–109(3) defines farm products as "crops or livestock". That definition leads to the conclusion that livestock (clearly sheep are livestock) are different from crops and therefore that the word "crops" in the security agreement does not cover sheep. If the litigation were between a trustee in bankruptcy and the secured creditor and if the debtor were still friendly with the secured creditor, he might testify that the parties intended the word "crops" to include sheep. Of course, we should take the farmer's testimony with a grain of salt. But if he so testified and was believed, presumably that is the way the contract should be read and even the trustee in bankruptcy should be bound, not so?

This too seems like a case in which the drafter prepared a document for one purpose (namely, granting security interests in crops) that was used for another (namely, granting a security interest in livestock). The loan officer made a mistake, but part of the fault may rest at the feet of the drafter who failed to understand the normal transaction. If, for example, the lender always takes security interests in livestock and crops together, the document is poorly drafted. Remember, you are a fool if you draft a legal document in a windowless room without a full understanding about the use to which the document will be put and the business circumstances that will prevail in its use.

D. On a loan application Debtor asked for a $500,000 loan and specified that the collateral would include a security interest in "all accounts receivable and inventory" of the debtor. When the security agreement was signed, it contained a form with a series of blocks to identify the kind of collateral claimed. As executed, the security agreement contained check marks next to the blocks marked "all equipment and machinery, furniture and fixtures" but there was none beside the block for inventory and none next to the block for accounts receivable. A financing statement was filed that described the collateral as "inventory and accounts receivable." On bankruptcy, does the trustee in bankruptcy or the secured creditor take the inventory and accounts? Is the debtor's testimony that the parties intended to cover inventory and accounts receivable admissible?

This is the same interpretive difficulty we saw in B, but with a twist. Here assume we are in bankruptcy and assume further that the trustee in bankruptcy claims that the debtor's testimony (against the trustee's position) should not be admitted on the ground that the trustee is a third party who should not be bound by independent and unreliable recollections of the other persons. In response, the secured creditor argues that neither the trustee nor any of the creditors the trustee represents could have been misled because the public filing properly disclosed the claim on inventory and accounts even though the private security agreement (by hypothesis not seen by any other creditor) was ambiguous. Should not the court listen to the creditor's and debtor's testimony and allow it to override the trustee in bankruptcy if it is persuasive? (If your answer is no, think how quickly you would have come to the opposite conclusion on a conventional contract in your first-year course on contract law. Why is this different?)

SECTION 3. THE CREATION OF SECURITY INTERESTS IN PROCEEDS

Under the 1972 version of Article 9, assume the creditor has an automatic security interest in proceeds of collateral even if the security agreement is silent on the question. Section 9–203(3) specifies: "unless otherwise agreed, the security agreement gives the secured party the rights to proceeds provided by section 9–306." That sentence in turn leads to UCC

9–306's definition of proceeds and to its description of the reach of the proceeds claim. Note in UCC 9–306(1) that proceeds include "whatever is received upon the sale, exchange, collection or other disposition of collateral or proceeds." Section 9–306(2) provides, however, that the security interest continues only in "any *identifiable* proceeds." It is obvious, is it not, that a secured creditor who has a perfected security interest in a dealer's inventory of automobiles, has a proceeds interest in the note and security interest given by a consumer when buying a specific automobile out of the dealer-debtor's inventory? That note and security interest i.e., chattel paper, UCC 9–105(1), is identifiable proceeds received in exchange for the collateral pursuant to 9–306(1) and (2); it can be tied to a particular transaction and to a particular automobile that was sold. So far, so good.

But one need not travel far down the proceeds road before the path becomes indistinct and the way less clear. Assume, for example, that our debtor-dealer sells a car for cash and that he deposits the cash in his general bank account that includes revenues from a variety of sources as well as some of his own personal funds. Clearly, the cash received was proceeds at the outset, but does it still remain "identifiable proceeds"?

Or consider the case in which the debtor is involved in an accident with the automobile and procures a tort recovery from the person at fault in the accident. Is that tort recovery "received upon the sale, exchange, collection or other disposition of the collateral"? If so, it is proceeds and covered by UCC 9–306; if not, the creditor has no secured claim in the tort recovery.

IN RE SAN JUAN PACKERS

United States Court of Appeals, Ninth Circuit, 1983.
696 F.2d 707.

PER CURIAM. This is a dispute between a secured creditor of a bankrupt food processor and a secured creditor of farmers from whom the food processor bought vegetables. The food processor, San Juan Packers, Inc., bought cans on credit from a can manufacturer, National Can Corporation, and granted the can manufacturer a floating lien on all of its inventory. In late summer, 1976, the food processor bought vegetables from many farmers, including the three involved in this litigation. These three farmers had obtained financing from Peoples State Bank and had granted the bank a security interest in their crops and the "proceeds" thereof.

The food processor filed a petition in bankruptcy after it had received the farmers' vegetables and processed and sold a portion of them, but before it had finished paying all purchase price installments due the farmers. Not having been paid by the food processor, the farmers did not pay the bank. The bank brought this adversary proceeding in bankruptcy court against all of the food processor's secured creditors to establish the priority of the bank's security interest in the farmers' vegetables and in the cash proceeds thereof. The parties agreed to the sale of all vegetables in the food processor's possession and creation of a fund from the proceeds to satisfy any judgment that might arise from this action.

The bankruptcy court found for the bank, and the can manufacturer appealed to the district court, which affirmed. The can manufacturer appeals to this court, advancing three contentions.

I.

The can manufacturer first contends that money received by the food processor for the farmers' vegetables are not "proceeds" to which the bank's security interest attached under its security agreements with the farmers.

The Uniform Commercial Code (UCC) provides that "[p]roceeds includes whatever is received when collateral or proceeds is sold, exchanged, collected or otherwise disposed of." Section 9–306(1). Under this definition, the money the food processor received for the farmers' vegetables is "proceeds" unless the vegetables ceased to be collateral when purchased by the food processor.

> " 'Collateral' means the property subject to a security interest. * * * " Section 9–105(1)(c). "Except where * * * Article [9] otherwise provides, a security interest continues in collateral notwithstanding sale * * * by the debtor unless his action was authorized by the secured party * * *." Section 9–306(2). Since the can manufacturer does not dispute the bankruptcy court's finding that the bank did not authorize the sale free of its security interest, and Article 9 does not otherwise provide, it would appear that the bank's security interest continued in the vegetables after their sale to the food processor, that the vegetables remained "collateral," and that whatever was received by the food processor when the vegetables were sold is "proceeds."

The can manufacturer points out that § 9–306(2) provides that a security interest continues, "notwithstanding sale * * * *by the debtor* and * * * in any identifiable proceeds including collections *received by the debtor* " (emphasis supplied), and argues that the bank's security interest was not saved by § 9–306(2) when the vegetables were sold and cash received by the food processor rather than by the farmers because the farmers and not the food processor were the "debtors." But under § 9–105(1)(d), the food processor *is* the "debtor":

> "(1) In this article, unless the context otherwise requires:
>
> "(d) 'Debtor' means the person who owes payment or other performance of the obligation secured, whether or not he owns or has rights in the collateral * * *. *Where the debtor and the owner of the collateral are not the same person, the term 'debtor' means the owner of the collateral in any provision of the Article dealing with the collateral,* the obligor in any provision dealing with the obligation, and may include both where the context so requires." (emphasis supplied).

Official Comment 2 to § 9–105 makes it clear that an owner of the collateral is a "debtor" whether he acquired his rights in the collateral at the time the security interest was created or at a later date:

> "In all but a few cases the person who owes the debt and the person whose property secures the debt will be the same. Occasionally, one person furnishes security for another's debt, *and sometimes property is transferred subject to a secured debt of the transferor which the transferee does not assume;* in such cases, under the second sentence of the definition, the term 'debtor' may, depending on the context, include either or both such persons." (emphasis supplied).

The can manufacturer protests that under this view the bank could follow these vegetables into the hands of the ultimate consumer.

But this is precisely what the plain language of the UCC requires.

* * *

II.

The can manufacturer's second argument is that by the terms of § 9–306(2) the bank's security interest continued only in "identifiable proceeds" and was lost because the food processor mixed together vegetables purchased from various farmers making it impossible to identify vegetables, or proceeds from the sale of vegetables remaining in the food processor's possession, as attributable to any particular farmer.

Section 9–315 of the UCC requires rejection of this argument. The bank had a perfected security interest in the farmers' vegetables, and those vegetables became part of a mass of vegetables in the hands of the food processor, so commingled that their identity became lost in the mass. By the express terms of § 9–315(1), where collateral loses its identity by commingling or processing, the security interest continues in the mass or product—and it is not disputed that the proceeds in the fund established in this case can be traced to commingled vegetables in the hands of the food processor.

* * *

III.

Finally, the can manufacturer argues that if § 9–315 is applied, the can manufacturer was entitled to share in the fund since the can manufacturer had a security interest in the vegetables in the food processor's possession grown by farmers other than the three in whose crops the bank had a security interest, and by the terms of § 9–315 each party whose collateral is commingled in the mass is entitled to a ratable share of the proceeds of the sale of the mass.

The bank resists application of § 9–315 on the ground, relied upon by the district court, that § 9–315(1) "requires the attachment of two security interests to the product or mass." The attachment of two security interests to the product or mass is an explicit condition only to the operation of § 9–315(2), not § 9–315(1). Moreover, this condition to the application of § 9–315(2) was satisfied because both the bank's interest in the vegetables of the three farmers with whom the bank had its security arrangement and the can manufacturer's security interest in the other vegetables in the food processor's inventory attached to the mass of each variety of vegetables when the vegetables of the same variety purchased from various farmers were commingled.

The bank contends further that § 9–315 does not apply because the vegetables were not sufficiently processed. The statute, however, refers to processing *and* commingling, both in the caption of the section and in § 9–315(1)(a). "Commingled" is not a term of art in this context; it simply means "to mix together," Webster's Third New International Dictionary 457 (1961), or "[t]o put together in one mass." Black's Law Dictionary 246 (5th ed. 1979). As the bank points out, Official Comment 3 to § 9–315 refers to commingling flour, sugar and eggs into cake mix, a process involving more than mere mixing, but there is no indication that the drafters meant to exclude simple mixing of fungible goods.

IV.

Application of § 9–315(2) does not, however, completely resolve this case. It is not clear from the record whether vegetables of the bank's three farmers were sold between the time these vegetables were delivered to the food processor and the time the food processor filed a bankruptcy petition. If such sales occurred and proceeds were not dissipated before bankruptcy, they are available to the secured parties subject to the provisions of § 9–306(4). Proceeds of sales made under the supervision of the bankruptcy court are, of course, not subject to § 9–306(4). Furthermore, there may be more than one § 9–315(2) ratio for each mass of vegetables because additional deliveries from farmers other than the three having security arrangements with the bank were subject to the can manufacturer's security interest; when such deliveries were added to the various masses of corn, peas, and carrots, the proportion of the security interest in each mass to which the can manufacturer was entitled increased.

The judgment appealed from is therefore vacated, and the case is remanded. * * *

Notes

1. How does the court sort out the commingled proceeds? In light of the foregoing opinion, can you think of any examples of proceeds that would not be "identifiable" in which a creditor accordingly would not have a proceeds interest?

2. Does UCC 9–306, when read in its entirety, contemplate that proceeds placed in a commingled bank account (that is, in which there are also placed funds not classified as proceeds) be regarded as identifiable? What clues do you get from § 9–306(2) and (4)?

Note

There is a nasty midwestern joke that goes as follows: How does one double the income of a farmer? The answer: Give him a second mailbox.

The bite in the joke arises partly from the fact that it hits too close to the truth. In 1983 direct government payments to farmers accounted for approximately 4.5 percent of the national gross farm income. These amounted to more than $9 billion in 1983; doubtless they have grown since. The payments come in many forms and for many reasons; for not planting a certain crop, for holding a certain crop off the market, for devoting certain acreage to conservation purposes, for shooting one's milk cows and for other reasons almost as numerous as the farmer's imagination. The following excerpts from the article by G.A. Marsh, Are PIK Payments "Proceeds" Under Article 9? Journal of Agricultural Taxation and Law 291 (1985–86), describe the courts' reaction to secured creditors' claims to such payments.

G.A. MARSH, ARE PIK PAYMENTS "PROCEEDS" UNDER ARTICLE 9?

7 Journal of Agricultural Taxation & Law 291, 296–300, 311–312 (1985–86).

* * *

Current government subsidy programs support both market prices of commodities and farm income levels. Although the programs vary from commodity to commodity and are subject to annual changes, the programs generally attempt to adjust production to demand through voluntary participation, while others involve government purchases of commodities.

Among the many support programs are the following: price support through government purchases, price support loan levels, target price and deficiency payments, set-aside programs, acreage limitations, diversion payments, quotas, export programs, and marketing orders. While only a recent variation of one of these programs will be examined in detail, the history of all of these programs is probably best described as a system where new ideas are discarded and old ideas are resurrected. Furthermore, it is not at all clear how much these programs have actually helped agricultural producers.

In 1981 and 1982, economic conditions of farmers worsened, caused in part by rising world agricultural production in the face of weakened demand. In the United States, stocks of nearly all major commodities rose tremendously, in some cases tripling the levels in storage over only a three-year period. Prices dropped dramatically, causing many farmers to face financial ruin. The problem was exacerbated by high interest rates and a generally weak economy. The poor economic conditions in the country not only contributed to a diminishing demand for some agricultural products, but also reduced the availability of nonfarm employment for farm families. Nonfarm employment had become an increasingly important source for debt repayment capacity among farmer-borrowers.

In response to the particular problems that were experienced in the early 1980s, the U.S. Department of Agriculture, acting under preexisting legislative authority, developed a Payment-in-Kind (PIK) Program for 1983. The commodities of corn, wheat, grain sorghum, upland cotton, and rice were involved in the program. PIK was developed to supplement already existing acreage reduction programs. Under the programs already in place before PIK, producers who planted one or more of the program crops, and who participated in and complied with acreage reduction and land diversion programs were eligible for program benefits. The benefits included land diversion payments, commodity loans, target price protection, and disaster payments. Those producers who participated in the acreage reduction and/or paid land diversion programs involving the subject crops could also participate in the PIK Program. Under PIK, producers could receive a quantity of pounds or bushels of the commodity from the Commodity Credit Corporation for an additional acreage reduction. The additional acreage reduction was the PIK acreage.

PIK ALTERNATIVES

Additional Reduction in Acreage

There were two alternatives available to farmers who chose to participate in the PIK plan. The first alternative under PIK required an additional reduction in the acreage of the crops permitted to be planted from 10–30 percent of the crop acreage base. The acreage base was the average number of acres a farmer devoted to production of that particular crop over a historical period. Farmers would then receive a fixed percentage of the average crop yield that they had experienced over a historical reference period—95 percent for wheat and 80 percent for other crops. This alternative was commonly referred to as "percent of base PIK."

Withdrawing Entire Crop Acreage

The second alternative was for the withdrawing of the entire crop acreage from production. Total land diversions in any county could not exceed 45 percent, and these bids were accepted only after the 10–30 percent elections were accepted. This alternative was commonly called "whole base PIK."

Participation in the PIK Program also required that the land withdrawn from production be devoted to conservation uses. Farmers had to plant a cover crop to control erosion.

The response of farmers to the PIK Program was unprecedented. Farmers qualifying for the PIK Program removed from production about 48 million of the 212 million acres expected to be planted in 1983.

* * *

In the attempt to address questions of the proper characterization of PIK benefits for Article 9 purposes, and whether those benefits were subject to security interests under security agreements that predated the program, the courts have rendered a number of puzzling and often conflicting decisions. These decisions fall along a wide spectrum. At one end are those cases where courts gave a narrow reading to both the relevant provisions of Article 9 and the financing statements—usually resulting in a holding in favor of the debtor or bankruptcy trustee. At the other end are those cases where the courts gave an expanded reading to both Article 9 and the security agreements—usually resulting in a decision in favor of secured creditors with security interests in crops. In nearly every case, the courts had some difficulty in the attempt to characterize the entitlements from this rather unusual program, where an individual received crops in exchange for a decision to refrain from growing crops.

Careful study of the cases suggests that the outcome would be determined based on whether the PIK entitlements were viewed as something like a "general intangible," or whether the entitlements were characterized as "proceeds" of crops. Where the characterization was the former, the creditors usually lost, absent a specific reference to general intangibles in the financing statement. Where the characterization was the latter, the secured creditor prevailed, even though this reading makes PIK commodities, the "proceeds" of crops that were never planted.

* * *

CONCLUSION

The frequent changes in government farm subsidy programs have been disruptive to existing relationships between borrowers and lenders. The implementation of the PIK Program for 1983, adopted by the USDA, proved to be no exception to the rule. Under the program, the Department of Agriculture entered into contracts with farmers under which the government provided quantities of grain in return for the farmer's agreement to set-aside acreage. Unlike many other farm programs providing disaster payments for destroyed crops or deficiency payments to correct for low prices received in the marketplace, the PIK Program provided for the delivery of crops in exchange for an agreement to refrain from growing crops. Due to the unique nature of the program, many of the security agreements existing at the time were not drafted in a manner that would give a lender a security interest in commodities received under the PIK Program. A number of courts were called upon to determine questions of the characterization of PIK benefits for Article 9 purposes, and to settle priority disputes between creditors and bankruptcy trustees.

Under Section 9–306 of the UCC, the proceeds of collateral "include whatever is received upon the sale, exchange, collection or other disposition of collateral or proceeds." The obvious problem in applying this language to PIK entitlements is that a payment received in exchange for an agreement not to plant does not constitute a sale, exchange, collection, or disposition of any existing collateral. No collateral exists because the acreage is idle. Therefore, the status of a creditor holding a security interest in crops and proceeds will depend on the interpretation of the language in Article 9, the loan documentation, and the characterization given the PIK payments.

A number of courts gave an expanded reading to the "proceeds" provision of the UCC, and upheld the rights of the secured creditors. These courts often glossed over the argument that since the crops had never come into existence, they could not have been "sold, exchanged, collected or disposed of" in any literal sense. Most of these courts relied on Article 9 cases dealing with farm subsidy programs that predated PIK. The farm subsidy programs in those cases were quite different from the PIK Program, and usually involved payments related to a planted crop. Reliance on those cases in addressing problems under the PIK Program seems unjustified, and results in an interpretation of "proceeds" that is contrary to a reading of the relevant Article 9 provisions.

The most precise treatment of PIK entitlements occurred in those cases where the courts demonstrated an understanding of the unique nature of the PIK Program, and an appreciation for reasonably precise descriptions in loan documentation. These courts could find no proceeds where there had been no collateral created from the first. Hence, the characterization of PIK entitlements was not as proceeds of crops, but as a general intangible or contract right.

These courts also avoided the inclination to find some apparent "intent" to cover farm subsidy payments, as had been demonstrated by several other courts. It is hard to imagine what a creditor's intent would be, given that the loan documentation made no mention of subsidy payments, and the program did not exist at the time the documentation was completed. Simply put, the better argument in these cases is that an agreement to grow nothing creates no collateral, and therefore no proceeds.

Question

Do you agree with Mr. Marsh's conclusion that PIK payments should not be regarded as proceeds where there was no "collateral created from the first"?

McLEMORE, TRUSTEE v. MID–SOUTH AGRI–CHEMICAL CORP.

United States Bankruptcy Court, Middle District of Tennessee, 1984.
41 B.R. 369.

KEITH M. LUNDIN, BANKRUPTCY JUDGE.

The trustee's complaint seeks to recover Payment-in-Kind ("PIK") certificates of entitlement owing to the debtors. The issues are: (1) whether PIK payments constitute crop "proceeds;" and (2) whether the debtors' assignment of PIK wheat payments to one of the defendants constitutes a preferential transfer. After consideration of the briefs, arguments and stipulations, the court holds that PIK entitlements are "proceeds," and the assignment of wheat PIK to Mid-South Agri-Chemical Corporation ("Mid-South") constituted a preferential transfer. However, Mid-South holds a properly perfected security interest in the debtors' corn PIK, the Farmers Home Administration ("FmHA") holds a perfected security interest in PIK for the debtors' wheat crop, and these security interests are enforceable post-bankruptcy.

* * *

I.

* * * On April 27, 1983, William Earl and Glenda F. Judkins ("debtors") filed a voluntary Chapter 11 petition. Prior to the filing, the debtors farmed several parcels of leased property in DeKalb County, Tennessee.

Mid-South is a creditor holding a security interest in the debtors' corn crop. Mid-South's security interest was perfected June 2, 1982 and extends to "proceeds" of the corn crop.

FmHA is a creditor holding a security interest in "all crops, annual and perennial, and other plant products now planted, growing or grown, or which are hereafter planted or otherwise become growing crops or other plant products" of the debtors. The FmHA perfected its security interest on June 23, 1982 and June 24, 1982. The financing statements covered all "proceeds" from the debtors' crops.

On January 28, 1983, the debtors executed a "Contract to Participate in the 1983 PIK Diversion Program" with the Commodity Credit Corporation ("CCC") covering four of their leased farms. A contract for the fifth farm was executed March 10, 1983. The contracts were approved March 18, 1983 and the debtors became entitled to deficiency and diversion payments.

On March 25, 1983, the debtors filed a "Payment-in-Kind Assignment and Power of Attorney" with the CCC designating Mid-South as their assignee for diversion payments, including payments due for the nonproduction of wheat. The debtors also compromised the outstanding balance of an earlier promissory note by executing a demand note to Mid-South.

The debtors thereafter received several installments under the PIK program. The remaining PIK certificates were delivered to the trustee to be sold. The trustee liquidated 7,657 bushels of corn for $25,153.24 and 829 bushels of wheat for $2,677.67.

II.

If PIK entitlements constitute "proceeds" to which a creditor's security interest in crops attaches although the crops are never planted then the creditors prevail over the trustee in this proceeding. Although the issue of whether PIK payments are "proceeds" is one of first impression in this district, other courts have held that crop subsidy and crop entitlement payments do constitute "proceeds" of the crops involved. In the leading case, *Pombo v. Ulrich (In re Munger),* 495 F.2d 511 (9th Cir.1974), the United States Court of Appeals for the Ninth Circuit explained that federal sugar beet abandonment payments were "proceeds" subject to security agreements covering the crops they replaced:

> Although resembling insurance payments, these subsidy payments flow not from private contract between the debtor and a third party, but rather from a government program designed to protect both the United States * * * and [farmers] * * * Abandonment payments, like the subsidy payments, * * * are an integral part of the * * * farming business and, when received, are within a broad reading of "proceeds." *Not to include such payments within the term "proceeds" would be to raise distinctions of form over the realities underlying this financing transaction, a result contrary to the intent of the Uniform Commercial Code.* (emphasis added).

Id. at 513. Other decisions, including several dealing directly with PIK entitlements, are in unanimous accord. * * *

Because any corn grown on the debtors' farm would have been covered by security interest, the crop substitute—benefits under the PIK program—should be treated the same; *In re Preisser,* 33 B.R. 65, 67 (Bankr.D.Colo.1983) (government benefits the debtor receives for the nonproduction of grain is a substitute for what would have been produced); *In re Nivens,* 22 B.R. 287, 291 (Bankr.N.D.Tex.1982) (subsidy payments are a substitute for crops and are "proceeds;" therefore, the creditor's security interest continues in deficiency and disaster payments).

This court agrees that PIK entitlements constitute "proceeds" of crop collateral, even if the crop was never planted.[2] Tenn.Code Ann. § 47–9–306(1) provides that: [quoting]

2. The court in *Kruse* made a distinction between subsidy payments to abandon or destroy crops and subsidy payments not to plant particular crops. This court does not share the application of such a distinction. The phrase "other disposition" is extremely broad and encompasses any type of disposition, actual or constructive. *In re Nivens,* 22 B.R. at 291 n. 4. The term "other disposition" is sufficiently broad to cover PIK payments received in lieu of the originally crop collateral. When a debtor contracts for PIK payments, the debtor precludes the creation of the corresponding crop collateral. Participation in the PIK program "disposes" of the debtor's crops by precluding their cultivation. This issue is irrelevant with regard to the PIK entitlements allocable to wheat in

The definition of "proceeds" should be given a flexible and broad interpretation. * * * Under federal agricultural regulations PIK entitlements are considered substitutes for the crops that otherwise would have been planted:

> Payments in kind are intended to compensate producers who have reduced their arrearages which would have otherwise been planted to the 1983 crops * * * Accordingly, quantities of these commodities which were made available as payment-in-kind are considered to be 1983 production.

48 Fed.Reg. 9, 233 (1983). The contract rights created when participation in the PIK program is approved are "substituted" for the crops that would have been harvested, but for participation in the program. The PIK payments are traceable to the crops subject to the defendants' security interests. The PIK entitlements are for specific crops, on specific acreage, and for specific production. Such a nexus between the entitlements and the original collateral indicates that participation in the PIK program was a substitute for the planting of the crop collateral.

A liberal construction of "proceeds" is necessary to avoid unintended interference with the objectives of federal agricultural subsidy programs. The trustee's interpretation would impair the effectiveness of the subsidy programs because encumbered crops would disqualify participation in federal subsidy programs or produce the anomalous result that the government would eviscerate its own security interest (and the interests of other "crop" financers) in crop collateral by approving a debtor's participation in subsidy programs.

> It would create an unconscionable means by which a farmer could defeat a creditor's security. If PIK payments were not proceeds, a farmer could abandon all farming activities in favor of program participation, thereby allowing him to dissipate the proceeds of the programs without any regard for their creditor's interests. Such a result cannot be permitted.

Wapakometa Production Credit v. Cupp, 38 B.R. at 956. Certainly this result was not intended and should not be judicially imposed. A flexible interpretation of the concept of "proceeds" promotes responsible management of farming operations by allowing alternatives to growing crops while simultaneously protecting creditors' security interests.

The defendants' security interests in crop "proceeds" survives the filing of the bankruptcy petition. 11 U.S.C.A. § 552 (West 1979) provides in relevant part:

> (b) Except as provided in sections 363, 506(c), 544, 545, 547, and 548 of this title, if the debtor and a secured party enter into a security agreement before the commencement of the case and *if the security interest created by such security agreement extends to property of the debtor acquired before the commencement of the case and to proceeds,* product, offspring, rents, or profits of such property, *then such security interest extends to such proceeds,* product, offspring, rents, or profits *acquired by the estate after the commencement of the case to the extent*

the instant case because a wheat crop was originally planted, but mowed under when the debtors contracted to participate in the PIK program.

> *provided by such security agreement* and by applicable nonbankruptcy law, except to the extent that the court, after notice and a hearing and based on the equities of the case, orders otherwise. (emphasis added).

The trustee has not alleged any defects in the security agreements or financing statements that would nullify the defendants' security interests. FmHA, therefore, has a continuing security interest in all of the debtors' crops and crop proceeds. Mid-South, however, has a first priority in the debtors' corn crop and corn proceeds by virtue of its prior perfected security interest. * * *.

[Some footnotes omitted.]

Notes

1. The trustee must have been a really low-down skunk to make the argument he did in this case. Not so?

2. Not all government subsidy programs are alike. Some are payments for crops destroyed. Some are payments for crops planted and then abandoned, and some are payments for leaving certain acreage fallow that previously had been devoted to the particular crop. Does the court conclude that the last version are proceeds of the crop? How can that be?

3. If one wished to take a direct security interest in the right to the payments in kind (PIK), how does he do that? Is the Payment In Kind a general intangible, an account or something else? Review UCC 9–105(1) & 9–106.

4. Assume that creditor had a perfected security interest in debtor's existing stock of "cows and proceeds." If the cows had calves, would they be subject to the security interest as proceeds? Review UCC 9–109(3). How would you modify the security agreement in order to make the answer to that question clear?

5. Ajax lent $50,000 to Happy Vending Co. (HV). HV gave a perfected security interest in "all game machines owned by debtor." When HV became bankrupt, the vending machines had $14,000 in them. Who gets the money, Ajax or HV's trustee?

Problem 3–6

Auto Dealer floor plans his cars with GMAC. Dealer sells a car out of inventory to Consumer for cash. He deposits the cash in his general bank account and later uses money from that account to purchase another car for his inventory. Assume that GMAC now asserts a claim in the second car as proceeds. Does GMAC have a good claim? See especially UCC 9–306(3).

Assume alternatively that the total funds in the bank account between the time of the deposit of the proceeds and the time of the challenge (a) stayed approximately the same; (b) declined to zero and returned to a positive amount. Do these call for different outcomes? GMAC is likely to have an alternative claim to the automobile and thus not to depend upon its proceeds claim, not so?

SECTION 4. DESCRIPTIONS IN THE SECURITY AGREEMENT—A PROPOSED REFORM

Evaluate the proposal set forth below.

SHANKER, A PROPOSAL FOR A SIMPLIFIED ALL–EMBRACING SECURITY INTEREST 14 U.C.C.L.J. 23, 25–29 (1981).

* * * Secured parties who wish a security interest in *all* of the debtor's personal property (and that includes most institutional lenders) now have a fairly sure way of obtaining it. Until now, the courts have refused to uphold a description stating "all personal property." Nevertheless, the secured parties' desire for an all-embracing lien can be accomplished merely by copying *all* of the collateral categories listed in Article 9. And the list is not that long. If I have counted correctly, it includes ten or eleven items, namely: consumer goods, equipment, farm products, inventory, fixtures, accounts, chattel paper, documents, instruments, and general intangibles. And, for good measure, it might not be a bad idea to add deposit accounts and cash to this list. One suspects that it will not be long before well-counseled secured parties will have learned this lesson. And, since they have learned it, this Article 9 list of collateral categories will soon become a standard boiler plate on most security documents.

If the law intends that security over all of the debtor's assets can be obtained (and, indeed, is now often being obtained) by simply copying from a boiler-plate list of words found in Article 9, then why even require it? At best, continuing to require this boiler-plate list can serve only as a trap for those who, by reason of inadvertence or lack of proper advice, fail to copy it precisely. And that seems a poor reason to penalize these unfortunate souls. Why not, then, remove the trap and, instead, simplify the process by amending Article 9 to declare that identification of collateral is no longer needed? Instead, the mere execution of a security agreement and financing statement (even though containing no collateral description whatsoever) would have the legal effect of giving to the secured party an all-embracing lien, that is, a security interest on all of the debtor's personal property. That is what most secured parties want, and that is what most of them are now getting.

This proposal is not nearly as startling as it may first sound. It follows the lead already taken by our Canadian neighbors who have adopted Article 9–type legislation. More important, the proposal simply recognizes that the law ought not require a lot of useless motion or formalistic ceremony in order to achieve a permissible objective.

There are important limitations on this proposal to obtain an all-embracing lien. First, the proposal will still require most nonpossessory security interests to be filed in order to achieve perfection. Thus, even though the precise category of collateral will not even be listed on the financing statement, knowledge by the secured party of the specific kind of collateral involved will be required to assure that he files it in the appropriate office. Further, this proposal will not prohibit the parties from limiting the collateral to something less than all of the debtor's personal property, if they conscientiously choose to do so. (Conditional sellers of a particular piece of equipment and banks financing only the inventory and accounts of the debtor are examples where such a choice might be made.) But, absent a deliberate decision to limit the collateral, the presumption would be, consistent with what is probably the fact, that all of the debtor's personal property is covered; and all third parties finding a financing statement on file would be charged with that knowledge.

Of course, the law itself will continue to put some limits on the extent to which all of the debtor's collateral would be swept into an all-embracing lien. For example, Section 9–204(2) of the Code will continue to limit the scope of an after-acquired property clause where consumer goods are involved, whereas Section [2.407 of the UCCC] * * * will continue to limit the collateral of sellers of consumer goods only to the goods which have been sold. But, absent such a limiting arrangement worked out by the parties themselves or by some rule of law, the rule would be that the secured party intended to obtain and legally would obtain a security interest that embraces all of the debtor's personal property; this would be so without the present necessity of typing onto his security documents the boiler-plate list of categories of collateral now found in Article 9. Thus, validity and priority of security interests will no longer depend on these endless (and largely useless) battles over the description found on the security documents—descriptions that are now becoming matters of boiler plate. Rather, these questions essentially would be determined simply by the order of perfection.

Social Policy Considerations

This is not to suggest that giving to secured parties this easy way of obtaining an all-embracing security interest is necessarily the wisest social policy. This proposal simply recognizes that the wisdom of this policy has already been accepted by Article 9. It urges only that this already accepted policy be implemented without the necessity of going through the useless motions now required—that is, mechanically copying the list of collateral now found in Article 9. And, an incidental advantage of the proposal is that it will save our judicial system a great deal of time, energy, and cost which is now being expended to litigate questions of whether collateral description is sufficient.

This kind of thinking is exactly what moved the UCC drafters to authorize the floating lien in the first place. They, in fact, recognized that the argument against even enacting a floating lien has much to be recommended.

> *This Article [9] decisively rejects it not on the ground that it was wrong in policy but on the ground that it was not effective.* In pre-code law there was a multiplication of security devices designed to avoid the policy; field warehousing, trust receipts, factors lien acts, and so on. * * *
>
> In almost every state it was possible before the code for the borrower to give a lien on everything he held or would have. There has no doubt been sufficient economic reasons for the change. *This Article in expressly authorizing the floating charge merely recognizes an existing state of things.* [Emphasis added.]

If that kind of thinking made sense when the floating lien was first authorized in the early 1950s, then it seems that the time has now come to take the next step—that is, to permit an all-embracing lien to be obtained without going through all the trouble, cost, and energy presently required to accomplish it. No effort has been made in this article to work out all of the details of this proposal or the specific statutory language needed to implement it. Rather, this article is presented to determine whether there is agreement that the basic idea makes sense. If there is marked disagreement with it, then, hopefully, this paper will stimulate a dialogue on what purpose is being served by the present approach. In particular, just what purpose continues to be served by requiring the boiler plating on security documents of a readily available list of words to achieve an objective which most want, which many already are obtaining, and which seems fully permissible under Article 9—namely, an all-embracing lien? [Footnotes omitted.] [Reprinted with permission from: Uniform Commercial Code Law Journal, Summer 1981, Vol. 14, No. 1. Copyright © 1981, Warren, Gorham & Lamont, Inc., 210 South Street, Boston, MA 02111. All Rights Reserved.]

SECTION 5. THE SECURITY AGREEMENT: DOING IT RIGHT

At least in law school, the study of law tends to become the examination of other people's errors. Law practice on the other hand is much more prophylactic. Your job is to do it right so there is no cataclysm. The security agreement that we have set out below is a well-drafted document. It was prepared by a skilled Detroit lawyer on behalf of a major regional lender. To get a better understanding of how one might avoid the pitfalls demonstrated in the cases in Sections 1 through 3 of this chapter, consider the various provisions in the security agreement. (Needless to say, the document set out below was designed for the creditor and was aimed at protecting its, and not the debtor's, interest.)

Note first the breadth of the debt described in the first paragraph. This security agreement covers not just the specific loan made on the date the security agreement is signed, but also those arising later. Can you think of a debt that might not be covered by this security agreement?

The document shows that the creditor is interested in much more than just the collateral. Read over the warranties and promises made by the debtor. Why do you suppose the creditor is interested in the prohibition against other encumbrances in 3.4? Will the provision concerning legal fees in 3.10 be effective?

Note that default can be caused by many events in addition to the failure by the debtor to pay money. Do you think 5.1(e) is valid under the Uniform Commercial Code? What about the anti-waiver clause contained in 5.6, can it too be waived? Note the use of the limited power of attorney in 5.8 as an aid to conveying title to a buyer at a foreclosure sale.

Presumably the agreement contemplates a line of credit or a series of periodic loans and repayments between the creditor and the debtor. What is the creditor obliged to lend under the agreement? What will determine the interest rate that the debtor is obliged to pay?

Problem 3–7

Answer the following questions by reference to the security agreement below.

1. Occasionally third parties, as in *Samuels,* assert that the debtor did not have good title to collateral. By hypothesis such parties are not signatories to the security agreement and thus cannot be directly bound by it. How might a

security agreement deal with this problem? How does this security agreement address it? See 2.2 and 3.3.

2. In the immediately preceding section we have dealt with the question of the identifiability of proceeds and their commingling. How does the security agreement address that problem? See 4.1.

3. In Chapter Six we will come to foreclosure. There we will deal with a series of thorny questions about the proper procedure one is to follow on repossession and resale: whether secured creditor has conducted a "commercially reasonable resale" is often the subject of litigation. Debtor will frequently claim that the creditor failed to give him adequate notice of the sale, failed to advertise the sale, etc. How does the security agreement deal with those problems? See 6.3 and 8. Will both of those sections stand up in court?

SECURITY AGREEMENT

(All Properties)

For value received, DEBTOR, INC., a Michigan corporation (the "Debtor"), hereby grants to LENDER, INC., a Michigan corporation (the "Secured Party"), a continuing security interest in all of Debtor's Accounts, Chattel Paper, Documents, Equipment, Fixtures, General Intangibles, Goods, Instruments and Inventory, all additions, attachments, accessories, parts, replacements, substitutions and renewals to or of such items, trade names, trade styles and goodwill, trademarks, copyrights and patents, and applications therefor, trade and proprietary secrets, formulae, designs, blueprints and plans, customer lists, literary rights, licenses and permits, tax refunds, notes and other receivables, insurance proceeds, returned or rebated insurance premiums, beneficial interests in trusts and minute books and other books and records, all other rights, properties and interests, of whatsoever nature and wheresoever located, of Debtor and the proceeds and products of all of the foregoing, in each case whether now owned or hereafter acquired (it being the intention of Debtor hereby to grant to the Secured Party a security interest in all personal property and fixtures of Debtor, whether now owned or hereafter acquired) (collectively, the "Collateral"), to secure payment of any and all indebtedness, obligations or liabilities whatsoever of Debtor to Secured Party, whether matured or unmatured, liquidated or unliquidated, direct or indirect, absolute or contingent, joint or several, due or to become due, now existing or hereafter arising and however evidenced, including without limitation the Note (collectively, the "Indebtedness").

1. DEFINITIONS. As used herein:

1.1 "Accounts," "Chattel Paper," "Documents," "Equipment," "Fixtures," "General Intangibles," "Goods," "Instruments" and "Inventory" shall have the meanings assigned to them in the Uniform Commercial Code on the date of this Agreement.

1.2 "Environmental Laws" shall mean any statute, code, ordinance, rule, regulation, permit, consent, approval, license, judgment, order, writ, decree, injunction or other authorization or mandate relating to the use, treatment, storage, disposal, manufacture, sale, transportation, shipment, generation, handling, emission, discharge or release of Hazardous Substances or otherwise relating to pollution or the protection of health, safety or environment.

1.3 "Event of Default" shall mean any of those conditions or events listed in Section 5.1 of this Agreement after the expiration of any applicable notice or cure periods.

1.4 "Hazardous Materials" shall mean any hazardous waste, solid waste, pollutant, contaminant, toxic substance or hazardous substance, including but not limited to any substance defined as hazardous or subject to control or regulation in the use, treatment, storage, disposal, manufacture, sale, transportation, shipment, generation, handling, emission, discharge or release of such material under any Environmental Law.

1.5 "Note" means the promissory note, dated ______, ____, from Debtor to Secured Party, and any amendments, renewals, substitutions or replacements thereof.

1.6 "Permitted Liens" shall mean:

(a) Liens and encumbrances in favor of the Secured Party;

(b) Existing liens described on a schedule annexed to this Agreement and acknowledged in writing by Secured Party;

(c) Liens for taxes, assessments or other governmental charges incurred in the ordinary course of business and not yet past due or being contested in good faith by appropriate proceedings;

(d) Liens not delinquent created by statute in connection with worker's compensation, unemployment insurance, social security and similar statutory obligations;

(e) Liens of mechanics, materialmen, carriers, warehousemen or other like statutory or common law liens securing obligations incurred in good faith in the ordinary course of business that are not yet due and payable; and

(f) Encumbrances consisting of zoning restrictions, rights-of-way, easements or other restrictions on the use of real property, none of which materially impairs the use of such property by the Debtor in the operation of the business for which it is used and none of which is violated in any material respect by any existing or proposed structure or land use.

1.7 The phrase "Uniform Commercial Code" means Act No. 174 of the Michigan Public Acts of 1962, as amended.

1.8 Except as otherwise herein provided, (a) all accounting terms not specifically defined in this Agreement shall be construed in accordance with generally accepted accounting principles, consistently applied, and (b) all other terms used herein shall have the meanings assigned to them in Article 9 (or, absent definition in Article 9, in any other Article) of the Uniform Commercial Code.

2. REPRESENTATIONS AND WARRANTIES. Debtor represents and warrants to Secured Party, on the date of this Agreement and on each date on which any of the Indebtedness shall be outstanding, that:

2.1 The Debtor is a corporation duly organized, validly existing and in good standing under the laws of the state described in the first paragraph of this Agreement, and has full power and authority to own its properties and to carry on its business as now conducted, and is in good standing and duly qualified to conduct business as a foreign corporation in each jurisdiction in which the ownership or leasing of its properties or the conduct of its business requires such qualification.

2.2 The Debtor has the full right, power and authority to execute and deliver this Agreement and to perform its obligations hereunder. This Agreement is the legal, valid and binding obligation of the Debtor and is enforceable in accordance with its terms, except as the enforcement thereof may be limited by laws of general application relating to bankruptcy, insolvency and the relief of debtors.

2.3 Neither the execution of this Agreement nor the consummation of the transactions contemplated herein will constitute or cause a breach or violation of the articles or certificate of incorporation, bylaws or other agreements or obligations binding upon the Debtor or affecting any of the Debtor's properties, or cause a lien or other encumbrance to attach to any of its properties, or require a consent of any person to prevent any such breach, violation, lien or encumbrance. No approval of or filing with any federal, state or local court, authority or administrative agency is necessary to authorize the execution and delivery of this Agreement by the Debtor or the consummation by the Debtor of the transactions contemplated herein.

2.4 All balance sheets, statements of income and retained earnings and changes in financial position, projections and other financial data of the Debtor which have been, or will be, furnished to the Secured Party for the purposes of, or in connection with, this Agreement and the transactions contemplated hereby:

(a) are true, complete and correct in all material respects;

(b) fairly present the properties, assets, financial position and results of operations of the Debtor as of the dates and for the periods stated therein or, if the same are projected or pro forma results, are reasonably expected to occur and are based on reasonable assumptions; and

(c) have been prepared to the extent applicable pursuant to and in accordance with generally accepted accounting principles, consistently applied.

2.5 The Debtor does not have any liabilities or obligations, whether accrued, absolute, contingent or otherwise, other than those set forth in financial statements furnished to the Secured Party in connection with this Agreement and those incurred by the Debtor in the ordinary course of its business.

2.6 The Debtor has not used Hazardous Materials on or affecting any premises occupied by the Debtor in any manner which violates any Environmental Law and, to the best of the Debtor's knowledge, no prior owner of any premises occupied by the Debtor or of any adjacent premises or any current or prior occupant thereof has used Hazardous Materials on or affecting any premises occupied by the Debtor in any manner which violates Environmental Laws. The Debtor has never received any notice of any violations (and is not aware of any existing violations) of any Environmental Laws by the Debtor or for which the Debtor may be responsible and, to the best of the Debtor's knowledge, there have been no actions commenced or threatened by any party against or with respect to the Debtor or such premises for noncompliance with any Environmental Laws. The Debtor has no accrued or contingent liability to any federal, state or local government or to any private party on account of or arising out of sewage, waste or hazardous waste disposal, air, water or land pollution or other environmental matters.

2.7 The Debtor has prepared in accordance with law and filed all tax returns required to be filed by it under the laws of the United States and any state, and has paid or established an adequate reserve in respect of all taxes, penalties, interest and related charges and fees for the periods covered by such returns.

2.8 The Debtor is in compliance with all applicable laws, including without limitation Environmental Laws and laws regulating the wages, hours or working conditions of employees.

3. COVENANTS AND AGREEMENTS. Debtor covenants and agrees as follows:

3.1 Debtor shall promptly notify Secured Party of any after-acquired Collateral which may be or become Fixtures under applicable law and shall provide Secured Party with consents or disclaimers filed by all persons having an interest in the real estate (including owners, mortgage holders and lessees) which either consent to the Secured Party's security interest and acknowledge the Secured Party's priority or which disclaim any interest in the Collateral.

3.2 Debtor shall keep adequate records of the Collateral and such other records as Secured Party shall determine to be necessary and allow Secured Party to examine, inspect and make abstracts from, or copy any of Debtor's books and records (relating to the Collateral or otherwise and whether printed or in magnetic or other machine readable form).

3.3 At the time any Collateral becomes subject to a security interest in favor of Secured Party, Debtor shall be deemed to have warranted that (i) Debtor is the lawful owner of such Collateral and has the right and authority to subject the same to a security interest in Secured Party; (ii) none of the Collateral is subject to any security interest other than Permitted Liens, and there are no financing statements on file, other than relating to Permitted Liens; (iii) Debtor acquired its rights in the Collateral in the ordinary course of its business; and (iv) the Collateral has been acquired for use primarily in business.

3.4 Debtor will keep the Collateral free at all times from any and all liens, security interests and encumbrances other than Permitted Liens. Debtor will not, without the prior written consent of Secured Party, sell or lease, or permit or suffer to be sold or leased, all or any part of the Collateral (whether in one transaction or in a series of related transactions), except sales of Inventory in the ordinary course of business. Secured Party or its agents or attorneys may at any and all reasonable times inspect the Collateral and may enter upon any and all premises where the same is kept or might be located.

3.5 Debtor agrees to furnish to the Secured Party annual and monthly balance sheets, statements of income and retained earnings and changes in financial position of the Debtor promptly after the end of each such fiscal period and such other information regarding the operations, business affairs and financial condition of the Debtor as the Secured Party may from time to time request and to permit the Secured Party and its employees, attorneys and agents to inspect all of the books, records and properties of the Debtor at any time upon reasonable request.

3.6 Debtor agrees to keep its insurable properties adequately insured and maintain insurance against fire, public liability, product liability and other risks customarily insured against by companies engaged in the same or a similar business to that of the Debtor, necessary worker's compensation insurance and such other insurance as may be required by law. All such policies shall contain a provision whereby they may not be canceled except upon thirty (30) days' prior written notice to the Secured Party. The Debtor agrees to deliver to the Secured Party at its request evidence satisfactory to the Secured Party that such insurance has been so procured and made payable to the Secured Party, as its interest appears, and that the Secured Party has been named as an additional insured with respect to liability insurance.

3.7 The Debtor agrees to pay promptly and within the time that they can be paid without interest or penalty all taxes, assessments and similar imposts and charges of every kind and nature lawfully levied, assessed or imposed upon the Debtor, and its property, except to the extent being contested in good faith.

3.8 The Debtor agrees to do or cause to be done all things necessary to preserve and keep in full force and effect the Debtor's corporate existence, rights and franchises and to comply with all applicable laws; maintain adequate records of its transactions and affairs and complete and accurate books of account; conduct and operate its business substantially as conducted and operated during the present and preceding calendar year; and maintain, preserve and protect all of its property (including, without limitation, the Collateral) used or useful in the conduct of its business and keep the same in good repair, working order and condition.

3.9 Debtor will do all acts and things, and will execute all writings requested by Secured Party to establish, maintain and continue the perfected security interest of Secured Party in the Collateral and will promptly on demand pay all costs and expenses of filing and recording, including the costs of any searches deemed necessary by Secured Party to establish and determine the validity and the priority of Secured Party's security interest.

3.10 Debtor will reimburse Secured Party for all expenses, including reasonable attorney fees and legal expenses, incurred by Secured Party in seeking to collect the Indebtedness or any part thereof, in defending the priority of Secured Party's security interest or in pursuing any of its rights or remedies hereunder, whether incurred in a state collection action or other proceeding, in a federal bankruptcy proceeding or in negotiations with the Debtor.

4. COLLECTION OF PROCEEDS

4.1 Debtor agrees to collect and enforce payment of all Accounts until the occurrence of an Event of Default or until the Secured Party shall direct Debtor to the contrary. From and after such occurrence or direction, Debtor agrees to (a) fully and promptly cooperate and assist Secured Party (or any other person as Secured Party shall designate) in the collection and enforcement of all Accounts, (b) hold in trust for Secured Party all payments received on Accounts and from the sale of any Inventory, all rights by way of suretyship or guaranty which Debtor has or hereafter acquires to enforce payment of Accounts and all rights in the nature of a mortgage, security interest or lien whereby Debtor may satisfy any Account out of property, (c) endorse and deliver to Secured Party all payments received by Debtor on Accounts or from the sale of Inventory in the form received by Debtor without commingling with any funds belonging to Debtor and (d) deliver to Secured Party all property in Debtor's possession or hereafter coming into Debtor's possession through enforcement of any such rights or interests.

4.2 Debtor authorizes Secured Party or any employee or agent thereof to indorse the name of Debtor upon any checks or other items which are received in payment of any Account and to do any and all things necessary in order to reduce the same to money.

4.3 Secured Party shall have no duty as to the collection or protection of Collateral or the proceeds thereof, nor as to the preservation of any rights pertaining thereto, beyond the use of reasonable care in the custody and preservation of Collateral in the possession of Secured Party.

5. DEFAULTS

5.1 The Debtor shall be in default of this Agreement upon the occurrence of any of the following conditions or events:

(a) If any of the Indebtedness shall not be paid when due;

(b) If any warranty or representation in connection with or contained in this Agreement, or if any financial data or other information now or hereafter furnished to the Secured Party by or on behalf of the Debtor, shall prove to be false or misleading in any material respect;

(c) If the Debtor shall fail to perform any of its obligations and covenants under, or shall fail to comply with any of the provisions of, this Agreement or any other agreement with the Secured Party to which the Debtor is a party and such failure shall not be cured by the Debtor or waived by the Secured Party within twenty (20) days after notice to the Debtor by the Secured Party.

(d) If the Debtor shall default in the due payment of any indebtedness, obligation or liability or in the due observance or performance of any term, covenant or condition in any agreement or instrument evidencing, securing or relating to such indebtedness, obligation or liability, or in the due observance or performance of any other material contract or undertaking binding on the Debtor, and such default shall continue beyond any grace periods applicable thereto.

(e) If there shall be rendered against the Debtor any judgment or decree which has become nonappealable and shall remain undischarged, unsatisfied by insurance and unstayed for more than twenty (20) days, whether or not consecutive; or if a writ of attachment or garnishment against the property of the Debtor shall be issued and levied in an action claiming $10,000 or more, and not released or appealed and bonded in a manner satisfactory to the Secured Party.

(f) If the Debtor shall voluntarily suspend transaction of its business, shall not pay its debts as they mature or shall make a general assignment for the benefit of creditors; or proceedings in bankruptcy or for reorganization or liquidation of the Debtor under the Bankruptcy Code of 1978 of the United States, as amended, or any successor act or code or under any other state or federal law for the relief of debtors shall be commenced by the Debtor or shall be commenced against the Debtor and shall not be discharged within thirty (30) days after commencement; or a receiver, trustee or custodian shall be appointed for the Debtor or for any substantial portion of its respective properties or assets.

5.2 Upon the occurrence of any Event of Default and the failure by the Debtor immediately to pay to the Secured Party all of the Indebtedness, Secured Party may at its discretion and without further notice to Debtor from time to time thereafter declare any or all of the Indebtedness to be immediately due and payable (if it is not otherwise already due and payable or payable on demand), and shall have and may exercise any one or more of the following rights and remedies:

(a) exercise all the rights and remedies upon default, in foreclosure and otherwise, available to secured parties under the provisions of the Uniform Commercial Code and other applicable law;

(b) institute legal proceedings to foreclose upon the lien and security interest granted by this Agreement, to recover judgment for all amounts then due and owing on the Indebtedness secured hereby and to collect the same out of any of the Collateral or the proceeds of any sale thereof;

(c) institute legal proceedings for the sale, under the judgment or decree of any court of competent jurisdiction, of any or all of the Collateral;

(d) personally or by agents or attorneys, enter upon any premises where the Collateral or any part thereof may then be located, and take possession of all or any part thereof and/or render it unusable; and, without being responsible for loss or damage to such Collateral, hold, store, and keep idle, or lease, operate, remove or otherwise use or permit the use of the Collateral or any part thereof, for such time and upon such terms as Secured Party may in its sole and complete discretion deem to be in its own best interest, or sell, lease and dispose of, or cause to be sold, leased and disposed of, all or any part of the Collateral at one or more public or private sales, leasings or other dispositions, at such places and times and on such terms and conditions as Secured Party may deem fit.

5.3 Debtor shall at any time at the request of Secured Party notify the account debtors or obligors of the security interest of Secured Party in any Accounts and direct payment thereof to Secured Party. Secured Party may, itself, upon the occurrence of any Event of Default, so notify and direct any such account debtor or obligor and may take control of any proceeds to which it may be entitled hereunder.

5.4 The proceeds of any sale or other disposition of Collateral authorized by this Agreement shall be applied, first, to all costs and expenses authorized by this Agreement or the UCC, and the balance shall be applied to the Indebtedness, first to interest and then to principal and the balance, if any, shall be paid to the Debtor or to such other person or persons as may be entitled thereto under applicable law. The Debtor shall remain liable for any deficiency, which it shall pay on demand.

5.5 Nothing herein is intended to preclude Secured Party from pursuing any other remedy provided by law for the collection of the Indebtedness or any portion thereof, or for the recovery of any other sum to which Secured Party may be or become entitled for the breach of this Agreement by Debtor, nor shall anything contained herein reduce in any way any rights of Secured Party contained in any other agreement between Debtor and Secured Party.

5.6 No waiver of default shall be effective unless in writing signed by an officer of Secured Party, and no waiver of any default or forbearance on the part of Secured Party in enforcing any of its rights under this Agreement shall operate as a waiver of any other default or of the same default on a future occasion or of any such right. No delay or omission in the exercise of any right, power or remedy accruing to the Secured Party upon any breach or default of the Debtor under this Agreement shall impair any such right, power or remedy, nor shall it be construed to be a waiver of any such breach or default, or an acquiescence therein.

5.7 Upon the occurrence of any Event of Default, Debtor agrees, upon request of Secured Party, to assemble the Collateral and make it available to Secured Party at any place designated by Secured Party which is reasonably convenient to Secured Party and Debtor and to deliver to Secured Party all accounting and other records pertaining to, and all writings evidencing, the Collateral or any portion thereof, together with all books, records and documents of the Debtor related thereto in whatever form kept by Debtor, whether printed, on magnetic tape or discs, or in other machine readable form, and all forms, programs, software and other materials and instructions necessary or useful to Secured Party in connection with such accounting and other records and Debtor agrees to direct its employees, agents, consultants and vendors, including but not limited to its accounting and data processing personnel and software vendors or licensors, to fully cooperate with the Secured Party to facilitate the Secured Party's effective utilization thereof.

5.8 Debtor hereby irrevocably appoints Secured Party (which appointment is coupled with an interest) the true and lawful attorney of Debtor (with full power of substitution) in the name, place and stead of, and at the expense of, Debtor:

(a) to demand, receive, sue for and give receipts or acquittances for any moneys due or to become due on any Account;

(b) with respect to any Collateral, to assent to any or all extensions or postponements of the time of payment thereof or any other indulgence in connection therewith, to the substitution, exchange or release of Collateral, to the addition or release of any party primarily or secondarily liable, to the acceptance of partial payments thereon and the settlement, compromise or adjustment thereof, all in such manner and at such time or times as Secured Party shall deem advisable;

(c) to make all necessary transfers of all or any part of the Collateral in connection with any sale, lease or other disposition made pursuant hereto;

(d) to execute and deliver for value all necessary or appropriate bills of sale, assignments, and other instruments in connection with any such sale, lease or other disposition of the Collateral;

(e) to endorse any item, howsoever received by Secured Party, representing any payment on or other proceeds or products of the Collateral; and

(f) to execute and file in the name of and on behalf of Debtor all financing statements or other filings deemed necessary or desirable by Secured Party to evidence or perfect the security interests herein granted.

6. MISCELLANEOUS

6.1 This Agreement shall in all respects be governed by and construed in accordance with the internal laws of the State of Michigan.

6.2 This Agreement and all the rights and remedies of Secured Party herein shall inure to the benefit of Secured Party's successors and assigns and to any other holder who derives from Secured Party title to or an interest in the Indebtedness or any portion thereof, and shall bind Debtor and the heirs, legal representatives, successors and assigns of Debtor.

6.3 Debtor hereby agrees that a written notice given to it at least five (5) days before the date of any act shall be deemed to be reasonable notice of such act and, specifically, reasonable notification of the time after which any private sale, lease or other disposition intended to be made hereunder is to be made. A notice shall be deemed to be given when delivered to Debtor or when placed in an envelope addressed to Debtor and deposited, with postage thereon prepaid, in a post office or official depository under the exclusive care and custody of the United States Postal Service.

6.4 A carbon, photographic or other reproduction of this Agreement shall be sufficient as a financing statement under the Uniform Commercial Code and may be filed by Secured Party as such in any filing office.

6.5 This Agreement constitutes the full and entire understanding and agreement among the parties with regard to the subject matter hereof. Neither this Agreement nor any term hereof may be amended, waived, discharged or terminated orally, except by a written instrument signed by the Secured Party.

7. STATEMENT OF BUSINESS NAME, RESIDENCE AND LOCATION OF COLLATERAL

Debtor warrants, covenants and agrees as follows:

7.1 Debtor's principal place of business is located in the County of ______, State of ______.

The mailing address is: ____
____.

7.2 Any other places of business of Debtor or locations of Collateral are indicated below:

7.3 Until Secured Party is advised in writing by Debtor to the contrary, all notices, requests and demands required hereunder or by law shall be given to, or made upon Debtor at the address indicated in Paragraph 6.1.

7.4 Debtor will give Secured Party prompt written notice of any change in Debtor's name, corporate existence and/or any of the above addresses.

7.5 Debtor's federal tax identification number is: ____-______.

8. JURY TRIAL WAIVER

DEBTOR AND BANK ACKNOWLEDGE THAT THE RIGHT TO TRIAL BY JURY IS A CONSTITUTIONAL RIGHT WHICH MAY BE WAIVED. DEBTOR AND BANK HEREBY KNOWINGLY, VOLUNTARILY AND IRREVOCABLY WAIVE THE RIGHT TO TRIAL BY JURY WITH RESPECT TO ANY AND ALL ACTIONS OR PROCEEDINGS REGARDING OR RELATING TO THE PERFORMANCE OR ENFORCEMENT OF, OR OTHERWISE ARISING OUT OF, THIS AGREEMENT OR THE INDEBTEDNESS.

IN WITNESS WHEREOF, the undersigned has signed this Security Agreement as of the ______ day of ______, ____.

DEBTOR, INC.

By ______________________
Its ______________________

SECTION 6. CREATING A SECURITY INTEREST IN STOCKS AND BONDS

It is commonplace to borrow against stocks and bonds. Customers borrow from their brokers; brokers borrow from banks, and it is important to have an inexpensive and certain mode of creating a valid security interest in stocks and bonds. Prior to the official 1977 amendments to Article 8 (and in the two states that have not yet enacted the 1977 amendments to Article 8), the classical security interest in stocks and bonds was created under UCC 9–203 by the debtor giving the creditor possession of the certificates. This satisfied the creation requisites of 9–203; it also satisfied the requirement of perfection under 9–305.

With the 1977 amendments to Article 8, UCC 9–305 has been modified to *exclude* "certificated securities" from its provisions. When those amendments apply to a transaction, one must proceed to 8–321 which treats "enforceability, attachment, perfection, and termination of security interests." One seeking to understand the mode of perfection under Article 8 is then led through a dizzying set of cross references to 8–313 and elsewhere. We will deal with problems associated with those in the next chapter. At this point, however, the student should understand why Article 8 was modified in 1977. In a sense, shares of stock are going through one full cycle from being completely intangible, to having tangible form, and now traveling back to complete intangibility. Initially, a shareholder's interest in a corporation was evidenced only by his name on the books of the corporation as the owner of a specific number of shares. Later it became useful to have certificates that evidenced those shares and the certificates were passed back and forth among shareholders, creditors (as pledgees), and others. The certificate was treated as representing the ownership in the share in the same way as a certificate of title represents ownership in a car or a note represents ownership of a debt.

As transactions multiplied and much transmission of data was done electronically, people began to realize that the certificates sometimes inhibited effective transfer of rights and imposed significant costs on the system. Thus, for example, it is common for a brokerage house customer to permit the brokerage house to keep all of the certificates representing his shares of stock in the broker's name and for the owner to hold no certificates. This enables the customer to direct the broker to make trades over the phone without the necessity of going to the safety deposit box, getting out the certificates, and assigning them to the broker in each case. If one is able to protect his computer memory better than he can protect certificates, he may also minimize theft losses by having only electronic or written records of stock ownership and doing away with certificates which must be safely kept. For all of these reasons, the next ten to fifteen years may witness the "decertification" of shares of stock. Already ownership rights to securities have become more "intangible."

This development, in turn, presents the question, how can one perfect a security interest in a share of stock that is not represented by a certificate or is represented by a certificate in the name of a trustee? If it is merely represented by the shareholder's name on the books of the corporation, presumably the right is something like a general intangible, not an instrument, as a certificated security would be. If it is a general intangible, perfection would call for a filing, yet those in the securities industry are not accustomed to searching UCC files and thus such a filing seems an inappropriate way to perfect a security interest. Because of that and for other reasons Article 8 was modified in 1977. At this writing Article 8 has been enacted in every state except Alabama and Vermont. We will give the students some exercise in its use in the next chapter. Article 8 is currently being revised and will probably be available for adoption by state legislatures in 1994.

In many cases the same act constitutes creation and perfection of a security interest under Article 8. Section 8–321(1) states that a security interest "is enforceable and can attach" only if it is transferred pursuant to 8–313(1). Section 8–313(1) contains ten separate subsections defining the acts necessary for a "transfer" and thus for the creation of a security interest. The nature of these acts depend upon whether there is a certificate outstanding, whether the certificate is held by a financial intermediary or by some other person, etc. For example, subsection 8–313(1)(a) provides that a transfer occurs with respect to a certificated security at the time when the person designated as a transferee (creditor, in our case) acquires possession. On the other hand, under subsection 8–313(1)(d), a transfer would occur at a time when a financial intermediary sends a person "confirmation of the purchase * * * [and] identifies [the security] as belonging to the purchaser * * *." There is not space here to examine the various circumstances under which securities may be held or to consider which of the particular subsections of UCC 8–313(1) fit with a particular form of ownership.

CHAPTER FOUR

PERFECTION OF THE SECURITY INTEREST

SECTION 1. INTRODUCTION

The word "perfection" is a classic term of art. It appears in Article 9 as a noun (perfection) and as a verb (to perfect), and the verb form in turn appears as an adjective (perfected). This terminology (which itself had some antecedents in commercial law) has now been widely adopted for limited purposes by the Bankruptcy Code, by the Internal Revenue Code, and in the future one can expect to see it robustly applied also to real property security devices.

By far the most important consequence of having a "perfected" as opposed to an "unperfected" security interest can be understood by examining UCC 9–301. That section subordinates unperfected security interests to the rights of lien creditors under the law. (Section 9–301(3) defines a lien creditor as a "creditor who has acquired a lien on the property involved by attachment, levy or the like.") Section 544 of the Bankruptcy Code gives each trustee in bankruptcy the rights of such a lien creditor at the date that a petition in bankruptcy is filed. Thus, the combination of those two sections means that virtually every unperfected secured creditor will be forced to give up his security interest to the trustee in bankruptcy and will be made to appear before the bar of justice as an unsecured creditor, a low form of life. If, on the other hand, a creditor is perfected, neither the lien creditor nor the trustee can use UCC 9–301 to defeat him and, in general, he prevails against such parties because of the broad protection given by UCC 9–201 and the absence of any overriding priority rule in Part Three. Of course, it is also important (though less so) that the perfected secured creditor generally prevails against other secured creditors and against certain subsequent purchasers. In sum, the importance of perfection is that it maximizes the protection that the secured creditor gets under Article 9 rules on what constitutes perfection set forth in Parts Three and Four of Article 9 and other law including the federal Bankruptcy Code. Although we have just alluded to a number of these priority rules, we will not study them in depth until the next chapter.

To state the consequences of perfection is to deal with the simplest part. The interesting questions in "perfection" cases between secured creditors and trustees in bankruptcy do not deal with such "no contest" clashes under sections 544 and 9–301. The creditor will typically stipulate that he loses to the trustee if he is found to be unperfected. The sport, and the subject of this chapter, revolves around the basic question: What must a secured creditor who has jumped through the hoops studied in the preceding chapter, and has thus created a security interest, do to become perfected?

One should begin with UCC 9–302. Although it does not say so in so many words, we believe that it might be paraphrased as follows: "The normal method of perfecting a security interest is by filing a financing statement. One who has filed a proper financing statement in the proper place is perfected, and except in the following cases, one who has not so filed is unperfected." Thus, the student should understand that filing a financing statement is the norm and that the provisions (a) through (g) in UCC 9–302(1) are exceptions to that general rule.

Reading UCC 9–302(1) will disclose that there are three basic methods of perfecting a security interest. The first is to file an appropriate financing statement. The second is to take possession of the collateral, i.e., set up a "pledge" (9–305). The third is to have "automatic perfection," i.e., to be perfected without having done any specific perfecting act. See if you can determine which of the sections of 9–302 provides for automatic perfection and which transaction is likely to be the most significant of those providing for automatic perfection.

After one has digested UCC 9–302 he should turn to the remaining perfection sections in Part Three, namely, UCC 9–303, 304, 305, and 306. We will study all of these in this chapter. Of greater significance and worthy of yet more study are all of the sections in Part Four of Article 9. These spell out what must be filed to perfect by filing, what must be contained in what must be filed and where the filing must be made. We will dig deeply into each of these sections in this chapter. Of particular interest are UCC 9–401 and 9–402.

Finally the student must consider UCC 9–105, 9–106 and 9–109 on the classification of various kinds of collateral. A quick examination of the sections in Part Three and Part Four reveals that a mode of perfection that may be sufficient and even necessary for one kind of collateral may be neither necessary nor sufficient for another. For example, filing or possession will perfect a security interest in goods, yet filing is wholly insufficient to perfect an interest in money, and possession will not perfect a security interest in accounts receivable. We will see why.

Having learned the general meaning and significance of perfection and having considered, however briefly, that one perfects, normally, by filing, sometimes by possession, and in certain special cases "automatically," the student should now ask why such acts are required of the secured creditor? Do they have anything to do with the creditor's rights against the debtor? It is true that a secured creditor earns no additional rights against his debtor after he has complied with UCC 9–203 by jumping through the other hoops under UCC 9–302, 9–401, etc. The function of perfection, of course, is to put third parties on notice of a possible security interest claimed by the creditor. By filing a public document (the financing statement) or by withholding possession of the debtor's assets from him, the perfecting creditor gives at least diligent third parties the opportunity to discover that security interest and take it into account in dealing with the debtor. The penalty the secured creditor pays for failing to give others the chance to discover his interest is that these other parties or their representative (the trustee in bankruptcy) acquire priority over an unperfected security interest, even a prior one. This raises the question of how one explains the various sections in UCC 9–302(1) that permit perfection automatically without notice. As to these, no such public notice or shift in possession to the creditor takes place. We will return to this puzzle.

In the sections that follow we will deal first with the most important mode of perfection, filing. Then we will cover legal issues raised by perfection, by possession, and by the automatic perfection rules. Throughout the chapter and at the end we will deal with a variety of related, but somewhat different, issues. For example, we must consider the question of choice of law in multistate transactions, and the special problems presented by securities, by proceeds, and by fixtures.

SECTION 2. CLASSIFYING THE COLLATERAL: A SUBSET OF PERFECTION ISSUES

UCC 9–105, 9–106, 9–107 and 9–109 all contain important definitions. Whether perfection of a security interest in consumer goods is automatic depends on its character as a purchase money security interest; that term is defined in UCC 9–107. In like fashion it is essential to consult the Code scheme of definitions of various kinds of collateral, UCC 9–105(1)(c), chattel paper, 9–105(1)(b), deposit account, 9–105(e), instrument, 9–105(i), account and general intangibles, 9–106, consumer goods, 9–109(1), equipment, 9–109(2), farm products, 9–109(3), and inventory, 9–109(4), etc. The requirements of perfection sometimes vary depending on the nature of the collateral.

To the unstudied eye, an account is apt to look much like chattel paper and only by examining the definitions can one be sure whether a particular security interest in such collateral is perfected or not under UCC 9–305. The same is true of the division between instruments and general intangibles. For most purposes the latter can never be perfected by possession and the former can be perfected only by possession. (Find the sections that say this.) Yet certain things (a vendor's interest in a land-sale contract, for example) might appear to some to be general intangibles and to others to be an instrument.

Note finally the particular definitions of kinds of goods in UCC 9–109. Do you see why the same refrigerator at different times during its life might be classified as inventory, consumer goods, or, possibly, as equipment? Note that those definitions do not arise from the attributes of the commodity, but from the use to which their owner, the "debtor," puts them. The same washing machine which is consumer goods in the hands of a private homeowner is inventory in the hands of the retailer and equipment in the hands of a commercial laundry.

Thus, the definitions are critical to perfection and the mode of perfection. Not only do they affect the way in which one perfects, they also affect the place where one might file a financing statement, and they might render a particular description (e.g., as inventory or equipment) to be appropriate or invalid. Consider the definitional problems posed by the following case and problem. A handy index to the definitions is to be found in Comment 5 to UCC 9–102.

IN RE K.L. SMITH ENTERPRISES, LTD.

United States Bankruptcy Court, District Colorado, 1980.
2 B.R. 280.

GLEN E. KELLER, JR., BANKRUPTCY JUDGE.

The facts are in large measure undisputed. The principal officer of the plaintiff over a number of years pioneered a method of housing laying hens and collecting eggs which is, by all accounts, unique in the industry. The chickens are housed in "egg production units," which are large, circular structures containing four concentric circles of caged hens, 10 tiers high. The circles revolve through the building, passing stations for feeding, watering, egg collection, and manure removal. The chickens pass a collection station, which consists of an elevator which the operator rides up and down among the tiers, hand collecting the eggs. After the eggs are collected, they are cooled and then processed by washing, spraying with a light oil to seal the shell, and "candling." The candling operation is nothing more than passing the eggs in a rotating fashion over a light to detect cracks or other defects which render the egg nonmarketable to the consumer trade. The eggs are then sized by weight and packaged in cartons. Where appropriate, the cartons of the customer, which have been preprinted, are used, and on other occasions, the eggs are packaged in 30–dozen cartons, where they are separated by layers of fiberboard. On some occasions, the Debtor does not put the eggs through the entire process of candling, washing, and oiling and sells the eggs as "nest run eggs," which puts the processing burden upon the purchaser.

The United Bank of Denver loaned the total principal sum of $2,400,000.00 to the Debtor on November 5, 1976. Four separate security agreements were executed in connection with this loan, two of which have specific application here. The first grants to the Bank a security interest in all inventory, accounts and contract rights of the Debtor, plus the proceeds therefrom. The second gives the Bank a security interest in all equipment and machinery of the Debtor. Appropriate financing statements were filed in the requisite offices to perfect the security interest in all of the described collateral.

The Bank became concerned about the Debtor's financial condition in the spring of 1979. Its concern became progressively more pronounced until, on September 21, 1979, the Bank forced the resignation of Kenneth L. Smith as the president and executive officer of the Debtor. The Bank then arranged for Mr. Norman Bell to serve as the Debtor's chief operating officer. Thereafter, and until November 23, 1979, Mr. Smith was not active in the operations of the Debtor's business and was without authority. The petition herein was filed November 23, 1979, and Mr. Smith thereupon resumed active operation of the Debtor's business.

The Debtor's primary customer for a number of years had been Safeway Stores, Inc. Safeway and the Debtor had a written contract, pursuant to which all of the Debtor's egg production meeting minimum standards was sold to Safeway. On September 24, 1979, Safeway Stores gave notice of its cancellation of the contract effective 30 days later in accordance with the termination clause in the contract. Safeway did continue to buy eggs, however, by sending inspectors to the egg facility and selecting eggs which would be purchased from time to time. On November 19, 1979, Safeway took delivery of an egg shipment which was not invoiced until November 24, 1979, pursuant to the routine billing practices of the Debtor. In addition to the receivable for the eggs shipped on November 19th, the Debtor had at the close of business on November 22nd other accounts receivable, which totaled, together with the Safeway account, a stipulated $40,192.50.

On November 24, 1979, an occasional customer of the Debtor, Mr. Gonzales, picked up a shipment of "nest run eggs" for resale in Mexico and paid the sum of $11,205.00 cash for such eggs. Mr. Gonzales, through his agent and interpreter, had spoken to the production foreman of the Debtor prior to November 16th to determine whether eggs might be available for his needs around the 16th of November. He was instructed that it was possible such delivery could be made. Due to travel difficulties and a storm, Mr. Gonzales did not arrive until the 24th of November. The arrangement with Mr. Gonzales had always been that he could purchase such "nest run eggs" as were available when he arrived to pick up delivery, and while he liked to obtain a full truckload, on a number of occasions, he had not been able to purchase a full truckload and had filled his truck with other merchandise, such as television sets or onions provided by other suppliers in the area.

After the filing of the petition herein, the Debtor delivered several shipments of eggs to Safeway, the last of which occurred on December 1, 1979. In December, as well, three flocks of chickens, totaling some 120,000 birds, were sold to the Campbell Soup Company. These hens had passed the age of prime laying capacity and no longer had utility in the production of eggs.

The Bank contends that the eggs are inventory within the meaning of its security instruments and that the chickens may be inventory or may in fact be equipment. It asserts that it, therefore, had a valid security interest in chickens and eggs. Notwithstanding the status of the chickens and eggs, it asserts a security interest in all of the sales to Safeway, which it claims to have been pursuant to contract; the sale to Mr. Gonzales, likewise asserted to have been pursuant to contract; and the sale of the chickens to Campbell Soup Company, which the Bank suggests may have been pursuant to contract as well. The Bank further claims a security interest in the accounts receivable as of the date of the filing of the petition, thus concluding that all of the cash in the Debtor's possession is "cash collateral," to which the Bank's security interest extends. The Debtor asserts that the chickens and eggs are "farm products" as that term is used in the Colorado version of the Uniform Commercial Code. 1973 CRS § 4-9-109. That section describes farm products as:

> "* * * crops or livestock or supplies used or produced in farming operations or if they are products of crops or livestock in their unmanufactured states (such as ginned cotton, wool-clip, maple syrup, milk, and eggs), and if they are in the possession of a debtor engaged in raising, fattening, grazing, or other farming operations. If goods are farm products they are neither equipment nor inventory."

It would thus seem that if eggs are products of "livestock," the hens themselves must be "livestock" within the meaning of that section. There does at least seem to be a biological connection. Official Comment to UCC § 9–109; United States v. Pete Brown Enterprises, Inc., 328 F.Supp. 600 (N.D.Miss.1971). The Bank has not disavowed the biological connection but asserts that in an operation such as this, where the sole business is the production of eggs, the eggs lose their characteristic as farm products and instead become inventory in the operation of a business. Great emphasis is placed by the Bank on the fact that there are no residents on the property of the Debtor and that while certain wheat was grown on adjacent land owned by the Debtor, it was not harvested. The Official Comment to UCC § 9–109 states:

> "Products of crops or livestock, even though they remain in the possession of a person engaged in farming operations, lose their status as farm products if they are subjected to a manufacturing process. What is and what is not a manufacturing operation is not determined by this Article. At one end of the scale some processes are so closely connected with farming—such as pasteurizing milk or boiling sap to produce maple syrup or maple sugar—that they would not rank as manufacturing. On the other hand an extensive canning operation would be manufacturing. The line is one for the courts to draw. After farm products have been subjected to a manufacturing operation, they become inventory if held for sale."

The pasteurization of milk or the boiling of sap seem to the court to be even more significant treatment of raw product than does the washing, candling, and spraying with oil of eggs. At the very least, they are in the same category, and the internal structure of the egg is not changed. The packaging of eggs in cartons does not seem to this court to be analogous to the "extensive canning operations" characterized by the Official Comment. Nearly all farm products must be packaged in some way for delivery to the farmer's customer. The facts that the packaging is done in the customer's package to eliminate a step in handling or that the operation is highly mechanized, do not seem to this court to disqualify the operation from the normal farm category. The language of the Code seems reasonably specific in its determination of what are farm products and does not appear to distinguish between the methods of producing the same product. The Bank's refreshing view that only conventional farming techniques which are unmechanized, unsophisticated, and labor intensive can produce farm products is unpersuasive. It is somewhat interesting to note that the loan at the Bank was made through its agricultural loan department.

The cases have uniformly found cattle feeding operations to be "farms" for the purposes of UCC § 9–109, although they are not farms in the traditional sense. See, for example, In re Charolais Breeding Ranches, Inc., 20 UCC Rep 193 (E.D.Wis.1976), where the court held that a tax shelter cattle feeding operation produced farm products, saying: "Although the bankrupt was not a farmer in the conventional sense, its business consisted of raising, breeding, and maintaining cattle." See also, Swift & Co. v. Jamestown National Bank, 426 F.2d 1099 (8th Cir. 1970).

* * * Similarly, in Mountain Credit v. Michiana Lumber & Supply, 31 Colo.App. 112, 498 P.2d 967 (1972), the court determined that a logging operation was not a "farming operation" within the meaning of 1973 C.R.S. § 4–9–401(1)(a). It was noted that trees could be farmed in a nursery setting, however. The construction of this statute, however, compels the conclusion that chickens are livestock and eggs are products of livestock. The statutory language is simply too clear. More importantly, the purposes of the Code could be badly abused. The Code was designed to provide a simple public explanation of claimed security interests so that the public might know under what conditions they were dealing with a debtor. To strain the statutory construction as sought by the Bank would seriously impair the public notice features which are the hallmark of the Uniform Commercial Code.

The court must conclude that the Bank has no security interest in the proceeds of either chickens or eggs, except to the extent such proceeds generated a prepetition "account" as defined in 1973 C.R.S. § 4–9–106 (1978 Supp). * * *

Problem 4–1

In each of the following cases a definitional section is critical in determining whether or not a secured creditor is perfected. Identify the section and identify the issue in that section which is relevant.

1. Debtor speaks to his banker about the purchase of an expensive stereo system that will cost approximately $1,200. Upon assurance that he will receive the loan, he buys the set and pays for it with $1,200 that belongs to his friend. Three days later he goes to the bank, signs a security agreement, gets the promised loan, and repays his friend. The bank does not file or take possession. Is it perfected?

2. Debtor goes to bank to borrow a large sum of money. Debtor offers as collateral four real estate mortgages covering a total indebtedness of $1,000,000 on which she is the creditor-mortgagee. She signs a proper security agreement and gives bank possession of the mortgages. (Assume there are no notes.) Is the bank perfected?

3. Instead of mortgages, in 2. above, assume that the borrower was holder of several notes representing total obligations of $100,000 and also the lessor under several leases of automobiles. She gives possession of these items to the bank in return for a loan. Is the bank perfected?

SECTION 3. PERFECTION BY FILING—WHERE TO FILE

The normal mode of filing under the UCC is to execute what is commonly known as a UCC–1; a standard form of what is meant by a UCC–1 is set out below. See UCC 9–402(1).

UNIFORM COMMERCIAL CODE FINANCING STATEMENT
(Approved by the Secretary of State and Michigan Association of Registers of Deeds)

INSTRUCTIONS:

1. TYPE OR PRINT All information required on this Form.
2. If dual filing is made, send the WHITE copies to the Secretary of State, Lansing, Michigan. Send the YELLOW copies to the local register of deeds. Retain PINK copies for files of the secured party and debtor.
3. Enclose filing fee.
4. IF ADDITIONAL SPACE IS NEEDED for any items on this Form, continue the items on separate sheets of paper (5" × 8"). One copy of these additional sheets should accompany the WHITE Forms, and one copy should accompany the YELLOW Forms. USE PAPER CLIPS to attach these sheets to the Forms (DO NOT USE STAPLES, GLUE, TAPE, ETC.) and indicate in Item 1 the number of additional sheets attached.
5. At the time of filing, the filing officer will return acknowledgement. At a later time, the secured party may date and sign the termination legend and use acknowledgement copy as a termination statement.
6. Both the WHITE and YELLOW Filing Officer copies must have original signatures. Only the debtor must sign the financing statement, and the signature of the secured party is not necessary, except that the secured party alone may sign the financing statement in the following 4 instances: Please specify action in Item 7 below.
   (1) Where the collateral which is subject to the security interest in another state is brought into Michigan or the location of the debtor is changed to Michigan.
   (2) "For proceeds if the security interest in the original collateral was perfected."
   (3) The previous filing has lapsed.
   (4) For collateral acquired after a change of debtor name, and a filing is required under MCLA 440.9402 (2) and (7); MSA 19.9402 (2) and (7).

---

1. No. of additional sheets	Liber	Page	For Filing Officer (Date, Time, Number, and Filing Office)
2. Debtor(s) (Last Name First) and address(es)	3. Secured Party(ies) and address(es)		
4. Name and address(es) of assignee(s) (if any)	CHECK ☒ if applicable 5. ☐ Products of collateral are also covered. 6. ☐ Collateral was brought into this state subject to a security interest in another jurisdiction.		

7. This financing statement covers the following types (or items) of property:

____

________________ ________________

________________ by ________________

Signature(s) of Debtor(s) (Signature of Secured Party or Assignee of Record)

[C206]

Financing Statement—Form UCC–1—Central Filing— 1972 Illinois Article 9

STATE OF ILLINOIS

UNIFORM COMMERCIAL CODE—FINANCING STATEMENT—FORM UCC-1

INSTRUCTIONS:

1. PLEASE TYPE this form. Fold only along perforation for mailing.
2. Remove Secured Party and Debtor copies and send other 3 copies with interleaved carbon paper to the filing officer. Enclose filing fee.
3. If the space provided for any item(s) on the form is inadequate the item(s) should be continued on additional sheets, preferably 5" x 8" or 8" x 10". Only one copy of such additional sheets need be presented to the filing officer with a set of three copies of the financing statement. Long schedules of collateral, indentures, etc., may be on any size paper that is convenient for the secured party.

This STATEMENT is presented to a filing officer for filing pursuant to the Uniform Commercial Code.

For Filing Officer (Date, Time, Number, and Filing Office)

Debtor(s) (Last Name First) and address(es)

Secured Party(ies) and address(es)

1. This financing statement covers the following types (or items) of property:

ASSIGNEE OF SECURED PARTY

2 ☐ Products of Collateral are also covered.

_____ Additional sheets presented.

_____ Filed with Office of Secretary of State of Illinois.

_____ Debtor is a transmitting utility as defined in UCC §9-105.

By: ______________________

Signature of (Debtor) (Secured Party)*

*Signature of Debtor Required in Most Cases:
Signature of Secured Party in Cases Covered By UCC §9-402 (2)

(1) Filing Officer Copy - Alphabetical

This form of financing statement is approved by the Secretary of State.

STANDARD FORM UNIFORM COMMERCIAL CODE - FORM UCC-1 - REV. 2-74

[B1132]

What information is available from the financing statement? Can one tell the interest rate? The principal amount of the loan? The terms of repayment? The duration? Can one be sure from the financing statement that there is any loan at all? The answer to these questions is "no," and the lesson to be learned is that the UCC calls *only* for "notice filing," that is for filing which merely puts third parties "on notice" that they may have to look further. The secured creditor is not required to file the security agreement (or loan application, etc.). This is to be contrasted with the *recording* of real estate mortgages where the operative document itself (the entire mortgage) is put on record and can be examined by any member of the public.

The question where to file divides into at least two questions. The first is in what state? The second, where within the state? The first question is answered largely by UCC 9–103, a provision we deal with in Section 7 infra. Here we are concerned mostly with where within the state one files. That is answered by UCC 9–401. Looking not at just one state, but at the various states, the issue is complicated by the fact that there are three alternatives to UCC 9–401. The student should read each of the alternatives with care and should note how they differ. Alternatives one to three progressively calls for more local filing. Only the third alternative calls for filing in more than one place, although a prudent creditor may, even under the first and second alternatives, choose to do more than one filing. Even a quick examination of 9–401 reaffirms the importance of definitions. For the purposes of the second and third alternative, farm products call for a local filing, but inventory does not. Fixture filings are local, but equipment filings are not. Note the third alternative does, however, call for a local filing in many cases in which the second alternative would call only for a state-wide filing. How does one explain these differences, and how does one explain the fact that the local filing is called for only in the case in which the debtor has but a single place of business in the state?

The notice filing provisions afford scope for overreaching on the part of the creditor. By filing a financing statement that covers "all farm products" the creditor can in effect cast a shadow over a given debtor's title to all of his significant personal property. To minimize that problem, section 9–208 gives the debtor a right to demand a more specific statement from his creditor concerning the amount of the debt and the identity of the collateral claimed by the creditor.

To test your understanding of UCC 9–401, consider the following problem.

Problem 4–2

(Assume that the second alternative to UCC 9–401 is in force except where the problem states otherwise.)

1. Debtor is a nurseryman who grows a substantial number of the shrubs, flowers and bushes that he sells at his nursery. He has a 100 acre plot on which he grows these items and has two greenhouses. In the front of one of the greenhouses he has a sales office and display room and outside of one of them during the summer months he sells various plants. Secured creditor filed a financing statement at the county seat of DeKalb County where the debtor's residence and the greenhouses and farm are located. He described in his financing statement the collateral as follows: "All nursery stock, all tractors, all farm equipment, all nursery equipment, one 530 Case backhoe, one tractor plow, one 24 disk." The nurseryman has now gone into bankruptcy and the trustee asks whether he can successfully challenge the security interest as it applies to the nursery stock. He estimates the value of the nursery stock to be in excess of $300,000. Some is maintained in pots in the greenhouses and on display; some in a holding area; and all of it is growing. At any given time the nurseryman reports that he has certain mature plants and others in various stages of development from one to seven years.

2. Debtor owned a ranch in central Kansas. He farmed that ranch and maintained both crops and a significant number of cattle on the ranch. From time to time he fattened cattle and sold them and at other times he purchased cattle and resold them without ever bringing them to his ranch. Bank's security agreement covered all "farm products, crops and farm implements."

The security agreement also contained the following clauses: "If marked here [X] debtor grants a security interest in all similar property owned by debtor during the period when the obligations are outstanding although such property may have been acquired or be natural increase after the date hereof.

"If marked here [X] the security interest will attach to all products and proceeds of the collateral but secured party does not hereby consent to the sale of collateral. * * *

"Debtor warrants that unless marked otherwise the collateral is used or being sought primarily for family or household purposes; but if marked here

[X] for farming operations;

[ ] for business operations; and

[ ] the collateral is being acquired with proceeds of the note * * * "

Bank filed a financing statement at the county seat where debtor's ranch was located. On debtor's bankruptcy he had 400 head of cattle on his ranch and was the owner of another 300 head that had been purchased the week prior to the bankruptcy and were being held at a local stockyard awaiting a sale that was to occur on the date following the day when the petition was filed. The trustee has asserted a claim to all of the cattle. If you were his counsel and he asked whether he would be successful, how would you advise him?

3. Assume that the debtor does business in a state with the third alternative to UCC 9–401. At the Secretary of State's office, Creditor filed a financing statement covering a large "International Td Dozer" worth more than $20,000. Creditor made no local filing. Trustee now argues that the creditor is unperfected. Is that so? The Dozer belonged to Yale Mining Corporation which did all of its mining in Lee County, Virginia, and in Harlan County, Kentucky. It leased equipment to other mining operators in other Virginia counties. The security agreement and the financing statement were signed and contained as an address of the debtor an address in Pennington Gap, Lee County, and it appears that shortly before the agreement was signed debtor had closed an office it had in Wise County and moved to Lee County. Debtor still retained a Post Office Box in Wise County and its registered agent for the purpose of service and a business bank account were at a bank in Wise County. On these facts, who gets the Dozer?

4. Bank takes a security interest in debtor's five race horses that are kept at Arlington Park in Illinois. Bank files a financing statement covering "horses" with the Secretary of State's office in Springfield, but does not do a local filing. Assuming that Illinois has the second alternative to UCC 9–401, is the bank perfected?

SECTION 4. PERFECTION BY FILING—WHAT TO FILE

An examination of UCC 9–402 and a consideration of the UCC–1 set out above show how little information needs to be included on a financing statement. It must have the names of the two parties, be signed by the debtor, give an address of the secured party and of the debtor, and contain a statement indicating the "types or describing the items of collateral." The security agreement can operate as the financing statement, but, except in consumer cases with very simple security agreements, that will not often be feasible. There is so little to be done, yet there are so many ways to go wrong. One cannot begin to imagine the ways in which a financing statement can be filled out incorrectly without reading some of the vast volume of cases that have now arisen under these sections. No person's imagination extends that far.

First, the creditor may omit something entirely. For example, the creditor may fail to get the debtor's signature or may omit the address itself. The description can and will be challenged if it is too narrow or too broad, but the most certain source of trouble for the creditor is the debtor's name. Is the name correct? Is it misspelled? Has the creditor used the corporate instead of the individual name or vice versa? Any one of these factors can render a financing statement invalid and cause the secured creditor to lose to a trustee in bankruptcy or other third party.

By far the most important requirement in UCC 9–402 involves the name of the debtor. The student should understand why that is so. It is only through indexing of the debtor's name that subsequent parties will find a financing statement. If others cannot find the financing statement, it is worthless. Thus, one can expect the trustee to examine the debtor's name with care and for the court to treat a trustee's complaint about errors in the debtor's name with real seriousness.

In fact name questions are likely to be much more complex than one can imagine at first blush. The first sentence of UCC 9–402(7) specifies the correct way to file where the debtor might plausibly be identified by either of two names, as for example, a partnership and a partner, a corporation run exclusively by one person, or any business organization that does business under another name. Note the apparent conflict between that sentence in UCC 9–402(7) and the first paragraph in Comment 7 to UCC 9–402. The statute seems to say what is sufficient, but not necessary; the Comment appears to say that compliance with the statute is both necessary and sufficient.

Yet more troublesome are the cases in which the debtor changes his, her or its name. In the consumer context a woman with an outstanding debt may assume her husband's name upon marriage or may take her original name upon divorce. Must the creditor file an amended financing statement? Business entities occasionally change their names. Must the creditor amend?

There is also the possibility of more fundamental business reorganization as when a sole proprietorship becomes a corporation. Of course, in the latter case one must worry not just about the proper mode of perfection, but about the efficacy of the underlying security agreement which by hypothesis has not been signed by a representative of the new organization.

In general UCC 9–402(7) and (8) are a bit of statutory leavening for the strict constructionists' judicial loaf. Many courts have been sticklers for absolute and strict compliance with the law regarding documents filed to give notice to third parties. In some cases this requirement has been carried to unseemly extremes and used to avoid financing statements that could not possibly mislead anyone. One suspects there is a deeper meaning to such judicial hostility to modestly defective filings. In several ways section 9–402(7) can serve as a shield against such hostility. In the first place it provides by implication that a financing statement filed in the old name continues effective even as to new collateral where the name change is not "seriously misleading." Even where the name change renders the old filing seriously misleading, section 9–402(7) provides that the filing remains effective as to collateral existing at the time of the name change and for that acquired within four months thereafter. Most important of all is the instruction in UCC 9–402(8), "a financing statement substantially complying with the requirements of this section is effective even though it contains minor errors which are not seriously misleading." That, presumably, is a direction from the legislature to the court to abandon fanatical insistence upon detail. After all, Article 9 was designed to "deformalize" the pre-Code law in these very respects.

IN RE LINTZ WEST SIDE LUMBER, INC.

United States Court of Appeals, Seventh Circuit, 1981.
655 F.2d 786.

CUDAHY, CIRCUIT JUDGE.

The Farmers & Merchants Bank of Fort Branch, Indiana seeks review of an order entered October 10, 1980, by the Honorable Gene E. Brooks, a United States District Judge, acting as a Judge of the Bankruptcy Court. This order granted the petition of J. Robert Duvall, trustee in bankruptcy for the estate of Lintz West Side Lumber, Inc., to set aside an earlier order entered by Judge Brooks, which authorized the abandonment of certain assets of the bankrupt. We affirm.

I.

Lintz West Side Lumber, Inc. ("Lintz Lumber" or the "bankrupt") was indebted to the Farmers & Merchants Bank (the "Bank") on two promissory notes totalling $90,000. To secure the indebtedness, the Bank obtained a security interest in the bankrupt's inventory and accounts receivable. The parties executed a security agreement to this effect, and the Bank prepared a financing statement which listed the debtor as:

Lintz, John Richard

Lintz, Mayella

2 Red Bank Road

Fort Branch, Indiana

The Bank filed the financing statement at the office of the Indiana Secretary of State and at the office of the Recorder of Gibson County, Indiana. * * *

On May 7, 1979, Lintz Lumber filed a voluntary petition in bankruptcy. * * * [In attacking the financing statement] the trustee argued that the statement, filed under the names of John and Mayella Lintz, rather than Lintz West Side Lumber, Inc., was insufficient to perfect the Bank's security interest because the difference in names would seriously mislead other creditors. * * *

[After the trial court decided against it,] the Bank subsequently instituted this appeal. * * * The Bank argues that the Uniform Commercial Code's system of "notice filing" was designed to assure that minor errors in the information provided on the financing statement would not defeat the perfection of a security interest. Since the bankrupt here is a close corporation located in a small town, the bank contends that a filing under the name of John and Mayella Lintz, the principal owners, directors and officers of the corporation, was sufficient to provide notice of the Bank's security interest to other creditors in the community.

Judge Brooks concluded, however, that the Bank's failure to include the correct name of the debtor corporation in the financing statement was seriously misleading because subsequent creditors had to depend upon a government official to search state records for the financing statement. *See* Anderson, *Uniform Commercial Code,* § 9–402:28 (1971); Ind.Adm.Rules and Reg. §§ 26–1–9–407–1 to 9. As a duly constituted corporation, Lintz West Side Lumber, Inc., is a legal entity separate and distinct from John and Mayella Lintz (whose names appear on the financing statement). A creditor would ordinarily, and could reasonably, assume that *corporate* assets would not be encumbered by a security interest filed under the names of these individuals despite the similarity in the names. Unless a creditor requested a search for the security interests held by others in the Lintz' personal property, the Bank's security interest would not be found. Under these circumstances, we cannot say that the names of the debtors were sufficiently similar to provide a creditor or official searching the records on behalf of a creditor with reasonable notice of the Bank's security interest.[7]

The Bank's argument that the security agreement was entered in good faith and without intent to defraud creditors does not alter this result. The bank's good faith is not at issue here. Moreover, good faith is only a necessary, not a sufficient, condition for perfection under the Uniform Commercial Code.

The Bank's allegation that no creditor in this case was actually mislead [sic] is similarly without merit. The district court noted that "Section 70(c) of the Bankruptcy Act clothes the trustee with the 'status of an ideal, imaginary creditor, irreproachable and without notice, and arms him with every conceivable right and power which under the applicable state law would be available to the most favored creditor who might have acquired a lien on the bankrupt's properties by legal or equitable proceedings.' Collier Bankruptcy Manual, *Trustees and Receivers in Bankruptcy Handbook,* § 13.-001; J. White and R. Summers, *Handbook of Law Under the Uniform Commercial Code,* § 24–3 page 867 (1972)." *In re Lintz West Side Lumber,* No. EV 79–205–B (Bankr.Ct. Oct. 10, 1980). The district judge, an expert in bankruptcy matters and presumably in the mechanics of perfection of security interests in personal property in Indiana, found that the trustee, as an ideal, hypothetical creditor of the bankrupt, can be considered to have been prejudiced by the Bank's seriously misleading financing statement. See *In re Thrift Shoe Co., Inc.*, 502 F.2d 1211 (9th Cir. 1974). After reviewing the record in this case, we are not persuaded that this finding is clearly erroneous. * * *

[Some footnotes omitted.]

Note

How do you suppose that the trustee learned that a secured creditor had filed an inadequate financing statement?

7. Both *In re Platt,* 257 F.Supp. 478 (E.D.Pa.1966) and *In re Hatfield Construction Company,* 10 UCC RS 907 (M.D.Ga.1971) are thus distinguishable from the instant case. In *Platt,* the court held that a financing statement filed under the name, Platt Fur Company, would not seriously mislead creditors of the true debtor, Henry Platt. Platt Fur Company, however, was an unregistered trade name for the business of Henry Platt and not a licensed corporate entity. In *Hatfield,* the financing statement securing assets of Hatfield Construction Company, a licensed corporation, was filed under the name of Wayne L. Hatfield. Although the court found that the financing statement was not seriously misleading, there is no indication that a government official was required to perform the search in that case. In addition, in both *Platt* and *Hatfield,* the court *affirmed* the determination of the bankruptcy judge.

IN RE GLASCO, INC.

United States Court of Appeals, Fifth Circuit, 1981.
642 F.2d 793.

RONEY, CIRCUIT JUDGE. The sole issue on appeal is whether a financing statement, filed with the Florida Secretary of State by a creditor, perfected a security interest in certain property of the bankrupt debtor. The bankruptcy court held the financing statement to be inadequate because it listed the debtor by the name in which it did business rather than its legal corporate name. The district court affirmed. Holding the debtor's name used in the financing statement was not seriously misleading, we reverse. * * *

Prior to its bankruptcy, the debtor engaged in the manufacture and sale of boats in Florida. Although its legal corporate name was "Glasco, Inc.," the debtor operated its business solely under the name, "Elite Boats, Division of Glasco, Inc."

Appellant, the Citizens Bank of Perry ("the bank"), was "floor planning" marine engines for the debtor. In 1977, in connection with this financing, the debtor executed promissory notes and a security agreement in the name of "Elite Boats, Division of Glasco, Inc." The bank, to perfect its security interest in the marine engines, timely filed a standard form UCC–1 financing statement with the Florida Secretary of State, as required by Florida law. The bank listed the debtor on the form as "Elite Boats, Division of Glasco, Inc." The form was signed at the bottom by an officer of the debtor, without any designation as to office, capacity or affiliation. A filing clerk in the Secretary of State's office indexed this financing statement under the name listed, but did not cross-index it under "Glasco, Inc."

Later in 1977, the debtor filed for bankruptcy. The trustee in bankruptcy, appellee here, inquired of the Secretary of State whether any financing statements had been filed under "Glasco, Inc." Since the trustee did not request a search under "Elite Boats" or "Elite Boats, Division of Glasco, Inc." as well, the bank's financing statement was not disclosed. With permission of the bankruptcy court and without notice to the bank, the trustee then sold the marine engines. The bank commenced this action against the trustee for the sale proceeds.

In granting the trustee's motion for summary judgment, the bankruptcy court held the financing statement to be improper because it did not list the debtor by its legal name, "Glasco, Inc." The court further held the Secretary of State had no duty to cross-index the financing statement under the debtor's legal name, and the trustee was not bound by its actual knowledge that the debtor did business as "Elite Boats, Division of Glasco, Inc." The district court affirmed. On appeal, the bank contends that (1) listing the debtor as "Elite Boats, Division of Glasco, Inc." was sufficient because it was not seriously misleading to future creditors; and (2) in any event, the Secretary of State should have cross-indexed under "Glasco, Inc."

To perfect a security interest in collateral, a creditor must file a financing statement which complies with the filing requirements of the Uniform Commercial Code, as adopted in Florida. Fla.Stat.Ann. §§ 679.9–401 et seq. (1966). The purpose of the filing system is to give notice to creditors and other interested parties that a security interest exists in property of the debtor. * * * Perfect accuracy, however, is not required as long as the financing statement contains sufficient information to "put any searcher on inquiry." * * * The emphasis of the Uniform Commercial Code is thus on commercial realities rather than on corporate technicalities. * * * Section 9–402(5) reflects this emphasis by providing: "A financing statement substantially complying with the requirements of this section is effective even though it contains minor errors which are not seriously misleading." * * *

The effect of errors in the listing of the debtor's name has been the subject of extensive litigation. * * * The decisions appear generally to turn on the particular factual circumstances involved. The case here, then, must be judged on its own facts, with the focus on whether potential creditors would have been misled as a result of the name the debtor was listed by in the bank's financing statement.

It is undisputed the debtor held itself out to the community and to creditors as "Elite Boats, Division of Glasco, Inc." Its checks, stationery, and bank account all bore the latter name. Apparently the same name was used in its bills, contracts and telephone listing, because there is no indication in the record the debtor ever used the name of just "Glasco, Inc.," or any other name. Thus, listing the debtor by the sole name in which it did business was not misleading, because any reasonably prudent creditor would have requested the Secretary of State to search under "Elite Boats" in addition to "Glasco, Inc." Of course, the trustee in bankruptcy is considered to be in the position of a hypothetical but prudent creditor. * * *

Siljeg v. National Bank of Commerce, 509 F.2d 1009 (9th Cir. 1975), is analogous. Siljeg involved a security interest in property of a corporate debtor which later merged into another company. The parties disputed whether the "true name" of the debtor was the pre-merger or post-merger name, for the purpose of determining the accuracy of the financing statement. In rejecting this focus of inquiry, the court held:

> "The issue to be determined is not the true name of the entity, but whether the filing was misleading. Filing under an assumed trade name is effective unless it is misleading * * * It is likely that the * * * corporation did business under only one name and it may well be that a filing under that name was not seriously misleading." 509 F.2d at 1012–13.

The court then remanded the case for consideration under this standard.

The trustee relies on several cases each involving an individual who is engaged in business under an assumed trade name. These cases generally hold that a financing statement listing only the trade name as the debtor will be insufficient to perfect a security interest effective against the individual. * * * There is a crucial distinction, however, between these cases and the case here. In the former, a single debtor is necessarily held out to the credit community under two names, that of the individual and of the business. The individual's credit for personal needs is unrelated to the business. A personal creditor would not necessarily be aware of the business or trade name, and thus may not discover security interests filed solely under the business name. In the present case, where the company does business only under one name, the opportunity for creditors to be misled is substantially reduced, even though that name is not the company's "true name." See Siljeg, supra, 509 F.2d at 1012.

We hold the listing of the debtor as "Elite Boats, Division of Glasco, Inc." rather than as "Glasco, Inc." was not seriously misleading. The financing statement was therefore in substantial compliance with the filing requirements under Florida law and was sufficient to perfect the bank's security interest.

Because of our holding on the first issue presented by the bank, we need not decide whether the Secretary of State had a duty to cross-index the financing statement under "Glasco, Inc." A creditor who has complied with the filing requirements does not bear the risk of improper indexing by the Secretary of State. * * *

Thus, the bank would have a perfected security interest whether or not the Secretary of State had breached a duty to cross-index.

Reversed.

TUTTLE, CIRCUIT JUDGE, dissenting. With deference, I dissent. The majority opinion treats this case as presenting a group of narrow issues arising under the filing provisions for perfection of security interests under the Uniform Commercial Code, Fla.Stat.Ann. § 679.9–401. The majority eschews technicality to reach what might be considered to be a common sense solution in finding a perfected security interest despite an irregularity in the filing. Because this superficially appealing result contains the seeds for future mischief I cannot concur.

The filing system under the Code revolves around the concept of "notice filing," where a filing is to " 'give the minimum information necessary to put any searcher on inquiry.' " In re Excel Stores, 341 F.2d 961, 963 (2d Cir. 1965); see UCC § 9–402, comment 2. To effectuate the Code's spirit of liberality and disdain for rigid technicality the drafters included the provision, now relied upon by the majority, that a financing statement is effective even if "it contains minor errors which are not seriously misleading." Fla.Stat. § 679.9–402(5). This provision clearly was designed to accomplish substantial justice and "to discourage the fanatical and impossibly refined reading of such statutory requirements in which courts have occasionally indulged themselves." UCC § 9–402, comment 8.

This provision of liberality, however, was never intended to vitiate the beneficial effects of having a single filing system for the benefit of both existing creditors and searchers of the files. In its decision which protects the rights of the bank-appellant, the majority has unfairly burdened the other persons who must rely upon the filing system. A variety of different types of errors may cause the name on the financing statement to be erroneous and result in an incorrect filing of the statement. In deciding whether an error is "seriously misleading" a court must apply an "appropriate sensitivity to the relevant factors." J. White & R. Summers, Handbook of the Law Under the Uniform Commercial Code § 23–16, 958 (2d ed. 1980). In this regard the Court of Appeals for the Second Circuit has held that a subsequent creditor might never search the filings under the trade name of "Landman Dry Cleaners" where the debtor's name was "Leichter." In re

Leichter, 471 F.2d 785, 787 (2d Cir. 1972). On the other hand, a filing under a trade name may be so similar to the debtor's real name that a searcher would be put on notice despite the technical error.

> The Referee found that a search of the public records under the name of Henry Platt would not have disclosed F.C.A.'s interest. Platt Fur Co. was an unregistered fictitious name for the business of Henry Platt. He also used Kenwell Fur Novelty Co. as a fictitious name.
>
> "The use of Kenwell as the debtor would clearly have left F.C.A. without a perfected security interest. However, the name Platt Fur Co. is sufficiently related to the name of the debtor, Henry Platt, to require those who search the records to make further investigation. Furthermore, the Referee found that the name was 'not seriously misleading,' the criterion for effectiveness under § 9–402(5)."

In re Platt, 257 F. Supp. 478, 482 (E.D. Pa. 1966).[1] The majority distinguishes cases such as Leichter as cases where the credit records of an individual's business should be distinguished from the credit records of the individual. The majority reasons that: "A personal creditor would not necessarily be aware of the business or trade name, and thus may not discover security interests filed solely under the business name. In the present case, where the company does business only under one name, the opportunity for creditors to be misled is substantially reduced, even though that name is not the company's 'true name.'" At 796. This distinction will not support the majority's result. The majority points to indications that the debtor always did business under the name "Elite Boats, Division of Glasco, Inc." and concludes that therefore any potential creditor would know to check under that non-legal name. But we are reviewing a case that was disposed of on a motion for summary judgment. Given this state of the record there may have existed creditors who would have perceived the debtor as simply "Glasco, Inc.," the legally proper title which, of course, it was. Surely the trustee could be taken to stand in the shoes of such an ideal creditor who had no notice. And in searching for "Glasco, Inc." one would not normally come across an item filed under the title of "Elite Boats." This is simply not a case where a searcher looking for the actual name would be put on notice by a filing under a similar trade name. A filing under the trade name in this case would not be filed near the actual name. Moreover, even if such creditors knew the trade name, they would still be justified to search only under the debtor's *legal* name. The terms of UCC § 9–402 require no more. Searching under a trade name would be completely unnecessary but for the majority's opinion. From now on in this Circuit, potential creditors must undertake to discover trade names and to conduct additional searches in order to avoid a judicial determination that they

1. The Florida law, amended subsequent to the beginning of this case, provides that: "A financing statement sufficiently shows the name of the debtor if it gives the individual partnership, or corporate names of the debtor, whether or not it adds other trade names or names of partners." Fla. Stat. Ann. § 679.9–402(6) (West. Supp. 1980). Leading commentators have inferred that this provision would alter the result of Platt: "With this provision on the books, the wise lawyer would advise Henry Platt and his creditors to use 'Henry Platt' as the name on the financing statement." White & Summers, supra, at 958. Although not the law in any state, the official comment to the revision behind this new Florida provision provides some insight on this situation: "Trade names are deemed to be too uncertain and likely not to be known to be the basis for a filing system." UCC § 9–402, comment 7.

lacked diligence. And even if they follow such precautions they might yet overlook one trade name and face potentially expensive litigation over whether they should have known about that trade name.

Of course, the majority's conclusion may yet be saved if the Secretary of State wrongly failed to carry out a duty to cross index the financing statement. A creditor who complies with the filing requirements may not bear the risk of errors by the filing officer. See UCC § 9–407, comment 1. This rule holds true because under the Code "Presentation for filing of a financing statement * * * constitutes filing under this chapter." Fla. Stat. § 679.9–403(1). See In re Royal Electrotype Corp., 485 F.2d 394, 395–96 (3d Cir. 1973); In re Fowler, 407 F. Supp. 799 (W.D. Okla. 1975). But those authorities do not aid the bank in the present case. The error lay in the bank's submission of the debtor's name as "Elite Boats, Division of Glasco, Inc." The filing officer dutifully filed the statement under precisely this name. The bank may argue that the filing officers usually cross index under all names given. For example, a financing statement using a "doing business as" listing of a debtor would be indexed under the legal name and the trade name. This argument by the bank differs from the position that the bank will not bear the risks of the filing officer's mistakes; rather this argument holds that the filing officer must correct the bank's errors. If the bank had clearly indicated two names separated by a notation such as "d.b.a.", its position would be stronger. But the fact remains that the bank's submission could very easily be taken to be *one* name especially by a clerk untrained in legal subtleties.[4] "A secured party does not bear the risk of improper filing or indexing *as long as his conduct does not lead to the error on the part of the filing officer.*" In re Fowler, 407 F.Supp. at 803 (emphasis added.)

Courts may have the opportunity to view a situation with perfect hindsight which is unavailable to participants in daily activities. The bank had the opportunity to submit the correct name of the debtor and failed to do so. A searcher versed in the operation of the UCC would know that the filing should be under the debtor's legal name. He would have no reason to look under a trade name, even if he is aware of the trade name's existence, because he should be able to rely on the bank to submit the legal name and not a trade name. Future creditors must now anticipate mistakes by would-be secured creditors in order not to be ensnared in the hindsight of courts. The trustee should prevail against the bank which is responsible for any confusion in this case.

I would affirm the district court's judgment. [Some footnotes omitted.]

Notes

1. Can you square *Lintz* and *Glasco?*

2. Should a court be willing to accept a less precise financing statement in a thinly populated rural area than it would accept in Los Angeles County?

4. The bank's argument that the filing officer should have recognized that there were two names on the form actually cuts against the bank. If it is so easy to see that "Elite Boats" is not a legal name then there is no reason or excuse for the bank's failure to submit the debtor's name as simply "Glasco, Inc."

3. Should the capacity of a subsequent search to turn up the financing statement be determinative of proper filing? What, for example, of the particularly diligent clerk who finds one that is improperly filed or of the inadequate computer cross-index that misses even those that would be obvious to a human searcher, such as one that omitted a period or a space?

4. Currently much searching is sometimes done by computer. In the future we can expect that nearly all UCC filing records will be maintained on computer memory and will be searched by computer. Note that the use of the computer as a searching device may restrict the search if the computer is programmed narrowly, but modern and developing computer technology may enhance the capacity of the searcher to find a misfiled or defective statement. For example, a computer can now be programmed to search not just under Christiansen, but also under names that sound the same, i.e., Christianson, Cristensen, Christenson etc. If collateral is also entered on the computer memory, the computer can do a cross indexing between the names and the kind of collateral and come up with a variety of alternatives.

5. Assume that you are a trustee in a case like *Glasco* and that you are contemplating the possibility of challenging a secured creditor's interest. What might be a first step in determining whether to proceed or not?

IN RE ALEXANDER

United States Bankruptcy Court, District of North Dakota, 1984.
39 B.R. 110.

WILLIAM A. HILL, BANKRUPTCY JUDGE. Phillip D. Armstrong, Trustee of the estates of Larry Alexander and John and Norma Alexander, requests that his interest in various of the Debtors' personal property be found superior to that of the Defendant, Farmers Home Administration. The Debtors filed petitions for relief under Chapter 7 of the Bankruptcy Code and were discharged in their bankruptcy proceedings on January 10, 1983.
* * *

John Alexander testified at the hearing held February 9, 1983, that he had refinanced his farming operation in 1978 through the Farmers Home Administration. The Farmers Home Administration required, however, that John Alexander execute a partnership agreement with his son, Larry, before it would enter into the refinancing arrangement. Although the partnership agreement was drawn up by the Farmers Home Administration and signed at its request, John Alexander testified that he and his son actually maintained separate farming operations. Each of the Alexanders had his own machinery, had his own seed, paid his own operating expenses, and filed his own tax returns.

The Farmers Home Administration filed a financing statement with the Register of Deed's office in Benson County, North Dakota, on February 6, 1979. The Debtors named in the financing statement were listed, as follows:

ALEXANDER DEBTOR(S) FARMS	SECURED PARTY	For Filing Officer
John J. Alexander Norma L. Alexander (Name) Larry J. Alexander (Name)	UNITED STATES OF AMERICA acting through FARMERS HOME ADMINISTRATION	File No: 251129 Date: 2/6/79 Time: 3:15 PM
Leeds, North Dakota 58346 (Mailing Address)	Box 207, Minnewaukan, N. D. (County Office Address) 58351	Filing Officer: RJF, pd3.00

The financing statement indicated that the Farmers Home Administration was claiming the following property as collateral for their loans:

> "Livestock, supplies, inventory, farm and other equipment and other farm products except growing and unharvested crops."

Armstrong contends that the financing statement filed by the Farmers Home Administration does not meet the requirements of NDCC § 41–09–41(1) and therefore is ineffective to perfect a security interest in the Debtors' property.

Section 41–09–41(1) of the North Dakota Century Code provides, in part:

> "A financing statement is sufficient if it gives the names of the debtor and the secured party, is signed by the debtor, gives an address of the secured party from which information concerning the security interest may be obtained, gives a mailing address of the debtor, and contains a statement indicating the types, or describing the items, of collateral."

Section 41–09–41 of the North Dakota Century Code codified section 9–402 of the Uniform Commercial Code. * * * The Eighth Circuit Court of Appeals, in a case involving the Minnesota statute codifying UCC § 9–402, stated that "a financing statement covers the collateral in question if it merely makes it reasonable for a subsequent creditor interested in the collateral to make further inquiries." Thorp Commercial Corp. v. Northgate Industries, Inc., 654 F.2d 1245, 1252 (8th Cir. 1981). A financing statement, therefore, must reasonably notify a creditor of prior interests in the Debtors' property.

In this instance, the financing statement filed by the Farmers Home Administration is sufficient to perfect a security agreement in machinery owned separately by the two Debtors, John and Larry Alexander. Although the financing statement was indexed under the name Alexander Farms, the court believes it reasonable that a creditor interested in the property of John and Larry Alexander within the largely rural county of Benson County, North Dakota, would examine all financing statements filed under the name Alexander. Further, the collateral listed in the financing statement of the Farmers Home Administration is not specified in overly broad terms. The term "farm and other equipment" is a reasonable notification that there may be a security interest claimed by FHA in the Debtors' farm machinery.

For the reasons stated,

It is ordered that the financing statement of the Farmers Home Administration is sufficient notice to perfect any security interest it may claim in the property of the Debtors.

Problem 4–3

Debtor, Smokee-Linc, Inc., a sausage manufacturer, executed a security interest in its accounts, equipment and inventory to secure a working capital loan from Centerville National Bank (CNB). CNB filed a financing statement covering the property at the Secretary of State's office. The UCC–1 filed by CNB listed "Smokee-Linc, Inc." as the debtor.

One month after CNB filed the UCC–1, Debtor filed for a corporate name change as required under the Corporation Code. The corporation name was changed to "Smokey Link, Inc." CNB was not notified of the change of corporate name.

Six months after CNB filed its UCC–1, Debtor filed in Chapter 11.

1. Assume that the Secretary of State files its UCC–1's in a central computing system. Whenever a filing search is requested, the computer searches for the debtor's name. Once this name is found, the computer prints out all filings under that name. The computer also prints out the filings under the three names alphabetically prior to and the three names alphabetically consecutive from the spot where the requested name should appear. On the date of the filing of the petition in bankruptcy, the trustee requested a filing search of "Smokey Link, Inc." and received the following names on the computer print out:

Smoker Heaven, Inc.

Smokers Anonymous, Inc.

Smoker's Nook, Inc.

Smokey Mountain Trails, Ltd.

Smoothee-Cream Ice Creams, Inc.

Smothers, Richard

Smothers, Thomas

The trustee argues that CNB is not perfected because the change in the debtor's name did not appear on the search and that the filing is therefore seriously misleading. Is she correct?

2. Assume that the Secretary of State does not have a computerized filing system. All filing searches are performed by those lower grade phenomena known as humans. Is it clear that CNB would not be perfected if a search requested by the trustee did not uncover the filing under "Smokee-Linc, Inc."?

Problem 4–4

1. Debtor had been doing business as and was incorporated as Mountainaire Chevrolet Inc. Bank filed a financing statement that appeared as follows:

The **FINANCING STATEMENT** is presented to a Filing Officer for filing pursuant to the Uniform Commercial Code

CREDIT UNION ACCOUNT NUMBER: 39495A-1

1. MATURITY DATE (IF ANY)

2. NUMBER OF ADDITIONAL SHEETS PRESENTED (IF ANY) (SEE INSTRUCTION 3)

FOR FILING OFFICER (DATE, TIME, NUMBER, AND FILING OFFICE)

3. DEBTOR(S) (LAST NAME FIRST) AND ADDRESS(ES):
Mountainaire Chevrolet, Inc.
1452 Crestlane Avenue
Glasgow, Kentucky

4. SECURED PARTY (IES) AND ADDRESS(ES):
Second National Bank of Glasgow
631 North Vermont
Glasgow, Kentucky

(APPLICABLE ONLY WHEN CHECKED) All household goods, furniture, and appliances belonging to the debtor or debtors now at the address stated above.

9 THIS FINANCING STATEMENT COVERS THE FOLLOWING TYPES (OR ITEMS) OF PROPERTY:
All inventory and Equipment

SIGNATURE(S) OF SECURED PARTY(IES): Second Nat'l Bank of Glasgow BY: Miles Luck, Loan Officer

SIGNATURE(S) OF DEBTOR(S): X Mountainaire Chevrolet, Inc. X Harry Reed, President

MCJL 421 (REV 4/81)

(4) FILE COPY - DEBTOR(S)

Subsequently the debtor changed its corporate name to Bud Long Chevrolet, Inc. by a proper filing with the commissioner of corporations in its state of incorporation. It thereafter went bankrupt. Assume that some of the assets in which the bank has a security interest (the equipment) had been purchased while the debtor was doing business as Mountainaire, but that all of the inventory of cars and parts had completely turned over in the year since the name change. Who takes the assets—the trustee in bankruptcy or the bank?

2. In the foregoing case assume that the principals of Mountainaire had sold their stock to a third party who had merged the Mountainaire Chevrolet into a pre-existing corporation by the name of Bud Long Chevrolet, Inc. Assume further that the bank continued to make loans to Bud Long Chevrolet, but as in the previous case it never filed a new financing statement, nor did it ever execute a new security agreement. Upon the dealer's bankruptcy, the bank is owed $1,000,000 and the collateral is worth $1,500,000. Who gets the collateral?

3. Assume that Mountainaire is merged into Bud Long Chevrolet Inc., but that Bud Long adopts as *its* name, "Mountainaire Chevrolet." Thus, we have a new corporation, but one doing business as, and actually bearing the name of, the old corporation. In that case are the old financing statements in the name of Mountainaire (a preexisting corporation) still effective to protect the security interest of the bank that continues to lend to the new company, Mountainaire? It is hard to see how anyone would be misled by the filing. On the other hand, there is no technical compliance with 9–401 and 9–402, and 9–402(7) does not reach this case.

If the debtor has become a new corporation, namely, Bud Long Chevrolet, the creditor has an additional problem that we consider in Chapter Three. There is no security agreement signed by and no grant of security from the person who is now claimed to be the "debtor." That difficulty may be solved not by the Uniform Commercial Code, but by the state corporation law. By the terms of the merger itself and by operation of law, the corporation into which Mountainaire was merged will have the obligations of Mountainaire, including the obligation on the security agreement. Note that 9–402(7) seems to contemplate more than simply name changes but also changes in "identity and corporate structure." Even so 9–402(7) appears only to cure defects in the filing, not defects in the grant of security under 9–203.

If the problem were changed so there was no merger, but merely the dissolution of a partnership and the transfer of the partnership assets to a corporation, then there might be real trouble under 9–203. That trouble would not necessarily be cured by the state corporation laws.

Note: Post Filing Changes

The immediately preceding problem illustrates some of the most common post filing changes. Doubtless the most common of all is the change in the name of the debtor. This could be a change in the name of an individual debtor, as for example, when a woman takes her husband's name or when she gets divorced and resumes her maiden name. Frequently it occurs with corporate name changes and that difficulty is compounded when there is a corporate merger or something beyond a name change. As we indicate above, section 9–402(7) goes only a small distance into the problem where there is a corporate merger or other change of business organization. The student should not think of this merely as a perfection problem under 9–402, but also as a conveyance problem under 9–203. Sometimes, but not always, the local corporation law will snatch the creditor's chestnuts out of the fire. Clearly problems of this sort should be on the check list any time there is merger, consolidation, or the purchase and sale of a company other than by purchase of the company's stock.

A second common post-perfection change is for the goods to move from one state to another, for the debtor's chief executive office to move from one state to another, or for either to move within a state. In Section 8 below we will examine UCC 9–103. That section and the cases under it provide a detailed body of rules for the interstate movement questions. UCC 9–401(3) deals with intrastate movement of headquarters or collateral.

A third problem, dealt with in Problem 4–2, and considered in detail in Section 3 with respect to proceeds, arises when the collateral itself changes form. At least one court has held that growing plants are farm products, but that when they are moved to the same debtor's retail place for sale, they become inventory. Collateral can be goods when purchased and become fixtures when later attached to real estate. We deal with these problems in Section 5. Section 9–306 on proceeds is a codification of the rules concerning perfection in the most common forms of collateral change.

What if the debtor sells the collateral subject to the secured creditor's security interest or without the secured creditor's assent. Must the secured creditor file anew under the name of the new owner? After all, creditors of the new owner will not be able to find a financing statement covering this collateral by searching under the name of the new owner. The answer is that a new filing is not required. See 9–402(7). The Permanent Editorial Board of the UCC is in accord, as stated in PEB Commentary No. 3—Sections 9–306(2) and 9–402(7).

IN RE COHUTTA MILLS, INC.

United States District Court, Northern District of Georgia, 1989.
108 B.R. 815.

HAROLD L. MURPHY, DISTRICT JUDGE.

FACTS AND PROCEDURAL HISTORY

Bankruptcy trustee Jones appeals the bankruptcy court's decision that the Small Business Administration (SBA) has a perfected security interest in personalty of bankruptcy debtor Cohutta Mills, Inc. The trustee had honored the SBA's claim to a security interest in realty, but objected to the SBA's claim to a security interest in personalty on the ground that it was not perfected.

The bankruptcy court held a hearing on the trustee's objection, where it heard argument from counsel and testimony from a representative of SBA, and received documentary evidence. The proof adduced shows that, in 1977, King's Tuft, Inc. borrowed money from Cohutta Banking Company (Cohutta Bank), and the loan was guaranteed by SBA. Cohutta Bank secured the note with equipment, machinery, and after-acquired property of King's Tuft and filed financing statements that perfected its interests.

In 1979, Cohutta Bank assigned the note and security interests to SBA, and filed statements reflecting those assignments.

Subsequently, to resolve financial problems of King's Tuft, its owners created a new corporation, Cohutta Mills, and transferred King's Tuft's assets to Cohutta Mills. On April 22, 1980, Cohutta Mills entered into an "Assumption Agreement" wherein it assumed King's Tuft's obligations under SBA's note. In the same document, SBA consented to the transfer on the condition that Cohutta Mills assumed those obligations. King's Tuft ceased to exist at that point.[1]

1. At the hearing, the trustee explained the situation as follows:

Cohutta Mills had the same president as King's Tuft and pursued the same line of business at the same location using the same machinery and equipment. SBA did not file new financing statements when the new corporation was formed, although it did send letters to King's Tuft's creditors. Approximately two years later, on August 16, 1982, SBA filed a continuation statement indicating that it retained a security interest in the property of King's Tuft. Cohutta Mills filed for bankruptcy on February 6, 1987.

* * *

THE PARTIES' ARGUMENTS

The trustee argues that SBA's interest is unperfected because SBA filed the continuation statement in the name of King's Tuft instead of Cohutta Mills. He stresses that Cohutta Mills was a new corporation, as opposed to [sic] change of name of King's Tuft, and reasons that a prospective creditor searching the files under the name of Cohutta Mills would not locate SBA's interest.

The trustee argues further that Cohutta Mills assumed SBA's note and *not* the security agreement and that, in any event, a security interest would not attach to after-acquired property of Cohutta Mills. Lastly, the trustee claims the SBA breached a contractual agreement to file financing statements in the name of Cohutta Mills.

SBA responds that it was not required to file a new financing statement when the property was transferred and that its continuation statement was effective. SBA contends further that this court cannot consider the trustee's argument concerning after-acquired property because the trustee did not develop a factual record thereon.

DISCUSSION

1. Did Cohutta Mills acquire King's Tuft's property subject to SBA's security interest?

"A security interest continues in collateral notwithstanding sale, exchange or other disposition thereof unless the disposition was authorized by the secured party in the security agreement or otherwise." Ga.Code Ann. § 11–9–306(2). In the instant case, SBA, the secured party, clearly authorized the disposition of the collateral from King's Tuft to Cohutta Mills. At

"There was an assumption agreement whereby King's Tuft transferred its debt to Cohutta Mills, Inc. And SBA signed off as one of the parties agreeing to this assumption. So, this takes place in April 22 of 1980.

"King's Tuft is no longer in business. They either, you know, went out of business on or about this period of time, dissolved. I checked the bankruptcy file. They did not file bankruptcy."

Hearing Transcript at 11–12. Mr. Turner, a loan specialist with SBA, testified that he understood the purpose of the transaction as follows:

"King's Tuft had encountered financial difficulty * * *. The president, Mr. Browen at that time, * * * was wanting to work out some type of situation. It, to the best of my recollection, was maybe do something in a new corporate name that would cut off some unsecured creditors carrying forward the assets of the King's Tuft Corporation subject to the indebtedness of the SBA loan."

Id. at 22. Mr. Turner testified further that the parties wanted to "restructure" the corporation to "gain a positive net worth position to allow them to obtain working capital financing." Id. at 23–24.

first glance, therefore, it would seem that the security interest did not continue in the collateral.

However, Ga.Code Ann. § 11–9–402(7) provides that "a filed financing statement remains effective with respect to collateral transferred by the debtor even though the secured party knows of or consents to the transfer." This language conflicts with § 9–306(2) insofar as it assumes that a security interest can remain perfected after a transfer even if the secured party has consented to, i.e., authorized, the transfer.

The conflict between these sections has been resolved in different ways by the courts:

> "Several decisions * * * hold that a transfer of collateral is not 'authorized' under § 9–306(2) if the secured party consents to the transaction on the condition that its security interest continues after transfer. See, e.g., Wegner v. Grunewaldt, 821 F.2d 1317, 1320–22 [3 UCC Rep Serv 2d 1700] (8th Cir.1987); Loeb v. Franchise Distributors, Inc. (In re Franchise Systems, Inc.), 46 B.R. 158 [40 UCC Rep Serv 689] (Bankr.N.D.Ga. 1985); Richmond Fixture & Equipment Co. v. Hyman (In re Southern Properties, Inc.), 44 B.R. 838 [40 UCC Rep Serv 1089] (Bankr.E.D.Va. 1984). These courts believe that treating such conditional consent as authorization under § 9–306(2) is highly artificial because to do so would give effect to one aspect of the consent while ignoring the other. They reconcile § 9–306(2) with § 9–402(7) by construing the latter as applying only to such conditional authorization. Other decisions arrive at the opposite result. Some do so because the lien is hidden after the conditional transfer from a potential creditor examining the records unless the record search includes the collateral's entire chain of title. See, e.g., Trustee Services Corp. v. East River Lumber Co., Inc. (In re Hodge Forest Industries, Inc.), 59 B.R. 801 [1 UCC Rep Serv 2d 974] (Bankr.D.Idaho 1986)."

In re Martin Specialty Vehicles,Inc., 87 B.R. 752, 761 [6 UCC Rep Serv 2d 337] (Bankr.D.Mass.1988). The Martin court adopted the former rule for the following reason:

> "Official Comment No. 8 to U.C.C. § 9–402 anticipates the necessity of searching the entire chain of title.[2] * * *. A construction of § 9–306(2) as excluding conditional assent from its operation and of § 9–402(7) as referring to such assent, therefore, not only puts the two statutes in harmony, but is also consistent with Official Comment 8 to § 9–402. This type of conditional consent should be distinguished from the situation where the secured party permits a sale on the condition that it be paid from the proceeds. There the condition relates to an event occurring after the transfer so that it can be logically separated from the consent. See, e.g., Moffat County State Bank v. Producers Livestock Association, 598 F.Supp. 1562 [40 UCC Rep Serv 314] (D.Colo.1984)."

2. Comment 8 reads as follows:

"Subsection (7) also deals with a different problem, namely whether a new filing is necessary where the collateral has been transferred from one debtor to another. This question has been much debated both in pre-Code law and under the Code. This Article now answers the question in the negative. Thus, any person searching the condition of the ownership of a debtor must make inquiry as to the debtor's source of title, and must search in the name of a former owner if circumstances seem to require it."

Id. at 761–62 (footnote added).

This court agrees that §§ 9–306(2) and 9–402(7) are best read as providing that a security interest terminates upon the transfer of the collateral unless the secured creditor unambiguously authorized the disposition subject to its security interest. Cf., Matter of Franchise Systems, 46 B.R. 158, 162 [40 UCC Rep Serv 689] (Bankr.N.D.Ga.1985), citing In re Matto's, Inc., 8 B.R. 485, 489 [30 UCC Rep Serv 1750] (Bankr.E.D.Mich.1981) (a security interest continues in collateral unless it is clear that the parties intended otherwise).

A review of the record reveals that SBA's consent to the transfer of the collateral was conditioned on the continuation of its security interest. The assumption agreement states that SBA was consenting to the "sale and transfer" of the assets subject to the "terms and conditions" of the note, "as modified, restated and renewed" pursuant to the assumption agreement. The agreement modified the note to the extent of redetermining the payment amounts and dates only. The note, which was attached to the assumption agreement as Exhibit A, recites that Cohutta Bank had transferred its "rights, titles, interest, powers and options in, to and under the within promissory note" to SBA. One of those "rights" was that upon nonpayment of the indebtedness, the creditor could proceed against the collateral. "Collateral," in turn, was defined as property hypothecated as security for the note.

The court concludes that all the parties unambiguously agreed that SBA's security interest would continue in the collateral. Cohutta Mills therefore acquired King's Tuft's property subject to SBA's security interests.

2. Was the Filed Financing Statement Effective to Perfect SBA's Security Interest in the Property After the Property had been Transferred to Cohutta Mills?

Under Georgia law, a financing statement, among other things, must give the correct name of the debtor. Ga.Code Ann. § 11–9–402(1). A financing statement that misnames the debtor is nevertheless effective so long as the error is not "seriously misleading." See § 11–9–402(8) ("A financing statement that substantially complies with the requirements of this Code section is effective even though it contains minor errors which are not seriously misleading." Conversely, if the financing statement misnames the debtor "so substantially that it is misleading, the filing has no effect and does not perfect the security interest."

If a financing statement is effective when filed but it becomes seriously misleading due to the subsequent name change or restructuring of the debtor, the secured party, under the second sentence of § 11–9–402(7), is nevertheless protected as to collateral covered through that time and, if applicable under the security agreement, to property acquired by the debtor through four months thereafter. § 11–9–402(7); Uniform Commercial Code § 9–402(7) comment 7 ("[t]he old financing statement, if legally still valid under the circumstances, would continue to protect collateral acquired before the change and * * * acquired within the four months.").

If, on the other hand, the financing statement is effective when filed but the collateral is transferred by the debtor, then, under the third sentence of § 11–9–402(7), the secured party's interest is perfected as to that collateral only. § 11–9–402(7) ("a filed financing statement remains effective with respect to collateral transferred by the debtor even though the secured party knows of or consents to the transfer.").

In sum, therefore, once the secured party files an effective financing statement, it is relieved, to a certain extent, of the burden of correcting misleading errors, and a prospective creditor is obligated to inquire into the debtor's source of title. Taylorville, 445 F.Supp. at 669; Franchise Systems, 46 B.R. at 162, quoting Uniform Commercial Code § 9–402(7) comment 8.

In the instant case, the financing statement was effective when filed in 1977 as it correctly named King's Tuft as the debtor. In 1980, however, when the collateral was transferred to Cohutta Mills, the statement became seriously misleading: because the two names are completely dissimilar, a searcher of Cohutta Mills' interests would not be alerted to inquire into King's Tuft's interests.

The effect of the filed financing statement is more difficult to resolve because the creation of Cohutta Mills was both a transfer of assets and a restructuring of King's Tuft's business to avoid financial problems. The UCC itself does not explain how a court should distinguish between those situations for purposes of § 9–402(7) and, as the Taylorville court noted, "[i]n practically all cases of transfer of secured collateral the transferee would have a different name, identity or corporate organization." Taylorville, 445 F.Supp. at 669.

* * *

In the instant case, based on the facts found by the bankruptcy court, which are not "clearly erroneous," the transaction in question seems closer to a restructuring of the corporation than a transfer of assets. Specifically, the bankruptcy court found that the two corporations had the same president and that Cohutta Mills pursued the same line of business at the same location using the same machinery and equipment as King's Tuft. Rather than merely a transfer of assets between two corporations, King's Tuft essentially became Cohutta Mills as a result of the transactions. The third sentence does not apply because the transfer was not between unrelated parties. See Bank of the West, 852 F.2d at 1168–71.

Under the second sentence of § 9–402(7), therefore, SBA's filed financing statement became seriously misleading upon the transfer of assets to Cohutta Mills, and covered property owned and acquired by Cohutta Mills through four months from the date of transfer only.

Having resolved that issue, the court must determine whether the continuation statement filed in the name of King's Tuft renewed SBA's perfected interest in that property.

* * *

Conclusions

When King's Tuft transferred its assets to Cohutta Mills, Cohutta Mills took the collateral subject to SBA's security interests. SBA's financing statement, which was on file in the name of King's Tuft, became seriously misleading at that time, with the legal consequence that SBA's security interest was perfected as to property owned and acquired by Cohutta Mills through four months after the transfer only.

The continuation statement, filed by SBA in 1982 in the name of King's Tuft, was seriously misleading when it was filed because the debtor at that time was Cohutta Mills. The continuation statement is therefore ineffective, which renders SBA's security interest in Cohutta Mills' property unperfected.

Accordingly, the decision of the bankruptcy court is reversed.

It is so ordered.

Note: Inadequacy of Filing

Your editors start with considerable skepticism about the arguments made by many who challenge financing statements. The most common competitor is the trustee in bankruptcy. The trustee is representing either himself and the unsecured creditors (in a Chapter 11) or the unsecured creditors (in a Chapter 7). We believe that very few of the persons represented by such trustees have been misled to their injury by defective filings. A few may have checked the files; a few more may have discovered what is in the files by reviewing a Dun and Bradstreet report on the debtor, but most would have extended credit to the debtor in blissful disregard of any public filings. Some will have done so with knowledge of the creditor's loan that is now being challenged. Others will have done so without any concern as to whether the debtor borrowed from the creditor in question. In short we suspect that most of those who challenge financing statements as defective have not been injured by reliance upon a defective filing. To the extent that we listen to their challenges and enrich them by avoiding the secured creditors' interests, we do so out of a latent hostility for secured creditors or, more rationally, as a prophylactic measure to encourage secured creditors to file accurately, thus to protect the few who do check the files.

Given this skepticism about the reliance of the challengers (and their representatives, such as the trustee), we would be relatively generous in accepting as valid financing statements that contain marked deviations from perfection requirements. Moreover, we think it appropriate for the court to consider the setting in which the case is to be found in analyzing whether security interests should be avoided or not. It is not too much to ask the secured creditor to determine how searches are made in the particular filing system in which he is filing, and to exercise particular care to insure that his financing statement conforms in those critical respects. Thus, if a search is done by computer and if the computer program is shorted out by periods or spaces in the name, we would expect the secured creditor to be particularly careful about spaces and periods in the name. Moreover, we would apply still different standards in different settings. If the filing is in a rural county in Nebraska where there are a handful of filings each year, and the total number of filings number only in the hundreds, we would accept more slovenly filings by comparison to those we would accept in Los Angeles County that run to hundreds every day and tens of thousands during a year's time. We are also taken with the common-sense approach in the *Glasco* case. If everyone is put on notice by a filing though it is not exemplary, shouldn't that be enough?

Most who study from this casebook will live to see all of the filing records computerized. Once the records are computerized, it will be possible to improve searches merely by modifying the searching program. Currently programs are in existence that will search under the name given by the searcher and by a variety of other spellings of the same name, and by phonetic spellings of it. Doubtless we have not seen the last of such program enhancement. As these search programs become more sophisticated and more likely to uncover even defective filings, such filings should be accepted as fulfilling their function.

One should not overlook the sections located further in the bowels of part 4 of Article 9, namely UCC 9–403 through 9–408. Particularly important is UCC 9–403. It tells, among other things, that a financing statement is good for a period of five years, and that debtor's insolvency proceedings in effect continue a filing. Moreover it has some intricate rules about continuation statements and their effect. Other sections provide for termination (9–404), assignment (9–405), and there is even a provision that alleviates the anxiety of one who really thinks he has a lease but files nevertheless (9–408). To get some understanding of the problems that untimeliness can cause consider the following case.

IN RE ADAM

United States Bankruptcy Court, District of North Dakota (1989).
96 B.R. 249.

Memorandum and Order

William A. Hill, Bankruptcy Judge.

The Chapter 7 trustee, armed with the avoiding powers of section 544 of the Bankruptcy Code, commenced the instant adversary proceeding on July 19, 1988, seeking to avoid Farmers Home Administration's (FmHA) security interest believed to be infirm by virtue of a continuation statement that failed to conform to the requirements of N.D.Cent.Code § 41–09–42(3) (U.C.C. § 9–403(3)). In issue are the cash proceeds stemming from the sale of the secured collateral including farm machinery and livestock. The parties have agreed that the issue as framed by the pleadings may be determined on stipulated facts, exhibits and briefs.

Findings of Fact

FmHA perfected a security interest in the Debtors' livestock, supplies, farm equipment, inventory and other farm products by filing a UCC–1 financing statement on January 27, 1971, as document file number 143390. Effectiveness was properly continued by the filing of continuation statements on September 8, 1975, and again on September 11, 1980. Both of these continuation statements refer to the original financing statement file number and the trustee does not challenge their validity.

On April 18, 1985, a third continuation statement was filed. However, instead of referring to the original financing statement by its filing number, it bore a file number referencing the 1980 continuation statement, to-wit: "This statement refers to original Financing Statement *# 14851* filed with *Register of Deeds* Date Filed *9–11–80*". The 1980 continuation statement referred to by the 1985 continuation statement does contain the original financing statement file number as well as its filing date.

The Debtors filed for relief under Chapter 7 on June 19, 1986.

CONCLUSIONS OF LAW

1.

The effectiveness of a filed financing statement lapses upon the expiration of five years from the date of filing and the security interest becomes unperfected unless a continuation statement is filed prior to lapse. N.D.Cent.Code § 41–09–41(2) (U.C.C. § 9–402(2)). *In re Hilyard Drilling Co., Inc.*, 840 F.2d 596, 599 (8th Cir.1988). N.D.Cent.Code § 41–09–42(3) (U.C.C. § 9–403(3)) provides:

> "A continuation statement may be filed by the secured party within six months prior to the expiration of the five-year period specified in subsection 2. Any such continuation statement must be signed by the secured party, identifying the original statement by file number, and state that the original statement is still effective * * *. Upon timely filing of the continuation statement, the effectiveness of the original statement is continued for five years after the last date to which the statement was effective.* * *"

The trustee charges that FmHA's security interest lapsed because it failed to conform to U.C.C. § 9–403(3) requirements in several respects. First, that it does not recite the original Financing Statement file number and secondly, that it was filed earlier than six months prior to the expiration of the original five-year period, as continued. FmHA argues that despite these perceived infirmities, the continuation statement substantially complies with the section 9–403(3) requirements and the infirmities ought to be regarded as "harmless error".

N.D.Cent.Code § 41–09–41(8) (U.C.C. § 9–402(8)) provides that a "financing statement substantially complying with the requirements of this section is effective even though it contains minor errors which are not seriously misleading". Minor errors which are not seriously misleading will not invalidate a financing statement or continuation statement which otherwise is in substantial compliance with statutory requirements. The materiality of minor errors in a continuation statement becomes relevant only in those situations where the continuation statement, on its face, substantially complies with section 9–403(3). Compliance with this section requires that a continuation statement (1) be filed within six months prior to the expiration of the original filing; (2) contain the signature of the secured party; (3) identify the original statement by file number; (4) state that original statement is still effective. If any of the foregoing are obviously missing, then there is no substantial compliance and the omission is fatal to the continuation statement's effectiveness. In the case of *In re Hilyard Drilling Co., Inc.,* 60 B.R. 500 (Bankr.W.D.Ark.1986), *aff'd,* 74 B.R. 125 (W.D.Ark. 1986), a secured creditor attempted to qualify a second financing statement as a continuation of an earlier financing statement. The court, noting the second financing statement failed to refer to the earlier financing statement, failed to state that the original financing statement was still effective and had not been filed within six months of the original financing statement, said that the second financing statement did not substantially comply with U.C.C. § 9–403(3) and thus could not come within the "harmless error" exception of section 9–402(8).

2.

Although the 1985 continuation statement in issue did not bear the original financing statement file number, it did bear the file number of the immediately preceding continuation statement which, in turn, bore file number as well as date of filing of the original financing statement. The reason for requiring a filing number reference is, of course, so that a party searching the record will be directed to the original financing statement. Several courts, considering erroneous file numbers on continuation statements, have held them to be nonetheless in substantial compliance with § 9–403(3) because the requisite notice is provided. In *In re Edwards Equipment Co.,* 46 B.R. 689, 692 (Bankr.E.D.Okla.1985), the continuation statement bore the file number of an amended financing statement rather than the original. The amended financing statement did, however, refer to the original financing statement by the correct file number. The court, pointing to the "notice concept", held that the error was not misleading because, "a creditor searching the index for this particular debtor is assuredly provided with information sufficient to be directed back to the original financing statement." Similarly, in *In re Vincent Gaines Implement Co., Inc.,* 71 B.R. 14 (Bankr.E.D.Ark.1986), a continuation statement referencing the original financing statement by an erroneous file number was found to be not seriously misleading because a searcher coming upon the continuation statement would be placed on notice to search the debtor index whereupon the correct file number would be discovered. Indeed, the Eighth Circuit in its appellate decision in the *Hilyard* case, *supra,* intimated that so long as a continuation statement gives an indication that it was filed for the purpose of continuing an earlier financing statement and provides some linkage to the original, it is in substantial compliance with U.C.C. § 9–403(3) and the omission of the original file number is harmless error. *In re Hilyard Drilling Co., Inc.,* 840 F.2d at 600. Because the 1985 continuation statement clearly references the previous 1980 continuation statement which, in turn, contains a file number reference to the original financing statement, it does provide definite linkage to the original financing statement sufficient to put an inquiring searcher on notice. In this respect the 1985 continuation statement is in substantial compliance with U.C.C. § 9–403(3) and the incorrect file number is not seriously misleading.

3.

The original financing statement was filed on January 27, 1971, with subsequent continuation statements being filed on September 8, 1975, September 11, 1980, and April 18, 1985. FmHA asserts that the previous continuation statement would have expired on September 11, 1985, and hence its April 18, 1985, continuation was within six months of expiration. FmHA in making this argument misconstrues the statutory method for calculating the time period necessary for effective continuation statement filings. Section 9–403(3) requires that a continuation statement be filed within six months prior to the expiration of five years from the date of filing of the *original financing statement.* Succeeding continuation statements must be filed within six months prior to the expiration of the original financing statement as continued. Cases are uniform in holding that extension periods occasioned by continuation statements do not commence on the filing date of a prior continuation statement, but rather from conclusion of the initial five-year financing statement period and the *end* of any subsequent five-year extension period. To be effective, a continuation statement must be filed within the six-month time period prescribed by section 9–403(3). The requirement is unambiguous and renders a prematurely filed continuation statement ineffective. FmHA calculates the five-year period from the date of the preceding 1980 continuation statement was filed which is incorrect. Commencing with the original financing statement filed January 27, 1971, each subsequent five-year period must be fully run out without regard to the filing date of intervening continuation statements. Thus, the original financing statement ran to January 27, 1976, continued by the September 8, 1975 continuation statement to January 27, 1981, and finally continued by the September 11, 1980 continuation statement to January 27, 1986. In order to effectively continue the financing statement beyond January 27, 1986, the continuation statement had to have been filed within six months preceding January 27, 1986, which is July 27, 1985. The April 28, 1985 filing was premature and clearly fails to meet one of the requirements of U.C.C. § 9–403(3). This failure cannot be overcome by resorting to U.C.C. § 9–402(8) because by this failure the continuation statement was not in substantial compliance with section 9–403(3). The effect of FmHA's failure to file its continuation statement within six months prior to the expiration of the original five-year period as run out by the 1975 and 1980 continuation statements renders it ineffective. *See Hilyard, supra.*

The Debtors' Chapter 7 petition was filed on June 19, 1986, and as of that date the trustee became vested with the status of a lien creditor with priority over any security interest that was unperfected as of that date. FmHA's security interest was unperfected on June 19, 1986, because the effectiveness of its financing statement lapsed on January 27, 1986, due to its failure to file its continuation statement in conformity with U.C.C. § 9–403(3).

Accordingly, the trustee has a first lien in the Debtors' livestock, supplies, farm equipment, inventory and other farm products which is paramount to the interest of FmHA which is unperfected and avoided. Further, that the trustee, in consequence of his priority position, shall be entitled to possession of all collateral and the proceeds thereof.

Judgment may be entered accordingly.

So ordered.

BOSTWICK–BRAUN COMPANY v. OWENS

United States District Court, Eastern District of Wisconsin, 1986.
634 F.Supp. 839.

DECISION AND ORDER

REYNOLDS, CHIEF JUDGE.

The plaintiff Bostwick–Braun Company ("Bostwick–Braun") seeks a declaratory judgment, pursuant to 28 U.S.C. §§ 2201, 2202 and Fed.Rule of Civ.Proc. 57, that it has a security interest in the personal property of a partnership called JoDan's Pro Hardware superior to the security interest of the defendant F & M Bank of Slinger ("F & M") and directing defendant Clifton G. Owens, Trustee in bankruptcy of the partnership, to disburse to plaintiff all proceeds from a sale of the property. Plaintiff is an Ohio corporation whose principal place of business is in Toledo, Ohio. Defendant F & M is a Wisconsin corporation whose principal place of business is in Slinger, Wisconsin. Defendant Trustee Clifton G. Owens is a resident of Wisconsin. The amount in controversy exceeds $10,000 exclusive of costs. This Court has jurisdiction, therefore, pursuant to 28 U.S.C. § 1332(a).

Bostwick–Braun moved for summary judgment in this court on August 28, 1985. That motion is fully briefed and ready for decision. The Court will grant Bostwick–Braun's motion.

Facts

On February 21, 1977, F & M Bank of Slinger properly filed at the Secretary of State's office a financing statement covering the personal property of Daniel Nordeen and Joanne Nordeen, partners in JoDan's Pro Hardware. On January 15, 1982, or almost four years and eleven months after filing its original financing statement, F & M filed another original financing statement covering the same personal property covered in its February 21, 1977, filing. F & M's January 15, 1982, filing did not refer in any way to the prior filing. F & M did not file at any time a document called a continuation statement with respect to its original 1977 filing.

On November 3, 1981, Bostwick–Braun properly filed at the Secretary of State's office a financing statement covering the same personal property of the JoDan Pro Hardware partnership.

On May 7, 1984, the partnership filed for voluntary bankruptcy under Chapter 7 of the Bankruptcy Code, 11 U.S.C. § 701 *et seq.* Both F & M and Bostwick–Braun filed claims against the estate as secured creditors.

On August 16, 1984, Trustee Clifton G. Owens notified parties in interest that he intended to pay over to Bostwick–Braun in satisfaction of its claim all the proceeds from a sale of the partnership's personal property. F & M filed an objection to the Trustee's proposal on August 24, 1984. The Trustee deposited proceeds of the sale, approximately $56,000, in a short-term, interest-bearing account pending determination of the two creditors' conflicting claims. Bostwick–Braun's and F & M's claims each exceed the proceeds of the sale.

F & M alleges, and for the purposes of this motion the Court will assume, that Bostwick–Braun had actual knowledge of F & M's prior security interest in the personal property of the debtor partnership.

Legal Analysis

While F & M had a perfected security interest in the personal property of the Nordeen partners before February 21, 1982, it allowed that interest to lapse by failing to file a continuation statement pursuant to Wis.Stats. § 409.403(3). F & M's filing on January 15, 1982, of a second original financing statement did not constitute substantial compliance with the statute. Bostwick–Braun's actual and constructive knowledge of F & M's prior security interest does not entitle F & M to equitable relief from the statute's requirements. Finally, Bostwick–Braun had perfected its security interest in the partners' personal property before F & M's interest lapsed, and since Bostwick-Braun's interest remained perfected at the time of the lapse, Bostwick-Braun's interest became senior to F & M's. Bostwick-Braun is, therefore, entitled to summary judgment on its claim to the proceeds from the sale of the partners' personal property.

Wis.Stats. § 409.403, U.C.C. § 9-403, provides that a security interest may be perfected for a five-year period by the filing of a financing statement and the tender of a filing fee. Section 409.403(2) provides as follows:

> [A] filed financing statement is effective for a period of 5 years from the date of filing. The effectiveness of a filed financing statement lapses on the expiration of the 5-year period unless a continuation statement is filed prior to the lapse * * * Upon lapse the security interest becomes unperfected, unless it is perfected without filing. If the security interest becomes unperfected upon lapse, it is deemed to have been unperfected as against a person who became a purchaser or lien creditor before lapse.

The original filing can be made effective for additional five-year periods by the filing of a continuation statement. Section 409.403(3) provides as follows:

> A continuation statement may be filed by the secured party within 6 months prior to the expiration of the 5-year period specified in sub. (2). Any such continuation statement must be signed by the secured party, identify the original statement by file number and state that the original statement is still effective * * *

The statute requires continuation statements to identify a still effective original filing so as to avoid confusion between competing claimants since priority among claims goes to the party who first files an original financing statement. The filing, therefore, of a second financing statement which fails to refer to an effective original filing does not bring a creditor into substantial compliance with § 409.403(3). *In re Hays,* 47 B.R. 546, 549 (Bankr. N.D.Ohio 1985); *Eastern Indiana Production Credit Ass'n v. Farmers State Bank,* 31 Ohio App.2d 252, 387 S.E.2d 824, 11 U.C.C.Rep.Serv. 664, 667 (1972).

Any notice of F & M's once perfected security interest Bostwick-Braun may have had as a junior secured creditor is irrelevant to the effect of F & M's failure to continue its interest. All courts which have decided the issue agree that, since the purpose of statutory filing requirements is, in most instances, to resolve notice disputes consistently and predictably by reference to constructive or statutory notice alone, U.C.C. § 9-403(3) precludes consideration of a junior creditor's actual notice of a now lapsed prior filing by a competing senior creditor. *Frank v. James Talcott, Inc.,* 692 F.2d 734, 739 (11th Cir.1982); *State Sav. Bank v. Onawa State Bank,* 368 N.W.2d 161, 164 (Iowa 1985); *Matter of Reda, Inc.,* 54 B.R. 871, 877-78 (Bankr.N.D.Ill. 1985).

F & M complains, understandably, that this result amounts to a windfall for Bostwick-Braun and appeals to the Court's equitable powers to reverse the effect of Wisconsin law. However, because F & M is a party accustomed to dealing with the requirements of commercial law, the Court cannot be as sympathetic to its appeal as it might otherwise be. The Court must be mindful too of interests beyond those represented here.

> Efforts by courts to fashion equitable solutions to mitigate the hardship on particular creditors of literal application of statutory filing requirements would have the deleterious effect of undermining the reliance which can be placed upon them. The harm would be more serious than the occasional harshness resulting from strict enforcement.

Uniroyal, Inc. v. Universal Tire & Auto Supply, 557 F.2d 22, 23 (1st Cir.1977); *see also Security Nat. Bank v. Dentsply Professional,* 617 P.2d 1340, 1343 (Okla.1980).

The fact that F & M's perfected security interest lapsed only affects the priority of F & M's interest with respect to third parties having perfected security interests themselves. F & M challenges Bostwick–Braun's claimed security interest on the basis that the text of the promissory note executed by Joanne and Daniel Nordeen on October 1, 1981, identifies the promissors as "C. DANIEL NORDEEN and JOANNE NORDEEN, d/b/a JoDan's Pro Hardware." Therefore, argues F & M, the note reflects only individual debt, not debt of the partnership, JoDan's Pro Hardware. F & M cites no authority in support of its argument.

F & M's reading of the October 1, 1981, promissory note is simply mistaken. The note is signed "JoDAN'S PRO HARDWARE By: (signature) C. Daniel Nordeen, Partner and Individually and By: (signature) Joanne Nordeen, Partner and Individually." There can hardly be serious dispute that the promissory note and security agreement on their face evince an intention by the parties to obligate the partnership. F & M has raised neither legal nor factual grounds to rebut such prima facie evidence. The note is, therefore, sufficient evidence of the partnership's debt.

ORDER

It is therefore ordered that the motion for summary judgment of plaintiff Bostwick–Braun Company is granted.

Note

The case makes clear that 9–403(2) allows an extension of perfection if a continuation statement is filed prior to lapse. But section 9–403(2) recognizes only continuation statements filed within the six month period prior to expiration of the original filing. To understand the reason for that rule put yourself in the position of a secretary of state. Absent such a rule, the filing officer would be inundated by countless continuation statements filed by nervous secured creditors who might find it in their interest to spend $5.00 to do a refiling every year rather than risk the possibility of letting any financing lapse.

Occasionally secured creditors file new financing statements instead of continuation statements. Such statements are effective to perfect the security interest from the time of filing, but they do not continue the old perfection. Superficially, one can distinguish the continuation statement from the financing statement because the former but not the latter makes explicit reference to an earlier filing. Still it is hard to construct a hypothetical in which a subsequent secured creditor would be informed by the continuation statement but would be misled to his injury by a newly filed financing statement. If the second secured creditor filed after the improper renewal, he is subordinate. If he filed after the first secured creditor's first filing and before the renewal, he has not yet been misled.

If that is not too clear, think about the following case. Secured Creditor 1 files on January 1, 1980; on January 1, 1984 Secured Creditor 2 checks the files, discovers Secured Creditor 1's filing and files itself. In December, 1984, Secured Creditor 1 files a new financing statement (when it should have filed a continuation statement instead). Secured Creditor 1 will be subordinate to Secured Creditor 2, but why? Secured Creditor 2 could have been misled to its injury by the mistake of Secured Creditor 1 only if Secured Creditor 2 made a second search, discovered the new financing statement (where there should have been a continuation statement), and concluded that it had priority because it was first to file. Thus, the only reliance we can imagine is a case in which the second creditor searches not merely when it does its first filing, but subsequently, or, having never searched in the first place and not having discovered the original filing, concludes upon a second search that it has priority as to the second advance.

Even when Secured Creditor 1 files a financing statement instead of a continuation statement one might argue that 9–312(5) gives the first creditor priority because it filed first and thereafter there was never a period when there was neither a filing nor perfection. See 9–312(5)(a).

But perhaps all of this is beside the point. Perhaps the only reason for disregarding a second financing statement is to protect the secretary of state against multiple filings of financing statements.

Questions

1. Even if the secured creditor in the *In re Adam* case had made the mistake that the secured creditor made in *Bostwick–Braun,* it would not have suffered, true?

2. What policy supports a rigid rule that prohibits either the substitution of the financing statement for a continuation statement or a provision that makes an early filed continuation statement invalid?

3. Assume that late in 1982 F & M's employee discovered the mistake and came to the filing officer with a continuation statement. He explained that there had been a mistake and asked that the continuation statement be substituted for the financing statement.

a. Would the filing officer accept the continuation statement?

b. Should the filing officer?

c. Is it ethical for a lawyer to make this request on behalf of F & M?

Statements of Continuation, Partial Release, Assignment, Termination or Amendment—Form UCC–3—1972 Illinois Article 9

STATE OF ILLINOIS
UNIFORM COMMERCIAL CODE
STATEMENTS OF CONTINUATION, PARTIAL RELEASE, ASSIGNMENT, ETC. – FORM UCC-3

INSTRUCTIONS:
1. PLEASE TYPE this form. Fold only along perforation for mailing.
2. Remove Secured Party and Debtor copies and send other 3 copies with interleaved carbon paper to the filing officer.
3. Enclose filing fee.
4. If the space provided for any item(s) on the form is inadequate the item(s) should be continued on additional sheets, preferably 5" x 8" or 8" x 10". Only one copy of such additional sheets need be presented to the filing officer with a set of three copies of Form UCC-3. Long schedules of collateral, etc., may be on any size paper that is convenient for the secured party.
5. At the time of filing, filing officer will return third copy as an acknowledgement.

This STATEMENT is presented to THE FILING OFFICER for filing pursuant to the Uniform Commercial Code.

Debtor(s) (Last Name First) and address(es)	Secured Party(ies) and address(es)	For Filing Officer (Date, Time, Number, and Filing Office)

This Statement refers to original Financing Statement No. ____________

Date filed: ____________, 19 ______ Filed with ____________

A. ☐ CONTINUATION..... The original financing statement between the foregoing Debtor and Secured Party, bearing the file number shown above, is still effective.

B. ☐ PARTIAL RELEASE.. From the collateral described in the financing statement bearing the file number shown above, the Secured Party releases the property indicated below.

C. ☐ ASSIGNMENT.......... The Secured Party certifies that the Secured Party has assigned to the Assignee whose name and address is shown below, Secured Party's rights under the financing statement bearing the file number shown above in the property indicated below.

D. ☐ TERMINATION........ The Secured Party certifies that the Secured Party no longer claims a security interest under the financing statement bearing the file number shown above.

E. ☐ AMENDMENT.......... The financing statement bearing the above file number is amended.
☐ To show the Secured Party's new address as indicated below.
☐ To show the Debtor's new address as indicated below.
☐ As set forth below:

____________ (Debtor)
(Signature of Debtor, if required)

____________ (Secured Party)

Dated ____________, 19 ______

By ____________
(Signature of Secured Party)

(1) Filing Officer Copy - Alphabetical   This form of Financing Statement is approved by the Secretary of State.
STANDARD FORM - UNIFORM COMMERCIAL CODE FORM UCC-3 REV 4-73 [B1142]

Problem 4–5

Bank Florida takes a security interest, makes a loan, and perfects the security interest in certain of debtor's equipment by a filing on December 1, 1984. On December 1, 1988, Tampa Bank & Trust takes and perfects a security interest in the same and additional equipment. Both security interests are properly perfected by filing and each security agreement is properly drawn to include after-acquired property. Tampa Bank & Trust is not a purchase money lender.

1. On March 1, 1989, Bank Florida files a continuation statement; on May 1, 1989, debtor goes into bankruptcy. In a bankruptcy trial late in 1990 who will be held to have priority in the equipment between Bank Florida and Tampa Bank & Trust?

2. What outcome if debtor does not file its bankruptcy petition until April 1990?

SECTION 5. PERFECTION IN FIXTURES

To understand the rules concerning perfection by filing with respect to fixtures, one must read UCC 9–313 together with UCC 9–401 and 9–402. Perhaps a small bit of history will help explain what will otherwise seem like a highly confusing set of rules. Under the 1962 version of Article 9, one first had to determine whether goods had become fixtures or not. If they had become fixtures, one filed a financing statement in the local office where a real mortgage on the property to which the fixtures were attached would have been filed. If he guessed wrong and the goods proved to be equipment and thus called for a statewide filing, the secured creditor was unperfected. The theory of the local filing was to include that filing in the real estate records and thus to alert parties who dealt with the real estate subsequent to the attachment of the fixture claim.

Unfortunately, nothing in the 1962 Code explicitly stated that this filing as to fixtures should be indexed *in the real estate records* to enable the real estate searcher to find it. Apparently, in some filing offices it was so indexed, and in others it was not. Moreover, if the creditor guessed wrong about the status of an item as a fixture or not, he was wholly unperfected if he filed in the wrong spot. Filing at the state capital was totally ineffective as to an item that later proved to be a fixture, and a local filing was totally ineffective as to an item that proved to be equipment.

In the 1972 version of Article 9, the drafters addressed these problems. First, they concluded that a secured creditor with an interest in a fixture should be offered two levels of protection. If he chose to be protected against subsequent *personal property* lenders, he could file as though the fixture were personal property (an ordinary Article 9 filing) and the Code would grant him protection. In the next chapter we will see how UCC 9–313(4) together with the other provisions of UCC 9–313 and 9–401 produced that result. If he also sought protection against subsequent *real estate* claimants such as purchasers and mortgagees, he was required to do a "fixture" filing. Fixture filing was defined in UCC 9–313 and provided for in UCC 9–401 and 9–402. The Code provides for the indexing of such a filing in the real estate records to enable a subsequent real estate searcher to find the fixture filing.

Those ignorant of this history, and even some who know of it, can easily read UCC 9–313, 9–401 and 9–402 to mean that one must do a fixture filing or be totally unperfected as to a fixture. That is not correct. Read UCC 9–401 with care. Note section 9–401(1)(b) (second alternative) provides for a local filing when "the collateral is timber to be cut or is minerals * * * or when the financing statement is filed *as a fixture filing.*" Note it provides always for local filing as to timber and minerals, but for a local filing as to fixtures only when there is "fixture filing," not in every case when the collateral is "fixtures." Thus it contemplates, and indeed permits, a filing as to fixtures under (1)(c) "in all other cases." If one wishes to have a perfected security interest (for protection against a subsequent trustee in bankruptcy under UCC 9–313(4)(d)), he may file as though the goods were equipment or consumer goods or whatever else they are if not fixtures (an ordinary Article 9 filing), and so have an interest with limited perfection, and limited protection, namely, protection against non-real estate payments. If all of that is not clear, read UCC 9–313 and 9–401 again.

What is a fixture? Section 9–313(1)(a) states that goods are fixtures "when they become so related to the particular real estate that an interest in them arises under the real estate law * * *." To one ignorant of the real estate law of a particular jurisdiction, that definition is useless. Even for one who has read the cases in Arkansas or New York or Florida, the definition is not likely to be helpful because the cases are likely to be in disarray. Only a foolish lawyer thinks he knows a fixture "when he sees one." While it is true that the size, weight, mode of attachment and degree of difficulty in removing a good attached in some way to the real estate are all likely to have an impact on a court's judgment whether a particular item has become a fixture or not, in thirty minutes in the library one can turn up cases that would call swimming pools goods, not fixtures, and define entirely mobile business machines as fixtures. The lesson for the planner is clear: the planner should never concern himself with trying to classify collateral as a fixture or not as a fixture! If there is some possibility that a good is a fixture, one should file as if it were *and* as if it were not.

After the fact (when *someone else* has not followed the advice given above) lawyers and judges must decide whether something is a fixture. Cases often state that the "intention of the parties determines whether something is a fixture." That test leaves a good deal to be desired, for the intention expressed at trial will invariably be self serving. Intentions expressed prior to the dispute are likely to be in a private document, not available for the observation of third parties who are asserting rights based upon the status of the collateral.

A few states follow the so called "institutional" doctrine for classifying collateral as fixtures. According to that doctrine, the proper test is to determine whether the item in question is somehow integral to the operation of something built on the real estate irrespective of its ease of movement. For example, a modest sized but critical machine important to the operation of a manufacturing or processing facility would be a fixture. Because UCC 9–313(1)(a) essentially incorporates the state common law defining fixture for the purpose of Article 9, one will have to look at the cases in the state in which the item is located to decide whether something is or is not a fixture. Unfortunately few courts have adopted the proposal of White and Summers which would have at least the virtue of certainty, if nothing else: "Anything that cannot be moved by one man in one hour armed with a crescent wrench is a fixture." The ensuing case grapples with the question how one determines whether an item is a fixture.

CUMMINGS, INC. v. BEARDSLEY

Supreme Court of Arkansas, 1980.
271 Ark. 596, 609 S.W.2d 66.

JOHN F. STROUD, JUSTICE. This is a suit filed in chancery court to foreclose the lien securing the balance of the purchase price and installation charge for two large illuminated motel and restaurant signs. Appellees filed a Motion for Summary Judgment which was granted by the trial court. We affirm the Chancellor as we agree that he properly granted the motion resulting in a dismissal of appellant's complaint.

In 1973, appellant contracted with Erect-O-Therm Structures, Inc., to fabricate and install two large signs on certain premises owned by Erect-O-Therm in Prescott, Arkansas. The signs were to advertise the location of the Stockholm Restaurant and Check Inn Motel. To secure the unpaid balance of the purchase price, Erect-O-Therm granted appellant a security interest in the signs by the execution of a security agreement describing them. A financing statement was filed with the Secretary of State of

Arkansas in 1974. The security agreement between appellant and Erect-O-Therm also provided that the signs were not to be so affixed or related to realty as to become a part of the realty. The larger of the two signs was hung some 80 feet from the ground on steel poles anchored in a concrete foundation four feet deep by 16 feet wide by 20 feet long. The smaller sign is supported by steel poles which rise 12 feet from their concrete foundation.

Subsequently, Erect-O-Therm experienced financial difficulties and apparently lost the motel and restaurant property, including the two signs, to Union Planters Bank of Memphis by virtue of the bank's foreclosure of a mortgage on that realty. Appellees Conrad and Lillemore Beardsley then acquired the property from Union Planters. On January 31, 1979, appellant brought this foreclosure suit against appellees for the unpaid balance of the purchase price in the amount of $20,355.35, plus 10% of that amount as attorney's fees, possession of the signs and a deficiency judgment against appellees for any deficit remaining after the proceeds of a resale of the signs are applied to the indebtedness. Appellees denied the material allegations of appellant's complaint by specifically alleging that they had not purchased the signs from appellant nor entered into any agreement with appellant, that they had no knowledge of any indebtedness for the signs nor had they assumed any such debt, and that the financing statement was filed in the wrong place. Appellees also filed a third party complaint against Union Planters, not involved in this appeal, where they allege that they should have judgment over against the bank for any damages they suffer in this suit inasmuch as the bank represented to them that the property was free of liens and encumbrances. Some nine months thereafter, appellees filed a motion for summary judgment which was submitted on the pleadings, deposition of an officer of the appellant company, deposition of appellee Conrad Beardsley, and briefs. From a granting of the motion appellants bring this appeal, urging that the court erred in granting the motion for summary judgment.

It is well-settled that summary judgment should be granted only when a review of the pleadings, depositions and other filings reveals that there is no genuine issue as to any material fact and the moving party is entitled to judgment as a matter of law. Rule 56, Arkansas Rules of Civil Procedure. In the present case, in its order of January 24, 1980, the trial court found as follows:

> 1. The Defendants, Conrad Beardsley and Lillemore Beardsley, did not purchase the signs and related property referred to in the complaint from the Plaintiff, and there is no genuine issue as to this fact.
>
> 2. The Defendants, Conrad Beardsley and Lillemore Beardsley, are not personally liable to the Plaintiff under the security agreement referred to in the complaint since these Defendants were not a party thereto and have not assumed the indebtedness referred to in said security agreement, and there is no genuine issue as to this fact.
>
> 3. As between the Plaintiff and Erect-O-Therm Structures, Inc., those parties agreed that the signs in question were not, and would not become fixtures, and so as between them the signs are not fixtures, but as between the Plaintiff and the Defendants, the signs, which include the supporting pipes, are fixtures. The Defendants were entitled to rely

on the filings in the Nevada County Circuit Clerk's office at the time they purchased property on which the signs are located on September 28, 1976. Ark.Stat.Ann. § 85–9–401 (addendum 1961) is the applicable statutory section since the filings involved in this case were made prior to the effective date of the 1973 amendment to Article 9 of the Uniform Commercial Code, and thereunder the proper place to file a security instrument in order to perfect securing interest was in the office where a mortgage on the real estate concerned would be filed or recorded. The Plaintiff filed its financing statement with the Secretary of State and not in the office of the Circuit Clerk of Nevada County, Arkansas, being the County where the real estate is located, and thus did not properly perfect its security interest in the signs as between it and the Defendants.

4. There are no genuine issues as to any material fact as between the Plaintiff and the Defendants, Conrad Beardsley and Lillemore Beardsley, d/b/a Check Inn and Check Inn; consequently, these Defendants are entitled to a judgment as a matter of law.

As to the trial court's first and second rulings, we agree there clearly is no genuine issue as to those matters. The copy of the security agreement attached to appellant's complaint reflects that the signs were purchased by Erect-O-Therm, not appellees, and that appellees were not a party to the agreement. There is nothing in the record to indicate, not even as an allegation, that appellees knew of or assumed the indebtedness when they purchased the motel and restaurant. The third ruling of the trial court, pertaining to the characterization of the signs as fixtures, is the only holding which appellant disputes. The trial court ruled that as between appellant and Erect-O-Therm the signs were not fixtures because of the provision in the security agreement which stated the signs would not be considered part of the realty. However, the trial court further held that, inasmuch as it was undisputed that appellees were not parties to the security agreement and were without knowledge of the aforementioned provision, the signs were fixtures as between appellant and appellees and there is no genuine issue as to that fact. These large signs anchored deep in concrete were so clearly fixtures, appellees had the right to rely on the records in the office of the Circuit Clerk of Nevada County, where filings covering fixtures are to be made, to determine if a lien was in existence at the time of their purchase. A good faith filing made in the wrong place (in this case the office of the Secretary of State) was not constructive notice to appellees as it is notice only to "any person who has knowledge of the contents of such financing statement." Ark.Stat.Ann. § 85–9–401(2) (addendum 1961).

* * * As noted previously, it was undisputed in the record that appellees were not in any way involved with the purchase of the signs from appellant; that they had not assumed the indebtedness referred to in the security agreement; that they had no knowledge of the agreement between appellant and Erect-O-Therm; and that appellant had not filed the financing statement in the Nevada County Circuit Clerk's office prior to appellees' purchase. As appellant failed to file the financing statement in Nevada County, as the security agreement was not determinative of the rights [and] obligations of appellees, and as the security agreement was the only proof offered by appellant to support his contention that summary judgment

should not lie, we cannot say that there was a genuine issue as to any material fact or that the trial court erred in granting appellees' Motion for Summary Judgment.

Affirmed. [Dissent omitted.]

Problem 4–6

1. Client plans to sell a radio transmission tower (pursuant to a "lease," in fact a security agreement), attached to the ground by guy wires covering eight acres and put on a concrete base that measures 10′ by 10′ and was 8′ deep. Would the radio tower be a fixture? Would you give your written opinion that it is?

2. In many cases courts state that if an item is found to be a fixture, the creditor will have to do a fixture filing in order to perfect its security interest to any degree. That statement is not correct. Consider the following examples by reading UCC 9–313 and 9–402 and determine in which cases the creditor is perfected and those in which he is not.

(a) Assume the court finds that the radio tower is a fixture and that the creditor has filed a UCC–1 with the Secretary of State's office. Debtor goes into bankruptcy. Does the trustee take the radio tower?

(b) Assume that the creditor does a fixture filing, the debtor goes bankrupt and the radio tower is found to be a fixture. Who wins now?

(c) Assume that the creditor does a fixture filing, but the radio tower is found not to be a fixture and that the debtor goes into bankruptcy. Who wins now?

What do you take to be the moral of this story? This is a wonderful case for the operation of Peskind's Law, not so? (This law says: "File everywhere possibly required.")

SECTION 6. PERFECTION BY POSSESSION

A. *What Is Possession?*

Section 9–305 authorizes perfection as to certain assets by the creditor's possession. These are letters of credit, goods, instruments, money, negotiable documents, and chattel paper. UCC 9–304(1) requires possession in certain circumstances. The Code does not define what is "satisfactory possession," but that issue is seldom presented. For example, in a field warehouse setting in which perfection depends upon possession by the field warehouseman and where the debtor's employees are permitted access to the warehouse goods, substantial questions about possession can easily arise. However, in modern practice a wise creditor will not rely solely upon the field warehouseman's possession for perfection. The creditor will have filed a financing statement as well. Whether the creditor's possession suffices is rarely a serious issue. In the most common pledge cases, the creditor bank plainly has possession of a certificate of deposit or other instrument. In other cases, the creditor locks up the debtor's airplane or the pawn shop has stuck the watch in a safe.

In at least one area, however, issues of possession may be significant. What, for example, of the case of an escrow agent who has possession of money or instruments on behalf of both parties. Is that possession adequate to perfect a security interest? Or what of the case in which two secured creditors claim an interest in a note and only one of them has possession? Unless the first acknowledges that he has possession on behalf of both of them, this can be troublesome. In the escrow case the courts have held the possession requirement has not been met in circumstances where the escrow agent is not the exclusive agent of the secured creditor, but is the agent of both the creditor and the debtor. Consider the following questions that might arise with respect to possession.

Problem 4–7

Secured creditors #1 and #2 both have security interests in debtor's certificate of deposit.

1. If the three execute an agreement stating that the debtor will hold possession "on behalf of secured creditors #1 and #2," will the security interest be perfected?

2. As an alternative, secured creditor #1 proposes simply that he hold possession and suggests that his possession will perfect the interest of both parties. How would you advise secured creditor #2?

The student should ask why certain forms of collateral are pledgeable and others are not. That clearly is the outcome under UCC 9–305, but why? Consider the following case.

M.M. LANDY, INC. v. NICHOLAS

United States Court of Appeals, Fifth Circuit, 1955.
221 F.2d 923.

[M.M. Landy, Inc. advanced money to Continental Charterers, Inc. and, as security, took an assignment of accounts receivable due Continental from the U.S. government. Also as security, Landy took possession of certain "warrants"—non-negotiable orders on the U.S. Treasury—payable to Continental which were to be in satisfaction of the government's debt. Continental became bankrupt and its trustee attacked Landy's security. The Referee in bankruptcy held that because certain filing requirements had not been met under the applicable federal and (pre-Code) state law, Landy's security was not perfected. Hence Continental's trustee prevailed. The Court of Appeals reversed, holding that filing was not necessary for perfection because Landy had taken possession of the warrants (a pledge); the case was remanded for further proof on an ancillary point. In the course of the opinion, the court discussed the concept of pledgeability.]

TUTTLE, CIRCUIT JUDGE.

* * *

Effectiveness of the Transaction as a Pledge.—Certain kinds of instruments represent obligations sufficiently that a delivery of them pledges the obligations. This was true of the common law specialty or sealed instrument; it is true of the commercial specialty or negotiable instrument. The idea of negotiability has now been extended to documents of title such as warehouse receipts and order bills of lading, and at the same time the idea of embodiment of a right to money has been and is being extended to certain non-negotiable choses. Stock certificates, insurance policies, and savings bank books may be the subject of pledges by delivery alone. Of course, not all written instruments embody the obligation; the delivery of an ordinary written contract, even if it is a memorandum necessary under the Statute of Frauds, is not a pledge of the obligation.

Williston proposed a rational distinction between the non-negotiable instruments which embody obligations and those which do not:

> "Certain contractual rights are embodied in instruments that are more than mere evidence of a claim and are popularly referred to and regarded as if they were themselves the obligations. To some extent the law has sanctioned this popular view, and there is a sound basis for it where by contract or custom, enforcement of a right is conditional on the surrender of the document evidencing the right. * * * The delivery of the document with donative intent transfers a right * * *. This is true of the gift of a policy of insurance, a savings bank book, a non-negotiable or unindorsed bill or note of a third person, a non-negotiable bond, a certificate of stock, or lottery ticket."

This distinction has been received with favor by all the leading text authorities. Brown, Personal Property § 59; 4 Collier, Bankruptcy (14th Ed.) ¶ 70.86; 2 Glenn, Fraudulent Conveyances and Preferences (Rev.Ed.) § 526. The Restatement of Contracts § 173(b)(iv) extends this concept of embodiment still further, to any "tangible token or writing, surrender of which is required by the obligor's contract for its enforcement." The Restatement of Security is more conservative, in that it would give this quality only to "indispensable instruments," which are defined in § 1, Comment *e*, as follows:

> "An indispensable instrument as used in the Restatement of this Subject means the formal written evidence of an interest in intangibles, so representing the intangible that the enjoyment, transfer or enforcement of the intangible depends upon possession of the instrument. If the instrument cannot be produced, the interest which it represents can be effectively asserted only by accounting for the absence of the instrument and obtaining as a substitute for it, either a duplicate or some form of court decree. Indispensable instruments include not only negotiable instruments such as promissory notes and bills of exchange, but also share certificates, bonds, interim certificates, savings bank books and insurance policies. Where the instrument is not an indispensable one, for example, a written assignment of a list of book accounts as security, the interest obtained by the assignee in the accounts is not a pledge."

Section 2, Comment *b,* and Illustration 7, recognize that non-negotiable indispensable instruments are not restricted to any special categories, and also recognizes [sic] a pledge interest even in a paper which might have value as evidence of a right, but is *not* indispensable to enforcing the right. In such a case the pledgee has a pledge interest in the paper, but not in the intangible right; such an interest is said to be in the nature of a "worrying asset." Section 8, Comment *a* points out that under the Uniform Warehouse Receipts Act, § 42, the Uniform Bills of Lading Act, § 33, and 49 U.S.C.A. § 112, a pledge of goods in the possession of a carrier or warehouseman may be created by delivery of a non-negotiable warehouse receipt or straight bill of lading to the pledgee, upon notification of the carrier or warehouseman. See also Restatement, Trusts, § 163; Restatement, Restitution, § 126, Comment *f*.

There are a considerable number of cases which support these principles contended for by the texts and Restatements. In Herman v. Connecticut Mutual Life Ins. Co., 218 Mass. 181, 105 N.E. 450, Ann.Cas. 1916A, 822, the assignee of an insurance policy who left the policy in the hands of an assignor, in reliance on fraudulent representations of the assignor, was held to have a claim inferior to that of a subsequent pledgee. In Talty v. Freedman's Savings & Trust Co., 93 U.S. 321, 23 L.Ed. 886, the security for a loan was a warrant of the City of Washington, D.C., certifying approval of the borrower's claim against the city. The Supreme Court recognized the lender's interest in this paper, presumably quite similar to the warrants in the present case, as a pledge. The case of Citizens State Bank v. O'Leary, 140 Tex. 345, 353, 167 S.W.2d 719, noted 21 Texas L.Rev. 642, involved the pledge of a "Certificate of Membership" in an unincorporated association, which entitled the member to certain income and $3,000 upon his retirement or death and the surrender and cancellation of the certificate. The certificate also provided that any assignment without the consent of the association would be void. The court held that a pledgee without the consent of the association has a valid security interest which cut off a prior assignment and unrecorded instrument called a mortgage. * * * [Footnotes omitted.]

Note

To return to our issue above, how should a secured creditor perfect a security interest in his debtor's (a mortgagee's) note and mortgage?

Problem 4–8

Bank (client) has inquired as to its rights with respect to a debtor who has recently filed in bankruptcy. Debtor had a savings account in an out-of-state bank containing $15,000. As security for a loan by bank, debtor gave possession of the passbook in the out-of-state bank that represented the account with the $15,000. Debtor's trustee in bankruptcy has asserted a right to the $15,000. Does bank have a perfected security interest? (Assume that Bank will defeat the trustee if that is so.) The case would be changed if the savings deposit were not in an out-of-state bank but were held in your client's bank. Why so? Do not overlook UCC 9–104.

B. *Rights and Duties of Parties to a Pledge*

In the case of possessory security, it is the secured party who has control of the collateral. In the absence of relevant contract provisions in the security agreement, to what degree must the secured party care for the pledged collateral? What freedom does he have to use and dispose of it? See UCC 9–207.

COOKE v. HADDON

Nisi Prius, 1862.
176 Eng.Rep. 103.

Trover, for four cases of champagne.

Pleas: not guilty and not possessed, and also a plea of lien.

Laxton and Eyre Lloyd for the plaintiff.

Barnard for the defendant.

The action was in trover for the recovery of four cases of champagne, deposited with defendant, a money-lender, by way of collateral security for a loan of money, for which, also, a bill of 25£ was given by the plaintiff. The sum actually received by the plaintiff was 18£, 19*s.*, and in respect of the bill several payments were, from time to time, made for interest, renewal, and in liquidation of the principal sum; but eventually a judgment was obtained against the present plaintiff, and execution was put into his premises in Farringdon street, where he kept a refreshment-room, for the balance, under which 11£, 7*s.* was realized. Plaintiff then called on defendant and demanded the champagne, and was by him referred to a person named Staff, in whose possession the wine was alleged by the defendant to be. Upon application to Staff, plaintiff was informed by that person that the return of the wine was impossible, as part of it had been drunk.

For the defence it was contended that the right of lien still subsisted, inasmuch as the full amount due upon the bill had not been realized under the execution, owing to a mistake of the defendant's attorney, by whom credit had been given in respect of a sum of 5£ twice over.

The learned Judge, in summing up, told the jury that when a deposit of goods was made by way of security for * * * a debt, it was the undoubted duty of the pledgee neither to use nor in any way to dispose of the goods so deposited, and that by so doing he would forfeit his lien. Here, therefore, the wine having been drunk, the plaintiff, independent of any question as to the amounts paid on account of the bill, was entitled to recover the value of the pledge. The other question for their determination was, as to damage, whether the payments which had at different times been made (the account between the parties being somewhat complicated) sufficed to discharge the debt.

The jury found a verdict upon both issues in favour of the plaintiff, assessing the value of the wine at 20£.

Notes

1. We sometimes hear of the borrower who is a credit drunk. Here it is the reverse. Would the case have come out the same way under UCC 9–207? Suppose the parties had signed a security agreement in which the pledgor had waived "all rights to the collateral." What result then? See Article 9 and Seasongood, *Drastic Pledge Agreements,* 29 Harv.L.Rev. 277 (1915). Would it be unprofessional to draft such a clause?

2. Suppose the wine had been destroyed by fire and that while the pledgor did not have insurance, the pledgee did. Assume that the pledgee's insuror paid the pledgee the full value of the wine, which proved to be equivalent to the amount that the pledgor owed the pledgee. Would the secured party still be entitled to collect the debt from the pledgor? Would the pledgee's insuror be entitled, via subrogation, to reimbursement from the pledgor? See UCC 9–207(2)(b). What result would occur if the following clause appeared in the security agreement between the pledgor and pledgee? "Pledgor hereby agrees that if he shall fail to procure insurance as agreed, the secured party's insuror

shall be entitled to collect from pledgor any indebtedness of pledgor to pledgee to the extent that insuror has paid insurance proceeds therefor to secured party."

What is the duty, if any, of a pledgee to convert debentures he holds as security? This question has arisen in several cases applying section 9–207 of the Code. One commentator has posed the problem in these terms:

> "The hybrid nature of a convertible debenture may require special treatment when this type of security is pledged as collateral. Like a debt, a debenture represents an obligation of the corporation to pay a sum certain at a future date, together with periodic interest. Thus, a debenture is similar to a bond having a minimum value and providing a fixed return on an investment. At the same time, a debenture grants the holder the option of converting the bond into common stock of the corporation at a fixed price prior to a predetermined redemption date. If debentures are called by a corporation prior to their redemption date, the question arises whether a pledgee-bank has a duty to the pledgor to convert the securities." [Footnote omitted.] Note, *Reasonable Care Under the U.C.C.: The Pledgee's Duty to Preserve Value of Convertible Debentures,* 59 Georgetown L.J. 240, 240–241 (1970).

The answer in one court, at least, was yes under UCC 9–207(1) and that damages under UCC 9–207(3) should be measured from the date that the debtor had a right to possession of the collateral rather than the date that the secured party should have converted. Traverse v. Liberty Bank & Trust Co., 5 UCC Rep.Serv. 535 (Mass.Sup.Ct.1967). But see Reed v. Central Nat'l Bank of Alva, 421 F.2d 113, 118 (10th Cir.1970), holding that damages should be measured by the difference in value just before and just after the negligent failure to convert.

CAPOS v. MID-AMERICA NATIONAL BANK OF CHICAGO

United States Court of Appeals, Seventh Circuit, 1978.
581 F.2d 676.

PELL, CIRCUIT JUDGE. Dr. Nicholas J. Capos brought this action against the Mid-America National Bank of Chicago (Mid-America) invoking at trial section 7 of the Securities Exchange Act of 1934, 15 U.S.C. § 78g, and Regulation U promulgated thereunder by the Federal Reserve Board, 12 C.F.R. § 221.1 et seq., and a common law theory that a bank holding stock as collateral for a loan has not only a right but a duty to foreclose on the collateral if its value should fall to the vicinity of the amount owed. After considering an extensive factual and documentary stipulation, deposition and live testimony of Capos and live testimony of a Mid-America official, the district court entered judgment against Capos on his complaint and for Mid-America on its counterclaim for principal and interest due. This appeal followed.

The salient facts are not complicated. In 1966 Capos purchased 5000 shares of stock in Diversified Metals Corporation (Diversified),[3] on the advice of his broker. Later that year, on further advice, he purchased 5000 additional shares with funds borrowed from the Michigan Avenue National Bank. The first 5000 shares were used as collateral, and Regulation U was explained to Capos at that time. In 1968, when the bank told Capos it wanted to sell the shares because their value was declining, Capos moved the loan to Mid-America. The April 10 Mid-America loan provided $50,591.83 to pay the loan at the Michigan Avenue National Bank, along with nearly $60,000 to pay income taxes. An earlier $10,000 working capital loan was consolidated therewith, and the entire $120,000 loan was secured by 6000 shares of Diversified, worth at the time about $360,000. No suggestion is made here that this transaction was other than in complete compliance with Regulation U.

In April 1969, Mid-America loaned Capos an additional $25,000 to pay income taxes, the loan being consolidated with the $120,000 previously owed. The Diversified stock then secured the entire loan, in compliance with Regulation U.

On July 25, 1969, Capos borrowed an additional $22,000 from Mid-America, secured by 4000 additional shares of Diversified stock with a value between $84,000 and $87,000. Capos and Mid-America executed a Form U–1 at the time, as required by 12 C.F.R. § 221.3(a), which stated that the proceeds were to be used for the "purchase of stock (regulated)." If, as the district court found, the purpose of the loan was to purchase margin stock, the loan violated Regulation U because the maximum loan value of the securing stock would have been $17,400. The premise of Capos' Regulation U theory is thus that Mid-America lent him $4600 more than it should have.

While the collateral originally was adequate, the situation changed dramatically in time. The value of Diversified stock fell from $60 per share on April 10, 1968, to approximately $21 per share on July 25, 1969. Unfortunately for all concerned, the slide continued. Although Mid-America at all pertinent times had the right to sell the collateral, it did not do so. Indeed, it was not until May 1972, when the value of the collateral had fallen to approximately $88,000, or $8.80 per share originally pledged [5] (the outstanding indebtedness being $147,000 at the time), that Mid-America proposed to sell the stock. Because Capos expressed optimism in Diversified and began a regular principal repayment plan, the stock was not sold. It eventually became worth $3.20 per share originally pledged, if indeed there was a market for the stock even at this price. The district court found, on ample evidence from Capos himself, that Capos had actual knowledge, at least on a week-to-week basis, of the price of the stock during the pertinent period.

* * *

3. The firm later changed its name to Diversified Industries, Inc. For convenience our reference to the firm will be simply as Diversified.

5. At some point, Diversified stock split, so the actual value per share may have been somewhat lower in May 1972. The figure per share originally tendered is useful for comparison.

II.

With regard to the common law theory, the district court thought that there was a duty on Mid-America to exercise reasonable care in preserving the value of the Diversified stock collateral, but concluded that the bank had not breached its duty, and that Capos' contributory negligence barred recovery in any event. We would have no difficulty affirming the court's judgment on the ground of contributory negligence if the underlying duty were that found by the district court to exist. Clearly Capos had equal opportunity with Mid-America to stay apprised of the declining value of the stock, and the district court's finding that Capos in fact did so, at least weekly, is fully supported by the evidence. At any point prior to the stock's value becoming less than the amount owed, Capos could have instructed the bank to sell the stock and liquidate the debt. Thereafter, he could have acquiesced in Mid-America's suggestion that the stock be sold. The loss in the stock's value was, quite simply, an investment loss, the investment was Capos', not Mid-America's, and any negligence in not cutting the losses was *at least* equally his.

Mid-America urges us to affirm the district court judgment on the alternative ground that a bank has no duty to its borrower to sell collateral stock of declining value. We think it appropriate to do so. It is the borrower who makes the investment decision to purchase stock. A lender in these situations merely accepts the stock as collateral, and does not thereby itself invest in the issuing firm. Nor, unless otherwise agreed, does the lender undertake to act as an investment adviser, although imposing a duty on the lender to sell the stock at the "reasonable" time would foist that role upon it. Not surprisingly, Illinois common law did not impose a duty on a pledgee to sell shares of stock at any time or liability for depreciation of the shares' value while in his possession. Rozet v. McClellan, 48 Ill. 345, 348 (1868).

The Uniform Commercial Code, which now governs these situations, provides:

> "A secured party must use reasonable care in the custody and preservation of collateral in his possession. In the case of an instrument or chattel paper reasonable care includes taking necessary steps to preserve rights against prior parties unless otherwise agreed."

Ill.Rev.Stat.1975, ch. 26 § 9–207(1). The Illinois Comments on this provision make it clear that the first sentence adopts the standard of care of the Restatement of Security, § 17 (1941), and that the second sentence adopts the standard of Restatement § 18. Restatement § 17 is in language quite similar to that used in § 9–207(1), but Official Comment a. is dispositive evidence that the duty imposed is not that urged by Capos:

> "The rule of reasonable care expressed in this Section is *confined to the physical care of the chattel,* whether an object such as a horse or piece of jewelry, or a negotiable instrument or document of title." (Emphasis added.)

The language of Restatement § 18 is much like that of the second sentence of § 9–207(1), and neither would appear to have any pertinence to the mere diminution in market value of securities. If there can be any doubt, Official

Comment a. to the Restatement provision ends it: "The pledgee is not liable for a decline in the value of pledged instruments, even if timely action could have prevented such decline."

We see no warrant in Illinois law for engrafting a new and significantly burdensome duty onto § 9–207(1). Although the district court's opinion referred to "harsh" results not in keeping with present day commercial realities if the statute's language is given its natural and apparently intended meaning, we see nothing harsh or unrealistic about requiring a borrower/investor to contract for investment advice if he wishes to receive it. As for the authorities relied upon by Capos and the district court,[9] they are readily distinguishable, as they involved failures to exercise rights to convert debentures into stock and a failure to present a note for payment (thus releasing a solvent indorser). Either situation falls within the second sentence of § 9–207(1), see Illinois Code Comment 2, whereas this case, as we have said, does not.

For the reasons set out herein, the judgment of the district court is affirmed. [Some footnotes omitted.]

Notes

1. Assume that the securities in *Capos* were convertible debentures. During the term of the loan and at a time when the debtor was on an extended vacation in Europe the debentures with a value of $100,000 (because the underlying stock was worth $100,000) were called. Being ignorant of the call, the bank did not tender the debentures. After the call date, the debentures were worth only $20,000 (that being the value of the debenture as a debt security only without the conversion feature). On debtor's return from Europe, she comes to you and asks whether she has a cause of action against the bank for failing to convert. At all times after the conversion feature ends, assume the debentures as dead instruments are worth $20,000. Assume that the stock into which it could have been converted was worth $100,000 on the conversion date, and $200,000 six months later when the loan became due, and $75,000 at the time of trial.

2. If Debtor can make a case under UCC 9–207, what are her damages?

3. If Debtor pledges stock to her stockbroker, can the stockbroker repledge them in a commingled pot with other securities to a bank? (See UCC 9–207(2)(e).)

C. Pledges of and Other Security Interests in Securities: The 1977 Amendments to Article 8

Securities present a special case for perfection by possession. For most of the twentieth century, rights in shares of stocks and in bonds have been represented by stock certificates and by pieces of paper called bonds. In the most common case, a stock certificate would be registered in the name of the true owner and his name would appear on the face of the stock certificate as the owner. That, of course, was not true of bearer bonds where the principal attribute of ownership was possession. In such cases, the debtor-owner

9. Reed v. Central National Bank of Alva, 421 F.2d 113 (10th Cir. 1970) (conversion rights); Grace v. Sterling, Grace & Co., 30 App.Div.2d 61, 289 N.Y.S.2d 632 (1968) (conversion rights); State Bank of Clinton v. Parkhurst, 155 Ill.App. 101 (1910) (presenting note for payment).

whose name appeared on the stock certificate could grant a perfected security interest by an agreement, written or oral, with his creditor and by transferring possession of the certificate to the creditor. In initial versions of Article 9 and Article 8 this transaction fits comfortably within UCC 9–203 and 9–305. Indeed, it probably represents the most frequent form of perfection by possession.

Increasingly since World War II, but particularly in response to the massive increase in the number of transactions since 1960, those who deal with securities and bonds have looked for ways to minimize the paperwork associated with the issuance and transfer of ownership rights in stocks and bonds. Ultimately this trend may cause the abolition of stock certificates entirely. Sometime in the 21st century we may find that stock certificates are merely a thought from a remote past and that ownership in corporations is indicated by identification on the books of the corporation, by notations in a computer memory somewhere, but not by pieces of paper with the owners' names specified on them.

As an intermediate step toward that conclusion it is now common for corporations to issue certificates in the "street name," that is in the name of a stockbroker with the understanding by all that the stockbroker is merely a nominee for the true owners, the customers of the brokerage house. Thus, for example, all of the shareholders of Merrill Lynch might own millions of shares of IBM, yet there might be only a few certificates outstanding, each for large amounts and each showing Merrill Lynch or its nominee as the apparent owner. In such cases the shareholder's interest in IBM is reflected exclusively by a Merrill Lynch computer memory and by the monthly statements and confirmations of purchase that he receives from Merrill Lynch. Both that case and the one that we foresee on the horizon where there is no certificate at all outstanding raise the question: How does one perfect a security interest in the customer-debtor's right in stock?

For the creditor the simplest method is to ask the debtor to procure a certificate in his name and to give the certificate to the creditor. This would today be a perfected interest under Articles 8 and 9. But if that is not done, the question arises: What is the debtor's interest and how is the creditor to perfect its security interest in the debtor's rights? If the certificate were in existence with the debtor's name on it, debtor's interest would be in the "instrument" under UCC 9–105. If his interest is properly portrayed as merely a claim against his stockbroker, it may well be no more than a general intangible.

In response to all of these problems the drafters of the Uniform Commercial Code proposed amendments to Article 8 in 1977. These amendments remove the entire perfection process with respect to securities from Article 9 and place it in Article 8. Moreover, they provide an intricate set of rules to deal with the various permutations described above in which the debtor is not in possession of a certificate bearing his name. As of this writing the 1977 revision to Article 8 has been adopted in every state except Alabama and Vermont. The Article is currently being revised and the revision will probably be available for adoption by state legislatures in 1994. It is important to understand how Article 8 works. It is also important to decide which cases involve securities and are therefore under Article 8 and which remain under Article 9.

Consider the definition of a certificated security in UCC 8–102(1).

(1) In this Article, unless the context otherwise requires:

(a) A "certificated security" is a share, participation, or other interest in property of or an enterprise of the issuer or an obligation of the issuer which is

(i) represented by an instrument issued in bearer or registered form;

(ii) of a type commonly dealt in on securities exchanges or markets or commonly recognized in any area in which it is issued or dealt in as a medium for investment; and

(iii) either one of a class or series or by its terms divisible into a class or series of shares, participations, interests, or obligations.

Problem 4–9

In which of the following cases is the asset involved a certificated or an uncertificated security subject to Article 8 and therefore not subject to Article 9?

1. The rights represented by a security held by Johnny in a closely held corporation. All of the other shares in the corporation are held by Lucille and Robert, Johnny's parents. These shares are not traded over the counter or on any exchange.

2. If in the foregoing case there is no certificate outstanding but Johnny is simply listed as the owner of a one-third interest in the corporation, is his interest now a security or not?

3. Chloe comes to the Bank with a document that shows her to be the owner of a $5,000 "limited partnership unit" in a Florida apartment development. The Bank is willing to make a loan, but would like a perfected security interest in that "unit." Is the right an Article 8 security or an interest outside of Article 8 and governed by Article 9?

Read the comments to 8–102 with care.

GENERAL ELECTRIC CO. v. TRACEY SERVICE CO., INC.

United States Court of Appeals, Third Circuit, 1984.
38 UCC Rep. 330, 729 F.2d 1446.

GIBBONS, CIRCUIT JUDGE. General Electric Company obtained a judgment against Tracey Service Company, Inc. and attempted to satisfy that judgment by levying a writ of execution on stock owned by the judgment debtor in its subsidiary, Tracey Mechanical, Inc. No certificates of stock could be found, and General Electric proceeded under Fed.R.Civ.P. 69 for supplementary relief requiring that Tracey Service Company, Inc. cause its subsidiary to issue a certificate evidencing ownership. The trial court directed Tracey Service Company, Inc. to execute a lost certificate affidavit, and on March 20, 1981 Tracey Mechanical, Inc. issued a certificate of stock in the name of the parent corporation. Counsel for General Electric Company obtained possession of the certificate and requested from the court an order directing the United States Marshal to seize it.

At this point Continental Bank intervened, making a claim of property. Continental's claim is predicated upon a security agreement executed by Tracey Service Company, Inc. on September 7, 1976, and on a Uniform Commercial Code financing statement filed on September 10, 1976. The security agreement grants Continental "a security interest in all accounts receivable * * * all Borrower's rights, powers and privileges with respect to any merchandise * * * and all general intangibles now owned or hereafter acquired, which means all personal property (including things in action) other than goods, accounts, contract rights, chattel paper, documents, and instruments, including but not limited to, records, ledgers, books, journals, check books, print-outs, blue prints, designs, computer programs, computer tapes, punch cards and other computer software, formulae, drawings, patents, trademarks, trade names and copyrights." The financing statement covers "[a]ll accounts receivable, contracts and contract rights, chattel paper, instruments, documents, all returned or rejected merchandise, and all general intangibles, all of the foregoing whether now owned or hereafter acquired and all cash and non-cash proceeds of the foregoing." Continental contends that the security agreement and financing statement give it a perfected security interest in Tracey Service Company, Inc.'s stock in its subsidiary, prior in time to the General Electric Company levy. Continental relies on the reference to "general intangibles" in both documents. It contends, further, that the stock certificate evidencing the Tracey Service Company, Inc. ownership of its subsidiary, issued on March 20, 1981, represents "proceeds" of a general intangible interest in the subsidiary within the meaning of the financing statement.

The trial court accepted the General Electric Company argument that although the financing statement includes proceeds of general intangibles, the security agreement does not cover such proceeds. Thus, the court reasoned, Continental's interest in the stock of Tracey Mechanical, Inc. depended on the reference in the security agreement to "instruments." As to these, the court held that the filing of the financing statement did not perfect Continental's security interest against third parties.

The financing statement covered proceeds, and 13 Pa. Cons. Stat.Ann. § 9306(c)(1) (Purdon 1983) provides that a security interest in proceeds becomes unperfected ten days after a debtor's receipt of proceeds unless:

> "(1) a filed financing statement covers the original collateral and the proceeds are collateral in which a security interest may be perfected by filing in the office or offices where the financing statement has been filed and, if the proceeds are acquired with cash proceeds, the description of the collateral in the financing statement indicates the type of property constituting the proceeds."

Continental's filed financing statement would seem to be within § 9306(c)(1) since it covers general intangibles, a security interest in which may be perfected by filing, and it contains a description of the proceeds as "instruments." The trial court reasoned, however, that 13 Pa. Cons. Stat.Ann. § 9203(a)(1) governed. That section provides that a security interest is not enforceable against the debtor or third parties unless:

"(1) the collateral is in the possession of the secured party pursuant to agreement, or the debtor has signed a security agreement which contains a description of the collateral * * *."

While the financing statement covered proceeds of general intangibles, the court concluded that the security agreement did not. Thus Continental's interest in Tracey Mechanical, Inc. terminated when the parent corporation's interest in it was converted from unissued stock—a general intangible—to issued stock, an instrument.

Perfection of a security interest in instruments requires that the secured party take possession. 13 Pa. Cons. Stat.Ann. § 9304(a). There is an exception in § 9304(a) for instruments which are proceeds of secured interests which may be perfected by filing, and a cross-reference to 13 Pa. Cons. Stat.Ann. § 9306(c). The latter section provides that proceeds become unperfected ten days after receipt by the debtor unless "the security interest in the proceeds is perfected before the expiration of the ten-day period." 13 Pa. Cons. Stat.Ann. § 9306(c)(3). Continental did not obtain possession of the stock certificate issued by Tracey Mechanical, Inc. within ten days, or indeed prior to the General Electric levy.

The judgment appealed from will, therefore, be affirmed.

BECKER, CIRCUIT JUDGE, concurring. While I concur in the judgment of the court, I would affirm on different grounds than the majority. Contrary to Judge Gibbons, I believe that Tracey Service's interest in Tracey Mechanical was at the time the security agreement was entered into an *instrument* under the Pennsylvania Uniform Commercial Code and not a general intangible, and that appellant therefore never had a security interest, perfected or otherwise, in the Mechanical stock,[1] but only a perfected security interest in general intangibles.[2] The problem with Continental's claim to the stock certificates is not so much that they represent unperfected proceeds of an earlier perfected security interest, but that Continental lacked a perfected security interest in the stock certificates in the first place.

The threshold question is whether Tracey's interest in Tracey Mechanical was represented by a stock certificate, and was, in UCC terms, an "instrument." Section 9–105(a) of the Uniform Commercial Code defines an instrument as a "negotiable instrument (defined in § 3–104), or a security (defined in § 8–102) or any other writing which evidences a right to the payment of money and is not itself a security agreement or lease and is of a type which is in ordinary course of business transferred by delivery with any necessary indorsement or assignment." Section 8–102, in turn, defines a security as "an instrument which: (i) is issued in bearer or registered form * * * and (iv) evidences a share, participation or other interest in property

1. Under 13 Pa.Cons.Stat.Ann. § 9203 (Purdon 1983), "a security interest is not enforceable against the debtor * * * with respect to the collateral and does not attach unless: (1) the collateral is in the possession of the secured party pursuant to agreement, or the debtor has signed a security agreement which contains a description of the collateral * * *." Since there can be absolutely no contention that Continental satisfies the first of these prerequisites, I examine its claim to the stock certificates based on a security agreement describing the collateral.

2. Were this a case where physical stock certificates were *never* issued by the corporation (rather than issued and lost), a creditor's claim to general intangibles would likely cover a debtor's equity interest in such a corporation.

or in an enterprise or evidences an obligation of the issuer." Subsequent parts of § 8–102 make reasonably clear that a security is conceived of as being represented by some form of writing.

Because of these definitional provisions, there can be little doubt that under ordinary circumstances Continental Bank would not even have a colorable claim in Tracey's stock certificates: Continental's security agreement claimed general intangibles and specifically disclaimed instruments.[3] The question arises as to whether a different result obtains here because the stock in Tracey Mechanical was not generally negotiable and the stock in Tracey Mechanical was eventually lost. I consider these matters in turn.

In In re Weber, 29 UCC RepServ 690 (Bankr. W.D. N.Y.1980), the court dealt with the issue of whether "Milk Certificates" issued by a dairy cooperative as evidence that the bearer had a claim against a reserve fund established by the cooperative were instruments under § 9–105(a) of the UCC. The court held that, despite the fact that the certificate was retirable at the sole discretion of the cooperative and that it was transferable only on the books of the corporation (i.e., that it was a registered security), it was an instrument nonetheless.

In Citizens National Bank of Orlando v. Bornstein, 374 So.2d 6 (Fla. 1979), the Florida Supreme Court dealt with the question of whether a non-negotiable certificate of deposit, ownership of which could be changed only by transfer on the books of the bank, was an instrument under the UCC. The court held that it was. "If the code drafters had intended to exclude non-negotiable instruments from coverage under section [9–105], they would not have added [the last clause] but would have limited it to include only 'negotiable instruments' as was done in article 3." The court also cited First National Bank in Grand Prairie v. Lone Star Life Ins. Co., 524 S.W.2d 525 (Tex.Civ.App.1975), as further authority for its holding. I find these cases persuasive and see no reason to believe that the Pennsylvania courts would decide the issue differently.

A second factor that might be offered to except this case from the ordinary rule, i.e., that the creditor must assert a claim to instruments where the debtor's equity interest in another corporation is represented by stock certificates, is that these certificates were lost. The problem with this argument, however, is that there is no evidence whatsoever that anyone knew the certificates were lost (or that the certificates were indeed lost) in 1976 when the security agreement was signed. If the creditor bank genuinely thought the certificates were lost, it did not take any steps that would be consistent with such a belief, such as requesting the debtor to obtain new stock certificates.

In sum, I would hold that where a corporation issues physical stock certificates, a creditor, in order to claim a security interest in a debtor stockholder's equity interest in that corporation, must follow the UCC procedures for instruments. I also conclude that the fact that stock in Tracey Mechanical was not negotiable, and that it was lost, does not alter the conclusion that Continental lacked a security interest in these certificates.

3. The fact that Continental's financing statement claimed instruments is, of course, irrelevant. See Pa.Cons.Stat.Ann. § 9–203(a)(1).

Problem 4–10

Rebecca has a large stock portfolio at E.F. Hutton. All of the shares are in the street name and she holds no certificates in her own name. Assume:

(a) That the state of Rebecca's residence has not enacted the 1977 version of Article 8. How should the bank perfect a security interest in her stock portfolio?

(b) That the state has enacted the 1977 version of Article 8. How then does the bank perfect?

Problem 4–11

Kelly Green is the registered owner and Commercial Credit the registered pledgee of the stock of Shamrock, Inc., all the stock of which is uncertificated. If Green wishes to use his interest in Shamrock as collateral for a loan from Manufacturer's Bank, and if Manufacturer's is willing to make the loan, how can Manufacturer's "perfect" an interest in Green's uncertificated shares? If Commercial later releases its security interest, what happens to Manufacturer's "perfection"?

SECTION 7. AUTOMATIC PERFECTION

UCC 9–302(1) contemplates at least six situations in which there will be automatic perfection. In most of those cases automatic perfection is granted because there is no significant prospect of a third party, and the parties very likely do not think of the transaction as a financing transaction. However two of them, namely the purchase money security interest in consumer goods under (1)(d) and the specialized security interest in (1)(b) (that incorporates UCC 9–304), do involve financing transactions and do have substantial significance.

Here for the first time the student meets the purchase money security interest. The automatic perfection in UCC 9–302(1)(d) depends on purchase money status. Purchase money status entitles a creditor to favored treatment in at least three separate settings. Under UCC 9–302(1)(d) the purchase money secured creditor is automatically perfected as to consumer goods without any filing or other act. Under UCC 9–312(3) and (4) the purchase money secured creditor enjoys priority over others who have filed prior to his filing. Under section 522(f) of the Bankruptcy Code, a purchase money secured creditor is immune from the attack that the trustee can otherwise make on certain perfected security interests.

The reasons for each of these three forms of special treatment are not necessarily identical. However, each in effect recognizes that the purchase money secured creditor is somehow superior to a conventional secured creditor. In the chapter on priority we will return to the question why should a purchase money secured creditor enjoy priority over others. Now it is enough to ask the question why such a creditor is given special treatment under UCC 9–302(1)(d) by way of automatic perfection status. Part of the basis for UCC 9–301(1)(d) is the reliance of the purchase money secured creditor. By taking a security interest in the assets sold or specifically financed by him, the creditor has in effect said, "I would not have made this loan, sold this commodity to the debtor without having a first security interest in it." In that sense he is unlike the conventional creditor who may have made an unsecured loan, and who, as times grew more perilous insisted upon a security interest as an afterthought. To some extent UCC 9–302(1)(d) may merely be a modern day equivalent of the conditional sale contract in consumer goods; it doubtless builds upon that history.

Moreover one can question the need for a filing in the case of security interests in consumer goods. Typically such goods depreciate rapidly; it would be uncommon for a *second* creditor to lend in reliance upon the value of a consumer's equity in most such items. The dollar amounts are frequently quite small. Furthermore, it would not be economic to require such secured creditors to perfect by filing. Why clutter the files at the county seats and in the state capital with such filings?

The student should read UCC 9–107 with care (the definition of a purchase money security interest). In all three areas where purchase money status is relevant the courts have had difficulty in determining how to distinguish purchase money from non-purchase money loans particularly in the setting in which the creditor takes a security interest in several assets of the debtor or makes several loans to the debtor or both. Note that UCC 9–107 requires that the purchase money lender made the loan "to enable" the debtor to acquire the asset. Can you think of settings in which the creditor might have difficulty in showing his loan enabled the debtor to acquire the asset? For one example consider the following case, a case whose facts have recurred in many jurisdictions with varying outcomes. As you read the case, consider the other alternatives that were open to the judge.

IN RE MANUEL

United States Court of Appeals, Fifth Circuit, 1975.
507 F.2d 990.

NICHOLS, ASSOCIATE JUDGE:

This case originated in the bankruptcy of James Lucius Manuel. On December 7, 1972, he purchased certain household furniture from appellant Roberts Furniture Co. On February 13, 1973, he purchased a television set, also from appellant. The purchase money security agreement he then signed referred to an unpaid balance of $573.32 from the first purchase, deducted $116.03 for refunds, leaving a prior unpaid balance of $457.29 which was added to the unpaid balance on the TV set, $174.07, making a total balance owed of $631.36. This agreement was never filed for perfection as Georgia law required, nor was perfection obtained by retaining possession. The agreement also failed to indicate the order in which purchases were paid off, and the amounts still due on each item and secured by the paid-up items. The apparent purpose of Roberts Furniture was to ensure that title to nothing passed until title to all passed. The February 13 purchase money agreement provided:

> "It is agreed that the contracts, whether one or more, heretofore entered into between Seller and Buyer, having an unpaid balance of $573.32 referred to as "prior balance" shall remain in full force and effect, that Seller's security interest in the goods sold thereunder shall remain perfected, until full payment for said goods has been made, and that the contract evidenced by this instrument shall have no effect on

the above mentioned existing contract except to modify the terms of payment thereof.

It is further agreed, however, that for the purposes of the payment of the said prior balance and total of payments on the contract evidenced by this instrument, that Buyer shall make one payment in the amount and for the period set forth below until the total of payments as set forth has been paid. Upon a default in the contract evidenced by this instrument the said existing contract shall also be deemed to be in default. Until all installment payments and all other amounts due hereunder, have been paid, Seller shall retain a security interest in the Goods and any and all equipment, parts, accessories, attachments, additions and other goods, and all replacements thereof, now or hereafter installed in, affixed to or used in connection with said Goods and, if Buyer sells or otherwise disposes of the Goods in violation of the terms of this agreement, in the proceeds of such sale or disposition. *Goods may secure all present and future liabilities, debts and obligations of whatever nature of BUYER to SELLER or its assigns."* (Emphasis supplied.)

Manuel filed a voluntary bankruptcy petition on May 3, 1973. Roberts Furniture claimed reclamation in bankruptcy on the basis of priority of their "Purchase Money Security Interest." The bankruptcy judge found that except for the TV set Roberts failed to acquire a Purchase Money Security Interest as defined by Georgia Code § 109A–9–107; that Roberts failed to perfect the security interest in any other manner provided by the Georgia and Uniform Commercial Codes; and that Section 70(c) of the Bankruptcy Act, 11 U.S.C. § 110, and Georgia Code § 109A–9–301(3) gave the bankruptcy trustee preference over Roberts' unperfected security interests.

The District Judge would have denied reclamation for the TV set also, except that the point was not preserved by cross appeal. Appellee now stipulates, contrary to the impression of the court below, that the combined value of all the involved merchandise is not equal to the debt owed Roberts Furniture Co. Nevertheless, we affirm.

I

* * *

The issue here is whether Georgia law would allow the arrangement below to be considered a Purchase Money Security Interest, which requires no filing for perfection. Georgia has enacted the Uniform Commercial Code. Georgia Code § 109A–9–107 defines a Purchase Money Security Interest: [court quotes 9–107] Georgia Code § 109A–9–302 provides the exceptions where filing is not required for perfection. One of the exceptions is:

* * *

(d) a purchase money security interest in consumer goods; * * *

There are other exceptions to the filing requirement, not here relevant. Otherwise, if not perfected by filing, under Georgia Code § 109A–9–301, the unperfected security interest is subordinate to the rights of "(1)(b) * * * a lien creditor * * *;" which term includes "(3) * * * a trustee in bankruptcy

* * *;" unless all the creditors had actual knowledge of the security interest, which is not contended here.

Roberts Furniture claims the exception for consumer goods. As the judges below noted, citing Allen v. Lokey, 307 F.2d 353 (5th Cir.1962), and National Silver Co. v. Nichols, 205 F.2d 52 (5th Cir.1953), the burden of proof to establish a security interest is upon the party seeking reclamation, and Roberts has not met that burden. The problem here begins with the fact that the security agreement filed with the court shows about $150 paid on about a $900 total debt, for 7 pieces of furniture and a TV set, with no clues as to what items are paid for and which are not, nor does any rule of first-bought, first-paid for appear.

A plain reading of the statutory requirements would indicate that they require the purchase money security interest to be in the item purchased, and that, as the judges below noted, the purchase money security interest cannot exceed the price of what is purchased in the transaction wherein the security interest is created, if the vendor is to be protected despite the absence of filing. Except as to the TV set, if at all, the interest here is not a "purchase money security interest" because it is not taken or retained by the seller of the collateral solely to secure all or part of *its* (emphasis supplied) price. Roberts attempted to make collateral secure debt other than its own price. The statutory exception does not reach the case.

The judges below drew their conclusion on the statutory language and on authority other than Georgia cases. Appellee has collected and cited to us a number of Georgia cases, which we have examined. We have no doubt that the Georgia courts will henceforward observe the express command of their legislature, but we find it unnecessary to analyze in detail cases which show no more than that they have hitherto done so, with respect to parts of the enactment here involved, other than those to be construed here. The District Judge refers to In re Simpson, 4 U.C.C.Rep. 243 (D.C.W.D.Mich. 1966). This referee in bankruptcy's opinion is well thought out, and documented with references to the Official Code Comment # 2, and to secondary authority. It was a case stronger for the vendor, than the one here, in that the farm machinery item in dispute was sold under the agreement which failed, in the referee's view, to create a purchase money security interest without filing, only because it included a clause making the item security, not only for its own price, but also for future advances. The entire discussion may be regarded as dictum since the referee ends up by holding that the vendor saved its security interest after all by recovering possession before the bankruptcy, without fraud on the creditors. In view of the wide circulation of the referee's opinion by the U.C.C. Reporting Service, the absence of contrary case authority, and its inherent reasonableness, we think our District Judge properly gave much weight to it.

The error of the belief below, that the value of the intended collateral exceeded the debt, is not fatal to the conclusion reached, though it does impair some of the reasoning, and prevents us from adopting the opinion below as our own.

We express no view as to whether a valid purchase money security interest was created with respect to the TV set. Nothing we say is to be taken as a holding as to that.

Affirmed.

Notes

1. How is the TV set distinguished from the other assets?

2. If the security agreement had contained a fifo clause, would that have cured the problem (that is, the first payments would first go to pay off the first item until it was free of the security interest; later payments for the next item, and so on, so that with the end payment for a particular item it would be freed from the security interest)?

Problem 4–12

Your client, Bank One, buys paper from a variety of consumer lenders. Often each document covers several items sold as in the *Manuel* case. The client has said that it is economically infeasible to write separate security agreements on each transaction, and asks whether the problem can be dealt with in some other way. What do you suggest?

Problem 4–13

Bank writes a letter of credit for its customer, Local Purchaser. The beneficiary is Swedish seller. In accordance with the agreement with customer, Bank has a security interest in the document and goods that are to be delivered under the letter of credit in return for its promise to pay against those documents. After the bank pays, it gives its customer the bills of lading to enable the customer to get possession of the goods. Unfortunately, a week after it has given the bills of lading to the customer and before the goods have arrived, the customer files a petition in Chapter 11. Does the bank have a right to the goods when they arrive or do the goods go into the bankruptcy estate, leaving the bank as an unperfected secured creditor?

What if the bank failed to take any action for three weeks after the bankruptcy petition had been filed?

SECTION 8. MULTIPLE STATE TRANSACTIONS, INCLUDING THE SPECIAL CASE OF THE AUTOMOBILE

When collateral is located in more than one state, or when the debtor has some association with more than one state, or when the collateral is moved or to be moved, the creditor must think of the law of several states to determine how to perfect a security interest. UCC 9–103 answers most of these questions. Note that it calls for perfection at the place where the goods are located for the most part, but it then gives a grace period if the goods are moved to another state. In certain circumstances (where the goods have no fixed situs), UCC 9–103 calls for perfection at the "location" of the debtor, itself sometimes uncertain.

Section 9–103 is the cursed offspring of our federal union. By having 50 states and 50 states laws governing commercial transactions, we must somehow have rules about where to perfect a security interest in a multistate transaction and about how to handle the many transactions in which more than one state is involved. Perfecting security interests in aircraft shows how simple life could be. By federal law all security interests in aircraft are perfected by a central filing in Oklahoma City. One need not worry about whether filing ought to be in Austin or Santa Fe or Sacramento.

For the foreseeable future, the problem of multi-state filing will be with us and thus 9–103 or something like it must be confronted. Although 9–103 speaks of "perfection and the effect of perfection or non-perfection", it is really about perfection. The "effects of non-perfection" are generally the same in one state as in another and mostly 9–103 should be regarded as not a general choice of law provision, but as a provision directed at a single question, namely, where to file. Should the financing statement be filed in Lansing or in Columbus, in Albany or in Concord? That is the question that 9–103 answers and almost everything else in 9–103 is superfluous.

Note that 9–103(1)(b) has provisions for pathological cases where the collateral is in motion during the attachment and perfection process. Subsection 9–103(1)(b) says that the governing law is that of the state where the collateral is located when the last event occurs on which is based the assertion of perfection. If, therefore, signing of a security agreement and filing of the financing statement do not occur simultaneously and in the period between one and another, the goods are moved from one state to another, one would have to ask the question where were the goods when the last event occurred.

The basic rule of law is stated in 9–103(1)(b): one files where the goods are located. If goods are in Indiana, filing is in Indianapolis or locally. If the goods are in Chicago, filing is in Springfield or locally. That rule alone must cover in excess of 90 percent of all the cases.

The first complication arises when goods are moved from one state to another. There the general rule is stated in 9–103(3)(d): there is normally a four-month grace period when the goods are moved from one jurisdiction to another. If there is no new perfection within the grace period, the security interest becomes unperfected. As we will see, there are some nasty little twists and complications in this rule as well.

Because of their special nature, some forms of personal property require special rules. Certificates of title get their own special rule in 9–103(2). Collateral that has no location, or at least no reliable permanent location, is covered by 9–103(3). This includes accounts, general intangibles and mobile goods. One should be clear that goods (such as a chair that could easily be carried from one state to another) are not for that reason "mobile." Almost all mobile goods have one thing in common, wheels. Accounts and general intangibles are like ghosts; they have no home. As to those and as to mobile goods, the filing is at the debtor's place of business. Generally, if the debtor has more than one, this is where the debtor's chief executive office is located. Under this rule all account filing against General Motors should be in Lansing, Michigan, even though the account might arise out of a sale of goods in Oklahoma or Georgia and even though General Motors is a Delaware corporation.

Whether we should keep the goods' location as the basic rule for filing or whether all filings ought to be moved to the debtor's location is now subject to debate. The new revision committee for Article 9 has proposed that 9–103(1)(b) be modified so that the general rule be the location of the debtor, not the location of the goods. In effect, this proposal would expand what is now 9–103(3) to include not merely mobile goods and general intangibles, but also goods in general. Which rule do you think is more sound?

Finally, one should note that there is an intrastate version of the "where to file debate." See UCC 9–401(3) and 9–401 alternative subsection (3).

KONKEL v. GOLDEN PLAINS CREDIT UNION

Supreme Court of Colorado, 1989.
778 P.2d 660.

VOLLACK, JUSTICE.

Golden Plains Credit Union (Golden Plains) appeals the judgment of the court of appeals in *Golden Plains Credit Union v. Konkel,* 759 P.2d 788 (Colo.App.1988), holding that the trial court erred in concluding that Golden Plains lost its security interest in a farm combine purchased in Kansas and subsequently moved and sold in Colorado. We affirm in part and reverse in part and remand the case to the court of appeals with directions to remand for further hearings.

I.

Golden Plains is a Kansas credit union. On May 4, 1978, it financed the purchase of two 1978 John Deere combines [1] by Duane Lewis, a farmer [2] and custom cutter.[3] In May 1978, Golden Plains filed a financing statement for the combines with the registrar of deeds in Hamilton County, Kansas, the county in which Lewis resided.

In the latter half of October 1979, Lewis transported the combines from Hamilton County, Kansas, to a farm he had recently purchased in Baca County, Colorado. On February 7, 1980, Lewis sold one of the combines in Colorado to Bud Konkel (Konkel), doing business as Konkel Equipment Company. Konkel made no effort to determine whether a financing statement describing Golden Plains' security interest in the combine was filed, nor did he have actual knowledge of Golden Plains' security interest. Konkel later sold the combine to a Colorado farmer.

In April 1984, Golden Plains filed a complaint in the Baca County District Court against Konkel for conversion of the combine, seeking its return or damages.[4] Golden Plains moved for summary judgment against Konkel on the ground that Golden Plains held a security interest in the combine at the time Konkel bought the combine from Lewis. Konkel moved for summary judgment against Golden Plains on the ground that Golden Plains lost its security interest in the combine in 1980 when it failed to file a

1. Lewis bought two combines in 1977. He traded them in for two 1978 combines in May 1978.

2. In his deposition, Lewis stated that he farmed 920 acres of land in Hamilton County, Kansas, in 1978, 600 of which he owned and 320 of which he rented. He also stated that he purchased and maintained an 1120-acre farm in Baca County, Colorado, in 1979.

3. In his deposition, Lewis stated that he had been a custom cutter of crops since 1970. In 1977, 1978, and 1979, he would cut crops in Oklahoma during the early part of the season, move the operation to Kansas and Nebraska, and finish the season in Colorado. He would then store the combines in Colorado during the winter.

4. After Golden Plains filed its complaint against Konkel, Konkel filed a third-party complaint against Lewis, alleging false representation at the time of the 1980 purchase.

second financing statement in Colorado within four months of the date Lewis moved the combine to Baca County.

The trial court granted Konkel's motion for summary judgment. It made no attempt to classify the combine under the Kansas version of the Uniform Commercial Code (UCC or Code). Instead, it held that Golden Plains lost its security interest in the combine four months after Lewis moved the combine to Baca County, Colorado, pursuant to section 84–9–103(1)(d) of the law of Kansas.

The court of appeals reversed the judgment of the trial court. It first found that Golden Plains had perfected its security interest in the combine in May 1978 by filing its financing statement in Hamilton County, Kansas. The court of appeals relied on *Sequoia Machinery, Inc. v. Jarrett,* 410 F.2d 1116 (9th Cir.1969), in concluding the combine was properly classified as "equipment used in farming operations" under section 84–9–401(1)(a) (1983) of the law of Kansas because the combine was "specifically designed to be used for farming functions." *Golden Plains Credit Union v. Konkel,* 759 P.2d at 790. The court of appeals noted that the proper place for a creditor to file a financing statement and thereby perfect its security interest in a combine is the office of the registrar of deeds in the county in which the debtor resided, a procedure that was followed in this case.

The court of appeals then concluded that the trial court erred in concluding that Golden Plains lost its security interest in the combine under section 84–9–103(1)(d)(i) four months after the combine was "brought into" Colorado. Instead, the court of appeals found that the applicable Kansas statute was section 84–9–103(3) (1983 & 1988 Supp.), governing "mobile goods." It noted that section 84–9–103(3)(a) and the Code commentary listed "commercial harvesting machinery" as an "excellent example" of mobile goods. It concluded that Golden Plains retained its security interest in the combine under section 84–9–103(3)(e) until four months after "a change of the debtor's location to another jurisdiction." The court of appeals remanded the case to the trial court for a factual determination of whether Lewis had "changed his location" within the meaning of section 84–9–103(3)(d) when he moved the combine to Colorado in October 1979.

We granted certiorari to determine two issues: first, whether Golden Plains properly perfected its security interest in the combine in May 1978; and second, assuming that Golden Plains had properly perfected its security interest in May 1978, whether Golden Plains lost its security interest in 1980 by failing to file a new financing statement in Colorado within four months of the time the debtor moved the combine to Baca County, Colorado.

II.

A.

Resolution of the first issue requires us to examine the efficacy of the "normal use test" in classifying collateral under the Kansas equivalent of section 9–401(1)(a) of the Code. Konkel argues that Golden Plains never perfected its security interest in the combine in May 1978 because Golden Plains did not file its financing statement in the Office of the Kansas Secretary of State. Implicit in this is the argument that the combine is equipment other than "equipment used in farming operations" within the meaning of section 84–9–401(1)(a) of the law of Kansas.[5] Golden Plains contends that this argument should not be addressed because it was raised for the first time before the court of appeals. Golden Plains argues that its security interest was properly perfected in May 1978 because the combine is "equipment used in farming operations" within the meaning of section 84–9–401(1)(a) of the law of Kansas.

While the thrust of the arguments in the district court hearing of October 23, 1985, centered on whether Golden Plains' security interest remained in effect after Lewis brought the combine to Colorado in the latter half of October 1979, Konkel's attorney did raise the issue of whether Golden Plains' security interest was properly perfected in May 1978. The attorney noted that equipment such as a combine may alternately be classified as farm equipment, requiring filing in the county of the debtor's residence, or commercial equipment, requiring filing with the Kansas Secretary of State. He argued that by classifying the combine as commercial equipment requiring filing with the Kansas Secretary of State, Golden Plains' filing in Hamilton County was "an erroneous filing, and [Golden Plains] [hasn't] continued that. That would be by operational [sic] law in '78–'83, five years." The lawyer cited *Mountain Credit v. Michiana Lumber & Supply, Inc.,* 31 Colo.App. 112, 498 P.2d 967 (1972), to support this argument. *Mountain Credit* concerns whether a creditor failed to perfect its security interest by filing a financing statement in the wrong place. From this, we conclude that the issue of perfection of Golden Plains' security interest in May 1978 was properly raised before the district court. We therefore must consider the merits of this argument.

Under Kansas law, the proper place to file a financing statement and thereby perfect a security interest is generally in the office of the secretary of state. Kan.Stat.Ann. § 84–9–401(1)(c) (1983 & 1988 Supp.). The practice of filing with the secretary of state, known as "central filing," however, is subject to a number of exceptions.[6] When the debtor is a resident of the state, the proper place to file a financing statement for collateral properly classified as "equipment used in farming operations," for example, is "in the office of the registrar of deeds in the county of the debtor's residence."[7] The

5. Konkel and Golden Plains agree that the combine is "equipment" within the meaning of section 84–9–109(2), which includes goods that are "used or bought for use primarily in business (including farming or a profession) or by a debtor who is a nonprofit organization or a governmental subdivision or agency or if the goods are not included in the definitions of inventory, farm products or consumer goods."

6. At the time this dispute arose, central filing was not required in Kansas for "equipment used in farming operations," "farm products," "accounts or general intangibles arising from or relating to the sale of farm products by the farmer," "consumer goods," or "crops." Kan.Stat.Ann. § 84–9–401(1)(a) (1983), *repealed and reenacted* (1984) (requiring central filing for "equipment used in farming operations," "farm products," and "crops"). In such cases the proper place to file a financing statement depended on whether the debtor was a Kansas resident. If the debtor was a Kansas resident, then the proper place to file was "in the office of the registrar of deeds in the county of the debtor's residence." If the debtor was not a Kansas resident, then the proper place to file was "in the office of the registrar of deeds in the county where the goods are kept." *Id.*

7. Although at the time this dispute arose a security interest in "equipment used in farming operations" could be perfected only by filing locally, the Kansas legislature amended section 84–9–401(1)(a) in 1984 by deleting the phrase "equipment used in farming operations" from the subsection relating to local filing. Ch. 345, sec. 1, § 84–9–401, 1983 Kan.Sess.Laws 1562, 1563. As a result, a security interest in such equipment

practice of filing in the county of the debtor's residence is known as "local filing." If the combine is properly classified as "equipment used in farming operations," then Golden Plains' local filing was sufficient to perfect its security interest in the combine. If the combine is properly classified as equipment other than equipment used in farming operations, however, then central filing would be required to perfect Golden Plains' security interest in the combine. In order to determine whether the court of appeals erred in concluding that central filing was not required to perfect Golden Plains' security interest, we must first classify the collateral. *In re Reier,* 53 B.R. 395, 396 (Bankr.S.D.Ohio 1985).

In jurisdictions such as Kansas that adopt the second alternative subsection (1) of section 9–401 of the UCC, the most difficult problem involving equipment not subject to a certificate of title law "is drawing the line between 'equipment used in farming operations,' which normally requires local filing, and commercial equipment, which normally requires central filing." B. Clark, *The Law of Secured Transactions Under the Uniform Commercial Code* ¶ 8.3[1][a], at 8–8 (1980). The problem arises because the UCC does not define the phrase "equipment used in farming operations." *See* 1 P. Coogan, W. Hogan, D. Vogts & J. McDonnell, *Secured Transactions Under the Uniform Commercial Code* § 6.03[2][a], at 6–34 (1989) ("[i]nartful drafting [of the phrase 'equipment used in farming operations'] has unintentionally produced a 'trap for the unwary' ").

As a result of this statutory ambiguity, courts have devised a number of tests to determine whether the collateral is properly classified as equipment used in farming operations. One such test is the "normal use test," which focuses on the inherent qualities of the collateral and the uses to which such collateral would normally be put. The leading case advocating the normal use test is *Sequoia Machinery, Inc. v. Jarrett,* 410 F.2d 1116 (9th Cir.1969). The normal use test has been adopted by a minority of jurisdictions. *See, e.g., In re Burgess,* 30 B.R. 364, 366 (Bankr.W.D.Okla.1983).

A second test is the "intended use test," which focuses on the use the debtor intended to make of the collateral as contemplated by the parties at the time of the sale. *See In re Collins,* 3 B.R. 144, 146 (Bankr.D.S.C.1980). A third test is the "actual use test," which focuses on the use the debtor actually made of the collateral. *See In re Yeager Trucking,* 29 B.R. 131, 134 (Bankr.D.Colo.1983) ("it is the use by the debtor, not any intended use by the creditor, that is controlling as to classification of the collateral"); *In re Butler,* 3 B.R. 182, 183–84 (Bankr.E.D.Tenn.1980) ("the purpose for which the goods are bought and used determines the category in which goods should be placed"). Most courts follow either the intended use test or the actual use test. *See generally* T. Crandall, R. Hagedorn, F. Smith, *Debtor–Creditor Law Manual* ¶ 7–06[3][d][i], at 7–87 (1985).

According to Professors White and Summers, the real debate in classifying "equipment used in farming operations" is between the actual use test and the intended use test rather than between those tests and the normal use test:

is now perfected under Kansas law by filing centrally rather than locally. *See* Balloun, *Survey of Kansas Law: Secured Transactions,* 32 U.Kan.L.Rev. 351, 368 (1984).

> How one resolves the intended use versus actual use dispute depends ultimately on whether he values more highly secured creditors' interests or third party creditors' interests. A secured creditor would like to rely upon the debtor's statement about his intended use at the time the loan is made. A careful creditor can procure the debtor's written statement about his intended use and can then file in the proper place according to that use. On the other hand, third party creditors will surely argue for the actual use test.

J. White & R. Summers, *Uniform Commercial Code* § 24–15, at 362 (3d ed. 1988).

Although the normal use test, intended use test, and actual use test each has some logical appeal, the Kansas legislature has demonstrated its preference for the actual use test. The 1983 Kansas commentary to section 84–9–109 (1983 & 1988 Supp.) [9] states that the key in classifying the collateral "is the use to which the debtor puts the goods, not any inherent quality of the goods themselves." Given this choice by the Kansas legislature, we must conclude that the court of appeals erred in concluding that the normal use test employed in *Sequoia Machinery* was the proper test to determine whether the combine was "equipment used in farming operations" within the meaning of section 84–9–401(1)(a) of the law of Kansas.[10]

While the prudent creditor in close cases such as this should file a financing statement both locally and centrally as insurance against an adverse judicial determination of the proper classification of a particular piece of equipment, *In re Burgess,* 30 B.R. at 366; B. Clark, *The Law of Secured Transactions Under the Uniform Commercial Code* ¶ 9.5, at 9–21 (1989); J. White & R. Summers, *Uniform Commercial Code* § 24–14, at 359 (3d ed. 1988), the Code does not demand dual filing. Where the financing statement must be filed to perfect a security interest depends on the proper classification of the collateral. The trial court did not classify the combine. On remand, it must decide whether Lewis in May 1978 actually used the combine as "equipment used in farming operations." If the answer to this question is "no," then Golden Plains failed to perfect its security interest and judgment must be entered for Konkel.

B.

If the trial court decides that Lewis' actual use of the combine in May 1978 was as "equipment used in farming operations," however, then the trial court must decide whether Golden Plains' security interest remained in effect after Konkel purchased the combine. Resolution of this issue requires

9. Section 84–9–109 governs the classification of collateral. It creates four such classifications: consumer goods; equipment; farm products; and inventory.

As the 1983 Kansas comments to section 84–9–109 recognizes: "The classification of goods is important in a number of situations, e.g., to answer questions of priority (84–9–312), in determining the proper place to file a financing statement (84–9–401), and in determining the rights of persons who buy from a debtor goods subject to a security interest (84–9–307)."

10. We need not decide and therefore express no opinion as to the appropriate test under Colorado law for determining whether a particular piece of machinery is "equipment used in farming operations."

a determination of whether the combine is an "ordinary good" [11] or a mobile good.

Konkel argues that Golden Plains' security interest lapsed under section 84–9–103(1)(d) when Golden Plains failed to file a financing statement in Colorado four months after Lewis brought the combine into Colorado. Golden Plains argues that its security interest remained in effect in February 1980 under section 84–9–103(3)(e) because Lewis did not "change" his "location" of Hamilton County, Kansas, when he moved the combine into Baca County, Colorado, in the latter half of October 1979.

Section 84–9–103(1), the Kansas equivalent of section 9–103(1) of the Code, resolves priority disputes among creditors from different states having an interest in "ordinary goods" moved from one state to another. A security interest in ordinary goods which is properly perfected in one state expires four months after it is brought into the second state "and is thereafter deemed to have been unperfected as against a person who became a purchaser" in the second state." Kan.Stat.Ann. § 84–9–103(1)(d)(i) (1983 & 1988 Supp.). This rule, known as the "carry-over perfection rule," gives secured creditors in one state a four-month grace period to relocate the ordinary goods and file a second financing statement. The grace period for ordinary goods begins to run from the time the collateral "is brought into" the second state. J. White & R. Summers, *Uniform Commercial Code* § 22–21, at 1057 n. 28 (1988). Failure to file a second financing statement during the four-month grace period, however, will cause the secured creditor to lose his or her priority and be subordinated to the interest of a purchaser of the ordinary goods during the grace period. *Massey–Ferguson Credit Corp. v. Wells Motor Co.,* 374 So.2d 319, 322 (Ala.1979); *Rockwell Int'l Credit Corp. v. Valley Bank,* 109 Idaho 406, 408, 707 P.2d 517, 519 (Idaho App.1985); U.C.C. § 9–103 comment 7. As one commentator describes the operation of section 9–103(1)(d):

> When ordinary goods are brought into another state subject to a perfected security interest, there is a carry over into the second state of the perfection obtained in the first state. This carry-over perfection is conditional, being conditioned upon the creditor's taking within the second state the steps required by that state to reperfect the security interest. If such steps are taken in the second state there is a perfection that continues according to the terms of the law of the second state. This perfection relates back to the initial acquisition of perfection in the first state.
>
> If the security interest is not perfected in the second state during the period of the carry-over perfection, it lapses retroactively and relative rights are determined as though such carry-over perfection had never existed.

8 R. Anderson, *Anderson on the Uniform Commercial Code* § 9–103:39, at 510 (1985) (footnotes omitted).

11. Under section 84–9–103(1)(a), what are colloquially known as "ordinary goods" are defined as "goods other than those covered by a certificate of title described in subsection (2), mobile goods described in subsection (3), and mineral described in subsection (5)."

In contrast to section 84–9–103(1), section 84–9–103(3), the Kansas equivalent of section 9–103(3) of the Code, resolves priority disputes among creditors from more than one state having an interest in "mobile goods" moved from one state to another. Mobile goods are defined in section 9–103(3)(a) as "goods which are mobile and which are of a type normally used in more than one jurisdiction." [12] A security interest in mobile goods which is properly perfected in one state expires four months after "a change in the debtor's location to another jurisdiction." Kan.Stat.Ann. § 84–9–103(3)(e). Under section 84–9–103(3)(d), a debtor is deemed to be "located" at his "place of business if he has one, at his chief executive office if he has more than one place of business, otherwise at his residence." Therefore, if the combine is properly characterized as a mobile good and Lewis was deemed to be located in Hamilton County, Kansas, then his transporting of the combine to Colorado in October 1979 would have no effect on his perfected security interest in Kansas and Konkel would take the combine subject to Golden Plains' security interest. If the combine is properly characterized as an ordinary good, however, then Konkel would take free of Golden Plains' security interest.

We agree with the analysis of the court of appeals that the combine is properly characterized under Kansas law as a mobile good. The court of appeals correctly noted that the definition of mobile goods in section 84–9–103(3)(a) expressly included "commercial harvesting machinery and the like." The court of appeals also properly recognized that the 1983 Kansas commentary to section 84–9–103 describes precisely the problem presented in this case:

> An excellent example of mobile goods, and one which is set forth expressly in [§ 84–9–103(3)], is commercial harvesting machinery. For example, if the debtor is a custom cutter headquartered in Wichita, [then] Kansas would be the proper place to file the financing statement even though the harvesting machinery goes from Texas to North Dakota during the cutting season.

For these reasons, we conclude that the combine Konkel purchased was a mobile good within the meaning of section 84–9–103(3)(a). Because the combine was properly characterized as a mobile good, the trial court erred in concluding that Golden Plains lost its security interest in the combine solely because Golden Plains failed to reperfect its security interest within four months of bringing the combine into Baca County, Colorado. When the collateral was "brought into" the second state is a relevant inquiry for ordinary goods but is an irrelevant inquiry for mobile goods. The relevant inquiry for mobile goods under Kansas law is whether the debtor has "changed his location," *see* Kan.Stat.Ann. § 84–9–103(3)(e), which in this case requires a determination of the debtor's place of "residence," *see* Kan.Stat.Ann. § 84–9–103(3)(d). The court of appeals correctly noted that this issue was not decided by the trial court. We leave that determination for the trial court on remand.

12. The definition of mobile goods also requires that the goods are not covered by a certificate of title under section 9–103(2)(a) and that the goods are either a debtor's equipment or his inventory that he leases to others. U.C.C. § 9–103(3)(a); J. White & R. Summers, *Uniform Commercial Code* § 22–23, at 1063 (1988). Both parties agree that neither of these requirements is at issue.

III.

On remand, the trial court must use the actual use test to determine whether Golden Plains properly perfected its security interest in the combine under Kansas law in May 1978. If it determines that the actual use of the combine was as "equipment used in farm operations," then the trial court must also determine if Lewis had "changed his location" under section 84–9–103(3)(d) at the time Konkel purchased the combine.

The judgment of the court of appeals is affirmed with respect to its decision that the combine was a mobile good. The judgment of the court of appeals is reversed with respect to its decision to require application of the "inherent use test." The case is remanded to the court of appeals with directions to remand to the trial court for further hearings.

Problem 4–14

Gamecock Porche Audi is a car dealer in Columbia, South Carolina. Volunteer Imports is a car dealer in Chatanooga, Tennessee. The two dealerships are separately incorporated, but they are both subsidiaries of a holding company known as Southeastern Imported Cars. Nations Bank financed the inventory of Gamecock and had a perfected security interest in all of its automobiles and other inventory. First American financed the inventory of Volunteer and had a perfected security interest in all of its assets. These security agreements had all the usual terms, including after-acquired property clauses. In March 1994, business was not good in Columbia. Gamecock decided to move fifteen new Porches it had on its South Carolina lot together with various parts to Volunteer. All of these assets were inventory and all were subject to Nations Bank's security interest. Their total value was $1,000,000. Nations Bank did not discover that these had been moved until Gamecock defaulted sometime late in the fall of 1994. It then went to Chatanooga where it discovered that half of the automobiles were still in the possession of Volunteer and that the other half had been sold to consumers. First American asserted first priority on the assets and proceeds and refused to allow Nations Bank to take any of them. Nations Bank commenced a lawsuit against First American (both Gamecock and Volunteer now having defaulted and both being on the verge of bankruptcy).

The transaction between Gamecock and Volunteer was a "sale" although it is unclear that any money passed hands. Assume for the purpose of the problem that Nations Bank's security interest would have carried over in the collateral in the hands of Volunteer but for the lapse that might have occurred because of the application of 9–103. (See also 9–306(2).) First American argues that Nations Bank's security interest lapsed.

1. Nations Bank argues that it had a perfected security interest for at least four months after the assets came into Tennessee. Since the rights of both First American and another lien creditor, who attached certain assets, arose within that four months, the rights of all of them were frozen during that time and Nations Bank's remains prior—so Nations Bank argues. How do you respond?

2. Assume that you represent Nations Bank who discovered the movement the week after it had occurred in March. Pending a lawsuit to seize the assets, what acts could Nations Bank take to continue its perfection in Tennessee? What if representatives of Gamecock and Volunteer were not cooperative?

3. Would your analysis of either of the above problems be changed if Gamecock, Volunteer or both had filed in Chapter 11 within four months after the assets had been moved from South Carolina to Tennessee?

Problem 4–15

The Dandy Printing Company has its principal place of business in New Mexico. First Bank loaned Dandy $100,000 for general expansion and, among other things, created and perfected (in New Mexico) a security interest in equipment, existing and after-acquired. Thereafter, Dandy entered into two transactions. First, Dandy contracted to purchase a book binding machine from a manufacturer in California for $50,000. When the machine was ready, Dandy sent its truck to California and brought the machine directly back to New Mexico. Five days after the machine was installed in Dandy's plant (you may assume that it is not a fixture), the manufacturer perfected a purchase money security interest in the machine by an appropriate filing in California. A month later the manufacturer filed a financing statement in Santa Fe. Second, Dandy purchased for cash in New Mexico ten aluminum containers for the shipment of books. Thereafter, the containers were transported to a branch office in Colorado where inventory was stockpiled to be shipped all over the country. Shortly thereafter Dandy borrowed $25,000 from Second Bank in Colorado for general purposes and, among other things, permitted Second Bank to create and perfect a security interest in the containers. It is now six months later and no further action has been taken by any of the parties to these transactions. Are either of these security interests effective?

Problem 4–16

Alfred was a resident of Muncie, Indiana when he bought a $40,000 mobile home from Muncie Mobile Home Sales whose only place of business was in downtown Muncie. Alfred paid $3,000 down and borrowed $37,000 from the seller. He granted a security interest to Muncie Mobile Home Sales; Muncie filed a financing statement on September 1, 1989, in Delaware County where Muncie is located. Shortly after the sale, Muncie sold Alfred's loan to Bank Indiana. Bank Indiana had filed a proper financing statement covering Muncie's inventory, intangibles, and proceeds. On September 15, Alfred installed his mobile home on a lot near Fort Wayne, Indiana, in Allen County. Comment on the accuracy of the following statements:

A. If Alfred goes into bankruptcy in November, 1989, the Bank will have a perfected security interest in the mobile home.

B. If Muncie Mobile Home Sales (but not Alfred) goes into bankruptcy in October, Bank will be entitled to payments from Alfred in preference to the claim of Muncie's trustee in bankruptcy.

C. If Muncie sells Alfred's security papers to Chicago Bank in October in violation of its agreement with and prior sale to Bank Indiana, Chicago Bank will have priority over Bank Indiana as to the payments.

Problem 4–17

Assume that Alfred moved not to Fort Wayne, but to Defiance, Ohio and located his mobile home on a lot in Defiance on October 1. On October 15 he sold the mobile home to Yale Bollinger, a local rock singer. Bollinger paid $40,000 to Alfred, who claimed to have good title. Bollinger borrowed $37,000 from Defiance Bank and gave it a security interest which Defiance Bank promptly perfected in Ohio.

If Bank Indiana discovers these events on November 1, will its rights in the mobile home be subordinate to the rights of Defiance Bank?

Note: Motor Vehicles, A Special Case

The certificate of title laws that now exist in all of the states in some form provide a mode of perfection that was in use in many states at the time of enactment of the Code, and which is entirely separate from the Code system of perfection. The drafters of Article 9 bowed to the certificate of title mode of perfection by adopting section UCC 9–302(3). That subsection in effect removes perfection as to most motor vehicles from the Article 9 filing system. In many states it was formerly possible and in some states, it may still be possible, to perfect certain security interests in titled vehicles under the UCC. Certificate of title legislation that allowed for optional perfection in certain cases under the UCC was known as an "incomplete" act whereas those that required certificate of title perfection were referred to as "complete" certificate of title acts. The trend has been toward complete title acts and away from incomplete ones.

This removal from Article 9 has left a few jagged edges. For example, it was not always clear whether a creditor could perfect a security interest in automobiles held by a dealer in inventory by a UCC filing or whether it was necessary to procure a certificate of title and get one's name on that certificate. That was particularly true in the case of used cars where a certificate would be outstanding (typically none would be outstanding with respect to a new car until its first sale). In section 9–302(3) the 1972 Code made it clear that an inventory financer of autos must perfect pursuant to Article 9 and nothing is required of such a party under certificate of title perfection rules.

Yet more clearly within Article 9 are the rules concerning the state of perfection and the continuation or not of perfection when an automobile is moved from one state to another or when the residence of the debtor changes. At least with respect to the continued perfection of the security interest section 9–103(2) gives most, if not all, of the answers. One should first read section 9–103(2) and *In re Nunley* with care and then answer the problems that follow.

IN RE NUNLEY

United States Bankruptcy Court, Eastern District of Tennessee, 1982.
21 B.R. 826.

CLIVE W. BARE, BANKRUPTCY JUDGE.

I

The dispute in this case between the plaintiff, Associates Commercial Corporation, and the defendants, the debtors [1] and their trustee, involves a 1979 Freightliner tractor truck. The plaintiff contends that it is the holder of a perfected security interest against the vehicle in question, whereas the trustee alleges that the security interest of the plaintiff is unperfected. The issue is whether or not the trustee may defeat the security interest of the plaintiff on the basis that: (i) the vehicle was *registered* in a jurisdiction other than the jurisdiction which *issued* the certificate of title for the

1. A default judgment has been entered against the debtors.

vehicle; (ii) no action was taken by the plaintiff secured creditor within the four-month period following removal, subsequent to the change of residence by the debtors from one jurisdiction to another and the concomitant removal of the vehicle into the jurisdiction of the debtor's new residence. See Va Code § 8.9–103(2), infra.

The parties are in agreement as to the following facts:

Earl Franklin Nunley purchased a 1979 Freightliner tractor truck, serial number CA213HL171013, on July 30, 1980, from Atlanta Freightliner Truck Sales and Service, Inc., Atlanta, Ga. A security agreement was executed by Nunley and assigned to Associates Commercial Corporation. Nunley had knowledge of this assignment as evidenced by the fact that he submitted monthly installment payments to Associates through their Georgia offices for a period of more than one year beginning in September of 1980. Associates forwarded the necessary documentation to the appropriate office in the Commonwealth of Virginia, which was the state of Nunley's residence when the tractor truck was purchased, for the purpose of obtaining a certificate of title reflecting the existence of Associate's first lien. (Nunley is a truck driver who leases his services to various carriers. His work requires that he drive his truck through many of the contiguous states.) A Virginia title certificate was issued on September 5, 1980, but the title certificate contained an erroneous serial number. (The serial number which appears on the certificate of title is CA21*4*HL171013. The correct serial number is CA21*3*HL171013.)

When Nunley purchased the vehicle in question, he was employed by Watkins Motor Lines, which informed him that he would have to register the tractor truck in either Florida or Georgia. A Florida Vehicle Registration Certificate bearing the correct serial number of the truck was issued on November 10, 1980. This registration expired on June 30, 1981.

In February of 1981, Nunley entered into a contract for the lease of his tractor truck and services with the Interstate Contract Carrier Corporation. His new employer informed him that he would be required to register his truck in either Illinois, Oklahoma or Utah. The debtor chose Oklahoma, and an Oklahoma registration was issued on May 11, 1981. The tractor truck was proportionally registered between the state of Oklahoma and 25 other states, including Tennessee and Virginia.

The debtors were residents of Virginia until August 5, 1981, when they moved to Tennessee. Associates was directly informed by Nunley of his change of residence. The debtors filed their chapter 7 bankruptcy petition on December 14, 1981, which was more than 120 days after their change of residence from Virginia to Tennessee.

The only action taken by Associates to perfect its security interest was the procurement of the Virginia certificate of title reflecting its first lien claim. Neither Associates nor Nunley sought issuance of a new title from any state in which the vehicle was reregistered and no state other than Virginia has issued a certificate of title covering the vehicle.

II

The plaintiff filed a complaint seeking relief from the automatic stay of 11 U.S.C.A. § 362 on February 9, 1982. The plaintiff alleged that: (1) the debtor had monetarily defaulted on a conditional sales contract assigned to the plaintiff; (2) plaintiff has a validly perfected security interest in a Freightliner tractor truck, the fair market value of which was less than the unpaid secured debt; (3) physical damage insurance on the security vehicle had been cancelled and the vehicle had been abandoned.

In his answer, the trustee denied that the plaintiff had a validly perfected security interest. The trustee alleged that the title certificate was ineffective since there was a variance between the actual serial number of the vehicle and the serial number reflected on the title certificate.[2] Additionally, the trustee alleged that "the subject vehicle was subsequently reregistered in the states of Florida and Oklahoma so as to require the proper notation in the respective states by the plaintiff in order to maintain the claim of a perfected security interest." [3]

The trustee takes the position that Virginia law is applicable in determining the outcome of this case. The trustee further believes that the outcome is to be determined by application of Va.Code § 8.9–103(2), which provides in apposite part:

> "(2) Certificate of title.
>
> "(a) This subsection applies to goods covered by a certificate of title issued under a statute of this state or of another jurisdiction under the law of which indication of a security interest on the certificate is required as a condition of perfection.
>
> "(b) Except as otherwise provided in this subsection, perfection and the effect of perfection or non-perfection of the security interest are governed by the law (including the conflict of laws rules) of the jurisdiction issuing the certificate until four months after the goods are removed from that jurisdiction and *thereafter until* the goods are *registered in another jurisdiction,* but in any event not beyond surrender of the certificate. After the expiration of that period, the goods are not covered by the certificate of title within the meaning of this section." (Emphasis added.)

The defendant trustee asserts that the reregistration in Florida and Oklahoma, which *preceded* the debtor's change of residence, coupled with the passage of more than 120 days from the date on which the debtors moved from Virginia to Tennessee and the accompanying removal of the collateral, cut off the perfected lien of the plaintiff, absent the issuance of a new title certificate in Tennessee within the four-month statutory period.

The plaintiff-lender, Associates, presents a tripartite argument. Initially, the plaintiff takes the position that the Virginia certificate of title serves to perfect its security interest and that "the debtors' multiple, nonresident registration of the truck" and subsequent move to Tennessee are inconsequential with regard to the perfection of the plaintiff's security interest in

2. In their briefs, the parties did not address the issue of the mistake in the serial number shown in the certificate of title. However, a single digit error in a financing statement, absent prejudice, is harmless.

* * *

3. By agreement of the parties, the vehicle has been sold by the trustee for $29,000.00, which was the highest bid at an advertised sale. The bid price, less expenses, has been paid by the plaintiff and deposited in an escrow account of the trustee pursuant to an order of the court.

the tractor truck. Secondly, the plaintiff argues that Va.Code § 8.9–103(2) is inapplicable to the instant facts since: (a) the motor vehicle in question was removed from as opposed to being brought into Virginia; (b) Va.Code § 8.9–302(4) provides that duration of a perfected security interest is governed by Va.Code § 46.1–68 through § 46.1–98.1. Finally, the plaintiff asserts that the perfection of its security interest in the tractor truck is continued even if Va.Code § 8.9–103(2) is controlling.

III

The starting point to resolve this conflict is T.C.A. § 47–9–103. Subsection (2) thereof provides in part:

"(2) If the chief place of business of a debtor is in this state, this chapter governs the validity and perfection of a security interest and the possibility and effect of proper filing with regard to general intangibles or with regard to goods of a type which are normally used in more than one (1) jurisdiction (such as automotive equipment, rolling stock, airplanes, road building equipment, commercial harvesting equipment, construction machinery and the like) if such goods are classified as equipment or classified as inventory by reason of their being leased by the debtor to others. Otherwise, the law (including the conflict of laws rules) of the jurisdiction where such chief place of business is located shall govern. If the chief place of business is located in a jurisdiction which does not provide for perfection of the security interest by filing or recording in that jurisdiction, then the security interest may be perfected by filing in this state."

The chief place of business of the secured debtor is in Tennessee. Consequently, the provisions of T.C.A. § 47–9–101 et seq. are apposite.

T.C.A. § 47–9–103(4) provides that:

"Notwithstanding subsections (2) and (3), if personal property is covered by a certificate of title issued under a statute of this state or any other jurisdiction which requires indication on a certificate of title of any security interest in the property as a condition of perfection, then the perfection is governed by the law of the jurisdiction which *issued* the certificate." (Emphasis added.)

Consequently, since Virginia does require indication on a certificate of title of any security interest in a motor vehicle, the laws of the Commonwealth of Virginia are applicable in this case. (The parties do not dispute this conclusion.)

Va.Code § 8.9–302 provides in pertinent part:

"(3) The filing of a financing statement otherwise required by this Article is not necessary or effective to perfect a security interest in property subject to

* * *

"(b) the following statutes of this state; §§ 46.1–68 through 46.1–98.1. * * *

"(4) Compliance with a statute or treaty described in subsection (3) is equivalent to the filing of a financing statement under this title, and a security interest in property subject to the statute or treaty can be perfected only by compliance therewith except as provided in section 8.9–103 on multiple state transactions. *Duration and renewal of perfection of a security interest perfected by compliance with the statute or treaty are governed by the provisions of the statute* or treaty; in other respects the security interest is subject to this title." (Emphasis added.)

The continuity and duration of the perfection of the security interest of Associates against the tractor truck is governed by Va Code § 46.1–68 et seq., unless Va Code § 8.9–103 is applicable.

The facts in the instant case are similar but not identical to the facts in a recent Sixth Circuit Court of Appeals decision. Uhle v. Parts and Trucks (In re Paige), 679 F.2d 601 (6th Cir. May 26, 1982) involved a debtor, a Michigan resident, who purchased a truck tractor in Indiana. A purchase money security agreement executed by the debtor was assigned to Associates Commercial Corporation, who is also the assignee of the security agreement involved in the subject dispute. The debtor drove as an interstate hauler for a company whose terminal was in Indiana and whose home office was in Minnesota. However, the debtor's employer also had a business office in Illinois. An agent of debtor's employer prepared an application for an Illinois certificate of title, which was subsequently issued. The certificate of title reflected the security interest of Associates. No financing statement was filed and no other certificate of title had been sought when Paige, the debtor, filed bankruptcy.

The Bankruptcy Court (Judge Nims) held that the security interest of Associates, although noted on the Illinois title certificate, was unperfected under Michigan law and invalid vis-à-vis the bankruptcy trustee. In re Paige, 3 B.R. 115 (Bankr. W.D.Mich.1980). The district court affirmed Judge Nims' holding in an unpublished order.

The court of appeals noted that the issue was simply whether or not the notation of the lien on the Illinois certificate of title served to perfect the security interest under Michigan law. The court of appeals concluded that Judge Nims erred in his interpretation of Mich.Stat.Ann. § 19.9103(4); M.C.L.A. § 440.9103(4), which is identical to T.C.A. § 47–9–103(4), quoted heretofore. The court of appeals based its conclusion on a literal reading of UCC § 9–103(4), which clearly provides that perfection is to be governed by the law of the certificating state if that state requires notation of a security interest on a certificate of title as a condition of perfection. The court noted that Illinois does require such a notation on a certificate of title and found Illinois law applicable, which meant that the security interest of Associates was properly perfected *vis-à-vis* the trustee.

In Paige, as in the instant case, the certificating state had adopted the 1972 version of the UCC. The respective destination states, Michigan and Tennessee, each have the 1962 version of the UCC as the source of law for commercial transactions. The only distinguishing fact which may be material is that there is no report of any registration in any state other than Illinois in the Paige case, whereas there were multiple registrations in the instant case, all of which *preceded* the removal of the vehicle from Virginia to Tennessee. This factor does not, in this court's opinion, preclude the application of the Paige decision to determine the outcome of the instant case.

The trustee cites Patti v. Barnett Bank (In re Hartberg), (Bankr. E.D.Wis.1979), in support of his position that the Associates' security interest is unperfected in the subject case. The debtors in Hartberg had purchased a vehicle in November of 1976, while residing in Florida. A security agreement was executed by the debtors in favor of Barnett Bank, and a Florida certificate of title was issued on December 10, 1976. The certificate of title, which reflected the security interest of the bank, was retained by Barnett Bank. In September of 1977, the debtors established a residence in Wisconsin, where the security automobile was registered on December 3, 1977. No certificate of title was issued by the State of Wisconsin. The debtors filed bankruptcy on July 3, 1978, which was 3 months after the debtors stopped making payments to Barnett Bank.

The bankruptcy trustee contended that the lien was never perfected in Wisconsin. Judge Hilgendorf agreed with the bankruptcy trustee. The holding of the case is that a secured creditor whose interest is noted on a certificate of title must take action within 4 months from the date of removal to continue the perfection of his interest in a motor vehicle which is removed from the certificating jurisdiction and *registered* in another jurisdiction.

The plaintiff does note in its brief, based on the following quotation from Hartberg, that the decision might have been different if the case had been decided under the provisions of the 1962 Code:

> "The original 1962 version of the Uniform Commercial Code relating to motor vehicles was substantially different from the 1972 official text which was adopted in Wisconsin in 1973. The 1962 Code was interpreted by most courts to grant priority to a lien holder whose lien was perfected by indication on the certificate of title regardless of where the automobile may have been taken and regardless of the period of time it remained in another jurisdiction." Hartberg, 25 UCC Rep.Serv. at 1432.

It is arguable that the decision in Hartberg is incorrect. The district court in the case of Strick Corp. v. Eldo-Craft Boat Co., Inc., 479 F.Supp. 720 (W.D.Ark.1979) interpreted "registered," as that term is employed in UCC § 9–103(2), to require the procurement of a certificate of title. The court noted:

> It is the opinion of this court that the section just quoted (UCC § 9–103(2)) continues in force the perfection of a security interest noted on a foreign certificate of title until a certificate has been issued by another jurisdiction." Strick, 479 F.Supp. at 725.

A more "customary" interpretation of registration is found in the district court's opinion in the case of In re Howard, 9 B.R. 957 (N.D.N.Y. 1981). The bankrupt had purchased a truck in November of 1978 from a Massachusetts dealer. The security interest of GMAC was duly noted on the Massachusetts title certificate. In January of 1979, the bankrupt moved from Massachusetts to New York. The security vehicle was registered in New York in July of 1979, but no title certificate was issued in conjunction with the registration. In a contest between GMAC, the secured creditor, and the bankruptcy trustee, the district court affirmed the decision of the bankruptcy court that the GMAC security interest was unperfected. The decision was based on the "plain language" of UCC § 9–103(2)(b) and the fact that the debtor's truck was reregistered in New York more than 4 months after its removal from Massachusetts.

This court's decision is governed by the Sixth Circuit's decision in Paige. The holding in Paige is that the perfection of a security interest in a motor vehicle which is brought into a jurisdiction which has adopted the 1962 version of the Uniform Commercial Code continues if the certificating state requires indication of the security interest on the certificate of title as a condition of perfection and the security interest is perfected in the jurisdiction which issued the certificate of title. Applying the holding of Paige to the instant facts, the court finds that the security interest of Associates is perfected by virtue of the Virginia certificate of title and that the interest is not unperfected as a result of the removal of the vehicle from Virginia to Tennessee. The statute under scrutiny herein, Va.Code § 8.9–103(2)(b) provides that:

> "[p]erfection and the effect of perfection or non-perfection of the security interest are governed by the law * * * of the jurisdiction issuing the certificate until four months after the goods are removed from that jurisdiction *and thereafter until the goods are registered in another jurisdiction.* * * * " (Emphasis added.)

There was in fact no registration of the vehicle in another jurisdiction *after* removal from Virginia to Tennessee. If there had been, the court would have been confronted with a different question. Since perfection of the interest of Associates is governed by the law of Virginia, the certificating state, that interest remains perfected because the Virginia certificate of title is valid and unsurrendered.

This Memorandum constitutes findings of fact and conclusions of law, Bankruptcy Rule 752.

Submit judgment. [One footnote omitted.]

Notes

1. What did the drafters intend with respect to a truck that was "registered" in many states? In a weak moment one of the drafters of Article 9 has suggested the drafters erred.

2. The first sentence in UCC 9–103(2)(b) is one of the most complex in the entire Uniform Commercial Code. Read it with care. Both the *Nunley* case and the problem that follows should give the student some understanding of its meaning.

Problem 4–18

In which of the following cases has the creditor become unsecured?

1. Debtor procures a certificate of title in Ohio, and lists secured creditor's name on it. Debtor moves to Pennsylvania and resides there for two years. Debtor retains his Ohio registration and certificate. At the end of two years, is debtor still perfected?

2. Assume in the foregoing example that the debtor procured a new certificate of title and relinquished his old one in Pennsylvania one week after he arrived there. Creditor discovers this and seeks to repossess the car 30 days after it has been removed from Ohio. Is the creditor unperfected?

3. Debtor buys a Porsche 928 for $45,000. Debtor pays $20,000 down and borrows $25,000 from Bank One in Columbus. Bank One properly perfects by getting its name noted on the certificate of title. Shortly after the car is purchased it is stolen off the street one night in Columbus. Five months later the car turns up in Birmingham, Alabama in the hands of a local doctor who claims to be a bona fide purchaser. The doctor displays an apparently clean Alabama certificate of title which was issued to him after he purchased the car from a used car dealer in Birmingham. It appears that the thief somehow procured a false or fraudulent clean certificate of title in Alabama and then sold the automobile under that title to the used car dealer. Assume that the car is now worth $27,000, that Bank One's debt still stands at $24,000 and that the Birmingham bona fide purchaser paid $30,000 for the car. Who gets what parts of the car among the Ohio owner, the Ohio Bank, and the Alabama purchaser? Is only a part of the answer provided by UCC 9–103? Assume that Bank One still has possession of the Ohio certificate of title.

Problem 4–19

Boscoe purchased a new car for $35,000 from Slick Motors. A certificate of title, duly noting Slick's security interest, was issued by State A where Boscoe resided. Six months later the car was stolen, taken to State B and, after some skillful fraud by the thief, a "clean" certificate of title was issued by State B. Shortly thereafter, the thief sold the car to Hume, a BFP, and delivered the clean certificate of title.

1. Assuming that State B has both the Uniform Act and the 1972 Official Text, what is the effect of this last transaction on the title of Boscoe and the security interest of Slick?

2. What provisions and procedures in the Uniform Act are designed to prevent the issuance of fraudulent certificates? If the state has in fact issued the fraudulent, but "clean" certificate, why shouldn't those who rely in good faith and pay value receive full protection?

SECTION 9. PERFECTION IN PROCEEDS

In the previous chapter we considered the nature of proceeds, how and in what circumstances a security interest attaches to proceeds and what "identifiable" proceeds are. Once one has resolved those issues, the questions of perfection are relatively clear, if somewhat complex. Here the student must read UCC 9–306(3) with care. Beware, it is easy to misread that subsection, particularly (3)(a). Consider the following problem.

Problem 4–20

In which of the following cases will Bank have a perfected security interest in the proceeds? In which cases will additional acts be required in order to continue its perfection?

1. Bank makes a secured loan to local corporation and files a financing statement covering inventory. It mentions neither "proceeds" nor any of the

items such as accounts or chattel paper. When inventory is sold, it produces cash, accounts receivable, and in some cases, chattel paper.

2. Assume that debtor retail merchant is a division of a larger corporation whose chief executive office is in another state. Now the Bank will be unperfected as to the accounts and chattel paper. True?

3. Assume now that the debtor uses some of the cash to purchase new inventory and some to purchase equipment. Assume further that the cash was deposited in a commingled bank account before it was drawn out to pay for that inventory and equipment. Ignoring the effect of any after-acquired property clause and relying exclusively on its proceeds claim, will the bank have a perfected proceeds interest now?

Problem 4–21

Assume that debtor sells collateral and takes his buyer's note. The note, of course, is proceeds and identifiable as such, and thus the security interest that formerly attached to the collateral attaches to the identifiable proceeds (buyer's note). Debtor goes into bankruptcy a month after he procures the buyer's note. Who takes the note: the trustee in bankruptcy or the secured creditor with the proceeds claim?

CITICORP (USA) v. DAVIDSON LUMBER CO.

United States Court of Appeals, Eleventh Circuit, 1983.
718 F.2d 1030.

Before GODBOLD, CHIEF JUDGE, RONEY and TJOFLAT, CIRCUIT JUDGES.

GODBOLD, CHIEF JUDGE:

Florida Steel Corp., a petitioning creditor of Davidson Lumber Co. and Davidson Timber Co., the "debtors," appeals from the judgment of the district court. That court held that a certificate of deposit (CD) constituted cash proceeds under Fla.Stat.Ann. Sec. 679.306(1) (West Supp.1983), and that therefore the appellees, Citicorp and Southeast Bank, had a continuing perfected security interest in the CD at issue, even though they were not in possession of the instrument. The district court's decision reversed the holding of the bankruptcy court, 19 Bankr. 871 (Bankr.S.B.Fla.1982), that the banks' security interest was unperfected. We reverse.

The banks shared a perfected security interest in various of the debtors' assets, including general intangibles, as collateral for the debtors' indebtedness of approximately $3 million. Shortly before various of the debtors' creditors filed an involuntary petition under chapter 7 of the Bankruptcy Code, the debtors received a federal tax refund of approximately $1.3 million. The banks had been aware that the debtors would receive this money, although the banks did not know exactly when. Without the knowledge of the banks, the debtors used this refund to purchase a CD of which the banks did not take possession.

In Florida security interests are governed by the Uniform Commercial Code. Under Florida law a perfected security interest in collateral continues in the proceeds generated by disposition of that collateral for at least 10 days. Fla.Stat.Ann. Sec. 679.306(3) (West Supp.1983). Continuation beyond the tenth day depends in part on how those proceeds are classified under Sec. 679.306. Section 679.306 provides in relevant part:

> (1) "Proceeds" includes whatever is received upon the sale, exchange, collection or other disposition of collateral or proceeds. Insurance payable by reason of loss or damage to the collateral is proceeds, except to the extent that it is payable to a person other than a party to the security agreement. Money, checks, deposit accounts, and the like are "cash proceeds." All other proceeds are "non-cash proceeds."
>
> (2) Except where this chapter otherwise provides, a security interest continues in collateral notwithstanding sale, exchange, or other disposition thereof unless the disposition was authorized by the secured party in the security agreement or otherwise, and also continues in any identifiable proceeds including collections received by the debtor.
>
> (3) The security interest in proceeds is a continuously perfected security interest if the interest in the original collateral was perfected, but it ceases to be a perfected security interest and becomes unperfected 10 days after receipt of the proceeds by the debtor unless:
>
> (a) A filed financing statement covers the original collateral and the proceeds are collateral in which a security interest may be perfected by filing in the office or offices where the financing statement has been filed and, if the proceeds are acquired with cash proceeds, the description of collateral in the financing statement indicates the types of property constituting the proceeds; or
>
> (b) A filed financing statement covers the original collateral and the proceeds are identifiable cash proceeds; or
>
> (c) The security interest in the proceeds is perfected before expiration of the 10–day period.
>
> Except as provided in this section, a security interest in proceeds can be perfected only by the methods or under the circumstances permitted in this chapter for original collateral of the same type.

The district court held that CD's are cash proceeds within the meaning of Sec. 679.306(1), and that therefore the banks' security interest in the CD remained perfected under Sec. 679.306(3)(b). Because the court's decision was based on its interpretation of Florida law, we have the fullest scope of review; the district court's interpretation of the Florida statute is not shielded by any presumption of correctness. *See Universal Minerals, Inc. v. C.A. Hughes & Co.,* 669 F.2d 98, 102 (3d Cir.1981); *see also International Horizons, Inc. v. Committee of Unsecured Creditors (In re International Horizons, Inc.),* 689 F.2d 996, 1002–05 (11th Cir.1982) (engaging in de novo review of district court's decision on choice of law on review of bankruptcy court).

Applying Sec. 679.306 to the present case, we find the banks had a temporarily perfected security interest in the CD for 10 days after it was acquired by the debtors. For that perfected security interest to continue, however, the banks had to fall within one of the three subsections of Fla.Stat.Ann.Sec. 679.306(3). The banks did not.

Neither of the parties argues that the banks' security interest continued to be perfected under Sec. 679.306(3)(a) or (c). Rather the issue presented is whether the CD constituted "identifiable cash proceeds" within the protection of Sec. 679.306(3)(b).

Cash proceeds are defined in Sec. 679.306(1):

> Money, checks, deposit accounts, and the like are "cash proceeds."

A CD is not a check or money. Likewise, a 1979 amendment to Fla.Stat. Ann.Sec. 679.105(1)(e) (West Supp.1983) explicitly provides that the term "deposit account" does not include CD's.

> "Deposit account" means [something] other than an account evidenced by a certificate of deposit. * * *

The 1979 amendment is particularly pertinent in the present case because the Sponsors' Notes to the amendment state:

> A definition of "deposit account" has been added to facilitate references to such accounts *in the section on proceeds* (s. 679.306).

(emphasis added). The narrow question we must decide is whether, as the banks argue, CD's fall within the "and the like" language of Sec. 679.306(1). It defies common sense, however, to suggest that the Florida legislature added the amendment excluding CD's from the definition of deposit accounts (one of the specified types of cash proceeds), and referred the reader to the section on cash proceeds, only to intend that CD's be treated as cash proceeds in the catch-all clause "and the like." The obvious legislative intent behind the amendment is that CD's are not cash proceeds.

The banks rely on *Citizens National Bank v. Bornstein,* 374 So.2d 6 (Fla.1979), in support of their argument that CD's are "like" checks and therefore are cash proceeds. This reads too much into the *Bornstein* opinion. It held that a CD is an "instrument." While checks may be instruments, so are promissory notes and bills of exchange, Fla.Stat.Ann. Sec. 673.104(2) (West 1966 & Supp.1983), neither of which is listed under Sec. 679.306(1) as identifiable cash proceeds.[1] *Bornstein* did not compare CD's to checks as the banks imply.

The banks argue that the result reached here would be "preposterous," because it "provides an opportunity for a debtor to conceal proceeds of

1. Generally, to perfect a security interest in an instrument the secured party must take possession of it. *See* Fla.Stat.Ann. Sec. 679.304 (West 1966 & Supp.1983). The banks admit that they did not take possession of the CD.

Under Sec. 679.306, checks represent a narrow departure from the general requirement of possession of instruments. That section provides that checks may be the object of a perfected security interest without possession when they are identifiable cash proceeds. Far from being "like" checks, however, CD's are similar to promissory notes. *Maxwell v. Agnew,* 21 Fla. 154 (1884). In *Southview Corp. v. Kleberg First Nat'l Bank,* 512 S.W.2d 817 (Tex.Civ.App.1974), the court explained:

> The promissory note theory of certificate of deposit has been incorporated into the Code as illustrated by the definition of a certificate of deposit: "[A] receipt of money with an engagement to repay it." * * * Following this definition of certificate of deposit, the Code makes such definition applicable to other chapters which would necessarily include Chapter 9. * * * In its usual and ordinary form, a certificate of deposit contains the elements of a promissory note, rather than of a mere receipt, and in general has that legal effect.

Id. at 819–20 (citations omitted). For this reason as well, the banks' argument that CD's are like checks must fail.

collateral from a secured creditor, to secretly convert that collateral into another form which requires perfection by taking possession, and then to effectively extinguish the right of that secured creditor by consciously withholding that collateral or keeping its existence a secret. * * * " Brief for Appellees at 18–19. This argument is misconceived. The Code gives secured creditors many methods of policing their debtors. By contractual agreement lenders may require their debtors to permit on-premises inspections of their books or they may insist that payments owed to the debtor by third parties must be sent directly to the lender. Fla.Stat.Ann. Sec. 679.502 (West Supp.1983). As Florida Steel points out, the banks might also have availed themselves of the Federal Assignment of Claims Act, 31 U.S.C. Sec. 203 (1976), *amended by* 31 U.S.C.A. Sec. 3727 (West 1983), which permits creditors to obtain directly from the government sums of money, such as tax refunds, which are liquidated claims owed by the government to the debtor. *See, e.g., King v. Gilbert,* 569 F.2d 398 (5th Cir.1978) (per curiam).

Because the district court misconstrued Sec. 679.306, we reverse its judgment and remand to the district court with instructions to affirm the judgment of the bankruptcy court.

Reversed and remanded.

SECTION 10. SECURING AN INTEREST WHEN THE COLLATERAL IS MULTIPLE ASSETS, I.E., CHATTEL PAPER

When one thinks of a simple security interest, one thinks of a debtor with some equipment or perhaps inventory who grants a security interest to a creditor. The creditor perfects that security interest by filing a financing statement. Perfection in that setting is quite simple and the creditor's principal concern is first that the collateral be worth more than the loan and second that the debtor not sell the collateral and sneak off in the night with the money.

When the collateral is not goods, but intangibles, an additional element of risk is present. In this case the secured creditor often has a claim upon a claim. The typical account receivable arises out of the debtor's sale of inventory to a person (the account debtor). There are now three persons involved in the transaction, the account debtor who owes money to the debtor and the debtor who owes money to the secured creditor. Perfection is still quite straightforward, but what if the account debtor has a defense against the debtor? Can the account debtor assert that defense against the secured creditor as well, or does the secured creditor take free of such defenses? Unless the secured creditor is a holder in due course or the defense arises out of another transaction, sections 9–206 and 9–318(1)(a) tell us that the account debtor can assert those defenses, and, therefore that the creditor must be concerned about these defenses. Of course, if 1,000 or 100,000 separate accounts are assigned by the debtor to the secured creditor, there is protection in numbers, for it is unlikely the defenses will arise in any significant number of the underlying transactions. Moreover, the secured creditor can insist on indemnity from the debtor against the account debtor's defenses. Nevertheless, there is an additional problem: whereas inventory does not assert defenses, an account debtor whose debts are the subject of security interests (accounts receivable) may do so.

Now let us complicate the problem further by making the Article Nine debtor not merely an unsecured creditor who has a right to the payment of an account, but a lessor or a secured creditor or a mortgagee who has taken a mortgage on the account debtor's real estate. In one common kind of case, the debtor sells a car to an account debtor and the account debtor signs a security agreement so that between the two of them, the ultimate "debtor" is a secured creditor and the ultimate "account debtor" is the debtor. The seller of the automobile who has taken the security interest now grants a security interest in its right to another secured creditor. Thus we have the relationship:

Bank (Secured Creditor)——>Car Dealer (Creditor, Debtor)——>
Buyer (Debtor, Account Debtor)

This transaction poses the difficulties presented by the transfer of an interest in an account, and some others as well. Note first the nomenclature. In our immediately preceding example the collateral was "accounts" (see 9–106). In this case the collateral is "chattel paper" (see 9–105(1)(b)). As in the former case, the person at the end of the line is an account debtor:

> "Account debtor" means the person who is obligated on an account, chattel paper or general intangible[.] (9–105(1)(a))

This transaction presents the same difficulty under 9–318(1) (concerning the account debtor's defenses) as does a security interest in the accounts, but it also presents the question how the secured creditor insures that it has a perfected security interest not only in the account debtor's promise to pay but also in the automobile or other asset that is the subject of the original lease or security agreement between the car dealer and the buyer. Understand that there are now two sets of creditors and two forms of collateral. As a secured creditor, the bank will doubtless wish to have protection against both sets and a perfected security interest in all of the collateral. To reiterate, assume that buyer (account debtor) has possession of the car and has creditors ranging from a credit card lender to the local utility. If the buyer defaults on some of these loans and goes into bankruptcy, these creditors will assert a claim against the car. Somehow there must be perfection of the security interest in the car that gives notice to those creditors. The car dealer, as the original secured creditor should have done what was necessary to perfect its security interest in the car. Usually this would be done by getting the dealership's name on the certificate of title. If the asset were an oil rig or something else, the seller would have to file a financing statement in the name of the account debtor. These acts would put the cluster of creditors who have lent money to the account debtor on notice of the car seller's security interest and would so have perfected it.

If the car dealer has a perfected security interest, the bank who takes a security interest in the chattel paper (a security interest in the security interest) is itself automatically perfected in the *car* under the terms of 9–302(2):

> If a secured party assigns a perfected security interest, no filing under this Article is required in order to continue the perfected status of the security interest against creditors of and transferees from the original debtor.

Read 9–302(2) carefully and note that it only protects creditors of and transferees from the "*original debtor.*"

But now there are other competitors, namely, the creditors of the car dealer (the creditors of the first secured creditor) the "debtor" in our transaction. The car dealer may have loans from other banks, may owe money to salesmen, suppliers, and other trade creditors, and somehow notice must be given to them that this asset (the stream of payments from account debtor and the claim in the account debtor's car) will not be available to them in case the car dealer defaults.

The bank has several ways to put the dealer's creditors on notice. First, it can simply file a financing statement in the name of the car dealer. A properly filed financing statement will put the car dealer's creditors on notice and will perfect the security interest in the car dealer's chattel paper. Alternatively the bank can take possession of the chattel paper. This too will perfect its interest.

To reiterate, the problem when there are multiple assets (in this case underlying goods and a promise to pay for those goods) is that the secured creditor must concern itself with two perfections against two sets of creditors. Normally the perfection against the creditors farthest downstream will already have occurred and 9–302(2) will give the secured creditor the benefit of that perfection in the underlying collateral, but that will not always be true. In any case, a diligent secured creditor should examine the perfection of its debtor in the underlying goods.

As the case below discloses and as the case in Chapter Seven will show, there are additional complications. First, the original transaction between the debtor and account debtor could be a lease or it could be a security agreement. In either case the asset that is transferred to the secured creditor is chattel paper, but as the case below will disclose, the perfection requirements may be quite different if the underlying deal is a "lease" and not a "security interest". As we will see in Chapter Seven distinguishing between true leases and security agreements is a complicated and difficult task.

An additional complication arises when the underlying transaction involves real estate and not personal property. Instead of a car dealer, the person seeking the loan from the bank may be a mortgagee of real estate. When this is so the parties will be stuck with one foot in the real estate law and one foot in Article 9. That transaction has some of the same qualities as taking a security interest in chattel paper and some others too. We reserve those problems for Chapter Seven.

Problem 4–22

Retail Merchant sells a $1500 stereo system for use in Buyer's home. Buyer signs a security agreement granting a security interest to Merchant. Merchant then transfers its rights in the chattel paper to Bank. Assume that Bank neither takes possession nor files a financing statement with respect to the chattel paper. Are the following propositions true?

a. If consumer-debtor goes into bankruptcy, Bank will have a perfected security interest in the stereo that will be superior to the claim of the consumer's trustee in bankruptcy and of his other creditors.

b. If Merchant goes into bankruptcy, Bank's claim to the chattel paper sold to it will be superior to the claim of Merchant's trustee.

c. If Bank had a perfected security interest in merchant's "inventory," it would fare better (1) in a; (2) in b.

IN RE LEASING CONSULTANTS, INC.

United States Court of Appeals, Second Circuit, 1973.
486 F.2d 367.

Before FRIENDLY and HAYS, CIRCUIT JUDGES, and JAMESON, DISTRICT JUDGE.

JAMESON, DISTRICT JUDGE:

Respondent-Appellant, First National City Bank (Bank), appeals from an order of the district court affirming, on a petition for review, the order of a referee in bankruptcy directing the Bank to turn over to the Petitioner-Appellee, George Feldman, Trustee in Bankruptcy (Trustee) of Leasing Consultants, Incorporated, (Leasing) the proceeds from the sale of equipment which had been leased by Leasing, located in New York, to Plastimetrix Corporation, located in New Jersey. The leases covering the equipment had been assigned to the Bank as security for a loan to Leasing.

The district court held, 351 F.Supp. 1390, on the basis of stipulated facts, that the perfection by the Bank by filing and possession in New York of its security interest in the lease/chattel paper was not a perfection of the Bank's security interest in Leasing's reversionary interest in the leased property, located in New Jersey. Consequently, the Trustee's lien was held superior to the Bank's unperfected security interest in the leased equipment.

SUMMARY OF FACTS

In March and June of 1969 Leasing entered into eight leases with Plastimetrix covering heavy equipment. The leased equipment was at all relevant times located in New Jersey. Leasing filed financing statements with the Secretary of State of the State of New Jersey covering each transaction, each statement bearing the legend: "THIS FILING IS FOR INFORMATIONAL PURPOSES ONLY AS THIS IS A LEASE TRANSACTION."

On December 15, 1969 Leasing entered into a "Loan and Security Agreement" with the Bank for the financing of its business of purchasing and leasing equipment. The agreement provided in part for the assignment of "a continuing security interest in the lease(s) and the property leased" as collateral security for advances and loans not to exceed 80% of aggregate unpaid rentals.

Pursuant to the security agreement Leasing borrowed money from the Bank in December, 1969 and February, 1970 and assigned as collateral security the eight Plastimetrix leases, each assignment covering all moneys due or to become due under the lease and the "relative equipment" described in the lease. The lease documents were delivered to the Bank.

On December 30 and 31, 1969 the Bank filed financing statements against Leasing with the Secretary of State of the State of New York and the Registrar of the City of New York, Queens County, where Leasing had its principal place of business.[1] No financing statements were filed by the Bank in New Jersey; nor did the Bank take possession of the leased equipment.

On October 14, 1970 Leasing was adjudicated bankrupt by the United States District Court for the Eastern District of New York. On October 30, 1970 Plastimetrix filed a petition under Chapter XI of the Bankruptcy Act in the United States District Court for the District of New Jersey.

The leases were in default and an offer was made to purchase the Bank's interest in the property for $60,000. On May 21, 1971 the Trustee, the Bank, and the purchaser entered into a stipulation providing for acceptance of the offer and execution of bills of sale by the Trustee and Bank covering all "right, title and interest" in the property, and that the sum of $60,000 "be substituted for the Property" and the "respective rights of the Trustee and of the Bank * * * be impressed upon and relegated to said fund of $60,000 with the same priority and to the same extent as they now have against the Property."

The Trustee petitioned the Referee in Bankruptcy for an order directing the Bank to turn over to the Trustee the sum of $60,000. Under stipulated facts the Trustee and Bank agreed that the question presented was solely one of law—involving the construction of Article 9 of the Uniform Commercial Code—and that the precise issue was:

> "Was the Bank required to file a financing statement against the Bankrupt with the Secretary of State of New Jersey in order to perfect a security interest in the leases assigned to it and the equipment leased thereunder by the Bankrupt to Plastimetrix?"

The Referee answered in the affirmative and ordered the Bank to turn over the $60,000, with interest, to the Trustee. On review the district court affirmed.

Decision of District Court

As the district court recognized, the aim of Article 9 of the Uniform Commercial Code, relating to "Secured Transactions", is "to provide a simple and unified structure within which the immense variety of present-day secured financing transactions can go forward with less cost and with greater certainty". Uniform Commercial Code, § 9–101, Official Comment. The drafters of this article eliminated many distinctions among security devices based on form alone. On the other hand, distinctions based on the type of property constituting the collateral were retained. Id.

Based on the stipulation of counsel, the court assumed that the agreements between Leasing and Plastimetrix were "true leases" and not "conditional sales agreements" or devices intended to create only a security interest.[2] Accordingly the court found that the Bank acquired "a security

1. The financing statement covered "continuing security interest in leases and any and all rents due and to become due thereunder, including all related equipment described therein, chattel paper represented thereby, accounts receivable therewith and proceeds arising therefrom."

2. Where a lease is intended as a security device the lessee usually becomes the owner or has the option to become the owner of the property at the end of the lease term. U.C.C. § 1–201(37). The lessor holds merely a security interest and has no reversionary right in the leased property.

interest in both the right to receive rental payments under the lease and in the reversionary interest in the underlying equipment."

The court held, and the parties agree, that the leases themselves were "chattel papers" (U.C.C. § 9–105(1)(b)) and that the Bank's security interest in the chattel paper was perfected by filing financing statements in New York and taking possession of the leases. U.C.C. § 9–304(1), 9–305, and 9–102(1).

The court held further: "By contrast, the machines themselves constituted 'equipment' located in New Jersey and hence, for perfection purposes, came within the scope of the New Jersey requirements." The Bank having failed to perfect its interest in the reversion in New Jersey, the court concluded that the Trustee "—a lien creditor within the meaning of Uniform Commercial Code § 9–301(3)—has priority over an unperfected security interest under § 9–301(1)(b)."

Emphasizing the distinction between rights under the chattel paper and the reversionary interest in the equipment, the court quoted from Professor Levie as follows:

> "In one situation the purchaser of a security agreement may have an advantage over the purchaser of a lease. Where [he] purchases equipment leases, he takes only an assignor's interest in the equipment lease itself. If [he] wishes to be secured by an interest in the goods as well, he must obtain a security interest * * * [in the goods] and perfect it." Levie, Security Interests in Chattel Paper, 78 Yale L.J. 935, 940 (1969).[3]

The district court concluded:

> "The distinction between the rights represented by the lease and those represented by the reversionary interest in the equipment is a real one, supported by logic and precedent. To ignore the distinction contributes neither to clarity nor uniformity under the Uniform Commercial Code. Moreover, it may mislead third party creditors. The simple solution for a bank in the situation of petitioner is to file notices as to its interest in the reversion in accordance with the law of the state where the equipment is located."

Contentions of Appellant

Appellant Bank contends that (1) whether the leases be considered "true leases" or security devices, the filing of the security interest in New York (where lessor and the chattel paper were located) covered all of the lessor's

3. The court continued:

"Practical considerations support this conclusion. The property leased was heavy manufacturing equipment. A potential creditor observing these complicated and non-portable machines should be entitled to believe that he could discover all non-possessory interests by consulting the files in the state where the equipment is located. The equipment was obviously of great value; the New Jersey files revealed only that the lessee held it under a lease. Since the lease agreement required each piece of equipment to have a plate affixed indicating that it was the 'property' of the lessor, judgment creditors of the lessor might assume that its reversionary interest in the equipment was of substantial value. Not being alerted to the diminution of value which would be effected by the creditor's security interest, they might then, for example, attach the lessor's interest, relying on an apparently unencumbered and valuable reversionary interest."

rights in the rentals and related equipment wherever located, without a separate filing against the equipment; or (2) alternatively, if a distinction is recognized between a "true lease" and a security device, appellant is entitled to an evidentiary hearing to determine whether the instruments were "true leases" or security interests in the equipment through the device of a lease; and (3) in any event, Leasing in fact had no "reversionary" interest in the property leased to Plastimetrix.

FAILURE TO FILE FINANCING STATEMENT IN NEW JERSEY

In contending that the filing and physical possession of the lease instruments in New York were sufficient to cover the leased equipment located in New Jersey, appellant argues that the "reversionary interest" of Leasing is "an intangible interest, sited at Leasing's domicile in New York, and not in New Jersey." If the reversionary interest in the equipment were characterized as a "general intangible", the Bank's security interest in the equipment would have been perfected when it filed with the New York Department of State and in the county in which Leasing had a place of business. N.Y.U.C.C. §§ 9–103(2), 9–401(1)(c) (McKinney 1964).

The policies of the Code, however, militate against such an interpretation. We agree with the district court that the reversionary interest is an interest in "goods" rather than an interest in intangibles, and that to perfect the security interest in the reversionary interest in the equipment it was necessary to file a financing statement in New Jersey where the equipment was located. N.J.Stat.Anno. 12A:9–102(1) (1962), 9–302, 9–401(1)(c) (Supp. 1972).

Obviously the leased property itself is "goods". We conclude, as did the district court, that the future reversionary interest is likewise an interest in goods, whether it represents "equipment" or "inventory" collateral. The drafters of the Code classified collateral mainly according to the nature or use of the underlying entity, rather than the character of its ownership at any given time. Significantly, the examples of "general intangibles" given in the Official Comment to § 9–106 are all types of property that are inherently intangible. And several Code sections and comments suggest that a collateral interest in "goods" remains such even when the goods are leased. See §§ 9–103(2); 9–109(4) and Official Comment 3; 9–304(3); N.Y.U.C.C. 9–109, Practice Commentary 2 (McKinney 1964) (Kripke).

We conclude accordingly that if the instruments were "true leases", the security interest in the leased equipment was not perfected because of the failure of the Bank to file financing statements in New Jersey.[4]

[The court concluded that the case should be remanded to determine whether the lease instrument was a "true lease" or intended as security. If the district court determined that the agreements were "true" leases, then it

4. Appellant alternatively contends that since "Leasing had assigned all of its interest in the machinery and equipment to the Bank" it had preferential rights to the equipment under "the law of bailment leases" regardless of the Code provisions. The assignment of the equipment from Leasing to the Bank, however, was expressly made "as security for any and all obligations of [Leasing] to the Bank under and pursuant to the Loan and Security Agreement * * *." This assignment clearly created a security interest in the Bank and made the requirements of Article 9 applicable to the Bank's interest in the equipment. U.C.C. § 9–102(1)(a).

will also be necessary to consider the effect of stipulations by the parties and whether the $60,000 fund "represents the sale of the leasehold as well as the sale of the reversionary interest in the equipment." The case was then remanded for determination of these and other matters. Hays, Circuit Judge, dissented. Some footnotes omitted.]

Notes

1. If you were to handle this transaction again on behalf of Citibank, what would you include in your security agreement and how would you perfect your security interest?

2. Did the lawyers, who apparently entered into a stipulation without appreciating its ramifications, commit malpractice?

3. If you knew that your opponent did not appreciate the significance of the stipulation about whether the security agreements were true leases or were not true leases and you nevertheless induced him to agree to the stipulation, would you have engaged in unethical conduct?

Problem 4–23

In *Leasing Consultants* how would the outcome have been changed if the documents labeled "leases" were really "security agreements"? Why did the filing in New Jersey by the lessor *not* perfect the security interest of the Bank?

CHAPTER FIVE
PRIORITIES

SECTION 1. INTRODUCTION

Perfection generally affords the secured creditor the maximum protection, i.e., priority, that the law allows. Yet as we noted earlier, and as will become clear in this chapter, the law does not always accord priority even to the prior perfected secured creditor. In this chapter we will consider the priorities between a perfected secured creditor on the one hand and a variety of challengers on the other. We will briefly consider the rights of the unperfected secured creditor as well.

Although the rules of priority to be learned here may sometimes apply elsewhere by analogy, students should not assume that they understand all, once they have studied these rules. It is possible, for example, to have a priority conflict between a real estate mortgagee and a mechanic's lienor, between two mechanic's lienors, between a tax lienor and a seller, and on and on. We will address none of the rules governing such conflicts in this chapter. Here, for the most part, we consider the priority rights of the perfected secured creditor under Article 9 against the world (gegen der Welt!).

The secured creditor, even the unperfected secured creditor, starts out from a general position of priority granted him by UCC 9–201. A secured creditor has the rights that his contract grants him not just against the debtor but against *everyone* * * * "except as otherwise provided by this act * * *." Most of what we will study in this chapter consists of the "other provisions" that in one way or another subordinate the secured creditor. Although UCC 9–201 will seldom be the end point of a lawyer's analysis, it should always be the beginning.

Next in importance is probably section 9–301. Its main effect is to subordinate an unperfected secured creditor to the rights of lien creditors and certain buyers. Third among the basic provisions is section 9–307 which subordinates even a perfected secured creditor to the rights of a buyer in the ordinary course in certain circumstances, and in some cases to others who do not even rise to the level of buyers in the ordinary course. Here is the first rude shock: even a perfected secured creditor may be subordinate to some buyers even though they know of the secured creditor's interest! Finally, among the basic provisions is UCC 9–312; it determines priority among secured creditors whose interests are in the same collateral. It is doubtless less important than UCC 9–301, but it is much more interesting and much more challenging intellectually. It is, however, somewhat like a house with many rooms, an attic filled with obscure relics.

The aforementioned four sections, 9–201, 9–301, 9–307 and 9–312 express some of the most fundamental ideas embodied in Article 9. First, those sections give bite to the perfection requirements (as for example by subordinating an unperfected secured creditor to the trustee in bankruptcy). Second, they carry out the general policy of Article 9 that a secured creditor who has checked the files only once, and has done a notice filing will then enjoy maximum priority allowed by law against other creditors and purchasers, including even as to after-acquired property and future advances (those rules are set out mostly in UCC 9–312(5)). It should be noted how by virtue of UCC 9–201's provisions granting general priority over purchasers, and by virtue of the modest concessions in 9–301(1)(c) to non-ordinary course buyers and in UCC 9–307(1) to ordinary course buyers, the sections together sustain the superiority of the perfected secured creditor over all but the most exceptional buyers and subsequent purchasers. Of course, section 9–312 recognizes that certain purchase money buyers should have priority even though they are second in time. Our study of UCC 9–312(3) and (4) will show how the statute meets various policies associated with purchase money lenders, and how the statute deals with them and their rights in proceeds in a detailed and intricate way.

Problem 5–1

A. Bank # 1 lends Debtor $50,000 and, on July 1, creates an enforceable security interest under UCC 9–203(1) in Debtor's factory equipment, UCC 9–109(2), "existing and after-acquired." See UCC 9–204(1). On July 15, C, an unsecured creditor, lends Debtor $25,000. On August 1, Bank # 1 perfected the security interest by filing a financing statement in the proper place. Read, again, UCC 9–302(1), 9–401(1) and 9–303(1). On October 1, D defaults to C, who sues, gets a judgment and, on December 1, obtains a judicial lien through execution upon the equipment. Bank # 1, declaring default, claimed priority over C in the equipment, which is worth $40,000. Who should prevail? See UCC 9–201 & 9–301(1).

B. On August 15, Bank # 2 lent D $25,000 and perfected a security interest by filing on the same date. On December 1, D defaulted on obligations to both banks and both claim priority in the equipment. Who has priority? See UCC 9–312(5).

C. On September 1, S sold D new factory equipment on credit for $25,000 and retained an enforceable security interest. The equipment was delivered to D on September 15. What must S do to obtain priority over Bank # 1 and Bank # 2? See UCC 9–107 & 9–312(4).

D. On October 1, D sold all of the equipment to B, another factory owner, for $50,000. B purchased in good faith and without knowledge of any outstanding security interests. B's check for $50,000 was placed in a safe in D's office. The sale of collateral without approval by the secured party was prohibited and constituted a default under the security agreement. Can Bank # 1 and Bank # 2 enforce their security interests in equipment against B? What about claims to the check? See UCC 9–306 & 9–307.

Note

This problem concerns the "shelter principle," a basic principle of commercial law. The shelter principle may be defined as a "right of ownership of personal property * * * [consisting] in part of the right to transfer it to others in the same form and with the same attributes, e.g., freedom of competing ownership interests or defenses or security interests that are not valid against the transferring owner." See PEB Commentary No. 6, Section 9–301(1).

The operation of the shelter principle may be illustrated as follows: Payee by fraud induced Maker to issue a promissory note to Payee. The fraud is a defense to the obligation of the Maker to pay under 3–305(a)(2). Payee then negotiated the note to Webber who took as a holder in due course. After the instrument became due, Webber negotiated it to Rose who had notice of the fraud. Though Rose could not be a holder in due course in Rose's own right, Rose succeeds to Webber's rights as a holder in due course and takes free of Maker's defense of fraud. The policy is to insure the holder in due course, Webber, a free market for the instrument. See 3–203(b) and Comment 4.

The shelter principle runs through the UCC and is explicitly recognized not only in Article 3 on negotiable instruments but also in 8–301(1) and 8–302(4) of Article 8 on Investment Securities, in 7–504(1) and 7–502(1) on Documents of Title, in 2–403(1) of Article 2 on Sales, and (at least) in 9–313(4)(b) of Article 9. Elsewhere in these teaching materials we also refer to the principle.

The problem that follows poses the question whether the shelter principle operates under section 9–301(1) of Article 9.

Problem 5–2

Assume that Howard sold an aircraft engine to King and took back a purchase money security interest which Howard did not immediately record as required for perfection under federal law. King thereafter sold the machine to Jackson who, because of Howard's failure to file, found no recorded security interest in the engine at the time of Jackson's purchase from King. Under 9–301(1)(c), Howard's security interest was therefore subordinate to Jackson's interest. At a later point, Howard recorded his security interest, so perfecting it. Still later, Jackson sold the engine to Fisher who had actual knowledge of the perfected interest. King defaulted and Howard claimed the engine from Fisher. Who prevails? See 9–301(1) and 9–403.

SECTION 2. PRIORITY AMONG COMPETING SECURITY INTERESTS IN THE SAME COLLATERAL, UCC 9–312

A. *Introduction—Future Advances*

The most important rule in UCC 9–312 is that embodied in 9–312(5). Basically it tells us that the Code priority is limited by the time of filing or, in some cases, the time of perfection. (Can you identify a case in which the time of filing is *not* the time of priority?) In effect, UCC 9–312 rejects the time the security interest *attaches,* the time a particular loan is *made,* and the time the debtor *acquired* an interest in the property as the operative event determining priority. Having filed, the secured creditor need not run back to check the files every time he makes an advance or every time the debtor acquires a new piece of property subject to the creditor's after-acquired property clause.

Moreover, there is no reference to being without notice when one wins the race to the place of filing. This tells us that our statute is a pure race statute.

Sometimes students confuse future advances (new loans) with after-acquired property (new assets). In most cases the rules as to both will be the same under UCC 9–312, but that is not true in all cases, and it is probably desirable to distinguish them. Consider the following examples which are chosen from comments 5 and 7 to UCC 9–312. As you read them, go back and read the statute and see whether you can make it say the things that the examples purport to disclose. If you cannot, you are not reading the statute correctly.

> Example 1. A files against X (debtor) on February 1. B files against X on March 1. B makes a non-purchase money advance against certain collateral on April 1. A makes an advance against the same collateral on May 1. A has priority even though B's advance was made earlier and was perfected when made. It makes no difference whether or not A knew of B's interest when he made his advance.
>
> The problem stated in the example is peculiar to a notice filing system under which filing may be made before the security interest attaches (see Section 9–402). The Uniform Trust Receipts Act, which first introduced such a filing system, contained no hint of a solution and case law under it was unpredictable. This Article follows several of the accounts receivable statutes in determining priority by order of filing. The justification for the rule lies in the necessity of protecting the filing system—that is, of allowing the secured party who has first filed to make subsequent advances without each time having, as a condition of protection, to check for filings later than his. Note, however, that his protection is not absolute: if, in the example, B's advance creates a purchase money security interest, he has priority under subsection (4), or, in the case of inventory, under subsection (3) provided he has properly notified A. * * *
>
> Example 2. A and B make non-purchase money advances against the same collateral. The collateral is in the debtor's possession and neither interest is perfected when the second advance is made. Whichever secured party first perfects his interest (by taking possession of the collateral or by filing) takes priority and it makes no difference whether or not he knows of the other interest at the time he perfects his own.

At common law in some cases one's priority dated not from the time of perfection but from the time the loan was made. In those jurisdictions the courts often distinguished between cases in which there was an "obligatory advance" (one in which the creditor was contractually bound to make) and those which were non-obligatory (where the creditor was free not to make the loan on the date he made it). Not surprisingly, in the former the courts sometimes dated the priority from the time the agreement had been made.

> Example 5. On February 1 A makes an advance against machinery in the debtor's possession and files his financing statement. On March 1 B makes an advance against the same machinery and files his financing statement. On April 1 A makes a further advance, under the original security agreement, against the same machinery (which is covered by the original financing statement and thus perfected when made). A has priority over B both as to the February 1 and as to the April 1 advance

and it makes no difference whether or not A knows of B's intervening advance when he makes his second advance.

A wins, as to the April 1 advance, because he first filed even though B's interest attached, and indeed was perfected, before the April 1 advance. The same rule would apply if either A or B had perfected through possession. Section 9–204(3) and the Comment thereto should be consulted for the validation of future advances.

The same result would be reached even though A's April 1 advance was not under the original security agreement, but was under a new security agreement under A's same financing statement or during the continuation of A's possession.

Problem 5–3

Answer each of the hypothetical questions below under the 1972 official text.

Ajax Sisters, a famous private banking concern, had filed a financing statement covering "accounts existing and after-acquired" of Neiman Marcus. You are counsel for Ajax and they ask you the following questions and pose to you the following cases:

1. If we file on January 15 with respect to accounts, as above, but neither lend nor make any agreement to lend at the time, and on January 20 a second creditor files and lends on the same account, will that lender have priority over us if we lend some money on January 30?

2. If in the foregoing example we make a series of non-obligatory advances to Nieman Marcus, will we continue to have priority over the intervening creditor or after we have knowledge of his loan, or will we be subordinated to the extent of our subsequent non-obligatory advances?

3. We are contemplating a loan to a large Atlanta department store to enable that store to purchase several new lines of appliances. We know that an Atlanta bank has already filed a financing statement that covers all of the inventory and accounts of that department store. Is there any way in which we can make a loan and set up a security arrangement so that we will have priority over the previously perfected Atlanta bank?

4. We contemplate lending as purchase money lenders on $50,000 of equipment that American Airlines will use as part of its fixed base operation in Dallas. We have two questions with respect to this equipment:

a. What steps must we take to ensure that we have priority over prior parties who have filed blanket financing statements covering existing and after-acquired equipment?

b. To the extent that this equipment is ultimately sold, will we have priority with respect to the accounts that it produces or will the prior filed general financier?

B. Purchase Money Priority

1. Purchase Money Security

In Chapter Four we already met the purchase money security interest when we considered the problem of the secured creditor who takes a "cross collateral clause" under which items purchased from the same seller at different times "cross collateralize" the prices of each other. *In re Manuel,* supra at p. 193 is such a case. Here we see the purchase money secured creditor in a different context, not as one asserting merely that he has perfected without filing, but asserting that he has priority over someone whose perfection pre-dates his. Section 9–312(3) and (4) are important purchase money provisions that grant priority to the purchase money lender with prior perfected security interests.

Why should one grant priority to a creditor that is later in time than the one whose interest is subordinated? There are at least two reasons for granting such priority, one historical and doctrinal, the other arising out of the policy to protect a debtor from creditor overreaching. The purchase money security interest has long been recognized in the sale of real estate where, for example, a seller would retain a mortgage when he sold his real estate to a buyer. Buyer would then grant a mortgage to a bank or a third party who would record the mortgage. In the priority dispute between the seller's prior but unrecorded mortgage and the bank's later and recorded mortgage, seller would often win. The rationale for this victory was that the seller's entire interest had not passed to the buyer and thus could never pass to the bank, for under the rule of *nemo dat qui non habet* (he who hath not cannot give), the bank could only get as good a title as its debtor had. That may have been a satisfactory explanation in the days when traditional conveyance law reigned; it is clearly not adequate to explain UCC 9–312(3) and (4).

A more modern justification for purchase money priority may be found in a desire to protect the *debtor* from the initial secured creditor's overreaching. If the security agreement with the first creditor contained a blanket description of the debtor's assets, including after-acquired collateral and a broad definition of debt, the debtor would become virtually indentured to the initial secured creditor. If that creditor refused to lend more money and also refused to grant a subordination agreement, the debtor would be unable to borrow to finance the purchase of a new asset from a second creditor willing to lend only against a security interest in that very asset having priority over the first creditor. The purchase money priority rule in effect frees the debtor from the reach of the first security agreement. By complying with UCC 9–312(3) or (4), the debtor can promise a subsequent purchase money lender that he will have priority over the first creditor as to the items newly purchased.

The issues for the lawyer under UCC 9–312(3) and (4) are similar to those seen above in *In re Manuel* and include some others as well. Here, as in *Manuel,* one must determine whether the loan by the creditor enabled the debtor to procure the asset. Here too one must determine the rights of the competing parties to the proceeds of the purchase money loan. The student should read UCC 9–312(3) and (4) with care. Note that the former grants priority only as to "identifiable cash proceeds" whereas the latter grants priority to "its proceeds." As part of the 1972 amendments to Article 9, these phrases were carefully chosen. What is the difference between them? Can you illustrate this difference?

Note finally that there is a notice requirement with respect to inventory in UCC 9–312(3) but no such requirement under UCC 9–312(4). The need for notice presumably arises out of the nature of inventory and accounts receivable loans. Typically these loans are "revolving loans" that involve continuous and periodic advances by the creditor as well as continuous and periodic payments by the debtor. Because these revolving loans contemplate such advances, there is a likelihood that a dishonest debtor might mislead his original creditor into making new advances based on another party's purchase money collateral. Hence the purchase money lender must notify the revolving loan financer of inventory to get priority. But because such advances are not usual with respect to non-inventory financing under UCC 9–312(4), the drafters saw no need for such notice.

Assume that you represent a creditor who has a perfected security interest in a retailer's inventory. Your client receives a notice that another party is going to claim a purchase money security interest in a new line of inventory. What action should your client take in order to protect its interest?

IN RE SMITH

United States Bankruptcy Court, Western District of Missouri, 1983.
29 B.R. 690.

PELOFSKY, BANKRUPTCY JUDGE.

* * * In this petition the Bank sought a determination of priorities as between it and FmHA as to certain collateral and for other relief. The Bank also filed Count II to a complaint, precisely which of the three then pending being unknown, again naming debtors and FmHA as defendants, seeking a determination of priorities and asking that the proceeds of the sale of cattle repossessed by FmHA be used to satisfy the Bank's debt.

* * *

The evidence shows that debtor Lloyd Smith was borrowing money from the Bank's predecessor in 1970. In August of 1976 the Bank took a security interest in "All livestock now owned and after acquired". No significant amount of money was advanced to debtors at this time. There is no evidence that debtors had any livestock in August of 1976. In March of 1979 debtors borrowed money from FmHA and executed a security agreement in favor of FmHA identifying cattle and hogs as collateral. Just prior to the advance a financing statement was filed and designated as security, inter alia, "* * * proceeds and products thereof: (a) * * * livestock * * *". Debtors deposited the funds in their account at the Bank and purchased the cattle and hogs called for in the security agreement.

During the period June 1981 through January 1982 debtors borrowed $20,222.59 from the Bank. During the period from April 17, 1981 through January 1982 debtors gave the Bank four financial statements. Debtors gave a statement in September of 1980 but this, the court finds, is too remote in time to be of probative value except that it also, as do the others, omits any reference to the FmHA debt. On August 24, 1981 the Bank filed a continuation statement of its 1976 UCC filing.

According to an affidavit filed by FmHA, an agent searched the UCC filings in Pulaski County on September 1, 1981 and found no continuation filing by the Bank. In late September 1981, debtors executed a security agreement in favor of FmHA identifying cattle and hogs as collateral. No financing statement was filed in connection with this security agreement. In March of 1982 FmHA foreclosed its security interest in the cattle and sold them, applying the proceeds against the loan. Debtors filed for relief under Chapter 7 of the Code on March 18, 1982, after the foreclosure. This adversary was filed shortly thereafter.

Section 400.9–312, R.S.Mo.1969, deals with "[p]riorities among conflicting security interests in the same collateral". The section provides, in part, that * * * [quoting 9–312(3) and (4)]

Section 400.9–109(3) R.S.Mo.1969 classifies goods as "[f]arm products" if they are " * * * livestock * * * used * * * in farming operations * * * If goods are farm products they are neither equipment nor inventory." The statutory comment notes that

> "4. Goods are 'farm products' only if they are in the possession of a debtor engaged in farming operations. Animals in a herd of livestock are covered whether they are acquired by purchase or result from natural increase."

The evidence shows that FmHA filed its financing statement prior to the funds being paid to debtor. Debtor used a substantial part of the money to purchase pigs and cattle. The purchases were made within two months of the advance. The purchase money security interest therefore was perfected when debtors received the collateral.

Debtors were engaged in farming at all times herein set out and § 400.9–109(3) excludes, therefore, these animals from the definition of inventory. The question of priority of creditors consequently is determined by reference to § 400.9–312(4). That section does not require notice to a creditor holding a prior filing in the same product with an after acquired clause and allows the creditor making a purchase money advance to have priority over the creditor holding "after acquired" rights. Thus, in May of 1979, FmHA had a priority in the purchased cattle over the claim of the Bank.

In its brief the Bank concedes that FmHA had a purchase money security interest in the collateral until September 27, 1981. The Bank argues that the security agreement dated September 28, 1981, destroyed that status and gave FmHA a security interest for an antecedent debt, thus restoring the Bank to its first filed priority status. There is no evidence that FmHA released its first security agreement or UCC filing or advanced new funds in return for execution of this September, 1981 security agreement. No financing statement was filed in connection with the 1981 security agreement.

There was no testimony explaining the 1981 agreement. It would appear that it was taken after the FmHA agent ran a lien search and discovered, or so it seemed, that the Bank lien had expired. The 1981 agreement may have been taken to identify the then existing security.

There are a number of reasons why execution of the 1981 security agreement is immaterial. The Bank had filed a continuation statement and the court so finds. The Bank is not charged with FmHA's failure to discover such a filing or the apparent failure of the Recorder to index or file. The

Bank continued to occupy a secured position in some respects. Nonetheless, as to the purchased cattle, FmHA's purchase money position was a priority without regard to the prior Bank filing and needed no subsequent action to maintain that priority even if the Bank's filing had lapsed.

The court concludes that execution of the 1981 security agreement, without more, is of no significance. The 1979 agreement was perfected and not altered by the subsequent agreement. Section 400.9–108 does not apply. In this instance the secured party made no advance, incurred no obligation, released no specific security interest and gave no value when the 1981 agreement was executed. [Citations omitted.]

The Bank also contends that the FmHA security agreement loses its purchase money character and priority as to cattle produced from those purchased. Calves which are bred are not purchased. They are "after acquired" in a general sense. The FmHA security agreement also covers all increases. The question then is whether cattle bred from security for a purchase money security interest are themselves purchase money security.

Section 400.9–107, R.S.Mo.1969, defines a purchase money security interest as one "taken by a person who by making advances ... gives value to enable the debtor to acquire rights in or the use of collateral if such value is in fact so used." Here there is no question that debtors used the FmHA advance to purchase cattle which they used for their benefit. The advance ultimately, through a natural process, also enabled debtors to have the use of calves, i.e., the products of the purchase money collateral.

The Uniform Commercial Code enables a security interest to follow collateral even if it is transformed. See § 400.9–314, R.S.Mo.1969, as to rules concerning accessions and § 400.9–315, R.S.Mo.1969, as to rules concerning commingled or processed goods. But these statutes, while preserving a security interest, do not resolve the issue as to whether the interest retains its purchase money character but there are clear suggestions that the character remains unchanged. See, for example, § 400.9–315(1)(b) which provides that a financing statement covering goods "also covers the product into which the goods have been manufactured, processed or assembled." See also Holzman v. L.H.J. Enterprises, Inc., 476 F.2d 949 (9th Cir. 1973) where the court held that inventory purchased from the sale of inventory subject to a purchase money security interest retained the character of purchase money security.

The purchase money security interest as an exception to the rules of priority of filing allows the creditor to have a security interest in identified collateral which it enabled the debtor to obtain. While such collateral may be transformed, as through manufacturing, it does not expand through its own effort. Cattle do (ignoring the biological act). The purchase money security interest is maintained by keeping the collateral intact or tracing the proceeds. Cattle as collateral expand by natural process.

In a case styled In re Ingram, 11 UCC Reporting Service 605 [468 F.2d 564] (5th Cir. 1972) the court held a security interest in progeny of leased cattle was not a purchase money security interest because the creditor only enabled the debtor to acquire "rights in and use of the breeder stock" and not the progeny. The suggestion in § 400.9–204, R.S.Mo.1969 is that since the debtor had no rights in unconceived progeny at the time the security agreement was executed, no security interest could attach and therefore the creditor acquired no rights in such unconceived animals.

The purchase money security interest priority is an exception to the general rule and should be construed narrowly even though the application to a cattle situation is inexact. Compare Index Store Fixture Co. v. Farmers' Trust Co., 536 S.W.2d 902 (Mo.App.1976). It must be remembered, in support of a narrow reading, that even the natural process of herd growth does not proceed without assistance not provided by the purchase money creditor. The result could be different if the evidence showed that some part of the purchase money collateral was sold and new animals purchased, but that is not the case here. Similarly this could be a variation if the calves only replaced cattle that had died. Again, while the herd has diminished here, there is no evidence that diminution occurred from the aging process.

The court concludes, therefore, that the purchase money security interest does not apply to the calves. FmHA is entitled to the proceeds of the sale of those cattle which retained purchase money character at the time of foreclosure but the Bank is entitled to the proceeds from the sale of any others.

The evidence shows that debtors purchased 19 cows and 20 pigs with the FmHA loan. FmHA sold 13 cows and 7 calves. Debtors owned no pigs at the time of the foreclosure. There is no evidence as to disposition of the other cows. The sale price was not allocated among the animals, although it appears that all of the cows could have been part of the purchase money herd. The parties are directed to confer and to advise the court whether a further hearing would be necessary to resolve the issue of allocation.

The court also reserves the question of the nondischargeability of the debt to the Bank until the issue of allocation is resolved. Further evidence may be necessary on that question.

Notes

1. The foregoing case was decided under the 1962 Code. Under UCC 9–312(4) of the 1972 Code, would it have come out differently? Are calves "proceeds"? In security agreements dealing with livestock one frequently sees reference to all livestock including "products." The reference to all livestock including "products" is presumably there because the secured creditor is uncertain whether calves, milk, and such fit the definition in 9–306(1). What do you think? What of PIK payments? Term agreements to purchase milk?

2. Assume that a creditor files a financing statement that covers all of the debtor's inventory. Over a period of time the inventory loan goes up and down and ultimately is paid off. A year later a new security agreement is executed between the parties and a new loan is made. Does this loan date to the earlier financing statement and achieve priority over an intervening loan?

3. Assume in 2 that the new loan had covered not just inventory, but also accounts receivable and in connection with the second security agreement an amendment to the original financing statement was filed to cover "accounts receivable and inventory." What would be the date of priority as to accounts?

Problem 5–4

Your client Finance Company does a great deal of purchase money lending. Some of that consists of lending to farmers as in *In Re Smith,* in which the

Company lends money for the acquisition of cattle and hogs and takes a security interest in those animals and in proceeds and products thereof. In other cases your client lends to retail merchants, takes a perfected security interest in their inventory, accounts receivable and proceeds. In most of these cases there is a prior perfected security interest that includes an after-acquired property clause, and it is critical to your client's interest to maintain priority over the earlier creditor. Having achieved purchase money status by complying with UCC 9–107, having given notice in compliance with UCC 9–312(3), and having filed in compliance with UCC 9–312(3) and (4), can you assure your client of priority, not only as to the original collateral but also to the proceeds in both cases? If not (and the answer should be no), how do you advise your client to conduct its business in order to minimize its risk?

Problem 5–5

The Great Outdoors Company operated five large department stores in Indiana. In 1986 Bank One took a security interest in all of the Great Outdoors inventory and proceeds and properly perfected that security interest by filing in Indianapolis. In 1988 Hart Schaffner & Marks lent the Great Outdoors $2,000,000 to finance the purchase of Hart Schaffner & Marks clothing. Hart Schaffner & Marks also filed a financing statement in Indianapolis and received a proper security agreement. This security agreement covered all Hart Schaffner & Marks clothing sold to the Great Outdoors together with accounts receivable arising from the sale of such clothing, all such proceeds and the like. In September 1990 Great Outdoors went bankrupt and at the time of its bankruptcy it held $1,200,000 of Hart Schaffner & Marks clothing, and $500,000 of accounts receivable arising from the sale of Hart Schaffner & Marks clothing. Who has priority between Bank One and Hart Schaffner & Marks in each of the following cases?

A. If Hart Schaffner & Marks gave no notice of its interest to Bank One.

B. If Hart Schaffner & Marks gave proper notice of its interest to Bank One.

C. Would Bank One's rights vis a vis Hart Schaffner & Marks be the same as to the first loan it made (before it knew of Hart Schaffner & Marks) and as to another $1,000,000 advance after it had learned of Hart Schaffner & Marks' security interest either by examining the records again or by receiving notice?

D. Assume bankruptcy occurred in 1992 and that Bank One's filing had lapsed because of the passage of five years, but that Hart Schaffner & Marks had examined the files and had seen Bank One's filing in 1988.

JOHN DEERE CO. v. PRODUCTION CREDIT ASSN. OF MURFREESBORO

Court of Appeals of Tennessee, Western Section, 1984.
686 S.W.2d 904.

NEARN, P.J. This appeal involves a dispute between two commercial lenders, John Deere Company and Production Credit Association (P.C.A.), over their interests in the proceeds from the sale of a piece of farm equipment purchased by James Willis. The Chancellor held that neither had priority over the other under Article 9 of the UCC (T.C.A. § 47–9–101, et seq.), and that their rights in the proceeds were pro rata, according to the amount each loaned to Willis.

The facts are not disputed. In a transaction prior to the one in question here, P.C.A. acquired a security interest in "all farm machinery and equipment, including but not limited to all tractors, tilling and harvesting equipment" owned by Willis and in all such property acquired in the future. The financing statement was properly filed on December 10, 1980. At that time, Willis owned a John Deere 6600 combine.

In September, 1981, this combine burned. The insurance proceeds on the combine were turned over to P.C.A. and applied to Willis' debt. Shortly thereafter, Willis borrowed $17,859.03 from P.C.A. to be used as a down payment on the purchase of a new combine and flex head from General Equipment Company (hereinafter "General").

To provide these funds, a sight draft made payable to General, drawn on a P.C.A. account and signed by Willis, was given to Willis by P.C.A. The face of the draft contained wording that it was to be used for the purchase of a John Deere 6620 combine, with a specific serial number. At the time of the issuance of this draft, P.C.A. did not obtain a new security agreement from Willis, nor was a new financing statement filed. However, the P.C.A. financing statement filed on December 10, 1980, contained both a future advances clause and an after-acquired property clause.

The same day that the sight draft was issued by P.C.A.—October 14, 1981—Willis signed a retail installment contract for the purchase of a new John Deere 6620 combine and a new John Deere 215 flex head from General for $59,000.00 less a down payment of $17,800.00. At the same time, he also signed a security agreement and financing statement in favor of General, which was properly filed on October 23, 1981. General accepted the draft of P.C.A. as down payment on the combine. Shortly after the transaction was completed between Willis and General, General assigned the security agreement and financing statement to the John Deere Company. John Deere accepted the assignment from General on October 29, 1981.

Subsequently, Willis defaulted on both the debts to P.C.A. and to John Deere. He voluntarily released the combine and flex head to P.C.A.. At the time of the default, the balance owed to Deere was $52,216.28 and the balance owed to P.C.A. was $17,859.03. Deere filed suit against Willis and P.C.A., seeking possession and sale of the combine, that the proceeds be paid into the court for a determination of the interests of P.C.A. and Deere and that a judgment for any deficiency be entered against Willis. P.C.A. surrendered the collateral with a reservation of its rights in the proceeds and filed a cross-claim against Willis and John Deere claiming a purchase money security interest in the combine in the amount loaned to Willis by P.C.A. for the down payment, $17,859.03. P.C.A. based its claim upon the draft dated September 14, 1981, issued by it to General and upon its original financing statement and security agreement filed in December, 1980. * * *

John Deere Company ... insists that P.C.A. could not have a purchase money security interest in the collateral based on the filing of their financing statement of December 1980 that contained an after-acquired property clause. We hold that P.C.A. does have a purchase money security interest in the collateral and because their financing statement was filed prior to Deere's, they also have priority over Deere's interest. We therefore must affirm in part and reverse in part.

* * * In order to perfect a security interest in farm equipment to insure that it will be superior to interests of third parties, the secured party must file a financing statement in the county of the debtor's residence. See T.C.A. § 47–9–401(1). If the value given is used by the debtor to purchase the collateral, then the secured party has a purchase money security interest in the collateral, which normally would give him priority over any other security interest in the same collateral, as long as he perfected his interest by filing a financing statement within twenty days of the debtor receiving possession of the collateral. See T.C.A. §§ 47–9–107(b) and 47–9–312(4).

In this case we have two secured parties fighting over the same collateral, now converted to money. It is undisputed that Deere has a perfected purchase money security interest in the collateral. It is also undisputed that P.C.A. gave the debtor money to purchase the collateral. The problem is that the security agreement and financing statement that P.C.A. is relying on were filed earlier, in another loan transaction. However, both of these instruments include an after-acquired property clause that we believe is sufficient to accomplish the purpose of giving P.C.A. a purchase money security interest in the combine. This is especially true in this case because the recorded financing statement specifically describes farm equipment. The purpose of the financing statement is to put third parties who check the filings on notice. We believe the financing statement P.C.A. had on file would have alerted Deere to the possibility that P.C.A. had an interest in the collateral. After thus being notified, it was incumbent upon Deere to look into the matter further if they wanted to make sure that they had the highest priority interest in the collateral. That is the purpose of notice filing. The burden is upon the party seeking a purchase money security interest to check recorded filings. Such task certainly should be performed when the credit advanced is substantially less than the purchase price of the collateral. Such fact clearly opens up the distinct possibility that someone else has advanced the debtor funds and will therefore be claiming a purchase money security interest in that collateral. * * * As far as we can determine from record, P.C.A. had a security agreement and a prior recorded financing statement and based thereon advanced to the debtor $17,859.03. The draft for $17,859.03 was given to the debtor, who in turn gave it to Deere, who applied it as a down payment for the new collateral. The undisputed testimony of P.C.A. was that no payments were made on the new loan. There is no difficulty in determining what portion of the loan was represented by the purchase money.

Additionally, P.C.A. is not claiming a purchase money security interest in the collateral any greater than the purchase money it loaned. They are claiming a purchase money security interest to the extent of the present consideration they advanced for the purchase of the combine, not for any prior loans they made. If they were, different results might be reached. See T.C.A. § 47–9–107, comment 2.

Therefore, we hold that P.C.A. has a purchase money security interest in the combine only up to the amount of the value they gave that was used for the purchase, that is, for $17,859.03. It is not our view that in all cases where a financing statement is filed and the lender has an after-acquired property clause in the financing statement that a *purchase money* security interest is retained in whatever the borrower purchases. A security interest yes, but the type will depend upon the circumstances. Where the funds are delivered by the lender for the specific purpose of purchasing specific equipment that is specifically covered by the prior financing statement of the parties, that security interest is a purchase money security interest when the funds are so used. Such are the provisions of T.C.A. § 47–9–107(b).

Deere asserts that a new financing statement had to be filed for P.C.A. to obtain a purchase money security interest in the combine. We see no reason for a second filing of a financing statement by P.C.A. to insure a purchase money security interest. The first filing was notice to the world of a security interest in farm equipment and after-acquired property, and any further notice filing would be, in our opinion, supererogation.

Since we hold that both parties have a perfected purchase money security interest in the combine, it must be determined which has priority.

Both interests attached at the same time, that is, when the debtor acquired rights in the collateral. P.C.A. had, in essence, a pre-filing and Deere's filing related back to the day the debtor obtained possession under T.C.A. § 47–9–312(4). Since this section does not assist us in determining which party has priority, we must look to the "clean up" section, § 47–9–312(5). Since both parties perfected by filing, the first to file has priority. See T.C.A. § 47–9–312(5)(a). Therefore, P.C.A.'s purchase money security interest is superior to Deere's.

Accordingly, P.C.A. is entitled to $17,859.03 of the disputed fund and John Deere is entitled to the balance.

The result is that the holding of the Chancellor that both P.C.A. and Deere possess purchase money security interest in the collateral is affirmed. However, his holding that the interests are held equally on a pro rata basis is reversed. Costs below are as there adjudged. Since the assessment of costs of appeal are not governed by the UCC, we adopt in principle the policy of the Chancellor and assess them on an equal, pro rata basis of one-half to each.

TOMLIN and HIGHERS, JJ. concur.

Problem 5–6

Consumer debtor has purchased ten items of hard goods from your client, Retail Appliance Mart. In each case the debtor executed a security agreement with your client; each was for the purchase price of the item sold. However, as the items mounted, the secured creditor was interested in having a security interest in the items previously purchased to support the amounts owed on items subsequently purchased and vice versa. Thus, each of the security agreements contain "cross-collateral clauses" in which the debt for one was secured by the asset purchased earlier and by assets purchased later. Moreover, the payments were consolidated because the debtor would have been hopelessly confused if each month he had to make a series of five or six different payments. Debtor is now threatening bankruptcy; his total outstanding balance is almost $12,000. His lawyer has made an offer. He has asked that the debt be written down to something under $10,000 in return for the debtor not going into bankruptcy. Debtor's lawyer makes two arguments against the retail seller's position. First, he argues that the bank no longer has a perfected security interest because perfection depends upon automatic perfection under UCC 9–302(1)(d). He argues that bank is not a purchase money lender because its cross-collateral clause keeps it from complying with UCC 9–107 inasmuch as the interest is not taken or retained by the seller, in the words of UCC 9–107 to secure all or part of "its" price.

For the same reason he argues that the debtor in bankruptcy will be able to shuck even a perfected security interest under Section 522(f) of the Bankruptcy Code because the security interest will no longer be a purchase money interest and it will be in items of household goods as to which the debtor would otherwise have an exemption.

Evaluate these arguments and determine whether you will advise your client to accept the offer. Advise your client how such problems might be avoided in the future.

Problem 5–7

United Bank of Littleton granted a secured loan to Drug Fair Inc., a retail drug store and pharmacy. The bank's security agreement and financing statement covered "all inventory, furniture, fixtures, equipment, accounts receivable, and machinery now owned or hereafter acquired." A year later Davis Brothers, a sales supplier of Drug Fair loaned $62,822 to Drug Fair, took a security interest in and filed a financing statement covering the following, "all drug and sundry inventory of debtor which debtor has purchased or may purchase from secured party and in which secured party has taken or will take a security interest." The security agreement and financing statement also covered "all prescription records." Davis gave no notice to United Bank of Littleton. Two years after Davis had filed its financing statement, a representative of United Bank discovered the financing statement by happenstance in connection with another search. Upon Drug Fair's bankruptcy, the trial court awarded Davis the inventory and the prescription records. United Bank has come to you to ask whether it has any basis for appeal. What do you think?

C. Monitoring Against Collateral Risks

It is easy for a lawyer or even a law student to acquire an exaggerated opinion of the importance of his work. The fear of subordination to another secured creditor because of failure to file is far down in the hierarchy of creditor concerns. More likely the creditor will be disappointed because the debtor commits fraud, the collateral declines in value or the documents are never executed at all. Some of those problems are considered in the discussion that follows.

ACCOUNTS

Accounts are mere rights to payment. Indeed, they are not even embodied in any unique piece of paper. That is, there is no such piece of paper that is the unique embodiment or exclusive representation of a specific account. We have already seen that for this reason an account cannot be the subject of a possessory security arrangement. All this foretells that an alleged account may not even exist, although the debtor may wave a sheet of paper around and proclaim its existence with Bishop-like solemnity. Assuming that the lender has satisfied himself that the *initial* accounts existed, he must be sure that subsequent advances under a floating lien are similarly secured. An occasional lender has been duped into lending against wholly fictitious accounts. See, e.g., Firestone Tire & Rubber Co. v. Central Nat'l Bank, 159 Ohio St. 423, 112 N.E.2d 636 (1953).

Even though it is real, an account is no more valuable than the account obligor's ability to pay. And in this world many an account obligor has become insolvent or very "slow pay". There is a story told along the banks of the Upper Mississippi of an accounts lender who lent large sums to his borrower (against the accounts) only to find that 111 of the 112 account obligors had taken bankruptcy in the preceding month prior to default. (The 112th owed an account only for $6.13.) Then, too, there are places where all the credit customers (or nearly all) of a given dealer are employed by the same employer. If that employer were to shut down, many of the employees would not be able to pay their bills and the collateral would be rendered worthless. If there is any risk of shut down, perhaps a lender should not lend to a dealer against such accounts.

Even if the account is real and the account obligor solvent, risks remain. For example, the obligor may have or acquire a defense against the obligee-assignor. As every first year law student of contracts learns, the account obligor can set up most such defenses not only against the obligee-assignor, but against the assignee-secured party as well. (On this, more later.)

How can a party with a floating lien in accounts protect against such risks? Review the material below:

KRIPKE et al., BUSINESS FRAUDS, THEIR PERPETRATION, DETECTION AND REDRESS, 20 Bus.Law. 83, 105, 106, 107–08, 109, 111–12 (1964).

"The third reason that I use this topic as an example of the problem of fraud on lenders is that accounts receivable financing is peculiarly susceptible to fraud unless expertly administered. Unlike the case where you discount promissory notes or trade acceptances or lend against them, the security in the accounts receivable field is an invoice—a unilateral piece of paper not signed by the account debtor whom you hope to charge, but prepared by the seller, his creditor. Moreover, the copy of the invoice which is submitted by the seller to the lender may not coincide at all with the copy of the invoice that the debtor himself receives. The lender may be deceived as to whether there is a solid agreement to pay or whether there is on the side a consignment arrangement or a sale-or-return arrangement or the like. Similarly, the invoice does not prove that the goods have been shipped and received; again, the opportunity for fraud is there. Finally, most accounts receivable financing is done on a non-notification basis, where the lender who is the assignee of the account has no direct contact with the account debtor. The assignor, the original seller, collects the account and is supposed to account for the collection to the lender. Because of that lack of direct contact, the possibility and the opportunity for a completely fabricated system of assignments of collateral—a Ponzi scheme—is there, and there is real potentiality for fraud.

* * *

"What can the financial community do in this potentially dangerous field to provide the financing that is so important to the economy, and at the same time, not get badly burned? The first recommendation is similar to the recommendation I made in the case of internal fraud—demand from your debtor certified reports of its financing condition by independent public accountants, because there is the first measure of protection. But, be sure that they are certified! One of the evils which the leaders of the accounting profession have been fighting against is the practice of some auditing firms of lending their name and their stationery to the publication of reports which are, in fact, not certified. * * *

* * *

"Suppose you have gotten accountants' certified statements, and you discover, nevertheless, that the statements were false, and you didn't have a fair picture of the financial condition of the borrower. Can you as a third-party lender, in this case, hold the public accountants responsible for their false statement of the condition of the company they examined? They didn't, of course, enter into any agreement with the lender—the question is whether they are liable to third parties for failure to perform their audit of the borrower properly.

* * *

"There will be very few cases in which the lender can make the showing necessary to put his loss back on the shoulders of the accountant. I go further than that. I was involved in one group of litigations against accountants arising out of fraudulent borrowing—and it is perhaps the only case in the history of a very honorable profession in which the contention made against the accountants was not merely that they had made a mistake in judgment or even that they had passed the shadowy line between negligence and gross negligence, but it was that they had deliberately and consciously failed to disclose the desperate financial condition of a dishonest debtor. I walked the streets of New York for weeks trying to find an accountant witness who would support that allegation. I could find plenty of accountants who would tell me that the conduct of the certifying accountants in that case was outrageous, but they would tell me so only privately. When it came to doing so in court, the profession closed ranks against the outsider like the medical profession does, and one could not find a witness. Thus, the remedy against accountants for the lender's loss is a very unlikely one.

"Let us now turn, as we did before on the subject of internal fraud, to the possibility that you can have insurance against this loss. There has been recently much litigation and much controversy on the question whether the type of surety bond which all bankers and all finance companies carry, namely, the banker's blanket bond, or the modified form of broker's blanket bond for finance companies, gives the lender coverage against fraudulent loss in this accounts receivable field. * * *

* * *

"This leaves the accounts receivable finance business, both as practiced by banks and as practiced by the specialized finance companies and factors, back to its own operating capabilities, without being able to put the loss on the accountants' shoulders or on a surety company. What have they done to protect themselves against these risks and how successfully have they done so? You may argue to me that it is obvious that they haven't been successful, or the surety companies wouldn't be withdrawing from the risk. This does not necessarily follow. There is a gray area here. For every *Estes* case or *Salad Oil* case that makes the newspapers, every experienced administrator of accounts receivable financing can cite you ten cases where his outside staff or his inside staff detected a fraud at the early stages. These finance companies have groups of what they call auditors. Perhaps they should not be called auditors, to avoid confusion with the independent public accountants. They might perhaps more properly be called inspectors. These staffs pay surprise visits to the financing clients, at intervals as frequent as 30 to 60 days. They are trained in accounting, but start with an attitude somewhat different from that of the public accountant, who is entitled to assume in the first instance, that his client is honorable. They are supposed to start with a quizzical or skeptical or even a suspicious attitude and to look for fraud, knowing that these frauds start not with someone who is known to be a bad moral risk but someone who, because of financial pressure, takes a little bit and converts himself into a bad moral risk. Thus, these inspectors employed by the lender make investigations that approximate the kind of detailed audit of all transactions which the public accountants have always said that they did not perform. These fellows check the books, check the delivery receipts, check the shipping receipts, reconcile the borrower's books with the lender's—all of this in a detailed fashion going far beyond that which time permits for the public accountant under the terms of his engagement. When they see something irregular—when they don't understand why the payables are so high in view of the fact that it is the purpose of accounts receivable financing to give a fellow a jump on his cash so that he will be current on his payables—when they see an inconsistency between the borrower's and the lender's books—when they see invoices that are created outside the regular numbering system, or typed on a different typewriter or written longhand—when they find the shipping clerk in possession of a pad of blank receipts signed by a trucker—when they see suspiciously large accounts—when they see a large receivable in the name of a company that looks like it simulates the name of a leading corporation—when they see their own loan checks with curiously irregular endorsements, *e.g.,* where the check didn't go through a bank account, but through a professional check cashier—all of these and many more red flags that are set forth on check lists six, eight or ten pages long of points to be checked, all of these become indications of fraud that the external auditing staff and the internal operating staff of a finance company are trained to watch. Even without the benefit of surety bond protection, these specialized techniques enable them to keep the losses down to manageable proportions. They have similar techniques for lending against inventory under warehouse receipts and it is of some interest that in the big *Salad Oil* fraud, only one finance company is involved in those hundreds of millions of dollars of loss and that one is involved not because it was directly deceived but because it lent money to someone else who was deceived.

"A question is forming as the demands for accounts receivable financing grow increasingly with the pressures on the working capital of small business, and the banks enter increasingly into this field—what are the banks going to do to overcome this peculiar susceptibility for fraud? One choice would be to set up their own auditing staffs with this special skill that I have just attempted to describe, but this is expensive and it necessitates a rate of charge somewhat in excess of that which banks are accustomed to charge. Or the banks can say, 'We'll deal only with the finest credits and not worry about fraud,' and then perhaps they may suffer the experience that this West Coast bank is now suffering with a million dollar accounts receivable fraud, from a good moral risk that turned sour.

"Finally, some of the banks are, in effect, buying the extra skills of the finance companies by entering into this field on a participation basis. The field is too new yet for anyone to determine just in which way the banks will finally resolve the problem of how they enter the field. It will be an interesting development. Above all, the message has to be that accounts receivable financing can only be successfully handled against this threat of fraud by building up techniques which go beyond the auditing of the independent public accountant and approach almost the detailed audit of individual transactions."

INVENTORY

The debtor can squander, damage, lose, secrete, etc., items of inventory. Or he may fail to care for it. And it may burn up, etc. If the inventory can be readily insured at economic rates, the secured creditor may want to insist on insurance. But insurance is either not available or too expensive for coverage of some risks. The possibilities are legion and the variations numerous. Consider, for example, the risk that a car dealer will borrow against an inventory that he represents to include cars that it in fact does not include. This is a pervasive risk. Below is one way one lender seeks to protect against this type of risk:

BIBOROSCH, FLOOR PLAN FINANCING, 77 Banking L.J. 725, 736–40 (1960).

"Except in the case of a sale, merchandise cannot be removed from the dealer's place of business for demonstration purposes without the bank's authorization. Merchandise on floor plan should be so stored as to allow reasonable accessibility for purposes of inspection. The agreement should include a provision that the bank's representative be permitted to inspect the dealer's inventory periodically at the bank's discretion. Seeking additional floor plan accommodation from another bank or finance company without prior discussion constitutes sufficient reason for discontinuing the floor plan arrangement.

"There are a number of different thoughts relating to the extent and frequency of checking dealer floor plan, but in the final analysis the procedure and manner of handling is a decision that rests with management. A collateral check is necessary for the bank's protection. This should be scheduled to keep the bank's exposure to a minimum, at the same time keeping in mind the effect that too frequent checking would have on dealer goodwill in relation to the risk involved (as well as the costs of a stepped up program). Common sense should weigh the benefits to be gained or lost by a plan that is economically unsound.

"In our bank an inspector calls on the dealer and obtains permission to make a physical inspection of the inventory listed on his floor plan checking report. He must personally see the serial or motor numbers on the merchandise and is not permitted to accept the 'say-so' of any other person who may volunteer to call the numbers to him. If for any reason the checking of the dealer's inventory is delayed by the dealer, the inspector must note this fact, together with the dealer's reasons in the 'remarks' section of the inspection report.

"In the case of automobiles, notations are made describing license plates on the cars. If the car or tires show any evidence of usage, this fact is also stated, and in all cases a record of the mileage is entered on the inspector's report. If a missing car is reported by the dealer as on hand at the dealer's branch location or off the floor or lot for any reason, full particulars must be given. When a car is sold and therefore not in the dealer's possession, a notation to this effect is also made for verification covering the period of delay in remitting payment. However, in nearly all instances the inspector will obtain a check from the dealer to be returned with his signed and dated report. This report should be studied and appropriate action taken with regard to the exceptions. When these have been cleared the report is filed and held available for future review of the dealer's performance record in the event exceptions become too frequent.

"Floor plan inspectors should never be assigned to call on the same dealer twice in succession because of the possibility of collusion. Furthermore, an excellent test check on an inspector's accurate or perfunctory performance is made possible by deliberately transposing or rearranging the last several numbers on his floor plan checking report covering a few of the items listed. Inspectors are also required to report new locations where merchandise is being stored in order to obtain a landlord's waiver. Reference should be made concerning potential fire or theft hazards. Comments by the dealer's employees concerning unethical sales practices or other important information should also be reported.

"It is customary to check floor plan once a month, but naturally not always on the same day. We follow this policy for every dealer. If, in our opinion, a dealer is not remitting proceeds as promptly as he should, we will check him again in four, five, or ten days. Some companies check dealers monthly until a favorable experience has been developed. If the circumstances warrant, the dealer may be moved up to a bimonthly basis, then to 90 days, and ultimately to a four, five, or six month basis for dealers of outstanding financial, moral, and operating stability.

"Other companies permit the use of stickers, written in ink and placed on windshields, to facilitate inspection of large inventories. Another policy, for desirable dealers, is the spot check system covering a certain percentage of the dealer's wholesale. If the inspection is in order, the balance of inventory is not checked.

"Checking appliance floor plan may pose a problem if the merchandise is in cartons stored on top of one another. In 1950 we ran into a situation where we found ourselves financing some empty containers. Many manufacturers place serial numbers on their cartons, either stenciled or in crayon, and some are tagged. We accept these figures after taking reasonable precautions that the cartons are sealed and we spot check several units in areas that are partially hidden or covered.

"In checking the floor plan of automobile dealers where there is an extremely large amount of wholesale outstanding, we have learned that a considerable amount of time can be saved by having the inspectors check the dealer's entire inventory in the order of accessibility, and then comparing this list with his floor plan checking report. By this means the inspectors do not have to peruse 20 to 40 sheets of serial numbers for every car inspected. This method has also disclosed some instances where factories have shipped cars to dealers but we had not paid for these automobiles. This enabled the dealer to sell from such shipments and withhold prompt remittance on the assumption that his inventory would not be checked for another 30 days.

"The consumer credit division records should be checked by the auditors each month to ascertain that there is an inspector's wholesale checking report on file for each dealer and that the same inspectors have not checked the same dealers on consecutive inspections.

"The auditors should make an independent physical inspection on a non-notification basis of all floor plan at least once a year on the dealer's premises. The list of floor plan, covering the account in question, should be prepared on the regular wholesale floor plan check reports assembled from the consumer credit department's ledger records, and the auditors should follow the same procedure as outlined for the regular inspectors.

"All wholesale floor plan accounts should be verified annually by direct confirmation with the dealers and, at that time, the following duties should be performed by the auditors.

"1. A trial balance of the ledger cards should be run by the dealer and verification of the total should be made with the dealer control cards and the general ledger control.

"2. Preparation of confirmation forms from information on the ledger records showing the dealer's name and address and loan balance as of the confirmation date. It is not necessary to confirm serial numbers in this case.

"3. It is impractical to run a trial balance of the floor plan notes because these are filed in loan folders together with other supporting papers, but a test check of the notes should be made against the ledger record from which a trial balance was taken.

"4. A test check of serial numbers should be made of merchandise on floor plan from the standpoint of the ledger records against trust receipts to ascertain that a trust receipt or other security agreement is on file and that merchandise represented by the serial numbers shown on the ledger records are recorded on the executed trust receipts.

"5. Dealer files should be checked to ascertain that proper filing has been made at the inception of the line of credit to show that we have a lien on any products floor planned for our dealer.

"6. Dealer files should be examined to establish that the bank has power of attorney to execute trust receipts, security agreements, chattel mortgages, and other documents in connection with the floor plan program, if that is company policy.

"7. A test check of the interest records should be made to ascertain that floor plan interest is billed properly and payment received. It is a customary practice to bill dealers for interest on a daily average balance basis.

"Inasmuch as wholesale credit is normally extended to dealers in order to obtain retail paper, it is recommended that precise records for every individual dealer covering wholesale collections be kept, and that these be related to the amount of retail paper received from the account. This particularly applies to automobile floor plan. By this means an average is established by totaling collections for the entire operation and total new car financing contracts submitted for discount. If a dealer's offerings are slightly below average, the account is still considered satisfactory or profitable if the deficiency in new retail volume is more than offset by used car installment contracts.

"In our analyses we maintain individual records for each dealer covering the amount of business received, the number of units discounted, the average amount of new car as well as used car deals, the number of repossessions and the total amount of losses per dealer, the number of rejections for each dealer account, and the number of contracts approved for each dealer but never submitted to us for discount. In connection with the latter, it is not uncommon for some dealers to call in two deals—one being an excellent piece of paper and the second a borderline deal. We like to reassure ourselves that the good credit is not used for window dressing to sell the marginal risk.

"This same procedure can be used as a practical approach if the bank floor plans heavy construction and road building equipment and boats. This system is not too realistic when applied to appliance financing because considerable merchandise is purchased on open account or by trade acceptances. It is good to note the average unpaid balance of appliance installment sale contracts to determine whether or not these balances are large enough to cover the cost of handling and to allow a reasonable profit."

SECTION 3. BUYERS OF GOODS, UCC 9–307(1) AND (2), 9–301

Read UCC 9–307(1) and 9–307(2). Read them twice. Now, which cases are governed by subsection (1) and which by subsection (2)? In fact, the provisions are mutually exclusive, but that certainly does not appear from a casual reading. In its early form section 9–307(1) started out with a prepositional phrase "In the case of inventory * * *." In effect the drafters were saying that if the goods were inventory in the hands of the *seller,* the buyer's rights were governed by subsection (1). If, on the other hand, the goods were consumer goods in the hands of the *seller,* the rights of a buyer were governed by subsection (2). Presumably, if the goods were equipment, they were governed by neither and the buyer was left to his meager fare in UCC 9–201 and 9–301(1)(c).

An academic critic of the Code pointed out that the reference to inventory in 9–307(1) was redundant because the idea that the seller had to have the goods in inventory was inherent in the idea of the "buyer in the ordinary course." Section 1–201(9) defines the buyer in the ordinary course as a person who buys from one "in the business of selling goods of that kind," i.e., from one who holds them as inventory. The criticism was correct, yet the redundancy in the former provision made it easier to understand.

It is easy to identify the standard buyer under each subsection. Mrs. Jones who purchases a television set from her local appliance or department store falls in subsection (1). Whether she buys for credit or with cash, she is buying in the ordinary course. She expects, the seller's secured creditor expects her, and the seller expects her to take free of the security interest that exists in favor of the secured creditor financing the store inventory. To say that Mrs. Jones should check the financing statements would be laughable. Given these expectations, it would be doubly mad to say that the security interest could carry over into the TV set in her hands. Thus the consumer retail buyer is the standard buyer covered by UCC 9–307(1). Not surprisingly, published cases arising under UCC 9–307 do not involve Mrs. Jones, but others whose status is not so clear.

Read carefully, section 9–307(2) represents a breach in the secured creditor's armour so narrow as to be insignificant. In the words of Professor Gilmore, it involves only sales "by amateurs to amateurs," and not all of those sales are covered by UCC 9–307(2), for if the security interest in seller's goods is perfected by a filed financing statement, even an amateur-to-amateur sale does not allow the buyer to take free of a security interest. The standard case here is the second hand sale by Mrs. Jones of her used television set to her neighbor. In that case the appliance store will have perfected its security interest in the television set automatically under UCC 9–302(1)(d), for it will be a purchase money security interest in consumer goods. Thus, in the words of the beginning prepositional phrase, the goods are "consumer goods" in the hands of the seller. They must also be consumer goods in the buyer's hands ("for his own personal, family or household purposes") and the security interest must have been perfected other than by filing.

Consider our amateur-to-amateur case of Jones and her neighbor Smith. Smith buys the television from Jones. Even if Smith had thought to check the files he would have found nothing because there was automatic perfection (of the retailer's security interest) without a filing. In such circumstances no one would seriously argue that Smith should be subordinate to the appliance store's security interest. Note how narrow the exception is, however. Goods must be consumer goods on both sides of the sale. If they are equipment in the hands of the seller, the initial prepositional phrase knocks them out of subsection (2). If the secured creditor has filed a financing statement, the buyer is deprived of the protection of the subsection.

Before we turn to the cases, the student should understand two additional limitations in UCC 9–307(1). Note first that one takes free only of a security interest "created by his seller." Thus, if the seller was not the debtor whose signature on the security agreement created the security interest, the buyer in the ordinary course does not take free of the security interest. Can you think of a case where that would be so?

Second, and most important, note the exception in the sentence for farm products, "other than a person buying farm products from a person engaged in farming operations * * *." The farm products exception in UCC 9–307(1) has been a festering sore. The case set out below is a representative example of a court tussle over that exception. Increasingly it has been drawn into question in the legislatures and in the courts. Some states (e.g., Tennessee) have abolished the exception. In one way or another the courts have avoided the exception in circumstances where it seemed appropriate to do so, even in cases in which the drafters might have thought otherwise. Recently even the Congress of the United States has become involved. A new federal law now will have the effect of overriding the farm products exception in some cases. We consider it below. But UCC 9–307(1) presents some highly relevant and hotly contested issues.

CHRYSLER CORP. v. ADAMATIC, INC.

Supreme Court of Wisconsin, 1973.
59 Wis.2d 219, 208 N.W.2d 97.

This action was commenced on October 21, 1970, by Appellant Chrysler Corporation, seeking to replevin certain goods which it had contracted to purchase from Defendant Adamatic, Inc. Respondent Lakeshore Commercial Finance Corporation was subsequently permitted to intervene on the basis that it claimed a perfected security interest in the goods in question. During the pendency of this action, Adamatic went into receivership and, consequently, Adamatic's receiver, Russell A. Eisenberg, was also permitted to intervene. On February 9, 1972, judgment was entered giving Chrysler possession of the goods but requiring it to pay certain sums to Lakeshore. Chrysler, Lakeshore, and the receiver have all appealed.

The facts of this lawsuit are largely undisputed.

Chrysler owns and operates a plant in Indianapolis, Indiana, where it manufactures alternators and other electrical components for the motor vehicles it assembles elsewhere. Construction of the alternators requires a "stator winder," a highly specialized machine which can wind copper wire around a component part known as the "stator." For several years Chrysler had been purchasing this equipment from an Ohio manufacturer but had been seeking to find a more efficient winding machine. Chrysler engineers discovered that Adamatic was producing an advanced machine at its Milwaukee plant which, while designed for a different purpose, potentially could be converted for use as a stator winder in the Chrysler plant. Chrysler's interest in utilizing the Adamatic machine led to the transactions forming the basis of this lawsuit.

In 1967, Adamatic had entered into various security agreements with Lakeshore, whereby the latter agreed to finance Adamatic's operations and in return took a security interest in Adamatic's inventory and various other assets. The security agreements were duly filed, and it is undisputed that

Lakeshore had a valid security interest in Adamatic's inventory at all relevant times.

Chrysler's first transaction with Adamatic, in March 1969, involved a contract calling for Adamatic to produce a prototype six-coil stator winder. Although the proposed machine was based on designs already formulated by Adamatic, it was to be custom built to Chrysler's specifications. The contract also required Adamatic to manufacture a "cell inserter," a separate machine, which was to be used in conjunction with the winder. The original purchase order quoted a price of $77,150 for the two units, but the price was later increased by $4,000 to cover an additional accessory for the cell inserter.

The agreement required Chrysler to make progress payments as the work neared completion. By the time the machines had been completed for shipment, Chrysler had paid 90 percent of the original purchase price. The remaining 10 percent was to be withheld until the goods were delivered and made to perform satisfactorily. Adamatic has never requested payment of this retainage, and it has not been paid.

On February 9, 1970, the completed winder and cell inserter were delivered to the Chrysler plant in Indianapolis. Although the cell inserter evidently performed to contract specifications, the six-coil winder failed to function well enough for production-line use. Over the next few months, Adamatic employees were in almost constant attendance at Chrysler's plant assisting Chrysler engineers in trying to get the winder working. Their attempts were unsuccessful, and on June 9, 1970, Chrysler sent a telegram to Adamatic threatening to cancel the second contract, executed in April 1970, between the parties if the winder could not be made to perform.

Finally, upon Adamatic's suggestion, it was decided to ship the units back to Milwaukee for additional work by Adamatic. By this time, Chrysler had decided that the six-coil winder should be converted for twelve-coil operation. On August 12, 1970, the cell inserter and six-coil winder were shipped back to Adamatic under a non-negotiable bill of lading. On August 20, 1970, Adamatic sent a quotation giving an additional price of $22,410 for the conversion. The quotation was accepted by Chrysler on a change order dated September 11, 1970. Subsequently, the parties executed a "Consigned Material Receipt Agreement," drafted by Chrysler, in which Chrysler purported to retain title to the goods.

Previously, in February, Chrysler had decided to enter into a second transaction with Adamatic involving additional machines of the same type. During that month, personnel from Lakeshore and Adamatic met with Chrysler in Detroit to discuss the financing of the second transaction. At that time, Chrysler was informed of Adamatic's shaky financial condition and the fact that Lakeshore held a security interest in Adamatic's inventory. Lakeshore told Chrysler that it was prepared to lend up to $300,000 to Adamatic if Chrysler would make progress payments on the proposed, second contract.

Chrysler's second contract with Adamatic was entered into in April 1970. A Chrysler purchase order requested Adamatic to produce three twelve-coil stator winders at a price of $83,646.43 per unit. The order, which was accepted by Adamatic, specified that the first machine was to be delivered on September 7, 1970, with the second and third twelve-coil winders to follow at thirty-day intervals. Chrysler agreed to make progress payments after the work was 25 percent complete, in an amount up to 80 percent of the value of the labor and materials put into the machines at that time.

In August 1970, Adamatic requested the first progress payment on the second contract. Chrysler sent an engineer to Milwaukee, who checked the work done and approved a progress payment of $105,761.55, representing 80 percent of the value which had been put into the machines. A payment in that amount was subsequently given to Adamatic, which immediately turned the money over to Lakeshore.

The six-coil winder had been returned in August, and by mid-September, 1970, the three twelve-coil winders were in various stages of construction. Adamatic's financial condition had long been shaky; by September, it had reached a perilous point. Its current balance sheet indicated a net deficit of $135,624.95. In addition, Adamatic had been delinquent for several months in making federal withholding tax payments to the Internal Revenue Service, and the I.R.S. was threatening Adamatic with a tax lien. Moreover, Adamatic was no longer able to pay its suppliers for parts going into the Chrysler machines, and construction was being slowed by suppliers who were withholding delivery. It appears that Adamatic was still operating only because Lakeshore was continuing to make cash advances sufficient to meet Adamatic's payroll.

On September 15, 1970, Lakeshore and Adamatic personnel met to discuss Adamatic's progress on the Chrysler contracts and the company's general financial prospects. At this time, Lakeshore advised Adamatic that it was in default and that unless it found some other source of financing, Lakeshore would be forced to liquidate its loan. Nevertheless, Lakeshore advanced an additional $30,000 to $50,000 to Adamatic, and by October 15, 1970, the loan balance was approximately $340,000. By the time of trial, however, Lakeshore had foreclosed on other secured assets still in Adamatic's possession, and Adamatic presently owes Lakeshore more than $200,000. It was stipulated that Adamatic was in default under its security agreements when this action commenced.

On October 12, 1970, Chrysler sent one of its engineers to Milwaukee in an attempt to expedite delivery of the twelve-coil winders, since the delivery dates for the first two machines had passed. He was told to return at the end of the week, when he could expect to receive the first machine. He returned on Friday, October 16th, and the following day the first twelve-coil winder was given a test run at the Adamatic plant. The machine was intended to handle two stators at once, but the tooling for one phase of the operation did not function. Moreover, the machine lacked a paint job and safety guards. Nevertheless, the engineer indicated that he would accept delivery and directed Adamatic to prepare the machine for shipment. Chrysler had arranged for a common carrier truck to be present that day, and the cell inserter was loaded on. Adamatic employees continued to work on the first twelve-coil winder during Saturday, October 17th, and on Sunday, the 18th, it operated properly. On Monday, October 19th, the truck returned, and the winder was skidded to the Adamatic dock for loading.

At this point, Lakeshore learned that Chrysler was trying to take delivery of the first twelve-coil winder. By telephone, Lakeshore's president directed Adamatic not to ship the machines. Accordingly, Adamatic personnel removed the cell inserter from the truck and moved the winder back into the plant.

Chrysler sought legal advice, and a meeting was held between the attorneys and representatives of Lakeshore and Chrysler on October 20, 1970. The participants in this meeting differ as to what transpired. According to Chrysler's witnesses, Lakeshore demanded that Chrysler renegotiate the price if it wanted delivery of the machines. Lakeshore's president testified, however, that he told Chrysler that Lakeshore had a perfected, security interest in the machines and was asserting its rights to possession.

Chrysler then commenced this replevin action to obtain possession of the machines. On October 21st, the sheriff seized the three twelve-coil winders and the cell inserter. At the time of the seizure, the first of the twelve-coil winders was substantially completed. The second was only about half finished, and the third was little more than a naked frame. The sheriff also seized the original six-coil winder, which had been completely stripped of usable parts after its return to Adamatic. In its original complaint, Chrysler declared the value of the goods to be $190,000 and put up a surety bond in twice that amount. Lakeshore immediately sought, and was granted, leave to intervene. Nevertheless, Lakeshore failed to file a sufficient redelivery bond, and the goods were turned over to Chrysler and removed to Indianapolis on or about October 27, 1950.

Adamatic, which had been insolvent for some time before the replevin, shortly thereafter went into receivership.

The trial of this action was held before a jury from November 16 to 23, 1971, and questions were submitted on a special verdict. The jury found that, as to the second contract for the twelve-coil winders, Chrysler had been a buyer in ordinary course of business. The jury further found that Lakeshore wrongfully caused Adamatic to detain the property involved in both transactions and that Chrysler's damages as a result of the detention were $40,000. It also found that Adamatic had been insolvent on the date this action commenced. The parties stipulated that issues regarding the first transaction (six-coil winder and cell inserter) were to be decided by trial judge, who determined that Chrysler had the right to possession of these machines.

The jury further found that the total value of the three twelve-coil winders was $220,000. It valued the cell inserter at $20,350, and the six-coil winder at $27,900. The trial judge changed the jury's answer with respect to the six-coil winder to $8,300 and reduced the finding of damages to Chrysler from $40,000 to $4,800.

Judgment was entered accordingly. The judgment essentially provided that Chrysler is entitled to all the goods involved in the action but denied Chrysler damages for the retention. For reasons not readily apparent, however, the trial judge ordered that Chrysler pay to Lakeshore (by way of the receiver) the value of the machines less the amounts which Chrysler had already paid Adamatic. In effect, he found that Chrysler held the goods subject to Lakeshore's security interest, despite the fact that he found Chrysler to be a buyer in ordinary course of business.

* * *

HEFFERNAN, JUSTICE.

It should be emphasized that the cause of action is for replevin. The action was brought by Chrysler to gain possession of the machines and for damages against Lakeshore for their wrongful detention. Although there is evidence in the record indicating a breach of contract by the manufacturer, Adamatic, no relief is sought for that. Lakeshore, on the other hand, asserts ownership of the machines because of its prior perfected security agreement with Adamatic. The receiver, representing the general creditors, bases its claim upon Lakeshore's rights as a secured creditor, but in addition asks for an accounting by Lakeshore for any excess which Lakeshore may receive from Chrysler. As an alternative only, the receiver argues that Chrysler's taking of the goods was an avoidable preference as against the unsecured creditors. No claim is asserted by either creditor against Chrysler for amounts unpaid on the contract price.

The legal issues fall into the natural division between the first contract involving the six-coil winder and the subsequent contract concerned with the three machines that are designated as twelve-coil winders.

THE FIRST CONTRACT—SIX-COIL WINDER

As recited in the statement of facts, the six-coil winder and the cell inserter were returned to Adamatic for alterations on August 12, 1970. Chrysler asserts, in respect to the six-coil winder, that it had title and possessory rights to the machine from the time it was first delivered to the Chrysler plant in February 1970. It asserts that the machine was returned to Adamatic on a bailment, by which Adamatic was to hold the winder for repair and alteration. Both creditors, Lakeshore and the receiver, assert that the return of the machine revested the title in Adamatic and made it subject to their claims.

Under sec. 402.401(1), Stats., subject to the provisions of ch. 409 and other limitations not applicable here, "title to goods passes from the seller to the buyer in any manner and on any conditions explicitly agreed on by the parties." The contract between Chrysler and Adamatic explicitly agreed that title to the six-coil winder and the cell inserter would vest in Chrysler upon the completion of manufacture and shipment to the Chrysler plant. Chrysler, therefore, obtained title to this machine when it was shipped from the Adamatic plant in early February 1970. At that time, under the terms of sec. 402.106(1), Stats., there was a completed sale. It is undisputed that this sale was in good faith and in the ordinary course of business. There is no claim that the original sale was in violation of Lakeshore's security interest or constituted a preference against the unsecured creditors.

In accordance with the provisions of sec. 409.307(1), Stats., Chrysler took the machines free of Lakeshore's security interest. The creditors, however, assert that Chrysler never "accepted" the goods or, if there were an initial acceptance, such acceptance was subsequently revoked. They rely upon sec. 402.401(4) for the proposition:

"A rejection or other refusal by the buyer to receive or retain the goods, whether or not justified, or a justified revocation of acceptance revests title to the goods in the seller. Such revesting occurs by operation of law and is not a 'sale.' "

This question was fully litigated, and the trial judge made the finding that Chrysler had title to the six-coil winder and the cell inserter at all times after their initial delivery to Chrysler. A review of the record reveals that this finding is fully supported by the applicable law and the evidence adduced at trial.

The fact that title passed when the goods were first delivered, however, does not ipso facto evince Chrysler's acceptance of them. A sale of goods does not necessarily imply the buyer's acceptance. White & Summers, Uniform Commercial Code, p. 249, sec. 8–2. While the delivery of the goods completed the sale, whether Chrysler accepted the machine depends on Chrysler's conduct after the delivery. Sec. 402.606, Stats., delineates conduct that constitutes the acceptance of goods. A buyer accepts goods if he notifies the seller that he accepts them, if he fails to make an effective rejection, or does an act inconsistent with the seller's ownership. There is no evidence that Chrysler expressly notified Adamatic that it was accepting the goods. On the other hand, Chrysler retained the six-coil winder for over six months without rejecting it. Under sec. 402.602, the rejection of goods must be made within a reasonable time after delivery and rejection will be ineffective unless the buyer seasonably notifies the seller.

No notification was ever given of the rejection of the six-coil winder. While there was evidence that Chrysler was displeased with the performance of the initial winder, there was no intimation that the winder was being rejected, although a letter from Chrysler to Adamatic carried the suggestion that, if the six-coil winder did not operate satisfactorily, the second contract—the contract for the three twelve-coil winders—would be cancelled. Chrysler in fact retained the six-coil winder for at least two months following the threat to cancel the other contract.

There was also evidence that Chrysler, during the period of possession, treated the six-coil winder as its own. It tagged the machine with a brass plate, giving it a Chrysler inventory serial number. Such conduct alone has been found to be evidence of acceptance. Julian C. Cohen Salvage Corp. v. Eastern Electric Sales Co. (1965), 205 Pa.Super. 26, 206 Atl.2d 331, 2 U.C.C.Rep. 432. The cell inserter was completely acceptable to Chrysler, but it, too, was returned to Adamatic. There is no contention that the mere return of the cell inserter constituted a rejection; rather, it was needed by Adamatic to run tests on other winders that were being manufactured. The documents that passed between Chrysler and Adamatic at about the time of the return of the six-coil winder and cell inserter show that Chrysler wished to retain title and possession of the machine and was returning it merely for adjustment and modification.

The questions of acceptance or rejection of goods are questions to be resolved by the finder of fact and depend upon the ascertainment of the intent of the parties. * * *

* * *

There is sufficient evidence to show that Chrysler acquired full title in the six-coil winder and cell inserter at the time of their initial delivery, and that Lakeshore's security interest could not re-attach to the goods in absence of a rejection by Chrysler. The rights acquired by Adamatic were those of a bailee, who had possessory interest for a limited purpose, but did not amount to "rights in the collateral." Sec. 409.204(1), Stats.; Cain v. Country Club Delicatessen of Saybrook, Inc. (1964), 25 Conn.Sup. 327, 203 Atl.2d 441, 2 U.C.C.Rep. 247. See, also, 1 Gilmore, Security Interests in Personal Property (1965), p. 353, sec. 11–5; 4 Anderson, Uniform Commercial Code (2d ed.), p. 179, sec. 9–204:7.

* * *

We hold that Chrysler, under the applicable law, was entitled to replevin of the six-coil winder and cell inserter. * * *

* * *

THE SECOND CONTRACT—TWELVE-COIL WINDERS

The situation in respect to the three twelve-coil winders is markedly different from that of the six-coil winder and the cell inserter. In respect to the twelve-coil winders, although there had been a contract entered into at an earlier time, the delivery of the goods was occasioned only by the replevin seizure itself. In the absence of Chrysler's claim, Lakeshore's right to the possession of the twelve-coil winders would be unquestioned.

It was conceded that Lakeshore had loaned substantial sums to Adamatic and, under ch. 409, Stats., had perfected a valid security interest in Adamatic's inventory. It was stipulated by the parties that, prior to the replevin, the twelve-coil winders were a part of that inventory. Had Chrysler not seized the machines under its claim of right, upon Adamatic's default Lakeshore could have taken possession of the machines under sec. 409.503 and sold them under the provisions of sec. 409.504 to satisfy, in part at least, Adamatic's obligations.

The mere physical transfer of the machines from Adamatic to Chrysler does not defeat Lakeshore's right to foreclose on the collateral. A perfected security interest gives the secured creditor rights in the goods themselves, and under the rule of sec. 409.201, Stats., those rights follow the collateral into the hands of subsequent owners.

Applying the principles of the Uniform Commercial Code, it is apparent that Chrysler took physical possession of the machines at a time when Lakeshore would ordinarily be entitled to their possession. Chrysler's possession of the goods is, therefore, subject to Lakeshore's security interest unless some other provision of the Code is sufficient to supersede the rights of Lakeshore.

Chrysler relies upon sec. 409.307(1), Stats., as an exception to the general rule that a purchaser is subject to an outstanding security interest. * * *

Chrysler claims to be "a buyer in ordinary course of business." That term is defined by sec. 401.201(9), Stats. * * *

Chrysler claims that it became a buyer in ordinary course of business at the time it originally contracted to purchase the twelve-coil winders. It further argues that Lakeshore's security interest was cut off at the time of entering into the contract and, at the time it took possession of the machines by replevin, its possession was free and clear of any claims of the secured creditor. Lakeshore and the receiver for the general creditors are united in disputing this claim. They argue that nothing less than a bona fide transfer of the goods could cut off the security interest, and that a replevin cannot constitute a transaction in ordinary course.

The initial question posed is whether one can become a buyer in ordinary course before a sale has occurred. While it is apparent that the contract was a contract to sell, only the position of the creditors can be reconciled with the language of the Uniform Commercial Code.

Under sec. 401.201(9), Stats., "buying" includes receiving goods under a pre-existing contract for sale. The statute is silent on the question of whether "buying" encompasses a situation where there has been a nonreceipt of the goods; but the enumeration in the statute, when reasonably construed, limits buying in ordinary course of business to those situations where a "sale," defined by sec. 402.106(1) as "the passing of title from the seller to the buyer for a price," has occurred. There is no contention that title passed to Chrysler prior to the physical transfer occasioned by the replevin, but, under sec. 401.201(9), the buyer in ordinary course must buy without knowledge that the sale is in violation of the rights of a third party. In the instant case Chrysler, at the time of the replevin, had full knowledge of the perfected security interest of Lakeshore.

The commentators who have written on sec. 401.201(9), Stats., shed but confused elucidation on whether one can become a buyer in ordinary course merely by entering into a contract to buy. Professor Gilmore notes that the Uniform Commercial Code, unlike prior uniform acts, does not require that a buyer actually take delivery to attain the status of buyer in ordinary course of business. 2 Gilmore, Security Interests in Personal Property, p. 696, sec. 26.6. * * *

It seems clear that, if there is a sale and the buyer has obtained title to the goods, his status as a buyer in ordinary course will not be defeated merely because he has not taken possession. Such is not our situation here, where Chrysler buttresses its claim as a buyer in ordinary course by asserting the replevin action was a part of the process by which title passed. Moreover, in the contract between the parties, delivery was envisaged as an integral part of the title-passing process.

Although both parties have treated all three twelve-coil winders as being "identified to the contract," the state of the record reveals grave doubt that this is really the fact. Only one machine was in a deliverable state. The other two, at the most, were but incompletely assembled component parts. While the Commercial Code, as pointed out above, does not require that in all cases the buyer actually take delivery in order to have a buyer in ordinary course of business status, sound policy considerations in the instant situation would seem to dictate that the rights of a secured creditor ought not be impaired in the absence of a physical transfer or assignment of the goods. We agree generally with the position submitted by the National

Commercial Finance Conference as amicus curiae. It points out that the Code generally gives preference to property interests which are evidenced either by recording or possession and that, to adopt the view of Chrysler, the financier of an inventory would no longer be able to rely on recorded interests and the status of his debtor's inventory. We recognize that this policy argument has been criticized by writers who contend that the commercial reality is that lenders rely not upon inventories or recorded instruments but rather upon the credit ratings of prospective debtors. * * *

* * *

This court, in Columbia International Corp. v. Kempler, *supra,* p. 559 of 46 Wis.2d, p. 469 of 175 N.W.2d, took a different position, stressing the policy of this jurisdiction—to place major reliance upon "apparent or ostensible ownership: People should be able to deal with a debtor upon the assumption that all property in his possession is unencumbered, unless the contrary is indicated by their own knowledge or by public records."

Thus, if Chrysler is to be afforded a status as a buyer in ordinary course of business, we conclude that such status must be determined as of the time he actually took possession of the goods.

The remedy of replevin is an unusual and drastic mode of recourse to secure the rights of a purchaser; and, from the viewpoint of common knowledge, it is almost absurd to argue that the acquisition of possession by replevin is in the ordinary course of business. It is certainly so in the instant case when we consider sec. 402.402, Stats. (the buyer's right of replevin) and sec. 402.716. Sec. 402.402(3)(a) provides:

> "Nothing in this chapter shall be deemed to impair the rights of creditors of the seller:
>
> "(a) Under the provisions of ch. 409 * * *."

The Commercial Code itself specifically negates Chrysler's contention that the replevin alone can in any way affect the rights of a prior secured creditor. Even if it be argued that these three machines were identified to the contract, sec. 401.201(37), Stats., states:

> " * * * the special property interest of a buyer of goods on identification of such goods to a contract for sale under s. 402.401 is not a 'security interest' * * *."

Chrysler thus makes the anomalous and unacceptable claim that its buyer's interest gives it a right superior to the holder of an antecedent perfected security interest.

Chrysler is not a buyer in ordinary course of business and holds the machines subject to the security interest of Lakeshore. From the viewpoint of equity, this is an unsatisfactory result, for the record shows that, prior to the replevin, Chrysler had substantially paid the contract price for all the goods involved. Our conclusion, however, is supported by the writings of distinguished commentators, who have pointed out that the Code itself affords but little protection for the prepaying buyer. The Code, however, gives broad latitude whereby a prepaying buyer, acting timely, can enter into suitable arrangements for his own protection.

In the instant case Chrysler was fully aware of the fact that it was not only a buyer but was financing the manufacturing process. It was for that reason it made progress payments on the basis of the work and materials as the manufacturing progressed. By proper negotiations with the other creditors, it might well have protected itself by obtaining a security interest in the goods it had contracted to buy. Lakeshore as a substantial creditor, interested in the well being of Adamatic, might well have been amenable to a Chrysler proposal that Lakeshore in part subordinate its security interest. In view of the size of this contract in proportion to the limited assets of the manufacturer, it was almost foolhardy for Chrysler to proceed in the face of the perfected security interest of Lakeshore.

Numerous law review articles discuss the problems posed for the prepaying buyer by the Code and various methods that may be used to obviate the very situation which resulted here. * * * The taking of the machines by Chrysler under the circumstances was unlawful. Lakeshore, not Chrysler, was entitled to possession of the twelve-coil winders.

Note

As the case above and the problems below demonstrate, courts have had difficulty in deciding when one becomes a buyer in the ordinary course. Must the buyer get title and possession or is it enough that the goods be merely "identified to the contract"? Or, more remote yet, that the buyer merely sign a contract to purchase?

In Daniel v. Bank of Hayward, 144 Wis.2d 931, 425 N.W.2d 416 (1988), the Wisconsin Supreme Court made a mistake. Out of sympathy for a foolish consumer buyer, it reversed the basic holding on that issue in *Chrysler v. Adamatic.* In *Daniel,* the court ruled that one could become a buyer much earlier in the transaction than it had found possible in the *Adamatic* case. Mr. and Mrs. Daniel had agreed to buy a van from a car dealer in the city of Hayward. They signed a contract to purchase a van that was to be assembled by General Motors according to their specifications. Shortly after they signed the contract and before their van had been manufactured, the Daniels signed over their existing motor home and delivered it to the dealership as a down payment. Apparently the dealer then sold the motor home, but it is unclear what the dealer did with the proceeds. The Bank of Hayward had a perfected security interest in all of the dealer's collateral and when the Daniels' van was delivered to the dealership, its security interest attached to the van, and, in fact, the "manufacturer's statement of origin" was sent directly to the bank and it apparently paid a sight draft directly to General Motors in payment for the Daniels' van.

Unfortunately, the day after the van was delivered to the dealer and before it was delivered to the Daniels, the bank seized all of the dealer's assets. The bank agreed to give the van to the Daniels but only after they agreed to pay the bank's full claim against the van. The Daniels then sued the bank on the theory they had become buyers in the ordinary course of the van and had so taken free of the bank's security interest. In reversing a lower court decision for the bank, the court found that the Daniels became "buyers" upon identification of the van to the contract—even before it had been delivered to the dealership and, of course, long before they had had possession.

Sympathy for the Daniels surely influenced the court; we wish the court had been made of sterner stuff. We question the wisdom of the Daniels' case. By opening the door to allow the pitiful Daniels to escape, we suspect Judge Abrahamson has allowed many undeserving parties to escape as well. Consider, for example, how the *Adamatic* case would come out if the *Daniel v. Bank of Hayward* rule were applied to it. Are we wrong?

Problem 5–8

Each of the following problems is based on the facts of a reported decision. How do you think the cases came out and how should they have come out?

1. Winnetka Motors agrees to buy two new automobiles from Birmingham Auto House, a dealer in an adjoining county. Winnetka pays for the cars at once and the parties agree that Auto House will hold them for a couple of weeks until Winnetka is ready for them. In the intervening two weeks Commercial Credit, the secured lender of Birmingham, does an inventory and finds that Birmingham has been selling automobiles and has not been remitting the proceeds and is thus in default. Commercial then repossesses all of Auto House's cars, including the two that have been sold to Winnetka. Winnetka sues Commercial for conversion and argues essentially that it had acquired prior rights because of UCC 9–307(1). How would you respond as Commercial's counsel?

2. Tanbro Fabrics Corp. is a textile manufacturer who purchases textiles from a mill and finishes them into dyed and patterned fabrics. In this case, Deering Milliken produced goods manufactured for Mill Fabrics. Under the agreement between Deering and Mill Fabrics, Deering was entitled to hold the goods and to retain a security interest in them until Mill Fabrics paid. Mill Fabrics resold the goods while they were still in Deering's warehouse to Tanbro. Tanbro paid Mill Fabrics and a month later demanded the delivery of the goods still in Deering's possession to it. Mill Fabrics in the meantime went bankrupt and accordingly Deering refused to deliver the goods. It asserted that it has a prior right in them to secure the debt owed by Mill Fabrics to it. Who gets the goods, Deering or Tanbro? If Deering is the winner, how would you advise Tanbro in the future? If Tanbro is the winner, how would you advise Deering?

Problem 5–9

Daisy Bank and Trust has a security interest in refrigerators, stoves, appliances and all other hard goods of Marie Louise, Inc., a department store. Assume that the security agreement purports to continue the security interest in the goods even after they have been sold. Now consider the following transactions in goods covered by the perfected security interest.

1. Wilbur buys a washing machine for cash. Wilbur takes free of Daisy's security interest. True or false?

2. Wilbur buys a washing machine on credit and signs a security agreement giving Marie Louise a security interest in the machine. Wilbur takes free of Daisy's security interest. True or false?

3. Wilbur buys a refrigerator on credit from Marie Louise and signs a security agreement. A month later Wilbur sells the refrigerator to his next-door neighbor, Charlotte. Identify the correct statement or statements:

   a. Charlotte takes free of the security interests of both Daisy and Marie Louise;

b. Charlotte takes free of Daisy's security interest because she qualifies under UCC 9–307(1);

c. Charlotte takes free of Marie Louise's security interest because of the application of UCC 9–307(1);

d. Charlotte does not qualify for the protection of UCC 9–307(1), nevertheless she takes free of both security interests.

LISBON BANK & TRUST CO. v. MURRAY

Supreme Court of Iowa, 1973.
206 N.W.2d 96.

McCormick, J. This appeal involves a problem under the Uniform Commercial Code arising out of a sale of cattle. Plaintiff Lisbon Bank and Trust Company loaned defendants to cross-petition (Glenn Meier and Joan Meier) $6620.00 on January 15, 1969, to purchase 48 Holstein heifers and received a duly perfected security interest in the cattle. On March 25, 1969, Glenn Meier sold 12 of the heifers to defendant Richard Murray for $2428.80. Subsequently the Meiers defaulted on their note and filed bankruptcy. The bank seeks in this action to collect $2428.80 from Murray on the theory he purchased the cattle subject to the bank's lien. Trial court found the sale was made free of the lien and dismissed the bank's petition. We affirm.

The determinative issue is whether the sale was authorized by the bank. Section 554.9306(2). The Code, provides:

> "Except where this Article otherwise provides, a security interest continues in collateral notwithstanding sale * * * by the debtor unless his action was authorized by the secured party in the security agreement or otherwise, and also continues in any identifiable proceeds including collections received by the debtor."

The Iowa Code commentators state this section was adopted from § 9–306 of the 1962 official text of the Uniform Commercial Code and compare this subsection with previous Iowa law:

> "Prior Iowa law was in accord that the lien of the secured party continued in the collateral after a sale thereof, Waters v. Cass County Bank, 65 Iowa 234, 21 N.W. 582 (1884), although the mortgagee could waive his lien by agreeing to the sale, Livingston v. Heck, 122 Iowa 74, 94 NW 1098 (1903)." 35B Iowa Code Annotated at 414.

The commentators add that the statute departs from former law by imposing a continuing lien on sale proceeds. However, as explained in the comment, where the lienholder authorizes the sale he waives his lien on the collateral under the Uniform Commercial Code just as under prior law.

We will assume the purchase in this case was by "a person buying farm products subject to a perfected security interest from a person engaged in farming operations" within the meaning of Code § 554.9307, under which other buyers in the ordinary course of business take free of a security interest even where the sale is unauthorized. See Uniform Commercial Code Comment, Iowa Code Annotated, at 431.

Trial court made a finding of fact that Glenn Meier had authority to sell the cattle. * * *

Sale may be authorized by the secured party "in the security agreement or otherwise." § 554.9306(2), The Code. The security agreement in this case did not authorize sale and therefore the bank cannot be held to have waived its security interest in the collateral unless it "otherwise" consented to the sale.

There was evidence the Meiers lived on a 33 acre tract near Lisbon where they bred sows, farrowed feeder pigs, grew hay and grazed livestock. The bank started loaning Glenn Meier money on his livestock operation in January 1968. Several loans covered by security agreements were made prior to January 15, 1969. At trial the bank acknowledged a general course of dealing, notwithstanding the security agreements, permitting him to sell collateral and apply the proceeds either to substitutions or on the notes. The bank admitted Meier accordingly sold hogs and horses on several prior occasions but denied he was authorized to sell cattle. There had been only one earlier cattle loan and those cattle had evidently not been sold at the time of the loan involved in this case. There was no evidence of any communication from the bank to Glenn Meier making any distinction as to cattle.

Glenn Meier told the bank at the time of the January 15, 1969, loan some of the cattle being purchased were bred, the others would be bred, and he intended to pasture them for six to 12 months on land owned by his father in Clinton County, selling them just before they calved. He hoped to pay the loan through enhancement in their value. The bank asserted it did not learn of the March 25, 1969, sale of 12 of the heifers to Murray until after the Meiers filed bankruptcy in May 1970.

However, it was undisputed that Glenn Meier took Murray's $2428.80 check to the bank the day after the sale. His version is that he told the bank's loan officer he sold some of the cattle and was permitted to deposit the money in his checking account rather than have it applied on the note. He said he spent the money on sows which became substitute collateral. The bank records show the check was deposited in his checking account. The bank loan officer denied Meier told him of the sale and said if he had the money would have been applied on the cattle loan. It was trial court's prerogative to pass on the credibility of the witnesses.

Both Glenn Meier and Murray testified Meier told Murray of the bank's security agreement on the cattle at the time of sale and Meier assured Murray he would take care of it.

Evidence of a course of dealing has relevance in interpreting agreements under the Uniform Commercial Code. Section 554.1205(1), The Code, defines course of dealing as "a sequence of previous conduct between the parties * * * which is fairly to be regarded as establishing a common basis of understanding for interpreting their expressions and other conduct." It may give particular meaning to and supplement or qualify terms of an agreement. § 554.1205(3), The Code.

A leading case on establishment of authority to sell secured farm products under the Uniform Commercial Code is Clovis National Bank v.

Thomas, 77 N.M. 554, 425 P.2d 726 (1967). There the security agreement expressly prohibited sale of the collateral without the prior written consent of the secured party. The court found the secured party had nevertheless as a matter of common practice permitted the debtor to make such sales without prior written consent. The secured party was held to have waived the requirement of written consent and its security interest. Clovis has been criticized for recognizing course of dealing as a basis for waiver of the requirement of written consent to sale. This is because the Uniform Commercial Code provides where express terms of an agreement and a course of dealing are inconsistent the express terms control. § 554.1205(4), The Code. See, generally, 47 Tex.L.Rev. 309, 313–314.

A different result was reached by the Nebraska Supreme Court in Garden City Production Credit Assn. v. Lannan, 186 Neb. 668, 186 N.W.2d 99 (1971). That case also involved a security agreement containing an express prohibition against sale without prior written consent. The Nebraska trial court had found waiver based on the secured party's failure despite knowledge of the sale to object to it until after the purchaser's check failed to clear.

We are not here confronted with a security agreement with a provision requiring written consent prior to sale, and we have a course of dealing which raises a question of fact as to the debtor's authority to sell. Clovis and Garden City each recognize, in accordance with the general rule, that a finding of authority to sell may be implied from a prior course of dealing at least in the absence of a security agreement prohibition against sale without written consent. * * *

This principle is unaffected by a finding such as was made here that the authority to sell was conditioned upon the debtor's agreement to apply the proceeds to the debt:

> "Where the sale of mortgaged property is made with the consent of a person authorized to give such consent, any failure of the mortgagor to live up to an agreement he made relating to accounting for the proceeds does not affect the waiver of the lien." United States v. Hansen, 311 F.2d 477, 480 (8 Cir. 1963).

* * *

If the authority had been conditioned on the purchaser making payment to the secured party, it appears the lien would not have been lost. * * * Waiver substitutes the personal obligation of the debtor for the collateral. * * * It was not so conditioned. And we are not here confronted with a situation where the purchaser had notice of any condition.

The fact the purchaser had actual notice of the security interest and was unaware it was waived does not alter the result. Waiver was between the bank and the Meiers. It was not necessary that it be communicated to the purchaser. Where sale is authorized the lien is divested and the purchaser takes the property free of it. * * *

In the present case there is substantial evidence from which the trier of fact could find the bank gave general authority to Glenn Meier to sell collateral subject to his duty to account for the proceeds. The bank acknowledges no complaint would have been made here had the proceeds been applied against the note. The bank lost because it trusted Glenn Meier to do what he had done before when he sold collateral. Murray trusted his assurance the sale was free of lien. As between the bank and Murray, the law imposes the risk of loss in these circumstances on the bank.

There is substantial evidence to support trial court's finding the bank consented to the sale. The case is affirmed.

Affirmed.

Problem 5–10

Assume that Rural Bank, having read the Lisbon Bank case, instructs its lawyer to draft a security agreement that will "solve the problem." Lawyer presents a security agreement with the following clauses:

1. *Debtor may not sell.* Debtor is expressly forbidden from selling the collateral under this security agreement without the prior written consent of the Bank. Upon any sale that is authorized by the Bank, Debtor shall procure payment directly to the Bank or jointly to the Bank and Debtor.

2. *No Waiver.* None of the provisions of this security agreement may be waived except in writing by an authorized officer of the Bank. No waiver or trade practice or course of performance in any past case will operate as a waiver in any future case. Thus, the fact that the Bank permits debtor to sell cattle or other products and keep the proceeds shall not be regarded as a grant of authority to do that in the future.

Assume that Debtor sells cattle and remits the proceeds on several occasions. On none of these occasions did he seek or get approval of the Bank. On the final occasion he sells all of his cattle for $220,000, departs to Las Vegas, where over the period of two weeks he loses the entire amount at the gaming tables. Bank is able to locate most of the livestock in the hands of purchasers. Will it be able to sue them for conversion, or replevy the livestock?

Problem 5–11

Assume that you are general counsel for a large Minneapolis bank. The bank comes to you with the following problem. A rather slovenly loan officer has managed to lend $1,000,000 to a large cattle dealer in the southern part of Minnesota. The loan officer from the bank was taken around various cattle yards to observe the cattle at the time of the loan and was informed that various of the cattle totalling in excess of 6,000 head were owned by the debtor. Loan officer did not check the brands nor make any other effort to confirm the actual number or the ownership of the debtor. It now appears that at the time the large loan was made, the debtor owned fewer than 100 head of cattle. Some of the property which he claimed to have under "oral lease" in fact was property of others not leased to him, and all of the cattle shown to the loan officer belonged to third parties.

During the six months when the loan was outstanding the farmer acquired a few hundred head of his own. In addition, he owned for a short period as many as 7,000 head which went through a very active cattle auction barn that he ran on his property. In the typical case he actually held title to these cattle for a short period of time and then sold them to third parties. Through his records all of the third parties can be identified and the total value of the cattle sold to them is approximately $800,000. Bank would like to pursue each of those buyers for conversion on the ground that its security interest attached to the cattle owned, however briefly, by the Debtor under the after-acquired property clause, and on the theory that these buyers did not take free under UCC 9–307. Note that there is no prior experience (as there was in *Lisbon*) and that the security agreement does not authorize the Debtor to sell cattle.

Bank would like your opinion about the probability of success in that lawsuit. Your junior associate has come up with the following tentative analysis:

> "The security agreement specifically attaches to after-acquired property and such terms are explicitly authorized by UCC 9–201, 9–203, and 9–204. It is conceded by all that the bank's debtor held title to these cattle for a period of time. When they were sold, those parties did not take free because of the exception in UCC 9–307 for farm products (sale was prior to 1987). It follows therefore the security interest traveled with the cattle into the hands of the third party and that the bank has a right to pursue those cattle. There is some chance that facts that are not now available to us may suggest that the bank gave the debtor authority to sell. Absent such facts, the security interest would continue in the cattle."

Would you act on this analysis?

Note: Federal Limitation on UCC 9–307(1)

By 1985 legislation, Congress has provided a mechanism which can override the "farm products" exception of UCC 9–307(1). Enacted within the Food Security Act of 1985, 7 U.S.C. § 1631 (Supp.1985), the statute grants federal protection to purchasers of farm products. In relevant part the statute provides:

> (d) Except as provided in subsection (e) and notwithstanding any other provision of Federal, State, or local law, a buyer who in the ordinary course of business buys a farm product from a seller engaged in farming operations shall take free of a security interest created by the seller, even though the security interest is perfected; and the buyer knows of the existence of such interest.

This general prohibition against lien enforcement is relatively straightforward. However, lengthy and complex exceptions may swallow the rule. The most important exceptions to the protection of purchasers of farm products are found in section 1631(e).

The first exception concerns buyers in the ordinary course with "actual knowledge" of the security interest. The general rule protects buyers with mere knowledge of the existence of a prior security interest. On the other hand, 1631(e)(1) provides that a buyer will take the purchased farm products subject to the existing security interest if the buyer receives written notice from the seller or secured party of the security interest within one year of sale and the buyer defaults on his obligation to pay for his purchase. At first blush the traditional notice system seems to have been turned on its head. No longer can a secured party depend on a centralized filing system for protection; if the secured party desires priority, he must send notice of his security interest to all potential purchasers of farm products from his debtor.

Of greater interest are the provisions creating a *second* filing system which permits the secured party to gain priority over purchasers of farm products. The second and third exceptions to 1631(d) concern the operations of a new creature called a "central filing system." Defined in 1631(c)(2), a central filing system is a centralized information system which registers secured creditors, debtors and purchasers of farm products. The central filing system is to be administered by the Secretary of State of each state, and each system is to be certified by the United States Department of Agriculture. Under the central filing system the Secretary of State periodically distributes all registered financing information to all registered buyers. If a state adopts a central filing system into its zoo of regulatory animals, an ordinary course purchaser of farm products will lose the general protections of 1631(d) if he is either not registered in the system or if he has received notice of a prior security interest from the Secretary of State. Thus, a state's enactment of a central filing system can return to the farm products exception originally contained in UCC 9–307(1).

Finally, a secured party in a non-central filing system jurisdiction may reduce the number of potential purchasers which he must notify if he requires his debtor to identify specifically all potential purchasers of the debtor's farm products. See 7 U.S.C. § 1631(h) (Supp.1985). If the debtor sells to a party not listed on the "accredited" purchaser list and neither gives prior notice to the secured creditor of the potential sale nor forwards the proceeds of the sale to the secured party, section 1631(b)(3) subjects the debtor to a fine of the greater of $5,000 or 15 percent of the proceeds of the sale. Note, however, that the *purchaser* will still receive the protection of 1631(d).

The basic effect of section 1631 is to shift the burden of informing. The purchaser's burden to seek out information regarding prior security interests is shifted either to the secured party (to notify all potential purchasers in non-central filing system states) or to the Secretary of State (to notify all registered purchasers in central filing system states).

The following note is a more elaborate description of the operation of the federal law and of its interaction with state law.

NOTE: *FARM PRODUCTS COLLATERAL:* STILL A PROBLEM?

1987 U.Ill.L.R. 241, 268–269 (1987).

* * * The exception to the general rule of section 1324(d) amply protects the secured party. Section 1324(e) provides lender protection through one of two optional schemes: a direct notice system or a central filing system. If a state does not adopt a central filing system, then the direct notice system applies to the sale of farm products that have been produced in that state.

A. Direct Notice System

The direct notice exception to the general rule of section 1324(d) states that a buyer of farm products takes subject to a security interest that the seller created if, within one year before the purchase, the buyer has received written notice from the secured party or the seller, *and* the buyer fails to perform the payment obligations contained in the written notice. The security agreement between the farmer and the secured party can require the farmer to furnish the secured party a list of the buyers, commission merchants, and selling agents to or through whom the farmer may sell his farm products. If the farmer sells to or through a person not on such a list without notifying the secured party in writing at least seven days in advance, or without accounting to the secured party for the proceeds of the sale within ten days after the sale, the farmer will be subject to a fine of the greater of $5,000 or fifteen percent of the sales price. Thus, the direct notice system allows the lender to protect himself by requiring the farmer to disclose to whom he will sell and by requiring that the buyer pay jointly to the farmer and lender or directly to the lender. The buyer protects himself by complying with the payment obligations contained in the secured party's written notice. This direct notice system is similar to several state legislatures' non-uniform amendments to the U.C.C. and a proposed system in earlier federal legislation.

B. Central Filing System

The central filing system exception to the general rule of section 1324(d) establishes a state-wide system whereby a secured party files an "effective financing statement" (EFS) with the Secretary of State. Buyers register with the Secretary of State in order to regularly receive a master list of security interests in farm products. Without registering, buyers may obtain EFS information within twenty-four hours after their inquiry. Under this system, the buyer takes subject to a security interest created by the seller if the buyer fails to register or inquire with the Secretary of State prior to the purchase *and* the secured party has filed an EFS with the Secretary of State covering the farm products being sold. The buyer also takes subject to a security interest created by the seller if the buyer receives a master list or EFS information covering the farm products being sold *and* the buyer does not secure a waiver or release of the security interest from the secured party by performing any payment or other obligation. Thus, under the central filing system, a lender protects himself by filing an EFS with the Secretary of State. The buyer protects himself by registering with the Secretary of State or by inquiring with the Secretary of State before purchase. If the master list or the Secretary of State discloses a security interest, the buyer must contact the secured party in order to obtain a waiver or release of the security interest. This central filing system is similar to those adopted earlier by a few states.

C. Interstate Sales

Occasions may arise where farm products are produced in one state and sold in another. If one state has adopted a direct notice system, and the other has adopted a central filing system, then the system of the state in which the farm products were produced applies. The necessary steps that a lender must take for protection are fairly clear. Assuming that a given product is produced in only one state, the lender follows either direct notice steps or central filing steps—depending on the system of the state where the farm products are produced. If the product is produced in a central filing state, the lender should file an EFS in that state. If the product is produced in a direct notice state, the lender should obtain a buyer's list from the farmer, and send those buyers direct notice.

The buyer also has to follow different steps to receive protection depending on where the product was produced, regardless of the system adopted in the state where the buyer is located. The buyer needs to ascertain from the seller the state in which the product was produced. If the product was produced in a direct notice state, the buyer is protected as long as he has received no notice, or complies with payment obligations in any notice received. If the product was produced in a central filing state, the buyer either must be registered in that state, or must inquire in that state. In addition, the buyer must contact any secured party, disclosed through a master list or inquiry, to ascertain and comply with conditions for waiver or release of the security interest.

In general, regardless of the debtor's residence, the secured party's location, or the buyer's location, the state in which the farm products were produced is the state whose system applies to the sale.

D. Analysis of the Preemption Options

The stated purpose of section 1324 is to remove a burden on interstate commerce in farm products that inhibited free competition in the market for farm products. As Congress explained:

> [C]ertain State laws permit a secured lender to enforce liens against a purchaser of farm products even if the purchaser does not know that the sale of the products violates the lender's security interest in the products, lacks any practical method for discovering the existence of the security interest, and has no reasonable means to ensure that the seller uses the sales proceeds to repay the lender.

Congress also found that "these laws subject the purchaser of farm products to double payment for the products, once at the time of purchase, and again when the seller fails to repay the lender."

Apparently, Congress's main concern was to correct the inability of buyers to protect themselves from the operation of the farm products exception. Congress, however, was also attempting to preserve some protection for the lender's security interest. Congress may also have been consciously attempting to severely restrict section 1324's preemptive power by using U.C.C. terminology and definitions resembling U.C.C. definitions. This might allow section 1324 to operate more easily within the pre-established framework of U.C.C. state law. Unlike the drafters of the U.C.C., Congress obviously was not concerned about uniformity of law; section 1324 allows states to choose one of two different schemes—the direct notice system or the central filing system.

* * *

Questions

1. Which of the two systems, direct notice or central filing, is the more efficient? Which is the more equitable? To answer those questions one needs to consider the burdens placed on the various parties in the two systems.

2. In an unquoted portion of the article, part of which was cited above, the author argues that the "central filing * * * may be the least costly solution that adequately protects both lenders and buyers." What is the basis for that conclusion?

SECTION 4. PRIORITY AMONG BUYERS OF INTANGIBLES, UCC 9–306, 9–308, 9–318, 9–309, 8–302

A. Chattel Paper, Instruments and the Like

The most renowned bona fide purchaser of intangible rights is barely mentioned in Article 9; he is the holder in due course of a negotiable instrument. We will meet that person in Chapter Twenty-Four, but it is not too soon to examine UCC 3–302 defining a holder in due course or UCC 3–305 specifying the rights of a holder in due course. Note that section 9–309 bows to those rights and to the rights of other lesser known bona fide purchasers such as the "due negotiatee" of a negotiable document of title under UCC 7–501 et seq., and the bona fide purchaser of a security under UCC 8–302. In addition, UCC 9–308 deals explicitly with competing claims to chattel paper and UCC 9–306(5) unravels priorities upon repossession of the underlying collateral.

Upon examination of UCC 3–302, 9–308, and the other sections, the student should be prepared to generalize from those sections and to ask why the law allows such a buyer necessarily second in time to have priority over someone who preceded him. Is the explanation no more than that this is the expectation of the parties that arises out of possession by the seller? Traditionally it has been thought desirable to allow a holder in due course to take free of other claims if the holder does nothing more than give new value to one who appears from the face of the instrument to be the owner. By such a method credit is easily and quickly extended and money was thought to flow readily from one place to another. In today's world where money is much more likely to pass over a wire than from hand to hand in response to a negotiable instrument, one might question the need for holder-in-due-course status.

Sections 9–308 and 8–302 rest on more specific commercial underpinnings. People do buy and sell chattel paper, and section 9–308 represents the drafters' judgment about the reasonable expectations of the various parties in that narrow setting. The same can be said about UCC 8–302, though a skeptic might argue that the section really represents only the buyer bank's interest and not that of customers on the selling end of the transaction.

Students should keep these questions in mind when they examine the cases and problems that follow. At minimum one needs to be able to answer the technical question: When will one lose to a subsequent party who may qualify under UCC 9–308 or 8–302? A good advocate will need also to address the policy question: when should such a person win, and why?

REX FINANCIAL CORP. v. GREAT WESTERN BANK & TRUST

Court of Appeals of Arizona, 1975.
23 Ariz.App. 286, 532 P.2d 558.

DONOFRIO, JUDGE.

This is an appeal from a judgment in favor of the appellee, Great Western Bank & Trust, on a motion to dismiss which was treated by the trial court as a motion for summary judgment under Rule 56 of the Arizona Rules of Civil Procedure, 16 A.R.S. The trial court considered all of the pleadings, affidavits, other matters of record, and the oral arguments of counsel and determined that there was no genuine issue of material fact, in reaching its judgment. For the reasons given below we affirm the judgment of the trial court.

* * * In December of 1971 appellant entered into an agreement with Liberty Mobile Home Centers, Inc., a dealer in mobile homes, under which appellant agreed to finance this dealer's inventory of mobile homes. The dealer delivered to appellant certain manufacturer's certificates of origin on mobile homes to secure repayment of the loans, and gave appellant a security interest in the vehicles by way of a security agreement between the parties. This appeal concerns four of those mobile homes. The four mobile homes were sold by the dealer in the regular course of his business to certain individuals on security agreement contracts. These four security agreement

contracts were then sold and assigned to the appellee, Great Western, in the ordinary course of its business for a certain sum which was paid to the dealer. Unfortunately, the dealer did not use these funds to pay off its outstanding loans owed to the appellant.

The basis for attacking a Rule 56 summary judgment ruling is that there were material factual issues disputed by the parties. All facts considered by the trial court appear in the pleadings, affidavits, depositions, and of course, oral arguments of the parties. On reviewing the record we are compelled to agree with the trial court that there were no material issues of fact, and that this was a question of law concerning the construction and application of A.R.S. § 44–3129 (UCC § 9–308) concerning the priority between certain secured creditors and purchasers of chattel paper.

A.R.S. § 44–3129 states:

> "A purchaser of chattel paper or a non-negotiable instrument who gives new value and takes possession of it in the ordinary course of his business and without knowledge that the specific paper or instrument is subject to a security interest has priority over a security interest which is perfected under § 44–3125 (permissive filing and temporary perfection). *A purchaser of chattel paper who gives new value and takes possession of it in the ordinary course of his business has priority over a security interest in chattel paper which is claimed merely as proceeds of inventory subject to a security interest (§ 44–3127), even though he knows that the specific paper is subject to the security interest.* Added Laws 1967, Ch. 3, § 5." (Emphasis added)

Since it was established that Great Western Bank had knowledge of the security interest claimed by Rex Financial Corporation in the four mobile homes, the second sentence of the foregoing section is the critical one for our purposes.

Appellant's first argument concerns the definition of "chattel paper" used in the above-mentioned sentence of A.R.S. § 44–3129. Appellant argues that the manufacturer's certificates of origin, which remained in its possession, were a part of the chattel paper and were necessary ingredients along with the security agreements purchased by Great Western to make up the "chattel paper" which must be possessed by the purchaser. We do not agree. A.R.S. § 44–3105(A)(2) defines "chattel paper" as: * * *. [quoting 9–105(1)(b)]

Appellant asserts that A.R.S. § 42–643 and § 28–325 of the Motor Vehicle Code contemplate that a manufacturer's certificate of origin is a part of the "transaction" where chattel paper is purchased as in A.R.S. § 44–3105(A)(2) above. We do not think that such comparison is relevant here. "Chattel paper" clearly must evidence "both a monetary obligation and a security interest in or a lease of specific goods." The manufacturer's certificates of origin do not meet this definition, and the trial court's construction of A.R.S. § 44–3105(A)(2) was correct in the application to this factual situation. It was undisputed that Great Western gave "new value" for the four security agreements it purchased from the dealer, all in accordance with § 44–3129.

The next requirement of § 44–3129 which is attacked by appellant is the requirement that the purchase of the chattel paper be "in the ordinary course of *his* business." (emphasis added) Appellant maintains that this refers to a practice which "should have been followed" and not to the practice of this particular purchaser of chattel paper. Again we do not agree. The plain language of the statute refers to *"his business"* (meaning the purchaser of the chattel paper). It is undisputed that this purchase was the normal means used at Great Western to obtain this type of chattel paper. As was stated in the deposition of Mr. McFadden, a representative of Great Western, he expected the *dealer* to disburse funds to appellant to pay off the loans for the "floor plan" financing that the dealer had obtained from appellant. The term "buyer in the ordinary course of business" with its requirements of good faith, as used elsewhere in the Uniform Commercial Code, is to be distinguished from the use here of "buyer in the ordinary course of *his* business." In fact, § 44–3129 (second sentence) allows the purchaser of the chattel paper to have priority even if he has knowledge of a prior security interest in the collateral. As noticed by White and Summers in their Treatise on the Uniform Commercial Code, " * * * the later party is favored on the assumption that chattel paper is his main course but merely the frosting on the cake for the mere proceeds claimant." White and Summers, Uniform Commercial Code, Sec. 25–17, p 951 (1972 Edition).

This brings us to the final issue raised by appellant: the fourth requirement of the second sentence of § 44–3129, that the security interest claimed by appellant is claimed "merely as proceeds of inventory subject to a security interest." We find Comment 2 to this section of the UCC (as found in the Final Report of the Permanent Editorial Board for the Uniform Commercial Code, Review Committee for Article 9, April 25, 1971) instructive on this issue. There it is stated:

> "Clause (b) of the section deals with the case where the security interest in the chattel paper is claimed merely as proceeds—i.e., on behalf of an inventory financer who has not by some new transaction with the debtor acquired a specific interest in the chattel paper. In that case a purchaser, even though he knows of the inventory financer's proceeds interest, takes priority provided he gives new value and takes possession of the paper in the ordinary course of his business."

We take this language to mean that the drafters of the Code contemplated a situation such as the instant one where the inventory financer, Rex Financial Corp., had a security interest in the collateral (mobile homes) and the proceeds upon sale. The record before us does not indicate that Rex entered into any new transaction with the debtor/dealer. The trial court had before it the security agreement between Rex and the dealer as well as the affidavit of Rex's president, and found that Rex's claim was merely to the proceeds of the inventory when sold. We do not find error in this construction and application of the term "mere proceeds of inventory" by the trial court. We think it is a reasonable interpretation of the record that the appellant, Rex, did not place a substantial reliance on the chattel paper in making the loan, but rather relied on the collateral (mobile homes) and the proceeds when the collateral was sold. The proceeds of the sale of these four mobile homes included the chattel paper sold by the dealer to Great Western. Rex could have protected itself by requiring all security agreements executed on sale of the mobile homes to be turned over immediately to Rex, or if sold, that all payments for the security agreements (chattel paper) be made to itself.

A case that aptly illustrates the operation of UCC § 9–308 (A.R.S. § 44–3129) is Associates Discount Corporation v. Old Freeport Bank, 421 Pa. 609, 220 Atl.2d 621 (1966). In that case a finance company which purchased chattel paper from an auto dealer (in a factual situation somewhat similar to ours) prevailed over a bank which had "floor planned" the inventory of the dealer. The court found that the bank's claim was a mere proceeds claim to the chattel paper and that UCC § 9–308 (second sentence) would operate to give priority to the purchaser of the chattel paper. The inventory financer's interest in the "proceeds" of the sale of the inventory had been shifted to the money paid by the purchaser of the chattel paper to the dealer. * * *

* * *

In any case, the construction and application of A.R.S. § 44–3129 (UCC § 9–308) to undisputed facts is a question of law for the trial court which was reasonably determined in the instant case.

Affirmed.

OGG, P.J. * * * and STEVENS, J. concur.

Notes

1. Assume that you are the inventory lender in a *Rex Financial* case and that you would like to have priority as to the chattel paper as well. How do you arrange that?

2. Assume a case like *Rex Financial,* but one in which the original secured creditor filed a financing statement listing "inventory and chattel paper." Assume further that its security agreement recited specifically that the creditor "relied upon" the chattel paper in making the loan. At trial the secured creditor argues two bases for a finding that it is not "merely" a proceeds claimant. First it points to the security agreement that specifics her reliance. Second it says that only a person without a financing statement representing chattel paper can be a "mere" proceeds claimant. If you represent the purchaser of the chattel paper, how do you respond to those arguments?

Problem 5–12

Bank has a perfected security interest in retailer's supply of mobile homes. It has a $500,000 loan outstanding that is secured by 20 mobile homes, each with a value of $25,000. Retailer's business does not go well and ultimately he declares bankruptcy. Upon his bankruptcy all concede that the 15 remaining new mobile homes go to the Bank with a perfected security interest in inventory. However, there are three additional mobile homes that have been repossessed and returned to the dealer's lot. As to these, there is chattel paper outstanding which was sold to a bona fide purchaser, Local Loan (for this purpose assume Local Loan had priority under UCC 9–308). Bank now argues that when the mobile homes were returned to the lot its security interest reattached and, as the first to file, it has priority. Local Loan argues that Bank's security interest was cut off under UCC 9–308 and that it does not reattach. Each of the two cites different portions of UCC 9–306(5) to support its case. What are those portions and who should win?

B. Repledged Collateral

A variety of priority conflicts can arise if the pledgee of stock or other collateral repledges the collateral to secure his own loan, sells it or otherwise gives an interest in the collateral to some third party. The pledgee's right to repledge collateral is explicitly recognized by UCC 9–207(2)(e) in the circumstances in which the repledge will be on terms "which do not impair the debtor's right to redeem it." The most common example of a case in which the repledge does not impair the debtor's right to redeem is the case in which the collateral is pledged for a loan of the same or lesser amount and of the same or lesser duration than the original loan. Presumably in such circumstances the repledgee will be willing to give up the collateral to the original pledgor upon the pledgor's payment of the second debt. The pledgor's payment of the pledgee's debt to the repledgee would presumably extinguish the obligation between them or reduce it pro tanto.

In the securities market it is commonplace for a customer of a stockbroker to pledge stock to secure margin borrowing from the broker. It is also common for the customer to authorize the stockbroker to repledge the stock to a bank or other financing institution and so to finance the stockbroker's operation. When the stockbroker goes broke and the bank appropriates the collateral to satisfy its debt, where is the customer? On this question, consider the following problems.

Problem 5–13

1. Mr. Barron was a customer of Ira Haupt and Co. He was a wheeler-dealer in the stock market and purchased "on the margin"—that is, he would sometimes put up $5,000 or $7,000 and Haupt would buy stock with a fair market value of $10,000. In effect, of course, Haupt was lending money to Barron and was in turn borrowing money from banks in order to make loans to his customers. In order to secure each loan with the other banks, Haupt put up Barron's stock as security for a longer term than pledged by Barron to Haupt. This stock was carried in the name of Haupt's nominee (street name) and it was endorsed to the bank at the time it was put up. Haupt now goes bankrupt as a result of the famous DeAngelis affair. Who gets the stock—Barron or the bank? You may assume that Barron signed an agreement with Haupt which contained terms essentially like the following:

> "This agreement covers all securities and other property whatsoever which you may at any time be carrying for the undersigned (either individually or jointly with others), or which may at any time be in your possession for any purpose including safekeeping, or to be held by you as security for all liabilities of the undersigned to you with the right on your part to transfer money or securities from any one of my accounts (other than from Regulated Commodity Accounts) to another when in your judgment such transfer may be necessary. You are hereby authorized, without notice to the undersigned, and without regard to whether you have in your possession or subject to your control at the time thereof either separately or together with securities and other property of other customers, either for the amount due you from the undersigned or for a greater sum."

See UCC 9–309, 8–301 et seq.

2. If the Barron/Haupt bank transaction had been undertaken with uncertificated securities, how would it come out? Assume that Barron borrowed from

Haupt to buy the stock but did not explicitly authorize Haupt to repledge the stock to a third party. Assume nevertheless that Haupt did so and that all the parties took the steps necessary under the new Article 8 to perfect their interests. On Haupt's bankruptcy who gets the stock, Barron or the bank?

C. Accounts, Money Earned and to Be Earned by the Sale of Goods and the Performance of Services

The word "account" stimulates images of thousands of transactions in which businesses or consumers buy sweaters, shirts, lumber, supplies or lawn mowers, and promise to pay for them in the future. In these transactions seller has fully performed its side of the bargain and the only remaining act is for the buyer to pay. Because the transactions are so numerous, any secured creditor taking a security interest in those accounts would not be much concerned about any particular buyer's defense against the seller.

The rules of priority of security interests in such accounts are quite straightforward. Section 9–312 applies in a conventional way. Section 9–102 makes clear that Article 9 governs whether the transaction between the lender and debtor is labeled a security interest in accounts receivable or a sale of those accounts. In either case priority would be dependent upon the time of attachment and perfection of a security interest and would be determined by 9–312. An account accompanied by a security interest in the underlying goods would turn into chattel paper and this would raise the issues discussed above under 9–308.

There is another universe of "accounts" that is almost completely separate from the one described above. This is the universe composed of construction contracts, defense production contracts, and the like. Here the buyer (often a state or local government, or a federal governmental agency, such as the Department of Defense) has an obligation to pay the debtor who is a construction company making a road or an airport or a manufacturing company making aircraft, ammunition or missiles. Under the 1962 Code these rights were not "accounts" but "contract rights" because they had not yet been earned by performance. Under the 1972 Code the two were combined and what formerly had been contract rights became a subclass of "accounts."

Notwithstanding that definitional change it is a mistake to think of the two kinds of accounts as the same. In many ways the rights to payment under the construction and manufacturing contracts are far more precarious than rights to payment under conventional consumer or business accounts. Moreover, the competitors of the secured creditor are likely to be different persons and the threats to the security come from different directions in the two settings.

Note the first significant difference between the two universes. In regard to conventional business accounts, the seller has completed its performance by delivering the goods to the buyer. But where the loan is made to a debtor construction company, the debtor may not have poured even the first yard of concrete. Months or even years of work may yet need to be done. Those months and years of work before payment carry with them daily opportunities for the construction company to default and for the state or governmental agency's assertion of a defense because of that default. Section 9–318(1)(a) tells that such defenses can normally be asserted (when they arise out of the same contract) by the account debtor not only against the debtor (construction company) but also against the bank that has taken a security interest in the right to payment. For that reason alone, the bank's right in these contract claims is more precarious than a similar right in a set of payments arising from completed sales.

A second characteristic of the latter universe is that the secured creditor has all or most of its eggs in one basket. If a contractor who has agreed to pave two gigantic runways defaults, all payments will stop. In classic accounts this ending will not occur. Even if the debtor has delivered shoddy goods in a number of transactions, the large numbers may protect the secured creditor and even a significant number of returns by buyers will not wipe out the security.

A final difficulty relates to bonding companies. With rare exceptions those who manufacture goods for the federal government and those who enter into construction contracts for state, local, or federal governments, must provide bonds to assure their performance and assure payment to those who deal with them (subcontractors). Bonding companies are contingent creditors and when they become actual creditors (upon default of the contractor and payment or performance by the bonding company) they are certain to compete with the bank for any payments owed to the debtor under the broken contract. As the following case will disclose, these companies typically assert rights outside of Article 9 and their rights are often recognized as superior to banks' Article 9 rights.

There are two types of bonds protecting different interests. The "payment" bond protects the owner from mechanic's liens and the like by assuring that laborers, subcontractors, and materialmen who contribute work and materials to the job will be paid. The "performance" bond assures that the bonding company will hire replacements to complete performance if the original contractor defaults.

The principal claim of the bonding companies will be subrogation. They will claim this equitable right to money to be paid for performance after default and for money already earned at the time of default that has been held back under the terms of the contract. This latter money is sometimes called a "retainage"; it commonly equals ten to fifteen percent of each payment. That is to say, the owner will pay only 85 to 90 percent of the amount due as progress payments at the time of performance and will hold back ten to fifteen percent against the possibility that performance has not been done properly and against the possibility that remaining performance will not be done properly. Although the bonding companies sometimes take assignments from their debtors, usually these companies do not assert claims as assignees or as secured creditors. Frequently a bank or other lender will already have filed a financing statement in the contractor's name before any bond is issued and a later bonding company would be subordinated to that claim in an Article 9 contest. On the other hand, bonding companies frequently win on the equitable battlefield.

To whom are the bonding companies subrogated? It depends. To the extent they pay materialmen, subcontractors, and such under their "payment" bond, they are subrogated to the rights of those persons. To the extent those persons held mechanics' liens or other priority claims, they might well have priority over everyone on the job. Obviously the bonding company will also have a right to assert the claims of the defaulted contractor, but—at least against a secured creditor—those claims would seem to do little or no good because by hypothesis the contractor has agreed to make payment to the secured creditor and has granted it security. The bonding company may also be subrogated to the rights of the owner (the state, local, or federal government). If that party would have the right to set off vis à vis the bank under 9–318(1)(a), then the bonding company could do so too.

The bonding companies have frequently described themselves as purchase money lenders. They, so they argue, advance money so that the project can be completed. Without their money the project would not be completed and—so the argument goes—there would be no asset or security for anyone. Thus, they claim the status of purchase money lenders who routinely enjoy priority over prior persons. The purchase money analogy goes only so far. The bank can also claim to be a purchase money lender, for if it had not advanced money, the first mile of concrete would not have been laid and to the extent the retainage has been earned by the laying of that mile of concrete, the bank will argue that it is entitled to the retainage over the rights of the bonding company. The following case traces the history of this continuing dispute. Its outcome is representative.

TRANSAMERICA INSURANCE COMPANY v. BARNETT BANK OF MARION COUNTY, N.A.

Supreme Court of Florida, 1989.
540 So.2d 113.

SHAW, JUSTICE.

* * *

Petitioner surety and Turner Construction, Inc., entered into an agreement whereby petitioner would provide surety bonds for construction projects which Turner contracted to perform for various government bodies. As required by section 255.05, Florida Statutes (1983),[1] Turner obtained payment and performance bonds for the benefit of each government body and for subcontractors and other persons supplying labor, material, and services in the construction projects. An indemnity agreement assigned accounts receivable to petitioner should Turner default. By its terms, the indemnity agreement constituted a security agreement without abrogating, restricting, or limiting the rights of petitioner under the agreement, under law, or in equity. Turner obtained a series of loans from respondent bank to finance its operations, in return for which Turner gave the bank a security interest in accounts receivable from the construction contracts. The bank's security interest was filed under the Uniform Commercial Code (U.C.C.) prior to the filing of petitioner's security interest.

Construction contracts customarily provide for progress payments to be made to contractors by the owner as construction proceeds. Two safeguards

1. All statutory references are to Florida Statutes (1983).

have been devised to protect owners against default by the contractor, both of which are involved here. The first is a contractual provision under which the owner retains a percentage of the progress payments for the purpose of curing or mitigating subsequent contractor default. The retainage is paid to the contractor upon satisfactory performance and/or payment, but neither the contractor nor its assignees or creditors have any claim on the funds until the contractor performs. The second safeguard is a requirement that the contractor obtain payment and performance surety bonds. Because of their importance, payment and performance bonds are mandatory under section 255.05 for government projects and are commonly employed by prudent private owners.

This case comes to us from a partial summary judgment which was affirmed in the district court. The trial court ruled that the bank's prior perfection of its security interests in Turner's accounts receivable from the construction contracts gave it priority over the claims of the surety based on equitable subrogation. The trial court order noted that it did "not operate as a determination that Turner was in fact owed any monies as a result of accounts receivable or funds earned but unpaid." Consistent with this disclaimer, it also appears that the trial court treated petitioner's equitable subrogation rights as if these rights arose solely from standing in the shoes of the contractor Turner [2] and not from standing in the shoes of the owner/obligee and laborers and materialmen involved in the construction projects. The district court adopted a similar analytical approach in its affirmance by rejecting what it called the "federal view" that sureties had priority by virtue of equitable subrogation arising from owner/obligees, laborers, and materialmen. Accordingly, the district court held: (1) the surety's assignment was a security interest subject to the filing and perfection requirements of the U.C.C.; (2) there is no good faith exception to U.C.C. filing requirements and it matters not whether the secured party who first perfects its interest knows of any other prior interests; and (3) the remedy of equitable subrogation is not available to a surety because of the filing requirements of the U.C.C.

The initial question is whether a surety's equitable subrogation rights are limited to rights it obtains by standing in the shoes of the defaulting contractor. On this point we agree with the court in *National Shawmut Bank v. New Amsterdam Casualty Co.*, 411 F.2d 843, 844–45 (1st Cir.1969).

> [T]here is confusion because the tendency is to think of the surety on Miller Act payment and performance bonds as standing in the shoes only of the entity it "insures"—the contractor. So long as this one-dimensional concept prevails, logic compels the surety to be assessed as merely one of the contractor's creditors, and to be subject to the system of priorities rationalized by the Uniform Commercial Code. But the surety in cases like this undertakes duties which entitle it to step into three sets of shoes. When, on default of the contractor, it pays all the

2. The trial court order recites "the equitable principle involved is that when one [the surety], pursuant to obligation, not a volunteer, fulfills the duties of another [the contractor], he is entitled to assert the rights of that other against third persons." The order also recites: "Based upon its prior compliance with the Florida Uniform Commercial Code, BARNETT has a superior claim to all accounts receivable and contract rights of *TURNER* which were earned or vested, but unpaid, as of the moment of the default by TURNER under any job or contract." (Emphasis added.)

> bills of the job to date and completes the job, it stands in the shoes of the contractor insofar as there are receivables due it; in the shoes of laborers and material men who have been paid by the surety—who may have had liens; and, not least, in the shoes of the government, for whom the job was completed.

The narrow view that a surety acts only for the contractor (principal) is inconsistent with the purpose of a surety bond: to protect the obligees. A surety who performs or pays on behalf of an obligee steps into the shoes of the obligee to the extent of performance or payment.

> Traditionally sureties compelled to pay debts for their principal have been deemed entitled to reimbursement, even without a contractual promise such as the surety here had. And probably there are few doctrines better established than that a surety who pays the debt of another is entitled to all the rights of the person he paid to enforce his right to be reimbursed.

Pearlman v. Reliance Ins. Co., 371 U.S. 132, 136–37, 83 S.Ct. 232, 235, 9 L.Ed.2d 190 (1962) (footnote omitted). These rights of the surety as subrogee are not inferior even to the rights of the obligee and may be asserted against the obligee. *Trinity Universal Ins. Co. v. United States,* 382 F.2d 317 (5th Cir.1967).

The district court held that the surety's assignment was a security interest under the U.C.C. We disagree for two reasons. First, the U.C.C. itself suggests that a surety's assignment from a contractor, should be excluded from the U.C.C. Section 679.104(6) excludes a transfer of a right to payment under a contract to an assignee who is also to do the performance under the contract. A surety's assignment is contingent on performance by the surety in the event the contractor defaults. This contingent assignment based on contractual performance contrasts sharply with the noncontingent assignment to a financier which does not call for performance and which is uncontrovertably a security interest. In this connection, we note that a draft provision of the U.C.C. which would have specifically subordinated a surety's assignment to a later perfected security interest was specifically rejected by the Editorial Board which drafted the U.C.C. *See In re J.V. Gleason Co.,* 452 F.2d 1219, 1221 nn. 5–6 (8th Cir.1971), and *National Shawmut Bank,* 411 F.2d at 846 n. 4. Contrary to the district court below, we see this rejection as evidence that the drafters of U.C.C. did not intend to upset the well-established rules governing the priority of a surety assignment. Respondent is attempting to obtain through court-made law what it and others similarly situated were unable to obtain in the drafting and adoption of the U.C.C. Second, even if we were to assume that a surety's assignment was a security interest, it does not follow that this would abrogate petitioner surety's rights under the doctrine of equitable subrogation. A security interest and equitable subrogation are not incompatible, indeed the surety contract here contained a provision that the assignments therein of a security agreement did not abrogate the surety's right to protect itself under other theories. This contractual provision is consistent with section 671.103 which provides that general principles of law and equity are applicable unless displaced by particular provisions of the U.C.C. Equitable subrogation arises from law, not from the provisions of a contract.

The district court acknowledged that statutes requiring filing or recording to give notice usually contain a "good faith" limitation. Nevertheless,

> [a]lthough, admittedly, it is not conclusively clear, it appears to us from the drafting history of U.C.C. § 9–312(5) (§ 679.312(5), Fla.Stat.), that a "good faith" limitation was intentionally omitted from the U.C.C. provision and, therefore, none should be implied by the courts.

Transamerica, 524 So.2d at 445. Although the point is not critical here, we note that section 671.203 imposes an obligation of good faith on performance or enforcement of every contract or duty within the U.C.C.

On the overall question of subrogation, the district court concluded that equitable subrogation was not available to a surety in Florida because sureties have ample opportunities to make contractual subrogation agreements with contractors, other contractor assignees, and with surety obligees and to file these assignments (security interests) under the U.C.C. As is obvious from our disposition of the other points above, we do not agree. Nonsurety assignees of a contractor in default have no enforceable claim on funds withheld by the owner/obligee because of contractor default. The interests of all concerned parties, whether they be contractors in default, nonsurety assignees, owners, or other obligees, are best served by prompt performance by the surety. Under these circumstances, it is appropriate to give priority to the claims of the surety, up to the limits of its performance. Section 671.102 provides that the code will be liberally construed and applied to promote its underlying purposes and policies, one of which is to make uniform the law among various jurisdictions. As Chief Judge Sharp pointed out in her dissent below,

> the overwhelming and essentially unanimous post-U.C.C. decisions in this country, federal as well as state courts, have held that (1) the surety's equitable right of subrogation is not a consensual security interest, (2) no U.C.C. filing is necessary to perfect the surety's interest, and (3) the surety's interest continues to be, as it was under pre-Code law, superior to the claim of a contract assignee, such as a bank.

White & Summers, Uniform Commercial Code § 22–5 (2d ed. 1980). Adopting the position of the district court would frustrate uniformity and create conflict in the application of U.C.C. This conflict of law would also exist in bankruptcy cases where equitable subrogation is recognized. *Pearlman; In re J.V. Gleason Co.; McAtee v. United States Fidelity & Guar. Co.,* 401 F.Supp. 11 (N.D.Fla.1975).

Petitioner also argues that its equitable subrogation rights to priority over the bank in individual contracts combine with common law setoff to give it priority over any excess construction funds from other contracts. We disagree for the reasons stated in Judge Sharp's dissent below. Priority based on equitable subrogation in one contract does not provide priority in excess funds from another contract. This does not mean, however, that an owner cannot prioritize its own common law right of setoff.

We quash the decision below and remand for further proceedings consistent with this decision.

It is so ordered.

EHRLICH, C.J., and OVERTON, MCDONALD, BARKETT and KOGAN, JJ., concur.

GRIMES, J., did not participate in this case.

SECTION 5. PRIORITY DISPUTES BEYOND SECTION 9-312, MULTIPLE CHAINS OF OWNERSHIP

By hypothesis all priority disputes involve multiple claims to the same asset. Many of the cases, such as those involving security interests in chattel paper and the like involve more than one creditor and more than one debtor. Even when these disputes involve multiple creditors and multiple debtors, most of the cases involve a single chain of ownership that might go from seller (secured creditor) to buyer (debtor) to second secured creditor (with an after-acquired property clause) to buyer number two, etc. Those cases can be quite complicated, but the priority rules in 9–301, 9–308, 9–312 et seq. generally resolve them with clarity and precision. Variations on these cases are raised in Problem 5–11 on p. 263 (having to do with 9–306(5) and the competition between the original inventory lender and the consumer finance lender when the financed collateral is repossessed and is back in the hands of the dealer), those arising under 9–307 (where a buyer purports to cut off the claims of a prior perfected secured creditor and then to grant a superior claim to another secured creditor), and those having to do with repledged collateral under 9–207. All of the latter cases involve a "single chain" of ownership and, however complicated, are directly addressed by the priority rules of Article 9.

Now consider a different problem that occurs only infrequently but that has tantalized students of personal property security law. This is the case in which Elijah in one corner of the forest grants a security interest in his inventory and equipment to Bank of America. Moses, on the other side of the forest, grants a security interest in his inventory and equipment to Citicorp. Each of these security agreements has an after-acquired property clause and each is subject to the provisions of 9–402(7). Assume that Moses merges with Elijah or alternatively, that Moses buys all of the assets of Elijah. In either case the perfected security interest of Bank of America carries over in the assets that now belong to Moses. Indeed, if the transaction was a corporate merger of Moses and Elijah, Moses might have liability on Elijah's security agreement with Bank of America. But Citicorp's security interest also attaches to this after-acquired property formerly of Elijah that now belongs to Moses and Citicorp clearly has acquired a perfected security interest in the assets that formerly belonged to Elijah.

Who has priority in the assets that formerly belonged to Elijah? If one applied 9–312(5) directly to the claims of Bank of America and Citicorp, pure happenstance would dictate whether Citicorp or Bank of America had filed first, and pure happenstance would determine their priority. To put the point another way, if Bank of America had searched under "Elijah" and Citicorp under "Moses," neither would have found the other's filing irrespective of the time of filing. Section 9–312 does not seem suited to this case. For a careful consideration of these questions, consider the following case.

BANK OF THE WEST v. COMMERCIAL CREDIT FINANCIAL SERVICES, INC.

United States Court of Appeals, Ninth Circuit, 1988.
852 F.2d 1162.

Appeals from the United States District Court for the Northern District of California. Before FARRIS, BRUNETTI and THOMPSON, CIRCUIT JUDGES.

* * *

THOMPSON, CIRCUIT JUDGE. * * *

* * *

FACTS

The district court's well-written opinion contains a thorough discussion of the complicated facts of this case. See Bank of the West v. Commercial Credit Fin. Servs., Inc., 655 F.Supp. 807, 810–12 [3 UCC Rep.Serv.2d 240] (N.D.Cal.1987). In its opinion, the court thoughtfully analyzed the evidence presented by both sides and meticulously set forth the events preceding this appeal in a chronological table accompanied by crossreferences to those portions of the record favoring each party. We have independently examined the substantial record on appeal. After this review, we are not left with a "firm and definite conviction" that the district court's findings of fact are erroneous. Accordingly, we adopt the district court's findings of fact and set out below a summary of those events pertinent to the issues on appeal.

On April 5, 1982, Bank of the West entered into a loan and security agreement with Allied Canners & Packers, Inc. ("Allied"), a wholly-owned subsidiary of Boles World Trade Corporation ("BWTC"). Bank of the West lent Allied $4,000,000 in exchange for a security interest in Allied's present and future-acquired inventory, accounts, and proceeds. The Bank perfected its security interest by filing a financing statement with the California Secretary of State on April 7, 1982.

In 1983, Allied's financial condition deteriorated and the Bank demanded repayment of the outstanding loan balance of $1,800,000. Allied persuaded the Bank to renegotiate the loan. This resulted in a restructuring agreement signed on January 13, 1984. Contemporaneously with the restructuring agreement, Allied signed a new security agreement granting Bank of the West a security interest in Allied's "present and hereafter acquired" accounts, inventory, and proceeds. As part of the loan renegotiations, there is evidence that BWTC suggested to Bank of the West that it would transfer a beverage wholesaling and importing business to Allied. See Bank of the West, 655 F.Supp. at 811.

In January 1984, another wholly-owned BWTC subsidiary, Boles & Co., Inc. ("BCI"), entered into a factoring agreement with CCFS. The factoring agreement provided that BCI would assign its accounts to CCFS. CCFS would then collect amounts due from account debtors; three days after collection, CCFS would remit to BCI the amounts collected, less a 1% commission, and less any prior advances, plus interest. Advances were to be made on accounts which remained uncollected 33 days following assignment. In the factoring agreement, BCI granted CCFS a security interest in its present and after-acquired accounts. In a separate security agreement to secure advances made to BCI pending collection of accounts, BCI also granted CCFS a security interest in BCI's present and after-acquired inventory and proceeds. CCFS properly perfected its security interests by filing a financing statement with the California Secretary of State on January 5, 1984.

To understand the issues on appeal, it is necessary to consider the complicated corporate structure of the affiliated companies owned by BWTC. BWTC, formerly called Boles & Co., Inc., owned several subsidiary corporations, which engaged in several different businesses. Before August 1983, the former Boles & Co. (now called BWTC) conducted a beverage importing and wholesaling business. On August 15, 1983, the board of directors of the original Boles & Co. voted to change its name to BWTC and to contribute the beverage business to one of its wholly-owned subsidiaries, Minerals Trading Corporation. On the same day, the directors of Minerals voted to change its name to Boles & Co., Inc. (referred to as BCI), and to accept the contribution of the beverage business assets from BWTC. Between August 1983 and June 30, 1984, BWTC again reorganized its subsidiaries and transferred the beverage business from BCI to Allied. Allied changed its name to Boles International Beverage Co. ("Allied/BIBCO") by vote of its board of directors on December 6, 1983, but did not file a certificate of amendment with the California Secretary of State to reflect this name change until June 11, 1984.

Much of the dispute in this case is over who owned the beverage business accounts factored by CCFS after January 13, 1984, the date on which Bank of the West signed the loan restructuring agreement with Allied/BIBCO. Bank of the West argues that at least by February 1, 1984, Allied/BIBCO was conducting the beverage business and that CCFS consequently was factoring accounts in which Bank of the West held a prior perfected security interest. The district court found that the beverage business was not finally transferred to Allied/BIBCO until July 1, 1984. See Bank of the West, 655 F.Supp. at 814 15. The court reviewed the extensive evidence presented by both sides and found that while BWTC may have intended to transfer the beverage business to Allied as early as October 1983, id. at 814, BWTC did not complete moving the beverage business to Allied/BIBCO until the end of June 1984. Id. at 815. Having examined the record, which is replete with conflicting testimony, vague assertions, and confused recollections, we cannot say that the district court's findings of fact are clearly erroneous. Accordingly, we accept the court's finding that between January 13 and June 30, 1984, BCI owned and operated the beverage business. In operating that business, BCI generated the accounts factored by CCFS. On July 1, 1984, the beverage business was transferred to Allied/BIBCO. Consequently, from and after that date, any accounts factored by CCFS were generated by sales of the beverage business inventory by Allied/BIBCO, or were accounts in existence at the time of the transfer.

C. *Resolving the Priority Dispute*

Having concluded that both Bank of the West and CCFS had perfected security interests in the inventory and accounts actually transferred from BCI to Allied/BIBCO, as well as the inventory and accounts acquired by Allied/BIBCO after the July 1, 1984 transfer, we must decide which of these security interests is entitled to priority. The district court resolved this question by looking to § 9312(5), which provides:

> "In all cases not governed by other rules stated in this section . . . priority between conflicting security interests in the same collateral shall be determined according to the following rules:
>
> "(a) Conflicting security interests rank according to priority in time of filing or perfection. Priority dates from the time a filing is first made covering the collateral or the time the security interest is first perfected, whichever is earlier, provided that there is no period thereafter when there is neither filing nor perfection.
>
> "(b) So long as conflicting security interests are unperfected, the first to attach has priority."

Cal.Com.Code § 9312(5).

By applying § 9312(5)(a) according to its literal language, the district court concluded that Bank of the West's security interest prevailed over that of CCFS. When BCI transferred the beverage business to Allied/BIBCO, Bank of the West's security interest attached under the after-acquired property clause in its security agreement. See Cal.Com.Code §§ 9203(1), 9204(1). When Bank of the West's security interest attached, it automatically became perfected pursuant to the earlier filed financing statement naming Allied as its debtor. See Cal.Com.Code § 9303(1). Bank of the West's financing statement was filed on April 7, 1982. CCFS's financing statement was filed January 5, 1984, and its security interest became perfected on January 10, 1984 when BCI executed the factoring and related security agreements. Section 9312(5) sets forth a "first to file or first to perfect" rule of priority. Because Bank of the West's financing statement was filed first, the district court concluded that the Bank's security interest prevailed over that of CCFS. Bank of the West, 655 F.Supp. at 817.

The situation we have described above has until this case been regarded by the commentators as only a hypothetical scenario. It is a scenario offered by the commentators, however, to illustrate a failure of the commercial code to resolve a priority dispute properly. See, e.g., B. Clark, The Law of Secured Transactions Under the Uniform Commercial Code ¶ 3.8[4] (1980); Harris, The Interaction of Articles 6 and 9 of the Uniform Commercial Code: A Study in Conveyancing, Priorities, and Code Interpretation, 39 Vand. L.Rev. 179, 222–25, 225 n. 182 (1986); Oldfather, Floor Plan Financing Under Article 9 of the Uniform Commercial Code, 14 U.Kan.L.Rev. 571, 582–84 (1966); Skilton, Security Interests in After–Acquired Property Under the Uniform Commercial Code, 1974 Wis.L.Rev. 925, 948. The difficulty noted by these commentators is this: Before the transfer from BCI to Allied, CCFS (the transferor's creditor) had a perfected security interest in the collateral. After the transfer, CCFS's perfected security interest suddenly is subordinated to the perfected security interest of Bank of the West (the transferee's creditor). CCFS, which had taken all steps required of it by the commercial code to announce its interest in the collateral *to potential creditors of the transferor* (BCI), now finds its security interest subordinated to that of the *transferee's* (Allied's) *creditor,* (Bank of the West), whose security interest came into play only because BCI made an unauthorized disposition of the collateral to which the Bank's security interest attached solely by operation of an after-acquired collateral clause. See B. Clark, supra, ¶ 3.8[4], at 3–53; Harris, supra, 39 Vand.L.Rev. at 222–25.

We agree with the commentators that applying § 9312(5) to resolve this priority dispute produces an unsatisfactory result. The principal reason that § 9312(5) fails to produce a proper result is that it does not appear the drafters contemplated what Professor Clark calls the "dual debtor dilemma." See B. Clark, supra, ¶ 3.8[4]. Certainly the official comments to the Uniform Commercial Code, which offer several illustrations of the operation of § 9312(5), do not address the situation in which the competing security interests are between creditors of *different* debtors. See Cal.Com.Code § 9312 Uniform Commercial Code Comments 4–8. In Mr. Coogan's seminal article, The New UCC Article 9, 86 Harv.L.Rev. 477 (1973), no mention of the dual debtor scenario is made in the thoughtful portion of the article addressing the drafters' reasons for adopting § 9312(5). See id. at 507–11. Because § 9312(5) does not contemplate the dual debtor scenario, we must resolve this priority dispute by returning to first principles.

As a general rule of construction, the commercial code "shall be liberally construed and applied to promote its underlying purposes and policies." Cal.Com.Code § 1102(1). The commercial code is intended to be flexible. "It is intended to make it possible for the law embodied in this Act to be developed by the courts in the light of unforeseen and new circumstances and practices. However, the proper construction of the Act requires that its interpretation and application be limited to its reason." Id. Uniform Commercial Code Comment 1. There are two reasons behind the rule of § 9312(5)(a). First, the "first to file or first to perfect" rule serves to modify the common law notion of "first in time, first in right." Harris, supra, 39 Vand.L.Rev. at 222. Section 9312(5) places a premium on prompt filing of financing statements as a means of protecting *future* creditors of the debtor. The financing statement alerts potential creditors that collateral against which they are contemplating making a loan already is encumbered. Thus, § 9312(5)(a) penalizes a creditor who has a security interest but who does not promptly file a financing statement by awarding priority to a later creditor who acquires a security interest in the same collateral and who more promptly files a financing statement. The "first to file or first to perfect" rule of § 9312(5)(a) thus addresses the problem of secret security interests that so concerned pre-Code courts. See id. But in the present case, the notice giving function of § 9312(5)(a) does not apply. Bank of the West is a creditor of another debtor entity, and the Bank's interest in the collateral arises solely out of an after-acquired property clause. Bank of the West cannot claim that it has relied to its detriment on the absence of a filed financing statement by CCFS.[7]

A second purpose behind § 9312(5)(a) is an implied commitment to a secured creditor who has filed a financing statement that, absent special

7. Indeed, there is evidence that as part of the restructuring agreement, the Bank agreed to subordinate its security interest to any institutional lender who financed the beverage business's accounts. CCFS gave BCI a subordination agreement to send the Bank when CCFS learned of the transfer. For reasons not clear in the record, the Bank did not execute the subordination agreement. The fact remains, however, that the Bank cannot argue that it was misled by the absence of a financing statement filed by CCFS.

considerations such as a purchase money security interest, see, e.g., Cal.Com. Code § 9312(3), (4), no subsequent creditor will be able to defeat the complying creditor's security interest. This notion finds support in comment 5 to § 9402(7), which reads in pertinent part: "The justification for this rule lies in the necessity of protecting the filing system—that is, of allowing the secured party who has first filed to make subsequent advances without each time having, as a precondition of protection, to check for filings later than his." Cal.Com.Code § 9312 Uniform Commercial Code Comment 5; see also Harris, supra, 39 Vand.L.Rev. at 223–24 (discussing same). This has been described as the "claim staking" function of the financing statement. See Knippenberg, supra, 52 Mo.L.Rev. at 61 & n. 22. What this means is that by filing a proper financing statement in the proper place, a secured creditor has staked a claim to its collateral and knows that, absent special considerations, its claim will prevail against *subsequently arising* interests in the same property. By complying with the Code, the creditor is relieved of much of the responsibility of monitoring its debtor's collateral—the Code has allocated the burden of discovering prior filed financing statements to later lenders. Cf.Cal.Com.Code § 9402 Uniform Commercial Code Comment 8 ("[A]ny person searching the condition of ownership of a debtor must make inquiry as to the debtor's source of title, and must search in the name of a former owner if the circumstances seem to require it.").

Applying § 9312(5)(a) to the present case serves neither of the rationales behind the "first to file or first to perfect" rule. The notice giving function is irrelevant because the creditor of a different debtor whose sole interest in disputed collateral arises from an after-acquired property clause has no incentive to check for financing statements against the property of another debtor. Certainly the burden is on a transferee's creditor to search the title to property, but this duty arises only when the transferee's creditor first appears on the scene after the transfer. Likewise, it makes no sense to use § 9312(5)(a) to defeat CCFS's perfected security interest when CCFS has taken all steps required of it by the Code to proclaim its interest in the collateral. CCFS is entitled to rely on the Code's promise that a creditor who fully complies usually may expect its security interest to be given priority in a dispute with another secured creditor. To apply § 9312(5)(a) to this case would produce an undesirable result that does not follow from the principles that the section is meant to promote.[8]

8. It is possible to argue, of course, that our analysis does violence to the interest of the transferee's creditor, whose security interest has been perfected by filing just the same as the transferor's creditor. But it is important to remember that the situation we consider is one in which the transferee's creditor's security interest attaches to the transferred collateral solely by operation of an after-acquired property clause. Although the Uniform Commercial Code expressly validates after-acquired property clauses, see Cal.Com.Code § 9204(1), these "floating liens" still have not been wholeheartedly accepted by the drafters.

"Subsection 1 makes clear that a security interest arising by virtue of an after-acquired property clause has equal status with a security interest in collateral in which the debtor has rights at the time value is given under the security agreement. That is to say: security interest in after-acquired property is not merely an 'equitable' interest; no further action by the secured party ... is required. This does *not* mean however *that the interest is proof against subordination or defeat* ...."

Cal.Com.Code § 9204(1) Uniform Commercial Code Comment 1 (emphasis added). To the extent our opinion results in holders of after-acquired property clauses not being able to prevail against the perfected security interest of a transferor's secured creditor, this is consistent with the drafters intention

We think the correct result is reached in this case by applying the common sense notion that a creditor cannot convey to another more than it owns. Put another way, the transferee, Allied, cannot acquire any greater rights in the beverage business's assets than its transferor, BCI, had in them. Cf.Cal.Com.Code § 2403(1) ("A purchaser of goods acquires all title which his transferor had or had power to transfer except that a purchaser of a limited interest acquires rights only to the extent of the interest purchased."); see also B. Clark, supra, ¶ 3.8[4] (suggesting principles of § 2403(1) apply to this situation); Harris, supra, 39 Vand.L.Rev. at 223, 225 n. 182 (same). Our analysis also finds direct support in the California Commercial Code. Section 9312(1) provides, "The rules of priority stated in other sections of this chapter ... shall govern where applicable." And § 9306(2) provides that a security interest follows collateral into the hands of a transferee when there is an unauthorized disposition by the transferor. See P. Coogan, W. Hogan, D. Vagts & J. McDonnel, Secured Transactions under the Uniform Commercial Code § 7.11A[2][p]. The drafters tell us that "[i]n most cases when a debtor makes an unauthorized disposition of the collateral, the security interest, under ... this Article, continues in the original collateral in the hands of the purchaser or other transferee. That is to say, ... the transferee *takes subject to the security interest* .... Subsection [9306(2)] codifies this rule." Cal.Com.Code § 9306(2) Uniform Commercial Code Comment 3. If the transferee (Allied) takes the transferred collateral subject to the transferor's creditor's (CCFS's) security interest, certainly the transferee's creditor (Bank of the West) can have no greater rights in the collateral than does its transferor (Allied). Because § 9402(7) preserves CCFS's perfected security interest in the collateral actually transferred as well as in the property acquired in the four months after the transfer, CCFS's security interest continues to be superior to Bank of the West's interest during this period, even though Bank of the West's interest also is perfected. This result is consistent with the principles of the filing system that we have previously discussed. If the notice giving function does not apply because Bank of the West has no reason to check for filings against BCI, the claim-staking function that protects CCFS should be enforced. CCFS has done all that the Code asks of it to protect its interest. Absent some countervailing consideration, CCFS should be entitled to rely on its perfected security interest.

* * *

CONCLUSION

BCI's transfer of the assets subject to CCFS's security interest was an unauthorized disposition of the collateral. Consequently, applying § 9306(2), CCFS's security interest followed the transferred assets into the hands of Allied. Because the transfer was in reality a change in corporate structure, CCFS's security interest remained perfected in all assets actually transferred as well as in those acquired by Allied in the four months after the transfer. See Cal.Com.Code § 9402(7) (second sentence). Because Allied/BIBCO's in-

in validating after-acquired property clauses but not granting them an assurance of absolute priority in all cases.

For an excellent analysis of the monitoring burdens placed on creditors as they relate to the second sentence of § 9402(7) and after-acquired property clauses, see Knippenberg, supra, 52 Mo.L.Rev. at 92–97.

terest in the assets transferred and those acquired in the four months thereafter is subject to CCFS's security interest, see Cal.Com.Code § 9306(2) Uniform Commercial Code Comment 3, Bank of the West can have no greater rights in the collateral than its debtor. Cf.Cal.Com.Code § 2403(1). Therefore, CCFS's perfected security interest is superior to that of Bank of the West. Because Bank of the West's security interest is subordinate to that of CCFS, CCFS could not have converted Bank of the West's property when it factored the post-transfer account. As a result, we reverse the decision of the district court and remand the case for entry of judgment in favor of CCFS.

Reversed and remanded.

Note: PEB Commentaries

The Permanent Editorial Board of the Uniform Commercial Code sometimes issues commentaries on unforeseen or similar issues. See P.E.B. Commentary No. 3 dealing with 9–402(7). For a trenchant analysis of the foregoing case and related issues, see Professor Kripke's letter to the Permanent Editorial Board dated April 6, 1989 and published in P.E.B. Study Group Document No. 3–5, October 11, 1990.

Problem 5–14

None of the following cases involve the multiple chain issue. Study them to see why.

1. Consumer grants a security interest on his TV set to seller who perfects by filing. Thief steals the TV and sells it to Buyer; Buyer grants a security interest to Bank One. Does 9–312(4) grant Bank priority? (We think the answer is no, but we do not think it arises out of the multiple chain issue.)

2. Appliance Dealer grants a security interest to Bank One in its inventory. Buyer purchases a TV set from Dealer and grants a security interest to Bank Two. (Bank Two prevails over Bank One but not because of 9–312. Again this is not a multiple chain case.)

3. Consumer buys a car and grants a properly perfected security interest to GMAC. Claiming to have clear title, consumer improperly sells the car to dealer. Dealer sells it to buyer two who gives a perfected purchased money security interest to Bank Two. (Bank Two loses to GMAC but not because of 9–312(5). Note the first sentence in 9–312(1) "the rules of priority stated in other sections of this part and the following sections will govern when applicable." That reference sends us to 9–307(1) for the key to this case.)

SECTION 6. PRIORITY WITH RESPECT TO FIXTURES, UCC 9–313

We might have dealt with the fixture issues in Chapter Seven on the ground that fixtures questions are essentially scope questions. Fixtures, of course, are items that started out their existence as personal property but that were then attached to personal property in such a way that they acquired some of the attributes of real estate while retaining some of those of personal property. They did not go through a complete metamorphosis in the way normal building materials might. Presumably normal building materials incorporated in the structure are neither personal property nor fixtures. For almost all purposes they have become real estate, will pass with a deed, be subject to a claim of a traditional mortgagee, and will for almost all purposes be treated like the dirt upon which they sit.

Fixtures, on the other hand, are things such as air conditioners, furnaces and the like. These are not so incorporated in the real estate that they are unquestionably a part of it; they still have a separate existence and, in most cases, could be detached and used elsewhere. Of course, the courts and the legislatures have long recognized the potential conflict between the claim of the real estate secured creditor (or purchaser) with regard to the fixture and the claim of a personal property secured lender to the fixture. Section 9–313 was incorporated in the Code to determine the priorities between personal property claimants on the one hand and real estate claimants on the other. Rarely does one see a competition between two real estate claimants to a fixture or between two personal property claimants to a fixture. The first of such conflict is probably not governed by UCC 9–313, but by the law of real estate, or in the case of two personal property claimants, by UCC 9–312.

For now we focus on UCC 9–313. Initially the student should read the section with care. It is quite complex, but the student should see parallels to section 9–312. Having studied the distinction between a "fixture filing" and a filing that is not a fixture filing but nevertheless perfects a security interest in a fixture, the student should now understand that UCC 9–313(4) requires in effect a real estate filing (a fixture filing) for one to enjoy the priority given under subsections (4)(a) and (b), but requires only a personal property filing to give the fixture claimant the priority specified in subsections (4)(c) and (d). The student should also see how 9–313 has dealt with the issue of fixtures owned by a lessee (subsection (5)) and with a construction mortgage (subsection (6)).

IN RE FINK

United States Bankruptcy Court, Western District of New York, 1980.
4 B.R. 741.

EDWARD D. HAYES, BANKRUPTCY JUDGE.

This is an action by the Trustee to avoid a security interest in a mobile house claimed by defendant, Endicott Trust Company of New York hereinafter referred to as "Endicott" and to preserve that lien pursuant to Bankruptcy Rule 611 as to defendant Wemco Corp. hereinafter referred to as "Wemco."

The facts appear to be as follows. The bankrupt, Pauline Fink, purchased a mobile home from Palmer Mobile Homes, Inc. on or about August 20, 1977. She entered into a retail installment contract. The security interest was transferred by assignment to Endicott on or about August 20, 1977. Endicott filed a financing statement which described the collateral as 24 × 52 1977 Bendix. Thereafter, the mobile home was delivered to Route 415 in the Town of Campbell which the bankrupt was leasing from Wemco. On August 24, 1977, the bankrupt contracted to purchase the real property on which the mobile home was placed from Wemco for $24,000. The realty consisted of about four acres and the only structure thereon was a store. The realty was transferred on December 1, 1977 by Wemco to the bankrupt and the bankrupt gave back to Wemco a purchase money mortgage for the full purchase price of $24,000.

The mobile home or modular home, which ever it may be, was delivered by Palmer Mobile Homes, Inc. and was placed on a foundation of concrete footers, concrete blocks and steel and wooden beams running the width and length of the building.

The details of construction follow. A foundation was evacuated. A septic tank was installed. Concrete footers were installed around the edge of the crawl space and at least one pillar of concrete blocks was erected in the center of the crawl space. Concrete blocks were installed and cemented to the footers. After this was done, the house was delivered to the lot in two sections (12′ × 52′) on steel cradles. The sections with cradles were then placed on the cement blocks. The house sections were bolted together. A roof cap was put on over the place in the roof where the sections were joined together and it was cemented and nailed down. Siding was put on the two ends of the house and nailed over the spot where the joinder of the section occurred to give the appearance of a continuous wall. The septic system was hooked up. Water lines were connected. An electrical line was connected to the store's system and the store's electrical system and capacity were increased. At this point, the top course of cinder blocks were placed in but not cemented to the course immediately below. No tie downs were used in the construction. The house even has an open fireplace, although this hangs on the side of the house. From the pictures in evidence, the house appears to be a normal ranch home without front or back steps.

Additional facts which were developed at the trial follow. Palmer, who installed the mobile home on the foundation, testified that he could remove and transport the home for about $500 by removing the roof cap and the siding and shingles from the end, disconnect water lines, electric septic tank and unbolt the sections of the house and transport it on the cradle of steel beams which support each section.

The officer of Wemco said that the house was constructed in the same fashion as any construction and that the attachment to realty was the same as in any stick built house.

Additionally, when Wemco transferred the property to the bankrupt, Fink, in December, 1977, the attorney for Wemco had the abstract redated. There was nothing on the abstract that gave Wemco any notice of an interest by Endicott in the house. Wemco, when it transferred the property to Mrs. Fink, took back a purchase money mortgage for $24,000.

The facts stated above raise the issue as to whether or not the home in question is a chattel that requires perfection by filing pursuant to New York State UCC 9–302(1)(d) or a fixture attached to real property that requires filing in accordance with New York State UCC 9–313(1)(a). Section 9–302(1)(d) of the Uniform Commercial Code holds that a financing statement must be filed to perfect a security interest in a motor vehicle. This section has been held to govern mobile homes * * *. UCC 9–313 requires a special filing where the item is a fixture. The filing must be in the office where a mortgage on real estate is filed and it must conform to the requirements of UCC 9–402(5) which requires that a financing statement filed as a fixture must show that it covers this type of collateral, must recite that it is to be indexed in the real estate records and the financing statement must contain a description of the real estate sufficient for its identification and it must show the name of the record owner.

If the home in question is considered to have ceased to be personalty and become a fixture by annexation to the real property, the filing made by Endicott was improper. The case turns upon whether the home is personalty or a fixture.

UCC § 9–313 states in part that "(1)(a) 'goods' are fixtures when they become so related to particular real estate that an interest in them arises under real estate law." The official comments which accompany this section say in part, "in cases where mobile homes or prefabricated steel buildings are erected by a person having an ownership interest in the land, the question into which category the buildings fall is one determined by local law." The definition of fixture is not an exact one. A recent law review article on the subject of fixtures under the UCC defines the term as follows:

> "A fixture is a former chattel which, because of its annexation to and association with realty, has become part and parcel thereof but which has not lost its separate physical identity. A fixture is neither personalty nor realty within a strict definition of those terms. Rather, it partakes of the characteristics of each, since prior to annexation it is movable and not associated with realty, but after annexation it loses its character as personalty and is deemed realty. Various definitions of fixture have been utilized, all of which emphasize the former chattel aspect and the annexation to realty." [1]

23 N.Y.Jur. Fixtures § 2 (1962) says as follows:

> "As a general rule, the true criterion of a fixture is based on the united application of three requisites: (1) actual annexation to the real property or something appurtenant thereto; (2) application to the use or purpose to which that part of the realty with which it is connected is appropriated; and (3) the intention of the party making the annexation to make a permanent accession to the freehold * * *".

In re Lido Beach Sewage Collection Dist., 40 Misc.2d 384, (County Ct. 1963), said at page 385:

> "Ordinarily for an article to become a fixture the following requisites must be met: Firstly, there must be annexation to the realty. Secondly, there must be adaptability of the article affixed to the use of the freehold. Thirdly, the intention of the party creating the annexation is to make the article a permanent accession to the freehold."

The two cases which have dealt with mobile homes in the context of UCC 9–313 are In re Foskett, 7 UCC Rep.Serv. 267 (W.D.Wisc.1970) and George v. Commercial Credit Corp., 440 F.2d 551 (7th Cir. 1971). They seem to follow the New York State tests set forth above. A recent 1979 Vermont Supreme Court case, Hartford Nat'l Bank & Trust Co. v. Godin, 398 Atl.2d 286, 26 UCC Rep.Serv. 221 (Vt.Sup.Ct.1979), also held a mobile home a fixture based on the same three tests set forth above.

1. Trade Fixture-Secured Transactions Under New York's Uniform Commercial Code, 44 Alb.L.Rev. 165, (1979).

Applying these principles to the case at bar, we find that the bankrupt contracted to purchase the mobile home at about the same time she entered into a contract to purchase the realty. She had a crawl space dug. She had footings installed and she had cinder block cemented to the footings to hold the home. The bankrupt installed a septic tank system, ran water and electric into the home. The bankrupt lived in the home.

Looking at the house, in the pictures that were taken of the house, it looks at least to the uninitiated eye like any other ranch house you might see erected in the country. There would be nothing to warn anyone that this was in fact a trailer or a motor vehicle. If it was a trailer, it came certainly in two parts and had to be separated into two parts to be moved along the road. Should someone wish to move the house, they would have to dismantle it, separate it into two parts, remove part of the roofing and remove five to six feet of the center strips of shingles at either end of the home. The house in the manner in which it was annexed to real property certainly meets the test set forth in the cases cited above. Therefore, this court finds that Endicott is an unsecured creditor and that their filing should have been under UCC § 9–313 rather than under UCC § 9–302(1)(d).

With regard to Wemco's interest, it is paramount to the trustee because Wemco had a filed mortgage agreement which is a lien upon the real property.

This Memorandum and Decision shall constitute Findings of Fact and Conclusions of Law in accordance with Rule 752 of the Rules of Bankruptcy Procedure.

Notes

1. The 1972 revisions to Article 9 did not become effective in New York until July 2, 1978. Why does the court apply the 1972 version of 9–313 to this case?

2. Assume that the value of the mobile home and real estate was more than enough to satisfy the mortgagee's claim. If there were $10,000 of value left over, how would that be divided between the trustee and Endicott?

a. under the 1972 version?

b. under the 1962 version? (Assuming that Endicott filed the UCC–1 form in the proper place for a personal property perfection, where would that be?)

Problem 5–15

1. Assume that Bank had financed the purchase of a washer, dryer and stereo, and that each was installed in debtor's house in such a way that under state law it would have become a fixture. Bank filed a financing statement covering these items in the personal property records, but not in the real estate records in the county where the debtor lived. Does Bank or the mortgagee have a better right in these?

2. Assume bank had taken a security interest only in debtor's mobile home. Bank inserted its name on the certificate of title and also filed in the personal property records in the county where the debtor resided at the time the mobile home was purchased. Debtor ultimately placed the mobile home in another county and moved into it. Subsequently Debtor went into bankruptcy and trustee now claims the mobile home. Who has priority?

Problem 5–16

Larry buys a farm from Moe in January by advancing a down payment of $80,000 and agreeing to pay off the remainder of $250,000 over 5 years. In February, Larry borrows $54,000 from Curly to pay for the installation of an irrigation well and pump. Curly receives a security interest in "all farming and irrigation equipment." Assume the security interest attaches to the pump before it is installed. In July, Larry is having trouble making his payments to Moe. They reach an agreement whereby Larry pays half of the July payment and the loan is rescheduled over 10 years. In November, Larry gives up farming and delivers a quitclaim deed to Moe in exchange for release from the debt.

1. Can Moe forbid Curly from removing the pump because he filed only in the personal property records in the county clerk's office?

2. If the 1962 version of Article 9 applies and assuming that Curly has priority over Moe under UCC 9–313(2), would the rescheduling agreement constitute a subsequent advance for the purpose of UCC 9–313(4)(c)? Would the delivery of the quitclaim deed in exchange for forgiveness of the loan make Moe a subsequent purchaser under UCC 9–313(4)(a)?

SECTION 7. SECURITY INTERESTS ARISING BY LABOR, ACCESSION, OR COMMINGLING, UCC 9–310, 9–314, 9–315

The sections cited above are in one sense analogous to the fixture rules. In the fixture cases typically one takes a security interest in an asset which then becomes a fixture and so becomes subject to a mortgage and to other real estate interests. Of course, the same thing can happen when a motor is installed in an automobile subject to an existing security interest, when a mechanic repairs an automobile or equipment and asserts a mechanic's lien for his work, or when goods are commingled or processed with other goods and two parties have security interests in different parts of the goods. UCC 9–314 on accession is closely analogous to UCC 9–313 and, in fact, bears a striking resemblance to UCC 9–313 as it existed in its 1962 incarnation. Section 9–315 in effect grants a prorata security interest in commingled goods. Section 9–310 governs a very small slice of mechanic's lien law. Note that section 9–310 grants priority over a prior perfected security interest but only to goods "in the possession" of the mechanic and only if the relevant mechanic's lien law does not expressly provide otherwise. Beware, for the law in some states explicitly states that the mechanic's lien is subordinate to an existing perfected security interest. The rule does not apply to all statutory lienors who might exist, but only to those who provide "services or materials" in the ordinary course of business.

A question not answered by UCC 9–314 or 9–315, but one that may be critical to the ultimate decision is the question whether the original secured creditor's security interest attaches to the accession or the commingled goods. Assume, for example, that a creditor has a security interest in a truck. After the security interest is granted the debtor causes the truck to be modified for logging operations by the addition of a new third axle, a loader, and a "jake brake." Unless the original security agreement covered accessions, it would not be clear that the original creditor even claimed an interest in those parts. In most cases, presumably, a well drafted security agreement will cover accessions and in the case of commingling will cover the end product either explicitly or by reference to proceeds or products. In *In re Lyford,* 34 U.C.C.Rep.Serv. 754, 22 B.R. 222 (Bkrtcy.D.Me.1982), the court concluded that such additions to a truck were accessions and were covered by the original security agreement. The court goes through an analysis not unlike that a court might use in determining whether goods attached to realty had become fixtures. Implicit in the court's analysis is the assumption that if the goods were not accessions, they would not have been covered by the original security agreement. That judgment, of course, would depend upon the language of the particular agreement.

Note that it will not always be obvious whether UCC 9–314 or 9–315 applies or, indeed, whether either of them does. Nor will it always be clear how to apply the applicable rule of priority. Consider the case that follows.

FIRST NATIONAL BANK OF BRUSH v. BOSTRON

Court of Appeals of Colorado, 1977.
39 Colo.App. 107, 564 P.2d 964.

STERNBERG, JUDGE.

The issues presented by this appeal are whether, under the Uniform Commercial Code, a perfected security interest in feed survives after consumption of the feed by cattle in which the secured party has no interest, and if so, whether the secured party is entitled to any of the proceeds from the sale of these cattle. We answer these questions in the negative and therefore affirm the judgment of the trial court.

One Eldon Weiss owned a ranch on which he raised cattle and feed crops. As a separate and distinct part of this operation Weiss entered into a joint venture with the defendant, Reinhold Bostron, under which Bostron was to supply the money and Weiss the labor necessary to raise Holstein heifers. The heifers were purchased by Bostron and Weiss with money borrowed from the plaintiff, First National Bank of Brush, which retained a perfected purchase money security interest in the animals. The Bostron-Weiss joint venture cattle were segregated from other cattle on the Weiss ranch. Feed for all the cattle, however, was commingled and fed to the animals Weiss owned individually and to those owned by the Bostron-Weiss joint venture. Intervenor, Colorado High Plains Agricultural Credit Corporation, held a perfected security interest given by Weiss, individually, in, among other things, "all feed now owned or hereafter acquired, all crops now growing or to be grown, proceeds and products of collateral."

The cattle raised by the joint venture were eventually sold at a loss, and consequently, even after paying most of the proceeds from the sale to First National Bank of Brush, there was a deficiency owing that bank. None of the proceeds from the sale of the Bostron-Weiss cattle were paid to the intervenor.

Plaintiff bank sued Weiss and Bostron to recover the remaining balance of the loan, and Colorado High Plains intervened claiming an interest in any recovery which the bank might obtain against Bostron. Weiss was adjudicated a bankrupt and proceedings against him in this action were stayed. Since the intervenor's security interest attached only to the feed owned by Weiss, its right of recovery, if any, from Bostron must be premised on the benefit which Bostron individually received from the joint venture as a result of the Weiss feed being fed to the joint venture cattle.

The provisions of the Uniform Commercial Code—Secured Transactions, § 4–9–101, et seq., C.R.S.1973, govern this case. Section 4–9–315, C.R.S.1973, provides:

"(1) If a security interest in goods [1] was perfected and subsequently the goods or a part thereof have become part of a product or mass, the security interest continues in the product or mass if:

"(a) The goods are so manufactured, processed, assembled, or commingled that their identity is lost in the product or mass; or

"(b) A financing statement covering the original goods also covers the product into which the goods have been manufactured, processed or assembled."

In light of the wording of this section, we conclude that cattle are neither a "product" nor a "mass" as these terms are used in the statute. The reference in subsection (a) to "manufactured, processed, assembled, or commingled" precludes any other interpretation. The feed which the cattle ate did not undergo any of these transformations, that is, it was not manufactured, processed, assembled or commingled with the cattle. Cattle consume food as motor vehicles do gasoline. Once eaten the feed not only loses its identity, but in essence it ceases to exist and thus does not become part of the mass in the sense that the code uses the phrase. Section 4–9–315, C.R.S.1973 (Comment 3), makes this evident:

"This section applies not only to cases where flour, sugar and eggs are commingled into cake mix or cake, but also to cases where components are assembled into a machine."

Feed as consumed by cattle is distinguishable from this notion of accession which the code's drafters visualized.

Moreover, since the financing statement did not specifically cover the product "into which the goods have been manufactured, processed or assembled" the language of § 4–9–315(1)(b), C.R.S.1973, does not support intervenor's claim.

Relying on § 4–9–306, C.R.S.1973, intervenor next contends that the cattle are proceeds of the feed as that term is defined in that portion of the code. The pertinent part of that statute states:

"(1) 'Proceeds' include whatever is *received* when collateral or proceeds is sold, exchanged, collected, or otherwise disposed of * * *

"(2) Except where this article otherwise provides, a security interest continues in collateral notwithstanding sale, exchange, or other disposition thereof by the debtor unless his action was authorized by the secured party in the security agreement or otherwise, and also continues in any identifiable proceeds * * *" (emphasis supplied)

1. There is no question but that the reference to goods in this section applies to the feed in question here. Section 4–9–105(f), C.R.S.1973, provides:

"'Goods' includes all things which are movable at the time the security interest attaches * * * 'Goods' also include the unborn young of animals and growing crops." See also § 4–2–105, C.R.S.1973.

This contention also is unavailing for several reasons. First, the trial court found that the intervenor lost its interest in the proceeds because it authorized the disposition of its collateral, i.e., the feed, by Weiss to the Bostron-Weiss joint venture. See Farmers National Bank v. Ceres Land Co., 32 Colo.App. 290, 512 P.2d 1174 (1973). This finding is supported by evidence in the record and therefore is dispositive. However, we also conclude that even if the intervenor had not authorized the use of the feed subject to its security interest by the joint venture, nevertheless intervenor's interest still would not have survived its consumption by the cattle.

Weiss *received* nothing when he disposed of the collateral by feeding it to the joint venture cattle. As noted in our discussion of § 4-9-315, C.R.S.1973, the collateral was consumed, and there are no traceable proceeds to which the security interest may be said to have attached. To interpret § 4-9-306, C.R.S.1973, as intervenor urges would extend the security interest of one in the position of the intervenor to the parts of the butchered animal, into the supermarket, and ultimately into the hands of the consumers. We cannot attribute such legislative intent to the General Assembly when it adopted this section of the UCC.

Intervenor's final contention is that by § 4-9-307(1), C.R.S.1973, it had an interest in the cattle which ate the feed. That section of the code provides:

> "A buyer in ordinary course of business * * * *other than a person buying farm products from a person engaged in farming operations* takes free of a security interest created by his seller even though the security interest is perfected and even though the buyer knows of its existence." (emphasis supplied)

Assuming, without deciding, that the joint venture was a buyer in the ordinary course of business from Weiss, a cursory reading of this portion of the code would suggest, as intervenor asserts, that its security interest continues into the cattle. However, the joint venture did not sell the feed; rather, it sold the cattle to which it was fed. As previously noted, in our analysis of § 4-9-315, C.R.S.1973, the collateral in which the security interest was initially taken is, after having been fed to the cattle, non-existent, and thus buyers of the cattle cannot reasonably be equated with buyers of the feed in which there exists a security interest.

In summary then, we hold that a security interest in feed does not in and of itself extend to the cattle which eat that feed by application of § 4-9-315, C.R.S.1973, nor do cattle which eat the feed constitute proceeds of the collateral by application of § 4-9-306, C.R.S.1973. We hold further that under the facts here, § 4-9-307(1), C.R.S.1973 does not extend the security interest in the feed after its ingestion by the cattle.

Judgment affirmed.

COYTE and ENOCH, JJ., concur.

Note

Assume that the manure produced in the debtor's feeding operation has considerable value and is routinely sold to others as fertilizer. Would the creditor with the security interest in the feed, have an interest in the proceeds or other interest in the manure?

Problem 5–17

Consider the following problems under UCC 9–310, 9–314, 9–315 as appropriate.

1. Assume that secured creditor One had a perfected security interest in debtor's 100 head of Brangus cattle. Secured creditor Two had a perfected security interest in debtor's 100 head of Hereford cattle, including two Hereford bulls. Upon debtor's bankruptcy, the inventory disclosed 30 Brangus, 25 Hereford, including the 2 bulls and 80 calves. At trial the testimony was conflicting, but it seems likely that at least 10 of the calves were offspring of the Hereford bulls mating with the Brangus cows and one witness testified that the flop ear which is an identifying characteristic of Brahman line descendents, including Brangus cattle, carry forward to the 1/32nd degree. Another testified, "When you've got a half-Brahman-cow-to-a-one-quarter-Brahman-cow cross with an Angus cow and then you put a Hereford bull in there with them, you're going to breed the ear off." Of the remaining calves it seemed that some were the offspring of Brangus cows who had been artificially inseminated and some were offspring of the Hereford who had been inseminated by the Hereford bulls. Assume that both secured creditors had a perfected security interest that included not only specific livestock originally covered, but also products and proceeds; that the party doing the artificial insemination has not been paid and asserts a lien under local law. How will the calves, cows and bulls be divided?

2. Bank has a perfected security interest in all of computer manufacturer's inventory, accounts receivable, present and after acquired. Seller of microchips also has a perfected security interest in the items sold by it to manufacturer including products and proceeds. Assume that the microchips are assembled in the computer in such a way that they are clearly identifiable, but cannot be removed without destroying the computer. The debt owed the microchip seller is $500,000. The value of the existing computers is $600,000. The bank has an unpaid debt of $3,000,000. Microchip seller asserts a first priority under UCC 9–314. Who will prevail? (Assume that the computers were sold under a stipulation that a security interest would attach to the proceeds in the same way as they would attach to the original items.)

3. Lessor obtained a security interest in a drilling rig leased to debtors Fred and Barbara Yost. Whayne Supply Company performed $2500 of repairs on the rig's Caterpillar engine, and properly perfected its material and service lien under Kentucky law. Several months after the repairs, the drilling rig was heavily damaged by fire and $75,000 of insurance proceeds were paid to and are now held by the lessor. Kentucky provides that one repairing machinery shall have a claim, but that the "lien shall not take precedence over a mortgage or bona fide sale and delivery." If you represented the lessor, how would you argue in this case? What responses might be made on behalf of Whayne?

SECTION 8. PRIORITY IN REPOSSESSED GOODS: A REPRISE

When Bank creates a security interest in Dealer's inventory, there is a substantial risk that it will be cut off by a sale to a buyer in the ordinary course of business. UCC 9–307(1). Dealer, however, may perfect a security interest in the goods sold to secure Buyer's obligation to Dealer. If Dealer receives chattel paper from Buyer, i.e., "non-cash" proceeds, UCC 9–306(1),

Bank will undoubtedly claim a perfected security interest in the chattel paper to secure Dealer's obligation to Bank. UCC 9–306(3). But remember, the chattel paper evidences Buyer's obligation to Dealer and a security interest to secure that obligation.

Suppose Buyer defaults and Dealer repossesses the goods. If Bank has been paid, there is no problem: Dealer will simply enforce the security interest in the goods to satisfy Buyer's obligation. But suppose Bank has not been paid. What are Bank's rights upon repossession? The answer to this and other questions is contained in UCC 9–306(5). Read it carefully and work the following problems. Review also Problem 5–12.

Problem 5–18

In the situation described above, what are Bank's claims, if any, to the repossessed collateral? Would they have priority over Dealer's interest?

Problem 5–19

Suppose that after Dealer sold the goods to B, a buyer in the ordinary course of business, but before they were repossessed, Finance Company perfected a security interest in the goods. Upon repossession, Bank, Dealer and Finance Company claim a perfected security interest in the goods. Is that claim correct? If so, which party has priority?

Problem 5–20

Suppose that Dealer, without Bank's consent, assigned the security interest and negotiated the note to Bank # 2 in the ordinary course of its business. Bank #2 knew of Bank's security interest. Upon Buyer's default, Bank # 2 repossessed the goods from Buyer. Which party has a perfected security interest with priority in the chattel paper? Which party has a perfected security interest with priority in the goods?

Problem 5–21

The facts are the same as in Problem 5–16 except that Dealer grants Bank # 2 a written security interest in the chattel paper and retains possession and Bank # 2 perfects the security interest by filing. Upon Buyer's default, Dealer repossessed the goods from Buyer. Which party has a perfected security interest with priority in the chattel paper? Which party has a perfected security interest with priority in the goods?

Bank will argue that under UCC 9–306(5), Bank # 2 must perfect a security interest in the repossessed goods to have priority. Do you agree?

CHAPTER SIX
DEFAULT AND FORECLOSURE

SECTION 1. INTRODUCTION

In this chapter we will explore default and its consequences. We will survey the problems involved in determining the nature and extent of any default and the various alternatives that may be open to the secured creditor when default does occur. The most important of these alternatives—so-called "foreclosure by sale"—is subjected to intensive analysis.

In the first several sections of this chapter, we will treat problems that arise in determining whether default has occurred. We will then survey the various remedies of the secured creditor on default. Most of these remedies are set forth in Part Five of Article 9 and include:

(1) negotiation and readjustment,

(2) creditor's right to judgment and execution,

(3) creditor's remedies under applicable real estate law,

(4) creditor's right to collect on intangibles and to repossess tangibles,

(5) strict foreclosure with respect to tangibles,

(6) foreclosure by sale with respect to tangibles, and right to any deficiency,

(7) suit on any negotiable paper.

See generally, White & Summers, Chapter 26.

SECTION 2. DEFAULT AND ACCELERATION

Default triggers the secured creditor's rights under Part 5 of Article 9. Despite that fact, one looks in vain for a definition of default in Article 9; instead the Article leaves this definition to the parties and to any bits of common law that may be available. However, UCC 1–208 deals with acceleration upon default and legislation in various states does restrict the creditor's power to declare default and to cause acceleration of indebtedness where the debtor is a consumer. When the debtor is not a consumer, the law generally permits the parties to establish the terms for acceleration and to define default by their agreement.

Invariably, security agreements contain acceleration clauses and lengthy, carefully drafted clauses to define default. Non-payment of the indebtedness is the first step in defining default in such clauses. A typical default clause will also take into account the possibility that the debtor will declare bankruptcy, will make an assignment for the benefit of creditors, will move the collateral or permit it to be damaged or destroyed. To sharpen your consideration of the problems presented to the creditor in defining default and acceleration, consider the following problems and consider particularly the clause (which we believe to be well drafted) included in the problem.

Problem 6–1

Polypol, Inc. is manufacturer of a variety of adult and children's toys. It manufactures a variety of dolls. Polypol purchases all of its raw materials on credit from Heathcliff, Inc., a wholesaler of metal, plastic, and wood products. Typically, Polypol will owe Heathcliff between $75,000 and $150,000 at any one time for materials delivered in the previous sixty days. Polypol has agreed to make payments every other month on the 10th for all purchases made up to thirty days preceding. To secure all indebtedness, Polypol has signed a security agreement with Heathcliff; the security agreement contains the following default and acceleration clause:

> Section 7. Events of Default; Acceleration. Any or all liabilities shall, at the option of Creditor and notwithstanding any time or credit allowed by any instrument evidencing any Liability, become immediately due and payable without notice or demand upon the occurrence of any of the following events of default: (a) default in the payment, when due and payable, of any amount due and payable hereunder or default in the payment or performances of any of the Liabilities; (b) default in the performance of any obligation or covenant contained or referred to herein; (c) any warranty, representation or statement made or furnished to Creditor by or on behalf of Debtor proves to have been false in any material respect when made or furnished; (d) failure of Debtor, after request by Creditor, to furnish financial information or to permit the inspection of its books and records; (e) any event which results in the acceleration of the maturity of the indebtedness of Debtor to others under any indenture, agreement or undertaking; (f) loss, theft, damage, destruction, sale or encumbrance to or of any of the Inventory, or the making of any levy, seizure or attachment thereof or thereon, or the entry of any judgment against Debtor; (g) death, dissolution, termination of existence, insolvency, business failure, appointment of a receiver of any part of the property of, assignment for the benefit of creditors by, or the commencement of any proceeding under any bankruptcy or insolvency laws by or against, Debtor or any guarantor or surety for any of the Liabilities of which, in the good faith opinion of Creditor, impairs Creditor's security or increases its risk.

How would you answer each of the following questions if you were counsel for Heathcliff? In answering the questions, one should consider not only the default clause and security agreement but also UCC 1–208 and 9–506 set forth below and the case that follows.

1. If Polypol were simply an assumed name of Hareton Earnshaw, sole proprietor doing business as Polypol, and Earnshaw died, would that be a default? (Some cases hold that the death of the debtor is not a default if no payments are due at the time of death and the security agreement is silent.)

2. The president of Heathcliff calls in a panic. He tells you that two large unsecured creditors of Polypol have levied on certain of Polypol's goods and will probably dispose of those goods within the next two or three days. He tells you that Polypol has not failed to make any payments but that Polypol will surely

default when its next payment comes due in 60 days if the goods allegedly seized by the other creditors are not available for its operation. He asks two questions:

(a) Is the levy by the other creditors a default?

(b) If it is not a default, are there any problems in the way of getting some use out of the goods so seized by levying creditors (assuming we have a prior security interest in the goods) between now and the time when Polypol defaults 60 days from now?

3. Earnshaw, the president of Polypol, and Linton, the president of Heathcliff, have a violent oral dispute about the quality of certain goods delivered by Heathcliff to Polypol. Linton calls to tell you of the fight and states that he wishes to commence legal proceedings for the collection of the entire indebtedness ($148,000) at once. He tells you that Polypol is not now in default (the next payment is due in 30 days) but that Earnshaw drove Linton off his place under threat of the use of force and will surely refuse to make any more payments. If you assume that the goods delivered by Heathcliff to Polypol were not defective, is Polypol now in default?

UCC § 1-208. Option to Accelerate at Will

A term providing that one party or his successor in interest may accelerate payment or performance or require collateral or additional collateral "at will" or "when he deems himself insecure" or in words of similar import shall be construed to mean that he shall have power to do so only if he in good faith believes that the prospect of payment or performance is impaired. The burden of establishing lack of good faith is on the party against whom the power has been exercised.

UCC § 9-506. Debtor's Right to Redeem Collateral

At any time before the secured party has disposed of collateral or entered into a contract for its disposition under Section 9-504 or before the obligation has been discharged under Section 9-505(2) the debtor or any other secured party may unless otherwise agreed in writing after default redeem the collateral by tendering fulfillment of all obligations secured by the collateral as well as the expenses reasonably incurred by the secured party in retaking, holding, and preparing the collateral for disposition, in arranging for the sale, and to the extent provided in the agreement and not prohibited by law, his reasonable attorney's fees and legal expenses.

KARNER v. WILLIS

Supreme Court of Kansas, 1985.
238 Kan. 246, 710 P.2d 21.

PRAGER, J.

This is a dispute between two judgment creditors and a garnishee bank over funds held by the bank in the defendant Lloyd's bank account. In answer to the garnishment, the garnishee bank responded that it had no funds of the defendant because it had exercised its right of setoff against the defendant's account. The plaintiff creditors contended that the setoff was wrongful. The district court held in favor of the bank. The plaintiffs then appealed, and the court of appeals affirmed in a published opinion in Karner

v. Willis, 10 Kan.App.2d 432, 700 P.2d 582 (1985). The supreme court granted the plaintiffs' petition for review.

The facts in the case were undisputed and essentially were as follows: On March 15, 1983, the plaintiffs, Herbert and Ruth Karner, obtained a judgment against the defendants, Willis and Lloyd, in the sum of $58,352.40 in the State of Oklahoma. Judgment was filed in the district court of Ellsworth County. On April 4, 1983, a duly authenticated copy of the Oklahoma judgment was filed in the district court of Ellsworth County. On August 3, 1983, an order of garnishment was issued by the district court of Ellsworth County directed to the Citizens State Bank of Ellsworth and the Kanopolis State Bank. Dale E. Hoosier, vice-president of Kanopolis State Bank, who received the garnishment, called the Ellsworth County sheriff's department and notified them that he had been served with a garnishment directed to the Citizens State Bank. The dispatcher of the sheriff's department notified the deputy of the mistake, and he immediately returned to the Kanopolis State Bank and exchanged the Citizens State Bank garnishment for the garnishment directed to the Kanopolis State Bank.

During the interim period, Dale E. Hoosier, acting on behalf of the Kanopolis State Bank, exercised a setoff against the account of the defendant debtor, Lloyd. In the court of appeals opinion, the Kansas statutes which control the right of a creditor bank to accelerate the maturity of a debt and to exercise a right of setoff against the debtor's account are discussed. Simply stated, K.S.A. 84–1–208 states that a contractual term providing that a party may accelerate payments or performance "when he deems himself insecure" or in words of similar import shall be construed to mean that he shall have the power to do so only if he *in good faith* believes that the prospect of payment of performance is impaired.

In the present case, the defendant debtor was indebted to the bank on a note which contained a provision which permitted the bank to accelerate the maturity of the debt if it deemed itself insecure. The trial court, in effect, found that the garnishee bank had acted in good faith in accelerating the debt and in setting off the note against the debtor's bank account.

The court of appeals viewed the basic issue on appeal to be whether there was substantial competent evidence in the record to support the findings of the trial court that, at the time the bank executed the setoff, it in good faith believed that the prospect of payment of the note was impaired. The court of appeals affirmed on the basis that "good faith" was a fact issue which the trial court resolved in the bank's favor, and found there was substantial competent evidence to support the trial court's findings.

When the trial court has made findings of fact and conclusions of law, the scope of appellate review is for this court to determine whether the trial court's findings are supported by substantial competent evidence. Woods v. Midwest Conveyor Co., 236 Kan. 734, Syl. ¶ 2, 697 P.2d 52 (1985). The appellate court will not weigh the evidence or pass upon the credibility of the witnesses. The reviewing court must review the evidence in the light most favorable to the party prevailing below. Marcotte Realty & Auction, Inc. v. Schumacher, 229 Kan. 252, 254, 624 P.2d 420 (1981).

At the hearing of this case, the only witness who testified was Dale E. Hoosier, the vice-president of the garnishee, Kanopolis State Bank. Hoosier testified that the day before the garnishment was served, the bookkeeper for the debtor depositor had been to the bank and requested signature cards to change the account name and signatures. Hoosier was aware of the Oklahoma judgment filed in Ellsworth County against the debtor earlier that year. At the time he made the setoff, he did not actually know whether the debtor was insolvent or not. The debtor had not been delinquent on any payments and was current on August 3, 1983, when the setoff was made. Mr. Hoosier testified that he deemed the bank was impaired in its security because the garnishment would have resulted in the sum of $40,000 being taken from the debtor's operating account as a farm implement dealer and, as a result, "he would have had no liquidity to operate." The bank records showed that on August 16, 1983, 13 days after the setoff, the bank loaned the debtor an additional $50,000, but in the interim period the debtor had paid $99,000 on the loan and pledged his used farm equipment as additional collateral.

In its opinion, the court of appeals recognized that there certainly was evidence presented that, viewed objectively, the bank was not insecure, but that the test of good faith dictated by K.S.A. 84–1–208 is subjective and requires only honesty in fact. Iola State Bank v. Bolan, 235 Kan. 175, 183, 679 P.2d 720 (1984); and K.S.A. 84–1–201(19). The court of appeals then applied the subjective test required by the statute and concluded that the trial court's finding of good faith was supported by substantial competent evidence. The majority of this court has concluded from the record that the court of appeals correctly determined the issue.

The judgment of the district court is affirmed. The judgment of the court of appeals is affirmed.

Herd, J., dissenting: I disagree with the majority holding that Kanopolis State Bank was acting in good faith when it deemed itself insecure on Ronald F. Lloyd's note and exercised its right of setoff against his checking and reserve accounts.

The evidence in this case consists of the testimony of Dale E. Hoosier, bank vice-president, the Lloyd note and the bank ledger.

Mr. Hoosier acknowledged that the bank officials knew an Oklahoma judgment in the amount of $58,352.40 had been properly filed of record in Ellsworth County against Mr. Lloyd. He testified the judgment did not make the bank deem itself insecure. He further testified that Mr. Lloyd's note with his bank was secured by a first mortgage on Ellsworth County real estate and did not mature until more than four months after the August 3 setoff. Hoosier also testified Lloyd was not delinquent in any note payments when the setoff was made. The bank ledger sheet shows that thirteen days after the setoff of $39,178.20 from Lloyd's account was applied on his note, and the bank loaned Lloyd an additional $50,000. Mr. Hoosier testified the reason he deemed the bank insecure with regard to Lloyd was because he knew a garnishment summons was going to be served on the bank to aid in satisfying the foreign judgment against Lloyd.

The bank argues the garnishment of Lloyd's bank accounts would have destroyed his liquidity and thus justifies its deeming itself insecure. This argument ignores the nature of the secured note. Neither the garnishment nor the foreign judgment affect the bank's security. As testified to, the bank was satisfied with the security for the Lloyd debt. The garnishment was seeking payment from Lloyd's unmortgaged assets. The bank's lending Lloyd an additional $50,000 thirteen days after the setoff is clear evidence it did not, in good faith, deem itself insecure.

A creditor has the power to accelerate debt payments when he deems himself insecure only if he in good faith believes the prospect of payment of the debt is impaired. K.S.A. 84–1–208. "Good faith" is defined at K.S.A. 84–1–201(19) as "honesty in fact in the conduct or transaction concerned."

While it is true, as the majority points out, that the test of good faith is a subjective one which must be considered from the viewpoint of the creditor, that does not mean a creditor can accelerate a note to maturity at its whim. As stated by the Utah Supreme Court in Clayton v. Crossroads Equipment Co., 655 P.2d 1125, 1128 (Utah 1982), "The obvious purpose of requiring that a secured party act in good faith is to impose the basic obligation of fair dealing, and to protect the purchaser from the mere whim or caprice of the secured party." If the good faith requirement of K.S.A. 84–1–208 is to have any meaning or purpose, we cannot allow the bank to use its acceleration and setoff authority to defeat a creditor's rights under the garnishment statute as Kanopolis State bank did here. This was the determination reached by the Indiana Court of Appeals in Universal C.I.T. Credit Corp. v. Shepler, 164 Ind.App. 516, 520–21, 329 N.E.2d 620 (1975). There, the Indiana court held that if the good faith provisions of Indiana Code Annotated §§ 26–1–1–208 and 26–1–1–201[19] * * * were to have any real effect, they must be modified to include a more objective standard, i.e., what would a "reasonable man" do under the same set of facts and circumstances. See also Williamson v. Wanlass, 545 P.2d 1145, 1149 (Utah 1976), where the Supreme Court of Utah recognized that acceleration is a harsh remedy which should be allowed only if there is some reasonable justification for doing so, such as a good faith belief that the prospect of payment is impaired as expressly provided in the U.C.C.

I would hold, as have courts of other jurisdictions, that in considering whether a creditor acted in good faith in deeming itself insecure, a secured party must show compelling facts of insecurity because the secured creditor is in a less precarious position than is an unsecured creditor. McKay v. Farmers & Stockmens Bank of Clayton, 92 N.M. 181, 183, 585 P.2d 325 (1978); Van Horn v. Van De Wol, Inc., 6 Wash.App. 959, 497 P.2d 252 (1972), 61 A.L.R.3d 241.

Here, the debtor's note with the bank was secured by a first mortgage on real estate. There is no evidence the collateral was impaired in any way. Nor is there any evidence the debtor was delinquent in payments on the note or that the prospect of payment was impaired. There is no evidence, compelling or otherwise, to support the bank's contention its setoff was in good faith. To be in good faith, the bank's action must have been in response to a bona fide belief, based on evidence, that its prospect of payment from Lloyd was impaired.

Finally, we find the reasoning of the Utah Supreme Court in Williamson v. Wanlass, 545 P.2d 1145, instructive. In *Williamson,* the debtor's promissory note was secured by a second mortgage on farm property which the debtors had purchased for $111,000. The court found that the holders of the promissory note failed to show a good faith belief that prospect of payment was impaired, justifying acceleration of the note under Utah Code Ann. 70A–1–208 (1980). The court made this finding notwithstanding the fact that the defendants were frequently late in making monthly installment payments on the note. The key factor was the fact that the plaintiffs had a second mortgage on extensive property and there was little doubt the note would be paid, principal and interest.

As in *Williamson,* here there is no evidence indicating an inability of the debtor to pay off the note, especially in light of the bank's first mortgage on Lloyd's Ellsworth County real estate. The debtor here was not delinquent in any payments, in contrast to the debtor in Williamson.

Under the construction given K.S.A. 84–1–208 by the majority opinion, any debtor who signs a standard note is vulnerable to acceleration of his note and setoff of his bank account upon the unsubstantiated statement of a bank that it deems itself insecure. In Iola State Bank v. Bolan, 235 Kan. 175, Syl. ¶ 8, 679 P.2d 720 (1984), we construed the good faith rule:

> "Where a bank knows sums deposited in the account of one of its depositors belong to a third party, it does not act in good faith when it applies such funds of the third party against the depositor's debts to the bank. Under such circumstances the third party has an action directly against the bank for conversion of the third party's funds from the debtor's accounts."

In Iola State Bank, the bank knew of outstanding checks from its delinquent borrower to various farmers for the purchase of grain but nevertheless set off the borrower's account, dishonoring his outstanding checks. We held the bank's action was not in good faith. Here, the bank knew of the judgment against its borrower and that a garnishment summons was en route to seize the bank account for application on the judgment. With this information, Kanopolis State Bank accelerated Lloyd's note and set off his bank account before the impending garnishment attached, even though the Lloyd note was not delinquent. This case is analogous to Iola State Bank, but stronger, because here the borrower's note was not delinquent. Thus, according to our own precedent, the Kanopolis State Bank lacked good faith in its set off of Lloyd's account.

I would reverse

HOLMES, J., joins the foregoing dissenting opinion.

SECTION 3. NEGOTIATION AND READJUSTMENT ON DEFAULT

It should not be assumed that, on default, all secured creditors always automatically and immediately seek payment in full by any available legal means. Realization on the collateral is, of course, one such means, and the secured creditor has contracted precisely for it. Even so, many a secured creditor will first try to work out some plan of voluntary repayment before resorting to his rights as a secured creditor. Indeed, he may excuse the default altogether. In the case of a default that signifies true difficulty in making payment, the secured creditor may be willing to reduce the amount of payments due, or extend time to the debtor. All this can be readily accomplished by modification of the basic security agreement.

Sometimes the debtor will be in difficulty with several creditors at the same time, who may then join together with the debtor to help him work out a satisfactory overall readjustment of his obligations.

SECTION 4. CREDITOR'S RIGHTS ON DEFAULT TO SEEK JUDGMENT AND EXECUTION

This remedy is the prime remedy of the *unsecured* creditor. It therefore may seem oddly out of place here. Yet UCC 9–501(1) expressly authorizes a secured creditor to "reduce his claim to judgment" as one way of proceeding, and UCC 9–501(5) states in full:

> "When a secured party has reduced his claim to judgment the lien of any levy which may be made upon his collateral by virtue of any execution based upon the judgment shall relate back to the date of the perfection of the security interest in such collateral. A judicial sale, pursuant to such execution, is a foreclosure of the security interest by judicial procedure within the meaning of this section, and the secured party may purchase at the sale and thereafter hold the collateral free of any other requirement of this Article."

Comment 6 to this section adds that a judicial sale pursuant to judgment and execution, though one of the methods of realizing contemplated by Article 9, is "governed by other law and not by this Article and the restrictions which this Article imposes on the right of a secured party to buy in the collateral at a sale under Section 9–504 do not apply."

The Code does not say what the creditor must do to obtain judgment and execution on the debt; state statutes and common law of ancient vintage specify these steps, and they vary somewhat from state to state. Generally, the creditor must first commence suit and obtain a judgment for the debt owed. After judgment the clerk of the court will, on request, issue a "writ of execution" (or the like). This writ recites that a judgment has been obtained and directs the sheriff or other appropriate officer to seize the property of the debtor and sell it to satisfy the judgment debt. With the writ in hand, the officer will levy against the debtor's property at his home or place of business (i.e., exercise dominion over it such that it is safely preserved for satisfaction of the debt). Finally, after giving public notice, the officer will sell the property at a public auction to the highest bidder and then turn proceeds necessary to satisfy the debt over to the creditor. The surplus, if any, goes to the debtor.

Given that Article 9 contemplates that even a *secured* creditor might choose judgment and execution over enforcement of his security interest, we should explain why he might so choose. First, this route allows the creditor to reach assets of the debtor in addition to the collateral (which may have declined in value). Second, by immediately procuring judgment and execution, the creditor eliminates the two step process of first selling the collateral and then suing for a deficiency (under UCC 9–504). Third, this route generally requires only that the creditor prove the debt and the default, whereas proceeding under Article 9 may give rise to other disputed issues. Fourth, the statute of limitations may, in an unusual case, dictate judgment and execution as a first step, for a deficiency proceeding might come too late. Cf. Associates Discount Corp. v. Palmer, 47 N.J. 183, 219 A.2d 858 (1966).

Fifth, the creditor might want to get the collateral quickly, yet under Article 9 be forbidden to act because the contemplated repossession would involve a breach of the peace. In such case, by filing a complaint and procuring a writ of attachment or by rapidly procuring judgment and execution, the creditor might be able to reach the collateral more quickly. Sixth, since officers of the court administer judgment and attachment or execution, the creditor eliminates the risk of incurring liability for improper foreclosure under UCC 9–504 and 9–507. Finally, UCC 9–501(5) allows the creditor to purchase the collateral at the sheriff's sale, something he usually cannot do at a private sale under UCC 9–504(3).

Despite the foregoing advantages, it is unusual for the secured creditor to pursue the judgment and execution route. Of course, if he does, he need not comply with Part Five of Article Nine. An illustrative example is C & T Recreation, Inc. v. Cannon Minnesota Corp., 367 N.W.2d 591 (Minn.App. 1985).

SECTION 5. INTANGIBLES AS COLLATERAL—CREDITOR'S RIGHT TO MAKE COLLECTIONS ON DEFAULT

We have seen such intangibles as accounts, contract rights, instruments and certain proceeds may be used as collateral. If so and the debtor defaults, may the secured creditor then look directly to the *debtor's obligor* for payment when the payment falls due? Sections UCC 9–502(1) and (2) are addressed to this general problem, and provide:

§ 9–502. Collection Rights of Secured Party

(1) When so agreed and in any event on default the secured party is entitled to notify an account debtor or the obligor on an instrument to make payment to him whether or not the assignor was theretofore making collections on the collateral, and also to take control of any proceeds to which he is entitled under Section 9–306.

(2) A secured party who by agreement is entitled to charge back uncollected collateral or otherwise to full or limited recourse against the debtor and who undertakes to collect from the account debtors or obligors must proceed in a commercially reasonable manner and may deduct his reasonable expenses of realization from the collections. If the security agreement secures an indebtedness, the secured party must account to the debtor for any surplus, and unless otherwise agreed, the debtor is liable for any deficiency. But, if the underlying transaction was a sale of accounts or chattel paper, the debtor is entitled to any surplus or is liable for any deficiency only if the security agreement so provides.

Note that the last sentence of UCC 9–502(2) provides an exception to the usual rule that a secured party must account to the debtor for any surplus after the collateral is disposed of and the proceeds applied to expenses and the outstanding debt. See UCC 9–504(2). Although Article Nine applies, in general to "any sale of accounts or chattel paper," (UCC 9–102(1)(b)), a "sale" in the disposition context has different consequences. How does one determine whether the debtor has "sold" the collateral or simply granted a security interest in it? The answer depends upon the amount of risk the secured party assumes if the accounts do not in fact exist (fraud) or the account debtor is unable to pay. If the secured party assumes all of the risk, the transaction is clearly a sale. If the secured party has "recourse" against the debtor, the transaction may be treated as intended for security if the debtor agreed, through warranties or otherwise, to assume substantially all of the risk. Whether risk allocation is intended as a sale or security turns on the facts of each case—a complex inquiry for which Article 9 provides little guidance. See Major's Furniture Mart, Inc. v. Castle Credit Corp., 602 F.2d 538 (3d Cir.1979) (transaction a "sale" where debtor assumes risk of both existence and collectibility of debt).

Problem 6–2

1. Bank has a perfected security interest in debtor's accounts receivable. It understands that it has the right to notify the account debtors and to make collections. However it is fearful that if it undertakes the collection process on its own, the debtor will go into bankruptcy during that process and the automatic stay will stop its collection activity and it will be forced to turn over the remaining accounts to the bankruptcy estate. Accordingly, creditor would like to give notice to the debtor that it intends to take the accounts in full satisfaction of the debt under UCC 9–505, and to cut off the debtor's entire interest 21 days after the notice is given.

2. How would you respond to the argument that one with a perfected security interest in accounts was obliged to sell those accounts under UCC 9–504 and could not simply collect them under UCC 9–502?

Problem 6–3

Your client, Commercial Credit, has loaned $500,000 to debtor and has taken a perfected security interest in debtor's inventory and accounts receivable. Debtor is now in default on the loan and you estimate the value of the accounts and inventory to be somewhere between $1,600,000 and $2,100,000. Bank has a perfected security interest securing a loan of $1,500,000 which has priority over your client's security interest.

1. If the loan to the Bank is not in default (and accordingly Bank is not proceeding to collect), what are the rights of your client, Commercial Credit?

2. If debtor defaults on Bank's loan and Bank commences proceedings under UCC 9–504 with respect to the inventory and UCC 9–502 with respect to the accounts, what are your client's rights and how does your client protect them?

Problem 6–4

Bank has a perfected security interest in all of the assets of a small company, including the inventory, equipment, accounts receivable, leases, and general intangibles. After default, Bank decides to take over the company by seizing all of the assets and taking them in full satisfaction of their debt under UCC 9–505. Bank's debt is $10 million and it estimates the total value of the company's assets to be $4 million. Accordingly, Bank informs the CEO that it intends to take over the company. The CEO leaves in a huff and never returns. The Bank then installs its CEO and continues the operation of the company. The Bank would like to get rid of the company; it makes the following proposal.

The Bank will send notice to the corporate debtor (all of whose stock is held by the departed CEO) of its intention to retain the assets under UCC 9–505. It will then put the company on the market and sell it as a going concern to a third party.

An associate in your office has pointed out that UCC 9–505 seems only to deal with collateral in the secured party's "possession." Will that cause problems if the CEO later comes back to challenge the disposition? If so, how does the bank proceed with the receivables and with other intangibles such as patents, copyrights, and trade secrets?

The problems become devilishly difficult when the collateral is chattel paper (UCC 9–105(1)(b)). Recall that chattel paper usually gives the creditor some interest in two kinds of collateral. In the first place it gives him a claim upon the account debtor's obligation to pay and in the second place it gives him some form of claim to the underlying collateral—at least in certain circumstances. Moreover, it is not always clear whether the transfer of the chattel paper carries with it any right in a reversionary interest that might exist in the debtor after the account debtor had ceased to pay on a lease or other non-purchase arrangement. In this connection, review *In re Leasing Consultants, Inc.*, Chapter Four, Section 10, supra.

SECTION 6. TANGIBLES—CREDITOR'S RIGHT TO REPOSSESSION ON DEFAULT EITHER FOR SETTLEMENT LEVERAGE OR AS A STEP IN FORECLOSURE

UCC 9–503 does not give the debtor a right to notice and a hearing prior to any repossession. That section provides:

> **§ 9–503. Secured Party's Right to Take Possession After Default**
>
> Unless otherwise agreed a secured party has on default the right to take possession of the collateral. In taking possession a secured party may proceed without judicial process if this can be done without breach of the peace or may proceed by action. If the security agreement so provides the secured party may require the debtor to assemble the collateral and make it available to the secured party at a place to be designated by the secured party which is reasonably convenient to both parties. * * *

Note, though, that the secured creditor may utilize self-help to repossess only "if this can be done without breach of the peace." Otherwise, he must resort to "judicial process"—replevin, a claim and delivery statute, or the like. Moreover, if the debtor has gone into bankruptcy, the secured creditor loses all rights of repossession.

STONE MACHINERY CO. v. KESSLER

Court of Appeals of Washington, 1970.
1 Wash.App. 750, 463 P.2d 651.

EVANS, CHIEF JUDGE.

Plaintiff Stone Machinery brought this action in Asotin County to repossess a D–9 Caterpillar Tractor which plaintiff had sold to defendant

Frank Kessler under conditional sales contract. Service of process was not made on the defendant but plaintiff located the tractor in Oregon and repossessed it. The defendant then filed an answer and cross-complaint in the Asotin County replevin action, alleging that the plaintiff wrongfully and maliciously repossessed the tractor, and sought compensatory and punitive damages under Oregon law. Trial was to the court without a jury and the court awarded defendant compensatory damages in the sum of $18,586.20, and punitive damages in the sum of $12,000 on defendant's cross-complaint.

The operative facts are not in serious dispute. Defendant Kessler purchased, by conditional sales contract, a used D–9 Caterpillar Tractor from the plaintiff Stone Machinery for the sum of $23,500. The unpaid balance of $17,500 was to be paid in monthly installments, with skip payments. The defendant's payment record was erratic and several payments were made late. However, payments of $3600 on March 29, 1966, and $1800 on July 18, 1966, put the contract payments on a current basis. The payment due on August 10, 1966 was not made and, on September 7, 1966, plaintiff's credit manager, Richard Kazanis, went to the defendant's ranch in Garfield, Washington, and demanded payment of the balance due on the contract or immediate possession of the tractor. At this time defendant had made payments on the purchase price totaling $17,200, including the trade-in. The defendant was unable to make full payment, or any payment at that time, and informed Mr. Kazanis that he would not relinquish possession of the tractor to him at that time, or at any time in the future, in the absence of proper judicial proceedings showing his right to repossess, and that "someone would get hurt" if an attempt was made to repossess without "proper papers." At that time the defendant informed Mr. Kazanis that he, the defendant, expected to be awarded a contract by the U.S. Bureau of Fisheries to do some work with the D–9 at their installation on the Grande Ronde River near Troy, Oregon, and that he would then be able to pay on the tractor.

On September 13, 1966, the plaintiff instituted this action in Asotin County, Washington, but the sheriff was unable to locate the tractor in that county. Thereafter, the plaintiff instituted another action in Garfield County, but the sheriff was unable to locate the tractor in that county. The evidence indicates that on September 24 Kessler took the tractor to Oregon to work the bureau of fisheries job.

On September 27, 1966, Mr. Kazanis, by use of an airplane, located the tractor on the Grande Ronde River, west of Troy, Wallowa County, Oregon. He then contacted the sheriff of Wallowa County and requested him to accompany them in the repossession of the tractor to prevent any violence by the defendant. The sheriff agreed to meet with Mr. Kazanis at Troy, Oregon, and on September 27, 1966, Mr. Kazanis in his private car, plaintiff's mechanic in a company pickup, and the plaintiff's truck driver in the company lo-boy truck, left Walla Walla, and the following morning met the Wallowa County Sheriff at Troy, where the sheriff was shown a copy of the conditional sales contract. The sheriff confirmed previous legal advice plaintiff had received that the plaintiff had the right to repossess the tractor (although not by the use of force) and thereupon the sheriff, in his official sheriff's car, followed by Mr. Kazanis in his private car, the mechanic in the pickup, and the truck driver in the lo-boy, proceeded to the scene where the defendant was operating the D–9 tractor in the Grande Ronde River approximately 7 miles west of Troy, pursuant to contract with the U.S. Bureau of Fisheries.

Upon arriving at the scene the sheriff, accompanied by Mr. Kazanis, walked to the edge of the river and motioned the defendant, who was working with the tractor in the river, to bring the tractor to shore. The sheriff was in uniform and wearing his badge and sidearms. The sheriff informed the defendant that the plaintiff Stone Machinery had a right to repossess the tractor, and stated, "We come to pick up the tractor." The defendant asked the sheriff if he had proper papers to take the tractor and the sheriff replied, "No." The defendant Kessler protested and objected to the taking of the tractor but offered no physical resistance because, as he testified, "he didn't think he had to disregard an order of the sheriff." The plaintiff's employee then loaded the tractor on the lo-boy and left for Walla Walla, Washington.

Within a few days the tractor was sold to a road contractor at Milton-Freewater, Oregon, for the sum of $7,447.80 cash, on an "as is" basis. The sale price represented the balance due on the contract, plus the plaintiff's charges for repossession.

Plaintiff's first assignments of error are directed to the following findings of the trial court:

XII

That the plaintiffs actions in repossessing the defendant's tractor on September 28, 1966, and the actions of the Wallowa County Sheriff, in aid of the plaintiffs, amounted to constructive force, intimidation and oppression, constituting a breach of the peace and conversion of defendant's tractor.

XIV

That the plaintiffs failed to show just cause or excuse for the wrongful act of repossession of the defendant's tractor on September 28, 1966.

XV

That the wrongful act of repossession, done intentionally on September 28, 1966, was malicious and was so wanton and reckless as to show disregard for the rights of the defendant, Frank Kessler.

* * *

Retaking possession of a chattel by a conditional seller, upon the default of the buyer, is governed by O.R.S. 79.5030 (U.C.C. 9–503):

Secured party's right to take possession after default. Unless otherwise agreed a secured party has on default the right to take possession of the collateral. In taking possession a secured party may proceed without judicial process *if this can be done without breach of the peace* or may proceed by action. (Italics ours.)

Defendant Kessler was admittedly in default for nonpayment of the August and September contract installments. By the terms of the above statute Stone Machinery had the right to take possession of the tractor without judicial process, but only if this could be done without a breach of the peace. The question is whether the method by which they proceeded constituted a breach of the peace.

No Oregon cases have been cited which define the term "breach of peace" so we must look to other authority. In Restatement of Torts 2d, § 116 (1965), the term is defined as follows:

> A breach of the peace is a public offense done by violence, or one causing or likely to cause an immediate disturbance of public order.

In the case of McKee v. State, 75 Okl.Cr. 390, 132 P.2d 173 (1942), breach of peace is defined (headnote 9, 132 P.2d 173), as follows:

> To constitute a "breach of the peace" it is not necessary that the peace be actually broken, and if what is done is unjustifiable and unlawful tending, with sufficient directness to break the peace, no more is required, nor is actual personal violence an essential element of the offense.

* * *

In the instant case it was the sheriff who said that he had no legal papers but that "We come over to pick up this tractor." Whereupon, the defendant Kessler stated, "I told him I was resisting this; there was an action started and I wanted to have a few days to get money together to pay them off." At this point defendant Kessler had a right to obstruct, by all lawful and reasonable means, any attempt by plaintiff to forceably repossess the tractor. Burgin v. Universal Credit Co., 2 Wash.2d 364, 98 P.2d 291 (1940). Had the defendant offered any physical resistance, there existed upon both the sheriff and plaintiff's agents a duty to retreat. See Westerman v. Oregon Auto. Credit Corp., 168 Or. 216, 122 P.2d 435 (1942). However, confronted by the sheriff, who announced his intention to participate in the repossession, it was not necessary for Kessler to either threaten violence or offer physical resistance. As stated by the court in Roberts v. Speck, 169 Wash. 613, at 616, 14 P.2d 33 at 34 (1932), citing from Jones on Chattel Mortgages § 705: (4th ed.)

> "The mortgagee becomes a trespasser by going upon the premises of the mortgagor, accompanied by a deputy sheriff who has no legal process, but claims to act *colore officii,* and taking possession without the active resistance of the mortgagor. To obtain possession under such a show and pretence of authority is to trifle with the obedience of citizens to the law and its officers."

Acts done by an officer which are such a nature that the office gives him no authority to do them are "*colore officii.*" See 7A Words & Phrases at 296 (Perm.Ed.), * * *.

In the instant case, when the sheriff of Wallowa County, having no authority to do so, told the defendant Kessler, "We come over to pick up this tractor", he was acting *colore officii* and became a participant in the repossession, regardless of the fact that he did not physically take part in the retaking. Plaintiff contends that its sole purpose in having the sheriff present was to prevent anticipated violence. The effect, however, was to prevent the defendant Kessler from exercising his right to resist by all lawful and reasonable means a nonjudicial take-over. To put the stamp of approval upon this method of repossession would be to completely circumvent the purpose and intent of the statute.

We hold there is substantial evidence to support the trial court's finding that the unauthorized actions of the sheriff in aid of the plaintiff amounted to constructive force, intimidation and oppression constituting a breach of the peace and conversion of the defendant's tractor.

* * *

Defendant Kessler was in default of his contract and had announced his intention to resist any attempted nonjudicial repossession. The words used in announcing his intention, namely, "someone would get hurt", were of such a nature as to justify the presence of a sheriff during any attempt at peaceable repossession although, as we have already held, this did not justify participation by the sheriff in the process of repossession. However, the fact that the sheriff did undertake to act *colore officii* in the repossession was not, under the circumstances, sufficient to support a finding that the plaintiff thereby displayed a particularly aggravated disregard for the rights of Kessler, within the meaning of Douglas v. Humble Oil & Refining Co., supra.

Judgment for compensatory damages is affirmed. Judgment for punitive damages is reversed.

Notes

1. Is this decision sound?
2. Can you explain how the damages were computed?

BLOOMQUIST v. FIRST NATIONAL BANK OF ELK RIVER

Court of Appeals, Minnesota, 1985.
378 N.W.2d 81.

FOLEY, J.

Debtor, Martin Bloomquist, appeals from a summary judgment and a deficiency judgment for creditor, First National Bank of Elk River. Debtor sued the bank asserting, inter alia, that the bank committed a breach of the peace when it repossessed collateral from the debtor's locked business without his consent. Debtor was unsuccessful in obtaining an injunction to enjoin the bank's sale of the collateral and the sale occurred before an appeal could be heard. The bank moved for summary judgment on the debtor's claims and sought a deficiency judgment on the notes arguing it had a right to "self-help" repossession. The trial court granted the bank summary judgment dismissing the debtor's claims and entered a deficiency judgment against the debtor. We reverse the summary judgment, vacate the deficiency judgment and remand for trial on the issue of damages for the conversion.

FACTS

Appellant, Martin Bloomquist (debtor) owned and operated an automobile repair service in Elk River, Minnesota. In the course of his business, debtor borrowed money from respondent First National Bank of Elk River (bank). Two notes are at issue here: (1) a promissory note dated July 14, 1983 in the amount of $11,540.20, which renewed a November 27, 1981 note for which all of debtor's business tools and equipment were given as security under a November 27, 1981 agreement, and (2) a promissory note in the amount of $3,505 dated November 23, 1982 for which a jeep with a snowplow was given as security.

On June 15, 1984 the bank sent debtor a letter demanding all note obligations be brought current by the end of June or "we will have to start action." The letter noted delinquencies of $1,405.00 on the equipment note and $1,790.68 on the jeep note.

Debtor paid the bank $470 on June 20, 1984. Mr. Wheaton, the bank's vice president, stated that in the next few weeks he visited debtor at his place of business, "informing him that unless the accounts were brought to date, repossession must take place." Debtor responded, "That will put me out of business." Wheaton replied, "I realize that." On one occasion Wheaton inventoried some of the equipment.

Debtor's version of the events is that Wheaton repeatedly threatened, "I will have to send in the boys and close you down." Debtor stated that he told Wheaton he would not give the bank his tools and that he was working on raising the money.

On about August 10, 1984, debtor offered the bank $600.00 but it was refused as inadequate. On August 20, 1984 the bank sent debtor a letter, noting the defaults, accelerating payment, demanding full payment, and concluding: "If payment is not made within the next three days the Bank will take possession of the secured goods. * * *"

On Saturday August 25, 1984, when debtor's business was closed, the bank's agents repossessed debtor's business tools and equipment. One of the bank's agents removed a cracked window pane, that was taped shut, to enter debtor's closed business. He then climbed through the window and opened the overhead garage door which had been secured with a deadbolt lock. The bank's agents, including the bank's vice president, the bank's attorney, an off-duty highway patrol officer and his son, then removed debtor's tools and equipment.

During the repossession, some of debtor's business tenants complained to bank agents that they could not just break and enter into debtor's business and remove his goods. Affidavits of these tenants indicate they protested the actions and were upset by what they observed. One tenant called the police after observing what she thought was a crime.

Debtor did not learn of the repossession until he arrived at his business on Monday morning and observed a repossession notice on a vehicle he was repairing. He denied consenting to the repossession and protested the bank's right to repossess. Within a few days, he commenced this suit claiming, inter alia, unlawful repossession and conversion, and seeking general, special and punitive damages.

During November 1984, debtor redeemed his jeep with snowplow. On January 5, 1985 the bank auctioned off the repossessed business tools and equipment for a total of $4,850. Debtor had sought to enjoin the sale, but the injunction was denied. An appeal to this court followed, but the sale occurred before the appeal could be heard.

Following the sale, debtor sought to amend his complaint disputing the method of sale and asserting other claims for damages. The bank moved for summary judgment on the issue of unlawful repossession and on its counterclaim for the balance due on the notes plus attorney's fees. The court granted the bank summary judgment—dismissing debtor's claims, and entered a deficiency judgment of $10,866.11, plus interest and attorney's fees against debtor. The court also granted the bank possession of debtor's "remaining shop equipment." Debtor appeals from the adverse judgments.

ISSUES

1. Did the bank commit a breach of the peace in repossessing collateral when its agents, without debtor's consent, entered debtor's locked business by removing a window pane?

2. Did the bank's sale of the repossessed goods constitute conversion as a matter of law?

ANALYSIS

Standard of review:

The function of a court reviewing summary judgment is to determine whether there are any genuine issues of material fact for trial, and whether the trial court erred in its application of the law. Betlach v. Wayzata Condominium, 281 N.W.2d 328, 330 (Minn.1979).

Trial court decision:

The trial court ruled as a matter of law that debtor's cause of action failed to state a claim for which relief might be granted based on its findings:

> "That because of Plaintiff's breach of the notes and security agreements with Defendant, Defendant had an absolute right to take possession of the tools and equipment which it repossessed on August 25, 1984.
>
> "That the First National Bank of Elk River did repossess the tools and equipment made the subject matter of this action in good faith in order to enforce its rights under the notes and security agreements given to it by Plaintiff Martin Bloomquist. That the repossession was by self help without Breach of Peace."

Statute at issue:

Minn.Stat. § 336.9–503 states:

> "Unless otherwise agreed a secured party has on default the right to take possession of the collateral. In taking possession a secured party may proceed without judicial process if this can be done *without breach of the peace* or may proceed by action * * *."

Wrongful repossession?

Debtor claims that creditor wrongfully repossessed his tools and equipment. Debtor claims that because he specifically told the bank he would not willingly give up his tools and equipment and since he never consented to the bank's entry into his business in any way, including in the security agreement, the bank had no authority to repossess and should have sought judicial relief. Moreover, the bank committed a breach of the peace when it repossessed by breaking and entering into the debtor's locked and closed business.

Creditor argues and the trial court agreed, that self-help repossession was appropriate because the debtor was in default. Therefore, debtor's breach of the notes gave creditor "an absolute right to take possession" of debtor's tools and equipment. Creditor notes that Minn.Stat. § 336.9–503 (1984) authorized self-help repossession if there is no breach of peace and the security agreement signed by debtor granted creditor the right to inspect the collateral. Creditor admits the agreement did not specifically authorize entry into debtor's business to repossess collateral.

We agree with debtor. Self-help repossession is not lawful where it requires or constitutes a breach of the peace. See Minn.Stat. § 336.9–503. Minnesota has not specifically delineated a test to determine whether a breach of the peace has occurred. However, we are guided by Minn.Stat. § 645.22 (1984) in construing this phrase.

> "Laws uniform with those of other states shall be interpreted and construed to effect their general purpose to make uniform the laws of those states which enact them." Id. * * *

State courts in Florida and Pennsylvania enunciate the following test or guidelines as helpful in determining whether a "breach of the peace" has occurred during the repossession of collateral:

> (1) Whether there was entry by creditor upon debtor's premises, and
>
> (2) Whether the debtor or one acting in his behalf consented to the entry and repossession.

Quest v. Barnett Bank of Pensacola, 397 So.2d 1020, 1023 (Fla.App.1981) (quoting White & Summers, Uniform Commercial Code 966 (1972)); see Walker v. Walthall, 121 Ariz. 121, 122, 588 P.2d 863, 864 (1978). In *Quest,* the Florida court explained that the debtor's express consent for creditor to enter an enclosed area must be freely and voluntarily given, and that implied consent only covers those activities that are within a fair and reasonable interpretation of the terms of the grant. The Arizona court, in *Walker,* noted that generally the facts of each case must be evaluated to determine if a breach of the peace has occurred.

Here, debtor repeatedly told the bank's vice president that he would not consent to a repossession. When a debtor has not consented to repossession and in fact, has specifically revoked any implied right to such repossession, a creditor is not entitled to the self-help remedy but must pursue a judicial remedy. *Quest,* 397 So.2d at 1023, see *Walker,* 121 Ariz. at 122, 588 P.2d at 864. Self-help repossession denies to the objecting debtor an opportunity to assert a defense to the repossession such as whether the parties' course of conduct has varied the agreements. See Cobb v. Midwest Recovery Bureau Co., 295 N.W.2d 232 (Minn.1980).

The case of Laurel Coal Co. v. Walter E. Heller & Co., Inc., 539 F.Supp. 1006 (W.D.Penn.1982) is nearly analogous to the instant case. In *Laurel,* the debtor's note was secured by a bulldozer. Upon the debtor's alleged default and failure to tender full payment as demanded, creditor repossessed the bulldozer by cutting a chain that secured a fence surrounding the debtor's business premises. The debtor sued, alleging that the self-help repossession was unlawful because it constituted a breach of the peace. The Pennsylvania court held "that the actual breaking of a lock or fastener securing property, even commercial property, constitutes a 'breach of the peace' * * *." Id. at 1007. The court also noted that, "even non-forceful repossessions may be found unlawful." Id. at 1008.

In the *Laurel* opinion, the Pennsylvania court cited with approval the earlier case of Stewart v. North, 65 Pa.Super. 195 (1916), which is factually similar to the instant case. In *Stewart,* the court held that breaking a window to unlock a door to a residence in order to repossess a piano was a breach of the peace constituting an unlawful repossession. See *Laurel* at 1007.

The case of Kimble v. Universal TV Rental, Inc., 65 Ohio Misc. 17, 417 N.E.2d 597 (1980) also supports our decision here. In *Kimble,* the Ohio court found that even though creditor and debtor had entered into an agreement providing for peaceable entry to recover goods, breaking into debtor's locked apartment and taking a rental TV set, without express or implied consent to do so, amounted to criminal acts and constituted a "breach of the peace" within the meaning of the Uniform Commercial Code. The Ohio court defined breach of the peace as a "violation of the public order, a disturbance of public tranquility, by an act or conduct inciting to violence or tending to provoke or excite others to breach the peace [*including*] *any violation of any law enacted to preserve peace and good order.*" Id. at 22, 417 N.E.2d at 602 (quoting 2 Anderson, Wharton's Criminal Law and Procedure, § 802 (1957)) (emphasis added).

Other cases supporting our holding include Thompson v. Ford Motor Credit Co., 324 F.Supp. 108 (D.S.C.1971) (no element of violence is needed in order for repossession of collateral to constitute a breach of the peace); Quest v. Barnett Bank of Pensacola, 397 So.2d 1020 (Fla.App.1981) (a breach of peace can occur if creditor damages debtor's property during the repossession); Dixon v. Ford Motor Credit Co., 29 Ill.Dec. 230, 72 Ill.App.3d 983, 391 N.E.2d 493 (1979) (a creditor's repossession in disregard of debtor's unequivocal oral protest may be found to be a breach of the peace); General Electric Credit Corp. v. Timbrook, 291 S.E.2d 383 (W.Va.1982) (an unauthorized entry into a debtor's dwelling to repossess collateral constituted a breach of the peace within the meaning of the UCC).

We note that the bank asks us to consider a number of cases where a breach of the peace is not found. See C.F. Adams Co. v. Sanders, 66 S.W. 815 (Ky.1902); Wirth v. Heavey, 508 S.W.2d 263 (Mo.App.1974); Global Casting Industries, Inc., v. Daley-Hodkin Corp., 105 Misc.2d 517, 432 N.Y.S.2d 453 (1980); Cherno v. Bank of Bablyon, 54 Misc.2d 277, 282 N.Y.S.2d 114 (Sup.Ct.Nassau Co. of 1967) aff'd 29 A.D.2d 767, 288 N.Y.S.2d 862 [4 UCC Rep 1185] (2d Dept.1968); North v. Williams, 120 Pa. 109, 13 A. 723 (1888); Harris Truck & Trailer Sales v. Foote, 58 Tenn.App. 710, 436 S.W.2d 460 (1968); Robertson v. Union Planters National Bank of Memphis, Tennessee, 561 S.W.2d 901 (Tex.Civ.App.1981). These cases do not control the instant case. All of these cases base their holding on the fact that the creditor entered the debtor's premises to repossess collateral, or repossess a motor vehicle, with debtor's express or implied consent.

The bank asserts that many of these same cases hold that there is no breach of the peace when the repossession occurs without violence or threat of violence. See e.g., *Harris Truck; Global Casting* (a breach of the peace is "a disturbance of public order by an act of violence, or by an act likely to produce violence. * * *" Id. 432 N.Y.S.2d at 455). The requirement of violence apparently represents a minority view. See, e.g., 6 Uniform Laws Annotated § 9–503, n. 15 (West 1981). This does not seem consistent with the commercial practices encouraged by the Minnesota Supreme Court and this court. See, e.g., *Cobb,* 295 N.W.2d, at 237–38; Steichen v. First Bank Grand, 372 N.W.2d 768 (Minn.Ct.App.1985). We believe the better view, expressed in the cases we have relied on, holds that no violence or threat of violence need occur before a breach of the peace may be found. See *Quest; Laurel: Thompson.* The Minnesota Supreme Court has already adopted the view in Berg v. Wiley, 264 N.W.2d 145, 150 (Minn.1978), that a non-violent, forcible entry to retake possession of a tenant's premises constitutes a breach of the peace.

Here it is uncontested that the bank's agents and their attorney entered debtor's closed and locked business without his consent. We are appalled at the course of conduct in this matter by the bank's officers and the bank attorney, their position is indefensible, and their actions in breaking and entering appellant's business premises were totally inappropriate since judicial process was readily available to enforce any claimed rights. The bank's breaking and entering debtor's business to repossess collateral constitutes a breach of the peace within the meaning of Minn.Stat. § 336.9–503, as a matter of law. See *Berg* (self-help repossession of premises was non-peaceable and wrongful as a matter of law where landlord retook possession in tenant's absence by picking the locks and locking her out).

Conversion

Our holding here requires a finding that the bank's sale of the unlawfully repossessed tools and equipment constitutes a conversion. See Kloos v. Gatz, 97 Minn. 167, 169–70, 105 N.W. 639, 640–41 (1906); see also Molm v. Barton, 27 Minn. 530, 8 N.W. 765 (1881).

> "To constitute conversion, there must be an execution of dominion over the goods which is inconsistent with and in repudiation of the owner's right to the goods or some act done which destroys or changes their character or deprives the owner of possession permanently or for an indefinite length of time."

Hildegarde, Inc. v. Wright, 244 Minn. 410, 413, 70 N.W.2d 257, 259 (1955).

We remand for trial on the issue of debtor's damages. The measure of damages for conversion is the fair market value of the repossessed goods at the time of the conversion, plus interest from that date. McLeod-Nash Motors, Inc. v. Commercial Credit Trust, 187 Minn. 452, 460, 246 N.W. 17, 20 (1932). Debtor also pled special damages and punitive damages. Debtor may be entitled to special damages including lost profits if he is able to prove the loss with reasonable certainty. See Cushing v. Seymour, Sabin & Co., 30 Minn. 301, 304–05, 15 N.W. 249, 250 (1883). Punitive damages are appropriately recovered in a wrongful repossession case. *Cobb* at 237–38; Steichen v. First Bank Grand, 372 N.W.2d 768, 772 (Minn.Ct.App.1985), pet. for rev.

denied, (Minn. October 18, 1985). "Punitive damages, where permitted by law, should be used as a deterrent against future unlawful conduct and as a warning that unlawful self-help repossession will not be condoned." *Steichen* at 773. These damage claims should be assessed by a jury at trial.

DECISION

The bank's repossession of collateral from debtor was unlawful because the bank committed a breach of the peace when its agents entered debtor's business without permission by removing a window pane to unlock the garage door. The subsequent sale of debtor's tools and equipment was therefore unauthorized and constitutes conversion as a matter of law.

We reversed the summary judgment, vacate the deficiency judgment, and remand for trial on the issue of damages for conversion, including a determination whether the bank is entitled to offset for the notes from compensatory damages and whether debtor is entitled to punitive and other damages.

Reversed and remanded for trial with deficiency judgment vacated.

Problem 6–5

Defendant Chrysler Credit Corporation appeals from a judgment entered against it and in favor of the plaintiffs in the amount of $20,000.

In July 1980, Jimmy McKinney bought a Dodge Mirada from Countywide Dodge for his wife's use. He negotiated and executed on behalf of McKinney Ceramic Tile Co., Inc., of which he was president and majority stockholder, a retail installment contract financing the automobile with Chrysler Credit Corporation. McKinney made only two payments pursuant to this agreement, because Countywide Dodge failed to repair the car to his satisfaction.

McKinney returned the car to Countywide Dodge on numerous occasions for repairs. The dealership successfully repaired most of the defects, but never succeeded in repairing a leak in the roof of the automobile. This leak was so bad that at times, after a rainshower, two inches of water was left standing in the front floor. Because of this repeated leaking, the car's interior had an offensive odor, and the leather interior was damaged.

Mr. McKinney visited the dealership time after time and, at one point in September, explained the problem to the owner of Countywide Dodge, who assured him it would be repaired. It was not. He then wrote letters to the dealership, Chrysler Corporation, and Chrysler Credit Corporation, notifying them that he would make no more payments on the vehicle until the leak was repaired. He received no response to these letters. Chrysler Credit later telephoned him about his failure to make the payments on the vehicle. Once again, he discussed the leak in the roof and was assured that it would be repaired. Soon thereafter, James Smith, a repossession agent of Chrysler Credit, contacted Mrs. McKinney about the car and the McKinneys' failure to make the payments on the note. Mrs. McKinney met Smith at a restaurant to discuss the matter. After a conversation, wherein Mrs. McKinney detailed to Smith the problem with the car, she and Smith reached an agreement. Mrs. McKinney testified as follows concerning the agreement:

> "He [Smith] told me that everything was fine, that all he had to do was to get me to take the car into the lot and it would be fixed. You know, they

would fix the leak in it. And, if they fixed the leak in it, then we would bring up the payment, which I agreed to."

Mrs. McKinney called their attorney from the restaurant. He spoke with Smith and confirmed the agreement not to repossess the car unless and until the McKinneys failed to bring the payments up to date following the repair of the vehicle's roof.

Mrs. McKinney and Smith then left the restaurant and drove to the dealership, where Mrs. McKinney surrendered the automobile to the dealership for repairs. The owner of the dealership confirmed the agreement to catch up the past due payments when the car was repaired.

A few days later, Chrysler Credit sent repossession notices to the McKinneys, advising them that the automobile had been repossessed and would be sold within five days after the receipt of those notices. The attorney for the McKinneys corresponded with Chrysler Credit, informing them of the agreement that repossession would not occur unless the repairs were made and the payments were not then brought up to date. Chrysler Credit did not respond to this letter.

The day after the repossession took place, Chrysler Credit called upon Countywide Dodge to pay off the McKinney account, pursuant to its recourse agreement, which it did.

Following these events, Countywide again made numerous attempts to repair the leaking roof in the car. Several times Mr. McKinney went in to the dealership and, each time, the roof leaked when tested. Later, Mr. McKinney was told to remove his personal belongings from the vehicle because it was no longer his car and was being sold. Thereupon Mr. McKinney filed suit against Chrysler Credit, Chrysler Corporation, and Countywide Dodge.

The trial court granted Countywide's motion for directed verdict at the close of the plaintiffs' case. The jury returned a verdict against Chrysler Corporation and in favor of the plaintiffs for breach of warranty. That verdict is not at issue in this appeal. The jury also returned a verdict against Chrysler Credit Corporation for $20,000.00 on a conversion claim.

1) On Appeal, what are the strongest arguments for both sides?

2) How would you decide the appeal?

Note: Other Legal Controls Upon Repossession

Upon default by a debtor, the secured party may seek to repossess the collateral through state statutory procedures granting replevin or detinue. These procedures are invoked before a judgment has been entered and customarily involve the issuance, upon an affidavit from the secured party, of a writ by a clerk of court to the sheriff to seize described property. Frequently, the secured party must post a bond. These statutory pre-judgment procedures pass muster under the Fourteenth Amendment to the United States Constitution if the debtor is entitled to a hearing on the merits within a reasonable time after repossession and before the collateral is sold. See, e.g., North Georgia Finishing, Inc. v. Di-Chem, Inc., 419 U.S. 601, 95 S.Ct. 719, 42 L.Ed.2d 751 (1975); Mitchell v. W.T. Grant Co., 416 U.S. 600, 94 S.Ct. 1895, 40 L.Ed.2d 406 (1974).

If self-help is exercised in a manner that breaches the peace, however, the debtor, as a practical matter, will not have a hearing on the merits until the secured party has sued for a deficiency judgment. By that time the collateral will have been sold and considerable costs incurred. Put differently, unless the debtor is able to enjoin the repossession, see UCC 9–507(1), the debtor's day in court, if available at all, comes after the alleged dirty work has been done.

The federal courts have held that in self-help cases the debtor is not protected by the Fourteenth Amendment: There is no "state action" that justifies granting the debtor procedural due process before the repossession. See, e.g., Flagg Brothers, Inc. v. Brooks, 436 U.S. 149, 98 S.Ct. 1729, 56 L.Ed.2d 185 (1978), holding that a warehouseman's proposed sale of goods entrusted to him for storage to enforce a statutory lien granted by the New York enactment of UCC 7–210 was not state action. See also, Adams v. Southern California First National Bank, 492 F.2d 324 (9th Cir.1973), cert. denied, 419 U.S. 1006, 95 S.Ct. 325, 42 L.Ed.2d 282 (1974) (self-help repossession under UCC 9–503 not subject to constitutional control).

What about additional protection under state law? You should check the constitution and statutes of the state where you intend to practice to determine whether any other controls are imposed upon self-help repossessions. If so, what are they? Do they apply to both commercial and consumer debtors? What remedies are available if the limitations are ignored by the secured party?

If there are no state constitutional or legislative limitations, the debtor may, in a proper case, be able to recover punitive damages for a "wrongful and outrageous" repossession. See, e.g., Chrysler Credit Corp. v. Turner, 553 So.2d 64 (Ala.1989) ($15,000 punitive damages for mere night-time repossession of car from driveway); MBank of El Paso v. Sanchez, 836 S.W.2d 151 (Tex.1992) ($1,000,000 punitive damages awarded to plaintiff whose auto with her in it was towed at high speeds and left with her in a repossession lot guarded by Doberman Pinschers until police rescued her).

SECTION 7. CREDITOR'S RIGHT TO RETAIN COLLATERAL IN SATISFACTION OF DEBT—"STRICT FORECLOSURE"

This option is, of course, not one that the secured creditor would generally want to elect unless the value of the collateral was equal to or greater than the amount of the outstanding indebtedness. It is an option that was recognized early in the law of real property security where it was called, and continues to be called "strict foreclosure." In this field, it had the effect of cutting off, by judicial decree, any right that the debtor might have to reacquire the realty. Such an interest was and is today called the debtor's "equity of redemption." Obviously, collateral would have highly uncertain value to a secured party taking it in satisfaction of the debt if the debtor might, *at any time thereafter,* require it by paying the indebtedness due. Hence, the law recognized the device of "strict foreclosure" whereby the secured party could go to court and, in effect, get an order cutting off the debtor's right to redeem should he not exercise it by a specified date. Observe that this device not only cut off the debtor's "equity of redemption"; it also cut off his "ownership equity"—the proportion of the property that was truly his. Thus the device did not certainly protect debtors against *forfeitures.* At the same time, it did not allow a creditor any deficiency, should the realty prove to be worth less than the outstanding indebtedness.

Section 9–505 provides:

Compulsory Disposition of Collateral; Acceptance of the Collateral as Discharge of Obligation

(1) If the debtor has paid sixty per cent of the cash price in the case of a purchase money security interest in consumer goods or sixty per cent of the loan in the case of another security interest in consumer goods, and has not signed after default a statement renouncing or modifying his rights under this Part a secured party who has taken possession of collateral must dispose of it under Section 9–504 and if he fails to do so within ninety days after he takes possession the debtor at his option may recover in conversion or under Section 9–507(1) on secured party's liability.

(2) In any other case involving consumer goods or any other collateral a secured party in possession may, after default, propose to retain the collateral in satisfaction of the obligation. Written notice of such proposal shall be sent to the debtor if he has not signed after default a statement renouncing or modifying his rights under this subsection. In the case of consumer goods no other notice need be given. In other cases notice shall be sent to any other secured party from whom the secured party has received (before sending his notice to the debtor or before the debtor's renunciation of his rights) written notice of a claim of an interest in the collateral. If the secured party receives objection in writing from a person entitled to receive notification within twenty-one days after the notice was sent, the secured party must dispose of the collateral under Section 9–504. In the absence of such written objection the secured party may retain the collateral in satisfaction of the debtor's obligation.

On all this, White and Summers have still more to say:

WHITE & SUMMERS, HANDBOOK OF THE LAW UNDER THE UNIFORM COMMERCIAL CODE 1209–1211 (3d ed. 1988).

Upon default and repossession, the secured creditor may wish to avoid the headache of resale and therefore accept the collateral in complete satisfaction of the debt under Section 9–505(2). By so doing he foregoes any right to a deficiency. This alternative of "strict foreclosure" was known to the common law and was available under the Uniform Conditional Sales Act. Sometimes the secured creditor will find strict foreclosure an attractive alternative to sale and suit for a deficiency. Presumably, when the value of the collateral is roughly equivalent to the amount of the outstanding debt, the secured creditor will choose strict foreclosure. Strict foreclosure has certain advantages over resale of the collateral or an action on the debt. In the first place, it may be accomplished with a modicum of effort on the part of the secured party. More important the secured creditor who strictly forecloses knows that the debtor or other parties cannot later plague him about the fairness of a resale price under Section 9–504. Section 9–505(2) authorizes strict foreclosure:

Thus, Section 9–505(2) presents an uncomplicated blueprint for strict foreclosure on default. First, the secured creditor must take possession of the collateral after default. Secondly, he is required to send a written notice to the debtor stating his intention to retain the collateral in satisfaction of the debtor's obligation, unless the debtor renounces his right to such notice after default. If the collateral is consumer goods, the foreclosing secured creditor must await the passage of twenty-one days without an objection from the debtor. If the collateral is consumer goods and the debtor has renounced his right to notice, the secured creditor may keep the goods, without ever having contacted any other creditor of the debtor claiming an interest in the collateral. However, if the collateral is not consumer goods, the secured creditor must send notice of intent to foreclose strictly to any other creditor of the debtor who has previously sent him written notice of a claim of an interest in the collateral. Then, if the unrenounced debtor or one of the other interested parties enters a written objection during the twenty-one days after the notice was sent, the secured party must dispose of the collateral under Section 9–504.

Furthermore, when the collateral is consumer goods and the debtor has paid 60 percent of the price, Section 9–505(1) provides that the secured creditor may not use strict foreclosure unless the debtor after default signs a statement renouncing his right to require the collateral resold in compliance with Section 9–504. This provision is based upon the supposition that a debtor who has paid 60 percent of the purchase price has built up equity in the goods, and that resale would result in a surplus. Hence in this situation the secured creditor may not strictly foreclose unless the debtor expressly renounces his right to demand resale.

Another potential problem for the secured party lies in the duration of the period when another party is entitled to object to strict foreclosure. Section 9–505(2) stipulates that the parties entitled to notice have twenty-one days "after the notice was sent" to object; thereafter the right of redemption and other rights are cut off. A wise secured party will give notice by registered or certified mail so that he can easily prove the time of sending.

Failure to give notice renders strict foreclosure invalid at least as to those entitled to receive notice who did not receive it. In re Sports Autos, Inc. involved a secured party who was also the president and sole shareholder of the debtor corporation. Without giving notice to the corporation or other secured creditors, he repossessed collateral worth approximately $90,000 more than the debt it secured and then set up essentially the same business under a different name. When the debtor's other creditors filed a petition for an involuntary declaration of bankruptcy, the Referee concluded that the secured party's failure to give notice deprived him of his right to retain the property.

In some cases debtors have attempted to force strict foreclosure upon an unwilling secured creditor.

SCHMODE'S INC. v. WILKINSON

Supreme Court of Nebraska, 1985.
219 Neb. 209, 361 N.W.2d 557.

CAPORALE, J.

Defendants-appellants, Mary and Ronald Wilkinson, doing business as M & R Trucking, challenge the deficiency judgment entered against them, jointly and severally, under Neb U.C.C. art. 9 (Reissue 1980), in favor of the plaintiff-appellee, Schmode's Inc., a Nebraska corporation. Among the Wilkinsons' assignments of error is the failure of the trial court to find that Schmode's elected to retain the collateral in satisfaction of the Wilkinsons' obligation. The record sustains that assignment, making it unnecessary that we address the remaining assignments. We reverse, remand, and direct that the cause be dismissed.

We note at the outset that this is an action at law. * * * The findings and disposition of the trial court therefore, the cause having been tried without a jury, have the effect of a jury verdict and will not be disturbed unless clearly wrong. * * *

Reviewed in accordance with that standard, the relevant facts are as follows.

Schmode's entered into a business transaction with Harco Leasing Company, Inc., whereby Schmode's sold to Harco a 1978 International tractor truck and a 1978 Hobbs trailer. Harco and the Wilkinsons then, on April 27, 1978, executed a conditional sales agreement, entitled "LEASING AGREEMENT," with respect to the truck, which obligated the Wilkinsons to pay Harco a principal amount, plus amortized interest and other charges, in 60 equal monthly installments and a larger 61st payment representing the truck's "residual value." On May 19, 1978, Harco and the Wilkinsons entered into a similar agreement with respect to the trailer, obligating the Wilkinsons to pay Harco a principal amount, plus amortized interest and other charges, in 60 equal monthly installments and a larger 61st payment representing the trailer's "residual value." Schmode's guaranteed Harco that if the Wilkinsons defaulted on their obligation such as to result in Harco's reclaiming the truck and trailer from the Wilkinsons, Schmode's would repurchase them from Harco.

The Wilkinsons defaulted, and on December 19, 1979, they delivered possession of the truck and trailer, collectively the collateral, to Schmode's.

The collateral was in need of repair and Schmode's restored it to sound mechanical condition, the restoration work being completed by May 3, 1980. The collateral was then placed on Schmode's lot in an attempt to sell it. As the collateral did not sell, Schmode's used it by leasing it to others through about mid-April of 1983, during which time it was operated a minimum of 204,000 miles.

Schmode's honored its agreement with Harco and paid the sums due Harco from the Wilkinsons. The parties do not dispute that Schmode's had a security interest in the collateral.

The collateral was publicly sold on April 28, 1983, pursuant to the trial judge's order. At the trial on the merits the trial judge found that the April 28 sale had not been commercially reasonable "because of the lapse of nearly three years and the use of said vehicles before the sale." The trial judge accordingly ruled that the Wilkinsons were entitled to setoffs for the damages they suffered due to the commercially unreasonable sale.

The Wilkinsons argue that Schmode's elected to retain the collateral in satisfaction of the obligation by keeping and leasing it for a period of almost

3 years after restoration and causing it to be operated for at least 204,000 miles, and therefore cannot obtain a deficiency judgment.

Neb. UCC § 9–505(2) (Reissue 1980) provides in relevant part:

> "In any other case involving consumer goods or any other collateral a secured party in possession may, after default, propose to retain the collateral in satisfaction of the obligation. Written notice of such proposal shall be sent to the debtor if he has not signed after default a statement renouncing or modifying his rights under this subsection."

Although we have not had occasion to deal with whether acts by a secured party other than the sending of notice may result in a § 9–505(2) election, other states with statutes virtually identical to ours have. There appear to be three different approaches.

One approach holds that an election under § 9–505(2) is impossible absent the service of notice on the debtor of the secured party's intent to retain the collateral in payment of the debt. Flickinger v. Genesee Corp., 71 A.D.2d 382, 423 N.Y.S.2d 73 (1979), typifies this view which seems to be premised on the notion that since the code provides a specific method for indicating that the secured party has elected to retain the collateral to satisfy the obligation, such an election cannot be implied from conduct not specified by the code. We reject this view on the ground that a secured party ought not be allowed to penalize a debtor by asserting the secured party's own failure to give the notice contemplated by § 9–505(2).

A second approach is that an election can be implied from an unreasonably prolonged retention of the collateral by the secured party and that the determination of what constitutes an unreasonable period of time is a question for the trier of fact. Service Chevrolet v. Sparks, 99 Wash.2d 199, 660 P.2d 760 (1983); Shultz v. Delaware Trust Co., 360 A.2d 576 (Del.Super.1976). This view appears to rest on the theory that to allow the secured party to retain the collateral for an unreasonably long time and then elect to sue the debtor on the underlying obligation would be unfair to the debtor.

The third approach requires that the secured party manifest an intent to accept the collateral in satisfaction of the obligation by some conduct other than an undue delay in disposing of the collateral. Nelson v. Armstrong, 99 Idaho 422, 582 P.2d 1100 (1978) (retaining farm equipment for 4½ months did not constitute an election); Jones v. Morgan, 58 Mich.App. 455, 228 N.W.2d 419 (1975) (keeping automobile for almost 2 years did not constitute an election); Tanenbaum v. Economics Laboratory, Inc., 628 S.W.2d 769 (Tex.1982) (taking back collateral at request of debtor that such be done in satisfaction of debt constituted election). This view rests, at least in part, on the notion that since the debtor is protected by other provisions in the code and because, at common law, the analogous concept of accord and satisfaction requires proof of the creditor's assent, in the absence of notice a clear manifestation of an election on the part of the creditor is required.

Under the circumstances of this case we need not choose at this time between the second and third approaches. Although we consider the question to be one of fact, we hold that in this case there is but one reasonable conclusion, and, therefore, as a matter of law, Schmode's, by using the collateral for a period of nearly 3 years after restoration by leasing and causing it to be operated for at least 204,000 miles, elected to retain the collateral in satisfaction of the Wilkinsons' obligation. The trial court was clearly wrong in not so holding.

We leave to another day and another case the question of whether under some circumstances the mere retention of collateral for an unreasonably long time may in and of itself imply a § 9–505(2) election.

The judgment is reversed and the cause remanded with directions to dismiss.

Reversed and remanded with directions to dismiss.

SECTION 8. CREDITOR'S RIGHT TO RESELL OR OTHERWISE DISPOSE OF THE COLLATERAL ON DEFAULT—"FORECLOSURE BY SALE"

Section 9–504 provides for foreclosure by sale. The jargon "foreclosure by sale," like "strict foreclosure" also derives from the law of real property. Foreclosure by sale may be explained as a legal invention designed to protect any ownership equity of the debtor from forfeiture, even though it, too, cuts off the debtor's "equity of redemption" (UCC 9–506). Of course, foreclosure by sale is a double-edged sword. Except as modified by regulatory law, if the UCC 9–504 foreclosure sale yields less than necessary to satisfy the debt, the debtor remains liable for the deficiency. See UCC 9–504(2).

We saw that in the land law, the "equity of redemption" was supposed to protect the debtor's "ownership equity" from forfeiture. But "strict foreclosure" evolved to protect the foreclosing secured party from the possibility that the debtor would later redeem. This protection for the secured creditor (the right of "strict" foreclosure) largely nullified the protection of the debtor's ownership equity given by his right to redeem. In a particular case, strict foreclosure might be invoked to cut off a quite substantial ownership equity of the debtor. This should seem doubly bad, for it not only deprived the debtor of his property, but gave the secured party a windfall as well. Hence, in came foreclosure by sale, which, among other things, was supposed to protect the debtor's ownership equity by (a) tending to assure a greater return from the collateral than just the amount of the debt due (a "surplus" representing debtor's "ownership equity") and (b) imposing a duty on the secured party to account to the debtor for such "surplus." Cf. UCC 9–504(2).

But, from the debtor's viewpoint, foreclosure by sale was and is a double-edged sword. Strict foreclosure, as such, left the secured party with no recourse if his collateral turned out to be worth less than the debt. Foreclosure by sale, on the other hand, brought with it the deficiency judgment, and foreclosure by sale could not, in and of itself, *assure* a return sufficient even to discharge the debt due, let alone provide a surplus representing any ownership equity of the debtor. As Professor Gilmore remarked:

"Sad experience has taught us that a power of sale, coupled with a right to a deficiency judgment can be harder on the debtor than strict foreclosure ever was. The surplus to be returned to the debtor after the sale is a glittering mirage; the deficiency judgment is the grim reality. Furthermore the person who buys at the sale today, nine times out of ten, is not our hero, the good faith purchaser for value, but the holder of the security interest who pays not in cash but by a credit against the debt."

2 GILMORE, SECURITY INTERESTS IN PERSONAL PROPERTY 1188–89 (1965).

From the creditor's point of view, what is at stake in any "realization" process is obvious enough: It is simply whether he is to be paid his due. But from the debtor's viewpoint, much more may be at risk, as Professor Gilmore indicates.

SECTION 9. SECTION 9–504(3): REQUIREMENTS OF COMMERCIAL REASONABLENESS AND THE EFFECTS OF NONCOMPLIANCE

Section 9–504(3) authorizes one who has repossessed collateral to resell it by public or private sale but it requires that "every aspect of the disposition including the method, manner, time, place and terms must be commercially reasonable." The Section goes on to require notice to the debtor (and certain others) in most circumstances. It is not surprising that UCC 9–504(3) has produced a great deal of litigation. Debtors have argued that sales are commercially unreasonable for the following reasons, among many others:

1. The price realized at the sale was too low.
2. The creditor waited too long to conduct the sale.
3. The creditor sold the goods in the wrong market (e.g. wholesale not retail).
4. The creditor failed to give the appropriate notice.
5. The creditor failed to do an adequate job of drumming up bidders at the sale, or to advertise properly the forthcoming sale.

In many circumstances the judgment of whether the sale was commercially reasonable was rather a subjective one, but the cases that follow will give the student a taste of the kinds of considerations that may be relevant. (See also White & Summers §§ 26–9 through 26–12.)

In reading the cases, the student should be mindful of these basic questions: Who is attacking the validity of the sale? On what grounds? And with what desired effect? Note that sometimes the party attacking the sale will be seeking affirmative recovery on a conversion theory or the like. At other times this party will merely be resisting a deficiency judgment. And there are still other possibilities.

A. Public or Private Proceedings?

The failure to hold a private rather than a public sale may itself be commercially unreasonable. For example, in United States v. Willis, 593 F.2d 247 (6th Cir.1979), the court held that it was commercially unreasonable in the circumstances of that case to hold a public rather than a private sale. The court stressed that a public sale is not inherently reasonable. The secured creditor had received private offers that were four times higher than the sum the auctioneer hired to conduct a public sale estimated the goods would bring. Article Nine does not define public and private sales. It is evident, though, that the Code drafters viewed a public sale as a sale open to the general public (or a segment thereof) and which is so advertised. By contrast, a private sale is not open to the general public and does not call for general advertisement. The Code explicitly attaches several consequences to the private-public sale distinction. First, UCC 9–504(3) provides that notice to the debtor and others in the case of a private sale need only provide reasonable notice of the time after which any private sale is to be made, but such notice in the case of a public sale must give reasonable notice of the time and place thereof. Second, section 9–504(4) says that the rights of a purchaser at a public sale may be somewhat greater than the rights of a purchaser at private sale. Third, section 9–504(3) allows the secured creditor to buy at a public sale but not at a private sale (except in special circumstances).

Comment 6 to 9–504 makes clear that "the policy adopted * * * [is] to encourage disposition by private sale through regular commercial channels." Doubtless such disposition does occur. But it is also now evident that very frequently secured creditors will first hold public sales at which they themselves buy in at or below the amount of the outstanding debt, after which they *then* resell "through regular commercial channels." Why might a secured creditor prefer this route rather than that of going directly to the private outlet in the first place? Should courts be careful to scrutinize such a process of public sale purchase and private resale on the part of the secured creditor?

*B. Was "Notice * * * Sent by the Secured Party to the Debtor"?*

Read UCC 9–504(3) again. Unless excused (under what circumstances?) or renounced by the debtor (how?), a notice "shall be sent by the secured party to the debtor * * *" When other than consumer goods are involved, the notice requirement may also include another secured party.

There are at least four problems lurking here: (1) Who is entitled to notice; (2) What should be the content of the notice; (3) When is the notice "sent;" and (4) What consequences flow from the failure to give a required notice?

CANADIAN COMMUNITY BANK v. ASCHER FINDLEY COMPANY

Court of Appeal, Second District, Division 5, 1991.
229 Cal.App.3d 1139, 280 Cal.Rptr. 521.

GRIGNON, ASSOCIATE JUSTICE.

This appeal is part of a complex web of litigation arising from a limited partnership tax shelter investment gone awry. The limited partners seek to reverse a judgment entered against them pursuant to a jury's general verdict rendered in connection with their agreement to assume certain obligations of the partnership. One of the questions presented in this appeal is whether a creditor's failure to comply with the notice and commercial reasonableness requirements of Commercial Code section 9504 necessarily bars a deficiency judgment against a limited guarantor of a note. We conclude that it does. We also consider the cross-appeal of the primary lender, which seeks reversal of the trial court's order setting aside and vacating the jury's general verdict in its favor and entering a different judgment in favor of the general partner and against the lender. * * *

* * *

Discussion

Appeal By The Limited Partners and The General Partner

California Commercial Code section 9504, subdivision 1, provides that, after default, a secured party may sell, lease, or otherwise dispose of any or all of the collateral securing the indebtedness. Following the disposition of the collateral, the debtor is liable for any deficiency. (*Id.* at subd. 2.) Section 9504 requires that notice of the disposition of the collateral be given to the debtor, and that any such disposition be conducted in a commercially reasonable manner. (*Id.* at subd. 3.) A commercially reasonable disposition is presumed to be in good faith and at the greatest possible market rate. (*Security Pacific National Bank v. Geernaert* (1988) 199 Cal.App.3d 1425, 1431, 245 Cal.Rptr. 712.) The requirements of section 9504 are strictly construed. "If the secured creditor wishes a deficiency judgment he must obey the law. If he does not obey the law, he may not have his deficiency judgment." (*Atlas Thrift Co. v. Horan* (1972) 27 Cal.App.3d 999, 1009, 104 Cal.Rptr. 315.) Failure to comply with either the notice requirement *or* the requirement of commercial reasonableness will act as an absolute bar to a deficiency judgment. (*Crocker National Bank v. Emerald* (1990) 221 Cal. App.3d 852, 270 Cal.Rptr. 699.) The protections of section 9504 may not be waived by a "debtor" prior to default. (Com.Code, § 9501, subd. 3.) Commercial Code section 9507 provides a right of action to recover losses caused by failure of the secured party to comply with section 9504 and defines "commercial reasonableness."

The jury in this matter returned special verdicts finding that: (1) pursuant to section 9504, CCB was required to but did not give notice of the disposition of the Rig to the General and Limited Partners and, further, that the Limited Partners were not estopped to assert such lack of notice; and (2) that the disposition of the Rig was not "commercially reasonable" within the meaning of section 9504.

The Limited Partners contend in this appeal that such special findings should have acted to bar the entry of judgment based on the jury's general verdict against them and for CCB in the amount of $1,771,200. Judgment was entered by the trial court on the general verdict because of the jury's additional special verdict that the General and Limited Partners failed to prove that CCB was obliged to credit the Rig disposition proceeds first against that part of the liability assumed by the Limited Partners under the Assumption Agreements. The trial court believed and instructed the jury [1]

1. The jury was instructed as follows: "... The Defendants and Cross-Complainants, Limited Partners, have the burden of establishing by a preponderance of the evidence all of the facts necessary to prove the following issue: [¶] That Canadian Commercial Bank (CCB) was required to credit money received from selling the drilling rig against the part of the loan assumed by the Limited Partners. [¶] If Plaintiff and Cross-Defendant CCB was required to credit money received from sale of the drilling rig against the part of the loan assumed by the Limited Partners, CCB has the burden of

that noncompliance with section 9504 procedures could be asserted only by a party who, in some way, suffered a loss caused by such noncompliance. If the Rig disposition proceeds were not to be first applied to the assumed portion of the liability, the trial court reasoned, then the amount of the Limited Partners' liability would not be affected by the amount of the disposition proceeds, and no loss would have occurred as a result of the noncompliance.

Are the Limited Partners Entitled to the Protections of Section 9504 as "Debtors"?

Is a guarantor a "debtor"?

CCB contends that a guarantor is not a debtor for purposes of section 9504 and, therefore, is not entitled to the statute's protections. Commercial Code section 9105, subdivision (d), defines a "debtor" as a person "... who owes payment or other performance of the obligation secured, whether or not he or she owns or has rights in the collateral and includes the seller of accounts or chattel paper. Where the debtor and the owner of the collateral are not the same person, 'debtor' means the owner of the collateral in any provision of the division dealing with the collateral, the obligor in any provision dealing with the obligation and may include both where the context so requires." (Com.Code, § 9105, subd. d.)

There is a split of authority among the districts of this Court of Appeal as to whether a guarantor is a "debtor" entitled to the protections of section 9504, and our Supreme Court has yet to consider this issue.[2] In *Rutan v. Summit Sports, Inc.* (1985) 173 Cal.App.3d 965, 219 Cal.Rptr. 381, the Third District, relying on a federal district court case from the Eastern District of Pennsylvania in which California law was applied, held that a guarantor was not a debtor and thus could waive the right to section 9504's notice of sale of collateral prior to default.[3] (*United States v. Kurtz* (E.D.Pa.1981) 525 F.Supp. 734, 745–746 affirmed (3d Cir.1982) 688 F.2d 827.) This reasoning was rejected by this District and the First and Fifth Districts in *Connolly v. Bank of Sonoma County* (1986) 184 Cal.App.3d 1119, 229 Cal.Rptr. 396; *C.I.T. Corp. v. Anwright Corp.* (1987) 191 Cal.App.3d 1420, 237 Cal.Rptr. 108, and

establishing by a preponderance of the evidence the following issues [re: notice, commercial reasonableness, and estoppel to claim lack of notice]." (BAJI 2.60 mod.) The jury was also instructed: "Limited partners are entitled to receive notice of a lender's intended sale or other disposition of a borrower's collateral if they prove that the lender is required to apply the money received from the sale or other disposition against the amount that they owe under the Assumption Agreements." (Instn. No. 103 citing *Brunswick Corp. v. Hays* (1971) 16 Cal.App.3d 134, 93 Cal.Rptr. 635; see *infra* and Com.Code, §§ 9105, subd. (1)(d) and 9507, subd. (1).)

2. One court has refused to apply California law on this issue because of the split in authority. In *American Honda Finance Corp. v. Bennett* (1989) 232 Neb. 21, 439 N.W.2d 459, the Nebraska Supreme Court considered whether the maker of a "continuing personal guaranty" of a security agreement governed by California law was entitled, as a "debtor," to the protections of section 9504. "... California law is unclear on whether a guarantor is entitled to notice. Further, no California court has determined what must be contained in a notice before it is valid." (*Id.* 439 N.W.2d at p. 462.)

3. In this case, under the terms of the Assumption Agreements, the Limited Partners did waive their right to section 9504's notice of sale of collateral prior to default. The protections of section 9504 may not be waived by a "debtor" prior to default. Thus, the determination of whether the Limited Partners are section 9504 debtors is critical to the resolution of the issues on this appeal.

American National Bank v. Perma-Tile Roof Co. (1988) 200 Cal.App.3d 889, 246 Cal.Rptr. 381.

The *Connolly* court surveyed the law of other jurisdictions and concluded that the overwhelming majority of sister-state courts had reached a conclusion opposite to *Rutan.* The *Connolly* court concluded that the notice requirement exists to provide a debtor an opportunity to bid at the sale, to safeguard his right of redemption and to permit him to reduce his liability by all practical means. (*Connolly v. Bank of Sonoma County, supra,* 184 Cal.App.3d at p. 1124, 229 Cal.Rptr. 396.) "Upon default, the guarantor becomes the primary debtor and is liable for any deficiency after sale or performance of other obligation. [Citations.] Accordingly, a guarantor has as much interest in protecting his rights during the sale or disposition of the collateral as does the primary debtor and therefore is equally entitled to notice." (*Ibid.*) *C.I.T. Corp.* endorsed the reasoning of *Connolly,* observing that "[the guarantor's] interest is at least as great as that of the debtor in seeing that a maximum amount is realized upon the sale of collateral." Similarly, the court in *Perma-Tile Roof Co.* also declined to follow *Rutan* and adopted the reasoning of *Connolly* and *C.I.T. Corp.* Recently, the Ninth Circuit Court of Appeals refused to follow *Rutan* in *In re Kirkland* (9th Cir.1990) 915 F.2d 1236, reasoning that as a federal court applying California law, it was "bound by the interpretation adopted by the majority of California appeals courts."

We are persuaded, along with the majority of California appellate courts which have considered this question, that a guarantor is a "debtor" for purposes of section 9504. Like the principal obligor, the guarantor "owes payment or other performance of the obligation secured." (Com.Code, § 9105, subd. d.) Like the principal obligor, the guarantor has an interest in preventing collusive or commercially unreasonable sales of collateral, so as to minimize his liability on the obligation secured. Like the principal obligor, the guarantor requires notice of the disposition so that he may redeem the collateral, or bid at sale, or produce other bidders at sale. We perceive no policy which would argue for differential treatment, generally, of guarantors and principal obligors in this respect.

Should Assumption Agreements Be Treated Differently than Guaranty Agreements?[4]

We also perceive no material differences between the Assumption Agreements at issue here and the guaranty agreements discussed in *Connolly, C.I.T. Corp.* and *Perma-Tile Roof Co.* We note that CCB does not argue that one who assumes a debt is materially different from one who guaranties a debt. In fact, there are only two differences between these types of contracts under California law. First, a guarantor has the right to proceed

4. The argument that the Commercial Code does not apply to the Assumption Agreements, because they do not constitute security instruments, is correct but misses the point. The Loan Agreement, pursuant to which the Rig was disposed *is* an instrument "which [was] intended to create a security interest in personal property." (Com. Code, § 9102(1)(a).) The issue is whether the Limited Partners are entitled, as section 9504 "debtors," under the Loan Agreement to invoke the protections of section 9504. Thus, whether the protections of the Civil Code have been waived or are otherwise not applicable to the Assumption Agreements as suretyship and not security agreements does not resolve the issue whether the Limited Partners, as "debtors," are independently entitled to the protections of the Commercial Code, as they apply to the Loan Agreement.

against his principal obligor for indemnification. (Civ.Code, § 2847.) A guarantor may waive this right. Here, in order to maximize the tax benefits of their investments, the Limited Partners became "obligors of last resort" without any rights against HBDA II, so that their assumed liability would be considered "at risk" and, therefore, tax deductible. Second, guarantors are also entitled to insist that the secured party proceed first against the collateral and/or the principal obligor before enforcing the guaranty. (Civ. Code, §§ 2845 and 2849.) A guarantor may also waive this right. Here, all such rights were waived by the Limited Partners in the Assumption Agreements, rendering them the primary obligors upon HBDA II's default. Thus, the Limited Partners' liability in this case was more like that of a primary obligor than a mere guarantor.

Should Limited Guaranties Be Treated Differently than Full Guaranties?

CCB contends that even if unlimited unconditional guarantors are entitled to section 9504 protection, limited guarantors should be protected only to the extent they can show a loss. CCB argues that the agreements at issue in *Rutan, Connolly, C.I.T. Corp.* and *Perma–Tile Roof Co.* were unlimited unconditional guaranties of the obligations of the principal and, therefore, not applicable to the limited guaranties involved in this case. They argue further that *Brunswick Corp. v. Hays, supra,* 16 Cal.App.3d 134, 93 Cal.Rptr. 635, on the other hand, involved a limited guaranty and, therefore, should be controlling here.

In *Brunswick,* the defendant had purchased from the plaintiff $239,056 in bowling equipment. The defendant made a $2,000 down payment with the balance owing over 96 months at 6 percent interest. Plaintiff retained a security interest in the bowling equipment. At plaintiff's request, defendant also provided a guaranty agreement which stated: "[n]otwithstanding any other provisions, the total amount of Guarantor's obligation hereunder shall be limited to the first four years' payments on the order contract totaling $118,528.16." (*Brunswick Corp. v. Hays, supra,* 16 Cal.App.3d at p. 136, 93 Cal.Rptr. 635.) Following default on the sales contract by defendant, plaintiff repossessed and sold the equipment at private sale for $147,000. Defendant refused to pay the deficiency of $90,056, contending that the disposition proceeds exceeded the guaranty amount and exonerated him from further payment.

The Court of Appeal disagreed, noting that the terms of the guaranty agreement constituted a waiver of defendant's right to insist, pursuant to Civil Code sections 2845 and 2849, that plaintiff give defendant the benefit of all security held and, thus, plaintiff's resort to the collateral did not constitute an exoneration of the principal obligation. The protections of the Civil Code pertaining to surety contracts may be waived. (*Wiener v. Van Winkle* (1969) 273 Cal.App.2d 774, 78 Cal.Rptr. 761.) The court held: "We conclude that in the absence of a specific provision to the contrary in the contract of guaranty, proceeds from the sale of the equipment could only be applied to exonerate the limited guaranty to the extent that the proceeds of the sale exceeded the amount of that portion of the original debt not covered by the limited guaranty." (*Brunswick Corp. v. Hays, supra,* 16 Cal.App.3d at p. 139, 93 Cal.Rptr. 635.) In other words, proceeds from the sale of the collateral would first be applied to the unguaranteed portion of the debt before reducing the guaranteed portion.

CCB argues that *Connolly, C.I.T. Corp.,* and *Perma–Tile Roof Co.* do not apply to the instant case, because the agreements at issue in those cases were unconditional guaranties of the entire amount of the principal obligation. In those instances, CCB contends, the debtor truly does have as much interest in the proper disposition of the collateral as does the principal obligor, as a higher price at sale will result in a dollar-for-dollar reduction in the liability of the guarantor. In this case, the Assumption Agreements operated as limited guaranties of the principal obligation, much like the agreement in *Brunswick.*

Brunswick is not controlling. *Brunswick* deals with the issue of exoneration of the principal debt and whether the disposition proceeds should be applied so as to effect an exoneration. The Commercial Code provisions at issue here were not even discussed in *Brunswick* because the defendant did not "attack the regularity of the sale." (*Brunswick Corp. v. Hays, supra,* 16 Cal.App.3d at p. 137, 93 Cal.Rptr. 635.) Thus, the most one could conclude from *Brunswick* 's application to the instant case is that the Rig disposition proceeds should first be applied to the unassumed portion of the Loan Agreement obligation, since there was no specific provision to the contrary in the Assumption Agreements. *Brunswick* simply does not answer the question whether a limited guarantor is entitled to a section 9504 notice and a duty of commercial reasonableness, if the disposition proceeds are applied first to the unguaranteed portion of liability.

CCB asks us to apply a gloss to *Brunswick,* constructed from the peculiar arithmetic of the transaction at issue in this matter.[5] CCB argues that the liability on the Rig exceeded $4 million, and the highest estimate offered at trial of the Rig's value was its insured value of $900,000 (with all other estimates in the $150,000 to $300,000 range). Therefore, the Rig's disposition could not have affected the Limited Partners' assumed liability of $1.7 million, since the unassumed portion of the liability, to which the proceeds were to be applied first, was approximately $2.3 million. This, they contend, distinguishes all other California cases which hold that guarantors are "debtors" under section 9504. We find this contention unpersuasive.

In many instances, a limited guaranty may nearly equal the total principal obligation. Surely a 90 percent guarantor has virtually the same interest in proper disposition of collateral as does the principal obligor. Additionally, if the value of the collateral is high enough, its disposition will affect the amount of the liability flowing from even a very small limited guaranty. In this case, if the Rig had held its construction value of $4 million, the manner of its disposition would have been of critical consequence to the Limited Partners. The interplay between the amount of the debt and the percentage of the debt guaranteed, as well as the market value of the collateral, is what will determine whether a limited guarantor will be adversely affected by a secured creditor's improper disposition of the collat-

5. The application of section 9504's strict requirements unquestionably works a harsh result in this case, because of the disparity between the value of the collateral and the debt. This is not a unique situation. See the similarly harsh result in *In re Kirkland, supra,* 915 F.2d 1236, where the line of credit involved $1,450,000, and a portion of the collateral was disposed of, without notice, for $59,000.

eral. Thus, we cannot say, as a general rule, that limited guarantors suffer no loss from noncompliance with section 9504. Furthermore, we cannot, by this decision, fashion a workable rule which protects some limited guarantors and not others. That is a job best left to our Legislature, should it be so inclined.

CCB urges this Court to recognize, *post facto,* that the fair market value of the Rig, even if obtained by sale, would not have relieved the Limited Partners from their liability on the Assumption Agreements. However, since the purpose of both the Uniform and California Commercial Codes is to create predictability and stability in the marketplace, it must provide rules which operate clearly and *prospectively.* One can imagine many situations, like the instant one, where, prior to sale, creditors, principal obligors, and debtors disagree as to the value of the collateral and therefore as to whether the guarantors, for example, will incur a loss if the collateral is disposed of improperly without notice. Such an ad hoc solution would invite unnecessary litigation. The alternative is to enforce section 9504's protections in all limited guarantee situations. We note that the requirements of that section are not burdensome and their uniform application works no hardship on secured creditors.[6]

Thus, we hold that limited guarantors are entitled to the protections of section 9504, including the absolute bar to a deficiency judgment upon noncompliance. The Limited Partners need not prove a "loss" from the Rig disposition in order to invoke the protections of section 9504. Whether they would be required to prove a "loss" in order to bring a cause of action for damages against CCB under section 9507 is irrelevant, since such proof has never been required by California courts with respect to section 9504.

In view of the foregoing, we find that the trial court's refusal to vacate the judgment and enter a new judgment in favor of the Limited Partners, based on the jury's special findings regarding lack of notice and commercial reasonableness under section 9504 was error, since the judgment as entered was not "consistent with or supported by the special verdict[s]". (Code Civ.Proc., § 663.) (See Discussion, *infra,* regarding the sufficiency of the evidence supporting those findings.) The jury's special verdict that the Limited Partners did not suffer a "loss" from the improper disposition of the Rig has no effect on CCB's noncompliance with section 9504 which constitutes an absolute bar to CCB's deficiency judgment against the Limited Partners. Because we reverse the general verdict against the Limited Partners, we need not address whether the verdict in favor of the General Partner acts to limit the liability of the Limited Partners, whether prejudgment interest was properly computed, or whether CCB was properly awarded attorney's fees and costs.

6. A similar argument—that section 9507 (damages for "loss") constitutes the exclusive remedy for noncompliance with section 9504—was raised and rejected in the context of principal obligors. Principal obligors simply need not prove a "loss" from noncompliance with section 9504 in order to invoke that section's absolute bar for noncomplying dispositions. (*Atlas Thrift v. Horan, supra,* 27 Cal.App.3d at p. 999, 104 Cal.Rptr. 315.) For the reasons stated, we see no reason to fashion a different rule for guarantors.

Cross-appeal By CCB

Sufficiency of the Evidence to Support the Special Findings re: Compliance with Section 9504

As noted above, the jury in this matter rendered a general verdict against the Limited Partners and in favor of CCB in the amount of $1,771,200. The jury also returned a general verdict in favor of CCB and against the General Partner in the amount of $1,168,686. The trial court entered judgment in favor of the General Partner in view of the special verdicts finding that CCB's disposition of its collateral had not been commercially reasonable, and that CCB had not complied with the notice provisions of section 9504 of the Commercial Code with respect to both the Limited Partners and the General Partner. CCB appeals from this order, contending that substantial evidence does not exist to support the special findings at issue. Because we have reversed the trial court's order denying the motion of the Limited Partners to vacate the judgment and enter a new judgment, we will address this issue as it now affects both verdicts against CCB.

In reviewing the sufficiency of evidence on appeal, all conflicts must be resolved in favor of the respondent, and all legitimate and reasonable inferences indulged to uphold the verdict, if possible. (*Crawford v. Southern Pacific Co.* (1935) 3 Cal.2d 427, 429, 45 P.2d 183.) Our power begins and ends with the determination as to whether there is *any* substantial evidence, contradicted or uncontradicted, which will support the conclusion reached by the jury. (*Ibid.*) We have no power to weigh the evidence, to consider the credibility of the witnesses, or to resolve conflicts in the evidence or in the reasonable inferences that may be drawn therefrom. (*Overton v. Vita–Food Corp.* (1949) 94 Cal.App.2d 367, 370, 210 P.2d 757.)

Substantial evidence unquestionably exists to support the special findings regarding notice and commercial reasonableness.[7] First, CCB concedes that the Settlement Agreement by which the Rig was leased to MDC was drafted in April and executed perhaps as late as May 1987, without notice to the General Partner or the Limited Partners. CCB argues that the option to purchase the Rig was not executed by MDC until December of that year, more than two months after a copy of the Settlement Agreement was delivered to counsel for the Limited Partners and the General Partner, and that the Rig was not "disposed" of until the option was exercised, consideration of $175,000 paid, and the bill of sale delivered. We disagree.

Section 9504, subdivision 1, expressly refers to the sale, *lease* or other disposition of collateral. Section 9504, subdivision 3, also refers to the sale or *lease* of collateral. "Subsection (1) does not restrict disposition to sale: the collateral may be sold, leased or otherwise disposed of...." (U.Com. Code com. to Com.Code, § 9504, 23C West's Ann.Cal.Code (1990 ed.); emphasis added.) Whether the Rig was sold upon MDC's exercise of its option following notice to the Limited Partners and the General Partner is irrelevant if the Partners were not given notice of the lease, which is plainly considered a "disposition" within the meaning of section 9504. The Settlement Agreement itself refers to the "Disposition" of the Rig. We conclude,

7. It appears from the record that any claim of ambiguity in these special verdicts has not been properly preserved for appeal. (*Nanny v. Ruby Lighting Corp.* (1952) 108 Cal.App.2d 856, 859, 239 P.2d 885.)

therefore, that substantial evidence exists to support the jury's special verdict that notice of the disposition of the collateral was not given.

We also find that substantial evidence exists to support the jury's special verdict that the disposition was not commercially reasonable, within the meaning of section 9504.[8] Evidence was adduced at trial which indicated that the Rig was sold at a below-market rate to the company whose wholly-owned subsidiary held a security interest in the Rig. The jury may have inferred from the Rig's construction cost of over $4 million (not including profit of $836,000) that the disposition price of $175,000 was substantially below market, despite adverse conditions in the oil drilling industry. Additionally, testimony was offered that the Rig had an insured value of $900,-000. One witness testified that he inquired of CCB about purchasing the Rig, and claimed to have mentioned a possible price of $300,000. Two witnesses testified that their inquiries regarding purchase of the Rig were rebuffed by CCB, which stated that the Rig could not be sold because of "legal problems." Finally, the jury may have inferred from the secrecy which surrounded the settlement negotiations and the fact that the Limited Partners and the General Partner learned of the Settlement Agreement only through formal discovery that the arrangement was a collusive one.

CCB offered expert and other testimony to establish that $175,000 was a commercially reasonable price for the Rig. CCB also offered testimony that the Rig was insured for an amount in excess of its market value because of the possibility of multiple partial losses, which was done with all MDC rigs. CCB also offered testimony to the effect that the comments regarding "legal problems" were harmless references to the bankruptcy court stay in effect rather than part of a collusive arrangement with MEC and MDC. The jury may, however, have disbelieved all of the evidence offered by CCB. Whether the evidence, which was believed by the jury and relied upon in arriving at the special verdicts at issue, was contradicted by CCB is immaterial.

DISPOSITION

The judgment in favor of CCB and against the Limited Partners is reversed. The trial court is ordered to vacate its order denying the motion to vacate the judgment and to enter a new order granting the motion, setting aside and vacating the judgment against the Limited Partners and in favor of CCB, and ordering entry of a new and different judgment in favor of the Limited Partners and against CCB. The judgment in favor of the General Partner and against CCB is affirmed. The order denying attorney's fees and costs to MEC is affirmed. The Limited Partners and the General Partner shall recover their costs on appeal. [Some footnotes omitted and renumbered—Eds]

ASHBY, ACTING P.J., and BOREN, J., concur.

Problem 6–6

On July 1, Bank lent Dobbs, the owner of a small business, $10,000 and perfected a security interest in equipment. Before the loan was made, however,

8. CCB does not contend that, and so we do not address whether, the granting of the motion for relief from stay by the bankruptcy court constitutes approval of the disposition in "any judicial proceeding" within the meaning of section 9507 and therefore establishes conclusively the commercial reasonableness of the disposition.

Bank insisted that Alice, Dobb's wealthy sister, sign the note as a guarantor. At that time, Alice signed a writing renouncing any right to notice under UCC 9–504(3) should Dobbs default and Bank enforce the security interest. At no time did Alice have any interest in Dobb's business.

On August 1, Finance Company lent Dobbs $5,000 and perfected a security interest in the equipment. On September 1, Dobbs defaulted and Bank repossessed the equipment. On September 5, Finance Company sent Bank a written notice that it claimed an interest in the collateral. Bank proposes to dispose of the equipment at a private sale. To whom should it send notice?

LEASING ASSOCIATES INC. v. SLAUGHTER & SON, INC.

United States Court of Appeals, Eighth Circuit, 1971.
450 F.2d 174.

MATTHES, CHIEF JUDGE.

Negotiations between Leasing Associates, Inc., a Texas corporation, hereinafter referred to as plaintiff, and Slaughter & Son, Inc., an Arkansas corporation, and F.E. Slaughter, as guarantor, hereinafter sometimes referred to as defendants, culminated in the execution of a leasing agreement dated May 10, 1967. Under the terms of the lease, Slaughter obligated itself to make certain payments to plaintiff and F.E. Slaughter guaranteed payment of all sums due under the instrument. Slaughter, as lessee under the agreement, took possession of a 1967 Chevrolet truck and a 1964 GMC Barco Log Loader.

A controversy developed between plaintiff and defendants over the fitness of the Chevrolet truck. Defendants repeatedly complained that the truck was defective and not fit for its intended use in hauling logs. Eventually, they discontinued making payments due under the lease. They returned the truck to plaintiff and thereafter, pursuant to proper notice from plaintiff to the defendants, the truck was sold by plaintiff.

The complaint in this action was filed on October 21, 1968 in the United States District Court for the Western District of Arkansas. Plaintiff sought a judgment for $10,001.42, representing the accrued and unpaid rent due on the truck, the amount expended by plaintiff for repairs, and the deficiency after giving credit for proceeds of sale. Defendants, on October 10, 1969, answered and counterclaimed for damages allegedly sustained because of the unfitness of the truck.

Defendants also defaulted in payments due on the log loader. In June, 1969, possession of that equipment was taken from defendants in a replevin proceeding filed in an Arkansas state court. The plaintiff obtained possession of the log loader on June 11, 1969. Pursuant to a notice to the defendants, the reasonableness of which is an issue on appeal, the log loader was sold for $500 on or about October 16, 1969.

On August 31, 1970, nearly two years after the filing of the original complaint, plaintiff filed its first amended complaint to recover, in addition to the amount allegedly due on the truck transaction, the amount it claimed to be due on the log loader transaction.

A jury trial resulted in a verdict in favor of plaintiff and against both defendants for $18,508.73, being the full amount prayed for.

* * *

II

Defendants' second point relates to that part of the judgment for $8,507.31, the amount due on the Barco log loader. Specifically, defendants' contention is that the court erred in admitting into evidence over their objection an exhibit purported to be a copy of a letter dated October 6, 1969, claimed to have been sent by plaintiff's credit manager to "Mr. F.E. Slaughter, F.E. Slaughter & Sons., Inc., Junction City, Arkansas." The argument is advanced that the proper foundation was not laid for admission of the exhibit, i.e., that evidence was insufficient to support a finding that the original of the letter had been sent to the above-named addressee via the United States mails.

Before we review the factual foundation bearing upon this question, we turn to the applicable provisions of the Uniform Commercial Code, as adopted in Arkansas, and case law pertinent to the issue. * * *

* * *

The sanction which makes the foregoing requirement [commercial reasonableness] viable is a rebuttable presumption that the value of any collateral sold without notice is equal to the debt. Therefore, as a prerequisite to the recovery of a deficiency judgment in Arkansas, the secured party has the burden of proving either the actual value of the collateral at the time of its sale after repossession, or proving that reasonable notice was sent (receipt need not be proven). * * *

In the present case, however, the plaintiff offered no proof that the $500 realized from the sale of the log loader was the fair and reasonable market value of that equipment. Therefore, if plaintiff failed to discharge its burden of proving that it gave reasonable notice as required it would be precluded from recovering the deficiency under attack.

There are two prongs to the notice question: (1) whether the mailing of a notice through regular mail channels will suffice to support a finding that reasonable notice was sent to the debtor; (2) whether the evidence here was sufficient to show as implicitly found by the jury that the letter of October 6 was in fact mailed.

Turning to the first of these, the Arkansas Supreme Court has been confronted with the identical question, that is, whether a notice in the form of a letter sent by regular United States mail was "reasonable notification," as required by Ark.Stat.Ann. § 85–9–504, supra. In reversing the trial judge, who had ruled that the letter constituted reasonable notice as a matter of law, the Supreme Court held that the evidence was sufficient to present a question of fact for the jury to resolve. Baber v. Williams Ford Co., 239 Ark. 1054, 396 S.W.2d 302 (1965). Thus, it appears that the *Baber* case definitely resolves the first phase of the notice issue in favor of the plaintiff.

We turn then to the more troublesome problem of whether the evidence was sufficient to say that the letter of October 6, 1969 was sent by placing the same in the mails. On this question, the evidence is sketchy and far from satisfactory.

The notice issue first entered the case near the end of the trial. Larry Slaughter, son of F.E. Slaughter, when asked on cross-examination by plaintiff's counsel whether he had received the letter of October 9, replied:

"Not that I can remember.

"Q. You have any knowledge of anyone in your company receiving this letter?

"A. Well, I don't know it if they did."

The foregoing is the only evidence pertaining to the receipt of the letter. F.E. Slaughter, to whom the letter was addressed, and who testified, was not interrogated as to receipt by him of the notice.

Following Larry Slaughter's testimony, plaintiff's counsel, apparently realizing plaintiff had the burden of proving that the notice had been sent, called Ernest M. Dillinger as a rebuttal witness.

The substance of this witness' testimony was that Exhibit 11 was a copy of the letter which he had written to Slaughter & Son, and that it was sent by regular mail. On cross-examination, Dillinger stated that he dictated the letter to his secretary, "she gave it to me for my signature and it went out in the normal course of business in my office as all mail does each day."

"Q. You assumed, then, that it went out? A. Yes, I assumed that it went out * * * I cannot prove it ever got inside the mailbox. All I can say is that it went out of our office in the normal course of business.

"Q. You assumed that it did? A. That's right.

"Q. You don't know whether it ever got past your secretary's desk, do you? A. Yes, it came back for my signature, I put it in my out box for the mail clerk to pick up and mail."

Whether the foregoing meager statements were of such qualitative nature as to provide an adequate foundation for admission into evidence of the carbon copy and the implicit finding by the jury that the original of the letter was actually mailed is, of course, governed by Arkansas law. The question brings into play reliance upon office custom or practice in mailing to show "reasonable notification." Our attention has not been directed to any Arkansas case and independent research has disclosed none that has specifically decided the circumstances in which such custom and practice can support a finding that a particular letter was mailed.

The most analogous Arkansas case is Dengler v. Dengler, 196 Ark. 913, 120 S.W.2d 340 (1938). There the evidentiary problem was whether defendant's testimony that she personally mailed a particular letter was sufficiently precise to warrant a presumption that the letter was received. Of importance here is the fact that the tenor of the Arkansas court's approach to the problem was cautiously to require clear proof of all the facts of a proper mailing, i.e., proper stamping, addressing and posting. Moreover, the Arkansas court's view of this type of evidence is clearly matched by its zealous protection of the debtor under Ark.Stat. § 85–9–504(3) in *Barker* and

Norton, supra. We therefore are constrained to approach this question with the narrow view of *Dengler,* that "the technicalities that make for justice may not be casually disregarded." 120 S.W.2d at 345.

As shown by *Annotations,* 25 A.L.R. 9, 13, supplemented at 85 A.L.R. 541, 544, and 30 Am.Jur.2d Evidence § 1119, the weight of authority holds the evidence here presented to be insufficient due to the failure to call the mailclerk to verify either that he mailed this particular letter or at least that it was his custom to mail such letters. Thus if Arkansas were to adopt the "majority rule," reversal would here be required. Conversely, it may be that the Arkansas court would share, as we do, Professor McCormick's view that testimony of the mailclerk would only be cumulative since, considering the modern volume of corporate correspondence, he could not be expected to remember posting a particular letter or emptying the mail tray on a particular day and probably could only reiterate the executive's description of the office practice. McCormick on Evidence, § 162, p. 343 n. 13 (1954). However, even if Arkansas law were in accord with the "minority view," a jury finding that clerical personnel performed their duties in properly posting the mail would be permissible only if there were clear testimony by the executive as to the customary practice in his office and his actions in compliance therewith. The problem in this case, however, is that plaintiff's sole witness on this point, Dillinger, proffered no description of the office practice from which a jury properly could determine whether his actions were in accord with it. He gave no indication as to who customarily did such basic acts as addressing, sealing, and stamping the envelopes and whether he could verify that he and his secretary had done such of those as was their customary duty before he signed the letter and placed it in the tray on his desk. His conclusory statement that "it went out in the normal course of business in my office as all mail does each day" is simply not enough. "The essential elementary facts may be shown by course of business properly proved, but an offer of [such] proof * * * must be directed to facts and not mere conclusions * * *." * * * While the plaintiff may "show the essential facts constituting transmission by mail by showing the course of business, it failed because there is no evidence in the record as to what this office routine may have been." * * * "That may be rather technical but the appellee relies upon a presumption which does not arise, unless the evidence itself discloses" the basic facts underlying it. * * *

Accordingly, whichever view Arkansas might be deemed to follow, we are constrained to hold that the evidence was not adequate to support the requisite jury finding that notification was placed in the United States mail.

In summary, we affirm the judgment of $10,001.42 as the deficiency due on the truck transaction. The remainder of the judgment, $8,507.31, is vacated and the claim for the balance due on the Barco Log Loader is remanded to the district court for another trial. One-half of the costs of printing the appendix and briefs shall be taxed against the plaintiff and one-half against the defendants.

STEPHENSON, CIRCUIT JUDGE concurring, with whom CHIEF JUDGE MATTHES and JUDGE BRIGHT join.

In concurring I add the comment that the issue here, which has occupied the busy time of the trial court and this court, should have been disposed of by the parties prior to trial through routine discovery and at the very latest during pretrial. [Footnotes omitted.]

Notes

The foregoing case illustrates a problem too often overlooked in law school, namely how does one prove his case in court; what specifically must he introduce into evidence; what questions must he ask of a witness, and what must the witness say? The creditor can fail to prove his case for a variety of reasons. In the first place, the secured party may have done everything correctly yet be unable to prove that because he has kept incomplete records or has destroyed the records. Secondly, even if the records are available, counsel for the secured party can bungle their introduction and so lose the case.

Each student should ask the following questions:

1. What pieces of documentary evidence should I introduce into evidence? (Security agreement? Notice? Copy of notice? Bill of Sale?)

2. What foundation must I lay for the documentary evidence and what witnesses can provide that foundation? (Will the credit manager be able to handle the entire thing or must I call the office manager?)

3. What witnesses must say what things to prove the necessary elements? (Need I call the repossessor? Or the Credit Manager?)

MALLICOAT v. VOLUNTEER FINANCE & LOAN CORP.

Tennessee Court of Appeals, 1966.
57 Tenn.App. 106, 415 S.W.2d 347.

McAmis, P.J. [What follows is merely an extract from the opinion.] After providing generally that the method, manner, time, place and terms of disposing of the collateral shall be 'commercially reasonable' the Act expressly requires that reasonable notification of the time and place of any public sale or reasonable notification of the time after which any private sale or other intended disposition is to be made shall be sent by the secured party to the debtor.

The requirement that the property be disposed of in a "commercially reasonable" manner seems to us to signify that the disposition shall be made in keeping with prevailing trade practices among reputable and responsible business and commercial enterprises engaged in the same or a similar business. It is general in scope and effect and is not mutually exclusive of the express requirement that notice of the intended disposition, whether by public or private sale, be sent to the debtor. The purpose of this notice, without doubt, is to enable the debtor to protect his interest in the property by paying the debt, finding a buyer or being present at the sale to bid on the property or have others do so, to the end that it be not sacrificed by a sale at less than its true value. Compare Range Motor Co. v. Tipton, 161 Tenn. 427, 33 S.W.2d 75, a suit under the Conditional Sales Statute.

In view of the undisputed proof in this case that the debtor did not receive the notice and that the secured creditor was aware that he had not received it, it is our opinion the creditor not only failed to show a compliance with the Act but that the record affirmatively shows a lack of compliance and a conscious disregard of the debtor's right to notice. The property was not perishable. The debtor lived in Knoxville where the creditor had its place of business and sold the property. In addition, the creditor had information as to where the debtor was employed and where his parents lived. Yet, the sale was allowed to proceed without any further effort to comply with the notice requirement.

In commenting on this provision of the Commercial Code, it is said at p. 788, 15 Am.Jur.2d, Commercial Code, Section 84:

> "Unless collateral is perishable or threatens to decline speedily in value or is of a type customarily sold on a recognized market, reasonable notification of the time and place of any public sale or reasonable notification of the time after which any private or other intended disposition is to be made shall be sent to the debtor. * * *"

The Act, T.C.A. § 47-1-201(26) reads:

> "A person 'notifies' or 'gives' a notice or notification to another by taking such steps as may be reasonably required to inform the other in ordinary course whether or not such other actually comes to know of it. * * *"

Under this provision of the Act, the Supreme Court of Arkansas held in Hudspeth Motors, Inc. v. Wilkinson, 382 S.W.2d 191 that a public sale of the property would not be invalidated because the debtor failed to receive the notice sent by mail until after the sale. This case is urged upon us in this case as supporting the judgment. We consider it inapposite, however, since the creditor in that case was unaware of the failure of the debtor to receive the notice in time. If interpreted as holding valid a sale where the creditor proceeds to sell the property knowing the debtor had never received the notice we would not be disposed to follow it.

The requirement of notice is for the benefit and protection of the debtor. This provision of the Act should be construed and applied in a manner to effectuate this salutary purpose and in the light of Tennessee law.

In Burden v. Burden, 44 Tenn.App. 312, 313 S.W.2d 566, it was said:

> "Notice which is a mere gesture is not notice. The means employed must be such as one desirous of actually informing the absent party might reasonably adopt. Mullane v. Central Hanover Bank & Trust Co., 339 U.S. 306, 70 S.Ct. 652, 94 L.Ed. 865."

* * *

Note: Effect of Secured Party's Failure to Comply With Article 9, Part 5 on Right to Deficiency

Assume that, after default, Secured Party has repossessed and disposed of the collateral. Secured Party applies the proceeds as directed in UCC 9-504(1) and brings suit to recover a deficiency as authorized by UCC 9-504(2). Debtor claims and is able to establish that the disposition was defective under UCC 9-504(3). No notice was sent and the manner of the resale was commercially unreasonable. It is probable that if the disposition had been proper, the amount of deficiency would have been reduced by 25%. Debtor, however, argues that compliance with UCC 9-504(3) should be a condition precedent to Secured Party's right to a deficiency. He asserts that the failure to give notice deprived Debtor of an opportunity to redeem the collateral under UCC 9-506 and that the commercially unreasonable resale so complicates the proof issue on damages that it would be unfair to require Debtor to prove loss under UCC 9–507(1). How should this argument be treated in commercial default cases?

Three views have emerged in the cases. The first, a pro-creditor position, follows the literal language of UCC 9–507(1): The secured party may recover the deficiency subject to a setoff for damages caused by the defective resale. The burden is on the Debtor to prove these damages. The second, a pro-debtor position, concludes that compliance with UCC 9–504(3) is a condition precedent to recovering a deficiency. This result is most likely to be reached when the defect is a failure of notice. The third, a compromise, holds that if a defective disposition has been established by Debtor, the value of the collateral is presumed to equal the outstanding debt unless Secured Party proves otherwise. This proof-shifting device forces Secured Party to show that the defect did not reduce the proceeds that could have been obtained if UCC 9–504(3) has been followed.

As this is written, the Study Committee for revision of Article 9 has proposed the codification of the rebuttable presumption theory. If this is ultimately incorporated in a revised Article 9, the secured creditor will have to prove the actual value that could have been realized on a commercially reasonable sale to recover as a deficiency the difference between the amount of the debt and this hypothetical recovery. At least two of us would have gone farther and would have put the burden of proof on the debtor to show any loss.

The newly promulgated revisions of Article 3 deal with the "guarantor as debtor." Revised subsections 3–605(g) and (i) appear to be in conflict with UCC 9–501(3) to the extent that the latter provision bars a debtor from waiving the requirements of UCC 9–504. Revised 3–605(g) and (i) read in full as follows:

> (g) Under subsection (e) or (f), impairing value of an interest in collateral includes (i) failure to obtain or maintain perfection or recordation of the interest in collateral, (ii) release of collateral without substitution of collateral of equal value, (iii) failure to perform a duty to preserve the value of collateral owed, under Article 9 or other law, to a debtor or surety or other person secondarily liable, or (iv) failure to comply with applicable law in disposing of collateral.
>
> * * *
>
> (i) A party is not discharged under this section if (i) the party asserting discharge consents to the event or conduct that is the basis of the discharge, or (ii) the instrument or a separate agreement of the party provides for waiver of discharge under this section either specifically or by general language indicating that parties waive defenses based on suretyship or impairment of collateral.

Note that subsection (i) explicitly authorizes a guarantor to consent either "specifically or by general language" to certain acts of the creditor. Among the acts under (g)(ii) is the "failure to perform a duty to preserve the value of the collateral" owed under Article 9 or other law or "failure to comply with applicable law in disposing of collateral." Thus, Section 3–605 seems to tell the guarantor and the creditor whose debt is guaranteed that the guarantor can waive a discharge that he might otherwise enjoy because the creditor "impaired the collateral" by failing to do a commercially reasonable resale, yet Section 9–501 seems to say that the debtor may not waive such rights. Which rule governs?

One escape would be to say that a guarantor is not a debtor for the purpose of part 5 of Article 9. The courts have rejected that argument.

Another is to treat the guarantor as a "debtor" asserting rights under UCC 9–504 and 9–507 and not a guarantor asserting rights to discharge under UCC 3–605. That interpretation would undermine the rights granted to a creditor who has a waiver under UCC 3–605(i). We do not have an answer to this conundrum, do you?

C. Was the Public Disposition Commercially Reasonable?

Assuming that the secured party's decision to conduct a public sale was commercially reasonable, when is the method by which that sale is conducted commercially reasonable?

SAVAGE CONSTRUCTION, INC. v. CHALLENGE–COOK BROS., INC.

Supreme Court of Nevada, 1986.
102 Nev. 34, 714 P.2d 573.

PER CURIAM:

FACTUAL AND PROCEDURAL BACKGROUND

In the spring of 1979, Challenge-Cook Bros., Inc. (Challenge-Cook) entered into negotiations with Savage Construction, Inc. (Savage) and John Tom Ross (Ross) for the purchase and sale of four cement mixers. These negotiations led to the contract purchase, by Savage, of the cement mixers. The installment contract provided that it should be interpreted under California law, which brings the contract under the California version of the Uniform Commercial Code. After the installment payments became delinquent, Challenge-Cook peacefully repossessed the equipment in September of 1981. Challenge-Cook then caused the publication of notice of a public sale, to be held October 15, 1981, in San Leandro, California, in three publications; October 4th, 11th and 14th in the Nevada Appeal, once on October 5th in the Inter-City Express and once October 9th in the Daily Pacific Builder. Challenge-Cook, the only bidder at the public sale, purchased the equipment for the amount of their own in-house appraisal of $39,500 per cement mixer. Within two weeks after the auction, Challenge-Cook sold two of the cement mixers for a combined cash price of $99,000, plus tax, and the other two cement mixers for a total of $94,000, plus tax, on a conditional sales contract. The record indicates that the source of at least one of these purchases was negotiating with Challenge-Cook before the auction regarding a retail purchase of the equipment; however, Challenge-Cook did not notify that potential purchase of the upcoming auction.

Challenge-Cook filed suit to recover a deficiency judgment. The case was tried to the court, which found Savage and Ross liable for the deficiency but, nevertheless, credited Savage and Ross with the price received by Challenge-Cook in its retail sale of the equipment.

Subsequent to the judgment, Savage and Ross filed a motion to retax and settle costs. This motion was denied. Challenge-Cook also filed a motion to alter or amend judgment. This motion as also denied. This appeal, seeking to set aside the deficiency judgment, followed. The cross appeal by Challenge-Cook requests the recomputation of the amount of the deficiency judgment.

The Appeal

Initially, we note that because the parties intended that California law govern this matter, we have deferred to the law of that jurisdiction.

Appellants first contend that the public auction that occurred after the repossession of the equipment was not "commercially reasonable." We agree. They point to a number of factors that support this position: the quality of the publicity, the price obtained at the auction, the price obtained at a subsequent retail sale that took place within two weeks of the auction, the number of bidders in attendance at the auction, and the respondent's failure to advise known potential purchasers of the scheduled auction. We will examine each of the factors individually.

The law is clear that "[t]he fact that a better price could have been obtained by a sale at a different time or in a different method from that selected by a secured party is not of itself sufficient to establish that the sale was not made in a commercially reasonable manner." Clark Equipment Co. v. Mastelotto, Inc., 87 Cal.App.3d 88, 96, 150 Cal.Rptr. 797 (1978). However, the conditions of the sale must be reasonably calculated to bring the fair market price that is equitable to both the debtor and the secured party. General Elec. Credit Corp. v. Bo-Mar Construction Co., 72 Cal.App.3d 887, 889, 140 Cal.Rptr. 417 (1977). Since a secured creditor is generally in the best position to influence the circumstances of sale, it is reasonable that the creditor has an enhanced responsibility to promote fairness.

The Quality of Publicity

Section 9504(3) of the California Commercial Code requires that "Notice of the time and place of a public sale shall also be given *at least five days before the date of sale* by publication once in a *newspaper of general circulation published in the county in which the sale is to be held.*" (Emphasis added.) In order to meet the requirements of Section 9504(3), Challenge-Cook was required to advertise the sale:

1. at least five days before the sale;
2. in a paper of general circulation; and
3. in a paper published in the county in which the sale is to take place.

The sale in the instant case took place in San Leandro, California. The publications used to meet the legal requirements were the Nevada Appeal, the Inter-City Express and the Daily Pacific Builder. There is no question that the advertisements used were timely. The Nevada Appeal, however, is not published in the county where the sale took place. The record shows that the other two papers were used without knowledge of circulation of readership.

Publicity is intended to encourage competitive bidding. The sources of advertising utilized by Challenge-Cook were notably inefficacious in light of the fact that Challenge-Cook was the only bidder at the auction.

The Price Obtained at the Auction and the Subsequent Retail Sale

A public auction need not bring in the highest possible price. See Clark Equipment Co., supra, 87 Cal.App.3d at 96, 150 Cal.Rptr. 797. However, the conditions of sale must be reasonably calculated to facilitate a sale at fair market value, whether wholesale or retail. See Bo-Mar, supra, 72 Cal. App.3d at 889, 140 Cal.Rptr. 417. So, in the instant case, the price received at the subsequent retail sale, held within two weeks of the auction sale, is an indicator of fair market value of the equipment. See Kobuk Engineering & Contracting Services, Inc. v. Superior Tank & Constr. Co-Alask, Inc., 568 P.2d 1007 (Alaska 1977).

Using the price received at the subsequent retail sales as an indicator of fair price, it is difficult for this court to justify the actions of the district court in computing Ross' and Savage's deficiency judgment. The district court held that the public auction was commercially reasonable. Yet appellants were given credit based on the subsequent retail sale. We find no basis for this in the law. If the public auction was commercially reasonable, it follows that the price received at the earlier sale should have been credited to appellants' remaining indebtedness. If the public auction was not commercially reasonable then, under California law, no deficiency judgment is allowed. See Atlas Thrift Co. v. Horan, 27 Cal.App.3d 999, 104 Cal.Rptr. 315 (1972).

The Number of Bidders in Attendance at the Auction

It is important to advertise a public sale properly in order to provide public notice to a potential buying audience, but the actual goal is to have bidders attend the auction. When no one attends the auction, there are many inferences that may be drawn. The lack of attendance and the purchase of collateral by a secured party does not necessarily indicate improper notice. In fact, the California Commercial Code permits a secured creditor, following repossession, to purchase collateral for himself "provided he acts in a good faith and commercially reasonable manner." Bo-Mar, supra, 72 Cal.App.3d at 889, 140 Cal.Rptr. 417. However, the fact that the same advertising efforts are used for many years and never produced anyone other than the secured party may indicate either a lack of good faith or inadequate and ineffective publication on the part of the secured party.

The Respondent's Failure to Advise Potential Buyers of the Auction

When a sale is being advertised to an open but unknown market, then the normal minimum legal requirements for commercial reasonableness of an auction may be sufficient. But when, as in the instant case, potential buyers are identified and not advised of the auction, then there is a breach of duty by the secured party. See Connex Press, Inc. v. International Airmotive, Inc., 436 F.Supp. 51 (D.C.Dist.Cal.1977).

Conclusion

We have carefully considered all the factors involved in Challenge-Cook's public auction. We have also considered the approach taken by the district court in determining the deficiency assessed against appellants. We conclude that the district court erred when it determined that the auction was commercially reasonable, but that appellants should be credited with the price received by Challenge-Cook from the subsequent retail sale. We also conclude that the respondent's public sale was not commercially reasonable for the reasons previously specified, and in particular, because potential buyers had been identified but were not advised of the upcoming auction sale. Therefore, the judgment of the district court is reversed and the case is remanded to the trial court for entry of judgment in favor of the appellants and a determination of costs and attorney's fees, if any.

Due to our disposition of this appeal, it is unnecessary to address the issue regarding appellant Ross' execution of a personal guaranty. Likewise, there is no need to consider those issues raised on cross-appeal and we make no decision with regard to them.

Notes

1. For another case holding that a public disposition was commercially unreasonable, see Smith v. Daniels, 634 S.W.2d 276, 278–79 (Tenn.App.1982). The court stated:

> Although the Code is careful to point out that a creditor's failure to procure the maximum possible price for collateral does not in and of itself make a sale commercially unreasonable, a sufficient resale price *is* the logical focus of the protection given debtors by these sections. See White & Summers, Uniform Commercial Code, § 26–11, p. 1115 (2d Ed.1980). This court's duty, then, is to determine from all the evidence contained in the record, presuming the chancellor's conclusions to be correct, whether the facts preponderate that appellee took all steps reasonably necessary to insure that the sale of the collateral would bring appellant a fair price.
>
> There are several factors which, taken together, caused this sale to be commercially unreasonable. First, no list was made of the equipment collateral that was repossessed. As a result, no definitive list was available at sale. We feel that it should be a bare minimum in repossession proceedings to keep a detailed and accurate list of exactly what has been reclaimed. Failure to do so creates the potential for all manner of abuses in the repossession process. With no clear record of what was available at sale, potential purchasers were handicapped in making their decisions. For the same reason, it is impossible for this court to adequately review the record and assess commercial reasonableness when we have no way of knowing for sure what was sold. Appellee erred in not making a list, for a simple lack of information directly affected the commercial reasonableness of the sale in this case.
>
> A second factor which materially affected the reasonableness of this sale was the manner in which it was advertised. In Mallicoat v. Volunteer Finance & Loan Corp., 57 Tenn.App. 106, 415 S.W.2d 347 (1966), this court stated that "[t]he requirement that the property be disposed of in a 'commercially reasonable' manner [signifies] that the disposition shall be made in keeping with prevailing trade practices among reputable and responsible business and commercial enterprises engaged in the same or a similar business."
>
> In this case, there is a conflict in testimony concerning the standard practices for sales of amusement equipment between appellee's witness, who is an employee of the general auction company that conducted this sale, and appellant's witness, who is one of the leading dealers in amusement equip-

ment in the state of Tennessee. Appellee's witness has participated in several sales of amusement equipment in his two years with Action Auction Company. This witness did not consider himself an expert in amusement equipment, was not personally familiar with individual types of the equipment, but felt that he could give a fair opinion as to what it was worth.

Appellant's witness is a regular and successful dealer in amusement equipment in the East Tennessee area, is personally familiar with individual types of amusement equipment, and considers himself an expert in the field. Under the authority of Mallicoat, we feel that more weight should be given to the testimony of appellant's witness because he is clearly better able to give information relevant to the prevailing trade practices in this type of business.

Appellant witness' testimony indicates with certainty that this sale was conducted in a commercially unreasonable manner. The sale was advertised twice in the Sevier County News five days and three days before the date of the sale, respectively. Notice was posted at the Sevier County Courthouse. Telephone calls were also made to amusement equipment dealers listed in the Knoxville "yellow pages." Appellant's expert testified that it was the standard practice in sales of this type to advertise in newspapers in each of the states major cities, to advertise in trade magazines, and to circulate flyers to dealers. We do not today specifically endorse or require that these steps be taken. It does, however, appear from this testimony that the specific advertising efforts made for this sale were inadequate to reach persons interested in the sale of this type of equipment and to assure that a reasonable price would be attained at sale. Appellee made inadequate advertising efforts in this case to protect the debtor's interests.

Other factors were present at this sale which contributed to its unreasonableness. The equipment was stored in such a way as to make individual inspection difficult and individual testing impossible. The warehouses had no electric lights or electricity, and the machines were stacked together in such a way that easy access was impossible. Finally, the equipment in this case was sold in bulk rather than individually. Appellant's expert testified that the standard method of sale was by the individual unit. We make no absolute requirement today that such equipment be sold individually, but compounded by the fact that no list of the merchandise was available and inspection was unduly hampered, we must hold that this sale was not commercially reasonable, and reverse the chancellor's finding as being against the preponderance of evidence.

Because appellee failed to conduct a commercially reasonable sale and a deficiency resulted, we must presume that a commercially reasonable sale would have satisfied appellant's debt. Commercial Credit Corp. v. Holt, 17 U.C.C. 316 (Middle Section, Court of Appeals, April 25, 1975). Appellee did not prove at trial before the chancellor by a preponderance of the evidence that the value of the resold collateral was less than the amount due on the note. Therefore, the chancellor's award of the deficiency judgment is reversed. Let all costs be taxed to appellee.

But see In re Zsa Zsa Limited, 352 F.Supp. 665, 671, 672 (S.D.N.Y.1972), affirmed 475 F.2d 1393 (2d Cir.1973), where the district court, in affirming the Referee's order confirming a public sale, stated that "the language of Section 9–507 reveals that the primary focus of commercial reasonableness is not the proceeds received from the sale but rather the procedures employed for the sale. * * *." In addition:

> Close scrutiny satisfies the court that the instant sale meets the requirement of commercial reasonableness, as that standard has developed for sales of collateral under the UCC. The sale herein had the benefit of judicial guidance. While the sale was not made pursuant to a detailed plan of the referee, the hearing before the referee did pass the plans through a judicial filter. When there has been such a hearing all interests have an opportunity to comment upon the arrangement for disposition of the collateral, and this should raise the presumption that the sale is commercially reasonable. Cf. § 9–507(2). Moreover, the conditions of the sale, as modified, were reasonable in terms of notice, manner, place, time, method and terms of sale. The code requires reasonableness; it does not make the secured party an insurer of a hypothetical expected return.

D. *Was the Private Disposition Commercially Reasonable?*

ATLAS CONSTRUCTION CO. v. DRAVO–DOYLE CO.

Court of Common Pleas, Pennsylvania, 1965.
3 UCC Rep.Serv. 124.

McKenna, J.

This case is before us on defendant's motion for judgment n.o.v., or, in the alternative, for a new trial. Also before the court is plaintiff's motion to mold the verdict.

The litigation arose out of a Security Agreement entered into on May 4, 1960, for the sale of a truck crane by defendant, a dealer in construction equipment and machinery, to plaintiff, a construction contractor. Plaintiff instituted suit to recover damages in the amount of $11,993.79 due to defendant's wrongful repossession and resale of the machinery after plaintiff defaulted on the payment of installments under the Security Agreement.

Defendant filed a counterclaim for $3,752.44, the deficiency due after applying the proceeds of the resale of the collateral to the unpaid balance of the Security Agreement.

The case came to trial on October 9, 1964. On October 13, 1964, the jury returned a verdict in favor of plaintiff, Atlas Construction Company in the amount of $10,333.79, and also found in Atlas' favor on the counterclaim.

Facts

As this matter is before us on defendant's motion for judgment n.o.v., the facts as hereinafter set forth appear in a light most favorable to plaintiff, the verdict winner.

On January 25, 1960, the parties entered into a rental contract for one 1959 Model 375 B.T. American Truck Crane. Under the Rental Agreement, plaintiff, lessee, had an option to purchase. On May 4, 1960 plaintiff exercised its option to buy and at that time a Security Agreement was signed. The Agreement called for a total contract price of $39,119.60. A sum of $7,400.00, which had been received as rent, was credited to the purchase price, and a cash down payment of $650.00 was made. The deferred balance, $31,069.60, was payable in twenty equal monthly installments of $1,553.48.

Atlas Construction Company maintained its offices in New Castle, Pennsylvania, and was primarily engaged in steel erection work. It used the truck crane for lifting and moving steel beams and arches. The machine was eleven feet high, weighed approximately 25 tons, and had a 95–foot boom. Though the crane was mounted on a truck and could be driven on the highway, the machine was not licensed as a motor vehicle, and a special state permit was required before it could be moved.

In the fall of 1961, plaintiff construction company, experiencing financial difficulties, defaulted on its payments on the crane. Defendant repossessed and moved it to Pittsburgh. On that occasion, however, the parties were able to agree upon an arrangement for the payment of installments, and the crane was returned to plaintiff.

Atlas again fell behind in its payments, and on February 25, 1962, agents of Dravo-Doyle repossessed the crane a second time. It was moved from Atlas' yard in New Castle to the property of one T. Bruce Campbell in West Middlesex, Pennsylvania, a distance of about ten miles. Plaintiff's President, Eugene Natale, was notified of this action, and was told that the equipment would be stored on Campbell's lot (T 10–11). On the same day a registered letter was sent by Dravo-Doyle to Natale, advising him that the repossessed crane would be disposed of by private sale after March 3, 1962. The registered letter bore the following address:

"Atlas Construction Company

Box 306

1025 Ryan Avenue

New Castle, Pennsylvania." (T 169)

Neither Natale, nor anyone else connected with Atlas received this letter, and on March 7, 1962, it was returned unclaimed to defendant's plant in Pittsburgh. On the same day defendant sent a second notice, by regular mail, to plaintiff. This was addressed to "Atlas Construction Company, 1025 Ryan Avenue, New Castle, Pennsylvania," and was received by Eugene Natale on March 8th. A copy of the registered letter of February 23rd was enclosed, along with a statement that Dravo-Doyle considered this earlier communication to be valid notification of the private sale of the repossessed equipment.

Subsequent to the repossession, defendant sold the crane to T. Bruce Sales Company, West Middlesex, Pennsylvania, a competitor of Atlas. Bruce Campbell, with whom the equipment was stored after repossession, was a principal of T. Bruce Sales Company. The resale price was $19,500.00.

The testimony conflicted as to the date of resale. Defendant produced a formal bill of sale for the crane, dated March 15, 1962. Plaintiff produced several records from defendant's files, however, which indicated that the sale to T. Bruce Sales Company was consummated on March 3rd (T 55, 75–76). Plaintiff also introduced a notation from a record in defendant's files, dated February 23, 1962, which stated that "Bruce Campbell will pay $2,000 down on a rental purchase option." (T 57).

Thomas Natale is the older brother of Eugene, and in 1962 was Vice President of Atlas Construction Company. This witness testified that within two days after the repossession, he contacted one Andrew Marapese, a general contractor, and told him that due to the repossession, Atlas would be willing to sell the truck crane. Marapese replied that he would be interested in buying, and said that he would discuss the matter with his partner, Walter P. Perman. On the afternoon of February 26th or 27th Marapese, Perman and Thomas Natale went to Campbell's lot in West Middlesex for the purpose of inspecting the equipment. When they arrived the crane was not present at the lot (T 39). Other testimony on behalf of the plaintiff indicated that the crane was absent from Campbell's premises at least three times during the period immediately following the repossession (T 106).

Both Marapese and Perman testified at the trial as to the price they were willing to pay for the crane. Marapese stated that they would have paid between $25,000.00 and $28,000.00 for the equipment (T 107), while Perman stated that they were prepared to pay "in the twenty bracket." (T 111).

Thomas Natale testified that he had several conversations with the President of Dravo-Doyle, Charles Hollingsworth, in the period immediately following the repossession. Natale stated that when he told Hollingsworth that he had a prospective purchaser for the crane, the latter replied:

> "* * * all right, Tom, you go ahead and make the preparation on it."

(T 36).

As of the date of repossession, plaintiff had paid a total of $22,663.30 on the crane, including the down payment of $8,050.00. The unpaid balance at that time was $16,456.21. Atlas' account had also been charged with a sum of $1,050.06, representing interest on past installments which had not been paid when due. After repossessing the equipment, defendant charged plaintiff's account with an additional $1,996.17, as expenses of repossession. Thus, the total amount shown on defendant's books as owing by plaintiff was $19,502.44.

Plaintiff filed the complaint in assumpsit on July 9, 1963, alleging that Dravo-Doyle's sale of the crane to Campbell violated the applicable provisions of the Uniform Commercial Code (Act of April 6, 1953, P.L. 3, § 9–101 et seq. as amended; 12A P.S. § 9–101 et seq.). As a result of the improper resale, plaintiff contended that it was deprived of the opportunity to protect its equity in the equipment by selling it to Marapese and Perman.

Plaintiff sought as damages the difference between $16,456.21, the unpaid balance on the contract, and $28,000.00, the amount which it is alleged that Marapese and Perman would have paid for the crane, a sum of $11,543.79. It is also claimed that when Dravo-Doyle repossessed the crane, it took a pick-up truck valued at $450.00, which had not been sold pursuant to the Security Agreement. Thus, Atlas claimed damages of $11,543.79, plus $450.00, or a total sum of $11,993.79.

Dravo-Doyle filed a counterclaim for damages in the amount of $3,752.44. Defendant alleged that when it repossessed the crane, it was unable to regain possession of four boom sections which had been sold pursuant to the Security Agreement. Consequently, when it resold to T.

Bruce Sales, it was obliged to replace these boom sections from its own stock. The value of these boom sections, $3,750.00, was thus deducted from the resale price of $19,500.00, and plaintiff was given credit for the difference of $15,750.00. As noted above, the amount shown as owing on Atlas' account with Dravo-Doyle was $19,502.44. Defendant's counterclaim for $3,752.44 was based on the difference between this amount and the $15,750.00 credit from the resale.

Discussion

1. *Defendant's Motion for Judgment n.o.v.*

Part 5 of Article 9 of the Uniform Commercial Code (12A P.S. § 9–501 et seq.) governs the rights and liabilities of the parties to this case. While recognizing that Dravo-Doyle was entitled to take possession of and to resell the crane upon default, plaintiff asserts that defendant failed to comply with the provisions of Section 9–504(3) of the Code, setting forth the obligations of a secured party in disposing of repossessed collateral. Briefly stated, this section requires that every aspect of the disposition of collateral be "commercially reasonable." This also provides that reasonable notification of the time after which a private sale is to take place must be sent by the secured party to the debtor.

Plaintiff's claim for damages is based upon Section 9–507(1) of the Code, which provides that the debtor has a right to recover from the secured party "any loss caused by a failure to comply with the provisions of this Part."

* * *

[The court held that the secured party had "sent" a proper notice even though it was not received by the debtor.]

Plaintiff also relies upon Section 9–504(3) of the Code and contends that considering all aspects of the disposition to Campbell, the jury could find that it was not carried out in a commercially reasonable manner. Emphasis is placed upon the fact that the resale price of $19,500.00 was substantially lower than the price of between $25,000.00 and $28,000.00 which Mr. Marapese was willing to pay for the crane. From this, it is argued that the resale price was unreasonably low.

In support of this contention, plaintiff introduced a publication known as the Green Guide Handbook, a loose-leaf book containing lists of average prices for new and used construction equipment, and published by the Equipment Guidebook Company (T 30). This book revealed that as of February, 1962, the average sale price for a 1959 Model 375 American Truck Crane was $23,200.00, plus $2,110.00 for booms and equipment, a total value of $25,310.00 (T 95–98).

The average prices listed in this book are competent evidence of value. Plaintiff's President stated (T 30) that the Green Guide is the recognized authority for market values. Charles Hollingsworth, the President of Dravo-Doyle, testified that his company keeps a copy of this book (T 90), and one of its salesmen admitted that he uses it on occasion as an indicator of equipment values (T 131).

In Family Finance Corp. v. Scott, 24 D. & C.2d 587 (1961), Judge Van der Voort of this court held that since the resale price of a repossessed automobile was substantially lower than its "Blue Book" value, a question was presented whether the sale upon repossession was commercially reasonable. The Green Book for construction equipment is comparable to the Blue Book for automobiles, and should be equally probative of market values.

It is true that Section 9–507(2) of the Code provides that:

"The fact that a better price could have been obtained by a sale at a different method than that selected by the secured party is not of itself sufficient to establish that the sale was not made in a commercially reasonable manner."

In the present case, however, there are factors in addition to the inadequate price, from which the jury could conclude that Dravo-Doyle's disposition of the crane was not commercially reasonable. George Hickson is a salesman for Dravo-Doyle, in charge of the promotion and sale of cranes (T 112). Hickson testified at the hearing that although his territory covered parts of Pennsylvania, Ohio, Maryland and West Virginia, he made no effort to contact a purchaser for the crane other than Campbell (T 140).

From the fact that the price received by Dravo-Doyle was substantially lower than the value of the equipment, as evidenced by Marapese's testimony and the Green Guide quotation, and from the fact that Dravo-Doyle contacted only one purchaser, the jury could conclude that defendant failed to take adequate steps to ensure that a fair price was received. Therefore the jury was justified in concluding that the sale was not "commercially reasonable."

The motion for judgment non obstante veredicto must be refused.

2. Defendant's Motion for a New Trial

It is contended that the court erred in excluding the testimony of one John H. Combs, Jr., who had been called to testify on behalf of defendant. Mr. Combs is employed by the Anderson Equipment Company, a competitor of Dravo-Doyle. He is presently the Treasurer of Anderson, and had previously served as Assistant Treasurer and Credit Manager of that Corporation.

Counsel for plaintiff requested an offer of proof as to the witness, whereupon the following conversation took place at sidebar (T 153–154):

"Mr. Wolfe: I propose to show by this witness that he is engaged in the same work as Dravo-Doyle Company, that he is familiar with the problems of the repossession of equipment, that he is familiar furthermore with the legal requirements concerned with respect to resale of repossessed equipment, and that in his experience notification on one-week's time of a private sale is reasonable and practiced in the trade.

"Mr. Libenson: I object to all of this witness' testimony.

"The Court: I think it is for the jury.

"Mr. Libenson: This is strictly for the jury.

"The Court: I will let in as to the notice. The rest is for the law and the jury.

"Mr. Libenson: If you let that in as to notice, this is extremely prejudicial. The Act says, 'Reasonable.' It is the jury's question. He has nothing to do with the sale or anything. If he testifies as to what prior practice was, it is extremely prejudicial because the jury will think it is accepted practice. There is no accepted practice. It is extremely prejudicial. I will move for withdrawal of a juror.

"Mr. Wolfe: You have to give the jury something to go on. * * *

* * *

* * * [Interest] should have been included in the verdict. We must, therefore, mold the jury's verdict to include interest, at six percent (6%), from February 23, 1962, until October 13, 1964, a period of thirty-two (32) months. The jury's verdict was $10,333.79, and interest thereon for thirty-two (32) months, totals $1,653.40. The verdict, as amended, will consequently total $11,987.19.

ORDER OF COURT

And now, June 7, 1965, upon consideration of the Motions for Judgment n.o.v. and for a New Trial filed by the defendant herein, it is ordered that the same be and they are hereby refused.

It is further ordered that Plaintiff's Motion to Mold the Verdict be granted and the verdict is hereby molded so as to include interest, in the sum of $1,653.40. The jury's verdict, as molded, will therefore be in the amount of $11,987.19.

Judgment to be entered on payment of the verdict fee.

Note: Planning for Commercial Reasonableness of the Resale

The secured creditor may get advanced court approval of the procedures and terms of a 9–504 resale. This approval will bind all parties. See 9–507(2). Moreover, courts have upheld clauses in the security agreement that purport to govern some or all aspects of a 9–504 disposition. Aetna Finance v. Culpepper, 171 Ga.App. 315, 320 S.E.2d 228 (1984) (nature of notice to debtor agreed to); Ford Motor Credit Co. v. DeValk Lincoln-Mercury, Inc., 600 F.Supp. 1547 (N.D.Ill.1985) (entire mode of disposition agreed to). Of course, if the debtor agrees, after default, to a mode of disposition, that will generally be conclusive. Sections 9–501 and 9–504 so provide. Becknell v. First National Bank in Little Rock, 740 F.2d 609 (8th Cir.1984).

E. Valuation of Collateral Where Disposition Unreasonable

CONTRAIL LEASING PARTNERS LTD. v. CONSOLIDATED AIRWAYS

United States Court of Appeals, Seventh Circuit, 1984.
742 F.2d 1095.

Appeals from the United States District Court for the Northern District of Indiana. Before POSNER and COFFEY, CIRCUIT JUDGES, and KELLAM, SENIOR DISTRICT JUDGE.

POSNER, CIRCUIT JUDGE. This diversity suit, which the parties agree is governed by the Uniform Commercial Code as codified in Indiana, raises a number of questions regarding a secured creditor's right to repossess and sell his collateral on the debtor's account.

In 1976 Consolidated Airways, Inc. sold a Grumman Gulf Stream commercial aircraft to Contrail Leasing Partners, Ltd. for $575,000—$60,000 down and the rest to be paid in monthly installments. Consolidated took back a chattel mortgage on the plane. Beginning with a missed payment in May 1978 Contrail defaulted, and in July Consolidated repossessed the plane and began trying to sell it to realize the unpaid balance on the mortgage. Consolidated made a deal to sell the plane to Emerald Airlines for $675,000, and on August 31 it sent Contrail a telegram notifying it that the sale would take place on or about September 5. Even though it had referred Emerald to Consolidated in the first place, Contrail notified Emerald that it objected to the sale; and fearing that the sale would become entangled in legal proceedings, Emerald backed out. Later the plane required substantial maintenance work which included rebuilding its propellers to comply with the Federal Aviation Administration's safety requirements. The work cost Consolidated a little more than $26,000. When the work was completed Consolidated notified Contrail (on March 23, 1979) that it planned to sell the plane at a public auction in two and a half weeks (April 9). Contrail brought this suit on March 26, before the sale, and moved for a preliminary injunction to prevent the sale. The motion was denied, and on April 6 Contrail filed a notice of lis pendens (litigation pending) with the FAA. At the sale, held as scheduled on April 9, Consolidated was the only bidder. It bid $515,000 for the plane, and became the owner. Contrail got nothing from the sale, because the sale proceeds were less than the sum of the unpaid balance of the mortgage plus various expenses that Consolidated claimed.

Contrail's case came on for trial. Fifteen months after the two-day trial ended, the district judge issued his opinion. In it he found that the sale had been commercially unreasonable and that the plane had been worth $625,000 on the day of the sale (to which had to be added the $38,000 that Consolidated had earned from leasing the plane during the period of repossession), and he concluded that Contrail was entitled to the difference between (1) the sum of these figures ($663,000) and (2) the amount owed to Consolidated on its mortgage plus the expenses Consolidated had incurred in the sale. The difference, as the judge calculated it, was $133,000, and he entered judgment for Contrail for that amount. Consolidated has appealed on the ground that $133,000 is too much, and Contrail has cross-appealed on the ground that it is too little because the plane was worth more than $625,000 on the date of the sale.

A creditor who, having repossessed the debtor's goods, sells them to satisfy his debt is entitled to retain so much of the proceeds of the sale as is necessary to pay off the debt. See UCC § 9–504, Ind.Code § 26–1–9–504. If he has incurred reasonable expenses in preparation for the sale he is entitled to deduct those as well. See UCC § 9–504(1)(a), Ind.Code § 26–1–9–504(1)(*l*). The district judge recognized this principle and therefore allowed Consolidated to deduct various expenses, but he misapplied the principle in two respects:

1. He did not allow Consolidated to deduct the interest that had accrued on the note secured by the chattel mortgage between the date of default, May 17, 1978, and the date of sale, April 9, 1979. The unpaid principal on May 17, 1978, was $403,056.90, and the note called for interest at the rate of one percent a month. The district judge did not explain why he had not credited Consolidated with this interest. Contrail conjectures that he meant to penalize Consolidated for its improper conduct regarding the sale, of which more presently. But there is no indication that this was what was in the judge's mind. Contrail had argued that Consolidated's behavior was so egregious as to entitle Contrail to punitive damages, and there is support in Indiana law for awarding punitive damages "where the debtor can clearly show that the secured party is intentionally and maliciously violating the rights of the debtor." Hall v. Owen County State Bank, 175 Ind.App. 150, 160 n. 10, 370 N.E.2d 918, 927 n. 10 (1977). But Contrail's request for punitive damages was turned down because the judge could find no malice or willfulness or other circumstances of aggravation in Consolidated's behavior. His opinion offers no ground for lopping off part of Consolidated's claim. His action is made more difficult to understand by the fact that he (quite properly) credited Contrail with the $38,000 that Consolidated had earned from leasing the plane during the period of repossession. Consolidated was able to generate that income for the debtor only because it had possession of the plane, and one of the costs of possession to Consolidated was going without the $403,000 that the debtor owed it. It was an opportunity cost, which is a real cost in law as in economics. See, e.g., Simmons v. United States, 698 F.2d 888, 898 (7th Cir.1983). Consolidated is entitled to recover that opportunity cost by charging interest for the period of repossession.

There is no suggestion that one percent a month for the 10 months of the repossession was an unreasonable charge for Consolidated's money; and it is not clear that it would make a difference if it were (provided it was not usurious). Though we have treated the interest as an expense of the creditor, it is more appropriately regarded as a part of the underlying debt (but it makes no difference which it is). The debt was unpaid principal plus one percent interest for every month the principal was unpaid; and it was the principal plus accrued interest that Consolidated was entitled to keep along with expenses when it sold the plane on August 9, 1979. Alternatively, the one percent a month can be viewed as prejudgment interest to which Consolidated was entitled under well settled principles illustrated by Indiana Telephone Corp. v. Indiana Bell Telephone Co., 171 Ind.App. 616, 634–35, 358 N.E.2d 218, 229 (1976), modified, 171 Ind.App. 638, 360 N.E.2d 610 (1977), since the principal was a definite amount and Contrail does not deny that one percent was the reasonable rate of interest in the circumstances.

2. Another cost incurred by Consolidated during the period of repossession was the money that it spent to rebuild the propellers. Some of the language in the district judge's opinion makes it appear that he intended to allow Consolidated that expense, but we are unable to find such an allowance in his final computation. The question is not, as Contrail would have it, whether the expense was necessary to keep the plane from being grounded, though there is much evidence that it was; the question is whether it was prudent. See UCC § 9–504(1)(a), Ind.Code § 26–1–9–504(1)(a). A pru-

dent expenditure could be expected to be reflected in the value of the plane at the date of sale. The plane the district judge valued at $625,000 as of April 9, 1979, was a plane with rebuilt propellers; and it is not suggested that Consolidated paid more to rebuild them than was necessary. Since Contrail was the beneficiary of the expenditure, Consolidated was entitled to deduct it from the proceeds that it paid over to Contrail.

If, pursuant to the parties' stipulation which was erroneously copied by the district court, we correct the principal amount on the date of the default to $403,056.90, and if we then add: $43,395.65, which is interest at one percent a month during the repossession period; $26,143.77, for the propeller work (on which interest is not sought); and finally the expenses (including a prior lien) allowed by the judge, which came to $122,649.67, then the grand total of what Consolidated should have been allowed to keep from the sale is $595,245.99—not, as the judge thought, $529,514.87. From this should be deducted the $38,000 in lease income that Consolidated earned on Contrail's account during the repossession period, for a net due Consolidated of $557,-245.99.

Further adjustments to this figure, relating to the issue of brokerage expense, will be considered later; but accepting its accuracy for the moment, one can see that if the sale was commercially reasonable, then since it yielded proceeds ($515,000) smaller than the amount due Consolidated, Contrail is entitled to nothing and Consolidated is entitled to the deficiency judgment it sought in a counterclaim that the district judge dismissed. But if the sale was commercially unreasonable, it becomes necessary to calculate the fair market value of the plane on April 9, 1979, and if that fair market value was more than what is due Consolidated, Contrail is entitled to the excess, plus (it is undisputed) interest since April 9, 1979.

* * *

[The court held that the disposition was commercially unreasonable.]

Although the sale was unreasonable, and Contrail was therefore entitled to the fair market value of the plane on the day of sale (minus whatever was due Consolidated), we do not think the district court's valuation of $625,000 can be sustained. True, there was some basis for this figure, even though in arriving at it the district court applied a pretty stiff discount of the $675,000 price for which Consolidated had agreed to sell the plane to Emerald Airlines ten months earlier—a price agreed on, moreover, before the extensive repair work that Consolidated undertook. But the testimony showed that the market for used Grumman Gulf Stream commercial aircraft is rather thin, and the fact that Emerald was willing to pay a high price in 1978 doesn't prove that anyone would have been willing to pay as high a price a year later—in 1982 Consolidated sold the plane for only $616,000. There was also testimony that similar Grumman Gulf Stream aircraft were sold during the late 1970's in the $400,000's, though these planes were not in such good condition as this one.

Although $625,000 may seem a fair if rough average of the various figures, it has three problems:

1. We cannot ignore Consolidated's argument that the relevant value is that of a plane against which a lis pendens has been filed, although the judge

ignored the argument in his opinion. (The fact that the opinion was written so long after the trial may explain why several issues were not discussed.) Contrail cannot walk away from the consequences of having filed a notice of lis pendens on the eve of sale. It had no valid reason to try to block the sale. It had an adequate remedy at law against Consolidated—the remedy it is pursuing in this case—if Consolidated failed to sell the plane in a commercially reasonable manner; for there is no suggestion that Consolidated is not good for any money it may owe Contrail. The only effect of filing the lis pendens was to make it less likely that a sale would command a good price. But it is not true, as Consolidated suggests, that the filing of the lis pendens drove the value of the plane to zero because no one but a creditor would pay for a plane so marked. When three years after the sale to itself Consolidated sold the plane for $616,000 the lis pendens was still on file—as it was when this case was argued. But on remand the district judge must make findings on the effect of the lis pendens on the plane's fair market value on the date of sale.

2. The judge did not explain why he gave no weight to two $750,000 offers for the plane made to Consolidated in or around March 1979. Although the complete terms of these offers are not in the record, the existence of the offers required the judge to explain why he chose the figure of $625,000, which was considerably lower. He may have a good explanation—the lis pendens perhaps, for it is unclear whether the offerors knew about it.

3. A point that cuts in the opposite direction—that suggests that $625,000 may have been too high an estimate—is that the judge did not (so far as appears anyway) allow for brokerage expense, which would have reduced the net proceeds of the sale to Contrail. In the aborted sale to Emerald Airlines, Consolidated had agreed to pay Emerald's broker a $35,000 commission, which works out to a shade over five percent. If Consolidated had found a buyer on April 9 at a price of $625,000, it might have had to pay a similar commission to the buyer's broker. The net proceeds from the sale would therefore have been less than $625,000. It makes no difference whether we say that the relevant market value was 95 percent of $625,000 (assuming a commission of five percent), or that it was $625,000 but that Consolidated is entitled to deduct a five percent brokerage commission as an expense of a commercially reasonable sale. In either event an additional adjustment is necessary. But we do not know what the adjustment should be.

Errors 2 and 3 could be offsetting. If the proper brokerage fee is five percent, and if the judge by disregarding the offers that Consolidated received in March 1979 undervalued the plane by five percent, then his estimate of $625,000 would be unchanged. But these are guesses. We do not know either percentage—or the bearing of the lis pendens. We do not even know whether the judge's valuation was net of brokerage—which leads to a further complication:

4. Consolidated may have been permitted to deduct certain expenses incurred in its sale to itself that it would not have incurred had it used a broker, in which event there would be double counting if it were allowed to deduct brokerage expense as well. Official Comment 2 to UCC § 9–507 states that the secured creditor is not required to resell the collateral at

retail rather than wholesale. Although it is true that Indiana has not enacted the official comments, as some states have, see, e.g., Piper Acceptance Corp. v. Yarbrough, 702 F.2d 733, 735 (8th Cir.1983) (Arkansas), no negative inference can be drawn; and even without the comment, it is pretty clear that § 9–507 does not require sale in a retail market. It provides that if the creditor "sells the collateral in the usual manner *in any recognized market therefor* * * * he has sold in a commercially reasonable manner." § 9–507(2), Ind.Code § 26–1–9–507(2) (emphasis added). Wholesale markets are recognized markets for most goods, including aircraft, as we know from the *Piper* case; and an ironclad rule against selling collateral at wholesale rather than retail would make no sense. Although retail prices tend to be higher than wholesale prices, this is because it costs more to sell at retail. Not only can there be, therefore, no presumption that the net gains to the seller are different at the two levels, but economic theory implies that returns at the two levels will tend toward equality, since until they are equalized dealers will have incentives to enter at the level where the higher returns are being earned and by entering will bid those returns down.

So the important thing is to match expenses with estimated value correctly. If the judge estimates a retail price, there should be a deduction for brokerage if retail sales of airplanes normally are made through brokers but not a deduction for expenses of a sale at wholesale; but if he estimates a wholesale price, then only the expenses associated with wholesale sales should be deducted.

To sum up, a remand is necessary to permit the district judge to clarify his findings. He must on remand reestimate the value of the plane (with the lis pendens) on April 9, 1979; specify whether that is a retail or a wholesale price; subtract from that price all pertinent expenses of sale, which we said earlier amount to $557,245.99—but the figure may have to be adjusted if the judge estimates a retail rather than a wholesale price; and award Contrail what is left after the subtraction, plus interest from April 9, 1979.

No costs will be awarded in this court, and Circuit Rule 18 shall not apply on remand.

Affirmed in part, reversed in part, and remanded with directions.

SECTION 10. RIGHTS OF THIRD PARTIES BEFORE AND AFTER THE DISPOSITION OF COLLATERAL

We have examined the rights of the debtor as the secured party declares default, repossesses and either retains or disposes of the collateral. What are the rights, if any, of third parties, i.e., creditors of or purchasers from the debtor, in the process?

Consider the following problems.

Problem 6–7

First Bank lent Debtor $25,000 and, on July 1, perfected a security interest in Debtor's equipment. The equipment's value was estimated to be $30,000. On August 1, Second Bank lent Debtor $10,000 and perfected a security interest in the equipment. First Bank learned of Second Bank's interest from Debtor, but did not declare a default under the security agreement. Six months later, Debtor defaulted on its obligation to First Bank, who peacefully repossessed the equipment. At that time, Debtor owed First Bank $20,000 and the collateral was valued at $25,000. Debtor then signed a written statement renouncing his right to object to any proposal by First Bank to retain the equipment under UCC 9–505(2) in full satisfaction of the obligation.

1. May First Bank retain the collateral in full satisfaction of Debtor's obligation without any obligation to account to Second Bank for any surplus? See UCC 9–505(2) & 9–507(1). See Blackhawk Production Credit Association v. Meridian Implement Co., 82 Ill.App.3d 93, 37 Ill.Dec. 387, 402 N.E.2d 277 (1980), suggesting that Second Bank has a potential claim under UCC 9–507(1).

2. Suppose, instead, that First Bank disposed of the collateral for $20,000 and settled with Debtor for an additional $500. Second Bank believes that the disposition was commercially unreasonable. Does Second Bank have any standing to complain? See Louis Zahn Drug Co. v. Bank of Oak Brook Terrace, 95 Ill.App.3d 435, 50 Ill.Dec. 959, 420 N.E.2d 276 (1981), holding that Second Bank has a potential claim under UCC 9–507(1).

3. What change did the 1972 revisions in UCC 9–505 and 9–504 make in the obligation of First Bank to give notice? What reasons were offered by the Permanent Editorial Board to justify the major shift in the burden of giving notice?

Problem 6–8

Suppose, in Problem 6–7, First Bank repossessed and disposed of the equipment in a commercially reasonable manner for $30,000. After application of the proceeds under UCC 9–504(1), a surplus of $7,500 was realized.

1. To whom should the surplus be paid, Debtor or Second Bank? See UCC 9–504(1)(c) & 9–504(2). What should Second Bank do to insure payment?

2. Suppose that First Bank paid the $7,500 to Debtor. What are Second Bank's rights against Debtor? Against First Bank? Does UCC 9–507(1) protect Second Bank here?

Problem 6–9

Assume, in Problem 6–7, that Debtor defaulted in its obligation to Second Bank but not First Bank. Second Bank, without actual knowledge of First Bank's security interest, peacefully repossessed the equipment and sold it in a commercially reasonable manner to Buyer for $20,000. After applying the proceeds, Second Bank paid a surplus of $7,500 to Debtor. Shortly thereafter, First Bank learned of this activity. What rights, if any, does First Bank have against Buyer? UCC 9–504(4)? Against Debtor? Against Second Bank?

CHAPTER SEVEN

SPECIAL PROBLEMS OF SCOPE

SECTION 1. INTRODUCTION

Section 9–102 contains an expansive definition of the transactions to which Article 9 applies. It applies not only to transactions that have relation to real property, but also to transactions that take the form of an absolute sale, and even to some that appear as leases or bailments. Moreover, the article governs aspects of analogous transactions such as consignments, and specifically treats real estate transactions involving fixtures. The process of defining the border between transactions within and those without Article 9 has been a continuous and difficult one for the courts. For example, the issue of "true lease" vs. security agreement has arisen in hundreds of courts in thousands of cases. To cite a second example, when is a bailment really a security interest? Then, too, the courts have recently begun to face the issue whether security in a mortgagee's interest and in rights under a land-sale contract are within Article 9. Numerous other scope issues have arisen, including the extent of the exclusions under UCC 9–104, and the federal government's obligation as a creditor to comply with the terms of Article 9. We will begin this chapter with the conventional lease versus security agreement issue. For reasons we will explain below, the new Bankruptcy Code has rekindled general interest in that question.

Next we will examine the status of the bailment and quasi-bailment and its relation to Article 9. When one puts goods in the hands of another for sale to third parties, that transaction looks much like and is in many ways the economic equivalent of an inventory loan. It has distinctive legal qualities, but it functions like a bank loan. The same might be said when one "bails" seed to a farmer for the production of a crop. By the same token some suggest that a purchaser of goods who has left them in the hands of his seller or an owner of goods who has given them to another for processing should be regarded merely as a creditor.

The borderline between real estate transactions and those under Article 9 has now been the scene of a host of new and troublesome problems. What law governs when a mortgagee (who holds a mortgage and the note of his debtor, mortgagor) comes to the bank and seeks to borrow against those? Is he to be treated like the holder of chattel paper or is this transaction exclusively under the real property law of a particular state? Section 9–102(3) and Comment 4 to 9–102, tell us that to some extent it is within Article 9. But to what extent?

Next we see competition between a bank asserting rights of setoff and others asserting security interests in bank accounts or in certificates of deposit. While it is clear from the exclusions in Article 9 that banks need not file a financing statement or take other Article 9 action to "perfect" a right to setoff, Article 9 still might establish the priority between setoff and another claim.

Finally we will consider some issues involving the federal government. Of course the federal government is not governed by state law but by its own law. Federal law determines the rights of Uncle Sam when he is the lender. Although the Supreme Court has chosen to apply Article 9 in many situations, the lower courts have been slow to follow the Supreme Court's direction and have been hesitant to treat the federal government as merely another lender. In the arena where the United States holds a tax lien, federal law clearly governs priority disputes with perfected security interests.

Scope issues often raise complex and sophisticated problems that presuppose an overall grasp of Article 9 if they are to be resolved satisfactorily. It is for this reason that we have postponed consideration of them until this point. Define the scope issue in the following problem.

Problem 7–1

Creditor, General Electric Credit Corporation, had a perfected security interest in a truck. The truck broke down and was taken for repairs to the shop of Great Lakes Energy Systems. Great Lakes installed a new motor in the truck but was never paid by the debtor. While the truck was still in the possession of Great Lakes, debtor filed a voluntary petition in bankruptcy. Thereupon Great Lakes removed the new motor from the truck and installed the old one. With the new motor, the truck is worth $26,000; without it, it is worth between $10,000 and $13,000. Must Great Lakes reinstall the motor and, if so, who gets the truck with the motor in it, General Electric, Great Lakes, or the trustee in bankruptcy?

Note: The Outlaws of Personal Property Security

Historically personal property security has been governed by state not federal law. With the adoption of Article 9, that state law became almost completely uniform. However, as we have seen, even Article 9 did not codify all the state law; for example, mechanic's liens were left on their own and certain other transactions were excluded by Section 9–104.

The thirty years since the widespread adoption of Article 9 have seen a troublesome development in the federal Congress. Repeatedly the Congress has enacted laws that have the intentional or incidental effect of granting some party, who has not complied with Article 9, priority over those who would otherwise have priority under Article 9. Scholars and state legislators can do little more than scold the Congress, but lawyers need to keep a wary eye for these off-record but superior claims. Below we discuss a number of them.

Among the explicit exceptions to the first-in-time priority rule are a multitude of state common law and statutory liens. Since these liens are nonconsensual, most are excluded from Article 9 coverage by sections 9–102 and 9–104 (except as provided in section 9–310, which provides for liens in favor of suppliers of services or materials with respect to goods in the supplier's possession). Possible state liens include landlord's, mechanic's, artisan's, processor's, repairmen's, construction, maritime, attorney's, employee's, materialmen's, lumberman's, and motion picture film liens. Examples of explicit federal liens include the priority liens given to certain suppliers of livestock and agricultural products. See Packers and Stockyards Act of 1921, 7 U.S.C.A. § 191; Perishable Agricultural Commodities Act of 1984, 7 U.S.C.A. § 499.

Criminal forfeiture laws have also touched secured creditors. What happens to bank's security interest in the favorite drug dealer's BMW that is seized by the Feds? See, e.g., Racketeer Influenced and Corrupt Organizations Act ("RICO"), 18 U.S.C.A. § 1961 et seq.; 21 U.S.C.A. § 881. In general, the forfeitures relate back to the time of the original (and *secret*) criminal act; subsequently perfected security interests are subordinate. Some statutes grant protection for secured creditors unaware of the illegal activity. See, e.g., RICO § 1963(*l*)(6)(B).

Environmental claims may interfere with a secured lender in several ways. A lender may find its collateral worthless because of contamination. The borrower may be unable to repay its debts because of environmental obligations. A secured creditor may see its interest subordinated under state environmental superliens or under the Bankruptcy Code (cleanup costs might be considered a necessary expense of preserving the property under 11 U.S.C.A. § 506(c)). Most frightening to lenders, however, was the possibility that holding a security interest in contaminated collateral could make the secured creditor jointly and severally liable for the entire cleanup as an "owner or operator" of the property. See, e.g., Comprehensive Environmental Response, Compensation and Liability Act (CERCLA), 42 U.S.C.A. § 9601 et seq. In 1992, the EPA published a rule that minimizes this latter fear. 40 C.F.R. § 300.1100. This rule provides clarification of what is generally known as the security interest exemption to CERCLA. As long as the lender does not participate in the management of the facility, most normal lending activities are protected by safe harbor provisions.

Although the federal tax lien, discussed earlier, is generally subordinate to prior perfected security interests, the United States Supreme Court has recently given a new weapon to the tax collector. Under Begier v. Internal Revenue Service, 496 U.S. 53, 110 S.Ct. 2258, 110 L.Ed.2d 46 (1990), a taxing body (state or local) gets absolute priority to the money in a debtor's bank accounts if it can show such funds to be properly related to so-called trust fund taxes collected by the debtor on behalf of the government. Trust fund taxes are a creature of Section 7501 of the Internal Revenue Code and include any taxes collected or withheld from others such as FICA, employment or excise taxes.

In *Begier* a bankruptcy trustee sought to recover the debtor's voluntary payment of trust fund obligations to the IRS as preferences. The Court struggled to define how extensive the nexus must be between the taxes collected and the funds paid to IRS. The Court eventually found that "any voluntary prepetition payment of trust-fund taxes out of the debtor's assets is not a transfer of the debtor's property." In other words, the debtor's voluntary payment of its tax obligations was sufficient to identify the funds to the statutory trust.

Although the case arose as a preference action, the reasoning applies to creditor priority disputes. It seems reasonable to conclude that a secured creditor has no greater rights in funds not owned by the debtor than a bankruptcy trustee would. No reported cases have squarely addressed this issue. In *Honey v. United States,* the Eighth Circuit declared that a "security interest in proceeds was superior to the interest of the IRS [in a debtor's account] to the extent that those funds actually were proceeds from the sale of inventory." 963 F.2d 1083, 1091 (8th Cir.1992). Of course, this begs the priority question because it is impossible for specific funds to be both a trust res and proceeds from collateral. The real issues are the tracing requirements applied to each claim and who bears the burden of proof.

Although a lender has a validly perfected security interest in inventory, it may find itself unable to foreclose on and dispose of the collateral. According to Citicorp Industrial Credit v. Brock, 483 U.S. 27, 107 S.Ct. 2694, 97 L.Ed.2d 23 (1987), if the goods were produced by the debtor in violation of the wage provisions of the Fair Labor Standards Act, (i.e., the debtor failed to meet its last payroll and so "paid" less than the minimum wage), this Act's prohibition upon interstate shipment of such goods applies to foreclosing creditors as well as the violating employer. Although the Supreme Court expressly stated that it was not granting a lien to the underpaid employees, the goods may not be sold unless the unpaid wages are paid. Maybe it is not a "lien" but it certainly walks and talks like one, doesn't it?

A similar problem arises for the inventory lender when the goods bear third party trademarks. If the licensing agreement between the debtor and the third party has expired or been terminated (not unlikely if the debtor is not paying its creditors), a foreclosing creditor may be unable to sell the goods without permission from (and additional payments to?) the trademark holder. Foreclosing on a debtor's equipment subject to patent licenses would require similar negotiations with the patent holder.

Beware, our list of personal property outlaws is not exhaustive.

SECTION 2. LEASES—SECURITY AGREEMENTS

The case that immediately follows considers whether the transaction involved is a mere lease of goods in which the lessor retains a residual interest in the goods and the lessee periodically pays rent for use of the goods for a term, or is instead a sale of goods with the seller retaining a security interest in the goods to secure payment of the purchase price that the buyer is to pay in installments over time. Whether a transaction is a lease or a secured installment sale can greatly change the legal consequences. If it is a lease, Article 2A (see Chapter Twenty-Three) applies. If it is really a secured installment sale although cast in the terminology of lease, Article 9 applies to the security aspects (and Article 2 to the sale aspects) of the transaction. If, for example, the "lessor" has failed to file a required financing statement, that party will lose to certain other creditors and the trustee in bankruptcy. If the transaction is a lease and thus governed by Article 2A, the lessor will have a significant residual interest in the goods, and third parties will generally take subject to the lease agreement more or less as written. Article 2A–103(1)(j) defines a lease in terms that exclude a security interest:

> Lease means a transfer of the right to possession and use of goods for a term or return for consideration, but a sale, including a sale or return, or retention or creation of a security interest is not a lease.

The case that immediately follows draws the line between a lease and a secured sale in light of the pre-Article 2A version of the Official Text of the Code which included, in section 1–201(37), an elaborate provision on this distinction. You should study the case not only in light of "old" section 1–201(37), but also in light of the newly revised section 1–201(37) appearing in the 1990 Official Text of the Code. This newly revised section is discussed in detail in Section Two of Chapter Twenty-Three at pp. 1046–1048 of this book. We advise that you consult that discussion after, rather than before, you have read the case. At that point you will want to determine whether the case would come out differently under the new section 1–201(37). You will also want to consider whether the new version disposes of the case more certainly than the old version.

IN RE MARHOEFER PACKING CO., INC.

United States Court of Appeals, Seventh Circuit, 1982.
674 F.2d 1139.

PELL, CIRCUIT JUDGE.

This appeal involves a dispute between the trustee of the bankrupt Marhoefer Packing Company, Inc., ("Marhoefer") and Robert Reiser & Company, Inc., ("Reiser") over certain equipment held by Marhoefer at the time of bankruptcy. The issue presented is whether the written agreement between Marhoefer and Reiser covering the equipment is a true lease under which Reiser is entitled to reclaim its property from the bankrupt estate, or whether it is actually a lease intended as security in which case Reiser's failure to file a financing statement to perfect its interest renders it subordinate to the trustee.

I

In December of 1976, Marhoefer Packing Co., Inc., of Muncie, Indiana, entered into negotiations with Reiser, a Massachusetts based corporation engaged in the business of selling and leasing food processing equipment, for the acquisition of one or possibly two Vemag Model 3007–1 Continuous Sausage Stuffers. Reiser informed Marhoefer that the units could be acquired by outright purchase, conditional sale contract or lease. Marhoefer ultimately acquired two sausage stuffers from Reiser. It purchased one under a conditional sale contract. Pursuant to the contract, Reiser retained a security interest in the machine, which it subsequently perfected by filing a financing statement with the Indiana Secretary of State. Title to that stuffer is not here in dispute. The other stuffer was delivered to Marhoefer under a written "Lease Agreement."

The Lease Agreement provided for monthly payments of $665.00 over a term of 48 months. The last nine months payments, totaling $5,985.00, were payable upon execution of the lease. If at the end of the lease term the machine was to be returned, it was to be shipped prepaid to Boston or similar destination "in the same condition as when received, reasonable wear and tear resulting from proper use alone excepted, and fully crated." The remaining terms and conditions of the agreement were as follows:

1. Any State or local taxes and/or excises are for the account of the Buyer.
2. The equipment shall at all times be located at

   Marhoefer Packing Co., Inc.
   1500 North Elm & 13th Street
   Muncie, Indiana

and shall not be removed from said location without the written consent of Robert Reiser & Co. The equipment can only be used in conjunction with the manufacture of meat or similar products unless written consent is given by Robert Reiser & Co.

3. The equipment will carry a ninety-day guarantee for workmanship and materials and shall be maintained and operated safely and carefully in conformity with the instructions issued by our operators and the maintenance manual. Service and repairs of the equipment after the ninety-day period will be subject to a reasonable and fair charge.

4. If, after due warning, our maintenance instructions should be violated repeatedly, Robert Reiser & Co. will have the right to cancel the lease contract on seven days notice and remove the said equipment. In that case, lease fees would be refunded pro rata.

5. It is mutually agreed that in case of lessee, Marhoefer Packing Co., Inc., violating any of the above conditions, or shall default in the payment of any lease charge hereunder, or shall become bankrupt, make or execute any assignment or become party to any instrument or proceedings for the benefit of its creditors, Robert Reiser & Co. shall have the right at any time without trespass, to enter upon the premises and remove the aforesaid equipment, and if removed, lessee agrees to pay Robert Reiser & Co. the total lease fees, including all installments due or to become due for the full unexpired term of this lease agreement and including the cost for removal of the equipment and counsel fees incurred in collecting sums due hereunder.

6. It is agreed that the equipment shall remain personal property of Robert Reiser & Co. and retain its character as such no matter in what manner affixed or attached to the premises.

In a letter accompanying the lease, Reiser added two option provisions to the agreement. The first provided that at the end of the four-year term, Marhoefer could purchase the stuffer for $9,968.00. In the alternative, it could elect to renew the lease for an additional four years at an annual rate of $2,990.00, payable in advance. At the conclusion of the second four-year term, Marhoefer would be allowed to purchase the stuffer for one dollar.

Marhoefer never exercised either option. Approximately one year after the Vemag stuffer was delivered to its plant, it ceased all payments under the lease and shortly thereafter filed a voluntary petition in bankruptcy. On July 12, 1978, the trustee of the bankrupt corporation applied to the bankruptcy court for leave to sell the stuffer free and clear of all liens on the ground that the "Lease Agreement" was in fact a lease intended as security within the meaning of the Uniform Commercial Code ("Code") and that Reiser's failure to perfect its interest as required by Article 9 of the Code rendered it subordinate to that of the trustee. Reiser responded with an answer and counterclaim in which it alleged that the agreement was in fact a true lease, Marhoefer was in default under the lease, and its equipment should therefore be returned.

Following a trial on this issue, the bankruptcy court concluded that the agreement between Marhoefer and Reiser was in fact a true lease and ordered the trustee to return the Vemag stuffer to Reiser. The trustee appealed to the district court, which reversed on the ground that the bankruptcy court had erred as a matter of law in finding the agreement to be a true lease. We now reverse the judgment of the district court.

II

The dispute in this case centers on section 1–201(37) of the Uniform Commercial Code, I.C. 26–1–1–201. In applying this section, the bankruptcy court concluded that "the presence of the option to renew the lease for an additional four years and to acquire the Vemag stuffer at the conclusion of the second four-year term by the payment of One Dollar ($1.00) did not, in and of itself, make the lease one intended for security."

The district court disagreed. It held that the presence of an option to purchase the stuffer for one dollar gave rise to a conclusive presumption under clause (b) of section 1–201(37) that the lease was intended as security. Although it acknowledged that the option to purchase the stuffer for only one dollar would not have come into play unless Marhoefer chose to renew the lease for an additional four-year term, the district court concluded that this fact did not require a different result. "It would be anomalous," said the court, "to rule that the lease was a genuine lease for four years after its creation but was one intended for security eight years after its creation."

Reiser, relying on Peter F. Coogan's detailed analysis of section 1–201(37), Coogan, Hogan & Vagts, Secured Transactions Under the Uniform Commercial Code, ch. 4A, (1981) (hereinafter "Secured Transactions Under U.C.C."), argues that the district court erred in construing clause (b) of that section as creating a conclusive presumption that a lease is intended as security where the lease contains an option for the lessee to become the owner of the leased property for no additional consideration or for only nominal consideration. It contends that by interpreting clause (b) in this way, the district court totally ignored the first part of that sentence which states that "[w]hether a lease is intended as security is to be determined by the facts of each case." Reiser claims that because the totality of facts surrounding the transaction indicate that the lease was not intended as security, notwithstanding the presence of the option to purchase the stuffer for one dollar, the district court erred in reversing the bankruptcy court's determination.

We agree that the district court erred in concluding that because the Lease Agreement contained an option for Marhoefer to purchase the Vemag stuffer at the end of a second four-year term, it was conclusively presumed to be a lease intended as security. However, in our view, the district court's error lies not in its reading of clause (b) of section 1–201(37) as giving rise to such a presumption,[2] but rather in its conclusion that clause (b) applies under the facts of this case.

2. This reading of section 1–201(37) is not without support in the reported cases. In Peco v. Hartbauer Tool & Die Co., 262 Or. 573, 500 P.2d 708 (1972), for example, the court noted that "[a]t first glance the provisions of * * * section [1–201(37)] may be somewhat confusing, probably because they are stated in the inverse order of impor-

The primary issue to be decided in determining whether a lease is "intended as security" is whether it is in effect a conditional sale in which the "lessor" retains an interest in the "leased" goods as security for the purchase price. 1C Secured Transactions Under U.C.C. § 29A.05[1][C], p. 2939. By defining the term "security interest" to include a lease intended as security, the drafters of the Code intended such disguised security interests to be governed by the same rules that apply to other security interests. *See* U.C.C., Art. 9. In this respect, section 1–201(37) represents the drafter's refusal to recognize form over substance.

Clearly, where a lease is structured so that the lessee is contractually bound to pay rent over a set period of time at the conclusion of which he automatically or for only nominal consideration becomes the owner of the leased goods, the transaction is in substance a conditional sale and should be treated as such. It is to this type of lease that clause (b) properly applies. Here, however, Marhoefer was under no contractual obligation to pay rent until such time as the option to purchase the Vemag stuffer for one dollar was to arise. In fact, in order to acquire that option, Marhoefer would have had to exercise its earlier option to renew the lease for a second four-year term and pay Reiser an additional $11,960 in "rent." In effect, Marhoefer was given a right to terminate the agreement after the first four years and cease making payments without that option ever becoming operative.

Despite this fact, the district court concluded as a matter of law that the lease was intended as security. It held that, under clause (b) of section 1–201(37), a lease containing an option for the lessee to purchase the leased goods for nominal consideration is conclusively presumed to be one intended as security. This presumption applies, the court concluded, regardless of any other options the lease may contain.

We think the district court's reading of clause (b) is in error. In our view, the conclusive presumption provided under clause (b) applies only where the option to purchase for nominal consideration necessarily arises upon compliance with the lease. *See* 1C Secured Transactions Under U.C.C. § 29.05[2][b] pp. 2947–49. It does not apply where the lessee has the right to terminate the lease before that option arises with no further obligation to continue paying rent. But see In re Royers Bakery, Inc., 1 U.C.C.Rep. 342 (Bankr.E.D.Pa.1963). For where the lessee has the right to terminate the transaction, it is not a conditional sale.[3]

tance. However, upon a careful reading of the entire section it is clear that the first question to be answered is that posed by clause (b)—whether the lessee may obtain the property for no additional consideration or for a nominal consideration. If so, the lease is intended for security. If not, it is then necessary to determine 'by the facts of each case' whether * * * the fact that the lease contains an option to purchase 'does not (of itself) make the lease one intended for security.'" Id. at 575, 500 P.2d at 709–10, quoting Ore.Rev.Stat. § 71–2010(37) (1969).

3. See S. Williston, The Law Governing Sales of Goods at Common Law and Under the Uniform Sales Act § 336, p. 528 (1909): It is, however, essential in order to make a conditional sale, in the sense in which that term is used ordinarily in statutes or elsewhere, that the buyer should be bound to take title of the property, or at least to pay the price for it. Therefore, a lease which provides for a certain rent in installments is not a conditional sale if the buyer can terminate the transaction at any time by returning the property, even though the lease also provides that if rent is paid for a certain period, the lessee shall thereupon become the owner of the property.

Moreover, to hold that a lease containing such an option is intended as security, even though the lessee has no contractual obligation to pay the full amount contemplated by the agreement, would lead to clearly erroneous results under other provisions of the Code. Under section 9–506 of the Code, for example, a debtor in default on his obligation to a secured party has a right to redeem the collateral by tendering full payment of that obligation.[4] The same right is also enjoyed by a lessee under a lease intended as security. A lessee who defaults on a lease intended as security is entitled to purchase the leased goods by paying the full amount of his obligation under the lease. But if the lessee has the right to terminate the lease at any time during the lease term, his obligation under the lease may be only a small part of the total purchase price of the goods leased. To afford the lessee a right of redemption under such circumstances would clearly be wrong. There is no evidence that the drafters of the Code intended such a result.

We therefore hold that while section 1–201(37)(b) does provide a conclusive test of when a lease is intended as security, that test does not apply in every case in which the disputed lease contains an option to purchase for nominal or no consideration. An option of this type makes a lease one intended as security only when it necessarily arises upon compliance with the terms of the lease.[5]

Applying section 1–201(37), so construed, to the facts of this case, it is clear that the district court erred in concluding that the possibility of Marhoefer's purchasing the stuffer for one dollar at the conclusion of a second four-year term was determinative. Because Marhoefer could have fully complied with the lease without that option ever arising, the district court was mistaken in thinking that the existence of that option alone made the lease a conditional sale. Certainly, if Marhoefer had elected to renew the lease for another term, in which case the nominal purchase option would necessarily have arisen, then the clause (b) test would apply. But that is not the case we are faced with here. Marhoefer was not required to make any payments beyond the first four years. The fact that, at the conclusion of that term, it could have elected to renew the lease and obtain an option to purchase the stuffer for one dollar at the end of the second term does not transform the original transaction into a conditional sale.

This fact does not end our inquiry under clause (b), however, for the trustee also argues that, even if the district court erred in considering the one dollar purchase option as determinative, the lease should nevertheless be considered a conditional sale because the initial option price of $9,968 is

4. Section 9–506 of the Code states:

Debtor's Right to Redeem Collateral

At any time before the secured party has disposed of collateral or entered into a contract for its disposition under Section 9–504 or before the obligation has been discharged under Section 9–505(2) the debtor or any other secured party may unless otherwise agreed in writing after default redeem the collateral by tendering fulfillment of all obligations secured by the collateral as well as the expenses reasonably incurred by the secured party in retaking, holding and preparing the collateral for disposition, in arranging for the sale, and to the extent provided in the agreement and not prohibited by law, his reasonable attorneys' fees and legal expenses.

5. This reading of clause (b) is in no way inconsistent with the plain language of that provision since, by its terms, it does not refer to the situation where there are alternate ways of complying with a lease, only one of which results in the nominal purchase option arising.

also nominal when all of the operative facts are properly considered. We agree that if the clause (b) test is to apply at all in this case, this is the option that must be considered. For this is the option that was to arise automatically upon Marhoefer's compliance with the lease. We do not agree, however, that under the circumstances presented here the $9,968 option price can properly be considered nominal.

It is true that an option price may be more than a few dollars and still be considered nominal within the meaning of section 1–201(37). Because clause (b) speaks of nominal "consideration" and not a nominal "sum" or "amount," it has been held to apply not only where the option price is very small in absolute terms, but also where the price is insubstantial in relation to the fair market value of the leased goods at the time the option arises.[7]

Here, however, the evidence revealed that the initial option price of $9,968 was not nominal even under this standard. George Vetie, Reiser's treasurer and the person chiefly responsible for the terms of the lease, testified at trial that the purchase price for the Vemag stuffer at the time the parties entered into the transaction was $33,225. He testified that the initial option price of $9,968 was arrived at by taking thirty percent of the purchase price, which was what he felt a four-year-old Vemag stuffer would be worth based on Reiser's past experience.

The trustee, relying on the testimony of its expert appraiser, argues that in fact the stuffer would have been worth between eighteen and twenty thousand dollars at the end of the first four-year term. Because the initial option price is substantially less than this amount, he claims that it is nominal within the meaning of clause (b) and the lease is therefore one intended as security.

Even assuming this appraisal to be accurate, an issue on which the bankruptcy court made no finding, we would not find the initial option price of $9,968 so small by comparison that the clause (b) presumption would apply. While it is difficult to state any bright line percentage test for determining when an option price could properly be considered nominal as compared to the fair market value of the leased goods, an option price of almost ten thousand dollars, which amounts to fifty percent of the fair market value, is not nominal by any standard.

Furthermore, in determining whether an option price is nominal, the proper figure to compare it with is not the actual fair market value of the leased goods at the time the option arises, but their fair market value at that time as anticipated by the parties when the lease is signed. 1C Secured Transactions Under U.C.C. § 29A.05[2][b], p. 2953. Here, for example, Vetie testified that his estimate of the fair market value of a four-year-old Vemag stuffer was based on records from a period of time in which the economy was relatively stable. Since that time, a high rate of inflation has caused the machines to lose their value more slowly. As a result, the actual fair market value of a machine may turn out to be significantly more than the

7. The trustee argues that the determination of whether the option price is nominal is to be made by comparing it to the fair market value of the equipment at the time the parties enter into the lease, instead of the date the option arises. Although some courts have applied such a test, the better approach is to compare the option price with the fair market value of the goods at the time the option was to be exercised.

parties anticipated it would be several years earlier. When this occurs, the lessee's option to purchase the leased goods may be much more favorable than either party intended, but it does not change the true character of the transaction.

We conclude, therefore, that neither option to purchase contained in the lease between Marhoefer and Reiser gives rise to a conclusive presumption under section 1–201(37)(b) that the lease is one intended as security. This being so, we now turn to the other facts surrounding the transaction.

III

Although section 1–201(37) states that "[w]hether a lease is intended as security is to be determined by the facts of each case," it is completely silent as to what facts, other than the option to purchase, are to be considered in making that determination. Facts that the courts have found relevant include the total amount of rent the lessee is required to pay under the lease, whether the lessee acquires any equity in the leased property, the useful life of the leased goods, the nature of the lessor's business, and the payment of taxes, insurance and other charges normally imposed on ownership. Consideration of the facts of this case in light of these factors leads us to conclude that the lease in question was not intended as security.

First, Marhoefer was under no obligation to pay the full purchase price for the stuffer. Over the first four-year term, its payments under the lease were to have amounted to $31,920. Although this amount may not be substantially less than the original purchase price of $33,225 in absolute terms, it becomes so when one factors in the interest rate over four years that would have been charged had Marhoefer elected to purchase the machine under a conditional sale contract.[8] The fact that the total amount of rent Marhoefer was to pay under the lease was substantially less than that amount shows that a sale was not intended.

It is also significant that the useful life of the Vemag stuffer exceeded the term of the lease. An essential characteristic of a true lease is that there be something of value to return to the lessor after the term. Where the term of the lease is substantially equal to the life of the leased property such that there will be nothing of value to return at the end of the lease, the transaction is in essence a sale. Here, the evidence revealed that the useful life of a Vemag stuffer was eight to ten years.

Finally, the bankruptcy court specifically found that "there was no express or implied provision in the lease agreement dated February 28, 1977, which gave Marhoefer any equity interest in the leased Vemag stuffer." This fact clearly reveals the agreement between Marhoefer and Reiser to be a true lease. See Hawkland, The Impact of the Uniform Commercial Code on Equipment Leasing, 1972 Ill.L.Forum 446, 453 ("The difference between a true lease and a security transaction lies in whether the lessee acquires an equity of ownership through his rent payments.") Had Marhoefer remained

8. The bankruptcy court found that Reiser was originally willing to sell Marhoefer the stuffer under a conditional sale contract the terms of which would have been $7,225 down and monthly installments of $1,224 over a twenty-four month period. The total payments under such an agreement would have amounted to $36,601, substantially more than the amount Marhoefer was required to pay over four years under the lease.

solvent and elected not to exercise its option to renew its lease with Reiser, it would have received nothing for its previous lease payments. And in order to exercise that option, Marhoefer would have had to pay what Reiser anticipated would then be the machine's fair market value. An option of this kind is not the mark of a lease intended as security.

Although Marhoefer was required to pay state and local taxes and the cost of repairs, this fact does not require a contrary result. Costs such as taxes, insurance and repairs are necessarily borne by one party or the other. They reflect less the true character of the transaction than the strength of the parties' respective bargaining positions.

IV

We conclude from the foregoing that the district court erred in its application of section 1–201(37) of the Uniform Commercial Code to the facts of this case. Neither the option to purchase the Vemag stuffer for one dollar at the conclusion of a second four-year term, nor the initial option to purchase it for $9,968 after the first four years, gives rise to a conclusive presumption under clause (b) of section 1–201(37) that the lease is intended as security. From all of the facts surrounding the transaction, we conclude that the agreement between Marhoefer and Reiser is a true lease. The judgment of the district court is therefore reversed. [Some footnotes omitted.]

Notes

1. If a court chooses to use the option price as a test of whether a lease is truly a lease or is merely a security agreement, should the court determine this price at the outset of the lease (and irrespective of the ultimate value of the property) or at the end of the lease (when the court knows the actual value of the property)?

2. Would any of the following factors be relevant in determining whether an arrangement should be treated as a lease or as a security agreement?

   a. Who received the investment tax credit.

   b. Whether any warranties were given by the lessor to the lessee.

   c. Who bore the responsibility for maintenance of the leased product.

3. In doing what the court calls "first tier" analysis, one must impute an interest or discount rate. How should a court do that?

Note: The Lease in Bankruptcy

The differential treatment accorded a "lease" on the one hand (under section 365 in bankruptcy) and a security agreement on the other (under 1129 and other sections in bankruptcy) means that the lease/security agreement controversy will continue and even intensify in bankruptcy cases under the 1978 Code.

Under sections 1129 and 1322, a plan can be imposed by the court on a secured creditor, even though the plan pays the secured creditor much less than his loan agreement calls for. This is the so-called "cramdown." Under a cramdown, however, the creditor is assured of payments equal to the present value of his collateral ("adequate protection"). Assume, for example, that an arrangement constituted a security agreement rather than a true lease, with the creditor having a security interest in a piece of equipment worth $50,000 which secured a $100,000 debt. Here, the secured creditor could be made to take payments with a present value of $50,000 and the remaining $50,000 could be treated as unsecured debt to be paid, perhaps, only a few cents on the dollar.

On the other hand, if the agreement were found to be a "lease," it would be governed by section 365 and the debtor would be faced with the choice of either returning the asset to the creditor or of complying explicitly with every term of the lease. Thus, in such a case, the debtor would presumably either return the equipment or, if it were particularly valuable, would be obliged to pay the full $100,000 in order to keep it. In effect, under a lease arrangement the lessor is entitled to realize the unique value of the lease to this particular debtor even though that value greatly exceeds the market value of the asset to others. If, in our hypothetical case, the value to the particular debtor of the collateral in question is only $50,000, obviously he would exercise his power under the Bankruptcy Code to reject the lease and procure similar equipment elsewhere for much less than $100,000. Thus, in In re Wikowski, 37 B.R. 352 (Bkrtcy.D.N.D. 1984), the court found that a "lease" was in fact a security agreement and thus concluded that the debtor farmer could keep his 120 head mini-swine nursery if he paid only its market value, even though that value was substantially less than the value of the remaining lease payments and even though the farmer may have valued the nursery much more highly.

SECTION 3. THE BORDER BETWEEN BAILMENT AND ARTICLES TWO AND NINE

Almost all of the conflicts between Article 2 and Article 9 deal in some way with the legal consequences arising from possession of goods by a given party. Some of these questions have grown up as discrete and well-recognized issues in the law of sales. For example, under a consignment the owner places goods in the hands of another for resale to third parties. This is an ancient practice, designed in some cases to allow the seller to maintain price control over the resale price. In other cases, the consignment is used as a device in effect to finance the retailer's business or to encourage the retailer to sell the consignor's goods by minimizing the retailer's risk. Because the consignor's interest is closely akin to a purchase-money seller's security interest, one might ask whether the creditors of the retailer should have rights prior to the consignor's interest, at least when the consignor has not put third parties on notice in any way. It is not surprising to find that section 2–326 of Article 2 which, when combined with UCC 9–114, treats the consignor for many purposes like a seller who retains a purchase money security interest.

Equally well recognized and developed is the doctrine set out in sections 2–702, 2–507 and 2–511 giving a defrauded seller the right to the return of his goods despite the fact that he has transferred possession to a buyer. The fraud in such cases is the buyer's receiving goods on credit while insolvent or after a representation of solvency. Yet here, too, one must ask whether the creditors of the buyer should have rights prior to the defrauded seller. Others such as the buyer's secured creditor with a floating lien, lien creditors, trustees in bankruptcy, and buyers in the ordinary course will certainly be ready to challenge the seller's right to the return of his goods.

The bailment cases give rise to a third well-recognized point of abrasion. Parties claiming as bailors may actually finance part of a debtor's operations. But should one who owns seed and "bails it" to a farmer be entitled to the crop produced (to repay the seed and harvesting loan) or should the crop go to a lender who has taken a specific security interest in the crop?

Finally, the courts have encountered a series of less well defined questions that partake partly of one and partly of another of the transactions described above. We will call one the "quasi consignment." Here an owner of goods puts them in the hands of a third party for processing and alternatively for their return or possibly for sale. Is this merely a bailment? A consignment? Something else? A similar case is one in which a purchaser buys goods and yet leaves them in the hands of the seller. This problem is governed in part by UCC 2–502, but some courts have used UCC 9–307 to deal with it. It resembles in some sense an ancient fraudulent conveyance in which it is argued that a buyer has allowed his seller to defraud subsequent creditors by permitting the seller to retain possession and thus apparent ownership of the property.

Because the typical transaction will often have attributes of more than one of the arrangements described above, each case is dependent to some extent on its own facts and each will form a basis for one party to argue for one of the doctrines described above and for another to argue a second and conflicting one. Thus, it is not uncommon to see a set of cases dealing with the problem, for example, under UCC 2–502 co-existing with cases that would appear to be in direct conflict, but decided under UCC 9–307. Each set fails to mention the other.

At the outset a student should examine the relevant Article 2 sections: UCC 2–326, 2–401, 2–402, 2–403, 2–502, 2–507, 2–511, 2–702, 2–711(3). The most directly relevant Article 9 sections should also be considered: UCC 9–102, 9–113, 9–114, 9–307. Having taken a quick look at those sections, the student is prepared to begin work on the problem and cases that follow.

Problem 7–2

Analyze the following problem under UCC 2–326.

Assume that General Electric sold a series of lamps, bulbs, and other electrical equipment to a retailer, Pettingale Electric. Most of these goods were on a "sale or return" basis. If they were not sold within 30 or 60 days, Pettingale had the right to return them to General Electric and get a refund of the money paid. General Electric did not file a financing statement under Article 9 and when Pettingale went into bankruptcy the trustee claimed the assets. In which of the following cases would General Electric win in competition with the trustee:

1. If General Electric had filed a financing statement six months prior to the filing of a petition.

2. If Pettingale did business under the name of "General Electric Supply Company."

3. If General Electric proved that a competing bank, who itself had lent more than half of the entire debt to Pettingale knew of General Electric's claim.

4. If General Electric introduced persuasive evidence that the purpose of its consignment was not to finance Pettingale, but to control the resale price and also to minimize tax liability.

SIMMONS FIRST NATIONAL BANK v. WELLS

Supreme Court of Arkansas, 1983.
279 Ark. 204, 650 S.W.2d 236.

HAYS, JUSTICE.

This suit presents the issue of whether the interest of a secured creditor in the inventory of a grain dealer is superior to that of a rice grower who subsequently deposits his rice with that dealer.

On May 1, 1980, Simmons First National Bank made a loan of $520,000 to Western Rice Mills, Inc., for which Western granted Simmons a security interest in all of its real and personal property, including all inventory and after acquired property. Western defaulted and in September of 1981, a receiver was appointed. Shortly thereafter, Harold Wells intervened, claiming ownership of certain rice and proceeds from the sale of rice, pursuant to a previous agreement with Western.

Wells had dealt with Western for a number of years, the standard arrangement being that Western would buy the rice outright from Wells, would mill it and then sell it. In April and May of 1981, because of financial difficulties, Western could not buy the rice outright from Wells. Wells and Western orally agreed instead that Western would mill the rice for a certain price and then market the rice at an agreed minimum price for Wells. The charge for milling would be deducted when Western sold the rice, and the remaining proceeds would go to Wells. In the interim, the rice was stored with Western.

The trial court, relying on the rationale of *In Re Sitkin Smelting and Refining, Inc.,* 639 F.2d 1213 (5th Cir.1981), found the arrangement between Wells and Western to constitute a bailment and found Ark.Stat.Ann. § 85–2–326 (Add.1961) inapplicable. Under this finding, the inventory lien of the bank did not extend to the rice or to the proceeds claimed by Wells.

Simmons argues for reversal that the Chancellor erred in finding that § 85–2–326 was inapplicable to the facts of this case. We agree and find that § 85–2–326 *is* applicable and we reverse as to those grounds.

The Chancellor mistakenly relied on *Sitkin,* whereby he found the arrangement to be a bailment and, apparently, found that that precluded the possibility of finding a consignment and § 85–2–326 applicable. We see two flaws in this analysis: first, the *Sitkin* case is factually distinguishable, the main issue there being whether the arrangement was a sale or a bailment. Second, even if a particular arrangement is found to constitute a bailment as opposed to a sale, that does not preclude a finding that there is also a consignment arrangement and, hence, § 85–2–326 is applicable.

In *Sitkin,* the issue was whether the bankruptcy court had erred in determining that possession of film entrusted to a bankrupt metal refiner, Sitkin, should be given to a secured creditor of the refiner rather than to the film manufacturer, Kodak, which had entrusted it to Sitkin. The arrangement between Sitkin and Kodak was basically that Sitkin would retain possession of film waste delivered to it by Kodak. But for Kodak's business purposes, not until the film had been reduced and destroyed and the silver content removed by Sitkin, would Kodak's ownership cease, and at that time a "settlement" would be made as to the amount owned by Sitkin. The court looked at a number of factors surrounding the transaction and found it to be a bailment and not a sale. The court also determined that the transaction was not a "sale or return" within the meaning of § 85–2–326 since the goods were not delivered for resale with an option to return. Although we are not convinced that the court was correct in finding a bailment and not a sale in *Sitkin,* that is irrelevant here.

Whether the arrangement in this case was a bailment or a sale is not determinative of the rights of the parties. Even if under the analysis of *Sitkin,* the trial court found a bailment and not a sale, the question of whether § 85–2–326 is applicable must still be answered. Western could have been a bailee for Wells and at the same time been a consignee under § 85–2–326. We emphasize the following language of § 85–2–326(3) which we find applicable to this fact situation: [quoting]

> The comment to this section reinforces the policy indicated by the language of this section:
>
> 2. Pursuant to the general policies of this Act which require good faith not only between the parties to the sales contract, but as against interested third parties, subsection (3) *resolves all reasonable doubts as to the nature of the transaction in favor of the general creditors of the buyer.* * * * (our italics).

Here, Wells delivered his goods, the rice, to Western for sale and Western maintained a place of business where it dealt in goods of that kind, under a name other than the name of the person making the delivery, Wells. With regard to the rights of creditors, it is irrelevant whether the transaction between the two parties was a bailment or a sale if the provisions of § 85–2–326(3) are also satisfied.

We find *In Re KLP, Inc. Finance Co. of America v. Morris,* 7 B.R. 256 (Bkrtcy.N.D.Ga.1980) more analogous to our case and it provides a more appropriate and clearer application of § 85–2–326. In *KLP,* the plaintiff had leased space from the debtor to store two organs. The organs were delivered to the debtor's warehouse where the debtor had traditionally dealt in organs and related goods. At the time of delivery, the agreement was modified to allow the debtor to secure offers for the purchase of the organs, subject to the debtor obtaining prior approval of the offers and sale by the plaintiff. When the debtor filed for bankruptcy, the plaintiff filed to recover the organs. The court ruled in favor of the Trustee whose status under the Bankruptcy Code is that of a hypothetical lien creditor who would have priority over a consignment seller who failed to comply with the requirements of UCC § 2–326. The following passage states the policy and reasoning behind UCC § 2–326:

> The applicable UCC provision, § 2–326, is not only one of the more important UCC sections, but is also one of the most unique provisions in the UCC article which governs the sale of goods. The uniqueness of the section lies primarily in the fact that the section applies to transactions which are not true sales at all, since the section governs agreements which somehow provide that "delivered goods may be returned by the buyer even though they conform to the contract." The section's impor-

tance lies primarily in the role it plays, along with the notice provisions of article nine, in giving disclosed claims to property priority over secret claims. To encourage disclosure of in rem claims is a central feature of any well-reasoned system of commercial law.

Of particular importance to the instant case is the fact that certain types of transactions are "deemed" by § 2–326(3) to constitute "consignment sales." The statute so characterizes a transaction when the following three circumstances are present:

(1) when goods are delivered for sale,

(2) when the "consignment buyer" maintains a place of business at which he deals in goods of the kind so delivered, and

(3) when the business name of the "consignment seller" is different than the business name of the consignment buyer.

If a transaction is so deemed to constitute a consignment sale, the consignment seller may obtain priority over the consignment buyer's creditors only by complying with the notice requirements of UCC § 2–326(3).

The facts of this case require us to examine § 85–2–326 for its applicability. The language of the statute and the commentary convince us that the reasoning of the court in *KLP* is sound. * * * Therefore, because we think the theory on which the case was tried would bring it within § 85–2–326, and since there was no evidence or argument that Wells complied with any of the requirements of § 85–2–326(3) so as to remove him from the provisions of that section, the priority of Simmons' interest would prevail on that issue.

* * *

FIRST STATE BANK OF WIGGINS v. SIMMONS

Supreme Court of Colorado, 1932.
91 Colo. 160, 13 P.2d 259.

CAMPBELL, J.

A full statement of the material facts in this case will not only shorten the discussion, but it is the best way to dispose of the controversy.

The Associated Seed Growers, a corporation, entered into a contract with M.L. Miller by the terms of which it delivered to him certain seeds and Miller agreed to act as bailee thereof for the purpose of raising a crop or crop of seeds therefrom which was to be redelivered to the seed company. Miller was to prepare the ground or soil for planting and was to plant approximately fifteen acres. The land on which the seed was planted belonged to a third party. Miller agreed to cultivate and care for the crop and harvest the same so as to secure the greatest possible return of seed suitable for seedmen's use and to sack all such seed that was grown and deliver the same to the seed company at Masters, Colorado. The parties in their agreement referred to this contract as a bailment. It expressly provides that the seed which was furnished by the seed company to Miller, and the entire seed crop produced therefrom, were at all times to be the property of the seed company and it had the right of possession of the same at any time, or, at its option, to harvest the crop or to cultivate the ground and deduct the cost of such cultivation from the compensation agreed to be paid to Miller for his services in planting and caring for the crop. The contract further provides that Miller shall have no right at any time to sell or dispose of the said stock seed furnished to him or the seed crop produced therefrom. As compensation for his services Miller was entitled to receive, and the seed company was required to pay him, at the rate of 7 cents per pound for the crop grown.

After this seed contract was made the defendant in error, here, Simmons, brought an action against Miller to recover on the latter's debt to him, and served a writ of garnishment upon the Associated Seed Company. The seed company made answer that there was owing to Miller under this seed contract the sum of $108.30. The plaintiff in error, the First State Bank of Wiggins, Colorado, intervened in this action and claimed the money which the seed company admitted it owed to Miller and based its claim upon a chattel mortgage given to it by Miller upon the crop produced.

The question for decision upon this review is whether the beans grown by Miller under the contract with the seed company are subject to the mortgage of the bank. Perhaps a better statement of the question is, did Miller have the right and power under his contract with the seed company to give a valid chattel mortgage on the prospective bean crop to the Wiggins Bank as against the claim and right which the seed company had thereto under its seed contract? We think Simmons' rights under his judgment against Miller are superior to that of the bank under its mortgage from Miller. Not only did the seed company and Miller designate the bean contract as a bailment, but a reading of the same makes it entirely clear that the transaction between the seed company and Miller was of that character. No property right in the crop to be grown passed under the contract from the seed company to Miller. It expressly provides that his interest under the contract is only the right to receive for his services to the seed company in caring for the crop a certain sum of money but it gave him no right whatever to the crop to be grown. In Morsch v. Lessig, 45 Colo. 168, 100 P. 431, we held that an owner is not affected by an unauthorized pledge of his goods by an agent to whom he has entrusted them. This contract between the Associated Seed Company and Miller was unquestionably a bailment. In Clay, Robinson & Co. v. Martinez, 74 Colo. 10, 218 P. 903, we held that the owner of bailed property is not estopped to deny the ownership of the bailee because he permits the latter to enter into contracts with third parties concerning the same. We also held in that case that every one deals with a bailee at his peril and, in the absence of special legislation to the contrary, one who deals with the bailee concerning the bailed property not only does so at his peril but is charged with notice of its real ownership. See, generally, 6 C.J. p. 1084 et seq.; 1 Bouv.Law Dict. p. 313 et seq.; 3 R.C.L. p. 71 et seq., §§ 35, 66.

Applying this recognized doctrine of bailment to the present case, we say that even though there might have been an equitable lien or assignment by Miller to the bank if the contract between the seed company and Miller was not a bailment, that doctrine is wholly inapplicable to the facts of this case, because the contract between the seed company and Miller constituted a bailment. Since no property right in and to the crop that was grown under this contract was ever acquired by Miller, he had no right or power, as against the rights of the seed company or its assignee, to give a chattel mortgage on the crop to the bank which was his creditor. The judgment is, therefore, affirmed.

Affirmed.

ADAMS, C.J., and ALTER, J., concur.

Notes

1. How would this case come out under the Code? In relation to a similar case, it has been said that: "The result seems pretty plainly contrary to the philosophy of the Commercial Code, but seems not to be overruled directly by any of its specific provisions." Bunn, *Financing Farmers,* 1954 Wis.L.Rev. 357, 363. Do you agree?

2. If the bailment device will not work under the Code, how might the financing buyer protect himself? Consider the following problem.

Problem 7–3

Farmer raises grapefruit. Nearby cannery cans grapefruit. F needs funds at the beginning and at the end of the growing season to pay for the care of his trees and for harvesting. C needs assurance that at the end of the growing season C will have enough harvested grapefruit to make the best possible use of C's canning facilities. Accordingly, in return for F's commitment to sell his crop to C, C is willing to advance funds to F to be used by F in growing and harvesting his crop, such money to be applied on the purchase price of the grapefruit when delivered to C. Assume that C has come to you "to set this thing up." First of all, what are the risks to C in such a venture? If we assume that C advances, say, $10,000 to F, what risks can materialize between the time of such advance and the date harvested grapefruit are to be delivered to C? The crop could fail for lack of care, or because of weather conditions. F could repudiate. F could harvest but wrongfully resell to a third party. An unsecured creditor of F could levy on the growing crop or on it as it is harvested. A secured creditor of F could foreclose. F could go bankrupt.

How might C maximize its protection against some or all of the foregoing hazards? What C most wants is as much legal assurance as is possible that C will actually get the grapefruit when harvested. As a buyer of goods under Article 2, C would potentially have rights under UCC 2–502(1) and UCC 2–716 to possession of the grapefruit *as against* F. But are these rights adequate, even as against F? As against third parties? Do these provisions give C sufficient rights against third parties? UCC 2–402(1) favors C as against unsecured creditors of F. But UCC 2–402(2) qualifies this, and UCC 2–402(3)(a) makes it plain that secured creditors are not affected by UCC 2–402(1). Moreover, C may lose to purchasers from F under UCC 2–403(2). What would you recommend?

Problem 7–4

1. United Steel Products was deeply in debt to Hoesch America, Inc. Ultimately they worked out their differences and an agreement was reached in which Hoesch would cancel its entire debt of $1,800,000 in return for U.S.P.'s transfer to it of its entire inventory. After that transfer had occurred and Hoesch had sold the steel, Maremont Corporation made a claim against Hoesch for approximately $400,000 of steel. Maremont claimed that it had purchased that steel from U.S.P. but in the downturn of the auto industry in 1983 had

allowed the steel to remain in the possession of U.S.P. for more than a year. Maremont produced invoices that show that the steel formerly owned by U.S.P. had been "delivered" to it and had been paid for. In fact the steel remained in U.S.P.'s inventory and was not marked in any particular way as separate from its inventory. Is Hoesch liable to Maremont on a conversion theory (or any other theory) for the value of the steel?

2. You are counsel for First Bank. It is contemplating the possibility of being the general financer of a clock manufacturer. As such it would take perfected security principally in inventory and accounts receivable of the manufacturer. An examination of the prospective debtor's operation discloses the following: frequently and in accordance with the practice in the clock trade, buyers prepay for clocks. Typically the clocks are manufactured and put in boxes. They often sit in inventory for weeks, and in some cases, months. The bank wishes to know whether it will have a right in the clocks superior or subordinate to the rights of the buyers. The clocks are generic, that is, they are not marked with any particular buyer's name nor are any specifically designed for particular buyers. However, the boxes in which the clocks are contained will typically be marked with the buyer's name. If the Bank insists upon a prior right in order to make the loan, what do you suggest?

For one of your editors' (White's) view about how these cases might be put together, consider the following:

Note: Ostensible Ownership and the Integrity of Article 9

We have already confronted the transaction in which one party signs a document entitled a "lease" which obliges him to make certain payments and gives him the option to purchase at the end of the term for a nominal consideration. The parties may frame their transaction so for a variety of reasons; never mind what they are for the time being. In UCC 9–102(1) and 1–201(37) the Code makes plain that substance is to govern form in such a transaction. A document masquerading as a lease is a security agreement. This is but one example of the function of UCC 9–102, which provides that Article 9 covers "any transaction (regardless of its form) which is intended to create a security interest in personal property * * *" Its purpose is to avoid the dismal history under which legislatures drafted laws to govern security arrangements and clever lawyers routinely escaped the grasp of such laws by devising ingenious documents that suited their clients' needs but did not fit the statutory definitions.

Many skirmishes have been fought over whether a lease was a "true lease" or a security agreement. It has always been implicit in such decisions that if one could convince the court that his document was a "true lease", he need not file a financing statement to recover the goods upon the lessee's bankruptcy. At least in the bona fide lease, the law has disregarded the fact that the debtor has possession; it has not required that the lessor make a public filing in order to protect his rights against third party claimants who might be misled by the lessee's possession.

Consider 9–102's application in a case once removed from the lease. In In re Medomak Canning Co., 25 UCC Rep.Serv. 437 (D.Me.1977), Underwood, a large New England food company, entered into an agreement with a smaller company,

Medomak Canning, under which the larger would supply ingredients, packaging and shipping material for the canning and packaging of certain foodstuffs and would pay a fixed fee for the canned goods when they were shipped at its direction to third parties. The exact nature of the transaction between the parties is unclear, for the large manufacturer was apparently attempting to set up the transaction as a sale and repurchase agreement whereas Medomak would have preferred to characterize the transaction as one in which it was simply processing Underwood's goods. With very little analysis of 9–102 the court assumed that upon Medomak's bankruptcy Underwood would have the right to the return of the approximately $100,000 of canned goods, raw materials and supplies if the contract were held to be one for processing and not for purchase and resale. Under UCC 9–102 that is far from clear. It is obvious from the opinion that at least Medomak's interest in the transaction was to achieve financing, for the court points out "it lacked the necessary capital to acquire approximately $100,000 worth of ingredients and packaging and shipping materials. * * *" Conceding that the transaction was in fact not a sale, Medomak's secured creditors who were competing with Underwood might have argued that they had superior rights nevertheless because the transaction was in effect one "intended to create a security interest in personal property," thus subject to Article 9 and no more than an unperfected security interest.

Before we analyze *Medomak,* consider a third case twice removed from the lease. In Chrysler Corp. v. Adamatic, Inc., 59 Wis.2d 219, 208 N.W.2d 97 (1973), reprinted p. 249, Chrysler had been financing the manufacture of certain equipment by a Milwaukee company that went bankrupt. At the time of the bankruptcy some of the machines were complete; others were in various states of manufacture. Two of the machines in Adamatic's possession had been previously delivered to Chrysler and been returned to Adamatic for further work. Chrysler argued that it was the "owner" not only of the delivered machines but of the others as well and thus could take the assets free of the after-acquired claim of the secured lender. Chrysler won only as to two machines which had been delivered and returned. As to the rest it was simply an unsecured creditor.

How does one square the cases? Bear in mind that in the first we have a true lease of equipment to be used in the lessee's business. In the second, we have the provision of inventory to be processed by another party and then either returned to the person furnishing the inventory or sent to a third party. Thirdly we have the purchase money financer who has neither possession nor a perfected security interest but simply argues that on completion, the title passes to him because of his prior payment.

At the outset we must reject the easiest answer. It would be easiest to say that all true owners who are not in possession must file public documents to show their ownership if they are to defeat competing creditors. Such a rule is so foreign to our general ideas of ownership that no one would agree to it. No one would say that a person must file a financing statement with respect to his own automobile in the repair shop to protect himself against the claims of the repairman's creditors. For that and other reasons we reject that result as outrageous.

Perhaps we should opt for the second easiest outcome, namely to say that the debtor's possession has no significance. Thus for example we would say that if Chrysler's contract with Adamatic provided for title to pass to Chrysler upon completion of the equipment, Chrysler would *ipso facto* enjoy superior rights.

The fact that Adamatic retained possession and that the goods thus remain the inventory of Adamatic would not give competing creditors any interest superior to Chrysler's. Surely we cannot tolerate that rule. We cannot tolerate it, for it would rip a huge gash in the fabric of Article 9. It would undermine the whole idea that a secured creditor can take a security interest in the debtor's inventory and, by checking the files and filing, make himself superior to almost all other claimants. So the second easiest result is also unacceptable.

Where then do we draw the line between the pure lease where we allow the lessor to retake the goods against even secured creditors notwithstanding the lessee's possession and the failure of the lessor to give public notice of his interest, and Chrysler's case on the other hand where, notwithstanding the underlying contract, we allow the other secured creditors to claim the machine in preference to Chrysler's claim that title passed to it upon completion? *Medomak* lies in this gray area and so does the consignment.

Consider some factors that one might weigh. First we might ask whether the transaction has attributes *known in the trade* (other than filing) which put competing creditors on notice of the owner's interest. Equipment leases are now widespread; surely no sensible creditor relies upon any person's possession of equipment without at least rudimentary inquiry into his rights in the goods. Exactly the same must be true of the many cars sitting in a repairman's shop and of the used clocks and watches in a jeweler's place of business. The other creditors' knowledge of the possessor's business puts them on notice of third party claims in various of those goods. A second telling factor may be the acts that the possessor expects to take with respect to the goods when he is finished with them. If he is to return them to the owner and that is known in the trade, it looks much less like a sale than if he is to pass them to third parties. Conceivably one might also be put on notice by the nature of the function to be performed. If for example large and expensive furnaces were in the plant of a person known to manufacture and install only small electric motors, that alone might be enough notice to other creditors to tell them that he was not the owner of the furnaces which were placed there for the installation of the motor and which were to be returned to the owner.

One might also look to analogous provisions of the Code to guide his judgment. Section 2–401 indicates that retention of title by a "seller" is nothing more than a security interest but that section is really not helpful, for it assumes the question, namely that there is a "buyer" and a "seller". More to the point is the idea of ostensible ownership, an idea grown in the common law and embodied in UCC 2–402(2). That doctrine tells that a creditor who is misled by a seller's continued possession after sale will have rights superior to those of the buyer. By the same token we let buyers override others' title interests in UCC 2–403 and security interests in UCC 9–307 in circumstances where the buyer is purchasing from inventory and would reasonably expect to receive clear title. UCC 2–326 draws a distinction between goods that are out "on approval" versus those that are "on sale or return". In the latter case the creditors of the possessor are likely to prevail, in the former they do not. Finally in Article 6 we find unsecured creditors with rights superior to those of a bulk purchaser in many cases. What are the unarticulated premises of these sections and how can they help in resolving the borderline secured transaction? First, they recognize what we have suggested above, namely that there are different expectations aroused by a debtor's possession of items that appear as his *inventory* than are aroused by his possession of *equipment.* Second, they reveal assumptions about the importance of the relative sophistication of the competing claimants. We find that the code subordinates relatively sophisticated persons such as bulk purchasers and buyers from farmers notwithstanding possession, but other less sophisticated claimants such as buyers in the ordinary course are given good title by the Code. We would suggest that these sections are no more than an explicit recognition and direct application of some of the general ideas and factors described above. They may serve as fruitful analogues, but neither they nor the factors described above are likely to provide certain answers.

Where does *Medomak* fall in all of this? It appears to us that it falls on the *Adamatic* side of the line. Financing the debtor was a clear purpose of the transaction. The collateral was inventory not equipment which could be expected to be returned to the original owner. The completed goods were to be shipped not back to Underwood but to various places at Underwood's direction. Moreover Underwood conceived of the transaction as a sale and repurchase and not simply as a lending for processing. Thus we think the case is wrong.

We are uncertain about the size of the gray area that lies between the true lease and the *Adamatic* case. However we are confident that this area is sizeable and that no certain answer can be given for the cases that fall within it. Consideration of the factors described above should assist a court in protecting the integrity of Article 9 and should tell it when it can safely uphold the owner, non-possessor's interest in the absence of compliance with Article 9 and without frustrating the expectations of other creditors. Nevertheless, *Medomak* illustrates that there will be hard cases on which reasonable persons will differ.

SECTION 4. THE RECLAIMING SELLER, UCC 2–702, ETC.

The Uniform Commercial Code, the Uniform Sales Act, and before that, the common law, have recognized the right of a limited class of unpaid sellers to the return of their goods in limited circumstances. This right of an unpaid seller contributes an exception to the general rule that a seller who does not specifically retain a security interest is no better off than an unsecured creditor of the buyer. That limited right of the unpaid seller to reclaim is set out principally in section 2–702 of the UCC:

> (1) Where the seller discovers the buyer to be insolvent he may refuse delivery except for cash including payment for all goods theretofore delivered under the contract, and stop delivery under this Article (Section 2–705).
>
> (2) Where the seller discovers that the buyer has received goods on credit while insolvent he may reclaim the goods upon demand made within ten days after the receipt, but if misrepresentation of solvency has been made to the particular seller in writing within three months before delivery the ten day limitation does not apply. Except as provided in this subsection the seller may not base a right to reclaim goods on the buyer's fraudulent or innocent misrepresentation of solvency or of intent to pay.
>
> (3) The seller's right to reclaim under subsection (2) is subject to the rights of a buyer in ordinary course or other good faith purchaser under this Article (Section 2–403). Successful reclamation of goods excludes all other remedies with respect to them.

The student should also read UCC 2–507 and 2–511, sections that have been construed to give cash sellers and sellers who receive checks on delivery rights similar to those enjoyed by credit sellers under UCC 2–702.

On their face, sections 2–702, 2–507 and 2–511 raise a series of technical, interpretative questions. What, for example, is necessary to constitute a written misrepresentation of solvency? Must the demand for return be made in writing or is an oral demand adequate to perfect the unpaid seller's rights under UCC 2–702? Does the ten day limitation embodied in UCC 2–702 also apply to UCC 2–507? What about the right to proceeds? We need not answer all of these questions here, but the student should be sensitive to them. Prior to enactment of the Bankruptcy Code in 1978, a series of cases had arisen concerning the rights of the trustee in bankruptcy vis a vis a seller reclaiming under 2–702. Routinely the trustee had argued that he was superior to the reclaiming seller either on the ground that he had a lien under 70c (now 544(a)) or that the UCC 2–702 right was, in fact, a form of statutory lien or a lien that first arose upon bankruptcy and so could be struck down under section 67 (now 546(b)). Congress sought to resolve these disputes by enacting 546(c). It reads in full as follows:

> Except as provided in subsection (d) of this section, the rights and powers of a trustee under sections 544(a), 545, 547, and 549 of this title are subject to any statutory or common-law right of a seller of goods that has sold goods to the debtor, in the ordinary course of such seller's business, to reclaim such goods if the debtor has received such goods while insolvent, but—
>
> (1) such a seller may not reclaim any such goods unless such seller demands in writing reclamation of such goods before ten days after receipt of such goods by the debtor; and
>
> (2) the court may deny reclamation to a seller with such a right of reclamation that has made such a demand only if the court—
>
> (A) grants the claim of such a seller priority as a claim of a kind specified in section 503(b) of this title; or
>
> (B) secures such claim by a lien.

Do you see how Congress has left threads hanging? Compare UCC 2–702 with § 546(c). Presumably the former was the template for the latter, but the template was substantially bent before it was used!

UNITED STATES v. WESTSIDE BANK

United States Court of Appeals, Fifth Circuit, 1984.
732 F.2d 1258.

JOHN R. BROWN, CIRCUIT JUDGE:

This statutory interpleader brought pursuant to 28 U.S.C. § 1335 was filed by the Small Business Administration (SBA) to determine the proper distribution of proceeds from a foreclosure sale. The fund represents the remaining assets of Texas Electronics Mart, Inc. (TEMI). In distributing the fund, the District Court determined that Westside Bank of San Antonio (Westside) held the only priority claim. The Court thus denied the priority status asserted by O'Sullivan Industries, Inc. (O'Sullivan) based on its right to reclaim the proceeds from the sale of goods it delivered to TEMI just prior to the foreclosure. O'Sullivan duly perfected this appeal. We hold that a seller of goods (here, O'Sullivan) retains a priority status to the extent of traceable proceeds from the sale of those goods where he has complied with all the requirements of Texas Business and Commerce Code Annotated § 2.702 (Vernon 1968) (the Texas UCC), and diligently pursued the right of reclamation created under that section. We therefore affirm in part, reverse in part, and remand for a determination of whether O'Sullivan diligently pursued its right to reclamation.

Factual Background

In April of 1976 TEMI executed a promissory note and security agreement in favor of Westside for the sum of $99,500. The note was guaranteed by the SBA. TEMI granted Westside a security interest in "all machinery, and equipment, fixtures, inventory and accounts receivable now owned, to be purchased with loan proceeds and hereafter acquired." The agreement included a future advance clause, a clause securing any legal fees incurred in enforcing the agreement, and a clause securing the interest due. Westside duly perfected its security interest.

In September of 1979, TEMI executed a second promissory note to Westside for the sum of $16,000. The note was collateralized with the 1976 security agreement through the future advance clause. At the time of trial, Westside asserted an outstanding claim on this note in the amount of $12,471.52.

Pursuant to the SBA guarantee, Westside assigned its rights under the first note to the SBA sometime in December, 1979.[3] The SBA declared the note delinquent and accelerated its maturity on December 14, 1979. In accordance with the security agreement, the SBA conducted a foreclosure sale of all TEMI's assets on January 21, 1980. After deducting the loan balance and expenses of the sale, the SBA deposited the remaining proceeds ($50,750.95) with the District Court for proper distribution among TEMI's creditors.

The District Court awarded Westside the sum of $17,666.60, representing its claim on the second note plus interest and attorney's fees. The Court, however, denied the priority right of reclamation asserted by O'Sullivan under Texas UCC § 2.702. The Court reasoned that any right of reclamation would be cut short by a prior secured lender's foreclosure. Because in this case the SBA had foreclosed, the Court found that O'Sullivan had no right to the proceeds from the sale of the goods. In disposing of the case on this basis, the District Court deemed it unnecessary to reach the issue whether O'Sullivan had complied with the statutory requirements for recla-

3. When a debtor defaults on a loan that the SBA has guaranteed, the lender may avoid the time, expense, and potential liability of foreclosure by assigning its rights under the loan to the SBA. The SBA then pays the lender the full amount of the loan and becomes subrogated to the rights of the lender, including any security interest or priority status the lender had attained. The UCC recognizes the utility of this practice and provides for it in § 9.504(c). Thus, when Westside assigned its rights under the first note to the SBA, both the SBA and Westside had a perfected security interest in TEMI's assets pursuant to the security agreement executed in April of 1976.

mation under § 2.702. The Court therefore distributed the remaining funds pro rata among O'Sullivan and TEMI's other general unsecured creditors.

THE RECLAMATION RIGHT

The right of reclamation is specifically created in favor of a credit seller by Texas UCC § 2.702. This right exists only in "specific and limited circumstances; it can be asserted only if an exacting procedure is followed; and the right can never be asserted to defeat the interest of certain third parties who have dealt with the defaulting buyer." *Matter of Samuels & Co., Inc.,* 526 F.2d 1238 (5th Cir.1976) (en banc), *cert. denied,* 429 U.S. 834, 97 S.Ct. 98, 50 L.Ed.2d 99 (1976).

In order for the right to arise, certain conditions must be met. First, the buyer must have received the goods on credit. There is no dispute that TEMI received the goods shipped by O'Sullivan on credit. Second, the buyer must receive the goods while insolvent. The District Court made no finding as to when TEMI became insolvent, but it did find that O'Sullivan did not know of TEMI's insolvency when it shipped the goods. Finally, the seller must learn of the buyer's insolvency and make demand for return of the goods within ten days from the date of delivery. The District Court found that O'Sullivan shipped furniture accessories valued at $36,756.94 on November 19 and 21, 1979, and that the shipments were received by TEMI on November 21 and 23, respectively. The Court determined that O'Sullivan learned of TEMI's insolvency sometime between November 21 and November 30. It also found that O'Sullivan made written demand for payment of the entire amount of TEMI's open account ($50,727.07) on November 30.

In addition to the demand made upon TEMI, O'Sullivan also made written demand upon Westside[6] through O'Sullivan's parent corporation, Conroy, Inc. The letter from Conroy also demanded payment for the full amount of TEMI's open account. This letter, however, also specified that it was a demand pursuant to § 2.702 of the Texas UCC. The goods were not returned, nor was payment made to O'Sullivan.

O'Sullivan filed suit against TEMI in state court on January 18, 1980 to enforce its right of reclamation. However, on January 21 the SBA foreclosure sale was conducted, and TEMI ceased to exist for all practical purposes as a business entity. This effectively terminated the state court litigation. In order to further protect the reclamation right it was asserting, O'Sullivan repurchased 797 of the 1,000 pieces of furniture from the November shipment at the foreclosure sale for a price of $27,500. On appeal, O'Sullivan continues to urge its priority status as to the full sales proceeds of $36,756.94. Alternatively, it urges priority status as to $27,500—the traceable proceeds from the goods O'Sullivan has sought to reclaim.

6. The record implies that O'Sullivan was unable to locate TEMI's principal officers. The issue presented is whether by November 30 Westside had assumed control of TEMI so as to become its fiduciary representative. If so, then written demand on Westside would be equivalent to written demand on TEMI. We find however, that there are insufficient facts in the record to determine this issue. Therefore, we remand for the limited purpose of resolving whether O'Sullivan's demands on Westside were tantamount to proper demand upon TEMI. *See* note 21, *infra. See also U.S. v. Terrey,* 554 F.2d 685 (5th Cir.1977) (where a creditor decides to liquidate collateral, he must act as the debtor's fiduciary in disposing of assets); *Tackett v. Mid-Continent Refrigerator Co.,* 579 S.W.2d 545 (Tex.Civ.App.1979) (secured party who repossesses property has duty to make commercially reasonable disposition on account for proceeds).

In determining that O'Sullivan's right to reclaim was terminated by the SBA foreclosure and therefore could not attach to proceeds, the District Court relied on *Matter of Samuels, supra.* We believe the Court's reliance was misplaced.

DISTINGUISHING SAMUELS

In *Samuels,* a divided *en banc* Court adopted Judge Godbold's dissent from the panel opinion, which held that an unpaid *cash* seller's right of reclamation is subordinate to a preexisting perfected security interest in the buyer's after acquired property. *Id.* at 1245. In so holding, the Court emphasized several important factors which are not present in the case before us. At the outset, the Court recognized that the reclaiming seller was a *cash* seller. *Id.* at 1244. Furthermore, he had not made a demand under § 2.702 until a full year after the delivery. The Court refused to find that his reclamation right had been timely exercised. *Id.* at 1245. Disturbed by the fact that in recognizing the cash seller's right to reclaim courts had extended the § 2.702 remedy, the Court refused to further extend the time within which the right could be exercised.

* * * [T]he meticulous analysis provided by *Samuels* regarding the interplay between Articles Two and Nine of the UCC is fully consistent with a finding in favor of O'Sullivan in the instant case. Turning first to the Texas UCC, § 2.401(a), the *Samuels* Court determined that the seller's interest was in the nature of a security interest. *Samuels, supra,* 526 F.2d at 1246. The Court went on to recognize that the UCC makes security interests that arise by operation of law under Article Two (such as the right of reclamation) subject to Article Nine. *Samuels, supra,* 526 F.2d at 1247. The Court found this crucial to the final outcome. It is not inconsistent with this reasoning for us to hold now that the express language of § 9.504, which makes the power of foreclosure "subject to Article Two," creates a duty in the foreclosing creditor to recognize and protect any Article Two interest of which the creditor is aware. Rather, such a holding reemphasizes the internal consistency of the UCC.

Finally, we find the fact that *Samuels* was a bankruptcy proceeding to be an important distinction. This is crucial because the *Samuels* Court treated the reclamation right there as an unperfected security interest. Under bankruptcy law, an unperfected security interest is cut short by the trustee's status as a hypothetical lien creditor against all assets in the debtor's estate from the date the petition is filed. In the instant case, bankruptcy was not pending; therefore, there is no hypothetical lien creditor to cut short O'Sullivan's interest, and none of TEMI's general creditors have attained that status.

THE RIGHT TO PROCEEDS

The issue whether a right of reclamation extends to proceeds has not been squarely addressed in Texas. For the reasons set out below, we hold that a seller's right of reclamation under § 2.702, if properly exercised, extends to traceable proceeds from the sale of goods where all prior interests in those goods have been fully satisfied. To hold otherwise would in many instances render the statutory remedy a nullity. In most instances, a buyer such as TEMI has granted a security interest in his after acquired property to at least one of his financing creditors. The seller is already second in priority to that lender. Furthermore, the right to reclaim goods does not arise unless the buyer is insolvent, a condition that makes foreclosure by the prior lender more than likely. Often there will be very little, if any, money left after the priority debts are paid. To hold that such a foreclosure terminates a reclaiming seller's rights to any remaining proceeds would in most cases emasculate the reclamation remedy. We recognize that Article Nine provides a means by which a seller can defeat prior liens, however, we are not faced with such a situation here. In enacting § 2.702 we believe that the Texas Legislature intended to provide an entirely separate remedy, outside the complexities of Article Nine. It is a remedy which enables a seller to maintain a priority status against the buyer's *unsecured* creditors in a situation such as this. We find support for this position in many contexts.

Priority Under the UCC

Turning first to the language of the statute, the seller's right is made subject to the rights of "a buyer in the ordinary course or other good faith purchaser or lien creditor under this chapter (Section 2.403)." Texas UCC § 2.702(c). Comment 3 to that section lists precisely those interests to which the seller's rights are made subject. Conspicuously missing are the buyer's general unsecured creditors. Quite the contrary, the comment expressly states that "this section constitutes preferential treatment as against the buyer's other creditors."

The Ninth Circuit has held that the Texas right of reclamation survives bankruptcy; thus the right of the trustee as a hypothetical lien creditor cannot supercede the right of the seller to reclaim despite the words of the statute. *Matter of Daylin,* 596 F.2d 853, 855–56 (9th Cir.1979). Citing *In re Telemart Enterprises, Inc.,* 524 F.2d 761 (9th Cir.1975), as authority, the *Daylin* Court further held that:

> Section 2.702 authorizes the exact equivalent of the common law remedy of rescission, and therefore sales described by that section result in a transfer of only voidable title. Consequently, the seller's right can only be cut off by a good faith purchaser for value.

Daylin, supra, 596 F.2d at 856 (citation omitted).

The District Court reasoned that O'Sullivan's right of reclamation was completely terminated when the SBA, as a prior lienholder, foreclosed. However, under the UCC system, the prior lienholder has several duties upon foreclosure of its lien that are designed to protect both the interests of the buyer and those of the buyer's other creditors. Texas UCC § 9.501 *et seq.* The SBA was charged with these duties when it became subrogated to Westside's position. Texas UCC § 9.504(e).

For example, a secured party's right to dispose of collateral is "subject to the chapter on sales (Chapter 2)," therefore, a seller's reclamation right, which is created under Chapter Two, is implicitly recognized as a limitation on the seller's ability to dispose of a debtor's assets. Texas UCC § 9.504(a). Furthermore, § 9.504(a) provides that after the lienholder satisfies its own claim, the proceeds of the sale must be applied to the satisfaction of any junior security interests if written demand is received. The record here clearly reveals that O'Sullivan made written demand on Westside, advising Westside of its § 2.702 claim prior to the foreclosure on TEMI's assets.

After junior interests are satisfied, the secured party must account to the debtor. "[W]here the secured party knows the collateral is owned by a person who is not the debtor, the owner of the collateral and not the debtor is entitled to any surplus." Texas UCC § 9.504(b), Comment 2.

If the nature of a seller's right of reclamation in Texas is that of an unperfected security interest, *see Matter of Samuels, supra,* 526 F.2d at 1244–46, then it seems clear that O'Sullivan was entitled to second priority status with regard to the proceeds after making demand. * * *

However, if O'Sullivan's interest is classified as the "equivalent" of a right to rescind, thereby enabling it to void the buyer's title, *Daylin, supra,* 596 F.2d at 856, then Westside was on notice that the goods in fact were owned by someone other than the debtor, and should have accounted to O'Sullivan for the proceeds. Finally, both the SBA and Westside implicitly recognized that O'Sullivan had retained an interest in the goods by giving O'Sullivan notice of the time and place of the foreclosure sale.

Bankruptcy Reform Act of 1978

While no bankruptcy petition was filed in the instant case, the treatment of a seller's right of reclamation under the new bankruptcy code provides a useful analogy. It is generally recognized that the UCC and the bankruptcy code were intended to provide a comprehensive and interrelated scheme for recognizing different property rights. Hence, the priority scheme of the UCC is incorporated into the bankruptcy code. The new code contains an express provision for dealing with the state UCC created right of reclamation in 11 U.S.C. § 546(c). The legislative history of that section makes clear that "the purpose of the provision is to recognize, in part, the validity of § 2–702 of the Uniform Commercial Code, which has generated much litigation, confusion, and divergent decisions in different circuits." House Judiciary Report No. 95–595 to accompany House Report 8200, 95th Cong., 1st Sess. (1977) pp. 371–72, U.S.Code Cong. & Admin.News 1978, pp. 5787, 6328.

While § 546(c) does not reverse the holding of *Samuels,* it does provide that the trustee's status as a hypothetical lien creditor is *subordinate* to the seller's right of reclamation. Furthermore, if the Court utilizes its power to deny the seller's right of reclamation, it must adequately protect the seller's interest by granting the seller's claim priority as an administrative expense or securing the claim with a lien. 11 U.S.C. § 546(c)(2). Thus, the post-*Samuels,* new bankruptcy code deals with a seller's right of reclamation as equivalent to a perfected security interest under Article Nine. *See* 11 U.S.C. § 363. Finally, the House Report indicates that Congress intended to extend the right of reclamation to proceeds:

> The right is subject however, to the power of the court to deny reclamation and protect the seller by granting him *a priority as an administrative expense for his claim arising out of the sale of the goods.*

House Report, *supra,* at 372, U.S.Code Cong. & Admin.News 1978, p. 6328. (emphasis added). Hence, we see that § 546(c) was intended to allow the reclaiming seller a priority claim against the *proceeds* from the sale of the goods when the Court chooses not to return the goods themselves. Clearly this constitutes "preferential treatment against the buyer's general unsecured creditors." *See* Texas UCC § 2.702 comment 3.

CONCLUSION

On the basis of all the foregoing, we hold that where a seller of goods has diligently asserted its right of reclamation and otherwise met the requirements of § 2.702, and where all prior lienholders have been fully satisfied, that seller's claim will be afforded priority status as against the buyer's general unsecured creditors. Furthermore, we hold that such a seller's priority will extend to proceeds that are traceable to the goods. We therefore reverse the District Court's holding as to this last point. * * * However, the District Court was clearly correct in granting Westside first priority to the interpleaded fund.

Affirmed in part, reversed in part and remanded.

[Some footnotes omitted.]

Notes

Is it obvious that a secured creditor's claim to after-acquired property is superior to the seller's rights under UCC 2–702?

Problem 7–5

Ronald's Steel Service Center sold steel to Regulation Manufacturing, a builder of truck bodies. Some steel it delivered on March 1, other it delivered on April 10, and still another shipment was shipped on April 8 and arrived at the buyer's loading dock on April 12. On April 17, Regulation filed in Chapter 11. Subsequently it developed that Regulation had been circulating inaccurate balance sheets that showed its finances to be much healthier than they were. It appears that Regulation's liabilities exceeded its assets about a month after its December balance sheet was circulated.

1. Ronald now asks whether it will be able to recover any of the steel from the trustee in bankruptcy. (You may assume that Ronald has taken no step to recover; that it is now April 24 and that there is no claim by a secured creditor.)

2. Contrary to the facts given above, assume that one of the competitors is a secured creditor who had a security interest in all of Regulation's inventory, including after-acquired property. If the secured creditor is not perfected, does that change the analysis?

SECTION 5. PERSONAL PROPERTY SECURITY INTERESTS IN REAL ESTATE TRANSACTIONS

Read UCC 9–102(3), Comment 4 to UCC 9–102 and section 9–104(j). If you now see the potential conflict and confusion among these three provisions you enjoy the beginning of wisdom. If you also realize that this conflict and confusion is compounded because the transactions to which the rules apply are so numerous and varied then you will have taken another major step forward. Consider some of the possibilities: a customer (a real estate mortgagee) might come to the bank seeking a loan and offering as security his debtor's mortgage and note. This is the case contemplated by Comment 4 to UCC 9–102. (It is also possible that the mortgagee might be a financial institution and might offer a bushelbasket full of notes and mortgages.) Still another debtor might, as a vendor, or as an assignee of a vendor, offer as security a vendor's interest under a real estate installment sale contract. In each of these cases one could argue that some part of the transaction is governed by Article 9. In almost all such cases, one could make a plausible argument that our bank should disregard Article 9 and should instead execute a document under the local real estate law and record something in the local real estate records.

In 1978 some of these problems were solved while still others were compounded by enactment of section 541(d) of the Bankruptcy Code. That section reads as follows:

> Property in which the debtor holds, as of the commencement of the case, only legal title and not an equitable interest, such as a mortgage secured by real property, or an interest in such a mortgage, sold by the debtor but as to which the debtor retains legal title to service or supervise the servicing of such mortgage or interest, becomes property of the estate under subsection (a)(1) or (2) of this section only to the extent of the debtor's legal title to such property, but not to the extent of any equitable interest in such property that the debtor does not hold.

Clearly this subsection was designed to cover the case in which the originator of mortgages (for example, a Savings and Loan) sells the interests in those mortgages to another party, but continues to service them. In effect, Congress is telling the trustee to keep his hands off such a transaction and to permit the purchaser of the mortgages to keep them in preference to the trustee's claims.

But here too lurk the seeds of controversy. Note that § 541(d) applies only to mortgages "sold." Does that mean that when one takes an interest in a mortgage that would be characterized not as a purchase or sale of the mortgage, but as a loan against it, § 541(d) does not apply? Observe also that although § 541(d) presumably subordinates the trustee (even his claim under § 544 when it is applicable), it does nothing to determine the priorities among purchaser or lender and other creditors not represented by the trustee.

One plausible way to approach the cases is to view the mortgagee's interest (and the vendor's interest and the lessor's interest) as essentially an interest in personal property, mostly an interest in a stream of promised payments. So viewed, such an interest, as security, would be collateral subject to Article 9 and other personal property rules. At the same time, use of the possessory interest as security—that of the mortgagor (and the lessee and the vendee) would be subject to the rules governing security in real estate. One wishing to take a security interest in the possessory end of things would have to comply with applicable real estate law and do a real estate recording. How should the cases set out below be analyzed and classified?

IN RE KENNEDY MORTGAGE CO.

United States Bankruptcy Court, District, New Jersey, 1982.
17 B.R. 957.

OPINION

WILLIAM LIPKIN, BANKRUPTCY JUDGE.

On March 9, 1981, an involuntary Petition for Relief was filed against the above named Debtor, Kennedy Mortgage Company (Debtor) and on the same day the Debtor consented to the Order for Relief under the provisions of the Bankruptcy Code, 11 U.S.C. 101 sequi.

Generally stated—the Debtor's principal activity was to process applications submitted to it for mortgages on real estate and for the advancement of the funds to the mortgage applicants necessary for completion of settlement. To that end, in addition to lending its own money, the Debtor entered into agreements with various banks and lending institutions for lines of credit whereby the Debtor was to be supplied with funds to carry out the mortgage settlements. The activity of the Debtor with such banks and lending institutions involved many mortgages totaling over forty (40) millions of dollars, as stated to me by the parties.

The banks with whom the Debtor established lines of credit are located in other States as well as New Jersey.

More specifically stated, as to the procedure followed between the Debtor and a lending bank, with whom the Debtor had an agreement establishing a line of credit, whereby the Debtor was put into actual receipt of funds, the transactions giving rise to the Complaint herein of the First National Bank of Boston (FNBB) are generally illustrative.

On August 19, 1980, FNBB and the Debtor entered into a Letter Agreement whereby FNBB agreed to extend to the Debtor a direct revolving warehousing line of credit not to exceed $10,000,000.00 and on that same date the Debtor executed its Demand Promissory Note in the principal sum of $10,000,000.00 with interest to float at the FNBB "Bank Rate". In conjunction therewith the Debtor executed a Letter of Credit and Security Agreement to the FNBB whereby the Debtor granted to FNBB a security interest in the mortgage notes and proceeds thereof to be pledged to FNBB to secure the Debtor's borrowings from FNBB pursuant to the Letter Agreement and the Demand Promissory note.

On February 13, 1981, the Debtor delivered to FNBB four (4) notes totaling the sum of $189,950.00 and on February 18, 1981, it delivered to FNBB a note for $44,150.00, a total of $234,100.00, upon which FNBB advanced to the Debtor the sum of $215,428.18 under the Letter Agreement and Note to it. Thus, the supplier of the funds, FNBB was given possession of the Notes executed by the five mortgagors arising out of the mortgage settlements.

At the time of the settlements the Debtor executed assignments of the mortgages to FNBB which were also delivered along with the original notes. The original mortgages were not delivered to FNBB because the Debtor delivered them to the proper office for recording. The Debtor also delivered various other papers as FNBB may have requested.

The assignments of the mortgages to FNBB were not recorded.

A bit of history is now in order as to the usual course of conduct of such financing by the lending banks. The financing by the so called "mortgage company", or mortgage broker, such as Kennedy, the Debtor, in this case, whereby the lending banks put up money to finance the mortgages is called "warehousing". The lenders have extended a line of credit to the mortgage company and within such limits lend money to the broker and then upon receipt of the note and unrecorded assignment of the mortgage "warehouse" the instruments for a period of time and then possibly sells them to investors in mortgages or transfers them into a pool of mortgages purchased by the Government National Mortgage Association known as "GNMA" or similar entities.

Consistent with such practice and procedures FNBB was in possession on March 9, 1981, the date of the commencement of proceedings in this Court, of the five notes and unrecorded assignments of mortgages as set forth above.

Thereafter, FNBB was advised by the Trustee that the notes were to be sold by the Trustee and become part of GNMA pool being formed by the North Carolina National Bank Mortgage Company (NCNB).[1] FNBB did transmit the instruments to NCNB in trust and upon sale of the pool the lien claimed by FNBB was to be transferred to the proceeds of sale, with the proceeds to be deposited in an escrow account. Consistent therewith I entered an Order dated March 19, 1981, and the notes and mortgages were sold to GNMA and the proceeds of the sale were deposited in an escrow account with the Fidelity Union Trust Company located in the State of New Jersey.

The sum on deposit associated with the 5 notes and mortgages is $222,395.00.

The parties in this estate, in the interest of preservation of the assets and administration of the Estate, had entered into a stipulation dated the same day, March 19, 1981, dealing with such matters, as in the present issue, whereby it was agreed in paragraph 11

> "There shall be paid to FNBB, IVB and Heritage the funds in their respective escrow accounts upon establishment of the validity and priority of their respective liens, but not more than the amount secured by such established liens."

The Order, to which I have referred, further provided, inter alia, that—

> "Interest on the Escrow accounts shall be payable as the interests of the parties shall appear as determined by the Court."

FNBB now seeks to have me determine that it had a valid lien upon the notes and mortgages and has a right to payment of $222,395.00 plus interest from the escrow account deposited with the National State Bank of Elizabeth.

Basically therefore this Complaint seeks a determination of its alleged lien upon the Escrow Fund to the extent of the 5 notes and mortgages which it sold into the GNMA pool. * * *

* * * On October 5, 1981, the FNBB filed a Motion for a Summary Judgment under the provisions of Bankruptcy Rule 756 (F.R.C.P. 56), supported by a brief and affidavits, alleging,

1. Purchase of notes and mortgages by GNMA is not on an individual basis. GNMA purchases such notes and mortgages in very large total numbers and sums and banks or mortgage brokers combine such instruments to make a "pool" of the required amount. In this instance the pool was three million ($3,000,000.00) dollars.

"There is no genuine issue as to any material fact and that FNBB is entitled to judgment as a matter of law (i) determining that FNBB has a validly perfected lien with respect to the five transactions at issue (and which became a part of a GNMA pool pursuant to a Stipulation and Order of this Court dated March 19, 1981, a copy of which is attached as Exhibit "A" to the Memorandum in support of this Motion,) and (ii) directing that Robert W. Larson, Trustee, pay to FNBB $222,395.00 from the Escrow Account established pursuant to said Stipulation and Order which contains the proceeds of sale of the notes subject to FNBB's lien, plus interest which has accrued on said escrow account and directing further that Robert W. Larson, Trustee, pay to FNBB an additional amount representing its attorneys fees, costs and per diem interest in excess of the amount in said escrow account."

At first blush, because of the indoctrination that is prevalent today in the commercial world where a creditor has not recorded its lien, pursuant to the requirements of the Uniform Commercial Code, it would appear that FNBB would not have rights superior to other creditors, and in this case superior to the Trustee of the Debtor Estate, who stands in the position of a judgment creditor holding a levy and lien on the Debtors assets. That would appear to be the fact in this case where FNBB obtained possession of a note payable by the mortgagor to the Debtor which note is only a promise to pay or acknowledgment of the debt in written form. The debt to the Debtor, represented by a note was secured by a mortgage, duly recorded, which protected the *Debtor* mortgagee, against any creditors of the *mortgagor.*

A mortgage instrument, though manifesting a lien on real estate, is, actually personal property as to the mortgagee, and in order to be effective in favor of the *mortgagee* as against other *creditors of the mortgagor* must be recorded in the proper office where the real estate is located. The rights of the creditors of the mortgagor are inferior to the rights of the mortgagee.

In this case the plaintiff received possession of the note which evidenced the debt and an assignment of the mortgage which it did not record.

The question therefore is—does the Trustee as a judgment creditor of the debtor, *mortgagee,* holding a lien and levy, have a superior right to the mortgages (and now their proceeds) over FNBB because the assignments to it were not recorded.

Great stress has been made of the fact that a decision which would deny FNBB a security interest in the mortgages would be upsetting to the commercial world.

It was disclosed that mortgage brokers arrange for placing of mortgages throughout the entire United States in the hundreds of millions of dollars and they obtain funds for such purposes from banks and other lending institutions and only surrender possession of the notes and deliver unrecorded assignments of the mortgages upon completion of the mortgage settlement. The bank and lending institutions warehouse the loans and sell them to investors or to GNMA or governmental agencies in blocks of millions of dollars. The method now used for financing of the mortgages would be seriously affected if every assignment had to be recorded. It would require searches of title and delay in transfers as well as involve considerable expense for recording and the recording of assignments. The easy access that mortgage brokers now have for a source of funds would be disrupted and reduce the availability of funds in the mortgage market. However, I cannot let that business practice be the sole and dominant factor in my decision in upholding the right of FNBB to the proceeds of a mortgage under an unrecorded assignment thereof, if the provisions of the Uniform Commercial Code and the Bankruptcy Code clearly dictate a different conclusion. If the Uniform Commercial Code or Bankruptcy Code or State Statutes dictated with certainty that an assignment of a mortgage on real estate be recorded in order to render the lien effective against creditors of the assignor then lending institutions would be obliged to record such assignments regardless of the cost and inconvenience. To hold otherwise would constitute judicial legislation on my part.

However, in determining the interpretation to be made of the pertinent statute, consistent with the limitations imposed upon a Court in determining the rights of litigants which flow from statutes, whereby the Court does not engage in judicial legislation, I am also mindful that the interpretation of such statutes does and should be considered in the light of modern business practices as stated in *Bristol Associates,* 505 F.2d 1056, 1062 (3 Cir.1974). Therein the Court held

> "While a uniform trade practice does not constitute proof that the legal consequences of the practice are what those in the field take them to be, neither can it be assumed that a legislature which passed the Code and which has considered and passed amendments to it on several occasions would let stand practices or beliefs which it disapproved. * * *
>
> Where language is susceptible of two reasonable meanings, a court, in the commercial field, should choose that interpretation which comports with current universal practices in the business world."

Consistent therewith, I am of the opinion that it is not necessary under the Uniform Commercial Code or the Bankruptcy Code or State Statutes for an assignee of a mortgage to record the assignment of the mortgage in order to have a secured status.

In interpreting and construing the applicable law the provision of the Uniform Commercial Code dealing with General Provisions must be observed wherein it is provided:

12A:1–102

(1) This Act shall be liberally construed and applied to promote its underlying purposes and policies.

(2) Underlying purposes and policies of this Act are

(a) to simplify, clarify and modernize the law governing commercial transactions;

(b) to permit the continued expansion of commercial practices through custom, usage and agreement of the parties;

(c) to make uniform the law among the various jurisdictions.

More particularly as to the Uniform Commercial Code sections which apply to this case dealing with Secured Transactions I observe the following provisions of 12A:9.

"102. Policy and Scope of Chapter [quoting] * * *

"Section 104—Transactions Excluded from Chapter.

This Chapter does not apply

(j) except to the extent that provision is made for fixtures in 12A:9–313, to the creation or transfer of an interest in or lien on real estate, including a lease or rents thereunder; (underlining added)

"Section 302. When Filing Is Required to Perfect Security Interest; Security Interests to Which Filing Provisions of This Chapter *Do Not Apply.*

(1) A financing statement must be filed to perfect all security interest *except* the following:

(a) a security interest in collateral in possession of the secured party under 12A:9–305;" (underlining added)

"304—A Security interest in chattel paper or negotiable documents may be perfected by filing. A security interest in instruments (other than instruments which constitute part of chattel paper) can be perfected only by the secured party's taking possession, except as provided in subsections (4) and (5)." (Underlining added)

"Section 305—*When Possession* by Secured Party Perfects Security Interest Without Filing.

A security interest in letters of credit and advices of credit * * * goods, instruments, negotiable documents or chattel paper may be perfected by the secured party's taking possession of the collateral. * * * A security interest is perfected by possession from the time possession is taken without relation back and continues only so long as possession is retained, unless otherwise specified in this Chapter."

The foregoing sections require a bifurcation in treatment of the note and the unrecorded assignment of the mortgage.

Clearly as to the note executed by the mortgagor to the Debtor the plaintiff, FNBB has a possessory lien thereon. No creditor including the Trustee of the Debtor Estate could claim a right to the obligation represented by the tangible note in the possession of FNBB.

In the *Matter of Bristol Associates, Inc.,* 505 F.2d 1056, 1061 (3d Cir. 1974) the court clearly resolved the question whether a promissory note falls within the scope of Article 9 by virtue of its status as an instrument. As stated therein possession of such an instrument creates a perfected lien in favor of the FNBB.

Under the provisions of Sections 302(1)(a) and 304(1) and 305, FNBB perfected its lien on the notes as security for the debt by reason of possession of the notes.

Does the U.C.C. require recording the assignment of the mortgage associated with the note? Can a creditor of the Debtor issue an execution upon the asset represented by the mortgage of record standing in the name of the Debtor as mortgagee? He can do so but the rights that would flow to such execution creditors would be limited by intervening rights of other parties such as the rights of FNBB arising out of the assignment of the mortgage even though the assignment was unrecorded. This conclusion is fortified by the expression of the Supreme Court of New Jersey in *Burke v. Hoffman,* 28 N.J. 467, 475, 147 A.2d 44 (1958) wherein the Court stated

> "A mortgage debt, although a chose in action is yet, where the subject of the security is land, 'an interest in land,' and priorities are governed by the rules applicable to interests in land, and not by the rules which govern interest in personalty.
>
> Pomeroy Ibid., ¶ 697. See also ¶ 712."

See also *Garnick v. Serewitch,* 39 N.J.Super. 486, 496, 121 A.2d 423 (Ch. 1956) wherein it was stated

"A mortgage is a lien or an interest in realty." * * *

The application for the reasons expressed in *Bristol Associates,* supra, dealing with subsection (j) of Section 12A:9–104 which relates to transactions to be excluded from Chapter 9, and subsection (3) of 12A:9–102 as interpreted by the comment 4 associated with subsection (3), which relates to an obligation secured by a transaction, are indicated in this case. Specifically dealing with 12A:9–102(3) as it relates to mortgages on real estate associated with notes which have been assigned the comment 4 reads as follows:

> "An illustration of subsection (3) is as follows:
>
> The owner of Blackacre borrows $10,000 from his neighbor, and secures his note by a mortgage on Blackacre. This Article is not applicable to the creation of the real estate mortgage. Nor is it applicable to a sale of the note by the mortgagee even though the mortgage continues to secure the note. However, when the mortgagee pledges the note to secure his own obligation to X, this Article applies to the security interest thus created, which is a security interest in an instrument even though the instrument is secured by a real estate mortgage. This Article leaves to other law the question of the effect on rights under the mortgage of delivery or non-delivery of the mortgage or of recording or non-recording of an assignment of the mortgagee's interest. See Section 9–104(j). But under Section 3–304(5) recording of the assignment does not of itself prevent X from holding the note in due course." (Underlining added)

In dealing with "*other law*"the law of the State of New Jersey is stated in *Rose v. Rein,* 116 N.J.Eq. 70, 73, 172 A. 510 (1934) which is in accord with *Leonard v. Leonia Heights Land Company,* 81 N.J.Eq. 489, 87 A. 645 (E. & A. 1913) wherein the court held that an unrecorded assignment of a mortgage is not void as against subsequent judgment creditors. The references to the various statutes in these two decisions may now be found in N.J.S.A. 46:16–1, which provides all deeds or instruments enumerated therein, which included mortgages and assignment of mortgages affecting real estate may be recorded in the office of the county recording offices wherein the real estate is situate.

The effect of recording instruments described in 46:16–1 is found in 46:21–1 wherein it is stated that such filing of record shall be notice to all subsequent creditors, purchasers and mortgagees of the execution of the deed or instrument so recorded and the contents thereof. In addition, 46:17–1 provides for the Registration of Mortgages in the office of the courts recording officer of the county in which the real estate is situate. Finally, as it concerns the issues before me, the provisions of N.J.S.A. 46:18–3 and 4 provide for an indexing record of assignment of mortgages and entry in books of records of assignments of mortgages.

The fact that assignments of mortgages may be recorded does not affect the validity of an assignment of a mortgage which has not been recorded. *Leonard v. Leonia Heights Land Company,* supra; *Clift v. Scheutz,* 83 N.J.Eq. 442 (Ch. 1914) 91 A. 815. The purposes of recording is to establish priorities and rights of individuals who are affected by chain of title or encumbrances on the real estate such as grantees of real estate from record title holders thereof or innocent mortgagors who are obligated to make payment on their mortgages.

As stated hereinabove, the nature of the property involved, namely a mortgage, though personal property of itself, represents an interest in real estate and therefore it is to be included as one of the included items covered by the Uniform Commercial Code under the provisions of Section 9–104(j) which, repeating, reads

> "This Chapter does not apply * * * (j) * * * to the creation of an interest in or lien on real estate * * * "

This construction given to this subsection is a commercially reasonable interpretation. *Bristol Associates,* supra 1063; *In re Middle Atlantic Stud Welding Co.,* 503 F.2d 1133 (3d Cir.1974).

The philosophy of all recording acts, be it as to personalty or realty, is to give notice to possible later purchasers, grantees, creditors and assignees of the status of title or prior interest of any entity in the property involved. In the instant case there was a valid recorded mortgage supported by a note evidencing an indebtedness by the owner of the property, the mortgagor, to the creditor, Debtor, Kennedy.

Any one seeking to buy the property or further encumber the property or obtain an assignment of the mortgage was on notice of a mortgage to Kennedy. They would be obliged to inquire of the owner by a declaration of no-setoff as to the amount admitted due and recognition by the mortgagor that no defense was claimed and that the lien was still in existence; an inquiry would be necessary of the mortgagee as to the amount outstanding on the indebtedness. Should an assignment of the mortgage not be of record then payment to the mortgagee in satisfaction of the mortgage by any one without knowledge of the assignment would be effective against the holder of the unrecorded assigned mortgage. However, the purposes of the recording statutes are being served, and under *Rose v. Rein,* supra and *Leonard v. Leonia Heights,* it is not necessary to record an assignment of the mortgage. Moreover, one important facet must now be recognized—a mortgage is security for a debt. Without the manifestation of the debt, usually evidenced by a note or bond, the mortgage instrument itself is subject to attack. The lien of a mortgage is regarded as no greater than the actual debt secured.

> "The mortgage is regarded primarily as a security; the debt is the principal fact, and the mortgage is collateral thereto."

Grennon v. Kramer, 111 N.J.Eq. 337, 340, 162 A. 758 (E. & A. 1932) 55 Am.Jur.2d 133. The existence of an obligation to be secured is an essential element of a mortgage.

* * *

As stated in Am.Jur.2d 133, "The existence of an obligation to be secured is an essential element of a mortgage. The mortgage has no efficacy if unaccompanied by a debt or obligation, either preexisting, created at the time, or contracted to be created. Accordingly, where the obligation secured fails, the mortgage is likewise commonly considered to be a nullity, and a mortgage or deed of trust in the nature of a mortgage given to secure an obligation void by positive prohibition of laws is of no force." [4]

In this case, the FNBB is the owner of the note, secured by the mortgage. Anyone interested in acquiring an interest in the mortgage would be obliged to obtain an interest in the debt. The Trustee in this case could not realize upon a mortgage if he did not own the obligation represented by the note. The failure to record the assignment of the mortgage would not be fatal to the right of FNBB to realize upon the mortgage as against parties such as judgment creditors of the Debtor because FNBB has a perfected lien on the note and the mortgage is only collateral to the note. The mortgage without the debt is of no effect.

For the foregoing findings of fact and conclusion of law, I find that FNBB has a perfected security interest in the five notes and mortgages and that the Trustee herein has no interest in the mortgages given to secure the notes. The notes and mortgages having been sold to GNMA through a pool, the plaintiff, FNBB has a lien upon the proceeds of such sale including the interest which has accrued thereon.

[Some footnotes omitted.]

IN RE MARYVILLE SAVINGS & LOAN CORP.

United States Court of Appeals, Sixth Circuit, 1984.
743 F.2d 413.

WELLFORD, CIRCUIT JUDGE.

Defendant trustee appeals the district court's determination that plaintiff bank had a perfected security interest in certain promissory notes and the deeds of trust that secured those notes. 31 B.R. 597. We Affirm in part and Reverse in part. Peoples Bank of Polk County, the plaintiff, is a bank organized under the laws of Tennessee. Prior to a name change, Peoples Bank of Polk County was known as Southern United Bank of Polk County. Maryville Savings and Loan Corporation, the debtor, is a corporation organized under the laws of Tennessee. Defendant McDonald is the trustee in bankruptcy of the debtor.

Debtor, through its duly authorized officers, executed a "Promissory Note, Security Agreement and Disclosure Statement" on June 10, 1981. The

4. I am not herein concerned with the question whether there is personal liability for the debt in the event of a deficiency between the value of the property and the amount due on the obligation after foreclosure. See 55 Am.Jr. 134, 135.

I emphasize that the question of equitable rights of mortgagors who make payments to the original mortgagee or to assignees with recorded assignments and who have no knowledge of the unrecorded assignment of the mortgage, or the rights of other assignees of the mortgage who also obtain the indicia of the debt and record their assignments are not involved in this case. The issue in this case relates only to the rights of FNBB as against the Trustee who stands in the shoes of a judgment creditor possibly holding a lien and levy on the assets of the Debtor.

document provided for the payment, upon demand, by debtor to plaintiff of the principal sum of $75,000, together with interest from the date of execution until the date of payment at the rate of 18% per annum. As collateral for the loan, debtor assigned to plaintiff all rights in certain promissory notes and deeds of trust encumbering real property located in Blount County, Tennessee. This assignment was accomplished by debtor's execution of a "General Assignment of Promissory Note and Trust Deeds." This assignment was duly recorded with the Register of Deeds of Blount County, Tennessee, on June 15, 1981, the usual manner for recordation in Tennessee of interests in real estate.

After the initial borrowing, debtor made certain payments on the principal amount and interest due under the note, bringing the balance due down to approximately $55,000. During January of 1982, debtor secured the advance of an additional $20,000 from plaintiff without the execution of another promissory note, and executed another "General Assignment of Promissory Notes and Trust Deeds," assigning all of its rights in additional notes and deeds of trust on real property to plaintiff. This document was also recorded with the Register of Deeds of Blount County, Tennessee, on January 28, 1982.

Typically, the deeds of trust provided that, among other things, "this conveyance shall secure the above described debt (the loan evidenced by a promissory note), and the interest thereon, or renewals ... thereof." The "deed of trust notes" recited that payment was due at the Maryville Savings and Loan Corporation. Each "Promissory Note, Security Agreement and Disclosure Statement" granted plaintiff a "security interest" in the underlying property or collateral, including "real or personal property," and the agreements were to be "interpreted according to the laws of the State of Tennessee, except where pre-empted by Federal law." The general assignments were "to establish a line of credit for Maryville Savings & Loan Corporation."

On March 18, 1982, debtor filed a Chapter 11 bankruptcy petition owing $75,000 plus interest on the note from plaintiff. Plaintiff initiated an adversary proceeding seeking a ruling that its security interest in the promissory notes and deeds of trust was perfected and that it therefore should recover the notes and the deeds of trust despite debtor's filing in bankruptcy. Defendant asserted that plaintiff's failure to take actual possession of the notes and deeds of trust prevented perfection of plaintiff's security interest under Uniform Commercial Code § 9–304(1), Tenn.Code Ann. § 47–9–304(1). Plaintiff argued that the transaction here was not covered by article nine of the U.C.C. because it involved a real estate transaction; as support, plaintiff cited U.C.C. § 9–104, Tenn.Code Ann. § 47–9–104, which provides:

> *Transactions excluded from chapter.*—This chapter does not apply:
>
> * * *
>
> (j) except to the extent that provision is made for fixtures in § 47–9–313, to the creation or transfer of an interest in or a lien on real estate * * *.

Defendant, on the other hand, relies upon U.C.C. § 9–102, Tenn.Code Ann. § 47–9–102, which provides:

(1) Except as otherwise provided in § 47–9–103 on multiple state transactions and in § 47–9–104 on excluded transactions, this chapter applies so far as concerns any personal property and fixtures within the jurisdiction of this state:

(a) to any transaction (regardless of its form) which is intended to create a security interest in personal property or fixtures including goods, documents, instruments, general intangibles, chattel paper, accounts or contract rights; and

(b) to any sale of accounts, contract rights or chattel paper.

* * *

(3) The application of this chapter to a security interest in a secured obligation is not affected by the fact that the obligation is itself secured by a transaction or interest to which this chapter does not apply.

The bankruptcy court, 27 B.R. 701, held that plaintiff failed to perfect its security interest in the notes and deeds of trust, but the district court reversed, holding that the recordation accomplished, although not in compliance with the U.C.C. as applicable in Tennessee, was sufficient.

In keeping with the parties' approach to this case, both the bankruptcy court and the district court assumed that article nine perfection requirements applied either to the entirety of this transaction or not at all—that is, it applied either to both the notes and the deeds or to neither. We conclude that this approach fails to give meaningful scope, depending on the result reached, either to § 9–102 or to § 9–104(j). Comment four to Tenn.Code Ann. § 47–9–102 illustrates the necessity in cases such as this to analyze the security interest created in the promissory note separately from the interest created in the deed of trust. That illustration reads, [quoting the "Blackacre"]

* * *

We are persuaded that §§ 9–102(3) and 9–104(j) may be reconciled by holding in this case that article nine be applied in regard to the promissory notes but *not* in regard to the deeds of trust.

This conclusion is bolstered by the Third Circuit's careful opinion in *In re Bristol Assoc., Inc.,* 505 F.2d 1056 (3d Cir.1974). In *Bristol,* a case involving Pennsylvania law, the court noted that amendments to the comments to U.C.C. § 9–102 made clear the drafters' intention that "only that portion of the package unrelated to the real property" be governed by article nine when "a promissory note and mortgage together become the subject of a security interest." 505 F.2d at 1061. *See also First Nat'l Bank of Boston v. Larson (In re Kennedy Mortgage Co.),* 17 B.R. 957, 963–65 (Bankr.D.N.J.1982). The Tennessee case law cited by plaintiff does not direct a contrary result.

The Tennessee Supreme Court in *May,** however, did hold that "the U.C.C. does not supercede the law in this state with respect to *liens upon real estate.*" 503 S.W.2d at 117 (emphasis added). Some authority has discussed whether a note pledged by a real estate mortgage given as security for a loan thereby becomes "realty paper" within the purview of article nine of the

* Commerce Union Bank v. May, 503 S.W.2d 112 (Tenn.1973).

U.C.C. Our attention has been called to no Tennessee case, however, that even discusses, much less adopts, this concept. We are not prepared to hold that in Tennessee the character of a note as personalty is transformed into a real estate interest merely because it is secured by a mortgage or deed of trust, or assigned as security together with a mortgage or deed of trust. Although the assignments in question did involve "transfers of interests in real property" because they involved deeds of trust, we cannot agree with the district court that the notes themselves constituted "liens upon real estate" nor adopted the character of real property. Both Tenn.Code Ann. § 47–9–102 and Tenn.Code Ann. § 47–9–104 purport to apply only to personal property and fixtures or to security interests in personal property.

In this case, then, we conclude that article nine applies to the plaintiff's security interest but only in the promissory notes themselves. Since plaintiff did not take possession of the notes, plaintiff's security interest in the notes was not perfected. *See* Tenn.Code Ann. § 47–9–304(1). On the other hand, we conclude that article nine does not apply to plaintiff's security interest in the deeds of trust. While defendant argues in his reply brief that plaintiff's security interest in the deeds of trust was not perfected even if article nine were held not to apply, he admits that he did not raise that issue below; plaintiff's security interest in the deeds of trust is therefore deemed to be a perfected interest. Accordingly, the judgment of the district court is Affirmed in part and Reversed in part.

Notes

1. Despite the Sixth Circuit's protestations to the contrary, its decision is in conflict with *In re Kennedy Mortgage Co.,* not so?

2. If you read the last paragraph in the opinion in *Maryville Savings,* consider how you would determine the priorities if you were the judge to whom the case was remanded. On a motion to reconsider, the court held that the notes, although arising from a real estate mortgage were subject to Article 9 and were, therefore, unperfected. In re Maryville Savings & Loan Corp., 760 F.2d 119 (6th Cir.1985).

Problem 7–6

1. Maltese was in the business of building and remodeling commercial and residential properties. It financed its operations by giving Bank a security interest in all of its present and future accounts, contract rights, general intangibles, chattel paper and their proceeds. Bank filed a financing statement at the Secretary of State's office in a jurisdiction that had the second alternative to 9–401. On Maltese's bankruptcy the trustee asserted that Bank did not have a perfected security interest on a series of payments totalling several hundred-thousand dollars that were due to Maltese from buyers of houses and condominiums on land-sale contracts. Does the Bank have a security interest and, if so, is it perfected?

2. Bohemian Savings and Loan Association of Cedar Rapids entered into a "loan participation and service agreement" of a bankrupt company, Columbia Pacific Mortgage. Columbia Pacific financed the construction and purchase of single family residences and then sold "participations" in its store of mortgages to such persons as Bohemian Savings. Bohemian had an 80 percent interest in a package of 49 mortgage loans in a total amount of $960,078. The trustee asserts

that he has a right to the mortgage payments to be made and also to the amount in his possession of $200,000 that was collected on foreclosure of several of the mortgages. He claims under 544(a)(3) of the Bankruptcy Code and asserts that Bohemian is nothing more than an unsecured creditor or, at best, an unperfected secured creditor. Assume that Bohemian made no filing, either in the real estate or in the personal property records. Who wins? Assume, however, that Columbia Pacific recorded the mortgages it received from the account debtors who owned the land. Who wins?

3. Bristol Associates was the lessor of certain store premises for a period of ten years. Early in the lease and in consideration for the loan, it gave Girard Bank and Trust a security interest in the lease. Girard did not record the security interest in the real estate records nor did it file any financing statement under Article 9. Ultimately Bristol went into bankruptcy and the trustee asserts that he has a right to the lease payments. Girard argues that 9–104(j) frees it from any obligation to record or to comply with the personal property laws. What do you think?

SECTION 6. PRIORITY OF BANK'S RIGHT OF "SETOFF"

Setoff is usually exercised by a bank, to set one debt off against another. In the most common circumstance debtor will owe bank a certain amount based on a loan and the debtor's deposit will itself be a loan by the bank back to the depositor. The setoff is merely the netting of the debt owed by the depositor to the bank against the bank's debt owed back to the depositor. The common law of setoff has a number of rules that we need not be concerned with here. For example, it requires that the debts on each side be mutual, i.e., that the same parties be on both sides on both debts, and that the amounts be unliquidated. Here we will assume that there is a right of setoff and we will take no time to examine the common law intricacies. Our concern is only with the question: To what extent does Article 9 govern setoff? Does it require some compliance with the Article 9 filing rules? Does Article 9 determine priority between a bank's setoff right and a secured creditor's security interest?

The starting point for analysis is UCC 9–104(i), which seems to exclude any consideration of the right of setoff from Article 9. That conclusion would seem to be supported by UCC 9–104(*l*), for it perhaps suggests that a security interest in a deposit account, a potential competitor with a setoff, is also outside of Article 9. This analysis would be too simple. One's certainty begins to crumble a bit when he looks at UCC 9–105(1)(e) that provides that accounts evidenced by a certificate of deposit are not deposit accounts. Presumably, therefore, security interests in certificates of deposit are governed by Article 9. Moreover, section 9–306 reveals that in certain cases bank accounts constitute proceeds and will often be governed by Article 9.

BROWN & WILLIAMSON TOBACCO CORP. v. FIRST NATIONAL BANK OF BLUE ISLAND

United States Court of Appeals, Seventh Circuit, 1974.
504 F.2d 998.

CLARK, ASSOCIATE JUSTICE.

This appeal, involving Sections 9–205 and 9–306(2) of the Uniform Commercial Code, arises from a judgment entered in favor of appellee,

Brown and Williamson Tobacco Corporation (B & W), for $70,724 and against appellant, First National Bank of Blue Island (Blue Island). We outline the facts here.

F.W. Koenecke & Sons, Inc. (Koenecke, Inc.), a tobacco wholesaler, was controlled by Robert Koenecke and his wife, Imogene. It bought tobacco products from various suppliers, including B & W, R.J. Reynolds Tobacco Corporation (RJR) and others. Its purchases from B & W were covered by a security agreement dated October 22, 1968, which, inter alia, assigned and granted to B & W a continuing security interest in all of Koenecke, Inc. current and future inventory of B & W products, accounts receivable arising from the sale of such products and all products and proceeds of the foregoing, all of which was referred to as "collateral". It further provided "* * * except for the sale of B & W cigarettes and other tobacco products in the ordinary course of business (Koenecke, Inc.) will not sell, assign or create or permit to exist any lien on or security interest in any collateral to or in favor of anyone other than B & W".

Koenecke, Inc. maintained a general checking account at Blue Island (No. 0–072–8) in which it deposited receipts from sales of tobacco products handled by it. Blue Island made loans both to Koenecke, Inc. and to Robert Koenecke and his wife personally. The first of these personal loans to the Koeneckes was on June 6, 1967, for $20,000 and paid on July 6, 1967, by Koenecke, Inc. On February 5, 1968, the Koeneckes borrowed $100,000 which was paid by Mr. Koenecke on April 9, 1968. On June 20, Koenecke, Inc. borrowed $82,000 which was paid by the company on September 17, 1968. On October 23, 1968, the Koeneckes borrowed $67,000 which was paid by the company on December 21, 1968. And on January 9, 1969, the Koeneckes borrowed $108,000, which was paid by the company on January 13, 1969. The proceeds of all of these loans were ultimately deposited in the bank account of Koenecke, Inc., No. 0–072–8.

Throughout the Fall of 1968 and continuing into 1969, Koenecke, Inc. suffered severe adverse publicity—especially through the press in Chicago—the gist of which was that its licensing arrangements were unlawful; its sales of cigarettes bore no Illinois revenue stamps; and some of its licenses were obtained through forgery. This had an adverse effect upon its sales.

On October 29, 1968, a $250,000 loan to Robert Koenecke and his wife was made by Blue Island on their personal, unsecured note. The proceeds of this loan were placed in the Koenecke, Inc. checking account No. 0–072–8, but the company did not sign, guarantee or endorse the same. The note was renewed on December 28, 1968 for 60 days. On February 10, 1969, Blue Island, becoming disturbed over Koenecke, Inc.'s finances, stopped honoring checks of Koenecke, Inc. that were drawn on uncollected funds deposited in checking account No. 0–072–8. Koenecke, Inc. was not notified of this action and, when it found out, it withheld making any further deposits in the account. At this time, there were several hundred thousand dollars in checks drawn against its general account, No. 0–072–8, which Koenecke, Inc. had issued to its suppliers, among whom were B & W and RJR. On February 17, 1969 representatives of RJR appeared in person at the bank, seeking collection of several previously dishonored checks. On that day there was a balance in the Koenecke, Inc. checking account No. 0–072–8 of

$713,586.52, of which $113,911 was attributable to sales by Koenecke, Inc. of B & W products which were covered by the security agreement.

On this same day—February 17th—the President and the Vice President of Blue Island spoke by telephone with Robert Koenecke and requested payment of the $250,000 note, although it was not due until February 26, 1969. Mr. Koenecke told Blue Island officers to pay the note from the corporate checking account of Koenecke, Inc., No. 0–072–8 and this was done by a debit memo of the bank on the next day. On February 18th he also directed Blue Island to debit Koenecke, Inc.'s account $40,000 and to issue a cashier's check in that amount to him. He endorsed the cashier's check to RJR.

On the 18th of February, upon the opening of Blue Island, there was a balance of $498,055.85 in the checking account No. 0–072–8 of Koenecke, Inc. and of this amount $70,724 was attributable to the proceeds of the sales of B & W products. Also on February 18th three representatives of B & W called personally on Blue Island to pay several checks drawn on Koenecke, Inc. account No. 0–072–8, but the bank refused because of a reported insufficiency of funds. During that same morning, representatives of RJR conferred with Blue Island officials and Robert Koenecke at the bank's offices in an attempt to collect an additional sum of several hundred thousand dollars for recent sales of its products to Koenecke, Inc. During a coffee break within the RJR meeting, Blue Island officers procured the signature of Robert Koenecke to the debit memo authorizing the payment of the Koeneckes' $250,000 note, but B & W was not advised thereof, although its representatives were in the bank. At the end of that day the checking account of Koenecke, Inc., No. 0–072–8 had a balance of only $3,317.49.

Koenecke, Inc. closed operations on February 24, 1969 and on March 13th a petition was filed to adjudicate Koenecke, Inc. bankrupt. On April 28, 1969, at a hearing on the bankruptcy matter, Vice President Mansfield of Blue Island, with some evasion, testified that at the direction of Mr. Koenecke, he had taken $252,567.70 from checking account No. 0–072–8 of Koenecke, Inc. and paid off with interest the personal note of Robert Koenecke and his wife due Blue Island on February 26, 1969. B & W elected not to participate in the bankruptcy, having decided to stand on its security. The Trustee in bankruptcy of Koenecke, Inc. sued Blue Island for some $530,000 covering several transfers of cash from Koenecke, Inc. to the bank. That suit was settled on November 23, 1970, for $100,000.

The bank raises four issues: (1) Did B & W lose its security interest by permitting the proceeds from the sale of its products to be commingled with other funds in the corporate account of Koenecke, Inc.; (2) Did B & W "cover" or trace its proceeds into the hands of the bank either as to depository or the ultimate transferee; (3) Did an action for conversion lie; (4) Was the transfer of the $252,567.70 to Blue Island from the account of Koenecke, Inc. a fraudulent one.

We decide the first two questions against the bank and affirm. The bank admits that "it sought and obtained preferred treatment for the payment of its $250,000 loan" but insists that its action constituted neither a conversion of B & W property nor a fraudulent transfer thereof. We find it unnecessary to pass on these issues since B & W had a perfected security interest in its "collateral" which was deposited in the Koenecke, Inc. checking account No. 0–072–8 and which it traced to the bank.

I. B & W Did Not Lose Its Security Interest:

Blue Island relies primarily upon the argument that B & W gave up its ability to identify its collateral when it permitted Koenecke, Inc. to commingle that collateral with other funds deposited in the latter's account No. 0–072–8. We find both the Uniform Commercial Code and the decided cases to the contrary. Section 9–205 of the Code specifically provides: "a security interest is not invalid * * * by reason of liberty in the debtor to use, commingle, or dispose of all or part of the collateral * * * or * * * of proceeds." And Section 9–306(2) adds: The security "also continues in any identifiable proceeds including collections received by the debtor."

Thus the Code "is explicit in preserving the priority of the secured party to the proceeds notwithstanding his consent to the sale of the primary collateral and further notwithstanding his consent to the debtor's unrestricted use and disposition of these proceeds so long as they remain identifiable." In re Mid State Wood Products Company, 323 F.Supp. 853, 857 (N.D.Ill.1971).

Blue Island urges us to follow a statement by Professor Grant Gilmore that proceeds cease to be identifiable when deposited in a bank account, so that the security interest is lost when such commingling occurs. *See* 2 G. Gilmore, Security Interests in Personal Property, § 27.4 at 735–36 (1965). Since Professor Gilmore was the principal draftsman and Reporter for Article 9 of the Code, his interpretation, though subsequently voiced, commands attention. Nevertheless, examining the language of the Code, in the light of its purpose, we conclude that the more reasonable implication is that the proceeds may be identifiable, and the security interest therein survive, even though commingled.

* * *

Universal C.I.T. Credit Corp. v. Farmers Bank of Portageville, 358 F.Supp. 317 (E.D.Mo.1973), upheld a security interest in cash from the sale of automobiles which had been deposited in the automobile dealer's general bank account. The court held that "proceeds are 'identifiable' if they can be traced in accordance with the state law. * * * The mere fact that the proceeds from the sales of the six automobiles were commingled with other funds * * * does not render the proceeds unidentifiable. * * *" 358 F.Supp. at 323–324. *See also* Associates Discount Corp. v. Fidelity Union Trust Co., 111 N.J.Super. 353, 268 A.2d 330 (1970); Girard Trust Corn Exchange Bank v. Lepley Ford, Inc., 25 Pa.D. & C.2d 395 (Pa.Ct.Comm.P. 1958). In Howarth v. Universal C.I.T. Credit Corporation, 203 F.Supp. 279, 282 (W.D.Pa.1962), the court at least assumed that if proceeds of collateral could be traced into a bank account, such proceeds would be deemed identifiable, and subject to the security interest. We are not persuaded by the contrary authority of Morrison Steel Co. v. Gurtman, 113 N.J.Super. 474, 274 A.2d 306 (1971).

Looking to Illinois law, it is clear in the different, but probably analogous, case of a fund impressed with a trust, such fund may be traced into a fund of commingled money, People v. Bates, 351 Ill. 439, 184 N.E. 597, 598 (1933), and it is conclusively presumed in equity that a trustee dissipates or spends his own funds first, before encroaching upon a trust fund. People v. People's Bank and Trust of Rockford, 353 Ill. 479, 187 N.E. 522, 525 (1933).

II. B & W Traced Its Collateral to Blue Island:

But Blue Island says that B & W did not trace or "cover" collateral into the hands of the bank. However a reading of the agreed stipulation of facts and of paragraph 3 of B & W's complaint which Blue Island admits to be true, shows the contrary.

There is no difficulty in tracing $70,724 of proceeds in which B & W had a security interest into the money in the checking account February 18, 1969. Blue Island has stipulated that Koenecke, Inc.'s checking account No. 0–072–8 had $498,055.85 in it on February 18 and that $70,724 thereof represented proceeds of sales of B & W products covered by the security agreement, calculated "through the application of generally accepted auditing and accounting principles."

Blue Island has stipulated further on that same day it transferred to itself, out of that same account, $252,567.70 in payment of Robert and Imogene Koenecke's personal note, not yet due. There were other transfers during the day amounting to $247,170.66 and at the close of business the balance was $3,317.49. The bank contends that the $70,724 has not been sufficiently identified as part of the $252,567.70 the bank transferred to itself, and it therefore must not be deemed to have had constructive notice of B & W's security interest therein.

Whether rationalized in terms of identifiability or of fairness in holding the bank to constructive notice, we think that the matter turns upon whether the transfer to Blue Island was a transfer in the ordinary course of business. Official Comment 2(c) to § 9–306 of the Code says as follows:

> Where cash proceeds are covered into the debtor's checking account and *paid out in the operation of the debtor's business,* recipients of the funds of course take free of any claim which the secured party may have in them as proceeds. What has been said relates to payments and transfers in ordinary course. The law of fraudulent conveyances would no doubt in appropriate cases support recovery of proceeds by a secured party from a transferee out of ordinary course or otherwise in collusion with the debtor to defraud the secured party. [Uniform Commercial Code Comment to Smith-Hurd Ill.Rev.Stat. ch. 26 § 9–306, p. 403 (emphasis added).]

Examination of the circumstances of the transfer persuades us that the transfer was clearly outside the ordinary course of business. At the beginning of the day, representatives of B & W appeared at the bank and sought the honoring of checks drawn to B & W on the Koenecke account, payment having been previously refused. Blue Island represented that the account did not contain adequate funds. Bank officers also met with RJR, also seeking payment for goods sold to Koenecke, Inc. During a coffee break in this meeting, Blue Island obtained a debit memorandum from Mr. Koenecke, authorizing the transfer to it. B & W representatives, still at the bank, were not informed.

There is no stipulation nor proof of the nature of the other transfers out of the account during the day nor the order in which they occurred. It seems likely, from the general situation, and we think fair to assume in the absence of proof, that they represented payment of checks which had been issued in the ordinary course of the business of Koenecke, Inc.

Therefore, we conclude that the funds subject to the B & W security interest were identifiable and the security interest continued in the money transferred to Blue Island. It seems fair and equitable to charge a party receiving a transfer from a general bank account outside the ordinary course of business with constructive notice of a security interest in funds therein.

[Footnotes omitted.]

Note

Section 9–306(2) provides for a security interest only in "identifiable proceeds." Did the drafters intend the amounts in a commingled bank account to be "identifiable"?

Problem 7–7

Spock Enterprises develops, produces, and markets children's toys. Spock has a $150,000 line of secured credit from Federation Bank and Trust. Federation has a security interest in Spock's inventory, accounts, equipment, general intangibles, and proceeds. On July 1, 1985 Spock opened an account at Vulcan Savings and Loan with $10,000. Assume that the $10,000 are identifiable proceeds subject to Federation's security interest. Vulcan lent Spock $5,000 without taking security. On August 1, 1985 a judgment creditor of Spock levied on the total balance in the Vulcan's account. During July, Spock's account with Vulcan showed the following activity:

Date	Transaction	Balance
7/1	Opening deposit	$10,000
7/9	Payment of monthly bills due 7/10	6,500
7/11	Deposit (sole stockholder's personal funds)	8,500
7/12	Deposit of Federation proceeds	10,500
7/13	Repayment to Vulcan of $5,000 loan	5,500
7/13	Deposit (sole stockholder's personal funds)	10,000
8/1	Judgment creditor levy (reduces account to)	0

Federation sued the judgment creditor for conversion. How much, if anything, should Federation win? Can Federation successfully recover anything from Vulcan?

Note: When Does a Setoff Occur?

Generally courts do not recognize a "setoff" as having occurred until the bank exercising the setoff has taken some overt act with respect to the account to be set off. For example, this act might constitute putting a memorandum in with the accounts payable or the actual debiting of the account in some way or placing a hold in the computer memory to show that there has been a set off. If the competing claimant serves notice or takes whatever other act is necessary before the bank takes the overt act to show the setoff, typically the competing claimant wins. This problem has been particularly troublesome for the banks in competing with the Internal Revenue Service over amounts deposited in account of debtors who suffer federal tax liens. In Peoples National Bank of Washington v. United States, 777 F.2d 459 (9th Cir.1985), the court ruled for the Internal

Revenue Service. The Internal Revenue Service levied on the account prior to the bank's taking any action to set off. Concluding that "an unexercised right of setoff does not terminate the depositor's property rights in an account," the court held for the Internal Revenue Service. Relying upon (and perhaps stretching) the Georgia law, the Court of Appeals for the Eleventh Circuit, came to the opposite conclusion in Trust Co. of Columbus v. United States, 735 F.2d 447 (11th Cir.1984). In that case the court relied on a term on the promissory note of the debtor that "delivered, pledged, assigned, conveyed, and transferred * * * all property * * * including accounts, monies, and deposits." The court concluded therefore that the promissory notes "created a valid and senior security interest in the bank which was wrongfully defeated by the government tax lien."

Note how weird this security agreement is. First, it is hermaphroditic; it is a security interest by the bank in the bank's own obligation to pay depositor, i.e., the deposit account. Second, it is a security interest that is outside of Article 9 if the security is in a deposit account, but within Article 9 if it is in a certificate of deposit. Finally, how one perfects a security interest outside of Article 9 or whether such security interests even continue to exist in a particular state after the adoption of Article 9 is subject to dispute. In any event, in this case it is hard to see any act of the bank that could be regarded as a perfecting act.

Problem 7–8

Assume that you represent a bank who fears that its right of setoff will be subordinated to some other bank's security interest or to a tax lien. Can you write a security interest that will be effective even though outside of Article 9? How should the bank perfect that interest?

SECTION 7. FEDERAL LAW

A. United States as a Lender

Section 9–104(a) excludes from Article 9's coverage "a security interest subject to any statute of the United States, *to the extent that* such statute governs the rights of parties to and third parties affected by transactions, in particular types of properties * * * ". (Italics supplied.) Comment 1 to 9–104 identifies the Ship Mortgage Act of 1920 and, to a limited extent, the Federal Aviation Act of 1958.

Even in the situations where the federal statutes have pre-empted Article 9's filing requirements, many courts have held that Article 9 governs some rights and liabilities because the federal statutes typically are not comprehensive. Although one perfects a security interest in an aircraft by a filing with the FAA in Oklahoma City, the courts generally hold that the mode of repossession and resale is governed by Article 9. To the extent that petitioners can move the Congress to fiddle with subjects governed by Article 9 rules, federal law will displace Article 9. The recent federal override of UCC 9–307 with respect to farm products is a case in point, see supra at p. 264.

An important intrusion of federal law into Article 9's domain occurs when the federal government contracts to lend. Although the Supreme Court has held that such contracts are governed by the federal common law (or by federal statutory or federal regulation where those are available), in 1979, in United States v. Kimbell Foods, Inc., 440 U.S. 715, 99 S.Ct. 1448, 59 L.Ed.2d 711 (1979), the Supreme Court held that a federal agency should normally be subject to state-law rules including Article 9's rules of perfection. Indeed, the Court explicitly adopted the Uniform Commercial Code as the federal common law. *In dictum* the Supreme Court recognized that some federal programs call for uniform law throughout the country, programs which variant state law "might frustrate."

The federal government is a lender in many settings. Thus, among other lender roles, it serves (1) as the Small Business Association, where it typically is a guarantor; (2) as a principal lender to farmers; (3) as a purchaser from and thus a financer of defense contractors. The government has been more successful at establishing its right to a special set of rules in its role as a defense purchaser than it has as a farm or small business lender.

IN RE AMERICAN POUCH FOODS, INC.

United States Court of Appeals, Seventh Circuit, 1985.
769 F.2d 1190, *cert. denied* 475 U.S. 1082, 106 S.Ct. 1459, 89 L.Ed.2d 716 (1986).

FAIRCHILD, SENIOR CIRCUIT JUDGE:

In a reorganization proceeding under Chapter 11 of the Bankruptcy Code the district court decided, in response to a complaint by the United States, that the United States held absolute title (and right to possession) to certain goods in the possession of the Debtor, American Pouch Foods, Inc. (Pouch). The court abstained from hearing Pouch's counterclaim. *In Re American Pouch Foods, Inc.,* 30 B.R. 1015 (D.C.N.D.Ill.1983). Pouch appeals. We affirm.

In January 1979, Pouch entered into a procurement contract with the United States Defense Logistics Agency (Government). The contract called for Pouch to produce combat rations, known as "Meals, Ready to Eat" (Food Pouches), for use by branches of the Armed Services. The contract gave Pouch the right to progress payments upon request, not more often than bi-weekly. The payments were limited to 90% of Pouch's cost incurred to the date of payment. The so-called title vesting clause of the progress payment part of the contract provided that title to all parts, materials, inventories, work in process and various other categories immediately vested in the Government.[1] Other provisions gave the Government the right to terminate for default (or for convenience of the Government) and to require delivery to it of completed supplies and manufacturing materials. The contract also provided that if, after notice of termination for default, it was determined that Pouch was not in default or that default was excusable, the rights and

1. The title vesting clause in the contract provided, in pertinent part:

(d) *Title.* Immediately, upon the date of this contract, title to all parts; materials; inventories; work in progress; * * * theretofore acquired or produced by the Contractor and allocable or properly chargeable to this contract under sound and generally accepted accounting principles and shall forthwith vest in the Government; and title to all like property thereafter acquired or produced by the Contractor and allocable or properly chargeable to this contract as aforesaid shall forthwith vest in the Government upon said acquisition, production or allocation. Notwithstanding that title to property is in the Government through the operation of this clause, the handling and disposition of such property shall be determined by applicable provisions of this contract such as: the Default clause and paragraph (h) of this clause; Termination for Convenience of the Government clause; and the Special Tooling clause. * * *

obligations of the parties would be the same as if the notice of termination had been for convenience of the Government.

After making approximately $13 million in progress payments the Government terminated the contract for default. The Government claimed that Pouch had not complied with required production schedules. On November 10, 1980, three days after the contract was terminated, Pouch filed a petition for reorganization under Chapter 11 of the Bankruptcy Code, 11 U.S.C. § 101 *et seq.* The Government claimed ownership and possession of all the property allocable to the contract in Pouch's possession or stored at warehouse facilities on its behalf. On December 5, 1980 the Government filed an adversary complaint in bankruptcy court to obtain possession.

Pouch filed an answer principally alleging wrongful termination of the contract and that the Government's title was a security interest not perfected as required by law and subordinate to the rights of the debtor and creditors. Pouch filed a counterclaim seeking damages arising from wrongful termination of the contract.

On February 9, 1981, the bankruptcy court held that, as a matter of law, the Government had absolute title to the property in question and was entitled to repossess it.

While the appeals were pending the bankruptcy court held that it had jurisdiction to hear Pouch's counterclaim even though the Armed Services Board of Contract Appeals had concurrent jurisdiction over the claim.

After the district court decided that questions of fact must be determined and remanded to the bankruptcy court, the Government filed a motion for reconsideration. In 1983, before that motion was decided, Pouch filed a motion in the district court to withdraw from the bankruptcy court the reference of the Government's adversary proceeding. That motion was granted.

Upon reconsideration the district court held that, as a matter of law, the Government had absolute title to all of the property covered by the title vesting clause. *In Re American Pouch Foods, Inc.,* 30 B.R. at 1023. The court also noted that if the Government only took a lien on the allocable property, to secure its progress payments, the lien would be paramount to any other liens. *Id.* The court decided to abstain from hearing Pouch's counterclaim because the issue was better brought before the Armed Services Board of Contract Appeals. *Id.* at 1024.

I

Pouch is a debtor in possession in a reorganization proceeding and as such claims, under 11 U.S.C. § 544(a)(1), the rights and powers of a creditor with a judicial lien. Pouch argues that the title vesting clause in the contract only gave the Government a security interest (lien) in the contract property and that Pouch's hypothetical lien has priority because the Government's lien was not perfected in compliance with the Illinois Commercial Code.

Pouch relies on *United States v. Kimbell Foods, Inc.,* 440 U.S. 715, 99 S.Ct. 1448, 59 L.Ed.2d 711 (1979). There the Supreme Court was confronted with the issue of "whether contractual liens arising from certain federal loan programs take precedence over private liens, in the absence of a federal statute setting priorities." 440 U.S. at 718, 99 S.Ct. at 1453 (footnote omitted). The loan programs involved were those of the Small Business Administration and Farmers Home Administration. The Court found it clear that priority of liens stemming from federal lending programs must be determined with reference to federal law. 440 U.S. at 726, 99 S.Ct. at 1457. After analysis of the character and purposes of the lending programs, the Court found it prudent in determining priority "to adopt the ready made body of state law as the federal rule of decision until Congress strikes a different accommodation." 440 U.S. at 740, 99 S.Ct. at 1464 (footnote omitted).

Pouch first contends that the title vesting clause in the Pouch contract creates only a security interest in the Government such as was clearly the case in *Kimbell Foods* and secondly that the principles applied in *Kimbell Foods* require application of the Illinois Commercial Code to determine priority here. It would follow that Pouch's statutory lien as debtor in possession would be superior to the lien of the Government.

We first consider whether the Government has title such that there is no question of priority of liens. The clear and precise language of the contract between Pouch and the Government granted the Government title. Pouch argues that, notwithstanding the language of the contract, given the intent of the parties, the many incidents and risks of ownership retained by Pouch under the contract, and modern theory in the law of secured transactions, the title vesting clause should not be interpreted literally as grant of title to the Government.

We acknowledge, generally, that contract language which purports to place title to goods in a party not in possession of them may well create only a security interest in that party. *See, e.g.,* Commercial Code provisions, Ill.Rev.Stat. ch. 26, §§ 1–201(37) (Supp.1985), 9–102 and 9–202 (1974). The terms of this contract left Pouch with many of the incidents and risks of ownership.

Thus there would be considerable reason to treat provisions like these, if found in a private contract, as creating a security interest. On the other hand, this is a contract for the procurement of materials for national defense, with its terms spelled out in the regulations of the Defense Department, 32 C.F.R. § 163.79, and a history suggesting a substantial reason for very literal interpretation of the title vesting language. * * *

[The court reviewed the history of the authorization for and characterization of advance payments under government contracts. The conclusion was that Congress intended to authorize progress payments in exchange for title rather than a lien or security interest. Furthermore, early judicial decisions supported a literal interpretation of the title vesting language.]

In *Marine Midland Bank v. United States,* 687 F.2d 395, 231 Ct.Cl. 496 (1982), the court read the title vesting clause as creating security for repayment (out of amounts due the contractor at final performance) of the progress payments, which the court deemed loans, rather than partial purchases. Having decided that the Government had only a security interest (as Pouch contends here) the court declined to apply the state U.C.C. as the federal rule of decision governing priority. Emphasizing the need for standardization and uniformity in Government procurement, as distinguished from the federal loan programs which were the subject of *Kimbell Foods, supra,* the court chose a rule that "the government's security interest under its title vesting procedures [is] paramount to the liens of general creditors." *Id.* 687 F.2d at 404. We would agree with the latter holding if the Government's interest were only a lien.

We acknowledge the reasonableness of the *Marine Midland* view if we were considering the title vesting provisions on a clean slate. We do not agree, however, that because the 1958 enactment of express authority to make progress payments removed the original motive for using a title vesting clause, the construction of the clause should change at the time of that enactment. *See* 687 F.2d at 401. Notwithstanding Judge Bennett's meticulous explication, we see no reason for departure from the consistent holdings before and after 1958 that the title vesting clause is to be taken literally.

We note, however, that application of the *Marine Midland* rule to the present case would produce the same result we reach, awarding possession to the Government. Pouch does not argue, nor does the record suggest, that the value of the goods exceeds the total of progress payments. *Cf.* 687 F.2d at 405.

In *United States v. Lennox Metal Manufacturing Co.,* 225 F.2d 302 (2nd Cir.1955) the court considered a contract providing for progress payments (there called partial payments) and containing a title vesting clause. The Government terminated the contract for default and sued the contractor to recover possession of the property and damages. The district court had found with adequate support that the contractor was not in default, and that foreclosed recovery of damages. The district court also denied recovery of possession.

Judge Frank wrote the opinion, stating his individual view in Part I. Part II, 225 F.2d beginning at 317, was agreed to by all three judges. The Government contended that upon failure to prove default by the contractor, it had nevertheless brought about a termination for convenience. The contract so provided. The court affirmed the denial of possession, holding in Part II that the Government's refusal to make larger progress payments had been inequitable and such conduct had disentitled it to equitable relief, *i.e.,* "the enforcement of an equitable lien on the [contractor's] property." 225 F.2d at 317. Evidently, although without explanation, the court interpreted the title vesting clause as creating only an equitable lien.

We do not agree. Our interpretation of the contract is that upon termination, whether for default or convenience, the Government becomes entitled to possession of the property to which it has title. The ultimate rights to pecuniary adjustment between the parties will depend upon the type of termination, but the Government is entitled to possession under either type. The Fifth Circuit has held that:

> [I]n cases involving termination of Government contracts, where the product is part of the national defense effort, the jurisdiction of the district courts does not embrace any issue beyond that of title, so long as the Government represents in its complaint that the contract had been terminated. To hold otherwise would permit a contractor to plead and

litigate factual issues surrounding the termination, and delay delivery of vitally-needed defense products.

United States v. Digital Products Corp., 624 F.2d 690, 692 (5th Cir.1980); *accord In Re Greenstreet, Inc.,* 209 F.2d 660, 667 (7th Cir.1954).

Lennox has not been followed, and has been criticized. Even if a court would apply equitable principles against the Government in a case where extreme unfairness were shown, circumstances of that type have not been suggested here.

* * *

The judgment appealed from is affirmed.

SWYGERT, SENIOR CIRCUIT JUDGE, dissenting.

Because this case concerns the rights of the United States arising under a nationwide federal program, there is no question that federal law governs. *United States v. Kimbell Foods, Inc.,* 440 U.S. 715, 726–27, 99 S.Ct. 1448, 1457–58, 59 L.Ed.2d 711 (1979). Yet, in defining the rule of decision that gives content to that federal common law, this court must often resort to State law, particularly where there is no express congressional directive to the contrary and where any other rule would disrupt commercial relations predicated on State law. *See id.* at 728–29, 740, 99 S.Ct. at 1458–59, 1464. I would apply Illinois' Uniform Commercial Code as the rule of decision and would hold that the United States owned only an unperfected security interest in the seized assets.

In *Kimbell,* 440 U.S. at 728–29, 740, 99 S.Ct. at 1458–59, 1464, the Supreme Court held that State law should apply as the rule of decision in a commercial dispute involving a nationwide federal program if (1) there is no congressional directive to the contrary, (2) the federal program in question need not be uniform in character nationwide, (3) the application of State law would not frustrate specific objectives of the program, and (4) the application of a federal rule would disrupt commercial relationships predicated on State law. The majority holds, under two alternative theories, that the first criterion was not satisfied in the case at bar.

First, the majority holds that by passing legislation in 1958 expressly authorizing "progress payments," *see* 10 U.S.C. § 2307(a)(1) (1982), Congress necessarily incorporated as binding federal law the past practices that defined the term. Because the United States had always purported to take absolute title—rather than a security interest—in the parts, work in process, and inventories of government contractors in return for progress payments, Congress must have intended to incorporate this practice into the law. *See ante* at 1193–96.

Yet, as the majority's thorough historical review demonstrates, *ante* at 1193–1194, the 1958 statute simply marked the culmination of Congress' long retreat from its former prohibition of advances of public money to government contractors in excess of the value of services already rendered or goods already delivered. It was Congress' intent to legalize the practice of advance payments in general. The statute and legislative history are silent on the question of whether the title-vesting clause that traditionally accompanied progress payments should be interpreted literally or as a *de facto* security interest. The only relevant concern of Congress was that the federal government be permitted to pay money in advance of contract performance; the specifics of defining the effect and ramifications of various contractual alternatives, such as progress payments, were left open.[1]

Congressional silence on such issues should not be interpreted as an invitation to the courts to fashion a uniform federal common law. The "guiding principle" in deciding whether to fashion rules of federal common law or to incorporate State law is that a "significant conflict between some federal policy or interest and the use of state law in the premises must first be specifically shown." *Wallis v. Pan American Petroleum Corp.,* 384 U.S. 63, 68, 86 S.Ct. 1301, 1304, 16 L.Ed.2d 369 (1966). It is not enough that Congress *could* have readily enacted a complete code of law governing these commercial transactions better than the available State law; the "latent federal power * * * to displace state law is primarily a decision for Congress," and Congress must explicitly indicate its intent to exercise this power. *See id.*

The second theory advanced by the majority, *see ante* at 1196, is that assuming the Government's interest should be defined as a security interest, pursuant to well-established principles of State commercial law, Congress has already provided by statute the governing law of priority. In authorizing liens to secure "advance" payments, Congress required that such liens be "paramount to any other lien." 10 U.S.C. § 2307(c) (1982). Despite the historical differences between "advance" and "progress" payments, Congress must have used the term "advance payments" in the generic sense to include all kinds of payments in advance of full contract performance. "[W]e can think of no reason why Congress could have intended less protection for the Government when making progress payments than when making advance payments." *Ante* at 1194.

I agree. Because Congress has expressly provided that government liens be paramount, this directive must be incorporated as a rule of priority. But one rule of priority does not make a commercial code. Congress provided no direction on a myriad of issues that must be decided in this case and in other commercial cases. There are no guidelines as to how to judge the validity of a government lien, when it attaches, or what prerequisites—such as perfection—must be met before a particular government lien can be enforced as a paramount lien. I would hold that State law provides the rule of decision in determining the creation, validity, and perfection of government liens.

It is not incongruous to hold that different sources of law govern various, but related, aspects of a single commercial transaction. *Kimbell* does not require that a commercial transaction be governed entirely by federal common law or entirely by State law. Indeed, the Supreme Court has stressed that "[e]ven where there is related federal legislation in an area * * * it must be remembered that 'Congress acts * * * against the background of the total *corpus juris* of the states.'" *Wallis,* 384 U.S. at 68, 86

1. Thus, in explaining its legalization of advance payments, the Senate Report simply cited the need for a "modernized code of procurement procedures." S.Rep. No. 2201, 85th Cong., 2d Sess., *reprinted in* 1958 U.S.Code Cong. & Ad.News 4021, 4024. Congress approved the principle of advance payments as consistent with modern commercial practice, but left to others the task of defining the specific rules governing advance payments.

S.Ct. at 1304 (quoting Hart & Wechsler, *The Federal Courts and the Federal System* 435 (1953)). In *Wallis* the Court adopted the kind of hybrid law I propose in the case at bar. The Court held that while federal law governs the ability of private parties to assign oil and gas leases, State law governs the validity of a particular transfer between two parties. Similarly, this court in *United States v. Meadors,* 753 F.2d 590, 592 (7th Cir.1985), selectively applied State law to only a few of the specific issues of commercial law presented in that case. Such hybrid law is consistent with our conception of federal regulation as often "interstitial in nature, enacted against a background of state law and building on state law relationships." Comment, *Adopting State Law as the Federal Rule of Decision: A Proposed Test,* 43 U.Chi.L.Rev., 823, 829 (1976); *accord* Mishkin, *The Variousness of "Federal Law": Competence and Discretion in the Choice of National and State Rules for Decision,* 105 U.Penn.L.Rev. 797, 804–05 (1957) ("Most pervasive, perhaps, is the principle that a decision to apply state law as a matter of federal judicial incorporation may frequently be made as to a single issue at a time.").

The first prong of *Kimbell* is therefore satisfied: there has been no congressional directive regarding what law should govern the creation, validity, and perfection of a government lien. Turning to the second prong, I would follow the Tenth Circuit's holding that the government's interest in a uniform federal law for military procurement would not be compromised by the incorporation of the Uniform Commercial Code ("UCC") as the rule of decision. *In re Murdock Machine & Engineering Co. of Utah,* 620 F.2d 767, 772–73 (10th Cir.1980). The need for uniformity is already satisfied by State law itself, inasmuch as every State except Louisiana has enacted the UCC. *See* J. White & R. Summers, *Handbook of the Law Under the Uniform Commercial Code* § 1 at 1 & n. 1 (2d ed. 1980). Here, as in *Kimbell,* 440 U.S. at 732–33 & n. 28, 99 S.Ct. at 1460–61 & n. 28, there is no evidence that the "minor variations" in Article 9 of the UCC from State to State would hinder the government's national program. That the government program here involves national defense does not alter this conclusion. I fail to see how the trivial inconveniences attending compliance with the essentially uniform recording requirements of the States somehow threaten national security. *Accord Murdock,* 620 F.2d at 772–73.

As for the third prong of *Kimbell,* it can be argued that destroying the priority of federal liens by subjecting the federal government to State recording requirements would frustrate a specific objective of the federal procurement effort: to ensure that federal liens are paramount to all others. It is true that incorporating State law as the rule of decision in the case at bar may effectively destroy the value of the Government's claim to the seized assets. Yet, if *noncompliance* with State recording laws would effectively defeat the Federal government's ability to claim a paramount lien, certainly *compliance* would not.[2] The Government's assertion at oral argument that incorporating the UCC into federal law would destroy the value of billions of dollars of government liens is an argument against retroactive application of

2. I would therefore hold that if the government executes a proper security agreement and if its lien attaches and is perfected, then the government holds a paramount lien—superior in priority even to the perfected security interests of other creditors.

such a rule, not an argument that the government would be unable to protect its interests under the UCC in the future.

There is no question that the fourth prong of *Kimbell* is satisfied. The application of a federal rule would disrupt commercial relationships predicated on State law. With an annual budget that will soon exceed $300 billion, *see* Boyd, *Leaders Report Budget Accord with President,* N.Y. Times, July 10, 1985, at 11, col. 5, the Defense Department has an enormous, brooding presence in the marketplace. Yet, it is not always obvious that the military is involved in a particular transaction. There is nothing inherent in the purchase of such pedestrian goods as food in the case at bar or steel in *Murdock* that alerts the seller to the military's presence. Thus, allowing the military to hold enormous secret liens wreaks havoc with the expectations of the business community. "Mindful of the burdens of time and expense such investigations [of the possibility of the military's interest in a transaction] would impose on our nation's commerce, and the injustice which would result by dealing government 'wild cards' to businessmen at random," I am "not inclined to create a special commercial law for the government's benefit." *Murdock,* 620 F.2d at 772.

I would therefore hold that State law provides the rule of decision governing the creation and perfection of the Government's security interest. As the majority apparently agrees, *see ante* at 1193, there can be little doubt that the title-vesting clause created a security interest. Illinois' UCC defines a secured transaction to include "any transaction (regardless of its form) which is intended to create a security interest in personal property or fixtures." Ill.Ann.Stat. ch. 26, § 9–102(1)(a) (Smith-Hurd 1974) ("Ill. UCC"). Thus, the Government's characterization of its interest as one of absolute title is irrelevant; it is the intent of the parties, not the form of the transaction, that is dispositive. Here, the many incidents of ownership conferred on Pouch combined with the federal contract officer's testimony that the purpose of the title-vesting clause was to secure performance, *see* Appellant's Brief at 26–27 (quoting Transcript), compel the conclusion that the parties intend the Government to take only a security interest.

It is undisputed that the Government failed to file a financing statement pursuant to Ill. UCC §§ 9–103, 9–302, 9–401–03. The Government therefore held only an unperfected security interest in the seized assets. *Id.* at § 9–303. To be sure, this did not render the security agreement invalid or unenforceable. And it can be argued that as long as the Government's security interest is valid under State law, the federal rule of priority should apply to render the Government's lien paramount. Yet, the federal statute is so sparse as to what prerequisites should be met to create a valid and enforceable paramount lien that I would define the State perfection requirement as such a prerequisite. Only in this way can federal legislation that is interstitial in nature be brought into harmony with the broad body of State law that remains in force and effect until expressly replaced with more comprehensive federal legislation. *See supra* at 1200.

I would hold then, that before the Government seized Pouch's assets, it held an unperfected security interest. As such, its rights were subordinate to those of a variety of other creditors, including the debtor-in-possession. *See* Ill. UCC §§ 9–301(1), (3).

It should be noted, however, that once the Government came into possession of the collateral, no creditor, regardless of its superior claim of right, could compel repossession. Such repossession would be inconsistent with the sovereignty of the United States. Rather, the remedy for those who held superior claims to the collateral is to sue for their proper share of the proceeds, because in destroying the value of their claims, the Government took their property without just compensation. *See* U.S. Const. amend. V; *Armstrong v. United States,* 364 U.S. 40, 80 S.Ct. 1563, 4 L.Ed.2d 1554 (1960); *United States v. Ansonia Brass & Copper Co.,* 218 U.S. 452, 471, 31 S.Ct. 49, 54, 54 L.Ed. 1107 (1910); *Marine Midland Bank v. United States,* 687 F.2d 395, 397–98, 231 Ct.Cl. 496 (1982), *cert. denied,* 460 U.S. 1037, 103 S.Ct. 1427, 75 L.Ed.2d 788 (1983).

I would therefore reverse and remand for further proceedings.

Note

Judge Swygert is right, is he not?

Problem 7–9

Welco Industries agreed to furnish electric motors and compressors to Wedj. Wedj was producing air conditioners under a government contract for the United States Army. Under an agreement between the parties entered in the presence of the government's administrative officer, the contracting officer had "agreed to approve government progress payments to Wedj Inc. for Welco material immediately on receipt at Wedj Inc." The parallel provision gave Wedj's promise to pay the full invoice price within 10 days of receipt. When Welco filed a writ of replevin in the state court in Pennsylvania, the federal government intervened to assert its rights, and had the case transferred to the federal court. Welco argued that under the Memorandum of Understanding, shipments to Wedj were subject to a "retention of title" until full payment had been made. The government contract with Wedj on the other hand provided that "immediately upon the date of this contract, title to all parts; materials, inventory; [and] work in progress * * * acquired or produced by the contractor and allocated or properly charged under this contract under sound and generally accepted accounting principles shall forthwith vest in the government." The government argued that the foregoing contract language applied and that the language transferred title to the compressors and other materials to the government.

1. If the federal government were not involved, would this merely be a case of an unperfected secured creditor who would lose to a subsequent purchaser? What sections would be particularly relevant under Article 9?

2. Assume that Welco had perfected its purchase money security interest and had given whatever notice that might be required under UCC 9–312(3). Would the federal government's claim then be subordinate?

B. The Federal Tax Lien

The federal tax lien (Internal Revenue Code sections 6321 through 6323) is unique for many purposes. Unlike many liens, it carries its own priority schedule.

The student should first understand when and how a tax lien is likely to arise. In a typical income tax case, the tax lien does not arise until after the tax has been "assessed," demand for its payment has been made, and that demand has not been satisfied. Typically, assessment cannot occur until the taxpayer has reported income due and not made payment of it, or until there has been an audit and an ascertainment of tax to be due by the Internal Revenue Service. The threat that brings the taxpayer to the tax court is the threat of "assessment" of the tax. Thus, in the usual proceeding before the tax court and on appeal, there has not yet been an "assessment" and therefore a tax lien cannot exist. The tax lien that a creditors' rights lawyer is most likely to see is not one that arose out of nonpayment of income taxes on the revenue of the debtor, but rather it is a lien arising because of the debtor's failure to withhold and pay over taxes on the salaries of employees.

When such a lien arises under 6321 and 6322, it attaches to all the debtor's property, wherever located, without the necessity for a filing. Under the basic priority rules, 6323(a), the federal tax lien is subordinate to "any purchaser, holder of a security interest, mechanics lienor, or judgment lien creditor until notice thereof" has been filed. Thus, at least in general, the federal tax lien conforms to the first-in-time first-in-right rule. A starting point for one's analysis is to ask whether the federal government has filed notice of the tax lien as provided in 6323(f). If that event has not yet occurred at the time a judgment lien arises or a security interest perfected, etc., a competing claimant typically will be victorious against the tax lien. Although there may be some difficulty and confusion about exactly where the IRS will file its notice, the general rule is not hard to understand or to apply.

A difficulty arises when the competing creditor is asserting a security interest in after-acquired property or a security interest based on an advance made after the filing of the notice of a tax lien or after the creditor's knowledge of the existence of a tax lien. In such cases, UCC 9–312 would grant priority to the first to file over a subsequent creditor despite the fact the security interest was in after-acquired property or that it depended upon a subsequent advance. But the same is true as against a federal tax lien only to a limited extent. That limited extent is spelled out most extensively in 6323(c) and 6323(d). These sections are quite complex, but the student should at least have a general idea about where and how they will apply. Consider the following problem.

Problem 7–10

1. Secured creditor takes and perfects a security interest in debtor's caterpillar tractor on March 1, 1988. On March 5, notice of a tax lien is filed. Who enjoys priority?

2. Bank has a perfected security interest in all of debtor's inventory and accounts receivable, including after-acquired accounts and inventory. Several years after the financing statement was filed and the security agreement was executed and at a time when the debtor had $2,000,000 of accounts and inventory and when $1,500,000 of the loan was outstanding, the federal government filed the notice of tax lien.

a. Who has priority at that point?

b. Assume that secured creditor makes two subsequent advances of $100,000 each. The first is made 20 days after the notice of tax lien is filed, and the second is made 60 days after. Which of the following statements is accurate:

(1) Neither of these advances will be protected under 6323(d).

(2) The first but not the second will be protected under 6323(c).

(3) Both will be protected under 6323(c) or 6323(a).

c. What if the Bank knew of the tax lien but not of the filing at the time it made both advances?

d. If Bank and the IRS both claim inventory and accounts that had been acquired by the debtor 90 days after the filing of the notice of tax lien, who would have priority?

RICE INVESTMENT COMPANY v. UNITED STATES

United States Court of Appeals, Fifth Circuit, 1980.
625 F.2d 565.

RANDALL, CIRCUIT JUDGE:

In October, 1973, Rice Investment Company ("Rice") loaned Handy Stop, Inc. (the "Debtor") $67,583.20. In connection with the loan, the Debtor executed and delivered to Rice a security agreement pursuant to which the Debtor granted to Rice a security interest in all of the Debtor's inventory then owned or thereafter acquired. A financing statement was filed in the office of the Secretary of State of the State of Texas on October 29, 1973. The Debtor made payments on its indebtedness to Rice from time to time. In March, 1975, $46,317.54 remained owing from the Debtor to Rice.

The Debtor incurred liabilities for withholding and FICA taxes for the third and fourth quarters of 1973 and the first quarter of 1974 in the total amount of $11,853.19. Assessments of the taxes were made during March, 1974. Thereafter, a notice of a federal tax lien in the amount of $8,521.51 was filed on April 26, 1974, for the third and fourth quarters of 1973, and a further notice of a federal tax lien in the amount of $4,587.59 was filed on August 5, 1974, for the first quarter of 1974. The Internal Revenue Service levied upon the Debtor's inventory on August 18, 1974. The outstanding tax liability of the Debtor, including interest, at that time was $13,514.18. The perishable inventory was sold by the United States on August 28, 1974 for $750, and the nonperishable items were sold on November 14, 1974 for $3,500.

In September, 1974, Rice brought suit against the United States under 26 U.S.C. § 7426 (1976) seeking recovery from the United States of the proceeds ($4,250) received by the United States from the sale of the Debtor's inventory. Rice's second amended complaint asserts that the lien of the United States under 26 U.S.C. § 6321 (1976) in the inventory of the Debtor was junior to the lien of Rice under 26 U.S.C. § 6323 (1976) (amended 1978; amendment not relevant to this appeal) and that the levy of the United States was therefore unlawful. During the proceedings, in response to interrogatories propounded by the United States, Rice acknowledged that it did not have any information in its possession by which it could determine the exact date on which the Debtor acquired the inventory which was seized by the Internal Revenue Service.[1] Further, Rice admitted, in its motion for summary judgment, that none of the actual inventory on hand in October, 1973, when the security agreement was entered into, was part of the inventory seized and sold on August 28, 1974, and November 14, 1974.

The question presented by this appeal is whether the federal tax lien filed by the United States on April 26, 1974,[2] pursuant to 26 U.S.C. § 6321, primes the security interest held by Rice in the inventory which was seized by the United States on August 18, 1974. We hold that the lien of the United States does prime the security interest of Rice in such inventory, and accordingly, we reverse the summary judgment granted by the district court and remand with instructions to enter summary judgment for the United States.

SOME HISTORY ON THE PROBLEM

* * *

Under 26 U.S.C. § 6321, every federal tax which is not paid on demand becomes a lien "upon all property and rights to property, whether real or personal, belonging to" the taxpayer. After-acquired property, such as the Debtor's property in this case, is reached by the lien. The lien is effective from the date of assessment of the tax and has aptly been described as a secret lien. When the lien was first created in 1866, it prevailed, even though secret, against a bona fide purchaser for value. In 1913, however, Congress extended protection to purchasers, mortgagees and judgment creditors, and in 1939, to pledgees, against federal tax liens of which notice had not been filed in a designated office. Further, recognizing the impracticability of searching for tax liens in some cases, Congress in 1939 provided priority over filed tax liens under certain conditions for purchasers of, and lenders secured by "securities" and in 1964, for purchasers of motor vehicles. However, as against the rest of the world, including the taxpayer himself, the federal tax lien was effective upon assessment without any need for public notice.

The most basic principle employed in the adjudication of the priority of competing liens is "the first in time is the first in right." When a federal tax lien is one of the liens involved, however, the Supreme Court added a gloss on that principle by requiring that in order to be "first in time," the nonfederal lien must first have become "choate," i.e., the identity of the lienor, the property subject to the lien and the amount of the lien must be established beyond any possibility of change or dispute. Further, the determination of whether "a lien has acquired sufficient substance and has become so perfected as to defeat a later-arising or later-filed federal tax lien" is a matter of federal law.

As the federal law on "choateness" developed, few liens prevailed in the battle against federal tax liens.

1. The Debtor's business consisted of a drive-in grocery store, and its inventory consisted of the perishable and nonperishable items customarily sold in such a store.

2. Since the amount of gross proceeds from the sale of the inventory ($4,250) is less than the amount of the lien ($8,521.51) as to which notice was filed on April 26, 1974, we concern ourselves here only with the lien filed on that date.

> Even mortgages and other contractual security interests, despite their specially favored position under the federal statute, were vulnerable before 1966 to subsequently filed federal tax liens to the extent that the security embraced after-acquired property or involved disbursements (whether optional or obligatory) yet to be made, including foreclosure expenses and other outlays for which a mortgagee normally is entitled to a lien with the same priority as the principal debt.

Plumb, *Federal Liens and Priorities—Agenda for the Next Decade,* 77 Yale L.J. 228, 231 (1967) (footnotes omitted).

Federal Tax Lien Act of 1966

Congress enacted the Federal Tax Lien Act of 1966 in an effort to conform the lien provisions of the Internal Revenue Code to the concepts developed in the Uniform Commercial Code. Another primary objective was to provide some limited but specific relief from the harshness of the choateness rule for, among others, commercial lenders whose loans and collateral may change daily.

Section 6323 of the Internal Revenue Code, as amended by the Federal Tax Lien Act of 1966, sets forth certain limitations on the validity and priority of federal tax liens imposed by § 6321 of the Internal Revenue Code as against certain persons, including the holder of a security interest in property which is the subject of such a lien. Subsection (c) of § 6323 is the provision designed to provide a safe haven for the holders of security interests arising in certain commercial financing arrangements. Subsection (c) provides, in relevant part, that

> even though notice of a lien imposed by section 6321 has been filed, such lien shall not be valid with respect to a security interest which came into existence after tax lien filing but which—
>
> (A) is in qualified property covered by the terms of a written agreement entered into before tax lien filing and constituting—
>
> (i) a commercial transactions financing agreement, * * * and
>
> (B) is protected under local law against a judgment lien arising, as of the time of tax lien filing, out of an unsecured obligation.

The balance of subsection (c) and subsection (h) define the terms used in subsection (c). Four of those definitions are relevant for our purposes—the definitions of "commercial transactions financing agreement," "qualified property," "commercial financing security" and "security interest." The term "commercial transactions financing agreement" is defined as

> an agreement (entered into by a person in the course of his trade or business)—
>
> (i) to make loans to the taxpayer to be secured by commercial financial security acquired by the taxpayer in the ordinary course of his trade or business, * * *
>
> but such an agreement shall be treated as coming within the term only to the extent that such loan or purchase is made before the 46th day after the date of tax lien filing or (if earlier) before the lender or purchaser had actual notice or knowledge of such tax lien filing.

The term "qualified property," when used with respect to a commercial transactions financing agreement, is defined to include "only commercial financing security acquired by the taxpayer before the 46th day after the date of tax lien filing." The term "commercial financing security" is defined to mean "(i) paper of a kind ordinarily arising in commercial transactions, (ii) accounts receivable, (iii) mortgages on real property, and (iv) inventory." Finally, subsection (h)(1) of § 6323 defines the term "security interest" as follows:

> The term "security interest" means any interest in property acquired by contract for the purpose of securing payment or performance of an obligation or indemnifying against loss or liability. A security interest exists at any time (A) if, at such time, the property is in existence and the interest has become protected under local law against a subsequent judgment lien arising out of an unsecured obligation, and (B) to the extent that, at such time, the holder has parted with money or money's worth.

Under subsection (c) of § 6323, the holder of a security interest competing for priority with a federal tax lien who is able to demonstrate that such security interest meets the requirements of subsection (c) and the related definition in subsection (h) achieves priority for such security interest over the federal tax lien by virtue of the introductory language of subsection (c) which renders the competing tax lien invalid as against such security interest. It is apparent, simply from reading subsections (c) and (h), that the holder of a security interest seeking to establish priority thereunder over a competing tax lien must clear several complex hurdles under such subsections, and the failure to clear any one of them leaves the holder outside the safe haven of subsection (c). In the case before the court, the United States argues that in view of Rice's admission that it did not have any information in its possession by which it could determine the date on which the Debtor acquired the inventory seized by the United States on August 18, 1974, Rice would be unable to carry its burden under § 6323 of proving that the inventory was "qualified property," i.e., property acquired by the Debtor before June 11, 1974 (the 46th day after the filing of the tax lien on April 26, 1974). We agree, and we hold that the security interest of the United States in the seized inventory is, accordingly, not invalid under § 6323 with respect to the security interest of Rice in such inventory. Our holding is based on the clear language of the statute, and is strongly supported by the equally clear legislative history. At least when the inquiry is solely whether an item of inventory is "qualified property," it is not necessary to resort to notions of "choateness" as a tool for statutory interpretation. In view of our holding, it is also unnecessary to analyze the status of Rice's security interest insofar as the other requirements of § 6323 are concerned, and we express no views with respect thereto.

* * *

Rice urges that we construe the "in existence" language contained in the definition of "security interest" in subsection (h) of § 6323 to cover not only the inventory of the Debtor in existence on the date of the filing of the tax lien, but also any inventory which thereafter replaced such inventory. Rice argues that such a construction is particularly appropriate where, as was the case here, there has been only a single advance by the lender. To accept Rice's argument, however, would be to ignore the clear language of subsection (c) which requires that, wholly apart from the date on which the loan is made (which is itself the subject of certain independent requirements under § 6323 concededly met here), the collateral must be "qualified property." It would also be to ignore the legislative history of the Federal Tax Lien Act of 1966 which evidences a clear intent not to give commercial lenders an infinite priority over the United States, but instead to limit such lenders to property acquired by the taxpayer debtor before the 46th day after the filing of the tax lien. Rice says that a decision in favor of the United States in this case will have the effect of requiring a secured lender to check each day to determine whether a federal tax lien has been filed with respect to each of its borrowers. While this may be something of an exaggeration, it is clear that subsection (c) of § 6323 requires a secured lender regularly to monitor the federal tax lien status of its borrowers because only the prompt ascertainment of the existence of a federal tax lien will put the secured lender in a position to protect its interest in the collateral. As this court noted in *Texas Oil & Gas,* "we realize that this disposition does not afford the protection that commercial lenders who deal with after-acquired property might prefer." 466 F.2d at 1053. But efforts to improve that protection should be directed to Congress and not to the courts.

BACK TO HISTORY

Since the security interest of Rice in the seized inventory is not entitled to priority over the federal tax lien under § 6323, Rice must demonstrate that it is entitled to priority under the federal law developed prior to the enactment of the Federal Tax Lien Act of 1966. However, it is clear that under the federal law on "choateness" described above, the federal tax lien filed by the United States on April 26, 1974, would be entitled to priority over the security interest of Rice in the inventory seized by the United States on August 18, 1974, because Rice, by its own admission, could not prove that the seized property was in existence and owned by the Debtor on the date the tax lien was filed, which would lead to the conclusion that the security interest of Rice in the seized inventory was not sufficiently choate on the date of the tax lien filing to prevail over the tax lien.

Our conclusion that Rice, having failed to secure a safe haven under § 6323, is left with the law on "choateness" and fails under that law is buttressed by this court's similar conclusion in *Texas Oil & Gas.* Having demonstrated, among other things, that the account receivable in that case did not constitute "qualified property" under § 6323, the court turned to a consideration of the status of the account under the federal law on "choateness":

> In the instant case, it is true that the bank had done all it could do under the Uniform Commercial Code to secure its interest in taxpayer-debtor's accounts receivable. However, that conclusion simply does not answer the case law as it has developed in the area of tax liens. However "complete" a lender's perfection may be under state recording laws and however "specific" state law might deem that interest to be, it is federal law that determines the extent to which that state determination will protect a private lien from a federal tax lien. It appears clear

> from the case law that an account receivable not yet "acquired" at the time of the filing of a tax lien because the final transaction creating the account receivable was not yet in existence cannot be considered choate, save for those accounts receivable now protected by section 6323(c).

Texas Oil & Gas, 466 F.2d at 1051.

In our case, while Rice may well have done all that it could do under the Texas Business & Commerce Code to perfect its security interest in the Debtor's after-acquired inventory, the security interest of Rice in inventory not yet acquired at the time of the filing of the tax lien cannot be considered choate for federal law purposes, and the federal tax lien prevails over such security interest.

Reversed and remanded with instructions to enter summary judgment for the United States.

[Some footnotes omitted.]

Note

Rice comes to you after the decision above and asks what advice you would give to avoid similar outcomes in future cases. What would you suggest?

Note: The "Choateness Doctrine"

Any lawyers who are deeply involved in tax lien litigation will have to wrestle with the "choateness doctrine." One might have hoped that the Federal Tax Lien Act had laid it to rest, but an examination of the *Rice* case and of others like it, shows that it lives on, albeit in a somewhat weakened form. Beware, we have merely opened your eyes to federal tax lien complexities.

Problem 7–11

A twin-engine Beech Baron worth $250,000 is subject to a tax lien and the IRS has filed a notice of tax lien. Owner sells the aircraft to Dealer for $230,000 but fails to reveal the existence of the filed tax lien and Dealer's search fails to turn up notice of it. Dealer then sells the aircraft to Buyer for $255,000. A year later Buyer trades in the Baron in connection with purchase of a larger aircraft. At that point the Internal Revenue Service discovers the location of the Baron and asserts a right to it.

1. Who has a better right to the Baron, the Internal Revenue Service or the Dealer and why?

2. Would the outcome be the same if the Dealer's competitor was a secured creditor who had taken a perfected security interest in the Baron from Owner?

3. Where should the Dealer have searched to find notice of the tax lien?

CHAPTER 8

THE SECURED CREDITOR IN BANKRUPTCY

SECTION 1. Introduction

Both the student and the Article 9 lender view the Bankruptcy Code as a frightening and forbidding presence. The student senses that the trustee in bankruptcy has complex rights derived from the Bankruptcy Code that are different from and in some ways much more far-reaching than those of the creditors. Many an Article 9 lender has not merely sensed those things; he has had his nose rubbed in them.

A. Some History

In 1978, Congress enacted the Bankruptcy Reform Act, Public Law 95–598, 92 Stat. 2549, which became law on October 1, 1979. This historic legislation repealed the Bankruptcy Act of 1898, as amended, and enshrined the new Bankruptcy Code in Title 11, U.S.C.A. In addition to simplifying and clarifying substantive bankruptcy principles that had evolved over the years, the Code established bankruptcy courts with comprehensive jurisdiction over all cases and civil proceedings arising in, or relating to, cases under the Code and upgraded and clarified the judicial status of the judges of the bankruptcy court. See 28 U.S.C.A. §§ 151–160, 1471–1482.

Since that time, the implementation of the Code has been marked by controversy, complexity, and confusion. The need for further congressional action was made clear by the Supreme Court in Northern Pipeline Construction Co. v. Marathon Pipe Line Co., 458 U.S. 50, 102 S.Ct. 2858, 73 L.Ed.2d 598 (1982), in which the court held that the broad jurisdiction granted to bankruptcy judges violated Article III of the Constitution. Ultimately, a new and complex jurisdictional system was developed by Congress and enacted into law in 1984 in the Bankruptcy Amendments and Federal Judgeship Act of 1984. Pub.L. No. 98–353, 98 Stat. 333. See King, *Jurisdiction and Procedure Under the Bankruptcy Amendments of 1984,* 38 Vand. L.Rev. 675 (1985). Other corrective amendments, some substantive, were also contained in the 1984 Act, and the process of amendment still continues. One must be aware, therefore, of the latest version of the statute, as well as that version in effect when the case in bankruptcy under study was commenced.

B. The Effect of Commencing a "Case" In Bankruptcy

A "case" in bankruptcy is commenced when a petition for relief is filed by or against a debtor with the bankruptcy court. Relief for a business debtor will be either a liquidation under Chapter 7 or a reorganization under

Chapter 11. See Code, Chapter 3, Subchapter 1. In Chapter 7 cases, a trustee, who represents the debtor's estate, will be selected. The trustee has numerous responsibilities and powers, including the capacity to sue and to be sued. In Chapter 11, the debtor will become the "debtor in possession" and, as such, exercise the trustee's rights. When we speak of "the trustee," we mean to include the debtor in possession in a Chapter 11 case.

After a case is commenced, a secured creditor under Article 9 may file a claim against the estate and request a determination, under Section 506, that the claim is secured by property in which the estate has an interest. Two important questions arise at this point: (1) Should the secured claim be allowed? If not (and we will see why this might occur), the claim is unsecured and the creditor, subject to the priorities of Section 507, must share pro rata with other unsecured creditors. (2) If the secured claim is allowed, is the value of the interest in property of the estate less than the amount of the allowed claim? If so, the creditor will be unsecured in the amount of the difference and must pursue that portion of the claim as an unsecured creditor. Valuation questions, therefore, may arise early in the proceedings.

Assume for now that the secured claim is allowed and that the value of the collateral—the property in which the estate has an interest—exceeds the amount of the claim. What are the immediate effects under the Bankruptcy Code of commencing a case? Here are some simple problems that can be answered by reference to the statute.

Problem 8–1

Assume that the Debtor filed a petition for relief under Chapter 7 (liquidation) on July 1, 1987.

1. On July 5, Debtor granted to Secured Party a security interest, enforceable under Article 9, in personal property owned by the Debtor and not previously encumbered. May the trustee avoid the security interest? See Section 549. Is the creation of a security interest a transfer? See Section 101(48).

2. On February 1, Secured Party created and perfected by filing a security interest in Debtor's inventory, existing and after-acquired, and proceeds. On July 5, Debtor acquired rights in inventory subject to the security interest. In addition, Debtor received proceeds from the sale in the ordinary course of business of inventory acquired before July 1. Does Secured Party have a security interest in the after-acquired property? In the proceeds? See Section 552.

3. On June 25, Debtor defaulted under the security agreement. On June 26, Secured Party, acting under Article 9, Part 5, peacefully repossessed all the inventory in Debtor's possession. On July 5, Secured Party sent Debtor a notice under UCC 9–504(3) that it intended to dispose of the inventory by private sale after July 15. Can the trustee block this disposition? See Section 362(a)(5). See also, Sections 541(a)(1) & 542.

4. Debtor's petition for relief in bankruptcy was a default under the security agreement. Can Secured Party thereafter repossess inventory subject to a security interest from Debtor? See Section 362(a)?

C. *Importance of Trustee in Bankruptcy*

Here we can examine but a small part of the Bankruptcy Code. Mostly we will consider the trustee's so-called avoidance rights (often called avoidance "powers"). Those are the rights that the trustee in bankruptcy can use to "avoid" a security interest or another transfer by the debtor. Although those rights are probably not the most important to be found in the Bankruptcy Code, they may be the most important from the point of view of the secured creditor. Whatever their weight in the bankruptcy scale, the right of the trustee in bankruptcy to avoid or, put another way, to enjoy ultimate priority over Article 9 secured creditors is a far greater source of concern to such creditors than the rights of competing secured creditors, of state-law lien creditors, or of purchasers.

Why are the rights of the trustee in bankruptcy so significant? First, they are significant because the trustee in bankruptcy is ubiquitous. For every competing secured creditor there are even more trustees in bankruptcy. For every competing state-law lien creditor there may even be a hundred trustees in bankruptcy. The competing secured creditor or other creditor arises only occasionally. A trustee in bankruptcy has the potential of arising with respect to every debtor of the Article 9 secured creditor, and springs into being instantly upon the filing of a petition in bankruptcy.

Secondly, the trustee is specially important because he always has rights that are simply not accorded to other competitors. Under section 544 he has the right of a lien creditor arising on the date the petition is filed. For our purposes this is the right granted by UCC 9–301(1)(b) to a state-law lien creditor to defeat an unperfected security interest. The trustee also can void preferences under section 547, can set aside certain perfected security interests under section 522(f) and can set aside a variety of transfers as fraudulent conveyances under section 548 or 544(b). All of these rights arise out of the federal law, but some depend in important respects upon state law. They are rights, however, that go beyond the rights of any individual state-law creditor and are bound in many cases to leave disappointed secured creditors strewn in the wake of their exercise. So the trustee is important not just because he is ubiquitous, but because he has very special rights.

The trustee is important for yet a third reason, namely, that he is not a member of the club. If one secured creditor gets into a dispute with another, it is conceivable, even likely, that they will be able to work out an arrangement that will suit both of them. They may find that they have mutual interests in this case or in another and thus that it is not in the interest of either to litigate. The trustee, on the other hand, is a professional representative of the unsecured creditors. By hypothesis he now deals with a dead, moribund, or badly faltering business, and unlike a solvent debtor or other secured creditor, he may have no long-term interest in working out a deal that is favorable to any given secured creditor. Thus, at least in liquidation, the trustee is willing to go to the mat, to litigate over his rights and to risk losing all against the prospect that he might win all.

Finally the trustee is more important than other competitors because he brings his own court with him. With few exceptions priorities between the trustee in bankruptcy and any secured creditor will be fought out, not in state courts, but in the federal bankruptcy court. They will be heard there by a bankruptcy judge who does nothing but hear such cases. Not only is this judge usually a sophisticated analyst of Article 9 and of the bankruptcy law, he is a judge with a stake in the bankruptcy process. Invariably he will be hostile to any whom he perceives to be at odds with what might be called the bankruptcy system. To the extent that the secured creditor presents himself as one who would rather not submit to the process but would instead prefer to deprive the others of some of the wherewithal (e.g. collateral) to play the bankruptcy game, the bankruptcy judge will not be receptive. Perhaps it is too strong to say that the bankruptcy court is a hostile environment for the secured creditors, but it is appropriate to say that this environment is not dedicated primarily to the secured creditors' interests. The bankruptcy court is clearly a place where the secured creditors' interests can be harmed or compromised in many ways and where secured creditors are unlikely to get their way by trying to fool or intimidate the judge.

We divide this chapter into two parts. In the first we will deal extensively and in depth with the avoidance rights of the trustee, sections 544, 547, 548, and others. In the second part we will deal in a more superficial way with some of the more subtle rights of the bankruptcy trustee. These are not rights to avoid the secured creditors' interests but merely to impede them, to bite at the secureds' heels in the hope of ultimately wearing them down to produce a compromise. These are the rights found in section 362 (the stay), in sections 1129 and 1325 (the cramdown), and in still other sections of the code.

The various forms of bankruptcy are identified by their "chapters." Chapter 7 contains the provisions for liquidation of an individual's or business's assets; Chapter 11 deals with reorganizations and Chapter 13 covers so called wage-earner plans. The students should not only understand this nomenclature, but also understand that many Chapter 11's are in fact merely prolonged liquidations and that a business can sometimes be run even after a Chapter 7 has been filed. In Chapter 13's and Chapter 7's there will always be an independent trustee. In Chapter 11 the debtor becomes the "debtor-in-possession" (sometimes called the "DIP") and himself has and asserts most of the rights of the trustee in bankruptcy. Thus, for the purpose of this course, when one sees a court talking about the rights of the "debtor-in-possession" he should think of that person as the trustee.

SECTION 2. TRUSTEE'S AVOIDANCE RIGHTS ("POWERS")

A. *The Basics*

It is familiar learning that subsection 544(a) of the Bankruptcy Act is the "strong-arm clause." This clause gives the trustee in bankruptcy the rights of a lien creditor as of the date the petition is filed in a voluntary case. The student should now understand how this section fits hand-in-glove with the lien creditor's rights to strike down unperfected security interests under UCC 9–301(1) and other state law.

Section 544(b) is a more obscure provision. It is a direct descendant of section 70e, the section involved in *In re Plonta* infra at p. 430. By reading *In re Plonta* and applying the Uniform Commercial Code and the Bankruptcy Code of 1978 to it, students should learn why 544(b) is no longer a very significant provision.

The other avoidance section that merits careful and detailed study is section 547 dealing with preferences. It allows a trustee in bankruptcy to recapture certain money and other assets that have been transferred out of the estate prior to the filing of the petition. Two "transfers" that will concern us in this course are the perfection of a security interest and the payment of a debt.

Sections 549, 550, 551 and 552 may be regarded as adjuncts to the more significant avoidance rights of sections 544 and 547. In addition we will consider section 548, a mini-fraudulent conveyance act, and section 558 which gives to the trustee the defenses that would have been available to the debtor.

Finally we will treat subsection 522(f), an avoidance right distinct from all the others. Under 522(f) the debtor may avoid a perfected security interest that could not have been attacked under any of the other provisions in certain circumstances where the debtor has the right to declare the asset as exempt under state law or under 522(d).

To get a grip on the basics the student should examine the lawyer's opinion in the following problem. The lawyer is sometimes, but not always, correct.

Problem 8–2

Assume that Gene Ovelli owns a small lumber mill that has been in financial difficulty for some months. During the current year, Ovelli has engaged in the transactions listed below.

1. January 8: Adams finances Ovelli's purchase of a $1000 piece of equipment from Jones, charges a usurious rate of interest and acquires a security interest duly created and perfected pursuant to Article 9 and which gives Adams a veto power over all of Ovelli's future dealings with others on credit.

2. January 10: First National Bank lent Ovelli $4000, and took Article 9 security in Ovelli's two cement mixers, but because of a slip-up, no financing statement was ever executed or filed.

3. June 11: Holt, who had lent $3000 to Ovelli a year previous pursuant to an unsecured note, became panicky and demanded that Ovelli give him security in a caterpillar that Ovelli owned free and clear. Ovelli and Holt duly executed a valid financing statement that referred to the caterpillar as "collateral" and Holt then duly filed it.

4. June 12: Stein who had lent $4000 to Ovelli pursuant to a secured obligation two years previously, but who had never filed a financing statement, filed a financing statement on June 12.

5. April 19: Brown, who had sold several power saws to Ovelli on unsecured credit, got a judgment against Ovelli and levied on the saws which the sheriff now has in his possession pending a scheduled judicial sale.

6. January 16: Ovelli transferred title to his new and unencumbered Cadillac sedan to his wife. At different times he has described this transfer as a gift out of love and affection for his wife or as a payment for her service

without pay at the lumbermill as a bookkeeper. Over the years she has done office work at the mill; she was never paid a formal salary for that work.

7. May 30: Costa, a cousin of Ovelli, lent Ovelli $5000 pursuant to an Article 9 security interest in lumber worth $6000 on Ovelli's premises. Costa did not, however, perfect this interest until June 7. Meanwhile, on June 5, Martin, an unsecured creditor of Ovelli (with a $500 claim) and armed with a judgment, levied on the lumber with knowledge of Costa's interest.

8. June 28: Adams lent Ovelli $5000 pursuant to a valid and contemporaneously perfected security interest in Ovelli's only remaining unencumbered personalty, a compressor worth $7500.

Against the foregoing background, Ovelli went to his lawyer, Drake, stated that his situation seemed hopeless, and that he wanted to "take bankruptcy" and start over.

Ovelli filed a petition in bankruptcy on July 3rd. Let us assume that the trustee in bankruptcy for Ovelli's estate has asked a lawyer, Fraser, to serve as his attorney during the course of the proceeding. The trustee has given Fraser a memorandum recording the eight transactions described above and asked what rights the trustee has, if any, in respect to each. Fraser's comments, gratuitous and otherwise, on some of the transactions follow:

1. *Trustee v. Adams.* Under section 558 the estate has the defenses of the debtor. Among those would be a claim in this case that the contract was usurious and arguably unconscionable.

2. *Trustee v. First National Bank.* This one we will challenge under section 544(a). It is a classic non-perfection-lien creditor situation in which the trustee beats the unperfected secured creditor by asserting the rights of a lien creditor under section 9–301 and section 544.

3. *Trustee v. Holt.* This is a classic section 547 case.

4. *Trustee v. Adams and Stein.* This too is a preference; or did the "transfer" occur before the 90 day term?

5. *Trustee v. Brown.* This one we could have challenged under the old section 67(a) that struck down almost all judicial liens that arose within four months of bankruptcy. I don't see a provision identical to that one in the Bankruptcy Reform Act. There must be one though.

6. *Trustee v. Mrs. Ovelli.* I wonder what we should do here. Certainly we should consider the use of section 548, but we may have difficulty in proving the facts under section 548. I think I will ask my associate if there are other bases upon which we could attack this transfer. What do you think?

7. *Trustee v. Costa and Martin.* We have lots of possibilities here it would seem. First I would think that we could strike Martin's claim down under section 547. Section 547 does not seem to help us against Costa because he perfected within 10 days. What about the possibility of subrogating ourselves to Martin's claim under section 544(b) directly? I wonder if the reference in section 544(b) to subrogation only to a creditor "holding an unsecured claim" deprives us of that right? Conceivably we can reassert Martin's claim under section 551, having struck it down, but does that mean we can unseat Ovelli only to the extent of $500?

8. *Trustee v. Adams and Stein.* I am tired, I will let the students work this one out.

B. Avoidance Rights, Less Basic

Section 544(b) of the Bankruptcy Code provides: "The trustee may avoid any transfer of an interest of the debtor in property or any obligation incurred by the debtor that is voidable under applicable law by a creditor holding an unsecured claim that is allowable under * * * this title. * * *"

IN RE PLONTA

United States Court of Appeals, Sixth Circuit, 1962.
311 F.2d 44.

CECIL, CHIEF JUDGE:

This is an appeal from the United States District Court for the Western District of Michigan, Southern Division. The controversy grows out of the bankruptcy of Eugene (Dean) W. Plonta. Sears, Roebuck and Co., the appellant, claims to be a secured creditor of the bankrupt Plonta. Wadsworth Bissell, trustee in bankruptcy, is the appellee. The parties will be referred to as the Bankrupt, Sears and Trustee, respectively.

The pertinent facts are not in dispute and may be stated as follows: The Bankrupt purchased a 22–foot cabin cruiser from Sears on a conditional sales contract April 30, 1956. The cruiser was in kit form and by agreement between the purchaser and seller, the boat hull, engine, parts and equipment were to be shipped for assembly to North Shore Marina, Incorporated, at Grand Haven, Ottawa County, Michigan. The various parts and equipment arrived at the marina about the middle of May, 1956. The boat was completed and given a trial run on July 3rd or 4th.

After the trial run, the boat remained at the marina for the installation of some additional items of equipment purchased by the Bankrupt and for which he paid the marina. On June 13, 1956, the Bankrupt executed and delivered a promissory note to Sears, for the balance of the purchase price and gave a chattel mortgage to Sears covering the boat and equipment as security for the payment of the note. The chattel mortgage was filed in the office of the Register of Deeds of Muskegon county, Michigan, June 21, 1956. The mortgage was not filed with the Register of Deeds of Ottawa county, the county in which North Shore Marina was located. At all times pertinent to this litigation, the Bankrupt was a resident of Muskegon county.

The installation of the additional equipment was completed about the middle of August. At this time, the Bankrupt took the boat to the Muskegon Yacht Club, in Muskegon county, docked it there one night and then returned it to North Shore Marina, in Grand Haven. It was then taken to a marina in Bear Lake channel, in Muskegon county, and left there two or three nights and again returned to Grand Haven. The Bankrupt traveled back and forth between North Shore Marina and Bear Lake channel until the latter part of August. At this time he was able to rent docking facilities in the channel. The boat remained here until October, when it was returned to the marina in Grand Haven and stored for the winter.

During the following year 1957, although the Bankrupt sometimes used the boat, it was continuously kept at the marina in Grand Haven for repairs and storage. On December 16, 1957, Sears repossessed the boat in foreclosure of its chattel mortgage and paid North Shore Marina its accumulated storage, repair and upkeep charges against the Bankrupt. About two hours after the repossession, the Bankrupt filed his petition in bankruptcy. The time relation between these two events was coincidental and not a race for priority. Subsequent to the repossession, Sears sold the boat for $2300, which was considered to be its fair and reasonable value.

The history of the litigation is as follows: On January 13, 1959, the Trustee filed a petition to require Sears to turn the $2300 over to the bankrupt estate. There was a hearing on this petition and the referee found from the facts above stated that the location of the boat for the purpose of filing a chattel mortgage, under Michigan Statutes Annotated 26.929, M.C.L.A. § 566.140, was Ottawa county, Michigan. He further found that the mortgage was invalid as to the Trustee for failure to file with the Register of Deeds, of Ottawa county, and ordered Sears to turn over $2300 to the estate. There was a petition for review of this order and on review the District Judge adopted the referee's findings of fact and conclusions of law and sustained his order.

Later counsel for Sears moved to set aside this order and for reconsideration of its petition for review. In the meantime, the Supreme Court of Michigan had decided the case of Schueler v. Weintrob, 360 Mich. 621, 105 N.W.2d 42, in which it was held that repossession by a mortgagee prior to the time of filing a petition in bankruptcy was in legal effect equivalent to filing in the county of location (M.S.A. 26.929) and deprived the Trustee in Bankruptcy of any rights under section 70, sub. c of the Bankruptcy Act. (Sec. 110, sub. c, Title 11, U.S.C.A.)

A motion was then filed on behalf of the Trustee for the court to receive additional testimony or remand the matter to the referee to take testimony concerning the extension of credit to the Bankrupt between the date of the execution of the mortgage on June 13, 1956, and the repossession of the property on December 16, 1957. The court sustained the motion and remanded the case to the referee for the purpose of taking further evidence. Upon hearing the referee found that within the interim period involved, Albert B. Doherty extended credit to the Bankrupt in the amount of $10, without knowledge of the mortgage and it was unpaid. The referee concluded that the existence of this interim creditor invalidated the mortgage as a security document pursuant to section 70, sub. e (Sec. 110, sub. e(1), Title 11 U.S.C.A.) of the Bankruptcy Act and that the benefits of the invalidity inured to all the general creditors of the Bankrupt. The turnover order of $2300 was again entered. On petition for review, the District Judge affirmed the order of the referee. In a subsequent order, the motion of Sears to vacate the original order of the court, dated October 20, 1960, was denied.

The first question presented for our consideration is whether, under the law of Michigan, the chattel mortgage should have been filed in Ottawa county, as well as Muskegon county. The Michigan Statute (M.S.A. 26.929) provides: "Every mortgage or conveyance intended to operate as a mortgage of goods and chattels which shall hereafter be made which shall not be accompanied by an immediate delivery and followed by an actual and continued change of possession of the things mortgaged, shall be absolutely void as against the creditors of the mortgagor, and as against subsequent purchasers or mortgagees in good faith, unless the mortgage or a true copy thereof shall be filed in the office of the register of deeds of the county where the goods or chattels are located, and also where the mortgagor resides * * *."

The referee found and concluded, from the facts as stated herein, that Ottawa county was the county of location and under the Michigan statute the mortgage should have been filed there.

* * *

We are bound by the finding of the referee and the District Judge that under the law of Michigan the mortgage was required to be filed in Ottawa county, unless such finding is clearly erroneous. * * *

The conclusion of the referee, affirmed by the trial judge, is amply supported by the evidence. His interpretation of the facts and the inference drawn therefrom as to the location of the boat was warranted and certainly not clearly erroneous.

The mortgage then was invalid, under the Michigan statute (M.S.A. 26.929) as to creditors of the Bankrupt. After the opinion of the court on the question of the necessity of filing the mortgage in Ottawa county, it seemed that Sears' security might be salvaged by the decision of the Supreme Court of Michigan, in Schueler v. Weintrob, 360 Mich. 621, 105 N.W.2d 42, to which reference is heretofore made.

Counsel for the appellant objected to having the case remanded to the referee for further consideration and a determination of the Trustee's rights under section 70, sub. e of the Bankruptcy Act. We find no merit to the appellant's claim that the court erred in remanding the case to the referee for further hearing. It was the duty of the District Judge to see that there was a full and complete discovery of all available evidence pertinent to any issues presented by the facts and law involved.

Section 70, sub. e(1) of the Bankruptcy Act (110, sub. e(1), Title 11, U.S.C.A.) provides: "A transfer made or suffered or obligation incurred by a debtor adjudged a bankrupt under this title which, under any Federal or State law applicable thereto, is fraudulent as against or voidable for any other reason by any creditor of the debtor, having a claim provable under this title, shall be null and void as against the trustee of such debtor."

The following facts, as found by the referee, are substantiated by the evidence: The mortgage was not filed in Ottawa county as required by the Michigan statute. Albert B. Doherty became a creditor in the amount of ten dollars July 20, 1957, when the mortgage was off record and his claim was provable against the Bankrupt under the Bankruptcy Act. The conclusion of the referee, sustained by the District Judge, that the mortgage being invalid under the Michigan statute as to interim creditor Doherty, was null and void as against the Trustee, is a correct application of the law. * * * Moore v. Bay, 284 U.S. 4, 52 S.Ct. 3, 76 L.Ed. 133.

So far as we have been able to ascertain the amount of the credit extended is immaterial and the validity or invalidity of the chattel mortgage is not affected by the size of the creditor's claim. Neither is it material that the debt was not scheduled or that the creditor did not know of the existence of the chattel; nor is it necessary to prove that the creditor would not have extended the credit if he had known of the mortgage. Counsel for the appellant have cited no authorities in support of these claims.

Finding no error in the record the judgment of the District Court is affirmed.

Notes

1. Which of the following is true:

A. If *Plonta* arose in modern day Michigan, which has enacted the 1972 amendments to Article 9, the trustee could prevail under subsection 544(a).

B. The trustee could not prevail under subsection 544(b).

C. The trustee might be successful in using section 547. See subsection 547(e)(2).

2. Note that subsection 544(b) requires the existence of an actual unsecured creditor who could avoid the transfer under applicable state law. In *Plonta,* Mr. Doherty with a $10 claim fulfilled that requirement. Suppose that Debtor, who owed Creditor $5,000, granted Creditor a security interest in collateral worth $100,000 in "consideration of the antecedent debt" and perfected it by filing. The transfer, however, was fraudulent because Debtor actually intended to defraud creditors. To what extent could the trustee, subrogated to Mr. Doherty's rights under subsection 544(b), avoid Debtor's transfer? (Note that a transfer with actual intent to defraud is fraudulent against existing and future creditors. Thus, the trustee—a future creditor—might also be able to avoid the transfer under sections 544(a) or 548.).

SECTION 3. PREFERENCES, SECTION 547

A. The Basics

We have touched on section 547 above. Because preferences offer interesting and intricate intellectual problems, they probably command more law school time than they deserve. Nevertheless, manipulating section 547 is fun; let us indulge ourselves.

The principal evil to be cured by the preference provision is that of preventing a debtor from favoring one creditor over others similarly situated through a transaction occurring within a short period prior to bankruptcy. Evidently Congress believed that one who sees bankruptcy on the horizon, and who is already insolvent, should not be free to favor one creditor over another, but should be required to treat all alike. Thus, the classic preference is the simple payment on the eve of bankruptcy of one creditor's debt when comparable payments are not being made to others.

A second common form of preference is to give property to a creditor, not in the form of money but in the form of a grant of a security interest to secure a prior loan on the eve of bankruptcy—"after thought" security. Certainly the granting of a valid security interest would have the same ultimate consequence as the payment of that creditor's debt.

Still different, is a preference given by means of the *perfection* of a previously created security interest within 90 days. One might think that the "transfer" between the creditor and the debtor should be deemed to have occurred at the time the security agreement was executed and the interest conveyed to the creditor. Such a creditor could argue that he was not an "after-thought" creditor, not a person who was particularly abusive, for he had achieved his grant of a security interest well before the 90–day period. Here we are assuming a case in which a security agreement was signed and the loan made long before the 90 days, but in which perfection occurred within 90 days. Section 547 condemns this transaction (though for different reasons) just as much as the one in which the security transfer, and its perfection, occurs after the loan and within the 90 days. True enough, the creditor here is not an after-thought creditor; he bargained for his transfer at a time when bankruptcy was not imminent. This creditor may be guilty of another kind of crime, however, namely that of holding an undisclosed security interest. If we uphold a security agreement that is executed long before the 90 days but perfected by a public filing for the first time on the eve of bankruptcy, we make it substantially easier for the debtor and a cooperating creditor to keep that transfer secret, to mislead other creditors into lending in the belief that the debtor has not granted a security interest, and thus ultimately to distort the distribution in bankruptcy. In this case the preference legislation is justified also as an attack on "secret liens." By putting the creditor at risk for 90 days *after* he perfects, the bankruptcy law renders the granting of such a secret lien much more risky than it would otherwise be.

Finally there are variations on the foregoing themes. They include the case in which the secured creditor's pot is filled by after-acquired property, property acquired for the first time within the 90 days. Before 1978, the secured creditor could argue that such a "transfer" occurred at the time of perfection, prior to the preference period, but that argument is no longer available and thus the trustee will be able to avoid some security interests to the extent that they attach to collateral acquired within 90 days of bankruptcy. A second variation on the earlier theme is the preference that occurs not by an intentional late filing, but by a mistaken late filing. This is the creditor who makes the loan and intends to perfect at once but who only perfects 20 to 30 days later, or conceivably several months later after he discovers, for example, that his first financing statement was not filed in the right place.

The student should now turn to section 547(b) which reads in full as follows:

> Except as provided in subsection (c) of this section, the trustee may avoid any transfer of an interest of the debtor in property—
>
> (1) to or for the benefit of a creditor;
>
> (2) for or on account of an antecedent debt owed by the debtor before such transfer was made;
>
> (3) made while the debtor was insolvent;
>
> (4) made—

(A) on or within 90 days before the date of the filing of the petition; or

(B) between ninety days and one year before the date of the filing of the petition, if such creditor at the time of such transfer was an insider;

(5) that enables such creditor to receive more than such creditor would receive if—

(A) the case were a case under chapter 7 of this title;

(B) the transfer had not been made; and

(C) such creditor received payment of such debt to the extent provided by the provisions of this title.

Note that the trustee must satisfy all five of the above tests in order to establish a voidable preference. If he fails on one, the transfer is not voidable. Several will seldom be disputed. First, the debtor is presumed to be insolvent within the 90 days; thus the trustee will invariably succeed under subsection (b)(3). Second, the transfer will almost always be "to or for the benefit of the creditor" and thus subsection (b)(1) will seldom be an issue. The same factors that control subsection (b)(2) are likely to control subsection (b)(4) and vice versa. Thus, for example, if the creditor can convince the court that the transfer occurred outside the 90 days, he may be simultaneously convincing the court that the transfer occurred at the same time as the giving of value and therefore that subsection (b)(2) is not violated. Invariably when a security interest is at stake, the time of the transfer will be critical.

The time of transfer is a technical matter governed for the purposes of section 547 by 547(e). That subsection reads in full as follows:

(e)(1) For the purposes of this section—

(A) a transfer of real property other than fixtures, but including the interest of a seller or purchaser under a contract for the sale of real property, is perfected when a bona fide purchaser of such property from the debtor against whom applicable law permits such transfer to be perfected cannot acquire an interest that is superior to the interest of the transferee; and

(B) a transfer of a fixture or property other than real property is perfected when a creditor on a simple contract cannot acquire a judicial lien that is superior to the interest of the transferee.

(2) For the purposes of this section, except as provided in paragraph (3) of this subsection, a transfer is made—

(A) at the time such transfer takes effect between the transferor and the transferee, if such transfer is perfected at, or within 10 days after, such time;

(B) at the time such transfer is perfected, if such transfer is perfected after such 10 days; or

(C) immediately before the date of the filing of the petition, if such transfer is not perfected at the later of—

(i) the commencement of the case; or

(ii) 10 days after such transfer takes effect between the transferor and the transferee.

(3) For the purposes of this section, a transfer is not made until the debtor has acquired rights in the property transferred.

Generally, the subsection gives a secured creditor a 10 day grace period in which to perfect. If he perfects within that time, the "transfer" is deemed to have occurred at the earlier point when the security agreement was signed or the loan made. The effect of such a relation back is to cause the transfer to occur simultaneously with value and thus for the transfer *not* to be for an antecedent debt. Note that the tests for perfection with respect to real estate and personal property are different.

The final condition, subsection (b)(5), finds its principal importance with respect to payments to secured creditors. The very idea of a preference is that one creditor gets more than he would get by virtue of the transfer than if there had been liquidation immediately prior to the transfer and he had to share with similarly situated creditors. If a creditor has a security interest that is perfected and that gives him a claim to collateral equal to the value of his debt, no payment to him will enable him to receive more money than he would have received under Chapter 7 (i.e., on liquidation) without the transfer. That is because the creditor would take 100 cents on the dollar on liquidation, namely the amount for which his collateral could be sold, and not more. To the extent that he receives a payment prior to liquidation his claim would be reduced and he would be entitled to only 100 cents on the remaining debt. Thus, if one assumes a secured creditor with a $100,000 claim and collateral worth $120,000, he will receive $100,000 on liquidation. A pre-bankruptcy payment up to $100,000 would not improve his position. Even though the payment came out of the estate, the estate would not be diminished because that payment would in turn free $100,000 of collateral for the other creditors. Hence he would not be receiving a preference.

After mastering the substantive provisions in section 547(b), one should turn to the exceptions in subsection 547(c). With the 1984 amendments, the exceptions have become so expansive that they may be more important than subsection (b) itself. Subsection (c)(1) might be looked upon as a loosening of the restraints imposed by subsection (b)(2) and in some sense that is an accurate way to consider it. For example, it would cover the case in which a creditor transferred goods to a debtor, the debtor paid by check, and the check cleared only a week or ten days later. On a strict reading of subsection 547(b) the transaction might constitute a voidable preference because the payment coming ten days later would be regarded as antecedent under (b)(2). Presumably (c)(1) would stretch the antecedency requirement at least this far and would take the transaction described out of section 547.

A more difficult question is whether subsection (c)(1) ever applies to extend the ten-day relation back rule for filing that is embodied in subsection 547(e)(2)(B). It seems doubtful that Congress intended subsection (c)(1) to change a quite specific and rigid requirement of ten days in subsection 547(e).

Many payments both to secured and unsecured creditors that would otherwise be voidable preferences will now be saved by subsection (c)(2). Students should study the subsection to see which payments within the 90–

day period might not qualify under subsection (c)(2). Surely it cannot be intended to save all payments. Prior to the 1984 amendments, subsection (c)(2) was of much more limited significance. As it existed prior to 1984, subsection (c)(2) applied only to payments made "not later than 45 days after the debt was incurred." Under that version only short-term obligations such as trade credit or utility obligations could conceivably be covered and payments to commercial lenders rarely fit within the 45–day rule. With removal of the 45–day limit in 1984, it is open season on payments of debt irrespective when the debt was incurred.

Subsection (c)(3) is designed to protect purchase money interests that might otherwise fall afoul of (b), and subsection (c)(4) is to cover the case in which the creditor receives a preference but then makes a subsequent loan. Quaere: what of a case under subsection (c)(4) in which the subsequent loan is secured by the collateral that has been in existence and has secured prior debts? Does such a loan fit within (c)(4) or is it excluded by the "not secured by an unavoidable security interest"?

Subsection (c)(5) is intricate and interesting but of limited significance. The student should read it with care.

Note that subsection (c)(6) is simply an exclusion to make sure that the special rules for statutory liens are not upset by section 547. Subsection (c)(7) is an important exception, added in 1984, that frees a variety of consumer transfers (payments, garnishment of wages) from the reach of the trustee.

Discussion with trustees, judges, and examination of the cases indicate that section 547 on preferences is substantially less significant in practice than a student might imagine. With the expansion of the exceptions in 1984, section 547 will likely become even less significant in practice than formerly.

In summary, the following analysis, in steps, is useful in applying section 547.

First, did the debtor make a transfer "of an interest of the debtor in property?" See subsections 101(48) & 547(b).

Second, if the answer is yes, when was the transfer made? See subsection 547(e). Note that if the transfer was a payment, it was made at the time it took effect between the parties. See subsection 547(e)(2)(A). If, however, the transfer was the grant of a security interest, it may be made later than the time it was effective between the parties. Thus, if a security interest attached on July 1 but was perfected by filing on July 15, the transfer was made—at the earliest—on July 15. Read subsection 547(e) carefully.

Third, was the transfer avoidable because all five conditions in 547(b) were satisfied?

Fourth, if the answer is yes, was the transfer saved by any of the five exceptions in subsection 547(c)? The exceptions to subsection 547(b) found in subsection 547(c) have been called the "safe harbor" provisions.

Please work the following problems.

Problem 8–3

Debtor, a small business, borrowed $10,000 from C1 on July 1 and $20,000 from C2 on July 15. The loans were unsecured. D issued C1 a note payable in six months and issued C2 a note payable on demand. D filed a voluntary case in bankruptcy on December 1 and it is stipulated that Debtor was insolvent from October 15 until December 1.

The trustee has identified the following transfers by Debtor as suspect and asks whether they can be avoided under subsection 547. The trustee asserts that they are all "unfair" grabs within the 90 day period and should be avoided.

1. On September 15, C1 persuaded D to grant a security interest in described collateral in consideration of the existing $10,000 debt. C1 perfected the security interest by filing on September 17. There is no question that the security interest is perfected under Article 9.

2. On October 20, C2 demanded payment of the note. Debtor paid C2 $10,000 by check on October 25.

3. On November 10, C3, another unsecured creditor, obtained a judgment against D and, on November 15, obtained a judicial lien on personal property under applicable state procedures.

Problem 8–4

Suppose, in Problem 8–3 above, that Debtor was insolvent from September 1 until December 1, the date the case was filed. On September 15, Debtor signed a contract to purchase a piece of equipment from Seller for $20,000. Debtor paid Seller $5,000 on September 15 and granted Seller an enforceable security interest in the equipment to secure the $15,000 balance, to be paid in two equal installments over the next six months. The equipment was delivered to Debtor on September 20. Seller perfected the security interest by filing a financing statement on September 28. On November 15, Debtor paid the first installment, some $7,500, to Seller.

The trustee argued that Debtor's grant of a security interest was a preference because it was not perfected until more than 10 days after it became effective between the parties. She cites subsection 547(e)(2)(B). In addition, the trustee claims that the installment payment, made on November 15, was clearly a preference under subsection 547(b).

The attorney for Seller made the following arguments:

1. Even if the transfer—the grant of a security interest—was made on September 28, it was saved from the clutches of subsection 547(b) by subsection 547(c)(3) or (c)(5).

2. Even though the payment—the first installment—was for an antecedent debt, it was saved by subsection 547(c)(2), if not 547(c)(1).

As bankruptcy judge, how would you rule?

B. The "Floating Lien" in Bankruptcy

Recall that Article 9 permits a secured party to create a security interest in existing and after-acquired collateral and proceeds in a single, written security agreement and to perfect that security interest by filing a single financing statement. If the financing statement is filed first, the security interest attaches to and is perfected in the after-acquired collateral when the debtor has "rights in the collateral." UCC 9–203(1) & 9–303(1).

An initial problem for the secured creditor with an after-acquired property clause in a Chapter 11 debtor's assets is posed by section 552(a) which reads as follows:

> Except as provided in subsection (b) of this section, property acquired by the estate or by the debtor after the commencement of the case is not subject to any lien resulting from any security agreement entered into by the debtor before the commencement of the case.

Subsection (b) of 552 gives back some of what is taken away under 552(a). Subsection (b) allows the security interest to attach to "proceeds, products, offspring, rents, or profits." Thus if new inventory is proceeds of old inventory and if, therefore, the secured creditor's claim does not depend exclusively on an after-acquired property clause, the security interest will attach. However, even the modest concession with respect to proceeds and products that is given by 552(b) is subject to the discretion of the court and does not apply if the court "based on the equities" of the case, orders otherwise.

As a practical matter, any debtor who contemplates a filing in Chapter 11 will need credit and will often look to its existing creditors as a source of that credit. Section 364 authorizes the debtor in possession to borrow (this borrowing is sometimes called "DIP lending") and, if necessary, section 364 authorizes the continuation of a security interest as to newly acquired collateral. See section 364(c)(2), (c)(3), and 364(d).

Property that was acquired within 90 days of the date of the petition in bankruptcy and so first came within the grasp of the after-acquired property clause will be claimed by the debtor in possession on the ground that the attaching of the security interest to that property was preferential. Outside of bankruptcy, priority against other secured creditors is determined by the time of the filing (UCC 9–312(5)(a)), yet it is clear that the security interest is effective between the debtor and secured creditor only at the time of attachment. Thus, under Article 9 at least, the transfer in an after-acquired property claim appears to be for an antecedent debt. Consider, however, UCC 9–108, a feeble attempt to weasel out of this box.

Under the Bankruptcy Act of 1898, the time when a transfer was made for purposes of avoidable preferences was not clearly defined. Section 60 did not say, as does subsection 547(e)(3), that for the "purposes of this section, a transfer is not made until the debtor has acquired rights in the property transferred." The result was a series of judicial opinions which stretched and pulled at the statutory language to preserve the "floating lien" from the preference attack, and an outpouring of literature on both sides of the controversy.

In the early versions of this casebook we included the principal case of Grain Merchants of Indiana, Inc. v. Union Bank and Savings Co., 408 F.2d 209 (7th Cir.1969). That case, decided under the Uniform Commercial Code but prior to the Bankruptcy Reform Act of 1978, held that a secured creditor had an unassailable security interest in after-acquired collateral. In that case the trustee challenged secured creditor's right to after acquired accounts receivable that had arisen within the preference period immediately preceding the debtor's filing. The trustee reasoned that no transfer could occur until the asset transferred came into existence and at that time the creditor was not making contemporaneous loan advances, ergo the after-acquired accounts receivable constituted preferential transfers.

Both in that case and elsewhere, the secured creditor's response to such an argument was that no other creditor had been injured or misled by the "turnover" of collateral, whether that collateral constituted inventory, accounts receivable, or something else. In *Grain Merchants* the secured creditor put forward several arguments. The central argument was that the transfer as defined in section 60, the predecessor to section 547, had occurred at the time the security interest became so far perfected that no lien creditor could have priority over it. Under Article 9 of the UCC the secured creditor maintained that this event occurred upon filing, an act that occurred years prior to the filing of the bankruptcy petition. The court accepted that argument, but this left others uncomfortable. For example, the argument would have validated the acquisition of after-acquired property in circumstances in which the creditor caused the debtor to build up his accounts receivable or inventory immediately prior to bankruptcy and thus arguably to prefer the secured creditor over others. Since the transfer would have been deemed to have occurred when the financing statement was filed, long before the four-month or ninety day period, there would be no preference even in that case. In response to these concerns, Congress passed 547(e)(3), a subsection that destroys the basic creditor argument in *Grain Merchants.* In addition the Congress added subsection 547(c)(5) which validates such after-acquired property clauses in circumstances in which there is no "buildup."

Grain Merchants' opinion also accepted a variety of other creditor arguments to which section 547 has not obviously responded. One argument is that the accounts receivable should themselves be looked at as a "single entity" that is transferred at the outset even though individual accounts come and go. If one regards the "property" as some metaphysical group of accounts and not as single accounts, then subsection 547(e)(3) does not necessarily invalidate such transfer. It seems to us, however, subsection 547(e)(3) should be read to reject this argument. It seems to contemplate the possibility that each item of inventory, each account receivable—commonly recognized as having an individual identity—is to be treated separately for the purpose of bankruptcy. Thus, we believe that 547(e)(3) rejects the "entity" theory.

A third argument appearing in the *Grain Merchants'* decision that probably has continued vitality is the "substitution of collateral doctrine." Presumably no preference occurs when a secured creditor within the preference period agrees to allow his debtor to substitute one asset as the collateral for another. In such case, contemporaneous value is given by the creditor's release of the original collateral in return for acquiring the new collateral. In *Grain Merchants,* the court indicated:

> "As existing accounts receivable were collected by Grain Merchants and deposited to its accounts at the bank, the funds from previously collected accounts were made available to the debtor, enabling it to continue in business and obtain new accounts receivable. * * * Here the newly arising accounts receivable may be considered as having been taken in exchange for the release of rights in the earlier accounts and for present consideration."

408 F.2d at 217.

Nothing in section 547 explicitly rejects the substitution theory and presumably it too has continuing vitality.

Problem 8–5

On July 1, Seller sold Debtor some equipment on credit. Seller created and perfected a security interest in Debtor's "equipment, existing and after-acquired," and Debtor agreed to pay the balance of the contract price on January 2. On September 1, Debtor owed Seller $25,000 and the value of Debtor's equipment was $25,000. On October 1, Debtor sold the equipment to Buyer for $25,000 and used the proceeds to purchase new equipment from another seller. On December 1, the date of bankruptcy, Debtor owed Seller $25,000 and the value of the new equipment was $27,500.

A. Trustee argues that the transfer of the security interest in the new equipment was a preference. Is he correct?

B. If subsection 547(c)(5) does not apply, do any of the other "safe harbor" provisions?

Problem 8–6

On July 1, Debtor signed a security agreement granting Secured Party a security interest in "inventory and accounts, existing and after-acquired." Secured Party filed a proper financing statement on that date. No value was give at this time. On September 15, Secured Party loaned Debtor $20,000 under the security agreement. On that date, the value of the collateral in which Secured Party had a perfected security interest was $15,000. On December 1, the date of bankruptcy, Debtor still owed Secured Party $20,000 and the value of the collateral, which had turned over completely, was $18,000. There was credible evidence that on November 15 the value of the collateral was $5,000 and that Debtor, at the urging of Secured Party, had built up the collateral by purchasing inventory from third parties on credit.

Is there a preference under subsection 547(c)(5)? If so, in what amount?

Problem 8–7

On July 1, Debtor granted Secured Party a written security interest in "inventory, accounts and proceeds, existing and after-acquired." Secured Party made a first advance of $5,000 and agreed to make additional advances over the next 12 months of $95,000, "in its sole discretion." A financing statement was filed on July 1.

On September 1, Debtor owed Secured Party $30,000 and the collateral was valued at $25,000. On December 1, the date of bankruptcy, Debtor owed Secured Party $25,000 and the value of the collateral which had completely turned over, was $23,000. Between September 1 and December 1, Secured Party had advanced an additional $5,000 and Debtor had paid $10,000 under the security agreement.

A. Was the transfer of inventory, clearly a preference under subsection 547(b), saved by subsection 547(c)(5)?

B. Was Debtor's payment of $10,000 a preference? See subsection 547(c)(2). If so, (and Secured Party must return the payment), how should this affect the determination of a preference under subsection 547(c)(5)?

IN RE LACKOW BROTHERS, INC.

United States Court of Appeals, Eleventh Circuit, 1985.
752 F.2d 1529.

HANCOCK, DISTRICT JUDGE:

This case involves an appeal by the Co-Trustees, William R. Roemelmeyer and Jeanette Tavormina (hereinafter referred to as Co-Trustees), of the bankrupt debtor, Lackow Brothers, Inc. (hereinafter referred to as Debtor), from a judgment entered by the bankruptcy court and affirmed by the district court in favor of Walter E. Heller & Company Southeast, Inc. (hereinafter referred to as Creditor). Co-Trustees brought an adversary proceeding in bankruptcy court to avoid a transfer of property made by Debtor to Creditor on the ground that the payments were preferential transfers voidable under 11 U.S.C. § 547(b). We affirm the lower court's determination that the payments were not preferential transfers pursuant to 11 U.S.C. § 547(b) and (c)(5).

Debtor was a manufacturer of moderately priced jewelry with inventory consisting primarily of gold jewelry. In September of 1980 Debtor and Creditor entered into an Inventory Loan Security Agreement and Accounts Financing Security Agreement under which Creditor received a promissory note and agreed to advance Debtor monies in exchange for a security interest in Debtor's inventory, goods, merchandise, accounts receivable, general intangibles and contract rights. On April 1, 1981, Debtor filed a voluntary petition under Chapter 11 of the Bankruptcy Code. After an unsuccessful attempt at reorganization, the case was converted to a Chapter 7 proceeding on August 4, 1981, at which time appellants were appointed Co-Trustees to liquidate Debtor's estate. On February 19, 1982, Co-Trustees filed a complaint alleging that Debtor had made preferential payments in the amount of $365,000 to Creditor within ninety days of the filing of the Chapter 11 petition. In order for the transfer to be avoided under section 547(b), the Co-Trustees had to prove that Creditor received more from these payments than it otherwise would have received in a Chapter 7 liquidation. The Creditor denied the allegations and affirmatively argued that the payments were specifically excluded from the Trustee's avoidance power under section 547(c)(5). In order to fall within this exception to preferential transfers, a creditor must prove that its financial position did not improve within the ninety days prior to bankruptcy.

In bankruptcy court, the Co-Trustees maintained that on the date of the filing of the petition Creditor was undersecured; therefore, according to *Barash v. Public Finance Corp.,* 658 F.2d 504 (7th Cir.1981), the payments made within ninety days of bankruptcy applied first to the unsecured component of Creditor's debt. The Co-Trustees premised this argument on the bankruptcy court's previous determination that the value of the pledged collateral on April 1, 1981 was $922,000. Undisputed evidence showed that on April 1, 1981, Debtor owed Creditor approximately 1.6 million dollars. If the Co-Trustees could get the bankruptcy court to readopt its April 1, 1981 determination of value then Creditor would have a secured claim in the amount of $922,000 and an unsecured claim in the amount of approximately

$678,000. Under *Barash, supra,* the $365,000 payment would apply toward the $678,000 unsecured claim and the bankruptcy court would have to avoid the preferential transfer.

Creditor relied on uncontradicted evidence of the "computer value" of the collateral on both the ninetieth day prior to bankruptcy (January 1, 1981) and on the date of bankruptcy (April 1, 1981), both to rebut the allegation of a preferential transfer under section 547(b) and affirmatively to prove the section 547(c)(5) exception. The computer printouts were routine accounting reports sent from Debtor to Creditor, upon which Creditor relied to advance additional funds. These records established that: (1) on January 1, 1981, the pledged collateral was worth approximately 4.7 million dollars while Debtor's obligation was approximately 1.9 million dollars; and (2) on April 1, 1981, the pledged collateral was worth approximately 3.9 million dollars and Debtor's obligation was approximately 1.6 million dollars. These values clearly establish that Creditor was fully secured. Hence, Creditor argued that it received no more than it would have received under Chapter 7 liquidation. Furthermore, since Creditor was fully secured on January 1 and April 1, its position did not improve within the ninety days prior to bankruptcy. Thus, the payments fell within the section 547(c)(5) preferential transfer exception.

Maintaining that the valuation of collateral must be determined on a case-by-case basis, the bankruptcy court refused to adopt its earlier value on April 1, 1981 and held that the proper valuation standard was the "ongoing concern" value of the collateral, as reflected in the routine accounting reports. The bankruptcy court concluded that Creditor did not improve its position by accepting Debtor's payments and therefore the payment was specifically excepted from preference under 11 U.S.C. § 547(c)(5).

On appeal to the district court, the Co-Trustees urged that the bankruptcy court erred in applying the "ongoing concern" value and that the correct standard to be applied was the "liquidation value." In asserting this position, Co-Trustees relied on Creditor's testimony that it had received 1.2 million dollars from the sale of Debtor's inventory and collection of the accounts receivable. Co-Trustees urged the adoption of this valuation standard since under it Creditor would be deemed undersecured and the payments would be preferential transfers pursuant to section 547(b). The district court, however, held that the liquidated value of the collateral, which was sold over six months *after* filing of bankruptcy would not accurately determine whether the Creditor's loan was secured during the ninety-day period *prior* to the filing of the petition; therefore, the "ongoing concern" was the only standard of valuation that could be adopted.

On this appeal the Co-Trustees urge us to find that the only proper standard of valuation in this case is the liquidation value and that payments should be avoided pursuant to section 547(b). The sole issue we must resolve is whether the district court was clearly erroneous in applying the "ongoing concern" value in determining Creditor had not received preferential payments under section 547(b) and in finding that Creditor's position had not improved under section 547(c)(5).

In this case the method used to value the collateral is crucial to determining whether the payments to Creditor in the ninety days prior to bankruptcy are subject to preference attack. Since Creditor had a "floating lien" on Debtor's inventory and accounts receivable, the section 547(c)(5) exception to preferential transfers applies and our inquiry should be whether Creditor's position "improved" relative to what it was preceding bankruptcy. To determine "improvement in position," Creditor's "position" is relevant on two different dates: January 1, 1981, ninety days before the filing of the Chapter 11 petition, and April 1, 1981, the date of the filing of the petition. Thus, the value of the accounts receivable and inventory must be calculated on these two dates. If the "ongoing concern" value is used, no "improvement in position" exists; however, if the liquidation value is used, improvement is apparent and the transfer should be avoided.

Section 506(a) of the Bankruptcy Code provides only general principles we should follow in determining what standard of valuation is proper in calculating the value of a creditor's secured claim: "* * * Such value shall be determined in light of the purpose of the valuation and of the proposed disposition or use of such property, and in conjunction with any hearing on such disposition or use or on a plan affecting such creditor's interest." 11 U.S.C. § 506(a). The legislative comments to this section do not give any further guidance except to reiterate that we are to determine value on a case-by-case basis, taking into account the facts of each case and the competing interests in the case. H.R.Rep. No. 545, 95th Cong., 1st Sess. 356 (1977) *reprinted in* 1978 U.S.Code Cong. & Ad.News 5787, 6312.

In an effort to provide some guidance to the courts in determining what value to use in calculating "improvement in position," Collier on Bankruptcy, a leading treatise in bankruptcy law, suggests that the liquidation value be used in a liquidation case under Chapter 7 and that the going concern value be used in a Chapter 9, 11, or 13 case. This advice is not set in cement, as Collier recognizes that other standards of value may be appropriate in certain cases. 4 Collier on Bankruptcy ¶ 547.41 at 129 (15th ed. 1984). Co-Trustees argue that Collier supports their position that the liquidation value should have been adopted in the bankruptcy and district courts as the value of the collateral on both January 1 and April 1, and therefore, that Creditor's position improved. We are convinced, however, that this case is one in which a standard of value other than the liquidation value is not only more appropriate, but is even mandatory.

The *only* evidence before this court showing what the monetary value of the accounts receivable and inventory was on January 1, 1981, is the value as shown on the computerized accounting reports. Despite Co-Trustees' argument on this appeal that the "computer value" is not credible, we have before us absolutely no evidence indicating that the accounting records were inaccurate or untrustworthy. The Co-Trustees did not challenge the accuracy of those records in the bankruptcy court. Moreover, the bankruptcy court specifically determined that these ongoing concern values were derived from Debtor's own routine accounting reports to Creditor in the regular course of business and that the values were properly admissible. The only evidence in the record of value for the ninetieth day prior to the filing of bankruptcy is the ongoing concern value; therefore, this is the *only* standard of valuation that can be applied to determine if Creditor's position improved between January 1 and April 1, 1981. The fact that Creditor sold Debtor's collateral for 1.2 million dollars six months *after* the Chapter 11 petition was filed does not shed much light on what the collateral was worth nine months earlier on the ninetieth day *before* filing of bankruptcy, especially taking into consideration the nature and type of the collateral. We agree with the district court's holding that the only standard of valuation that could be applied in this case to any degree of accuracy would be the "ongoing concern" standard. See *Matter of Lackow Bros., Inc.,* 19 B.R. 601 (S.D.Fla.1982).

Co-Trustees also rely on *In re Adams,* 2 B.R. 313 (M.D.Fla.1980) and *Matter of Cooper,* 7 B.R. 537 (N.D.Ga.1980) to support their argument that the liquidation value is the *only* proper value to use in this case. Neither of these cases concern the value of inventory or accounts receivable, nor do they involve property values at a point in time *prior* to bankruptcy. We hold that these cases simply do not apply to this appeal.

We conclude that the holdings of the bankruptcy court and the district court were not clearly erroneous in using the ongoing concern value to determine that pursuant to section 547(c)(5) Creditor had not improved his position between the ninetieth day prior to bankruptcy and the actual date the petition was filed. We therefore affirm. [Footnotes omitted.]

Notes

1. Do you agree with the following assertions: (A) The creditor in In re Lackow did not need to rely on subsection 547(c)(5) to avoid the preference—subsection 547(b)(5) would work just as well; (B) In addition to subsection (c)(5), subsection 547(c)(2) would work just as well.

2. Suppose it is clear that payments during the 90 day period were made when the debt exceeded the value of the collateral (the debtor was under-secured) but that the secured party was over-secured at the time of bankruptcy. Are the payments preferential? Or, suppose the payments were made when oversecured but the secured party was undersecured at the time of bankruptcy. What is the critical time for section 547(b), the time of payment or the time of bankruptcy? Cf. Barash v. Public Finance Corp., 658 F.2d 504 (7th Cir.1981), cited in *In re Lackow,* which held, among other things, that where the secured party was under-secured at both critical points, any payments made during the 90 day period should be allocated to the unsecured part of the obligation and were preferences unless saved by subsection 547(c)(1) or (2).

Problem 8–8

Alfred's Building Materials was a seller of air conditioning, air conditioning ducts and equipment. Skilled Trades was a local contractor in the business of installing air conditioning and heating systems. In the summer of 1986 Skilled Trades ordered approximately $8,000 worth of air conditioning equipment and ducting to be installed in the Church of Christ located in Buchanan, Michigan. Alfred's had heard word on the street that Skilled Trades was having difficulty making its payments on its trade debt and told Skilled Trades that it was hesitant to undertake the usual 30 or 90 days credit on such a sale. Accordingly, representatives of Skilled Trades talked to the Board of Trustees of the church who agreed to pay $8,000 when the equipment was delivered. Alfred's maintained that the agreement between it and Skilled Trades was for a "C.O.D. Delivery." In fact, the materials were delivered in three lots to the job site during the last week in October and the first two weeks of November, 1986. The accompanying invoices were marked "C.O.D." Upon delivery, the church, in accordance with its agreement, issued three checks totalling $8,000 to Skilled

Trades. On November 17, Skilled Trades issued its check for $7,175.45. Skilled Trades had the check certified on that date, and on that date or the next mailed it to Alfred's. Alfred's in turn deposited the check in its account and the check was paid on November 25, 1986.

Skilled Trades filed a petition in Chapter 7 on December 10, 1986. The trustee has asserted a right to the return of the $7,175.45 on the ground that it constitutes a voidable preference. What result?

Problem 8–9

Albert, a high living bachelor who had entered several disastrous financial transactions, owned a Porsche 928 free and clear. As his creditors closed in upon him he decided to pay off a debt to his brother-in-law by transferring the Porsche to him. He owed his brother-in-law in excess of $50,000, money he had borrowed for an unsuccessful oil and gas partnership. Three weeks before he filed in Chapter 7 he transferred his Porsche to his brother-in-law in full satisfaction of the debt. The brother-in-law promptly resold the car to a local car dealer for $31,000. The brother-in-law then disappeared and has not been seen since. The car dealer has since adopted the car as his personal car and is driving it. The trustee in Albert's Chapter 7 asks whether he can recover the car from the car dealer. What do you think? What if local dealer had not used the car as his own, but had resold it to a local doctor?

C. Proceeds in Bankruptcy

At the date of bankruptcy, a secured party may claim a security interest in identified proceeds from the disposition of the original collateral. This claim, even though supported under UCC 9–306, is subject to the trustee's avoidance powers. Thus, if the security interest in proceeds was not perfected it would be vulnerable under subsection 544(a) and UCC 9–301(1)(b). Or if the security interest in proceeds was perfected but, in combination with other collateral improved the secured party's position under subsection 547(c)(5), it might be avoided as a preference. Subsection 552(b) states, however, that unless otherwise avoidable if the debtor acquired the original collateral before the commencement of the case, the security interest extends to proceeds "acquired by the estate after the commencement of the case to the extent provided by such security agreement and by applicable non-bankruptcy law * * *."

A recurring problem involves attempts to trace proceeds, particularly cash proceeds, see UCC 9–306(1), which have been commingled with other funds in deposit accounts. If state law tracing rules cannot identify the actual asset in which the security interest is claimed, some courts have disallowed the claim. See, e.g., Elliott v. Bumb, 356 F.2d 749 (9th Cir.1966) cert. denied 385 U.S. 829, 87 S.Ct. 67, 17 L.Ed.2d 66 (1966). The "intermediate balance test" has been upheld in bankruptcy. In re Martin, 25 B.R. 25 (Bankr.N.D.Tex.1982). Under this test, proceeds which are traced into a commingled account are presumed to remain there until all funds have been withdrawn. New deposits, however, are presumed not to replenish the proceeds unless they are actually proceeds from the disposition of collateral.

An unresolved controversy has arisen over the application of UCC 9–306(4) in bankruptcy. In this subsection, Article 9 attempts to provide a specific tracing rule for application in insolvency proceedings. Read that subsection carefully.

Problem 8–10

Secured Party created and perfected a security interest in Debtor's "inventory and accounts, existing and after-acquired, and proceeds" on July 1. On September 1, Debtor owed Secured Party $25,000 and the value of the collateral, including proceeds, was $20,000. On December 1, the date of bankruptcy, Debtor still owed Secured Party $25,000. The value of the inventory and accounts was $20,000. In addition, Debtor has a deposit account in which cash proceeds from the sale of inventory have been commingled with other funds.

As of November 21, there was a $100 balance in the account.

On November 22, Debtor deposited $10,000 received from the sale of inventory.

On November 24, Debtor withdrew $10,000 and lost it all in the futures market.

On November 28, Debtor deposited $10,000 received from the sale of factory equipment.

On December 1, Debtor declared bankruptcy.

A. How much can Secured Party claim under the Intermediate Balance Test?

B. How much can Secured Party claim under UCC 9–306(4)?

C. Is the amount claimed under UCC 9–306(4) a preference under section 547 of the Bankruptcy Code? (See the next case).

Note

As we have shown elsewhere the courts have made mincemeat out of parts of 9–306. First, they have routinely held that one can use cockamamie tracing presumptions such as fifo, lifo, and jessel's bag, to "identify" proceeds in a bank account where proceeds of a loan have been commingled with other money. We doubt that is what the drafters had in mind when they gave a security interest in "identifiable" proceeds under 9–306(2), but that is now water over the dam.

How do those cases interact with 9–306(4) which was specifically designed for proceeds, mostly proceeds in a bank account, at the time of insolvency? It appears that the drafters intended to allow a ten day presumptive right in commingled bank accounts under (d)(ii) to the exclusion of all other claims. Since the courts have now recognized the claims in commingled accounts as "identifiable" when one applies fifo or some other such rule, one wonders whether the drafters would now reinterpret section 9–306(4)(d)(ii).

Even within its bounds 9–306(4)(d)(ii) has suffered greatly at the hands of judges. Some have held it is preferential, In re Gibson Products of Arizona, 543 F.2d 652 (9th Cir.1976); others have misinterpreted it by capping the proceeds claim at the level of proceeds "deposited" as opposed to proceeds "received by the debtor" as the statute plainly states. Consider the following problem.

Problem 8–11

Within ten days prior to bankruptcy, Ames Department Stores collected over $5,000,000 in cash, checks, and credit card receivables from third parties. All but an insignificant percentage of these amounts came from the sale of goods that were subject to Mellon Bank's perfected security interest. Mellon Bank has received no payments within 10 days and has no claim under 9–306(4)(a), (b), or (c). On the eleventh day before bankruptcy, Ames had $1,000,000 in its bank account at Pittsburgh National Bank and on the date of bankruptcy it had $2,000,000 in that account.

1. What part of the PNB bank account can Mellon claim under 9–306(4)(d)(ii)?

2. If all of the $2,000,000 in the account were proceeds, would the result be different?

3. What if only $1 of the $1,000,000 deposited within ten days was proceeds?

4. Mellon fails to prove that any of the money in the account was proceeds, but argues that it was the trustee's responsibility to prove that the money came from other sources. What result?

Note: Rights of the Secured Creditor in Bankruptcy, In General

Surprisingly there is no manifesto anywhere in the many pages of the Bankruptcy Code that explicitly recognizes the rights of a perfected secured creditor in bankruptcy. No general provision says the Bankruptcy Code respects the secured creditor's rights; nothing says that the secured creditors' assets cannot be taken, and nothing in the Code gives the secured creditor complete protection against loss.

Yet it is correct to say that the basic rights of a perfected secured creditor are recognized and respected in bankruptcy. Upon liquidation in Chapter 7, the secured creditor has the right to the return of its collateral or its value. Upon confirmation of a plan under Chapter 11, it has a right to the same (section 1129(a)(7)(A)(ii)), and if the secured creditor opposes the plan, has a right to secured "deferred cash payments" with a present value equal to the value of its collateral, or, alternatively, to the proceeds on sale of its collateral, or to the "indubitable equivalent." So, *in general,* the rights of the secured creditor are protected in bankruptcy. Its rights cannot be voted away by others and it should leave bankruptcy with the same collateral as it arrived with or with money equal to the value of those assets.

When does the Bankruptcy Code not protect, and how might bankruptcy injure the secured creditor? Unless the secured creditor's claim is oversecured (i.e., unless the value of the collateral exceeds the amount of the debt), the Code does not give the secured creditor "lost opportunity cost." In layman's terms this means that interest accruals and, *a fortiori* interest payments, stop. Section 362 bars repossession of collateral, its sale, and the reinvestment of the proceeds of sale with another debtor. Assume, for example, a creditor with a $1,000,000 debt and a perfected security interest in $1,000,000 of collateral owned by LTV. LTV entered bankruptcy in July of 1986; as this is written in 1993, LTV is still in bankruptcy. That means that our hypothetical secured creditor will have lost forever six years' return on its $1,000,000. If that $1,000,000 could have been lent to another at 10 percent a year, the return, uncompounded, would have been more than $600,000. Such lost opportunities are particularly significant in large bankruptcies such as LTV that linger in the bankruptcy court for years.

If the Bankruptcy Code does not protect against lost opportunity costs, at least it protects against loss of value in the collateral. Assume, for example, that our LTV creditor has a security interest in equipment that is declining in value. Because of section 362, secured creditor would be stayed from repossessing the collateral. But section 362(d) requires the stay to be lifted (and the collateral returned) unless the debtor somehow makes up for its decline in value. In the words of the Code, the debtor must provide "adequate protection" as defined by section 361. The debtor might do this by giving additional collateral to the creditor, by making payments equal to the depreciation, or by some other means.

Before we go farther, perhaps we should see who is and who is not a secured creditor in bankruptcy. Section 506(a) defines a secured creditor as one who has a security interest in a particular asset—but only to the extent of the value of that asset. Thus, if our LTV creditor had a $1,000,000 debt secured by an asset that was worth $500,000, the creditor would have two claims, one an unsecured claim for $500,000 (to be included in one class) and a second a $500,000 secured claim (to be included in another). Properly, our creditor is a secured creditor in bankruptcy only to the extent of $500,000. In Article 9 we are accustomed to calling everyone who has a security interest a "secured creditor" irrespective of the value of the collateral; that is not the way the term is used in the Bankruptcy Code.

Now turn to the many humiliations that the secured creditor may suffer in bankruptcy. This will show why some secured creditors would quarrel with the description of bankruptcy we have set out above. Some secured creditors would describe bankruptcy as death by one thousand cuts. We have already mentioned the first provision that confronts the secured creditor. This is the automatic stay, section 362. After the petition is filed, it prohibits any collection activity; it prohibits perfection, repossession, resale (if there has already been repossession), and a galaxy of other acts that a secured creditor might wish to take to put pressure on the debtor. Section 549 prohibits payments to the secured creditor as well as to other creditors. Upon bankruptcy, the secured creditor can neither repossess nor receive payments.

A second consequence of bankruptcy, also discussed above, is the lost opportunity for reinvestment. This refusal to recompense the lost opportunity is stated in section 502(b)(2), implied in 506(b), and affirmed in United Savings Assoc. of Texas v. Timbers of Inwood Forest Assoc., 484 U.S. 365, 108 S.Ct. 626, 98 L.Ed.2d 740 (1988).

Consider further indignities that may befall the secured creditor as time passes in bankruptcy. First, section 1129 (generally defining rights and obligations of the parties in making a plan under Chapter 11), provides for a vote, but in certain cases allows the debtor to "cram down" a plan over the opposition of most of its creditors. True, the secured creditor must get at least what it would get on liquidation under Chapter 7, i.e., the value of its collateral, but it is assured no more. Moreover, it is not assured the return of his collateral but only the cash value of the collateral as agreed or as found by the court. One need not be the least bit neurotic to see the great room for mischief in the judge's determination of the value of various assets.

Over the objection of the creditor, the debtor may choose to "deaccelerate" and reinstate the old loan (see section 1124(2)) and having done so, treat the creditor (all the time protesting to the contrary) as though the creditor had voted for the plan (see 1129(a)(8)(B)).

Parallel to the rights in Chapter 11 and Chapter 13 that allow the debtor essentially to "buy" the collateral for the price determined by the court, section

722 allows an individual debtor to buy back his personal property (usually his car) for its value even though the debt securing it greatly exceeds its value. Compare this to the right of redemption under 9–506, where the debtor would be required to pay the entire debt in order to redeem.

Finally, one should note other and more complicated avoidance rules that we have not discussed above. Fraudulent conveyances (whose ramifications go far beyond Article 9) can be set aside under sections 544(b) and 548. In addition, section 522(f) avoids certain non-possessory, non-purchase money security interests in household furnishings and the like. These can apply even in circumstances where the security interest was fully perfected prior to bankruptcy.

The foregoing should make the student respectful of the complications hidden in the Bankruptcy Code. In theory the Code respects and protects perfected security interests. In practicc the Bankruptcy Code greatly diminishes the rights of the secured creditor would enjoy outside of bankruptcy. If the truth were known, we predict it would show that bankruptcy also greatly diminishes the value a security interest would have outside of bankruptcy. The largest threat comes with the possibility of avoidance of the security interest under 544 or 547 or one of the other sections, but as we have suggested above, other less dramatic but no less debilitating wounds await the secured creditor when the debtor goes bankrupt.

BOOK TWO

SALES

PART ONE

INTRODUCTORY MATERIALS

CHAPTER NINE

NATURE AND SCOPE OF ARTICLE 2 ON SALES

SECTION 1. WHY DO SALES AND CONTRACTS FOR SALE TAKE PLACE?

Sales law evolved in response to disputes between private parties over agreements to transfer the ownership of personal property, usually goods, for a price. As in all areas of private law, the transaction, whether a sale or a contract to sell, came first and the law of sales followed. Indeed, it is probable that the various bodies of specialized commercial law, such as negotiable instruments, developed in response to the particular needs of the parties before the need for a general law of contracts occurred to anyone. See G. Gilmore, The Death of Contract 11–12 (1974).

If not compelled by law, why do sales occur? One answer is that in an exchange economy sales have to take place. To put this abstractly, a productive unit in a modern economy specializes in making one or but a few types of goods. Such a unit does not make enough of everything to satisfy all its own needs. It is not self sufficient and must engage in exchanges with other productive units.

But why such specialization in the first place? First, since men and organizations have different capacities and abilities, it becomes economical to match capacities and abilities with productive tasks for which they are best suited. Second, since different regions differ in natural resources and climate it becomes economical to put regions to work on productive activities for which they are best suited. Third, even if capacities, abilities, resources and climates were undifferentiated, it would still be advantageous to have specialization and therefore to have an exchange economy, whether the advantage comes from a greater quantity of production, time saved or improved quality through concentration of effort. See A. Smith, The Wealth of Nations 7–9 (Mod.Lib.Ed.1937).

A variety of factors, then, begets specialization and specialization begets exchanges—sales. According to Ian Macneil, four conditions should exist for an economy based upon exchange to flourish: (1) Specialization of labor and exchange; (2) A sense by individuals of their capacity for choice and the consequences of its exercise; (3) An awareness of the continuum between past, present, and future; and (4) A social matrix which reinforces the exercise of choices made with an eye to the future. Macneil, *The Many Futures of Contracts,* 47 S.Cal.L.Rev. 691, 696–712 (1974).

But the sale, a completed exchange, is one thing and a contract to sell in the future quite another. One might imagine a very simple society in which sales of goods took place but never pursuant to prior contracts to sell. In a complex industrialized society such as ours, however, contracts to sell and to buy goods are essential to planned economic activity. A manufacturer, for example, must have raw materials, and it must be able to rely on receiving them at designated times and places if it is to operate efficiently. For such reason it will make agreements to purchase raw materials, and recognition of these agreements, frequently of long duration, will make it more certain that its business will function as planned.

Another factor is required for a market directed economy to flourish: The legal system must permit and facilitate the acquisition, use and transfer of private property. Article 2 of the UCC is, with a minimum of regulation, devoted to this support function.

SECTION 2. A ROADMAP TO THE SALES ARTICLE OF THE UCC

As part of his essential background, the user of Article Two needs a basic roadmap to the 104 provisions involved. The presentation here will be in terms of stages of the modern mercantile sales deal, which is typically for future delivery of goods on credit, and therefore a deal that progresses from initial agreement through performance to discharge. The discrete stages along the way are typically these: agreement; post-agreement—pre-shipment; the stage of getting the goods (or documents therefor) to the buyer; receipt and inspection, and payment. The overwhelming majority of deals progress all the way through to payment without incident. But a significant proportion do not, and these break down at different stages, in different ways, and for different reasons. Thus, what follows here will be "pathologically oriented" in the respect that, at each stage, the focus will be on the *kinds* of things that can go wrong.

One caveat: Because the discussion in this section is by way of prelude, it is necessarily general and to some extent oversimplified. Also, it is not comprehensive. In each of these respects, so, too, a roadmap.

A. The Agreement Stage

Perhaps the most drastic of all things that can go wrong is for the parties to assume that they have made a binding contract only to find that in law they have not. This is much less of a risk, however, under Article 2 than it is in general contract law. This is so for two reasons. First, Article 2 makes contract formation easier than it is in the general law. Formalities are delimited. See, UCC 2–201 and 2–203. The consideration doctrine is modified with a bias toward contract formation. See UCC 2–205, and 2–209(1). The requirement that an acceptance must be precisely within the terms of an offer to constitute an acceptance is abolished. See UCC 2–207, and 2–206(1)(a). A non-conforming shipment of goods in response to a unilateral offer is, under certain circumstances, nonetheless an acceptance. UCC 2–206(1)(b). Contracts can be formed by mere conduct alone, even though the precise moment of making is undetermined. UCC 2–204(1) and (2).

Second, Article 2 includes a general provision to the effect that a contract for sale does not fail for indefiniteness if the parties have intended to make a contract and there is a reasonably certain basis for giving an appropriate remedy. UCC 2–204(3). Further to this, the Article includes many "gap-filler" provisions which come into play to fill gaps in agreements that might otherwise fail under general contract law for indefiniteness. See UCC 2–204(3), 2–305, 2–306, 2–307, 2–308, 2–309, 2–310, 2–311, 2–503, 2–504, 2–507, and 2–511.

In addition to failures of contract formation, disputes may arise over (1) whether a term is or is not a part of the contract and (2) whether a given term is to be interpreted in one way rather than another. These kinds of disputes can arise at any stage, but it is appropriate to allude to them here. On whether a term is or is not a part of the contract, the parol evidence rule of UCC 2–202 governs. Under Article 2, lawyers and judges will resolve problems of interpretation and construction in part by reference to UCC 1–102 on rules of construction, UCC 1–205 on course of dealing and usage of trade, and UCC 2–208 and 2–207(3) on course of performance or practical construction.

The alert, careful lawyer should, through draftsmanship and advice, be able to reduce if not eliminate altogether any risks that the parties will fail to make a binding contract or even that significant disputes over interpretation will arise.

B. The Post-Agreement—Pre-Shipment Stage

A seller will either have the goods on hand, or have to manufacture them or acquire them elsewhere. In any of these events, there is often a time lapse between the date when the contract is made and the time when the goods are sent to the buyer. During this period, the buyer may repudiate, or the seller may repudiate, or it may become clear that one of the parties will not later be able to perform.

UCC 2–610 and 2–611 deal with repudiation. Assume it is the buyer who repudiates. The seller can call off the deal. See UCC 2–610(b) and 2–703(f). Or it can also seek damages under UCC 2–706 or 2–708 as appropriate. Can it choose to go forward with the transaction and force the goods on the buyer? Yes, under limited circumstances. See UCC 2–704(1)(a) and 2–709(1)(b).

UCC 2–704(2) gives the *manufacturing* seller flexibility in the event of repudiation.

Now let us assume that the seller repudiates at this stage. What are the buyer's rights? Again, the buyer, too, may call off the deal, UCC 2–610(b), 2–711(1), or it may also have damages. UCC 2–711(1), 2–712, 2–713. Can it choose to go forward with the transaction and force the goods out of the seller? See UCC 2–610(b) and 2–711(2)(a) and (b). As with most "goods oriented" remedies, this alternative may put the buyer in conflict with creditors of and purchasers from the seller. If the buyer has a prior perfected Article 9 security interest, it would prevail over most such third parties. Otherwise, the buyer must rely on its right, if any, to specific performance or replevin as specified in UCC 2–716, and this right is generally subject to third party interests.

A closer look at the parties' damages remedy is in order. Can it be combined with other remedies? Yes. The Code does not favor "election" doctrines. (Even cancellation does not extinguish a right to damages. See UCC 2–720). Are there any significant parallels between the seller's damages remedy and that of the buyer? Yes. Both can go into the market and "fix" damages against the other party, so to speak. See UCC 2–706(1) and 2–712(1) and (2). Yet neither is *required* to do this. Both can simply sue for damages for repudiation and get the full market-contract-price differential rather than the differential between contract or market and a substitute transaction consummated by the "reselling" seller or "covering" buyer. See UCC 2–708(1) and 2–713. Can the parties get consequential damages? It is clear that the buyer can. See UCC 2–715.

The rights of a party to call off the deal, to get damages, or to go forward with the deal, are the basic remedial options. They are carefully analyzed in detail in Peters, *Remedies for Breach of Contracts Relating to the Sale of Goods Under the Uniform Commercial Code: A Roadmap for Article Two,* 73 Yale L.J. 199 (1963).

After the agreement and prior to shipment, other things can go wrong besides repudiation. It may emerge that one of the parties will not, later, at the appointed time, be *able* to perform. In such circumstances, UCC 2–609 allows the aggrieved party to demand adequate assurances of performance. Failure to provide such assurances within a reasonable time is classed as a "repudiation." Prospective inability to perform will, when it exists, entitle the aggrieved party to pursue the same general remedial options as may be available upon repudiation.

Insolvency should be mentioned as a special form of prospective inability to perform which inherently introduces third parties. When opposing third party interests are in the picture, "going forward" with the deal becomes less desirable to the seller where the buyer is insolvent, and less freely available to the buyer where the seller is insolvent. Compare UCC 2–702(1) and 2–502(1).

Casualty to goods identified to the contract is another kind of event that can occur after contract and prior to shipment. In some circumstances, it will excuse the seller. See UCC 2–613. The topic of casualty and attendant risk of loss problems will be considered in the next section.

C. The Stage of Getting the Goods or Documents Therefor to the Buyer

Many commercial contracts call for the seller to deliver the goods to the buyer at the buyer's town or place of business. For the time, manner and place of delivery, *absent* such contractual stipulation, see UCC 2–309, 2–307, 2–308, 2–503 and 2–507.

Here the primary focus is on seller's performance. Several basic things can go wrong with it at this stage. The seller may deliver late, or at the wrong place, or in improper manner.

Also, the seller who is required or authorized to send the goods to the buyer must, unless otherwise agreed, make a "proper contract" of carriage and notify the buyer of shipment. See UCC 2–504. The seller may simply fail to do this, thereby incurring liability to the buyer. Of course, the rights of the buyer upon default at this stage vary with the nature of the default. Can the buyer always call the deal off? No. See e.g., the last paragraph of UCC 2–504, 2–612, 2–614, and 2–615. But it will generally be entitled to damages. See UCC 2–711.

The carrier may fail to perform *its* obligations. The duties of such a carrier will be specified in the contract of carriage (bill of lading) and in Article 7 of the Code, where the deal is intrastate. If interstate, the Federal Bill of Lading Act governs. The carrier will be liable for damages caused by improper loading for which it is responsible. See UCC 7–301(4). The carrier may negligently cause damage to the goods for which liability lies under UCC 7–309. Or the carrier may simply fail to follow instructions thereby causing loss. For example, the seller may have a right to stop the goods in transit under UCC 2–705 and the carrier may fail to honor stoppage instructions. Here, though, the seller rather than the buyer would be the aggrieved party.

The goods in transit may be lost or damaged (with or without the carrier's fault). The carrier's insurance will often cover most of the loss. But "risk of loss" problems can arise. Generally, risk passes upon tender at destination when the contract calls for delivery at the buyer's city. See UCC 2–509(1)(b). Hence, as between seller and buyer, seller would be responsible for loss occurring during carriage in such a deal. It should be noted that UCC 2–510 says, among other things, that a seller cannot pass the risk of loss *re* non-conforming goods.

If, before risk passes to the buyer, the goods "suffer" total casualty, without fault of either party, then under UCC 2–613 the seller will be excused from the contract if the contract was one which required for its performance goods identified when the contract was made.

The foregoing discussion has centered on deals for goods only. What if the contract calls for delivery of a document of title to the buyer in exchange for the buyer's cash payment on the spot or his signature to a time draft? See UCC 2–503(5). Most of the main kinds of things that can go wrong in procuring and transmitting documents can be readily inventoried. As procured, the document may fail to describe the goods properly. See UCC 7–301. Or it may not be in correct form. See UCC 2–503(5)(a). The document may be lost or stolen. See UCC 7–601. Or it may get into the wrong hands, and, if negotiable, and the transferee takes by due negotiation, then the transferee will generally get title to the document and to the goods. See UCC 7–501 and UCC 7–502. But see UCC 7–503. Or the document may be altered. See UCC 7–306.

D. The Receipt-Inspection Stage

This, in commercial deals, is, to seller and buyer alike, the crucial stage. Here the seller will typically lose any control he has over the goods. Here the buyer will, usually for the first time, inspect and decide whether to accept or reject. Naturally, the buyer will generally prefer to inspect before paying. Blind payment puts him at a disadvantage: when the goods turn out not to be conforming, he finds himself a potential plaintiff, whereas, if there is to be litigation at all, it is generally better to be a potential defendant who has first inspected and then rejected the goods for nonconformity. The blindly paying buyer is also at a disadvantage in the respect that it, as plaintiff, must assume the risk of the seller's insolvency in regard to satisfaction of any judgment it gets against a defaulting seller. Further, the buyer who pays blindly may find that it has assumed control over and therefore responsibility for the goods. See generally, Honnold, *The Buyer's Right of Rejection,* 97 U.Pa.L.Rev. 457 (1949).

Contracts often specifically provide for a right of the buyer to inspect before payment or acceptance. But what if the contract is silent? UCC 2–513 says that the buyer has a right to inspect before payment or acceptance unless it has contracted it away. One way the buyer can give up this right is by agreeing to pay "against documents" covering the goods. UCC 2–513(3)(b), 2–512, 2–310.

What are the ways a seller can fail to perform at this stage (other than "failures of delivery" already considered)? In the main, the seller may fail to tender goods to which he has title, or fail to tender goods that are of the right quantity or of the right quality. These latter two kinds of breaches are not uncommon, as breaches go. And they both may take a variety of forms, depending on the nature of the goods. Similarly, the seller may tender non-conforming *documents* covering goods.

What is the general standard of performance to which the seller is held? The contract is the first touchstone. But, in general contract law, it is familiar that under the doctrine of substantial performance, some departures from the contract are permitted with the result that the non-performing party can still recover "on the contract." Is it the same under the Code? Generally, no. UCC 2–601 seemingly requires "perfect tender." As to quality, the warranty provisions of Article 2 (UCC 2–312—2–315) determine the relevant standard of performance as to quality to the extent the contract is silent. The perfect tender doctrine is, however, modified by UCC 2–508, 2–612, and other provisions.

Assuming the seller has failed to make perfect tender, and that he cannot rely on the doctrine of substantial performance, what are the buyer's rights? Its basic damages remedy has already been outlined. See UCC 2–712 and 2–713. The emphasis here should be on the buyer's "goods-oriented" options. If the buyer wishes, it may reject. UCC 2–601. To do so, it has to jump through the right hoops. UCC 2–602, 2–605. If it is a merchant, it may have duties in regard to care and disposition of the goods. UCC 2–603, 2–604. The buyer may, however, want the seller to perform—to send goods that do conform. It *may* be entitled to specific performance or replevin under UCC 2–716.

What if the buyer has accepted the goods (UCC 2–606) and has later discovered a defect, or has accepted the goods with seller's assurances that non-conformities would be corrected, but such has not occurred? Has the buyer forever lost its right to throw the goods back at the seller? No. See

UCC 2–608. But the buyer, again, must jump through the right hoops. See UCC 2–608(2) and 2–607(3)(a).

Such revocation of acceptance, along with rejection, leaves the buyer free, too, to pursue damages. See UCC 2–608(3), 2–711(1), and 2–714.

Finally, the buyer may choose to retain non-conforming goods and recover damages. See UCC 2–714(1) and (2). But, if it is to take this avenue, it must give notice of the breach under UCC 2–714(1). In commercial cases, this avenue is more common than in consumer cases where the defect in the goods often makes them of no value at all, and the buyer's main concern is to get damages for breach of warranty, often consequential damages of a personal injury or property damage character. See 2–715(2)(b). Most of Article 2 litigation is warranty of quality litigation, consumer and non-consumer. The Code's basic warranty provisions, to be treated intensively later, are UCC 2–313, 2–314, 2–315, 2–316, 2–317, and 2–318.

To turn, now, to non-performance by the *buyer* at the receipt-inspection stage. It may fail to provide proper facilities for presentation of the goods for inspection. See UCC 2–503(1). It may make a wrongful demand for inspection. See UCC 2–513(3)(b). It may fail to follow contractual or statutorily prescribed procedures for inspection. See UCC 2–513(1). It may "impose" unagreed upon standards of conformity. It may deny the seller's right to cure. UCC 2–508. It may deny any right of the seller to supply less than perfectly conforming goods. UCC 2–612(2). It may mistakenly think the goods do not conform. It may fail to jump through prescribed rejection hoops. UCC 2–602. It may fail to take over the goods and care for or dispose of them as required under UCC 2–603 and UCC 2–604. Perhaps most significant in the usual run of cases, it may refuse, for some reason, to pay at this time as agreed or as required in the absence of agreement. See UCC 2–507(1).

The appropriate maneuver for the seller will vary with the nature of the buyer's breach and the course of action the buyer takes. Often the seller will want and will be entitled to damages, a general remedy already outlined at the post-agreement stage. See UCC 2–703. Here the focus will be on (1) the seller's "goods oriented" remedies assuming the buyer is retaining the goods, and (2) the seller's right to the price, whether or not the buyer retains the goods.

Generally, if the buyer is refusing payment, and payment is due at this stage, the seller will be entitled to replevy the goods from the buyer under UCC 2–507(2) and 2–511. As with most goods-oriented remedies, third parties may enter the picture and defeat the aggrieved party. As against creditors, UCC 2–702 controls. As against buyers from the buyer, UCC 2–403 must be consulted. And, of course, as in all situations, any relevant cases. But the seller could retain a security interest in the goods of high priority entitling it to defeat almost all third parties except "buyers in ordinary course of business." See UCC 9–107, 9–201, 9–307(1).

And when is the seller entitled to the price against a buyer in breach at this stage? If the buyer has accepted the goods (UCC 2–606) and has not properly rejected them or justifiably revoked his acceptance of them, then the seller may have the price. UCC 2–709. The seller may also get the price in two other, more restricted, situations under UCC 2–709(1).

E. The Payment Stage

The overwhelming majority of transactions pass on through the payment stage without incident. But some hang up at this stage, too. Payment due on delivery has already been treated. But in the overwhelming majority of commercial deals, and in a substantial proportion of consumer deals, payment is strung out over some period *after* the buyer comes into possession of the goods. Breakdowns in the payment process in deals of this nature will now be considered. All citations are to the 1990 Revisions of Articles 3 and 4.

If the deal is silent on payment, then payment is due on tender of delivery. UCC 2–507. C.O.D. deals and transactions calling for payment of a draft upon presentation of documents may be thought of as assimilations of cash deals.

Credit must be agreed upon. Terms vary. Extension of credit may be *secured* under Article 9. Also, a buyer may be required to sign a time draft, thus giving the seller or his transferee the advantages of having a signed negotiable instrument to sue on. See UCC 3–301, 3–305(a).

A buyer may fail to pay because of insolvency. In this situation, the seller will, again, be interested in goods-oriented remedies. Its right to recover the goods from the buyer under Article 2 is quite limited. UCC 2–702(2). What is more, this right is itself "subject to" the claims of certain parties under UCC 2–702(3).

The buyer may undertake to pay by drawing a check to seller's order. A check is a negotiable instrument if in proper form (UCC 3–104). A check orders the drawer's bank to pay the payee or to the payee's order or to bearer. The buyer-drawer's bank may refuse to honor the check, for any one of a variety of reasons but most commonly because the check over-draws the buyer's account.

Assume the check is dishonored. What action could the seller take? It could sue the buyer on the underlying obligation. See UCC 3–310(b). But it could not recover from the bank, for a check is not an assignment (UCC 3–408) and a party is not liable on an instrument unless its signature appears thereon. UCC 3–401. Nor is the seller recognized as a third party beneficiary of the contract of deposit between buyer's bank and buyer. It is possible, on the right facts, that bank would be liable to seller on a tort theory, such as conversion. See UCC 3–420.

If the buyer was not the drawer of the check, but simply was indorsing over a check made to him to seller, seller might be a holder in due course under UCC 3–302 and, in an action against the drawer, immune from most ordinary defenses (e.g., failure of consideration, fraud) that a drawer might have against someone suing him on the instrument. See UCC 3–414 and 3–305. Similarly, the seller might be a holder in due course against an indorser and immune from such defenses. See UCC 3–305. To hold such a drawer or indorser liable, though, the seller would have to give notice of dishonor etc. as required by UCC 3–414(b), 3–415, and Part 5 of Article 3. There is the further possibility that the seller will be entitled to recover from a transferor of the instrument on a "warranty" theory. See UCC 3–416(b).

To recapitulate: Upon dishonor of a check given in payment for goods, the seller might have recovery against the buyer on the underlying obligation, or against the buyer and possibly other parties "on the instrument," or possibly against a transferor on a "warranty" theory.

So much for how things might go upon dishonor. What if the buyer's bank does not dishonor the check, but rather, fails to pay the proper party, i.e., the seller, or fails to pay the proper amount? Such events can occur in a variety of ways. We shall at this juncture consider only two situations. Assume the buyer draws a check to seller, but is interrupted and does not sign it as drawer. A thief steals the check, forges buyer's signature, and then takes the check to X who cashes it, giving thief the money. X presents the check to buyer's bank and buyer's bank honors it. Later, the forgery is discovered. Buyer's bank is not entitled to charge drawer's account, because the item is not "properly payable." UCC 4–401(a). But drawer-buyer is not, of course, discharged from liability to seller and still must pay. Can the bank retrieve its loss from X? See UCC 3–418.

The seller may be a wrongdoer. What if the seller alters the amount of the check upward and the bank pays? Again, drawer-buyer's account is not chargeable as to the excess unless he negligently contributed to the alteration. UCC 4–401, 3–406. The seller, if he can be found, can be prosecuted. And the bank can recover against seller.

So much for a *sample* of the kinds of things that can go wrong in the payment process where a check is used.

An intermediary bank or carrier may fail to perform its obligations in the payment process. The carrier in a C.O.D. deal may fail to pick up the cash. The bank in a documentary deal may (a) fail to secure proper payment from the buyer upon tender of the documents, or (b) fail to procure buyer's signature to a time draft as agreed. See UCC 4–501, 4–502, and 4–503. The moral for the seller is dual: utilize reliable intermediaries and deal with sound buyers.

What is the plight of a buyer who puts a check in the process of payment or signs a draft or pays cash on a sight draft and thereafter immediately discovers that the goods fail to conform? Is there anything he can do, through prompt action, to "undo" what he has done? These questions will be treated in the context of specific cases.

Conclusion

This concludes what is intended only to be a *general outline* of the main stages of the unfolding sale transaction, of the *kinds* of things that can go wrong at each stage, and of the generally relevant law bearing thereon. The remaining chapters of Book Two on Sales are generally presented according to the foregoing "stage" scheme of organization. Every problem and principle considered in this chapter will be treated again, usually in depth. What the student should now have is: (1) a general overview of the modern commercial sales transaction on credit as it progresses from the agreement stage through performance and payment, (2) some sense of the nature of the things that can go wrong at each stage, (3) a *functionally* useful roadmap through the structure of Article 2, and (4) some idea of how Articles 3, 4, 7, and 9 may bear on sales transactions. Obviously, this section of this chapter should be studied and reviewed. Properly digested, it can equip the student to appreciate more fully what lies ahead.

Before leaving the Article 2 Roadmap, four developments should be kept in mind.

First, in addition to the 1990 Revisions of Articles 3 and 4, a new Article 4A, Funds Transfers, has been promulgated. This Article regulates the electronic transfer of funds between commercial parties through banks and the Federal Reserve. It is another way to pay for goods sold. An excellent overview is found in the Prefatory Note to Article 4A.

Second, a new Article 2A, Leases has been promulgated. The focus of 2A is on the lease of goods, a transaction that is neither a sale nor a secured transaction. Article 2A is treated in Chapter 23.

Third, the Vienna Convention on the International Sale of Goods (CISG) became effective in the United States in January, 1988. When applicable, CISG, as federal law, preempts Article 2. For helpful analysis, see J. Honnold, Uniform Law for International Sales Under the 1980 United Nations Convention (2d ed. 1991). For a brief comparison of CISG with Article 2, see Winship, *Domesticating International Commercial Law: Revising U.C.C. Article 2 in Light of the United Nations Sales Convention,* 37 Loyola L.Rev. 43 (1991).

Fourth, Article 2 is now being revised by the National Conference of Commissioners on Uniform State Laws. The target date for completion is August, 1995. For background to the revision process, see Leary & Frisch, *Is Revision Due for Article 2?,* 31 Vill.L.Rev. 399 (1986); American Bar Association Task Force, *An Appraisal of the March 1, 1990, Preliminary Report of the Uniform Commercial Code Article 2 Study Group,* 16 Del.J. of Corporate Law 981–1325 (1991) (hereafter Task Force); PEB Study Group, *Uniform Commercial Code, Article 2 Executive Summary,* 46 Bus.Lawyer 1869 (1991). One of your co-authors serves as Reporter for the Article 2 revision.

SECTION 3. THE SCOPE OF ARTICLE 2

To what disputes does Article 2 apply, either directly or by analogy? Section 2–102 provides that "unless the context otherwise requires, this Article applies to transactions in goods. . . ." Article 2, however, "does not apply to any transaction which although in the form of an unconditional contract to sell or present sale is intended to operate only as a security transaction . . ." See UCC 2–102.

Section 2–102 raises more questions than its text answers.

What, for example, are goods? Under UCC 2–105(1) and 2–107 goods are defined as "things . . . which are movable at the time of identification to the contract for sale" and excludes "money in which the price is to be paid, investment securities . . . and things in action." Thus, in a contract for sale, a stereo is goods but an account receivable is not. Compare UCC 9–102(1)(b) & 9–105(1)(h).

When are goods identified to the contract? The question is answered in UCC 2–501. What difference does it make whether goods are identified? Goods must be "existing and identified before any interest in them" can pass to a buyer, UCC 2–105(2), whether that interest be title, UCC 2–401, or a "special" property interest, UCC 2–501(1). The importance of these property interests will be explored later. Note that an attempt to sell "future" goods, i.e., goods that are neither existing nor identified, operates as a "contract to sell."

What is a "transaction" in goods? Section 2–106(1) provides that "In this Article unless the context otherwise requires 'contract' and 'agreement' are limited to those relating to the present or future sale of goods." Thus, where those words are used in Article 2, the transaction is a sale or a contract to sell goods. But the word "transaction" is not clearly defined. Could it include a lease or a bailment? What about a gift?

When does the context "otherwise" require? For example, if the "transaction" is other than a contract for sale, should the context be invoked to broaden or narrow the scope of Article 2? If the use of context broadens scope, should all or part of Article 2 be applied?

Finally, if Article 2 does not directly apply, can it be extended by analogy to the dispute before the court? The comments if not the text of the UCC support this extension, see Comment 1, UCC 1–102, but the question remains when it is proper for a court to apply legislation to a dispute concededly beyond the scope intended by the legislature. See, generally, D. Murray, *Under the Spreading Analogy of Article 2 of the Uniform Commercial Code,* 39 Fordham L.Rev. 447 (1971).

In approaching these questions, remember that there are two kinds of Code limitations on the seemingly unlimited scope of the word "transactions." First, there are other Articles, e.g., Article 7, on bailments for storage or carriage, which may supercede the specific provisions of Article 2. Secondly, many of the specific provisions of Article 2 are themselves cast in terms of "seller" and "buyer" or limited to "contracts for sale." It would thus appear that some provisions of Article 2 might apply to a non-sales situation, e.g., UCC 2–202, 2–206, 2–207, 2–210, 2–302, & 2–316, while other provisions are, seemingly, limited to sales, e.g., UCC 2–205, 2–312, 2–313, 2–314 & 2–315.

Here are some problems and cases. As you study them, ask "What difference does it make whether Article 2 applies?"

Problem 9–1

(1) F orally agreed to sell B his wheat crop yet to be planted for $3 a bushel. Bad weather sharpened the demand for wheat. Before the crop was planted, F repudiated the agreement with B and sold the crop to C for $4 a bushel. B sued F for damages. F defended, invoking the statute of frauds. UCC 2–201. B argued that UCC 2–201 does not apply. What result? See UCC 2–102, 2–105 and 2–201.

(2) S agreed to sell B timber standing on S's land to be severed by S. S severed half of the timber but before B could haul it away, all timber, standing or severed, that B agreed to buy was destroyed by fire. B argued that the Code's risk of loss provisions applied. See UCC 2–102, 2–107(1) and 2–509. Is B correct? What change did the 1972 Official Text make in UCC 2–107?

(3) S owned a building which he contracted to sell to B who was to remove it from its concrete foundation, put it on skids, and drag it away. Before removal, S repudiated. Does Article 2 govern B's remedial rights? See UCC 2–107(1), 2–

711 and 2–713. (In Foster v. Colorado Radio Corporation, 381 F.2d 222 (10th Cir.1967), the court applied the Code's remedial provisions only to the goods involved in a combined real estate and personal property sale.)

BARCO AUTO LEASING CORP. v. PSI COSMETICS, INC.

Civil Court of the City of New York, 1984.
125 Misc.2d 68, 478 N.Y.S.2d 505.

EDWARD H. LEHNER, JUDGE.

The issue in this case is whether a lessor's disclaimer of all warranties in an automobile lease is enforceable where a vehicle to be used for business purposes failed to operate properly within a short period after delivery.

This action is against the corporate lessee and the individual grantors (officers of the corporate defendant) for breach of an automobile lease, seeking to recover the accelerated unpaid rental for the remainder of the lease term plus attorneys' fees. Defendants' answer sets forth a general denial and a counterclaim for loss of business resulting from an inability to attend certain business meetings due to the defective nature of the vehicle. Before the court is plaintiff's motion for summary judgment.

On September 27, 1982 defendant PSI Cosmetics, Inc. entered into an automobile lease agreement with plaintiff for the rental of a 1982 Renault. Defendants assert in their papers that: on November 28, 1982 the engine began to smoke and the car was towed to a nearby authorized Renault dealership where it took over three months to repair what was said to be a burned out motor; during this period defendants continued to make all rental payments despite being deprived of the use of the vehicle; upon picking up the vehicle from the repair shop Mr. Golumbia was informed that after driving the vehicle an additional 300 to 600 miles, he should have it retorqued; three days after this work was done the engine again began to burn, and the automobile was rendered inoperative and towed to plaintiff's lot. As a result of this experience Golumbia allegedly missed an important business meeting, resulting in the cancellation of a $40,000 contract, thereby providing the basis for the counterclaim.

The agreement, printed on plaintiff's standardized form without any typed or handwritten riders, contains myriad procedural safeguards by which the lessor seeks to insulate itself. The lease provides that the lessor retains title and a security interest in the vehicle. There is no option to purchase granted to the lessee, who waives "counterclaim, set off, reduction, abatement, deferment or any other kind of defense because of * * * unsatisfactory performance of the vehicle or for any reason whatever. * * *" Repairs and replacement of parts are made the responsibility of the lessee. Further insulation is provided for the lessor by a disclaimer of any warranties, except for the manufacturer's standard warranty. The implied warranties of merchantability and of fitness for a particular use are conspicuously disclaimed (UCC §§ 2–316(2); 1–201(10)).

Although not raised in their answer, defendants contend in their papers that both the warranty disclaimer and the waiver of counterclaims are unconscionable and that, as to the action for the unpaid balance, plaintiff has failed to mitigate its damages in that it failed to sell the automobile.

* * *

The first issue that must be decided is whether Article 2 of the Uniform Commercial Code and the implied warranties which it provides apply to the automobile lease herein. If so, what remains to be resolved is whether the warranty disclaimer is unconscionable.

Several cases in this jurisdiction have applied UCC Article 2 to the leasing of chattels * * *.

Judicial approaches to the applicability of Article 2 to leases has been "placed along a spectrum measuring willingness to depart from the sale construct." Note, Disengaging Sale Law from the Sale Construct: A Proposal to Extend the Scope of Article 2 of the UCC, 96 Harv.L.Rev. 470, 475 (1982).

The "exclusionary" view requires strict adherence to the premise that Article 2 applies only to paradigmatic sales, thereby excluding lease transactions as well as hybrid sales-plus-services contracts from coverage.

The "analogy" approach advocates that Article 2 be applied to transactions held not to be paradigmatic sales, but only when the transactions closely resemble such sales. Murray, Under the Spreading Analogy of Article 2 of the Uniform Commercial Code, 39 Ford.L.Rev. 447, 451 (1971). This has been the approach of the courts in this state. See: *Uniflex, Inc. v. Olivetti Corp. of America,* 86 A.D.2d 538, 445 N.Y.S.2d 993 (1st Dept.1982) (leases); *Aguiar v. Harper & Row Publishers Inc.,* 114 Misc.2d 828, 832, 452 N.Y.S.2d 519 (Civ.Ct.N.Y.Co.1982) (sales-plus-services). Thus, Article 2 is said to be "attended by a penumbra or umbrella of influence in areas of contract law not specifically within the literal definition of sales under section 2–102", Lupiano, J., dissenting in *Leasco Data Processing Equipment Corp. v. Starline Overseas Corp.,* 74 Misc.2d 898, 903, 346 N.Y.S.2d 288 (App.T. 1st Dept.1973), aff'd 45 A.D.2d 992, 360 N.Y.S.2d 199, mot. for lv. to appeal dismissed, 35 N.Y.2d 963, 365 N.Y.S.2d 179, 324 N.E.2d 557 (1974). See also Restatement, Contracts Second, § 208 (1981), Comment *a.*

Related to the analogy approach is the "policy" approach which further departs from a rigid adherence to the sales model by the selective application of particular provisions of Article 2 whenever the policies underlying such provisions are appropriate to the transaction in issue. Note, The Uniform Commercial Code as a Premise for Judicial Reasoning, 65 Colum.L.Rev. 880 (1965). See, e.g. *Dillman and Associates Inc. v. Capitol Leasing Co.,* 110 Ill.App.3d 335, 66 Ill.Dec. 39, 442 N.E.2d 311, 316 (1982); *Walter E. Heller & Co. v. Convalescent Home of the First Church of Deliverance,* 49 Ill.App.3d 213, 8 Ill.Dec. 823, 365 N.E.2d 1285 (1977).

The most inclusive approach is a more complete departure from the sales construct, focusing on the Article 2 scope provision in § 2–102 ("transactions in goods"). Although the article is replete with terms such as "sale", "seller", and "buyer" [See: Lousin, Leases, Sales and the Scope of Article 2 of the U.C.C. in Illinois, 67 Ill.B.J. 468, 470 n. 20 (1979)], such language is nowhere to be found in § 2–102. An argument for such approach, as applied to lease transactions, is that it recognizes the modern economic realities of less-than-full-title property interests, rejecting the use of location of title as a basis for resolving issues. In eschewing the prevailing analysis of the analogy approach, it is said to avoid ad hoc determinations and the intellectually questionable pigeonholing of facts so that the transaction will more closely resemble a sale. Note, 96 Harv.L.Rev. 470; Murray, supra. Thus, unlike the analogy approach, it does not perpetuate the use of the "covert tools" in decision-making which the draftspersons of the UCC had hoped to avoid. See: UCC § 2–302, Official Comment 1; Llewelyn, The Common Law Tradition 365 (1960); Ackerman, Reconstructing American Law 22 (1984).

Though eloquently advocated, Note, 96 Harv.L.Rev. 470; Murray, supra, the inclusive approach has not been accepted. While it has been noted that "transactions in goods" encompasses a far wider area of activity than a "sale", e.g. *Hertz Commercial Leasing Corp. v. Transportation Credit Clearing House,* supra, 59 Misc.2d 226, at 230, 298 N.Y.S.2d 392, this has been more in the way of judicial lip service. The cases in New York have not specifically relied on the language of the Article 2 scope provision alone, most preferring instead to analyze the underlying facts of the transaction in issue in order to determine whether it sufficiently approximates a sale. See: Annotation, What Constitutes a Transaction, a Contract for Sale, or a Sale Within the Scope of UCC Article 2, 4 A.L.R. 4th 85, 109–118 (1981).

Therefore, much as this court might prefer to indulge in the flexible and inclusive approach in determining whether the lease transaction herein is subject to the provisions of Article 2, the inquiry will be limited to an analysis of the transaction in order to determine whether or not it is analogous to a sale.

The agreement provides for rental payments over a four year period totalling $9153.12. No information has been submitted as to the fair market value of the car at the time that the lease was entered into, nor as to what portion of the price represents finance charges. The lessee is responsible for insurance coverage, repairs and replacement of parts; it bears the risk of damage or loss of the vehicle; and it agrees to indemnify the lessor for any claims. Lessor retains title to the vehicle and a security interest. The agreement is denominated "an agreement of lease only." Finally, there is no option to purchase although the agreement states that such option may be provided by a purchase rider.

In determining the answer to the similar problem of whether a lease of personal property is intended to be a security interest the UCC has adopted a simple test: "Whether a lease is intended as security is to be determined by the facts of each case; however * * * an agreement that upon compliance with the terms of the lease the lessee shall become or has the option to become the owner of the property for no additional consideration or for a nominal consideration does make the lease one intended for security." (UCC § 1–201(37)). The absence of a purchase option does not foreclose the inquiry as to whether a particular transaction is a lease or a security interest; the court merely goes on to consider any other relevant factors in order to make its determination.

The same reasoning applies in determining whether a particular lease transaction is governed by Article 2. Thus, in *Uniflex, Inc. v. Olivetti Corp. of America,* supra, where there was no option to purchase, no provision for a renewal term at a nominal rental, and lessee was required to return the equipment at the end of the initial term, the First Department held that an issue of fact existed as to the nature of the lease since the price for the rental was far in excess of the cost of the equipment. Defendant's affirmative defense based on the four year statute of limitations for the sale of goods (UCC § 2–725) rather than the six year period for contracts (CPLR § 213 subd. 2) was therefore reinstated.

Although the court lacks information as to the value of the car, the relationship of consideration to actual value, while an important factor, is not the only one. While the lessor retains title and a security interest, the fact that the lessee is saddled with both the risks and headaches of ownership suggests that there is no significant economic difference between full title ownership and the instant lease. Therefore the court concludes that the transaction at bar is governed by the provisions of Article 2 of the UCC, and that the lease is subject to the implied warranties of merchantability and of fitness for a particular purpose (UCC §§ 2–314, 2–315) unless they have been effectively disclaimed.

The form of the disclaimer of warranties herein complies with the requirements of UCC § 2–316(2). The question remains as to whether or not such disclaimer is unconscionable, since it is nonetheless subject to judicial scrutiny under UCC § 2–302. * * * See: White and Summers, Uniform Commercial Code 475–481 (2d ed. 1980).

* * *

Since it cannot be determined whether or not this agreement is enforceable without affording both sides the "opportunity to present evidence as to its commercial setting, purpose and effect" (UCC § 2–302 subd. 2), plaintiff's motion for summary judgment on the issue of liability under the agreement is denied.

UCC § 2–302 gives the court the power to refuse to enforce an unconscionable agreement. It does not, however, provide damages to a party who enters into such agreement. *Pearson v. National Budgeting Systems Inc.*, 31 A.D.2d 792, 297 N.Y.S.2d 59 (1st Dept.1969); *Vom Lehn v. Astor Art Galleries Ltd.*, 86 Misc.2d 1, 11, 380 N.Y.S.2d 532 (Sup.Ct. Suffolk Co.1976). Accordingly, defendants' counterclaim for damages is dismissed.

Note: Leases and Article 2

Barco Auto Leasing Corp. was decided before the promulgation of Article 2A. Assuming that the transaction was a lease rather than a sale of goods (is that what the court decided?), the challenge was to develop a method to apply Article 2, with its provisions on warranties and disclaimers, to the lease. That method is called extension by analogy. Review *Barco.* How does the court justify extension by analogy? What law would govern if extension by analogy was not proper?

After the promulgation of Article 2A, the distinction between sales and leases is less important, at least where warranty disputes are involved. Article 2A has detailed provision on warranties, disclaimers and unconscionability, see UCC 2A–108, 2A–209 through 2A–216, and most are consistent with their counterparts in Article 2.

Nevertheless, the distinction between a lease of and a security interest in goods is still very important. If the transaction is a sale rather than a lease under revised UCC 1–201(37), then any interest in the goods retained by the purported lessor until the purported lessee has paid the "rent" will be treated as a security interest and will be unperfected unless the purported lessor either files a financing statement or otherwise complies with the notice requirements of Article 9. If the transaction is a "true" lease, however, Article 9 does not apply.

These issues are treated more fully in Chapter 23.

COAKLEY & WILLIAMS, INC. v. SHATTERPROOF GLASS CORP.

United States Court of Appeals, Fourth Circuit, 1983.
706 F.2d 456, *appeal after remand*, 778 F.2d 196 (1985), cert. denied, 475 U.S. 1121, 106 S.Ct. 1640, 90 L.Ed.2d 185 (1986).

MURNAGHAN, CIRCUIT JUDGE:

The strategy of experienced trial lawyers is to avoid, in all but the clearest case, a defense on the basis of a Federal Rules of Civil Procedure 12(b)(6) motion contending that there has been a "failure to state a claim upon which relief can be granted." At so early a stage, all factual inferences must be made in favor of the plaintiff; the facts must be viewed as the plaintiff most strongly can plead them.

Hence, the issues presented to the district court, the foundation underlying much of the law which may govern at subsequent stages of the case, will be addressed in circumstances which may well prove unduly favorable to the plaintiff. With little or no chance of prevailing, the defendant, in filing a 12(b)(6) motion, risks educating the plaintiff to aspects of the case which might otherwise be overlooked or at least not arise in circumstances so predispositive to the plaintiff's side of things.

The present case illustrates the proposition. On an appeal from a dismissal under 12(b)(6) the accepted rule is "that a complaint should not be dismissed for failure to state a claim unless it appears beyond doubt that the plaintiff can prove no set of facts in support of his claim which would entitle him to relief." *Conley v. Gibson,* 355 U.S. 41, 45–46, 78 S.Ct. 99, 101–102, 2 L.Ed.2d 80 (1957). Liberal construction in favor of the plaintiff is mandated. *Jenkins v. McKeithen,* 395 U.S. 411, 421, 89 S.Ct. 1843, 1848, 23 L.Ed.2d 404 (1969). We state as "facts" the allegations and inferences most favorable to the plaintiff.

Washington Plate Glass Company had a contract "to furnish and install aluminum and glass curtain wall and store front work" [3] on a building located in Lanham, Maryland being built by Coakley & Williams, Inc., the plaintiff. To accomplish its contractual undertaking, Washington purchased the glass spandrel required from the defendant, Shatterproof Glass Corp. Still other materials needed for the project, predominantly aluminum, it appears were acquired in part at least elsewhere.

3. The contract referred to "Spandrel glass to be ¼" gold reflective glass with 1" rigid insulation fastened to curtain wall members approximately 1–½" behind glass spandrel." In addition the agreement called on Washington to provide, *inter alia*: a Texas Aluminum 400 series wall system, vision glass, aluminum objects of several kinds, steel anchor clips, field fasteners, and porcelain enamel panels.

The contract price under the Coakley and Washington agreement amounted to $262,500, subsequently increased by amendment to $271,350.[4] The glass purchased by Washington from Shatterproof cost $87,715.00,[5] with the proviso that units were "to be properly marked for field installation."

The work progressed and the contract for the aluminum and glass curtain wall and storefront work was completed in March of 1974. Discoloration of the glass ensued, and Coakley complained. To remedy the situation, Washington agreed to replace the glass at no cost to Coakley, and did in fact replace a substantial portion of the glass. Shatterproof supplied the replacement glass and reimbursed Washington for the cost of re-installation, accomplished in April of 1977.

By December of 1977, the glass had again discolored, and complaints began to flow from Coakley to Washington and Shatterproof in or about December 1978. Shatterproof declined to replace a second time. On January 14, 1981, Coakley filed suit against Shatterproof in the Circuit Court for Montgomery County, Maryland alleging breach of implied warranties of merchantability and fitness for a particular purpose. Reliance was placed on certain provisions of the Maryland Uniform Commercial Code, Annotated Code of Maryland, § 1–101 et seq. Removal to the United States District Court for the District of Maryland followed, and Shatterproof sought dismissal under Fed.R.Civ.P. 12(b)(6).

A hearing on the 12(b)(6) motion followed at which Shatterproof contended (1) that the U.C.C. was inapplicable, (2) that lack of privity was fatal to the claim, and (3) that the statute of limitations had run prior to commencement of the action. We now have the case before us on appeal from an order granting the 12(b)(6) motion and dismissing the case solely on the grounds that the U.C.C. was not applicable.

Whether the U.C.C. applies turns on a question as to whether the contract between Washington and Coakley involved principally a sale of goods, on the one hand, or a provision of services, on the other. U.C.C. § 2–314 creates an implied warranty "that the *goods* shall be merchantable" to be "implied in a contract for their sale." Section 2–315 establishes an implied warranty "that the *goods* shall be fit" for a particular purpose, "[w]here the seller at the time of contracting has reason to know [the] particular purpose." (Emphasis added.)

Consequently, unless there has been a buyer of goods, the U.C.C. warranties of merchantability and of fitness for a particular use do not

4. Of that increase of $8,850, the bulk ($8,000) reflected specification of ASG Reflectoview Tru-Therm, 1 lite coated with 20 GI Gold and temperal monolithic spandrel 1/4" 20 GI Gold to match. The remaining $850 increase was due to a change in the corner configuration from aluminum panel to 1/4" Gold Reflectiveview glass.

5. The complaint is silent as to dollar amounts assignable to the additional materials. Obviously, the more they cost, the less the amount of the contract price attributable to services. We are not inclined to rely on statements of counsel at the time of argument in lieu of well-pleaded allegations. Counsel for Coakley asserted that the evidence would show that the cost of materials was substantially in excess of the cost of installation, *i.e.* more than $130,000. Even without counsel's arguments as a basis, it is still appropriate to recognize that such a possibility is in no way foreclosed by the allegations in the complaint. The plaintiff, at the early 12(b)(6) stage, is entitled to the benefit of the doubt.

apply. Furthermore, unless there has been a buyer of goods,[9] the elimination of a requirement of privity would not have been achieved.[10] Accordingly, both questions (1) as to the availability of the warranties and (2) as to the amenability of Shatterproof, who was not in privity with Coakley, to suit by Coakley, come down to whether the transactions between Washington and Coakley was a sale of goods or the provision of services.

To resolve that question, we must address ourselves to a welter of cases reaching varying results depending on the considerations deemed to predominate in each particular case.[11] It should not pass unnoticed that all were decided at summary judgment or beyond. No case involving the issue appears to have been disposed of at the Rule 12(b)(6) or demurrer stage. They emphasize, in particular, three aspects which may, or may not, constitute indicia of the nature of the contract: (1) the language of the contract, (2) the nature of the business of the supplier, and (3) the intrinsic worth of the materials involved.

A distillation of the cases produces an inescapable conclusion that, on the facts in their present pro-plaintiff posture,[15] a reasonable viewing of them would permit a factfinder to conclude that the contract between Washington and Coakley predominantly concerned a sale of goods, and consequently was governed by the U.C.C. A Rule 12(b)(6) motion simply cannot serve to dispose of the case.

As to the first of the emphasized aspects, the contract between Washington and Coakley speaks in terms of furnishing and installing a wall and performing storefront work. Clearly, at the very outset of performance Washington had the responsibility to bring to the affected premises the materials which ultimately would form the glass curtain wall and store front. The U.C.C. in § 2–105 defines "goods" as "*all* things (including specially manufactured goods) which are movable at the time of identification to the contract for sale other than the money in which the price is to be paid, investment securities (Title 8) and things in action." (Emphasis added.) That at least creates an uncertainty to be resolved only by a full

9. Under U.C.C. § 2–103(1)(a), the term "buyer" is defined, in unexceptional terms, as "a person who buys or contracts to buy goods."

10. *See* U.C.C. § 2–314(1)(b): "Any previous requirement of privity is abolished as between the *buyer* and the seller in any action brought by the *buyer*." (Emphasis added.) Absent compliance with § 2–314(1)(b), the lack of privity would have been fatal to Coakley's maintenance of the cause of action. *E.g., Vaccarino v. Cozzubo,* 181 Md. 614, 31 A.2d 316 (1943).

If the transaction was one for goods, Coakley was self-evidently the buyer. Shatterproof was the seller of goods in a transaction in which the intermediary, Washington, not Coakley, was the buyer. However, Washington's purpose in buying was to apply the items purchased to uses benefitting Coakley.

11. *E.g., Bonebrake v. Cox,* 499 F.2d 951, 960 (8th Cir.1974) (The appeal was from an adjudication on the merits, following a full trial, and reached the conclusion that a contract to supply and install bowling equipment dealt predominantly with goods, even though the amount of services involved was substantial. "The test for inclusion or exclusion [in or from the provisions of the U.C.C.] is not whether they are mixed, but, granting that they are mixed, whether their predominant factor, their thrust, their purpose, reasonably stated, is the rendition of service, with goods incidentally involved (*e.g.,* contract with artist for painting) or is a transaction of sale, with labor incidentally involved (*e.g.,* installation of a water heater in a bathroom). The contract before us, construed in accordance with the applicable standards of the Code, is not excluded therefrom because it is 'mixed,' * * * ").

15. We, of course, have no way of knowing what will actually be developed when the parties are put to their respective proofs.

factual presentation to determine whether the nature of the Washington business was predominantly the provision of goods or the furnishing of services. The fact that Coakley was a building contractor specializing in construction is not sufficient to provide a completely definitive answer. While often, and perhaps customarily, a contractor is engaged in the provision of services, the scope of a contractor's work is not necessarily monolithic and, in the present circumstances, it becomes a question of unresolved fact whether Coakley, for the purposes of the single relationship to which we are restricted, was a buyer of goods.

In this connection, it is not irrelevant that Coakley has alleged that the purchases by Washington from Shatterproof included anchor clips and field fasteners. At the early stage at which we find ourselves, the allegation requires us to indulge the inference urged by counsel for Coakley that putting the glass in place was a simple snap-on process requiring little expenditure of time or labor. One can readily imagine, without the advantage of specificity deriving from a full trial on the merits, that the contract largely contemplated the provision of precast panels as goods, without the installation being nearly so extensive or significant as the supplying of the glass itself.

The fact that the contract does not follow a standard, routine or regularized form, coupled with the plaintiff's contention that standard form contracts are virtually universal for construction (i.e., generally, service) contracts, operates to leave open the possibility of a finding that the contract is more one for goods than would be the customary construction contract.

Turning to the second point, the nature of Washington's business, the fact that Washington was a dealer and not a manufacturer does not have any particularly dispositive significance. Many retailers of goods function in the role of middleman. Shatterproof sold Washington materials in a transaction which unquestionably, on the sparse record before us at the preliminary stage at which we find ourselves, was a sale of goods, and the question comes down essentially to whether those materials or the services which Washington also provided under its contract with Coakley predominated. Without full consideration of as yet unascertained facts that question is simply not ripe for resolution. It is one of fact, not law; at least it is at this early stage.

Third, the complaint affords no realistic, and certainly no dispositive, information as to the value of the spandrels et al. in case of breakup into the component parts of the glass curtain wall and store front work. That can only be determined by further development of the record, and is, in all events, but one of several factors which must be evaluated in conjunction with all the others in resolving the ultimate factual issue: did Washington and Coakley deal primarily with goods or services?

Accordingly, Coakley has alleged enough to survive a motion to dismiss under Fed.R.Civ.P. 12(b)(6). Nor, at the other extreme, has it alleged too much, permitting sure ascertainment that services, not goods, were the gravamen of the transaction. Coakley should, therefore, be permitted to show, unless the statute of limitations bars recovery, that it was a buyer of goods and, therefore, entitled to proceed under the U.C.C. provisions.[17]

* * *

[The court held that the claim was not barred under the statute of limitations, UCC 2–725.]

Accordingly, the judgment is reversed and the case remanded for further proceedings not inconsistent with this opinion.

Reversed and remanded.

[Some footnotes omitted.]

Notes

1. After trial, the trial court determined that services rather than goods predominated in the transaction and held that the plaintiff was not entitled to claim breach of the implied warranty of merchantability imposed by UCC 2–314. This result was affirmed on appeal, 778 F.2d 196 (4th Cir.1985).

2. The either-or effect of the "predominate purpose" test was rejected in Anthony Pools v. Sheehan, 295 Md. 285, 455 A.2d 434 (1983), cited by the principal case in footnote 17. Where services predominate, if the goods supplied (a diving board) were unmerchantable and caused loss (personal injuries), Article 2 could be applied both to impose an implied warranty of merchantability and to determine whether a clause purporting to disclaim the implied warranty of merchantability was enforceable. The court stressed that the goods had to be supplied under a commercial transaction, rather than a contract for professional services, and must "retain their character * * * after completion of the performance promised * * *" Note, however, that the goods were supplied to a consumer who suffered personal injuries. Should that make a difference in the analysis?

ADVENT SYSTEMS LTD. v. UNISYS CORP.

United States Court of Appeals, Third Circuit, 1991.
925 F.2d 670.

OPINION OF THE COURT

WEIS, CIRCUIT JUDGE.

In this diversity case we conclude that computer software is a good within the Uniform Commercial Code; in the circumstances here a non-

17. Following argument on January 13, 1983 of the instant case, the Maryland Court of Appeals, on January 25, 1983, handed down its decision in *Anthony Pools, a Division of Anthony Industries, Inc. v. Sheehan,* 295 Md. 285, 455 A.2d 434 (1983). That case involves the somewhat different, although related, question of whether, in the case of a hybrid goods and services transaction, a disclaimer of an implied warranty of merchantability was unenforceable, as to the goods component of a contract predominantly for services, because such disclaimers are not legally permitted where there is a sale of consumer goods. U.C.C. § 2–316.1. The disclaimer was held unenforceable on the grounds that consumer goods retained their status as goods despite the fact that the contract was predominantly for services. The all or nothing contention that, the contract being predominantly one for services, none of the items covered by it should be treated as goods was rejected.

The Maryland Court of Appeals expressly reserved judgment as to whether U.C.C. § 2–316.1's ban on implied warranty disclaimers would also extend to consumer goods used up in the course of rendering the consumer service. At the very least, the result in *Anthony Pools* does nothing to question the soundness of the conclusion we have reached.

exclusive requirements contract complies with the statute of frauds; and expert testimony on future lost profits based on prior projections is suspect when actual market performance data are available. Because the district court ruled that the Code did not apply, we will grant a new trial on a breach of contract claim. We also decide that a parent corporation is privileged in disrupting prospective contractual negotiations of its subsidiary with another party and therefore will affirm a judgment in favor of the defendant on a tortious interference count.

Plaintiff, Advent Systems Limited, is engaged primarily in the production of software for computers. As a result of its research and development efforts, by 1986 the company had developed an electronic document management system (EDMS), a process for transforming engineering drawings and similar documents into a computer data base.

Unisys Corporation manufactures a variety of computers. As a result of information gained by its wholly-owned United Kingdom subsidiary during 1986, Unisys decided to market the document management system in the United States. In June 1987 Advent and Unisys signed two documents, one labeled "Heads of Agreement" (in British parlance "an outline of agreement") and, the other "Distribution Agreement."

In these documents, Advent agreed to provide the software and hardware making up the document systems to be sold by Unisys in the United States. Advent was obligated to provide sales and marketing material and manpower as well as technical personnel to work with Unisys employees in building and installing the document systems. The agreement was to continue for two years, subject to automatic renewal or termination on notice.

During the summer of 1987, Unisys attempted to sell the document system to Arco, a large oil company, but was unsuccessful. Nevertheless, progress on the sales and training programs in the United States was satisfactory, and negotiations for a contract between Unisys (UK) and Advent were underway.

The relationship, however, soon came to an end. Unisys, in the throes of restructuring, decided it would be better served by developing its own document system and in December 1987 told Advent their arrangement had ended. Unisys also advised its UK subsidiary of those developments and, as a result, negotiations there were terminated.

Advent filed a complaint in the district court alleging, *inter alia,* breach of contract, fraud, and tortious interference with contractual relations. The district court ruled at pretrial that the Uniform Commercial Code did not apply because although goods were to be sold, the services aspect of the contract predominated.

A jury found for Unisys on the fraud count, but awarded damages to Advent in the sum of $4,550,000 on the breach of contract claim, and $4,350,000 on the count for wrongful interference with Unisys U.K. The district court granted judgment n.o.v. to defendant on the interference claim but did not disturb the verdict awarding damages for breach of contract.

On appeal Advent argues that the Distribution Agreement prohibited Unisys from pressuring its UK subsidiary to terminate negotiations on a corollary contract. Unisys contends that the relationship between it and Advent was one for the sale of goods and hence subject to the terms of statute of frauds in the Uniform Commercial Code. Because the agreements lacked an express provision on quantity, Unisys insists that the statute of frauds bans enforcement. In addition, Unisys contends that the evidence did not support the damage verdict.

* * *

II.

Software and the Uniform Commercial Code

The district court ruled that as a matter of law the arrangement between the two parties was not within the Uniform Commercial Code and, consequently, the statute of frauds was not applicable. As the district court appraised the transaction, provisions for services outweighed those for products and, consequently, the arrangement was not predominantly one for the sale of goods.

In the "Heads of Agreement" Advent and Unisys purported to enter into a "joint business collaboration." Advent was to modify its software and hardware interfaces to run initially on equipment not manufactured by Unisys but eventually on Unisys hardware. It was Advent's responsibility to purchase the necessary hardware. "[I]n so far as Advent has successfully completed [some of the processing] of software and hardware interfaces," Unisys promised to reimburse Advent to the extent of $150,000 derived from a "surcharge" on products purchased.

Advent agreed to provide twelve manweeks of marketing manpower, but with Unisys bearing certain expenses. Advent also undertook to furnish an experienced systems builder to work with Unisys personnel at Advent's prevailing rates, and to provide sales and support training for Unisys staff as well as its customers.

The Distribution Agreement begins with the statement, "Unisys desires to purchase, and Advent desires to sell, on a non-exclusive basis, certain of Advent hardware products and software licenses for resale worldwide." Following a heading "Subject Matter of Sales," appears this sentence, "(a) Advent agrees to sell hardware and license software to Unisys, and Unisys agrees to buy from Advent the products listed in Schedule A." Schedule A lists twenty products, such as computer cards, plotters, imagers, scanners and designer systems.

Advent was to invoice Unisys for each product purchased upon shipment, but to issue separate invoices for maintenance fees. The cost of the "support services" was set at 3% "per annum of the prevailing Advent user list price of each software module for which Unisys is receiving revenue from a customer." Services included field technical bulletins, enhancement and maintenance releases, telephone consultation, and software patches, among others. At no charge to Unisys, Advent was to provide publications such as installation manuals, servicing and adjustment manuals, diagnostic operation and test procedures, sales materials, product brochures and similar items. In turn, Unisys was to "employ resources in performing marketing efforts" and develop "the technical ability to be thoroughly familiar" with the products.

In support of the district court's ruling that the U.C.C. did not apply, Advent contends that the agreement's requirement of furnishing services did not come within the Code. Moreover, the argument continues, the "software" referred to in the agreement as a "product" was not a "good" but intellectual property outside the ambit of the Uniform Commercial Code.

Because software was a major portion of the "products" described in the agreement, this matter requires some discussion. Computer systems consist of "hardware" and "software." Hardware is the computer machinery, its electronic circuitry and peripheral items such as keyboards, readers, scanners and printers. Software is a more elusive concept. Generally speaking, "software" refers to the medium that stores input and output data as well as computer programs. The medium includes hard disks, floppy disks, and magnetic tapes.

In simplistic terms, programs are codes prepared by a programmer that instruct the computer to perform certain functions. When the program is transposed onto a medium compatible with the computer's needs, it becomes software. The process of preparing a program is discussed in some detail in *Whelan Associates, Inc. v. Jaslow Dental Laboratory, Inc.*, 797 F.2d 1222, 1229 (3d Cir.1986), *cert. denied,* 179 U.S. 1031, 107 S.Ct. 877, 93 L.Ed.2d 831 (1987) and *Apple Computer, Inc. v. Franklin Computer Corp.*, 714 F.2d 1240 (3d Cir.1983), *cert. dismissed,* 464 U.S. 1033, 104 S.Ct. 690, 79 L.Ed.2d 158 (1984). *See also* Rodau, *Computer Software: Does Article 2 of the Uniform Commercial Code Apply?,* 35 Emory L.J. 853, 864–74 (1986).

The increasing frequency of computer products as subjects of commercial litigation has led to controversy over whether software is a "good" or intellectual property. The Code does not specifically mention software.

In the absence of express legislative guidance, courts interpret the Code in light of commercial and technological developments. The Code is designed "[t]o simplify, clarify and modernize the law governing commercial transactions" and "[t]o permit the continued expansion of commercial practices." 13 Pa.Cons.Stat.Ann. § 1102 (Purdon 1984). As the Official Commentary makes clear:

> "This Act is drawn to provide flexibility so that, since it is intended to be a semi-permanent piece of legislation, it will provide its own machinery for expansion of commercial practices. It is intended to make it possible for the law embodied in this Act to be developed by the courts in the light of unforeseen and new circumstances and practices."

Id. comment 1.

The Code "applies to transactions in goods." 13 Pa.Cons.Stat.Ann. § 2102 (Purdon 1984). Goods are defined as "all things (including specially manufactured goods) which are moveable at the time of the identification for sale." *Id.* at § 2105. The Pennsylvania courts have recognized that " 'goods' has a very extensive meaning" under the U.C.C. *Duffee v. Judson,* 251 Pa.Super. 406, 380 A.2d 843, 846 (1977); *see also Lobianco v. Property Protection, Inc.,* 292 Pa.Super. 346, 437 A.2d 417 (1981) ("goods" under U.C.C.

embraces every species of property other than real estate, choses in action, or investment securities.).

Our Court has addressed computer package sales in other cases, but has not been required to consider whether the U.C.C. applied to software per se. *See Chatlos Systems, Inc. v. National Cash Register Corp.,* 635 F.2d 1081 (3d Cir.1980) (parties conceded that furnishing the plaintiff with hardware, software and associated services was governed by the U.C.C.); *see also Carl Beasley Ford, Inc. v. Burroughs Corporation,* 361 F.Supp. 325 (E.D.Pa.1973) (U.C.C. applied without discussion), *aff'd* 493 F.2d 1400 (3d Cir.1974). Other Courts of Appeals have also discussed transactions of this nature. *RRX Industries, Inc. v. LabCon, Inc.,* 772 F.2d 543 (9th Cir.1985) (goods aspects of transaction predominated in a sale of a software system); *Triangle Underwriters, Inc. v. Honeywell, Inc.,* 604 F.2d 737, 742–43 (2d Cir.1979) (in sale of computer hardware, software, and customized software goods aspects predominated; services were incidental).

Computer programs are the product of an intellectual process, but once implanted in a medium are widely distributed to computer owners. An analogy can be drawn to a compact disc recording of an orchestral rendition. The music is produced by the artistry of musicians and in itself is not a "good," but when transferred to a laser-readable disc becomes a readily merchantable commodity. Similarly, when a professor delivers a lecture, it is not a good, but, when transcribed as a book, it becomes a good.

That a computer program may be copyrightable as intellectual property does not alter the fact that once in the form of a floppy disc or other medium, the program is tangible, moveable and available in the marketplace. The fact that some programs may be tailored for specific purposes need not alter their status as "goods" because the Code definition includes "specially manufactured goods."

The topic has stimulated academic commentary[2] with the majority espousing the view that software fits within the definition of a "good" in the U.C.C.

Applying the U.C.C. to computer software transactions offers substantial benefits to litigants and the courts. The Code offers a uniform body of law on a wide range of questions likely to arise in computer software disputes: implied warranties, consequential damages, disclaimers of liability, the statute of limitations, to name a few.

The importance of software to the commercial world and the advantages to be gained by the uniformity inherent in the U.C.C. are strong policy arguments favoring inclusion. The contrary arguments are not persuasive, and we hold that software is a "good" within the definition in the Code.

2. Among the articles and notes that have reviewed extant caselaw are: Boss & Woodward, *Scope of the Uniform Commercial Code; Survey of Computer Contracting Cases,* 43 Bus.Law. 1513 (1988); Owen, *The Application of Article 2 of the Uniform Commercial Code To Computer Contracts,* 14 N.Kentucky L.Rev. 277 (1987); Rodau, *Computer Software: Does Article 2 of the Uniform Commercial Code Apply,* 35 Emory L.J. 853 (1986); Holmes, *Application of Article Two of the Uniform Commercial Code to Computer System Acquisitions,* 9 Rutgers Computer & Technology L.J. 1 (1982); Note, *Computer Software As A Good Under the Uniform Commercial Code: Taking a Byte Out of the Intangibility Myth,* 65 B.U.L.Rev. 129 (1985); Note, *Computer Programs as Goods Under the U.C.C.,* 77 Mich.L.Rev. 1149 (1979).

The relationship at issue here is a typical mixed goods and services arrangement. The services are not substantially different from those generally accompanying package sales of computer systems consisting of hardware and software. *See Chatlos Systems, Inc. v. National Cash Register Corp.,* 479 F.Supp. 738, 741 (D.N.J.1979); *Beasley Ford,* 361 F.Supp. at 328.

Although determining the applicability of the U.C.C. to a contract by examining the predominance of goods or services has been criticized, we see no reason to depart from that practice here. As we pointed out in *De Filippo v. Ford Motor Co.,* 516 F.2d 1313, 1323 (3d Cir.), *cert. denied,* 423 U.S. 912, 96 S.Ct. 216, 46 L.Ed.2d 141 (1975), segregating goods from non-goods and insisting "that the Statute of Frauds apply only to a portion of the contract, would be to make the contract divisible and impossible of performance within the intention of the parties."

We consider the purpose or essence of the contract. Comparing the relative costs of the materials supplied with the costs of the labor may be helpful in this analysis, but not dispositive. *Compare RRX,* 772 F.2d at 546 ("essence" of the agreement) *with Triangle,* 604 F.2d at 743 ("compensation" structure of the contract).

In this case the contract's main objective was to transfer "products." The specific provisions for training of Unisys personnel by Advent were but a small part of the parties' contemplated relationship.

The compensation structure of the agreement also focuses on "goods." The projected sales figures introduced during the trial demonstrate that in the contemplation of the parties the sale of goods clearly predominated. The payment provision of $150,000 for developmental work which Advent had previously completed, was to be made through individual purchases of software and hardware rather than through the fees for services and is further evidence that the intellectual work was to be subsumed into tangible items for sale.

We are persuaded that the transaction at issue here was within the scope of the Uniform Commercial Code and, therefore, the judgment in favor of the plaintiff must be reversed.

* * *

Notes

1. *Arguments people make ...* Arguments against the application of Article 2 to computer transactions can be classified as follows:

(a) The transaction is a lease of software and hardware rather than a sale. If so, see UCC 1–201(37), Article 2A would apply to a lease of goods and could be extended by analogy to cover any services. See UCC 2A–102, Comment.

(b) The transaction is a license of software and hardware rather than a sale or a lease. If so, then neither Article 2A nor Article 2 apply unless extended by analogy. See Burkert v. Petrol Plus, Inc., 216 Conn. 65, 579 A.2d 26 (1990) (common law applied). But see Step–Saver Data Systems, Inc. v. Wyse Technology, 939 F.2d 91 (3d Cir.1991), which applied Article 2 to a license of computer terminals and software.

(c) Software is not goods, because professional services dominate. Despite the potential of this argument under the predominate purpose test, it is rarely accepted by the courts. See Ritter, *Software Transactions and Uniformity: Accommodating Codes Under the Code,* 46 Bus.Law. 1825 (1991). See also, Lousin, *Cases on the Scope of Article 2,* 46 Bus.Law. 1855 (1991).

(d) Where services predominate in the development of software but the hardware is clearly goods, courts should divide the transaction and treat movable goods under Article 2 and the services under the common law. This argument is made and *Advent Systems Ltd.* is criticized for not following it in Schlinsog, *Advent Systems Ltd. v. Unisys Corp.: UCC Governs Software Transactions,* 4 Software L.J. 611, 620–627 (1991). According to the author, this approach avoids both the manipulation and the all-or-nothing approach of the predominate purpose test.

(e) Transactions in computer software and hardware are uniquc, and should be governed by a special statute. See Boss, *Developments on the Fringes: Article 2 Revisions, Computer Contracting, and Suretyship,* 46 Bus.Law. 1802, 1811–1816 (1991).

Problem 9–2

The National Conference of Commissioners on Uniform State Laws has prepared a tentative redraft of UCC 2–102 and submitted it for comment. What is your opinion?

§ 2–102. Scope; Certain Security and Other Transactions Excluded From This Article.

(1) Unless the agreement or context otherwise requires, this Article applies to contracts for the sale of goods, including contracts where the sale of goods predominates. Regardless of whether the sale of goods predominates, this Article also applies to:

(a) Any dispute relating to the goods supplied under the contract, and

(b) any contract where the seller agrees to service, repair or replace goods after delivery to the buyer.

(2) Unless the agreement or the provisions of this Article otherwise require, this Article does not apply to the following transactions in goods:

(a) leases, Article 2A,

(b) contracts in the form of a sale which operate only as security agreements, Article 9,

(c) licenses,

(d) bailments, and

(e) gifts.

(3) If there is a conflict between this Article and Articles 2A or 9, Articles 2A and 9 govern.

(4) Except as otherwise provided in this Act, any provision of this Article, if relevant in principle and appropriate in the circumstances, may be applied by analogy to a sale of personal property other than goods or a transaction in goods not governed by this Article.

SECTION 4. SOME BASIC CONCEPTS IN ARTICLE 2

A. *Introduction*

The present form of Article 2, Sales, emerged from a careful and critical review of the 1952 Official Text by the New York Law Revision Commission in 1953–54, and was promulgated in the 1958 Official Text of the Uniform Commercial Code. The principal draftsperson in the early drafts of Article 2 and its predecessor (the Revised Uniform Sales Act), and its most effective champion until his death in 1962, was Professor Karl N. Llewellyn. (The drafts of Llewellyn's efforts from 1940–44 to revise the Uniform Sales Act are reproduced in E. Kelly, Uniform Commercial Code Drafts (1984), Vols. I and II.) Work under the joint auspices of the National Conference of Commissioners on Uniform State Laws and the American Law Institute began on January 1, 1945. See Schnader, *A Short History of the Preparation and Enactment of the Uniform Commercial Code,* 22 U.Miami L.Rev. 1, 5 (1967).) In a real sense, Article 2 is "Karl's Kode:" His ideas and approach to commercial law, even though imperfectly achieved, tended to dominate the final product. For useful discussion, see W. Twining, Karl Llewellyn and the Realist Movement (1973). See also Wiseman, *The Limits of Vision: Karl Llewellyn and the Merchant Rules,* 100 Harv.L.Rev. 465 (1987). Compare Casebeer, *Escape from Liberalism: Fact and Value in Karl Llewellyn,* 1977 Duke L.J. 671 with Danzig, *A Comment on the Jurisprudence of the Uniform Commercial Code,* 27 Stan.L.Rev. 621 (1975). See also, Williams, *Book Review,* 97 Harv.L.Rev. 1495 (1984).

According to Richard Danzig, Llewellyn did not regard law as a "body of deduced rules, or as an instrument chosen by social planners from among a universe of alternatives." Rather, he "saw law as an articulation and regularization * * * of a generally recognized and almost indisputably right rule ... inherent in, but very possibly obscured by, existing patterns of relationships." For him, law was "immanent" or "imbedded" in any situation and it was the task of the law authority, usually a judge, to discover it. Under this view, the task of the legislature is to prescribe standards, such as commercial reasonableness, on how to find the law and leave the task of particularization, i.e., finding the "situation sense," to the court. *Danzig,* supra, at 624–27. In the rejection of rules and the search for standards which responded to the behavior patterns of the disputants in context, Llewellyn was clearly in step with Arthur L. Corbin and other so-called "Realists." See Speidel, *Restatement Second: Omitted Terms and Contract Method,* 67 Cornell L.Rev. 785, 786–92 (1982).

Article 2 was also influenced by the nature of the problems and actors with which it deals. According to Danzig: "Commercial law is at the margin of public law. It deals with a subcommunity ('merchants'), whose members occupy a status position distinct from society at large, whose disputes are often resolved by informal negotiation or in private forums, whose relationships tend to continue over time rather than ending with the culmination of single transactions, and whose primary rules derive from a sense of fairness wide-spread—if imprecisely defined—within the commercial community." *Danzig,* supra, at 622–23.

B. Agreement, Not Promise, as the Foundation Stone

Students of commercial law have already learned a great deal about the concept of promise in the first year course in contracts. The Restatement (Second) of Contracts even defines a contract as "a promise or a set of promises for the breach of which the law provides a remedy, or the performance of which the law in some way recognizes as a duty." It is true that the analysis of commercial arrangements in terms of the concept of promise fits the facts of many contracts, including many involving the sale of goods. But the analysis fails to fit many other contracts, very felicitously, including some for the sale of goods, thus suggesting that there must be a more fundamental concept. That concept, as we will see, is the concept of agreement, and it is this that is the true foundation stone of Article Two.

Here we will offer some illustrative examples of features of consensual arrangements for the sale of goods that are more felicitously analyzable in terms of agreement rather than the exchange of promises as such. First, in the law of sales many express warranties arise by virtue of the seller's "affirmations of fact," not promises as such. UCC 2–312 expressly so states. Second, many other obligations in the law of sales arise in particular cases by virtue of tacit assumptions, custom, trade usage, course of dealing and course of performance. In such instances, there is rarely anything resembling an express promise, and the concept of an implied in fact promise seldom fits the facts more than fictionally. Third, many sale of goods transactions are not discrete, "one-shot," affairs but occur over time within longer term relationships. Many features of these relationships are not the subject of express promises (or even implied ones) yet they generate important obligations, obligations themselves shored up by the code doctrine of good faith and fair dealing to which we will soon turn. The broad structures of such relationships often pre-exist so that when the parties enter into a particular relation general obligations attendant upon such a relation attach. Finally, countless discrete, "one-shot," exchanges take place each day in which no promises are made on either side yet the law imposes obligations on both parties. "Over the counter" sales and supermarket sales are only the most familiar of these. In all of the foregoing examples, the most fundamental concept at work is that of agreement, not promise (and even agreement does not account for everything). The Code itself recognizes the primacy of agreement. In Article One, agreement and contract are defined in these terms:

1–201 General Definitions

(3) "Agreement" means the bargain of the parties in fact as found in their language or by implication from other circumstances including course of dealing or usage of trade or course of performance as provided in this Act (Sections 1–205 and 2–208). Whether an agreement has legal consequences is determined by the provisions of this Act, if applicable; otherwise by the law of contracts (Section 1–103). (Compare "Contract").

(11) "Contract" means the total legal obligation which results from the parties' agreement as affected by this Act and any other applicable rules of law. (Compare "Agreement.")

C. *The Article Two "Merchant" Concept*

Article Two includes fourteen provisions in which the term "merchant" appears. UCC 2–104(1) defines merchant to mean:

> A person who deals in goods of the kind or otherwise by his occupation holds himself out as having knowledge or skill peculiar to the practices or goods involved in the transaction or to whom such knowledge or skill may be attributed by his employment of an agent or broker or other intermediary who by his occupation holds himself out as having such knowledge or skill.

The fourteen sections which employ the term "Merchant" are: 2–103(1)(b) (good faith); 2–201(2) (statute of frauds); 2–205 (firm offer); 2–207 ("battle of the forms"); 2–209(2) (modification, rescission and waiver); 2–312(3) (warranty of title); 2–314(1) (implied warranty of merchantability); 2–327(1)(c) (sale on approval); 2–402(2) (rights of creditors of sellers); 2–403(2) (entrusting); 2–509(3) (risk of loss); 2–603(1) (rightful rejection); 2–605(1)(b) (waiver of buyer's objections); and 2–609(2) (adequate assurance of performance).

Section 2–314 imposing an implied warranty of merchantability on merchants, and section 2–201 on the statute of frauds seem to have generated the most litigation over who qualifies as a merchant.

LOEB & COMPANY, INC. v. SCHREINER

Supreme Court of Alabama, 1975.
294 Ala. 722, 321 So.2d 199.

ALMON, JUSTICE.

This is an appeal from a judgment of the Circuit Court of Lowndes County. The court decreed that the plaintiff and the defendant entered into an oral contract for the purchase and sale of one hundred fifty bales of cotton but that the contract was unenforceable under the Alabama Uniform Commercial Code because the defendant was not a "merchant" as that term is used and defined.

The plaintiff-appellant, Loeb and Company, Inc., is engaged in the marketing of raw cotton. James L. Loeb of Montgomery is President of the company and has bought cotton from the defendant-appellee, Charles Schreiner, for the past four or five years. Charles Schreiner is a cotton farmer and has been engaged in the farming of cotton and other crops since 1963.

Following a conversation on the 18th or 20th of April, 1973, with regard to the price paid by appellant company to Marlowe Reese, a neighbor of appellee, appellee telephoned appellant on April 23 and asked if the price paid Reese was available to him. He received from the president of appellant company a statement that he would pay appellee the same price. Appellant maintained at trial that appellee orally contracted with him during the telephone conversation to sell appellant company one hundred fifty bales of cotton. Appellee admitted that there were negotiations but maintained that he never agreed to sell the one hundred fifty bales.

The date, parties, terms and conditions of the alleged contract to sell were confirmed in the records of appellant company on April 23, 1973, and two copies of a confirming statement were mailed to appellee. Appellee received the confirming statement but neither signed it nor returned it, nor in any manner took exception to it until four months later when appellant telephoned him inquiring the whereabouts of the statement. In the meanwhile the price of raw cotton had risen from the price in the alleged contract of 37¼ cents to the middle 80 cents.

When appellant company telephoned appellee and inquired about the confirming statement, appellee said that he did not intend to sign and return it and told appellant to discuss the matter with his attorney.

The trial court found that there was an oral contract but that the contract was unenforceable under the Alabama Uniform Commercial Code because the appellee was not a merchant as that term is used in Tit. 7A, §§ 2–104 and 2–201, Code of Alabama, 1940, Recompiled 1958.

Tit. 7A, § 2–201 is the section which sets out the statute of frauds for Article 2 of the Uniform Commercial Code. It governs all contracts for the sale of "goods." Cotton is included within the definition of "goods" as defined by the Code. *Cox v. Cox,* 292 Ala. 106, 289 So.2d 609 (1974). § 2–201 provides in pertinent part as follows:

> "Except as otherwise provided in this section a contract for the sale of goods for the price of $500 or more is not enforceable by way of action or defense unless there is some writing sufficient to indicate that a contract for sale has been made between the parties and signed by the party against whom enforcement is sought or by his authorized agent or broker. A writing is not insufficient because it omits or incorrectly states a term agreed upon but the contract is not enforceable under this paragraph beyond the quantity of goods shown in such writing.
>
> "(2) *Between merchants* if within a reasonable time a writing in confirmation of the contract and sufficient against the sender is received and the party receiving it has reason to know its contents, it satisfies the requirements of subsection (1) against such party unless written notice of objection to its contents is given within ten days after it is received." (Emphasis added).

Appellant contends that the trial court erred in finding that the appellee cotton farmer was not a merchant and that § 2–201(2) was not applicable. If appellee is not a "merchant," § 2–201 would act as a bar to the enforcement of the contract in question. However, if appellee is a "merchant," he would be liable on the contract because he did not within ten days give notice of objection to appellant's confirming statement. Tit. 7A, § 2–104(1) defines "merchant" as follows:

> "(1) 'Merchant' means a person who deals in goods of the kind or otherwise by his occupation holds himself out as having knowledge or skill peculiar to the practices or goods involved in the transaction or to whom such knowledge or skill may be attributed by his employment of an agent or broker or other intermediary who by his occupation holds himself out as having such knowledge or skill."

Only a few courts have considered the question of whether a farmer is a "merchant." In *Cook Grains v. Fallis,* 239 Ark. 962, 395 S.W.2d 555 (1965), the Arkansas Supreme Court held that a soybean farmer was not a merchant when he was merely trying to sell the commodities he had raised. The court stated that there was not

> "* * * a scintilla of evidence in the record, or proffered as evidence, that appellee is a dealer in goods of the kind or by his occupation holds himself out as having knowledge or a skill peculiar to the practices of goods involved in the transaction, and no such knowledge or skill can be attributed to him." 239 Ark. at 964, 395 S.W.2d at 556.

In *Oloffson v. Coomer,* 11 Ill.App.3d 918, 296 N.E.2d 871 (1973), the Third Division of the Appellate Court of Illinois stated in dictum that a farmer in the business of growing grain was not a "merchant" with respect to the merchandising of grain. However, in *Campbell v. Yokel,* 20 Ill.App.3d 702, 313 N.E.2d 628 (1974), the Fifth District of the Appellate Court of Illinois dealt with a case that involved an action against some soybean farmers on an alleged breach of an oral contract for the sale of soybeans. The court held that the soybean farmers, who had grown and sold soybeans for several years were "merchants" when selling crops and were therefore barred by § 2–201(2) from asserting the statute of frauds as a defense.

One court has suggested that whether or not a farmer is a "merchant" within the meaning of § 2–104 should turn upon whether or not he has engaged in a particular type of sale in the past. In *Fear Ranches, Inc. v. Berry,* 470 F.2d 905 (10th Cir.1972), a breach of warranty case, the court held that where the defendant cattle farmers made a sale to a non-meatpacker for resale when they had previously sold all of their cattle to meatpackers, they were not "merchants" with respect to the sale to the non-meatpacker. The court felt that the sale of cattle for resale was a sale of a different type of goods and made up a different type of business than the sale of cattle to meat-packers.

We hold that in the instant case the appellee was not a "merchant" within the meaning of § 2–104. We do not think the framers of the Uniform Commercial Code contemplated that a farmer should be included among those considered to be "merchants."

In order for a farmer to be included within the § 2–104 definition of "merchants," he must do one of the following:

1. deal in goods of the kind;
2. *by his occupation* hold himself out as having knowledge or skill peculiar to the practices or goods involved in the transaction; or
3. employ an agent or broker or other intermediary who by his occupation holds himself out as having such knowledge or skill.

Since the farmer in the instant case did not qualify as a merchant under 3 above, he would have to qualify under 1 or 2. It is not sufficient under 2 that one hold himself out as having knowledge or skill peculiar to the practices or goods involved, he must *by his occupation* so hold himself out. Accordingly, a person cannot be considered a "merchant" simply because he is a braggart or has a high opinion of his knowledge in a particular area.

We conclude that a farmer does not solely *by his occupation* hold himself out as being a professional cotton merchant.

The remaining thing which a farmer might do to be considered a merchant is to become a dealer in goods. Although there was evidence which indicated that the appellee here had a good deal of knowledge, this is not the test. There is not one shred of evidence that appellee ever sold anyone's cotton but his own. He was nothing more than an astute farmer selling his own product. We do not think this was sufficient to make him a dealer in goods.

The official comment to § 2–104 states in part as follows:

> "This Article assumes that transactions between *professionals* in a given field require special and clear rules which may not apply to a *casual or inexperienced seller or buyer.* It thus adopts a policy of expressly stating rules applicable 'between merchants' and 'as against a merchant', wherever they are needed instead of making them depend upon the circumstances of each case as in the statutes cited above. This section lays the foundation of this policy by defining those who are to be regarded as professionals or 'merchants' and by stating when a transaction is deemed to be 'between merchants'." (Emphasis added).

Although a farmer might sell his cotton every year, we do not think that this should take him out of the category of a "casual seller" and place him in the category with "professionals."

If indeed the statute of frauds has, as claimed, permitted an injustice, it is a matter which addresses itself to the legislature.

The judgment is due to be and is hereby

Affirmed.

HEFLIN, C.J., and MERRILL, MADDOX, FAULKNER, JONES, SHORES and EMBRY, JJ., concur.

Note

Contra: Colorado–Kansas Grain Co. v. Reifschneider, 817 P.2d 637 (Colo. App.1991) (farmer a merchant under UCC 2–201(2)).

HILLINGER, THE ARTICLE TWO MERCHANT RULES: KARL LLEWELLYN'S ATTEMPT TO ACHIEVE THE GOOD, THE TRUE, THE BEAUTIFUL IN COMMERCIAL LAW 73 Geo.L.J. 1141, 1146–1148, 1174, 1175, 1176–1180 (1985).

We are experiencing a merchant muddle that stems from a fundamental misunderstanding about the nature and purpose of the Article 2 merchant rules. They are not what we thought they were. Their intended purpose and function suggest a different approach both to the merchant rules themselves and to their application to nonmerchants.

This article demonstrates that the Article 2 merchant rules were never intended to codify merchant custom and trade usage. Llewellyn, the principal draftsman of Article 2, invented the merchant rules. The necessity that mothered his invention was his passionate desire to make "commercial law and practice clear, sane, *and safe.*" The merchant rules are statutory expressions of Llewellyn's drafting creed that "[s]impler, clearer, and better adjusted rules, built to make sense and to protect good faith, make for more foreseeable and more satisfactory results both in court and out." Llewellyn sculpted the merchant rules to bring "the beautiful" to commercial law and commercial practice.[28] To Llewellyn's eye, legal beauty lay in functional rules—rules that could guide businessmen in conducting their business affairs, rules that could assist them in their "trouble shooting, trouble evasion and forward planning." Llewellyn drafted the merchant rules to apprise businessmen, attorneys, and courts of the peculiar obligations of businessmen. Their clarity, rationality and certainty in application would protect decent businessmen and promote sound, reasonable, and decent business practices.

The idea of separate merchant rules for businessmen sprang from Llewellyn's pragmatism. Llewellyn believed businessmen needed rules on which they could rely, rules that would produce predictable results. The existence of predictable rules would make commercial activity more rational and would thereby encourage its expansion. Moreover, Llewellyn believed the policies and considerations involved in a mercantile situation differed from those in a nonmercantile situation, and that a unitary approach to sales rules would inevitably muddle policies and rationales. This result would jeopardize the predictability he so wanted to create for businessmen. Under a single rule, governing both businessmen and nonbusinessmen, a court trying to protect Aunt Tilly might manipulate, distort, or misconstrue the rule, making uncertain its later interpretation or application to Tilly, Inc. Rules fashioned specifically for a commercial setting, and insulated from nonmercantile considerations, would thus protect the rules' predictability for businessmen. One set of sales rules for businessmen and another for Aunt Tilly would eliminate the possibility of undermining the commercial rule to do justice to Aunt Tilly.

Yet Llewellyn did not intend to preclude judicial application of the merchant rules to nonmerchants in every instance. If application to a nonmerchant would not jeopardize the rule's certainty and predictability, Llewellyn wanted the courts to apply the merchant rule to nonmerchants. Indeed, a provision in the 1949 draft expressly so provided.

* * *

In concluding that good commercial law and practice required special commercial rules, Llewellyn was not concluding that the commercial rules could have no application to a noncommercial context. Section 1–102(3) of the 1949 draft makes that clear: "A provision of this Act which is stated to be applicable 'between merchants' or otherwise to be of limited application need not be so limited when the circumstances and underlying reasons justify extending its application."

* * *

Had the 1949 provision authorizing liberal application of the merchant rules to nonmerchants survived and been enacted, the question of merchant status would not have assumed its current importance. Courts could have sidestepped many status questions by concluding that merchant status was ultimately irrelevant, and the reasons underlying the merchant rule—reasonableness, soundness, and decency—would justify its application to the nonmerchant. Unfortunately, the drafters finally bowed to merchant critics and eliminated section 1–102(3), apparently as a political concession to save the embattled Article 2 merchant distinction itself.

* * *

The farmer cases involving statute of frauds defenses all involve a similar plot. Farmer periodically calls Grain Elevator Company to check on current grain prices. During one call Farmer likes what he hears and the parties conclude a contract on the phone, the grain to be delivered some months later. Shortly after the oral deal, Grain Elevator Company prepares and sends a written confirmation of the phone deal to farmer. Farmer does not respond. Grain Elevator Company then contracts to sell Farmer's grain to a third party. At the time scheduled for delivery, the price of grain has skyrocketed, and not surprisingly, Farmer no longer likes the contract price. He sells his grain to someone else at the higher market price. Farmer's breach forces Grain Elevator Company to cover at the current market price to meet its contractual obligations. It ultimately sues Farmer to recover its loss.

Farmer appears in court outfitted in bib overalls and cowboy boots that cast off a faint perfume of manure. Farmer inevitably makes two responses to Grain Elevator Company's contract action: (1) "We never made a contract" and, (2) "Even if we did, I am a farmer, not a merchant, and therefore, the contract is unenforceable because I never signed anything." Grain Elevator Company always responds that Farmer is a merchant and the statute is therefore satisfied because Farmer never responded to its confirmation letter. As Article 2 is presently understood, the result of the litigation turns on the issue of the farmer's status.

In treating this question, some courts have concluded that the terms "farmer" and "merchant" are mutually exclusive: farmers are "tillers of the soil," while merchants are "traders in goods." The evidence indicates Llewellyn did not consider most farmers to be merchants for purposes of the statute of frauds. In a comment to an early draft, Llewellyn discussed the apple farmer who marketed three to six hundred bushels a year. Although such a farmer would give the implied warranty of merchantability (because he would qualify as a "goods" merchant), he would not be subject to section 2–207's rule that additional minor terms stated in a confirmation became part of the parties' contract (a "practices" merchant provision), because invocation of section 2–207(2)

> depends upon the established practice of regular merchants to attend and reply promptly to correspondence. No such practice exists among small farmers * * * his occupation does not hold him out as familiar with any practice "of the kind involved" or as having the general knowledge or skill in that aspect of a person in trade.

In defending the inapplicability of the statute of frauds to transactions under five hundred dollars, Llewellyn discussed farmers and merchants separately, noting that in regard to such transactions, a merchant is protected by his normal procedure of reducing transactions to written sales slip or confirmation; a farmer is protected by his standing in the community.

In some of his articles, Llewellyn distinguished the horse and haystack from "wares-in-commerce," arguing the commercial sales rules that had evolved from horse and haystack deals were unsuited for the new world of modern commerce. One may surmise that Llewellyn intended to leave farmers with their haystack law and to give businessmen new "wares-in-commerce" law. This theory would explain why Llewellyn repeatedly distinguished merchants from farmers and housewives in his testimony before the New York Law Revision hearings.

Although Llewellyn probably would have agreed that a farmer is not an Article 2 "practices" merchant, he would have been upset with the consequences that flow from this conclusion. Courts that have held the farmer not to be a merchant have applied section 2–201(1) (the nonmerchant rule) and refused to enforce the contract. Llewellyn would have wanted the courts to apply section 2–201(2)'s confirmation letter exception despite the farmer's nonmerchant status, because the purpose and policies behind the merchant exception would justify such application. Llewellyn designed section 2–201(2) to accommodate oral deals that the decent businessman confirmed promptly in accordance with sound business practice. He intended section 2–201(2) to serve as a bulwark against one party's indecent speculation at the expense of the other. Here, Farmer's questionable conduct as contrasted with Grain Elevator Company's sound and good business practice of sending out a confirmation letter would justify the application of section 2–201(2). No harm could come to the merchant rule by invoking it in that situation and its application would produce a just and satisfactory result.

Other courts, confronted with the farmer situation, have concluded the farmer is a merchant; one court emphasized that the statutory definition, rather than common sense, controlled. Although these courts have interpreted the merchant definition to include those whom Llewellyn probably did not intend to include, their "misconstruction" enabled them to achieve the result Llewellyn would have wanted, through application of the merchant rule. In short, had 1–102(3) been enacted, courts could have dismissed many "Who is a merchant?" questions with a glib "Who cares?" If the policy fits, the merchant rule should govern. Given the merchant rules' inherent reasonableness, the policy would fit more often than not.

The loss of section 1–102(3) and a basic misunderstanding about the underlying purpose of the Article 2 merchant rules have created a flaw in Article 2's bifurcated system. Courts assume the existence of an Article 2 barrier, which precludes application of the merchant rules to situations involving only one merchant or only nonmerchants. Courts either respect the barrier, often reaching poor results, or surmount it by various means to reach the proper results. Those who are unquestionably nonmerchants suffer most. They can never find refuge in the Article 2 merchant rules. This situation is especially ridiculous because there does not appear to be anything intrinsically commercial about most of the Article 2 merchant rules. The merchant rules for firm offers, the statute of frauds, risk of loss, and so on, are edicts issuing forth from the temple of reason, not the marketplace. The merchant rules embody good sense, not just good commercial sense.

Compared with the nonmerchant rules, the merchant rules seem enlightened. The merchant rules impose only the mildest, most modest of responsibilities, such as the duty to open one's mail and respond to it promptly. The merchant's failure to abide by these duties often results in equally innocuous consequences. For example, the businessman who fails to reply to a confirmation letter simply loses his statute of frauds defense against contract enforcement. The businessman who fails to read or respond to the offeree's letter of acceptance is bound by *minor* additional contract terms contained in the acceptance. These are rules which, in most instances, could apply to the common man with little fear of judicial distortion or doctrinal confusion. In fact, it may be said that what's good for businessmen in Article 2 is good for the rest of us. [Reprinted from Volume 73 of the Georgetown Law Journal by permission of Professor Ingrid M. Hillinger, © 1985.]

D. Power to Contract Out of Article Two

It is one thing for a lawyer and his client to find themselves properly within Article Two of the Code. It is quite another for the relevant Code provisions therein to be controlling in the face of contrary agreement of the parties. For many are not. Article Two, like prior law, grants broad freedom of contract. Scope for the lawyer's role as planner is therefore very great. And, as Llewellyn once stressed:

> "[I]n the normal modern case the first measure of the parties' rights is * * * the contract * * *, only an analysis which stresses the contract first and hammers on the necessity of keeping it in mind as the framework of all that follows, is adequate to teaching * * * only by emphasis, from the beginning, on the contract, can one bring to due honor the problem of draftsmanship * * *." Llewellyn, Cases and Materials on Sales xiv–xv (1931).

It should be noted that the "contract" to which Llewellyn refers may be one of three basic kinds. First, it may be fully negotiated between the parties and its terms reduced to writing. This is the least common form. Second, the contract may take the form of a signed standardized printed agreement. This is a very common form. Third, because the parties agree only on the barest essentials of goods and price, the contract may consist largely of "terms" supplied by statute. This is the most common form. Much of Article Two can be viewed as a statutorily standardized contract which comes into play to the extent the agreement of the parties is silent.

Regardless of the form of the contract, the lawyer will need to know his or her freedom of contract: that is, what Article Two allows, does not allow, and supplies absent contrary agreement. And the good commercial lawyer who is in a position to structure things in advance for his client will be especially alert to the kinds of things that might go wrong with his client's deal as it progresses from stage to stage.

To the lawyer, perhaps the most fundamental distinction here is that between planning and drafting the affirmative business content of a deal, and planning and drafting, *prophylactically* as it were, for things that can go wrong. With regard to the former, the businessman is dominant, though the lawyer contributes as draftsman. *Re* the latter, the lawyer is at the fore. The businessman supplies "business" specifications, e.g., nature, quality and quantity of goods, payment terms and the like, and the lawyer drafts in these, but his most distinctive contributions are frequently not here; rather, they are to try to envision the unfolding transaction as it progresses from stage to stage, to identify the kinds of things that can go wrong at each stage, and then to bring her preventive and remedial sophistication to bear on these possible eventualities *in advance at the agreement stage.*

But while the *contract is,* by virtue of the broad freedom granted in UCC 1–102(3), *primary,* and Article Two secondary, it does not, of course, follow that just any clause the lawyer drafts will stand up under Article Two, (and even if it will stand up under Article Two, other, non-Code law, may sometimes be invoked to strike it down). So far as *Code* limitations on freedom of contract are concerned, it is useful to differentiate four kinds applicable within Article 2. First, there is the type of *specific* Article Two provision that is itself not variable by agreement. Second, Article 2, in UCC 2–302, generally invalidates unconscionable contracts and unconscionable contract clauses. Third, UCC 1–203 imposes an "obligation of good faith" in the performance or enforcement of every contract or duty within the Act. Fourth, UCC 1–103 provides that certain equitable principles shall be controlling. The first kind of limitation will be considered in a general way in the present section, the second, third, and fourth in subsequent sections of this chapter.

The provisions of Article Two fall into three categories: (1) those which themselves explicitly state that they can be varied by agreement, (2) those which themselves *explicitly* state that they can not be varied by agreement, and (3) those which are not thus flagged one way or the other at all. The first kind poses no problems for the draftsman of a sales contract. The second kind he or she must identify and keep in mind. See, e.g., UCC 2–616(3), 2–718(1), 2–209(3), 2–318, 2–725(1), and 1–204(1). But provisions of the third type (unflagged either way) pose a real problem, for it is *clear* that some of these provisions cannot be varied by agreement, despite the general green light in UCC 1–102(3). Examples are UCC 2–201 on the Statute of Frauds, UCC 2–719(3) protecting "underdogs", and such third party protection provisions as UCC 2–702, 2–502, and 2–403. Yet within this same broad category of unflagged provisions are some that clearly can be varied by agreement. See, for example, the Code provisions on recoverable damages for breach, UCC 2–713, 2–714 and 2–718. The problem, then, is this: If, as is plainly the case, our third category of unflagged provisions includes some which can be varied by agreement and some which cannot, by what criteria are we to determine which is which?

Problem 9–3

Consider the validity of the following clauses which purport to vary the effect of the sections cited.

(1) "Pursuant to this basic agreement, the parties shall make subsequent agreements for the purchase and sale of lumber, each such subsequent agreement to constitute a binding contract only when and if the parties have fully

agreed to all material terms." See UCC 2–204(2), (3), and various gap-filler provisions in Part 3 of Article 2.

(2) "In the event that buyer discovers a nonconformity upon delivery of said goods, buyer shall not be required to notify seller thereof, provided that buyer commences any legal proceedings therefor against seller within two years of discovery of said breach." See UCC 2–607(3)(a) and 1–102(3).

(3) "In the event buyer defaults hereunder, seller shall be entitled to recover the agreed price for said goods whether or not Article Two of the Uniform Commercial Code so provides." See UCC 2–709.

E. Legal Controls on Article Two Contractual Behavior: Unconscionability and Good Faith

Below we discuss and consider UCC 2–302, providing that unconscionable contract clauses are invalid, and UCC 1–203, imposing a general obligation of good faith. You have already met both of those sections in your first year course in contracts. It is sometimes said that the unconscionability limitation on freedom of contract applies at the formation stage whereas the good faith limitation applies only to the performance or enforcement stage. Yet that good faith may have some bearing on issues normally resolved at the formation stage is quite evident, as with section 2–305(2) which provides that "A price to be fixed by the seller or by the buyer means a price for him to fix in good faith." Indeed, good faith may even have a bearing on liability for acts or omissions of one party as early as the negotiation stage. Of course, this would have to be via UCC 1–103 on supplemental general principles, for UCC 1–203 itself only imposes an obligation of good faith in the "performance" and "enforcement" of the contract. Similarly, the student will do well to entertain the possibility that unconscionability may have a bearing at *post* formation stages: See, e.g., UCC 2–309.

ZAPATHA v. DAIRY MART, INC.

Supreme Judicial Court of Massachusetts, 1980.
381 Mass. 284, 408 N.E.2d 1370.

WILKINS, JUSTICE.

We are concerned here with the question whether Dairy Mart, Inc. (Dairy Mart), lawfully undertook to terminate a franchise agreement under which the Zapathas operated a Dairy Mart store on Wilbraham Road in Springfield. The Zapathas brought this action seeking to enjoin the termination of the agreement, alleging that the contract provision purporting to authorize the termination of the franchise agreement without cause was unconscionable and that Dairy Mart's conduct was an unfair and deceptive act or practice in violation of G.L. c. 93A. The judge ruled that Dairy Mart did not act in good faith, that the termination provision was unconscionable, and that Dairy Mart's termination of the agreement without cause was an unfair and deceptive act. We granted Dairy Mart's application for direct appellate review of a judgment that stated that Dairy Mart could terminate the agreement only for good cause and that the attempted termination was null and void. We reverse the judgments.

Mr. Zapatha is a high school graduate who had attended college for one year and had also taken college evening courses in business administration and business law. From 1952 to May, 1973, he was employed by a company engaged in the business of electroplating. He rose through the ranks to foreman and then to the position of operations manager, at one time being in charge of all metal finishing in the plant with 150 people working under him. In May, 1973, he was discharged and began looking for other opportunities, in particular a business of his own. Several months later he met with a representative of Dairy Mart. Dairy Mart operates a chain of franchised "convenience" stores. The Dairy Mart representative told Mr. Zapatha that working for Dairy Mart was being in business for one's self and that such a business was very stable and secure. Mr. Zapatha signed an application to be considered for a franchise. In addition, he was presented with a brochure entitled "Here's a Chance," which made certain representations concerning the status of a franchise holder.[1]

Dairy Mart approved Mr. Zapatha's application and offered him a store in Agawam. On November 8, 1973, a representative of Dairy Mart showed him a form of franchise agreement, entitled Limited Franchise and License Agreement, asked him to read it, and explained that his wife would have to sign the agreement as well.

Under the terms of the agreement, Dairy Mart would license the Zapathas to operate a Dairy Mart store, using the Dairy Mart trademark and associated insignia, and utilizing Dairy Mart's "confidential" merchandising methods. Dairy Mart would furnish the store and the equipment and would pay rent and gas and electric bills as well as certain other costs of doing business. In return Dairy Mart would receive a franchise fee, computed as a percentage of the store's gross sales. The Zapathas would have to pay for the starting inventory, and maintain a minimum stock of saleable merchandise thereafter. They were also responsible for wages of employees, related taxes, and any sales taxes. The termination provision, which is set forth in full in the margin,[2] allowed either party, after twelve months, to terminate the agreement without cause on ninety days' written notice. In the event of termination initiated by it without cause, Dairy Mart agreed to repurchase the saleable merchandise inventory at retail prices, less 20%.

1. It included the following statements: "* * * you'll have the opportunity to own and run your own business * * *"; "We want to be sure we're hooking up with the right person. A person who sees the opportunity in owning his own business * * * who requires the security that a multi-million dollar parent company can offer him * * * who has the good judgment and business sense to take advantage of the unique independence that Dairy Mart offers its franchisees * * * We're looking for a partner * * * who can take the tools we offer and build a life of security and comfort * * *".

2. "(9) The term of this Limited Franchise and License Agreement shall be for a period of Twelve (12) months from date hereof, and shall continue uninterrupted thereafter. If DEALER desires to terminate after 12 months from date hereof, he shall do so by giving COMPANY a ninety (90) day written notice by Registered Mail of his intention to terminate. If COMPANY desires to terminate, it likewise shall give a ninety (90) day notice, except for the following reasons which shall not require any written notice and shall terminate the Franchise immediately:

"(a) Failure to pay bills to suppliers for inventory or other products when due.

"(b) Failure to pay Franchise Fees to COMPANY.

"(c) Failure to pay city, state or federal taxes as said taxes shall become due and payable.

"(d) Breach of any condition of this Agreement."

The Dairy Mart representative read and explained the termination provision to Mr. Zapatha. Mr. Zapatha later testified that, while he understood every word in the provision, he had interpreted it to mean that Dairy Mart could terminate the agreement only for cause. The Dairy Mart representative advised Mr. Zapatha to take the agreement to an attorney and said "I would prefer that you did." However, he also told Mr. Zapatha that the terms of the contract were not negotiable. The Zapathas signed the agreement without consulting an attorney. When the Zapathas took charge of the Agawam store, a representative of Dairy Mart worked with them to train them in Dairy Mart's methods of operation.

In 1974, another store became available on Wilbraham Road in Springfield, and the Zapathas elected to surrender the Agawam store. They executed a new franchise agreement, on an identical printed form, relating to the new location.

In November, 1977, Dairy Mart presented a new and more detailed form of "Independent Operator's Agreement" to the Zapathas for execution. Some of the terms were less favorable to the store operator than those of the earlier form of agreement.[3] Mr. Zapatha told representatives of Dairy Mart that he was content with the existing contract and had decided not to sign the new agreement. On January 20, 1978, Dairy Mart gave written notice to the Zapathas that their contract was being terminated effective in ninety days. The termination notice stated that Dairy Mart "remains available to enter into discussions with you with respect to entering into a new Independent Operator's Agreement; however, there is no assurance that Dairy Mart will enter into a new Agreement with you, or even if entered into, what terms such Agreement will contain." The notice also indicated that Dairy Mart was prepared to purchase the Zapathas' saleable inventory.

The judge found that Dairy Mart terminated the agreement solely because the Zapathas refused to sign the new agreement. He further found that, but for this one act, Dairy Mart did not behave in an unconscionable manner, in bad faith, or in disregard of its representations. There is no evidence that the Zapathas undertook to discuss a compromise of the differences that led to the notice of termination.

On these basic facts, the judge ruled that the franchise agreement was subject to the sales article of the Uniform Commercial Code (G.L. c. 106, art. 2) and, even if it were not, the principles of unconscionability and good faith expressed in that article applied to the franchise agreement by analogy. He further ruled that (1) the termination provision of the agreement was unconscionable because it authorized termination without cause, (2) the termination without cause violated Dairy Mart's obligation of good faith, and (3) the termination constituted "an unfair method of competition and unfair and deceptive act within the meaning of G.L. c. 93A, § 2."

3. In his testimony, Mr. Zapatha said that he objected to a new provision under which Dairy Mart reserved the option to relocate an operator to a new location and to a requirement that the store be open from 7 A.M. to 11 P.M. every day. Previously the Zapathas' store had been open from 8 A.M. to 10 P.M. There were other provisions, such as an obligation to pay future increases in the cost of heat and electricity, that were more burdensome to a franchisee. A few changes may have been to the advantage of the franchisee.

1. We consider first the question whether the franchise agreement involves a "transaction in goods" within the meaning of those words in article two of the Uniform Commercial Code (G.L. c. 106, § 2–103, as appearing in St.1957, c. 765, § 1), and that consequently the provisions of the sales articles of the Uniform Commercial Code govern the relationship between the parties. The Zapathas point specifically to the authority of a court to refuse to enforce "any clause of the contract" that the court finds "to have been unconscionable at the time it was made." G.L. c. 106, § 2–302, as appearing in St.1957, c. 765, § 1.[4] They point additionally to the obligation of good faith in the performance and enforcement of a contract imposed by G.L. c. 106, § 1–203, and to the specialized definition of "good faith" in the sales article as meaning "in the case of a merchant * * * honesty in fact and the observance of reasonable commercial standards of fair dealing in the trade." G.L. c. 106, § 2–103(1)(b), as appearing in St.1957, c. 765, § 1.[5]

We need not pause long over the question whether the franchise agreement and the relationship of the parties involved a transaction in goods. Certainly, the agreement required the plaintiffs to purchase goods from Dairy Mart. "Goods" for the purpose of the sales article means generally "all things * * * which are movable." G.L. c. 106, § 2–105(1), as appearing in St.1957, c. 765, § 1. However, the franchise agreement dealt with many subjects unrelated to the sale of goods by Dairy Mart. About 70% of the goods the plaintiffs sold were not purchased from Dairy Mart. Dairy Mart's profit was intended to come from the franchise fee and not from the sale of items to its franchisees. Thus, the sale of goods by Dairy Mart to the Zapathas was, in a commercial sense, a minor aspect of the entire relationship. We would be disinclined to import automatically all the provisions of the sales article into a relationship involving a variety of subjects other than the sale of goods, merely because the contract dealt in part with the sale of goods. Similarly, we would not be inclined to apply the sales article only to aspects of the agreement that concerned goods. Different principles of law might then govern separate portions of the same agreement with possibly inconsistent and unsatisfactory consequences.

We view the legislative statements of policy concerning good faith and unconscionability as fairly applicable to all aspects of the franchise agree-

4. General Laws c. 106, § 2–302, as appearing in St.1957, c. 765, § 1, reads as follows:

"§ 2–302. Unconscionable Contract or Clause

"(1) If the court as a matter of law finds the contract or any clause of the contract to have been unconscionable at the time it was made the court may refuse to enforce the contract, or it may enforce the remainder of the contract without the unconscionable clause, or it may so limit the application of any unconscionable clause as to avoid any unconscionable result.

"(2) When it is claimed or appears to the court that the contract or any clause thereof may be unconscionable the parties shall be afforded a reasonable opportunity to present evidence as to its commercial setting, purpose, and effect to aid the court in making the determination."

5. Generally throughout the Uniform Commercial Code, "good faith" is defined to mean "honesty in fact in the conduct or transaction concerned." G.L. c. 106, § 1–201(19). The definition of "good faith" in the sales article includes a higher standard of conduct by adding a requirement that "merchants" observe "reasonable commercial standards of fair dealing in the trade." G.L. c. 106, § 2–103(1)(b). There is no doubt that Dairy Mart is a "merchant" as defined under the sales article. See G.L. c. 106, § 2–104.

ment, not by subjecting the franchise relationship to the provisions of the sales article but rather by applying the stated principles by analogy. * * * This basic common law approach, applied to statutory statements of policy, permits a selective application of those principles expressed in a statute that reasonably should govern situations to which the statute does not apply explicitly. See Note, Article Two of the Uniform Commercial Code and Franchise Distribution Agreements, 1969 Duke L.J. 959, 980–985.

2. We consider first the plaintiffs' argument that the termination clause of the franchise agreement, authorizing Dairy Mart to terminate the agreement without cause, on ninety days' notice, was unconscionable by the standards expressed in G.L. c. 106, § 2–302.[6] The same standards are set forth in Restatement (Second) of Contracts § 234 (Tent.Drafts Nos. 1–7, 1973). The issue is one of law for the court, and the test is to be made as of the time the contract was made. G.L. c. 106, § 2–302(1), and comment 3 of the Official Comments. See *W.L. May, Co. v. Philco-Ford Corp.,* 273 Or. 701, 707, 543 P.2d 283 (1975). In measuring the unconscionability of the termination provision, the fact that the law imposes an obligation of good faith on Dairy Mart in its performance under the agreement should be weighed. See *W.L. May, Co. v. Philco-Ford Corp., supra* at 709, 543 P.2d 283.

The official comment to § 2–302 states that "[t]he basic test is whether, in the light of the general commercial background and the commercial needs of the particular trade or case, the clauses involved are so one-sided as to be unconscionable under the circumstances existing at the time of the making of the contract. * * * The principle is one of prevention of oppression and unfair surprise * * * and not of disturbance of allocation of risks because of superior bargaining power." Official Comment 1 to U.C.C. § 2–302.[7] Unconscionability is not defined in the Code, nor do the views expressed in the official comment provide a precise definition. The annotation prepared by the Massachusetts Advisory Committee on the Code states that "[t]he section appears to be intended to carry equity practice into the sales field." See 1 R. Anderson, Uniform Commercial Code § 2–302:7 (1970) to the same effect. This court has not had occasion to consider in any detail the meaning of the word "unconscionable" in § 2–302. Because there is no clear, all-purpose definition of "unconscionable," nor could there be, unconscionability must be determined on a case by case basis (see *Commonwealth v. Gustafsson,* 370 Mass. 181, 187, 346 N.E.2d 706 [1976]), giving particular attention to whether, at the time of the execution of the agreement, the contract provision could result in unfair surprise and was oppressive to the allegedly disadvantaged party.

We start with a recognition that the Uniform Commercial Code itself implies that a contract provision allowing termination without cause is not per se unconscionable. See *Corenswet, Inc. v. Amana Refrigeration, Inc.,* 594

6. The agreement permitted immediate termination on the occurrence of certain conditions which are not involved in this case.

7. The comment has been criticized as useless and at best ambiguous (J. White & R. Summers, The Uniform Commercial Code, 116 [1972]), and § 2–302 has been characterized as devoid of any specific content. Leff, Unconscionability and the Code—(The Emperor's New Clause, 115 U.Pa.L.Rev. 485, 487–489 [1967]). On the other hand, it has been said that the strength of the unconscionability concept is its abstraction, permitting judicial creativity. See Ellinghaus, In Defense of Unconscionability, 78 Yale L.J. 757 (1969).

F.2d 129, 138 (5th Cir.1979) ("We seriously doubt, however, that public policy frowns on any and all contract clauses permitting termination without cause."); *Division of Triple T Serv., Inc. v. Mobil Oil Corp.*, 60 Misc.2d 720, 730, 304 N.Y.S.2d 191 (1969), aff'd 34 A.D.2d 618, 311 N.Y.S.2d 961 (N.Y. 1970). Section 2–309(3) provides that "[t]ermination of a contract by one party except on the happening of an agreed event requires that reasonable notification be received by the other party and an agreement dispensing with notification is invalid if its operation would be unconscionable." G.L. c. 106, § 2–309, as appearing in St.1957, c. 765, § 1. This language implies that termination of a sales contract without agreed "cause" is authorized by the Code, provided reasonable notice is given. * * * There is no suggestion that the ninety days' notice provided in the Dairy Mart franchise agreement was unreasonable.

We find no potential for unfair surprise to the Zapathas in the provision allowing termination without cause. We view the question of unfair surprise as focused on the circumstances under which the agreement was entered into.[8] The termination provision was neither obscurely worded, nor buried in fine print in the contract. Contrast Williams v. Walker-Thomas Furniture Co., 350 F.2d 445, 449 (D.C.Cir.1965). The provision was specifically pointed out to Mr. Zapatha before it was signed; Mr. Zapatha testified that he thought the provision was "straightforward," and he declined the opportunity to take the agreement to a lawyer for advice. The Zapathas had ample opportunity to consider the agreement before they signed it. Significantly, the subject of loss of employment was paramount in Mr. Zapatha's mind. He testified that he had held responsible jobs in one company from 1952 to 1973, that he had lost his employment, and that he "was looking for something that had a certain amount of security; something that was stable and something I could call my own." We conclude that a person of Mr. Zapatha's business experience and education should not have been surprised by the termination provision and, if in fact he was, there was no element of unfairness in the inclusion of that provision in the agreement. * * *

We further conclude that there was no oppression in the inclusion of a termination clause in the franchise agreement. We view the question of oppression as directed to the substantive fairness to the parties of permitting the termination provisions to operate as written. The Zapathas took over a going business on premises provided by Dairy Mart, using equipment furnished by Dairy Mart. As an investment, the Zapathas had only to purchase the inventory of goods to be sold but, as Dairy Mart concedes, on termination by it without cause Dairy Mart was obliged to repurchase all the Zapathas' saleable merchandise inventory, including items not purchased from Dairy Mart, at 80% of its retail value. There was no potential for forfeiture or loss of investment. There is no question here of a need for a reasonable time to

8. As we shall note subsequently, the concept of oppression deals with the substantive unfairness of the contract term. This two-part test for unconscionability involves determining whether there was "an absence of meaningful choice on the part of one of the parties, together with contract terms which are unreasonably favorable to the other party." *Williams v. Walker-Thomas Furniture Co.*, 350 F.2d 445, 449 (D.C.Cir.1965). See *Corenswet, Inc. v. Amana Refrigeration, Inc.*, 594 F.2d 129, 139 (5th Cir.1979). The inquiry involves a search for components of "procedural" and "substantive" unconscionability. See generally Leff, Unconscionability and the Code—The Emperor's New Clause, 115 Pa.L.Rev. 485 (1967). * * *

recoup the franchisees' initial investment. See * * * Gellhorn, Limitations on Contract Termination Rights—Franchise Cancellations, 1967 Duke L.J. 465, 479–481. The Zapathas were entitled to their net profits through the entire term of the agreement. They failed to sustain their burden of showing that the agreement allocated the risks and benefits connected with termination in an unreasonably disproportionate way and that the termination provision was not reasonably related to legitimate commercial needs of Dairy Mart. * * * To find the termination clause oppressive merely because it did not require cause for termination would be to establish an unwarranted barrier to the use of termination at will clauses in contracts in this Commonwealth, where each party received the anticipated and bargained for consideration during the full term of the agreement.

3. We see no basis on the record for concluding that Dairy Mart did not act in good faith, as that term is defined in the sales article ("honesty in fact and the observance of reasonable commercial standards of fair dealing in the trade"). G.L. c. 106, § 2–103(1)(b). There was no evidence that Dairy Mart failed to observe reasonable commercial standards of fair dealing in the trade in terminating the agreement. If there were such standards, there was no evidence of what they were.

The question then is whether there was evidence warranting a finding that Dairy Mart was not honest "in fact." The judge concluded that the absence of any commercial purpose for the termination other than the Zapathas' refusal to sign a new franchise agreement violated Dairy Mart's obligation of good faith. Dairy Mart's right to terminate was clear, and it exercised that right for a reason it openly disclosed. The sole test of "honesty in fact" is whether the person was honest. * * * We think that, whether or not termination according to the terms of the franchise agreement may have been arbitrary, it was not dishonest.[9]

The judge concluded that bad faith was also manifested by Dairy Mart's introductory brochure, which made representations of "security, comfort, and independence." Although this brochure and Mr. Zapatha's mistaken understanding that Dairy Mart could terminate the agreement only for cause could not be relied on to vary the clear terms of the agreement, the introductory brochure is relevant to the question of good faith. However, although the brochure misstated a franchisee's status as the owner of his own business, it shows no lack of honesty in fact relating to the right of Dairy Mart to terminate the agreement. Furthermore, by the time the Zapathas executed the second agreement, and even the first agreement, they knew that they would operate the franchise, but that they would not own the assets used in the business (except the goods to be sold); that the franchise agreement could be terminated by them and, at least in some circumstances, by Dairy Mart; and that in fact the major investment of funds would be made by Dairy Mart. We conclude that the use of the brochure did not warrant a finding of an absence of "honesty in fact." See

9. Under G.L. c. 106, § 1–203, "[e]very contract * * * imposes an obligation of good faith *in its performance or enforcement*" (emphasis supplied). We shall assume that an act of termination falls within the "performance" of the agreement. See Baker v. Ratzlaff, 1 Kan.App.2d 285, 288, 564 P.2d 153 (1977). But see Summers, "Good Faith" in General Contract Law and the Sales Provisions of the Uniform Commercial Code, 54 Va.L.Rev. 195, 252 (1968).

Corenswet, Inc. v. Amana Refrigeration, Inc., 594 F.2d 129, 138 (5th Cir.1979); *Mason v. Farmers Ins. Cos.*, 281 N.W.2d 344, 347 (Minn.1979).[10]

4. Although what we have said disposes of arguments based on application by analogy of provisions of the sales article of the Uniform Commercial Code, there remains the question whether the judge's conclusions may be supported by some general principle of law. The provisions of the Uniform Commercial Code with which we have dealt by analogy in this opinion may not have sufficient breadth to provide protection from conduct that has produced an unfair and burdensome result, contrary to the spirit of the bargain, against which the law reasonably should provide protection. See Restatement (Second) of Contracts § 231 (Tent.Drafts Nos. 1–7 1973); Corbin, Contracts § 654A (C.K. Kaufman 1980 Supp.).[11]

The law of the Commonwealth recognizes that under some circumstances a party to a contract is not free to terminate it according to its terms. In *Fortune v. National Cash Register Co.*, 373 Mass. 96, 104–105, 364 N.E.2d 1251 (1977), we held that where an employer terminated an at will employment contract in order to deprive its employee of a portion of a commission due to him, the employer acted in bad faith. There, the employer correctly argued that termination of the employee was expressly permitted by the contract, and that all amounts payable under the terms of the contract at the time of termination had been paid. We concluded, however, that the law imposed an obligation of good faith on the employer and that the employer violated that obligation in terminating the relationship in order to avoid the payment of amounts earned, but not yet payable. The Legislature has limited the right of certain franchisors to terminate franchise agreements without cause.[12] On the other hand, the Legislature

10. It has been suggested that, despite the limited definition of good faith in the Code, in some contexts the general obligation of good faith in § 1–203 can be used to import an objective standard of "decency, fairness or reasonableness in performance or enforcement" into a contract to which it applies. Farnsworth, Good Faith Performance and Commercial Reasonableness Under the Uniform Commercial Code, 30 U.Chi. L.Rev. 666, 668 (1963). Good faith in this sense can be regarded as an "excluder," barring varied forms of unreasonable conduct in different circumstances. See Summers, "Good Faith" in General Contract Law and the Sales Provisions of the Uniform Commercial Code, 54 Va.L.Rev. 195, 196 (1968). Rather than stretch the Code definition of good faith beyond the plain meaning of the words used to define good faith, we prefer, as we are about to do, to analyze the question of fairness and reasonableness independently of the Code.

11. The unconscionability provision of G.L. c. 106, § 2–302, concerns circumstances determined at the time of the making of the agreement and relates only to the unconscionability of a term or terms of the contract. The "good faith" obligation of G.L. c. 106, § 1–203, deals with "honesty in fact," a question of the state of mind of the merchant or of his adherence to whatever reasonable commercial standards there may be in his trade. A merchant's conduct might not be dishonest and might adhere to reasonable standards, if any, in his trade and thus might be in good faith under § 1–203, and yet be unfair and unreasonably burdensome.

12. See G.L. c. 93B, § 4(3)(e), (4) concerning the cancellation or nonrenewal of a motor vehicle dealer's franchise and requiring good cause for manufacturer's or distributor's action; G.L. c. 93E, §§ 5, 5A, requiring cause for a supplier's termination or nonrenewal of a gasoline station dealer's agreement and imposing an obligation on the supplier to repurchase merchantable products sold to the dealer.

New Jersey has a Franchise Practices Act of general applicability that "prohibits a franchisor from terminating, cancelling or failing to renew a franchise without good cause which is defined as the failure by the franchisee to substantially comply with the requirements imposed on him by the franchise. N.J.S.A. 56:10–5." *Shell Oil Co. v. Marinello*, 63 N.J. 402, 409, 307 A.2d 598, 602 (1973), cert. denied, 415 U.S. 920, 94 S.Ct. 1421, 39 L.Ed.2d 475 (1974). Although the act applied only prospectively (N.J.S.A.

has not adopted limitations on the right to terminate all franchise agreements in general, and its failure to do so is understandable because of the varied nature of franchise arrangements, where such varying factors exist as the relative bargaining power of the parties, the extent of investment by franchisees, and the degree to which the franchisee's goodwill, as opposed to that of the franchisor, is involved in the business operation. Further, in recognition of a general duty of good faith and fair dealing in business transactions under the law of the Commonwealth, c. 93A of the General Laws imposes on any person who engages in the conduct of any trade or commerce an obligation not to use any "unfair or deceptive acts or practices," as defined in G.L. c. 93A, § 2(a), as appearing in St.1967, c. 813, § 1, in dealing with another person who engages in any trade or commerce. G.L. c. 93A, § 11, as amended through St.1979, c. 72, § 2.

We thus analyze the case before us in terms of whether in terminating the agreement Dairy Mart failed to act in good faith in a broader sense than the term is used in G.L. c. 106, § 1–203, or dealt unfairly with the Zapathas, and whether Dairy Mart engaged in any unfair or deceptive act or practice. Much of what we said in discussing unconscionability and bad faith in terms of the Uniform Commercial Code applies here and need not be repeated. There is no showing that Dairy Mart usurped funds to which the Zapathas were reasonably entitled. Certainly Dairy Mart did not deprive the Zapathas of income that they had fairly earned, as the employer attempted to do in the *Fortune* case. We know nothing of any goodwill that the Zapathas had developed in their own name. There was no showing that, by their special efforts, the Zapathas built up the business at the Springfield store. As far as the record shows, they would lose no financial investment on termination and would not be left with unsaleable inventory or special purpose supplies and equipment. * * *

We are most concerned, as was the judge below, with the introductory circular that Dairy Mart furnished Mr. Zapatha. The judge ruled that the introductory circular contained misleading information concerning the Zapathas' status as franchisees. However, we cannot find in that document any deception or unfairness that has a bearing on the right of Dairy Mart to terminate the agreement as it did. A representative read the termination clause to Mr. Zapatha before the Zapathas signed the agreement. Mr. Zapatha declined an invitation to take the agreement to a lawyer. He understood individually every word of the termination clause. Moreover, when Dairy Mart terminated the agreement, it offered to negotiate further, and the Zapathas did not take the opportunity to do so.

Unless we were to take the position that termination without cause of a franchise agreement of the character involved here is prohibited invariably by the law of the Commonwealth, a position we decline to adopt * * *, Dairy

56:10–8), in the *Marinello* case the New Jersey Supreme Court applied the expressed public policy to bar termination of a service station operator's franchise in the absence of good cause, as so defined.

The special status of service station operators has prompted some courts to adopt common law rules requiring good cause for termination in spite of contract language that seemed to allow termination without cause. See *Arnott v. American Oil Co.*, 609 F.2d 873, 880–884 (8th Cir.1979), cert. denied, ___ U.S. ___, 100 S.Ct. 1852, 64 L.Ed.2d 272; *Atlantic Richfield Co. v. Razumic,* 480 Pa. 366, 390 A.2d 736 (1978); *Ashland Oil, Inc. v. Donahue,* 223 S.E.2d 433 (W.Va.1976).

Mart lawfully terminated the agreement because there was no showing that in terminating it Dairy Mart engaged in any unfair, deceptive, or bad faith conduct.

Judgments reversed.

[Some footnotes omitted. Those retained have been renumbered. Eds.]

SUMMERS, "GOOD FAITH" IN GENERAL CONTRACT LAW AND THE SALES PROVISIONS OF THE UNIFORM COMMERCIAL CODE, 54 Va.L.Rev. 195, 199–202 (1968).

What is the best way to determine a judge's meaning when he uses the phrase "good faith"? In the case law taken as a whole, does the term have a single general meaning of its own, or perhaps several such meanings? (The answers to these questions are closely linked.) Sometimes what a judge means by good faith will be instantly obvious, but frequently it will not be. When not, it may be that he is using the phrase loosely. But even if he is using it with care, there may still be unclarity. He might indicate only that, in a given context, parties are to act in good faith or that a party did or did not act in good faith, without elaborating at all. Or he might elaborate without communicating in any specific way—for example, by laying down some very general definition of good faith, such as acting "honestly" or "being faithful to one's duty or obligation." The analyst of such an opinion is likely to inquire: What is the meaning of good faith itself? He seems to assume that the phrase has some general meaning or meanings, one of which the judge presumably intends.

One of the principal theses of this Article is that in cases of doubt, a lawyer will determine more accurately what the judge means by using the phrase "good faith" if he does not ask what good faith itself means, but rather asks: What, in the actual or hypothetical situation, does the judge intend to rule out by his use of this phrase? Once the relevant form of bad faith is thus identified, the lawyer can, if he wishes, assign a specific meaning to good faith by formulating an "opposite" for the species of bad faith being ruled out. For example, a judge may say: "A public authority must act in good faith in letting bids." And from the facts or the language of the opinion it may appear that the judge is, in effect, saying: "The defendant acted in bad faith because he let bids only as a pretense to conceal his purpose to award the contract to a favored bidder." It can then be said that "acting in good faith" here simply means: letting bids without a preconceived design to award the contract to a favored bidder.

If good faith had a general meaning or meanings of its own—that is, if it were either univocal or ambiguous—there would seldom be occasion to derive a meaning for it from an opposite; its specific uses would almost always be readily and immediately understood. But good faith is not that kind of doctrine. In contract law, taken as a whole, good faith is an "excluder." It is a phrase without general meaning (or meanings) of its own and serves to exclude a wide range of heterogeneous forms of bad faith. In a particular context the phrase takes on specific meaning, but usually this is only by way of contrast with the specific form of bad faith actually or hypothetically ruled out. Aristotle was one of the first to recognize that the function of some words and phrases is not to convey general, "extractable" meanings of their own, but rather is to exclude one or more of a variety of things. He thought "voluntary" was such a word. And the late Professor J.L. Austin of Oxford made much of "excluders."

Note: Good Faith in the Uniform Commercial Code

In the 1990 Official Text of Article 1, UCC 1–203 generally provides that "[e]very contract or duty within this Act imposes an obligation of good faith in its performance or enforcement" and UCC 1–201(19) provides, unless the context otherwise requires, that good faith "means honesty in fact in the conduct or transaction concerned." In the 1990 Official Text of Article 2, UCC 2–103(1)(b) states that "unless the context otherwise requires * * * good faith, in the case of a merchant, means honesty in fact and the observance of reasonable commercial standards of fair dealing in the trade." There are no changes in these provisions from the previous Official Texts.

Other Articles of the 1990 Official Text, however, reveal a tendency to expand the content if not the scope of the good faith duty. For example, Article 2A, in UCC 2A–103(3), adopts for leases of goods the Article 2 definition of good faith, with its distinction between merchants and non-merchants. UCC 2A–103(3) also adopts Article 2's definition of merchant, and since most commercial lessors will be merchants, the so-called objective test of good faith will dominate.

More importantly, Article 3, in UCC 3–103(a)(4), provides that good faith means "honesty in fact and the observance of reasonable commercial standards of fair dealing." This definition applies to merchant and non-merchant alike and focuses on the "fairness of conduct" rather than the lack of ordinary care or "reasonable commercial standards of fair dealing in the trade." Compare UCC 2–103(1)(b). The Article 3 definition of good faith is incorporated into Article 4, UCC 4–104(b), and replicated in Article 4A, UCC 4A–105(6).

Questions about good faith for the revision of Article 2 include: (1) Should the duty of good faith be imposed upon pre-contract relationships as well as upon performance and enforcement of the contract? (2) Should the objective definition of good faith be revised to conform with that in Article 3? (3) Should the objective definition apply to all sellers and buyers, not just merchants? Keep these question in mind as we work through Article 2.

For an excellent analysis of the good faith and unconscionability issues in *Zapatha* and similar cases and much, much more, see Rau, *Implied Obligations in Franchising: Beyond Terminations,* 47 Bus.Law. 1053 (1992). For a more cosmic view of good faith in contract performance, see Burton & Andersen, *The World of Contract,* 75 Ia.L.Rev. 861 (1990).

Problem 9–4

(1) Frank is a book wholesaler in New York City, John a book retailer in a University town where a great law school exists. John has a lot of used copies of a great commercial law casebook about to be superseded by a fourth edition, a fact known to John but not to Frank. John sells a large number of the books to Frank without disclosing the foregoing fact. Later, Frank discovers the fact and seeks to rescind. What result? Assume John's non-disclosure does not constitute "fraud" under tort law. Assume, too, that John has broken no warranty. See UCC 1–203 and 1–201(19). Does UCC 1–203 apply? Is this the only relevant

provision? Among other things, what of UCC 1–103? To make effective use of UCC 1–103, what kind of extra-Code case law would you hope to find?

(2) For three years, Ice, Inc., a small ice manufacturer, has been selling roughly 25 tons of ice a month to the Sam McGee Storage, Co., pursuant to a contract one clause of which empowers McGee to order "such ice as it requires." On January 20, McGee, having decided to expand its operations, ordered three hundred tons of ice from Ice, Inc. for February. Ice, Inc., of course, could not supply this amount, and so notified McGee. McGee then declared itself "free to buy all our needs from Prime, Inc., a manufacturer more our size." Ice, Inc. has come to you for advice. What would you advise? Among other things, see UCC 1–203, 1–201(19), 2–306, 2–103(1)(b) and 2–311(1).

(3) Rowan brokered custom-made (new and old) cars, a very special market. Martin, his best customer, wanted a special car for which he was willing to pay dearly $15,000 provided he could get it in time to drive it in the Grand Nationale. Tucker, an always-do-well "consumer" known to Rowan, had such a car which he agreed to sell Rowan for $13,000. Later and just before the Grand Nationale, Tucker, having learned of Rowan's resale price to Martin, insisted that Rowan pay $14,500 "or the deal is off." Rowan finally agreed, got the car, resold it to Martin for $15,000 and then came to you for advice. Does he have any recourse against Tucker? Among other things, see UCC 2–209(1) and relevant comments, 1–203, 1–201(19).

(4) Milk-O-Wheat, Inc. wanted to buy some grain. It had never dealt with seller before, but nonetheless placed a binding order with seller for 100 tons of wheat "delivery no later than August 2, our terminal." One hundred tons of good wheat arrived but not until August 4, due to an unexpected railway disaster. The delay did not slow up Milk-O-Wheat's operations any, but it rejected anyway, since the market had fallen and it was possible to get such wheat much more cheaply elsewhere. You are to assume that in the trade, prompt deliveries are expected, for usually the buyer is relying on such for the efficient conduct of his operations. Seller comes to you for advice. What would you advise? Among other things, see UCC 2–601, 2–508, 2–504, 1–203, 1–201(19), and 2–103(1)(b).

SECTION 5. SUPPLEMENTAL GENERAL PRINCIPLES

Section 1–103 of the Uniform Commercial Code provides:

> Unless displaced by the particular provisions of this Act, the principles of law and equity, including the law merchant and the law relative to capacity to contract, principal and agent, estoppel, fraud, misrepresentation, duress, coercion, mistake, bankruptcy, or other validating or invalidating cause shall supplement its provisions.

Equitable principles (not displaced) generally remain intact under the foregoing provision, *even in the face of contrary contractual provisions.* Thus, the parties cannot contract out of the bearing of most equitable notions having to do with estoppel, fraud, misrepresentation, duress, coercion, mistake and the like. See, generally, Summers, *General Equitable Principles Under Section 1–103 of the Uniform Commercial Code,* 72 Nw.U.L.Rev. 906 (1978).

Problem 9–5

(1) Section 2–509(3) of Article Two provides: "In any case not within subsection (1) or (2), the risk of loss passes to the buyer on his receipt of the goods

if the seller is a merchant, otherwise the risk passes to the buyer on tender of delivery". Assume the buyer hires the seller to build a boat mast. After the mast is under way, it occurs to the seller that the work should be insured. The buyer represents that insurance he already has covers the work, and, relying on this the seller does not insure. After completion but before delivery, the mast is destroyed by fire and the buyer discovers that his policy does not cover the mast. The seller sues the buyer for the price under section 2–709. The buyer defends by citing section 2–509(3) under which the risk of loss was on the seller, and denies liability. What result? Assume the preamble to the contract between buyer and seller recites that their agreement is the sole controlling law governing the rights of the parties. Would this affect the result? Cf. Mercanti v. Persson, 160 Conn. 468, 280 A.2d 137 (1971).

(2) Seller was in the business of selling lumber to various parties, including Buyer. Buyer knew Seller was operating "close to the margin". Buyer stopped payment of checks issued to pay for the lumber sold and delivered to Buyer and offered to pay only a sum $2000 less than that due under the contract "in full settlement." Seller told Buyer that if Seller failed to get the money, "he would be ruined financially." Buyer told Seller that he, Buyer, had "taken steps to stop payment of money due Seller from other parties too". Seller then agreed to the settlement at $2000 less. Is the settlement valid? Would it make any difference if the settlement recited that the agreement was in all respects a valid and binding contract? Cf. Vine v. Glenn, 41 Mich. 112, 1 N.W. 997 (1879).

PART TWO

THE AGREEMENT STAGE

CHAPTER TEN

CONTRACT FORMATION

SECTION 1. INTRODUCTION

A classic function of courts and contract law is to determine when parties negotiating for an agreed exchange have concluded an enforceable bargain. At what point have they crossed the line beyond which neither party can withdraw without liability for breach?

Under the Restatement, Second, of Contracts, the answer depends upon concepts with which you should now be familiar. First, contract is defined as a "promise or a set of promises for the breach of which the law gives a remedy. * * * " Section 1. Not all promises, however, are contracts. In bargain transactions, defined in Section 3 of the Restatement, Second as an agreed exchange of promises or performances, there must be a "bargain in which there is a manifestation of mutual assent to the exchange and a consideration." Section 17(1). According to Section 22(1), the manifestation of mutual assent to an exchange "ordinarily takes the form of an offer or proposal by one party followed by an acceptance by the other party or parties. * * *" (An offer is defined as a "manifestation of willingness to enter into a bargain, so made as to justify another person in understanding that his assent to that bargain is invited and will conclude it." Section 24. An acceptance of an offer is defined as a "manifestation of assent to the terms thereof made by the offeree in a manner invited or required by the offer." Section 50(1).)

To constitute consideration, "a performance or a return promise must be bargained for," Section 71(1), i.e., "sought by the promisor in exchange for his promise and * * * given by the promisee in exchange for that promise." Section 71(2).

How does Article 2 conform to the Restatement, Second formula, "Offer plus acceptance plus consideration = contract?"

First, contract "means the total legal obligation which results from the parties' agreement as affected by this Act and any other applicable rules of law." UCC 1–201(11). In contract formation disputes, the relevant provisions of "this Act" are found in Article 2, Part 2, as supplemented by UCC 1–103.

Second, agreement means the "bargain of the parties in fact as found in their language or by implication from other circumstances including course of dealing or usage of trade or course of performance as provided in this Act (Sections 1–205 and 2–208)." Note that the definition of "bargain * * * in fact" does not include a requirement that there be a promise. Further, although the concept of bargain is consistent with an agreed exchange, there is no explicit requirement that the exchange be bargained for. In short, although the agreement may contain promises and the exchange may be bargained for, there is no explicit requirement of either a promise or consideration to satisfy the definition. See Murray, *The Article 2 Prism: The Underlying Philosophy of the Uniform Commercial Code,* 21 Washburn L.J. 1 (1981).

Third, UCC 2–204 is the key formation section in Article 2, Part 2. Read it, please. Note that UCC 2–204(1) and (2) sweep away technical rules on how and when the contract is made: Important evidence will be "conduct by both parties which recognizes the existence of such a contract." Further, UCC 2–204(3) provides a standard to deal with disputes where one party withdraws before all of the material terms have been agreed: "Even though one or more terms are left open a contract for sale does not fail for indefiniteness if the parties have intended to make a contract and there is a reasonably certain basis for giving an appropriate remedy." Thus, there are no rules specifying the quantity of agreement that must be reached before a contract can be formed. Rather, the issue turns on what the parties have "intended" and whether the court can fill the "gaps" with reasonable certainty when giving an appropriate remedy. By "intended," UCC 2–204(3) presumably means an intention to conclude the bargain without further agreement, rather than an intention that the bargain be legally binding. Compare Restatement, Second 21 ("neither real nor apparent intention that a promise be legally binding is essential to the formation of a contract. * * * ").

Read Article 2, Part 2, including the Comments and then work through the following materials.

SECTION 2. OFFER AND ACCEPTANCE—UCC 2–204, 2–205 AND 2–206

In the following problems, first formulate the statutory issues posed and then resolve them as best you can from the Code.

Problem 10–1

S, a retailer, sold personal computers manufactured by M. After preliminary negotiations, B, a corporation, mailed to S a printed form prepared by B inviting S to make an "offer" to sell 10 described personal computers for $25,000. The form contained five paragraphs of printed matter, inserted on a single page between blank lines to be filled in at the top and a signature line at the bottom. The third paragraph above the signature line provided: THIS OFFER WILL BE HELD OPEN FOR 30 DAYS AFTER RECEIPT BY THE OFFEREE. S filled in the blanks as requested by B, signed the form, dating it May 30, 1987, and returned it to B, who received it on June 3, 1987. On June 15, 1987, S notified B by telegram that the offer was revoked: A better deal had been worked out with C for the personal computers. On June 16, 1987, B telegraphed to S an acceptance of the offer, which was received the same day. B insists that there was a contract. Is B correct? Start with UCC 2–205.

Problem 10–2

S, a manufacturer, had a quantity of used computer hardware which it was willing to sell with a limited warranty for $50,000. On June 1, B, a retailer, examined the equipment and discussed terms. An oral agreement was reached on all terms except price. On June 5, B mailed S a signed offer to purchase the equipment for $40,000 and enclosed a $4,000 check as a down payment. S received the offer and check on June 7 and, on June 8, deposited the check in its business account. S did not communicate with B. On June 10, S received an offer from C to purchase the equipment for $50,000 cash. The offer was accepted the same day. On June 11, S informed B that its offer had been rejected and mailed to B a cashier's check for $4,000.

B claims that a contract was formed on June 8 when S deposited the check. B supports its claim with the following arguments: (1) The offer should be construed as inviting an acceptance "in any manner and by any medium reasonable in the circumstances," and depositing the check was a reasonable manner of acceptance, UCC 2–206(1)(a); (2) Depositing the check was a "reasonable mode of acceptance" under UCC 2–206(2); and (3) The sending by B and the deposit by S of the check was "conduct by both parties which recognizes the existence of a contract," UCC 2–204(1), or demonstrated that the "parties have intended to make a contract" under UCC 2–204(3).

Which, if any, of these arguments should the court accept?

Problem 10–3

S, a manufacturer of fertilizer, and B, a farmer, had done business for 10 years. When fertilizer was needed, B would order by telegram a specific quantity and quality and S would fill the order at S's current wholesale price, shipping the goods to B by carrier FOB point of shipment. Frequently, S would ship less or more than what B ordered, but the deviation would never exceed 15%. B invariably accepted and paid for what was actually shipped without objection. On July 10, 1987, a time of price instability in the fertilizer market, B telegraphed to S an order for 500 bags of a specified fertilizer "for prompt shipment." The wholesale price on that date was $18 per bag. On July 12, 1987, S shipped 400 bags of fertilizer to B and mailed an invoice for the wholesale price on that date, $20.00. On July 15, 1987, while the goods were still in transit and the wholesale price was $25.00 per bag, S notified B that the offer had been rejected and diverted the shipment to C, who agreed to pay $26 per bag.

B claimed that there was a contract for the sale of 500 bags of fertilizer on July 12, 1987 at $20.00. B relied upon UCC 2–206(1)(b), asserting that this was precisely the case contemplated in Comment 4. Is B correct?

MID–SOUTH PACKERS v. SHONEY'S, INC.

United States Court of Appeals, Fifth Circuit, 1985.
761 F.2d 1117.

Before WILLIAMS, JOLLY, and HILL, CIRCUIT JUDGES.

PER CURIAM:

This diversity action on a Mississippi contract is before us following the district court's entry of summary judgment in favor of plaintiff Mid-South

Packers, Inc., (Mid-South) and against defendant Shoney's, Inc., (Shoney's). We affirm.

I.

The facts, as viewed in the light most favorable to Shoney's, are as follows. In the spring of 1982, Mid-South and Shoney's engaged in negotiations for the sale by Mid-South to Shoney's of various pork products including bacon and ham. A business meeting was held between representatives of the two companies on April 17, 1982, at the offices of Mid-South in Tupelo, Mississippi. The discussion concerned prices and terms at which Mid-South could supply bacon and ham to Shoney's. At this meeting, Mid-South submitted a letter styled "Proposal" that set forth prices and terms at which Mid-South would supply Shoney's with various types of meat. The letter also provided that Shoney's would be informed forty-five days prior to any adjustment in price. The letter contained neither quantity nor durational terms. Shoney's expressed neither assent to nor rejection of the prices outlined in the letter. Shoney's estimated its needs from Mid-South at 80,000 pounds of meat per week. The legal effect of the letter proposal is the center of the controversy.

In July 1982, Shoney's began purchasing goods from Mid-South. The transactions were initiated by Shoney's, either through purchase orders or through telephone calls. On the day following each shipment, Mid-South sent invoices to Shoney's containing additional provisions for payment of both fifteen percent per annum interest on accounts not paid within seven days and reasonable collection costs, including attorney's fees. Shoney's bought vast quantities of bacon from Mid-South until August 12, 1982. On that date, Mid-South informed Shoney's at a meeting of their representatives that the price for future orders of bacon would be raised by $0.10 per pound, due to a previous error in computation by Mid-South. Shoney's objected to the price modification, apparently in reliance on the forty-five day notice provision contained in the disputed letter proposal. After negotiations, Mid-South agreed to increase the price by only $0.07 per pound. Shoney's neither agreed nor refused to purchase at the new price. Mid-South's new proposal was never reduced to writing.

On the first Shoney's purchase order sent after the August 12 meeting, Shoney's requested shipment at the old lower price. When Mid-South received the purchase order its representative, Morris Ates, called Shoney's representative, Ray Harmon, and advised Harmon that Mid-South would only deliver at the new higher price. The uncontradicted testimony of Ates is that Harmon told Ates to ship the bacon and to note the higher price on Shoney's purchase order. The bacon was shipped, and an invoice at the new price followed as did Shoney's payment, also at the new price.

From August 18 until October 5, 1982, Shoney's placed numerous orders for goods, including bacon, with Mid-South. Some if not all of these orders involved telephone conversations between representatives of the two companies, at which time Mid-South again quoted its increased selling price. The telephone conversations were followed by written purchase orders from Shoney's which quoted both the new price from Mid-South and a price computed at the original amount of $0.07 less per pound. In all cases, the orders were filled by Mid-South and invoiced at the new price. These invoices also included the additional terms providing for interest on delinquent accounts and reasonable collection costs. Shoney's paid Mid-South's quoted prices in all instances except the final order. On the final order before Shoney's began purchasing from another supplier, Shoney's offset the amount due on the invoice by $26,208, the amount allegedly overcharged on prior orders as a result of the $0.07 price increase.

Mid-South then brought this action to recover the amount offset plus interest and reasonable collection costs, including attorney's fees, as provided in the invoices. Shoney's admits that it owes $8,064.00 of the offset to Mid-South, inasmuch as this amount is attributable to orders placed after the expiration of the forty-five day notice period which, Shoney's contends, commenced on August 12 when Mid-South asked for the price increase.

II.

Shoney's contends that it accepted the proposal of Mid-South to supply it meat by placing orders with Mid-South, thereby forming a binding contract between the parties. Shoney's characterizes the contract as a "requirements contract" and asserts that the quantity term under the contract was that amount it reasonably and in good faith required. Accordingly, Shoney's argues that the notice provision contained in the letter proposal contractually bound Mid-South to notify Shoney's forty-five days before increasing its prices.

Mid-South asserts that the proposal was at most a "firm offer." Mid-South argues that under Miss.Code Ann. § 75–2–205 (1972), Uniform Commercial Code § 2–205, (hereinafter referred to as U.C.C. or the Code), a firm offer is irrevocable despite a lack of consideration "during the time stated or if no time is stated for a reasonable time; but in no event may such period of irrevocability exceed three (3) months." Thus, Mid-South contends that under any construction of the document, the offer must have expired three months after April 17, 1982, the date of the letter proposal, or on approximately July 17, 1982; therefore, it asserts the right on August 12, 1982, to increase the selling price without notice.

The district court, on consideration of cross summary judgment motions, adopted Mid-South's theory, holding that no long-term requirements contract was created and that each purchase order constituted a separate contract for the amount stated at the price required by Mid-South.

Requirements contracts are recognized in Mississippi and are not void for indefiniteness. Miss.Code Ann. § 75–2–306(1). However, an essential element of a requirements contract is the promise of the buyer to purchase exclusively from the seller either the buyer's entire requirements or up to a specified amount. * * * Absent such a commitment, the requirements contract fails for want of consideration. * * *

Ray Harmon, Shoney's agent in the transaction, maintained that Shoney's at all times had the right to purchase goods from suppliers other than Mid-South, that Shoney's continued to purchase from Mid-South because it was satisfied with its service and the quality of its goods, and that the purchase orders sent by Shoney's to Mid-South beginning in July 1982 "would have been the only commitment (Shoney's) would have made." Mid-South agrees that Shoney's had the right to change suppliers. Thus, by

Shoney's own admission, no requirements contract could have arisen from the April 17 letter proposal and the meeting at which it was discussed.

Under the Code, the letter proposal and surrounding negotiations constituted, at most, a "firm offer" which was irrevocable, without consideration, only for a period of three months commencing on April 17 and ending on July 17, 1982. Miss.Code Ann. § 75–2–205.[2] Thus, Mid-South had the right, after July 17, to raise its offered price as it did and the district court was correct in so holding.

The district court was also correct in holding that each purchase order stood on its own as a contract between Shoney's and Mid-South. More specifically, Mid-South's letter proposal was its offer in the sense that it was a promise to sell at the listed prices, justifying Shoney's in understanding that its assent, *i.e.,* its purchase orders or telephone calls, would close the bargain. *Boese-Hilburn Co. v. Dean Machinery Co.,* 616 S.W.2d 520 (Mo.App. 1981); *Propane Industrial, Inc.,* 429 F.Supp. at 219; 1 A. Corbin, Contracts § 11 at 25 (1963); 1 S. Williston, Contracts § 24A (3d ed.1957); Restatement (Second) of Contracts § 24 (1981) (offer as promise). Thus, each time Shoney's manifested its assent, in telephone calls or purchase orders to Mid-South, a new and independent contract between the parties was created. *See Coastal Chemical Corporation v. Filtrol Corporation,* 374 F.2d 108, 109 (5th Cir.1967) (Mississippi law); 1A A. Corbin, Contracts § 157 at 40–46 (where the theory here espoused is discussed at length).

Mid-South's offer, held open in its discretion at least after July 17, was properly revoked and replaced by the offer of a seven-cent price increase at the August 12 meeting. *Cf.* 1A A. Corbin § 157 at 46. Shoney's accepted this new offer for the first time on August 18 when Harmon, having been informed by Ates that Mid-South would not sell except at the new price, ordered shipment. Thereafter, Shoney's created separate contracts and obligated itself to pay the new price each time it mailed purchase orders with that price noted on them.[3] Shoney's practice of also noting the old price on the purchase orders had no contractual significance since Harmon admitted that the practice was "a tracking procedure" used by Shoney's internally in order to determine the difference between the old price and the new. Ates' testimony is uncontradicted that Harmon also told him this.

In addition, Harmon admitted that Shoney's ordered at and paid the new price with the intention of causing Mid-South to believe that Shoney's had accepted the new price so that the shipments would continue; and Mid-South attached precisely that significance to Shoney's conduct. Shoney's secretly harbored intent to later deduct the difference between the old and new price could not bind Mid-South. *See, e.g., Hotchkiss v. National City Bank,* 200 Fed. 287, 293 (S.D.N.Y.1911) (Hand, J.), *aff'd* 231 U.S. 50, 34 S.Ct.

2. Section 75–2–205 provides, in part:

An offer by a merchant to buy or sell goods in a signed writing which by its terms gives assurance that it will be held open is not revocable, for lack of consideration, during the time stated or if no time is stated for a reasonable time, but in no event may such period of irrevocability exceed three (3) months.

3. The purchase orders also contained a column entitled "amount" which showed the total purchase price arrived at by multiplying the per unit price by the quantity ordered. On most of the post-August 12 purchase orders, Shoney's used the new higher price in computing the amount total.

20, 58 L.Ed. 115 (1913) (only manifested assent is binding); Restatement (Second) of Contracts §§ 20(2)(a), 201(2)(a) (1981) (same). Conduct may bind a party to a contract if it "show[s] agreement." Miss.Code Ann. § 75–2–204(1); § 75–2–207(3). "Agreement" of the parties must be manifested either in language or conduct in the circumstances. Miss.Code Ann. § 75–1–201(3). The only manifestations Shoney's made were those consistent with assent to Mid-South's new offer. Finally, the parties' "course of performance" is consistent only with Mid-South's expressed offer and Shoney's expressed acceptance of the new price. Miss.Code Ann. § 75–1–205(3)–(4); *Cf.* Miss.Code Ann. § 75–2–202(a).

Shoney's remedy under the circumstances was either to reserve whatever right it might have had to the old price by sending its purchase orders with an "explicit reservation," Miss.Code Ann. § 75–1–207, or to find a supplier who would sell at an acceptable price. No rational theory of the law of contracts could permit Shoney's to manifest acceptance of Mid-South's new offer, thus inducing performance, and then revoke that acceptance and demand compliance with the terms of the prior, withdrawn offer. *See* Miss.Code Ann. § 75–2–606(1)(b); § 75–2–607(1). Hence, the entire $26,208 offset by Shoney's is due and owing Mid-South and the district court's judgment, to this extent, was proper.

* * *

[The Court held that Mid-South's invoices containing additional provisions for payment and attorney fees were "confirmations" under UCC 2–207(1) and that the "additional" terms became part of the agreement under UCC 2–207(2).]

Affirmed. [Some footnotes omitted.]

Note: Conduct and Mutual Intent to Contract

When does conduct by both parties support a mutual intent to contract, even though material terms have not been agreed? The issue was raised with disputed results in a complex litigation between Bethlehem Steel Corporation and Litton Industries. After extensive negotiations, Litton agreed to construct a newly designed ore vessel for Bethlehem at a fixed price. Thereafter, the parties agreed in writing that Bethlehem should have an option, for a stated period of time, to have Litton construct up to five additional ore vessels of the same design at a stated base price of $20.4 million. If Bethlehem exercised an option, the base price was subject to escalation to be agreed by the parties for both labor and material costs under stated indices, with the escalation computed to the date a contract was executed. Despite Litton's initial requests, Bethlehem refused to exercise the option or to negotiate over price. After Litton closed its shipyard, however, Bethlehem sought to exercise the option for three additional vessels. Both parties negotiated over the escalated price but, despite apparent good faith efforts, were unable to agree. Bethlehem then sued Litton for $95,000,000 in damages, claiming that despite the failure to agree on price, the parties intended to contract for the three vessels, see UCC 2–204(3), and that the court should supply a reasonable, escalated price, see UCC 2–305(1).

The trial court treated the intention issue as a question of fact and concluded that, given the importance of the escalation clause to the contract, the complexity of the determinations involved, and the rapid inflation underway, the parties did not intend to contract unless an agreement could be reached on price. This decision was reversed, on appeal, by a three judge panel, Bethlehem Steel Corp. v. Litton Industries, Inc., 35 UCC Rep.Serv. 1091 (Pa.Super.1982). On rehearing, a panel of seven judges reversed the decision of the three judge panel and reinstated the decision of the trial court to the effect that there was no contract. 321 Pa.Super. 357, 468 A.2d 748 (1983). The "panel of seven's" decision was affirmed by an equally divided Supreme Court in Bethlehem Steel Corp. v. Litton Industries, Inc., 507 Pa. 88, 488 A.2d 581 (1985).

The supreme court justices voting to affirm the decision of the trial court stressed: (1) the writings of the parties were ambiguous and many terms were left open; (2) there was competent evidence to support the conclusion that the conduct of the parties was inconsistent with an intent to be bound; (3) there was no reasonably certain basis for giving an appropriate remedy; and (4) the "option" was not supported by consideration.

Justice Zappala, speaking for the justices voting to find a contract concluded, on the other hand, that Litton had acted in bad faith in negotiating over the escalation provision. Despite Bethlehem's willingness to consider a number of price indices, Litton, according to Justice Zappala, "did not intend to develop any language regarding a proposed ship construction contract" and "prevented execution of a ship construction contract by failing to bargain in good faith on the open terms." 488 A.2d at 600. On his view, this was a breach for which Bethlehem was entitled to damages.

SECTION 3. OFFER AND ACCEPTANCE—THE BATTLE OF THE FORMS AND UCC 2–207

Every student knows of the "mirror-image" rule of general contract law: An "acceptance" which varies the terms of an offer is not an acceptance at all, but a counter-offer. This is an old rule, and it makes some sense. But consider its application to the following hypothetical case: Seller sends a written offer to Buyer offering to sell processed rubber at a stated price. Buyer replies by ordering a quantity of rubber from Seller within the terms of Seller's offer, except that Buyer's order form states at the bottom in conspicuous type: "The acceptance of this order you must in any event promptly acknowledge." Seller fails promptly to acknowledge, but ships the rubber. When the rubber arrives, Buyer refuses it, having preferred to buy elsewhere, say because the price has fallen. Seller sues Buyer for breach of contract. Buyer defends claiming that because of his "acknowledgment clause" in his order form, this form was not an acceptance, but was a counter-offer which was never accepted since Seller did not acknowledge promptly. Held: for Buyer, citing the mirror-image rule. Cf. Poel v. Brunswick-Balke-Collender Co., 216 N.Y. 310, 110 N.E. 619 (1915).

There have been such decisions. And they can be traced to the influence of the mirror-image rule. If such decisions are objectionable, then they are peculiarly objectionable in the commercial field, for the scope for such decisions there is great. This is so because of the widespread and long-standing practice whereby many sellers and buyers of goods use their own standard forms in doing business: Seller sends an offer on a form containing printed terms; Buyer "accepts" using his own form with printed terms, or vice versa. Any reasonably close correspondence between the two sets of terms is, in many lines of business, sheerest coincidence. Yet, the parties nonetheless go forward with their transactions. When something goes wrong, in the unusual case, then is there a contract? If so, on what terms—Seller's? Buyer's? Courts applying the mirror-image rule, willy-nilly, might say there is no contract at all, and not even reach the second of these questions. Objections to this solution have been several, as some students once noted:

NOTE, 111 U.Pa.L.Rev. 132, 133 (1962).

"At common law and under the Uniform Sales Act, a purported acceptance which modifies the terms of the offer is a rejection and a counter-offer. Although this rule is supposed to promote certainty in the terms of the agreement, businessmen frequently undertake performance in reliance on the mistaken assumption that such an "acceptance" has created a contract. Moreover, in the context of modern business practice of using standard forms to transmit and acknowledge orders, the rule encourages a "battle of forms"—a constant effort by businessmen to gain an advantage in their transactions by qualifying their obligations by means of forms containing unilaterally beneficial conditions. In addition, the rule provides a loophole for parties wishing to extricate themselves from unfavorable deals which in commercial understanding have been closed." [Footnotes omitted.]

The Official Text of section 2–207 went through still more changes until it took its present form in the 1962 Official Text, which continues to be the form set forth below. (Revisions in the Official Comments were made in 1966.)

§ 2–207. Additional Terms in Acceptance or Confirmation

(1) A definite and seasonable expression of acceptance or a written confirmation which is sent within a reasonable time operates as an acceptance even though it states terms additional to or different from those offered or agreed upon, unless acceptance is expressly made conditional on assent to the additional or different terms.

(2) The additional terms are to be construed as proposals for addition to the contract. Between merchants such terms become part of the contract unless:

(a) the offer expressly limits acceptance to the terms of the offer;

(b) they materially alter it; or

(c) notification of objection to them has already been given or is given within a reasonable time after notice of them is received.

(3) Conduct by both parties which recognizes the existence of a contract is sufficient to establish a contract for sale although the writings of the parties do not otherwise establish a contract. In such case the terms of the particular contract consist of those terms on which the writings of the parties agree, together with any supplementary terms incorporated under any other provisions of this Act.

Problem 10–4

Review the final version of UCC 2–207. It contemplates contract formation by at least three routes. Route A consists of that part of subsection (1) up to the comma. Route B is that which appears after the comma in subsection (1).

Route C is found in UCC 2–207(3). Before going farther in this Chapter, answer the following questions.

1. May a contract be formed *via* Route B by conduct? If so, does Route B overlap with Route C?

2. To which of these routes does UCC 2–207(2) relate?

3. Which route is intended to change the "mirror image" rule?

4. Does any route purport, under some circumstances, to preserve the "mirror image" rule? What circumstances?

5. How would you state the general goals of UCC 2–207?

Problem 10–5

[The facts are taken from Roto–Lith, Ltd. v. F.P. Bartlett & Co., 297 F.2d 497 (1st Cir.1962).]

After negotiations, on October 23 Buyer sent Seller a written order to purchase a drum of "N–132–C" emulsion, stating "End use: wet pack spinach bags." All concede that this was an offer. On October 26, Seller sent Buyer an acknowledgment of the order and on October 27, shipped the goods. The acknowledgment, which arrived no later than the goods, was Seller's standard form for these transactions. On the front in conspicuous type, all warranties express or implied were disclaimed and the sale was made "subject to the terms on the reverse side." On the reverse side, conspicuous language stated that Buyer assumed the risk "for results obtained from use of these goods, whether used alone or in combination with other products." Also, Seller limited its liability to "replacement of any goods that materially differ from the Seller's sample order on the basis of which the order for such goods was made." Finally, language on the reverse provided that "If these terms are not acceptable, Buyer must so notify Seller at once."

Buyer accepted, used and paid for the emulsion without objection. Later, the spinach bags failed to hold, resulting in extensive consequential losses. Buyer claimed that the emulsion was not merchantable and sued Seller for direct and consequential damages. Buyer argued that there was a contract for sale but it did not include the terms in Seller's acknowledgment. Seller argued that a contract was formed when Buyer accepted the goods and that the contract contained the clauses in the acknowledgment form. Accordingly, Seller breached no warranty and, in any event, limited its liability to replacement of the goods.

What result under UCC 2–207. First use the "route" analysis in *Problem 10–4* and then compare your analysis with that of the court in the next case.

Note: Arbitration and UCC 2–207.

Arbitration clauses are frequently involved in "battle of the forms" disputes. When the underlying contract evidences a "transaction involving commerce" the Federal Arbitration Act, 9 U.S.C.A. §§ 1–16 applies. See Id. § 2. This was the case in Dorton v. Collins & Aikman Corp., 453 F.2d 1161 (6th Cir.1972), where Collins appealed the district court's refusal to stay the litigation pending arbitration under 9 U.S.C.A. § 3. The issue on appeal was whether Dorton had agreed to the arbitration clause contained on the reverse side of Collins acknowledgment form, and the court held yes unless the clause materially altered the contract. UCC 2–207(2)(b). The court remanded the case to the district court to make that determination.

The determination on remand is tricky. The United States Supreme Court, in interpreting Section 2 the Federal Arbitration Act, has held that state law on contract formation may not discriminate against or single out for different treatment a claimed federal right to arbitrate. Put differently, a state court, in interpreting UCC 2–207, must treat an arbitration clause in a standard form the same way that it would treat any other clause in a standard form. Thus, an interpretive rule that an arbitration clause was *per se* a material alteration or must be expressly assented to but which did not apply to, say, a disclaimer clause, would be highly suspect.

Accepting that as a matter of federal law there must be consistency in treatment under UCC 2–207, there is still some disagreement over what the test for "material alteration" should be. Should it be a quantitative test, a question of unfair surprise or some combination of both? Suppose, for example, that arbitration is regarded as a substantial deviation from the usual judicial remedies, but because of an extended course of dealing between the parties, one party knows or has reason to know that an arbitration clause will be included in the other's standard form. Is that party bound in the absence of express assent? One court has held "yes" on the grounds that there was implied assent to the clause and no unfair surprise. See Schulze & Burch Biscuit Co. v. Tree Top, Inc., 831 F.2d 709 (7th Cir.1987). But, again, a final solution is far from clear.

One of your editors has an explanation why parties arguing immateriality seldom win. The fact that a lawyer earning $200 an hour is standing before an appellate court arguing for the inclusion of a particular term is a mute disaffirmance of his case. If the term were not material, why would the client pay so much money to present the issue to an appellate court? In that editor's view, those who argue for the inclusion of a term because it does not cause material change are mostly doomed to failure, whether they are arguing for an arbitration provision or some other.

For a more complete discussion, see I. MacNeil, R. Speidel & T. Stipanowich, Arbitration Under the Federal Arbitration Act: Law, Practice and Procedure § 17.5 (1994).

J. WHITE AND R. SUMMERS, HANDBOOK OF THE LAW UNDER THE UNIFORM COMMERCIAL CODE 27–31 (2d ed. 1980).

Assume that buyer sends a purchase order which provides that any dispute will be governed by arbitration. Seller responds with an acknowledgement which provides that any dispute will not be resolved by arbitration. If the *bargained* terms on the purchase order and acknowledgement agree, we would find that the seller's document is a definite and seasonable expression of acceptance under 2–207 and that a contract has been formed by the exchange of the documents. We would thus bind the welsher who seeks to get out of the contract before either performs.

Assume that the seller then ships the goods, the buyer receives and pays for them, and the parties fall into dispute about their quality. Does the contract call for arbitration or does it not? * * *

* * * [T]he seller can argue that his acceptance is only an acceptance of the terms on which the two documents agree, and they did not agree on arbitration, nor do Code gap fillers provide for arbitration. This argument finds no explicit support in 2–207, but one of us (White) thinks it finds some support in part of Comment 6. * * *

In the end, how would our hypothetical case come out under the Code? One of us (White) would turn to [Official Comment 6] and find that the two terms cancel one another. On this view the seller's form was only an acceptance of terms in the offer which did not conflict with any terms in the acceptance. Thus the ultimate deal would not include an arbitration clause unless the course of performance (2–208), course of dealing (1–205), or usage of trade (1–205) supplies one. The Code does not expressly authorize this result, but it does not bar it either.

The other of us (Summers) believes that Comment 6 is not applicable. In his view it applies only to variant terms on *confirming* forms, not to variant terms on forms one of which is an offer and the other an acceptance under 2–207(1) (a distinction itself drawn in Comment 1). Thus the buyer's arbitration clause controls, for the seller's no-arbitration clause, as a *different* term embodied in the accepting form, simply falls out; 2–207(2) cannot rescue it since that provision applies only to *additional* terms. White answers that, among other things, this reading gives the sender of the first form (the buyer here) an unearned advantage. Summers does not agree that the "advantage" is entirely unearned. The recipient of the first form at least had an opportunity to object to its contents. Moreover, Summers believes that White's approach is relatively more unfair to the offeror than Summers's approach is to the offeree. According to Summers, the offeror has more (even if only a little more) reason to expect that his clause will control than the offeree has to expect that his will. After all, when the offeree sends his form he will have already received a form from the offeror, and offerees know full well that forms of different parties rarely coincide. But even if the offeror's advantage is to some extent unearned, the text of 2–207, according to Summers, appears more or less plainly to authorize it, and if the drafters intended the White approach, they could have easily drafted the section accordingly.

What if the "different" term comes into being partly by operation of a Code gap filler provision * * * rather than by virtue of a conflict of terms specified in the two forms (as in our hypothetical case)? For example, in Air Products & Chemicals, Inc. v. Fairbanks Morse, Inc.,[12] the seller's accepting form limited consequential damages. The buyer's offering form was silent on this subject but the buyer appears to have urged that the relevant Code gap filler (2–714(3)) "impliedly" provided for full consequential damages, that the seller's term was therefore a "different" term under 2–207(1), and that *it* alone thus fell out, thereby preserving the buyer's Code-provided right to full consequential damages. The Court ultimately reached this result (though not on precisely this reasoning). In light of the text, Summers concurs, though he is concerned that this reading may give the sender of the offering form too much of an overall advantage. (Summers would redraft the statute.)

12. 58 Wis.2d 193, 206 N.W.2d 414, 12 UCC Rep. Serv. 794 (1973).

Consider this further variation. Assume for example that the form offer contains an otherwise valid disclaimer of warranties and that the acceptance contains a conflicting *express* warranty. According to White, neither become part of the contract under 2–207(1) despite the fact that the contract is formed. Likewise neither enters the contract through 2–207(2) because the term in the acceptance is a different, not an additional term. Moreover by its terms 2–207(3) does not apply to this case but applies only to the case where "the writings of the parties do not otherwise establish a contract." Is it possible, nonetheless, that an *implied* warranty enters the contract directly as a gap filler without reference to 2–207(3)? White believes that it does and that indeed most of the gap fillers do not depend upon 2–207 to enter the contract. He says there are many contracts adequately formed by an offer and an acceptance which a gap filler dealing with price or warranty or terms of delivery would enter without any reference to 2–207. On White's view, that seems the proper result in this case. He thinks that the court in Bosway Tube & Steel Corp. v. McKay Machine Co. reached just this result by applying both 2–207(1) and 2–207(3). It seems to him that the court's result is correct (but that it is technically incorrect in finding that 2–207(3) can apply to a case in which the court has already found a 2–207(1) contract).

On White's analysis the foregoing outcome favors neither party. But if the buyer-offeror's argument be accepted, the offeror will almost always get his own terms. If, on the other hand, the *Roto-Lith* decision be followed, and the second document is not an acceptance or is expressly conditional and therefore cannot "operate" as an acceptance, the second party will almost always get his own terms because the second document will constitute a counteroffer accepted by performance. White believes that neither of these results is sound, and would not give either party a term when their documents conflict as to that term. The Code may then provide a term substantially identical to one of those rejected. So be it. At least a term so supplied has the merit of being a term that the draftsmen considered fair.

Summers does not read the cases as does White. More important, Summers believes White misreads 2–207, both in text and in spirit. Summers would, in the foregoing further hypothetical case, uphold the otherwise valid disclaimer as to both express and implied warranties. [Some footnotes omitted.] [For the revision of this text in light of subsequent cases, see J. White & R. Summers, Uniform Commercial Code 31–36 (3d ed. 1988).]

Vermont Law School

South Royalton, Vermont 05068

Telephone: (302) 763–8303

September 10, 1980

Professor Robert S. Summers
Cornell University Law School
Ithaca, NY 14853

Dear Professor Summers:

I have meant for a long time to write you and your collaborator, Professor White, to express my admiration for your handbook on the Code. I often consult it and always with profit.

I have most recently been reading your admirable discussion of § 2-207. Let me say at the outset that I thoroughly approve of your decision to let the disagreement between you and White on the proper construction of that abominable section hang out instead of papering it over.

I do think that insufficient attention has been paid to the tangled drafting history of § 2-207. (I am not about to reveal any ''secret history''; I had nothing to do with the drafting of § 2-207 at any stage and I cannot remember ever having discussed it with Karl Llewellyn.) The point is that as late as the 1952 draft of the Code, § 2-207 consisted only of what are now subsections (1) and (2). Subsection (3) was added in response to criticisms of the New York Law Revision Commission (which were probably based on suggestions by John Honnold, who acted as a consultant on Article 2 for the Commission). The 1952 version of § 2-207 was bad enough (particularly in the (2)(b) reference to ''material alteration'') but the addition of subsection (3), without the slightest explanation of how it was supposed to mesh with (1) and (2), turned the section into a complete disaster. To make matters worse, the 1952 Comment (which had presumably been drafted at a much earlier point by Llewellyn) was never adequately revised to take the new subsection (3) into account. (Beginning in 1949 or 1950, Llewellyn refused to have anything to do with the Article 2 Comments, which were thereafter periodically updated by an anonymous hack in the Philadelphia office of the American Law Institute. It might be interesting to check back through earlier drafts of the Code to see how the text and Comment of § 2-207 evolved through 1952.) The later (1966) revisions of the Comment, which you attribute to Braucher, were band-aid jobs.

My principal quarrel with your discussion of § 2-207—and all the other discussions I have read—is that you treat the section much too respectfully—as if it had sprung, all of a piece, like Minerva from the brow of Jove. The truth is that it was a miserable, bungled, patched-up job—both text and Comment—to which various hands—Llewellyn, Honnold, Braucher and my anonymous hack—contributed at various points, each acting independently of the others (like the blind men and the elephant). It strikes me as ludicrous to pretend that the section can, or should, be construed as an integrated whole in the light of what ''the draftsman'' ''intended.'' (I might note that, when subsection (3) was added, Llewellyn had ceased to have anything to do with the Code project.) One of the chores which we hire courts (and commentators) to perform is to clean up the messes which statutory draftsmen leave behind them. The proper approach to § 2-207, which is arguably the greatest statutory mess of all time, is to take it light-heartedly (or, as Professor Corbin used to say, cheerfully).

Which brings me to the ''infamous'' Rotolith case * * *. On the facts of the case with respect to the October shipment as Judge Aldrich stated them, I think it would have been outrageous to have saddled the seller with warranties which (as the buyer knew) he had expressly (and quite reasonably) disclaimed. I grant you that the opinion does considerable violence to the statutory language, even in the 1952 version * * *. Even so, I find it hard to conceive of a situation in which the commission of statutory mayhem was more justifiable or more necessary. Surely, when the legislature goes mad, the courts can (and should) restore us to sanity.

In the 1950's I used to go around the country peddling the Code. On one occasion I had to explain Article 2 to a group of ''corporate counsel'' in California—they represented airplane manufacturers and similar great enterprises. When I finished with § 2-207, they were, so far as I could tell, appalled. They were not so much concerned with the obvious drafting ambiguities as they were with the (equally obvious) intent to bind contracts at the earliest possible point. They evidently preferred not to be bound (whether their clients were selling or buying) until all the formalities had been accomplished, the last i dotted, the last t crossed. Perhaps, as Stuart Macaulay has suggested, businessmen don't really want binding contracts. Perhaps there was something to be said for the common law rules of offer and acceptance. At all events: Down with § 2-207.

Yours,

Grant Gilmore
Professor of Law

jlm

DAITOM, INC. v. PENNWALT CORP.

United States Court of Appeals, Tenth Circuit, 1984.
741 F.2d 1569.

Before BARRETT, DOYLE and LOGAN, CIRCUIT JUDGES.

WILLIAM E. DOYLE, CIRCUIT JUDGE.

I. STATEMENT OF THE CASE

This is an appeal from the grant of summary judgment against Daitom, Inc. (Daitom), the plaintiff below. The result was dismissal by the United States District Court for the District of Kansas of all three counts of Daitom's complaint.

Daitom had brought this diversity action in federal court on March 7, 1980 against Pennwalt Corporation and its Stokes Vacuum Equipment Division (Pennwalt). Counts I and II of Daitom's complaint alleged breach of various express and implied warranties and Count III alleged negligent design and manufacture by Pennwalt of certain rotary vacuum drying machines sold to and used commercially by Daitom in the production of a vitamin known properly as dextro calcium pantothenate and commonly as Vitamin B–5.

Daitom is a Delaware chartered corporation having its principal place of business in Kansas. It was formed to implement a joint venture between Thompson-Hayward Chemical Company, Inc. of Kansas City, Kansas and Daiichi-Seiyakii Co., Ltd., of Tokyo, Japan. Pennwalt is a Pennsylvania chartered corporation with its principal place of business in Pennsylvania.

Daitom requests a reversal of the district court's grant of summary judgment against Daitom on all counts of its complaint and seeks a remand for a trial on the merits.

We have concluded that there should be a reversal with respect to Counts I and II, together with a remand to the district court for a trial on the merits of those claims. On the other hand, we have concluded that there should be an affirmance of the summary judgment against Daitom on Count III of its complaint.

II. FACTS

The essential facts so far as they pertain to the issues presented in this appeal are as follows.

For the purpose of implementing its joint venture, Daitom planned to construct and operate a manufacturing plant to commercially produce dextro calcium pantothenate. The design of the plant was undertaken and handled on behalf of Daitom by Kintech Services, Inc. (which company will be referred to as Kintech), an engineering design firm located in Cincinnati, Ohio. Kintech had the responsibility not only for designing the plant; it also was responsible for investigating various means of drying the product during the production process, and for negotiating the purchase of certain equipment to be used in the plant. Included in the equipment was automated drying equipment to be used in removing methanol and water from the processed vitamin as part of the purification process.

There were numerous tests made and conducted at Kintech's request by equipment manufacturers. Kintech formulated specifications for the automated drying equipment. (This is referred to as Kintech Specification 342, Record, Volume I, at 59–65). On behalf of Daitom, Kintech invited various vendors to bid on the needed equipment.

Pennwalt, on September 7, 1976, submitted a proposal for the sale of two rotary vacuum dryers with dust filters and heating systems to dry dextro calcium pantothenate. The typewritten proposal specified the equipment to be sold, the f.o.b. price, and delivery and payment terms. A pre-printed conditions of sale form was also attached to the proposal and explicitly made an integral part of the proposal by the typewritten sheet.

Kintech recommended to Daitom that Pennwalt's proposal be accepted and on October 5, 1976, well within the thirty-day acceptance period specified in the proposal, Daitom issued a purchase order for the Pennwalt equipment. The purchase order consisted of a pre-printed form with the identification of the specific equipment and associated prices typewritten in the appropriate blank spaces on the front together with seventeen lengthy "boilerplate" or "standard" terms and conditions of sale on the back. In addition, on the front of the purchase order in the column marked for a description of the items purchased, Daitom typed the following:

Rotary vacuum dryers in accordance with Kintech Services, Inc. specification 342 dated August 20, 1976, and in accordance with Stokes proposal dated September 7, 1976.

The two rotary vacuum dryers and the equipment that went along with them were manufactured by Pennwalt and delivered to Daitom's plant in early May 1977. For the reason that there had been no construction of Daitom's plant, the crated equipment was not immediately installed. Instead, it was stored outside in crates. On June 15, 1978, the dryers were finally installed and first operated by Daitom. Daitom notified Pennwalt of serious problems with the operation of the dryers on June 17, 1978.

Daitom's contention was that the dryers suffered from two severe defects: 1) they were delivered with misaligned agitator blades causing a scraping and damaging of the dryer interiors and an uneven distribution of the products being dried; and 2) they were undersized necessitating an overloading of the dryers and a "lumping up" of the product rendering it unsuitable for further use. Pennwalt's repair personnel visited the Daitom plant to investigate the alleged operating difficulties, but Daitom contends the dryers were not repaired and have never performed as required under the specifications and as represented by Pennwalt. This was the basis for the lawsuit.

This suit was brought in federal court on March 7, 1980, after Pennwalt's alleged failure to correct the difficulties with the dryers. On Pennwalt's motion, the district court granted summary judgment against Daitom on all three counts of its complaint. The court dismissed Counts I and II after applying section 2–207 of the Uniform Commercial Code (U.C.C.) and finding that Daitom's breach of warranties claims were barred by the one-year period of limitations specified in Pennwalt's proposal. The court further concluded that alleged damages in Count III for the negligent design and manufacture of the dryers were not available in tort; the sole remedy being in an action for breach of warranties which here was barred by the period of limitations. Consequently, summary judgment was granted against Daitom. Daitom's subsequent motion for reconsideration was denied by the district court on June 3, 1982, and following that, this appeal took place.

III. Discussion

A. *The Issues*

It is to be noted that the district court granted summary judgment against Daitom on Counts I and II of the complaint, finding the breach of warranties claim barred by the one-year period of limitations which was set forth in Pennwalt's proposal. In ruling against Daitom the court followed a three step analysis. First, it concluded that pursuant to U.C.C. § 2–207(1), a written contract for the sale of the rotary dryers was formed by Pennwalt's September 7, 1976 proposal and Daitom's October 5, 1976 purchase order accepting that proposal. Second, the court found that the one year period of limitations specified in Pennwalt's proposal and shortening the typical four-year period of limitations available under the U.C.C. became part of the contract of sale and governed the claims for breach of warranties. Thus, the court accepted the proposal that was contained in the documents that had been submitted by the defendant-appellee. Third, the court concluded that the one-year period of limitations was not tolled by any conduct of Pennwalt's, so that consequently, Daitom's claims were barred because they were brought after the expiration of the one year limitations period. The view we have of the submission and response is that the approval was initial and general and contemplated further discussion and improvement.

The circumstances surrounding the delivery of this equipment and what occurred thereafter is of high importance. The equipment was delivered in crates and boxes, and at that time Daitom had no plant. Instead of seeking to protect the equipment in some way, Pennwalt simply delivered the boxes and left. The documents which were part of the delivery provided for this one-year period of limitations specified in the Pennwalt proposal. Seemingly, this conduct on the part of Pennwalt in making a quick delivery and quick departure took hold in connection with the motion for summary judgment, the court ruling that more than one year had passed before they were able to try out the machinery and discover the defects. The suggestion is made as to how this machinery could have been utilized or contested because of the conditions that were present. Why, then should the one-year limitations period, created by Pennwalt, be allowed to take effect?

Daitom has challenged the district court's findings as to the terms which became a part of the contract. Daitom argues that its October 5, 1976 purchase order did not constitute an acceptance of Pennwalt's September 7, 1976 proposal. Instead, Daitom claims that its purchase order explicitly made acceptance conditional on Pennwalt's assent to the additional or different terms in the purchase order. As a consequence, Daitom argues, pursuant to U.C.C. § 2–207(1),[1] the exchanged writings of the parties did *not* form a contract, because Pennwalt failed to assent to the additional or different terms in the purchase order. The most relevant additional or different terms Daitom alleges were in *its* purchase order were the terms reserving all warranties and remedies available in law, despite Pennwalt's limitation of warranties and remedies in its proposal. In a sense Pennwalt argues it enjoyed an exclusive right to set the conditions.

Daitom argues that on their face the writings failed to create a contract, and, instead, that a contract was to be formed by *the conduct* of both parties, pursuant to § 2–207(3), and the resulting contract consisted of the terms on which the writings agreed, together with "any supplementary terms incorporated under any other provision of [the UCC]." Therefore, Daitom concludes, the resulting contract governing the sale of the rotary dryers incorporated the U.C.C. provisions for express warranties (§ 2–313), implied warranties (§§ 2–314, 2–315), and a four year period of limitations.

As an alternative argument, Daitom contends that even if its October 5, 1976 purchase order did constitute an acceptance of Pennwalt's September 7, 1976 proposal and did form a contract, all conflicting terms between the two

1. The parties, throughout this litigation and through their briefs, agree that the law of Pennsylvania governs their warranty claims. The parties further agree that Pennsylvania has adopted the provisions of the Uniform Commercial Code and that for the purpose of this action the Pennsylvania statute does not modify the U.C.C. provisions. See 13 Pa.C.S.A. § 2207 (Purdon's 1984). Therefore, throughout this memorandum the relevant code sections will be referred to only by the U.C.C. numeral designation.

writings were "knocked out" and did not become part of the resulting contract, because of their being at odds one with the other. Therefore, Daitom concludes once again that the resulting contract consisted of only those terms in which the writings agreed and any supplementary or "gap-filler" terms incorporated under the provisions of the U.C.C.; specifically §§ 2–313, 2–314, 2–315, 2–725.

Daitom makes a further argument which has some appeal and that is that even if the one-year period of limitations specified in Pennwalt's proposal became a part of the sales contract, it was tolled by Pennwalt's wrongful conduct, which included fraudulent concealment of the equipment's defects and failure of the essential purpose of the limited remedies. Since this court's decision does not rely on the question of the tolling of the limitations period, we will not devote detailed argument to this.

* * *

C. *The Writings and the Contract*

The trial court concluded that the parties' exchanged writings formed a contract. Thus, there was not a formal single document. Pennwalt's September 7, 1976 proposal constituted the offer and Daitom's October 5, 1976 purchase order constituted the acceptance.

It is essentially uncontested that Pennwalt's proposal constituted an offer. The proposal set forth in some detail the equipment to be sold to Daitom, the price, the terms of shipment, and specifically stated that the attached terms and conditions were an integral part of the proposal. One of those attached terms and conditions of sale limited the warranties to repair and replacement of defective parts and limited the period of one year from the date of delivery for any action for breach of warranty.[3]

The proposal was sent to Kintech and forwarded to Daitom with a recommendation to accept the proposal. Daitom sent the October 5, 1976 purchase order to Pennwalt. This purchase order constituted an acceptance of Pennwalt's offer and formed a binding contract for the sale only pursuant

3. Paragraph 5 of the terms and conditions of sale stated in full (emphasis added):

6. WARRANTIES:

a. Seller warrants that at the time of delivery of the property to the carrier, it will be, unless otherwise specified, new, free and clear of all lawful liens and security interests or other encumbrances unknown to Buyer. If, within a period of one year from the date of *such delivery* any parts of the property (except property specified to be used property or normal wear parts) fail because of material or workmanship which was defective at the time of such delivery, Seller will repair such parts, or furnish parts to replace them f.o.b. Seller's or its supplier's plant, provided such failure is due solely to such defective material or workmanship and is not contributed to by any other cause, such as improper care or unreasonable use, and provided such defects are brought to Seller's attention for verification when first discovered, and the parts alleged to be so defective are returned, if requested, to Seller's or its supplier's plant. *No action for breach of warranty shall be brought more than one year after the cause of action has accrued*

SELLER MAKES NO OTHER WARRANTY OF ANY KIND, EXPRESS OR IMPLIED, INCLUDING ANY WARRANTY OF FITNESS OF THE PROPERTY FOR ANY PARTICULAR PURPOSE EVEN IF THAT PURPOSE IS KNOWN TO SELLER.

In no event shall Seller be liable for consequential damage.

b. Because of varied interpretations of standards at the local level, Seller cannot warrant that the property meets the requirements of the Occupational Safety and Health Act.

to 2–207(1), despite the statement of terms additional to or different from those in the offer.[4] But these terms were not without meaning or consequence. However, the acceptance was not expressly conditioned on Pennwalt accepting these additional or different terms.

There is a provision which Daitom contends made the acceptance expressly conditional on Pennwalt's accepting the additional or different terms which appeared in the pre-printed, standard "boilerplate" provisions on the back of the purchase order. It stated:

> Acceptance. Immediate acceptance is required unless otherwise provided herein. It is understood and agreed that the written acceptance by Seller of this purchase order or the commencement of any work performance of any services hereunder by the Seller, (including the commencement of any work or the performance of any service with respect to samples), shall constitute acceptance by Seller of this purchase order and of all the terms and conditions of such acceptance is *expressly limited to such terms and conditions, unless each deviation is mutually recognized therefore in writing.* (Emphasis added.)

This language does not preclude the formation of a contract by the exchanged writings pursuant to § 2–207(1). Nor does it dictate the adoption of a conclusion holding that as a result the acceptance provided the applicable terms of the resulting contract. First, it is well established that a contract for the sale of goods may be made in any manner to show agreement, requiring merely that there be some objective manifestation of mutual assent, but that there must be. There is not a contract until it takes place. See U.C.C. § 2–204; *Ore & Chemical Corporation v. Howard Butcher Trading Corp.,* 455 F.Supp. 1150, 1152 (E.D.Pa.1978). Here there is such an objective manifestation of agreement on essential terms of equipment specifications, price, and the terms of shipment and payment, all of which took place before the machinery was put to any test. The purchase order explicitly referred to and incorporated on its front Kintech's equipment specifications and Pennwalt's proposal. But we are unwilling to hold such a typewritten reference and incorporation by Daitom brings the matter to a close. The acceptance and warranty terms as provided for by the above excerpted acceptance clause, does manifest a willingness on all essential terms to accept the offer and form a contract. *Cf., Daitom v. Henry Vogt Machine Co.,* No. 80–2081 (D.Kan., unpublished 2/22/82) (In that case the court held that under identical factual circumstances and involving the identical purchase order form language, such typewritten reference and incorporation of the offer constituted a written modification of the purchase order's boilerplate acceptance terms to conform to those in the offer.) This was, of course, before an attempt was made to use the equipment.

4. The principal additional or different terms referred to the reservation of warranties. Specifically:

> (8) WARRANTY. The Seller warrants that the supplies covered by this purchase order will conform to the specifications, drawings, samples, or other descriptions furnished or specified by buyer, and will be fit and sufficient for the purpose intended, merchantable, of good material and workmanship, and free from defect. The warranties and remedies provided for in this paragraph * * * shall be in addition to those implied by or available at law and shall exist not withstanding [sic] the acceptance by Buyer of all or a part of this applies with respect to which such warranties and remedies are applicable.

Second, the boilerplate provision does not directly address the instant case. The purchase order is drafted principally as an *offer* inviting acceptance. Although this court recognizes that the form may serve a dual condition depending on the circumstances, the imprecision of language that permits such service detracts from Daitom's argument of conditional acceptance.

Third, the courts are split on the application of § 2–207(1) and the meaning of "expressly made conditional on assent to the additional or different terms." *See Boese-Hilburn Co. v. Dean Machinery,* 616 S.W.2d 520 (Mo.App.1981). *Roto-Lith Ltd. v. F.P. Bartlett & Co., Inc.,* 297 F.2d 497 (1st Cir.1962) represents one extreme of the spectrum, that the offeree's response stating a term materially altering the contractual obligations solely to the disadvantage of the offeror constitutes a conditional acceptance. The other extreme of the spectrum is represented by *Dorton v. Collins & Aikman Corporation,* 453 F.2d 1161 (6th Cir.1972), in which case the court held that the conditional nature of the acceptance should be so clearly expressed in a manner sufficient to notify the offeror that the offeree is unwilling to proceed with the transaction unless the additional or different terms are included in the contract. The middle of the spectrum providing that a response merely "predicating" acceptance on clarification, addition or modification is a conditional acceptance is represented by *Construction Aggregates Corp. v. Hewitt-Robins, Inc.,* 404 F.2d 505 (7th Cir.1968), *cert. denied,* 395 U.S. 921, 89 S.Ct. 1774, 23 L.Ed.2d 238 (1969).

The facts of this case, Daitom asserts, are not of a character that would suggest that there had been an unequivocal acceptance. The defendant-appellee was aware that the machinery had not even been tried. Once it was tried, it broke down in a very short time. It is hard to see a justifiable acceptance, Daitom asserts, when the buyer does not even know whether it works, and, in fact, learns after the fact, that it does not work. This fact alone renders the "contract" to be questionable.

The better view as to the meaning and application of "conditional acceptance," and the view most likely to be adopted by Pennsylvania, is the view in *Dorton* that the offeree must explicitly communicate his or her unwillingness to proceed with the transaction unless the additional or different terms in its response are accepted by the offeror. * * *

Having found an offer and an acceptance which was not made expressly conditional on assent to additional or different terms, we must now decide the effect of those additional or different terms on the resulting contract and what terms became part of it. The district court simply resolved this dispute by focusing solely on the period of limitations specified in Pennwalt's offer of September 7, 1976. Thus, the court held that while the offer explicitly specified a one-year period of limitations in accordance with § 2–725(1) allowing such a reduction, Daitom's acceptance of October 5, 1976 was silent as to the limitations period. Consequently, the court held that § 2–207(2) was inapplicable and the one-year limitations period controlled, effectively barring Daitom's action for breach of warranties.

While the district court's analysis undertook to resolve the issue without considering the question of the application of § 2–207(2) to additional or different terms, we cannot accept its approach or its conclusion. We are unable to ignore the plain implication of Daitom's reservation in its boilerplate warranties provision of all its rights and remedies available at law. Such an explicit reservation impliedly reserves the statutory period of limitations; without such a reservation, all other reservations of actions and remedies are without effect.

The statutory period of limitations under the U.C.C. is four years after the cause of action has accrued. UCC § 2–725(1). Were we to determine that this four-year period became a part of the contract rather than the shorter one-year period, Daitom's actions on breach of warranties were timely brought and summary judgment against Daitom was error.[5]

We realize that our conclusion requires an inference to be drawn from a construction of Daitom's terms; however, such an inference and construction are consistent with the judicial reluctance to grant summary judgment where there is some reasonable doubt over the existence of a genuine material fact. *See Williams v. Borden, Inc.*, 637 F.2d 731, 738 (10th Cir. 1980). When taking into account the circumstances surrounding the application of the one-year limitations period, we have little hesitation in adopting the U.C.C.'s four-year limitations reservation, the application of which permits a trial on the merits. Thus, this court must recognize that certain terms in Daitom's acceptance differed from terms in Pennwalt's offer and decide which become part of the contract. The district court certainly erred in refusing to recognize such a conflict.[6]

The difficulty in determining the effect of different terms in the acceptance is the imprecision of drafting evident in § 2–207. The language of the provision is silent on how different terms in the acceptance are to be treated once a contract is formed pursuant to § 2–207(1). That section provides that a contract may be formed by exchanged writings despite the existence of additional or different terms in the acceptance. Therefore, an offeree's response is treated as an acceptance while it may differ substantially from the offer. This section of the provision, then, reformed the mirror-image rule; that common law legal formality that prohibited the formation of a contract if the exchanged writings of offer and acceptance differed in any term.

Once a contract is recognized pursuant to § 2–207(1), § 2–207(2) provides the standard for determining if the additional terms stated in the acceptance become a part of the contract. Between merchants, such *additional* terms become part of the resulting contract *unless* 1) the offer expressly limited acceptance to its terms, 2) the additional terms materially alter the contract obligations, or 3) the offeror gives notice of his or her objection to the

5. Daitom filed its complaint on March 7, 1980. While the parties dispute when the cause of action accrued and the period of limitations began to run, resolution of the dispute is unnecessary if this court concludes the four-year limitations period controls. Even if it is found the action accrued in May 1977 on delivery of the dryers to Daitom's plant, the four-year period of limitations had not expired on March 7, 1980 when the complaint was filed.

6. There is some indication in its memorandum and order that had the district court considered the effect of the conflicting terms, it would have applied § 2–207(2)(b) and concluded that the terms in Pennwalt's offer controlled because Daitom's conflicting terms would have materially altered the content. Memorandum and Order at 11. Because we hold, *infra*, that conflicting terms should not be analyzed pursuant to § 2–207(2), this conclusion of the district court is also in error.

additional terms within a reasonable time. Should any one of these three possibilities occur, the *additional* terms are treated merely as proposals for incorporation in the contract and absent assent by the offeror the terms of the offer control. In any event, the existence of the additional terms does not prevent a contract from being formed.

Section 2–207(2) is silent on the treatment of terms stated in the acceptance that are *different,* rather than merely additional, from those stated in the offer. It is unclear whether "different" terms in the acceptance are intended to be included under the aegis of "additional" terms in § 2–207(2) and, therefore, fail to become part of the agreement if they materially alter the contract. Comment 3 suggests just such an inclusion.[7] However, Comment 6 suggests that different terms in exchanged writings must be assumed to constitute mutual objections by each party to the other's conflicting terms and result in a mutual "knockout" of both parties' conflicting terms; the missing terms to be supplied by the U.C.C.'s "gap-filler" provisions.[8] At least one commentator, in support of this view, has suggested that the drafting history of the provision indicates that the word "different" was intentionally deleted from the final draft of § 2–207(2) to preclude its treatment under that subsection.[9] The plain language, comments, and drafting history of the provision, therefore, provide little helpful guidance in resolving the disagreement over the treatment of different terms pursuant to § 2–207.

Despite all this, the cases and commentators have suggested three possible approaches. The first of these is to treat "different" terms as included under the aegis of "additional" terms in § 2–207(2). Consequently, different terms in the acceptance would never become part of the contract, because, by definition, they would materially alter the contract (i.e., the offeror's terms). Several courts have adopted this approach. *E.g., Mead Corporation v. McNally-Pittsburg Manufacturing Corporation,* 654 F.2d 1197 (6th Cir.1981) (applying Ohio law); *Steiner v. Mobil Oil Corporation,* 20 Cal.3d 90, 141 Cal.Rptr. 157, 569 P.2d 751 (1977); *Lockheed Electronics Company, Inc. v. Keronix, Inc.,* 114 Cal.App.3d 304, 170 Cal.Rptr. 591 (1981).

The second approach, which leads to the same result as the first, is that the offeror's terms control because the offeree's different terms merely fall out; § 2–207(2) cannot rescue the different terms since that subsection applies only to *additional* terms. Under this approach, Comment 6 (apparently supporting a mutual rather than a single term knockout) is not

7. Comment 3 states (emphasis added):

Whether or not *additional or different* terms will become part of the agreement depends upon the provision of subsection (2).

It must be remembered that even official comments to enacted statutory text do not have the force of law and are only guidance in the interpretation of that text. *In re Bristol Associates, Inc.,* 505 F.2d 1056 (3d Cir.1974) (while the comments to the Pennsylvania U.C.C. are not binding, the Pennsylvania Supreme Court gives substantial weight to the comments as evidencing application of the Code).

8. Comment 6 states, in part:

Where clauses on confirming forms sent by both parties conflict each party must be assumed to object to a clause of the other conflicting with one on the confirmation sent by himself * * *. The contract then consists of the terms expressly agreed to, terms on which the confirmations agree, and terms supplied by the Act, including subsection (2).

9. See D.G. Baird & R. Weisberg, *Rules, Standards, and the Battle of the Forms: A Reassessment of § 2-207,* 68 Va.L.R. 1217, 1240, n. 61.

applicable because it refers only to conflicting terms in confirmation forms following *oral* agreement, not conflicting terms in the *writings* that form the agreement. This approach is supported by Professor Summers. J.J. White & R.S. Summers, *Uniform Commercial Code,* § 1-2, at 29 (2d ed. 1980).

The third, and preferable approach, which is commonly called the "knock-out" rule, is that the conflicting terms cancel one another. Under this view the offeree's form is treated only as an acceptance of the terms in the offeror's form which did not conflict. The ultimate contract, then, includes those non-conflicting terms and any other terms supplied by the U.C.C., including terms incorporated by course of performance (§ 2-208), course of dealing (§ 1-205), usage of trade (§ 1-205), and other "gap fillers" or "off-the-rack" terms (e.g., implied warranty of fitness for particular purpose, § 2-315). As stated previously, this approach finds some support in Comment 6. Professor White supports this approach as the most fair and consistent with the purposes of § 2-207. *White & Summers, supra,* at 29. Further, several courts have adopted or recognized the approach. *E.g., Idaho Power Company v. Westinghouse Electric Corporation,* 596 F.2d 924 (9th Cir.1979) (applying Idaho law, although incorrectly, applying § 2-207(3) after finding a contract under § 2-207(1)); *Owens-Corning Fiberglas Corporation v. Sonic Development Corporation,* 546 F.Supp. 533 (D.Kan.1982) (Judge Saffels applying Kansas law); *Lea Tai Textile Co., Ltd. v. Manning Fabrics, Inc.,* 411 F.Supp. 1404 (S.D.N.Y.1975); *Hartwig Farms, Inc. v. Pacific Gamble Robinson Company,* 28 Wash.App. 539, 625 P.2d 171 (1981); *S.C. Gray, Inc. v. Ford Motor Company,* 92 Mich.App. 789, 286 N.W.2d 34 (1979).

We are of the opinion that this is the more reasonable approach, particularly when dealing with a case such as this where from the beginning the offeror's specified period of limitations would expire before the equipment was even installed. The approaches other than the "knock-out" approach would be inequitable and unjust because they invited the very kind of treatment which the defendant attempted to provide.

Thus, we are of the conclusion that if faced with this issue the Pennsylvania Supreme Court would adopt the "knock-out" rule and hold here that the conflicting terms in Pennwalt's offer and Daitom's acceptance regarding the period of limitations and applicable warranties cancel one another out. Consequently, the other provisions of the U.C.C. must be used to provide the missing terms.

This particular approach and result are supported persuasively by the underlying rationale and purpose behind the adoption of § 2-207. As stated previously, that provision was drafted to reform the infamous common law mirror-image rule and associated last-shot doctrine that enshrined the fortuitous positions of senders of forms and accorded undue advantages based on such fortuitous positions. *White & Summers, supra* at 25. To refuse to adopt the "knock-out" rule and instead adopt one of the remaining two approaches would serve to re-enshrine the undue advantages derived solely from the fortuitous positions of when a party sent a form. Cf., 3 Duesenberg & King at 93 (1983 Supp.). This is because either approach other than the knock-out rule for different terms results in the offeror and his or her terms always prevailing solely because he or she sent the first form. Professor Summers argues that this advantage is not wholly unearned, because the offeree has an opportunity to review the offer, identify the conflicting terms and make his or her acceptance conditional. But this joinder misses the fundamental purpose of the U.C.C. in general and § 2–207 in particular, which is to preserve a contract and fill in any gaps if the parties intended to make a contract and there is a reasonable basis for giving an appropriate remedy. UCC 2–204(3); 2–207(1); 2–207(3). Thus, this approach gives the offeree some protection. While it is laudible [sic] for business persons to read the fine print and boilerplate provisions in exchanged forms, there is nothing in § 2–207 mandating such careful consideration. The provision seems drafted with a recognition of the reality that merchants seldom review exchanged forms with the scrutiny of lawyers. The "knock-out" rule is therefore the best approach. Even if a term eliminated by operation of the "knock-out" rule is reintroduced by operation of the U.C.C.'s gap-filler provisions, such a result does not indicate a weakness of the approach. On the contrary, at least the reintroduced term has the merit of being a term that the U.C.C. draftpersons regarded as fair.

We now address the question of reverse and remand regarding Counts I and II. The result of this court's holding is that the district court erred in granting summary judgment against Daitom on Counts I and II of its complaint. Operation of the "knock-out" rule to conflicting terms results in the instant case in the conflicting terms in the offer and acceptance regarding the period of limitations and applicable warranties cancelling. In the absence of any evidence of course of performance, course of dealing, or usage of trade providing the missing terms, §§ 2–725(1), 2–313, 2–314, 2–315 may operate to supply a four-year period of limitations, an express warranty,[10] an implied warranty of merchantability, and an implied warranty of fitness for a particular purpose, respectively. The ruling of the district court on Counts I and II does not invite this kind of a broad inquiry, and thus, we must recognize the superiority in terms of justice of the "knock-out" rule. Consequently, the ruling of the district court on Counts I and II must be reversed and the matter remanded for trial consistent with this court's ruling.

* * *

[The court held that there was no Cause of Action in tort where an allegedly defective product caused only economic loss.]

Accordingly, the district court correctly concluded that Daitom's requested damages are not recoverable in tort. The court's summary judgment ruling against Daitom on Count III, therefore, should be affirmed. As explained above, we reverse the trial court with respect to Counts I and II. The cause is remanded for further proceedings consistent with this opinion.

BARRETT, CIRCUIT JUDGE, dissenting:

I respectfully dissent. Insofar as the issue of contract formation is concerned in this case, we are confronted with a "battle of the forms" case involving the interpretation and application of U.C.C. 2–207. I would affirm.

Pennwalt's proposal of September 7, 1976, was an "offer." It was submitted to Daitom in response to solicitations initiated by Daitom and it

10. Daitom alleges that several letters from Pennwalt expressly warrantied the performance of the rotary dryers. *E.g.*, Pretrial Order, Record Volume II at 59, para. 12, 13, 14, 15.

contained specific terms relating to price, delivery dates, etc., and its terms were held "open" for Daitom's acceptance within 30 days. In my view, Daitom accepted the offer with its purchase order. That order repeated the quantity, model number, and price for the items as those terms appeared in the Pennwalt proposal and, by reference, it incorporated four pages of specifications attached to Pennwalt's proposal or "offer." The purchase order did contain some different and additional language from that contained in Pennwalt's proposal. However, the Code has rejected the old mirror image rule. Thus, I agree with the district court's finding/ruling that a contract was formed in the circumstances described.

I also agree with the district court's conclusion that the terms of Pennwalt's proposal constituted the "terms of the contract." I do not agree, as Daitom argues, that its "acceptance" was made "conditional" upon Pennwalt's assent to the additional/different terms set forth in Daitom's purchase order. The court correctly found no such *express* condition in Daitom's acceptance.

The "knock-out" rule should not, in my view, be reached in this case. It can be applied only if, as Daitom argues and the majority agrees, the "conflicting terms" cancel each other out. The "knock-out" rule does have substantial support in the law, but I do not believe it is relevant in this case because the *only* conflicting terms relate to the *scope* of the warranty. In this case, it is not an important consideration because, pursuant to the express time limitations contained in Pennwalt's "offer," Daitom lost its right to assert any warranty claim. There was no term in Daitom's purchase order in conflict with the express one-year limitation within which to bring warranty actions. I agree with the district court's reasoning in rejecting Daitom's contentions that the one-year limitation period should not apply because (1) the term failed of "its essential purpose" of providing Daitom with a limited remedy under U.C.C. § 2–719(2) and (2) the time-limit was tolled due to Pennwalt's alleged fraudulent concealment of the defect. I concur with the trial court's finding that Daitom made no showing that the one-year limitation period was unreasonable because of some act of Pennwalt. As to the fraudulent concealment allegation, the court properly observed that Daitom did not plead this claim with the particularity required and, further, that the alleged fraudulent acts were not independent of the alleged breaches proper.

[Some footnotes omitted.]

Note: How Should UCC 2–207 Be Revised?

Upon reading the endless cases and commentary on Section 2–207, it seems clear that some revision is in order. But what? Should Article 2 return to the common law "mirror image" rule? This is the approach of Article 19(2) of the Convention on the International Sale of Goods, at least where additional or different terms materially alter the terms of the offer. Or should a revision be drafted that more clearly achieves the objectives of Section 2–207, which were to (1) preserve some contract where intended by the parties despite the presence of additional or different terms in the writings and (2) avoid unfair surprise when one party attempts to include additional or different terms to which the other has not expressly agreed to in the contract. As a practical matter, in most cases the question is what are the terms of the contract, not whether a contract was created.

If the latter path is taken, the revision should, at a minimum, deal with the following problems.

First, suppose the parties have reached an oral agreement which, but for the statute of frauds, is enforceable as a contract. One party then sends a written confirmation of the oral agreement which contains additional or different terms. How should that confirmation be treated? Is it a repudiation of the oral agreement or simply a proposal for modification? If the latter, when do the additional or different terms become part of the agreement? The issue is further complicated by the statute of frauds. How should additional or different terms in a confirmation which is essential to satisfying the statute of frauds under UCC 2–201(2) be treated? A plausible answer is that if the confirmation is sufficient under Section 2–201(2), the parties must still prove what the agreement is and Section 2–207 is relevant to the process.

Second, by what standard is it determined whether an offeree's response with additional or different terms accepts an offer, especially where there is no conduct by both parties expressing an intention to contract? A closely related question is the language that the offeree must use to state that it will not contract unless the offeror agrees to the additional or different terms.

Third, if there is no contract after an exchange of writings, by what standard is it determined whether the offeree's terms become part of the agreement? Is it enough if the offeror accepts goods tendered by the offeree without objecting to the additional or different terms?

Fourth, if there is a contract, whether through an exchange of writings or mutual conduct, what terms does it include? If the additional or different terms of either party are not initially included, by what standard is it determined whether they are subsequently included?

Fifth, should it make any difference whether the terms are material or nonmaterial? If so, to what should materiality refer, the terms of the offer purportedly accepted or the principles of Article 2 itself?

Sixth, should the distinction between additional and different terms be preserved?

Review Problem 10–5 and the *Daitom* case just considered. How should they be resolved under each of the two proposed revision of Section 2–207 set forth below? Which revision do you prefer? What further changes would you make?

SECTION 2–207. ADDITIONAL TERMS IN ACCEPTANCE OR CONFIRMATION.

[Reporter's Note. Two versions of Section 2–207 have been drafted. Alternative A uses the structure of existing Section 2–207 and attempts to amplify and clarify in light of apparent objectives, academic commentary and judicial decisions. Alternative B develops a different structure that attempts to simplify and present a focused solution to the unfair surprise issue.]

Alternative A

(a) A definite acceptance that is sent within a reasonable time creates a contract even though it states terms additional to or different from those offered unless acceptance is clearly and conspicuously made conditional on assent to the additional or different terms.

(b) A written confirmation of a previous agreement which states terms additional to or different from those agreed upon does not operate as a repudiation of the agreement unless the confirmation is clearly and conspicuously made conditional on assent to the additional or different terms.

(c) The additional or different terms must be construed as proposals for modification of a contract formed under subsection (a) or a previous agreement. Between merchants, these terms become part of the contract or previous agreement unless:

(1) the offer clearly and conspicuously limits acceptance to the terms of the offer;

(2) the terms materially alter the contract or previous agreement;

(3) notification of objection to the terms has previously been given or is given within a reasonable time after notice of them is received; or

(4) in the case of different terms, the parties exchange written confirmations of a previous agreement which contain different terms.

(d) Conduct by both parties which recognizes that the parties have intended to conclude an agreement is sufficient to establish a contract for sale although the writings of the parties do not otherwise establish a contract or no contract was formed under subsection (1) or by any previous agreement. In this case, the terms of the contract consist of those on which the writings or symbols of the parties agree, together with any supplementary terms incorporated under subsection (c) or any other provisions of this Act.

(e) Additional or different terms not made part of the contract under subsections (c) or (d) do not become part of the agreement unless the party against whom they operate knows or has reason to know of them and manifests assent to the writings or symbols.

Alternative B

(a) If writings or symbols are exchanged and contain varying terms, whether additional or different, or are sent in confirmation of and vary a previous agreement, a contract exists if the requirements of Section 2–204 are satisfied and there is a reasonable basis for giving an appropriate remedy.

(b) If a contract is formed under subsection (a), the varying terms do not become part of the agreement unless the party against whom they operate knew or had reason to know that the terms, whether material or immaterial variations, were included in the writings or symbols of the other party and manifested assent to them.

(c) If a contract is formed under subsection (a), the terms include those upon which the writings or symbols agree and those included under subsection (b), those to which the parties have otherwise agreed, and any supplementary terms incorporated pursuant to other provisions of this Act.

SECTION 4. THE STATUTE OF FRAUDS

A. *History and Purposes*

A statute of frauds imposes additional conditions upon the enforceability of agreements which otherwise qualify as contracts. In general, there must be a writing consistent with the existence of a contract, specifying some if not all of the terms, and signed or authenticated by the party to be charged. The UCC has several such statutes of frauds, see, e.g., UCC 1–206, 8–319 (contract for sale of securities), 9–203(1) (creation of enforceable security interest), including UCC 2–201, which governs contracts for the "sale of goods for the price of $500 or more." UCC 2–201(1).

At least three justifications for the statute of frauds have been asserted. First, the statute avoids fraudulent or perjured claims that some contract was in fact made. Second, the statute avoids fraudulent or perjured claims regarding the terms of a contract admittedly made. Third, the statute serves a useful purpose in so far as it contributes to the business habit of making a writing. See Vold, *The Application of the Statute of Frauds Under the Uniform Sales Act,* 15 Minn.L.Rev. 391, 393–94 (1931).

The first two justifications have long been criticized as anachronistic. The conditions existing in 17th Century England—uncontrolled jury discretion, restrictions upon the competency of witnesses and immature contract doctrine—no longer obtain. See Willis, *The Statute of Frauds—A Legal Anachronism,* 3 Ind.L.J. 427, 429–31 (1928). Attacks of this sort, plus the opportunity provided by the statute for "technical unmeritorious defenses" induced Parliament, in 1954, to repeal the statute of frauds provision in the British Sale of Goods Act. See Grunfield, *Law Reform (Enforcement of Contracts) Act,* 1954, 17 Mod.L.Rev. 451 (1954).

The third justification is more difficult to undercut. According to Professor Vold, the "cases that justify the statute are * * * the thousands of uncontested current transactions where misunderstanding and controversy are avoided by the presence of a writing which the statute at least indirectly aided to procure. * * *" *Vold,* supra. But see Comment, *The Statute of Frauds and the Business Community: A Re-Appraisal in Light of Prevailing Practices,* 66 Yale L.J. 1038 (1957) (reliance on an oral order rather than the practice of employing writings is prevalent practice). Karl Llewellyn agreed with Vold's assessment, see Llewellyn, *What Price Contract? An Essay in Perspective,* 40 Yale L.J. 704, 746–48 (1931), and his views were influential in the drafting of UCC 2–201.

What justifications exist for UCC 2–201? Should the statute of frauds in Article 2 be repealed? Keep these questions in mind as you work through the following simple problems.

B. *Illustrative Problems and Cases*

The following problems and cases illustrate some of the issues that have arisen over the scope and application of UCC 2–201.

Problem 10–6

On February 1, S, a farmer, entered into an oral contract with B, a grain dealer, to plant his fields in corn and to harvest and deliver the output for $2.30 per bushel by October 1. B immediately resold the corn to C, a cereal producer, for $2.60 per bushel. On April 1, before the fields had been planted, S informed B that he had entered into a written contract with D, another dealer, to sell his output of corn for $3.00 per bushel. B claimed a breach of contract, but S's lawyer stated that the alleged contract was not enforceable because of the statute of frauds. As B's lawyer, identify and assess all arguments that the transaction was not within the scope of UCC 2–201(1).

Problem 10–7

Suppose that on April 1, S had written and signed the following note to B: "The rising corn futures prices makes it necessary for me to cancel our deal. Sorry. Perhaps we can do business again next year." B's lawyer argues that if the oral transaction was within the scope of UCC 2–201(1), that statute was satisfied by the note. B is also prepared to prove that the parties had done business for 10 years and that S had always sold B the output from his land. As S's lawyer, identify and assess all of the arguments to the contrary.

Problem 10–8

Suppose that on February 1, B had written S a signed letter asking whether S would be willing to sell his output of corn "again this year." In response, S had hand written but not signed the following note, which was delivered by a family member: "George. Output is fine, but no deal until we agree on a fair price." On February 5, B (George) visited S on the farm and an oral agreement to sell the output of corn at $2.30 per bushel was reached. On February 7, B mailed the following letter to S, which was received by S on February 9: "Dear Silas. This is to confirm our agreement for the sale of corn at $2.30 per bushel, delivery by October 1. George." S did not respond to the letter. On April 1, S wrote the following signed note to B: "Dear George: We never had a deal. I have sold my output to D. (s) Silas." B's lawyer makes two arguments: (1) The statute of frauds was satisfied by application of UCC 2–201(2); (2) When all of the writings are considered, the statute of frauds has been satisfied. How would you rule?

NEBRASKA BUILDERS PROD. CO. v. INDUSTRIAL ERECTORS, INC.

Supreme Court of Nebraska, 1992.
239 Neb. 744, 478 N.W.2d 257.

HASTINGS, C.J. Appellant, Nebraska Builders Products Co. (Nebraska Builders), brought this action against the appellee, The Industrial Erectors, Inc. (Industrial), to recover the excess costs of substitute performance on an alleged purchase contract for cranes. Nebraska Builders appeals from a judgment of the trial court declaring that there was no enforceable contract between the parties but that, instead, the parties contemplated a written contract which was never executed. We reverse, and remand for further proceedings.

* * *

The record reflects the following facts: In early 1985, the Omaha Public Power District (O.P.P.D.) invited bids for the construction of a service center near Elkhorn, Nebraska. William Hawkins, on behalf of Nebraska Builders, an Omaha-based company engaged in the business of selling construction products, obtained the plans and specifications which identified supplies, materials, and equipment to be used in the construction of the service center. Nebraska Builders intended to submit its bid as a subcontractor or material supplier to the companies bidding for the general contract for the construction of the service center later that year. Hawkins identified many items in the plans and specifications which Nebraska Builders could potentially supply for the project, including several types of crane systems. Previously, Nebraska Builders had purchased such cranes from Industrial. Industrial is a Chicago-based company which manufactures various types of cranes and also sells cranes manufactured by others.

Hawkins contacted Timothy Brennan, Industrial's sales manager, in February 1985, to inquire if Industrial was interested in submitting a bid on the cranes. Brennan traveled to Omaha on February 28, 1985, to review the plans and specifications for the crane systems. Brennan obtained the information necessary to prepare a bid, including Section 11520 of the specifications—Material Handling and Associated Equipment. The specifications were very detailed, specifying manufacturer, model number, electrical requirements, capacity, speed, control system, and other performance characteristics. Variance in equipment had to be approved in writing by the project engineer pursuant to a procedure set forth in the specifications. Both Brennan and Hawkins were aware of this procedure.

On March 12 or 13, 1985, Brennan telephoned Hawkins and told him that Industrial would sell and install the crane systems as per specifications for a total sum of $449,920, which consisted of $399,935 for materials and $49,985 for installation. Brennan stated that there were some minor exceptions to the specifications, but those could be worked out with the O.P.P.D. engineer. Nebraska Builders submitted a bid based, in part, on Industrial's bid. On March 26, 1985, Brennan confirmed the telephone conversation with a letter to Hawkins stating Industrial's proposal.

By this letter, exhibit 14, Industrial "propose[d] to furnish all Crane Systems, Jib Cranes and Monorail Systems per Specification No. 11520 dated 2/26/85 including the three Addendums." Then followed a detailed listing of the specific items which Industrial agreed to furnish at a total material cost of $399,935, plus $49,985 if Industrial was to install the listed equipment.

William Hawkins contacted Hawkins Construction Company (Hawkins Construction), the general contractor with the lowest bid, to see if Nebraska Builders was the low bidder on any of the items Hawkins Construction had bid on. This conversation led to a period of negotiations between Industrial and Nebraska Builders. During the negotiations, Nebraska Builders put together a "package bid" and gave Hawkins Construction a lump-sum price on several items, including the cranes. Nebraska Builders alleges that upon its request Industrial reduced its bid twice. Industrial disputes the second reduction and argues that the bid was only once reduced, by $4,500. However, exhibit 46 consists of a series of adding machine tapes including notations admittedly made by Brennan of Industrial. These tapes indicate a second reduction of $26,937, with additions of $2,400 for each interlock device. As testified to by Hawkins, there were four interlock devices, and this total reduction was therefore $17,337.

At the time Nebraska Builders submitted its package bid to Hawkins Construction, William Hawkins had reviewed Industrial's proposal and knew that the items proposed were different models made by different manufacturers than those called for in the specifications; however, the proposal stated that Industrial would furnish all crane systems as required by Section 11520 of O.P.P.D.'s specifications. Hawkins was also aware that any deviations needed specific approval. He was not concerned about the deviations since O.P.P.D. was required to accept alternatives if they were of equal quality. Since Industrial was in the business of manufacturing and selling cranes and had stated that the proposal was per specifications and any deviations from the specifications were "minor," Hawkins believed that the cranes set forth in Industrial's proposal were of equal quality, and thus, approval of the deviations would not be a problem.

During early May, Hawkins was informed by Hawkins Construction that Nebraska Builders' bid on the crane systems, as well as on various other items, was accepted. Hawkins testified that he immediately telephoned Industrial to accept Industrial's offer. He does not remember whether he talked to Brennan or Jerry Cole, the president of Industrial. Brennan testified that he did not have that conversation with Hawkins. Cole did not testify at the trial.

Although Brennan denies his having the conversation in which Nebraska Builders accepted Industrial's bid, Industrial and Nebraska Builders exchanged correspondence concerning the variance approval and exceptions to the specifications between May 31 and August 9, 1985. In a letter dated May 31, 1985, Brennan assured Nebraska Builders that Industrial had adhered to all of O.P.P.D.'s specifications in preparing its bid and that all equipment "will be equal to or better than" the equipment specified in the plans and specifications. Brennan also sent a letter dated June 10, 1985, which starts as follows: "This letter is to confirm our telecon regarding the above subject." The above-named subject in the letter was "Jib Crane, Monorails and Crane Equipment." The letter states further that Industrial is "trying to alleviate the confusion of the materials that Industrial is supplying." Brennan went on to describe the cranes "to be furnished" and concluded by stating that he hoped "this letter will alleviate any confusion regarding the materials to be furnished and we look forward to working with you on this project." The O.P.P.D. engineers for the district ultimately approved Twin City Monorail (Twin City) and Crane Manufacturing & Service Corporation, Industrial's subcontractors, as crane manufacturers.

During this same time period, Industrial repeatedly requested Nebraska Builders to issue a purchase order, written contract, or letter of intent. Nebraska Builders denied these requests, stating that a written contract would be forthcoming upon its signing a contract with Hawkins Construction. Nebraska Builders never provided Industrial with a written contract. Industrial, in turn, did not issue any written contract or purchase order to any of its suppliers and, in fact, told one supplier that a written purchase order could not be given until Industrial received one from Nebraska Builders.

Despite the fact that there was no written contract, Brennan visited Nebraska Builders' office on August 8, 1985, on behalf of Industrial. Industrial also prepared and submitted shop drawings showing the recommended foundation design and bolt locations for the various floor-mounted jib cranes included in Industrial's proposal.

Brennan sent Hawkins a letter dated July 23, 1985, to confirm a verbal conversation concerning a list of deviations from the specifications, which deviations, if changed to meet the specifications, would constitute an additional cost of an unspecified amount to Industrial's bid. Hawkins testified that he was confused when he received the letter because he had not spoken to Brennan about any deviations to the specifications other than when he got Industrial's oral bid in March 1985. Hawkins discussed the letter with Brennan during Brennan's trip to Omaha on August 8, 1985. Brennan stated that he had not included in Industrial's bid the hoists for the jib cranes and that he had forgotten to include the footwalks and handrails for the largest overhead crane. Hawkins told Brennan that he expected Industrial to supply everything called for in the specifications in accordance with its bid.

Brennan had prepared another letter, dated August 7, 1985, which purported to confirm a telephone conversation between Hawkins and Brennan. The letter informed Hawkins that in order to provide the cranes in accordance with the specifications "with no exceptions" there would be an additional cost of $167,500 to the original quotation. Brennan testified that the letter was never sent to Hawkins. Brennan further stated that he could not recall the telephone conversation referred to in his letter to Hawkins.

In September 1985, Brennan told Hawkins that Twin City, the company from which Industrial was to purchase some of the cranes, did not want to furnish the cranes. According to Brennan, Twin City felt that the specifications had been drawn up for one manufacturer.

Hawkins became concerned that Industrial was not going to perform under the alleged contract. He telephoned Cole, Industrial's president, to discuss his concerns. Cole assured Hawkins that he would discuss the matter with Twin City and attempt to get it resolved. Brennan informed Hawkins sometime between October 7 and 9 that Twin City had taken several exceptions to the specifications and that as a result Twin City's price to Industrial was going to increase by more than $100,000.

Hawkins went to Chicago on October 14, 1985, to meet with Brennan and Cole to discuss Industrial's problem with Twin City. During the meeting, Brennan and Cole showed Hawkins a breakdown of the original bid and the new costs in view of Twin City's price increase. Hawkins was informed that strict compliance with the specifications would increase the original bid by approximately $150,000, which included extra costs for the jib crane hoists and Twin City's price increase. Hawkins told Industrial that a price increase was not possible. Brennan stated that Industrial would not perform without the price increase. Discussions between Industrial and Nebraska Builders terminated. Nebraska Builders claims to have obtained performance of the contract elsewhere at an additional cost of $136,136.11.

Industrial and Nebraska Builders had no written agreement regarding the time of performance, necessity or amount of a performance bond, time of payment, or whether Industrial would be bound by the terms and conditions of the general contract. However, some of these items were discussed in

Industrial's proposal letter. Nebraska Builders and Industrial contemplated entering into a written agreement which would have addressed such concerns. Hawkins testified that Nebraska Builders has a standard subcontract form which includes such terms as a complete description of work, approved variances, price, terms of payment, time of performance, performance bond, and adherence to the terms of the general contract.

The parties stipulated at trial that the dispute would be governed by the Uniform Commercial Code. Following a trial and submission to the court without a jury, judgment was entered in favor of Industrial.

* * *

The last issue argued by Industrial is that Nebraska Builders' action is barred by the statute of frauds. Section 2–201 of the U.C.C. states the formal requirements of the statute of frauds:

> "(1) Except as otherwise provided in this section a contract for the sale of goods for the price of five hundred dollars or more is not enforceable by way of action or defense unless there is some writing sufficient to indicate that a contract for sale has been made between the parties and signed by the party against whom enforcement is sought or by his authorized agent or broker. A writing is not insufficient because it omits or incorrectly states a term agreed upon but the contract is not enforceable under this paragraph beyond the quantity of goods shown in such writing.
>
> * * *
>
> "(3) A contract which does not satisfy the requirements of subsection (1) but which is valid in other respects is enforceable * * * (b) if the party against whom enforcement is sought admits in his pleading, testimony or otherwise in court that a contract for sale was made, but the contract is not enforceable under this provision beyond the quantity of goods admitted * * *."

Since the value of the cranes exceeds $500, the statute of frauds is applicable. Therefore, we turn to the question whether the requirements of the statute of frauds have been met. In the case Veik v. The Tilden Bank, 200 Neb. 705, 265 N.W.2d 214 (1978), a letter was found to be sufficient to satisfy the requirements of the statute of frauds. This court stated that a writing will be sufficient to avoid the U.C.C. statute of frauds if the writing evidences a contract for the sale of goods, is signed by the party against whom enforcement is sought, and specifies a quantity. The required writing need not contain all the material terms of the contract. According to comment 1 to § 2–201, the writing needs only to afford a basis for believing that the offered oral evidence rests on a real transaction.

Several writings can be pieced together to satisfy the requirement, even though the writings taken alone would not have been sufficient. See, Reich v. Helen Harper, Inc., 3 U.C.C.Rep.Serv. (Callaghan) 1048 (N.Y.City Civ. Dec. 27, 1966) (a sales confirmation and an invoice sent by the seller's agent to the buyer, combined with a letter by the buyer criticizing the quality of the goods, satisfy the writing requirement of § 2–201(1)); Waltham Truck Equip. Corp. v. Massachusetts Equip. Co., 7 Mass.App. 580, 389 N.E.2d 753 (1979) (three separate letters signed by a representative of the buyer can be read together to satisfy the statute of frauds, even though two letters indicated a dispute as to one of the terms of the contract).

In the case at bar, the proposal letter and the followup letters indicate that a contract was formed. The proposal letter of March 26, 1985, begins with the following sentence: "This letter is to confirm our telecom regarding the above subject [i.e., 'Jib Cranes and Monorails']." The letter states the quantity of the goods to be furnished; the items, 14 cranes and 1 monorail, are listed in detail. After the alleged phone conversation in which Nebraska Builders accepted Industrial's bid, a correspondence between the two parties emerged concerning the materials to be furnished. A letter sent by Brennan dated May 31, 1985, assures Nebraska Builders that Industrial has adhered to the plans and specifications required by O.P.P.D. In a subsequent letter dated June 10, 1985, Brennan states that Industrial is "trying to alleviate the confusion of the materials that Industrial *is supplying.*" (Emphasis supplied.) The letter refers to the included brochures, which "show that the equipment *to be furnished* meets the standards and quality [required by O.P.P.D.]." (Emphasis supplied.) The letter ends as follows: "We hope this letter will alleviate any confusion regarding the materials to be furnished and *we look forward to working with you on this project.*" (Emphasis supplied.)

On August 9, 1985, Brennan sent another letter to Nebraska Builders in which he "assume[s] that the hoist/trolley units will be furnished by others or would be an adder to the *contract.*" (Emphasis supplied.) Finally, on August 15, 1985, Brennan sent Hawkins a letter in which he recommends a certain foundation for the bolt setting of the mast-type jib crane. The letter includes several drawings. The drawings were returned to Industrial with notes and corrections on them made by Nebraska Builders' architect.

The three requirements of the statute of frauds § 2–201 are satisfied when the five letters are read together. First, the letters clearly evidence a sale of goods. Second, the writings are signed by the authorized agent of the party against whom enforcement is sought. In the case at hand, enforcement of the contract is sought against Industrial, and the letters are all signed by Brennan, who had the authority to contract on behalf of Industrial. Last, the quantity of the goods to be sold is indicated in the letter dated March 26, 1985, which describes in detail 14 cranes and 1 monorail.

The agreement is also enforceable, since the case falls within the statute of frauds exception of § 2–201(3)(b). According to § 2–201(3)(b), oral contracts may be enforced absent a writing "if the party against whom enforcement is sought admits in his pleading, testimony or otherwise in court that a contract for sale was made * * *." Comment 7 to § 2–201 states that "it is no longer possible to admit the contract in court and still treat the statute as a defense."

Section 2–201(3)(b) contains the following three requirements: There must be an admission; the admission must be made by the party against whom enforcement of the oral contract is sought; and the admission must be made in court.

An admission within the meaning of § 2–201(3)(b) can be made "when the party denying the existence of the contract and relying on the statute takes the stand and, without admitting explicitly that a contract was made, testifies to facts which as a matter of law establish that a contract was formed." See Lewis v. Hughes, 276 Md. 247, 256–57, 346 A.2d 231, 236 (1975).

A compelled or involuntary admission of the existence of an oral contract, obtained during cross-examination at trial, may be relied upon to satisfy § 2–201(3)(b). See, Lewis, supra; Dangerfield v. Markel, 252 N.W.2d 184 (N.D.1977), appeal after remand 278 N.W.2d 364 (N.D.1979); Meylor v. Brown, 281 N.W.2d 632 (Iowa 1979); Franklin Cty. Co–op v. MFC Services (A.A.L.), 441 So.2d 1376 (Miss.1983); M & W Farm Serv. Co. v. Callison, 285 N.W.2d 271 (Iowa 1979). The statutory requirement can be satisfied by way of pleadings, bills of particulars, depositions, affidavits, admissions pursuant to notices to admit, and oral testimony, including admissions made on cross-examination. See Reissman Int'l Corp. v. J.S.O. Wood Products, 10 U.C.C.Rep.Serv. (Callaghan) 1165 (N.Y.Civ. June 6, 1972).

Brennan made the following admission while being cross-examined:

> "Q At the meeting on October 14th in Chicago you specifically told Mr. Hawkins, did you not, either you or Mr. Cole, that Industrial Erectors would not perform or supply any cranes on this project unless it received compensation somewhere in the neighborhood of $150,000.00 more than that set forth in its bid, isn't that correct?
>
> "A I believe it was stated, if the order was to be as per specified with the electrical circuitry and everything else, that there would be an increase *to the contract.*"

Since Industrial disputes the fact that there was a meeting of the minds, and Brennan's testimony establishes the existence of a contract, his testimony should be considered an admission.

This case is very similar to Ursa Farmers' Cooperative v. Trent, 58 Ill.App.3d 930, 374 N.E.2d 1123 (1978). In Trent, the defendant denied the making of a contract, but admitted at trial that he had testified during a discovery deposition: " 'Whoever I talked to, I contracted 2500 bushels of beans' " and " 'I signed up for 2500 bushels of beans at [$]4.01.' " Id. at 931, 374 N.E.2d at 1124. The court held that the trial court properly concluded that the defendant had made an in-court admission of an oral contract for the sale of beans. We hold that similarly in this case Brennan's testimony, considering the circumstances presented at trial, established the existence of an oral contract.

We do not hereby hold that an admission is made whenever the defendant utters the magic words contract or agreement. We acknowledge the possibility that laypeople might misuse legal terminology. We therefore suggest that if a party denying the existence of a contract uses contractual terminology, the court should look at the other evidence presented by the defendant. The record in this case shows that Brennan admitted submitting variance approval documents to Nebraska Builders shortly after the alleged agreement occurred. He also admitted that he sent a letter advising Nebraska Builders that Industrial would adhere to the specifications. In addition, Brennan testified that he visited Omaha and was looking for more commitment from Nebraska Builders in the form of a letter of intent or purchase order. Brennan's conduct indicates that an agreement between the parties existed. See Quaney v. Tobyne, 236 Kan. 201, 689 P.2d 844 (1984) (an admission can be established through verbal admission and conduct). In light of Brennan's conduct we consider the testimony previously quoted to be an admission, and not an inadvertently mistaken use of legal terminology.

The second requirement, that the admission be made by the party against whom enforcement is sought, is also satisfied, since Brennan made the admission on behalf of Industrial.

Last, the admission must be made in court. In Wilke v. Holdrege Coop. Equity Exchange, 200 Neb. 803, 265 N.W.2d 672 (1978), this court held that the exception of § 2–201(3)(b) did not apply to a letter of compromise written by plaintiff's attorney to the manager of the defendant, since the admission was not made in the pleading, testimony, or otherwise in court. The case at hand, however, is distinguishable from Wilke, since Brennan admitted to a contract during his testimony at trial. In Farmland Service Coop, Inc. v. Klein, 196 Neb. 538, 244 N.W.2d 86 (1976), we held that a letter confirming the oral agreement was not within the exceptions enumerated in § 2–201(3). The letter in Farmland Service Coop was referred to in a deposition, but never offered or received into evidence. The admission in the case at bar, however, was made by Brennan during his cross-examination at trial and thus offered into evidence. As a result the case falls within the exception to the statute of frauds, and Industrial can therefore not use § 2–201 as a defense. The rationale is that the statute of frauds was not designed to protect a party who made an oral contract, but, rather, to aid a party who did not make a contract though one is claimed to have been made orally with him. See Reissman Int'l Corp., supra.

The district court's finding that no contract existed was based on an erroneous application of the law controlling this case. As previously mentioned, the parties stipulated at trial that the case was governed by the U.C.C. Even if the parties had not made this stipulation, the case should have been decided under the U.C.C., since the predominant factor of the alleged contract was the sale of goods. See Mennonite Deaconess Home & Hosp. v. Gates Eng'g Co., 219 Neb. 303, 363 N.W.2d 155 (1985) (to determine whether a contract which involves both the sale of goods and services falls within the coverage of the U.C.C., the court looks at the predominant factor of the contract). Therefore, the judgment is reversed and the cause remanded for further proceedings consistent with this opinion.

Reversed and remanded for further proceedings.

THOMSON PRINTING MACHINERY CO. v. B.F. GOODRICH CO.

United States Court of Appeals, Seventh Circuit, 1983.
714 F.2d 744.

Before Wood and Cudahy, Circuit Judges, and Grant, Senior District Judge.

Cudahy, Circuit Judge.

Appellant Thomson Printing Company ("Thomson Printing") won a jury verdict in its suit for breach of contract against appellee B.F. Goodrich

Company ("Goodrich"). The district court concluded, however, that as a matter of law the contract could not be enforced against Goodrich because it was an oral contract, the Statute of Frauds applied and the Statute was not satisfied. Because we conclude that the contract was enforceable on the basis of the "merchants" exception to the Statute of Frauds, we reverse.

Introduction

Thomson Printing buys and sells used printing machinery. On Tuesday, April 10, 1979, the president of Thomson Printing, James Thomson, went to Goodrich's surplus machinery department in Akron, Ohio to look at some used printing machinery which was for sale. James Thomson discussed the sale terms, including a price of $9,000, with Goodrich's surplus equipment manager, Ingram Meyers. Four days later, on Saturday, April 14, 1979, James Thomson sent to Goodrich in Akron a purchase order for the equipment and a check for $1,000 in part payment.

Thomson Printing sued Goodrich when Goodrich refused to perform. Goodrich asserted by way of defense that no contract had been formed and that in any event the alleged oral contract was unenforceable due to the Statute of Frauds. Thomson Printing argued that a contract had been made and that the "merchants" and "partial performance" exceptions to the Statute of Frauds were applicable and satisfied. The jury found for Thomson Printing, but the district court entered judgment for Goodrich on the grounds that the Statute of Frauds barred enforcement of the contract in Thomson's favor.

Historical Background

In 1671, in Old Marston, Oxfordshire, England, defendant Egbert was sued by plaintiff John over an alleged oral promise by Egbert to sell to John a fighting cock named Fiste. John's friend, Harold, claimed he overheard the "deal" and by that dubious means John won, though in fact there apparently was no deal. In 1676 courts did not allow parties to a lawsuit to testify so Egbert could not testify to rebut Harold's story. Compounding the problem was the fact that courts then could not throw out jury verdicts manifestly contrary to the evidence. So, in response to the plight of the Egberts of this world and to the recurring mischief of the Johns, as well as to combat possible "fraude and perjurie" by the Harolds, Parliament passed in 1677 a "statute of frauds" which required that certain contracts for the sale of goods be in writing to be enforceable.[1]

The "Merchants" Exception

A modern exception[2] to the usual writing requirement is the "merchants" exception of the Uniform Commercial Code, Ohio Rev.Code Ann. § 1302.04(B) (Page 1979) (U.C.C. § 2–201(2)), which provides:

1. This historical background is based on J. White & R. Summers, Handbook of the Law Under the Uniform Commercial Code 50 (2d ed. 1980) (footnotes omitted). *See generally* E.A. Farnsworth, Contracts ch. 6 (1982).

2. An exception of longstanding, which was also argued here, is the "partial performance" exception. We express no opinion on the application of this exception.

> Between merchants if within a reasonable time a writing in confirmation of the contract and sufficient against the sender is received and the party receiving it has reason to know its contents, it satisfies the [writing requirement] against such party unless written notice of objection to its contents is given within 10 days after it is received.

We must emphasize that the only effect of this exception is to take away from a merchant who receives a writing in confirmation of a contract the Statute of Frauds defense if the merchant does not object. The sender must still persuade the trier of fact that a contract was in fact made orally, to which the written confirmation applies.

In the instant case, James Thomson sent a "writing in confirmation" to Goodrich four days after his meeting with Ingram Meyers, a Goodrich employee and agent. The purchase order contained Thomson Printing's name, address, telephone number and certain information about the machinery purchase.[3] The check James Thomson sent to Goodrich with the purchase order also had on it Thomson Printing's name and address, and the check carried notations that connected the check with the purchase order.[4]

Goodrich argues, however, that Thomson's writing in confirmation cannot qualify for the 2–201(2) exception because it was not received by anyone at Goodrich who had reason to know its contents.[5] Goodrich claims that Thomson erred in not specifically designating on the envelope, check or purchase order that the items were intended for Ingram Meyers or the surplus equipment department. Consequently, Goodrich contends, it was

3.

Complete Erection Service Miehle Factory Trained Erectors Sales and Service No. 8756

THOMSON PRINTING MACHINERY CO.
MAINTENANCE • REPAIRING • REBUILDING

1936 to 1940 Augusta Boulevard • Chicago, Illinois 60622 • Phone 227–8600

BF GOODRICH COMPANY
500 S. MAIN STREET
AKRON, OHIO 44318

Date 4–14–79

Order No. ______

PURCHASE ORDER

1 # 70 MIEHLE C & C WITH BERRY LIFT
1 # 3/0 MIEHLE TWO COLOR PRINTING PRESS
1 STAUDE MASTER GLUER & ASSORTED PARTS

PACKAGE PRICE $9000.00
DEPOSIT $1000.00
BALANCE UPON REMOVAL $8000.00

CERTIFICATE OF INSURANCE BEING MAILED
BY CRITCHELL–MILLER AGENCY

4. The notations in the upper left hand corner of the check were "1 70 C & C, 1 3/0 T.C. and 1 Staude Master Gluer." See PX 1. Compare these notations with the Purchase Order the check accompanied, *supra,* note 3.

5. The district court found that both parties were merchants for the purpose of 2–201(2). We agree. "For purposes of [2–201(2)] almost every person in business would, therefore, be deemed to be a 'merchant' * * * since the practices involved in the transaction are non-specialized business practices such as answering mail." U.C.C. § 2–104, Comment 2.

unable to "find a home" for the check [6] and purchase order despite attempts to do so, in accordance with its regular procedures, by sending copies of the documents to several of its various divisions. Ingram Meyers testified that he never learned of the purchase order until weeks later when James Thomson called to arrange for removal of the machines. By then, however, the machines had long been sold to someone else.

We think Goodrich misreads the requirements of 2–201(2). First, the literal requirements of 2–201(2), as they apply here, are that a writing "is received" and that Goodrich "has reason to know its contents." There is no dispute that the purchase order and check were received by Goodrich, and there is at least no specific or express requirement that the "receipt" referred to in 2–201(2) be by any Goodrich agent in particular.

> These issues are not resolved by [2–201(2)], but it is probably a reasonable projection that a delivery at either the recipient's principal place of business, a place of business from which negotiations were conducted, or to which the sender may have transmitted previous communications, will be an adequate receipt.

3 R. Duesenberg & L. King, Bender's UCC Service § 2–204[2] at 2–70 (1982).

As for the "reason to know its contents" requirement, this element "is best understood to mean that the confirmation was an instrument which should have been anticipated and therefore should have received the attention of appropriate parties." *Perdue Farms, Inc. v. Motts, Inc.,* 459 F.Supp. 7, 20 (N.D.Miss.1978) (quoting from Bender's UCC Service, *supra,* § 2–204[2] at 2–69). "The receipt of a spurious document would not burden the recipient with a risk of losing the [Statute of Frauds] defense * * *." *Id.* In the case before us there is no doubt that the confirmatory writings were based on actual negotiations (although the legal effect of the negotiations was disputed), and therefore the documents were not "spurious" but could have been anticipated and appropriately handled.

Even if we go beyond the literal requirements of 2–201(2) and read into the "receipt" requirement the "receipt of notice" rule of 1–201(27), we still think Thomson Printing satisfied the "merchants" exception. Section 1–201, the definitional section of the U.C.C., provides that notice received by an organization

> is effective for a particular transaction * * * from the time when it would have been brought to [the attention of the individual conducting that transaction] if the organization had executed *due diligence.*

U.C.C. § 1–201(27) (emphasis supplied). The Official Comment states:

> reason to know, knowledge, or a notification, although "received" for instance by a clerk in Department A of an organization, is effective for a transaction conducted in Department B only from the time when it was *or should have been* communicated to the individual conducting that transaction.

U.C.C. § 1–201(27), Official Comment (emphasis supplied).

6. The check itself was deposited pending clarification in a Goodrich "liability" account.

Thus, the question comes down to whether Goodrich's mailroom, given the information it had, should have notified the surplus equipment manager, Ingram Meyers, of Thomson's confirmatory writing. At whatever point Meyers should have been so notified, then at that point Thomson's writing was effective even though Meyers did not see it. *See* 2 A. Squillante & J. Fonseca, WILLISTON ON SALES § 14–8 at 284 (4th ed. 1974) ("the time of receipt will be measured as if the organization involved had used due diligence in getting the document to the appropriate person").

The definitional section of the U.C.C. also sets the general standard for what mailrooms "should do":

> An organization exercises due diligence if it maintains reasonable routines for communicating significant information to the person conducting the transaction and there is reasonable compliance with the routines.

U.C.C. § 1–201(27). One cannot say that Goodrich's mailroom procedures were reasonable as a matter of law: if Goodrich had exercised due diligence in handling Thomson Printing's purchase order and check, these items would have reasonably promptly come to Ingram Meyers' attention. First, the purchase order on its face should have alerted the mailroom that the documents referred to a purchase of used printing equipment. Since Goodrich had only one surplus machinery department, the documents' "home" should not have been difficult to find. Second, even if the mailroom would have had difficulty in immediately identifying the kind of transaction involved, the purchase order had Thomson Printing's phone number printed on it and we think a "reasonable routine" in these particular circumstances would have involved at some point in the process a simple phone call to Thomson Printing. Thus, we think Goodrich's mailroom mishandled the confirmatory writings. This failure should not permit Goodrich to escape liability by pleading non-receipt. *See* WILLISTON ON SALES, *supra,* § 14–8 at 284–85.

We note that the jury verdict for Thomson Printing indicates that the jury found as a fact that the contract had in fact been made and that the Statute of Frauds had been satisfied. Also, Goodrich acknowledges those facts about the handling of the purchase order which we regard as determinative of the "merchants" exception question. We think that there is ample evidence to support the jury findings both of the existence of the contract and of the satisfaction of the Statute.

The district court, in holding as a matter of law that the circumstances failed to satisfy the Statute of Frauds, was impressed by James Thomson's dereliction in failing to specifically direct the purchase order and check to the attention of Ingram Meyers or the surplus equipment department. We agree that Thomson erred in this respect, but, for the reasons we have suggested, Goodrich was at least equally derelict in failing to find a "home" for the well-identified documents. Goodrich argues that in the "vast majority" of cases it can identify checks within a week without contacting an outside party; in the instant case, therefore, if Goodrich correctly states its experience under its procedures, it should presumably have checked with Thomson Printing promptly after the time it normally identified checks by other means—in this case, by its own calculation, a week at most. Under the particular circumstances of this case, we therefore think it inappropriate to set aside a jury verdict on Statute of Frauds grounds.

The district court's order granting judgment for Goodrich is reversed and the cause is remanded for further proceedings consistent with this opinion.

Reversed and remanded.

Problem 10–9

IBM and Epprecht entered an oral agreement allegedly for the production by Epprecht of 50,000 print-head assemblies for computers. The assemblies were to conform to particular specifications prepared and furnished by IBM. IBM issued purchase orders for 7,000 assemblies, 4,000 of which were accepted and 3,000 of which were rejected by IBM. IBM paid the price of the assemblies accepted but, claiming quality problems, refused to pay anything for the rejected assemblies and cancelled the agreement. Epprecht, alleging the facts stated above, sued for damages caused by IBM's "wrongful" rejection of 3,000 units. IBM moved for a summary judgment on the basis of UCC 2–201. Epprecht argued that the summary judgment should be denied: Although there was no writing, the statute of frauds was satisfied under UCC 2–201(3)(a) & (c). Epprecht cited Impossible Electronic Techniques, Inc. v. Wackehnut Protective Systems, Inc., 669 F.2d 1026, 1036–37 (11th Cir.1982), where the court stated that the "statute exempts contracts involving 'specially manufactured' goods from the writing requirement because in these cases the very nature of the goods serves as a reliable indication that a contract was indeed formed." Further: "Where the seller has commenced or completed the manufacture of goods that conform to the special needs of a particular buyer and thereby are not suitable for sale to others, not only is the likelihood of a perjured claim of a contract diminished, but denying enforcement to such a contract would impose substantial hardship on the aggrieved party. * * * The unfairness is especially acute where * * * the seller has incurred substantial, unrecoverable expense in reliance on the oral promise of the buyer. * * * The crucial inquiry is whether the manufacturer could sell the goods in the ordinary course of his business to someone other than the original buyer. If with slight alterations the goods could be so sold, then they are not specially manufactured; if, however, essential changes are necessary to render the goods marketable by the seller to others, then the exception does apply." How should the court rule?

LIGE DICKSON CO. v. UNION OIL CO. OF CAL.

Supreme Court of Washington, 1981.
96 Wash.2d 291, 635 P.2d 103.

DORE, JUSTICE.

The Ninth Circuit Court of Appeals certified the following question to us:

> Under the law of the State of Washington, may an oral promise otherwise within the statute of frauds, Wash.Rev.Code § 62A.2–201, nevertheless be enforceable on the basis of promissory estoppel? *See* Restatement (Second) of Contracts § 217A. *See generally Klinke v. Famous Recipe Fried Chicken, Inc.,* 94 Wash.2d 255, 616 P.2d 644 (1980).

Our answer to this question is "no". Analysis and elaboration follow.

The business relationship between plaintiff Lige Dickson Company (or its predecessor partnership) and defendant Union Oil Company of California is long standing, dating from 1937. Plaintiff was a general contractor and purchased its oil-based products from defendant. In 1964, defendant encouraged and aided plaintiff in entering the asphalt paving business. From 1964 through 1973, with one exception, plaintiff purchased all its liquid asphalt from defendant. In the ordinary course of business, plaintiff telephoned orders to defendant, plaintiff was invoiced, and all bills were paid. Plaintiff and defendant never executed a written contract providing for the sale and purchase of liquid asphalt.

From 1964 until late 1970, the defendant's price for liquid asphalt remained constant. In December 1970, all of the suppliers of liquid asphalt in the Tacoma area raised their prices. Responding to this in May or June of 1971, plaintiff requested, and defendant provided, an oral guarantee against further increases insofar as would affect those contracts which committed the plaintiff to manufacture and sell asphalt paving at fixed, agreed sums. A list was made of the plaintiff's contracts and the parties computed the amount of liquid asphalt needed to fulfill them. At the same time, defendant promised plaintiff that any upward change in price would be applicable only to contracts which plaintiff entered into after the price increase.

At trial, an official of defendant conceded that by November 1973 there was an unwritten custom in the liquid asphalt business in the Tacoma area, well known and acted upon by suppliers, and users, that any increase in price of liquid asphalt would not be applicable to manufacturers' then-existing contracts. From mid-1971 until November 1973, defendant's sales representatives visited plaintiff and ascertained tonnage of liquid asphalt needed for plaintiff to fulfill existing paving contracts and also promised plaintiff that the price for that liquid tonnage would be protected.

Nevertheless, in November 1973 defendant wrote to plaintiff that the price of liquid asphalt was rising by $3 per ton and plaintiff was informed on December 6 and 13, 1973 of further increases. The new prices were to be applicable to all purchases made after December 31, 1973. This was plaintiff's first notification that defendant was abandoning the parties' price protection agreement. In addition, the new prices were on a "verbal, indefinite basis * * * subject to change" with or without notice.

Without a firm supplier, plaintiff was unable to seek new paving contracts during the first part of 1974. What liquid asphalt was available was used by plaintiff to complete existing contracts. Plaintiff incurred a total increased out-of-pocket cost of $39,006.50 in acquiring liquid asphalt to perform existing contracts.

Plaintiff brought suit against defendant in the United States District Court for Western Washington for breach of contract. The trial court found that there was an oral contract between the parties, but the statute of frauds, RCW 62A.2–201 rendered the contract unenforceable. The cause was appealed to the Ninth Circuit which certified the question quoted above to this court.

The facts as outlined above are contained in the District Court's Findings of Facts which were made part of the record before this court. In the Ninth Circuit appeal, defendant has assigned errors to certain of these findings. These contentions, however, are not before us. We do not need certainty in the facts to answer the pure question of law presented for our determination. The Ninth Circuit has retained jurisdiction over all matters but the narrow question of law certified here.

The Restatement (Second) of Contracts § 217A (Tent.Drafts Nos. 1–7, 1973)[3] (hereinafter § 217A) authorizes enforcement of a promise which induced action or forbearance by a promisee notwithstanding the statute of frauds. Adoption of § 217A was before this court in *Klinke v. Famous Recipe Fried Chicken, Inc.,* 94 Wash.2d 255, 616 P.2d 644 (1980).

In *Klinke,* the plaintiff had been induced by defendant to leave his employ in Alaska and to move to Washington to establish a food franchise. Defendant had promised plaintiff that defendant would qualify and register in Washington as a dealer in franchises. After plaintiff's move, defendant failed to secure the proper dealer registration and later abandoned its efforts to do so. The plaintiff claimed $200,000 in lost time and wages and other damages. On summary judgment, the trial court dismissed the case because RCW 19.36.010(1)[4] voids unwritten contracts which cannot be performed in one year. The Court of Appeals reversed the trial court based on two theories. *Klinke v. Famous Recipe Fried Chicken, Inc.,* 24 Wash.App. 202, 600 P.2d 1034 (1979). First, defendant's failure to reduce the agreement with plaintiff to a writing, and plaintiff's reliance on such promise, estopped defendant from asserting the statute of frauds as a defense. Restatement of Contracts, §§ 90, 178, comment f (1932). Second, the Court of Appeals adopted § 217A. On review of that decision, we refused to adopt § 217A but affirmed the court's reversal on its first theory. We stated:

> The unforseen application of section 217A to areas of law outside the scope of the facts of this case convinces us that it would be unwise to

3. The Restatement (Second) of Contracts § 217A (Tent.Drafts Nos. 1–7, 1973) reads:

"Enforcement by Virtue of Action in Reliance

"(1) A promise which the promisor should reasonably expect to induce action or forbearance on the part of the promisee or a third person and which does induce the action or forbearance is enforceable notwithstanding the Statute of Frauds if injustice can be avoided only by enforcement of the promise. The remedy granted for breach is to be limited as justice requires.

"(2) In determining whether injustice can be avoided only by enforcement of the promise, the following circumstances are significant:

"(a) the availability and adequacy of other remedies, particularly cancellation and restitution;

"(b) the definite and substantial character of the action or forbearance in relation to the remedy sought;

"(c) the extent to which the action or forbearance corroborates evidence of the making and terms of the promise, or the making and terms are otherwise established by clear and convincing evidence;

"(d) the reasonableness of the action or forbearance:

"(e) the extent to which the action or forbearance was foreseeable by the promisor."

[§ 139 in final version. Ed.]

4. RCW 19.36.010 states, in part:

"In the following cases, specified in this section, any agreement, contract and promise shall be void, unless such agreement, contract or promise, or some note or memorandum thereof, be in writing, and signed by the party to be charged therewith, or by some person thereunto by him lawfully authorized, that is to say: (1) Every agreement that by its terms is not to be performed in one year from the making thereof * * *"

adopt that section now unless necessary to effectuate justice. That is not mandated by the facts of this case.

Klinke v. Famous Recipe Fried Chicken, Inc., 94 Wash.2d 255, 262, 616 P.2d 644 (1980).

Plaintiff in the subject case urges us to now adopt § 217A as being "necessary to effectuate justice". Plaintiff focuses on the parties' long-standing relationship and defendant's responsibility "in great part" for introducing plaintiff into the asphalt paving business. Plaintiff also asserts that defendant's price protection agreement and assurances encouraged (i.e., induced?) plaintiff to make bids and enter into contracts.

Defendant asks this court to distinguish the statute of frauds at issue in *Klinke* from the statute of frauds contained within the Uniform Commercial Code (U.C.C.) at issue here.[5] Such distinction has been recognized.

> The statute of frauds requirements may vary as to the nature of the agreements involved, and a close examination of the subject matter of the oral promise in question is therefore warranted. For example, if the oral promise in question concerned the sale of goods, the attorney would want to be aware of the requirements set out in UCC § 2–201(3) which states the circumstances under which a contract for the sale of goods may be enforceable notwithstanding the statute of frauds * * * It should be pointed out that where there exists, in statute or in case law, clearly established means under which a contract dealing with a particular subject matter may be rendered enforceable notwithstanding the statute of frauds, the courts may be hesitant to apply promissory estoppel in such a manner as to enlarge upon those means of avoiding the statute.

Annotation Comment Note.—Promissory Estoppel as Basis for Avoidance of Statute of Frauds, 56 A.L.R.3d 1037, 1045 (1932). (Footnotes omitted.) The Ninth Circuit Court of Appeals has held, in interpreting and applying California law, that U.C.C. § 2–201 cannot be overcome through the application of the doctrine of promissory estoppel. *C.R. Fedrick, Inc. v. Borg-Warner Corp.,* 552 F.2d 852 (9th Cir.1977). The Kentucky Supreme Court reached the same conclusion based upon the U.C.C.'s internal method of avoiding § 2–201's hardship. *C.G. Campbell & Son, Inc. v. Comdeq. Corp.,* 586 S.W.2d 40 (Ky.App.1979). It reasoned that the statutory avoidance of § 2–201 found in § 2–201(3) was as far as the legislature was willing to go and

> any attempt by the courts to judicially amend this statute which is plain on its face would contravene the separation of powers mandated by the Constitution.

Campbell at page 41.

On the other hand, the Iowa Supreme Court reached the opposite result in *Warder & Lee Elevator, Inc. v. Britten,* 274 N.W.2d 339 (Iowa 1979). That

5. The Uniform Commercial Code as adopted in Washington is found at RCW Title 62A. Reference to U.C.C. § 2–201 and

court found that U.C.C. § 1–103[6] provided the authority for the use of promissory estoppel to defeat the statute of frauds. That section provides, *inter alia,* that "unless displaced by the particular provision of this chapter" estoppel and other validating or invalidating doctrines shall supplement the U.C.C. The court reasoned that the exceptions to the statute of frauds found at § 2–201(3)(a)–(c) are "definitional" and were not meant to displace equitable and legal principles otherwise applicable to contract actions.

> If [2–201] were construed as displacing principles otherwise preserved in [1–103], it would mean that an oral contract coming within its terms would be unenforceable despite fraud, deceit, misrepresentation, dishonesty or any other form of unconscionable conduct by the party relying upon the statute. No court has taken such an extreme position. Nor would we be justified in doing so. Despite differences relating to the availability of an estoppel defense, courts uniformly hold "that the Statute of Frauds, having been enacted for the purpose of preventing fraud, shall not be made the instrument of shielding[,] protecting, or aiding the party who relies upon it in the perpetration of a fraud or in the consummation of a fraudulent scheme." 3 Williston on Contracts § 553A at 796 (Third Ed. Jaeger, 1960).

Warder & Lee Elevator, Inc. v. Britten, supra at page 342.

Defendant asks us to adopt the view of the dissent in *Warder & Lee Elevator, Inc. v. Britten, supra.* The thrust of the dissent is that § 1–103 allows estoppel to supplement the U.C.C. "unless displaced by the particular provisions of this chapter"; and § 2–201 contains its own limiting language in that the statute of frauds applies "except as otherwise provided *in this section.*" (Italics ours.) Further, the dissent noted that a party to an oral contract who has been defrauded has available the equitable remedy of restitution. In such a case, the recovery is based on the wrong, not on a contract.

From the limited record before us in the subject case, it appears that equitable estoppel is not available to the plaintiff. There seems to be neither allegation nor proof of fraud or deceit. Plaintiff's only remedy may be based upon breach of the oral contract. *Nonetheless,* we must hold that promissory estoppel cannot be used to overcome the statute of frauds in a case which involves the sale of goods.

The Uniform Commercial Code was adopted to regulate commercial dealings. Uniformity among different jurisdictions in decisions concerning commerce was a major motivation behind development of the U.C.C. By so doing, it was hoped that this area of the law would become clearer and disputes would be more readily resolved. These policies are enunciated in the U.C.C., in part, as follows:

> 62A.1–102 Purposes; rules of construction; variation by agreement
> * * *

§ 1–103 in this opinion are intended to refer to Washington's corresponding sections.

6. Washington's version of § 1–103, found at RCW 62A.1–103, reads:

"Unless displaced by the particular provisions of this Title, the principles of law and equity, including the law merchant and the law relative to capacity to contract, principal and agent, estoppel, fraud, misrepresentation, duress, coercion, mistake, bankruptcy, or other validating or invalidating cause shall supplement its provisions."

(2) Underlying purposes and policies of this Title are

(a) to simplify, clarify and modernize the law governing commercial transactions;

* * *

(c) to make uniform the law among the various jurisdictions.

It was hoped that commercial transactions could take place across state boundaries without the stultifying effect caused by differences in states' laws.

> The Uniform Commercial Code, hammered out by lawyers, judges and law teachers dedicated to clarity and good business sense in commercial law, has brought together into one coherent statement the best laws and practices prevalent in the United States.

American Bar Association, *Uniform Commercial Code Handbook,* "The Uniform Commercial Code," at 1 (1964).

> Because of the federal system, the American lawyer, probably more than any other, has been conscious of the disadvantages of differing laws. Internally he has tried to do something about it.

American Bar Association, *Uniform Commercial Code Handbook,* "The Uniform Commercial Code," at 19 (1964).

If we were to adopt § 217A as applicable in the context of the sale of goods, we would allow parties to circumvent the U.C.C. *See Warder & Lee Elevator, Inc. v. Britten, supra,* (Reynoldson, C.J., dissenting). For example, to prove justifiable reliance (an element of promissory estoppel), the promisee may offer evidence of course of dealing between the parties, as plaintiff did in this case. The Official Comments to RCWA 62A.1–205(4) state that the statute of frauds

> restrict[s] the actions of the parties, and * * * cannot be abrogated by agreement, or by a *usage of trade* * * *

RCWA 62A.1–205 at 71. (Italics ours.)

Notwithstanding our appreciation of plaintiff's dilemma, we cannot help but foresee increased litigation and confusion as being the necessary result of the eroding of the U.C.C. if § 217A is adopted in this case. We join the other courts which limit the doctrine of promissory estoppel from overcoming a valid defense based on the statute of frauds contained within the Uniform Commercial Code. By so doing, we make no comment on the applicability of § 217A to defeat the raising of the statute of frauds as a defense under RCW 19.36.010.

BRACHTENBACH, C.J., and DOLLIVER, WILLIAMS, STAFFORD, DIMMICK and UTTER, JJ., concur.

ROSELLINI, JUSTICE (concurring specially).

I agree with the majority that, in order to preserve the integrity of the Uniform Commercial Code, the question submitted by the Ninth Circuit Court of Appeals must be answered in the negative. It is evident that the legislature gave careful thought to the circumstances which would justify exceptions to the requirement of a written contract, and those exceptions are set forth in the act itself. They do not include circumstances which in other areas of law might invoke the doctrine of promissory estoppel.

While the code makes no provision for relief under the theory of promissory estoppel, it does provide an exception to the requirement of a writing

> if the party against whom enforcement is sought admits in his pleading, testimony or otherwise in court that a contract for sale was made, but the contract is not enforceable under this provision beyond the quantity of goods admitted; * * *

RCW 62A.2–201(3)(b).

There is in the district court's findings some suggestion that there may have been such an admission here. If that were the case, the code itself would provide a remedy.

HICKS, J., concurs.

[Some footnotes omitted.]

Note

Contra: B & W Glass, Inc. v. Weather Shield Mfgr., Inc., 829 P.2d 809 (Wyo.1992).

CHAPTER ELEVEN

THE POTENTIALLY ADVERSE BEARING OF "PRE-CONTRACT" FACTS AND EVENTS UPON THE AGREEMENT

SECTION 1. INTRODUCTION

Suppose the seller and buyer have concluded a bargain which is enforceable as a contract under Article 2, Part 2. The bargain is reduced to writing and signed by both parties. After performance commences, a dispute erupts over the obligations under the contract. The dispute may involve either the scope of the agreement in fact or the meaning of terms clearly within the scope of agreement. In either case, there is an honest disagreement.

How does Article 2 deal with disputes of this sort? For example, one party, to support an argument about the scope or meaning of the agreement, will undoubtedly seek to introduce evidence beyond the "four corners" of the writing. Can the other party exclude this evidence and, if so, under what circumstances?

The starting place is the definition of agreement in UCC 1–201(3): Agreement means "the bargain of the parties in fact as found in their language or by implication from other circumstances including course of dealing or usage of trade or course of performance as provided in this Act (Sections 1–205 and 2–208.)" Under this expansive definition, agreement may not be limited to the terms in the writing: It may include terms derived from trade usage, a prior course of dealing between the parties or the negotiations leading up to the particular bargain at stake. Thus, as the *Columbia Nitrogen* case, infra at page 498, reveals, one party may seek to supplement a price term contained in the writing by a usage or practice of the trade. See UCC 1–205(2).

If the statutory conditions for admissibility are satisfied, the next question is whether the parties, by agreement, have attempted to limit the scope of their bargain. Have they, for example, attempted to "contract out" of relevant trade usage or the expectations created by a prior course of dealing? If so, should that attempt be recognized by the court? See UCC 1–205(4), where an ordering principle is stated. Similarly, did both parties intend that their writing be a partial or total integration of their agreement, i.e., did they intend to exclude from the writing terms that were in fact agreed prior to or contemporaneously with its adoption? If so, the stage is set for application of the infamous parol evidence rule, UCC 2–202.

Finally, if the scope of agreement is determined, how are disputes over the meaning of terms to which the parties agreed to be resolved? What does the UCC say with regard to contract interpretation disputes and the evidence which is relevant to their resolution?

These questions will occupy our attention in this Chapter. For background see *Chen, Code, Custom and Contract: The Uniform Commercial Code as Law Merchant*, 27 Tex. Int'l. L.J. 91 (1992).

SECTION 2. PRE–CONTRACT FACTS OR EVENTS WHICH VARY, SUPPLEMENT OR GIVE MEANING TO THE AGREEMENT

COLUMBIA NITROGEN CORP. v. ROYSTER CO.

United States Court of Appeals, Fourth Circuit, 1971.
451 F.2d 3.

BUTZNER, CIRCUIT JUDGE.

Columbia Nitrogen Corp. appeals a judgment in the amount of $750,000 in favor of F.S. Royster Guano Co. for breach of a contract for the sale of phosphate to Columbia by Royster. Columbia defended on the grounds that the contract, construed in light of the usage of the trade and course of dealing, imposed no duty to accept at the quoted prices the minimum quantities stated in the contract. It also asserted an antitrust defense and counterclaim based on Royster's alleged reciprocal trade practices. The district court excluded the evidence about course of dealing and usage of the trade. It submitted the antitrust issues based on coercive reciprocity to the jury, but refused to submit the alternative theory of non-coercive reciprocity. The jury found for Royster on both the contract claim and the anti-trust counterclaim. We hold that Columbia's proffered evidence was improperly excluded and Columbia is entitled to a new trial on the contractual issues. With respect to the antitrust issues, we affirm.

I.

Royster manufactures and markets mixed fertilizers, the principal components of which are nitrogen, phosphate and potash. Columbia is primarily a producer of nitrogen, although it manufactures some mixed fertilizer. For several years Royster had been a major purchaser of Columbia's products, but Columbia had never been a significant customer of Royster. In the fall of 1966, Royster constructed a facility which enabled it to produce more phosphate than it needed in its own operations. After extensive negotiations, the companies executed a contract for Royster's sale of a minimum of 31,000 tons of phosphate each year for three years to Columbia, with an option to extend the term. The contract stated the price per ton, subject to an escalation clause dependent on production costs.

Phosphate prices soon plunged precipitously. Unable to resell the phosphate at a competitive price, Columbia ordered only part of the scheduled tonnage. At Columbia's request, Royster lowered its price for diammonium phosphate on shipments for three months in 1967, but specified that subsequent shipments would be at the original contract price. Even with this concession, Royster's price was still substantially above the market. As a result, Columbia ordered less than a tenth of the phosphate Royster was to ship in the first contract year. When pressed by Royster, Columbia offered to take the phosphate at the current market price and resell it without brokerage fee. Royster, however, insisted on the contract price. When Columbia refused delivery, Royster sold the unaccepted phosphate for Columbia's account at a price substantially below the contract price.

II.

Columbia assigns error to the pretrial ruling of the district court excluding all evidence on usage of the trade and course of dealing between the parties. It offered the testimony of witnesses with long experience in the trade that because of uncertain crop and weather conditions, farming practices, and government agricultural programs, express price and quantity terms in contracts for materials in the mixed fertilizer industry are mere projections to be adjusted according to market forces.*

Columbia also offered proof of its business dealings with Royster over the six-year period preceding the phosphate contract. Since Columbia had not been a significant purchaser of Royster's products, these dealings were almost exclusively nitrogen sales to Royster or exchanges of stock carried in inventory. The pattern which emerges, Columbia claimed, is one of repeated and substantial deviation from the stated amount or price, including four instances where Royster took none of the goods for which it had contracted. Columbia offered proof that the total variance amounted to more than $500,000 in reduced sales. This experience, a Columbia officer offered to testify, formed the basis of an understanding on which he depended in conducting negotiations with Royster.

The district court held that the evidence should be excluded. It ruled that "custom and usage or course of dealing are not admissible to contradict the express, plain, unambiguous language of a valid written contract, which

* One witness testified, in part, as follows:

"The contracts generally entered into between buyer and seller of materials has always been, in my opinion, construed to be the buyer's best estimate of his anticipated requirements for a given period of time. It is well known in our industry that weather conditions, farming practices, government farm control programs, change requirements from time to time. And therefore allowances were always made to meet these circumstances as they arose."

"Tonnage requirements fluctuate greatly, and that is one reason that the contracts are not considered as binding as most contracts are, because the buyer normally would buy on historical basis, but his normal average use would be per annum of any given material. Now that can be affected very decidedly by adverse weather conditions such as a drought, or a flood, or maybe governmental programs which we have been faced with for many, many years, seed grain programs. They pay the farmer not to plant. If he doesn't plant, he doesn't use the fertilizer. When the contracts are made, we do not know of all these contingencies and what they are going to be. So the contract is made for what is considered a fair estimate of his requirements. And, the contract is considered binding to the extent, on him morally, that if he uses the tonnage that he will execute the contract in good faith as the buyer. * * *"

"I have never heard of a contract of this type being enforced legally. * * * Well, it undoubtedly sounds ridiculous to people from other industries, but there is a very definite, several very definite reasons why the fertilizer business is always operated under what we call gentlemen's agreements. * * *"

"The custom in the fertilizer industry is that the seller either meets the competitive situation or releases the buyer from it upon proof that he can buy it at that price * * *. [T]hey will either have the option of meeting it or releasing him from taking additional tonnage or holding him to that price. * * *"

And this custom exists "regardless of the contractual provisions."

"[T]he custom was that [these contracts] were not worth the cost of the paper they were printed on." [451 F.2d at 7, n. 3]

by virtue of its detail negates the proposition that the contract is open to variances in its terms. * * * "

A number of Virginia cases have held that extrinsic evidence may not be received to explain or supplement a written contract unless the court finds the writing is ambiguous. E.g., Mathieson Alkali Works v. Virginia Banner Coal Corp., 147 Va. 125, 136 S.E. 673 (1927). This rule, however, has been changed by the Uniform Commercial Code which Virginia has adopted. The Code expressly states that it "shall be liberally construed and applied to promote its underlying purposes and policies," which include "the expansion of commercial practices through custom, usage and agreement of the parties. * * * " Va.Code Ann. § 8.1–102 (1965). The importance of usage of trade and course of dealing between the parties is shown by § 8.2–202, which authorizes their use to explain or supplement a contract. The official comment states this section rejects the old rule that evidence of course of dealing or usage of trade can be introduced only when the contract is ambiguous. And the Virginia commentators, noting that "[t]his section reflects a more liberal approach to the introduction of parol evidence * * * than has been followed in Virginia," express the opinion that Mathieson, supra, and similar Virginia cases no longer should be followed. Va.Code Ann. § 8.2–202, Va.Comment. See also Portsmouth Gas Co. v. Shebar, 209 Va. 250, 253 n. 1, 163 S.E.2d 205, 208 n. 1 (1968) (dictum). We hold, therefore, that a finding of ambiguity is not necessary for the admission of extrinsic evidence about the usage of the trade and the parties' course of dealing.

We turn next to Royster's claim that Columbia's evidence was properly excluded because it was inconsistent with the express terms of their agreement. There can be no doubt that the Uniform Commercial Code restates the well established rule that evidence of usage of trade and course of dealing should be excluded whenever it cannot be reasonably construed as consistent with the terms of the contract. Division of Triple T Service, Inc. v. Mobil Oil Corp., 60 Misc.2d 720, 304 N.Y.S.2d 191, 203 (1969), aff'd mem., 311 N.Y.S.2d 961 (1970). Royster argues that the evidence should be excluded as inconsistent because the contract contains detailed provisions regarding the base price, escalation, minimum tonnage, and delivery schedules. The argument is based on the premise that because a contract appears on its face to be complete, evidence of course of dealing and usage of trade should be excluded. We believe, however, that neither the language nor the policy of the Code supports such a broad exclusionary rule. Section 8.2–202 expressly allows evidence of course of dealing or usage of trade to explain or supplement terms intended by the parties as a final expression of their agreement. When this section is read in light of Va.Code Ann. § 8.1–205(4), it is clear that the test of admissibility is not whether the contract appears on its face to be complete in every detail, but whether the proffered evidence of course of dealing and trade usage reasonably can be construed as consistent with the express terms of the agreement.

The proffered testimony sought to establish that because of changing weather conditions, farming practices, and government agricultural programs, dealers adjusted prices, quantities, and delivery schedules to reflect declining market conditions. For the following reasons it is reasonable to construe this evidence as consistent with the express terms of the contract:

The contract does not expressly state that course of dealing and usage of trade cannot be used to explain or supplement the written contract.

The contract is silent about adjusting prices and quantities to reflect a declining market. It neither permits nor prohibits adjustment, and this neutrality provides a fitting occasion for recourse to usage of trade and prior dealing to supplement the contract and explain its terms.

Minimum tonnages and additional quantities are expressed in terms of "Products Supplied Under Contract." Significantly, they are not expressed as just "Products" or as "Products Purchased Under Contract." The description used by the parties is consistent with the proffered testimony.

Finally, the default clause of the contract refers only to the failure of the buyer to pay for delivered phosphate. During the contract negotiations, Columbia rejected a Royster proposal for liquidated damages of $10 for each ton Columbia declined to accept. On the other hand, Royster rejected a Columbia proposal for a clause that tied the price to the market by obligating Royster to conform its price to offers Columbia received from other phosphate producers. The parties, having rejected both proposals, failed to state any consequences of Columbia's refusal to take delivery—the kind of default Royster alleges in this case. Royster insists that we span this hiatus by applying the general law of contracts permitting recovery of damages upon the buyer's refusal to take delivery according to the written provisions of the contract. This solution is not what the Uniform Commercial Code prescribes. Before allowing damages, a court must first determine whether the buyer has in fact defaulted. It must do this by supplementing and explaining the agreement with evidence of trade usage and course of dealing that is consistent with the contract's express terms. Va.Code Ann. §§ 8.1–205(4), 8.2–202. Faithful adherence to this mandate reflects the reality of the marketplace and avoids the overly legalistic interpretations which the Code seeks to abolish.

Royster also contends that Columbia's proffered testimony was properly rejected because it dealt with mutual willingness of buyer and seller to adjust contract terms to the market. Columbia, Royster protests, seeks unilateral adjustment. This argument misses the point. What Columbia seeks to show is a practice of mutual adjustments so prevalent in the industry and in prior dealings between the parties that it formed a part of the agreement governing this transaction. It is not insisting on a unilateral right to modify the contract.

Nor can we accept Royster's contention that the testimony should be excluded under the contract clause:

> "No verbal understanding will be recognized by either party hereto; this contract expresses all the terms and conditions of the agreement, shall be signed in duplicate, and shall not become operative until approved in writing by the Seller."

Course of dealing and trade usage are not synonymous with verbal understandings, terms and conditions. Section 8.2–202 draws a distinction between supplementing a written contract by consistent additional terms and supplementing it by course of dealing or usage of trade. Evidence of additional terms must be excluded when "the court finds the writing to have been intended also as a complete and exclusive statement of the terms of the agreement." Significantly, no similar limitation is placed on the introduction of evidence of course of dealing or usage of trade. Indeed the official comment notes that course of dealing and usage of trade, unless carefully negated, are admissible to supplement the terms of any writing, and that contracts are to be read on the assumption that these elements were taken for granted when the document was phrased. Since the Code assigns course of dealing and trade usage unique and important roles, they should not be conclusively rejected by reading them into stereotyped language that makes no specific reference to them. Cf. Provident Tradesmen's Bank & Trust Co. v. Pemberton, 196 Pa.Super. 180, 173 A.2d 780. Indeed, the Code's official commentators urge that overly simplistic and overly legalistic interpretation of a contract should be shunned.

We conclude therefore that Columbia's evidence about course of dealing and usage of trade should have been admitted. Its exclusion requires that the judgment against Columbia must be set aside and the case retried.

* * *

[After affirming the district court's charges to the jury on modification and damage issues and judgment on the anti-trust issue, the court remanded the case for a new trial.]

[Footnotes omitted.]

Notes

1. To achieve the outcome in Columbia Nitrogen, the moving party was required: (1) to prove the existence and scope of the trade usage "as facts", UCC 1–205(2); (2) to prove that both parties were in the trade or, if not, that they were or "should be" aware of the usage, 1–205(3); (3) to persuade the court to admit the usage for a proper purpose, i.e., to "give particular meaning to and supplement or qualify" the terms of the agreement, UCC 1–205(3); (4) to survive a possible claim that the established usage was unreasonable, UCC 1–205, Comment 6; and (5) to persuade the court that the usage can be "construed wherever reasonable as consistent" with any express terms purporting to "contract out" of the usage. UCC 1–205(4). The outcome in the *Columbia Nitrogen* case has been criticized:

> The court's attempt to demonstrate a possible consistent interpretation is a strained exercise in semantic quibbling that * * * boggles the reasonable mind. The opinion reads so poorly because the court did not address the correct issue * * * the inquiry should have examined the relationship of the usage of trade to the facts of the case. That 'contracts' have been treated as 'fair estimates' is not enough: additional facts must be known about the types of contracts so regarded. * * * The * * * opinion, however, did not discuss relevance and only stated some of the facts about the usage of trade. The facts that are detailed in the opinion require further inquiry because they indicate that the disputed contract was unlike the contracts treated as estimates in the trade. Kirst, *Usage of Trade and Course of Dealing: Subversion of the UCC Theory,* 1977 U.Ill.L.F. 811, 844–45 (footnotes omitted).

Do you agree?

2. Shell Oil entered long-term contracts for the supply of Nanakuli's asphalt requirements on the Island of Oahu, Hawaii. Under the 1969 contract, the price was to be Shell's posted price at the time of delivery. In January, 1974, Shell raised the price from $44 to $76 per ton. Nanakuli, however, had previously committed 7,200 tons of asphalt to paving contractors at prices calculated at the $44 per ton price. When Shell charged $76 per ton for the asphalt, Nanakuli refused to pay this price and claimed that it was entitled to "price protection" under a usage of the asphalt paving trade in Hawaii and that this usage was incorporated into the contract. Price protection required that Shell hold the price on all tonnage committed in reliance upon the $44 per ton price prior to the price increase. The jury returned a verdict of $220,000 for Nanakuli on the ground that Shell had breached the contract by failing to protect the $44 price. The federal district judge set aside the verdict and granted Shell's motion for judgment n.o.v. The Ninth Circuit Court of Appeals vacated the district court's decision and reinstated the jury verdict.

In a long, complex opinion, which was clearly sympathetic to the UCC's emphasis on context, the Court held, inter alia, that: (1) the trial judge did not abuse his discretion in defining the applicable trade as the asphalt paving trade, rather than the purchase and sale of asphalt alone; (2) the "price protection" usage in that trade was established and Shell was or should have been aware of it; (3) the usage was reinforced by the conduct of Shell in the performance of the contract with Nanakuli; and (4) the jury could have reasonably construed the price protection usage as consistent with the express price term in the contract and a clause purporting to exclude all prior "oral" agreements from the writing.

The court stated that the agreement must be examined in "light of the close, symbiotic relations between Shell and Nanakuli on the island of Oahu, whereby the expansion of Shell on the island was intimately connected with the business growth of Nanakuli." In addition, the UCC "looks to the actual performance of a contract as the best indication of what the parties intended those terms to mean." Finally, the court concluded that "price protection" was consistent with the express price term "as long as it does not totally negate it." The usage "only came into play at times of price increases and only for work committed prior to those increases on non-escalation contracts." It was, therefore an "exception to, rather than a total negation of, the express price term" which was known to Shell and constituted an "intended part of the agreement, as that term is broadly defined by the Code. * * *" Nanakuli Paving & Rock Co. v. Shell Oil Co., Inc., 664 F.2d 772 (9th Cir.1981). The Nanakuli court cited and discussed Columbia Nitrogen as a "leading case" in a group of federal decisions that "usually have been lenient in not ruling out consistent additional terms or trade usage for apparent inconsistency with express terms." The court, however, noted Professor Kirst's criticism of *Columbia Nitrogen* for failing to examine the relationship of the trade usage to the facts of the case, but concluded that this objection had been met in *Nanakuli.* See, generally, Kastley, *Stock Equipment for the Bargain in Fact: Trade Usage, "Express Terms," and Consistency Under Section 1–205 of the Uniform Commercial Code,* 64 N.Car.L.Rev. 777, 788–791 (1986).

3. It is clear that particular parties can "contract out" of a general usage of trade which otherwise would be part of the agreement. UCC 1–205(4). Draft a one sentence clause which, in your judgment, would be effective to exclude the usages involved in the *Columbia Nitrogen* and *Shell Oil* cases.

ALASKAN NORTHERN DEVELOPMENT, INC. v. ALYESKA PIPELINE SERVICE CO.

Supreme Court of Alaska, 1983.
666 P.2d 33, *cert. denied*, 464 U.S. 1041, 104 S.Ct. 706, 79 L.Ed.2d 170 (1984).

James J. White,* Ann Arbor, Mich., * * * for appellant.

Before BURKE, C.J., and RABINOWITZ, MATTHEWS and COMPTON, JJ.

OPINION

COMPTON, JUSTICE.

Alaska Northern Development, Inc. ("AND") appeals a judgment in favor of Alyeska Pipeline Service Co. ("Alyeska") in a dispute involving contract formation and interpretation. For the reasons stated below, we affirm.

I. FACTUAL AND PROCEDURAL BACKGROUND

In late October or early November 1976, David Reed, a shareholder and corporate president of AND, initiated discussion with Alyeska personnel in Fairbanks regarding the purchase of surplus parts. The Alyeska employees with whom Reed dealt were Juel Tyson, Clarence Terwilleger and Donald Bruce.

After a series of discussions, Terwilleger indicated that Reed's proposal should be put in writing so it could be submitted to management. With the assistance of AND's legal counsel, Reed prepared a letter of intent dated December 10, 1976. In this letter, AND proposed to purchase "the entire Alyeska inventory of Caterpillar parts." The place for the purchase price was left blank.

Alyeska responded with its own letter of intent dated December 11, 1976. The letter was drafted by Bruce and Tyson in consultation with William Rickett, Alyeska's manager of Contracts and Material Management. Again, the price term was absent. The letter contained the following language, which is the focus of this lawsuit: "Please consider this as said letter of intent, *subject to the final approval of the owner committee.*" (Emphasis added.)

Reed was given an unsigned draft of the December 11 letter, which was reviewed by AND's legal counsel. Reed then met with Rickett, and they agreed on sixty-five percent of Alyeska's price as the price term to be filled in the blank on the December 11 letter. Rickett filled in the blank as agreed and signed the letter. In March 1977, the owner committee rejected the proposal embodied in the December 11 letter of intent.

AND contends that the parties understood the subject to approval language to mean that the Alyeska owner committee[1] would review the proposed agreement only to determine whether the price was fair and reasonable. Alyeska contends that Reed was never advised of any such

* Could this person be one of the editors of this casebook?

1. The owner committee is composed of the owner oil companies of Alyeska, a joint venture.

limitation on the authority of the owner committee. In April 1977, AND filed a complaint alleging that there was a contract between AND and Alyeska, which Alyeska breached. The complaint was later amended to include counts for reformation and punitive damages.

Alyeska moved for summary judgment on the punitive damages and breach of contract counts. The superior court granted summary judgment in favor of Alyeska on the punitive damages count. The court initially denied Alyeska's motion for summary judgment on the breach of contract claim; however, based on a review of the case after discovery had closed, the court announced at a hearing on September 26, 1980, that it would reverse its earlier ruling and grant Alyeska's motion. The court confirmed this ruling at a hearing on November 5, 1980, after consideration of AND's Motion for Clarification.

The superior court explained its rationale for granting summary judgment against AND on the breach of contract claim as follows. The court recognized that AND predicated its breach of contract claim on the theory that Reed's letter of December 10th was an offer and that Rickett's letter of December 11th was an acceptance of that offer. Viewed in that light, the court addressed "four theoretical possibilities in analyzing the interplay between the December 11th letter and the December 10th letter." First, the writings could be construed as an offer with a responding promise to pass the offer on to the owner committee, which was responsible for making such determinations. Second, the letters could be construed as an offer and a counter-offer that AND rejected. Third, the letters could be considered as an offer with a responding counter-offer containing, among other things, the unlimited right of the owner committee to review and approve. The court ruled that if the letters were ultimately found to fall into one of these three categories, AND would not prevail, either because the offer embodied in the December 10 letter was never accepted, or because the owner committee never approved the proposal.

The only way in which AND might prevail was on the fourth possibility, i.e., the letters could be construed as an offer followed by a counter-offer limiting the authority of the owner committee to review only the contract price. The court ruled that AND could not establish a breach of contract claim under the fourth construction of the letters because the parol evidence rule barred the admission of extrinsic evidence that might limit the scope of the owner committee's approval power.[2] The only recourse for AND, therefore, was to seek reformation of the December 11 letter that limited the owner committee approval clause.

The case proceeded to trial on the reformation claim. After a six-week trial, the superior court concluded that AND had failed to establish that a specific agreement was not properly reduced to writing and therefore rejected its request to reform the December 11 letter. Attorney's fees were awarded to Alyeska.

On appeal, AND does not challenge the superior court's denial of reformation. Instead, it contends that the superior court erred in granting

2. AND also predicated its breach of contract claim on the existence of a prior oral agreement. The superior court implicitly rejected this theory in its analysis of the parol evidence rule.

summary judgment on the breach of contract and punitive damages counts, erred in denying a trial by jury on the reformation count, erred in not permitting cross-examination for purposes of impeachment, and erred in awarding attorney's fees to Alyeska.

II. Application of the Parol Evidence Rule

The superior court held that the parol evidence rule of the Uniform Commercial Code, section 2–202, codified as AS 45.02.202,[3] applied to the December 11 letter and therefore no extrinsic evidence could be presented to a jury which limited the owner committee's right of approval. AND contends that the court erred in applying the parol evidence rule. We disagree.

In order to exclude parol evidence concerning the inclusion of additional terms to a writing, a court must make the following determinations. First, the court must determine whether the writing under scrutiny was integrated, i.e., intended by the parties as a final expression of their agreement with respect to some or all of the terms included in the writing. Second, the court must determine whether evidence of a prior or contemporaneous agreement contradicts or is inconsistent with the integrated portion. If the evidence is contradictory or inconsistent, it is inadmissible. If it is consistent, it may nevertheless be excluded if the court concludes that the consistent term would necessarily have been included in the writing by the parties if they had intended it to be part of their agreement. AS 45.02.202; *Braund, Inc. v. White,* 486 P.2d 50, 56 (Alaska 1971); U.C.C. § 2–202 comment 3 (1977).

A. *Was the December 11 Letter a Partial Integration?*

An integrated writing exists where the parties intend that the writing be a final expression of one or more terms of their agreement. *Kupka v. Morey,* 541 P.2d 740, 747 n. 8 (Alaska 1975); Restatement (Second) of Contracts § 209(a) (1979). Whether a writing is integrated is a question of fact to be determined by the court in accordance with all relevant evidence. Restatement (Second) of Contracts § 209 comment c (1979).

In granting summary judgment on the breach of contract claim, the superior court stated that it had carefully considered all relevant evidence, including oral and written records of all facets of the business deal in question, to arrive at its finding that the agreement was partially integrated.[4] After the six-week trial on the reformation issue, the superior court reaffirmed this finding:

3. AS 45.02.202 provides:

Final written expression; parol or extrinsic evidence. Terms with respect to which the confirmatory memoranda of the parties agree, or which are otherwise set out in a writing intended by the parties as a final expression of their agreement with respect to the terms included in the writing, may not be contradicted by evidence of a prior agreement or of a contemporaneous oral agreement, but may be explained or supplemented

(1) by course of dealing or usage of trade (AS 45.01.205) or by course of performance (AS 45.02.208); and

(2) by evidence of consistent additional terms unless the court finds the writing was intended also as a complete and exclusive statement of the terms of the agreement.

4. At the hearing on AND's Motion for Clarification, the superior court stated:

[I]t seems to me absolutely conclusive on this evidence, and I'm making this as a finding of fact, that this agreement is partially integrated, and I'm not making it by reference only to the four corners of the—of the writings but reference to all the extrinsic evidence that has been proffered to me, read everybody's deposition, consid-

35. The plaintiff initially contends that the letter of December 11, 1976 (the letter) was not integrated or partially integrated and therefore the court was in error in granting summary judgment in favor of defendant on the contract counts of the plaintiff's complaint on September 26, 1980.

36. After considering the evidence submitted at trial, the court reaffirms its prior conclusion that the letter was integrated as to the Owners Committee's approval clause.

37. The parties intended to write down their discussions in a comprehensive form which allowed Reed to seek financing and allow the primary actors (Tyson, Bruce, Terwilleger, Rickett) to submit the concept embodied by the letter to higher management * * *.

38. There are three subjects upon which plaintiff seeks reformation. * * * As to the first, [limiting the Owner Committee to a consideration of price] which has been plaintiff's primary focus, the court finds that such reference was integrated such that the parole [sic] evidence rule would bar any inconsistent testimony. Testimony that the owners were limited to "price" in their review is inconsistent.

* * *

41. With respect to the Owners Committee's approval clause, according to the plaintiff's contention the owners were entitled to review the transaction, on whatever basis, only one time. This was testified to by both Mr. Reed and argued by plaintiff in closing. * * * It was also conceded in closing that the review by the owners, on whatever standard, would occur prior to any formal contract being negotiated and executed. * * * This is also consistent with the testimony of each of the participants.

42. In addition, Mr. Reed, in consultation with Ed Merdes and Henry Camarot, his attorneys, tendered the letter of March 4, 1977, as a document which could serve as "the contract". * * * The March 4 letter contains no further reference to the Owners Committee's approval function * * *. Therefore, I find that as to the Owners Committee's approval * * * the letter of December 11 constitutes an integration or partial integration * * *. This having been established, the analysis outlined by the court on September 26, 1980, when granting defendant's motion for summary judgment on the contract claims is applicable. [Citations omitted.]

After reviewing the record, we cannot say that this finding of a partial integration was clearly erroneous.

AND contends that the "clearly erroneous" standard used for reviewing findings of fact issued after a trial does not apply because the breach of contract claim was dismissed by summary judgment. Under the circum-

ered in detail all the processes of negotiations, everything that was said and done by everybody as related by them up till the time that Rickett included the language in the letter and turned it over to Reed. So we're not here talking about the for [sic] corners or ambiguity or anything like that. We're talking about all the extrinsic evidence, meaning on balance to a conclusion more probable than not that this is a partially integrated agreement.

stances of this case, we believe that the clearly erroneous standard applies rather than the standard of review used in summary judgment cases because the summary judgment ruling was not a final judgment for purposes of appeal.

Rule 54(b) of the Alaska Rules of Civil Procedure provides in relevant part:

> When more than one claim for relief is presented in an action * * * the court may direct the entry of a final judgment as to one * * * of the claims * * * upon an express determination that there is no just reason for delay and upon an express direction for the entry of judgment. In the absence of such determination and direction * * * the order or other form of decision is subject to revision at any time before the entry of judgment adjudicating all the claims and the rights and liabilities of all the parties.

In the pre-trial conference, the superior court indicated that it would make a Rule 54(b) determination if the parties so desired. The parties did not request a Rule 54(b) determination and none was made. During this conference, the court also made it clear that it was willing at the reformation trial to hear all evidence bearing on contract formation, including the negotiations leading up to the letters of intent and the meaning the parties placed on these negotiations and letters. The court emphasized that it was "not cutting out anybody on presenting extrinsic evidence * * * [and] that under Rule 54 the court can, until the end of the case * * * change any decision it's previously reached."

AND contends that the superior court's determination that the only issue at trial concerned reformation "necessarily foreclosed a variety of factual and legal issues on contract formation and interpretation," but does not indicate what evidence it was foreclosed from presenting on these issues. Our review of the record indicates that the integration issue was fully explored by AND during the trial.

After six weeks of testimony, during which time the court had the opportunity to view the demeanor and to judge the credibility of the witnesses, the superior court entered written findings of fact and conclusions of law. As shown in the portion quoted above, these findings reviewed and reaffirmed the findings made in the court's prior summary judgment ruling. Accordingly, the appropriate standard of review is the same as for any other finding of fact, i.e., that the superior court's findings of fact must be upheld unless "clearly erroneous." Alaska R.Civ.P. 52(a). As stated above, the finding of partial integration was not clearly erroneous; therefore, we find no merit in AND's contentions to the contrary.

B. *Does the Excluded Evidence Contradict the Integrated Terms?*

Having found a partial integration, the next determination is whether the excluded evidence contradicts the integrated portion of the writing. Comment b to section 215 of the Restatement (Second) of Contracts is helpful in resolving this issue.[5] Comment b states:

5. Restatement (Second) of Contracts § 215, which parallels the rule stated in U.C.C. § 2–202, reads: "Except as stated in the preceding Section, where there is a binding agreement, either completely or partially integrated, evidence of prior or contempo-

> An earlier agreement may help the interpretation of a later one, but it may not contradict a binding later integrated agreement. Whether there is a contradiction depends * * * on whether the two are consistent or inconsistent. This is a question which often cannot be determined from the face of the writing; the writing must first be applied to its subject matter and placed in context. The question is then decided by the court as part of a question of interpretation. Where reasonable people could differ as to the credibility of the evidence offered and the evidence if believed could lead a reasonable person to interpret the writing as claimed by the proponent of the evidence, the question of credibility and the choice among reasonable inferences should be treated as questions of fact. But the asserted meaning must be one to which the language of the writing, read in context, is reasonably susceptible. If no other meaning is reasonable, the court should rule as a matter of law that the meaning is established.

According to comment b, therefore, a question of interpretation may arise before the contradiction issue can be resolved. If the evidence conflicts, the choice between competing inferences is for the trier of fact to resolve. *Alyeska Pipeline Service Co. v. O'Kelley,* 645 P.2d 767, 771 n. 2 (Alaska 1982). The meaning is determined as a matter of law, however, if "the asserted meaning [is not] one to which the language of the writing, read in context, is reasonably susceptible." Restatement (Second) of Contracts § 215 comment b (1979). See also J. Calamari & J. Perillo, The Law of Contracts §§ 3–12, 3–13 (2d ed. 1977).

AND contends that the superior court erred in granting summary judgment because the evidence conflicted as to the meaning of the owner committee approval clause. It concludes that under *Alyeska* it was entitled to a jury trial on the interpretation issue. Alyeska contends, and the superior court ruled, that a jury trial was inappropriate because, as a matter of law, AND's asserted meaning of the clause at issue was not reasonably susceptible to the language of the writing. The superior court stated:

> The Court is making the * * * ruling that the offer of evidence to show that Rickett's letter really meant to limit owner committee approval to the price term alone * * * is not reasonably susceptible—or the writing is not reasonably susceptible to that purpose. And therefore, that extrinsic evidence operates to contradict the writing, not specific words in the writing, but the words in the context of the totality of the writing and the totality of the extrinsic evidence.

We agree that the words used in the December 11 letter are not reasonably susceptible to the interpretation advanced by AND. Therefore, we find no merit to AND's contention that it was entitled to a jury trial on the interpretation issue.

After rejecting the extrinsic evidence for purposes of interpretation, the superior court found AND's offered testimony, that the owner committee's approval power was limited to approval of the price, to be inconsistent with and contradictory to the language used by the negotiators in the December

raneous agreements or negotiations is not admissible in evidence to contradict a term of the writing."

11 letter. AND contends that the offered testimony did not contradict, but rather explained or supplemented the writing with consistent additional terms. For this contention, AND relies on the standard articulated in *Hunt Foods & Industries, Inc. v. Doliner,* 26 A.D.2d 41, 270 N.Y.S.2d 937 (N.Y.App. 1966). In *Hunt Foods,* the defendant signed an option agreement under which he agreed to sell stock to Hunt Foods at a given price per share. When Hunt Foods attempted to exercise the option, the defendant contended that the option could only be exercised if the defendant had received offers from a third party. The court held that section 2–202 did not bar this evidence from being admitted because it held that the proposed oral condition to the option agreement was not "inconsistent" within the meaning of section 2–202; to be inconsistent, "the term must contradict or negate a term of the writing. A term or condition which has a lesser effect is provable." *Id.* 270 N.Y.S.2d at 940.

The narrow view of consistency expressed in *Hunt Foods* has been criticized. In *Snyder v. Herbert Greenbaum & Associates, Inc.,* 38 Md.App. 144, 380 A.2d 618 (Md.App.1977), the court held that the parol evidence of a contractual right to unilateral rescission was inconsistent with a written agreement for the sale and installation of carpeting. The court defined "inconsistency" as used in section 2–202(b) as "the absence of reasonable harmony in terms of the language *and* respective obligations of the parties." *Id.* 380 A.2d at 623 (emphasis in original) (citing U.C.C. § 1–205(4)). *Accord: Luria Brothers & Co. v. Pielet Brothers Scrap Iron & Metal, Inc.,* 600 F.2d 103, 111 (7th Cir.1979); *Southern Concrete Services, Inc. v. Mableton Contractors, Inc.,* 407 F.Supp. 581 (N.D.Ga.1975), *aff'd mem.,* 569 F.2d 1154 (5th Cir.1978).

We agree with this view of inconsistency and reject the view expressed in *Hunt Foods.*[6] Under this definition of inconsistency, it is clear that the proffered parol evidence limiting the owner committee's right of final approval to price is inconsistent with the integrated term that unconditionally gives the committee the right to approval. Therefore, the superior court was correct in refusing to admit parol evidence on this issue.[7]

* * *

[The court also held that the trial court was correct to deny a jury trial on the reformation issue and to grant a summary judgment against AND on the punitive damage issue.]

Notes

1. In the absence of a "merger" clause, how does the court determine whether the writing was "intended by the parties as a final expression of their

6. *Hunt Foods* was implicitly rejected in *Johnson v. Curran,* 633 P.2d 994, 996–97 (Alaska 1981) (parol evidence concerning an early termination right based on nightclub owner's dissatisfaction with the band's performance was inconsistent with parties' written contract specifying definite time without mention of any right of early termination and thus inadmissible).

7. Our affirmance of the superior court's holding that the proposed version is inconsistent with the integrated clause obviates discussion of whether the addition, if consistent, would have been included in the December 11 letter. Furthermore, we decline to reach AND's contentions regarding the applicability of U.C.C. § 2–207 because AND never raised the § 2–207 argument at the superior court level. *See, e.g., Jeffries v. Glacier State Telephone Co.,* 604 P.2d 4, 11 (Alaska 1979).

agreement" as to some or all of the terms? UCC 2–202. Put differently, how does one evaluate the decision in the *Alaska Northern* case that the writing was intended to be a partial integration with regard to the "approval" clauses? The question is important, for in the absence of any integration, the term limiting the power to reject would be part of the agreement, whether included in the writing or not.

UCC 2–202 and the comments are silent on this question. It may be useful to indulge a presumption, see UCC 1–201(31), that a writing which "reasonably appears to be a complete agreement" is "an integrated agreement unless it is established by other evidence that the writing did not constitute a final expression." Restatement, Second, Contracts 209(3). See Intershoe, Inc. v. Bankers Trust Co., 77 N.Y.2d 517, 569 N.Y.S.2d 333, 571 N.E.2d 64 (1991) (form and content of currency trade confirmation support integration in the absence of other evidence). Since there was no "other" persuasive evidence in the *Alaska Northern* case, the determination that the parties intended a partial integration at least seems sound. What constitutes "other" evidence? According to Comment (c) to Restatement § 209, incompleteness of the writing may be shown by "any relevant evidence, oral or written, that an apparently complete writing never became fully effective, or that it was modified after initial adoption."

2. If the writing is integrated in whole or in part, terms in that writing "may not be contradicted by evidence of any prior agreement or of a contemporaneous oral agreement. * * *" UCC 2–202. Accord: Restatement, Second, Contracts § 215. But if there is a partial integration, as in *Alaska Northern,* the writing may be supplemented "by evidence of consistent additional terms." UCC 2–202(b). Section 216(2) of the Restatement, Second, Contracts puts the matter more affirmatively: "An agreement is not completely integrated if the writing omits a consistent additional term. * * *" We now return to a question that has dominated the trade usage cases: What is a consistent additional term? Is the "absence of reasonable harmony" test applied in *Alaska Northern* the same as the test expressed in Comment 3 to UCC 2–202, i.e., that the term, if agreed upon, "would certainly have been included in the document * * *?" Or, must the "consistent additional agreed term" be one "as in the circumstances might naturally be omitted from the writing?" Section 216(2)(b). For still another application of the "absence of reasonable harmony" test, See ARB. Inc. v. E–Systems, Inc., 663 F.2d 189 (D.C.Cir.1980) (after review of extrinsic evidence, "merger" clause held to express genuine intention of parties).

3. What is the effect of a "merger" clause providing that the writing is the "final and complete agreement of the parties" and that there are "no understandings, agreements, or obligations unless specifically set forth in the writing?" Assuming that the clause is not unconscionable, Seibel v. Layne & Bowler, Inc., 56 Or.App. 387, 641 P.2d 668 (1982) (ordinary consumer unfairly surprised by fine-print merger clause in standard form contract), and assuming that the clause or the contract was not induced by fraud, see UCC 1–103 and Franklin v. Lovitt Equipment Co., 420 So.2d 1370 (Miss.1982), and assuming that there was no other evidence establishing a contrary intention, the UCC answer seems clear: The writing may neither be contradicted by evidence of "any prior agreement or of a contemporaneous agreement" nor "supplemented * * * by evidence of consistent additional terms." UCC 2–202.

May, however, the total integration be "explained or supplemented * * * by course of dealing or usage of trade * * * or by course of performance?" Despite some ambiguity in UCC 2–202, the answer appears to be yes, subject to the limitations imposed by UCC 1–205(4). Thus, evidence of a prior course of dealing has been admitted to explain or supplement the terms of an integrated writing, see e.g., Ralph's Distributing Co. v. AMF, Inc., 667 F.2d 670 (8th Cir.1981), and evidence of trade usage and a prior course of dealing that was thought to "contradict" terms in the writing has been excluded. See, e.g., General Aviation, Inc. v. Cessna Aircraft Co., 915 F.2d 1038 (6th Cir.1990); General Plumbing & Heating, Inc. v. American Air Filter, 696 F.2d 375 (5th Cir.1983). We return, then, full circle to the test of consistency raised in the trade usage cases.

Problem 11–1

Fiber Industries sold fiber to carpet manufacturers for use in the making of carpets. Salem Carpet bought trademark fiber from Fiber Industries on an order-by-order basis. There was no written agreement other than the individual purchase orders. Both Salem's purchase order form and Fiber Industries acknowledgment form contained "merger" clauses, which provided that the form "contains all the terms and conditions of the purchase agreement and shall constitute the complete and exclusive agreement between Seller and Purchaser." In August, 1980 Fiber Industries announced that it was withdrawing from the carpet industry, but that it would supply all customers in an "orderly fashion" until the phase-out was complete. Salem accepted a final order of fiber at a contract price of $407,128.40, but refused to pay the full amount because of losses suffered as a result of Fiber Industries' withdrawal from the market. Salem claimed that there was a "customary practice" in the carpet industry obligating Fiber Industries to fill all orders made by Salem during the projected market life of any carpet style which utilized fiber manufactured by Fiber Industries. Salem was prepared to establish a usage that the "carpet manufacturer will continue to make its branded fiber available for the useful life of the carpet style or for sufficient time to allow the carpet manufacturer to produce and sell sufficient carpet to recoup the large start-up expenses incurred in introducing and marketing a new line of branded carpet."

Assume that both contract forms were silent on the issue. Assume, further, that the usage could be established. Under UCC 1–205(4) and 2–202, should the court admit evidence of the usage as part of the agreement?

FRIGALIMENT IMPORTING CO. v. B.N.S. INTERNATIONAL SALES CORP.

United States District Court, Southern District of New York, 1960.
190 F.Supp. 116.

FRIENDLY, CIRCUIT JUDGE.

The issue is, what is chicken? Plaintiff says "chicken" means a young chicken, suitable for broiling and frying. Defendant says "chicken" means any bird of that genus that meets contract specifications on weight and quality, including what it calls "stewing chicken" and plaintiff pejoratively terms "fowl". Dictionaries give both meanings, as well as some others not relevant here. To support it, plaintiff sends a number of volleys over the net: defendant essays to return them and adds a few serves of its own. Assuming that both parties were acting in good faith, the case nicely illustrates Holmes' remark "that the making of a contract depends not on the agreement of two minds in one intention, but on the agreement of two sets of external signs—not on the parties' having *meant* the same thing but on their having *said* the same thing." The Path of the Law, in Collected Legal Papers, p. 178. I have concluded that plaintiff has not sustained its burden of persuasion that the contract used "chicken" in the narrower sense.

The action is for breach of the warranty that goods sold shall correspond to the description, New York Personal Property Law, McKinney's Consol.Laws, c. 41, § 95. Two contracts are in suit. In the first, dated May 2, 1957, defendant, a New York sales corporation, confirmed the sale to plaintiff, a Swiss corporation, of

> "U S Fresh Frozen Chicken, Grade A, Government Inspected, Eviscerated 2½–3 lbs. and 1½–2 lbs. each
> all chicken individually wrapped in cryovac, packed in secured fiber cartons or wooden boxes, suitable for export
> 75,000 lbs. 2½–3 lbs. .... at $33.00
> 25,000 lbs. 1½–2 lbs. .... at $36.50
> per 100 lbs. FAS New York
> scheduled May 10, 1957 pursuant to instructions from Penson & Co., New York."

The second contract, also dated May 2, 1957, was identical save that only 50,000 lbs. of heavier "chicken" were called for, the price of the smaller birds was $37 per 100 lbs., and shipment was scheduled for May 30. The initial shipment under the first contract was short but the balance was shipped on May 17. When the initial shipment arrived in Switzerland, plaintiff found, on May 28, that the 2½–3 lbs. birds were not young chicken suitable for broiling and frying but stewing chicken or "fowl"; indeed, many of the cartons and bags plainly so indicated. Protests ensued. Nevertheless, shipment under the second contract was made on May 29, the 2½–3 lbs. birds again being stewing chicken. Defendant stopped the transportation of these at Rotterdam.

This action followed. Plaintiff says that, notwithstanding that its acceptance was in Switzerland, New York law controls under the principle of Rubin v. Irving Trust Co., 1953, 305 N.Y. 288, 305, 113 N.E.2d 424, 431; defendant does not dispute this, and relies on New York decisions. I shall follow the apparent agreement of the parties as to the applicable law.

[The court first determined that the contract language offered no assistance in determining the meaning of the word, "chicken", which standing alone was ambiguous.]

Plaintiff's next contention is that there was a definite trade usage that "chicken" meant "young chicken." Defendant showed that it was only beginning in the poultry trade in 1957, thereby bringing itself within the principle that "when one of the parties is not a member of the trade or other circle, his acceptance of the standard must be made to appear" by proving either that he had actual knowledge of the usage or that the usage is "so generally known in the community that his actual individual knowledge of it may be inferred." 9 Wigmore, Evidence (3d ed. 1940) § 2464. Here there was no proof of actual knowledge of the alleged usage; indeed, it is quite plain that defendant's belief was to the contrary. In order to meet the alternative requirement, the law of New York demands a showing that "the usage is of so long continuance, so well established, so notorious, so universal and so reasonable in itself, as that the presumption is violent that the parties contracted with reference to it and made it a part of their agreement." Walls v. Bailey, 1872, 49 N.Y. 464, 472–473.

Plaintiff endeavored to establish such a usage by the testimony of three witnesses and certain other evidence. Strasser, resident buyer in New York for a large chain of Swiss cooperatives, testified that "on chicken I would definitely understand a broiler." However, the force of this testimony was considerably weakened by the fact that in his own transactions the witness, a careful businessman, protected himself by using "broiler" when that was what he wanted and "fowl" when he wished older birds. Indeed, there are some indications, dating back to a remark of Lord Mansfield, Edie v. East India Co., 2 Burr. 1216, 1222 (1761), that no credit should be given "witnesses to usage, who could not adduce instances in verification." 7 Wigmore, Evidence (3d ed. 1940), § 1954; see McDonald v. Acker, Merrall & Condit Co., 2d Dept. 1920, 192 App.Div. 123, 126, 182 N.Y.S. 607. While Wigmore thinks this goes too far, a witness' consistent failure to rely on the alleged usage deprives his opinion testimony of much of its effect. Niesielowski, an officer of one of the companies that had furnished the stewing chicken to defendant, testified that "chicken" meant "the male species of the poultry industry. That could be a broiler, a fryer or a roaster", but not a stewing chicken; however, he also testified that upon receiving defendant's inquiry for "chickens", he asked whether the desire was for "fowl or frying chickens" and, in fact, supplied fowl, although taking the precaution of asking defendant, a day or two after plaintiff's acceptance of the contracts in suit, to change its confirmation of its order from "chickens," as defendant had originally prepared it, to "stewing chickens." Dates, an employee of Urner-Barry Company, which publishes a daily market report on the poultry trade, gave it as his view that the trade meaning of "chicken" was "broilers and fryers." In addition to this opinion testimony, plaintiff relied on the fact that the Urner-Barry service, the Journal of Commerce, and Weinberg Bros. & Co. of Chicago, a large supplier of poultry, published quotations in a manner which, in one way or another, distinguish between "chicken," comprising broilers, fryers and certain other categories, and "fowl," which, Bauer acknowledged, included stewing chickens. This material would be impressive if there were nothing to the contrary. However, there was, as will now be seen.

Defendant's witness Weininger, who operates a chicken eviscerating plant in New Jersey, testified "Chicken is everything except a goose, a duck, and a turkey. Everything is a chicken, but then you have to say, you have to specify which category you want or that you are talking about." Its witness Fox said that in the trade "chicken" would encompass all the various classifications. Sadina, who conducts a food inspection service, testified that he would consider any bird coming within the classes of "chicken" in the Department of Agriculture's regulations to be a chicken. The specifications approved by the General Services Administration include fowl as well as broilers and fryers under the classification "chickens." Statistics of the Institute of American Poultry Industries use the phrases "Young chickens" and "Mature chickens," under the general heading "Total chickens," and the Department of Agriculture's daily and weekly price reports avoid use of the word "chicken" without specification.

* * *

[The court next reviewed arguments that the defendant's meaning of the word "chicken" was supported by definitions in Department of Agriculture regulations, by its inability to obtain young chickens at the agreed contract price and by plaintiff's conduct after the first shipment was received.]

When all the evidence is reviewed, it is clear that defendant believed it could comply with the contracts by delivering stewing chicken in the 2½–3 lbs. size. Defendant's subjective intent would not be significant if this did not coincide with an objective meaning of "chicken." Here it did coincide with one of the dictionary meanings, with the definition in the Department of Agriculture Regulations to which the contract made at least oblique reference, with at least some usage in the trade, with the realities of the market, and with what plaintiff's spokesman had said. Plaintiff asserts it to be equally plain that plaintiff's own subjective intent was to obtain broilers and fryers; the only evidence against this is the material as to market prices and this may not have been sufficiently brought home. In any event it is unnecessary to determine that issue. For plaintiff has the burden of showing that "chicken" was used in the narrower rather than in the broader sense, and this it has not sustained.

This opinion constitutes the Court's findings of fact and conclusions of law. Judgment shall be entered dismissing the complaint with costs. [Footnotes omitted.]

Note

Why, you ask, did we include this "old saw?" Here are a few reasons.

First, the case demonstrates that the UCC parol evidence rule has little to do with issues of interpretation. Rather, extrinsic evidence is admissible to assist the trier of fact in determining the meaning of a term which is part of the agreement. See Farnsworth, *Meaning in the Law of Contracts,* 76 Yale L.J. 939 (1967); Corbin, *The Interpretation of Words and the Parol Evidence Rule,* 50 Cornell L.Rev. 161 (1965).

Second, the case supports the attack by the "realists" on the belief that words have a "plain meaning" that can be determined from the four corners of a writing. As Chief Justice Traynor put it, the "* * * test of admissibility of extrinsic evidence to explain the meaning of a written instrument is not whether it appears to the court to be plain and unambiguous on its face, but whether the offered evidence is relevant to prove a meaning to which the language of the instrument is reasonably susceptible." Pacific Gas and Elec. Co. v. G.W. Thomas Drayage & Rigging Co., 69 Cal.2d 33, 69 Cal.Rptr. 561, 564, 442 P.2d 641, 644 (1968). See UCC 2–202, Comment 1(b).

Third, the case illustrates the wide range of facts, including trade usage, that may be relevant to interpretation disputes. It is consistent with the UCC's position that the "meaning of the agreement of the parties is to be determined by the language used by them and by their action, read and interpreted in the light of commercial practices and other circumstances." UCC 1–205, Comment 1. It also illustrates that even with access to evidence from the commercial context, the plaintiff failed to establish that his meaning of "chicken" should prevail.

According to the Restatement, in order for the plaintiff to prevail, he would have to establish that either (a) he did not know the different meaning attached by the defendant to "chicken" and the defendant knew the meaning attached by the plaintiff, or (b) the plaintiff had no reason to know of the different meaning attached by the defendant and the defendant had reason to know the meaning attached by the plaintiff. Section 201, Restatement, Second, Contracts. See also, 202–203, 219–223. Does the Restatement test square with the outcome in the "chicken" case? Does the UCC provide any guidance on what the plaintiff must establish to prevail? (We think that the answer is no.)

Fourth, (and finally), the case shows that even though the purpose of the claimed trade usage was proper—to give meaning to the term "chicken"—the plaintiff failed to prove the usage. Review the facts and Judge Friendly's opinion to determine why the proof failed and consider the following note.

Note: Proof of Trade Usage and Other Context Evidence

Trade usage and other context evidence are facts to be established by the moving party, i.e., the party seeking to persuade the court that his interpretation of the scope or meaning of the agreement should prevail. UCC 1–205(2). Since these facts are normally not presumed to exist, see UCC 1–201(31), the plaintiff has the "burden of establishing" them, i.e., he must persuade the "triers of fact that the existence of the fact is more probable than its non-existence." UCC 1–201(8). The moving party, therefore, has both the burden of production and the burden of persuasion. These burdens are normally satisfied, if at all, through expert witnesses and documents, see UCC 1–205(2), in an atmosphere where objections to the expert's qualifications, the authenticity of documents and hearsay and relevance are routine. See, e.g., C. McCormick, Evidence 13 (2d ed. 1972); McElhaney, *Expert Witnesses and the Federal Rules of Evidence,* 28 Mercer L.Rev. 463 (1977). The pitfalls in this process are illustrated by the "Chicken" case.

But there are more problems for the moving party. According to Professors Allen and Hillman, a "comprehensive set of proof rules would establish who must bear the burden of pleading, of persuasion, and of producing evidence, and would define the appropriate contours of judicial comment on the evidence." Allen & Hillman, *Evidentiary Problems In—And Solutions For—the Uniform Commercial Code,* 1984 Duke L.J. 92, 98. They suggest that if the Drafters had stopped with the burden of persuasion rule in UCC 1–201(8) and the burden of production rule in UCC 1–201(31), the "Code's approach to proof problems, if liberally construed, would have been nearly adequate." The Code "could have been interpreted to place on plaintiffs and moving parties the burdens of production and persuasion on all issues—the normal rule—unless it specifically allocated one or the other burden by using the terminology of either section 1–201(8) or 1–201(32)." Further, trial judges "could then have determined pleading requirements and the scope of their authority to comment on the evidence by referring to their jurisdiction's procedural law." Id.

The questions in particular cases, such as proof of trade usage, are (1) whether other Code provisions are inconsistent with these general principles of production and persuasion and, if so, (2) whether the Code contains rules of proof that describe how the burdens should be allocated and provide guidance on pleading or the conditions under which a judge may comment on the evidence. In areas other than proof of trade usage, Professors Allen and Hillman answer the two questions "yes" and "no" and conclude that these failures, as manifested in judicial opinions, have interfered with a basic purpose of the Code to promote clarity and consistency in commercial dealings. Id. at 98–105.

The potential for trouble exists in the trade usage areas as well. Suppose, for example, that a buyer of steel seeks to establish a trade usage that a written contract for goods described as "36 inch steel" is satisfied by steel with a width between 36″ and 37″. (For such a case, see Decker Steel Co. v. Exchange Nat'l Bank of Chicago, 330 F.2d 82 (7th Cir.1964). Here are some trouble spots for which the Code has no answers.

(1) At what point in the plaintiff's case does the burden of production shift to the defendant and what proof must the defendant adduce to satisfy that intermediate burden?

(2) Suppose the defendant, by way of affirmative defense, attacks the established usage as unreasonable or unconscionable. Comment 6 to UCC 1–205 states that the "very fact of commercial acceptance makes out a prima facie case that the usage is reasonable, and the burden is no longer on the usage to establish itself as being reasonable." What does this mean for the burdens of production and persuasion?

(3) Finally, suppose the defendant raises express written language purporting to totally integrate the writing, UCC 2–202, or to exclude the usage. Is there a presumption that the writing expresses the intention of both parties? If so, do both the burden of production and the burden of persuasion shift to the plaintiff? How are those burdens satisfied?

In order to clarify the rules governing the proof of facts in a trial under the Code, Professors Allen and Hillman propose the following addition:

"Section 1–210. Rules Governing the Proof of Facts at Trial

(1) Definitions

(a) A burden of production is a requirement that a party produce sufficient evidence on an issue to avoid a directed verdict on that issue. The phrases "to presume" or "prima facie case," and any derivations thereof, shall be interpreted to refer to a burden of production, unless expressly provided otherwise.

(b) A burden of persuasion is a requirement that a party convince the finder of fact to a previously specified level of certainty of the truth of an issue. The phrases "to establish" or "to show" and any derivations thereof shall be interpreted to refer to a burden of persuasion, unless expressly provided otherwise.

(2) General Provisions

(a) Pleading. Unless expressly provided otherwise, all pleading matters shall be governed by the Rule (or Code) of Civil Procedure.

(b) Burden of Production and Persuasion. Unless expressly provided otherwise or unless the interests of justice clearly require otherwise, plaintiffs and moving parties shall bear the burden of production and persuasion on all contested issues. The justification for any judicial exception must be specifically provided by the trial court and is subject to review on appeal. A question of fact upon which allocation of a burden of production or persuasion is conditioned shall be decided by the court for the purpose of allocating the burden of production or persuasion.

(c) Standard of Persuasion. Unless expressly provided otherwise or unless the interests of justice clearly require otherwise, a burden of persuasion is satisfied if the party, bearing it convinces the fact finder that the existence of the fact is more probable than its non-existence, and a burden of production is satisfied if the court determines that a reasonable person could so find. The justification for any judicial exception must be specifically provided by the trial court and is subject to review on appeal.

(d) Peremptory Instruction or Ruling. The trial court may remove an issue from the consideration of the jury if reasonable persons with an understanding of the commercial practices involved would not disagree about the matter.

(e) Order of Proof. The trial court may require the presentation of evidence in the order that it determines would best facilitate the trial process.

(f) Judicial Comment on the Evidence. After the close of the evidence and arguments of counsel, the court may fairly and impartially sum up the evidence or examine the implication of the evidence, or both, for the benefit of the jury. Notice of intended comment shall be provided to counsel, and an opportunity to respond with evidence or argument shall be permitted."

Id. at 105–06.

CHAPTER TWELVE

THE EFFECT OF OPEN TERMS AND RESERVED DISCRETION

SECTION 1. INTRODUCTION: THE UCC AS A SOURCE OF SUPPLETIVE TERMS

In the bargain envisioned by the drafters of the First Restatement of Contracts, promulgated in 1931, the transaction was a relatively discrete exchange and the parties were expected to agree on all of the material terms before a contract was formed. Thus, if material terms, such as quantity or price, were left open or to be agreed, the odds were strong that a court would hold that no enforceable contract was created until there was agreement. Examples of this approach include Transamerica Equip. Leasing Corp. v. Union Bank, 426 F.2d 273 (9th Cir.1970); Walker v. Keith, 382 S.W.2d 198 (Ky.1964); Wilhelm Lubrication Co. v. Brattrud, 197 Minn. 626, 268 N.W. 634 (1936).

In the bargain envisioned by the drafters of Article 2, prepared in the years after World War II, the transaction is not limited to a discrete exchange where promises are made. As we have seen, the definition of agreement, UCC 1–201(3), employs a broader theory of relevant behavior: the bargain can be derived from the particular parties' past, present and future conduct, as well as the practices and usages of others engaging in exchange in the same trade or market. In short, Article 2 allows for relational as well as discrete exchange. See Macneil, *Relational Contract: What We Do and Do Not Know,* 1985 Wis.L.Rev. 483, 485–91. Thus, the parties may, by choice or because of complexity, intend to conclude a bargain without agreeing on every material term. Even in a discrete exchange, they may leave an important term, such as the price, open, or to be agreed, or to be fixed by one of the parties. In exchanges of longer duration or where circumstances are expected to change in unanticipated ways, this technique is especially salutary. It obviates the need for complete risk allocation at the time of contracting and puts a premium on negotiation and adjustment in the light of change.

Section 2–204(3) does not require complete agreement on material terms. Rather, it incorporates standards that permit the parties to conclude a contract "even though one or more terms are left open" if they have "intended to make a contract" and there is a "reasonably certain basis for giving an appropriate remedy."

The first question, then, is to decide whether the parties intended to conclude the bargain and, thus, to "make" a contract, when a material term is left open or to be agreed. What factors are relevant to this determination of intent? If the parties did so intend, the second question is whether there is a "reasonably certain basis for giving an appropriate remedy?" Article 2, Part 3, itself, provides many terms to fill "gaps" in the agreement. Study these "off the rack" gap fillers now, for in many cases they will furnish the basis for certainty of remedy.

Another permitted technique is to leave discretion for fixing or defining the terms of performance to one of the parties. Thus, the agreement may provide that the price is to be the price fixed by the seller at the time of delivery, or that the quantity ordered is to be the buyer's requirements. Similarly, the buyer may agree to use "best efforts" to market a product or to purchase described goods "if satisfied" or both parties may agreed to negotiate over an open term in the future. What effect will reserved discretion by one party have on the enforceability of the agreement? Will the illusory character of the deal mean that there was not consideration? If not, what controls should be imposed upon the exercise of that discretion? See UCC 1–203 (good faith duty in performance and enforcement of the contract). For now, work these simple problems, using the provisions of Article 2, Part 3.

Problem 12–1

A. Seller, a dealer in Delaware Cobbler Potatoes, sells existing goods from cold storage. On February 1, Seller agreed, in a writing signed by both parties, to sell Buyer "1,000 sacks of Delaware Cobbler Potatoes." The writing contained no other terms except the following clause: "The parties to this agreement intend to make a contract and consider themselves bound to this writing." On March 15, Seller, without justification and before any potatoes were identified, repudiated the agreement. Buyer promptly "covered," i.e., purchased 1,000 sacks of Delaware Cobblers for $10 a sack on the open market, in full compliance with UCC 2–712. The market price had been $7 per sack on February 1. What damages, if any, can Buyer recover under UCC 2–712?

B. Suppose, in A above, the writing stated that Seller agreed to sell Buyer "Delaware Cobbler Potatoes for $7 per sack with delivery no later than March 15." Seller failed to deliver. On March 15 the market price for Delaware Cobblers was $10 per sack. What damages, if any, can Buyer recover under UCC 2–713?

C. One last problem. Suppose, in A above, that the writing stated that Seller agreed to sell 1,000 sacks of Delaware Cobbler potatoes, delivery by March 15, at a price "to be fixed by the seller." The market price on February 1 was $7 per sack. On March 15, Seller tendered delivery of the goods and fixed a price of $20 per sack. The current market price was $12 and rising. Buyer rejected the tender and "covered" under UCC 2–712 for $13 per sack. Both parties claim that the other breached the contract. Who should prevail?

Note: "Gap" Filling and Default Rules

Article 2 imposes three controls on the power of courts to fill "gaps" in the agreement and, thus, to supply terms for the parties.

First, the issue must arise outside of the scope of the parties' agreement, express or implied, as fairly interpreted. UCC 1–201(3). For example, trade usage may be introduced to supplement terms of the agreement, but it is not a "gap" filler. It is part of the parties' agreement.

Second, the parties must intend to conclude the bargain even though some terms have not been agreed. Experience suggests that the more important and complex the term, the less likely it is that the requisite intention is present. The best evidence of this intention is "conduct by both parties which recognizes the existence of such a contract." UCC 2–204(1).

Third, even if the parties so intended, the terms to be supplied by the court are defined by the statutory provisions in Article 2, Part 3, which, in turn, are rooted in standards of reasonableness. See, for example the following "gap" fillers: UCC 2–304(1) (price payable in money or otherwise); 2–305(1) (price is a "reasonable price" at the time for delivery); 2–306(1) (no unreasonably disproportionate quantity can be supplied or ordered); 2–307 (all goods must be tendered in a single delivery); 2–308 (place where delivery to be made); 2–309 (time for delivery and duration of contract are a "reasonable" time); 2–310 (when and where payment is due); 2–312—2–318 (warranties); and 2–319—324 (delivery terms). See, generally, Speidel, *Restatement, Second: Omitted Terms and Contract Method,* 67 Cornell L.Rev. 785 (1982), suggesting that the Code has led the courts to the waters of commercial reasonableness without instructing them how to drink.

Remember, these "gap" fillers are supplied in the absence of agreement. The parties have power to fill in the gaps themselves. Similarly, most of Article 2's principles of liability, performance and remedy can be varied by agreement. See, e.g., UCC 1–103(2), 2–718(1) and 2–719. Thus, many commentators have described both the "gap" fillers and the legal principles in computer terminology: They are "default" rules that operate in the absence of contrary agreement. The question is what should these default rules be?

Since the commentators are, in the main, concerned with economic analysis, the answer depends upon efficiency. What default rules have the best chance to reduce the transaction costs involved in bargaining for, performing and enforcing the contract? This is a matter of some dispute. Should it be a rule that most parties would have probably agreed to if able to engage in costless bargaining or should it be a rule, somewhat arbitrary, that is the easiest for the parties to bargain around? The former is a more complex, reasonable rule that lowers transaction costs when the parties accept it without bargaining, but increases them if the parties bargain in fact. The latter minimizes transaction costs if the parties in fact bargain around it, but increases them if the parties are forced to live with a rule that neither probably would have wanted. According to David Charny, this requires one set of default rules when it is probable that the parties will bargain and another set for cases where it is probable that they will not. See Charny, *Hypothetical Bargains: The Normative Structure of Contract Interpretation,* 89 Mich.L.Rev. 1815 (1991). See also, Goetz & Scott, *The Limits of Expanded Choice: An Analysis of the Interactions Between Express and Implied Terms,* 73 Cal.L.Rev. 261 (1985).

To further complicate analysis, other commentators have urged rules that deviate from what most parties would have wanted by requiring one party with a strategic advantage in bargaining to reveal critical information to the other. These so-called "penalty" default rules decrease transaction costs if the relevant information is disclosed *ex ante* contracting and penalize the non-disclosing party if it is not. See, e.g., Ayres & Gertner, *Filling Gaps in Incomplete Contracts: An Economic Theory of Default Rules,* 99 Yale L.J. 87 (1989). Still further, other commentators have begun to debate the appropriate default rules for relational contracts. See, e.g., the articles by Clayton P. Gillette, Douglas G. Baird, and Robert E. Scott in 19 J. of Legal Stud. 535–616 (1990).

In light of this debate, how would you characterize the "default" rules in Article 2, Part 3? Are they responsive to what reasonable parties would probably have agreed or are they designed to facilitate ease in bargaining around? Can you identify a "penalty" default rule in Article 2, Part 3? [Hint. What is the effect of omitting a quantity term?] Should the revision of Article 2 pay more attention to these questions?

SECTION 2. DISPUTES OVER QUANTITY AND PRICE

A. *Introduction*

A problem for the attorney asked to plan a long-term contract for the sale of goods is to draft an agreement which is legally enforceable and preserves flexibility in the areas thought by the client to be the most troublesome or uncertain during performance. The seasoned practitioner may say that the real challenge is to achieve realistic flexibility and risk allocation rather than legal enforceability. This is discussed further in Macneil, *Contracts: Adjustment of Long-term Economic Relations Under Classical, Neoclassical and Relational Contract Law,* 72 Nw.U.L.Rev. 854 (1978) (difficulties in planning long-term supply contract).

The lawyer must understand the client's business needs and risks, assess the probability of changed circumstances, draft appropriate clauses and, in negotiating with the other side, be capable of achieving a mutually satisfactory agreement. This challenge is strikingly posed when problems of quantity and price are involved. Goldberg, *Price Adjustments in Long-Term Contracts,* 1985 Wisconsin L.Rev. 527; Note, *Requirements Contracts: Problems of Drafting and Construction,* 78 Harv.L.Rev. 1212 (1965).

Remember, the statute of frauds, UCC 2–201(1), states that a "contract is not enforceable * * * beyond the quantity of goods shown * * *" in the writing "signed by the party against whom enforcement is sought. * * *" A commitment to supply output or to buy requirements, however, is a quantity term which, because it can be interpreted and limited under UCC 2–306, satisfies the statute of frauds. For effective criticism of the statute of fraud's quantity policy, see Bruckel, *The Weed and the Web: Section 2–201's Corruption of the Code's Substantive Provisions—The Quantity Problem,* 1983 U.Ill.L.F. 811.

B. *Quantity*

Our primary concern in this subsection is with "output" and "requirements" contracts. Here is a "warm-up" problem on the interpretation of UCC 2–306.

Problem 12–2

Seller, a wholesale dealer in plywood, and Buyer, a producer of pine veneer, entered into a five year contract under which Buyer agreed to purchase 50,000 square feet of plywood per year at $1.00 per square foot. Terms on the time and method of shipment and payment were also agreed. The written contract was dated July 1, 1993.

A. On July 1, 1996, the market price of plywood had climbed to $4.00 per square foot. The increase was due, primarily, to sharpened demand for forest products. Buyer was operating at full capacity and Seller could resell all of the plywood obtained from the manufacturers. Seller, however, was unhappy with its arrangement with Buyer. Buyer, no softy, said: "Tough. You assumed the risk!" Is Buyer correct?

B. Assume the same facts except that Buyer agreed to purchase its annual "requirements" of plywood from Seller at $1.00 per square foot. The contract did not explicitly say "all of our requirements exclusively from Seller." Furthermore, the contract did not provide for estimates of quantity or maximum-minimum quantities which Buyer could not exceed. Buyer's annual requirements for the first three years were 25,000, 32,500 and 35,000 square feet. During the fourth year, with the market price at $4.50 per square foot, Buyer requested a total of 60,000 square feet, the capacity of its production facility. Seller objected and Buyer, still no softy, said: "Tough. You assumed the risk!" Seller's lawyer responded by quoting to buyer's lawyer during negotiations from Billings Cottonseed, Inc. v. Albany Oil Mill, Inc., 173 Ga.App. 825, 328 S.E.2d 426, 429, 430 (1985):

> Appellant's argument that a valid requirements contract was established by partial performance on its part is also without merit. Ordinarily, partial performance renders enforceable a contract unenforceable for lack of consideration and mutuality by supplying the lack of mutuality. * * * There can be no partial performance in the context of a requirements contract, however, for it is the promise of exclusivity that provides the consideration to the seller. * * * The promise to buy alone is not sufficient performance, for without exclusivity the purchaser's promise is merely to buy when he wants and the promise of the seller becomes merely an invitation for orders. * * * Thus, the requisite mutuality is not supplied." (Citations omitted.)

What arguments should Buyer make at this point? Should they prevail? See, particularly, Bruckel, *Consideration in Exclusive and Nonexclusive Open Quantity Contracts Under the U.C.C.: A Proposal for a New System of Validation,* 68 Minn.L.Rev. 117 (1983), who rejects the exclusivity requirement.

C. In light of hindsight, what is the best contractual arrangement for an enterprise selling plywood to a producer with a finite capacity, in a period where prices are expected to rise due primarily to increased demand for the product:

(1) Fixed-price plus "requirements," with an upper limit on quantity;

(2) Fixed-price plus an agreement to sell all or a specified part of the seller's "output" of plywood exclusively to the buyer;

(3) An "open" or market price plus either a requirements or an output agreement;

(4) Either separate contracts or short term, i.e., one year, arrangements with fixed prices and fixed quantities;

(5) Other?

ORANGE & ROCKLAND, etc. v. AMERADA HESS CORP.

Supreme Court of New York, Appellate Division, 1977.
59 A.D.2d 110, 397 N.Y.S.2d 814.

MARGETT, JUSTICE.

This action, for damages as a result of an alleged breach of a requirements contract, raises related but distinctly separate issues as to whether the plaintiff buyer's requirements occurred in good faith and whether those requirements were unreasonably disproportionate to the estimates stated in the contract.

In a fuel oil supply contract executed in early December, 1969, defendant Amerada Hess Corporation (Hess) agreed to supply the requirements of plaintiff Orange and Rockland Utilities, Inc. (O & R) at plaintiff's Lovett generating plant in Tompkins Cove, New York. A fixed price of $2.14 per barrel for No. 6 fuel oil, with a sulphur content of 1% or less, was to continue at least through September 30, 1974, with the price subject to renegotiation at that time. Estimates of the amounts required by plaintiff were included in the contract clause entitled "Quantity". Insofar as those estimates are relevant to the instant controversy, they were as follows:

1970—1,750,000 barrels

1971—1,380,000 barrels

1972—1,500,000 barrels

1973—1,500,000 barrels

The estimates had been prepared by plaintiff on December 30, 1968, as part of a five-year budget projection. The estimates anticipated that gas would be the primary fuel used for generation during the period in question.[1] This was a result of the lower cost of gas and of the fact that gas became readily available for power generation during the warmer months of the year as a result of decreased use by gas customers. Plaintiff expressly reserved its right to burn as much gas as it chose by the inclusion, in the "Quantity" provision of the requirements contract, of a clause to the effect that "[n]othing herein shall preclude the use by Buyer of * * * natural gas in such quantities as may be or become available".

Within five months of the execution of the requirements contract, the price of fuel oil began to ascend rapidly. On April 24, 1970 the market price of the oil supplied to plaintiff stood at between $2.65 and $2.73 per barrel. On May 1, 1970 the price was in excess of $3 per barrel. The rise continued and was in excess of $3.50 per barrel by mid-August, and more than $4 per barrel by the end of October, 1970. By March, 1971 the lowest market price was $4.30 per barrel—more than double the price set forth in the subject contract.

Coincident with the earliest of these increases in the cost of oil, O & R proceeded to notify Hess, on four separate dates, of increases in the fuel oil requirements estimates for the year. By letter dated April 16, 1970, O & R notified Hess that it was expected that over 1,460,000 barrels of oil would be consumed over the period April–December, 1970. Since well over 600,000 barrels of oil had been consumed during the first three months of the year, the total increase anticipated at that time was well in excess of 300,000 barrels over the estimate given in the contract.

1. For example, it was projected that in 1970 gas would generate 14,047,545,000,000 BTU while oil would be used to generate 10,810,740,000,000 BTU. The comparable ratios for the following years are: 1971—1⅝; 1972—1⁶⁄₉; 1973—⁹⁄₅.

Eight days later, by letter dated April 24, 1970, O & R furnished Hess with a revised estimate for the period May through December, 1970. The figure given was nearly 1,580,000 barrels which, when combined with quantities which had already been delivered or were in the process of delivery during the month of April, exceeded the contract estimate by over 700,000 barrels—a 40% increase.

The following month the estimates were again increased—this time to nearly one million barrels above the contract estimate. Hess was so notified by letter dated May 22, 1970. Finally, a letter dated June 19, 1970 indicates a revised estimate of more than one million barrels in excess of the 1,750,000 barrels mentioned in the contract; an increase of about 63%.

On May 22, 1970, the date of the third of the revised estimates, representatives of the two companies met to discuss the increased demands. At that meeting O & R's president allegedly attributed the increased need for oil to the fact that O & R could make more money *selling* gas than burning it for power generation. Hess refused to meet the revised requirements, but offered to supply the amount of the contract estimate for the year 1970, plus an additional 10 percent.

The June 19, 1970, letter referred to above recited that the Hess position was "wholly unacceptable" to O & R. It attributed the vastly increased estimates to (a) an inability to burn as much natural gas as had been planned and (b) the fact that O & R had been "required" to meet higher electrical demands on its "own system" and to furnish "more electricity to interconnected systems" than had been anticipated.

Thereafter, for the remainder of 1970, Hess continued to supply the amount of the contract estimates plus 10 percent. A proposal by Hess, in October, 1970, to modify the existing contract by setting minimum and maximum quantities, and by setting a price keyed to market prices, was ignored by O & R. Although the proposed modification set a price 65 cents lower than the market price, it was more advantageous for O & R to insist on delivery of the estimated amounts in the December, 1969 contract (at $2.14 per barrel) and to purchase additional amounts required at the full market price.

During the remainder of the contract period Hess continued to deliver quantities approximately equal to the estimates stated in the subject contract. O & R purchased additional oil for its Lovett plant from other suppliers. The contract between Hess and O & R terminated one year prematurely by reason of an environmental regulation which took effect on October 1, 1973 and which necessarily curtailed the use of No. 6 fuel oil with a sulphur content as high as 1%. During the period 1971 through September, 1973 O & R consistently used more than double its contract estimates of oil at Lovett.[2]

2. The Hess contract estimated 1971 usage at 1,380,000 barrels. In fact, 1,301,045 barrels were supplied that year by Hess and 1,844,947 barrels were supplied by other companies, for a total of 3,145,993 barrels. The contract estimate for 1972 was 1,500,000 barrels; a total of 3,325,037 barrels was purchased by O & R. The contract estimate for the first nine months of 1973 was 1,125,000 barrels (75% of the 1,500,000 listed in the contract as an estimate for all of 1973); 2,401,979 barrels were received by O & R during that nine-month period.

This action was commenced in mid–1972. O & R's complaint seeks damages consisting of the difference between its costs for fuel oil during the period in question and the cost it would have incurred had Hess delivered the total amount used by O & R at the fixed contract price of $2.14 per barrel. The trial was conducted in September, 1975 before Mr. Justice Donohoe, sitting without a jury. In an opinion dated March 8, 1976, Trial Term held that plaintiff should be denied any recovery on the ground that its requirements were not incurred in good faith. Specifically, Trial Term found that plaintiff's greatly increased oil consumption was due primarily to (a) increases in sales of electricity to other utilities and (b) a net shift from other fuels, primarily gas, to oil. The former factor was condemned on the premise that "[i]ndirectly, O & R called upon Hess to supply the demands for electricity to the members of the [New York Power] Pool. O & R then shared the savings in the cost of fuel with the other members of the Pool". The latter factor was not elaborated on to any great degree. Trial Term did, however, infer that O & R seized "the opportunity to release its reserve commitment of gas" and thereby reaped very substantial profits.

Although Trial Term stated in its opinion that one of the questions before it was whether plaintiff's demands were unreasonably disproportionate to the estimates set forth in the contract, it failed to reach this question in the light of its conclusion that plaintiff had failed to act in good faith. Plaintiff contends on this appeal (1) that Trial Term's finding of an absence of good faith is unsupported by the record and (2) that since its requirements for the entire term of the contract were less than twice total contract estimates, its demands were not "unreasonably disproportionate" as a matter of law. We reject both contentions upon the facts of this case and affirm Trial Term's dismissal of the complaint.

It is noted at the outset that the parties agreed, pursuant to their contract, that New Jersey law should apply. The governing statute is section 2–306 (subd. [1]) of the Uniform Commercial Code (UCC), which provides, in relevant part:

> "A term which measures the quantity [to be supplied by a seller to a purchaser of goods] by the * * * requirements of the buyer means such actual * * * requirements as may occur in good faith, except that no quantity unreasonably disproportionate to any stated estimate or in the absence of a stated estimate to any normal or otherwise comparable prior * * * requirements may be * * * demanded" (N.J.Stat.Ann., 12A:2–306, subd. [1], [matter in brackets added]).

There is, as Trial Term observed, a good deal of pre-Code case law on the requirement of "good faith". It is well settled that a buyer in a rising market cannot use a fixed price in a requirements contract for speculation. * * * Nor can a buyer arbitrarily and unilaterally change certain conditions prevailing at the time of the contract so as to take advantage of market conditions at the seller's expense * * *.

There is no judicial precedent with respect to the meaning of the term "unreasonably disproportionate" which appears in subdivision (1) of section 2–306 of the UCC. Obviously this language is not the equivalent of "lack of good faith"—it is an elementary rule of construction that effect must be given, if possible, to every word, clause and sentence of a statute. * * * The phrase is keyed to stated estimates or, if there be none, to "normal or otherwise comparable prior" requirements. While "reasonable elasticity" is contemplated by the section (see Official Comment, par. 2 to UCC § 2–306), an agreed estimate shows a clear limit on the intended elasticity, similar to that found in a contract containing minimum and maximum requirements (see Official Comment, par. 2 to UCC § 2–306). The estimate "is to be regarded as a center around which the parties intend the variation to occur" (supra).

The limitation imposed by the term "unreasonably disproportionate" represents a departure from prior case law, wherein estimates were generally treated as having been made simply for the convenience of the parties and of no operative significance (Note, Requirements Contracts under the Uniform Commercial Code, 102 U.Pa.L.Rev. 654, 660–661; Note, Requirements Contracts: Problems of Drafting and Construction, 78 Harv.L.Rev. 1212, 1218; cf. Shader Contr. v. United States, 276 F.2d 1, 149 Ct.Cl. 535). It is salutary in that it insures that the expectations of the parties will be more fully realized in spite of unexpected and fortuitous market conditions (see Note, Requirements Contracts under the Uniform Commercial Code, 102 U.Pa.L.Rev. 654, 666–667, supra). Thus, even where one party acts with complete good faith, the section limits the other party's risk in accordance with the reasonable expectations of the parties.

It would be unwise to attempt to define the phrase "unreasonably disproportionate" in terms of rigid quantities. In order that the limitation contemplated by the section take effect, it is not enough that a demand for requirements be disproportionate to the stated estimate; it must be *unreasonably* so in view of the expectation of the parties. A number of factors should be taken into account in the event a buyer's requirements greatly exceed the contract estimate. These include the following: (1) the amount by which the requirements exceed the contract estimate; (2) whether the seller had any reasonable basis on which to forecast or anticipate the requested increase * * *; (3) the amount, if any, by which the market price of the goods in question exceeded the contract price; (4) whether such an increase in market price was itself fortuitous; and (5) the reason for the increase in requirements.

Turning once again to the facts of the instant case, we conclude that, at least as to the year in which this controversy first arose, there was ample evidence to justify a finding of lack of good faith on plaintiff's part. Even through the thicket of divergent and contrasting figures entered into exhibit at trial, the following picture emerges: non-firm sales[3] from plaintiff's Lovett plant, presumably in large part to the New York Power Pool, increased nearly sixfold from 67,867 megawatt hours in 1969 to 390,017 megawatt hours in 1970. The significance of that increase in *non-firm* sales lies in the fact that such sales did not enter into the budget calculations which formed the basis of the estimates included in the contract. Even assuming that a prudent seller of oil could anticipate some additional requirements generated by non-firm sales, an increase of the magnitude which occurred in 1970 is unforeseeable. That increase, of 322,150 mega-

3. Non-firm sales are to be contrasted with "firm" sales, which are synonymous with predictable sales. Firm sales include predictable sales to O & R's own customers and sales pursuant to contract with other utilities.

watt hours, translates into the equivalent of over 500,000 barrels of oil.[4] The conclusion is inescapable that this dramatic change in plaintiff's relationship with the New York Power Pool came about as a result of the subject requirements contract, which insured it a steady flow of cheap oil despite swiftly rising prices.[5] O & R's use of the subject contract to suddenly and dramatically propel itself into the position of a large seller of power to other utilities evidences a lack of good faith dealing.[6]

In addition to this massive increase in sales of power to other utilities, the evidence indicates that at about the time O & R was demanding roughly one million barrels of oil in excess of the 1970 contract estimate, there was an internal O & R proposal to release gas to a supplier which represented the equivalent of 542,000 barrels of oil. An internal O & R memorandum dated May 26, 1970 (four days after the meeting at which Hess refused to supply the one million additional barrels demanded) recommended that in view of the Hess position, the proposed release be cancelled. Significantly, O & R never did burn as much oil as had been demanded in May and June, 1970. Its total usage for the year was 2,294,845 barrels—471,155 barrels less than its maximum demand. This was explained, by O & R officials, in part, on the ground that their "gas department" had made a "pessimistic estimate" which did not turn out to be quite true.

Thus it appears that in May, 1970 Hess refused an O & R demand of roughly one million barrels in excess of the contract estimate, which demand was occasioned by greatly increased sales to other utilities and a proposed release of gas which might otherwise normally have been burned for power generation.[7] The former factor is tantamount to making the other utilities in the State silent partners to the contract * * *, while the latter factor amounts to a unilateral and arbitrary change in the conditions prevailing at the time of the contract so as to take advantage of market conditions at the seller's expense. Hess was therefore justified in 1970 in refusing to meet

4. A figure of 515,400 barrels of oil is arrived at by multiplying the increase in sales of non-firm megawatt hours (322,150) by a very conservative conversion factor of 1.6.

5. Notwithstanding the fact that Hess failed to supply all that was demanded by O & R, it is apparent that even with a mix of Hess and non-Hess oil, plaintiff's costs of producing electricity with oil would have been lower than those of any companies purchasing oil on the open market or with "floating" contracts. This observation is underscored by the fact that O & R found it more advantageous to purchase the balance of its "requirements" on the open market (over and above the contract estimates which Hess was supplying) rather than to renegotiate the contract at a price 65 cents lower than posted market prices.

6. "[A] sudden expansion of the plant by which requirements are to be measured would not be included within the scope of the contract as made but normal expansion undertaken in good faith would be within the scope of this section." (Official Comment, par. 2 to UCC § 2–306.)

7. While there was testimony by O & R officials to the effect that this gas, supplied by the Home Gas Company, could not be burned at the Lovett plant because that gas was only transmitted to another geographical sector of O & R's territory, it strains credulity to believe that the interstate pipeline system is so parochial that releases in one sector would not affect operations in another sector. Home Gas Company was, in fact, a subsidiary of the Columbia Gas Transmission Company at the time, and Columbia Gas was burned at the Lovett plant. Furthermore, plaintiff's contention is belied by (a) the May 26, 1970 memo which linked the proposed release to oil deliveries at Lovett and (b) a revised calculation from O & R's gas department, dated May 19, 1970, which allocated Home gas between O & R's two geographical divisions for the purpose of showing gas availability for electrical generation.

plaintiff's demands, by reason of the fact that plaintiff's "requirements" were not incurred in good faith.

With respect to subsequent years however, the record is ambiguous as to the cause of plaintiff's drastically increased requirements. Non-firm sales from Lovett actually declined slightly in 1971 and 1972 although they were still greatly in excess of 1969 sales.[8] If one takes 1969 as a base year, increased non-firm sales from Lovett in 1971 amounted to the equivalent of about one-half million barrels of oil[9], while in 1972 they amounted to the equivalent of just over 300,000 barrels.[10] Comparable figures for 1973 are impossible to arrive at with any degree of confidence because sales figures in the record are for the full year, while defendant's obligation to supply oil extended through only three-quarters of the year. In any event, it is apparent that O & R's tremendously expanded use of oil during the period subsequent to 1970 cannot be explained solely by reference to increased sales to other utilities. In 1971 oil use exceeded the contract estimate by over 1,750,000 barrels; the 1972 figure was in excess of 1,825,000 barrels; and for the first nine months of 1973 the increase was more than 1,275,000 barrels.[11]

It appears that a large portion of the difference between actual use and contract estimates during this period can be attributed to a rather large decline in plaintiff's "actual take" of gas as opposed to the estimates of gas availability which were made in 1968 (and which were used in the computation of the December 30, 1968 budget). This decline, with the equivalent figure in barrels of oil,[12] was as follows:

8. In 1971 total sales from Lovett amounted to 387,874 MWH; firm sales were 17,294 MWH. Assuming these firm sales were all generated at Lovett, total non-firm sales would have been 370,580 MWH—down slightly from the 390,017 MWH sold on a non-firm basis in 1970. In 1972 total sales from Bowline (a new generating plant), from Lovett, and from gas turbines amounted to 722,329 MWH. Firm sales for the year were 423,734, of which 374,327 MWH were generated at Bowline. Assuming that the remaining 49,407 MWH in firm sales were generated at Lovett (and not by the gas turbines), that plant's non-firm sales for the year would have amounted to 256,320 MWH.

We have focused on non-firm sales in our analysis because the record does not reveal whether firm sales during this period were taken into account in the preparation of the December 30, 1968 budget projection which formed the basis of the contract estimates. If they were, they would be meaningless in attempting to explain the tremendous increase in plaintiff's oil requirements.

While there was evidence that electrical power is "fungible" and that allocation of sales to various plants is an "accounting function", the testimony at trial did establish that the allocation is performed in a sufficiently rational manner. We therefore decline to attribute all O & R sales to the Lovett plant.

9. We choose the increase over 1969 rather than the absolute figure for sales because a certain amount of power pool sales, based on O & R's past experience, would be reasonably foreseeable. In 1971, non-firm sales from Lovett amounted to 370,580 MWH (see n. 8), an increase of 303,007 MWH over the 67,867 MWH sold on a non-firm basis in 1969. If we multiply this increase by the very conservative conversion factor of 1.6, we arrive at a barrel equivalent of 484,811.

10. This calculation is made in exactly the same manner as the one for 1971. The increase in sales of non-firm power amounts to 188,453 MWH (256,320 MWH less 67,867 MWH) and application of the conversion factor results in a barrel equivalent of 301,525.

11. This figure is arrived at by subtracting three-quarters of the contract estimate from total oil deliveries during the first nine months of 1973.

12. One barrel of oil is equivalent in heating value to 6 Mcf of gas.

Estimate (Mcf)	Actual Take (Mcf)	Decrease	Equiv. Barrels of Oil
1971—40,615,000	34,518,000	6,097,000	1,016,167
1972—43,661,000	36,274,000	7,387,000	1,231,167
1973 (9 mos) 34,034,700	25,783,000	8,251,700	1,375,283

Even allowing for the fact that O & R's actual system requirements were slightly lower during this period than the estimated system requirements (thus theoretically leaving more gas available for electric generation), it is clear that the decline from the estimates in gas received by O & R was a very major factor in plaintiff's increased use of oil during this period.

The record is unclear as to why this decline came about. Plaintiff introduced into evidence a Public Service Commission memorandum which indicates that gas supplies available to interstate transmission companies had become extremely tight. However plaintiff failed to call one witness who was expert in its gas operations and who could testify as to the link, if any, between this general shortage and plaintiff's operations. While an unfavorable inference may be drawn when a party fails to produce evidence which is within his control and which he is naturally expected to produce, we decline to speculate as to causes of the decline in gas received by plaintiff. In any event, such speculation is not necessary for resolution of this appeal.

We hold that under the circumstances of this case, any demand[13] by plaintiff for more than double its contract estimates, was, as a matter of law, "unreasonably disproportionate" (UCC, § 2-306, subd. [1]) to those estimates. We do not adopt the factor of more than double the contract estimates as any sort of an inflexible yardstick.[14] Rather, we apply those standards set forth earlier in this opinion, which are calculated to limit a party's risk in accordance with the reasonable expectations of the parties.

Here, as noted, plaintiff's requirements during the period 1971 through September, 1973, were more than double the contract estimates. Defendant had no reasonable basis on which to forecast or anticipate an increase of this magnitude. Indeed the contract suggests the parties contemplated that any variations from the estimate would be on the downside—else why did plaintiff expressly reserve for itself the right to burn as much as it chose? The market price of the grade of oil supplied had more than doubled by March, 1971. It stayed at or above $4.00 per barrel for the rest of the applicable period and had reached nearly $5.00 per barrel by the end of September, 1973. The record is silent as to whether defendant had any reason to anticipate this enormous increase in oil prices. Finally, the increase in requirements was due in part to plaintiff's increased sales to other utilities and also due to a significant decline in anticipated deliveries of gas, the cause of which was inadequately explained by plaintiff. The quantities of oil utilized by plaintiff during the period subsequent to 1970

13. There is no indication in the record that O & R continued to supply Hess with up-dated "requirements" demands after June 19, 1970. In fact, it can be inferred from a fair reading of the record that O & R entered into a contract with another supplier to furnish amounts required in excess of the amounts Hess was willing to supply. Nevertheless, we assume for the sake of argument that there was a continuing "demand" by plaintiff for its total requirements.

14. Interestingly, plaintiff would have us hold as a matter of law that where an actual requirement varies "only by a factor of two from a stated estimate", it is not unreasonably disproportionate to such estimate.

were not within the reasonable expectations of the parties when the contract was executed, and accordingly we hold that those "requirements" were unreasonably disproportionate to the contract estimates (see UCC, § 2–306, subd. [1]).

Judgment of the Supreme Court, Rockland County, entered June 4, 1976, affirmed, with costs.

Notes

1. Since 1977, there has been little litigation of significance on the issues decided in Orange & Rockland. See Homestake Mining Co. v. Washington Public Power Supply System, 476 F.Supp. 1162, 1167–69 (N.D.Cal.1979) (bad faith for buyer under requirements contract to insist on goods not needed for the particular business activity referred to in contract). For commentary, see White & Summers, Section 3–8; Note, *Requirements Contracts, "More or Less," Under the Uniform Commercial Code,* 33 Rutgers L.Rev. 105 (1980). For discussions of the good faith issue in flexible quantity contracts, see Burton, *Breach of Contract and the Common Law Duty to Perform in Good Faith,* 94 Harv.L.Rev. 369, 381–84, 395–97 (1980); Muris, *Opportunistic Behavior and the Law of Contracts,* 65 Minn.L.Rev. 521, 556–65 (1981).

2. The court in Orange & Rockland used factors existing and events foreseeable at the time of contracting to determine whether the buyer's orders were "unreasonably disproportionate" to the stated estimates. Where the estimates did not apply, however, the court used motives and factors existing at the time the requirements were ordered to determine whether the buyer's conduct was in bad faith. The buyer lost on both counts. Suppose, however, that the amounts ordered were unreasonably disproportionate to the stated estimates but the buyer's actual requirements were in good faith. Which limitation upon the exercise of discretion should prevail under UCC 2–306(1)?

3. *Going Out of Business.* Suppose the buyer claims that its actual requirements for the goods described in the contract were non-existent or drastically reduced from prior years. Such a decision appears to be justified if made in good faith. UCC 2–306(1). As one court put it, the "seller assumes the risk of all good faith variations in the buyer's requirements even to the extent of a determination to liquidate or discontinue the business." It might be said that the buyer's duty to buy is conditioned upon the existence of actual requirements. Further: "The rule is based on a reliance on the self-interest of the buyer, who ordinarily will seek to have the largest possible requirements. Protection against abuse is afforded by penetrating through any device by which the requirement is siphoned off in some other form to the detriment of the seller. The requirement of good faith is the means by which this is enforced and self-interest in its undistorted form is maintained as the standard." HML Corporation v. General Foods Corporation, 365 F.2d 77 (3d Cir.1966) (burden on seller to prove bad faith). See Comment, *And Then There Were None: Requirments Contracts and the Buyer Who Does Not Buy,* 64 Wash.L.Rev. 871 (1989).

What, then, is bad faith in this setting? What if the decision is not to curtail losses but simply to make more profits on an alternative line of production? Inferences of bad faith abound when the seller has some demand for its output or the buyer still has some requirements and the decision is "merely to curtail losses." UCC 2–306, Comment 2. A leading case is Feld v. Henry S. Levy & Sons, Inc., 37 N.Y.2d 466, 373 N.Y.S.2d 102, 106, 335 N.E.2d 320, 323 (1975), where the court concluded that an "output" seller was justified in a good faith cessation of a single operation rather than entire business "only if its losses from continuance would be more than trivial". A cessation "merely to curtail losses" would be improper. Should the amount of loss from continued performance be the major issue? How much is too much? One of your co-authors believes that the standards derived from the Comments to UCC 2-306 are impossible to apply.

EMPIRE GAS CORP. v. AMERICAN BAKERIES CO.

United States Court of Appeals, Seventh Circuit, 1988.
840 F.2d 1333.

Appeal from the United States District Court for the Northern District of Illinois.

Before POSNER, FLAUM, and KANNE, CIRCUIT JUDGES.

POSNER, CIRCUIT JUDGE. This appeal in a diversity contract case presents a fundamental question—surprisingly little discussed by either courts or commentators—in the law of requirements contracts. Is such a contract essentially a buyer's option, entitling him to purchase all he needs of the good in question on the terms set forth in the contract, but leaving him free to purchase none if he wishes provided that he does not purchase the good from anyone else and is not acting out of ill will toward the seller?

Empire Gas Corporation is a retail distributor of liquefied petroleum gas, better known as "propane." It also sells converters that enable gasoline-powered motor vehicles to operate on propane. The sharp rise in gasoline prices in 1979 and 1980 made American Bakeries Company, which operated a fleet of more than 3,000 motor vehicles to serve its processing plants and bakeries, interested in the possibility of converting its fleet to propane, which was now one-third to one-half less expensive than gasoline. Discussions between the companies resulted in an agreement in principle. Empire Gas sent American Bakeries a draft of its standard "Guaranteed Fuel Supply Contract," which would have required American Bakeries to install a minimum number of conversion units each month and to buy all the propane for the converted vehicles from Empire Gas for eight years. American Bakeries rejected the contract and Empire Gas prepared a new one, which was executed on April 17, 1980, and which was "for approximately three thousand (3,000) [conversion] units, more or less depending upon requirements of Buyer, consisting of Fuel Tank, Fuel Lock Off Switch, Converter & appropriate Carburetor & Small Parts Kit," at a price of $750 per unit. American Bakeries agreed "to purchase propane motor fuel solely from EMPIRE GAS CORPORATION at all locations where EMPIRE GAS has supplied carburetion and dispensing equipment as long as EMPIRE GAS CORPORATION remains in a reasonably competitive price posture with other major suppliers." The contract was to last for four years.

American Bakeries never ordered any equipment or propane from Empire Gas. Apparently within days after the signing of the contract American Bakeries decided not to convert its fleet to propane. No reason has been given for the decision.

Empire Gas brought suit against American Bakeries for breach of contract and won a jury verdict for $3,254,963, representing lost profits on

2,242 conversion units (the jury's estimate of American Bakeries' requirements) and on the propane fuel that the converted vehicles would have consumed during the contract period. The judge added $581,916 in prejudgment interest.

* * *

The heart of this case is the instruction concerning American Bakeries' obligation under the contract. If there were no legal category of "requirements" contracts and no provision of the Uniform Commercial Code governing such contracts, a strong argument could be made that American Bakeries agreed to buy 3,000 conversion units or *slightly* more or *slightly* less, depending on its actual needs, and hence that it broke the contract by taking none. This is not only a semantically permissible reading of the contract but one supported by the discussions that the parties had before the contract was signed (and these discussions are admissible to explain though not to change the parties' undertakings), in which American Bakeries assured Empire Gas that it was planning to convert its entire fleet. American Bakeries insisted on adding the phrase "more or less depending upon requirements of Buyer" just in case its estimate of 3,000 was off, and this is quite different from supposing that the phrase was added so that American Bakeries would have no obligation to buy any units at all.

The parties agree, however, that despite the negotiating history and the inclusion in the contract of a specific estimate of quantity, the quoted phrase sorted the contract into the legal bin labeled "requirements contract" and thereby brought it under the governance of § 2–306(1) of the Uniform Commercial Code, which provides:

> "A term which measures the quantity by the output of the seller or the requirements of the buyer means such actual output or requirements as may occur in good faith, except that no quantity unreasonably disproportionate to any stated estimate or in the absence of a stated estimate to any normal or otherwise comparable prior output or requirements may be tendered or demanded."

Over American Bakeries' objection the judge decided to read the statute to the jury verbatim and without amplification, remarking to the lawyers,

> "Now, I have nothing to do with the fact that there may be some ambiguity in 2–306. If there is ambiguity, well, that is too bad. This is the law that the legislature has adopted. With due respect to all these great judges that [American Bakeries' counsel] has cited and these great academic lawyers he has called to my attention, well, good, they have a lot of time to mull over these problems.
>
> "But I have the problem of telling this jury what the law is, and the law is right here, right here in this statute, and I have a good deal of faith in this jury's ability to apply this statute to the facts of this case."

* * *

The interpretive question involves the proviso dealing with "quantity unreasonably disproportionate to any stated estimate." This limitation is fairly easy to understand when the disproportion takes the form of the buyer's demanding more than the amount estimated. If there were no ceiling, and if the price happened to be advantageous to the buyer, he might increase his "requirements" so that he could resell the good at a profit. See, e.g., Crane v. C. Crane & Co., 105 Fed. 869, 872 (7th Cir.1901); Weistart, Requirements and Output Contracts: Quantity Variations Under the UCC, 1973 Duke L.J. 599, 640–41; cf. Utah International, Inc. v. Colorado–Ute Electric Ass'n, Inc., 425 F.Supp. 1093, 1100–01 (D.Colo.1976). This would place him in competition with the seller—a result the parties would not have wanted when they signed the contract. So the "unreasonably disproportionate" proviso carries out the likely intent of the parties. The only problem is that the same result could easily be reached by interpretation of the words "good faith" in the preceding clause of § 2–306(1), thus making the proviso redundant. But redundancies designed to clarify or emphasize are common in legal drafting; and anyway the Uniform Commercial Code has its share of ambiguities, see Wisconsin Knife Works v. National Metal Crafters, 781 F.2d 1280, 1288 [42 UCC Rep Serv 830] (7th Cir.1986).

The proviso does not distinguish between the buyer who demands more than the stated estimate and the buyer who demands less, and therefore if read literally it would forbid a buyer to take (much) less than the stated estimate. Since the judge did not attempt to interpret the statute the jury may have read it literally, and if so the judge in effect directed a verdict for Empire Gas. The stated estimate was for 3,000 units; American Bakeries took none; if this was not unreasonably disproportionate to the stated estimate, what buyer shortfall could be?

So we must decide whether the proviso should be read literally when the buyer is demanding less rather than more than the stated estimate. There are no cases on the question in Illinois, and authority elsewhere is sparse, considering how often (one might think) the question must have arisen. But the clearly dominant approach is not to construe the proviso literally, but instead to treat the overdemanding and underdemanding cases differently. We think this is right. We also note that it was the common law approach: "the seller assumes the risk of all good faith variations in the buyer's requirements even to the extent of a determination to liquidate or discontinue the business." HML Corp. v. General Foods Corp., supra, 365 F.2d at 81; see also Fort Wayne Corrugated Paper Co. v. Anchor Hocking Glass Corp., 130 F.2d 471, 473 (3d Cir.1942).

Granted there is language in the Official Comments (not official in Illinois, be it noted) which points to symmetrical treatment of the overdemanding and underdemanding cases: "the agreed estimate is to be regarded as a center around which the parties intend the variation to occur." UCC § 2–306, comment 3. But there is no elaboration; and the statement is in tension with the statement in comment 2 that "good faith variations from prior requirements are permitted even when the variation may be such as to result in discontinuance," for if that principle is sound in general, why should it cease to be sound just because the parties included an estimate of the buyer's requirements? A tiny verbal point against the symmetrical interpretation is the last word of the proviso—"demanded." The statement that "no quantity unreasonably disproportionate to any stated estimate * * * may be * * * demanded" is more naturally read as applying to the case where the buyer is demanding more than when he is reducing his demand below the usual or estimated level.

More important than this verbal skirmishing is the fact that the entire proviso is in a sense redundant given the words "good faith" in the main clause of the statute. The proviso thus seems to have been designed to explicate the term "good faith" rather than to establish an independent legal standard. And the aspect of good faith that required explication had only to do with disproportionately *large* demands. If the buyer saw an opportunity to increase his profits by reselling the seller's goods because the market price had risen above the contract price, the exploitation of that opportunity might not *clearly* spell bad faith; the proviso was added to close off the opportunity. There is no indication that the draftsmen were equally, if at all, concerned about the case where the buyer takes less than his estimated requirements, provided, of course, that he does not buy from anyone else. We conclude that the Illinois courts would allow a buyer to reduce his requirements to zero if he was acting in good faith, even though the contract contained an estimate of those requirements.

This conclusion would be greatly strengthened—too much so, as we shall see—if the only purpose of a requirements contract were to give the seller a reasonably assured market for his product *by forbidding the buyer to satisfy any of his needs by buying from another supplier.* (An output contract, also dealt with in § 2–306(1), gives the buyer a reasonably assured source of supply by forbidding the seller to sell any of his output to any other buyer.) The buyer's undertaking to deal exclusively with a particular seller gives the seller some, although far from complete, assurance of having a market for his goods; and of course he must compensate the buyer for giving up the opportunity to shop around for a better deal from competing sellers.

* * *

Both extreme interpretations—that the buyer need only refrain from dealing with a competitor of the seller, and that the buyer cannot go significantly beneath the estimated quantity except in dire circumstances—must be rejected, as we shall see. Nevertheless the judge should not have read the "unreasonably disproportionate" proviso in § 2–306(1) to the jury. The proviso does not apply, though the requirement of good faith does, where the buyer takes less rather than more of the stated estimate in a requirements contract.

This error in instructions requires reversal and a new trial on liability unless it is clear either that American Bakeries acted in good faith or that it acted in bad faith, since the statute requires the buyer to take his "good faith" requirements from the seller, irrespective of proportionality. The Uniform Commercial Code does not contain a definition of "good faith" that seems applicable to the buyer under a requirements contract. Compare § 2–104(1) with § 2–103(1)(b). Nor has the term a settled meaning in law generally; it is a chameleon. See, e.g., Bosco v. Serhant, Nos. 86–2918 et al., slip op. at 11 [836 F2d 271] (7th Cir. December 2, 1987); In re TCI Ltd., 769 F.2d 441, 445 (7th Cir.1985). Clearly, American Bakeries was acting in bad faith if during the contract period it bought propane conversion units from anyone other than Empire Gas, or made its own units, or reduced its purchases because it wanted to hurt Empire Gas (for example because they were competitors in some other market). Equally clearly, it was not acting in bad faith if it had a business reason for deciding not to convert that was independent of the terms of the contract or any other aspect of its relationship with Empire Gas, such as a drop in the demand for its bakery products that led it to reduce or abandon its fleet of delivery trucks. A harder question is whether it was acting in bad faith if it changed its mind about conversion for no (disclosed) reason. There is no evidence in the record on why it changed its mind beyond vague references to "budget problems" that, so far as appears, may have been nothing more than a euphemism for a decision by American Bakeries not to allocate funds for conversion to propane.

If no reason at all need be given for scaling back one's requirements even to zero, then a requirements contract is from the buyer's standpoint just an option to purchase up to (or slightly beyond, i.e., within the limits of reasonable proportionality) the stated estimate on the terms specified in the contract, except that the buyer cannot refuse to exercise the option because someone offers him better terms. This is not an unreasonable position, but it is not the law. Among the less important reasons for this conclusion are that option contracts are dealt with elsewhere in the Code, see § 2–311, and that the Official Comments to § 306 state that "a shut-down by a requirements buyer for lack of orders might be permissible where a shut-down *merely to curtail losses* would not." UCC § 2–306, comment 2 (emphasis added). More compelling is the Illinois Code Comment to § 2–306, which states that "this section * * * is but a codification of prior Illinois decisional law," which had made clear that a requirements contract was more than a buyer's option.

* * *

The statement of an estimate invites the seller to begin making preparations to satisfy the contract, and although no reliance expense was incurred by the seller in this case, a seller is entitled to expect that the buyer will buy something like the estimated requirements unless it has a valid business reason for buying less. More important than the estimate (which was not a factor in the Illinois cases just cited) is the fact that ordinarily a requirements contract is terminated after performance has begun, rather than before as in the present case. Whether or not the seller can prove reliance damages, the sudden termination of the contract midway through performance is bound to disrupt his operations somewhat. The Illinois courts interpret a requirements contract as a sharing of risk between seller and buyer. The seller assumes the risk of a change in the buyer's business that makes continuation of the contract unduly costly, but the buyer assumes the risk of a less urgent change in his circumstances, perhaps illustrated by the facts of this case where so far as one can tell the buyer's change of mind reflected no more than a reassessment of the balance of advantages and disadvantages under the contract. American Bakeries did not agree to buy conversion units and propane for trucks that it got rid of, but neither did Empire Gas agree to forgo sales merely because new management at American Bakeries decided that its capital would be better employed in some other investment than conversion to propane.

* * *

The essential ingredient of good faith in the case of the buyer's reducing his estimated requirements is that he not merely have had second thoughts about the terms of the contract and want to get out of it. See Wilsonville Concrete Products v. Todd Building Co., 281 Ore. 345, 352, 574 P.2d 1112, 1115 [23 UCC Rep Serv 590] (1978); Royal Paper Box Co. v. E.R. Apt Shoe Co., 290 Mass. 107, 195 N.E. 96 (1935); Fort Wayne Corrugated Paper Co. v. Anchor Hocking Glass Corp., supra, 130 F.2d at 473–74; White & Summers, supra, at 126. Whether the buyer has any greater obligation is unclear, see id. at 126–27, but need not be decided here. Once it is decided (as we have) that a buyer cannot arbitrarily declare his requirements to be zero, this becomes an easy case, because American Bakeries has never given any reason for its change of heart. It might seem that once the district judge decided to instruct the jury in the language of the statute, American Bakeries was foreclosed from arguing that it had scaled down its requirements in good faith; a reduction to zero could never be proportionate if, as the instruction implied, the proviso on disproportion applies to reductions as well as increases in the buyer's takings. But the judge did not make this decision until the instructions conference. Until then American Bakeries had every opportunity and incentive to introduce evidence of why it decided not to convert its fleet to propane. It introduced none, and even at the argument in this court its counsel could give no reason for the change of heart beyond a hint that it was due to a change in management, which would not be enough by itself to justify a change in the buyer's requirements.

Even though Empire Gas had the burden of proving breach of contract and therefore (we may assume) of proving that American Bakeries acted in bad faith in reducing its requirements from 3,000 conversion units to zero (see HML Corp. v. General Foods Corp., supra, 365 F.2d at 83; but see Utah International, Inc. v. Colorado–Ute Electrical Ass'n, Inc., supra, 425 F.Supp. at 1100), no reasonable jury could have failed to find bad faith, and therefore the error in instructing the jury on proportionality was harmless. Empire Gas put in evidence, uncontested and incontestable, showing that American Bakeries had not got rid of its fleet of trucks and did have the financial wherewithal to go through with the conversion process. * * *

* * *

The judgment is affirmed except for the award of prejudgment interest. Modified and affirmed.

KANNE, CIRCUIT JUDGE, dissenting. I agree with the majority that the error in giving the instruction regarding the "unreasonably disproportionate" proviso in Illinois' Uniform Commercial Code § 2–306(1) requires a reversal and new trial, "unless it is clear either that American Bakeries acted in good faith or that it acted in bad faith * * *." The fundamental problem is that there was no evidence of either good or bad faith as those terms are normally defined.[1] For different reasons neither Empire Gas nor American Bakeries produced evidence of American Bakeries' honesty or

1. Section 1–201(19) which applies to all sections of the Code defines good faith as "honesty in fact in the conduct or transaction concerned." Section 2–103, which applies to sales, defines good faith as "honesty in fact and the observance of reasonable commercial standards of fair dealing in the trade."

dishonesty or fair or unfair dealing in regard to its reduction of its requirements to zero.

As in Massey–Ferguson, Inc. v. Helland, 434 N.E.2d 295, 299 [33 UCC Rep Serv 1532] (Ill.App. 2 Dist.1982), " * * * the material testimony in this case did not reveal any lies, deceit, overreaching or other examples of dishonesty in fact in the transaction * * * nor was any evidence adduced regarding reasonable commercial standards of fair dealing in the trade." In Massey–Ferguson, the Illinois Appellate Court found that a plaintiff's failure to introduce specific evidence as to bad faith constituted a failure to carry its burden of proof on the issue of bad faith.

The majority in the case before us assumes that Empire Gas bears the burden of proof on the issue of American Bakcries' bad faith. The majority then presumes that Empire meets this burden of showing bad faith by simply presenting evidence that "American Bakeries had not got rid of its fleet of trucks and did have the financial wherewithal to go through with the conversion." I do not agree that from this scant evidence "no reasonable jury could have failed to find bad faith," and thus the district court's failure to instruct the jury properly on this issue was not harmless error. In reality, at trial, Empire Gas was never required to shoulder—let alone carry—any actual burden of proof on bad faith.[2] The majority thus transforms the seller's theoretical burden of proof on bad faith (unarticulated to the jury) into an actual presumption of the buyer's bad faith (articulated post-trial).

Empire Gas, if actually put to the test, may or may not be able to produce evidence of bad faith. Likewise, we do not know whether American Bakeries would be able to produce evidence to support a good faith reduction to zero. Absent the majority's presumption, at trial no one knew, at least based on the evidence, that it had become American Bakeries' burden to go forward with proof of its good faith.

Clearly American Bakeries' reduction of its requirements for conversion units from 3,000 to zero was "unreasonably disproportionate" on its face. However, the court (correctly I believe) holds today that what appears to be a buyers' unreasonably disproportionate reduction of requirements is not enough to determine liability under § 2–306—evidence of a buyer's good or bad faith is also necessary.

It is not this standard, but its practical application to the trial of this case, which causes me to part company with my brethren.

If, as the majority apparently holds—the seller has the burden of proof on the issue of the buyer's bad faith—I would reverse and remand for new trial because Empire Gas did not bear that burden and the trial record

2. The district court actually rejected the instruction tendered by American Bakeries which articulated Empire's burden of proof regarding bad faith. American Bakeries' tendered Instruction No. 19 reads in pertinent part as follows:

" * * *

"The buyer must exercise good faith in determining its requirements. Good faith means honesty in fact in the conduct or transaction concerned.

"Even if an estimate is stated in a requirements contract, the buyer need not order more goods than the buyer in good faith determines it requires. This is so even if such good faith requirements are substantially less than a previously stated estimate or even if the buyer has no requirements at all."

discloses no facts ordinarily found necessary by Illinois courts to prove bad faith.

If, on the other hand, the majority actually holds (again correctly I believe)—a buyer's assertion of an unreasonably disproportionate reduction in his requirements creates a bad faith presumption which may be rebutted by the buyer's proof of good faith—I would also reverse and remand for a new trial because this new rebuttable presumption of bad faith was not the Illinois rule under which the trial was conducted.

Note: Best Efforts in Exclusive Dealing Relationships

UCC 2–306(2) provides that a "lawful agreement by either the seller or the buyer for exclusive dealing in the kind of goods concerned imposes unless otherwise agreed an obligation by the seller to use best efforts to supply the goods and by the buyer to use best efforts to promote their sale."

An exclusive dealing relationship is a continuing, highly interdependent agency, franchise or contract for distribution. It facilitates the manufacturer's effort to market the goods. It is common for the distributor to agree to order requirements as generated by "best efforts" from and to deal exclusively in some defined territory with the manufacturer. When the agreement to use "best efforts" is coupled with exclusive dealing, there is consideration. Hunt Foods, Inc. v. Phillips, 248 F.2d 23 (9th Cir.1957). There is some risk, however, that the arrangement, because of its restriction upon competition, will run afoul of the antitrust laws. See L. Sullivan, Anti-Trust 163–66 (1977). In any event, the arrangement must be lawful under state and federal law and an agreement by the distributor to make best efforts must exist. See Gerard v. Almouli, 746 F.2d 936 (2d Cir.1984) (no best efforts agreement where condition precedent fails). UCC 2–306(2) presumes that the "best efforts" agreement exists unless the parties have otherwise agreed. See Tigg Corp. v. Dow Corning Corp., 962 F.2d 1119 (3d Cir.1992) (requirements contract with exclusive dealing clause imposes best efforts duty on buyer).

What are "best efforts" when the duty is part of the agreement? Beyond the requirement that the distributor make an honest effort in the particular setting, there is disagreement among the courts. For a leading case and some helpful analysis, see Bloor v. Falstaff Brewing Corp., 601 F.2d 609 (2d Cir.1979) and Goetz & Scott, *Principles of Relational Contracts,* 67 Va.L.Rev. 1089 (1981).

C. The Price Term

In a market directed economy, the sale price is the result of seller costs, buyer demand, information available to and negotiations between the parties and the quality of competition in the relevant market area. Since price is a material term in any sale, the determination of what price was agreed, as well as the method for ascertainment, is important when disputes arise.

Sections 2–204(3) and 2–305 are the key UCC sections. Review them and work through the following materials.

IN RE GLOVER CONSTRUCTION CO., INC.

United States Bankruptcy Court, Western District of Kentucky, 1985.
49 B.R. 581.

MERRITT S. DIETZ, BANKRUPTCY JUDGE. Simple contract elements—the offer, acceptance and "meeting of the minds" that bind bargaining parties to their promises—rarely play a part in today's complex bankruptcy litigation. But the outcome of the case at hand depends exactly on the basic question of whether the parties, in the extensive course of their dealings, ever really had an enforceable agreement between them.

In the fall of 1981, the debtors, Glover Construction Company, Inc. and Glover Contracting Company, Inc. (Glover), and the plaintiff, Fleetwash Systems, Inc. (Fleetwash), began negotiating for a contract whereby Fleetwash would furnish Glover with vehicle washing equipment for installation on a construction project at Fort Knox, Kentucky. In February of 1982 the parties executed a "contract"[1] for the purchase of the equipment. The terms of this "purchase order" called for a total price of $370,000 and payments by Glover of "net 30th of month following month in which material is delivered". The purchase order also contained the following language concerning the equipment's price:

> Terms: (Options) 10% Down Payment upon approval by owner $37,000.00. 2% Discount on 370,000.00 = $7,400.00 off Final Payment.
>
> 25% Down Payment upon approval by Owner $92,500.00. 5% Discount on 370,000.00 = 18,500.00 off Final Payment. 60% Annual Interest Rate.

Immediately after the signing of the purchase order, Glover and Fleetwash began quarreling as to the exact meaning of the above quoted terms. Fleetwash has constantly maintained that the contract called for Glover to make *either* a 10% or 25% down payment before they were to ship the contract materials. Glover, however, has consistently argued that the contract merely granted Glover the *option to earn a discount by making either a 10% or 25% down payment* and that the only mandatory payment terms were those calling for "Net 30th of month following month in which material is delivered". The conduct of the parties following the signing of the purchase order as well as their testimony at the trial showed that neither party intended to be bound by the terms of the purchase order unless the other party agreed to their interpretation of the price/payment provisions.

In September of 1982, Glover offered to make a 25% down payment on the vehicle washing equipment if Fleetwash would provide Glover with releases of liens on the equipment from both Fleetwash and its suppliers. Fleetwash could only provide Glover with a release of its own against the equipment, and Glover did not make the down payment.

On November 10, 1982 Glover filed a petition for reorganization under Chapter 11 of the Bankruptcy Code. Robert C. Glover was appointed debtor in possession and Glover continued work on the Fort Knox project. A trustee was appointed by this court for the limited purpose of collecting and disbursing Glover's progress payments.

In February of 1983, one year after the signing of the original purchase order, Fleetwash offered to deliver a portion of Glover's order if Glover

1. Although the parties stipulated that they entered into a contract, the facts indicate that a valid contractual relationship never existed. See note 3 infra and accompanying text.

would "walk the invoice through [the U.S. Army Corps of Engineers' billing procedures]". The total invoice price of this shipment was $144,200. At the time Fleetwash made this partial shipment, the two parties still had not agreed on the price and payment terms. Glover received the equipment and submitted to the U.S. Army Corps of Engineers a pay request covering the Fleetwash invoice. The Army approved the pay request and issued a check in the net amount of $129,780 [2] to the trustee who still holds these funds. Glover objected to the disbursement of these funds to Fleetwash on a number of grounds, and the present action ensued.

* * *

The initial issue we must address is whether the parties had a valid contract for the sale of the vehicle washing equipment. Although the parties stipulated that they entered into a contract with the signing of the purchase order on February 15, 1982, it is an ancient and unchallenged principle of contract law that for there to be a valid contract there must first be agreement as to the essential terms of that contract.[3] This rule has been modified to some extent by the Uniform Commercial Code (UCC) and its "gap-filler provisions". The provision of Kentucky's [4] version of the UCC which deals with open price terms, KRS 355.2–305, provides that:

> "(1) The parties, if they so intend can conclude a contract for sale *even though the price is not settled.* In such a case the price is a *reasonable price* at the time for delivery if
>
> * * *
>
> "(b) the price is left to be agreed by the parties and they fail to agree
>
> * * *
>
> "(4) *Where, however the parties intend not to be bound unless the price be fixed or agreed and it is not fixed or agreed there is no contract.* In such case the buyer must return any goods already received or if unable so to do must pay their *reasonable value* at the time of delivery" * * * [emphasis added]

In the present case the parties entered into the purchase order without having agreed on the contract's price and payment terms. Kentucky's version of the UCC would ordinarily supply the price terms of the contract, except that the parties to this action clearly intended not to be bound to the terms of the purchase order unless their interpretation of the price terms was accepted by the opposing party. Both KRS 355.2–305(4) and pre-UCC case law [5] state that in such a case *there is no contract between the parties.*

2. All payment by the Army Corps of Engineers were subject to a 10% retainage.

3. Smith v. Hilliard, 408 S.W.2d 440 (Ky. 1966); Vidt v. Burgess, 136 S.W.2d 1080 (Ky. 1940); Dean v. Meter, 8 Ky.Opin. 746 (Ky. 1874).

4. As a general rule of law the place of performance of the contract governs the rights of the parties absent a clear showing of contrary intent. Smith v. Stone, 202 F.Supp. 11 (E.D.Ky.1962). In this case the parties intended to have the purchase order "governed and construed according to the laws of the state of Kentucky" since that language was included as a choice of law provision in the order form.

5. Herman v. Jackson, 405 S.W.2d 9 (Ky. 1966); Thompson v. Hunters Ex'r et al., 269 S.W. 266 (Ky.1954); Marshall's Adm'r v. Webster, 155 S.W.2d 13 (Ky.1941).

Due to this finding [6] we need not consider the parties' lengthy, if misplaced, arguments on the issues of breach and damages.[7] Our ruling that no contract existed between Glover and Fleetwash does not preclude payment to Fleetwash for goods delivered to Glover. KRS 355.2–305(4) provides that where there is no contract "the buyer must return any goods already received or if unable so to do must pay their reasonable value at the time of delivery [to the seller]". We therefore must determine the reasonable value of the goods.

Although neither the UCC, applicable case law nor White & Summers define what constitutes "reasonable value", in our opinion the term "reasonable value" as used in this context is merely a codification of the doctrine of restitution [8] as the basis of recovery in cases involving a quasi-contract, or contract implied in law.[9] The term "reasonable value" is not to be considered synonymous with the term "reasonable price", although it is possible—and certainly a commercial ideal—that an item's reasonable value and reasonable price might coincide.

At trial both parties offered extensive evidence as to the value of the equipment. Fleetwash, arguing that the parties intended to contract but merely left open the price and payment terms, placed the reasonable price of the equipment at approximately $137,000. Glover, on the other hand, produced three estimates of value ranging from $32,000 to $34,000.

After carefully reviewing all estimates of the value of the vehicle washing equipment delivered to Glover by Fleetwash, and considering the credibility and reliability of all witnesses as well as the circumstances surrounding their estimates, it is our opinion that the reasonable value of the equipment in question is $43,000. Our basis for this particular figure comes from a letter written by Melvin Wiegand, Vice President of Fleetwash, to the attorney who was representing them in the Chapter 11 reorganization of their predecessor brother-sister corporation, Wiegand Engineering, before a bankruptcy court in Texas. In that letter Fleetwash told its attorney that it would invoice Glover in the net amount of $123,000 for the equipment it sent to be installed at the Fort Knox construction site. The letter went on to say that "This transaction will result in an income of approximately $80,000. * * *" It is our opinion that this letter which indicates the reasonable value to be $43,000 is entitled to more weight by

6. "Whether an agreement has been concluded, in most cases, is a question to be determined by the trier of fact." KRS 355.2–305, Kentucky Commentary (1983). In this case our determination on this issue is clearly factual and is subject to the "clearly erroneous" standard of review. See In re Calhoun, 715 F.2d 1103, 1110 (6th Cir.1983).

7. See White & Summers, Uniform Commercial Code § 3–7, p. 117 (2d ed. 1980).

8. Black's Law Dictionary, (5th ed. 1979) defines restitution as:

"act of restoring; * * * the act of making good or giving equivalent for any loss, damage or injury; * * * restoration of status quo and is amount which would put plaintiff in as good a position as he would have been if *no contract had been made* and restores to plaintiff [the] value of what he parted with in performing [the] contract * * * a person who has been unjustly enriched at the expense of another is required to make restitution to the other. [emphasis added]

9. A contract implied in law or quasi contract indicates a duty imposed by law, "without mutual assent, for the purpose of affording a remedy or right of recovery where money or property or services were received under such circumstances that in equity and good conscience the recipient [must] pay for them." Thompson v. Hunter's Ex'r, 269 S.W.2d at 269.

this court than either of the self-serving estimates prepared by interested parties in anticipation of litigation *before this court,*[10] or the hopelessly confused estimate presented by the Army Corps of Engineers.[11] This award of $43,000 covers both the 2-wheeled vehicle washing systems as well as the miscellaneous hose station equipment, since from a review of the limited cost data provided by Fleetwash, it is clear that an award of $43,000 for the vehicle washing systems alone would be over-generous. In fact, in making this award we are being extremely generous to Fleetwash by accepting the value estimate contained in their letter to their Texas bankruptcy counsel, instead of placing the reasonable value of the equipment at the figure urged by Glover. This award is in line with the restitutional nature of the "reasonable value" language of KRS 355.2–305(4) since, by Fleetwash's own admission, this amount should place them in as good a position as they would have occupied if they had never made the shipment to Glover.

Therefore it is the opinion of this court that the parties to the purchase order in controversy, Fleetwash and Glover, never agreed as to the meaning of the price and payment terms of the order and did not intend to be bound by the terms of the order unless the other party acquiesced to their interpretation of the price and payment terms. Further the court finds that, in light of the fact that no contract existed between the parties, Fleetwash is entitled to the reasonable value of the goods they delivered to Glover, which we set at $43,000.

An appropriate order reflecting these findings of fact and conclusions of law will be entered by the court.

Notes

1. Consider three questions: (1) What method did the parties adopt to determine the price, see UCC 2–305(1)(b); (2) When that method failed, what evidence persuaded the court that the parties did not intend to be bound unless the price was agreed; and (3) What difference, if any, exists between the price if the parties had intended to be bound, UCC 2–305(1), and the restitution remedy invoked because they did not so intend, UCC 2–305(4)? Review the discussion of the Bethlehem Steel-Litton litigation, supra at 507. See also, Flowers Baking Co. of Lynchburg, Inc. v. R–P Packaging, Inc., 229 Va. 370, 329 S.E.2d 462, 465 (1985), where the court, in concluding that there was no intention to contract, stated: "While it is true that the UCC has greatly modified the rigors of the common-law rules governing the formation of contracts, it remains a prerequisite that the parties' words and conduct must manifest an intention to be bound. Although they may make a contract which deliberately leaves material terms open for future determination, no contract results where their words and conduct demonstrate a lack of intention to contract. * * * Such a lack is not remedied by evidence of custom and usage in the trade * * * or by a written

10. We arrived at a reasonable value of the equipment from this letter by subtracting the expected income from the net invoice amount. For a full text of the letter and the pro forma invoice on the 2 wheeled vehicle wash systems see Appendix A [omitted].

11. The Army Corps of Engineers estimate of the value of the equipment Fleetwash sold Glover, would generally be given much weight by this court. However due to the confused manner in which their evaluation was prepared, the third-hand nature of their representative's testimony at trial and the fact that the Army Corps of Engineers had to "clarify", by unsworn letter, the testimony another representative gave at a deposition on this matter led this court to attach very little weight to their estimate.

memorandum purporting to confirm oral discussion which did not in themselves amount to an agreement * * *"

2. Under UCC 2–305(1), the same questions are posed if "nothing is said as to price" or the "price is to be fixed in terms of some agreed market or other standard as set or recorded by a third person or agency and it is not so set or recorded:" (1) Did the parties intend to "conclude a contract even though the price is not settled;" (2) If not, what remedies are available under UCC 2–305(4); and (3) If so, what is a "reasonable price at the time for delivery?" The pre-Code law is reviewed in Prosser, *Open Price in Contracts For the Sale of Goods,* 16 Minn.L.Rev. 733 (1932); Comment, *UCC Section 2–305(1)(c): Open Price Terms and the Intention of the Parties in Sales Contracts,* 1 Valpo.L.Rev. 381 (1967).

Problem 12–3

In 1963, S, a producer of iron ore, and B, a manufacturer of steel, entered a 25 year contract for the supply of iron ore. S was obligated to deliver between 1,000 and 1,500 tons per month by rail. B agreed to pay the regular net contract rate for a ton of iron ore as published every three months in a trade Journal entitled "Iron and Steel World." The contract provided that in the event "Iron and Steel World" ceased publication, "the parties shall mutually agree upon a rate for such iron ore, taking into consideration the contract rate being charged for one ton of iron ore by similarly situated parties." No provision for arbitration or mediation was made in the contract.

The relationship prospered. For a time, a representative of S served on B's board of directors and the parties frequently met to discuss economic developments and how the profits of both could be improved. In 1988, the contract was renewed for another 20 years, and S agreed to pay a 5% surcharge for each ton accepted to help B pay for new equipment purchased to deal exclusively with iron ore from S's mines.

In 1993, with the steel industry picking up steam, "Iron and Steel World" ceased publication. At the same time, S was approached by another steel manufacturer with a much more attractive proposal for a long-term contract. S and B negotiated a price for the first six months of 1993, but S refused to negotiate thereafter and terminated the contract. S argued either that the parties did not intend to contract if "Iron and Steel World" failed to publish a net price for iron ore or that if they did so intend the contract failed for indefiniteness. Either way, the contract was at an end. B argued that the requisite intention to contract was present in the parties course of performance and that other objective evidence existed in the market from which a price could be determined. Moreover, B urged the court to order S to comply with the contract by negotiating over a price and if no agreement was reached to either fill the gap with a "reasonable price" or appoint a mediator.

What result? The problem is taken from the case of Oglebay Norton Co. v. Armco, Inc., 52 Ohio St.3d 232, 556 N.E.2d 515 (1990), where the court adopted B's arguments.

TCP INDUSTRIES, INC. v. UNIROYAL, INC.

United States Court of Appeals, Sixth Circuit, 1981.
661 F.2d 542.

Before ENGEL, KEITH and KENNEDY, CIRCUIT JUDGES.

CORNELIA G. KENNEDY, CIRCUIT JUDGE.

TCP Industries, Inc. (TCP) filed this breach of contract action against

Uniroyal, Inc. (Uniroyal) to recover profits lost when Uniroyal refused to purchase butadiene pursuant to an April 1, 1974 contract. Uniroyal counterclaimed seeking damages from TCP and Donald C. Fresne (Fresne), its president and principal shareholder, for fraud, breach of an earlier 1970 contract, and breach of the 1974 contract. The jury returned a verdict for TCP in the amount of $1,045,650 and judgments of no cause of action on Uniroyal's three counterclaims. Uniroyal appeals. The parties agree that the Uniform Commercial Code applies. They did not object to the District Court's application of Michigan law, the law of the forum.

Butadiene is a petrochemical product extracted from gas and oil and principally used in the production of synthetic rubber. TCP does not produce butadiene but has since 1966 acted as a middleman in arranging sales of the product from El Paso Products Company (El Paso), a Texas refinery, to Uniroyal. TCP sold to Uniroyal at the same price it purchased butadiene from El Paso. Historically, its sole profit was limited to a commission or a reseller's discount of two-tenths (2/10) of a cent per pound which El Paso paid TCP out of El Paso's price.

On November 3, 1970, TCP and Uniroyal entered into the 1970 contract. That contract covered the period of April 1, 1971 through March 31, 1974 and provided for the annual sale of 50 million pounds of butadiene at 8.00 to 8.25 cents per pound, depending on place of delivery. The contract restricted any price increase to the third year of the contract and then only to passing on those escalations in El Paso's production costs specifically related to increased labor or natural or butane gas costs which El Paso passed on to TCP. The contract also included a meet or release clause which provided that if Uniroyal received a bona fide offer from another producer to sell it at least 10,000,000 pounds of butadiene at a lower price, then TCP would have to meet that price within 30 days or release Uniroyal from its obligation to purchase such amount under the contract.

El Paso continued to sell butadiene to TCP which resold it to Uniroyal under these conditions until September 1973, six months before the expiration of TCP's contract with Uniroyal, when, unknown to Uniroyal, TCP's three year contract with El Paso expired. El Paso thereupon advised TCP that it would continue to sell it butadiene but that its reseller's discount would be discontinued and TCP should look for its profits solely from its markup to Uniroyal.

In October 1973, TCP increased its price to Uniroyal by .00247 per pound. In February 1973, El Paso increased its price to TCP by 3.5 cents to 11.75 cents per pound. TCP passed this price increase on to Uniroyal along with an additional increase of almost three cents. On March 1, 1974, TCP initiated another one cent per pound increase.[1] Uniroyal continued to accept and pay for butadiene at the increased prices. The parties agree and it is undisputed that except for El Paso's 3.5 cent increase passed along by

1. These figures have been taken from the pretrial order. Although there are discrepancies between these figures and those found in the briefs, exhibits and transcripts of the proceedings, the parties do not dispute that the total amount in controversy is $301,679.

TCP in February, the remaining increases were contrary to the express provisions of the written contract, and resulted in an overcharge to Uniroyal of $301,679.

During the same period that TCP was raising the price of butadiene under the 1970 contract, the parties were negotiating the terms of the 1974 contract. These negotiations were conducted in an atmosphere described by those in the industry as nothing less than chaotic. Price controls for butadiene expired in early 1974. Because of the shortage of crude oil due to the Arab oil embargo, a greater proportion of the supply of oil was being used to produce fuel oil rather than petrochemicals such as butadiene. Butadiene sellers were refusing to take on new customers. Since Uniroyal could not make synthetic rubber without butadiene, TCP's 50 million pound annual supply was extremely valuable and Uniroyal adopted measures to ensure itself of this dependable supply of butadiene. After several months of bargaining, Uniroyal and TCP entered into a new contract which represented a dramatic departure in form and substance from their previous agreements. This contract did not have a price escalation clause but instead contained the following pricing provision:

> The price for butadiene purchased hereunder shall be $0.1347 per pound F.O.B. point of origin. The price for butadiene is subject to change providing Texas Chemical gives no less than fifteen days notice.

The 1974 contract did not contain a meet or release clause for the first two years of its four year term.

Soon after signing, TCP informed Uniroyal that the price would increase from 13.7 cents on April 1, 1974, to 20.75 cents on July 1, and to 22.55 cents on October 1. By November 1974, the shortage of butadiene had eased and producers were ready to take on new customers. That month Uniroyal took only 489,000 pounds of butadiene as opposed to an average of 3,642,000 pounds in each of the previous seven months. Uniroyal took no butadiene from December 1974 through February 1975, first saying that it needed no butadiene and then explaining that the price was too high. Uniroyal again started to purchase in March 1975 at about 19.0 cents per pound. The parties agreed to reserve their rights against each other under the contract.

* * *

[The court affirmed the jury verdict denying Uniroyal's counterclaim for an alleged breach of the 1970 contract.]

THE 1974 CONTRACT

Uniroyal also argues that the evidence was insufficient to support the jury's finding that TCP was entitled to the price it set under the 1974 contract. The contract contained the following pricing provision:

> The price for butadiene purchased hereunder shall be $0.1347 per pound F.O.B. point origin. The price for butadiene is subject to change providing Texas Chemical gives no less than fifteen days notice.

The District Court held this language ambiguous and permitted parol evidence. Uniroyal claims that TCP was limited by the parties' prior course of dealing to passing on to Uniroyal changes in the prices charged to TCP by El Paso. Uniroyal contends that if TCP was not limited to passing through

El Paso's price, then it failed to set a reasonable price in accordance with M.C.L.A. § 440.2305.

In the usual case, the question of the parties' intentions when a price term is left open is a question for the trier of fact. Official Comment 2, M.C.L.A. § 440.2305. The jury was presented with considerable evidence that the parties vigorously negotiated the 1974 contract. Fresne testified that he told Wills that he wanted the right to unilaterally set the price at the high end of the market. He explained that this was a major reason for the six month negotiation period. TCP negotiated the deletion of the standard meet or release clause during the first two years of the four year contract and refused to include Uniroyal's suggested right to cancel clause if the price charged for butadiene was unacceptable. Also persuasive that the prior course of dealing as to pricing did not govern the 1974 contract was that the pricing language of the 1970 contract was not carried over to, and in fact was changed dramatically in the 1974 contract. The parties intentionally deleted the explicit and elaborate formula for pricing (the escalation clause) found in the 1970 contract and in its place required that TCP give Uniroyal 15 days notice prior to implementing a price increase. If the parties had intended to continue the explicit pricing terms of the 1970 contract, or had intended that only El Paso's increases to TCP would be passed along to Uniroyal, such language could have again been utilized. In fact, that specific language was deleted. The jury was presented with sufficient evidence that the "subject to change" provision of the 1974 contract did not limit TCP's price increases to passing through El Paso's increased costs.

Nor do we accept Uniroyal's alternative argument. M.C.L.A. § 440.2305 governs the open price term of the 1974 contract. The pertinent provisions provide:

> (1) The parties if they so intend can conclude a contract for sale even though the price is not settled. In such a case the price is a reasonable price at the time for delivery if
>
> (a) nothing is said as to price; or
>
> (b) the price is left to be agreed by the parties and they fail to agree; or
>
> (c) the price is to be fixed in terms of some agreed market or other standard as set or recorded by a third person or agency and it is not so set or recorded.
>
> (2) A price to be fixed by the seller or by the buyer means a price for him to fix in good faith.

Official Comment 3, referring to subsection (2), states:

> [D]ealing with the situation where the price is to be fixed by one party rejects the uncommercial idea that an agreement that the seller may fix the price means that he may fix any price he may wish by the express qualification that the price so fixed must be fixed in good faith. Good faith includes observance of reasonable commercial standards of fair dealing in the trade if the party is a merchant. (Section 2–103).

M.C.L.A. § 440.2103(1)(b) defines "good faith" in the case of a merchant as "honesty in fact and the observance of reasonable commercial standards of fair dealing in the trade."

Neither the Code nor the Official Comments to the Code require that a merchant-seller price at fair market value under a contract with an open price term, but specify that prices must be "reasonable" and set pursuant to "reasonable commercial standards of fair dealing in the trade."

> When there is a gap as to price, 2–305 directs the court to determine 'a reasonable price,' provided the parties intended a contract. Note that the section says 'a reasonable price' and not 'fair market value of the goods.' In many instances these two would not be identical. For example, evidence of a prior course of dealing between the parties might show a price below or above market. Without more, a court could justifiably hold in these circumstances that the course of dealing price is the 'reasonable price.'

J. White & R. Summers, *Uniform Commercial Code,* § 3–7, 117 (2d ed. 1980). Similarly, the price might be reasonable although not set pursuant to "reasonable commercial standards of fair dealing." An example would be where the party sets the open price at a reasonable retail price although reasonable commercial standards of fair dealing would require that the price be set at a reasonable wholesale rate. In the instant case the price was set within the wholesale range. The only issue is whether a spot market price within that range was reasonable vis-a-vis the existence of a long term contract price and whether that is a question of fact or of law.

At all times under the 1974 contract TCP sold or offered to sell butadiene to Uniroyal at prices within the range of those reported in the *Chemical Marketing Reporter,* a domestic publication specifically providing information on the butadiene market. The parties stipulated that the following price ranges appeared in the *Chemical Marketing Reporter* for the period April 1, 1974 to March 31, 1976.

April, 1974—June, 1974	12–17 cents
July, 1974—September, 1974	16–25 cents
October, 1974—January, 1975	17½–25 cents
February, 1975—March, 1976	18–22 cents

TCP's prices of 20.75 cents on July 1, 1974, and 22.25 cents on October 1, 1974, while tending toward the high end, were always well within the above range. Although Jesse Owens of El Paso initially testified that 22.25 cents per pound was not a "fair" price for the period of November 1974 through March 1975, he later explained that this conclusion was based on El Paso's long term contracts all of which contained a meet or release clause, the effect of which is to keep prices competitive to within ½ cent per pound. TCP, however, had negotiated with Uniroyal to omit such a clause during the first two years of the contract and include it for the final two years. On the other hand, Ralph Ericsson, president of a company which produces an annual survey of the world-wide butadiene industry, testified that during the last six months of 1974 butadiene prices were rising as high as 28.5 on a straight pass through basis. In his opinion, TCP's price was commercially reasonable under all the circumstances. Thus, there was evidence from which the jury could have reasonably found that TCP's price for butadiene under the 1974 contract was commercially reasonable and set in good faith. Uniroyal too narrowly defines good faith and commercial reasonableness when it contends that as a matter of law TCP met neither because it set its price in accord with total market prices including the spot market rate [rather] than pricing solely on long term contract prices.

While taking testimony on the market price of butadiene the District Court allowed Ralph Ericsson, qualified as an expert in the production and pricing of butadiene, to testify as to the meaning of the pricing clause contained in the 1974 contract. Over objection, Ericsson testified that he had never seen a price clause exactly like that one and that "the way I read this contract, the seller had the right to set the price and the buyer was obligated to accept that price." Following admission of this evidence, the District Court instructed the jury that the testimony was admitted for such value as the jury might wish to give it. Subsequently, Uniroyal's timely motion for new trial on this basis was denied.

Absent any need to clarify or define terms of art, science, or trade, expert opinion testimony to interpret contract language is inadmissible. * * * Here the witness was not testifying about a technical term which needed explaining. Since the witness had never seen a contract without a meet and release clause or cancellation clause where there was an open pricing provision the witness could not testify to the meaning given under such a contract by the trade. The question of what the contract clause meant was a factual one for the jury to determine from the testimony presented. *Loeb v. Hammond,* 407 F.2d 779, 781 (7th Cir.1969).

While we find that the District Court erred in admitting this testimony we note that no error in the admission or exclusion of evidence is ground for reversal or granting a new trial unless refusal to take such action appears to the court to be inconsistent with substantial justice. * * * Considering the entire record we do not find that the District Court's denial of Uniroyal's motion for new trial on the grounds of Ericsson's improper testimony was inconsistent with substantial justice.

* * *

The judgment of the District Court is affirmed.

Note

UCC 2–305(2) provides that a "price to be fixed by the seller or the buyer means a price for him to fix in good faith." In Au Rustproofing Center, Inc. v. Gulf Oil Corp., 755 F.2d 1231 (6th Cir.1985), Au contracted with Gulf to be a Gulf dealer for a period of ten years. Gulf agreed to pay Au a special allowance of two cents per gallon on all gasoline purchased at a "tankwagon" price to be set without contractual restriction by Gulf. After the 1973 oil crisis ruptured the market, Gulf suspended the special discount and charged Au a "tankwagon" price that was not competitive with other suppliers in the relevant market area. As a result, Au's gross margins substantially declined. In the ensuing litigation, the court held, inter alia, that Gulf had no duty to fix competitive gasoline prices for its dealers: "* * * (A)lthough Gulf assumed the implied duty of a party controlling the price to set a reasonable price * * * the record does not establish that the high price Gulf charged to Au was so unreasonable that it negated Gulf's substantial performance of the implied duty. * * * Gulf is required to fix a price in good faith. * * * Good faith includes observance of reasonable commercial standards of fair dealing in the trade or the general range of market prices. * * * Au contends that because its competitors sold gasoline for less than Au could buy it from Gulf, Gulf's prices were unreasonable. * * * In our view, this contention is insufficient to establish that prices set by Gulf contravened reasonable commercial standards in the gasoline market or otherwise constituted bad faith or commercially unreasonable behavior." Id. at 1235–36. But see Nanakuli Paving & Rock Co. v. Shell Oil Co., Inc., 664 F.2d 772 (9th Cir.1981) (Seller with discretion to fix price acted in bad faith in failing to follow "price protection" usage and to give reasonable notice of price increase).

Problem 12–4

B manufactures precious metal products and provides refining services. On July 1, 1979, S delivered 1,600 ounces of sterling silver to B under a contract for sale. B was to process the metal to determine its silver content and fix the price by multiplying the amount of silver by the market price on that day. S understood that B's normal processing time was four to six weeks. Due to B's negligence, however, the silver was misplaced and not found and processed until November 1. During this period, the per ounce price of silver was on the rise: On July 1 it was $17.25, on August 1 it was $18.50, on August 15 it was $20 and on November 1 it was $28. S, citing UCC 2–305(3), claims that it can cancel the contract and recover the silver and sell it on the open market. B argues that the case is governed by UCC 2–305(2): Thus, there was an enforceable contract even if B acted in bad faith and the price should be a reasonable price at the time when B should have completed the processing and fixed the price.

How should the court rule?

V. GOLDBERG, PRICE ADJUSTMENT IN LONG–TERM CONTRACTS, 1985 Wis.L.Rev. 527, 531–34.

* * *

II. The Economics of Price Adjustment

A. The Benefits of Price Adjustment

Business firms have ample incentives to include some form of price adjustment mechanism in their contracts even if both parties are risk neutral. Firms do not generally enter into multi-year contracts because of their concern for the future course of prices. Rather, they enter into the agreements to achieve the benefits of cooperation. Having entered into such an agreement, the parties have to make some decision regarding the course of prices during the life of the agreement. That is, price adjustment will probably be ancillary to the main purposes of the agreement.

Price adjustment can be difficult and costly. Why then bother? Why not simply establish a price or a schedule of prices for the duration of the agreement? I will suggest four reasons that might lead business firms to consider using some form of price adjustment. First, if the contract concerns a complex product that will be continuously redefined during the life of the contract, a price adjustment mechanism can price the "amendments" to the original agreement. Examples include cost-plus pricing of sophisticated defense hardware and complex construction projects. Second, to properly coordinate their behavior, the parties want correct price signals. If the price of an input were below the market price (and if the buyer could not resell at a price greater than the contract price) the buyer would have an incentive to use "too much" of the input. Since this should be anticipated at the formation stage, the costs of poor coordination are borne by both parties. This is a pure "moral hazard" problem akin to an insured person consuming too much health care because the post-insurance price is too low.

Two other reasons are, analytically at least, more interesting: reduction of pre-contract search and post-agreement jockeying. In both these explanations, the success of price adjustment depends upon its ability to reduce the variance of outcomes. The reduced variance is not, however, valued directly. Rather, it enables the parties to curtail mutually harmful behavior, thereby increasing the value of the agreement to both parties.

A contract establishes gains to be divided between the parties; a fixed-price contract determines the distribution of these gains. The parties could attempt to increase their share of the gains before signing the contract by improving their information on the future course of costs and prices. The more they each spend on this search, the smaller the pie. *Ceteris paribus,* the larger the variance of the outcomes, the more resources would be devoted to this effort. The parties, therefore, have an incentive to incorporate into the initial agreement a device that would discourage this wasteful searching. Price adjustment mechanisms can do precisely that by reducing the value of the special information. This argument applies even for standardized commodities sold in thick markets.

If after the firms enter into a long-term agreement the contract price fails to track changing market conditions, the loser will be reluctant to continue performance. It could breach and suffer the legal and reputational consequences, but other, less severe, alternatives to willing compliance exist. A buyer could, for example, insist upon strict compliance with quality standards. The aggrieved party could read the contract literally—"working to the rules" as in labor disputes or in centrally planned economies. This is a variation on the pure moral hazard story. The incorrect price induces the aggrieved party to expend resources in attempting to renegotiate the terms of the agreement. The costs can arise directly from the effort to renegotiate or indirectly through strategic bargaining. That is, the loser might threaten to engage in acts which impose costs upon the other party but do not constitute a legal breach. These costs are a result of the failure to coordinate behavior in the face of changed circumstances. These costs would be unimportant if the parties had easy access to market alternatives; *ceteris paribus,* the more isolated from alternatives the contracting parties are, the more significant are the potential losses from poor coordination. Again, to the extent that the parties can anticipate these problems at the formation stage, the value of the exchange is reduced. If the probability of wasteful behavior increases as the divergence between contract price and the opportunity cost of the aggrieved party widens, price-adjustment rules which narrow the gap become increasingly attractive.

B. *The Mechanics of Price Adjustment*

The easiest way to adjust the price is to index. But what should the parties be indexing? The overall price level? Input costs? Market price? Ideally the parties would index the market price. The payoff from indexing, after all, is from the reduction in the divergence between the contract price and the market price. However, practical exigencies usually lead parties to index other prices as proxies. Indeed, in a long-term contract there often is no unique external market price. The implications of this fact will become clearer in the discussion of *Alcoa v. Essex* below.

Cost changes will be a reasonably good proxy for changes in the market price if demand does not fluctuate too much or if industry supply is very elastic. However, changes in input prices are not necessarily the same as changes in input costs. If the relative prices of inputs change, the firm has an incentive to alter factor proportions to take advantage of the new price relationships. Also, if factor productivity changes, the connection between input prices and costs deteriorates. Nevertheless, indexing to input prices is common.

While indexing would be the easiest price adjustment mechanism to implement, it has the obvious disadvantage of tracking changing conditions imperfectly. The poorer the correlation between the index and what it is supposed to be tracking, the less attractive it will be. Another relatively simple mechanical rule is permitting one party to solicit outside offers with the other party having the right of first refusal. This allows better tracking of that party's opportunity cost, but it discourages making relation-specific investments. That is, the direct costs of price adjustment would be low, but the indirect costs of discouraging entering into a long-term relationship in the first place might be quite high. Cost-plus pricing tracks cost changes more closely, but is more subject to manipulation; it also gives the seller poorer incentives to control costs, and requires that the parties devote more resources to monitoring performance.

Negotiation is, of course, always an option. Even if the contract explicitly utilizes one of the methods mentioned in the previous paragraph or unambiguously states that the contract is a fixed price agreement, one party could propose that the price be renegotiated. The contract price, the clarity of the legal rule, and the costs of invoking the legal rule provide the background against which the renegotiation might take place.

Renegotiation allows use of accurate, current information in revising the contract; but reopening the contract could result in cost-generating strategic behavior, especially if one of the parties is vulnerable to the threat of nonrenewal. Renegotiation is not a zero-sum affair with one side's gains offset by the other's loss. In exchange for an increased price, for example, a seller could offer a contract extension and the prospect of not working to the letter of the contract. (A threat, after all, is just a promise with the sign reversed.)

The contract could explicitly establish the conditions under which renegotiation is to take place. It could require renegotiation at fixed intervals or have it triggered by specific events (for example, a rise in a price index of more than 20%). Gross inequity clauses call for renegotiation if the contract price is too far out of line, but typically do not spell out the criteria for determining when a gross inequity exists. The parties could agree to renegotiate in good faith and determine what would happen if the negotiations break down. The failure to negotiate a new price could result in continued performance at the current price, termination, mediation or arbitration, and so forth.

There are, in sum, a lot of mechanisms available for adjusting price within a long-term contract. All are imperfect. Their relative costs and benefits will determine which, if any, the parties should choose.

* * *

[Footnotes omitted.]

CHAPTER THIRTEEN

EXCUSE FROM OR ADJUSTMENT OF THE CONTRACT FOR CHANGED CIRCUMSTANCES

SECTION 1. INTRODUCTION

The question, "Who bears what risks arising from changed circumstances in a contract for sale?" is intriguing and eternal. If the "risk events" have been identified in the bargaining process and explicitly allocated in the agreement, the answer is clear: if the agreement is otherwise enforceable, i.e. not unconscionable or avoidable for fraud, and the language, reasonably interpreted, supports a particular risk allocation, then that allocation should prevail. Thus, an agreed fixed price in a contract for sale is thought to allocate the risk for both parties that, during performance, the market price for similar goods will go up or down.

But suppose there is neither an agreed nor a "tacit" risk allocation, yet the person seeking relief has made an unconditional promise. The seller agrees to deliver the goods by December 1 and the agreement says nothing about the risk that a strike may close the seller's major source of supply. When, if ever, should a court grant some relief from changed circumstances? What form should that relief take? The UCC provides a starting point for answers in Sections 2–613 through 2–616. Or, suppose that the parties, in response to changed circumstances, agree to modify or adjust the contract. When should a court enforce an agreed adjustment? The starting point here is UCC 2–209.

These problems have arisen with distressing frequency in the topsy-turvey economy of the last 20 years. We will take a brief look at some of them here. Since many of the cases involve changed circumstances which affect a price mechanism agreed to by the parties, there will be some necessary overlap with the price issues covered in Chapter Twelve. But the excuse issue is distinct and two of us, at least, believe that it deserves separate treatment. For deep background, see Wladis, *Impracticability as Risk Allocation: The Effect of Changed Circumstances Upon Contract Obligations for the Sale of Goods*, 22 Ga.L.Rev. 503 (1988).

SECTION 2. RELIEF FROM CHANGED CIRCUMSTANCES

Problem 13–1

S, an art dealer, owned a etching by Picasso. B, a collector, examined it at S's gallery and, after negotiations, S agreed to sell it to B for $75,000. Under the written contract for sale, B was to return with a cashier's check the next day and pick up the etching. B returned check in hand but, alas, the Picasso was destroyed by fire during the night. What are the rights and duties of the parties? See UCC 2–613 and 2–509. Suppose, instead, that the Picasso, unknown to S, had been stolen and was replevied by the true owner rather than destroyed by fire? Are the cases of changed circumstances?

WICKLIFFE FARMS, INC. v. OWENSBORO GRAIN CO.

Court of Appeals of Kentucky, 1984.
684 S.W.2d 17.

DUNN, JUDGE.

This is an appeal from a summary judgment in favor of appellee, Owensboro Grain Company, entered in the Daviess Circuit Court September 9, 1982, as amended September 29, 1982. The action arises out of a contract to sell No. 2 white corn and the defense of impossibility of performance resulting from a drought.

The appellant, Wickliffe Farms, Inc., in business since 1971, farms several contiguous farms in Muhlenberg County. Of the approximate 1980 acres it farms, the corporation owns about 250 acres, Reynolds Wickliffe, its president and principal shareholder, owns about 1000 acres, and Reynolds' father's estate, the J.W. Wickliffe Estate, owns 730 acres.

The Corporation had done business with the appellee, Owensboro Grain, since 1975, primarily thru Reynolds Wickliffe, representing the corporation, and Julian G. "Sonny" Hayden, employed by Owensboro Grain as a grain merchandiser.

In February, 1980, Wickliffe contacted Hayden by telephone and they orally agreed that the corporation would deliver 35,000 bushels of No. 2 white corn at $3.70 per bushel to Owensboro Grain between December 15, 1980, and January 31, 1981. The agreement was confirmed in a writing executed by Owensboro Grain and signed by Wickliffe on behalf of the corporation. The agreement, prepared by Owensboro Grain, was on its standard "fill in the blanks" form as to quantity, the grain commodity, the price, the routing, and shipment date. It was dated February 29, 1980, and identified the corporation as the accepting party. It contained no additional language of any significance other than the following part of a small print "force majeure" clause unilaterally favoring Owensboro Grain:

> All agreements, undertakings, obligations or liabilities hereunder, made or to be kept and performed by Owensboro Grain Company, are made and shall be kept and performed subject to and contingent upon strikes, embargoes, fires, accidents, war restrictions, acts of God, or other conditions over which Owensboro Grain Company has no control and any inability on its part to keep, perform or satisfy the agreements, undertakings, obligations or liabilities hereunder caused or brought about by reason of any of the foregoing conditions shall, at the option of Owensboro Grain Company, render this contract null and void and the parties hereto shall have no further rights or obligations hereunder * * *

Owensboro Grain's principal business is dealing in the Chicago Board of Trade market area by purchasing grain for future delivery and by arranging an immediate sale of it to consumers or exporters at a margin of profit the market will competitively allow. In reference to his employer's business generally and to the instant transaction specifically, Hayden testified: "* * * my orders from the stockholders are to buy it, sell it, or hedge it. In this case you have to sell it because you can't hedge it."

In keeping with this practice, immediately after the contract was executed for Wickliffe to deliver the No. 2 white corn in the future, Owensboro Grain sold the 35,000 bushels, along with white corn similarly purchased from other farmers, to C.B. Fox, an exporter, at a price that guaranteed a 20 to 25 cent profit.

Unfortunately, in the summer of 1980, Muhlenburg County, together with the rest of western Kentucky, suffered a severe drought. Wickliffe's No. 2 white corn crop was severely damaged as were the crops of the other farmers in the area. Consequently, Wickliffe was unable to produce sufficient No. 2 white corn to fulfill its contract. In January, 1981, it delivered its entire crop, 18,718.57 bushels, to Owensboro Grain and was paid the agreed amount of $3.70 per bushel.

As a result of the short delivery, Owensboro Grain was required to purchase the amount of the shortage at $5.54 per bushel, the then market price, to satisfy its obligation to C.B. Fox entered into as a result of its futures contract with Wickliffe. The total amount spent to make up the bushels' deficit was $29,306.57. This amount was not withheld as a "set off" when it paid Wickliffe for the corn it managed to deliver, but $19,157.07 was withheld from amounts owed Wickliffe for purchase of corn and soybeans in January and February, 1982, by Owensboro Grain.

Wickliffe sued Owensboro Grain in the Daviess Circuit Court for the amount of the sale of the corn and soybeans. Owensboro Grain counterclaimed for its loss resulting from the partial non-delivery of No. 2 white corn in 1981. The trial court entered summary judgment in favor of Owensboro Grain on its counterclaim, later amended to include interest.

On appeal, as well as in the trial court, Wickliffe primarily relies on the defense of impossibility of performance caused by the severe drought, a "force majeure." We agree with the trial court that this defense is not applicable since the contract did not specify the land on which the corn was to be grown. Hence, we affirm.

There is no disagreement that the provisions of § 2–615 of the Uniform Commercial Code (U.C.C.) (1978), adopted as KRS 355.2–615, address the issue before us; also, there is no disagreement that there is no Kentucky law interpreting KRS 355.2–615, particularly with reference to U.C.C. § 2–615 comment 9 (1978), which in pertinent part is as follows:

> The case of a farmer who has contracted to sell crops *to be grown on designated land* may be regarded as falling within * * * this section, and he may be excused, when there is a failure of the specific crop. * * *

We have carefully considered Wickliffe's argument that the contract was one-sided or unconscionable because it contained no specific "force majeure" clause in its favor as it did in favor of Owensboro Grain and conclude the argument is without merit. We reach a like conclusion on

Wickliffe's position that an "adhesion contract" resulted from the "fill in the blanks" form of the contract.

Wickliffe's principal argument is that the defense of impossibility provided by KRS 355.2–615 should be available to it due to the fact that it was contemplated by both parties that the No. 2 white corn was to be grown on its 2000 contiguous acres in Muhlenburg County and, that the adverse weather of the 1980 summer was a condition that was unforeseen and unforeseeable by the parties, and which rendered Wickliffe's performance impossible, and, pursuant to the statute, thereby excused his obligation to fully perform.

Nowhere in the contract, however, is there any reference to any specific acreage upon which the crop was to be grown. Wickliffe urges that KRS 355.2–202 permits contradiction of the written terms of the parties' intention by admission of proof of a contemporaneous oral agreement. This statute provides:

> Terms with respect to which the confirmatory memoranda of the parties agree or which are otherwise set forth in a writing intended by the parties as a final expression of their agreement with respect to such terms as are included therein may not be contradicted by evidence of any prior agreement or of a contemporaneous oral agreement but may be explained or supplemented
>
> (a) by course of dealing or usage of trade (KRS 355.1–205) or by course of performance (KRS 355.2–208); and
>
> (b) by evidence of consistent additional terms unless the court finds the writing to have been intended also as a complete and exclusive statement of the terms of the agreement.

This argument ignores the fact that to be admissible, the proof must come within the provisions of subparagraph (b) of the statute that requires the parol evidence be of additional terms consistent with the written contract. Here there is no consistency between Wickliffe's claim that the corn was to be produced off a particular part of a 2000 acre farm and a contract providing for nothing other than buying and selling 35,000 bushels of No. 2 white corn. There was no proof before the trial court, parol or otherwise, offered or proffered by Wickliffe, to establish that both parties contemplated and agreed upon a contract to sell the corn from any particularly designated acreage.

The undisputed admissible material facts before the trial court prove the ordinary "futures contract" of an agreement to buy and sell a quantity of grain at a given price per bushel, to be delivered at a future date, the purchaser thereafter arranging a "back to back" sale of the commodity. The sellers in such a transaction gamble the market price will not be greater at the time of delivery and the buyers gamble that it will not be lower. All Owensboro Grain was interested in was buying 35,000 bushels of No. 2 white corn from Wickliffe at $3.70 per bushel and nothing more. Its business was not to speculate either in the weather, crop yield or fluctuation of market price. It guaranteed its profit by selling immediately. Wickliffe's only interest was to sell it. It chose to contract to deliver the corn at a given price at a given future date and failed to do so.

Since there exists no issue of material fact and Owensboro Grain is entitled to judgment as a matter of law, the trial court committed no error in granting summary judgment on Owensboro Grain's counterclaims. *Shah v. American Synthetic Rubber Corp.*, Ky., 655 S.W.2d 489 (1983).

The Daviess Circuit Court summary judgment and amended summary judgment are affirmed.

All concur.

Notes

1. Should it matter whether the corn was planted on the seller's 2,000 acres before or after the contract was formed? See UCC 2–613. Under either UCC 2–613 or 2–615(a), why must the seller prove an agreement to sell the corn from designated acres? For example, in Alimenta (U.S.A.), Inc. v. Gibbs Nathaniel (Canada) Ltd., 802 F.2d 1362 (11th Cir.1986), a dealer in rather than a grower of peanuts was granted relief under 2–615(a) when a drought hit the regional growing areas. The expected peanut crop was reduced by 35%. The court, among other things, held that the seller's failure to insist upon a clause relieving it from the risk of drought did not mean that it assumed, as a matter of law, a "greater obligation" by agreement under 2–615(a). See also, Alimenta (U.S.A.), Inc. v. Cargill, Inc., 861 F.2d 650 (11th Cir.1988), where on similar facts the court granted relief under 2–615(a) and excluded evidence of the size and financial responsibility of the seller. This evidence was irrelevant to the statutory question under 2–615(a) whether "performance as agreed" was made impracticable by the drought.

2. If excuse is granted under UCC 2–613, the contract is avoided if the "loss is total." UCC 2–613(b). If the loss is partial or the goods no longer conform to the contract, the buyer is given a statutory option either to avoid the contract or to accept the goods with a price adjustment. UCC 2–613(b).

Under UCC 2–615, the adjustment process is more complicated. If delay or non-delivery of the entire performance is excused under UCC 2–615(a), the seller must give the buyer seasonable notification, UCC 2–615(c). The buyer then has the options set forth in UCC 2–616(1), including the right to "terminate and thereby discharge any unexecuted portion of the contract."

In excused cases of delay or non-delivery in "part," however, the seller "must allocate production and deliveries among his customers but may at his option include regular customers not then under contract as well as his own requirements for further manufacture" and this may be done in "any manner which is fair and reasonable." UCC 2–615(b). Note that the seller must now notify the buyer of the delay and the "estimated quota * * * made available for the buyer," UCC 2–615(c).

The buyer's option under UCC 2–616(1) with regard to an allocation "justified" under UCC 2–615(b) is either to terminate the contract or to "modify the contract by agreeing to take his available quota in substitution." But see UCC 2–616(2), imposing a duty on the buyer to act "within a reasonable time not exceeding thirty days." A seller who fails to allocate deliveries in a fair and reasonable manner cannot assert the defense of commercial impracticability under UCC 2–615. Roth Steel Products v. Sharon Steel Corp., 705 F.2d 134 (6th Cir.1983). A buyer who fails to exercise the statutory options within a reasonable time loses the opportunity to preserve an adjusted contract for future performance. See UCC 2–616(2); Federal Pants, Inc. v. Stocking, 762 F.2d 561

(7th Cir.1985) (contract lapses with respect to any deliveries affected). See Bugg, *Crop Destruction and Forward Grain Contracts: Why Don't Sections 2–613 and 2–615 of the UCC Provide More Relief*, 12 Hamline L.Rev. 669 (1989).

Note: Failure of Seller's Source of Supply—Herein of the Force Majeure Clause

Section 261 of the Restatement, Second of Contracts provides a test for "discharge" that parallels UCC 2–615(a): "Where, after a contract is made, a party's performance is made impracticable without his fault by the occurrence of an event the non-occurrence of which was a basic assumption on which the contract was made, his duty to render that performance is discharged, unless the language or the circumstances indicate the contrary." This test is particularized for certain distinctive events. Thus, Sections 262 and 263 provide that the death or incapacity of a person whose existence or capacity is required for performance, or the destruction or deterioration of a thing necessary for performance, "makes performance impracticable" and, thus, are events "the non-occurrence of which was a basic assumption on which the contract was made." Compare UCC 2–613.

But what happens when a source of supply deemed necessary by the seller for performance of the seller's contract with the buyer fails? Under the Restatement, this is swept up under the general principle in Section 261 with a corollary that "a party generally assumes the risk of his own inability to perform his duty." Thus: "Even if a party contracts to render a performance that depends on some act by a third party, he is not ordinarily discharged because of a failure by that party because this is also a risk that is commonly understood to be on the obligor." See Section 261, Comment (e); Illustration 13.

An exception to this has been established in cases interpreting UCC 2–615(a). Thus, where a particular supplier is specified in the contract, assumed by the parties to be the exclusive source of supply, and fails to perform, the seller is excused, provided that it: (1) employed all "due measures" to assure that the agreed supplier would perform, and (2) turned over to the buyer any rights against the supplier corresponding to the seller's claim of excuse. UCC 2–615, Comment 5. In Zidell Explorations, Inc. v. Conval International, Ltd., 719 F.2d 1465 (9th Cir.1983), the court held that a failure to tender rights against the seller did not constitute a per se violation of the duty of good faith: Rather, the jury must determine in all the facts and circumstances whether the seller had satisfied its responsibility under Comment 5.

Frequently, a seller will attempt to protect itself against failures in a contemplated source of supply, whether agreed to be exclusive or not, by a force majeure clause. Such clauses vary in scope and content from industry to industry. A common form may look like this:

> "Neither party shall be liable for * * * loss, damage, claims or demands of any nature whatsoever due to delays or defaults in performance caused by impairment in any manner of seller's source of supply by (list causes or events) or by any other event, whether or not similar to the causes specified above * * *, which shall not be reasonably within the control of the party against whom the claim would otherwise be made."

When a force majeure clause is invoked, the following questions must be answered:

(1) Are the events specified and the relief sought within the scope of the clause;

(2) If so, was the event within the control or due to the fault or negligence of the party seeking relief, see PPG Indus. Inc. v. Shell Oil Co., 919 F.2d 17 (5th Cir.1990);

(3) If not, did the party seeking relief exercise reasonable efforts after the event occurred to secure performance as agreed from some source, see Nissho-Iwai Co., Ltd. v. Occidental Crude Sales, Inc., 729 F.2d 1530 (5th Cir.1984); and

(4) Is relief under a force majeure clause restricted in any way by UCC 2-615(a)? Put differently, if the parties clearly agree to expand the scope of excuse available under UCC 2–615(a), should the agreement be enforced? In Interpetrol Bermuda Ltd. v. Kaiser Aluminum International Corp., 719 F.2d 992 (9th Cir.1983), the answer was yes, subject to the requirement of conscionability and the good faith duty to seek an alternative source of performance. In addition, the court held that where excuse was based upon the force majeure clause rather than UCC 2–615, there was no requirement that the seller assign its rights against the defaulting source of supply to the buyer:

* * *

> We agree with the district court that comment 5 does not control in this case. Kaiser was not excused under § 2–615 and could not have been. Section 2–615 applies only when the events that made the performance of the contract impracticable were unforeseen at the time the contract was executed. See Taylor-Edwards Warehouse & Transfer Co. v. Burlington Northern, Inc., 715 F.2d 1330, 1336 (9th Cir.1983). The extensive negotiations over the force majeure clause, discussed above, indicate that the parties not only foresaw the risk that Oxy Crude would default but also bargained over which party would bear the loss in that event. Accordingly, it would violate fundamental principles of contract law, to use § 2–615 of the UCC to rewrite the contract to which the parties agreed. UCC § 2–615, comment 8 (§ 2–615 inapplicable if "contingency in question is * * * included among the business risks which are fairly to be regarded as part of the dickered terms. * * *").
>
> Although there has been some doubt expressed as to whether the Code permits parties to bargain for exemptions broader than those available under § 2–615,[7] at least one circuit has concluded they may. See Eastern Air Lines, Inc. v. McDonnell Douglas Corp., 532 F.2d 957, 990 (5th Cir.1976). See also Olson v. Spitzer, 257 N.W.2d 459 (S.D.1977) (exculpatory clause valid for defining events which excuse seller's performance). We agree with the Fifth Circuit. Comment 8 to § 2–615 plainly indicates that parties may "enlarge upon or supplant" § 2–615.[8] While exculpatory clauses phrased in

7. See Hawkland, The Energy Crisis and Section 2–615 of the Uniform Commercial Code, 79 Com.L.J. 75 (1974).

8. Comment 8 to § 2–615 provides that:

"The provisions of this section are made subject to assumption of greater liability by agreement and such agreement is to be found not only in the expressed terms of the contract but in the circumstances surrounding the contracting, in trade usage and the like. Thus the exemptions of this section do not apply when the contingency in question is sufficiently foreshadowed at the time of contracting to be included among the business risks which are fairly to be regarded as part of the dickered terms, either consciously or as a matter of reasonable, commercial interpretation from the circumstances * * *. The exemption otherwise present through usage of trade under the present section may also be expressly negated by the language of the agreement. Generally express agreements as to exemptions designed to enlarge

general language should not be construed to expand excuses not provided for by the Code, circumstances surrounding a particular agreement may indicate that the parties intended to accord the seller an exemption broader than is available under the UCC.[9] Eastern Air Lines, 532 F.2d at 990–91. We have already decided that the force majeure clause agreed to by Kaiser and InterPetrol was intended to excuse Kaiser prior to shipment of the crude from the Persian Gulf if Kaiser's supplier failed to deliver for any reason. We now hold that it was permissible for them to make such an agreement. Thus, if InterPetrol is to prevail on its claim that it succeeds to Kaiser's rights, it must do so on grounds apart from the Code.

California courts have read into force majeure clauses an implied covenant of good faith. Terry v. Atlantic Richfield Co., 72 Cal.App.3d 962, 964, 140 Cal.Rptr. 510, 511 (1977); see Milton v. Hudson Sales Corp., 152 Cal.App.2d 418, 427, 431, 313 P.2d 936, 942 (1957). This common law covenant of good faith is applicable to force majeure clauses such as the one agreed to by Kaiser and InterPetrol. If the common law requirement of good faith implies a requirement that a seller turn over to its buyer the seller's rights against a defaulting supplier, then the district court erred in granting Kaiser's motion to dismiss.

InterPetrol failed to cite any instance under the common law, under circumstances similar to those of this case, where a buyer succeeded to the rights of the seller against a defaulting supplier.[10] The common law has not provided to a disappointed buyer the rights called for by InterPetrol.

We see no reason to now create a right which has not been recognized by the common law. There is a certain amount of economic wisdom in permitting a seller, consistent with the limiting provisions of the Code,[11] to contract out of liability. In a relatively free and fluid wholesale market, a seller should be entitled to utilize the power of his position to contract to his best advantage. That might include, as here, the extraction of a force majeure clause from a buyer. If the seller's supplier is not able because of market forces to require a similar provision in the agreement between seller and supplier, the result is that the seller is excused but the supplier is not. Yet we see no reason to award the windfall of recovery against the supplier to the buyer, who agreed to excuse the seller, instead of the seller, who was able to insist on better protections. When a trader is able to bargain for such favorable conditions, the natural trend will be for traders in the less favorable positions of buyer and supplier to move into the less competitive and therefore more contractually secure part of the market.

We find no reason to transfer the benefit of Kaiser's superior negotiating position to InterPetrol by giving InterPetrol Kaiser's rights against Trako and Oxy Crude. We do find that it serves the forces of natural

upon or supplant the provisions of this section are to be read in the light of mercantile sense and reason, for this section itself sets up the commercial standard for normal and reasonable interpretation and provides a minimum beyond which agreement may not go."

9. Force majeure clauses are, of course, limited by those sections of the Code prohibiting agreements which are manifestly unreasonable, in bad faith or unconscionable. See §§ 1–102(c), 1–203 and 2–302. See also Eastern Airlines, 532 F.2d at 991 n. 96; Transatlantic Financing Corp. v. United States, 363 F.2d 312, 315 n. 3 (D.C.Cir.1966).

10. InterPetrol did not rely on third-party beneficiary concepts at trial and did not attempt to raise the theory on appeal.

11. See supra note 9.

market adjustments not to transfer Kaiser's rights. We therefore affirm the decision of the district court.[12]

* * *

[719 F.2d at 999–1001]

Note: The ALCOA Case

In Aluminum Company of America v. Essex Group, Inc., 499 F.Supp. 53 (W.D.Pa.1980), the facts of which are elaborated in the extract from *Goldberg,* infra at 616, the parties entered in 1967 into a 17 year contract under which ALCOA was to process alumina supplied by Essex into molten aluminum to be used by Essex in the manufacture of aluminum wire products. The long-term contract, called a "toll conversion service contract," was to be performed at a plant owned by ALCOA in Indiana. As part of the pricing mechanism, the parties agreed upon an escalation clause, developed by the noted economist Alan Greenspan, which varied with actual production costs at the plant. The clause was developed on the basis of past cost patterns and reflected projected cost variations that would give ALCOA a target profit of $.04 per pound.

In 1973, during the energy crisis, electricity costs at the Indiana plant began to escalate well beyond the projections in the price escalation clause. Even though the contract was profitable up to this time, it was estimated that ALCOA would lose $60 million over the balance of the contract due to a 500% variation between indexed and actual costs. At the same time, Essex was enjoying an apparent windfall gain by reselling converted aluminum for which it paid ALCOA $.364 per pound on the open market for $.733 per pound. When efforts by ALCOA to obtain an agreed price adjustment from Essex failed, ALCOA sued to obtain relief from the escalation clause and a reformation of the contract so that Essex must pay the actual costs incurred at the plant. Essex counterclaimed for breach damages and the issues were joined.

In an unprecedented decision, the court concluded that ALCOA was entitled to "some relief" from the changed circumstances and that the relief should be an equitable reformation of, rather than discharge from, the contract. The court, without the agreement of the parties, devised its own adjustment formula to fill the gap in the agreement. Essex appealed but the parties settled the dispute by agreement before the case could be heard.

Since the contract between ALCOA and Essex was characterized as for services rather than the sale of goods, UCC 2–615 was not directly applicable. The court, however, blended the doctrine of mutual mistake, commercial impracticability and frustration of purpose to achieve a result that, in part, could have been reached under UCC 2–615. The court's analysis was consistent with the four steps required to deal with UCC 2–615's "basic assumption" test:

First, did the seller assume by agreement a greater obligation than the degree of excuse normally available under UCC 2–615? If so, excuse should be denied. ALCOA's answer was no.

Second, if a greater obligation was not assumed, was the event that materialized a "contingency the non-occurrence of which was a basic assumption on

12. Our holding is based in part on the fact that Kaiser and InterPetrol were in relatively similar positions in the petroleum market. We have not considered circumstances involving traders from different levels in the hierarchy of the petroleum distribution network. We note too that InterPetrol was not obligated to other buyers to deliver oil it expected to get from Kaiser.

which the contract was made?" If not, excuse should be denied. ALCOA's answer was yes: Both parties assumed at the time of contracting that the escalation clause was reasonable and the changed circumstances were not foreseen as likely to occur.

Third, if so, did the contingency make "performance as agreed * * * impracticable?" If the answer is yes, then the seller is entitled to "some relief." ALCOA's answer was yes: A $60 million loss over the balance of a commercial contract made continued performance "commercially senseless and unjust," particularly where Essex was realizing "windfall" profits.

Fourth, if the seller is entitled to "some relief," what form should that relief take, discharge of the executory contract or preservation of the contract under a court-imposed price adjustment? The Code's answer is not clear. ALCOA's answer was to delete the existing price escalation clause, which had failed its intended purpose, and to impose in the gap a new price term which was thought to respond to the changed circumstances. For more discussion, see Speidel, *Court-Imposed Price Adjustments Under Long-Term Supply Contracts,* 76 Nw. U.L.Rev. 369 (1981).

ALCOA, to date, stands as the high (or low) water mark in disputes under UCC 2–615. Under circumstances comparable to ALCOA, i.e., rising costs of performance or sharply higher prices, other courts have denied any relief to the seller under UCC 2–615(a). See, Iowa Elec. Light and Power Co. v. Atlas Corp., 467 F.Supp. 129, 134 (N.D.Iowa 1978), rev'd on other grounds 603 F.2d 1301 (8th Cir.1979); Louisiana Power & Light v. Allegheny Ludlum Industries, 517 F.Supp. 1319 (E.D.La.1981); Missouri Public Serv. Co. v. Peabody Coal Co., 583 S.W.2d 721 (Mo.App.1979), cert. denied 444 U.S. 865, 100 S.Ct. 135, 62 L.Ed.2d 88 (1979). Under the opposite circumstances, i.e., a sharply reduced demand and, thus, lower prices for the product, buyers have fared no better than sellers. Although the courts, citing Comment 9, concede that UCC 2–615(a) protects buyers, little mercy has been shown to the buyer who, in the light of changed circumstances, has agreed to take goods at a quantity in excess of current needs and pay a price substantially in excess of market. See Northern Illinois Gas Co. v. Energy Cooperative, Inc., 122 Ill.App.3d 940, 78 Ill.Dec. 215, 225, 461 N.E.2d 1049, 1059 (1984), where the court said: "* * * (A)s any trader knows, the only certainty of the market is that prices will change. Changing and shifting markets and prices from multitudinous causes is endemic to the economy in which we live. Market forecasts by supposed experts are sometimes right, often wrong, and usually mixed. If changed prices, standing alone, constitute a frustrating event sufficient to excuse performance of a contract, then the law binding contractual parties to their agreements is no more." Accord: Northern Indiana Public Service Co. v. Carbon County Coal Company, 799 F.2d 265 (7th Cir.1986), where the court, speaking through Judge Posner, stated:

> Since impossibility and related doctrines are devices for shifting risk in accordance with the parties presumed intentions, which are to minimize the costs of contract performance, one of which is the disutility created by risk, they have no place when the contract explicitly assigns a particular risk to one party or the other. As we have already noted, a fixed-price contract is an explicit assignment of the risk of market price increases to the seller and the risk of market price decreases to the buyer, and the assignment of the latter risk to the buyer is even clearer where, as in this case, the contract places a floor under price but allows for escalation. If, as is also the case here, the buyer forecasts the market incorrectly and therefore finds himself

locked into a disadvantageous contract, he has only himself to blame and so cannot shift the risk back to the buyer by invoking impossibility or related doctrines. * * * Since 'the very purpose of a fixed price agreement is to place the risk of increased costs on the promisor (and the risk of decreased costs on the promisee),' the fact that costs decrease steeply * * * cannot allow the buyer to walk away from the contract."

V. GOLDBERG, PRICE ADJUSTMENT IN LONG–TERM CONTRACTS, 1985 Wis.L.Rev. 527, 534–42.

* * *

III. Alcoa v. Essex *

A. The Facts

In 1967, Alcoa and Essex entered into a twenty year agreement in which Alcoa agreed to convert Essex's alumina into molten aluminum at Alcoa's Warrick, Indiana plant. Essex purchased its alumina from an Alcoa subsidiary under a second long-term contract. The trial judge insisted that the two contracts were separate and that by design Alcoa's left hand did not know what the right hand was doing. After conversion the molten aluminum would be loaded into crucibles owned by Essex and taken by truck to Essex's nearby fabricating plant built specifically to receive it. The contract was for 50 million pounds per year and included options for three additional blocks of 25 million pounds each. (By 1973, the parties had deleted the last two blocks.) Hence, the contract quantity at the time the litigation arose was 75 million pounds per year.

The initial contract price was 15 cents per pound, composed of a "demand charge" of five cents per pound,[22] and a "production charge". The latter included a fixed component of four cents per pound (which was the "profit" on the plant constructed to fulfill this contract) and three cents each for non-labor (primarily fuel) and labor costs. The former was indexed by the Industrial Component of the Wholesale Price Index and the latter by Alcoa's average hourly labor cost at the Warrick plant. The contract included a ceiling price of 65% of the price of a specified type of aluminum as reported in a trade journal; however, it did not specify a minimum price.

The demand charge was to be paid regardless of whether Essex took any aluminum. In effect, Essex "rented" a portion of Alcoa's Warrick plant at a fixed rate of $7.09 million per year ($4.09 million for the demand charge and $3 million for the fixed charge) and paid a service fee of six cents per pound that was indexed.

Problems arose following the large increase in fuel prices in 1973. In the ensuing years the market price of aluminum and the cost of producing it

* Aluminum Co. of America v. Essex Group, Inc., 499 F.Supp. 53 (W.D.Pa.1980).

22. Actually, this price was to be adjusted to cover increased construction costs at the Warrick plant when new blocks of aluminum capacity were ordered. The price of the first block (50 million pounds) was 5.27 cents per pound and the price for the second block was 5.82 cents per pound. These prices would remain constant for the life of the contract.

in Warrick increased far more rapidly than did the contract price. By 1979, Essex received aluminum from Alcoa under the contract at 36 cents per pound and resold some of it in the open market at 73 cents. Non-labor production costs rose from 5.8 cents to 22.7 cents in 1973–78, while the wholesale price index less than doubled. Alcoa attempted to renegotiate the price as early as 1975. In 1978, the dispute went to trial.

The trial court ruled in Alcoa's favor. Indexing non-labor production costs to the Wholesale Price Index was deemed a "mutual mistake" because it tracked those costs so badly. The court also accepted Alcoa's alternative theories of impracticability and frustration. The court reformed the contract, since rescission would result in a windfall for Alcoa and deprive Essex of the benefits of its long-term supply contract. The court rewrote the price term of the contract to include a minimum price assuring Alcoa a one cent per pound "profit".

The disputed contract represented only a small part of the business of Alcoa and Essex. Alcoa's sales and total assets in 1979 were each almost $5 billion.[23] By the time of trial, Essex had been acquired by United Technologies, another multi-billion dollar firm. Despite its losses on this contract, Alcoa's overall profits in 1979 were around $500 million; its rate of return on equity in 1978 exceeded 14 percent for the first time in 22 years.[24] This is not, clearly, a case in which a bad contract jeopardized the survival of a firm, as in *Westinghouse.* Rather, it is more instructive to view this contract as a poor performer in the firm's much larger portfolio of contracts, a portfolio which was performing very well overall.

B. The $75 Million Misunderstanding

The court placed considerable emphasis on the fact that projected losses from 1977 to 1987 were in the range of $75 million. This is one of those funny numbers that means nothing, but could end up as a fundamental part of the *Alcoa* doctrine, were one to emerge. Alcoa was excused because they stood to lose $75 million; we won't excuse X because it cannot prove that it will lose such a large amount. (As I will note below, the *Alcoa* judge distinguished another case on precisely this ground.) It is, therefore, useful to look at how the court determined the magnitude of the loss.

The "profits" are the revenue minus the actual production costs minus the demand charge (the 5 + cents per pound). The court assumed something (the decision does not make it quite clear what) about future costs and prices for the remaining life of the contract and then added them up. There are three obvious problems with this. First, the future profits are undiscounted. A dollar lost in 1984 is just as important as a dollar lost in 1979. Second, the estimates are based on guesses about the future course of prices; there is nothing wrong with guesses, but time has a way of transforming guesses into facts.[25] But these are quibbles. The most important point is that the estimate, even if done right, is irrelevant.

What does Alcoa lose if it must fulfill the contract? It loses the chance to sell the aluminum to someone else. That is the true measure of the loss,

23. *The Fortune Directory,* Fortune, May 5, 1980, pp. 274, 276.

24. *Aluminum's Bosses Are Beaming,* Forbes, Nov. 27, 1978, at 40.

25. In fact, aluminum prices fell sharply in the early 1980's. That price decline undoubtedly facilitated settlement of the dispute.

and in this case it is considerably greater than the figure cited by the judge. In the year the suit was brought the loss was over thirty cents per pound, over $20 million. The original cost of construction of the plant is a red herring equivalent to "par value" for a stock, a vestige of the past with no economic content.

The error is important. In an earlier case,[26] the court refused to allow Gulf Oil to escape its obligation to deliver jet fuel under a five-year contract despite the fact that the price index utilized had inadequately tracked the course of oil prices. The court held that the cost data presented were insufficient to ascertain how much it cost Gulf to produce a gallon of jet fuel, and, therefore, Gulf had failed to prove that it had suffered losses on the contract. The *Alcoa* judge applied the "negative accounting profit" test in distinguishing this decision from *Alcoa.*

When faced with a claim of changed circumstances, courts or arbitrators should not look to accounting cost data to determine the merits of the claim. The relevant question is whether the difference between the contract price and the aggrieved party's next best option is large enough to warrant relief. An accounting cost or profit standard is an invitation to produce a lot of information with a low expected value.

C. *Alcoa's Mistake*

In retrospect, of course, Alcoa made a big mistake. However, the mistake singled out by the court to justify reformation of the contract was not the most important one. The failure of the price index to accurately measure the change in fuel prices accounted for only about ten to twelve cents of the difference between the contract price and the market price for aluminum in 1979 (that difference being over 30 cents). The main problem was that the contract did not track changing demand conditions and the demand for aluminum was soaring in the late 1970's.

Moreover, the contract was not designed to adjust to large changes in the overall price level. Sixty percent of the initial contract price (the demand charge plus the fixed "profit") was unadjusted for the life of the contract. A very simple example gives an indication of the type of problem this could cause. Suppose that the price level rises about 7% per year (doubling roughly every ten years); assume that the factors of production remain equally productive and that they continue to be used in the same proportions. The indexed production costs would then rise from six cents per pound to 24 cents per pound in the twentieth year. However, the remaining costs are unindexed, so the final contract price would rise only to (24 + 9 =) 33 cents. To keep the real price of aluminum constant the contract price would have had to increase to 60 cents.

The relevant question is not whether Alcoa made what turned out to be a bad decision. They did. But was it a bad decision at the time they made it? The answer to that is less certain. When I began this project it seemed clear that Alcoa could have, and should have, done better. At a minimum, I thought, they should have indexed the remaining 60% of the costs. However, a more careful look leads me to believe that it is a much closer question.[30]

26. Eastern Air Lines v. Gulf Oil Corp., 415 F.Supp. 429 (S.D.Fla.1975).

30. The question of whether Alcoa had made a mistake is unrelated to the court's

This long-term contract is in many respects similar to a lease or sale of part of Alcoa's Warrick production capacity to Essex. A fixed rental for long-term leases is not uncommon. Moreover, if one firm sells a durable asset to another, it is the rule rather than the exception, that the price is not to be readjusted after the sale has taken place. It can be argued, then, by analogy, that this component of the long-term contract that looks so much like a lease should also be at a fixed price.

If the contract price of a long-lived asset were to be readjusted to better track the market price, the parties would expend less resources today in pursuit of special information. If this benefit were great; we would expect the parties to incorporate price adjustment arrangements in their sales and leases of assets. However, the benefits will often be very small. Information regarding the future price level, for example, is already incorporated in the term structure of interest rates. It is not necessarily *accurate* information, ex post; however, the key question is whether it is *improvable* information, ex ante. Incorporating a general price index, therefore, need not result in reduced information costs.

The lease/sale analogy, however, has difficulties. A pure lease or sale is similar to a contract for a standardized commodity because further coordination between the two parties is unnecessary; the only issue is whether price adjustment reduces the initial price search. However, the more the outcomes depend upon future coordination by the parties, the less likely they will use a fixed price contract.[31] For example, shopping center leases in which the lessor engages in activities which generate business for the tenants will base at least part of the compensation on a percentage of the gross (which automatically provides for some price adjustment). If Alcoa were leasing the plant to Essex and allowing Essex to operate it, the fixed price arrangement would be routine. The fact that operation of the plant was in Alcoa's hands reduced the likelihood that a fixed price would be successful. The increased divergence between the contract price and Alcoa's best alternative would induce Alcoa to engage in strategic behavior, thereby reducing the value of the contract to both parties.

However, it is unlikely that indexing capital costs would result in a more accurate contract price. I would speculate that the pre-1973 experience would confirm that indexing this cost component to the general price level, construction costs, or any other conceivable cost-based measure would have resulted in a poorer fit between the market and contract price.[32]

Instead of using a cost-based price adjustment, the parties could have attempted to track market conditions by, for example, indexing to a particu-

finding of mutual mistake. I am only trying to determine whether the price adjustment mechanism in this contract was a reasonable one under the circumstances.

31. This discussion is highly speculative since I am only dimly aware of the adjustment mechanisms actually used in long-term leases. I should note that a common device is to use short-term agreements with fixed prices so that the price can be renegotiated on a regular basis. Such arrangements might also include an expectation, legal or otherwise, of renewal on reasonable terms.

32. Note that this is a different argument than the one accepted by the court. It emphasized how closely the wholesale price index had tracked one component of costs in the pre-contract period. I am claiming that there did not exist an index that would have closely tracked another, and larger, component of costs.

lar aluminum price.[33] Using output prices to index is not without problems. First, other goods with published prices that are sufficiently close to the output that we are attempting to index might not exist. Second, the observable external prices are typically list prices, not transaction prices. If these diverge, the index suffers. It is plausible that the two would diverge in a concentrated industry like aluminum since list prices typically change more slowly in such industries.[34] Further, if the contract price were linked to the list price of a type of Alcoa's aluminum, then Alcoa would have an incentive, however modest, to set the list price in excess of the transaction price.

Even if list prices were accurate measures of transaction prices, a more fundamental difficulty remains. The parties do not necessarily confront the same external price. That is, the relevant price to each party is its opportunity cost—the net price it could get from the next best trading partner. In a market for a standardized commodity, the list price and these two opportunity costs would be roughly the same. However, in a long-term contract in which the parties deliberately isolate themselves from the external market, these three prices are more likely to diverge. Generally, the more isolated the contracting parties are from market alternatives, the poorer the relationship between these three prices is likely to be. Thus, while the parties might desire to index their agreement to a published market price, the very nature of a long-term contract makes it likely that the index price would not perform its function adequately. It is, therefore, not at all obvious that indexing the contract to changes in the published price of a particular type of output would be in the interest of the two parties.

In the instant case, Alcoa's opportunity cost is the net price it could receive by using the Warrick capacity to produce ingot for export to other customers. Essex's opportunity cost is the price of delivered aluminum ingot. There is no a priori reason to believe that these will be close to each other. However, for an index to work it is not necessary that the prices be close, only that they move together over time. Whether these two opportunity costs (and the market price for aluminum ingot) move together over time is an empirical question which I intend to explore in a later paper.

Essex chose to incorporate the output price information in the form of a maximum price. Alcoa, however, was not willing to pay (by agreeing to a lower initial contract price) for a price minimum. The failure to do so might well have been a mistake ex ante, but it is at least plausible that a ceiling

33. Note that in the previous paragraph I treated the capital cost as a historical cost. Alternatively, we could adjust to reflect the value of the fixed plant as it changes during the life of the structure. Thus, the cost of using the plant to fill this contract must include the opportunity cost of using the plant for other purposes (namely supplying aluminum to someone else). If the capital had a wide variety of other uses (for example, retail space or small vans), such an adjustment might be sensible. If, however, the capital was highly idiosyncratic, as in this case, its value would closely track changing market conditions. If these could be indexed accurately it would almost surely be unproductive to index the market value of capital either instead of or in addition to the market price of the output.

34. For example, in 1979 Business Week reported list prices for ingot of 66 cents per pound while the spot price was 75 cents. This is a bit misleading, however, because of the existence of price controls at the time. *Aluminum Wastes No Time Raising Prices,* Bus.Wk., Oct. 15, 1979, at 36.

indexed to published prices would be more valuable to Essex than a similarly indexed floor would have been to Alcoa. Alcoa's superior knowledge of the aluminum industry might make Essex suspicious of the manner in which costs were indexed. A bias in favor of Alcoa, because of Alcoa's superior knowledge, would make a bound on the index relatively more valuable to Essex.

Conceivably, therefore, Alcoa's failure to index plant costs or include a minimum price was not an error ex ante. Looking at the new contract may provide some insight on this issue. We know that the parties rejected the judicially imposed minimum price based on ex ante accounting costs. But we do not know whether that was a reason for rejection and we do not know what replaced it. I would speculate that the new contract includes a minimum and that the minimum depends upon output prices. If so, that would suggest that Alcoa had erred initially.

IV. Resolution of Price Adjustment Disputes

Suppose that contracting parties assign the task of resolving price adjustment disputes to an outsider (a court or an arbitrator). The outsider can be asked to resolve two very different questions: (a) have conditions changed sufficiently to justify relief; and (b) what form should relief take—what will the new price (or price formula) be? Since the parties bear the costs of producing the evidence, they must reckon the expected costs of producing evidence on production costs, accounting profits, market prices, opportunity costs, and so forth, and weigh these against the expected benefits (in terms of reducing the costs arising from the divergence of contract price from market price). These evidentiary costs provide the backdrop for subsequent renegotiation. Thus, for example, if a standard required that one party spend a lot to produce evidence to forestall price revision, its opposite party could use those potential costs as a bargaining chip in renegotiation.

For determining whether relief is justified, accounting cost data of the sort relied upon by the Alcoa judge are largely beside the point. The relevant question is whether the difference between the contract price and the aggrieved party's next best option is large enough to warrant relief. The requisite price differential would vary across contracts. There is no "magic number": if price goes up by at least *X%* or losses total at least $*Y*, adjust the price. A large divergence between the market and contract price for a standardized commodity, for example, would have little adverse effect on the expected value of a contract; it would, therefore, be unlikely that the parties would benefit from revision. Conversely, if a modest price divergence would generate considerable joint costs, revision could be effective. The problem is complicated by the fact that making relief easy to obtain generates additional joint costs as well. Rational parties might easily find that the potential benefits from price revision come at too high a cost.

This is especially true if there is no obvious standard for determining a new contract price. My initial presumption was that if a reasonable measure of the output price were available, the parties would want the arbitrator to use this to guide his decision. Further consideration has led me to conclude that this might not be very helpful. A simple example illustrates the problem. Suppose that when the contract was written Alcoa would have received 10 cents a pound for its aluminum on the open market, Essex would have paid 20 cents per pound, and the contract price was fifteen cents. When the case is litigated, Alcoa could sell at 50 cents and Essex buy at 70, and the contract price is 35 cents. What should the contract price be? Even if this information were costlessly produced and absolutely accurate, are the parties better off putting the decision in the hands of an arbitrator? What decision rule would they want him to apply? When the opportunity costs of the buyer and seller diverge, it is not at all clear what should guide the arbitrator in setting a new price. Thus, the possible divergence not only impairs the value of a published price as an index, but makes it more difficult for the parties to rely upon outsiders (arbitrators and judges) to revise the price. [Some footnotes omitted.]

* * *

INTERNATIONAL MINERALS & CHEMICAL CORP. v. LLANO, INC.

United States Court of Appeals, Tenth Circuit, 1985.
770 F.2d 879; *cert. denied,* 475 U.S. 1015, 106 S.Ct. 1196, 89 L.Ed.2d 310 (1986).

* * *

[International (IMC) agreed to purchase natural gas from Llano under a ten year contract, scheduled to terminate on June 30, 1982. IMC sought a declaratory judgment that it was excused from its obligation to "take or pay" for an agreed minimum quantity of natural gas during the last eighteen months of the contract, due to more stringent regulation by the New Mexico Environmental Improvement Board of particle emissions from existing combustion evaporators in IMC's plant. Under EIB Regulation 508, IMC was ultimately required to shut down the combustion evaporators, which had consumed approximately 60% of its natural gas requirements. Llano counterclaimed for $3,564,617.12, the amount that it claimed was due under the contract for gas for which IMC should have paid.

The trial court held: (1) UCC 2–615 was not applicable to buyers unless the contract was "conditioned on a definite and specific venture or assumption. * * * "; and (2) The "force majeure" and "adjustment of minimum bill" clauses in the contract, Paragraphs 15 and 16 set out below, did not excuse performance unless it became absolutely impossible or illegal to purchase the minimum amount of gas. On the facts, the trial court denied relief to IMC and concluded that IMC was liable for the contract price for gas it should have taken, even though Llano had been able to sell the gas elsewhere for a higher price.

IMC appealed and the court limited its consideration to whether IMC was excused under either UCC 2–615 or Paragraphs 15 and 16 of the contract.]

BARRETT, CIRCUIT JUDGE.

* * *

The pertinent portions of the contract are as follows:

Now, therefore, in consideration of the premises and of the mutual covenants and agreements hereinafter set forth, the parties do hereby bargain, contract and agree as follows:

1. *SUPPLY OF NATURAL GAS:* Subject to the terms and conditions of this Contract, Seller will sell and deliver to Buyer and Buyer will take, purchase and pay for the entire fuel requirements of Buyer's Plant, provided that Buyer may at its option procure and maintain a supply of standby fuel to be used only to such extent as may be necessary when the gas supply from Seller may be interrupted or curtailed, as hereinafter provided, and in such other amounts as may be necessary from time to time to test such standby facilities and fuel.

* * *

6. *DELIVERY REQUIREMENTS:* During the term of this Contract, unless Seller agrees in writing to the contrary, the minimum daily deliveries that Seller shall make to Buyer and Buyer shall take from Seller shall be 4800 million BTU's per day except as hereafter provided. The maximum daily deliveries that Seller shall be required to make to Buyer shall be 133% of the average daily requirements of Buyer's Plant for the preceding 365 days provided, however, Seller shall at no time be required to deliver in excess of 6400 million BTU's per day unless Seller agrees in writing to the contrary.

Buyer does not contemplate reducing its operations, but on the contrary contemplates the increase thereof from the present daily requirements. In order to meet unanticipated contingencies, it is agreed that in the event Buyer during the term of this Contract reduces its operation by closing a portion of its plant, it shall have the right upon six months notice in writing to reduce the minimum requirements to a figure equal to 70% of the stated minimum of 4800 million BTU's per day. In the event of such reduction in minimum requirements, Seller's price to Buyer then in effect under the terms hereof shall be increased by ½¢ per million BTU's, but not in excess of the highest price for a like quantity of gas then being paid by any potash company in the area.

7. *MINIMUM ANNUAL PURCHASE:* During the term of this Contract, commencing with the first year, Buyer agrees to take from Seller a volume of gas having a BTU content of not less than 355 times the minimum daily deliveries specified in Section 6 hereof. Buyer agrees to pay Seller for such minimum volume of gas at the price set forth in Section 5 hereof provided that if Buyer fails during any calendar year to take such minimum volume of gas, then the deficiency between the volume actually taken and Buyer's minimum purchase obligation shall be paid at the price in effect during the calendar year in which such deficiency occurs.

Billing for any payment due by reason of a deficiency in Buyer's takings of gas hereunder during a particular calendar year shall be included on the bill rendered to Buyer for gas delivered to Buyer during the month of December in the calendar year in which such deficiency occurred and payment therefore shall be made in the manner provided for monthly bills in Section 11 hereof. Failure on the part of Seller to so bill Buyer for any such deficiency payment shall not constitute a waiver hereof by Seller.

* * *

15. *FORCE MAJEURE:* Either party shall be excused for delay or failure to perform its agreements and undertakings, in whole or in part, when and to the extent that such failure or delay is occasioned by fire, flood, wind, lightning, or other acts of the elements, explosion, act of God, act of the public enemy, or interference of civil and/or military authorities, mobs, labor difficulties, vandalism, sabotage, malicious mischief, usurpation of power, depletion of wells, freezing or accidents to wells, pipelines, permanent closing of Buyer's operations at its Eddy County mine and refinery, after not less than six (6) months notice thereof to Seller, or other casualty or cause beyond the reasonable control of the parties, respectively, which delays or prevents such performance in whole or in part, as the case may be; provided, however, that the party whose performance hereunder is so affected shall immediately notify the other party of all pertinent facts and take all reasonable steps promptly and diligently to prevent such causes if feasible to do so, or to minimize or eliminate the effect without delay. It is understood and agreed that settlement of strikes or other labor disputes shall be at the sole discretion of the party encountering the strike or dispute.

Nothing contained herein, however, shall be construed as preventing the Buyer from discontinuing the operation of the plant for such periods of time as may be required by Buyer to perform necessary overhaul operations on plant properties or to accomplish preventative maintenance operations on such plant properties, which the Buyer may determine as necessary to safeguard its investment in the plant.

16. *ADJUSTMENT OF MINIMUM BILL:* In the event that Seller is unable to deliver or Buyer is unable to receive gas as provided in this Contract for any reason beyond the reasonable control of the parties, or in the event of force majeure as provided in Section 15 hereof, an appropriate adjustment in the minimum purchase requirements specified in Section 7 shall be made.

(Pl.Exh. 3, Def.Exh. C8b).

The contract may be characterized as a requirements contract, with an important limitation: Pursuant to paragraph 6, the buyer (IMC) is obligated to take, at a minimum, a daily average of 4800 million BTU's of gas. Pursuant to paragraph 7, if the buyer does not take this minimum amount, the buyer is obligated to pay for the minimum amount of gas anyway. These provisions are known in the industry as "take or pay" provisions, the purpose of which is to compensate the seller for being ready at all times to deliver the maximum amount of gas to the buyer and to eliminate the risk that the seller would face in a pure requirements contract were the buyer's requirements to drop too low. *See, e.g., Utah International, Inc. v. Colorado—Ute Electric Association,* 425 F.Supp. 1093 (D.Colo.1976) ("take or pay" coal purchase contract); *Mobile Oil Corporation v. Tennessee Valley Authority,* 387 F.Supp. 498 (N.D.Ala.1974) ("take or pay" electricity contract). The harshness of the "take or pay" provisions in this contract are to some extent ameliorated by the "force majeure" provision of paragraph 15 and the "adjustment of minimum bill" provision of paragraph 16; paragraphs 15 and 16 are discussed below.

* * *

On a fundamental level, this case is one of contract construction. Our primary objective, as always, in the construction or interpretation of a contract is to ascertain the intention of the parties. *Schultz & Lindsay Construction Co. v. State,* 93 N.M. 534, 494 P.2d 612, 613 (1972); *Yankee Atomic Electric Company v. New Mexico and Arizona Land Company,* 632 F.2d 855, 858 (10th Cir.1980) (interpreting New Mexico law.) We assume that the parties intended a reasonable interpretation of the language. *Smith v. Tinley,* 100 N.M. 663, 674 P.2d 1123, 1125 (1984). Accordingly, the legal context in which the contract was made will be relevant. As mentioned above, paragraphs 15 and 16 ameliorate the harshness of the "take or pay" provisions in that either party's duty of performance may be excused upon the occurrence of certain contingencies. As we examine the language of paragraphs 15 and 16, an appropriate area to look for guidance is the common law doctrine of impossibility/impracticability, codified at Section 2–615 of New Mexico's Uniform Commercial Code (N.M.Stat.Ann. § 55–2–615 (1978)), which was the law in New Mexico at the time the parties contracted and which remains the law today. While it is a basic premise of both Section 2–615 and the Uniform Commercial Code in general that the parties may allocate risks and penalties between themselves in any manner they choose, N.M.Stat.Ann. §§ 55–1–102 and 55–2–615 (1978), the Code and the common law upon which it is based remain a significant backdrop.

We first consider the effect of paragraph 15, the "force majeure" provision, on IMC's duty of performance under the circumstances of this case. Specifically, Paragraph 15 provides that either party is excused from performance if failure or delay in performance is "occasioned" by such events as fire, flood, act of God, interference of civil and/or military authorities, etc. The party seeking to be excused from performance must provide the other party with immediate notice of all pertinent facts and take all reasonable steps to prevent the occurrence. It also appears that the seller is entitled to six months notice before the buyer can be excused. We agree with the trial court that paragraph 15 does not operate to excuse IMC, although our conclusion is based on a somewhat different rationale. First, IMC's notice to Llano was inadequate in that no reasons were given as to why gas consumption would be decreased. Adequate notice was required to trigger the protections of the provision. Second, even if we assume *arguendo* that Rule 508 prevented IMC from taking the gas, Rule 508 would still pose no obstacle to IMC's ability to pay. Since this is a "take or pay" contract, the buyer can perform in either of two ways. It can either (1) take the minimum purchase obligation of natural gas (and pay) or (2) pay the minimum bill. It is settled law that when a promisor can perform a contract in either of two alternative ways, the impracticability of one alternative does not excuse the promisor if performance by means of the other alternative is still practicable. *Ashland Oil And Refining Co. v. Cities Service Gas Co.,* 462 F.2d 204, 211 (10th Cir.1972); *Glidden Company v. Hellenic Lines, Limited,* 275 F.2d 253, 257 (2d Cir.1960); Restatement (Second) of Contracts § 261, comment f (1981). Paragraph 15 does not compel a different result; it would at most excuse IMC from its duty to "take," not from its duty to "pay."

Paragraph 16, the "minimum bill" provision, however, affords the buyer additional protection. It provides that, in the event the buyer is "*unable* to receive gas as provided in the Contract for any reason *beyond the reasonable control* of the parties * * * " (emphasis added), then "an appropriate adjustment in the minimum purchase requirements specified in Section [paragraph] 7 shall be made." Paragraph 7, in turn, provides for a minimum bill based on the difference between the buyer's minimum purchase obligation and the gas actually taken. It follows that an adjustment of the buyer's minimum purchase requirements made pursuant to paragraph 16 would have the effect of lowering the buyer's minimum bill under paragraph 7. Llano's contention that paragraph 16 provides for a reduction in IMC's minimum purchase obligation but not its minimum bill obligation (Appellee's Brief at 4) is thus quickly disposed of.

The determinative question, then, is: Did the promulgation of Rule 508 constitute an event beyond the reasonable control of IMC that rendered IMC "unable" to receive its minimum amount of gas under the contract?

A simplistic, literal interpretation of the word "unable" would, in our view, be inappropriate and lead to absurd results: IMC could never be "unable" to take Llano's gas; IMC could always take the gas and vent it into the air, even if its facilities were completely destroyed. The word "unable" appears here as a term in a contract, prepared by businessmen and attorneys; thus, it is appropriate to construe the term in light of the common law as it existed in New Mexico when the contract was entered into. For our purposes, then, "unable" is synonymous with "impracticable," as that term is used in the common law and in Section 2–615.

The term "impracticable" has, over the years, acquired a fairly specific meaning. Although earlier cases required that performance be physically impossible before the promisor would be excused, strict impossibility is no longer required. *See* Restatement of Contracts (Second) § 261, comment d (1981). The New Mexico Supreme Court has described the doctrine of impracticability as follows:

> Regarding the meaning of "impossibility" as used in the rules that excuse the non-performance of contracts, it is stated:
>
> "As pointed out in the Restatement of Contracts, the essence of the modern defense of impossibility is that the promised performance was at the making of the contract, or thereafter became, impracticable owing to some extreme or unreasonable difficulty, expense, injury, or loss involved, rather than that it is scientifically impossible. * * * The important question is whether an unanticipated circumstance has made performance of the promise vitally different from what should reasonably have been within the contemplation of both parties when they entered into the contract. If so, the risk should not fairly be thrown upon the promisor." *Wood v. Bartolino,* 48 N.M. 175, 146 P.2d 883, 886, (1944), *quoting* 6 Williston on Contracts, § 1931.

Cf. Gulf Oil Corporation v. Federal Power Commission, 563 F.2d 588, 599 (3d. Cir.1977), *cert. denied* 434 U.S. 1062, 98 S.Ct. 1235, 55 L.Ed.2d 762 (1978)

("The crucial question in applying that doctrine to any given situation is whether the cost of performance has in fact become so excessive and unreasonable that the failure to excuse performance would result in grave injustice. * * * "); *Mineral Park Land Co. v. Howard,* 172 Cal. 289, 156 P. 458, 460 (1916) ("a thing is impracticable when it can only be done at an excessive and unreasonable cost").

Performance will be excused when made impracticable by having to comply with a supervening governmental regulation. N.M.Stat.Ann. § 55–2–615 (1978); Restatement of Contracts (Second) § 264 (1981). Thus, for example, in the case of *Kansas City, Missouri v. Kansas City, Kansas,* 393 F.Supp. 1 (W.D.Mo.1975), the court held that the defendant city's obligation to accept the plaintiff city's sewage was excused by the enactment of the Federal Water Pollution Control Act Amendments of 1972. The federal act imposed new requirements with regard to the treatment of sewage that was discharged into the Missouri River; the court found that the added expense of such treatment would impose a significant, unreasonable burden on the defendant. *Accord City of Vernon v. City of Los Angeles,* 45 Cal.2d 710, 290 P.2d 841 (1955).

Inasmuch as there was no technically suitable way for IMC to comply with the EIB's Regulation 508 without shutting down the Ozarks and changing to the SOP, with the concomitant decrease in natural gas consumption, we hold that the adjustment provision of paragraph 16 of the contract was triggered. IMC was unable, for reasons beyond its reasonable control, to receive its minimum purchase obligation of natural gas between January 1, 1981 and June 30, 1982; thus, the minimum bill should have been adjusted appropriately. IMC should not be required to pay for any natural gas it did not take under the contract.

Llano contends that there was no supervening legal impracticability in this case because IMC was not required to be in final compliance until December 31, 1984, and that IMC cooperated with the EIB and came into compliance too early. The argument here is that, notwithstanding the interim standards contained in the schedules of compliance, IMC should have stalled in its negotiations with the state regulatory agency, which would have resulted in the pollution of air until the last minute. We must reject this contention on two grounds: First, as a matter of policy, individuals and corporations who cooperate with local regulatory agencies and comply with the letter and spirit of legally proper regulations, environmental or otherwise, are to be encouraged. Stalling tactics are not regarded favorably. Second, as a matter of law, government policy need not be explicitly mandatory to cause impracticability. Thus, for example, in *Eastern Air Lines, Inc. v. McDonnell Douglas Corporation,* 532 F.2d 957 (5th Cir.1976), an aircraft manufacturer was excused from its contractual obligation to deliver commercial jet airliners on certain scheduled dates because it had voluntarily complied with government requests to expedite production of military equipment needed for the war in Vietnam. Similarly, in the maritime context, shipowners have been excused from contractual obligations because they have anticipated governmental intrusion. *The Kronprinzessin Cecilie,* 244 U.S. 12, 37 S.Ct. 490, 61 L.Ed. 960 (1917) (German ship was justified in returning to New York rather than completing a voyage to Great Britain and France on the eve of the outbreak of hostilities in World

War I); *The Clavaresk,* 264 F. 276 (2d Cir.1920) (shipowner may anticipate and need not resist government requisition of his ship for wartime service in order to be excused from performance of a charter agreement). There is, we recognize, a limit to the extent to which an individual can seek refuge in the context of a case such as this by cooperating with the government: "any action by the party claiming excuse which causes or colludes in inducing the governmental action preventing his performance would be in breach of good faith and would destroy his exemption." Official Comment 10, N.M.Stat. Ann. § 55–2–615 (1978). Here, Regulation 508 was promulgated by the EIB as part of New Mexico's State Implementation Plan mandated by the Clean Air Act. Regulation 508's existence and its enforcement mechanism is designed to eliminate pollution of the environment, thus serving the public health and welfare. IMC's recognition of the public benefit goal and its willingness to cooperate in eliminating pollution can hardly be termed improper collusion.

For the reasons described above, the judgment of the trial court in favor of Llano is reversed. The case is remanded with direction that the court enter a declaratory judgment in accordance with this opinion.

Note: Take or Pay Contracts

International Minerals featured a "take or pay" contract under which the buyer agreed to either "take" the gas when produced and pay for it or "pay" for the gas without taking it, with the producer holding it for "make up" deliveries in the future. As one court put it:

> The purpose of the take or pay clause is to apportion the risks of natural gas production and sales between the buyer and seller. The seller bears the risk of production. To compensate the seller for that risk, the buyer agrees to take, or pay for if not taken, a minimum quantity of gas. The buyer bears the risk of market demand.

Universal Resources Corp. v. Panhandle E. Pipe Line Co., 813 F.2d 77, 80 (5th Cir.1987). The courts have held that such clauses are not unconscionable at the time of contracting and are agreements for alternative performance rather than liquidated damage clauses. Thus, the failure to "take" is not itself a breach of contract by the buyer. In order for a buyer to breach such an alternative performance contract, the buyer must *both* fail to take *and* fail to pay. See, on alternative performance contracts, 5 *Corbin on Contracts* sections 1079–1087. It follows that "The * * * take or pay clause is a promise [of performance] in the Agreement, not a measure of damages after breach. * * *" Universal Resources Corp. v. Panhandle Eastern Pipe Line Co., 813 F.2d 77, 80 n. 4 (5th Cir.1987). Where the buyer is in breach, the UCC does not allow the seller to recover the price, i.e., the face amount under the "or pay" clause because the terms of UCC 2–709 on price actions are not met, and a seller is not allowed specific performance of the price term under 2–716 (which applies only to buyers). Rather, the seller's UCC remedy is under UCC 2–708. (One court has taken a different view and allowed the producer to recover the full amount of the "or pay" clause as if it were a liquidated damages clause. See Prenalta Corp. v. Colorado Interstate Gas Co., 944 F.2d 677 (10th Cir.1991)).

Depending upon the market and the exercise of bargaining power, "take or pay" contracts may also contain a force majeure clause similar to that in *International Minerals* or other clauses allocating risk, such as a "market out" clause. Under a "market out" clause, the buyer, usually a pipeline, can terminate the contract if a more favorable long term price for gas can be found from another source and the producer is unwilling or unable to match it. See Caggiano, *Understanding Natural Gas Contracts,* 38 Oil & Gas Q. 267, 267–278 (1989).

In the absence of a "market out" or similar clause, the courts have been unwilling to excuse the buyer, commonly a pipeline, in the face of dramatic declines in market prices for gas from the wellhead, even when resulting from deregulatory acts by the FERC, the Federal Energy Regulatory Commission. The reasoning seems to be that the "take or pay" clause allocates such risk to the buyer, thereby foreclosing excuse under UCC 2–615(a), and that the language of the force majeure clause was not intended to cover shifts in market price or demand. See, e.g., Kaiser–Francis Oil Co. v. Producer's Gas Co., 870 F.2d 563 (10th Cir.1980); Golsen v. ONG Western, Inc., 756 P.2d 1209 (Okl.1988). Query whether this analysis is really applicable given the highly regulated nature of the industry, with market swings attributable to de-regulatory acts that were not really foreseen when the parties originally entered their take-or-pay contracts many years earlier. We now offer some further background. Historically, there have been three main actors in the market: (1) The utilities selling to the public and acquiring their gas from a pipeline pursuant to a "minimum take" clause with the pipeline, (2) the pipelines supplying the utilities and in turn buying their gas from the producers pursuant to "take or pay" clauses, and (3) the producers. Taken together, the minimum take clause between utility and pipeline, and the take or pay clause between pipeline and producer generally functioned to assure consumers a reliable supply of gas.

In the 1970's gas fell into short supply, and the government decided to deregulate gas prices. By the first years of the 1980's, there was a large increase in gas prices. Many consumers then switched to other fuels, but gas prices did not fall, given that the utilities were bound under long term minimum take clauses with pipelines, and pipelines were bound under long term take or pay clauses with producers. At least for the short term, normal market forces were not at work.

FERC, the Federal Energy Regulatory Commission, then stepped in beginning in 1984 and issued orders that excused utilities from their minimum take obligations to pipelines yet required pipelines to carry the gas of others in competition with their own. But FERC did not, however, excuse the pipelines from take or pay obligations to producers. Thus, the pipelines lost, to a large extent, their long term sales market for gas, yet remained bound to producers. In such circumstances, should the pipelines be allowed to invoke force majeure clauses or UCC 2–615?

Problem 13–2

Softstuff, a coal producer, manufactures coke for steel production. Coke is made by subjecting coal to extreme heat in specially constructed ovens or batteries. Bitum is a steel maker. In May, 1988, the parties began to negotiate over a 10 year coke supply contract. It was agreed that Bitum was to take and pay for 20,000 tons of coke per month. This was, in effect, Softstuff's output from its coke batteries. In addition to agreements on quality, the parties agreed that Bitum was to pay a base price of $42 per ton, subject to escalation based upon externally compiled cost indices. These indices reflected the average costs incurred by coke producers rather than the actual costs of Softstuff's operation.

At the time of negotiation, the demand for coke was strong and the market price per ton was $41. The parties discussed the question of price stability over a ten year period. Softstuff "hoped" that strong demand would continue but Bitum was more pessimistic. Bitum proposed and Softstuff rejected a clause giving Bitum the option to terminate the contract at the end of any year wherein the market price of coke was 30% lower than the adjusted contract price for three or more months. There was no trade usage on price adjustment and the parties had not done business with each other before.

After further negotiations, the parties concluded a contract which, among other things, contained the following clause:

EXCUSE FOR BUYER

1. If because of Buyer's reduced blast furnace production, Buyer's requirements for coke cease or are reduced to a point where it is not practical for Buyer to purchase coke pursuant to this agreement, Buyer shall be released from its future obligations hereunder for the period of such cessation or reduction without any liability whatsoever upon Buyer giving Seller 90 days advance written notice.

2. Buyer's failure to comply or delay in compliance with the terms and conditions of this agreement shall be excused if due to any of the following which render performance commercially impracticable: act of God, fire, flood, strike, work stoppage, labor dispute, accident or mill interruption, complete or partial blast furnace relining, temporary failure of supply of iron ore, pellets or flux, any action by governmental authority, including ecological authorities, or any other cause beyond Buyer's reasonable control.

On January 15, 1989, Softstuff shipped and Bitum accepted and paid for the first 20,000 ton installment of coke at the base contract price. This pattern of performance continued under January 15, 1993, when Bitum notified Softstuff in writing that due to a "collapse in the market for coke and steel products" the contract is "hereby terminated in 90 days." At that time, the escalated contract price for coke was $50 per ton. The market price for comparable coke, however, had dropped to $25 per ton and the demand for Bitum's steel products had dropped 60% since the time of contracting. After an unsuccessful effort to negotiate a modification, Bitum reaffirmed that, after the 90 days period had expired, it would not accept any more coke under the contract.

In August, 1993, Softstuff sued Bitum for breach of contract. The sole question for you is whether Bitum is excused from performance under either paragraph of the EXCUSE FOR BUYER clause.

SECTION 3. ENFORCEABILITY OF AGREED ADJUSTMENTS

The parties to a dispute over contract performance frequently settle the matter by agreement. In one type of settlement, claims are adjusted, payments are made and the contract is discharged. These settlements are sometimes described as an accord and satisfaction. In another type of settlement, contract duties are adjusted in a bargain under which performance is to continue. These settlements are called contract modifications. In both, the enforceability of the settlement may be subsequently attacked on the grounds of fraud, lack of consideration or duress. You have encountered both types in the course on contracts.

In this Section we will focus upon agreed modifications made in response to changed circumstances. The key provision is UCC 2–209.

Problem 13–3

A. Suppose, in Problem 13–2 supra, that before Bitum attempted to terminate the contract under the Excuse clause, Bitum explained the changing market situation and its impact on Bitum to Softstuff and requested Softstuff to consider and to negotiate over a proposed modification of the contract. Bitum suggested that the contract be adjusted in either of two ways for the remaining six years: (1) Keep the pricing structure but permit Bitum to order "requirements;" or (2) Keep the quantity term but permit Bitum to pay the market price of coke at the time of delivery. Bitum argued that S had, at a minimum, a duty to negotiate in good faith over the proposed adjustment, citing UCC 2–209, 1–203, 2–103(1)(b), and Comments 6 & 7 to 2–615. Softstuff declined, contending that unless the contract required it (and it did not), there was no duty to negotiate PERIOD. S cited Missouri Public Serv. Co. v. Peabody Coal Co., 583 S.W.2d 721 (Mo.App.1979), cert. denied 444 U.S. 865, 100 S.Ct. 135, 62 L.Ed.2d 88 (1979), where the court concluded: "Where an enforceable, untainted contract exists, refusing modification of price and seeking specific performance of valid covenants does not constitute bad faith or breach of contract * * *."

How should B respond?

B. Suppose, after negotiations, Softstuff agreed to substitute "market price" for escalated price for the duration of the contract. Thereafter, Softstuff determined that market price would not cover its production costs and claimed that the modification was not enforceable, citing UCC 2–209(1). What result? See the next case.

ROTH STEEL PRODUCTS v. SHARON STEEL CORP.

United States Court of Appeals, Sixth Circuit, 1983.
705 F.2d 134.

[In November, 1972, Roth contracted to purchase 200 tons of "hot rolled" steel per month from Sharon through December, 1973. The price was $148 per ton. Sharon also "indicated" that it could sell "hot rolled" steel on an "open schedule" basis for $140 and discussed the "probability" that Sharon could sell 500 tons of "cold rolled" steel at prices varying with the type ordered. At that time, the steel industry was operating at 70% of capacity, steel prices were "highly competitive" and Sharon's quoted prices to Roth were "substantially lower" than Sharon's book price for steel. In early 1973, market conditions changed dramatically due to the development of an attractive export market and an increased domestic demand for steel. During 1973 and 1974, the steel industry operated at full capacity, steel prices rose and nearly every producer experienced substantial delays in filling orders. In March, 1973, Sharon notified all purchasers, including Roth, that it was discontinuing price concessions given in 1972. After negotiations, the parties agreed that Roth would pay the agreed price until June 30, 1973 and a price somewhere between the agreed price and Sharon's published prices for the balance of 1973. Roth was initially reluctant to agree to this modification, but ultimately agreed "primarily because they were unable to purchase sufficient steel elsewhere to meet their production requirements." Sharon was supplying one-third of Roth's requirements and all other possible suppliers were "operating at full capacity and * * * were fully booked." The parties proceeded under this modification during the balance of 1973, although Sharon experienced difficulties in filling orders on time. During 1974, the parties did business on an entirely different basis. Roth would order steel, Sharon would accept the order at the price "prevailing at the time of shipment." During 1974 and 1975, Sharon's deliveries were chronically late, thereby increasing the price to Roth in a rising market. Roth, however, acquiesced in this pattern because it believed Sharon's assurances that late deliveries resulted from shortages of raw materials and the need for equitable allocation among customers and because there was "no practical alternative source of supply." This acquiescence was jolted in May, 1974 when Roth learned that Sharon was allocating substantial quantities of rolled steel to a subsidiary for sale at premium prices. After several more months of desultory performance on both sides, Roth sued Sharon for breach of contract, with special emphasis upon the modified contract for 1973. Sharon raised several defenses, including impracticability and, in the alternative, the agreed modification. The district court, after a long trial, held, *inter alia,* that Sharon was not excused from the 1973 contract on the grounds of impracticability and that the modification was unenforceable. A judgment for $555,968.46 was entered for Roth.

On appeal, the court of appeals affirmed the district court's decision on the impracticability, modification and other issues, but remanded the case for factual findings on whether Roth gave Sharon timely notice of breach. On the impracticability defense under UCC 2–615(a), the court held that "Sharon's inability to perform was a result of its policy accepting far more orders than it was capable of fulfilling, rather than a result of the existing shortage of raw materials." In refusing to enforce the modification of the 1973 contract, the court had this to say.]

CELEBREZZE, SENIOR CIRCUIT JUDGE.

* * *

C. In March, 1973, Sharon notified its customers that it intended to charge the maximum permissible price for all of its products; accordingly, all price concessions, including those made to the plaintiffs, were to be rescinded effective April 1, 1973. On March 23, 1973, Guerin [Roth's vice pres.] indicated to Metzger [Sharon's sales manager] that the plaintiffs considered the proposed price increase to be a breach of the November, 1972 contract. In an effort to resolve the dispute, Guerin met with representatives of Sharon on March 28, 1973 and asked Sharon to postpone any price increases until June or July, 1973. Several days later, Richard Mecaskey, Guerin's replacement, sent a letter to Sharon which indicated that the plaintiffs believed that the November, 1972 agreement was enforceable and that the plaintiffs were willing to negotiate a price modification if Sharon's cost increases warranted such an action. As a result of this letter, another meeting was held between Sharon and the plaintiffs. At this meeting, Walter Gregg, Sharon's vice-president and chairman of the board, agreed to continue charging the November, 1972 prices until June 30, 1973 and offered, for the remainder of 1973, to charge prices that were lower than Sharon's published prices but higher than the 1972 prices. Although the plaintiffs initially rejected the terms offered by Sharon for the second half of 1973, Mecaskey reluctantly agreed to Sharon's terms on June 29, 1973.

Before the district court, Sharon asserted that it properly increased prices because the parties had modified the November, 1973 contract to reflect changed market conditions. The district court, however, made several findings which, it believed, indicated that Sharon did not seek a modification to avoid a loss on the contract. The district court also found that the plaintiffs' inventories of rolled steel were "alarmingly deficient" at the time modification was sought and that Sharon had threatened to cease selling steel to the plaintiffs in the second-half of 1973 unless the plaintiffs agreed to the modification. Because Sharon had used its position as the plaintiffs' chief supplier to extract the price modification, the district court concluded that Sharon had acted in bad faith by seeking to modify the contract. In the alternative, the court concluded that the modification agreement was voidable because it was extracted by means of economic duress; the tight steel market prevented the plaintiffs from obtaining steel elsewhere at an affordable price and, consequently, the plaintiffs were forced to agree to the modification in order to assure a continued supply of steel. See e.g. Oskey Gasoline & Oil Co. v. Continental Oil Co., 534 F.2d 1281 (8th Cir.1976). Sharon challenges these conclusions on appeal.

The ability of a party to modify a contract which is subject to Article Two of the Uniform Commercial Code is broader than common law, primarily because the modification needs no consideration to be binding. ORC § 1302.12 (UCC § 2–209(1)). A party's ability to modify an agreement is limited only by Article Two's general obligation of good faith. * * * In determining whether a particular modification was obtained in good faith, a court must make two distinct inquiries: whether the party's conduct is consistent with "reasonable commercial standards of fair dealing in the trade," * * * and whether the parties were in fact motivated to seek modification by an honest desire to compensate for commercial exigencies; * * * ORC § 1302.01(2) (UCC § 2–103). The first inquiry is relatively straightforward; the party asserting the modification must demonstrate that his decision to seek modification was the result of a factor, such as increased costs, which would cause an ordinary merchant to seek a modification of the contract. See Official Comment 2, ORC § 1302.12 (UCC § 2–209) (reasonable commercial standards may require objective reason); J. White & R. Summers, Handbook of Law under the UCC at 41. The second inquiry, regarding the subjective honesty of the parties, is less clearly defined. Essentially, this inquiry requires the party asserting the modification to demonstrate that he was, in fact, motivated by a legitimate commercial reason and that such a reason is not offered merely as a pretext. * * * Moreover, the trier of fact must determine whether the means used to obtain the modification are an impermissible attempt to obtain a modification by extortion or overreaching. * * *

Sharon argues that its decision to seek a modification was consistent with reasonable commercial standards of fair dealing because market exigencies made further performance entail a substantial loss. The district court, however, made three findings which caused it to conclude that economic circumstances were not the reason that Sharon sought a modification: it found that Sharon was partially insulated from raw material price increases, that Sharon bargained for a contract with a slim profit margin and thus implicitly assumed the risk that performance might come to involve a loss, and that Sharon's overall profit in 1973 and its profit on the contract in the first quarter of 1973 were inconsistent with Sharon's position that the modification was sought to avoid a loss. Although all of these findings are marginally related to the question whether Sharon's conduct was consistent with reasonable commercial standards of fair dealing, we do not believe that they are sufficient to support a finding that Sharon did not observe reasonable commercial standards by seeking a modification. In our view, these findings do not support a conclusion that a reasonable merchant, in light of the circumstances, would not have sought a modification in order to avoid a loss. For example, the district court's finding that Sharon's steel slab contract [26] insulated it from industry wide cost increases is correct, so far as it goes. Although Sharon was able to purchase steel slabs at pre-1973 prices, the district court's findings also indicate that it was not able to purchase, at those prices, a sufficient tonnage of steel slabs to meet its production requirements.[27] The district court also found that Sharon experienced substantial cost increases for other raw materials, ranging from 4% to nearly 20%. In light of these facts, the finding regarding the fixed-price contract for slab steel, without more, cannot support an inference that Sharon was unaffected by the market shifts that occurred in 1973. Similarly, the district court's finding that Sharon entered a contract in November, 1972 which would yield only a slim profit does not support a conclusion that Sharon was willing to risk a loss on the contract. Absent a finding that the market shifts and the raw material price increases were foreseeable at the time the contract was formed—a finding which was not made—Sharon's willingness to absorb a loss cannot be inferred from the fact that it contracted for a smaller profit than usual. Finally, the findings regarding Sharon's profits are not sufficient, by themselves, to warrant a conclusion that Sharon was not justified in seeking a modification. Clearly, Sharon's initial profit on the contract [28] is an important consideration; the district court's findings indicate, however, that at the time modification was sought substantial future losses were foreseeable.[29] A party who has not actually suffered a

26. Sharon was a party to a contract with United States Steel which allowed it to make monthly purchases of slab steel ranging from a minimum of 25,000 tons per month to a maximum of 45,000 tons per month. It was also a party to a contract with Wierton Steel which allowed it to purchase slab steel in amounts varying between 10,000 to 20,000 tons per month. Both of these contracts were entered prior to 1973, at a very attractive price. When the market strengthened in 1973, however, Sharon was unable to obtain the maximum monthly tonnages permitted under these contracts; U.S. Steel delivered only 30,000 tons per month and Wierton 10,000 tons per month.

27. The district court found that Sharon suffered a continuing shortage of slab steel. It found that in 1972 (when Sharon was operating at substantially less than full capacity) it received 602,277 tons of slab steel; that in 1973, it received 506,596 tons of slab steel; and that in 1974 it received 373,898 tons. Thus, the record is clear that Sharon was in a difficult position. As demand for steel increased, and as Sharon's mills began to work at a higher capacity, its supply of slab steel steadily diminished.

28. The district court noted that in the first three months of 1973, Sharon made $3,089.00 on sales to Roth and lost $263.00 on steel sold to Toledo. Although Sharon lost significant sums of money on its contract with the plaintiffs, Sharon enjoyed overall profits in 1973, with net earnings of $11,566,000 on net sales of $338,205,000.

29. The evidence indicates, and the district court found, that with the exception of hot rolled sheets Sharon absorbed a loss on every rolled steel product which it sold to the defendants in 1973, even though the modified prices were in effect during the third and the fourth quarters.

loss on the contract may still seek a modification if a future loss on the agreement was reasonably foreseeable. Similarly, the overall profit earned by the party seeking modification is an important factor; this finding, however, does not support a conclusion that the decision to seek a modification was unwarranted. The more relevant inquiry is into the profit obtained through sales of the product line in question. This conclusion is reinforced by the fact that only a few product lines may be affected by market exigencies; [30] the opportunity to seek modification of a contract for the sale of goods of a product line should not be limited solely because some other product line produced a substantial profit.

In the final analysis, the single most important consideration in determining whether the decision to seek a modification is justified in this context is whether, because of changes in the market or other unforeseeable conditions, performance of the contract has come to involve a loss. In this case, the district court found that Sharon suffered substantial losses by performing the contract *as modified.* See note 29, supra. We are convinced that unforeseen economic exigencies existed which would prompt an ordinary merchant to seek a modification to avoid a loss on the contract; thus, we believe that the district court's findings to the contrary are clearly erroneous. * * *

The second part of the analysis, honesty in fact, is pivotal. The district court found that Sharon "threatened not to sell Roth and Toledo any steel if they refused to pay increased prices after July 1, 1973" and, consequently, that Sharon acted wrongfully. Sharon does not dispute the finding that it threatened to stop selling steel to the plaintiffs. Instead, it asserts that such a finding is merely evidence of bad faith and that it has rebutted any inference of bad faith based on that finding. We agree with this analysis; although coercive conduct is evidence that a modification of a contract is sought in bad faith, that prima facie showing may be effectively rebutted by the party seeking to enforce the modification. * * * Although we agree with Sharon's statement of principles, we do not agree that Sharon has rebutted the inference of bad faith that rises from its coercive conduct. Sharon asserts that its decision to unilaterally raise prices was based on language in the November 17, 1972 letter which allowed it to raise prices to the extent of any general industry-wide price increase. Because prices in the steel industry had increased, Sharon concludes that it was justified in raising its prices. Because it was justified in raising the contract price, the plaintiffs were bound by the terms of the contract to pay the increased prices. Consequently, any refusal by the plaintiffs to pay the price increase sought by Sharon must be viewed as a material breach of the November, 1972 contract which would excuse Sharon from any further performance. Thus, Sharon reasons that its refusal to perform absent a price increase was justified under the contract and consistent with good faith.

This argument fails in two respects. First, the contractual language on which Sharon relies only permits, at most, a price increase for cold rolled steel; thus, even if Sharon's position were supported by the evidence, Sharon would not have been justified in refusing to sell the plaintiff's hot rolled steel

30. Apparently, Sharon's record overall profit was the result of other operations. It obtained a pre-tax profit of less than one percent on its total sales of rolled steel.

because of the plaintiffs' refusal to pay higher prices for the product. More importantly, however, the evidence does not indicate that Sharon ever offered this theory as a justification until this matter was tried. Sharon's representatives, in their testimony, did not attempt to justify Sharon's refusal to ship steel at 1972 prices in this fashion. Furthermore, none of the contemporaneous communications contain this justification for Sharon's action. In short, we can find no evidence in the record which indicates that Sharon offered this theory as a justification at the time the modification was sought. Consequently, we believe that the district court's conclusion that Sharon acted in bad faith by using coercive conduct to extract the price modification is not clearly erroneous. Therefore, we hold that Sharon's attempt to modify the November, 1972 contract, in order to compensate for increased costs which made performance come to involve a loss, is ineffective because Sharon did not act in a manner consistent with Article Two's requirement of honesty in fact when it refused to perform its remaining obligations under the contract at 1972 prices.[31]

* * *

Notes

1. Section 89 of the Restatement, Second, of Contracts provides: "A promise modifying a duty under a contract not fully performed on either side is binding (a) if the modification is fair and equitable in view of circumstances not anticipated by the parties when the contract was made; or (b) to the extent provided by statute; or (c) to the extent that justice requires enforcement in view of material change of position in reliance on the promise." Is Roth consistent with the Restatement?

2. Following the logic of UCC 2–209(1) and the comments, Roth invalidated the modification because of Sharon's bad faith rather than because of economic duress. In fact, the court, in note 31, suggested that proof of coercive means will not necessarily invalidate a modification made in good faith. Exactly what is bad faith in the Sixth Circuit?

3. Economic duress may be invoked to invalidate a modification where one party has made a "wrongful" threat to withhold delivery of needed goods, the threatened party can not obtain substitute goods from another source and the ordinary remedy of an action for breach of contract is not adequate. See Austin Instrument, Inc. v. Loral Corp., 29 N.Y.2d 124, 324 N.Y.S.2d 22, 272 N.E.2d 533 (1971). Professor Hillman, for one, favors this approach. See Hillman, *Contract Modification Under the Restatement (Second) of Contracts,* 67 Cornell L.Rev. 680 (1982). Could the modification in Roth be invalidated for economic duress? See Kelsey-Hayes Co. v. Galtaco Redlaw Castings Corp., 749 F.Supp. 794 (E.D.Mich. 1990), holding that UCC 2–209(1) does not preempt the common law of economic duress.

31. The district court also found, as an alternative ground, that the modification was voidable because the plaintiffs agreed to the modification due to economic duress. See, e.g., Oskey Gasoline & Oil Co. v. Continental Oil, 534 F.2d 1281 (8th Cir.1976). Because we conclude that the modification was ineffective as a result of Sharon's bad faith, we do not reach the issue whether the contract modification was also voidable because of economic duress. We note, however, that proof that coercive means were used is necessary to establish that a contract is voidable because of economic duress. Normally, it cannot be used to void a contract modification which has been sought in good faith; if a contract modification has been found to be in good faith, then presumably no wrongful coercive means have been used to extract the modification.

Note: Modifications and the Statute of Frauds

Assume that S and B enter an oral contract to sell 10 units of goods for $400. The statute of frauds does not apply because the price is less than $500. UCC 2–201(1). Suppose that the parties, before any performance has occurred, modify the contract by adding 10 more units of goods for $400. This agreement modifying the contract is clearly enforceable under UCC 2–209(1). But now UCC 2–209(3) comes into play: "The requirements of the statute of frauds * * * (Section 2–201) must be satisfied if the contract as modified is within its provisions." Without question, the "contract as modified" is within UCC 2–201(1), even though neither the original contract nor the modification were for a price of "$500 or more." Thus, it would appear that the modification must meet the requirement of a writing in UCC 2–201(1) or satisfy the exceptions listed in UCC 2–201(3). In addition, the modification should be in writing if it falls within UCC 2–201(1) on its own or if it changes the quantity term of an original contract that fell within UCC 2–201. A literal reading of this somewhat murky provision does not, however, support the conclusion that if the original contract was within UCC 2–201, any modification must also be in writing. See White & Summers 53–59.

The murkiness is not abated as one reads further. UCC 2–209(4) provides: "Although an attempt at modification or rescission does not satisfy the requirements of subsection * * * (3) it can operate as a waiver." A waiver of what, the requirement of UCC 2–201(1) itself? Not likely. And what "operates" as a waiver? Article 2 does not say.

At common law, the concept of waiver was frequently invoked to excuse conditions precedent to a contractual duty to perform. Suppose, for example, that the contract provided that before the buyer had a duty to pay for goods delivered, they must be inspected and certified by a designated third party. In theory, the buyer has no duty to pay until the condition is satisfied. But if, with knowledge that no certificate had been issued, the buyer elected to accept and pay for the goods, the condition was waived. This was waiver by "election." Similarly, if B, before delivery, represented to S that the certificate would not be required and B relied upon that representation, the condition would be excused. This was waiver by estoppel. The former waived conditions which had already failed and the latter waived conditions which had not. See Restatement, Contracts (Second) 84. Although both types of waiver modified or discharged conditions in the contract, they did not affect the right of the waiving party to damages for defective performance:

Only a modification supported by consideration or other valid reasons for enforcement could do that. See National Utility Service, Inc. v. Whirlpool Corp., 325 F.2d 779 (2d Cir.1963).

With this sketchy background, look again at UCC 2–209(2), (4), and (5) and resolve the following problem. (Taken from Wisconsin Knife Works v. National Metal Crafters, 781 F.2d 1280 (7th Cir.1986)). See also, Newell, *Cleaning up UCC Section 2–209*, 27 Idaho L.Rev. 487 (1990).

Problem 13–4

After negotiations, B mailed to S a written order for the purchase of 281,000 "spade bit blanks," for use in the manufacture of spade bits. The goods were to be delivered in installments by the dates stipulated in the purchase order. In addition, the purchase order contained, inter alia, the following "condition" of purchase: "No modification of this contract shall be binding upon Buyer unless made in writing and signed by Buyer's authorized representative. Buyer shall have the right to make changes in the Order by a notice, in writing, to seller." Seller accepted the purchase order in a written acknowledgment and commenced to manufacture the bits.

S was consistently late in tendering delivery. B, however, accepted the late deliveries without declaring a breach or invoking the written modification condition. After accepting 144,000 blanks, however, B, invoking the delivery schedule in the purchase order, cancelled the contract for breach and sued S for damages. (There was some evidence that B cancelled because of a dispute with a sub-purchaser of the completed spade bit rather than S's delays.)

You are clerk to the trial judge. She asks you for a memo on the following questions:

(1) Was the "no modification" condition in the purchase order enforceable against Seller, see UCC 2–209(2);

(2) If so, did B's conduct of accepting S's late deliveries "operate as a waiver" of either the contract delivery schedule or the "no modification" condition, see UCC 2–208(3), 2–209(4);

(3) If the conduct did operate as a waiver, how is UCC 2–209(5) relevant to the dispute? For assistance, see Cassidy Podell Lynch, Inc. v. SnyderGeneral Corp., 944 F.2d 1131 (3d Cir.1991) (course of performance waives "no oral modification" clause.

Note: Arbitration of Disputes Arising Under Long-Term Supply Contracts

Arbitration is an informal method of dispute resolution which occurs, in most cases, outside of the judicial process. It depends upon an enforceable agreement between the parties to submit existing or future disputes to arbitration.

The scope of the arbitrator's power to decide is determined by that agreement: It may include "all" disputes between the parties of any kind whatever or be limited to particular disputes, such as the failure to agree upon an adjustment or the excusability of one or both parties due to commercial impracticability.

Arbitration clauses are frequently found in long-term supply contracts, where the incentive of the parties to preserve the relationship while disputes over performance are being resolved is high. Whether an arbitration clause is part of the agreement, however, is frequently disputed in litigation involving the "battle of the forms." See Chapter Ten, Section 3, supra.

Assume that the contract includes a "reopener" clause, which envisions three steps: (1) If changed circumstances not foreseeable as likely to occur substantially affect performance, either party may request the other to agree to an adjustment in the contract; (2) The parties shall negotiate over the requested adjustment in good faith; (3) If the parties fail to agree, the dispute shall be submitted to arbitration where the arbitrator shall determine whether changed circumstances justifying the requested adjustment existed and, if so, what the adjustment should be.

Suppose that the buyer invoked the clause and, after negotiations with the seller, no agreed modification was reached. The buyer then filed a demand for arbitration and the seller refused. In fact, when the buyer refused to pay for goods under the contract until the dispute was resolved, the seller cancelled and sued for breach of contract in a *state court.* What should the buyer do?

In this all too familiar situation, the steps are likely to look like this.

1. The buyer must determine whether state or federal law governs the dispute over arbitration. The issue is less important on matters of substance, i.e. the enforceability of agreements to arbitrate future disputes, since most commercial states have modern, comprehensive arbitration statutes, such as the Uniform Arbitration Act. Uniform Arbitration Act §§ 1–25 (1955) 7 U.L.A. 4 (1978). But the question is crucial in deciding where to sue to compel arbitration and determining what procedures will govern. Let us assume that the dispute is subject to the United States Arbitration Act, 9 U.S.C.A. §§ 1–14 (1982), and that any litigation will be commenced in the United States District Court and be subject to the Federal Rules of Civil Procedure.

2. The buyer should sue in the federal district court to stay the seller's suit for breach of contract and to compel arbitration under the contract. This is the critical early point in the arbitration, for the court must decide such questions as whether the arbitration clause is enforceable and, if so, whether the parties have agreed to arbitrate the dispute in question. If the answer to either question is no, then the suit to stay and compel is dismissed. If the answer to both questions is yes, then the federal court will issue a preemptive order to the state court to stay the law suit and issue an order to the seller to commence arbitration. The order to compel arbitration is, in effect, a decree of specific performance. See, e.g., Sharon Steel Corporation v. Jewell Coal & Coke Co., 735 F.2d 775 (3d Cir.1984).

3. If the parties have been ordered to arbitrate, the next steps are to select the arbitrators, schedule hearings on the issues to be resolved and conduct the arbitration. Frequently, the American Association of Arbitration (the AAA) will provide material assistance in this process through furnishing lists of potential arbitrators, providing rules and procedures to be followed during the arbitration and facilitating the process from beginning to end. See G. Goldberg, A Lawyer's Guide to Commercial Arbitration, 35–59 (2d ed. 1983).

4. Under American law, an arbitrator's decision on questions of fact and law is binding on the parties, unless judicial review is sought and one of the narrow grounds for overturning an award is satisfied. These grounds go to the honesty of the arbitrators and the integrity of the process rather than to the merits of the dispute. Thus, if the parties agree to arbitrate a clearly defined dispute subject to the rules and procedures of the AAA and one party, thereafter, refuses to arbitrate, the courts will compel arbitration, subject to limited attacks at the threshold upon the arbitrability of the dispute and, thereafter, confirm and enforce the award, subject to attacks upon the honesty of the arbitrators and the integrity of the process.

See, in general, Ian MacNeil, Richard Speidel & Thomas Stipanowich, Arbitration Under the Federal Arbitration Act: Law, Practice and Procedure (1994).

PART THREE

THE POST–AGREEMENT—PRE–SHIPMENT STAGE

CHAPTER FOURTEEN

BUYER'S BREACH—A SURVEY OF SELLER'S REMEDIES

SECTION 1. A GENERAL INTRODUCTION TO CODE REMEDIES

Before the time for the seller's performance has arrived, the buyer might repudiate, commit a "total" breach of an installment contract, fail to make an advance payment when due, or the like. In such circumstances, the seller will want to know (1) whether his own performance is excused and (2) to what remedies he may resort.

In Chapter Fourteen, after a preliminary consideration of the nature and significance of the buyer's wrongful conduct, we will survey the various remedies open to the seller. In Chapter Fifteen, we will reverse the position of the parties, and consider the various remedies open to the buyer when the seller repudiates or commits a total breach of an installment contract. These two chapters have been structured to afford the student maximum opportunity to compare seller's remedies and buyer's remedies in comparable situations. Article 2 invites this kind of analysis, for it grants seller and buyer alike a wide range of parallel remedies. Thus, the seller's action for the price (UCC 2–709) is parallel to the buyer's action for specific performance (UCC 2–716). So, too: the respective rights of seller and buyer to damages based on contract-market price differentials (UCC 2–708 and 2–713) and the respective rights of seller and buyer to enter into substitute transactions and measure their losses accordingly (UCC 2–706 and 2–712). A comprehensive analysis appears in Sebert, *Remedies Under Article Two of the Uniform Commercial Code: An Agenda for Review,* 130 U.Pa.L.Rev. 360 (1981). The seminal article is Peters, *Remedies for Breach of Contracts Relating to the Sale of Goods Under the U.C.C.: A Roadmap for Article Two,* 73 Yale L.J. 199 (1963). See also R. Anderson, Damages Under the Uniform Commercial Code (1988); Scott, *The Case for Market Damages: Revisiting the Lost Profits Puzzle,* 57 U.Chi.L.Rev. 1155 (1990).

Before going further, we should note and respond to the budding heresy (believed by White) that contract and sales remedies are without practical significance. See, generally, White, *Contract Law in Modern Commercial Transactions, An Artifact of Twentieth Century Business Life?,* 22 Washburn L.J. 1 (1982). According to White, the student who knew of the infrequency of suit (businessmen want to preserve relations), the modesty of sums recovered (*Hadley v. Baxendale* and all that) and the increasing resort to alternative forms of dispute resolution (arbitration) might be tempted to include contract and sales remedies among those things one has to study to get through law school but which have little relevance thereafter. In support of this thesis, the studies of Professor Stewart Macaulay might be cited, e.g., *Non-Contractual Relations in Business: A Preliminary Study,* 28 Am.Sociol.Rev. 55 (1963), which suggest that commercial parties themselves iron out most contract and sales disputes on their own on the basis of common sense and economics.

Even so, Speidel and Summers believe that it hardly follows that the student can ignore the remedial side of the coin. In the first place, not all contract recoveries are inconsequential or piddling. If the contract is a large one which has a long term, even a modest contract-market differential can produce a whopping sum of money. Moreover, a modest relaxation of *Hadley v. Baxendale* and a willingness of the courts to compensate sellers for lost profits and lost volumes could cause an important change in the picture.

More important, however, is the fact that the impact of contract remedy doctrine cannot properly be measured by the frequency of litigation. For surely, the predicted damage and specific performance awards that courts would grant play an important role in the negotiation of every contract dispute which is handled by lawyers. In such cases we bargain at least in part on the basis of the lawyer's judgment about what damages will be awarded at trial. Thus both the lawyer who is going to negotiate a settlement on behalf of an aggrieved client and the lawyer who is going to advise his client how best to extricate himself from a situation in which he or the opposing party has broken a contract need to know the variety of available remedies and the merits and demerits of each.

SECTION 2. IMPAIRING SELLER'S EXPECTATION OF FULL PERFORMANCE: PROSPECTIVE INABILITY; REPUDIATION, AND INSTALLMENT CONTRACTS

A. *Insolvency and Prospective Inability—UCC 2–609*

UCC 2–609(1) provides that a contract for sale "imposes an obligation on each party that the other's expectation of receiving due performance will not be impaired." This obligation is breached when one party gives the other "reasonable grounds for insecurity" with regard to the promised performance. At this point, the aggrieved party "may in writing demand adequate assurance of due performance and until he receives such assurance may if commercially reasonable suspend any performance for which he has not already received the agreed return." Comment 2 to UCC 2–609 stresses that the right to suspend performance includes "any preparation therefor." If the other party, upon receipt of a "justified" demand, fails "to provide within a reasonable time not exceeding thirty days such assurance of due performance as is adequate under the circumstances of the particular case," it has repudiated the contract and the aggrieved party may take appropriate remedial action, including cancellation. Between merchants, the reasonableness of grounds for insecurity and adequacy of any assurance offered "shall be determined according to commercial standards." UCC 2–609(2).

Thus, an aggrieved party may suspend his performance even though the other party's conduct is short of breach or repudiation but the aggrieved party cannot cancel the contract until the mandatory communication procedure fails to produce "adequate assurance." In this process, a high incidence of consensual adjustment and continued performance is likely, particularly when the generality of the standards in UCC 2–609 is taken into account. On the other hand, if adjustment does not occur and one party has suspended his performance or cancelled the contract, the other may claim that such action was not justified. Within this framework, courts and lawyers will have to give some content to the phrases "reasonable grounds for insecurity" and "adequate assurance of due performance." For good background discussion, see Wardrop, *Prospective Inability in the Law of Contracts,* 20 Minn. L.Rev. 380 (1936); 6 Corbin, Contracts §§ 1259–1261 (1962); Note, *A Right to Adequate Assurance of Performance in All Transactions; UCC 2–609 Beyond Sales of Goods,* 48 S.Cal.L.Rev. 1358 (1975). See also, Robertson, *The Right to Demand Adequate Assurance of Due Performance Under UCC Section 2–609 and Restatement (Second) of Contracts Section 251,* 38 Drake L.Rev. 305 (1988–89).

Suppose that under a written contract for the sale of goods the seller is to deliver in a single lot on March 1 and the buyer is to pay the full contract price on April 1. The buyer's basic obligation here is to accept and pay for the goods in accordance with the contract, UCC 2–301, and it is in this regard that grounds for insecurity may arise. Except insofar as the seller has rights under UCC 2–702(2), however, once the buyer has accepted the seller's tender of delivery, the seller can reduce any insecurity he feels about subsequent payment of the price only by exercising rights he may have under an Article 9 security interest—rights he may not have. As a practical matter, UCC 2–609 itself affords little protection to a seller who has fully performed his obligation before the alleged ground for insecurity arises.

Before delivery, however, UCC 2–609 is available and in some cases this availability is spelled out with precision for both seller and buyer alike. See UCC 2–210(5) and UCC 2–611(2). From the seller's point of view, two situations are described which justify protective action. When, in an installment contract, the buyer's default in past due payments is not sufficient to justify a cancellation, the seller may withhold delivery of goods then due until payment for past deliveries is received. UCC 2–612(3), Comment 7. When the seller, in a credit transaction, discovers the buyer to be insolvent (as defined in UCC 1–201(23)), he may "refuse delivery except for cash including payment for all goods theretofore delivered under the contract, and stop delivery" under UCC 2–705. This latter remedy finds firm support in §§ 53(1)(a) and 54(1) of the Uniform Sales Act and in prior case law. See, e.g., Leopold v. Rock-Ola Mfg. Corporation, 109 F.2d 611 (5th Cir.1940). However, it has been held that insolvency alone does not justify cancellation of the contract. Keppelon v. W.M. Ritter Flooring Corp., 97 N.J.L. 200, 116 A. 491 (1922).

Short of the situations noted above, exactly what constitutes either reasonable grounds for insecurity or adequate assurance of due performance is less clear. Resolve the following problem, giving careful attention to the comments to UCC 2–609.

Problem 14–1

S agreed to manufacture special equipment for B. Delivery was to be in installments, with payment for each installment within 15 days of delivery. S commenced performance but, before any deliveries were made, S began to hear unfavorable comments about B's credit. After a quick check, the following facts emerged: (1) Dun & Bradstreet had recently reduced B's credit rating; (2) B's working capital was fully stretched out and some suppliers were experiencing delays in payment; (3) B had recently changed banks, and the "word" was out that B's financial condition was "extended" and that care should be exercised before extending credit; and (4) B's overall financial condition had worsened since the date of the contract.

A. You represent S. On the day before the first delivery was due, S called you for a conference. With the credit information on the table, S stated that unless you could persuade him otherwise, he would refuse to deliver the goods unless B paid cash. What would you recommend? See UCC 1–201(23), 2–702(1), 2–609.

B. Assume that you persuade S to exercise caution and talk to B before taking action. S, therefore, gives B a written demand for "adequate assurance" and temporarily suspends the first delivery. UCC 2–609(1). B, in response, establishes solvency and claims that the current situation is "temporary." B, however, states that long-term viability depends upon getting prompt delivery of the equipment, which is needed in the business, on credit. If there are delays, no assurances can be given.

Does this constitute "adequate assurance" of due performance? What else could S reasonably demand? On this last point, consider the following opinion by Cummings, Circuit Judge, concurring in Pittsburgh-Des Moines Steel Co. v. Brookhaven Manor Water Co., 532 F.2d 572, 583–84 (7th Cir.1976):

"Although I agree with the result reached in the majority opinion, I differ with the reasoning. Reasonable men could certainly conclude that PDM had legitimate grounds to question Brookhaven's ability to pay for the water tank. When the contract was signed, the parties understood that Brookhaven would obtain a loan to help pay for the project. When the loan failed to materialize, a prudent businessman would have 'reasonable grounds for insecurity.' I disagree that there must be a fundamental change in the financial position of the buyer before the seller can invoke the protection of UCC § 2–609. Rather, I believe that the Section was designed to cover instances where an underlying condition of the contract, even if not expressly incorporated into the written document, fails to occur. See Comment 3 to UCC § 2–609. Whether, in a specific case, the breach of the condition gives a party 'reasonable grounds for insecurity' is a question of fact for the jury.

"UCC § 2–609, however, does not give the alarmed party a right to redraft the contract. Whether the party invoking that provision is merely requesting an assurance that performance will be forthcoming or whether he is attempting to alter the contract is a mixed question of law and fact, depending in part upon the court's interpretation of the obligations imposed on the parties. In this case, PDM would have been assured only if significant changes in the contract were made, either by receiving Betke's personal guarantee, by attaining escrow financing or by purchasing an interest in Brookhaven. The district court could probably conclude as a matter of law that these requests by PDM demanded more than a commercially 'adequate assurance of due performance.'"

Note that a demand by the seller for an assurance that exceeds the buyer's obligation under the contract may be a repudiation. See Scott v. Crown, 765 P.2d 1043 (Colo.App.1988).

Note: Scope of Seller's Reclamation Rights

The Code protects a credit seller against specified events within the control of the buyer that occur before delivery. If the buyer commits a breach of contract, the seller may, at a minimum, withhold delivery of the goods involved, UCC 2–703(a), or, in a proper case, stop delivery by a carrier or other bailee to the buyer, UCC 2–705(1). If the buyer becomes insolvent, the seller may "refuse delivery except for cash" under UCC 2–702(1) or "stop delivery" under UCC 2–705(1). Where the buyer gives reasonable grounds for insecurity short of a breach or insolvency, the seller may, if commercially reasonable, "suspend any performance for which he has not already received the agreed return." UCC 2–609(2). The first two cases, at least, illustrate what the common law called a seller's possessory lien and what the Code calls a possessory security interest arising under Article 2. See UCC 1–201(37) & 9–113. So long as the seller retains actual or constructive possession of the goods after default by the credit buyer, it can enforce the security interest in the goods under Article 2, free from, or with priority over, the claims of the buyer's other creditors.

If the goods have been delivered to the buyer, however, the matter becomes more complicated. For now, note the following principles, to which we will return in Chapter 22, Section 4(c).

(1) If the seller retains "title" until payment, the effect is to create a non-possessory security interest, which is within the scope of Article 9. See UCC 1–201(37), 2–401(1), & UCC 9–102(1). Although the security interest is enforceable against the buyer, i.e., the seller could repossess the goods from the buyer, see UCC 9–203(1), 9–501(1) & 9–503, it will be subject to the claims of lien and secured creditors of the buyer unless "perfected" by filing a financing statement and otherwise entitled to priority. See UCC 9–201, 9–301(1), 9–302(1) & 9–312(5).

(2) If the seller does not retain title but the buyer was insolvent at the time of delivery, the seller has a limited claim to reclamation under UCC 2–702(2) & (3). Note that even if all the conditions of subsection (2) are met, the rights of a "buyer in ordinary course or other good faith purchaser" may have intervened.

(3) If the seller did not retain title and the buyer was not insolvent at the time of delivery, the seller has no interest in or claim to the goods upon default by the buyer. The seller has, in effect, only an unsecured claim for the price. UCC 2–709(1).

Problem 14–2

Suppose, in Problem 14–1, above, that on July 1, S shipped a carload of equipment to B by public carrier "FOB the place of shipment." (For what this means, see UCC 2–319(1)(a), 2–503(2) & 2–504). The carrier issued a non-negotiable bill of lading, naming B as "consignee," i.e., the person entitled to the goods under the document. On July 2, while the goods were still in transit, B resold the goods for cash to C, a good faith purchaser for value. On July 3, before receipt of the goods by B, S learned from reliable sources that B was insolvent. The goods were scheduled to arrive by 10 pm on July 3, but could not be picked up until July 5.

A. Can S on July 3 stop delivery of the goods under UCC 2–705?

B. If S can stop delivery against B, under what circumstances, if any, will C, a good faith purchaser for value, nevertheless take free of S's security interest in the goods? See UCC 2–401, 2–403 & 9–307. Is it clear that if S properly stops delivery under UCC 2–705 as against B and before C obtains possession of the goods, C will take subject to S's security interest? For a case holding that seller's stop order, which was received before buyer received the goods but after an acknowledgement by a warehouse, was too late, see In re Pester Refining Co., 66 B.R. 801 (Bkrtcy.D.C.Iowa 1986).

B. Buyer's Repudiation

In the first year course in contracts, considerable attention is usually given to the cognate problems of determining whether a contracting party has repudiated or materially broken an installment contract. Accordingly, our treatment here will be an abbreviated one, emphasizing the relevant Code provisions and the role of the lawyer called upon to advise the seller on what to do in the face of the buyer's conduct. The consequences of an erroneous decision by the lawyer can be catastrophic. The seller's lawyer may advise that the buyer has repudiated or materially broken an installment contract, and that seller is free to cease his own performance and seek damages. If this advice proves incorrect, the seller will turn out to be the wrongdoer, and, accordingly, liable in damages. For such a case, see Teeman v. Jurek, 251 N.W.2d 698 (Minn.1977). In such a case he may just choose another lawyer to defend him. It should be added that the lawyer who renders advice in this context does not always have weeks to do research in the library. His client, the seller, may, be manufacturing the goods, and may want to know *now* what course of action he is free to take in the face of buyer's conduct.

What constitutes a "repudiation"? Although UCC 2–610 uses this word, the Code nowhere defines it. And in real life, it is a lucky and unusual lawyer whose client reports that the other contracting party has repudiated by such unequivocal language as "I repudiate" or "kiss my foot." A more common circumstance finds the other party slowly slipping down that incline into bankruptcy while believing and fully expecting that he will "have the money in just a few days," or that he will "have the goods in just a week." Another common cause for the same lawyer's headache is the chiseler—the fellow who asks for more than the contract clearly entitles him to, but not enough more to make his request outrageous. But see Toppert v. Bunge Corp., 60 Ill.App.3d 607, 18 Ill.Dec. 171, 377 N.E.2d 324 (1978) (semi-outrageous conduct).

As we have seen, the client's situation (and therefore his lawyer's) in such a case is greatly eased by UCC 2–609 which gives the right to demand assurance of performance from the other party and causes failure of assurances to be forthcoming to become a repudiation after "a reasonable time not exceeding thirty days." In some cases clients will be unwilling to twiddle their thumbs for 30 days and the lawyer will be called upon to determine whether a communication from the other party constitutes a repudiation.

The comments to UCC 2–610 give some guidance. Comment 1 reads in part as follows: "* * * anticipatory repudiation centers upon an overt communication of intention or an action which renders performance impossible or demonstrates a clear determination not to continue with performance." Comment 2 continues:

> It is not necessary for repudiation that performance be made literally and utterly impossible. Repudiation can result from action which reasonably indicates a rejection of the continuing obligation. And, a repudiation automatically results under the preceding section on insecurity when a party fails to provide adequate assurance of due future performance within thirty days after a justifiable demand therefor has been made. Under the language of this section, a demand by one or both parties for more than the contract calls for in the way of counter-performance is not in itself a repudiation nor does it invalidate a plain expression of desire for future performance. However, when under a fair reading it amounts to a statement of intention not to perform except on conditions which go beyond the contract, it becomes a repudiation.

Obviously, courts and lawyers will resort to extra-Code case law for guidance in deciding whether or not a given buyer has repudiated. See Restatement, Second, Contracts § 251.

Problem 14–3

In the Spring of 1992, Seller, a lumberyard, contracted to sell a quantity of specially selected hardwood to Buyer, a furniture manufacturer, at a fixed price. The lumber was to be shipped "fob Seller's lumberyard" within 10 days of demand by Buyer. No time for the demand was specified in the agreement. In May, 1992, Seller inquired when the demand would be made and was informed by Buyer "within the next few weeks." At the end of June, Seller, pressed for cash and storage space, requested by letter that Buyer "help us out" by placing the order quickly. When there was no response, Seller telegraphed that "much as we hate to we must ask for some relief" and requested a conference to "straighten the matter out." Buyer replied that it would be glad to have a conference but "if it is in regard to taking any lumber, we would say that we are not in a position, and do not intend to take any lumber this year and probably not until next Fall." Seller telegraphed that the response was "totally unacceptable" and demanded that Buyer take immediate delivery. Two weeks passed without a response. At this time the market price for the hardwoods was over 20% below the contract price.

Your client is furious and wants to cancel the contract, resell the hardwood and "sue those * * * for damages." And he wants action "right now."

A. Has the Buyer repudiated the contract? If you have doubts, what quick steps should be taken to minimize the risk? (Don't overlook the possibility that the Buyer is in breach because a reasonable time for making the demand has expired. See UCC 2–309(1) & 1–204.)

B. If Buyer has repudiated, what remedial options are available? See UCC 2–610, 2–611 & 2–703.

C. Suppose that the date for delivery had been set for December 1 and that the Buyer repudiated on July 3. If the seller cancelled the contract and immediately sued for damages, what would be the measure of damages? See UCC 2–708 & 2–723.

Note: Interaction Between UCC 2-609 and UCC 2-610

Suppose Seller and Buyer are in a long-term contract and the market price has plummeted well below the contract price. There are no redetermination clauses in the contract and Seller has refused to negotiate over a price adjustment. The prospects for relief under UCC 2-615(a) or any theory are very slim. Is there any alternative for Buyer other than to perform and take the loss or to breach and take a judgment for damages?

One possibility is to invoke UCC 2-609. But Buyer cannot demand adequate assurance of due performance from Seller unless "reasonable grounds for insecurity" have arisen. UCC 2-609(1). This is unlikely in a falling market, since Seller will probably have both the capacity and incentive to perform. Such a demand is also perverse, since Buyer's true objective is to avoid rather than to secure Seller's performance. Thus, unless Buyer can show objective circumstances generating the insecurity, the use of UCC 2-609(1) is doomed to failure. See, e.g., Universal Resources Corp. v. Panhandle Eastern Pipe Line Co., 813 F.2d 77 (5th Cir.1987), rehearing denied, 821 F.2d 1097. See also, United States v. Great Plains Gasification Associates, 819 F.2d 831 (8th Cir.1987), where Buyer had no reasonable grounds and, even so, demanded more by way of assurance than Seller was obligated to provide.

Another possibility for Buyer is to find an interpretation question in the contract and state to Seller that there will be no further performance until the interpretation question is resolved by a court. Buyer may also seek a declaratory judgment and should make it clear to Seller that Buyer will perform the contract in full in accordance with the court's interpretation. Will this provide Buyer with a "safe harbor" until the dispute is resolved?

The answer should be no if there is not a good faith dispute. The courts will have little sympathy if Buyer has manufactured the dispute in an effort to avoid the contract. Even if there is a good faith dispute, UCC 2-610 does not say whether this communication is a repudiation. There is some risk that a court will conclude that Buyer's qualified statement that it will not perform until the good faith dispute is resolved but then will perform in full is a repudiation. See Record Club of America v. United Artists Records, 643 F.Supp. 925 (S.D.N.Y. 1986). But see In re Chateaugay Corp., 104 B.R. 637 (S.D.N.Y.1989), holding that the qualified statement was not a repudiation.

One solution is to provide a narrow definition of actionable repudiation in the revised Article 2. This would protect Buyer's qualified repudiation and provide a safe-harbor where there is a good faith dispute. In addition, a narrow definition would reduce uncertainty, tend toward preserving the contract and facilitate communication between the parties. But as one commentator has observed, this revision would simply shift the problem from UCC 2-610 back to UCC 2-609, with its open ended phrases. See Note, *Proposed Amendments to Article 2 of the Uniform Commercial Code: The Tangled Web of Anticipatory Repudiation and the Right to Demand Assurances,* 40 U.Kan.L.Rev. 287 (1991).

The question, then, is whether UCC 2-609 needs a revision for more predictability and certainty and, if so, exactly what should the revision be? For example, if Buyer's qualified statement is not a repudiation under a revised UCC 2-610, does it give "reasonable grounds for insecurity" under 2-609(1)? If so, does Buyer give "adequate assurance" if it states that the contract will be fully performed as interpreted by the court? One would hope so, but if a court, in its discretion, concludes not, then conduct which is not a repudiation under UCC 2-

610 becomes a repudiation under UCC 2–609(4). Obviously, that is a result to be avoided.

C. Buyer's Substantial Impairment of the Value to the Seller of His Installment Contract With the Buyer

What is an installment contract and what difference does it make to the seller and buyer?

Under UCC 2–612(1), an installment contract "requires or authorizes the delivery of goods in separate lots to be separately accepted, even though the contract contains a clause 'each delivery is a separate contract' or its equivalent." Compare UCC 2–307; Stinnes Interoil, Inc. v. Apex Oil Co., 604 F.Supp. 978 (S.D.N.Y.1985) (whether parties intended installment deliveries or delivery in a single lot is question of fact).

Under an installment contract, payment is due "at the time and place at which the buyer is to receive the goods" unless "otherwise agreed." UCC 2–310(a). Suppose that the buyer fails to pay for an installment when due or repudiates the duty to pay for a single installment? What are the seller's remedies? Can, for example, the seller cancel the contract under UCC 2–703(f), and sue for damages?

Consider, first, a failure to pay a single installment when due. Under UCC 2–703, where the buyer "wrongfully * * * fails to make a payment due on or before delivery * * * then with respect to any goods directly affected and, if the breach is of the whole contract (Section 2–612), then also with respect to the whole undelivered balance, the aggrieved seller may * * * (f) cancel." UCC 2–612(3) provides that there is a "breach of the whole" whenever a "default with respect to one or more installments substantially impairs the value of the whole contract * * *" Thus, the answer is clear: No cancellation unless there is a breach of the "whole" under the substantial impairment standard set in UCC 2–612(3).

Suppose that the buyer fails to pay an installment due after delivery? UCC 2–703 appears to limit the remedy of cancellation to the failure to make payments due "on or before delivery." UCC 2–709(1)(a), however, provides the usual remedy: When the "buyer fails to pay the price as it becomes due the seller may recover * * * the price (a) of goods accepted. * * *" Thus, when the buyer has accepted the goods (and taken possession) and the price then becomes due, the seller is expected to enforce the contract by suing for the price rather than to cancel. Furthermore, UCC 2–709(1) appears to foreclose acceleration of a contract to pay in installments: An action to recover the price is proper when the buyer "fails to pay the price as it becomes due." Thus, if the seller had delivered all the goods in exchange for a promise to pay the price in installments and the buyer failed to pay one or more, the seller's remedy appears to be limited to an action for the price on each installment as the breach occurs.

What about a repudiation by the buyer of an installment not yet due? UCC 2–612(3) is limited to a "default with respect to one or more installments * * *" In common parlance, a repudiation is not a default. Does this mean that the seller can cancel the entire contract? The answer is no. Do you see why? Read UCC 2–610 and 2–703. Unless the repudiation "with respect to a performance not yet due" substantially impairs the value of the contract to the other, the aggrieved party, here the seller, may not resort to the remedies for breach in UCC 2–703.

Here, now, is one of the "great" cases on "material" breach in installment contracts.

PLOTNICK v. PENNSYLVANIA SMELTING & REFINING CO.

United States Court of Appeals, Third Circuit, 1952.
194 F.2d 859.

HASTIE, CIRCUIT JUDGE.

This litigation arises out of an installment contract for the sale of quantities of battery lead by a Canadian seller to a Pennsylvania buyer. The seller sued for the price of a carload of lead delivered but not paid for. The buyer counterclaimed for damages caused by the seller's failure to deliver the remaining installments covered by the contract. The district court sitting without a jury allowed recovery on both claim and counterclaim. This is an appeal by the seller from the judgment against him on the counterclaim. The ultimate question is whether the buyer had committed such a breach of contract as constituted a repudiation justifying rescission by the seller.

Suit was brought in the District Court for the Eastern District of Pennsylvania. Federal jurisdiction is based on diversity of citizenship. Consequently, the conflict of laws rules of the forum, Pennsylvania, are invoked to solve the choice of law problem. Klaxon Co. v. Stentor Electric Mfg. Co., 1941, 313 U.S. 487, 61 S.Ct. 1020, 85 L.Ed. 1477. This involves no difficulty since familiar conflict of laws doctrine accepted generally and in Pennsylvania tells us that legal excuse for the non-performance or avoidance of a contract is to be determined in accordance with the law of the place of performance. Restatement, Conflict of Laws, Pa.Annot. § 358 (1936). Beyond this, the parties agree, and correctly so, that Pennsylvania is the place of performance in this case. Therefore, we apply the substantive law of Pennsylvania, particularly the Uniform Sales Act, to determine the legal consequences of the operative facts.

Uncontested findings of fact show that the contract in question was the last of a series of agreements, several of them installment contracts, entered into by the parties between June and October, 1947. Under these contracts, numerous shipments of lead were made by the seller in Canada to the buyer in Philadelphia. The seller frequently complained, and with justification, that payments were too long delayed. On the other hand, several shipments were not made at the times required by the contracts. However, by the end of March 1948, all contracts other than the one in suit had been fully performed by both parties. In this connection, it was the unchallenged finding of the district court that both parties waived the delays which preceded the buyer's breach involved in this suit. The earlier delays are relevant only insofar as they may reasonably have influenced either party in its interpretation of subsequent conduct of the other party.

The contract in suit was executed October 23, 1947 and called for deliveries aggregating 200 tons of battery lead to be completed not later than

December 25, 1947. The agreed price was 8.1 cents per pound, or better if quality warranted. The court found that it was the understanding of the parties that at least 63 percent of the price should be paid shortly after each shipment was delivered and the balance within four weeks after that delivery. This finding is not contested.

Under this contract a first carload was delivered November 7, 1947. About 75 percent of the price was paid six days later. A second carload was received January 8, and about 75 percent of the price was paid 10 days later. Final adjustments and payments of small balances due on these two carloads were completed March 30, and these shipments are not now in dispute. The earliest shipment immediately involved in this litigation, the third under the contract, was a carload of lead received by the buyer on March 23, 1948. This delivery followed a March 12 conference of the parties. They disagree on what transpired at that conference. However, about 290,000 pounds of lead were then still to be delivered under the contract which stated December 25, 1947 as the agreed time for the completion of performance. And shortly after the conference, one carload of 43,000 pounds was delivered. No part of the price of this third carload has been paid. It is not disputed that plaintiff is entitled to the price of this shipment and his recovery on his claim in this suit vindicates that right.

On April 7, the buyer, who had been prodding the seller for more lead for some time, notified the seller that unless the balance of the lead should be delivered within thirty days he would buy in the open market and charge the seller any cost in excess of 8.1 cents per pound. On April 10, the seller replied refusing to ship unless the recently delivered third carload should be paid for. On May 12, buyer's attorney threatened suit unless the undelivered lead should be shipped promptly and at the same time promised to pay on delivery 75 percent of the price of this prospective shipment together with the full price of the third installment already received. Seller's solicitor replied on May 22 that seller regarded the contract as "cancelled" as a result of buyer's failure to pay for lead already delivered. At the same time the letter stated the seller's willingness to deliver at the originally agreed price if the overdue payment should be made by return mail and a letter of credit established to cover the price of the lead not yet shipped. Buyer's attorney replied on May 25 that buyer had withheld the price of the third carload "only as a set-off by reason of the failure of your client to deliver" and that buyer would place the overdue payment in escrow and would accept the remaining lead if shipped to Philadelphia "sight draft attached for the full invoice price of each car". On May 27, seller's solicitors reiterated the position stated in their March 22 letter and on June 2 seller notified buyer that the Canadian government had imposed export control on lead. The district court found, and it is here admitted, that between October 1947 and May 1948 the market price of battery lead increased from 8.1 cents to 11½ cents per pound.

The court concluded that the failure of defendant to make a down payment of at least 63 percent of the price of the third carload constituted a breach of contract but "not such a material breach of the contract as to justify plaintiff in refusing to ship the balance due under the contract within the meaning of section 45 of The Sales Act". This was the decisive conclusion of law which the seller has challenged.

Section 45 of the Sales Act as in force in Pennsylvania provides in relevant part as follows: "Where there is a contract to sell goods to be delivered by stated instalments, which are to be separately paid for, and * * * the buyer neglects or refuses to * * * pay for one or more instalments, it depends in each case on the terms of the contract, and the circumstances of the case, whether the breach of contract is so material as to justify the injured party in refusing to proceed further * * * or whether the breach is severable, giving rise to a claim for compensation, but not to a right to treat the whole contract as broken." Pa.Stat.Ann. Tit. 69, § 255 (Purdon, 1931).

We are dealing, therefore, with a situation in which the controlling statute explicitly makes the circumstances of the particular case determine whether failure to pay the price of one shipment delivered under an installment contract justifies the seller in treating his own obligation with reference to future installments as ended. Our problem is how to determine the legal effect of non-payment in a particular case.

We think the key is to be found in the rational basis of the statute itself. The flexibility of the statute reflects the impossibility of generalization about the consequences of failure to pay promptly for installments as delivered. Yet, the commercial sense of the statute yields two guiding considerations. First, nonpayment for a delivered shipment may make it impossible or unreasonably burdensome from a financial point of view for the seller to supply future installments as promised. Second, buyer's breach of his promise to pay for one installment may create such reasonable apprehension in the seller's mind concerning payment for future installments that the seller should not be required to take the risk involved in continuing deliveries. If any such consequence is proved, the seller may rescind. Moreover, the Pennsylvania decisions indicate that these embarrassments and apprehensions are normal consequences of non-payment; but the cases also make it clear that they are not necessary consequences. American Tube & Stamping Co. v. Erie Iron & Steel Co., 1924, 281 Pa. 10, 125 A. 304; G.B. Hurt, Inc., v. Fuller Canneries Co., 1920, 269 Pa. 85, 112 A. 148; Cf., Helgar Corp. v. Warner's Features, Inc., 1918, 222 N.Y. 449, 119 N.E. 113.

In this case there is no evidence that the delay in payment for one carload made it difficult to provide additional lead. To the contrary, seller admits that throughout the period in controversy he had sufficient lead on hand for the full performance of this contract. He could have delivered had he chosen to do so. His excuse, if any, must be found in reasonable apprehension as to the future of the contract engendered by buyer's behavior.

The district court's finding number 16, with which seller takes issue, is a direct negation of the claim of reasonable apprehension upon which seller seeks to establish under Section 45 of the Sales Act his asserted "right to treat the whole contract as broken." It reads as follows: Plaintiff's claim of fear that the defendant would not pay for the balance of battery lead due under Contract No. 5794 at the contract price was without foundation and unreasonable."

In considering the propriety of this finding, it is to be borne in mind that the point here is not the absence of legal justification for the withholding of an overdue payment but rather whether, under the circumstances, that withholding gave the seller reason to believe that there was likelihood of continuing or additional default when and after he should deliver the rest of the lead in accordance with his promise. The substantiality of this alleged apprehension must be judged in the light of the uncontroverted finding that no impairment of buyer's credit had been shown. Moreover, the market was rising and all of the evidence indicates that buyer needed and urgently requested the undelivered lead. Indeed, as early as March 1, before the delivery of the carload for which payment was withheld, the buyer had complained quite urgently of the non-delivery of the entire balance of some 290,000 pounds overdue since December. Thereafter, when the seller shipped 43,000 pounds, about one-seventh of what was due, the buyer insisted that he was withholding payment because of the delay in delivery of the overdue balance. The court's finding that buyer had waived any claim for damages for delay up to that time does not alter this factual picture or its rational implications. In these circumstances, the trial court was justified in concluding that buyer's explanation of his conduct merited belief and that seller had no valid reason to be fearful that payment would not be forthcoming upon full delivery.

The clincher here is provided by the additional evidence concerning the possibility of delivery with sight draft attached. While there is no specific finding on the point, the evidence, including testimony tendered on behalf of seller, shows without dispute that at the beginning of this series of contracts, the seller had the privilege of shipping on sight draft but elected not to do so. And just before the collapse of the efforts of the parties to work out their difficulties amicably, the buyer specifically proposed that the seller assure himself of prompt payment by the use of sight drafts accompanying shipments. It is again important that at this time the market was substantially higher than the contract price and that seller was advised of buyer's urgent need for lead to meet his own commitments. In such circumstances it is incredible that the buyer would refuse to honor sight drafts for the contract price. These facts considered together leave no basis for reasonable apprehension concerning payment.

There is one other relevant and important fact. Throughout the controversial period the seller, with a stock of lead on hand adequate for the full performance of this contract, was using this lead in a rising market for sales to other purchasers at prices higher than agreed in the present contract. The inference was not only allowable but almost inescapable that desire to avoid a bad bargain rather than apprehension that the buyer would not carry out that bargain caused the seller to renounce the agreement and charge the buyer with repudiation. Rescission for such cause is not permissible. See Truitt v. Guenther Lumber Co., 1920, 73 Pa.Super. 445, 450.

It follows that the seller has failed to establish justification for recision under Section 45 of the Sales Act and that judgment for the buyer on the counterclaim was proper.

The judgment will be affirmed.

Notes

1. How should Plotnick be analyzed and decided under the UCC? See Cassidy Podell Lynch, Inc. v. Snyder General Corp., 944 F.2d 1131 (3d Cir.1991),

holding that buyer's failure to pay one installment did not alone justify cancellation and that concerns over future payments should be resolved through a demand for adequate assurance under UCC 2–609(1).

2. As a law professor, Ellen A. Peters was highly critical of UCC 2–612, especially as it applied to the buyer's remedies upon breach by an installment seller. She called it a "law professor's delight" in that it required "wandering through a maze of inconsistent statutory standards and elliptical cross references." Peters, *Remedies for Breach of Contracts Relating to the Sale of Goods Under the Uniform Commercial Code: A Roadmap for Article Two,* 73 Yale L.J. 199, 223–27 (1963). As a Justice on the Supreme Court of Connecticut, she had an opportunity to apply UCC 2–612(3) to a default by the buyer in payment.

In Cherwell-Ralli, Inc. v. Rytman Grain Co., Inc., 180 Conn. 714, 433 A.2d 984 (1980), the buyer fell behind in payment for nineteen accepted shipments under an oral installment contract with the seller. Nevertheless, the buyer demanded adequate assurance of due performance, based upon a concern that the seller would close its plant due to product shortages. The seller gave adequate assurances, stating that deliveries would continue if the buyer paid his account. The buyer issued a check for some of the arrearage but then, because of renewed but unfounded concerns about the seller's capacity to perform, stopped payment. The parties reached an impasse in discussions over payment and performance and, ultimately, the seller closed its plant because it could not deliver the goods and cancelled the contract. The seller sued for the price of goods accepted and the buyer counterclaimed for damages caused by the seller's failure to deliver the balance of the installments.

The Supreme Court affirmed the trial court's decision that the buyer, not the seller, had breached the contract. The court, speaking through Justice Peters, reached the following conclusions: (1) On the facts, the improper order to stop payment of the check coupled with the substantial arrearages in payment was a breach which impaired the value of the "whole" contract under UCC 2–612(3); (2) If the breach is of the "whole," the seller may cancel the contract without invoking the adequate assurance provisions of UCC 2–609; (3) The seller did not reinstate the contract by bringing suit to recover the price of past installments: UCC 2–612(3) does not apply where the seller has cancelled and sued for past installments due; (4) The trial court was correct in concluding that the buyer had no "reasonable grounds for insecurity," either before or after the check was issued; and (5) Implicitly, the seller could cancel the contract even though the breach related to payments due after delivery and the buyer did not repudiate its obligation to make future payments.

Note: Cancellation as a Remedy for Breach

As you have seen, the Code gives the seller a number of useful, if not risky, "self-help" remedies. Under UCC 2–609, the seller, if he satisfies the requisite conditions and procedures, may "suspend any performance for which he has not already received the agreed exchange." If the buyer is discovered to be insolvent, the seller may "refuse delivery except for cash * * * and stop delivery under this Article * * *." UCC 2–702(1). Similarly, the seller, under UCC 2–703, may withhold delivery or stop delivery by any bailee of goods "directly affected" by the buyer's breach. These remedies protect the unperformed balance of the seller's obligation but are not inconsistent with the ultimate completion by both parties of the exchange. The disruption may be adjusted and the contract performed.

The remedy of cancellation, however, is more drastic. UCC 2–703(f). Cancellation occurs "when either party puts an end to the contract for breach by the other." UCC 2–106(4). Cf. UCC 2–309 and 2–106(3) (termination occurs when either party "pursuant to a power created by agreement or law puts an end to the contract otherwise than for its breach"). How does an aggrieved party "cancel" a contract? The Code prescribes no procedure and requires no notice to the other party. Thus, if the seller determines that the buyer has breached, decides to cancel rather than to suspend performance or negotiate and takes action inconsistent with continued performance, e.g., resells identified goods, the cancellation is effective. See Mott Equity Elevator v. Svihovec, 236 N.W.2d 900 (N.D.1975). The effect of a cancellation is that the seller "retains any remedy for breach of the whole contract or any unperformed balance." UCC 2–106(4). But see UCC 1–107, where "any claim or right arising out of an alleged breach can be discharged in whole or in part without consideration by a written waiver or renunciation signed and delivered by the aggrieved party." Presumably, a written cancellation without more would not be a renunciation under UCC 1–107. See Goldstein v. Stainless Processing Co., 465 F.2d 392 (7th Cir.1972).

Even if the cancellation is effective, such drastic action must be justified under UCC 2–703. UCC 2–612 imposes one important limitation in installment contracts. And even if the buyer has repudiated, it must be with respect to "a performance not yet due the loss of which will substantially impair the value of the contract to the other. * * * " UCC 2–610. This question figures prominently in the cases. See, e.g., Pillsbury Co. v. Ward, 250 N.W.2d 35 (Iowa 1977) (buyer's unilateral extension of delivery date in rising soybean market substantially impaired the value of the contract to the seller).

Efficient though it may be, there are some limitations upon the remedy of "self help." In Kelly v. Miller, 575 P.2d 1221 (Alaska 1978), the seller, after the buyer had failed to pay the price due on goods delivered, moved in and "repossessed" them. The court, in a dispassionate opinion, found that "in repossessing the tractor without judicial process * * * " the seller had "fashioned his own remedy." Frontier ingenuity notwithstanding, no security interest had been retained under Article 9, there was no right to reclamation under UCC 2–702 and the seller was not entitled to replevin. The consequences? The seller's "failure to seek the remedy provided him under [UCC 2–709] combined with his resort to a remedy not recognized, so far as we have discovered, at either law or equity, precludes him from recovering damages for any loss he may have suffered as a result of [the] breach of contract."

Yet the seller still has the goods! What recourse, if any, is available to the buyer? Cf. UCC 9–507(2).

SECTION 3. SELLER'S ACTION FOR THE PRICE

Read UCC 2–709. Note that when the buyer "fails to pay the price as it becomes due the seller may recover * * * the price (a) of goods accepted. * * * " When goods are accepted is determined under UCC 2–606. See, e.g., Swift & Co. v. Rexton, Inc., 187 Conn. 540, 447 A.2d 9 (1982) (acceptance inferred from buyer's conduct). This is a neat, clean and efficient remedy. The seller gets cash for the goods without the loss of any business volume and the buyer assumes the burden of taking over and disposing of the goods. It is, loosely speaking, like specific performance, although the seller must ultimately proceed in rem, i.e., against the buyer's property. See Schumann

v. Levi, 728 F.2d 1141 (8th Cir.1984) (equitable remedy of specific performance and Code's action for the price are "virtually identical").

If, however, the buyer has breached before accepting the goods or incurring the risk of loss, the seller is entitled to recover the price only "if the seller is unable after reasonable effort to resell them at a reasonable price or the circumstances reasonably indicate that such an effort will be unavailing." UCC 2–709(1)(b). Why should the seller have the burdens of possession and disposition? According to Professor Llewellyn:

> * * * But then decently admeasured damages are all a seller needs, and are just what a seller needs, when the mercantile buyer repudiates. It is, indeed, social wisdom * * * (to require the seller) in most cases which have not involved shipment to a distant point, to dispose of whatever goods may have come into existence or into his warehouse; that is its business, and the buyer's prospective inability has already been evidenced. To force such goods on the buyer, where they are reasonably marketable by the seller, is social waste. * * *

Llewellyn, Through Title to Contract and A Bit Beyond, 25 N.Y.U.L.Q.Rev. 158, 176–177 (1938).

Problem 14–4

Simpka v. Volta: A Continuing Drama

BASIC FACTS:

Simpka manufactured office equipment and has its principal place of business in Ohio. Simpka sells in a 10–state market in the Northeast. The market is competitive and favors low cost and durability rather than style. Volta, a stock broker in New York City, is building a new building to house its expanding operations. It will require a wide assortment of office equipment, both standard and specially manufactured. After defining its needs, Volta negotiated with a number of office equipment firms, including Simpka. Volta decided in favor of Simpka and, on May 1, contracted for the following:

> The order is for for two lots: (1) Standard items; 200 desks, 200 chairs, 400 regular chairs, for $120,000, and (2) Custom furniture made to Volta's specifications; 20 desks, 20 desk chairs, 20 tables and 20 easy chairs, for $80,000. Standard goods are to be shipped "fob Ohio" in four equal installments on June 1, July 1, September 1 and October 1. Custom goods are to be shipped in one installment not later than November 1. Payment is due for each installment within 30 days of delivery to the carrier.

Simpka v. Volta: Scene 1

Assume it is now December 1. Volta has accepted all four shipments of standard furniture and has paid for two. Volta has refused to purchase the custom furniture, which Simpka had already manufactured and identified to the contract. Simpka informs you that it could resell the custom furniture in the 10 state market for $40,000 and that it was at least possible that a higher price, not more than $50,000, could be obtained farther West. Simpka, angry at Volta, would like to hold the completed furniture and recover the $80,000 price. Simpka, however, will not pursue this remedy unless you give him an opinion that the odds are at least even that he will win the law suit. A Summer Associate has given you the extract, below, from Foxco Indus., Ltd. v. Fabric

World, Inc., 595 F.2d 976, 983–84 (5th Cir.1979). Will you give Simpka such an opinion?

"UCC § 2–709(1)(b), that portion of § 2–709 which would apply here, provides that an action for the price of goods may be maintained "if the seller is unable after *reasonable* effort to resell them at a *reasonable* price or the circumstances *reasonably* indicate that such effort will be unavailing." Ala.Code tit. 7, § 2–709(1)(b) (1977) (emphasis added). The Official Comment to § 2–709 states, in pertinent part, that:

"2. The action for the price is now generally limited to those cases where resale of the goods is impracticable * * *

"3. This section substitutes an objective test by action for the former 'not readily resalable' standard. An action for the price under subsection (1)(b) can be sustained only after a 'reasonable effort to resell' the goods 'at reasonable price' has actually been made or where the circumstances 'reasonably indicate' that such an effort will be unavailing."

Ala.Code tit. 7, § 7–2–709, Official Comment (1977). As was recognized in Multi-Line Manufacturing, Inc. v. Greenwood Mills, Inc., 123 Ga.App. 372, 180 S.E.2d 917 (1971), a case involving the cancellation of a contract to purchase fabric, the language of § 2–709(1)(b) "clearly evinces legislative intent that these matters ordinarily should be subject to determination by a jury * * * " Id. at 373, 180 S.E.2d at 918. Thus, we will reverse only if, as a matter of law, there was no way in which the jury could find that Foxco was unable, after reasonable effort, to resell the fabric at a reasonable price or that it was reasonably clear that an effort to resell would have been fruitless.

"The evidence at trial clearly established that all of Foxco's goods were specially manufactured for the customer who ordered them and that it was difficult for Foxco to resell fabric manufactured for one purchaser to another buyer. Further, it was normally very difficult to sell Foxco's spring fabric after the spring buying season had ended; the precipitous decline of the knitted fabric market presented an additional barrier to resale. It was not until the next spring buying season returned that Foxco, in September 1975, finally sold a portion of the goods identified to Fabric World's October 1974 order.

"Fabric World argues that Foxco made no effort whatsoever to resell the goods during the months that intervened (between the contract breach and Foxco's eventual disposition of the fabric in September 1975) despite the presence of some market for the goods in that interim period. Thus Fabric World concludes, the requisites of § 2–709(1)(b) were not satisfied. Under § 2–709(1)(b), however, Foxco was required only to use *reasonable* efforts to resell its goods at a *reasonable* price. From the time of Fabric World's breach to September 1975 there was a 50% decline in the market price of this material. We cannot say that the jury was precluded from finding that Foxco acted reasonably under the circumstances or that there was no reasonable price at which Foxco could sell these goods. Fabric World breached its contract with Foxco, and the jury was entitled to a charge which gave Foxco the full benefit of its original bargain. * * * "

Simpka v. Volta: Scene 2

Suppose that on June 1 Simpka had tendered and Volta had accepted all of the standard items. Volta paid $30,000 on July 1. If Volta fails to pay on August 1, what is Simpka's remedy? Suppose Volta failed to pay and repudiated the contract on September 1. Could Simpka cancel the contract, accelerate the obligation and sue for the price of all goods accepted? See UCC 2–610(b) and 2–709(1).

SECTION 4. SELLER'S RIGHT TO "CONTRACT-MARKET" DAMAGES

If the seller is not entitled to the price under UCC 2–709, what other remedies are available?

One option is to resell the goods under UCC 2–706, whether they were identified to the contract before or after the buyer's breach. See UCC 2–703(c) & 2–704. When the conditions established in UCC 2–706 are satisfied, the seller may recover the "difference between the resale price and the contract price together with any incidental damages * * * but less expenses saved in consequence of the buyer's breach." UCC 2–706(1).

Another option, whether the goods have been resold or not, is to seek damages for "non-acceptance or repudiation" under UCC 2–708. See UCC 2–703. But the measures of damages under UCC 2–708 are strikingly different: Subsection (1), an objective standard, measures loss by the difference between the market price and the contract price while Subsection (2), a subjective standard, allows recovery of the "profit (including reasonable overhead) which the seller would have made from full performance by the buyer. * * * " on the particular contract in dispute.

These options pose two important questions: (1) What limitations, if any, are imposed upon a seller's decision to pursue a particular remedy; and (2) Once a proper remedy has been selected, how are damages to be measured?

Consider, first, UCC 2–708(1). The contract price-market price measure can be fraught with inappropriateness and difficulty. Further, it may either over-or under-compensate the seller. Should it be repealed? Should it be explicitly limited by the "expectation" compensation policy expressed in UCC § 1–106(1)?

Problem 14–5

Simpka v. Volta: Scene 3

Back to Simpka-Volta. Assume that the contract was for only the standard items and the deal was signed on March 1. The price and delivery schedule are unchanged. Volta repudiated on April 3.

A. On April 5, Simpka accepted Volta's repudiation, cancelled the contract and sued for damages under UCC 2–708(1). See UCC 2–610(b). The case came to trial in the next year and the following evidence was introduced: (1) The aggregate market price on April 5 in Ohio of the four lots was $110,000; (2) Also in Ohio, the market value of the June 1 installment was $24,000, the July 1 installment was $27,000, the September installment was $30,000 and the October installment was $29,000; (3) In New York, the prices are the same except for the October lot, which was $24,000.

Assuming that Simpka has not resold the goods, to what damages is Simpka entitled under UCC 2–708(1)? On the time and place for tender, see UCC 2–503.

B. Assume that, on April 3, Simpka decided to wait to see whether Volta would retract the repudiation. UCC 2–611. Simpka waits until July 15, then cancels the contract and sues for damages under UCC 2–708(1). If Simpka does not resell, will its damages be the same as in A, above?

C. What if Simpka had resold on April 5 for $100,000? Is Simpka bound by this decision? See UCC 2–706. If the UCC 2–708(1) measure was more than $20,000, could Simpka pursue that remedy? See the next case.

TRANS WORLD METALS, INC. v. SOUTHWIRE CO.

United States Court of Appeals, Second Circuit, 1985.
769 F.2d 902.

[In April, 1981 the parties entered into a contract for the sale of 12,000 metric tons of primary aluminum, to be delivered in monthly installments of 1,000 metric tons from January through December, 1982. The contract price was $.77 per pound, or a total price of $20.4 million. Seller shipped 750 metric tons in January, 1982 and the balance of the first installment in early February. Between April, 1981 and March, 1982, the market price of aluminum dropped "dramatically." On March 4, 1982, Buyer, without discussing the late first installment or issuing additional delivery instructions, cancelled the contract because of Seller's default. In Seller's suit for damages, the jury concluded that Buyer had accepted all deliveries and even if late, there was no substantial impairment of the value of either the first installment or the whole contract. Thus, buyer had repudiated the contract. This conclusion was affirmed on appeal.

The jury awarded Seller damages of $7,122,141.84, consisting of $6,702,-529 for Buyer's repudiation of the balance of the contract and $419,232.84 for the installment accepted. The district court added prejudgment interest of $1,304,804.88 and entered a judgment for $8,426,946.72. The propriety of this damage award under the UCC was attacked on appeal.]

NEWMAN, J.

* * *

II.

Southwire complains that the damage award, calculated by the difference between contract and market prices, gave Trans World an unwarranted windfall. Southwire favors an alternative measure of damages based on the rate of profit earned by Trans World on the first month's completed shipments projected over the twelve-month life of the contract. Such a measure, Southwire argues, would better estimate the amount Trans World would have made had the contract been completed. We reject this alternative as contrary to the Uniform Commercial Code.

Seller's damages for repudiation are governed by section 2–708 of the Uniform Commercial Code. Subsection 1 of this section sets forth the general rule that damages are to be calculated by the difference between the contract and market prices:

(1) Subject to subsection (2) and to the provisions of this Article with respect to proof of market price (Section 2–723), the measure of damages for non-acceptance or repudiation by the buyer is the difference between the market price at the time and place for tender and the unpaid contract price together with any incidental damages provided in this Article (Section 2–710), but less expenses saved in consequence of the buyer's breach.

N.Y.U.C.C. Law § 2–708(1). The drafters of the Uniform Commercial Code recognized that this measure would not adequately compensate certain types of sellers, generally referred to as "lost volume sellers." *See* J. White & R. Summers, Uniform Commercial Code § 7–9, at 274–76 (2d ed. 1980) ("White & Summers"). Therefore, an alternative measure of damages was provided for those sellers who would be *inadequately* compensated by the standard contract/market price differential:

(2) If the measure of damages provided in subsection (1) is inadequate to put the seller in as good a position as performance would have done then the measure of damages is the profit (including reasonable overhead) which the seller would have made from full performance by the buyer, together with any incidental damages provided in this Article (Section 2–710), due allowance for costs reasonably incurred and due credit for payments or proceeds of resale.

N.Y.U.C.C. Law § 2–708(2). This measure of damages is often preferred by sellers who have not acquired the goods to be sold prior to the buyer's repudiation because such sellers often would be undercompensated by the contract/market price measure of damages.[3]

Southwire argues that the "lost profits" measure should also apply when the seller would be *overcompensated* by section 2–708(1). We disagree. We do not doubt that the contract/market price differential "will seldom be the same as the seller's actual economic loss from breach." White & Summers § 7–7, at 269; *see* Peters, *Remedies for Breach of Contracts Relating to the Sale of Goods Under the Uniform Commercial Code: A Roadmap for Article Two,* 73 Yale L.J. 199, 259 (1963). However, nothing in the language or history of section 2–708(2) suggests that it was intended to apply to cases in which section 2–708(1) might overcompensate the seller. *See* White & Summers § 7–12, at 283. Nor has Southwire cited any New York case that interprets section 2–708(2) as Southwire urges us to interpret it. As a federal court sitting in diversity, we will not extend the application of this state law.

3. Professors White and Summers refer to such sellers as "jobbers."

> By "jobber" we refer to a seller who satisfies two conditions. First, he is a seller who never acquires the contract goods. Second, his decision not to acquire those goods after learning of the breach is commercially reasonable under 2–704. * * * Since he has no goods on hand to resell, he cannot even resell on the market at the time of tender and so recoup the amount necessary to make him whole by adding such proceeds to his 2–708(1) recovery. Thus the only recovery which grossly approximates the "jobber's" economic loss is a recovery based on lost profits.

White & Summers § 7–10, at 278. In a case involving a commodity like aluminum that fluctuates rapidly in price—as compared to standard-priced goods like cars, *see* 67 Am. Jur.2d *Sales* § 1129—the lost profits of a selling jobber may well be adequately reflected by the contract/market price differential.

Nor are we convinced that Trans World has been overcompensated. No measure other than the contract/market price differential will award Trans World the "benefit of its bargain," that is, the "amount necessary to put [it] in as good a position as [it] would have been if the defendant had abided by the contract." *Western Geophysical Co. of America, Inc. v. Bolt Associates, Inc.,* 584 F.2d 1164, 1172 (2d Cir.1978) (quoting *Perma Research & Development Co. v. Singer Co.,* 402 F.Supp. 881, 898 (S.D.N.Y.1975), *aff'd,* 542 F.2d 111 (2d Cir.), *cert. denied,* 429 U.S. 987, 97 S.Ct. 507, 50 L.Ed.2d 598 (1976)). The contract at issue in this case is an aluminum supply contract entered into eight months prior to the initial deliveries called for by its terms. The last of the anticipated deliveries of aluminum would not have been completed until a full twenty months after the negotiations took place. It simply could not have escaped these parties that they were betting on which way aluminum prices would move. Trans World took the risk that the price would rise; Southwire took the risk that the price would fall. Under these circumstances, Trans World should not be denied the benefit of its bargain, as reflected by the contract/market price differential.[4] *Cf. Apex Oil Co. v. Vanguard Oil & Service Co.,* 760 F.2d 417 (2d Cir.1985) (defaulting seller obliged to pay damages based on contract/market price differential).

The decision primarily relied upon by Southwire is distinguishable from this case. *Nobs Chemical, U.S.A., Inc. v. Koppers Co., Inc.,* 616 F.2d 212 (5th Cir.1980), involved a seller acting as a middleman. The seller in Nobs had entered into a second fixed-price contract with its own supplier for purchase of the goods to be sold under the contract sued upon; its "market price" thus had been fixed in advance by contract. Because the seller had contractually protected itself against market price fluctuation, the Fifth Circuit concluded that it would have been unfair to permit the seller to reap a riskless benefit. As that Court noted, "the difference between the fallen market price and the contract price is [not] necessary to compensate the plaintiffs for the breach. Had the transaction been completed, their 'benefit of the bargain' would not have been affected by the fall in the market price. * * * " *Id.* at 215. Whether or not we would have reached the same result in *Nobs,* here the benefit of the bargain under a completed contract would have been affected by the fall in aluminum prices.[5] Because Trans World accepted the risk that prices would rise, it is entitled to benefit from their fall.

III.

Southwire raises a number of further points on appeal. The first involves the proper determination of the market price for purposes of calculating the contract/market price differential. The jury relied upon Trans World's damage calculations, which were based on the market price as reflected by bids received on April 26 (and projections discussed below).

4. Southwire presented no evidence and made no claim concerning any expenses saved by Trans World as a result of Southwire's breach. Such expenses, if established, would have reduced the recoverable damages. N.Y.U.C.C. Law § 2–708(1); *see Katz Communications, Inc. v. The Evening News Association,* 705 F.2d 20, 26–27 (2d Cir.1983).

5. Although Trans World had available to it about 78,000 tons of aluminum at the time of the breach, Trans World had corresponding obligations to deliver about 76,000 tons of aluminum to buyers other than Southwire. Absent any indication that Trans World had "identified" any of this metal to the Southwire contract, *see* N.Y.U.C.C. Law § 2–501(b), we cannot say, as could the court in *Nobs,* that a change in the market price would not affect the seller's "benefit of the bargain."

Southwire argues that because the contract was repudiated on March 4, the market price figure used to calculate damages should be the March 4 price. We do not agree. The measure of damages set forth in section 2–708(1) is "the difference between the market price *at the time and place for tender* and the unpaid contract price." N.Y.U.C.C. Law § 2–708(1) (emphasis added); *cf. id.* § 2–713(1) (*buyer's* damages for repudiation by *seller* measured by contract/market price differential "at the time when the buyer learned of the breach"). Thus, the pertinent market price date is not the date of repudiation but the date for tender.

We would accept Southwire's argument that the date Trans World learned of the repudiation would be the correct date on which to calculate the market price had this action been tried *before* the time for full performance under the contract. *See* N.Y.U.C.C. § 2–723(1) (market price at time aggrieved party learned of repudiation used to calculate damages in action for anticipatory repudiation that "comes to trial before time for performance with respect to some or all of the goods"). However, where damages are awarded *after* the time for full performance, as in this case, the calculation of damages under section 2–708(1) should reflect the actual market price at each successive date when tender was to have been made under the repudiated installment contract. This was the rule prior to enactment of the Uniform Commercial Code. *United States v. Burton Coal Co.,* 273 U.S. 337, 340, 47 S.Ct. 351, 352, 71 L.Ed. 670 (1927) (following repudiation of supply contract, "seller may recover the difference between the contract price and the market value at the times when and the places where deliveries should have been made"); *L.W. Foster Sportswear Co. v. Goldblatt Brothers, Inc.,* 356 F.2d 906, 910 & n. 6 (7th Cir.1966) (recognizing same standard under pre-U.C.C. law and U.C.C. § 2–708); *see* 67A Am.Jur.2d *Sales* § 1115, at 505 n. 19 (2d ed. 1985); *id.* § 1118, at 510 n. 50. New York did not intend to deviate from this measure of damages upon adoption of the Uniform Commercial Code: The Official Comment to section 2–708 indicates that the "prior uniform statutory provision is followed generally in setting the current market price at the time and place for tender as the standard by which damages for non-acceptance are to be determined." N.Y.U.C.C. Law § 2–708 Official Comment 1. The "prior uniform statutory provision" indicated that where " 'there is an available market for the goods * * * [damages should be measured by] the difference between the contract price and the market or current price * * * when the goods ought to have been accepted, or, if no time was fixed for acceptance, then at the time of the refusal to accept.' " *Id.* § 2–708 Practice Commentary (quoting Sales Act § 64 (McKinney's Personal Property Law § 145)).

We therefore conclude that when calculating damages for a buyer's repudiation of an installment contract by the contract/market price differential, "time * * * for tender" under section 2–708(1) is the date for each successive tender of an installment, as specified in the contract. *See* 67A Am.Jur.2d *Sales* § 1118, at 510 ("[W]here the breach is of an installment contract, damages should be measured by the market price at the time of each delivery." (footnote omitted)). In this case the successive dates for tender were the last day of each month in 1982, at which time Trans World was authorized to invoice that month's shipments even if such shipments had not been "released" by Southwire's delivery instructions. A contract/market price differential should have been calculated for each month during 1982.

We recognize that the jury relied upon a damage calculation prepared for Trans World that did not use actual market prices for each month of scheduled tenders. Instead, Trans World's expert took the actual price for April 1982 and projected forward from that date "anticipated" increases of $15 per metric ton for each month thereafter. Though the use of such an estimate was inappropriate because the actual market price for each successive month was known by the date of the trial, Southwire has no basis for complaint. Trans World's projected monthly market prices were closer to the contract price than were the actual market prices. Trans World therefore received less in damages using its expert's projection than it would have received using the correct measure. Furthermore, Southwire did not preserve at trial the factual issue as to the correct market price on each successive date of tender. Southwire did not object to Trans World's use or the accuracy of projected prices nor otherwise raise the issue with the jury, relying instead on its unsuccessful effort to convince the jurors that the contract/market price differential was not an appropriate method for calculating damages. Having failed to preserve the point for appeal, Southwire may not now raise the issue for the first time. *See, e.g., Schmidt v. Polish People's Republic,* 742 F.2d 67, 70 (2d Cir.1984).

* * *

We have considered Southwire's remaining claims and find them to lack merit. The judgment of the District Court is affirmed.

Notes

1. Given the remedial objectives of UCC 1–106(1) and the general duty of good faith in the "enforcement" of the contract, UCC 1–203, was the seller overcompensated under UCC 2–708(1)? Retrace the statutory steps to the seller's victory: UCC 2–610(b), 2–703(e), 2–708(2) (rejected by the court), and 2–708(1). Relying on *Nobs Chemical,* which was distinguished in the principal case, the court in Union Carbide Corporation v. Consumers Power Co., 636 F.Supp. 1498 (E.D.Mich.1986), held that a seller who was a middleman and who did not, under the pricing arrangement, bear the risk of fluctuations in the market price, could not use UCC 2–708(1) when that measure resulted in overcompensation. The court interpreted the word "inadequate" in UCC 2–708(2) to mean "incapable or inadequate to accomplish the stated purpose of the UCC remedies of compensating the aggrieved person but not overcompensating that person or specifically punishing the other person." In short, where the measure of damages in UCC 2–708(1) fails fairly to measure the damages suffered by the plaintiff, that formula is "inadequate" and, to avoid a penalty, UCC 2–708(2) should be applied. *Nobs Chemical* and its progeny are criticised in Scott, supra at 640 at 1168–69, 1175–79. He argues that if the parties knew *ex ante* contract that UCC 2–708(2) rather than UCC 2–708(1) would be applied, there would be a different price for the goods.

2. In *Trans World Metals* the case came to trial *after* the time for performance had passed. Thus, UCC 2–723(1), which measures damages at the time when the seller "learns of the repudiation," did not apply. As such, the court felt free to measure market damages at the "time and place for tender," UCC 2–708(1), even though that time was significantly after Seller learned of the breach.

Is there any support for the proposition that when the buyer repudiates the seller's damages should be limited to the difference between the contract price for the entire undelivered balance and the market price determined at a commercially reasonable time after the repudiation? See UCC 2–610(a). What are the advantages and disadvantages of adopting such a rule?

Note: Measuring Damages for Breach of Take or Pay Contracts

One of the major indoor sports in the Rocky Mountains and in the southwest has been litigation between gas producers and pipelines over contracts by the latter to purchase natural gas from the former. For reasons described above at p. 628, in almost all of these cases, the pipelines have found their contracts to be uneconomic. The pipelines have lost their long-term buyers yet they remain bound to the sellers. Until recently, pipelines had a further difficulty, namely, the obligation under federal regulation to sell all or almost all of their gas at a fixed price that is computed based upon the aggregate cost of their gas. That meant that pipelines might be obliged to purchase gas at an escalated price under the contract with the producer in a situation where any resale of that gas on the spot market might be below the price at which they could legally sell. In the period from the mid–1980s through the early 1990s, this market has been characterized by repeated attempts on the part of the pipelines to renegotiate their contracts and, where that was not possible, to escape the contracts on various grounds.

Assuming for the purpose of the argument that the purchaser pipeline has broken its contract, that the contract extends indefinitely into the future (possibly for the life of the reservoir), and contains a minimum price of $5 per mcf that escalates at 8 percent per year, how would one compute the damages? Assume, for the sake of argument, that the spot price at the time of breach was $1.30 per mcf and that there was only a sparse long-term market. Assume that the long-term market called for prices based on spot plus a premium of 10 or 15 percent. In that regime how does one compute damages under 2–708(1) and 2–723?

First, for deliveries due before the case comes to trial, the court might apply 2–708(1). On the other hand, a plaintiff might point to 2–723(1). That provides "*any* damage based on market price" should be determined according to the price of the goods prevailing when the aggrieved party learned of the breach, if the case comes to trial before tender with respect to "some or all of the goods." Thus the plaintiff might argue that the plain language of 2–723 calls for the sale of *all* of the gas if any of it would have been delivered after trial. Under that reading of 2–723 one would use the contract market difference at the time of repudiation for all of the transactions, even though several years had passed between the breach and the trial.

Ignoring for the moment any problem associated with deliveries prior to the time of trial, how does one apply section 2–723(1) in our hypothetical case? The court in Manchester Pipeline Co. v. Peoples Natural Gas Co., 862 F.2d 1439 (10th Cir.1988) held that the subtrahend in the formula should be the price in the long-term market, not the spot price. That holding makes sense if there is a long-term market and if it is the market to which the sellers would normally look for substitute sales. As this is written in 1993, there is almost no long-term market. Because of the continued changes in federal regulations and because of the uncertainty engendered by those changes and by the large price swings, few parties are willing to sign long-term contracts.

Could a producer argue that 2–723 calls for a "snapshot" on the date of repudiation and that the proper measure of damage is the difference between the contract price that would have been charged on that date minus the spot market on that date, multiplied by the total units of gas to be sold over the last contract? A greedy producer might even argue for escalation of the minuend (the contract price) while he held the subtrahend (the spot price on that date) constant.

An additional complication has to do with discounting amounts that would be paid in the distant future. Section 2–723 does not mention discount to present value; some might argue that one merely takes the contract market difference on that date, multiplies it by the number of units and awards that amount to the plaintiff as damages. But that amount would overcompensate the plaintiff because much of its profit from a 20 year contract would not have been paid for years. Clearly those amounts should be discounted to present value. Once there is agreement some amount needs to be discounted, there awaits a yet more bitter fight over the proper annual percentage for discounting.

Some plaintiffs in these circumstances have argued for the price under 2–709, but those arguments have been rejected on the ground that the goods are not identified to the contract. A better reason to deny the price is that the gas could be resold—even if identified to this contract. There is always a spot market at some price where a producer can sell its gas. Under FERC rules the pipeline must carry the gas even in competition with its own.

In a few cases plaintiffs have recovered under 2–708(2), but if the plaintiff is a producer it is not a lost volume seller and any recovery under 2–708(2) should be no more than the contract price minus some amount for the proceeds of an actual or eventual resale. Unless the proceeds of resale are subtracted, or the "net profit" is computed some other way, section 2–708(2) will over compensate and will eliminate the seller's incentives to mitigate.

SECTION 5. SELLER'S RIGHT TO RESELL AND "FIX" DAMAGES

In the *Trans World Metals* case, the seller did not have aluminum conforming or identified to the contract on hand at the time of the breach. Suppose, however, that conforming aluminum in sufficient quantities was within the seller's possession or control. See UCC 2–704(1). If an action for the price is not possible, UCC 2–709(1)(b), the seller should consider the remedy of resale under UCC 2–706, a provision which permits the seller to resell and authoritatively fix his damages based upon the difference between the contract price and what is realized from the resale contract. Lost volume problems aside, this recovery normally places the seller in the position he would have occupied if the buyer had fully performed.

Read UCC 2–706 carefully and work the next problem.

Problem 14–6

Simpka v. Volta: Scene Four

In June, Simpka made the first shipment of standard furniture and received a $30,000 payment from Volta. Volta, however, was dissatisfied with the shipment and a dispute over quality simmered over the summer, with Simpka withholding delivery. On September 14, Volta repudiated the entire contract, including the custom furniture. Assume that Volta's repudiation was a total breach of contract. Simpka has three installments of standard furniture, for which Volta agreed to pay $90,000, and the custom furniture, for which Volta agreed to pay $80,000, on hand and identified to the contract. Simpka would like to resell all of that furniture, either in Ohio or New York, and obtain the maximum damages under UCC 2–706. It is now October 1 and you have the following facts before you:

1. The cost of shipping each installment of standard furniture from Ohio to New York is $6,000. The cost of shipping the custom furniture is $10,000.

2. The market price of the custom furniture in Ohio on September 14 was $75,000. It is expected to remain constant for the balance of the year. The market price of the custom furniture in New York on September 14 was $70,000. It is uncertain how that market will perform in the future.

3. The market price of an installment of standard furniture on September 14 was $30,000 in Ohio and $33,000 in New York. On October 1, the respective prices were $27,000 in Ohio and $30,000 in New York. It is estimated that on November 1, the respective prices will be $22,500 in Ohio and $27,000 in New York and that on December 1 the respective prices will be $18,000 in Ohio and $27,000 in New York.

A. Develop a plan to resell all of the furniture that has the best chance to maximize damages and satisfy UCC 2–706.

B. What remedy, if any, is available if the conditions of UCC 2–706 are not satisfied? See Comment 2, UCC 2–706. How should you plan for this contingency? Remember, some courts have held that a seller who acts in bad faith is limited to the damages that should have been recovered under UCC 2–706 if all the conditions had been met. See Note: Seller's Remedial Choices, infra at p. 670.

C. If, upon resale, you satisfy the conditions of UCC 2–706, are you foreclosed from using UCC 2–708(1)? Have you made an election of remedies? See Comment 1, UCC 2–703.

AFRAM EXPORT CORP. v. METALLURGIKI HALYPS, S.A.

United States Court of Appeals, Seventh Circuit, 1985.
772 F.2d 1358.

POSNER, CIRCUIT JUDGE.

The appeal and cross-appeal in this diversity breach of contract suit raise a variety of interesting issues, in particular of personal jurisdiction and contract damages.

Afram Export Corporation, the plaintiff, is a Wisconsin corporation that exports scrap metal. Metallurgiki Halyps, S.A., the defendant, is a Greek corporation that makes steel. In 1979, after a series of trans-Atlantic telephone and telex communications, the parties made a contract through an exchange of telex messages for the purchase by Metallurgiki of 15,000 tons of clean shredded scrap, at $135 per ton, F.O.B. Milwaukee, delivery to be made by the end of April. Metallurgiki apparently intended to use the scrap to make steel for shipment to Egypt, pursuant to a contract with an Egyptian buyer. Afram agreed to pay the expenses of an agent of Metallurgiki—Shields—to inspect the scrap for cleanliness before it was shipped.

The scrap for the contract was prepared, in Milwaukee, by Afram Metal Processing Company. Both Afram Metal Processing and the plaintiff Afram

Export are wholly owned subsidiaries of Afram Brothers. All three are Wisconsin corporations, and have the same officers and directors. Unless otherwise indicated, when we say "Afram" we mean "Afram Export."

Shields arrived to inspect the scrap on April 12. He told Afram that the scrap was clean but that Metallurgiki would not accept it, because the price of scrap had fallen. Sure enough, Metallurgiki refused to accept it. Afram brought this suit after selling the scrap to other buyers. Metallurgiki unsuccessfully challenged the court's jurisdiction over it, then filed a counterclaim alleging that Afram had broken the contract and had thereby made it impossible for Metallurgiki to fulfill its contract with the Egyptian purchaser.

After a bench trial, the district judge gave judgment for Afram for $425,149 and dismissed the counterclaim. 592 F.Supp. 446 (D.Wis.1984). Metallurgiki has appealed from the judgment for Afram, and Afram has cross-appealed, contending that the judge should have given it the full damages it sought based on the difference between the contract price and the cover price—$483,750—plus incidental damages of $40,665, prejudgment interest, the costs of a so-called public sale, and attorney's fees for defending against the counterclaim.

* * *

* * * Afram claims that it sold all of the scrap rejected by Metallurgiki at a public sale on June 15, 1979, and that its damages should therefore be based on the price of that sale, which was $102.75 per ton. The district judge disagreed. He found that two-thirds of the scrap had been sold at a substantially higher price to Luria Brothers on June 4 ($118—actually somewhat less, because Afram defrayed some freight costs) and the other third to International Traders on September 15 at a price of $103. Afram points out that the sale on June 4 actually was made by its affiliate, Afram Metal Processing Company, and further argues that since all Afram scrap is sold from the same pile in Milwaukee it is arbitrary to treat the first sale after the breach of contract as the cover transaction, rather than the sale that Afram designated as that transaction.

We agree with the district judge that the sale on June 4 was a cover transaction, even though the nominal seller was a different corporation from the plaintiff. Not only are both corporations wholly owned subsidiaries of another corporation, not only do all three corporations have the same officers and directors, but the record indicates substantial commingling of assets and operation of the three corporations as a single entity. Shortly after Metallurgiki's rejection, Zeke Afram, an officer of both Afram Export (the party to the contract with Metallurgiki) and Afram Metal Processing (the nominal owner of the scrap sold on June 4), called Luria Brothers and explained that he had extra scrap for sale because of a buyer's breach; apparently he did not bother to indicate which Afram corporation he was calling on behalf of. The June 4 sale followed shortly. The conversation and the timing of the sale are powerful evidence that the breach enabled the sale—that it would not have occurred but for the breach—and hence that the revenue from the sale must be subtracted from the contract price to determine Afram's loss. Cf. *Servbest Foods, Inc. v. Emessee Industries, Inc.*, 82 Ill.App.3d 662, 668–72, 37 Ill.Dec. 945, 951–53, 403 N.E.2d 1, 7–9 (1980).

But this does not dispose completely of the issue of the cover price. If the sale on June 15 was "made in good faith and in a commercially reasonable manner," it fixed Afram's damages on the remaining one-third of the scrap. UCC § 2–706(1), Wis.Stat. § 402.706(1). The question may seem less than earthshaking since the June 15 sale price and the September sale price which the district court used as the cover price for the remaining third were only 25¢ per ton apart. But the bona fides of the June 15 sale casts additional light on the intercorporate relations of the Afram group and hence on the proper interpretation of the sale to Luria Brothers. In any event, the district judge was entitled to find that neither condition in section 2–706(1) was satisfied. Cf. *Coast Trading Co. v. Cudahy Co.,* 592 F.2d 1074, 1080–81 (9th Cir.1979). The June 15 "sale" was about as pure a bookkeeping transaction—as empty of economic significance—as can be imagined. Cf. *Milbrew v. Commissioner of Internal Revenue,* 710 F.2d 1302, 1305 (7th Cir.1983). It consisted of a transfer of the scrap on the books of one affiliated corporation to the books of another. The transferor and transferee were not only under common ownership but were operated as if they were limbs of a single organism. The scrap itself was not moved; it remained on the scrap heap till sold later on. No invoice or check for the sale was produced at trial. The inference that the sale was designed simply to maximize the enterprise's damages, leaving it free to resell the scrap at higher prices later on, is overpowering. The sale of the scrap three months later to International Traders at a (slightly) higher price provided better evidence of what the enterprise actually lost, so far as the scrap not sold to Luria Brothers is concerned, by Metallurgiki's breach of contract.

The next issue relates to incidental damages, which the Uniform Commercial Code allows a seller who is the victim of a breach of contract to recover in addition to the difference between sale price and cover price. UCC § 2–706(1), Wis.Stat. § 402.706(1). Incidental damages are "any commercially reasonable charges, expenses or commissions incurred in stopping delivery, in the transportation, care and custody of goods after buyer's breach, in connection with return or resale of the goods or otherwise resulting from the breach." UCC § 2–710, Wis.Stat. § 402.710. Afram says it borrowed $2.5 million from a bank of which $2.025 million was to finance the purchase of the junked cars that it shredded in order to produce scrap in the form called for by the contract with Metallurgiki. It has calculated the interest (some $40,000) that it paid between the date of breach and the date of cover on the amount of the loan used to finance the cars. But it can recover this interest, if at all, only as incidental damages, and not as consequential damages, for under the Uniform Commercial Code consequential damages are a buyer's not a seller's remedy. See UCC § 2–715, Wis. Stat. § 402.715; *Nobs Chemical, U.S.A., Inc. v. Koppers Co.,* 616 F.2d 212, 216 (5th Cir.1980).

The line between incidental and consequential damages is rather unclear. It may help in locating it to notice that in many cases of consequential damages, a buyer who is the victim of a seller's breach of contract is seeking damages for consequences that he could have avoided or minimized at lower cost than the contract breaker. *EVRA Corp. v. Swiss Bank Corp.,* 673 F.2d 951, 957 (7th Cir.1982). In the case that established the common law's position that consequential damages are not recoverable without special notice to the seller, *Hadley v. Baxendale,* 9 Ex. 341, 156 Eng.Rep. 145 (1854), the defendant, a carrier, broke a contract with the plaintiff to deliver the plaintiff's mill shaft to the manufacturer of the shaft for repair. Because the plaintiff had no spare shaft, it was forced to shut down the mill; and it sought the profits that it lost during the period of shut-down caused by the defendant's delay in delivering the shaft. The court refused to award these damages. They could easily have been avoided by the plaintiff's having a spare shaft, which prudence dictated that a mill owner have anyway. This omission could not fairly be charged to the seller. It was not—as the prerequisite for obtaining consequential damages in a contract case has come to be called, see, e.g., Farnsworth, Contracts § 12.14, at p. 876 (1982)—"foreseeable" by him, because a seller is not charged with foreseeing the buyer's imprudence.

This would be the same case, only in the unusual setting of a seller's seeking consequential damages, if Metallurgiki's breach of contract had precipitated Afram into bankruptcy because Afram was paying back-breaking interest on the loan that it had taken out to enable it to fulfill its obligations under the contract. Afram would be responsible for arranging its affairs in such a way as not to be abnormally vulnerable to a breach of contract; excessive leverage would be the counterpart to Hadley's failure to keep a spare shaft on hand. At the other end of the spectrum, reasonable expenses incurred by Afram in putting the scrap in a form where it would be salable to a substitute buyer would be recoverable as incidental damages; virtually by definition, such expenses could not be avoided by greater prudence on the seller's part.

The actual case is somewhere in the middle, but if we had to decide exactly where, we probably would disagree with the district judge, who regarded this as a case of consequential rather than incidental damages. Although knowledge of the details of the seller's financial arrangements is not chargeable to the buyer, it is obvious to the buyer and unavoidable by the seller that the seller will incur an interest cost (explicit or implicit, as we shall see) in the interval between the breach of the contract and the cover sale; and the party who is better able to avoid this expense and who therefore should bear the risk of its occurrence is the contract-breaking buyer, not the seller. The cases therefore allow the seller to recover the additional interest expense as incidental damages. See, e.g., *Bulk Oil (U.S.A.), Inc. v. Sun Oil Trading Co.,* 697 F.2d 481, 482–84 (2d Cir.1983); *Hofmann v. Stoller,* 320 N.W.2d 786, 792–93 (N.D.1982); *Gray v. West,* 608 S.W.2d 771, 781 (Tex.Civ.App.1980).

The district judge also suggested that there was no damage, incidental or consequential: "presumably the interest costs for the money to purchase the junk cars would be recovered when the scrap which they had become was sold to some purchaser," so that Afram would be made "whole as to this cost of raw materials through the award of the difference between the contract price and the resale price." But this implies that the price charged to the substitute buyers, Luria Brothers and International Traders, would be calculated on a cost-plus basis, and thus include the additional interest expense that Afram incurred because of Metallurgiki's breach of contract. Prices in competitive markets are not determined on that basis, however; and so far as the record shows the market for steel scrap is competitive. The prices that Luria Brothers and International Traders were willing to pay for Afram's steel scrap depended on how much these buyers would have had to pay for the product from competing sellers, not on how much extra interest Afram had to pay because of the delay in selling its scrap.

Nevertheless we agree with the district court's conclusion that Metallurgiki is not liable for the interest that Afram seeks. All the record contains is the computation of interest. There is no evidence that Afram would have repaid the loan, or $2.025 million of it, on payment of the contract price by Metallurgiki, had that happy event occurred. The loan agreement was not placed in evidence, and since the loan is for more than the amount used to buy the junked cars, there is no presumption that it would have been paid back as soon as the contract for which the junked cars had been bought was fulfilled. Indeed, we do not even know whether the loan was repaid when Afram resold the scrap to Luria Brothers and International Traders. For purposes of computing prejudgment interest, a separate item of damages is discussed next. Afram kept on calculating interest, at the same rate (prime plus .5 percent) as the interest rate on the loan, right up to the date of trial; this is consistent with Afram's not having repaid the loan when it resold the scrap.

So far as the proof shows, then, Afram is not really complaining about an extra interest expense; it is complaining about losing the use of part of the money it borrowed from the bank, the part that was tied up in the junked cars longer than it would have been had Metallurgiki not broken the contract. This of course is a genuine loss; it is what economists call an "opportunity cost," and courts now understand that an opportunity cost is a real cost. See, e.g., *Simmons v. United States,* 698 F.2d 888, 898 (7th Cir.1983). In this case it would be measured by the interest or profit that Afram could have obtained from investing, or using elsewhere in its business, the money that it would have gotten from Metallurgiki by the end of April if Metallurgiki had not broken the contract, but that as a result of the breach it did not get till June and September.

But a forgone profit from exploiting a valuable opportunity that the breach of contract denied to the victim of the breach fits more comfortably under the heading of consequential damages than of incidental damages. The profits that Afram might have made from using that $2.025 million elsewhere in its business are like the milling profits that Hadley might have made if the carrier had not delayed in delivering the mill shaft for repair. Afram has not tried to establish its lost profits from the temporary loss of the use of the $2.025 million; all it is seeking is the extra interest it had to pay. But its theory is one of opportunity cost, as it makes clear in its brief by stating that it would be entitled to interest as incidental damages even if it had not used borrowed money to pay for the junked cars. Afram is correct that it would incur an opportunity cost whether it used its own money or used money that it had borrowed; in either event it would lose the use of money that it could deploy elsewhere at a profit. But we do not think the law has evolved to the point where every time a buyer breaks a contract, the seller is entitled to the time value of the money tied up in the contract, as incidental damages. All the seller is entitled to is an out-of-pocket interest expense that would not have been incurred but for the breach. We have found no case where (so far as we are able to determine from the statement of facts in the case) the seller was able to recover interest on a general business loan not tied to the subject matter of the sale, but we have found two cases that imply he may not. See *Schiavi Mobile Homes, Inc. v. Gironda,* 463 A.2d 722, 727 (Me.1983); *S.C. Gray, Inc. v. Ford Motor Co.,* 92 Mich.App. 789, 811–12, 286 N.W.2d 34, 43–44 (1979).

* * *

Thus we affirm the judgment of the district court except with respect to the denial of prejudgment interest to Afram, as to which we remand the case for a determination of the amount of prejudgment interest to which Afram is entitled at the statutory rate of five percent. Wis.Stat. § 138.04; *Kilgust Heating Div. v. Kemp,* 70 Wis.2d 544, 550, 235 N.W.2d 292, 295–96 (1975). No costs in this court.

Affirmed in part, reversed in part, and remanded.

Notes

1. Why was the public resale on June 15 at $102.75 per ton improper? Should the September resale price of $103 per ton be used to measure damages under UCC 2–706(1)? UCC 2–708(1)? See Apex Oil Co. v. Belcher Co. of New York, Inc., 855 F.2d 997 (2d Cir.1988) (resale of fungible goods in fluctuating market six weeks after breach not commercially reasonable).

2. According to the court, Afram was not a "lost volume" seller—but for the breach, Afram could not have resold the scrap. How, then, are the proceeds from the resale to be treated under UCC 2–706(1)?

3. Exactly how did Judge Posner classify and treat the interest payments made by Afram after the breach on an obligation incurred much earlier? If they are neither incidental nor consequential damages, what are they—fixed or "overhead" costs? In Ernst Steel Corp. v. Horn Construction Division, Halliburton Co., 104 A.D.2d 55, 481 N.Y.S.2d 833 (1984), the court stated: "In an appropriate case a seller is entitled to recover commercially reasonable finance and interest charges incurred as a result of a buyer's breach as a proper item of incidental damages * * * For the most part, however, interest expenses have only been awarded to sellers for indebtedness specifically identified to goods intended for resale to the breaching party and who, as a result of the breaching, cannot repay the loans."

4. Article 2 does not explicitly provide that the seller may recover consequential damages caused by a buyer's breach. Compare UCC 2–715(2). But does it foreclose such a recovery? Suppose that the buyer had promised to pay $100,000 on August 1 for scrap delivered on July 1 and knew that the seller needed prompt payment to renew an advantageous contract with another supplier. Despite assurances that payment would be made, the buyer did not pay and the contract was not renewed. The seller, although making reasonable efforts, was unable to obtain alternative financing. It is clear, is it not, that this is a proper case for a consequential damage claim under general contract law? See UCC 1–103; Restatement, Second, Contracts § 351, Comment (e). Does UCC 1–106(1) preclude access to the common law?

Note: Seller's Remedial Choices—Cumulation or Election?

Comment 1 to UCC 2–703 states that the section "rejects any doctrine of election of remedies as a fundamental policy" and stresses that the "index" is "essentially cumulative in nature" and includes "all of the available remedies for breach." Whether the choice or pursuit of one remedy "bars another depends entirely on the facts of the individual case." Thus, UCC 2–709(3) provides that a seller who pursues an action for the price and is "held not entitled" to it "shall nevertheless be awarded damages for non-acceptance under * * *" UCC 2–708. Similarly, Comment 2 to UCC 2–706 states that a failure to act properly under this section deprives the seller "of damages here provided and relegates him to that provided in Section 2–708." The primary risk of pursuing a particular remedy and failing is, apparently, one of evidence: will the record support a claim for damages under UCC 2–708? A case in point is B & R Textile Corp. v. Paul Rothman Indus., 101 Misc.2d 98, 420 N.Y.S.2d 609 (1979), aff'd, 27 UCC Rep.Serv. 994 (N.Y.Sup.Ct.1979), where the buyer argued that the seller's reliance upon the price received in a resale where the required notice was not given constituted an election of remedies. This argument was rejected by a court, which held that the seller's prompt resale generated a price which, when supported by evidence of other sales contemporaneously made by the seller, established the "market price" under UCC 2–708(1). See also, Cole v. Melvin, 441 F.Supp. 193 (D.S.D.1977), where a defective resale left a thin but adequate record from which to establish the market price. The point for the litigator is clear: develop, if possible, the "fall back" evidence necessary to satisfy UCC 2–708(1).

Some policy questions lurk on the fringes. Suppose the seller pursues the resale remedy and complies fully with UCC 2–706. If, thereafter, it sues for higher damages under UCC 2–708(1) will damages be limited by UCC 2–706(1)? At least one court has so held. See Tesoro Petroleum Corp. v. Holburn Oil Co., Ltd., 145 Misc.2d 715, 547 N.Y.S.2d 1012 (Sup.Ct. N.Y.1989). Or, suppose the seller arguably should have resold under UCC 2–706 but failed to do so. Will a recovery under UCC 2–708(1) be reduced by what could have been obtained on a resale? The answers to these questions may become clearer after we have considered the so-called "lost volume" problem and the application of UCC 2–708(2) in the next section. At least one court, however, has held that if the seller is *not* a "lost volume" seller and has conducted a commercially unreasonable resale under UCC 2–706(1), the recovery under UCC 2–708(1) will be limited by what the seller *should* have received in damages if the resale had been proper. The seller's apparent bad faith in the resale limited the recovery to "actual losses" and precluded any windfall gains permitted under the formula in UCC 2–708(1). See Coast Trading Co. v. Cudahy Co., 592 F.2d 1074 (9th Cir.1979).

SECTION 6. SELLER'S RIGHT TO "PERSONALIZED" DAMAGES—UCC 2–708(2)

In the scheme of things, UCC 2–708(2) appears to be the seller's remedy of last resort. An assumption is that if conforming goods can be identified before or after the breach, the seller will prefer either an action for the price under UCC 2–709 or damages based upon a resale under UCC 2–706. If those remedies fail, the seller can resort to damages under UCC 2–708. But which part of 2–708, subsection (1) with its contract-market price formula, or subsection (2) which awards the "profit (including reasonable overhead) which the seller would have made from full performance by the buyer * * *?"

The Code answer is that UCC 2–708(1) should be applied unless the measure of damages is "inadequate to put the seller in as good a position as performance would have done. * * *" As we have seen, however, if subsection (1) puts the seller in a better position than subsection (2), and does not, when the policy of UCC 1–106(1) is considered, overcompensate, then the buyer cannot limit the seller to the profits that would have been made on their particular contract. This analysis, with its emphasis upon an objective measure of damages, reinforces the residual character of UCC 2–708(2), with its emphasis upon a particularized measure.

Accepting this analysis for the moment, the critical questions for the lawyer and judge are: (1) When should UCC 2–708(2) be used to measure the seller's damages; and (2) When applicable, how should those damages be measured? These questions have generated a continuing flow of law review commentary, much of which attempts to apply rather complex if not sophisticated economic analysis. For a recent example, see Note, *Lost-Profits Damage Awards Under Uniform Commercial Code Section 2–708(2),* 37 Stan. L.Rev. 1109 (1985). For a clear and sensible analysis, see Sebert, *Remedies Under Article Two of the Uniform Commercial Code: An Agenda for Review,* 130 U.Pa.L.Rev. 360, 383–407 (1981). See also Scott, supra at p. 640 at 1165–68, 1179–86.

Problem 14–7

Simpka v. Volta—Scene Five

On July 1, Volta contracted to purchase office furniture, to be manufactured by Simpka, from Dolt, a distributor. The price was $90,000. Dolt then placed an order for the furniture with Simpka for $80,000, with delivery to Volta no later than October 1. On August 15, Volta, without justification, repudiated the contract with Dolt. Dolt promptly canceled the order with Simpka, who had not started to work on the goods, for a customary cancellation charge of $1,000.

D comes to you for advice. The market price of the furniture at the "time and place for tender", October 1, under UCC 2–708(1) was estimated to be $90,000. D had incurred $2,000 in expenses between July 1 and August 15. D would have paid S $80,000 for the furniture and spent another $1,500 to prepare the goods for delivery if V had not repudiated. These expenditures, however, were not made.

A. Which section should be used to measure D's damages? Why?

B. If UCC 2–708(2) is applicable, how should Dolt's damages be measured?

R.E. DAVIS CHEMICAL CORP. v. DIASONICS, INC.

United States Court of Appeals, Seventh Circuit, 1987.
826 F.2d 678.

Before BAUER, Chief Circuit Judge, CUDAHY and FLAUM, Circuit Judges.

CUDAHY, Circuit Judge.

Diasonics, Inc. appeals from the orders of the district court denying its motion for summary judgment and granting R.E. Davis Chemical Corp.'s summary judgment motion. Diasonics also appeals from the order dismissing its third-party complaint against Dr. Glen D. Dobbin and Dr. Galdino Valvassori. We affirm the dismissal of the third-party complaint, reverse the grant of summary judgment in favor of Davis and remand for further proceedings.

I.

Diasonics is a California corporation engaged in the business of manufacturing and selling medical diagnostic equipment. Davis is an Illinois corporation that contracted to purchase a piece of medical diagnostic equipment from Diasonics. On or about February 23, 1984, Davis and Diasonics entered into a written contract under which Davis agreed to purchase the equipment. Pursuant to this agreement, Davis paid Diasonics a $300,000 deposit on February 29, 1984. Prior to entering into its agreement with Diasonics, Davis had contracted with Dobbin and Valvassori to establish a medical facility where the equipment was to be used. Dobbin and Valvassori subsequently breached their contract with Davis. Davis then breached its contract with Diasonics; it refused to take delivery of the equipment or to pay the balance due under the agreement. Diasonics later resold the equipment to a third party for the same price at which it was to be sold to Davis.

Davis sued Diasonics, asking for restitution of its $300,000 down payment under section 2–718(2) of the Uniform Commercial Code (the "UCC" or the "Code"). Ill.Rev.Stat. ch. 26, para. 2–718(2) (1985). Diasonics counterclaimed. Diasonics did not deny that Davis was entitled to recover its $300,000 deposit less $500 as provided in section 2–718(2)(b). However, Diasonics claimed that it was entitled to an offset under section 2–718(3). Diasonics alleged that it was a "lost volume seller," and, as such, it lost the profit from one sale when Davis breached its contract. Diasonics' position was that, in order to be put in as good a position as it would have been in had Davis performed, it was entitled to recover its lost profit on its contract with Davis under section 2–708(2) of the UCC. Ill.Rev.Stat. ch. 26, para. 2–708(2) (1985). Section 2–708 provides:

* * *

Diasonics subsequently filed a third-party complaint against Dobbin and Valvassori, alleging that they tortiously interfered with its contract with Davis. Diasonics claimed that the doctors knew of the contract between Davis and Diasonics and also knew that, if they breached their contract with Davis, Davis would have no use for the equipment it had agreed to buy from Diasonics.

The district court dismissed Diasonics' third-party complaint for failure to state a claim upon which relief could be granted, finding that the complaint did not allege that the doctors intended to induce Davis to breach its contract with Diasonics. The court also entered summary judgment for Davis. The court held that lost volume sellers were not entitled to recover damages under 2–708(2) but rather were limited to recovering the difference between the resale price and the contract price along with incidental damages under section 2–706(1). Ill.Rev.Stat. ch. 26, para. 2–706(1) (1985). Section 2–706(1) provides:

* * *

Davis was awarded $322,656, which represented Davis' down payment plus prejudgment interest less Diasonics' incidental damages. Diasonics appeals the district court's decision respecting its measure of damages as well as the dismissal of its third-party complaint.

II.

We consider first Diasonics' claim that the district court erred in holding that Diasonics was limited to the measure of damages provided in 2–706 and could not recover lost profits as a lost volume seller under 2–708(2). Surprisingly, given its importance, this issue has never been addressed by an Illinois court, nor, apparently, by any other court construing Illinois law. Thus, we must attempt to predict how the Illinois Supreme Court would resolve this issue if it were presented to it. Courts applying the laws of other states have unanimously adopted the position that a lost volume seller can recover its lost profits under 2–708(2).[2] Contrary to the result reached by the district court, we conclude that the Illinois Supreme Court would follow these other cases and would allow a lost volume seller to recover its lost profit under 2–708(2).

We begin our analysis with 2–718(2) and (3). Under 2–718(2)(b), Davis is entitled to the return of its down payment less $500. Davis' right to restitution, however, is qualified under 2–718(3)(a) to the extent that Diasonics can establish a right to recover damages under any other provision of Article 2 of the UCC. Article 2 contains four provisions that concern the recovery of a seller's general damages (as opposed to its incidental or consequential damages): 2–706 (contract price less resale price); 2–708(1) (contract price less market price); 2–708(2) (profit); and 2–709 (price). The problem we face here is determining whether Diasonics' damages should be measured under 2–706 or 2–708(2). To answer this question, we need to engage in a detailed look at the language and structure of these various damage provisions.

The Code does not provide a great deal of guidance as to when a particular damage remedy is appropriate. The damage remedies provided under the Code are catalogued in section 2–703, but this section does not indicate that there is any hierarchy among the remedies. One method of approaching the damage sections is to conclude that 2–708 is relegated to a role inferior to that of 2–706 and 2–709 and that one can turn to 2–708 only after one has concluded that neither 2–706 nor 2–709 is applicable.[6] Under

2. *See, e.g., Comeq, Inc. v. Mitternight Boiler Works, Inc.,* 456 So.2d 264, 267–69 (Ala.Sup.Ct.1984); *Autonumerics, Inc. v. Bayer Ind., Inc.,* 144 Ariz. 181, 191, 696 P.2d 1330, 1340 (Ariz.App.Ct.1984); *Capital Steel Co. v. Foster & Creighton Co.,* 264 Ark. 683, 689, 574 S.W.2d 256, 259–60 (Sup.Ct.1978); *National Controls, Inc. v. Commodore Business Machines, Inc.,* 163 Cal.App.3d 688, 696–99, 209 Cal.Rptr. 636, 641–43 (1st Dist. 1985); *Snyder v. Herbert Greenbaum & Assocs., Inc.,* 38 Md.App. 144, 153–54, 380 A.2d 618, 624–25 (1977); *Teradyne, Inc. v. Teledyne Ind., Inc.,* 676 F.2d 865, 868 (1st Cir. 1982) (applying Massachusetts law); *Neri v. Retail Marine Corp.,* 30 N.Y.2d 393, 397–99, 334 N.Y.S.2d 165, 167–70, 285 N.E.2d 311, 313–14 (1972); *Lake Erie Boat Sales, Inc. v. Johnson,* 11 Ohio App.3d 55, 56, 463 N.E.2d 70, 71–72 (1983); *Famous Knitwear Corp. v. Drug Fair, Inc.,* 493 F.2d 251, 253–54 (4th Cir.1974) (applying Virginia law); *Islamic Republic of Iran v. Boeing Co.,* 771 F.2d 1279, 1289–90 (9th Cir.1985) (applying Washington law), *cert. dismissed,* ___ U.S. ___, 107 S.Ct. 450, 93 L.Ed.2d 397 (1986).

6. Evidence to support this approach can be found in the language of the various damage sections and of the official comments to the UCC. *See* § 2–709(3) ("a seller who is held not entitled to the price under

this interpretation of the relationship between 2–706 and 2–708, if the goods have been resold, the seller can sue to recover damages measured by the difference between the contract price and the resale price under 2–706. The seller can turn to 2–708 only if it resells in a commercially unreasonable manner or if it cannot resell but an action for the price is inappropriate under 2–709. The district court adopted this reading of the Code's damage remedies and, accordingly, limited Diasonics to the measure of damages provided in 2–706 because it resold the equipment in a commercially reasonable manner.

The district court's interpretation of 2–706 and 2–708, however, creates its own problems of statutory construction. There is some suggestion in the Code that the "fact that plaintiff resold the goods [in a commercially reasonable manner] does *not* compel him to use the resale remedy of § 2–706 rather than the damage remedy of § 2–708." Harris, *A Radical Restatement of the Law of Seller's Damages: Sales Act and Commercial Code Results Compared,* 18 Stan.L.Rev. 66, 101 n. 174 (1965) (emphasis in original). Official comment 1 to 2–703, which catalogues the remedies available to a seller, states that these "remedies are essentially cumulative in nature" and that "[w]hether the pursuit of one remedy bars another depends entirely on the facts of the individual case." *See also State of New York, Report of the Law Revision Comm'n for 1956,* 396–97 (1956).[7]

Those courts that found that a lost volume seller can recover its lost profits under 2–708(2) implicitly rejected the position adopted by the district

this Section shall nevertheless be awarded damages for non-acceptance under the preceding section [§ 2–708]"); UCC comment 7 to § 2–709 ("[i]f the action for the price fails, the seller may nonetheless have proved a case entitling him to damages for non-acceptance [under § 2–708]"); UCC comment 2 to § 2–706 ("[f]ailure to act properly under this section deprives the seller of the measure of damages here provided and relegates him to that provided in Section 2–708"); UCC comment 1 to § 2–704 (describes § 2–706 as the "primary remedy" available to a seller upon breach by the buyer); *see also Commonwealth Edison Co. v. Decker Coal Co.,* 653 F.Supp. 841, 844 (N.D.Ill.1987) (statutory language and case law suggest that "§ 2–708 remedies are available only to a seller who is not entitled to the contract price" under § 2–709); Childres & Burgess, *Seller's Remedies: The Primacy of UCC 2–708(2),* 48 N.Y.U.L.Rev. 833, 863–64 (1973). As one commentator has noted, 2–706

> is the Code section drafted specifically to define the damage rights of aggrieved reselling sellers, and there is no suggestion within it that the profit formula of section 2–708(2) is in any way intended to qualify or be superior to it.

Shanker, *The Case for a Literal Reading of UCC Section 2–708(2) (One Profit for the Reseller),* 24 Case W.Res. 697, 699 (1973).

7. UCC comment 2 to 2–708(2) also suggests that 2–708 has broader applicability than suggested by the district court. UCC comment 2 provides:

> This section permits the recovery of lost profits in all appropriate cases, which would include all standard priced goods. The normal measure there would be list price less cost to the dealer or list price less manufacturing cost to the manufacturer.

The district court's restrictive interpretation of 2–708(2) was based in part on UCC comment 1 to 2–704 which describes 2–706 as the aggrieved seller's primary remedy. The district court concluded that, if a lost volume seller could recover its lost profit under 2–708(2), every seller would attempt to recover damages under 2–708(2) and 2–706 would become the aggrieved seller's residuary remedy. This argument ignores the fact that to recover under 2–708(2), a seller must first establish its status as a lost volume seller. * * *

The district court also concluded that a lost volume seller cannot recover its lost profit under 2–708(2) because such a result would negate a seller's duty to mitigate damages. This position fails to recognize the fact that, by definition, a lost volume seller cannot mitigate damages through resale. Resale does not reduce a lost volume seller's damages because the breach has still resulted in its losing one sale and a corresponding profit.

court; those courts started with the assumption that 2–708 applied to a lost volume seller without considering whether the seller was limited to the remedy provided under 2–706. None of those courts even suggested that a seller who resold goods in a commercially reasonable manner was limited to the damage formula provided under 2–706. We conclude that the Illinois Supreme Court, if presented with this question, would adopt the position of these other jurisdictions and would conclude that a reselling seller, such as Diasonics, is free to reject the damage formula prescribed in 2–706 and choose to proceed under 2–708.

Concluding that Diasonics is entitled to seek damages under 2–708, however, does not automatically result in Diasonics being awarded its lost profit. Two different measures of damages are provided in 2–708. Subsection 2–708(1) provides for a measure of damages calculated by subtracting the market price at the time and place for tender from the contract price.[9] The profit measure of damages, for which Diasonics is asking, is contained in 2–708(2). However, one applies 2–708(2) only if "the measure of damages provided in subsection (1) is inadequate to put the seller in as good a position as performance would have done. * * * " Ill.Rev.Stat. ch. 26, para. 2–708(2) (1985). Diasonics claims that 2–708(1) does not provide an adequate measure of damages when the seller is a lost volume seller.[10] To understand Diasonics' argument, we need to define the concept of the lost volume seller. Those cases that have addressed this issue have defined a lost volume seller as one that has a predictable and finite number of customers and that has the capacity either to sell to all new buyers or to make the one additional sale represented by the resale after the breach. According to a number of courts and commentators, if the seller would have made the sale represented by the resale whether or not the breach occurred, damages measured by the difference between the contract price and market price cannot put the lost volume seller in as good a position as it would have been in had the buyer performed.[13] The breach effectively cost the seller a "profit," and the seller can only be made whole by awarding it damages in the amount of its "lost profit" under 2–708(2).

We agree with Diasonics' position that, under some circumstances, the measure of damages provided under 2–708(1) will not put a reselling seller in as good a position as it would have been in had the buyer performed because the breach resulted in the seller losing sales volume. However, we disagree

9. There is some debate in the commentaries about whether a seller who has resold the goods may ignore the measure of damages provided in 2–706 and elect to proceed under 2–708(1). Under some circumstances the contract-market price differential will result in overcompensating such a seller. *See* J. White & R. Summers, *Handbook of the Law under the Uniform Commercial Code* § 7–7, at 271–73 (2d ed. 1980); Sebert, *Remedies under Article Two of the Uniform Commercial Code: An Agenda for Review,* 130 U.Pa.L.Rev. 360, 380–83 (1981). We need not struggle with this question here because Diasonics has not sought to recover damages under 2–708(1).

10. This is also the position adopted by those courts that have held that a lost volume seller can recover its lost profits under 2–708(2). *See, e.g., Snyder,* 38 Md.App. at 153–54, 380 A.2d at 624–25.

13. According to one commentator,

> Resale results in loss of volume only if three conditions are met: (1) the person who bought the resold entity would have been solicited by plaintiff had there been no breach and resale; (2) the solicitation would have been successful; and (3) the plaintiff could have performed that additional contract.

Harris, *supra* p. 682, at 82 (footnotes omitted).

with the definition of "lost volume seller" adopted by other courts. Courts awarding lost profits to a lost volume seller have focused on whether the seller had the capacity to supply the breached units in addition to what it actually sold. In reality, however, the relevant questions include, not only whether the seller could have produced the breached units in addition to its actual volume, but also whether it would have been profitable for the seller to produce both units. Goetz & Scott, *Measuring Sellers' Damages: The Lost–Profits Puzzle,* 31 Stan.L.Rev. 323, 332–33, 346–47 (1979). As one commentator has noted, under

> the economic law of diminishing returns or increasing marginal costs[,] . . . as a seller's volume increases, then a point will inevitably be reached where the cost of selling each additional item diminishes the incremental return to the seller and eventually makes it entirely unprofitable to conclude the next sale.

Thus, under some conditions, awarding a lost volume seller its presumed lost profit will result in overcompensating the seller, and 2–708(2) would not take effect because the damage formula provided in 2–708(1) does place the seller in as good a position as if the buyer had performed. Therefore, on remand, Diasonics must establish, not only that it had the capacity to produce the breached unit in addition to the unit resold, but also that it would have been profitable for it to have produced and sold both. Diasonics carries the burden of establishing these facts because the burden of proof is generally on the party claiming injury to establish the amount of its damages; especially in a case such as this, the plaintiff has easiest access to the relevant data. *Finance America Commercial Corp. v. Econo Coach, Inc.,* 118 Ill.App.3d 385, 390, 73 Ill.Dec. 878, 882, 454 N.E.2d 1127, 1131 (2d Dist.1983) ("A party seeking to recover has the burden not only to establish that he sustained damages but also to establish a reasonable basis for computation of those damages.") (citation omitted); *see also Snyder,* 38 Md.App. at 158–59 & n. 7, 380 A.2d at 627 & n. 7.[14]

One final problem with awarding a lost volume seller its lost profits was raised by the district court. This problem stems from the formulation of the measure of damages provided under section 2–708(2) which is "the profit (including reasonable overhead) which the seller would have made from full performance by the buyer, together with any incidental damages provided in this Article (Section 2–710), due allowance for costs reasonably incurred and due credit for payments or *proceeds of resale.*" Ill.Rev.Stat. ch. 26, para. 2–708(2) (1985) (emphasis added). The literal language of 2–708(2) requires that the proceeds from resale be credited against the amount of damages awarded which, in most cases, would result in the seller recovering nominal damages. In those cases in which the lost volume seller was awarded its lost profit as damages, the courts have circumvented this problem by concluding that this language only applies to proceeds realized from the resale of uncompleted goods for scrap. *See, e.g., Neri,* 30 N.Y.2d at 399 & n. 2, 334 N.Y.S.2d at 169 & n. 2, 285 N.E.2d at 314 & n. 2; *see also* J. White & R. Summers, *Handbook of the Law under the Uniform Commercial Code* § 7–

14. As some commentators have pointed out, the cost of calculating a loss of profit may be very high. Goetz & Scott, *supra,* at 353 ("the complexity of the lost-volume problem suggests that the information costs of exposing an overcompensatory rule are relatively high").

13, at 285 ("courts should simply ignore the 'due credit' language in lost volume cases") (footnote omitted). Although neither the text of 2–708(2) nor the official comments limit its application to resale of goods for scrap, there is evidence that the drafters of 2–708 seemed to have had this more limited application in mind when they proposed amending 2–708 to include the phrase "due credit for payments or proceeds of resale." [15] We conclude that the Illinois Supreme Court would adopt this more restrictive interpretation of this phrase rendering it inapplicable to this case.

We therefore reverse the grant of summary judgment in favor of Davis and remand with instructions that the district court calculate Diasonics' damages under 2–708(2) if Diasonics can establish, not only that it had the capacity to make the sale to Davis as well as the sale to the resale buyer, but also that it would have been profitable for it to make both sales. Of course, Diasonics, in addition, must show that it probably would have made the second sale absent the breach.[16]

* * *

IV.

Accordingly, we affirm the district court's dismissal of the third-party complaint, reverse the grant of summary judgment in favor of Davis and remand for further proceedings consistent with this opinion.

Affirmed in part, reversed in part and remanded.

[Some footnotes omitted.]

Notes

1. After remand and trial, R.E. Davis again appealed from a judgment of the district court in favor of Diasonics. R.E. Davis Chemical Corp. v. Diasonics, Inc., 924 F.2d 709 (7th Cir.1991). The Court of Appeals affirmed that Diasonics was a lost volume seller under the test announced in the first opinion, even though it had failed to identify the exact unit sold or the buyer to whom that unit was sold. The court also affirmed the trial court's calculation of lost profits under UCC 2–708(2), [$453,050, less the $300,000 deposit] but reversed and remanded with regret on the ground that the trial court erroneously excluded evidence of additional expenses that Diasonics would have incurred if Davis had fully performed its part of the bargain. The court stated that "Diasonics is entitled to the benefit of its bargain, no more, no less."

2. In *Davis,* the seller was a lost volume manufacturer who actually resold an MRI presumably intended for the breaching buyer. Without regard to the proceeds of the so-called second sale, the seller was entitled to lost profits under UCC 2–708(2) for breach of the first sale. Accord: National Controls, Inc. v. Commodore Business Machines, Inc., 163 Cal.App.3d 688, 209 Cal.Rptr. 636 (1985). If there was no lost volume, Davis would receive credit for the proceeds

15. In explaining its recommendation that 2–708 be amended to include the requirement that due credit be given for resale, the Enlarged Editorial Board stated that its purpose was "to clarify the privilege of the seller to realize junk value when it is manifestly useless to complete the operation of manufacture." Supplement No. 1 to the 1952 Official Draft (1955), *quoted in* Harris, *supra* p. 682, at 98.

16. *See supra* p. 683 n. 13; *see also* Schlosser, *Damages for the Lost–Volume Seller: Does an Efficient Formula Already Exist?* 17 U.C.C.L.J. 238, 245 & n. 20 (1985); Sebert, *supra* p. 683 n. 9, at 387–88.

of any resale by Diasonics. See Van Ness Motors, Inc. v. Vikram, 221 N.J.Super. 543, 535 A.2d 510 (1987). Otherwise, Diasonics would be put in a better position than if there had been full performance.

3. Suppose Diasonics was a "middleman" or who obtained MRI's for resale from the manufacturer rather than manufacturing them itself. See the *Neri* case, discussed in *Davis*. The lost volume analysis has been applied here as well, even if the seller never has finished goods on hand and does not resell. According to Professor Sebert, because the middleman does not have finished goods on hand, "UCC 2–708(2) is the only Code damages provision that produces sensible results for such a seller; all of the other damage provisions contemplate the existence of finished goods." Sebert, supra at p. 640, 130 U.Pa.L.Rev. at 385.

Problem 14–8

Simpka v. Volta—Scene Six

On March 1, Simpka contracted to manufacture custom furniture for Volta for $80,000, delivery f.o.b. Ohio no later than November 1. On May 1, Volta repudiated without justification. Simpka had commenced to manufacture the furniture but no item was completed. The market price of the furniture in Ohio was $60,000. The market price in New York was $55,000. The economy was in a mild recession, and the respective market prices in November were expected to be $40,000 in Ohio and $35,000 in New York.

A. A summer associate has given you the following memo: "It is clear that Simpka could complete the manufacture, UCC 2–704(2), and attempt to resell the custom furniture. See UCC 2–706(2), stating that it is 'not necessary that the goods be in existence or that any or all of them have been identified to the contract before the breach.' If a resale can be made, damages can be recovered under UCC 2–706(1), or, if there is lost volume, under UCC 2–708(2). If a resale cannot be made, Simpka can recover the price from Volta. UCC 2–709(1)(b). I recommend that we advise Simpka to complete the manufacturing process." Do you agree?

B. Suppose, in the exercise of reasonable commercial judgment, Simpka stopped the manufacturing process. UCC 2–704(2). (1) Simpka had components on hand purchased for the contract which cost $20,000. These components were scrapped for $15,000. (2) Simpka had incurred other performance costs ("variable" costs) of $15,000 which could not be salvaged. (3) Because of the breach, Simpka did not have to incur other performance of "variable" costs, estimated to be $25,000. What damages should Simpka recover under UCC 2–708(2)? Who has the burden of establishing that "overhead" is or is not reasonable?

Note: Who Is a Lost Volume Seller?

The assumption underlying the "lost volume" problem is simple to state: If a seller had the capacity to and probably would have made a second sale regardless of the buyer's breach, the goal of UCC 1–106(1) will be frustrated if the profit the seller would have made on the first sale is offset by the proceeds of the second sale. Embracing this assumption, *R.E. Davis* and the authorities cited therein have used UCC 2–708(2) to protect the profit on the first sale without regard to the proceeds of any resale.

In so doing, most courts have adopted a simple test for determining lost volume: If, in the relevant time period, the seller had the capacity to make a second sale and, after the breach, in fact made a resale, the requirement is satisfied. Rejected is the view, advocated by some commentators, that lost volume exists when the seller satisfies three conditions: (1) The buyer who purchased the resold entity would have been solicited by the seller had there been no breach; (2) The solicitation would have been successful; and (3) The seller could have performed the additional contract. Harris, *A Radical Restatement of the Laws of Seller's Damages: Sales Act and Commercial Code Results Compared,* 18 Stan.L.Rev. 66, 80–83 (1965). In refusing to "require proof of a complex economic relationship," one court was satisfied by proof that the seller "would have made the sale to the resale purchaser even if" the buyer had performed, that the seller "resold the parts, and that it had an existing inventory of these parts." Islamic Republic of Iran v. Boeing Co., 771 F.2d 1279 (9th Cir.1985) (Washington law).

In addition, most courts have ignored (if not rejected) the claim by some that even if a second sale could have been made, it would not, in all probability, have been profitable. See Goetz & Scott, *Measuring Seller's Damages: The Lost-Profits Puzzle,* 31 Stan.L.Rev. 323 (1979). Why? The argument is summarized by Professor Sebert supra page 640:

> One foundation of the Geotz and Scott argument is the accepted proposition that economically efficient entities, whether they be manufacturers or retailers, attempt to operate at a level of output where marginal cost equals marginal revenue. Economic theory also posits that these efficient sellers are likely to be producing at a level where marginal costs are rising as additional units are produced or sold, and that marginal revenue is likely to be falling, or at best remaining constant, because the increased supply caused by additional production or sales will cause the market price to fall. Based upon these traditional economic concepts, Goetz and Scott argue that, even if the seller had the capacity to do so, a seller operating at the level where marginal cost equals marginal revenue would not have produced the additional goods to sell to buyer 2 if buyer 1 had not breached. In a world of rising marginal costs and static or declining marginal revenue, it would not have been efficient for the seller to produce or obtain additional goods to sell to buyer 2 because the marginal cost of those goods would exceed the marginal revenue received from their sale and the seller would have lost money. Thus, Goetz and Scott suggest that the sale to buyer 2 is a sale that the efficient seller normally would not have made, and therefore the seller is not a lost volume seller.
>
> Sebert at 389–90. *

Professor Sebert rejects Goetz and Scott's presumption that the seller is not a lost volume seller, "even though a seller has the capacity to make an additional sale and even though the resale buyer probably would have bought from the seller had the original buyer not breached" without rejecting the possibility that the resale merely replaces the original sale because of the assumed rising marginal costs. He proposes the following approach: "* * * (O)nce the seller shows that he had the capacity to make an additional sale and

* Another argument by Goetz and Scott, summarized by Sebert, is that a seller normally will not have lost volume because the buyer's breach will cause an increase in demand for the seller's product, offsetting any losses suffered because of the buyer's breach. The assumptions are that the breach indicates that the buyer did not want the goods, and that a sale by the buyer would likely be to someone who otherwise would have bought from the seller. "Because the buyer who breaches can no longer resell the goods, that breach will permit the seller to make an additional sale to a customer who otherwise would have bought from the breaching buyer." Sebert at 392. This argument has been criticized as misrepresenting the problem when the seller is a retailer. Goldberg, *An Economic Analysis of the Lost-Volume Seller,* 57 S.Cal.L.Rev. 283, 288–90 (1984).

that the resale buyer probably would have bought from him anyway, I would place the burden of proof on the breaching buyer to show that the seller would not have made an additional sale because of rising marginal costs." Sebert at 391.

How does the decision in *R.E. Davis* vary this analysis?

ROBERT E. SCOTT, THE CASE FOR MARKET DAMAGES: REVISING THE LOST PROFITS PUZZLE

57 U.Chi.L.Rev. 1155, 1192–96 (1990).

* * *

c) Solving the lost volume problem under the UCC. The lost volume problem clearly remains vexing. I have argued that the optimal damage rule would compensate the plaintiff seller for any market price shift as well as for the selling efforts "consumed" in the effort to secure the breached contract. Under the optimal default rule, therefore, damages would be less than the estimated profits per contract (the recovery presumptively available under § 2–708(2)), but more than market damages plus post-breach incidental expenses (the recovery presumptively available under §§ 2–708(1) and 2–710). The challenge is to find a consistent interpretation of the various UCC provisions that better approximates the optimal default rule for lost volume cases.

Many courts and commentators would permit lost volume sellers to seek damages under § 2–708(2). This approach appears consistent with the statutory language and with the drafters' apparent belief that volume sales require careful attention to the position the seller would have achieved upon performance. But, as the discussion above has shown, a lost profits rule in lost volume claims invites excessively large awards. The award of lost profits is not a good proxy for the lost selling efforts. A significant portion of those "profits" covers sale completion costs and fixed overhead that the breaching buyer does not consume. Thus, recovery under § 2–708(2) of "the profit (including reasonable overhead) which the seller would have made from full performance" will always exact a cancellation penalty from the buyer in a sum greater than most parties would have stipulated had they bargained over the issue in advance. Moreover, § 2–708(2) specifies, *in addition,* that seller is entitled to "any incidental damages [under § 2–710]." Because the selling costs recovered under the guise of lost profits include post-breach and post-contract selling activities, this language specifically invites courts to grant sellers a double recovery for post-breach incidental costs.

Permitting recovery of lost profits for volume sellers under § 2–708(2) thus places on the retail buyer (often a consumer) the daunting burden of establishing the amount by which the *estimated* profits exceed the actual selling costs consumed in securing the breached contract. Viewed simply as a question of procedural efficiency, this outcome seems perverse. The plaintiff-seller enjoys the comparative advantage in assembling and presenting evidence of the selling costs attributable to the breach. A default rule that shifts the burden to the buyer both increases the costs and reduces the accuracy of legal enforcement. Indeed, it is likely that expected enforcement costs will exceed any anticipated returns from litigating the accuracy of an award under § 2–708(2). If so, the ultimate effect of using § 2–708(2) to compensate lost volume sellers will be to institutionalize a severe and socially wasteful cancellation policy. First, a lost profits rule gives most sellers more protection against cancellation than they could plausibly want. Second, the amount of the insurance coverage is based on factors (such as seller's costs) that buyers cannot determine except at great cost. The resulting uncertainty degrades product quality with no benefit accruing to either party.

Consider the alternative rule: volume sellers receive market damages under § 2–706 or § 2–708(1) together with incidental damages under § 2–710. The recovery of any shift in the market price between contract and delivery is not problematic. The issue turns solely on the calculation of incidental damages. Recall that the volume seller's expectancy upon signing the contract is the opportunity to complete the deal at the time of performance. Performance would have earned seller that opportunity; breach has foreclosed it. To satisfy the full performance compensation principle, seller must receive damages equal to the lost contractual opportunity. The value of the foregone opportunity, however, is not measured by the value of the contract per se, but by the pro rata selling costs consumed in dealing with the breaching buyer.

The statutory language of § 2–710 seems broad enough to embrace post-contract as well as post-breach reliance costs. The costs consumed in securing the breached contract could be recoverable as "expenses * * * incurred * * * in connection with return or resale * * * *or otherwise resulting from the breach.*" Nevertheless, courts have generally awarded volume sellers only the post-breach expenses incurred in reselling the goods. This general rule should be qualified in several respects, however. First, volume sellers who choose to recover market damages rather than lost profits never request, much less prove, the selling costs attributable to the breached contract. Second, courts have explicitly limited the recovery of incidental damages to post-breach expenses only for claims brought under § 2–708(2), which may reflect the intuition that the plaintiff is seeking a double recovery. In short, the barriers to using § 2–710 to compensate the losses of a volume seller may be much lower than is commonly assumed. If sellers must introduce those costs via § 2–710, the procedural efficiency of the damage rule increases; sellers in general enjoy the comparative advantage in establishing uncompensated selling costs.

The preceding argument may prove too much, however. It is quite possible, especially in the case of the retail volume seller, that one cannot tease the ideal default rule out of the UCC's statutory language, especially with its judicial gloss. There are several reasons, however, to prefer the inadequacies of market damages to the excesses of lost profits. Certain default rules are set not because they represent the ultimate allocations preferred by most bargainers, but rather because they best induce one party to share important information with the other. Consider the familiar foreseeability limitation on consequential damages embodied in *Hadley v. Baxendale.*[122] Limiting damages for the unforeseeable consequences of

122. 9 Ex 341, 156 Eng Rep 145 (1854).

breach induces the promisee to disclose to the promisor private information concerning the consequences of breach, thus stimulating the transmission of mutually beneficial information between the bargainers.

This information-forcing dimension may explain the common-law preference for market damages even in the context of volume sales. The market damages rule induces the seller to bargain for a more appropriate cancellation rule. By allocating the risk of cancellation to the party who possesses the key information concerning the costs of breach, the UCC would motivate specially designed provisions to cope with the lost volume problem.

Even those parties who are not induced to opt out of the market damages rule would be better off than they would be under a lost profits regime. There are strong reasons to believe that most parties would assign the risk of a lax cancellation rule to the seller rather than place the equivalent risk of a harsh rule on the buyer. At least in the retail context, sellers are better able to spread the risk than customers. Moreover, the market damages rule, whatever its inadequacies, enjoys the great advantage of clarity. Both parties can better evaluate the expected deviation from the ideal than they could under the more complex and less certain lost profits rule.

* * *

[Some footnotes omitted.] [Reprinted with Permission of the Author and the University of Chicago Law Review.]

CHAPTER FIFTEEN

SELLER'S REPUDIATION AND THE LIKE—A SURVEY OF BUYER'S REMEDIES

SECTION 1. INTRODUCTION

There are three "garden" varieties of breach by a seller; repudiation, failure to deliver and a tender of delivery which does not conform to the contract. This chapter will feature the buyer's remedies which are responsive to the first two varieties, namely, permissible action when the expectation of receiving due performance is impaired, UCC 2–609, claims to goods in the possession of the seller, UCC 2–716 and 2–502, and damages, either after "cover" under UCC 2–712 or under the formula in UCC 2–713. Note that where the seller makes a non-conforming tender and the buyer "rightfully rejects or justifiably revokes acceptance," the buyer may claim damages under UCC 2–712 or 2–713. UCC 2–711(1). The special problems involved in the buyer's remedies of rejection, UCC 2–601, and revocation of acceptance, UCC 2–608, however, prompt us to defer their consideration to Chapter Eighteen. Similarly, we have deferred for more extensive treatment the non-conformity called breach of warranty and the remedies available to a buyer who has accepted defective goods and, for one reason or another, does not revoke acceptance under UCC 2–608. These important remedies include "direct," UCC 2–714(2), "incidental," UCC 2–715(1), and "consequential," UCC 2–715(2) damages. At the same time, we will examine the extent to which a seller can disclaim warranties, UCC 2–316, and the parties can alter by agreement code remedies normally available. UCC 2–719.

It is useful to identify the functional parallels between seller's and buyer's remedies. Compare UCC 2–703 and 2–711. And see UCC 2–702 and 2–502, 2–709 and 2–716, 2–706 and 2–712, 2–708 and 2–713, and 2–710 and 2–715(1). The parallelism is conscious, but there is one important difference from the buyer's perspective. Although the buyer, like the seller, is in business to make a profit (and, undoubtedly, most buyers are also sellers), the purchase contract is designed to obtain goods which will be used in the overall business enterprise. The better the price, the quicker the delivery, and the higher the quality, then the more likely that the overall business will be profitable. Consequently, unless the buyer's plans have changed, an immediate concern upon breach by the seller will be replacement of the goods or inducing the seller to perform. Higher costs and delays in this replacement process both deprive the buyer of the benefit of his bargain and affect overall profitability. Thus, if the goods have not been tendered, the most important remedies will be specific performance, 2–716, or cover, 2–712, and, if delay is involved, recovery of consequential damages under UCC 2–

715(2). The "formula" in UCC 2–713(1) is a residual remedy which is used when specific performance is not available and relief for "cover" in UCC 2–712(1) is, for whatever reason, not pursued. Some have urged that UCC 2–713 be repealed. See Childres, *Buyer's Remedies: The Danger of Section 2–713,* 72 Nw.U.L.Rev. 837 (1978). Whatever the value of this "residual" remedy, one thing is clear: since the buyer's contract, unlike the seller's, is not complicated by "lost volume" problems, there is, perhaps, a sounder basis for concluding that a buyer who did cover or should have covered is foreclosed from using UCC 2–713(1) when that would provide a higher recovery. Even if this option is preserved, the buyer cannot recover consequential damages caused by the breach which could have been "reasonably * * * prevented by cover or otherwise." UCC 2–715(2)(a). We will consider these possibilities in the balance of this chapter.

SECTION 2. WHEN HAS SELLER REPUDIATED? COMMITTED A MATERIAL BREACH OF AN INSTALLMENT CONTRACT?

Just as the Code does not define what constitutes a repudiation by a buyer so it does not define what constitutes a repudiation by a seller. The same open-endedness permeates the "adequate assurance" provisions of UCC 2–609, and the impact of breach upon installment contracts, UCC 2–612. In many situations, relevant criteria will be similar for seller and buyer alike. Thus, if either party threatens to cease performance unless the other agrees to a performance not fairly within the scope of the original agreement, a repudiation may have occurred. For illustrations, compare Louis Dreyfus Corp. v. Brown, 709 F.2d 898 (5th Cir.1983), where the court held that a farmer repudiated a contract to deliver grain, with Bill's Coal Co., Inc. v. Board of Public Utilities of Springfield, Mo., 682 F.2d 883 (10th Cir.1982), where the court held that a supplier's bad faith interpretation of the price term was not a repudiation and the buyer's cancellation, therefore, was a breach. See also Kaiser-Francis Oil Co. v. Producer's Gas Co., 870 F.2d 563 (10th Cir.1989) (buyer refuses to perform unless seller agrees to modify "take or pay" clause.)

In long-term gas supply contracts, buyers have attempted to minimize the effect of fixed price provisions by invoking UCC 2–609. The buyer suspends its duty to pay and sends a written demand for adequate assurance of due performance to the seller. The benefits of a temporary suspension, however, are over shadowed by the risk that there was in fact no "reasonable grounds" for insecurity. Thus, in Universal Resources Corp. v. Panhandle Eastern Pipe Line Co., 813 F.2d 77 (5th Cir.1987), *rehearing denied,* 821 F.2d 1097 (5th Cir.1987), the court found no objective evidence from either the seller's words or conduct or the market for natural gas to justify a fear that seller would be unable or unwilling to perform the contract. Buyer, in effect, relied upon hypothetical rather than real grounds. Similarly, in United States v. Great Plains Gasification Assoc., 819 F.2d 831 (8th Cir. 1987), the buyer had no objective grounds to believe that the seller would abandon services and, in any event, demanded assurance in excess of what the seller was required to perform under the contract. Possible buyer's are induced to play "games" with UCC 2–609 because neither applicable contract clauses nor UCC 2–615 grant them relief from changed market circumstances. The cost of losing the game is, at a minimum, liability for the suspended payments plus interest and, at a maximum, a repudiation of the contract.

In the *Plotnick* case, supra at p. 649, the court assessed the significance of the buyer's late payment partly in terms of whether it impaired the seller's capacity to continue performance. A court might ask similar questions about a seller's late delivery. See UCC 2–612(2). But such symmetry will not be found in all cases and there will be borderline situations. For a helpful discussion, see Jackson, *"Anticipatory Repudiation" and the Temporal Element of Contract Law: An Economic Inquiry into Contract Damages in Cases of Prospective Non-Performance,* 31 Stan.L.Rev. 69, 75–101 (1978).

Problem 15–1

The Tivoli Manufacturing Co., a manufacturer of air compressors, contracted with the Ace Supply Co. to furnish at a fixed price a large quantity of specially tooled valves for use in the compressors. Ace agreed to deliver the valves in 6 equal installments at 3 month intervals. Tivoli stated that the installments were geared to a long range production schedule and a projected increase in demand for the compressors. Tivoli furnished design drawings to assist Ace in "tooling up," gave Ace 6 months of lead time, and advanced 25% of the contract price. Two weeks before the first installment was due, Tivoli appeared in your office with the following letter from Ace:

> Gentlemen:
>
> As suggested in our telephone conversation of last week, our engineers misread the design drawings which you furnished us.
>
> We must, therefore, retool our original model value at considerable extra expense and some delay. We regret that we will be unable to meet the first installment, scheduled for delivery in two weeks. We will make every effort to meet the second installment three months hence and to deliver the quantity promised in the first installment before the contract delivery schedule is completed.
>
> Yours sincerely,
>
> Ace Supply Co.

Tivoli states that it would like to cancel the contract and get back the 25% advance. Upon close questioning, you discover: 1) the delay in delivery will "wreak havoc" with Tivoli's production schedule and existing contractual commitments; 2) if the contract were cancelled, Tivoli would purchase 50% of the valves ordered from Ace from another manufacturer who guaranteed full performance in 4 months; 3) Tivoli's estimated demand for the compressors was about 50% too high; 4) in Tivoli's judgment, Ace would "probably" meet the next installment and make up the late deliveries. What is your advice?

SECTION 3. BUYER'S RIGHT TO GET THE GOODS—SPECIFIC PERFORMANCE AND REPLEVIN

Suppose, in Problem 15–1, that Ace repudiated the entire contract with Tivoli because it received an offer to purchase all of the compressor valves on hand and its output of similar valves during the next 12 months at a price that was "too good to refuse." Also, Ace estimated a 35–50% increase in the cost of production over the next year. At the time of repudiation, Ace had on hand 25% of the total quantity ordered by Tivoli. The valves were conforming and identified to the contract. Tivoli needs the valves "yesterday" to meet production orders and estimates that it will take four months and 30% more money to establish a reliable source of supply. In short, Tivoli wants both the valves Ace has on hand and the future output of conforming valves at the agreed price until the quantity ordered has been satisfied.

Problem 15–2

You represent Tivoli in this matter and your client wants results. Which of the following alternatives is best suited to your client's interest and most likely to be successful?

1. Suspend performance and wait under UCC 2–610 and try to negotiate the matter with Ace. Offer more money and couple that with appropriate "non-legal" pressures.

2. Replevin of the valves under UCC 2–716(3). See Tatum v. Richter, 280 Md. 332, 373 A.2d 923 (1977) (replevin of used Ferrari).

3. Seek specific performance of the contract and an order restraining Ace from selling the existing goods and future output to third parties. See UCC 2–716(1); Kaiser Trading Co. v. Associated Metals & Minerals Corp., 321 F.Supp. 923 (N.D.Cal.1970), appeal dismissed 443 F.2d 1364 (9th Cir.1971).

4. Recover the goods under UCC 2–502.

LACLEDE GAS CO. v. AMOCO OIL CO.

United States Court of Appeals, Eighth Circuit, 1975.
522 F.2d 33.

Ross, C.J.

The Laclede Gas Company (Laclede), a Missouri corporation, brought this diversity action alleging breach of contract against the Amoco Oil Company (Amoco), a Delaware corporation. It sought relief in the form of a mandatory injunction prohibiting the continuing breach or, in the alternative, damages. The district court held a bench trial on the issues of whether there was a valid, binding contract between the parties and whether, if there was such a contract, Amoco should be enjoined from breaching it. It then ruled that the "contract is invalid due to lack of mutuality" and denied the prayer for injunctive relief. The court made no decision regarding the requested damages. Laclede Gas Co. v. Amoco Oil Co., 385 F.Supp. 1332, 1336 (E.D.Mo.1974). This appeal followed, and we reverse the district court's judgment.

On September 21, 1970, Midwest Missouri Gas Company (now Laclede), and American Oil Company (now Amoco), the predecessors of the parties to this litigation, entered into a written agreement which was designed to provide central propane gas distribution systems to various residential developments in Jefferson County, Missouri, until such time as natural gas mains were extended into these areas. The agreement contemplated that as individual developments were planned the owners or developers would apply to Laclede for central propane gas systems. If Laclede determined that such a system was appropriate in any given development, it could request Amoco to supply the propane to that specific development. This request was made in the form of a supplemental form letter, as provided in the September 21 agreement; and if Amoco decided to supply the propane, it bound itself to do so by signing this supplemental form.

Once this supplemental form was signed the agreement placed certain duties on both Laclede and Amoco. Basically, Amoco was to "[i]nstall, own, maintain and operate * * * storage and vaporization facilities and any other facilities necessary to provide [it] with the capability of delivering to [Laclede] commercial propane gas suitable * * * for delivery by [Laclede] to its customers' facilities." Amoco's facilities were to be "adequate to provide a continuous supply of commercial propane gas at such times and in such volumes commensurate with [Laclede's] requirements for meeting the demands reasonably to be anticipated in each Development while this Agreement is in force." Amoco was deemed to be "the supplier," while Laclede was "the distributing utility."

For its part Laclede agreed to "[i]nstall, own, maintain and operate all distribution facilities" from a "point of delivery" which was defined to be "the outlet of [Amoco] header piping." Laclede also promised to pay Amoco "the Wood River Area Posted Price for propane plus four cents per gallon for all amounts of commercial propane gas delivered" to it under the agreement.

Since it was contemplated that the individual propane systems would eventually be converted to natural gas, one paragraph of the agreement provided that Laclede should give Amoco 30 days written notice of this event, after which the agreement would no longer be binding for the converted development.

Another paragraph gave Laclede the right to cancel the agreement. However, this right was expressed in the following language:

> "This Agreement shall remain in effect for one (1) year following the first delivery of gas by [Amoco] to [Laclede] hereunder. Subject to termination as provided in Paragraph 11 hereof [dealing with conversions to natural gas], this Agreement shall automatically continue in effect for additional periods of one (1) year each unless [Laclede] shall, not less than 30 days prior to the expiration of the initial one (1) year period or any subsequent one (1) year period, give [Amoco] written notice of termination."

There was no provision under which Amoco could cancel the agreement.

For a time the parties operated satisfactorily under this agreement, and some 17 residential subdivisions were brought within it by supplemental letters. However, for various reasons, including conversion to natural gas, the number of developments under the agreement had shrunk to eight by the time of trial. These were all mobile home parks.

During the winter of 1972–73 Amoco experienced a shortage of propane and voluntarily placed all of its customers, including Laclede, on an 80% allocation basis, meaning that Laclede would receive only up to 80% of its previous requirements. Laclede objected to this and pushed Amoco to give it

100% of what the developments needed. Some conflict arose over this before the temporary shortage was alleviated.

Then, on April 3, 1973, Amoco notified Laclede that its Wood River Area Posted Price of propane had been increased by three cents per gallon. Laclede objected to this increase also and demanded a full explanation. None was forthcoming. Instead Amoco merely sent a letter dated May 14, 1973, informing Laclede that it was "terminating" the September 21, 1970, agreement effective May 31, 1973. It claimed it had the right to do this because "the Agreement lacks 'mutuality.' "[1]

The district court felt that the entire controversy turned on whether or not Laclede's right to "arbitrarily cancel the Agreement" without Amoco having a similar right rendered the contract void "for lack of mutuality" and it resolved this question in the affirmative. We disagree with this conclusion and hold that settled principles of contract law require a reversal.

I.

* * *

We conclude that there is mutuality of consideration within the terms of the agreement and hold that there is a valid, binding contract between the parties as to each of the developments for which supplemental letter agreements have been signed.

II.

Since he found that there was no binding contract, the district judge did not have to deal with the question of whether or not to grant the injunction prayed for by Laclede. He simply denied this relief because there was no contract. Laclede Gas Co. v. Amoco Oil Co., supra, 385 F.Supp. at 1336.

Generally the determination of whether or not to order specific performance of a contract lies within the sound discretion of the trial court. Landau v. St. Louis Public Service Co., 364 Mo. 1134, 273 S.W.2d 255, 259 (1954). However, this discretion is, in fact, quite limited; and it is said that when certain equitable rules have been met and the contract is fair and plain "specific performance goes as a matter of right." Miller v. Coffeen, 365 Mo. 204, 280 S.W.2d 100, 102 (1955), quoting, Berberet v. Myers, 240 Mo. 58, 77, 144 S.W. 824, 830 (1912). (Emphasis omitted.)

With this in mind we have carefully reviewed the very complete record on appeal and conclude that the trial court should grant the injunctive relief prayed. We are satisfied that this case falls within that category in which specific performance should be ordered as a matter of right. See Miller v. Coffeen, supra, 280 S.W.2d at 102.

Amoco contends that four of the requirements for specific performance have not been met. Its claims are: (1) there is no mutuality of remedy in the contract; (2) the remedy of specific performance would be difficult for the court to administer without constant and long-continued supervision; (3)

1. While Amoco sought to repudiate the agreement, it resumed supplying propane to the subdivisions on February 1, 1974, under the mandatory allocation guidelines promulgated by the Federal Energy Administration under the Federal Mandatory Allocation Program for propane. It is agreed that this is now being done under the contract.

the contract is indefinite and uncertain; and (4) the remedy at law available to Laclede is adequate. The first three contentions have little or no merit and do not detain us for long.

* * *

[The court, after stressing that the agreement was for the buyer's requirements and was supported by consideration, rejected summarily the notion that "both parties be mutually entitled to * * * specific performance in order that one of them be given that remedy by the court." The defendant's right to performance can be protected by a conditional decree. The argument that specific performance would require excessive supervision was rejected on the ground that the rule invoked was "discretionary" and frequently ignored where the public interest, here providing propane to retail customers, was manifest. Finally, the court concluded that the court could determine the terms of performance with "reasonable certainty." The "requirements" feature offered no problem to enforcement. Nor did the fact that the contract stated no "definite time of duration:" the evidence established that the last subdivision should be converted to natural gas in 10 to 15 years and this set "a reasonable time limit on performance."]

It is axiomatic that specific performance will not be ordered when the party claiming breach of contract has an adequate remedy at law. Jamison Coal & Coke Co. v. Goltra, 143 F.2d 889, 894 (8th Cir.), cert. denied, 323 U.S. 769, 65 S.Ct. 122, 89 L.Ed. 615 (1944). This is especially true when the contract involves personal property as distinguished from real estate.

However, in Missouri, as elsewhere, specific performance may be ordered even though personalty is involved in the "proper circumstances." Mo.Rev.Stat. § 400.2–716(1); Restatement of Contracts, supra, § 361. And a remedy at law adequate to defeat the grant of specific performance "must be as certain, prompt, complete, and efficient to attain the ends of justice as a decree of specific performance." National Marking Mach. Co. v. Triumph Mfg. Co., 13 F.2d 6, 9 (8th Cir.1926). Accord, Snip v. City of Lamar, 239 Mo.App. 824, 201 S.W.2d 790, 798 (1947).

One of the leading Missouri cases allowing specific performance of a contract relating to personalty because the remedy at law was inadequate is Boeving v. Vandover, 240 Mo.App. 117, 218 S.W.2d 175, 178 (1949). In that case the plaintiff sought specific performance of a contract in which the defendant had promised to sell him an automobile. At that time (near the end of and shortly after World War II) new cars were hard to come by, and the court held that specific performance was a proper remedy since a new car "could not be obtained elsewhere except at considerable expense, trouble or loss, which cannot be estimated in advance."

We are satisfied that Laclede has brought itself within this practical approach taken by the Missouri courts. As Amoco points out, Laclede has propane immediately available to it under other contracts with other suppliers. And the evidence indicates that at the present time propane is readily available on the open market. However, this analysis ignores the fact that the contract involved in this lawsuit is for a long-term supply of propane to these subdivisions. The other two contracts under which Laclede obtains the gas will remain in force only until March 31, 1977, and April 1, 1981, respectively; and there is no assurance that Laclede will be able to receive any propane under them after that time. Also it is unclear as to whether or not Laclede can use the propane obtained under these contracts to supply the Jefferson County subdivisions, since they were originally entered into to provide Laclede with propane with which to "shave" its natural gas supply during peak demand periods. Additionally, there was uncontradicted expert testimony that Laclede probably could not find another supplier of propane willing to enter into a long-term contract such as the Amoco agreement, given the uncertain future of worldwide energy supplies. And, even if Laclede could obtain supplies of propane for the affected developments through its present contracts or newly negotiated ones, it would still face considerable expense and trouble which cannot be estimated in advance in making arrangements for its distribution to the subdivisions.

Specific performance is the proper remedy in this situation, and it should be granted by the district court.

CONCLUSION

For the foregoing reasons the judgment of the district court is reversed and the cause is remanded for the fashioning of appropriate injunctive relief in the form of a decree of specific performance as to those developments for which a supplemental agreement form has been signed by the parties. [Some footnotes omitted.]

Notes

1. Laclede Gas is one of the few cases under UCC 2–716(1) which both grants specific performance of a contract to sell goods and attempts to justify the decision on grounds of "other proper circumstances." More recently, specific performance with ancillary injunctive relief in long-term contracts for the supply of natural resources for energy has been granted without discussion. Iowa Elec. Light and Power Co. v. Atlas Corp., 467 F.Supp. 129, 138 (N.D.Iowa 1978), reversed on other grounds 603 F.2d 1301 (8th Cir.1979) (uranium oxide); Missouri Public Serv. Co. v. Peabody Coal Co., 583 S.W.2d 721 (Mo.App.1979), cert. denied 444 U.S. 865, 100 S.Ct. 135, 62 L.Ed.2d 88 (1979) (bituminous coal). A useful history of UCC 2–716 and a comparison with the Restatement, Second of Contracts, is Greenberg, *Specific Performance Under Section 2–716 of the Uniform Commercial Code: "A More Liberal Attitude" in the "Grand Style,"* 17 N.Eng.L.Rev. 321, 344–53 (1982).

2. Should specific performance rather than damages be the preferred remedy in all cases of breach of contract? Put differently, if it were clear that specific performance (1) best protected the promisee's subjective value in the contract; (2) minimized if not avoided consequential damages; and (3) decreased the overall costs of judicial administration or the parties' post-breach negotiations, what are the arguments for the current rule, i.e., damages are preferred unless they are inadequate? An argument for specific performance "on demand" is made in Ulen, *The Efficiency of Specific Performance: Toward A Unified Theory of Contract Remedies,* 83 Mich.L.Rev. 341 (1984). Should a court enforce an agreement that specific performance is the appropriate remedy, without regard to UCC 2–716(1)?

3. *Specific performance under CISG.* Article 45(1)(a) of the Convention provides that if "the seller fails to perform any of his obligations under the contract or this Convention, the buyer may: (a) exercise the rights provided in

articles 46–52." Article 46(1) provides that the "buyer may require performance by the seller of his obligations unless the buyer has resorted to a remedy which is inconsistent with this requirement." Thus, the buyer appears to have power to demand specific performance as a matter of right. See Walt, *For Specific Performance Under the United Nations Sales Convention,* 26 Tex.Int'l L.J. 211 (1991). Article 28, however, provides that a court is not bound to order specific performance "unless the court would do so under its own law in respect of similar contracts for sale not governed by this Convention." Thus, in cases where the Convention applies, a United States court would not be required to order specific performance if that remedy was not available under UCC 2–716(1).

Problem 15–3

Suppose, in *Laclede Gas,* supra, that because of unanticipated events, the supplier's cost of production rose dramatically during performance of the contract. The supplier, in good faith, proposed a reasonable prospective modification, which the buyer, without negotiation, rejected. Upon repudiation by the supplier, the buyer sought specific performance plus injunctive relief. In response, the supplier made the following argument:

> "May it please the court. We concede that at law our client would not be excused from performance under UCC 2–615 and that the buyer has stated a case for specific performance under UCC 2–716(1). We also concede that the law of this jurisdiction is that the buyer had no duty to negotiate over or agree to our proposed modification, no matter how reasonable. These are harsh outcomes 'at law.'
>
> "Specific performance, however, is an equitable remedy to be granted in the discretion of the court. UCC 2–716(2) provides that a decree of specific performance 'may include such terms and conditions as to payment of the price, damages, or other relief as the court may deem just.' Comment 7 to UCC 2–615, although not directly on point, suggests that good faith may 'justify and even * * * require' a 'good faith inquiry seeking a readjustment of the contract terms to meet the new conditions.' Our proposed modification was fair and equitable in light of the changed circumstances. If the buyer had accepted it, the result would clearly be enforceable under UCC 2–209(1). Thus, your honor, we contend that it would be unjust to grant specific performance in this case without a price adjustment for the balance of the contract. We, therefore, urge the court to condition any decree for specific performance upon the buyer's consent to the reasonable modification which we have proposed."

How should the court rule?

SECTION 4. BUYER'S RIGHT TO "MARKET-CONTRACT" DAMAGES

Note first that UCC 2–713 instructs the court to use the market price "at the time when the buyer learned of the breach," and except in cases of rejection or revocation of acceptance indicates that the place for tender is the place to measure damages. The cognate provision for the seller's damages, UCC 2–708(1), directs the use of the "time and place for tender."

The meaning of the words "when the buyer learned of the breach" is likely to cause trouble only in the anticipatory repudiation situation, as we will see below. Professor Patterson suggested in the New York Law Revision Commission Reports that it was no more than a codification of the New York common law:

PATTERSON, 1 N.Y.LAW REV.COMM.REP. 697–699 (1955) "*Case law on Section UCC 2–713.*

"Since the 'ordinary' measure of damages for non-delivery by the seller (as defined in § 2–711(1)(b)) is the contract price less the market value of the goods, under the Uniform Sales Act enacted in New York in 1911, and even long before that year, we need not multiply New York citations to support that formula. The chief differences between Section 2–713 and the present statute are those relating to the *time when* and the *place where* market value is to be determined. * * *

"*Time when market value determined.*

"The present New York statute (P.P.L., § 148(3)) fixes the market value as of the time when the goods 'ought to have been delivered' or, if no time was fixed for delivery, 'at the time of refusal to deliver.' The proposed statute would make 'the time when the buyer learned of the breach' determine the market price. This is *apparently* a change in New York law; but actually it probably is not a change in the law as applied by New York courts. In at least two New York cases it was held that the market value was to be measured as of the time when the buyer knew of the default.* However, the Court of Appeals' language included 'should have known,' which would be different from the time when the buyer 'learned' of the breach. These cases do not purport to depart from the ordinary rule except where 'special circumstances' justify allowing the buyer a longer time to cover by a second buying in the market. Yet in one case an instruction that damages be measured by the price paid for similar goods bought by the buyer 'within a reasonable time after breach' (to allow him a reasonable time to cover), was held reversible error. In this case it seems that the buyer learned of the breach at once. Ordinarily, it is believed, no significant lag would occur. The purpose of Section 2–713(1), which applies (§ 2–711) only as an alternative to cover (§ 2–712) is presumably to prevent the buyer's getting any more damages by waiting for the market to go down ("speculating at the seller's expense," some courts would say) after he learns of the breach; if the market goes up further, the buyer will have to pay more and yet will recover only the difference (market minus contract price) when he first learns of the breach. The buyer is thus encouraged to 'cover' promptly. However, under Section 2–712 the buyer may cover 'without unreasonable delay' after the *breach* (*not* "learning of the breach"), which means that the buyer could *delay* after (learning of) the breach and *then* fix damages. Then could not a buyer, after learning of the breach on May 1, wait until May 15, when he purchases a larger quantity of the same goods, and then have his option to fix damages on May 1, asserting his purchase on

* Professor Patterson describes the two New York cases as follows:

Perkins v. Minford, 235 N.Y. 301, 139 N.E. 276 (1923) (action by buyer for breach by seller in shipping at Cuban port (F.O.B.) a quantity of sugar 200,000 lbs. less than seller contracted to ship; buyer did not know of breach until much later, and this is a "special circumstance" under § 148 calling for variation from ordinary damage rule, time of breach); Boyd v. Quinn, 8 Misc. 169, 41 N.Y.Supp. 391 (1896) (contract to ship goods by rail from Peoria, Ill., to New York; buyer didn't know, until he inquired of seller and received seller's refusal, that seller had defaulted).

May 15 at a lower price was *not* a 'cover'; or, if the price goes up, to claim that his purchase on May 15 was a 'cover' not unreasonably delayed (§ 2–712) and fix damages at the higher price then prevailing? Should the alternative statement in Section 2–711(1) be tightened to avoid this?"

Problem 15–4
Volta v. Simpka Revisited

Review the facts of *Volta v. Simpka,* Problem 14–4. Suppose that Simpka was to ship the custom furniture in two installments on October 1 and October 15. The first installment, consisting of 60% of the goods, was shipped f.o.b. Ohio on October 1, arrived in New York on October 12 and was rejected by Volta for manufacturing defects on October 15. The second installment was never shipped by Simpka. At trial, the court found that Volta "learned of the breach" on the first installment on October 15 and "learned" of the breach on the second installment on October 20. Assume that the contract price on the first shipment was $48,000 and was $32,000 on the second. Neither side claims that UCC 2–712 governs the case.

The market price for goods comparable to the first installment on October 15 was $60,000 in New York and $50,000 in Ohio. The market price for comparable goods to the second installment on October 20 was $28,000 in Ohio and $40,000 in New York. You may assume that the total cost of shipment from Ohio to New York would have been $4,000, but since the first installment was shipped "for buyer's account," no payment has as yet been made.

How much in damages, if any, should the court award to Volta?

Problem 15–5
More Simpka v. Volta

In June, 1986 the *Simpka-Volta* contract was modified to provide that all of the furniture, both standard and custom, was to be shipped in one lot on March 1, 1987. The contract price was increased to $220,000. On July 1, 1986, however, Simpka repudiated the contract in unequivocal terms and no shipments were ever made under the contract. When the case came to trial in February, 1988, Volta made the following argument: "Our damages should be measured on either July 1, 1986, when we learned of the repudiation, or May 1, 1987, when we purchased furniture in substitution (covered) on the open market." The evidence revealed the relevant market prices for comparable goods during this time frame as follows:

July 1–31, 1986	$260,000
August 1–December 31, 1986	200,000
March 1, 1987	220,000
May 1, 1987	280,000

Simpka would like the damages to be measured as of March 1, 1987, the date the goods were to be delivered. You represent Simpka. Develop the strongest arguments you can to support Simpka's position. Then read the next case.

COSDEN OIL v. KARL O. HELM AKTIENGESELLSCHAFT

United States Court of Appeals, Fifth Circuit, 1984.
736 F.2d 1064, *rehearing denied*, 750 F.2d 69 (1984).

REAVLEY, CIRCUIT JUDGE.

* * *

II. TIME FOR MEASURING BUYER'S DAMAGES

Both parties find fault with the time at which the district court measured Helm's damages for Cosden's anticipatory repudiation of orders 05, 06, and 07. Cosden argues that damages should be measured when Helm learned of the repudiation. Helm contends that market price as of the last day for delivery—or the time of performance—should be used to compute its damages under the contract-market differential. We reject both views, and hold that the district court correctly measured damages at a commercially reasonable point after Cosden informed Helm that it was cancelling the three orders.

Article 2 of the Code has generally been hailed as a success for its comprehensiveness, its deference to mercantile reality, and its clarity. Nevertheless, certain aspects of the Code's overall scheme have proved troublesome in application. The interplay among sections 2.610, 2.711, 2.712, 2.713, and 2.723, Tex.Bus. & Com.Code Ann. (Vernon 1968), represents one of those areas, and has been described as "an impossible legal thicket." J. White & R. Summers, *Uniform Commercial Code* § 6–7 at 242 (2d ed. 1980). The aggrieved buyer seeking damages for seller's anticipatory repudiation presents the most difficult interpretive problem.[6] Section 2.713 describes the buyer's damages remedy:

> Buyer's Damages for Non-Delivery or Repudiation
>
> (a) Subject to the provisions of this chapter with respect to proof of market price (Section 2.723), the measure of damages for non-delivery or repudiation by the seller is the difference between the market price *at the time when the buyer learned of the breach* and the contract price together with any incidental and consequential damages provided in this chapter (Section 2.715), but less expenses saved in consequence of the seller's breach.

(emphasis added).

Courts and commentators have identified three possible interpretations of the phrase "learned of the breach." If seller anticipatorily repudiates, buyer learns of the breach:

(1) When he learns of the repudiation;

(2) When he learns of the repudiation plus a commercially reasonable time; or

(3) When performance is due under the contract.

6. The only area of unanimous agreement among those that have studied the Code provisions relevant to this problem is that they are not consistent, present problems in interpretation, and invite amendment.

See, e.g., First National Bank of Chicago v. Jefferson Mortgage Co., 576 F.2d 479 (3d Cir.1978); *Cargill, Inc. v. Stafford,* 553 F.2d 1222 (10th Cir.1977); J. White & R. Summers § 6–7 at 240–52; Note, *U.C.C. § 2–713: Anticipatory Repudiation and the Measurement of an Aggrieved Buyer's Damages,* 19 Wm. & Mary L.Rev. 253 (1977).

We would not be free to decide the question if there were a Texas case on point, bound as we are by *Erie* to follow state law in diversity cases. We find, however, that no Texas case has addressed the Code question of buyer's damages in an anticipatory repudiation context. Texas, alone in this circuit, does not allow us to certify questions of state law for resolution by its courts. *See United Services Life Insurance Co. v. Delaney,* 396 S.W.2d 855 (Tex.1965).

We do not doubt, and Texas law is clear, that market price at the time buyer learns of the breach is the appropriate measure of section 2.713 damages in cases where buyer learns of the breach at or after the time for performance. This will be the common case, for which section 2.713 was designed. *See* Peters, *Remedies for Breach of Contracts Relating to the Sale of Goods Under the Uniform Commercial Code: A Roadmap for Article Two,* 73 Yale L.J. 199, 264 (1963). In the relatively rare case where seller anticipatorily repudiates and buyer does not cover, * * * the specific provision for anticipatory repudiation cases, section 2.610, authorizes the aggrieved party to await performance for a commercially reasonable time before resorting to his remedies of cover or damages.

In the anticipatory repudiation context, the buyer's specific right to wait for a commercially reasonable time before choosing his remedy must be read together with the general damages provision of section 2.713 to extend the time for measurement beyond when buyer learns of the breach. Comment 1 to section 2.610 states that if an aggrieved party "awaits performance beyond a commercially reasonable time he cannot recover resulting damages which he should have avoided." This suggests that an aggrieved buyer can recover damages where the market rises during the commercially reasonable time he awaits performance. To interpret 2.713's "learned of the breach" language to mean the time at which seller first communicates his anticipatory repudiation would undercut the time that 2.610 gives the aggrieved buyer to await performance.

The buyer's option to wait a commercially reasonable time also interacts with section 2.611, which allows the seller an opportunity to retract his repudiation. Thus, an aggrieved buyer "learns of the breach" a commercially reasonable time after he learns of the seller's anticipatory repudiation. The weight of scholarly commentary supports this interpretation. *See* J. Calamari & J. Perillo, *Contracts* § 14–20 (2d ed. 1977); Sebert, *Remedies Under Article Two of the Uniform Commercial Code: An Agenda for Review,* 130 U.Pa.L.Rev. 360, 372–80 (1981); Wallach, *Anticipatory Repudiation and the UCC,* 13 U.C.C.L.J. 48 (1980); Peters, *supra,* at 263–68.

Typically, our question will arise where parties to an executory contract are in the midst of a rising market. To the extent that market decisions are influenced by a damages rule, measuring market price at the time of seller's repudiation gives seller the ability to fix buyer's damages and may induce seller to repudiate, rather than abide by the contract. By contrast, measuring buyer's damages at the time of performance will tend to dissuade the buyer from covering, in hopes that market price will continue upward until performance time.

Allowing the aggrieved buyer a commercially reasonable time, however, provides him with an opportunity to investigate his cover possibilities in a rising market without fear that, if he is unsuccessful in obtaining cover, he will be relegated to a market-contract damage remedy measured at the time of repudiation. The Code supports this view. While cover is the preferred remedy, the Code clearly provides the option to seek damages. *See* § 2.712(c) & comment 3. If "[t]he buyer is always free to choose between cover and damages for non-delivery," and if 2.712 "is not intended to limit the time necessary for [buyer] to look around and decide as to how he may best effect cover," it would be anomalous, if the buyer chooses to seek damages, to fix his damages at a time before he investigated cover possibilities and before he elected his remedy. *See id.* comment 2 & 3; *Dura-Wood Treating Co. v. Century Forest Industries, Inc.,* 675 F.2d 745, 754 (5th Cir.), *cert. denied,* 459 U.S. 865, 103 S.Ct. 144, 74 L.Ed.2d 122 (1982) ("buyer has some time in which to evaluate the situation"). Moreover, comment 1 to section 2.713 states, "The general baseline adopted in this section uses as a yardstick the market in which the buyer would have obtained cover had he sought that relief." *See* § 2.610 comment 1. When a buyer chooses not to cover, but to seek damages, the market is measured at the time he could have covered—a reasonable time after repudiation. *See* §§ 2.711 & 2.713.

Persuasive arguments exist for interpreting "learned of the breach" to mean "time of performance," consistent with the pre-Code rule. *See* J. White & R. Summers, *supra.* § 6–7; Anderson, *supra.* If this was the intention of the Code's drafters, however, phrases in section 2.610 and 2.712 lose their meaning. If buyer is entitled to market-contract damages measured at the time of performance, it is difficult to explain why the anticipatory repudiation section limits him to a commercially reasonable time to await performance. *See* § 2.610 comment 1. Similarly, in a rising market, no reason would exist for requiring the buyer to act "without unreasonable delay" when he seeks to cover following an anticipatory repudiation. *See* § 2.712(a).

The interplay among the relevant Code sections does not permit, in this context, an interpretation that harmonizes all and leaves no loose ends. We therefore acknowledge that our interpretation fails to explain the language of section 2.723(a) insofar as it relates to aggrieved buyers. We note, however, that the section has limited applicability—cases that come to trial before the time of performance will be rare. Moreover, the comment to section 2.723 states that the "section is not intended to exclude the use of any other reasonable method of determining market price or of measuring damages. * * *" In light of the Code's persistent theme of commercial reasonableness, the prominence of cover as a remedy, and the time given an aggrieved buyer to await performance and to investigate cover before selecting his remedy, we agree with the district court that "learned of the breach" incorporates section 2.610's commercially reasonable time.[11]

* * *

11. We note that two circuits arrived at a similar conclusion by different routes. In *Cargill, Inc. v. Stafford,* 553 F.2d 1222 (10th Cir.1977), the court began its discussion of

[Some footnotes omitted.]

ALLIED CANNERS & PACKERS, INC. v. VICTOR PACKING CO.

Court of Appeal of California, First District, 1984.
162 Cal.App.3d 905, 209 Cal.Rptr. 60.

[In early September, 1976, Victor agreed to sell Allied 375,000 pounds of raisins for October, 1976 delivery at 29.75 cents per pound. Victor knew that Allied had contracted to resell the raisins to foreign purchasers. Allied expected to gain a profit of $4,462.50 on the resale transaction. On September 9, 1976, heavy rains severely damaged the region's raisin crop, including that of Victor. When Victor was unable to obtain raisins from other sources, it repudiated the contract with Allied on September 15, 1976. The regulated market for raisins did not reopen until October 18, 1976, at which time the price was 87 cents per pound. In the meantime, Allied's resale buyers had either agreed to rescind their contracts without liability or failed to assert claims for damages by the time of trial.

Allied sued Victor for damages under UCC 2–713(1), measured by the difference between the contract price, 29.75 cents per pound, and the market price at the time and place for delivery, 87 cents per pound. The trial court concluded that Allied was an exporter rather than a buyer for its own account. Accordingly, Allied could not use UCC 2–713 and was limited to its actual loss on the transaction, $4,462.50. The Court of Appeal, however,

damages by embracing the "time of performance" interpretation urged by Professors White and Summers. *Id.* at 1226. Indeed, the court stated that "damages normally should be measured from the time when performance is due and not from the time when the buyer learns of repudiation." *Id.* Nevertheless, the court

> conclude[d] that under § 4–2–713 a buyer may urge continued performance for a reasonable time. At the end of a reasonable period he should cover if substitute goods are readily available. If substitution is readily available and buyer does not cover within a reasonable time, damages should be based on the price at the end of that reasonable time rather than on the price when performance is due.

Id. at 1227. The *Cargill* court would employ the time of performance measure only if buyer had a valid reason for not covering.

In *First Nat'l Bank of Chicago v. Jefferson Mortgage Co.,* 576 F.2d 479 (3d Cir.1978), the court initially quoted with approval legislative history that supports a literal or "plain meaning" interpretation of New Jersey's section 2–713. Nevertheless, the court hedged by interpreting that section "to measure damages within a commercially reasonable time after learning of the repudiation." *Id.* at 492. In light of the unequivocal repudiation and because cover was "easily and immediately * * * available * * * in the well-organized and easily accessible market," *id.* at 493 (quoting *Oloffson v. Coomer,* 11 Ill. App.3d 918, 296 N.E.2d 871 (1973)), a commercially reasonable time did not extend beyond the date of repudiation.

We agree with the *First National* court that "the circumstances of the particular market involved should determine the duration of a 'commercially reasonable time.'" 576 F.2d at 492; *see* Tex.Bus. & Com.Code § 1.204(b). In this case, however, there was no showing that cover was easily and immediately available in an organized and accessible market and that a commercially reasonable time expired on the day of Cosden's cancellation. We recognize that § 2.610's "commercially reasonable time" and § 2.712's "without unreasonable delay" are distinct concepts. Often, however, the two time periods will overlap, since the buyer can investigate cover possibilities while he awaits performance. *See* Sebert, *supra,* at 376–77 & n. 80.

Although the jury in the present case did not fix the exact duration of a commercially reasonable time, we assume that the jury determined market price at a time commercially reasonable under all the circumstances, in light of the absence of objection to the form of the special issue.

held that Allied was a buyer with forward resale contracts and that the buyer's remedies in the Code applied.

The court first reviewed Sections 2–712 through 2–715.

* * *

ROUSE, ASSOCIATE JUSTICE

Sections 2–712 and 2–713 of the Uniform Code are sometimes referred to as "cover" and "hypothetical cover," since the former involves an actual entry into the market by the buyer while the latter does not. (See Childres, *Buyer's Remedies: The Danger of Section 2–713* (1978) 72 Nw.U.L.Rev. 837, 841 [applying those terms] (hereafter cited as *Buyer's Remedies*); Peters, *Remedies for Breach of Contracts Relating to the Sale of Goods Under the Uniform Commercial Code: A Roadmap For Article Two* (1963) 73 Yale L.J. 199, 259 [market under section 2–713 is "purely theoretical"] (hereafter cited as *Remedies for Breach of Contracts*).) It has been recognized that the use of the market price-contract price formula under section 2–713 does not, absent pure accident, result in a damage award reflecting the buyer's actual loss. (*Buyer's Remedies, supra,* at pp. 841–842; *Remedies for Breach of Contracts, supra,* at p. 259; *Market Damages, supra,* 92 Harv.L.Rev. 1395 et seq.; * White & Summers, Uniform Commercial Code, *supra,* at p. 224.)

For example, in this case it is agreed that Allied's actual lost profit on the transaction was $4,462.50, while application of the market-contract price formula would yield damages of approximately $150,000. In *Market Damages, supra,* Simon and Novack describe the courts as divided on the issue of whether market damages, even though in excess of the plaintiff's loss, are appropriate for a supplier's breach of his delivery obligations and observe: "Strangely enough, each view has generally tended to disregard the arguments, and even the existence, of the opposing view. These two rival bodies of law, imposing in appearance, have passed each other like silent ships in the night." (92 Harv.L.Rev. 1395, 1397.) In *Buyer's Remedies, supra,* Professor Childres similarly points out that the courts have generally not undertaken any real analysis of the competing considerations involved in determining the correct measure of damages in such circumstances. (72 Nw.U.L.Rev. 837, 844 et seq.) We will undertake such an analysis.

Professors White and Summers, after noting their belief that "the Code drafters did not by [section 2–713] intend to put the buyer in the same position as performance would have" (White & Summers, Uniform Commercial Code, *supra,* at p. 224), advance two possible explanations for the section. First, they suggest that it is simply a historical anomaly: "Since cover was not a recognized remedy under pre-Code law, it made sense under that law to say that the contract-market formula put buyer in the same position as performance would have *on the assumption that the buyer would purchase substitute goods.* If things worked right, the market price would approximate the cost of the substitute goods and buyer would be put 'in the same position. * * *' But under the Code, 2–712 does this job with greater precision, and 2–713 reigns over only those cases in which the buyer does not purchase a substitute. Perhaps the drafters retained 2–713 not out of a

* Simon & Novack, *Limiting the Buyer's Market Damages to Lost Profits: A Challenge to the Enforceability of Market Contracts*, 92 Harv.L.Rev. 1395 (1979).

belief in its appropriateness, but out of fear that they would be dismissed as iconoclasts had they proposed that the court in noncover cases simply award the buyer any economic loss proximately caused by seller's breach." (*Ibid.*)

They conclude, however, that probably the best explanation for section 2–713 "is that it is a statutory liquidated damage clause, a breach inhibitor the payout of which need bear no close relation to plaintiff's actual loss." (White & Summers, Uniform Commercial Code, *supra,* at p. 225.) They then observe that this explanation conflicts with the policy set forth in section 1–106, which provides in subdivision (1): "The remedies provided by this code shall be liberally administered *to the end that the aggrieved party may be put in as good a position as if the other party had fully performed* but neither consequential or special nor penal damages may be had except as specifically provided in this code or by other rule of law." (Emphasis added.) They find section 2–713 consistent, however, with a belief that plaintiffs recover too little and too infrequently for the law of contracts to be effective, and offer no suggestion for resolution of the conflict. (*Ibid.*)

In her article *Remedies for Breach of Contracts, supra,* then-Professor Peters states: "Perhaps it is misleading to think of the market-contract formula as a device for the measurement of damages. * * * An alternative way of looking at market-contract is to view this differential as a statutory liquidated damages clause, rather than as an effort to calculate actual losses. If it is useful in every case to hold the party in breach to some baseline liability, in order to encourage faithful adherence to contractual obligations, perhaps market fluctuations furnish as good a standard as any." (73 Yale L.J. 199, 259.) She does not discuss the conflict between the market-contract formula and the "only as good a position as performance" policy embodied in section 1–106.

Simon and Novack state: "While it is generally recognized that the automatic invocation of market damages may sometimes overcompensate the plaintiff, a variety of arguments have been employed by commentators and courts to justify this result: the desirability of maintaining a uniform rule and of facilitating settlements; the public interest in encouraging contract performance and the proper functioning of the market; the prevention of defendant's unjust enrichment; the restoration of the very 'value' promised to plaintiff; and the inherent difficulty and complexity of proving actual economic losses not encompassed within the contract terms." (Fns. omitted; *Market Damages supra,* 92 Harv.L.Rev. 1395, 1403.) That a defendant not be unjustly enriched by a bad faith breach is a concern widely shared by commentators and courts. (*Id.,* at p. 1406, fn. 51, and cases there cited.)

Viewing section 2–713 as, in effect, a statutory provision for liquidated damages, it is necessary for us to determine whether a damage award to a buyer who has not covered is ever appropriately limited to the buyer's actual economic loss which is below the damages produced by the market-contract formula, and, if so, whether the present case presents a situation in which the damages should be so limited.

One view is that section 2–713 of the Uniform Code, or a substantively similar statutory provision, establishes the principle that a buyer's resale contract and damage claims made thereunder are irrelevant to an award of damages, and that damages therefore cannot be limited to a plaintiff's actual economic loss. (See 11 Williston, Contracts (3d ed. 1968) § 1388 [Uniform Code]; *Coombs and Company of Ogden v. Reed* (1956) 5 Utah 2d 419, 303 P.2d 1097 [Uniform Sales Act]; *Brightwater Paper Co. v. Monadnock Paper Mills* (1st Cir.1947) 161 F.2d 869 [Massachusetts Sales Act then in effect]; *Goldfarb v. Campe Corporation* (1917) 99 Misc. 475, 164 N.Y.S. 583 [New York Sales Act then in effect].) Simon and Novack, while favoring that view, concede that it can be argued that the provision of section 1–106 that an aggrieved party be put " 'in as good a position as if the other party had fully performed' " calls for an opposite conclusion. (*Market Damages, supra,* 92 Harv.L.Rev. 1395, 1412–1413, fn. 71.)

Although we find no cases discussing the interaction of section 1–106 and section 2–713, we note that some pre-Uniform Code cases held that a limitation to actual losses should be placed upon the market price-contract price measure of damages under general contract principles. (See, e.g., *Foss v. Heineman* (1910) 144 Wis. 146 [128 N.W. 881]; *Isaacson v. Crean* (1917) 165 N.Y.S. 218; *Texas Co. v. Pensacola Maritime Corporation* (5th Cir.1922) 279 Fed. 19.) One author on the subject has apparently concluded that such a limitation is appropriate under the Uniform Code when the plaintiff-buyer has a resale contract and the existence of the resale contract is known to the defendant-seller: "It may be supposed * * * that the buyer was bound by a contract made before the breach to deliver to a third person the very goods which the buyer expected to obtain from the seller, and the price under the resale contract may be less than the market price at the time of the breach. If the reason generally given for the rule permitting the recovery of additional damage because of an advantageous resale contract existing and known to the defendant when he contracted be applied, namely, that such consequential damages are allowed because the parties supposedly contract for them, it would follow that in every case the damage that the defendant might normally expect to follow from breach of his contract should be recovered even though the plaintiff actually suffered less damage than the difference between the contract price and the market price." (4 Anderson, Uniform Commercial Code (3d ed. 1983) § 2–711:15, pp. 430–431.)

The only California case directly applying section 2713 is *Gerwin v. Southeastern Cal. Assn. of Seventh Day Adventists* (1971) 14 Cal.App.3d 209, 92 Cal.Rptr. 111. There the plaintiff had contracted to purchase bar and restaurant equipment which he planned to use in a hotel he had recently acquired. The seller failed to deliver the equipment, and plaintiff, who had not covered, was awarded damages of $15,000 as the difference between the contract price and the market price of the equipment. The plaintiff had not covered because substitute items were not available at prices within his financial ability. (*Id.,* at pp. 218–219, 92 Cal.Rptr. 111.) Presumably, after recovering his damage award, the plaintiff in *Gerwin* paid it out to purchase other equipment. That case is inapposite to the present case because the plaintiff there had no resale contract which limited his liability and defined the actual profit he expected to make through the acquisition of the items covered by the sales contract.

We conclude that in the circumstances of this case—in which the seller knew that the buyer had a resale contract (necessarily so because raisins would not be released by RAC unless Allied provided it with the name of the buyer in its forward contract), the buyer has not been able to show that it will be liable in damages to the buyer on its forward contract, and there has been no finding of bad faith on the part of the seller—the policy of section 1106, subdivision (1), that the aggrieved party be put in as good a position as if the other party had performed requires that the award of damages to the buyer be limited to its actual loss, the amount it expected to make on the transaction. We note that in the context of a cover case under section 2712, a Court of Appeal has recently approved the use of section 1106 to limit damages to the amount that would put the plaintiff in as good a position as if the defendant had performed. (*Sun Maid Raisin Growers v. Victor Packing Co.* (1983) 146 Cal.App.3d 787, 792, 194 Cal.Rptr. 612.)

We need not determine in this case what degree of bad faith on the part of a breaching seller might warrant the award of market-contract price damages without limitation, in circumstances otherwise similar to those involved here, in order to prevent unjust enrichment to a seller who deliberately breaches in order to take advantage of a rising market. Although Allied implies that Victor was guilty of bad faith here because after its breach it allowed another packer to acquire reserve raisins to which it was entitled at 36.25 cents per pound, rather than acquiring the raisins and delivering them to Allied, the record is simply not clear on Victor's situation following the rains. It does appear clear, however, that, as the trial court found, the rains caused a severe problem, and Victor made substantial efforts to persuade RAC to release reserve raisins to it in spite of its failure to get its check to RAC before 8:30 a.m. on September 10, 1976. We do not deem this record one to support an inference that windfall damages must be awarded the buyer to prevent unjust enrichment to a deliberately breaching seller. (Compare *Sun Maid Raisin Growers v. Victor Packing Co., supra,* 146 Cal.App.3d 787, 194 Cal.Rptr. 612 [where, in a case coincidentally involving Victor, Victor was expressly found by the trial court to have engaged in bad faith by gambling on the market price of raisins in deciding whether to perform its contracts to sell raisins to Sun Maid].)

The judgment is affirmed. Each party is to bear its own costs on appeal.

KLINE, P.J., and SMITH, J., concur.

Notes

1. Accord: H–W–H Cattle Co., Inc. v. Schroeder, 767 F.2d 437 (8th Cir. 1985). But see Apex Oil Co. v. Vanguard Oil & Service Co., Inc., 760 F.2d 417, 424 (2d Cir.1985), where the court rejected the seller's contention that the buyer, a broker who intended to resell the oil to another customer, could not use the formula in UCC 2–713(1). The court, speaking through Judge Newman, offered the following reasons:

> The formula makes sense when an end user sues the breaching seller because, even if the end user elects not to go into the market and cover, thus demonstrating its out-of-pocket loss, it still has lost the value of having the product. However, in this case, Apex was not an end user, but rather a broker who planned to resell the product to another customer. In the absence of proof that Apex had a customer willing to purchase the oil, it seems fictional to hold that Apex has "lost" the difference between the market price and contract price. However, Vanguard's arguments fail to consider the UCC formula from the perspective of the breaching seller, who

always has the option of going into the market and buying products to satisfy its obligation to the buyer. Since Vanguard elected not to cover and thus fix its loss, it saved an amount equal to the difference between the market price and the contract price. The UCC formula reflects a policy judgment that it makes more sense to award the amount of that saving to the buyer than to permit the non-performing and non-covering seller to retain it. Whether that policy decision should be legislatively limited to buyers who demonstrate some prospect of foregone opportunity for profitable resale is not for us to say.

2. A "middleman" or "jobber," other than a consignee, is both a buyer and a seller. Review the treatment of this functionary when seeking damages as a seller. See supra Chapter Fourteen. What conclusions can you draw as to the availability of the standard damages formulas in UCC 2–708(1) and UCC 2–713(1) to the "jobber?"

Problem 15–6

In April, 1993, Buyer, a cooperative, contracted to buy seller's seasonal output of sunflower seeds at $13 per hundred pounds. It was estimated that seller would grow between 80 and 85 thousand pounds, with delivery in three installments between December, 1993 and March, 1994. Buyer resold the seeds to Dealer for $13, and was to retain a $.55 per pound handling charge for each pound received from Seller and delivered to Dealer. After part performance, Seller repudiated in January, 1994. The market price had nearly doubled. By March 31, 1994, Seller had sold 80,000 pounds of sunflower seed to another dealer for the prevailing market price of $26 per pound.

Buyer sued seller for damages under UCC 2–713(1), measured by the difference between the contract price and the market price, some $13 per pound. Seller, citing *Allied Canners & Packers,* supra, argued that Buyer's recovery should be limited to $.55 per pound, the fee that would have been earned upon full performance by Seller. Seller relied upon UCC 1–106(1) as a limitation on UCC 2–713(1) and stressed that since Buyer's profit was fixed, it assumed no risk on fluctuating market prices. There was no evidence on how the dispute, if any, between Buyer and Dealer was resolved.

After trial, a judgment was entered for Buyer. The trial judge's memo made several points. See Tongish v. Thomas, 16 Kan.App.2d 809, 829 P.2d 916 (1992), *affirmed,* 25 Kan. 728, 840 P.2d 471 (1992).

First, in interpreting Article 2, if general and specific provisions cannot be harmonized, the specific should prevail. Since UCC 1–106(1) and UCC 2–713(1) are arguably inconsistent, UCC 2–713(1) controls as a matter of statutory interpretation.

Second, *Allied Canners,* a minority decision, can be distinguished on the facts. Moreover, the case has been criticized as ignoring "the clear language of § 2–713's compensation scheme to award expectation damages in accordance with the parties' allocation of risk as measured by the difference between contract price and market price on the date set for performance." Schneider, *UCC Section 2–713: A Defense of Buyer's Expectancy Damages,* 22 Cal.W.L.Rev. 233, 266 (1986).

Third, lost profit damages are inappropriate in cases where the seller has repudiated and the buyer has protected itself against market fluctuations. Since lost profits reflect the value of a completed exchange, they create instability before delivery and give the seller an incentive to breach the contract if the market fluctuates to its advantage. Damages under § 2–713, on the other hand, tend to discourage breach by the seller. Scott, *The Case for Market Damages: Revisiting the Lost Profits Puzzle,* 1155, 1174–78 (1990).

You represent Seller. On appeal, what arguments should you make? How should the case be decided?

SECTION 5. BUYER'S RIGHT TO COVER AND "FIX" DAMAGES

Cover, like resale (UCC 2–706), is an important Code innovation. It is an intelligent legal response to the legitimate needs of the ordinary buyer who, when faced with the seller's breach, must look elsewhere for the goods. Under the standard contract-market differential formula, an aggrieved buyer who repurchased to fulfill his needs was taking real pot luck. If, as was likely to be the case, the court measured the market at a time or place other than those at which he purchased, the contract-market paid too much or too little. UCC 2–712 will change all that.

Professor Honnold in the New York Law Revision Commission Reports has described the relation of the cover provision to the prior law in New York as follows:

HONNOLD—1 N.Y.LAW REV.COMM.REP. 569, 570 (1955)

(2) *Effect of "cover" in determining damages under Uniform Sales Act*

Under Section 67(1) and (3) of the Uniform Sales Act (P.P.L., § 148(1)(3)) the basic test for the measurement of damages recoverable by buyer is "the difference between the contract price and the *market or current* price of the goods at the time or times when they ought to have been delivered * * * ". The Uniform Sales Act says nothing about "cover," and has no provision which gives binding effect to the price paid by buyer in buying substitute goods.

However, in one situation, at least, some decisions have given controlling effect to buyer's repurchase. If buyer purchases substitute goods for *less* than market price, this repurchase price may be the maximum amount on which damages can be measured. The Code would give a different result, since under Section 2–711(1), buyer is afforded a choice between damages based on "cover" (§ 2–712) and damages based on market price (§ 2–713).

The amount paid by buyer has been held an insufficient basis for proof of his damages if there was a current market for the goods; market price must be proved as the basis for computing damages. This rule has been criticized as unduly harsh to the wronged party, and it has at least one qualification: where the goods in question *are not* readily marketable, the price paid by buyer to secure the goods from another seller will be controlling. Under the Code, as we have seen, a buyer who "covers" need not prove the market price.

The conditions which one must meet to comply with UCC 2–712 are like those of UCC 2–706: at least superficially simple and unspecific.

One must purchase: 1) reasonably and in good faith;
2) without unreasonable delay; and
3) in substitution.

On reflection a few problems appear. The first is the recurring problem: what is the reasonable time and what is a commercially reasonable purchase? If the buyer routinely purchases separate lots of goods and now seeks to allocate one of those routinely purchased lots to this contract's cover, what result? A third problem is the question whether cover, if made, is the exclusive measure of damages. A fourth is, how does one adjust for the difference between cover items and those contracted for—what if the contract calls for AM radios but AM–FM radios are procured as cover?

Problem 15–7

Return again to *Simpka-Volta.* Assume that Simpka missed the first delivery of standard furniture and, on June 15, mailed an unequivocal repudiation of the entire contract. On November 15, Volta replaced, from a supplier in Ann Arbor, the standard furniture for $150,000 and the custom furniture for $100,000. The shipment was f.o.b. New York. Volta claims $50,000 damages under UCC 2–712. Simpka's lawyer has responded with the following arguments:

1. UCC 2–712 is not available, since there was an unreasonable delay in the repurchase. The time starts running from the date of repudiation, not from the date upon which the contract would have been performed.

2. Even so, the $50,000 damages should be reduced by the $5,000 transportation cost which the second seller paid from Ann Arbor. Volta would have had to pay those costs under the repudiated f.o.b. point of shipment contract.

3. In fact, the market for the standard furniture was lower than the contract price. The goods which Volta purchased in New York were Grade A and the contract called for Grade B furniture, merchandise of lesser quality.

What damages?

Problem 15–8

Assume that Simpka fails to perform the contract; a series of negotiations considering possible alternatives are conducted between Volta and Simpka, and these eventually break down in January. At that time Volta purchases nearly identical replacement furniture in the New York market for $188,000. Volta now sues Simpka under UCC 2–713 for the contract-market differential at the time of performance. Assume that the court has ruled in this particular case that the "time when the buyer learned of the breach" was the times of the respective deliveries to be made by Simpka and has further found that the contract market differential at those times is a total of $20,000.

Simpka's counsel has argued that the January purchase constituted a cover and that such cover is the exclusive measure of damages. In support of his argument Simpka's counsel cites comment 5 to UCC 2–713 which reads as follows:

> The present section provides a remedy which is completely alternative to cover under the preceding section and applies only when and to the extent that the buyer has not covered.

Volta has hired Professor (now Justice) Ellen Peters as its counsel, and she makes the following argument in response to the contention that UCC 2–712 is the exclusive remedy.

PETERS, REMEDIES FOR BREACH OF CONTRACTS RELATING TO THE SALE OF GOODS UNDER THE UNIFORM COMMERCIAL CODE: A ROAD-MAP FOR ARTICLE TWO, 73 Yale L.J. 199, 260–61 (1963).

"Comment 5 is clear enough; but nothing supporting this position can be found in the text of 2–713. However, 2–711, which lists the buyer's rights upon rightful rejection, states its alternatives in a sequence consistent with Comment 5: 'the buyer may * * * "cover" and have damages under the next section [which contains the cover-contract formula] * * *; or * * * recover damages for non-delivery [the market-contract formula].' Section 2–711 is clear that a buyer need not cover unless he so chooses, but seemingly requires damages to be measured by cover if cover has been effectuated. In the case of a seller suing for non-acceptance, there is no parallel limitation, either in comment or text. The only possible explanation for such a difference in the treatment of buyers and sellers would have to be derived from inequalities in the statements of the other half of the option, the market-contract formulae. Perhaps the seller needs a freer hand when he resells than the buyer who covers because the seller's market-contract formula is so erratic a measure of damages.

"But the history of the development of these remedies over the various drafts of the Uniform Commercial Code suggests a quite different explanation. Until the 1957 version, 2–713 on seller's remedies prefaced his right to recover damages for non-acceptance with 'so far as any goods have not been resold.' At that point then, the market-contract formula was equally conditional for both buyers and sellers, the buyer's rights then being identical in text and comment to their present 1962 statement. The 1957 amendment, deleting this language, was promulgated, according to the Report of the 1956 Recommendations of the Editorial Board, at the suggestion of the New York Law Revision Commission 'to make it clear that the aggrieved seller was not required to elect between damages under Section 2–706 and damages under Section 2–708.' This comment is instructive on two counts: it indicates a purpose to safeguard alternative remedies, and, more important, it characterizes the amendment as a clarification rather than as a change. The latter point might be dismissed as mere face-saving on the part of the revision committee but for the fact that changes are called changes in other comments. If the committee's characterization is correct, the reference to resale, even in the old 2–703 on seller's remedies, was addressed not to the existence of a resale but to whether the resale was being relied upon to measure damages. But if this is an accurate reading of the old 2–703, it is equally appropriate to a free choice among the buyer's remedies under 2–711.

"A non-restrictive reading of the various remedies sections to preserve full options to use or to ignore substitute transactions as a measure of damages makes more sense than Comment 5 for a number of reasons. It preserves a parity of remedy for buyers and sellers. It is consistent with a number of other Code sections which frown on premature election of remedies. It is a good deal easier to administer, since it would be most difficult to ferret out from a reluctant complainant information about transactions sufficiently related to the contract in breach to qualify as cover or resale. Finally, preservation of the option encourages recourse to actual market substitutes, since it guarantees to the injured party that he will not lose a remedy in the event of an unusually favorable substitute contract. It is thus consistent with the Code's overall interest in keeping goods moving in commerce as rapidly as possible."

What should Volta receive? For cases permitting recovery under UCC 2–713(1) despite evidence that the buyer had covered, see Ralston Purina Co. v. McFarland, 550 F.2d 967 (4th Cir.1977); Interior Elevator Co. v. Limmeroth, 278 Or. 589, 565 P.2d 1074 (1977). But see Neibert v. Schwern Agri-Production Corp., 219 Ill.App.3d 188, 161 Ill.Dec. 841, 579 N.E.2d 389 (1991) (UCC 2–713 applies only when and to the extent that buyer has not covered).

FERTICO BELGIUM S.A. v. PHOSPHATE CHEMICALS EXPORT ASSOCIATION, INC.

New York Court of Appeals, 1987.
70 N.Y.2d 76, 517 N.Y.S.2d 465, 510 N.E.2d 334, 3 UCC2d 1812.

BELLACOSA, J. A seller (Phoschem) breached its contract to timely deliver goods to a buyer-trader (Fertico) who properly sought cover (under the Uniform Commercial Code that means acquiring substitute goods) from another source (Unifert) in order to avoid breaching that buyer-trader's obligation to a third-party buyer (Altawreed). The sole issue involves the applicable principles and computation of damages for breach of the Phoschem-to-Fertico contract.

We hold that under the exceptional circumstances of this case plaintiff Fertico, as a buyer-trader, is entitled to damages from seller Phoschem equal to the increased cost of cover plus consequential and incidental damages minus expenses saved (UCC § 2–712[2]). In this case, expenses saved as a result of the breach are limited to costs or expenditures which would have arisen had there been no breach. Thus, the seller Phoschem is not entitled to a credit from the profits of a subsequent sale by the first buyer-trader Fertico to a fourth party (Janssens) of nonconforming goods from Phoschem. Fertico's letter of credit had been presented by Phoschem and honored so, under the specific facts of this case, Fertico had no commercially reasonable alternative but to retain and resell the fertilizer. This is so despite Fertico's exercise of cover in connection with the first set of transactions, i.e., Phoschem to Fertico to Altawreed. The covering buyer-trader may not, however, as in this case, recover other consequential damages when the third party to which it made its sale provides increased compensation to offset additional costs arising as a consequence of the breach.

In October 1978 appellant Fertico Belgium S.A. (Fertico), an international trader of fertilizer, contracted with Phosphate Chemicals Export Association, Inc. (Phoschem), a corporation engaged in exporting phosphate fertilizer, to purchase two separate shipments of fertilizer for delivery to Antwerp, Belgium. The first shipment was to be 15,000 tons delivered no later than November 20, 1978 and the second was to be 20,000 tons delivered by November 30, 1978. Phoschem knew that Fertico required delivery on the specified dates so that the fertilizer could be bagged and shipped in satisfaction of a secondary contract Fertico had with Altawreed, Iraq's agricultural ministry. Fertico secured a letter of credit in a timely manner with respect to the first shipment. After Phoschem projected a first shipment delivery date of December 4, 1978, Fertico advised Phoschem, on November 13, 1978, that the breach as to the first shipment presented "huge problems" and cancelled the second shipment which had not as of that date been loaded, thus ensuring its late delivery. The first shipment did not actually arrive in

Antwerp until December 17 and was not off loaded until December 21, 1978. Despite the breach as to the first shipment, Fertico retained custody and indeed acquired title over that first shipment because, as its president testified, "[w]e had no other choice" (Rec. on App., at 597–598) as defendant seller Phoschem had presented Fertico's $1.7 million letter of credit as of November 17, 1978, and the same had been honored by the issuer (see, UCC § 5–114).

Fertico's predicament from the breach by delay of even the first shipment, a breach which Phoschem does not deny, was that it, in turn, would breach its contract to sell to Altawreed unless it acquired substitute goods. In an effort to avoid that secondary breach, Fertico took steps in mid-November to cover (UCC § 2–712) the goods by purchasing 35,000 tons of the same type fertilizer from Unifert, a Lebanese concern. The cost of the fertilizer itself under the Phoschem-to-Fertico contract was $4,025,000, and under the Unifert-to-Fertico contract $4,725,000, a differential of $700,000. On the same day Fertico acquired cover, November 15, 1978, Fertico's president traveled to Baghdad, Iraq to renegotiate its contract with Altawreed. In return for a postponed delivery date and an additional payment of $20.50 per ton, Fertico agreed to make direct inland delivery rather than delivery to the seaport of Basra. Fertico fulfilled its renegotiated Altawreed contract with the substitute fertilizer purchased as cover from Unifert.

In addition to the problems related to its Altawreed contract, Fertico was left with 15,000 tons of late-delivered fertilizer which it did not require but which it had been compelled to take because Phoschem had received payment on Fertico's letter of credit. This aggrieved international buyer-seller was required to store the product and seek out a new purchaser. Fertico sold the 15,000 tons of the belatedly delivered Phoschem fertilizer to another buyer, Janssens, on March 19, 1979, some three months after the non-conforming delivery, and earned a profit of $454,000 based on the cost to it from Phoschem and its sale price to Janssens.

In 1981 Fertico commenced this action against Phoschem seeking $1.25 million in damages for Phoschem's breach of the October 1978 agreement. A jury returned a verdict of $1.07 million which the trial court refused to overturn on a motion for judgment notwithstanding the verdict. The Appellate Division vacated the damage award, ordered a new trial on the damages issue only and ruled, as a matter of law, (1) that the increased transportation costs on the Altawreed contract were not consequential damages; (2) that the higher purchase price paid by Altrawreed to Fertico was an expense saved as a consequence of the Phoschem breach; and (3) that the Fertico damages had to be reduced by the profits from the Janssens' sale (Fertico Belgium S.A. v. Phosphate Chemicals Export Assoc. Inc., 120 A.D.2d 401, 501 N.Y.S.2d 867. Fertico appealed to this court on a stipulation for judgment absolute. We disagree with propositions (2) and (3) in the Appellate Division ruling, and conclude that the Uniform Commercial Code and our analysis support a modification and reinstatement of $700,000 of the damage award in a final judgment resolving this litigation between the parties.

Failure by Phoschem to make delivery on the contract dates concededly constituted a breach of the contract (White and Summers, Uniform Commercial Code § 6–2, at 207). The Uniform Commercial Code, § 2–711, gives the non-breaching party the alternative of either seeking the partial self-help of cover along with recovery of damages (UCC § 2–712), or of recovering damages only for the differential between the market price and the contract price, together with incidental and consequential damages less expenses saved (UCC § 2–713; see also, Productora e Importadora de Papel, S.A. de C.V. v. Fleming, 376 Mass. 826, 383 N.E.2d 1129. Fertico exercised its right as the wronged buyer-trader to cover in order to obtain the substitute fertilizer it required to meet its obligation under its Altawreed contract (see, UCC § 2–712, Comment 1).

A covering buyer's damages are equal to the difference between the presumably higher cost of cover and the contract price, plus incidental or consequential damages suffered on account of the breach, less expenses saved (UCC § 2–712[2]). Fertico is thus entitled to a damage remedy under this section because its cover purchase was made in good faith, without unreasonable delay, and the Unifert fertilizer was a reasonable substitute for the Phoschem fertilizer (UCC § 2–712[1]; Reynolds v. Underwriters Bank, 44 N.Y.2d 568, 572–573, 406 N.Y.S.2d 743, 378 N.E.2d 106).

Fertico's additional costs for delivering the fertilizer inland rather than at a seaport would usually constitute consequential damages because they resulted from Phoschem's breach, because Phoschem knew that Fertico would incur damages under its separate contract obligation and because the damages were not prevented by the cover (UCC § 2–715[2]). The increased costs attendant to the Altawreed contract are consequential damages because they did not "arise within the scope of the immediate [Phoschem–Fertico] transaction, but rather stem from losses incurred by [Fertico] in its dealings [with Altawreed] which were a proximate result of the breach, and which were reasonably foreseeable by the breaching party at the time of contracting" (Petroleo Brasileiro, S.A. Petrobras v. Ameropan Oil Co., 372 F.Supp. 503, 508. Ordinarily, an award for consequential damages occasioned by the seller's breach would be necessary to put a buyer like Fertico in as good a position as it would have been had there been no breach (UCC § 1–106; see, Neri v. Retail Marine Corporation, 30 N.Y.2d 393, 334 N.Y.S.2d 165, 285 N.E.2d 311; 3 Hawkland, Uniform Commercial Code Series § 2–715:01, at 389). Inasmuch as Altawreed compensated Fertico for the additional delivery costs, Fertico was insulated from any loss in that respect as a result of Phoschem's breach, thereby eliminating this category of potential damages. On this question of consequential damages, the appellate division was correct.

The additional compensation to Fertico, an international trader, from Altawreed is not, however, an expense saved as a consequence of the seller Phoschem's breach for which Phoschem is entitled to any credit (UCC § 2–712[2]). In most instances, and particularly in this case, saved expenses must be costs or expenditures which would be anticipated had there been no breach (see, Productora e Importadora de Papel, S.A. de C.V. v. Fleming, 376 Mass. 826, 839, 383 N.E.2d 1129, 1137, supra). For example, if a seller were to breach a contract to deliver an unpackaged product to the buyer and the buyer were to cover with the same product prepackaged, the cost of packaging which the buyer would have had to perform is an expense saved as a consequence of the breach (see, 3 Hawkland, Uniform Commercial Code Series § 2–712:02, at 362). The increased remuneration from Altawreed was compensation for the additional shipment responsibilities incurred by Fertico, not a cost or expenditure anticipated in the absence of a breach, and therefore was erroneously analyzed and credited in Phoschem's favor by the Appellate Division.

The third prong of the damages analysis relates to the profit made from the independent sale of the Phoschem fertilizer to Janssens. The Appellate Division erred in offsetting this profit against the damages otherwise suffered since that court mistakenly concluded that the sale stemmed from and was dependent upon Phoschem's breach. This offset, on these peculiar facts, would severely disadvantage Fertico, a trader in fertilizer who both buys and sells, and who would have pursued such commercial transactions had there been no breach by Phoschem. It would be anomalous to conclude that had it not been for Phoschem's breach Fertico would not have continued its trade and upon such reasoning to counterpoise the profits from the Janssens' sale against the damages arising from Phoschem's breach. Inasmuch as the facts here are exceptional because Fertico met its sub-sale obligations with the cover fertilizer and yet acquired title and control over the late-delivered fertilizer from Phoschem, our decision does not fit squarely within the available Uniform Commercial Code remedies urged by the dissent. Thus, strict reliance on Neri v. Retail Marine Corp. (30 N.Y.2d 393, supra) and on Hawkland's Commentary (3 Hawkland, Uniform Commercial Code Series § 2–714:05, at 384), as undertaken by the dissent, does not provide an adequate resolution to the particular problem presented in this case.

Fertico learned of Phoschem's breach after Phoschem had negotiated Fertico's $1.7 million letter of credit, which constituted complete payment for the first shipment. With no commercially reasonable alternative, Fertico took custody of the first shipment but cancelled the second (UCC § 2–601[c]), having previously notified Phoschem of its breach (UCC § 2–607). The loss resulting to Fertico by having to acquire cover, even in the face of its acceptance of a late delivered portion of the fertilizer, is properly recoverable under § 2–714(1) (3 Hawkland, Uniform Commercial Code Series § 2–714:05, at 384–385). At the same time, Uniform Commercial Code § 1–106 directs that the remedies provided by the Uniform Commercial Code should be liberally administered so as to put the aggrieved party in as good a position as if the other party had fully performed. Had Phoschem fully performed, Fertico would have had the benefit of the Altawreed transaction and, as a trader of fertilizer, the profits from the Janssens' sale as well. "Gains made by the injured party on other transactions after breach are never to be deducted from the damages that are otherwise recoverable, unless such gains could not have been made had there been no breach" (5 Corbin, Contracts, § 1041, at 256; see also, Steen Industries, Inc. v. Richer Communications, Inc., 226 Pa.Super. 219, 314 A.2d 319). Fertico's profit made on the sale of a non-specific article such as fertilizer, of which the supply in the market is not limited, should not therefore be deducted from the damages recoverable from Phoschem (5 Corbin, Contracts, § 1041, at 258–260; see also, Neri v. Retail Marine Corp., 30 N.Y.2d 393, 401, 334 N.Y.S.2d 165, 285 N.E.2d 311 supra).

Fertico was concededly wronged by Phoschem's breach and Fertico resorted to Uniform Commercial Code remedies which are rooted in what we perceive to be the realities of the marketplace. Fertico did what reasonable traders would do and would like to do in mitigating risks inflicted in this case by Phoschem and in exerting its commercial resourcefulness. That is, it took steps to save its business, its customers, its good will and its deals and ultimately to also recover appropriate damages from a wrongdoer. That did not produce a "windfall" or a "double benefit" to the aggrieved party as the dissenting opinion asserts. The result we reach today countenances no such thing. On the contrary, to deprive the buyer-trader Fertico of its rightful differential damages of $700,000 and to credit this transactionally independent profit to Phoschem would perversely enrich the wrongdoer at the expense of the wronged party, a result those in the marketplace would find perplexing and a result which the generous remedial purpose of the Uniform Commercial Code does not compel or authorize. The dissent's characterization of the recovery by an injured party of damages for a breach of contract as a "benefit" is wrong, since that functionally attributes a kind of lien against the independently pursued benefit derived out of that separate transaction.

Accordingly, the order of the appellate division affirming liability but vacating, on the law, the damage award and remanding the matter for a new trial on the issue of damages, as appealed to this court on a stipulation for judgment absolute, should be modified and damages awarded to Fertico in the amount of $700,000 in accordance with this opinion.

WACHTLER, C.J. and SIMONS, KAYE, and HANCOCK, JJ., concur.

TITONE, J., dissents with an opinion in which ALEXANDER, J. concurs.

TITONE, J. (dissenting). At issue in this appeal is the relationship among the various remedies that Article 2 of the Uniform Commercial Code provides for buyers aggrieved by sellers' defaults. Central to the analysis is the principle that the Code's remedies "shall be liberally administered to the end that the aggrieved party may be put in *as good a position* as if the other party had fully performed" (UCC § 1–106[1] [emphasis supplied]). Here, the majority has concluded that the aggrieved buyer may retain both cover damages and the profit from the resale of the late-delivered goods, in effect, securing the benefit of its bargain twice. Since that result is not required by, and indeed is not even consistent with, the purpose of the Code's generous remedial provisions, I must respectfully dissent.[1]

I begin with the premise that an aggrieved buyer who has purchased substitute goods and sued for "cover" damages under UCC § 2–712 has impliedly rejected the seller's nonconforming performance and, consequently, holds the seller's goods only as security for any pre-payments made to the seller (see UCC §§ 2–706[6] –711[3]). I find the contrary position—that an aggrieved buyer may compatibly resort to cover and also retain and resell the nonconforming goods for its own account—to be legally insupportable and economically unsound. The "cover" remedy represents a recognition by the Code's drafters that a buyer aggrieved by a breach or repudiation "may not be made whole by the mere recovery of damages, because he is left,

1. My disagreement with the majority lies only in its conclusion that the appellate division erred by offsetting Fertico's damage award against the profit Fertico obtained on the resale of Phoschem's goods. I agree completely with the majority's conclusion concerning the proper application of the $20.50 per ton additional reimbursement that Fertico obtained from Altawreed.

thereby, in a position in which he does not have the goods he wants" (3 Hawkland, Uniform Commercial Code Series § 2–712:01, pp. 359–360). The Code's "cover" provision, which authorizes the buyer to purchase equivalent goods in the open market and then sue the breaching seller for any price differential (see UCC § 2–712), was intended as a practical method of furnishing the buyer with a fair substitute for the goods it bargained for but did not receive. Thus, from an economic standpoint, the buyer receives the full benefit of his bargain when he obtains cover damages under UCC § 2–712. Allowing the buyer to retain and resell the goods in addition obviously leads to a windfall, since the buyer is receiving more than the benefit of the transaction it bargained for.

Moreover, the language of the Code makes clear that the buyer cannot both sue for cover and accept the goods. UCC § 2–712(1) defines "cover" as a purchase of goods "*in substitution for* those due from the seller" (emphasis supplied) and authorizes an aggrieved buyer to resort to cover only "[a]fter a breach within [UCC § 2–711(1)]," which specifically states that cover "under [UCC § 2–712(1)]" is available when "the seller fails to make delivery * * * or the buyer rightfully rejects or justifiably revokes acceptance" (UCC § 2–711[1]). Finally, any doubt about the applicability of the cover remedy referred to in UCC § 2–711 is dispelled by Comment 1: "The remedies listed here are those available to a buyer *who has not accepted the goods or who has justifiably revoked his acceptance*" (emphasis supplied).

In short, consistent with its purpose, the cover remedy is, by its terms, available only in situations where the buyer either does not have the needed goods because of nondelivery or cannot use the goods that were delivered because of a defect in the seller's performance. In all other situations, the aggrieved buyer must resort to the remedies provided in UCC § 2–714, which concerns nonconforming goods that have been accepted (see UCC § 2–711, official comment 1). While there are instances in which an accepting buyer may also seek cover damages under UCC § 2–714(1), even the commentary the majority cites makes clear that the cover remedy is not intended to be used with respect to those nonconforming goods that the buyer has received *and accepted;* rather, the remedy is properly used only to replace the portion of needed goods the buyer either does not have or does not take (3 Hawkland, supra, § 2–714:05, pp. 384–385).[2]

Viewed within the framework of these basic principles, cases such as this one involving late delivery are not difficult to resolve. As in cases where there has been a total failure to deliver, the buyer in late-delivery cases may reject the untimely performance and cover with substitute goods.

2. The commentary cited by the majority states, in pertinent part:

"Where the buyer accepts goods that are nonconforming because of a deficiency in quantity or a late delivery, subsection 2–714(1) gives him the right to damages for 'the loss resulting in the ordinary course of events from the seller's breach as determined in any manner which is reasonable.'

"*In the case of a shortage of quantity,* the buyer usually will establish his damages by covering. That is to say, he will go into the market and buy goods to substitute for those that the seller wrongfully failed to deliver. * * * *In the case of a late shipment* that otherwise conforms to the contract, the *accepting* buyer has no need to cover * * *"

(3 Hawkland, supra § 2–714:05, pp. 384–385) (emphasis supplied). In other words, while cover is not precluded when there has been a partial acceptance of a nonconforming shipment, it is used only to replace goods that were either not delivered or not accepted.

Additionally, unlike the buyer aggrieved by a total failure to deliver, the buyer aggrieved by a late delivery has the alternative option of accepting the belatedly-delivered goods and retaining for itself any profit realized on resale. However, contrary to Fertico's claims, the aggrieved buyer may not pursue both courses simultaneously, since it would then benefit twice from what was a single bargain—a result that is unacceptable under UCC § 1–106 (see Melby v. Hawkins Pontiac, 13 Wash.App. 745, 537 P.2d 807 [alternative remedies may be pursued under UCC, but not where double recovery would result]).

The majority has attempted to rationalize that result here by relying on a damages rule that has previously been applied only to aggrieved seller. The rule permits a seller who regularly deals in goods of a particular type to sue the breaching buyer for lost profit even though the wrongfully rejected goods have been sold to another buyer without loss. The rule applies only where the seller has an *unlimited* supply of *standard-price* goods (see Neri v. Retail Marine Corp., 30 N.Y.2d 393, 399–400, 334 N.Y.S.2d 165, 285 N.E.2d 311; 3 Hawkland, supra, § 2–708:04, 331–332). In those situations, "it may safely be assumed that" the seller would have made two sales instead of one if the buyer had not breached, and, consequently, it can fairly be said that the buyer's breach deprived the seller of an opportunity for additional profit (3 Hawkland, supra, 332). Thus, traditional remedies such as resale or market price differential are "inadequate to put the seller in as good a position as performance would have done," and the seller may sue for the lost profit (UCC § 2–708[2]).

The Code, however, does not contain an analogous provision allowing aggrieved buyers to recover profits from lost sales, and there is good reason for that omission, since neither of the conditions necessary for application of the sellers' lost profit remedy may be satisfied in the case of an aggrieved buyer. First, a party in the position of a buyer cannot, by definition, be said to have an unlimited supply of the goods at his disposal for resale, even where the goods are fungible, the buyer who intends to resell must go into the marketplace to acquire the goods in the first instance.[3] Second, a buyer who must go into the market to obtain goods will ordinarily not be able to rely on the availability of a "standard price"; rather, unlike the seller who has an unlimited supply of standard-price goods in its inventory, the reselling buyer remains at the mercy of the wholesale market's price fluctuations. Because of these differences, it *cannot* "be safely assumed" that the aggrieved buyer-dealer would have made a second sale at a particular profit were it not for the seller's breach. To the contrary, the occurrence of and profit on a second transaction would depend on such other, unrelated variables as the availability and wholesale market price of the goods at the time the buyer-dealer went into the market to acquire them. Thus, the rationale for the seller-dealer's lost-profit remedy is simply inapplicable to buyer-dealers.

Indeed, this case illustrates the difficulty of applying the seller's lost-profit remedy to aggrieved buyers. Were it not for Phoschem's breach,

3. Indeed, it seems somewhat ironic to recognize, on the one hand, the buyer's right to go into the marketplace and acquire "cover" goods at an increased cost and, on the other hand, treat the buyer as a party in the position of a seller with an unlimited supply of goods at its disposal.

Fertico would have delivered the 15,000 tons of fertilizer it had purchased from Phoschem to Altawreed and would have had to go into the marketplace again to acquire an additional 15,000 tons if it wished to make a second sale to Janssens. In this respect, Fertico's position here is really no different in principle from that of an aggrieved seller which had only one set of goods at its immediate disposal. In both instances, the breach of a prior agreement is what has made the goods available for a second sale (cf. 5 Corbin, Contracts § 1041, p 256). And, while a second sale may have been theoretically possible even without the breach, the uncertainties occasioned by the buyer/seller's need to return to the marketplace for more goods of the same kind preclude the assumption, implicit in the majority's holding (see also Neri v. Retail Marine Corp., supra), that the second sale and its accompanying profit would have been made on the same terms even if no breach had occurred.

Finally, I cannot agree with the majority's reliance on the supposedly "exceptional" circumstance that Fertico both "met its sub-sale obligations with cover fertilizer and * * * acquired title and control over the late delivered fertilizer". First, the basis for and significance of the majority's conclusion that Fertico acquired title to the goods is left unclear. Certainly, the fact that Fertico had already paid for the goods cannot be controlling, since the Code clearly does not equate payment and receipt of the goods with passage of title. To the contrary, the Code expressly contemplates and accounts for these situations by permitting a wronged buyer who has rejected to retain and resell the goods in its possession to recover any down payment (UCC §§ 2–706[6], –711[3]). The Code also requires in these situations, however, that the buyer account to the breaching seller for any additional profit it has made on the resale (UCC § 2–706[6]). Nothing in the majority opinion satisfactorily explains why this remedy is insufficient.[4]

Furthermore, the majority's emphasis on the asserted "exceptional facts" is unpersuasive because under the terms of the majority's holding the outcome in a given case would turn, in large measure, on the fortuity of which party had possession of the goods after the breach. In the case of a simple late delivery the buyer will ordinarily have possession after the breach. Under the majority's holding, that buyer may *both* obtain cover damages *and* resell the seller's goods, retaining any profit for itself. In the case of a complete failure to deliver, however, the seller will ordinarily have possession of the goods after the breach. Under the Code, the buyer in such a case may obtain *either* cover damages *or* the goods (if they have been specifically identified to the contract), but not both (UCC § 2–716[3]). Thus, the buyer aggrieved by a late delivery is placed in a substantially better position than a buyer aggrieved by a complete failure to deliver, although there is no apparent legal or commercial justification for the distinction. Even more seriously, a seller who completely repudiates is placed in a more advantageous position than one who merely delivers late. While both must pay cover damages, the repudiating seller may resell the undelivered goods in its possession for its own account—an option unavailable to the seller who has delivered, albeit late. Since I cannot agree with a rule of law that

4. That retention and resale of Phoschem's goods was the most "commercially reasonable alternative" does not alter Fertico's obligation under the Code to hold any profits made on the resale for Phoschem's account (UCC §§ 2–706[6], 2–711[3]).

ultimately imposes a greater penalty on the less serious of two similar breaches, I dissent and vote to affirm.

Notes

1. What do you think of the following analysis of *Fertico.*

"This is a close case. When one reads the majority opinion, she begins to nod her head in agreement and then finds herself doing the same thing when reading the dissent. The real question is to compare the plaintiff's economic status at the end of all the relevant transactions with the economic status that the plaintiff would have enjoyed had the defendant not breached the contract. The majority assumes that if the contract had been performed, the plaintiff would have made the intended resale to the Iraqi buyer, and also the second resale to the other buyer. The dissent suggests that this is only speculation. The dissent indicates that it is likely that if the American seller had not breached, the European buyer would not have sought substitute goods in Lebanon to fulfill its contract with the Iraqis and in fact would have had only one sale. If that is what would have happened, the dissent is correct. If, on the other hand, the European reseller would have had both resales, then the majority seems correct.

In these circumstances, it should be the responsibility of the defendant (who seeks to reduce the plaintiff's damages) to show that it is more probable than not the plaintiff would *not* have had both sales, would not have enjoyed the second resale profit, and thus that the second resale profit (as a child of the breach) should be used to reduce the plaintiff's recovery. The burden should be put on the defendant to come forward with that kind of evidence at the trial. Although it is not certain from the appellate opinion, it seems the defendant did not do that but simply made a legal argument on appeal. If that is what happened, the dissent is correct."

2. *Other Sources of Cover.*

Section 2–712(1) provides that upon breach by the seller "the buyer may 'cover' by making in good faith and without unreasonable delay any reasonably purchase of or contract to purchase goods in substitution for those due from the seller." Must that purchase be from a third party selling substitute goods in the open market, or can the buyer cover by making a purchase from the breaching seller or by manufacturing the goods itself?

In Kelsey–Hayes Co. v. Galtaco Redlaw Castings Corp., 749 F.Supp. 794 (E.D.Mich.1990), the court held without much discussion that the breaching seller was a proper source for cover under UCC 2–712(1). The seller had repudiated because of financial considerations but offered to continue production at a slightly higher price until the buyer could find an alternative source of supply. The buyer accepted the offer without reserving any rights under the breached contract. The court concluded that the purchase may be viewed as a "successful effort" to cover, even though the buyer bought the same goods from the sale seller on different terms. On balance, the decision favored the seller more than the buyer because the court rejected the buyer's claim that the agreed cover contract was entered under duress. Thus, the "cover" contract, in the form of a modification, was enforced and the buyer's damages were limited to the difference between the contract price and the higher price in the "cover" contract.

In Dura–Wood Treating Co. v. Century Forest Industries, Inc., 675 F.2d 745 (5th Cir.1982), the court held that under proper circumstances the "cover" remedy was satisfied when the buyer manufactured the goods itself. Upon seller's breach of a contract to deliver creosote treated hardwood cross-ties, the buyer obtained price quotations from other suppliers and concluded that it could produce the ties internally at a lower price than it could purchase substitutes on the open market. That price, however, was higher than the contract price and the seller objected that UCC 2–712(1) required a "cover" from a third party. The court, recognizing that UCC 2–712(1) "read literally" appears to require cover from an outside source, nevertheless held that an internal cover was sufficient where it put the buyer in the same position as full performance would have done and enabled the buyer to obtain needed goods. The court then affirmed the district court's finding that the buyer acted in good faith, covered within a reasonable time and provided a reasonable substitute. Although the factual questions raised by an internal cover are complex, other courts are in accord with the *Dura–Wood* decision. See, e.g., Cives Corp. v. Callier Steel Pipe & Tube, Inc., 482 A.2d 852, 858 (Me.1984).

Note that the cases discussed above support unique covers actually undertaken by the buyer. But suppose the buyer had failed to follow these interesting paths? One consequence is that damages under UCC 2–712(1) are not available. The buyer must sue under UCC 2–713(1). More importantly, the failure to cover may affect the buyer's ability to recover consequential damages under Section 2–715(2)(a), which provides that consequential damages are recoverable "which could not reasonably be prevented by cover or otherwise." Do you think that a refusal by the buyer to cover from the breaching seller or by internal production would be reasonable? See the next Section.

SECTION 6. CONSEQUENTIAL DAMAGES FOR BREACH BY DELAY OR NONDELIVERY

A commercial buyer may have different objectives in contracting to buy goods: (1) As a jobber or distributor, to resell goods in the same condition as delivered by the seller; (2) As a manufacturer, to use the goods as part of a product to be manufactured and resold; and (3) As a manufacturer, to use the goods as equipment to maintain or expand its capacity to produce goods for resale. Thus, a jobber would purchase, say, a completed woodstove for resale to consumers while a manufacturer would purchase either steel to be incorporated into a stove to be manufactured or equipment with which to manufacture the stove.

In each case, an unexcused delay or a failure to deliver by the seller results in two potential sources of damages, "direct" damages measured by the contract price and either the market price, UCC 2–713, or the cost to cover, UCC 2–712, and "consequential" damages, measured by the buyer's loss from being unable to use the goods. UCC 2–715(2)(a). Frequently, the buyer claims as consequential damages the net profits that would have been made if the goods had been delivered on time.

There are four traditional limitations upon the recovery of consequential damages. Three limitations are explicit in UCC 2–715(2)(a): (1) The loss must result from or be caused by the breach; (2) The loss must result from "general or particular requirements and needs" of the buyer "of which the seller at the time of contracting had reason to know * * *: and (3) The loss must be one "which could not reasonably be prevented by cover or otherwise." A fourth limitation, applicable to all claims for damages, is that the loss must be proved by the plaintiff with reasonable certainty. To prevail in a claim for consequential damages, the plaintiff must satisfy all four limitations.

For now, consider the following problem and case. We will return to the consequential damages problem in connection with the buyer's claim for damages with regard to accepted goods, infra at Chapter Twenty-One, Section 3.

Problem 15–9

On May 1, F, a farmer, sold B, a dealer, 2,000 bushels of # 1 yellow corn, just planted in F's fields, for $3.00 a bushel. Delivery was promised no later than October 15. On May 15, B resold the corn to C, a cereal manufacturer, for $4.00 a bushel. Due to a drought in other parts of the country, the market price for # 1 yellow at the time of delivery was $5.00 per bushel. F failed to deliver and C demanded delivery from B of 1,000 bushels at $4.00 per bushel.

1. What should B do to maximize damages against F?

2. Suppose, after negotiations, C agreed to release B from the contract upon payment of $500. B paid the $500.

3. Suppose on May 15, B had been able to resell the corn to C for $6.00 a bushel even though the prevailing market price for futures was $4.00. What damages?

HYDRAFORM PRODUCTS CORP. v. AMERICAN STEEL & ALUMINUM CORP.

Supreme Court of New Hampshire, 1985.
127 N.H. 187, 498 A.2d 339.

SOUTER, JUSTICE.*

The defendant, American Steel & Aluminum Corporation, appeals from the judgment entered on a jury verdict against it. The plaintiff, Hydraform Products Corporation, brought this action for direct and consequential damages based on claims of negligent misrepresentation and breach of a contract to supply steel to be used in manufacturing woodstoves. American claims that prior to trial, the Superior Court (Nadeau, J.) erroneously held that a limitation of damages clause was ineffective to bar the claim for consequential damages. American further claims, inter alia, that the Trial Court (Dalianis, J.) erred (a) in allowing the jury to calculate lost profits on the basis of a volume of business in excess of what the contract disclosed and for a period beyond the year in which the steel was to be supplied; (b) in allowing the jury to award damages for the diminished value of the woodstove division of Hydraform's business; (c) in failing to direct a verdict for the defendant on the misrepresentation claim; and (d) in allowing Hydraform's president to testify as an expert witness. We hold that the trial court properly refused to enforce the limitation of damages clause, but we sustain the other claims of error and reverse the judgment.

* Now Associate Justice of the United States Supreme Court.

Hydraform was incorporated in 1975 and began manufacturing and selling woodstoves in 1976. During the sales season of 1977–78 it sold 640 stoves. It purchased steel from a number of suppliers until July 1978, when it entered into a "trial run" contract with American for enough steel to manufacture 40 stoves. Upon delivery of the steel, certain of Hydraform's agents and employees signed a delivery receipt prepared by American, containing the following language:

> "Seller will replace or refund the purchase price for any goods which at the time of delivery to buyer were damaged, defective or not in conformance with the buyer's written purchase order, provided that the buyer gives seller written notice by mail of such damage, defect or deviation within 10 days following its receipt of the goods. *In no event shall seller be liable for labor costs expended on such goods or other consequential damages."*

(Emphasis added.)

When some of the deliveries under this contract were late, Hydraform's president, J.R. Choate, explained to an agent of American that late deliveries of steel during the peak season for manufacturing and selling stoves could ruin Hydraform's business for a year. In response, American's agent stated that if Hydraform placed a further order, American would sheer and stockpile in advance, at its own plant, enough steel for 400 stoves, and would supply further steel on demand. Thereafter Hydraform did submit a purchase order for steel sufficient to manufacture 400 stoves, to be delivered in four equal installments on the first days of September, October, November and December of 1978.

American's acceptance of this offer took the form of deliveries accompanied by receipt forms. The forms included the same language limiting American's liability for damages that had appeared on the receipts used during the trial run agreement. Hydraform's employees signed these receipts as the steel was delivered from time to time, and no one representing Hydraform ever objected to that language.

Other aspects of American's performance under the trial run contract reoccurred as well. Deliveries were late, some of the steel delivered was defective, and replacements of defective steel were tardy. Throughout the fall of 1978 Mr. Choate protested the slow and defective shipments, while American's agent continually reassured him that the deficient performance would be corrected. Late in the fall, Mr. Choate finally concluded that American would never perform as agreed, and attempted to obtain steel from other suppliers. He found, however, that none could supply the steel he required in time to manufacture stoves for the 1978–79 sales season. In the meantime, the delays in manufacturing had led to cancelled orders, and by the end of the season Hydraform had manufactured and sold only 250 stoves. In September, 1979, Hydraform sold its woodstove manufacturing division for $150,000 plus royalties.

In December, 1979, Hydraform brought an action for breach of contract, which provoked a countersuit by American. In January, 1983, American moved to dismiss Hydraform's claims for consequential damages to compensate for lost profits and for loss on the sale of the business. American based the motion on the limitation of damages clause and upon its defense that

Hydraform had failed to mitigate its damages by cover or otherwise. In February, 1983, Hydraform's pretrial statement filed under Superior Court Rule 62 disclosed that it claimed $100,000 as damages for lost profits generally and $220,000 as a loss on the sale of the business. Later in February, 1983, the superior court permitted Hydraform to amend its writ by adding further counts, which included claims for fraudulent and negligent misrepresentation. Hydraform did not, however, proceed to trial on the claim of fraud.

In April, 1983, *Nadeau,* J., denied American's motion to dismiss the claims for consequential damages. He relied on the Uniform Commercial Code as adopted in New Hampshire, RSA chapter 382–A, in ruling that the limitation of damages clause was unenforceable on the alternative grounds that the clause would have been a material alteration of the contract, *see* RSA 382–A:2–207(2)(b), or was unconscionable or was a term that had failed of its essential purpose, *see* RSA 382–A:2–719(2) and (3). He further concluded that, under the circumstances of the case, the failure to cover, if proven, would not bar consequential damages.

The case was tried to a jury before *Dalianis,* J. American's exceptions at trial are discussed in detail below. At the close of the evidence, American objected to the use of a verdict form with provision for special findings, and the case was submitted for a general verdict, which the jury returned for Hydraform in the amount of $80,245.12.

* * *

Since the clause was not enforceable, the trial court allowed the jury to consider Hydraform's claims for lost profits in the year of the contract, 1978, and for the two years thereafter, as well as its claim for loss in the value of the stove manufacturing business resulting in a lower sales price for the business in 1979. American argues that the court erred in submitting such claims to the jury, and rests its position on three requirements governing the recovery of consequential damages.

First, under RSA 382–A:2–715(2)(a) consequential damages are limited to compensation for "loss resulting from general or particular requirements and needs of which the seller at the time of contracting had reason to know * * *" This reflection of *Hadley v. Baxendale,* 156 Eng.Rep. 145 (1854) thus limits damages to those reasonably foreseeable at the time of the contract. *See Gerwin v. Southeastern Cal. Ass'n of Seventh Day Adventists,* 14 Cal. App.3d 209, 220, 92 Cal.Rptr. 111, 118 (1971); *Petrie-Clemons v. Butterfield,* 122 N.H. 120, 124, 441 A.2d 1167, 1170 (1982). To satisfy the foreseeability requirement, the injury for which damages are sought "must follow the breach in the natural course of events, or the evidence must specifically show that the breaching party had reason to foresee the injury." *Salem Engineering & Const. Corp. v. Londonderry School Dist.,* 122 N.H. 379, 384, 445 A.2d 1091, 1094 (1982). Thus, peculiar circumstances and particular needs must be made known to the seller if they are to be considered in determining the foreseeability of damages. *Lewis v. Mobil Oil Corporation,* 438 F.2d 500, 510 (8th Cir.1971).

Second, the damages sought must be limited to recompense for the reasonably ascertainable consequences of the breach. *See* RSA 382–A:2–715, comment 4. While proof of damages to the degree of mathematical certainty is not necessary, *Smith v. State,* 125 N.H. 799, 805, 486 A.2d 289, 294 (1984), a claim for lost profits must rest on evidence demonstrating that the profits claimed were "reasonably certain" in the absence of the breach. *Whitehouse v. Rytman,* 122 N.H. 777, 780, 451 A.2d 370, 372 (1982). Speculative losses are not recoverable.

Third, consequential damages such as lost profits are recoverable only if the loss "could not reasonably be prevented by cover or otherwise." § 2–715(2)(a). *See* § 2–712(1) (*i.e.,* by purchase or contract to purchase goods in substitution for those due from seller). In summary, consequential damages must be reasonably foreseeable, ascertainable and unavoidable.

Applying these standards, we look first at the claim for lost profits for the manufacturing season beginning in September, 1978. There is no serious question that loss of profit on sales was foreseeable up to the number of 400 stoves referred to in the contract, and there is a clear evidentiary basis for a finding that Hydraform would have sold at least that number. There was also an evidentiary basis for the trial court's ruling that Hydraform acted reasonably even though it did not attempt to cover until the season was underway and it turned out to be too late. American had led Hydraform on by repeatedly promising to take steps to remedy its failures, and the court could find that Hydraform's reliance on these promises was reasonable up to the time when it finally and unsuccessfully tried to cover.

Lost profits on sales beyond the 400 stoves presents a foreseeability issue, however. Although American's agent had stated that American would supply steel beyond the 400 stove level on demand, there is no evidence that Hydraform indicated that it would be likely to make such a demand to the extent of any reasonably foreseeable amount. Rather, the evidence was that Mr. Choate had told American's agent that the business was seasonal with a busy period of about four months. The contract referred to delivery dates on the first of four separate months and spoke of only 400 stoves. Thus, there appears to be no basis on which American should have foreseen a volume in excess of 400 for the season beginning in 1978. Lost profits for sales beyond that amount therefore were not recoverable, and it was error to allow the jury to consider them.

Nor should the claims for profits lost on sales projected for the two subsequent years have been submitted to the jury. The impediment to recovery of these profits was not total unforeseeability that the breach could have effects in a subsequent year or years, but the inability to calculate any such loss with reasonable certainty. In arguing that a reasonably certain calculation was possible, Hydraform relies heavily on *Van Hooijdonk v. Langley,* 111 N.H. 32, 274 A.2d 798 (1971), a case that arose from a landlord's cancellation of a business lease. The court held that the jury could award damages for profits that a seasonal restaurant anticipated for the three years that lease should have run. It reasoned that the experience of one two-month season provided sufficient data for a reasonably certain opinion about the extent of future profits. The court thus found sufficient certainty where damages were estimated on the basis of one year of operation and profit, as compared with no operation and hence no profit in the later years.

Hydraform's situation, however, presents a variable that distinguishes it from *Van Hooijdonk*. In our case the evidence did not indicate that American's breach had forced Hydraform's stove manufacturing enterprise out of business, and therefore the jury could not assume that there would be no profits in later years. Without that assumption the jury could not come to any reasonably certain conclusion about the anticipated level of sales absent a breach by American. The jury could predict that Hydraform would obtain steel from another source and would be able to manufacture stoves; but it did not have the evidence from which to infer the future volume of manufacturing and sales. Thus, it could not calculate anticipated lost profits with a reasonable degree of certainty.

There is, moreover, a further reason to deny recovery for profits said to have been lost in the later years. Although Hydraform's pretrial statement disclosed that Hydraform claimed $100,000 in lost profits, it did not indicate that the claim related to the seasons beginning in 1979 and 1980. Since the pretrial statement also listed a claim for loss of the value of the business at the time of its sale in 1979, we believe that the statement could reasonably be read as claiming lost profit only for the one year before the business was sold. Therefore the claim for profits in 1979 and 1980 should have been disallowed for failure to disclose the claim as required by Superior Court Rule 62.

We consider next the claim for loss in the value of the business as realized at the time of its sale in 1979. As a general rule, loss in the value of a business as a going concern, or loss in the value of its good will, may be recovered as an element of consequential damages. *See Salem Engineering & Const. Corp. v. Londonderry School Dist.*, 122 N.H. at 384, 445 A.2d at 1094; *Salinger v. Salinger,* 69 N.H. 589, 591–92, 45 A. 558, 559–60 (1899); *see also J. Story, Partnership* § 99, at 169–70 (6th ed.1868).

In this case, however, it was error to submit the claim for diminished value to the jury, for three reasons. First, to the extent that diminished value was thought to reflect anticipated loss of profits in future years, as a capitalization of the loss, it could not be calculated with reasonable certainty for the reasons we have just discussed. Second, even if such profits could have been calculated in this case, allowing the jury to consider both a claim for diminished value resting on lost profits and a claim for the lost profits themselves would have allowed a double recovery. *See Westric Battery Co. v. Standard Electric Co., Inc.,* 522 F.2d 986, 989 (10th Cir.1975). Third, to the extent that diminished value was thought to rest on any other theory, there was no evidence on which it could have been calculated. There was nothing more than Mr. Choate's testimony that he had sold the business in September of 1979 for $150,000 plus minimum royalties, together with his opinion that the sales price was less than the business was worth. This testimony provided the jury with no basis for determining what the business was worth or for calculating the claimed loss, and any award on this theory rested on sheer speculation.

In summary, we hold that the jury should not have been allowed to consider any contract claim for consequential damages for lost profits beyond those lost on the sale of 150 stoves, the difference between the 400 mentioned in the contract and the 250 actually sold. Nor should the trial court have allowed the jury to consider the claim for loss in the value of the business.

* * *

Reversed.

Note: Punitive Damages for Seller's Breach by Repudiation or Non-delivery

Under what circumstances, if any, could Hydraform recover punitive damages for American Steel's breach of contract?

UCC 1–106(1) provides that "penal damages" may not be recovered "except as specifically provided in this Act or by other rule of law." There is nothing in the UCC which "specifically" authorizes punitive damages for any breach of a contract for sale. What about "other" rules of law? Compare UCC 1–103.

In the absence of legislation preempting the UCC, an accepted starting place is Section 355 of the Restatement, Second, of Contracts: "Punitive damages are not recoverable for a breach of contract unless the conduct constituting the breach is also a tort for which punitive damages are recoverable." Thus, if the breach is not "also" a tort, punitives are not recoverable. Even so, the breach which is a tort must, in the view of some courts, be "wilful" and "accompanied by fraud, malice, wantoness or oppression." McIntosh v. Magna Systems, Inc., 539 F.Supp. 1185, 1190 (N.D.Ill.1982). In most cases, this exacting test will not capture a breach that is simply negligent or a breach that is wilful where the objective is to recapture a gain that was foregone in the bargaining at the time of contracting. Moreover, the duty of good faith imposed by general contract law, see Section 205 of the Restatement, Second, Contracts, is classified as a term of the contract. Thus, bad faith in the performance or enforcement of the contract, however defined, is a breach of the bargain for which contract remedies are available. See Sections 5(2), 235(2) and Comment (b). See also, Speidel, *The Borderland of Contract,* 10 N.Ky.L.Rev. 163, 180–81, 188–93 (1983).

A court could, however, decide that a "bad faith" breach was a tort which, if egregious, would support an award of punitive damages. California courts have done so in the context of insurance, and this result has been accepted in many states. Insurance contracts, however, contain elements not normally present in a commercial contract for sale between professional sellers and buyers. See Louderbach & Jurika, *Standards for Limiting the Tort of Bad Faith Breach of Contract,* 16 U.S.F.L.Rev. 187 (1982), who note the existence of a "special" relationship, with elements of unequal capacity, dependence and trust, between the individual insured and a corporate insurer. The absence of these special dimensions in commercial transactions has lead most courts to conclude that tort damages, including punitives, are not appropriate, regardless of the nature or purpose of the breach.

A possible portent of things to come is Seaman's Direct Buying Service, Inc. v. Standard Oil Co., 36 Cal.3d 752, 206 Cal.Rptr. 354, 686 P.2d 1158 (1984), where the Supreme Court of California, in a dispute between commercial parties, stated without clearly holding that a "party to a contract may incur tort remedies when, in addition to breaching the contract, it seeks to shield itself from liability by denying, in bad faith and without probable cause, that the contract exists." 206 Cal.Rptr. at 363, 686 P.2d at 1167. *Seaman's,* with its potential for converting all bad faith breaches into torts, has received much critical comment. See, e.g., Comment, *Extending the Bad Faith Tort Doctrine to General Commercial Contracts,* 65 B.U.L.Rev. 355 (1985). Although its future is uncertain, the nose of the punitive damage camel is clearly under the contract tent.

PART FOUR

THE STAGE OF GETTING THE GOODS OR DOCUMENTS TO THE BUYER

CHAPTER SIXTEEN

RISK OF LOSS

SECTION 1. THE BASIC GROUND RULES

There are many slips between the cup and the lip. One is that goods which have been identified to the contract for sale are destroyed or damaged before delivery without the fault or negligence of either party. Which party, seller or buyer, bears the risk of this loss?

The question is important. If the risk of loss has passed, the buyer must, unless insured, absorb the loss and pay the contract price. See UCC 2–709(1)(a). If the buyer has insured them, the insurance company will indemnify the buyer to the extent obligated under the policy and, through equitable or contractual subrogation, assert any claims that the buyer might have against third parties who caused the loss.

If the risk of loss has not passed, the seller, unless insured, must absorb the loss and, unless excused from performance, tender delivery of substitute goods. Again, if the goods are insured, the insurance company will indemnify the seller and, in all probability, assert any claims the seller may have against third parties through subrogation. When is the seller with the risk excused from performance because the goods were lost or damaged? The answer in most cases will be found in UCC 2–613 and 2–615, which you should review at this time.

When does the risk of loss pass? Section 22 of the Uniform Sales Act, which was enacted in 37 states, provided that the goods remained at the seller's risk until the "property" was transferred to the buyer. Thereafter, the risk was on the buyer "whether delivery had been made or not * * *." Section 18, however, provided that the property in "specific or ascertained goods" passed from the seller when the contract intended it to be transferred and Section 19 stated a series of five rules for ascertaining such intention when it was not otherwise made clear.

As the following excerpt reveals, the "property" or "title" approach to risk of loss was thought both to promote confusion and to ignore commercial realities.

LLEWELLYN, 1 HEARINGS BEFORE THE NEW YORK LAW REVISION COMMISSION ON THE UNIFORM COMMERCIAL CODE 96–97, [160–61] (1954).

"May I say one other thing in that connection, and say it without any hesitancy at all for the record? The number of lawyers who have an accurate knowledge of sales law is extremely small in these United States. My brother Bacon has taught sales law for 28 years. When he says it isn't too difficult to determine where the court will decide the title is or isn't or is going to be or should be, he is speaking a truth within limits for people who have taught sales law for 28 years. I submit to you, sir, that there are not many of them.

"The ordinary lawyer, except for odds and ends of people who have specialized in this field, finds sales law as uncertain and as confused as you yourselves found it, if you are lawyers, when you finished the course in sales and wondered what the deuce you were going to do about an examination in confusion, dealing apparently with confused material and perhaps a confused professor.

"It is a body of law in which we just do not know our way around, and the thing that has been criticized, the elimination of the passing of title or the place where it is to pass, as the vital, focal factor for the courts to think about, is one of the great clarifications that has been offered to the law of these United States over many years.

"The way in which one comes to see that is not by praising the Code. The way in which one comes to see that is to turn to the only body of truly commercial sales law which operates almost entirely without use of the concept of title. There you have a body of sales law which is clean, clear, guidesome, which it is almost impossible to misconstrue, and which practically pays no attention to title at all. That is the law of the C.I.F. contract, and the inspiration of the law of the C.I.F. contract is the inspiration at least to try to bring it home to ordinary sales law, that just doesn't happen to be overseas and confined to a few people; that is what has led to the plan of the Code, working in terms of the facts, what the parties really thought about, and what the issues really are.

"So that, far from giving any excuse on behalf of the drafting staff or the supporting organizations for the elimination of the title concept as the center of the sales chapter, we bring it before you as what we conceive to be a true contribution and a true opportunity to bring a difficult, useful and troubled body of law within the compass of anybody, anytime, anyhow.

"Speaking to you, sir, as one law teacher to another, I suggest that this is going to be a great contribution to the law students of the United States. I think they can really learn their sales, and learn it fast, if you will give them Article 2."

The Code rejected title as the test for determining when the risk of loss has passed: "Each provision of this Article with regard to the rights, obligations and remedies of the seller, the buyer, purchasers or other third parties applies irrespective of title to the goods except where the provision refers to such title." UCC 2–401. Thus, title may be relevant to the scope of an insurance policy or the evidence of state taxation, but not to risk of loss.

See, e.g., House of Lloyd, Inc. v. Director of Revenue, 824 S.W.2d 914 (Mo.1992) (risk of loss and title pass at different times). See also UCC 2–403.

The primary provisions dealing with risk of loss are UCC 2–509 and 2–510. Note that the test is flexible rather than rigid and is keyed to the agreement of the parties and the stage of performance thereunder. More particularly, the risk is tied, in most cases at least, to which party has possession of or control over the goods. Two assumptions appear to underlie this approach: (1) The party in possession or in control is in the "best" position, cost considered, to minimize or avoid loss; and (2) The party in possession or in control is more likely to have insurance against losses that could not be avoided. In short, parties in control of goods are thought to be what economists call the "least cost loss avoiders" and the best insurers against risk. See Note, *Risk of Loss in Commercial Transactions: Efficiency Thrown Into the Breach,* 65 Va.L.Rev. 559 (1979). Thus, the Code sought to minimize the cases where the risk passed to the buyer before the goods changed hands—cases where the risk of loss was not on the party with possession and control and where the one with the risk would often not be insured for the loss. A useful discussion is Howard, *Allocation of Risk of Loss Under the UCC: A Transactional Evaluation of Sections 2–509 and 2–510,* 15 U.C.C.L.J. 334 (1983).

SECTION 2. RISK OF LOSS UNDER THE CODE IN THE ABSENCE OF BREACH

A. Seller Has No Obligation to Ship Goods; Goods in Possession of Bailee

Unless otherwise agreed, the seller has no obligation to ship the goods to the buyer. The place of delivery is the "seller's place of business or if he has none his residence." UCC 2–308(a). What the seller must do to tender delivery to the buyer is spelled out in UCC 2–503(1). If at the time of contracting, identified goods are in the possession "of a bailee and are to be delivered without being moved," what the seller must do to tender delivery is spelled out in UCC 2–503(4). See UCC 2–308(b). For the importance of this, read UCC 2–509(2) & (3) and work through the following materials.

Problem 16–1

Sam purchased a new VCR for $500 in June, 1993. In November, 1993, Sam, pressed for cash, advertised the VCR for sale. On Friday, Bob visited Sam's condo, inspected the unit and, after some negotiations, agreed to buy it for $300, with $150 down and the balance on delivery. Bob asked when he could take the VCR. Sam said he wanted it over the weekend to tape the Bear's game and that he would call Bob at work on Monday to set up a time "after work on Monday." Bob agreed. On Sunday evening, a self-appointed neighborhood "resource reallocator" forcibly entered Sam's condo and "removed" the VCR. When informed, Bob stopped payment on the $150 check. Sam argued that the VCR was Bob's and that he still owed Sam the entire $300. Neither party was insured. Who should prevail?

Problem 16–2

After negotiations and inspection, B agreed in writing to purchase identified, new factory equipment for $15,000. The agreement provided, in part, that the price was due "when goods received by the purchaser" and that delivery was to be to "purchaser's truck within 4 weeks of contract date, seller to give purchaser 7 days notice of delivery." Two weeks later, S notified B in writing that the goods were "in a deliverable state and at your disposal." The notice was received on a Friday. Over the weekend and before B took possession, vandals broke into S's plant and seriously damaged the machinery. B refused to take delivery, claiming that the risk of loss was on S. Neither party was insured. Who prevails?

SILVER v. WYCOMBE, MEYER & CO., INC.

Civil Court of the City of New York, 1984.
124 Misc.2d 717, 477 N.Y.S.2d 288.

DAVID B. SAXE, JUDGE.

This action by an insurance company, as subrogee, to recover proceeds paid to its insured, Martin Silver, was tried before the court on stipulated facts.

Plaintiff, through his agent, Elsie Simpson, an interior decorator, ordered custom furniture from defendant Wycombe, Meyer & Co., Inc. (Wycombe). The furniture was manufactured by codefendant Jackson-Allen Upholstery Corp. (Jackson-Allen), a subsidiary of defendant Wycombe, at its factory in Catasauqua, Pennsylvania. On or about February 23, 1982, Wycombe sent invoices to plaintiff advising that the furniture was ready for shipment. Plaintiff thereupon tendered payment in full and directed Wycombe to ship one room of furniture but to hold the other until instructed further. Accordingly, one room of furniture was shipped to plaintiff. But before any instructions were received as to the second room of furniture, it was destroyed in a fire which was not due to any negligence on the part of defendants. Fireman's Fund Insurance Co. paid plaintiff for the loss and seeks to recover the proceeds from defendants on the theory that the risk of loss never passed to the buyer, its insured.

In the absence of contrary agreement by the parties, risk of loss under the Uniform Commercial Code is determined by the manner in which delivery is to be made (U.C.C. 2–509). The original order, documented by defendant Wycombe's order form, indicates a price of $7053 "+ del'y," and all invoices provide for shipment to plaintiff's home "Truck prepaid." It is clear that the provisions of U.C.C. 2–509 Subdiv. (1) govern the issue of when risk of loss passes to the buyer "where the contract requires or authorizes the seller to ship the goods by carrier * * *" Where the contract requires the seller to deliver the merchandise at a particular location, risk of loss passes upon tender of the goods at that location (U.C.C. 2–509(1)(b)) and where the contract does not require the seller to deliver the goods to a particular destination, it passes upon their delivery to the carrier (par. (a)). Where the contract provides for delivery at the seller's place of business or at the situs of the goods, risk of loss passes upon actual receipt by the buyer, if seller is a merchant, and otherwise upon tender of delivery (U.C.C. 2–509(3)).

Under the facts of the case at bar, the terms of the contract as it regards delivery are not stated. It is apparent, however, that regardless of the particular agreement between buyer and seller, defendants have set forth no facts sufficient to place the risk of loss upon plaintiff under any of the cited U.C.C. provisions. Indeed, the Official Comment 3 to U.C.C. 2–509 makes it clear that "a merchant seller cannot transfer risk of loss and it remains upon him until actual receipt by the buyer, even though full payment has been made and the buyer has been notified that the goods are at his disposal" (Note 3).

Defendants, however, advance the novel theory that, because of plaintiff's request that they hold the furniture subject to further instruction, they became mere bailees of the goods and that the provisions of U.C.C. 2–509(2) should govern this case. They argue that the invoices informing plaintiff that the furniture was ready for shipment constitute acknowledgment of the buyer's right to possession, transferring the risk of loss pursuant to U.C.C. 2–509(2)(b) to the buyer.

This position is entirely without merit. The provisions of U.C.C. 2–509(2) contemplate a situation in which goods are in the physical possession of a third party who will continue to hold them after consummation of the sale. Therefore, this is not a provision appropriately applied to the circumstances at bar which anticipate the passing of title *and* physical possession more or less simultaneously. Furthermore, bailment requires *delivery* of the goods to the bailee (see Black's Law Dictionary, 4th ed., p. 179, 1968). Having concluded that defendants failed to establish delivery of the furniture to plaintiff, by no stretch of the imagination may plaintiff be said to have redelivered it to defendants for safe-keeping.

Defendants cannot transform what is clearly a sale of goods into a bailment simply because they acceded to the buyer's request to postpone delivery. The agreement between buyer and seller clearly contemplates delivery at the buyer's home and, under the Uniform Commercial Code, risk of loss remains upon a merchant seller until he completes his performance with reference to the physical delivery of the goods (U.C.C. 2–401(2); U.C.C. 2–509(3) and Note 3 to U.C.C. 2–509; *Ramos v. Wheel Sports Center,* 96 Misc.2d 646, 409 N.Y.S.2d 505, Civ.Ct., Bx.) It may be that defendant Jackson-Allen is a bailee for defendant Wycombe, but this Court is not required to rule on and makes no determination of this question.

Accordingly, judgment for plaintiff in the amount demanded in the complaint together with costs, disbursements and interest from April 13, 1982.

Notes

1. Under what circumstances, if any, can a merchant seller become a "bailee" for purposes of UCC 2–509(2)?

2. Note that the buyer's insurance company had indemnified the buyer for loss of the goods and sued the seller as a subrogee. Why did the insurer argue that risk of loss had not passed to the buyer? If the risk had passed, upon what theory could the insurer recover from the seller?

JASON'S FOODS, INC. v. PETER ECKRICH & SONS, INC

United States Court of Appeals, Seventh Circuit, 1985.
774 F.2d 214.

POSNER, CIRCUIT JUDGE.

The jurisdictional question that led us to order a limited remand in *Jason's Foods, Inc. v. Peter Eckrich & Sons, Inc.*, 768 F.2d 189 (7th Cir.1985), has been answered by the district judge: the defendant's principal place of business is Indiana, so there is diversity jurisdiction, and we can proceed to the merits of the appeal. Section 2–509(2) of the Uniform Commercial Code as adopted in Illinois (whose law, the parties agree, governs this diversity suit) provides that where "goods are held by a bailee to be delivered without being moved, the risk of loss passes to the buyer * * * (b) on acknowledgment by the bailee of the buyer's right to possession of the goods." Ill.Rev. Stat. ch. 26, ¶ 2–509(2). We must decide whether acknowledgment to the *seller* complies with the statute. There are no reported cases on the question, either in Illinois or elsewhere. Three commentators have opined that acknowledgment must be to the buyer, but without discussion. See Nordstrom, Handbook of the Law of Sales 404–05 (1970); Howard, *Allocation of Risk of Loss Under the UCC: A Transactional Evaluation of Sections 2–509 and 2–510,* 15 UCC L.J. 334, 347 n. 42 (1983); Comment, *Risk of Loss Under Section 2509 of the California Uniform Commercial Code,* 20 UCLA L.Rev. 1352, 1358 n. 30 (1973). There is a hint of the same position, again without explanation, in Latty, *Sales and Title and the Proposed Code,* 16 Law & Contemp.Prob. 3, 14 (1951); Note, *Risk of Loss Under the Uniform Commercial Code,* 7 Ind.L.Rev. 711, 726 (1974), and Note, *Commercial Transactions: Risk of Loss: What Does the Code Mean by Bailee?,* 21 Okla.L.Rev. 310 (1968). The defendant submitted in the district court an affidavit from a professor of commercial law at Ohio State University (Professor Clovis), who also concluded, also without elaboration, that acknowledgment must be to the buyer. The plaintiff did not question the admissibility of expert testimony on a pure issue of domestic law—though well it might have. See, e.g., *Marx & Co. v. Diners' Club, Inc.*, 550 F.2d 505, 510–11 (2d Cir.1977); *Loeb v. Hammond,* 407 F.2d 779, 781 (7th Cir.1969); *United States v. Zipkin,* 729 F.2d 384, 387 (6th Cir.1984). An alternative procedure would have been for the district judge to invite a disinterested expert on commercial law to submit a brief as *amicus curiae.* See Code of Judicial Conduct for United States Judges, Canon 3(A)(4) and commentary thereto.

On or about December 30, 1982, Jason's Foods contracted to sell 38,000 pounds of "St. Louis style" pork ribs to Peter Eckrich & Sons, delivery to be effected by a transfer of the ribs from Jason's' account in an independent warehouse to Eckrich's account in the same warehouse—which is to say, without the ribs actually being moved. In its confirmation of the deal, Jason's notified Eckrich that the transfer in storage would be made between January 10 and January 14. On January 13 Jason's phoned the warehouse and requested that the ribs be transferred to Eckrich's account. A clerk at the warehouse noted the transfer on its books immediately but did not mail a warehouse receipt until January 17 or January 18, and it was not till Eckrich received the receipt on January 24 that it knew the transfer had taken place. But on January 17 the ribs had been destroyed by a fire at the warehouse. Jason's sued Eckrich for the price. If the risk of loss passed on January 13 when the ribs were transferred to Eckrich's account, or at least before the fire, Jason's is entitled to recover the contract price; otherwise not. The district judge ruled that the risk of loss did not pass by then and therefore granted summary judgment for Eckrich.

Jason's argues that when the warehouse transferred the ribs to Eckrich's account, Jason's lost all rights over the ribs, and it should not bear the risk of loss of goods it did not own or have any right to control. Eckrich owned them and Eckrich's insurance covered any ribs that it owned; Jason's had no insurance and anyway, Jason's argues, it could not insure what it no longer owned. (The warehouse would be liable for the fire damage only if negligent. Cf. *Refrigeration Sales Co. v. Mitchell-Jackson, Inc.,* 770 F.2d 98 (7th Cir.1985).) Finally, Jason's points out that the draftsmen of the Uniform Commercial Code were careful and deliberate. Both subsections (a) and (c) of section 2–509(2)—the subsections that surround the "acknowledgment" provision at issue in this case—provide that the risk of loss passes to the buyer on or after "his receipt" of a document of title (negotiable in (a), nonnegotiable in (c)). If the draftsmen had meant that the acknowledgment of the buyer's right to possession of the goods—the acknowledgment that is subsection (b)'s substitute for a document of title—must be to the buyer, they would have said so.

Eckrich argues with great vigor that it cannot be made to bear the loss of goods that it does not know it owns. But that is not so *outré* a circumstance as it may sound. If you obtain property by inheritance, you are quite likely to own it before you know you own it. And Eckrich's position involves a comparable paradox: that Jason's continued to bear the risk of loss of goods that it knew it no longer owned. So the case cannot be decided by reference to what the parties knew or did not know; and neither can it be decided, despite Jason's' urgings, on the basis of which party could have insured against the loss. Both could have. Jason's had sufficient interest in the ribs until the risk of loss shifted to Eckrich to insure the ribs until then. You do not have to own goods to insure them; it is enough that you will suffer a loss if they are lost or damaged, *Hawkeye-Security Ins. Co. v. Reeg,* 128 Ill.App.3d 352, 83 Ill.Dec. 683, 470 N.E.2d 1103 (1984); *Prince v. Royal Indemnity Co.,* 541 F.2d 646, 649 (7th Cir.1976), as of course Jason's would if the risk of loss remained on it after it parted with title. See generally Stockton, *An Analysis of Insurable Interest Under Article Two of the Uniform Commercial Code,* 17 Vand.L.Rev. 815, 816–21 (1964). Section 2–509(2) separates title from risk of loss. Title to the ribs passed to Eckrich when the warehouse made the transfer on its books from Jason's' account to Eckrich's, but the risk of loss did not pass until the transfer was "acknowledged."

Thus, as is usually the case, insurability cannot be used to guide the assignment of liability. (The costs of insurance might sometimes be usable for this purpose, as we shall see, but not in this case.) Since whoever will be liable for the loss can insure against it, the court must determine who is liable before knowing who can insure, rather than vice versa. If acknowledgment to the seller is enough to place the risk of loss on the buyer, then Eckrich should have bought insurance against any losses that occurred afterward. If acknowledgment to the buyer is necessary (we need not decide whether acknowledgment to a third party may ever suffice), Jason's should have bought insurance against any losses occurring until then.

The suggestion that the acknowledgment contemplated by subsection (b) can be to the seller seems very strange. What purpose would it serve? When Jason's called up the warehouse and directed that the transfer be made, it did not add: and by the way, acknowledge to me when you make the transfer. Jason's assumed, correctly, that the transfer was being made forthwith; and in fact there is no suggestion that the warehouse clerk ever "acknowledged" the transfer to Jason's. If the draftsmen of subsection (b) had meant the risk of loss to pass when the transfer was made, one would think they would have said so, and not complicated life by requiring "acknowledgment."

A related section of the Uniform Commercial Code, section 2–503(4)(a), makes acknowledgment by the bailee (the warehouse here) a method of tendering goods that are sold without being physically moved; but, like section 2–509(2)(b), it does not indicate to whom acknowledgment must be made. The official comments on this section, however, indicate that it was not intended to change the corresponding section of the Uniform Sales Act, section 43(3). See UCC comment 6 to § 2–503. And section 43(3) had expressly required acknowledgment to the buyer. See, e.g., *Peelle Co. v. Industrial Plant Corp.,* 120 N.J.L. 480, 200 A. 1007 (1938). Rules on tender have, it is true, a different function from rules on risk of loss; they determine at what point the seller has completed the performance of his side of the bargain. He may have completed performance, but if the goods are still in transit the risk of loss does not shift until the buyer receives them, if the seller is a merchant. See UCC § 2–509(3) and UCC comment 3 to section 2–509. In the case of warehouse transfers, however, the draftsmen apparently wanted risk of loss to conform to the rules for tender. For comment 4 to section 2–509 states that "where the agreement provides for delivery of the goods as between the buyer and seller without removal from the physical possession of a bailee, the provisions on manner of tender of delivery apply on the point of transfer of risk." And those provisions as we have said apparently require (in the case where no document of title passes) acknowledgment to the buyer. The acknowledgment need not, by the way, be in writing, so far as we are aware. Jason's could have instructed the warehouse to call Eckrich when the transfer was complete on the warehouse's books. See *Whately v. Tetrault,* 29 Mass.App.Dec. 112, 5 UCC Rep.Serv. (Callaghan) 838 (1964). That is why Jason's' case is not utterly demolished by the fact that the document of title—that is, the warehouse receipt—was not received by Eckrich till after the fire. Acknowledgment in a less formal manner is authorized; indeed, section 509(2)(b) would have no function if the only authorized form of acknowledgment were by document of title, whether negotiable or nonnegotiable.

The second sentence of comment 4 to section 509 is also suggestive: "Due delivery of a negotiable document of title covering the goods or acknowledgment by the bailee that he holds for the buyer completes the 'delivery' and passes the risk." The reference to a document of title is to subsections (a) and (c); and in both of those cases, of course, the tender involves notice to the buyer. It would be surprising if the alternative of acknowledgment did not.

All this may seem a rather dry textual analysis, remote from the purposes of the Uniform Commercial Code, so let us shift now to the plane of policy. The Code sought to create a set of standard contract terms that would reflect in the generality of cases the preferences of contracting parties at the time of contract. One such preference is for assignments of liability—or, what amounts to the same thing, assignments of the risk of loss—that create incentives to minimize the adverse consequences of untoward events such as (in this case) a warehouse fire. There are two ways of minimizing such consequences. One is to make them less painful by insuring against them. Insurance does not prevent a loss—it merely spreads it—but in doing so it reduces (for those who are risk averse) the disutility of the loss. So if one of the contracting parties can insure at lower cost than the other, this is an argument for placing the risk of loss on him, to give him an incentive to do so. But that as we have seen is not a factor in this case; either party could have insured (or have paid the warehouse to assume strict liability for loss or destruction of the goods, in which event the warehouse would have insured them), and so far as the record shows at equal cost.

The other method of minimizing the consequences of an unanticipated loss is through prevention of the loss. If one party is in a better position than the other to prevent it, this is a reason for placing the risk of loss on him, to give him an incentive to prevent it. It would be a reason for placing liability on a seller who still had possession of the goods, even though title had passed. But between the moment of transfer of title by Jason's and the moment of receipt of the warehouse receipt by Eckrich, neither party to the sale had effective control over the ribs. They were in a kind of limbo, until (to continue the Dantesque image) abruptly propelled into a hotter region. With Jason's having relinquished title and Eckrich not yet aware that it had acquired it, neither party had an effective power of control.

But this is not an argument for holding that the risk of loss shifted at the moment of transfer; it is just an argument for regarding the parties' positions as symmetrical from the standpoint of ability either to prevent or to shift losses. In such a case we have little to assist us besides the language of subsection (b) and its surrounding subsections and the UCC comments; but these materials do point pretty clearly to the conclusion that the risk of loss did not pass at the moment of transfer.

When did it pass? Does "acknowledgment" mean receipt, as in the surrounding subsections of 2–509(2), or mailing? Since the evidence was in conflict over whether the acknowledgment was mailed on January 17 (and at what hour), which was the day of the fire, or on January 18, this could be an important question—but in another case. Jason's waived it. The only theory it tendered to the district court, or briefed and argued in this court, was that the risk of loss passed either on January 13, when the transfer of title was made on the books of the warehouse, or at the latest on January 14, because Eckrich knew the ribs would be transferred at the warehouse sometime between January 10 and 14. We have discussed the immateriality of the passage of title on January 13; we add that the alternative argument, that Eckrich knew by January 14 that it owned the ribs, exaggerates what

Eckrich knew. By the close of business on January 14 Eckrich had a well-founded expectation that the ribs had been transferred to its account; but considering the many slips that are possible between cup and lips, we do not think that this expectation should fix the point at which the risk shifts. If you were told by an automobile dealer from whom you bought a car that the car would be delivered on January 14, you would not take out insurance effective that day, without waiting for the actual delivery.

Finally, Jason's' argument from trade custom or usage is unavailing. The method of transfer that the parties used was indeed customary but there was no custom or usage on when the risk of loss passed to the buyer.

Affirmed.

Notes

1. At common law, if the goods were identified and in the possession of a bailee, title and, thus, risk of loss, passed at the time of sale even though the buyer was not entitled to take possession. See Tarling v. Baxter, 6 B. & C. 360, 108 Eng.Rep. 484 (KB 1827). Compare UCC 2–401(3). In *Jason's Foods,* the court held that even though title had passed, the risk of loss did not pass until the bailee acknowledged to the buyer the buyer's right to take possession. Do you agree? Compare UCC 2–705(2)(b).

2. The "bailee" in *Jason's Foods* was a warehouseman, i.e., a "person who by a warehouse receipt * * * acknowledges possession of goods and contracts to deliver them." UCC 7–102(1)(a). A warehouse receipt, UCC 1–201(45), is a document of title which "in the regular course of business * * * is treated as adequately evidencing that the person in possession of it is entitled to receive, hold and dispose of the document and the goods it covers." UCC 1–201(15). In *Jason's Foods,* the warehouse receipt issued but not received by the buyer before the fire was not negotiable. See UCC 7–104(1). See UCC 2–509(2)(c) & 2–503(4)(b). Note that the buyer must actually receive the written delivery order and, under UCC 2–503(4)(b), risk of loss remains on the seller "until the buyer has had a reasonable time to present the document or direction * * *." These sections further reinforce Judge Posner's analysis, do they not? Does UCC 2–509(2)(b) even apply to the case where a warehouseman regularly acknowledges a buyer's right to possession by a non-negotiable document of title?

3. The warehouseman's duty of care is stated in UCC 7–204(1).

4. *The Case of the Lost Propane.* Even though the goods are in the possession of a bailee at the time of contracting, the parties may agree that the bailee is to ship or deliver the goods to the buyer rather than simply acknowledge that the buyer is entitled to possession. If so, risk of loss is governed by either UCC 2–509(1) or (3) rather than UCC 2–509(2). In Commonwealth Petroleum Co. v. Petrosol Int'l, Inc., 901 F.2d 1314 (6th Cir.1990), the goods were propane stored in underground tanks in the possession of a Bailee. After Buyer paid the price and Bailee acknowledged Buyer's right to possession but before any tender of delivery by Bailee, the propane was destroyed. The court, after extensive litigation, ultimately held that the parties had not agreed that Bailee was to ship or deliver the goods to Buyer and left the risk of loss on Buyer under UCC 2–509(2)(b). In short, the goods were to be delivered "without being moved."

Problem 16–3

Red Feather, a fine yearling, won her first race. A pleased Owner (much pleased) shipped her back to the stable by common carrier, taking a non-negotiable bill of lading naming O as the consignee. While the horse was in transit, O sold her to B for $10,000. Owner accepted a check for $10,000, handed B the non-negotiable bill of lading and stated "she's all yours." Two hours later, Red Feather was killed in an accident while still in the carrier's possession.

A. B stopped payment on the check and insisted that the risk of loss remained on S. Is B correct?

B. Suppose that, unknown to either party, Red Feather was dead at the time of the contract. What result? See UCC 2–613.

B. Shipment Contracts

Probably the most common transaction in which risk of loss disputes will arise involves contracts that require or authorize the seller to ship the goods to the buyer by carrier. It is also likely that the agreement will use certain delivery terms, such as "FOB seller's plant," FAS or CIF. See UCC 2–319 & 2–320. The Code drafters were aware of the common business understanding of these terms and consciously adapted the risk of loss provisions to them. Compare UCC 2–319(1) and 2–509(1). For what the seller must do under these terms to tender delivery, see UCC 2–503 & 2–504.

In most cases, the meaning and consequences of these delivery terms is clear. In an FOB point of origin or shipment contract, the buyer pays the cost of transportation and bears the risk of loss while the goods are in transit. UCC 2–319(1)(a) and 2–509(1)(a). In an FOB point of destination contract, the seller pays the cost of transportation and bears the risk while the goods are in transit. UCC 2–319(1)(b) and 2–509(1)(b). But occasionally there is some confusion.

Problem 16–4

From its mill in Fortuna, California, Seller, Raylo Lumber, received a written order for lumber sent by Buyer, Oregon Pacific Lumber, from its place of business in Portland Oregon. The order provided in part:

> To Raylo Lbr. Co. Ship to Oregon–Pacific Lumber Co. Council Bluffs, Iowa Rate 1.20 (show on bill of lading) Routing SP UP (via Colby, Kansas) Shipment One week Terms: Regular 2% ADF 10 days Please Show Oregon–Pacific Lumber Co. as Shipper * * * Thoroughly Air Dried White Fir—WCLA Rules No. 15 Constr. & Btr., Allow. 25% standard ALS S4S EE DET—Clean Bright Stock one (1) Carload.

Two days later, Seller loaded a railroad car provided by the carrier with conforming lumber and sealed the door. Later that day, Seller prepared an invoice for Buyer as follows: "Shipped to Oregon–Pacific Lumber Company Council Bluffs, Iowa * * * F.O.B. delivered $1.20 rate. * * * 31,152′ White Fir, A.D. 2 × 4 STD. & BTR. S4S at $84.00 Per M—$2,616.77." Later that day, Seller prepared a non-negotiable bill of lading naming Buyer as both Consignor and Consignee and presented it to an agent of the railroad. The agent signed the bill of lading and Seller immediately mailed the bill and the invoice to Buyer.

Before the bill and invoice were received and before Carrier picked up the load car from siding, fire broke out without the fault of Seller and the goods were destroyed. B argued that risk of loss had not passed before the fire. More specifically, B argued that the term "F.O.B. delivered" in context meant that S had agreed to deliver the goods "at a particular destination" and that risk of loss would not pass until the goods were "duly tendered" at that destination. See UCC 2–509(1)(b). Is that argument correct? See UCC 2–319(1), 2–509(1), 2–503 and the comments.

COOK SPECIALTY CO. v. SCHRLOCK

United States District Court, Eastern District of Pennsylvania, 1991.
772 F.Supp. 1532.

MEMORANDUM

WALDMAN, District Judge.

Defendant Machinery Systems, Inc. ("MSI") contracted to sell plaintiff a machine known as a Dries & Krump Hydraulic Press Brake. When the machine was lost in transit, plaintiff sued defendants to recover for the loss. Presently before the court is plaintiff's Motion for Summary Judgment and defendant MSI's Cross–Motion for Summary Judgment.

* * *

II. FACTS

The pertinent facts are not contested and are as follow.

Plaintiff entered into a sales contract with defendant MSI for the purchase of a Dries & Krump Press Brake in August of 1989 for $28,000. The terms of the contract were F.O.B. MSI's warehouse in Schaumburg, Illinois. Defendant R.T.L., also known as Randy's Truck Lines, ("the carrier") was used to deliver the press brake from the defendant's warehouse to the plaintiff in Pennsylvania. MSI obtained a certificate of insurance from the carrier with a face amount of $100,000 and showing a $2,500 deductible (*See* dfdt. ex. D.)

On October 20, 1989, the carrier took possession of the press brake at MSI's warehouse. While still in transit, the press brake fell from the carrier's truck. The carrier was cited by the Illinois State Police for not properly securing the load. Plaintiff has recovered damages of $5,000 from the carrier's insurer, the applicable policy limit for this particular incident. The machine was worth $28,000.

III. DISCUSSION

This dispute is governed by the Uniform Commercial Code ("UCC") provisions regarding risk of loss. The parties agree that there is no meaningful distinction between the pertinent law of Pennsylvania and Illinois, both of which have adopted the UCC.

The term "F.O.B., place of shipment," means that "the seller must at that place ship the goods in the manner provided in this Article (section 2–504) and bear the expense and risk of putting them into the possession of the carrier." 13 Pa.C.S.A. § 2319. Thus, MSI bore the expense and risk of putting the machine into the carrier's possession for delivery. At the time the carrier takes possession, the risk of loss shifts to the buyer. The UCC provides:

> Where the contract requires or authorizes the seller to ship the goods by carrier.
>
> a) if it does not require him to deliver them at a particular destination, the risk of loss passes to the buyer when the goods are duly delivered to the carrier. * * *

13 Pa.C.S.A. § 2509.

Goods are not "duly delivered" under § 2–509, however, unless a contract is entered which satisfies the provisions of Section 2–504. *See* 13 Pa.C.S.A. § 2509, Official Comment 2. Section 2–504, entitled "Shipment by Seller" provides that:

> Where the seller is required or authorized to send the goods to the buyer and the contract does not require him to deliver them at a particular destination, then unless otherwise agreed he must
>
> a) put the goods in the possession of such a carrier and make such a contract for their transportation *as may be reasonable having regard to the nature of the goods* and other circumstances of the case.

13 Pa.C.S.A. § 2504 (emphasis added).

Plaintiff argues that the contract MSI made for the delivery of the press brake was not reasonable because defendant failed to ensure that the carrier had sufficient insurance coverage to compensate plaintiff for a loss in transit. Plaintiff thus argues that the press brake was never duly delivered to a carrier within the meaning of section 2–509 and accordingly the risk of loss never passed to plaintiff.

Plaintiff relies on two cases. In the first, *La Casse v. Blaustein,* 93 Misc.2d 572, 403 N.Y.S.2d 440 (Civ.Ct.1978), the defendant seller shipped calculators to the plaintiff buyer, a college student, in two cartons by fourth class mail. The buyer authorized the seller to spend up to $50 for shipping and insurance. The seller spent only $9.98 and insured each carton, valued at $1663, for $200. The seller wrongly addressed one of the cartons, and inscribed a theft-tempting notation on it. The New York County Civil Court held that the defendant had improperly arranged for transportation of the calculators.

La Casse is the only reported case which suggests that a seller's failure to obtain adequate insurance may breach his duty to make a reasonable contract for shipment under § 2–504. The dearth of support for plaintiff's position is instructive. A leading UCC authority has remarked: "Under this subsection [§ 2–504], what constitutes an 'unreasonable' contract of transportation? *Egregious* cases do arise." *See* J. White and R. Summers, *Uniform Commercial Code* § 5–2 (1988). The only such "egregious case" identified by White and Summers is *La Casse,* where "the package was underinsured, misaddressed, shipped by fourth class mail, and bore a 'theft-tempting' inscription." White and Summers, *supra,* at § 5–2.

The actions taken by the defendant in *La Casse* were utterly reckless. Moreover, unlike the defendant in that case, MSI did not undertake the responsibility to insure the shipment, and did not ship the press brake at a lower cost than the plaintiff expressly authorized it to pay.

Plaintiff also relies on *Miller v. Harvey,* 221 N.Y. 57, 116 N.E. 781 (1917). This pre-Code case is inapplicable. In *Miller,* by failing to declare the actual value of goods shipped on a form provided for that purpose, the seller effectively contracted away the buyer's rights against the carrier. Official Comment 3 to section 2–504 states:

> [i]t is an improper contract under paragraph (a) for the seller to agree with the carrier to a limited valuation below the true value and thus cut off the buyer's opportunity to recover from the carrier in the event of loss, when the risk of shipment is placed on the buyer.

Thus, a contract is improper if the seller agrees to an inadequate valuation of the shipment and thereby extinguishes the buyer's opportunity to recover from the carrier. That is quite different from a seller's failure to ensure that a carrier has sufficient insurance to cover a particular potential loss, in which case the carrier is still liable to the buyer.

Plaintiff's focus on a single sentence of Official Comment 3 ignores the explicit language of the statute which defines reasonable in the context of "having regard to the nature of the goods," 13 Pa.C.S.A. § 2504, and the portion of the Comment which states:

> Whether or not the shipment is at the buyer's expense the seller must see to any arrangements, *reasonable in the circumstances,* such as refrigeration, watering of live stock, protection against cold * * * and the like. * * *

Id., Official Comment 3.

The clear implication is that the reasonableness of a shipper's conduct under § 2–504 is determined with regard to the mode of transport selected. It would be unreasonable, for example, to send perishables without refrigeration. *See Larsen v. A.C. Carpenter, Inc.,* 620 F.Supp. 1084, 1119 (E.D.N.Y. 1985). No inference fairly can be drawn from the section that a seller has an obligation to investigate the amount and terms of insurance held by the carrier.

The court finds as a matter of law that MSI's conduct was not unreasonable under section 2–504. MSI obtained from the carrier a certificate of insurance and did nothing to impair plaintiff's right to recover for any loss from the carrier. Accidents occur in transit. For this reason, the UCC has specifically established mercantile symbols which delineate the risk of loss in a transaction so that the appropriate party might obtain insurance on the shipment. The contract in this case was "F.O.B." seller's warehouse. Plaintiff clearly bears the risk of loss in transit.

There are no material facts in dispute and MSI is entitled to judgment as a matter of law.

Notes

In shipment contracts, the risk of loss passes at the time the seller completes or "duly" tenders delivery at the point to which the goods are to be delivered. UCC 2–509(1). In FOB point of shipment contracts, UCC 2–319(1)(a), the critical tender section is UCC 2–504. Although the seller must do a number of things to tender delivery, obtaining insurance for the buyer's account is not one of them. Compare UCC 2–320 (C.I.F. term). For a case holding that the goods were not "duly" tendered where the seller failed to provide prompt notice of shipment in an FOB point of shipment contract, see Rheinberg-Kellerei GMBH v. Vineyard Wine Co., Inc., 53 N.C.App. 560, 281 S.E.2d 425 (1981). Does this position seem sound?

Note: Liability of Overland Carrier for Goods Lost or Damaged in Shipment

As we have seen, in an FOB place of shipment contract, risk of loss passes to the buyer when the seller "duly" tenders the goods to a carrier, whether that carrier be a truck, airplane, railroad or vessel. In addition, under the documents issued by the carrier, the buyer is the person "entitled" to the goods. See UCC 7–102(1)(b) & 7–403(4). Thus, if the goods are lost or damaged in transit, the buyer or its insurance company as subrogee has both the standing and the incentive * to bring suit against the carrier. Kumar Corp. v. Nopal Lines, Ltd., 462 So.2d 1178 (Fla.App.1985), holds that plaintiffs with standing to sue the carrier include the party with the risk of loss or his agent and an insurance subrogee.

The common law liability of the overland carrier has been described as follows:

DOBIE, BAILMENTS AND CARRIERS 325 (1914)

"By the common law, the common carrier is, with certain exceptions, an insurer of the goods intrusted to him. According to the very early cases, the only exceptions to the common carrier's liability as an insurer of the safe delivery of the goods were: 1) the act of God; and 2) the public enemy. To these, however, our native justice and the genius of our jurisprudence have added: 3) the act of the shipper; 4) public authority; and 5) the inherent nature of the goods."

The common-law liability of common carriers, however, was subject to contractual limitations and exclusions inserted by carriers in the relevant documents.

The current status of carrier liability is determined under federal and state legislation and international treaties that, in turn, depend upon the type of carrier and the scope of its operation. Thus, the liability of international air carriers is determined by the Warsaw Convention, ratified by the United States in 1934, 49 Stat. 3000 (1934), T.S. No. 876, and the liability of vessels engaged in "foreign trade" is regulated by the Carriage of Goods by Sea Act, enacted by Congress in 1936. 49 Stat. 1207 (1936), 46 U.S.C.A. §§ 1300–15. A general survey appears in Sorkin, *Changing Concepts of Liability,* 17 Forum 710 (1981).

The liability of domestic overland carriers in interstate commerce, i.e., railroads and truckers, is regulated by the 1906 Carmack amendments to the Interstate Commerce Commission Act of 1887, as reenacted in 1980 without substantial change. 49 U.S.C.A. § 11707. The statute is, essentially, a codification of the carrier's insurer liability at common law with the important benefit

* Several things make the carrier an appealing defendant. First, it is likely that it causes or has the potential for causing more loss, destruction and damage than any other party associated with a typical sales transaction. Second, the carrier is almost always solvent. Third, it is easy to prove a case against a carrier. Finally, the carrier, as a public service enterprise, is obliged to deal with all persons and cannot readily use economic pressure of withholding services to forestall a suit. Ed.

to the shipper that efforts to exclude or modify the scope of statutory liability by agreement are void. As the statute has been interpreted by the courts, the person entitled under the document states a *prima facie* case against the carrier by showing that the goods were delivered in good condition and arrived in a damaged condition and the amount of damages. To escape liability, the carrier has what is described as a "substantial double burden:" It must show both that it was free from negligence and that the damage to the cargo was due to one of the excepted causes relieving the carrier of liability at common law, i.e., act of God, public enemy, act of shipper himself, act of public authority or an inherent vice in the goods. See Martin Imports v. Courier–Newsom Exp., Inc., 580 F.2d 240, 242 (7th Cir.1978), cert. denied 439 U.S. 983, 99 S.Ct. 574, 58 L.Ed.2d 655 (1978). The leading case in this line is Missouri P.R. Co. v. Elmore & Stahl, 377 U.S. 134, 84 S.Ct. 1142, 12 L.Ed.2d 194 (1964). For an illustrative interpretation, see Oak Hall Cap and Gown Co. v. Old Dominion Freight Line, Inc., 899 F.2d 291 (4th Cir.1990).

The liability of domestic overland carriers in intrastate commerce is determined by Article 7 of the UCC, more particularly, UCC 7–309. See UCC 7–103; Starmakers Pub. Corp. v. Acme Fast Freight, Inc., 615 F.Supp. 787 (S.D.N.Y. 1985) (Carmack Act preempts UCC where interstate shipments are concerned). Subsection 7–309(1), which is poorly drafted, starts by imposing a duty of ordinary care on the carrier, but then states that the subsection "does not repeal or change any law or rule of law which imposes liability upon a common carrier for damages not caused by its negligence." Thus, in the many states where the common law liability of a carrier as insurer was recognized, the carrier could be liable even though exercising reasonable care. Subsection 7–309(2) gives limited effect to provisions in the bill of lading limiting liability: The carrier can limit liability to the value of the goods stated in the document but "no such limitation is effective with respect to the carrier's liability for conversion to its own use."

As one might expect, there has been no litigation of significance involving UCC 7–309.

SECTION 3. EFFECT OF BREACH ON RISK OF LOSS—UCC 2–510

UCC 2–510 modifies the risk of loss principles established by UCC 2–509 in certain circumstances where one of the parties is in breach. The consequences of this modification are twofold.

First, in some cases the breaching party will have to absorb the loss of or pay for lost, stolen or destroyed goods where, but for the breach, the risk of loss would have been on the other party. Thus, UCC 2–510 reallocates the risk of loss because one party breached the contract and negates the assumptions made ex ante about who was in the best position to insure. This reallocation has been questioned on policy grounds in McCoid, *Allocation of Loss and Property Insurance,* 39 Ind.L.J. 647 (1964).

Second, UCC 2–510 operates, in some circumstances, as an anti-subrogation clause: It places the risk on the non-breaching party's insurance company in circumstances where but for the insurance contract the risk of loss would be on the breaching party. Thus, under UCC 2–510(2), a buyer who, because of the seller's breach, rightfully revokes acceptance may treat the risk of loss as having rested on the seller "to the extent of any deficiency in his effective insurance coverage." Because of the statute, the insurance company must pay if there is no deficiency and, apparently, is precluded from any recovery as a subrogee against the seller. See Comment 3, which states: "This section merely distributes the risk of loss as stated and is not intended to be disturbed by any subrogation of an insurer."

What is the point of all this? One commentator has suggested that UCC 2–510 is of "dubious origin," has little practical impact on the way that insurance companies do business and "serves no practical purpose save the harassment of the legal mind." King, *UCC Section 2–510—A Rule Without Reason,* 77 Com.L.J. 272 (1972). Nothing has emerged since 1972 to cast serious doubt on this conclusion. Professor Howard, in *Allocation of Risk of Loss Under the UCC: A Transactional Evaluation of Sections 2–509 and 2–510,* 15 U.C.C.L.J. 334, 355–68 (1983), questions whether a commercial breach in the absence of bad faith is important enough to undercut the importance of insurance.

Here are some simple problems.

Problem 16–5

On June 1, S contracted to sell B 10 units of described goods for $10,000. S agreed to ship the goods "FOB point of shipment" by June 15 and B agreed to pay in full within 30 days of receipt. S had insurance on the goods until they were delivered to the carrier. B had insurance on the goods when "title" passed to him, i.e., at the "time and place of shipment." UCC 2–401(2)(a). S's insurance covered the current market value of the described goods. B's insurance covered 50% of the current market value of the goods.

A. S delivered the goods to the carrier on June 16 (they were shipped on June 17) and failed to give B any notice of the shipment. Review UCC 2–504. The goods were totally destroyed in transit on June 19. B, citing UCC 2–510, argues that the risk of loss was on S. Consequently, B had no liability for the price. Is B correct? See UCC 2–601 (right of rejection), 2–508 (cure) and 2–606 (acceptance).

B. Suppose, in (A) above, that the goods were not destroyed in transit. Rather, they were tendered by the carrier and accepted by B and taken to its plant. See UCC 2–606. The next day, the goods were destroyed without B's fault or negligence. Who has the risk of loss?

C. Continuing this exercise, suppose in (B) above, that after B accepted the goods, inspection at the plant revealed a latent, substantial defect which justified revocation of acceptance under UCC 2–608(1). B promptly notified S of the revocation. UCC 2–608(2). The next day, before S could send instructions, the goods were destroyed without the fault or negligence of B. Assuming that B, at the time of loss, had no liability for the price, see UCC 2–608(3), who has the risk of loss?

D. In light of these problems, what recommendations would you make for revision of UCC 2–510(1) & (2)? What problems, if any, do you see in the operation of UCC 2–510(3)?

SECTION 4. RISK OF LOSS AND INSURANCE

A. Some General Principles

As previously noted, the risk of loss rules in UCC 2–509 were designed, in part, to conform to assumptions about which party, seller or buyer, was in the best position, cost considered, either to prevent or to insure against loss of or damage to the goods. As Judge Posner put it in JASON'S FOODS, supra:

> "The Code sought to create a set of standard contract terms that would reflect in the generality of cases the preferences of contracting parties at the time of contract. One such preference is for assignments of liability—or, what amounts to the same thing, assignments of the risk of loss—that create incentives to minimize the adverse consequences of untoward events such as * * * a warehouse fire. There are two ways of minimizing such consequences. One is to make them less painful by insuring against them. Insurance does not prevent a loss—it merely spreads it—but in doing so it reduces (for those who are risk averse) the disutility of the loss. So if one of the contracting parties can insure at lower cost than the other, this is an argument for placing the risk of loss on him, to give him an incentive to do so. * * * The other method of minimizing the consequences of an unanticipated loss is through prevention of the loss. If one party is in a better position than the other to prevent it, this is a reason for placing the risk of loss on him, to give him an incentive to prevent it. It would be a reason for placing liability on a seller who still had possession of the goods, even though title had passed. * * * " 774 F.2d at 218.

The Code, however, has very little to say about insurance. UCC 2–501 states some but not all the circumstances where the seller and buyer will have an insurable interest in the goods. Thus, the "buyer obtains a special property interest and an insurable interest in goods by identification of existing goods as goods to which the contract refers even though the goods so identified are non-conforming and he has an option to return or reject them * * *," UCC 2–501(1), and the "seller retains an insurable interest in the goods so long as title to or any security interest in the goods remains in him. * * *," UCC 2–501(2). But UCC 2–501(3) provides that "Nothing in this section impairs any insurable interest recognized under any other statute or rule of law." Thus, UCC 2–501 is a one-way ratchet provision: it can expand, but not contract the scope of insurable interest. For the scope of insurable interest in property insurance cases, one may consult Stockton, *An Analysis of Insurable Interest Under Article Two of the Uniform Commercial Code,* 17 Vand.L.Rev. 815 (1964). See also, Pinzur, *Insurable Interest: A Search for Consistency,* 46 Ins.Counsel J. 109 (1979). Beyond insurable interest and the anti-subrogation rule of UCC 2–510, however, one must look elsewhere when disputes over insurance arise.

To sharpen the issues, read the following fact situation and puzzle over a few questions.

Problem 16–6

Repuenzel contracted to sell 1,000 pistons to Cicero for $10,000, $2,000 of which was paid upon contracting and the balance of which is due 30 days after delivery. Repuenzel created and perfected a security interest in the goods under Article 9 and shipped the goods "FOB place of Shipment," taking a non-negotiable bill of lading naming Cicero as consignee. During transit the goods were totally destroyed by fire. The contract for sale said nothing about risk of loss or insurance.

1. Which party has the risk of loss?

2. Which, if any, party has an insurable interest in the goods while in transit?

3. Standard fire insurance policies, with riders, have limited applicability to goods to be shipped to the buyer under a contract for sale. For the seller, personal property is likely to be defined as "property sold but not removed" from the building. For a buyer, coverage begins for "personal property * * * in cars on tracks when such cars are on the premises or within 100 feet of buildings described; in the open or in vehicles on the premises; on sidewalks, streets, alleys, or detached platforms when within 50 feet of buildings described."

Given these limitations, additional protection must be purchased by sellers and buyers with insurable interests while the goods are in transit. Read through the excerpts from the two types of policies which follow. Is Repuenzel's security interest covered by the Manufacturer's Output Policy? Is Buyer's ownership interest protection under the Transportation—All Risks Form?

MANUFACTURER'S OUTPUT POLICY

1. *Interest and Property Insured:* Except as hereinafter excluded, this policy insures:

(a) The interest of the Insured in all personal property owned by the Insured;
(b) The interest of the Insured in improvements and betterments to buildings not owned by the Insured;
(c) The interest of the Insured in, and legal liability for personal property of others in the actual or constructive custody of the Insured;
(d) Personal property of others
  (1) Sold by the Insured which the Insured has agreed prior to loss to insure for the account of the purchaser during course of delivery;
  (2) In the custody of the Insured which the Insured has agreed prior to loss to insurer;
  (3) Sold by the Insured under an installation agreement whereby the Insured's responsibility continues until the installation is accepted by the purchaser.

2. *Interest and Property Excluded:* This policy does not insure:

(a) Currency, money, notes, securities, growing crops or standing timber;

(b) Property while covered under import or export ocean marine policies;

(c) Animals, aircraft or watercraft;

(d) Property sold by the Insured under conditional sale, trust agreement, installment payment, or other deferred payment plan;

(e) Loss resulting from interruption of business or other consequential loss extending beyond the direct physical loss of or damage to the insured property.

3. *Perils Insured:* This policy insures against all risks of direct physical loss of or damage to the insured property from any external cause (including general coverage and salvage charges on shipments covered while waterborne) except as hereinafter excluded.

* * *

9. *Specific Insurance:* Other insurance in name of and for the benefit of the Insured may be permitted or may be required to be effected applying specifically to any location covered by this policy. Such other insurance is hereinafter referred to as specific insurance. Where specific insurance has been required by the Company, the Insured agrees to effect and keep in force specific insurance in the specified amount until otherwise agreed to in writing by the Company, and in failure thereof this Company shall not be liable for that part of any loss which would have been recoverable or due thereunder had such specific insurance been in force, whether valid or not and whether collectible or not. With respect to any specific insurance, this policy shall be considered as excess insurance and shall not apply or contribute to the payment of any loss until the amount due from all such specific insurance whether collectible or not shall have been exhausted. Under the policy the Insured is to be reimbursed to the extent of the difference between the amount recoverable or due from any specific insurance whether collectible or not and the amount of loss otherwise recoverable hereunder, not exceeding however, the difference between the limit of liability under this policy at any specified location and the amount of specific insurance at such specified location for loss or damage arising out of the perils insured against by such specific insurance.

10. *Other Insurance:* Except as to specific insurance as defined in Section 9 of this policy, this policy shall not cover to the extent of any other insurance whether prior or subsequent hereto in date, and by whomsoever effected, directly or indirectly covering the same property, and this Company shall be liable for loss or damage only for the excess value beyond the amount due from such other insurance.

The Company agrees to advance to the Insured as a loan the amount which would have been collectible under this policy except for the provisions of this Section, such loan to be repayable only to the extent of and at the time of the Insured's collection from such other insurance.

* * *

15. *Assistance and Cooperation of the Insured:* The Insured shall cooperate with the Company and, upon the Company's request, shall attend hearings and trials and shall assist in effecting settlements, securing and giving evidence, obtaining the attendance of witnesses and in the conduct of suits. Other than as provided in Section 16 of this policy, the Insured shall not, except at his own cost voluntarily make any payment, assume any obligation or incur any expense.

* * *

19. *Carriers or Bailees:* This insurance shall not inure directly or indirectly to the benefit of any carrier, nor without the affirmative consent of the Insured, to the benefit of any other bailee. The Insured may accept without prejudice to this insurance the ordinary bills-of-lading used by common carriers, including released or partially released value bills-of-lading, and the Insured may waive subrogation against railroads under Side Track Agreements, and except as otherwise provided, the Insured shall not enter into any special agreement with carriers otherwise releasing them from their common law or statutory liability. The Company shall not be liable for any loss or damage which, without its consent, has been settled or compromised by the Insured.

20. *Company's Right of Recovery:* In the event of any payment under this policy, the Insured shall execute and deliver instruments and papers and do whatever else is necessary to secure the subrogation rights of the Company. The Insured shall do nothing after loss to prejudice such rights. However, the Company specifically waives its rights of subrogation against all the subsidiary and affiliated companies of the Insured. Any release from liability, other than as provided in Section 19, entered into prior to loss hereunder by the Insured shall not affect this policy or the right of the Insured to recover hereunder. At the option of the Company, the Insured will execute a loan agreement, to the extent of any loss collectible under this policy. Said loan will bear no interest and will be repayable only in the event and to the extent of the net recovery effected from any party believed to be liable for said loss. Upon payment of any loss or advancement or loan of moneys concerning the loss, the Insured will at the Company's request and expense make claim upon and institute legal proceedings against any party which the Company believes to be liable for such loss, and will use all proper and reasonable means to recover the same, under the exclusive direction and control of the Company.

21. *Company's Options:* In the event of loss hereunder it shall be the option of the Company to take all, or any part, of the property at the agreed or appraised value, and also to repair, rebuild or replace the property destroyed or damaged, with other of like kind and quality, within a reasonable time, on giving notice of its intention so to do within thirty days after the receipt of the Proof of Loss herein required. There can be no abandonment to the Company of any property.

If branded or labeled merchandise covered by this policy is damaged and the Company elects to take all or any part of the property at the agreed or appraised value, the Insured may at his own expense stamp "salvage" on the merchandise or its containers or may remove the brands or labels, if such stamp or removal will not physically damage the merchandise.

TRANSPORTATION—ALL RISKS FORM

ASSURED CICERO CORP.

Loss, if any, payable to assured or order.

On goods and merchandise, including packages, consisting principally of PISTONS shipped by or to the assured at assured's risk within the limits of the Continental United States and Canada (excluding Alaska).

VALUATION: The said goods and merchandise shall be valued at actual invoice cost, including prepaid or advanced freight, if any, together with such costs and charges (including the commission of the assured as selling agent, but excluding duty), as may have accrued and become legally due thereon. In the event of there being no invoice, the valuation of the merchandise insured hereunder shall be the actual cash market value of the property insured at point of destination on the date of disaster.

This policy insures shipments consisting of the property insured for the following amounts in any one loss:

$15,000. while in the custody of any Truckman or Trucking Company,
$15,000. while in the custody of any Railroad or the Railway Express Agency (including while on ferries and/or railroad cars on transfers or lighters),

$1,000.= while in the custody of Air Carriers or Air Express Companies, $15,000. during transportation to and from conveyances or premises of the above described carriers, in motor trucks or trailers operated by the Assured, (excluding theft, embezzlement, conversion or any wrongful act on the part of the assured, his servants or employees).

In no event shall this Company be liable for more than $30,000. in any one casualty, either in case of partial or total loss, or salvage charges, or any other charges, or expenses, or all combined.

Insurance hereunder attaches when the goods leave factory, store or warehouse at initial point of shipment, and covers continuously thereafter, including while on docks, wharves, piers, bulkheads, in depots, stations and/or on platforms of common carriers, all while in due course of transportation, until same are delivered at factory, store or warehouse at destination.

THIS POLICY INSURES AGAINST

All Risks of loss or damage to the insured property from any external cause (including General Average and/or salvage charges and expenses), except as herein excluded.

THIS POLICY DOES NOT INSURE

(a) Accounts, bills, deeds, evidences of debt, currency, money, coins, bullion, notes, securities, stamps, jewelry, precious stones or fine arts;

(b) Against loss or damage resulting from inadequate packing or improper preparation for shipment or from insecure stowage when not stowed by the carrier;

(c) Against loss or damage by vermin or against loss or damage by leakage, evaporation, shrinkage, breakage, marring, scratching, heat or cold, or by being scented, moulded, rusted, soured, or changed in flavor unless caused by fire, lightning, windstorm, flood, explosion or collision, derailment or overturning of vehicle while on land, or collision or crashing of aircraft while in flight, or by the vessel, craft or lighter being stranded, sunk, burned or in collision while waterborne.

(d) Against loss or damage resulting from delay or loss of market, howsoever caused;

(e) Against loss or damage caused by strikes, locked-out workmen, or persons taking part in labor disturbances, or arising from riot, or civil commotion;

Against loss or damage caused by or resulting from:

(f) (1) hostile or warlike action in time of peace or war, including action in hindering, combating or defending against an actual impending or expected attack, (a) by any government or sovereign power (de jure or de facto), or by any authority maintaining or using military, naval or air forces; or (b) by military, naval or air forces; or (c) by an agent of any such government, power, authority or forces;

(2) any weapon of war employing atomic fission or radioactive force whether in time of peace or war;

(3) insurrection, rebellion, revolution, civil war, usurped power, or action taken by governmental authority in hindering, combating or defend-

ing against such an occurrence, seizure or destruction under quarantine or customs regulations, confiscation by order of any government or public authority, or risks of contraband or illegal transportation or trade.

(g) Export shipments laden on board export conveyance or under the protection of marine insurance, whichever first occurs;

(h) Import shipments until fully discharged from import conveyance and then only after marine insurance has ceased to cover;

(i) Shipments by parcel post and/or mail.

Premium Readjustment and Report of Shipments. The premium charged under this policy is based on an estimate of $300,000. value of shipments made during the period insured, and the Assured warrants to report to this Company at the end of ______________ (Policy year, unless otherwise specified) the actual value of all shipments (in accordance with the valuation clause contained in this policy) covered hereunder during the period for which such report is required, and upon the total of all reported shipments exceeding in the aggregate the said estimate of $300,000., the Assured agrees to pay this Company additional premium at the rate of .05 per $100, such additional premium to become due and payable to this Company immediately upon the furnishing of the aforesaid report or reports; but in the event of the actual shipments falling short of the said estimate of $______ then this Company will return premium at the same rate on the deficiency, but no return premium shall become due or payable until the expiration of this policy; it being understood that by the acceptance of this readjustment clause, the reinstatement clause in the body of this policy is waived.

* * *

Claim Against Carrier. In the event of any loss or damage to the goods and/or merchandise insured hereunder the assured shall immediately make claim in writing against the carrier or carriers involved.

Insurer's Right to Institute Legal Proceedings in Name of Insured. It is expressly agreed that upon payment of any loss or advancement or loan of moneys concerning the same, that the Assured will at the request and expense of the Company, and through such counsel as the Company may designate, make claim upon and institute legal proceedings against any carrier, bailee, or other parties believed to be liable for such loss, and will use all proper and reasonable means to recover the same.

Impairment of Carrier's Liability. Any act or agreement by the Assured, prior or subsequent hereto, whereby any right of the Assured, in the event of loss or damage, to recover the full value of, or amount of damage to, any property insured hereunder, against any carrier, bailee or other party liable therefor, is released, impaired or lost, shall render this policy null and void, but the Insurer's right to retain or recover the premium shall not be affected. It shall, however, be permissible for the Assured, without prejudice to this insurance, to release any carrier to the extent of not less than Fifty Dollars ($50.) per package where the weight of the package does not exceed 100 pounds, or fifty cents per pound, actual weight, where the weight of the shipment exceeds 100 pounds. This Company is not liable for any loss or damage, which without its consent, has been settled or compromised by the Assured.

4. Reread the two insurance policies, reprinted above. To what extent do they confer subrogation rights to "collateral" sources, i.e., contract rights that the seller or buyer may have against each other?

Remember, if a loss occurs within the scope of the policy and all conditions precedent are satisfied, the insurer's liability is for the amount of the actual loss and no more. This principle of indemnification is designed, primarily, to control the insurer's incentive to realize a net gain from the receipt of insurance proceeds. See Keeton, Insurance Law § 3.1(b) (1971). Subrogation often supports the principle of indemnity, since the insurance company, upon paying the insured, steps into the insured's shoes and tries to assert claims of that insured against some other person (the carrier, the other party to the contract, some third party, etc.) for the loss for which it has paid. In theory, at least, subrogation rights and the return from enforcement ought to figure into the calculation by the insurer of the premiums to be charged.

According to conventional doctrine, there are two kinds of subrogation, legal or equitable and contractual. The former arises by operation of law and the latter is created by contract between the insurer and the insured. See Jorski Mill & Elevator Co. v. Farmers Elevator Mut. Ins. Co., 404 F.2d 143, 147 (10th Cir.1968). The source of subrogation determines the scope of the right. Thus, if B with the risk of loss is insured and the goods are damaged by the negligence of a third party, the insurer, upon paying B, is subrogated by operation of law to any tort claims that B may have against the third party. See, e.g., Home Ins. Co. v. Bishop, 140 Me. 72, 34 A.2d 22 (1943). But what about contract rights that either seller or buyer may have against the other? Here's the rub, for some courts have labeled contract rights as "collateral" sources for subrogation and have required a contract clause specifically granting the right. Put another way, subrogation imposed by operation of law is sometimes held not to reach these collateral rights.

> The difficulty * * * lies in the fact that the problem is basically one of allocation of the burden of loss as between an insurer and an innocent third party. And in the case of "equitable" or "legal" subrogation the equities in favor of the insurer are simply not so decisive as they are when the third party is a tort-feasor.

United States Fidelity & Guar. Co. v. Slifkin, 200 F.Supp. 563, 569 (N.D.Ala. 1961).

5. Suppose that Cicero, with the risk of loss, is insured but Repuenzel, with a security interest and an insurable interest, is not insured. If the goods are destroyed without Cicero's fault or negligence and the insurer pays, does Repuenzel have any enforceable claim to the insurance proceeds? Or is the seller now unsecured with a claim only for the unpaid price?

The answers are no and yes, unless (1) The contract for sale required Cicero to obtain insurance for the benefit of Repuenzel and Cicero had complied, or (2) Repuenzel's claim is enforceable under UCC 9–306(1).

In the absence of a contractual obligation to insure, see Royal Zenith Corp. v. Citizens Publications, Inc., 179 N.W.2d 340 (Iowa 1970), casualty insurance is invariably treated as personal to the insured—it is intended to indemnify Cicero's loss (a matter of contract between Cicero and his insurer) not Repuenzel's. See Quigley v. Caron, 247 A.2d 94 (Me.1968). As a matter of planning, therefore, Repuenzel should insist that either Cicero obtain insurance for its benefit or Repuenzel should obtain a policy covering goods sold on a conditional sales contract to the extent of unpaid balances.

What about UCC 9–306(1)? The 1972 Official Text of UCC 9–306(1) provides that "Insurance payable by reason of loss or damage to the collateral is proceeds, except to the extent that it is payable to a person other than a party to the security agreement." This provision overruled decisions under the 1962 Official Text to the contrary, see *Note,* 65 Mich.L.Rev. 1514 (1966), but has some definite limitations: If the proceeds are payable to someone other than Repuenzel or, as cash proceeds, fall into the many pitfalls of maintaining a perfected security in proceeds under UCC 9–306, the security will dissipate.

(6) Suppose Repuenzel, with an insurable interest, is insured to the full value of the goods and Cicero, with the risk of loss, has no insurance. If the goods are destroyed and Repuenzel is paid in full, can Cicero have the benefit of that insurance? Put differently, can Cicero have a credit for the insurance against any price still owed to Repuenzel? If the answer is yes, then Repuenzel's insurer would be denied any right to subrogation to collateral sources granted by contract.

Most courts, after balancing the equities, have answered the question in the negative. See, e.g., Lancaster v. The Bailey Co., 41 B.R. 164 (Bkrtcy.D.C.Tenn. 1984). For a contrary and definitely minority view, see In re Future Mfg. Corp., 165 F.Supp. 111 (N.D.Cal.1958). There have been no recent decisions of significance.

B. Carrier Liable to Insured Party With Risk of Loss: Conflicts Between Insurance Companies

Suppose that Cicero, insured and with the risk of loss, obtains a judgment against the carrier under the Carmack Act, supra, for the value of the goods destroyed. Cicero's insurer, who has paid Cicero, has participated in the litigation as subrogee. What additional problems are posed because the contest is, in essence, between two insurance companies, that of Cicero and that of the carrier?

SORKIN, ALLOCATION OF THE RISK OF LOSS IN THE TRANSPORTATION OF FREIGHT—THE FUNCTION OF INSURANCE, 40 Fordham L.Rev. 67, 85–87 (1971).

* * *

IV. The Role of Insurance in Allocation of the Risk of Loss

Although common carriers subject to the Carmack Amendment of the Interstate Commerce Act are held to a high standard of liability, there are some exceptions and limitations to a carrier's liability. Furthermore, the amount of damages sustained is always a potential issue. If the loss or damage is substantial, the carrier will contest the claim, provided it can find a legal basis upon which to do so. Consequently, most commercial shippers are insured against loss or damage to their property during the course of its transportation.

"The shipper's insurance company may be considered as a potential third-party upon whom the ultimate economic burden of the risk of loss or damage should be placed, since the insurance company receives its compensation specifically for assuming the risk of loss or damage, whereas the carrier's compensation is based primarily on the cost of transportation. However, equity and economic burden have usually not been determining factors in allocating the risk of loss between the shipper's insurer and the carrier. The judicial resolution of the problem has historically been based upon the law of contracts and the interpretation of the Interstate Commerce Act.

A. Benefit of Insurance Clauses in Bills of Lading

For over a century the standard form of carrier bill of lading has provided, in effect, that if a shipper of merchandise has purchased insurance against loss or damage to the shipper's goods during the course of their transportation, and if the shipper's goods are lost or damaged, the carrier shall receive the benefit of such insurance. The intended result of such a clause is that the carrier will not be liable for the loss or damage to the extent that the shipper or owner is compensated by his insurance carrier. Judicial recognition of the validity of such benefit of insurance clauses has been established.

An insurer who pays the loss of a shipper is ordinarily subrogated to the shipper's rights. However, if the insured has contracted with the carrier giving the carrier the benefit of any insurance available to the shipper in case of loss or damage, then it has long been held that the insurer loses its right of subrogation. The shipper who insures his goods against loss or damage during their transportation is involved in at least two separate contracts—the contract between the shipper and the common carrier (the bill of lading), and the contract between the shipper and the insurance company (the policy). To counterbalance the benefit of insurance clause in the bill of lading, the insurance companies changed their policies and added a provision which stated that if an insured shipper entered into an agreement giving a carrier the benefit of the shipper's insurance, then the insurance policy issued to the shipper would be void.

The courts, when faced with both the bill of lading provision giving the carrier the benefit of the shipper's insurance and the insurance policy declaring the policy void upon the shipper's acceptance of such a bill of lading provision, concluded that both agreements were effective, i.e., the shipper could agree with the carrier to give the carrier the benefit of the shipper's insurance, but since the insurance was void the carrier received nothing and the shipper could not receive the insurance proceeds. This, of course, was harmful to the shipper and of no benefit to the carrier. The legal draftsmen of the insurance companies were victorious in their word war with the carriers' scriveners.

The bill of lading was then amended to provide that the carrier was to have the benefit of the insurance effected by the shipper 'so far as this shall not avoid the policies or contracts of insurance.' Thus, if the insurance policy stated that the policy would be void if the carrier could get the benefit of insurance, the bill of lading provision stated that in such event the carrier would not get the benefit of the shipper's insurance. The draftsmen for both sides had created a state of equilibrium, except in those cases where an insurance company neglected to provide that the policy would be void if the carrier received the benefit of the shipper's insurance. Thus the determination whether the ultimate burden of loss should be borne by the carrier or the shipper's insurer was made on the basis of interpretation of conflicting contracts without consideration of the economic justification of placing the burden either on the carrier or the insurer and without consideration of its effect upon interstate commerce." [Footnotes omitted]

TOWMOTOR CO. v. FRANK CROSS TRUCKING CO.

Superior Court of Pennsylvania, 1965.
205 Pa.Super. 448, 211 A.2d 38.

[Shipper sued common carrier Towmotor for damages to a vehicle which had been injured while in the possession of the carrier. Defendant responded that plaintiff had been fully insured, had recovered its loss from its insurance company, and under the terms of the bill of lading it was entitled "to the benefit of plaintiff's insurance." The court went on as follows, quoting first from the clause in the bill of lading.]

JACOBS, J.

* * *

"Any carrier or party liable on account of loss or damage to any of said property shall have the full benefit of any insurance that may have been effected upon or on account of said property so far as this shall not avoid the policies or contracts of insurance: Provided that the carrier reimburse the claimant for the premium paid thereon."

The plaintiff in its reply admits that the above quoted clause was included in the bill of lading. It further admits that the vehicle was insured by Aetna and that Aetna paid it the sum of $3,190.33 but avers that payment was made in the form of a loan rather than in payment of the loss, and asserts in its defense the following quoted condition of the Aetna policy:

"1. Carrier-Bailee. This insurance shall in no wise inure directly or indirectly to the benefit of any carrier or other bailee, and the Assured agrees that in case any agreement be made or accepted with any carrier or bailee by which it is stipulated that such or any carrier or bailee shall have, in case of any loss for which said carrier or bailee may be liable, the benefit of this insurance or exemption in any manner from responsibility grounded in the fact of this insurance, then and in that event this Company shall be discharged of any liability for such loss hereunder, but this policy in these and all cases of loss or damage by perils insured against shall be liable and owe actual payment for (only) what cannot be collected from carrier or bailee."

Aetna's policy as well as the release given to Aetna by plaintiff, provide that Aetna shall be subrogated to the rights of the plaintiff to recover for such loss from the persons, firms or corporations who have caused the loss.

If it were not for the benefit of insurance clause in the bill of lading this case would be easily decided. In general a common carrier of goods is regarded as an insurer against all losses. Arabian American Oil Company v. Kirby & Kirby, Inc., 171 Pa.Super. 23, 90 A.2d 410. No exception to the general rule has been averred by the defendant and unless the benefit of insurance clause is sufficient to save it, it is liable for the loss. The benefit of insurance clause in the bill of lading and the clauses referring to such benefit in the insurance policy are the result of the efforts of the insurance companies to shift the common law liability of the carriers on one hand and, on the other hand, to protect against such shifting of liability. We will endeavor to interpret the result of such legal maneuvering.

A benefit of insurance clause such as the one contained in the bill of lading in this case is valid because the carrier itself might have insured against the loss, even though occasioned by its own negligence. Luckenbach v. W.J. McCahan Sugar Refining Co., 248 U.S. 139, 39 S.Ct. 53, 63 L.Ed. 170. The important words in the benefit of insurance clause above quoted are "so far as this shall not avoid the policies or contracts of insurance." Absent those words, should the insurer pay the loss it would lose the benefit of the claim against the carrier to which it would otherwise be subrogated and the carrier would go free. However, when we read the above quoted words in connection with the provisions of the insurance policy we come to another conclusion.

* * *

The benefit of insurance clause not being available to the defendant, it is liable for the loss. Although the plaintiff is the shipper and has been paid for the loss, judgment may properly be entered in its favor. Both the insurance policy and the release given by plaintiff specifically provide that the insurer shall be subrogated to the rights of plaintiff and may sue in plaintiff's name. Any recovery will inure to the benefit of the insurance company.

Judgment affirmed.

FLOOD, J., absent.

Notes

1. In Salon Serv., Inc. v. Pacific & Atlantic Shippers, 24 N.Y.2d 15, 298 N.Y.S.2d 700, 246 N.E.2d 509 (1969), a conflict identical to that in *Towmotor* was manifest in the shipper's bill of lading from the carrier and the insurance policy from its insurer. In affirming the decision of the appellate division, the Court of Appeals, speaking through Judge Burke, held that the "benefit of insurance" clause in the bill of lading was invalid under Section 2 of the Interstate Commerce Act. Enforcing the clause would result in a prohibited rate discrimination because the carrier would, indirectly, receive greater compensation from a shipper who had effected insurance than from one who had not. The court quoted from National Garment Co. v. New York, C. & St.L.R. Co., 173 F.2d 32, 38 (8th Cir.1949):

> "Insurance for the benefit of a carrier is of value to the carrier from the beginning of the transportation and, in the event of transportation without loss, which we assume is the usual case, the carrier has received the compensation forbidden by the Interstate Commerce Act at the expense of the shipper. In the event of loss the carrier, if it so elects, returns to the shipper the cost of the compensation which it was forbidden by the Act to receive in the first place, avoids its liability as a carrier, and deprives the insurer of its rights under a valid contract." 246 N.E.2d at 511.

CHAPTER SEVENTEEN

"DOCUMENTARY" AND OTHER SALES INVOLVING DOCUMENTS OF TITLE: POSSIBLE BREAKDOWNS

SECTION 1. INTRODUCTION—DOCUMENTS OF TITLE

When buyers and sellers deal with each other, the goods will often be either (1) as yet unmanufactured, (2) located at the seller's place of business, (3) located at the place of business of the seller's supplier, (4) located in an independent warehouse, or (5) located somewhere else away from the buyer's place of business. Most sellers do not have their own trucking, rail, or waterway facilities. They must, therefore, turn to independent carriers to deliver the goods they sell. When goods are sold while in warehouses, (as is often true in deals made on the commodity exchanges) sellers must also rely on the services of independent warehousemen to make delivery (physically or through "attornment"). These independent third parties—carriers and warehousemen—typically issue "bills of lading" and "warehouse receipts," respectively, covering goods received from shippers and storers. In so doing, these bailees assume certain special obligations both under the terms of such documents and under applicable statutes, as we will see.

In the parlance of commercial lawyers, bills of lading and warehouse receipts (see the forms at pp. 753–754) are called "documents of title." UCC 1–201(15) defines document of title as follows:

> (15) "Document of title" includes bill of lading, dock warrant, dock receipt, warehouse receipt or order for the delivery of goods, and also any other document which in the regular course of business or financing is treated as adequately evidencing that the person in possession of it is entitled to receive, hold and dispose of the document and the goods it covers. To be a document of title a document must purport to be issued by or addressed to a bailee and purport to cover goods in the bailee's possession which are either identified or are fungible portions of an identified mass.

As we will see (Section 4 below), documents of title may be "negotiable" or "non-negotiable." It is now pertinent to list the main functions of these pieces of paper issued by carriers and warehousemen. A bill of lading or warehouse receipt serves:

1. As a receipt for the goods received by the bailee from the shipper or storer.

2. As a contract between the bailor and bailee for the transportation and/or storage of the goods.

3. As a kind of legal substitute for the goods themselves when the document is negotiable—the law says that *generally:* "title to the goods moves with title to the negotiable document."

4. As a means whereby the seller may either (a) himself retain a security interest in the goods until they are paid for or (b) readily create a security interest in the goods in favor of his own bank or other lender.

All of these functions of bills of lading and warehouse receipts are quite important. The importance of the function depends on the nature of the transaction involved—on how documents of title are utilized in the transaction. In the next section, one basic transaction pattern will be described.

The "front side" of a typical negotiable bill of lading looks like this:

FORM 35

7

THIS SHIPPING ORDER must be legibly filled in, in ink, in indelible pencil, or in carbon, and retained by the Agent

RECEIVE subject to the classifications and tariffs in effect on the date of the issue of this Shipping Order, the property described below in apparent good order, except as noted contents and condition of contents of packages unknown, marked, consigned and destined as indicated below, which said company (the word company being understood throughout this contract as meaning any person or corporation in possession of the property under the contract agrees to carry to its usual place of delivery of said destination, if on its own road or its own water line, otherwise to deliver to another carrier on the route to said destination. It is mutually agreed, as to each carrier of all or any of said property over all or any portion of said route to destination, and as to each party at any time interested in all or any of the said property, that every service to be performed hereunder shall be subject to all the conditions not prohibited by law, whether printed or written, herein contained, including the conditions on the back hereof, which are hereby agreed to by the shipper and accepted for himself and his assigns. **The surrender of the original ORDER Bill of Lading property indorsed shall be required before the delivery of property. Inspection of property covered by this bill of lading will not be permitted unless provided by law or unless permission is indorsed on this original bill of lading or given in writing by the shipper.**

131—CHICAGO AND NORTH WESTERN RAILWAY CO.—131

BILL OF LADING DATE	BILL OF LADING NO.	INVOICE NO.	CUSTOMER'S NO.

CAR INITIALS AND NUMBER	KIND	WEIGHT IN TONS			LENGTH OF CAR		MARKED CAPACITY OF CAR		LOAD LIMIT OF CAR
		GROSS	TARE	NET	ORDERED	FURNISHED	ORDERED	FURNISHED	

T TRLR. **O** INIT. **F** & NO. **C**	LENGTH	PLAN NO. / TRANSF. TO CAR	DATE	WAYBILL NO.

TO NO.	STATION	STATE OR PROV.	STATE CODE	AT NO. ( ) B/A ( )	STATION	STATE OR PROV.	STATE CODE
( )							

ROUTE (Show each Junction and Carrier in route order to destination of waybill)
131 C & NW

ROUTE CODE NO.

FULL NAME OF SHIPPER

CODE NO.

SHOW "A" IF AGENT'S ROUTING OR "S" IF SHIPPER'S ROUTING

CONSIGNED TO
ORDER OF

ORIGIN AND DATE, ORIGINAL CAR, TRANSFER FREIGHT BILL AND PREVIOUS WAYBILL REFERENCE AND ROUTING WHEN REBILLED.

NOTIFY

AT STATE OF COUNTY OF

DESTINATION

SHIPPER'S SPECIAL INSTRUCTIONS

Received $__________ to apply in prepayment of the charges on the property described hereon.

__________ Agent or Cashier.

Per__________ (The signature here acknowledges only the amount prepaid.)

WEIGHED

AT__________

GROSS__________

TARE__________

ALLOWANCE__________

NET__________

IF CHARGES ARE TO BE PREPAID, WRITE OR STAMP HERE "TO BE PREPAID".

WHEN SHIPPER IN THE UNITED STATES EXECUTES THE NO-RECOURSE CLAUSE OF SECTION 7 OF THE BILL OF LADING, INSERT "YES".

*If the shipment moves between two ports by a carrier by water, the law requires that the bill of lading shall state whether it is "carrier's or shipper's weight".

Indicate by symbol in Column provided ★ how weights were obtained for L.C.L. Shipments only. R – Railroad Scale. S – Shipper's Tested Weights. E – Estimated – Weigh and Correct. T – Tariff Classification or Minimum.

NO. PKGS.	DESCRIPTION OF ARTICLES, SPECIAL MARKS AND EXCEPTIONS	COMMODITY CODE NO.	★	*WEIGHT (Subject to Correction)	RATE	FREIGHT	CHARGES ADVANCED	PREPAID

DO NOT USE THIS SPACE

Subject to Section 7 of Conditions, if the shipment is to be delivered to the consignee without recourse on the consignor, the consignor shall sign the following statement. The carrier shall not make delivery of this shipment without payment of freight and all other lawful charges.

Signature of Consignor

Note—Where the rate is dependent upon value, shippers are required to state specifically in writing the agreed or declared value of the property. The agreed or declared value of the property is hereby specifically stated by the shipper to be not exceeding

PER

DATE__________

AGENT__________

SHIPPER__________ PER__________ PER__________

The reverse side of both the negotiable and nonnegotiable bill of lading form contains about two acres of fine print called "contract terms and conditions."

SECTION 2. "DOCUMENTARY SALES"—THE STANDARD PATTERN

Documents of title may be used in a variety of ways in a sales transaction. In *one* type of transaction called the "documentary sale," the buyer agrees to pay cash in exchange for documents. Besides documents of title (usually bills of lading) this transaction also involves the use of what is called a "sight draft." A sight draft is a draft (see UCC 3–104(e)) drawn up by a seller which orders the buyer to pay so much in cash "at sight" to the party presenting the draft. Below is an illustrative sight draft:

$ 1,000.00 August 7 (1978)

At Sight Pay to

the order of Repeunzel Auto Parts

One thousand and no/100-------------- Dollars

Value received and charge the same to account of

TO Cicero's Automotive, Inc.

) Repeunzel /for

No. 28601) Repeunzel Auto Parts, Inc.

[C3044]

Now, how might the above piece of paper, and a document of title such as a bill of lading actually be put to functional use together in real life transactions? Professor Farnsworth has offered this account of the standard transaction pattern in the so-called "documentary sale". References to the 1990 official text have been inserted between brackets in the original text of his discussion.

FARNSWORTH, DOCUMENTARY DRAFTS UNDER THE UNIFORM COMMERCIAL CODE, 22 Bus.Law. 479–487 (1967).

"*Introduction.* The Uniform Commercial Code has as a premise 'that "commercial transactions" is a single subject of the law, notwithstanding its many facets.' * * *

"No better transaction could be chosen to illustrate this recognition than the use of the documentary draft, since it involves the sale of goods, which is dealt with in Article 2 (Sales), a draft, which is dealt with in Article 3 (Commercial Paper), its collection, which is dealt with in Article 4 (Bank Deposits and Collection), and a bill of lading, which is dealt with in Article 7 (Warehouse Receipts, Bills of Lading and Other Documents of Title), in addition to being subject to Article 1 (General Provisions). If a letter of credit were involved, it would also be subject to Article 5 (Letters of Credit) and if the buyer were to finance his purchase by a trust receipt it would also be subject to Article 9 (Secured Transactions: Sales of Accounts, Contract

Rights and Chattel Paper). This discussion will not, however, be concerned with either letters of credit or secured transactions.

"Because the documentary draft has long been a feature of both domestic and international sales transactions, the terminology and the rules relating to documentary drafts are relatively well established. * * * This article will be in two parts: first, a description of a typical sales transaction involving a documentary draft with an analysis of the relevant provisions of the code; and second, a discussion of some variations from this standard pattern in the light of the provisions of the Code. Before either, however, a brief discussion of terminology is appropriate.

"*Terminology.* The term 'draft,' used by the Code to replace the older term 'bill of exchange,' in this discussion refers to the order drawn by the seller on the buyer of the goods (UCC 3–104(1)(b), (2)(a)) [UCC 3–104(a), (e)]. The term 'documentary draft' is used for a draft, whether negotiable or non-negotiable, with accompanying documents or other papers to be delivered when the draft is honored (UCC 4–104(1)(f)) [UCC 4–104(a)(6)]. By 'document' is meant a 'document of title' (UCC 7–102(1)(e)), including a 'bill of lading, dock warrant, dock receipt, warehouse receipt or order for the delivery of goods, and also any other document which in the regular course of business or financing is treated as adequately evidencing that the person in possession of it is entitled to receive, hold and dispose of the document and the goods it covers' (UCC 1–201(15)). The most significant of these for present purposes is the 'bill of lading,' which is defined as 'a document evidencing the receipt of goods for shipment issued by a person engaged in the business of transporting or forwarding goods, and includes an airbill' (UCC 1–201(6)). It may be a negotiable bill if by its terms the goods are to be delivered to bearer or to order or, where recognized in overseas trade, if it runs to a named person or assigns; otherwise it is a non-negotiable bill, the term used by the Code in preference to the traditional synonym 'straight' bill (UCC 7–104). These, then are the essential terms; now to the transaction.

Part I. The Basic Transaction

"*Purpose of the Transaction.* Many domestic and some foreign sales of goods are made on open credit, with payment to be made in 30, 60 or 90 days. But credit must be bargained for and a seller lacking faith in the buyer's credit may refuse to agree to a credit term. In the absence of such an agreement, the Code provides that the buyer must pay when he receives the goods (UCC 2–310(a)). In the simplest case, where the seller and the buyer carry out the exchange face to face, five consequences follow. First, the seller is assured of payment when he gives up control of the goods. Second, the buyer is assured of control of the goods when he pays. Third, the seller finances the transaction only until the goods leave his hands. Fourth, the buyer finances the transaction only after the goods reach his hands. And fifth, the buyer can inspect the goods before he pays (UCC 2–513(1)).

"When the parties are at a distance the situation changes and some means must be found to give each party a measure of the advantages which he enjoys in the simple face-to-face exchange. The traditional method is the documentary exchange, calling for payment by the buyer against a draft with a bill of lading attached. The immediate purpose of this discussion is to inquire into how the Uniform Commercial Code affects such a transaction.

"*The Agreement.* If the buyer's obligation, in the absence of a contrary agreement, is to pay against the delivery of goods, what contract terms suffice to vary this obligation and to oblige him to pay against documents? Since the Code provides no general words of art for this purpose, such conventional formulae as 'sight draft against bill of lading' will continue to suffice. Furthermore, where the goods are sold 'C.I.F.' (cost, insurance and freight), 'C. & F.' (cost and freight), 'F.O.B. vessel' (free on board vessel) or 'F.A.S.' (free along side), 'unless otherwise agreed the buyer must make payment against tender of the required documents and the seller may not tender nor the buyer demand delivery of the goods in substitution for the documents' (UCC 2–319(4), 2–320(4)). The reason is that these terms contemplate shipment to a distant port where the documents will arrive well ahead of the goods, and so a documentary exchange is presumed unless negated by the agreement. The rule does not apply to ordinary 'F.O.B.' (free on board) contracts which do not have these characteristics.

"*Shipment of the Goods.* When the parties have agreed to a documentary exchange, the seller will ordinarily place the goods in the hands of a carrier, obtaining a negotiable bill of lading to his own order. According to the Code, the effect of this 'shipment under reservation' is to reserve in him 'a security interest in the goods' (UCC 2–505(1)(a)). Beyond this, the bill of lading must satisfy the requirements of the sales article, Article 2, of the Code (UCC 7–509). For one example, where the contract contemplates overseas shipment and unless otherwise agreed, under an 'F.O.B. vessel' term, the seller must procure an 'on board' bill of lading, one stating that the goods have actually been loaded, whereas under a 'C.I.F.' or 'C. & F.' term a 'received for shipment' bill of lading, which falls short of stating that the goods have been loaded, is enough (UCC 2–323). For another example, unless otherwise agreed, under an 'F.O.B. point of shipment' contract, the seller must make such a contract for the transportation of the goods as is reasonable in the light of their nature and the other circumstances (UCC 2–504(a)). Although duplicate bills of lading, clearly marked as such, are regularly issued in this country, bills are not issued in sets of multiple originals for domestic trade. The Code expressly prohibits their issuance in sets except where customary in overseas transactions (UCC 7–304(1); see also UCC 7–402).

"The seller, having obtained the negotiable bill of lading to his own order, then attaches it, together with an invoice and any other documents required by the contract, to a sight, or demand, draft for the amount due him drawn by him as drawer upon the buyer as drawee to the seller's own order. The Code allows drafts to be drawn in sets, although their use is in practice confined to foreign trade, where an original may be drawn to go with each of the multiple originals of a bill of lading which has been issued in a set (UCC 3–801) [omitted in Revised Article 3]. The seller then indorses the draft and bill of lading and takes them to his bank. For the moment, it will be assumed that the bank takes the documentary draft for collection; the situation when it discounts will be discussed presently.

"*Collection of the Draft.* The bank, known as a 'collecting bank' (UCC 4–105(d)) [UCC 4–105(5)] and more specifically as the 'depositary bank' (UCC 4–105(a)), [UCC 4–105(2)] is required to 'present or send the draft and accompanying documents for presentment' (UCC 4–501), which it will normally do by forwarding them through 'customary banking channels' (UCC 2–308(c), 2–503(5)(b)). Most important, it will treat the draft as a 'collection' item rather than a 'cash' item. Checks, the most common items handled by banks, are dealt with in bulk as 'cash' items on the assumption that they will be honored in the overwhelming majority of cases; provisional credits are entered immediately for a check at all stages of the collection process and automatically become final without further action upon payment by the drawee bank (UCC 4–213(2)) [UCC 4–215(c)]. Documentary drafts, on the other hand, are handled as 'collection' items and dealt with individually, rather than in bulk, and since no assumption is made that they will be honored, no credits, not even provisional credits, are given until the item has been paid by the buyer. Ultimately the draft will reach the 'presenting' bank (UCC 4–105(e)) [UCC 4–105(6)], which will undertake to present the documentary draft to the buyer.

"The presenting bank will know the identity and location of the buyer, who will be indicated on the bill of lading as the person to be notified of the arrival of the goods (cf. UCC 7–501(6)) as well as on the draft as the drawee. Unless otherwise instructed, the bank may make presentment to the buyer by sending him a written notice that it holds the item (UCC 4–210(1) [UCC 4–212(a)]; see also UCC 2–503(1), (5) and Comment 3 to UCC 2–308). In the event that the buyer does not honor the draft before the close of business on the third banking day after the notice was sent, the bank may treat it as dishonored (UCC 4–210(2)) [UCC 4–212(b)]. The buyer may, however, within this time require exhibition of the draft and documents by the bank so that he can determine whether it is properly payable (UCC 4–210 [UCC 4–212], 3–505(1)(a), 3–506(2)) [UCC 3–501(b)(2)(i). UCC 3–506 was omitted in Revised Article 3]. If direct presentment is made to the buyer, instead of presentment by notice, it must be made at the place specified in the draft, or if there be none at his place of business or residence (UCC 3–504(2)(c)) [3–501(b), 3–111], and he then has until the close of business on that day to pay (UCC 3–506(2)) [omitted]. Absent contrary instructions, a collecting bank may have an additional day 'in a good faith effort to secure payment'; it may also be excused for delay caused by circumstances beyond its control (UCC 4–108) [UCC 4–109].

"As already pointed out, under the face-to-face transaction, which the documentary exchange is designed to supplant, the buyer had the right to inspect the goods before paying for them (UCC 2–513(1)). Since the goods will normally travel much more slowly than the documents, they will not ordinarily be available for inspection at the time that the buyer is required to pay under the rules just discussed. Therefore, absent agreement to the contrary, the buyer has no right to inspect the goods before he pays when the contract provides for payment against documents of title, except in the case, to be discussed later, where payment is due only after the goods are to become available for inspection (UCC 2–513(3)(b); see also UCC 2–310(b)). Indeed, the negotiable railway bill of lading typically bears the legend: 'Inspection of property covered by this bill of lading will not be permitted unless provided by law or unless permission is indorsed on this original bill of lading or given in writing by the shipper.' The Code goes on to provide that where, as in the transaction under discussion, the contract calls for payment before inspection, even the nonconformity of the goods does not, with rare exceptions, excuse the buyer from paying (UCC 2–512(1)). But it makes it clear that such payment does not amount to an acceptance of the goods by the buyer and that the buyer retains his right to inspect the goods upon delivery and all of his remedies against the seller for breach of contract (UCC 2–512(2)). He merely loses the opportunity of inspection before payment, an opportunity that gave him advantage of refusing to pay, rather than the disadvantage of having to sue to recover his payment, in the event of a non-conformity.

"Since the draft under discussion is a sight draft, the buyer is called upon to pay, rather than to accept it, before he gets the documents. Only when the draft is payable more than three days after presentment may the presenting bank release the documents against the buyer's acceptance rather than his payment (UCC 2–514, 4–503(a)) [UCC 4–503(1)]. Payment may be easily effected if the buyer offers cash or if the presenting bank happens to be one in which the buyer has an account. Short of this, the Code permits the presenting bank to take a cashier's check (a check drawn by a bank on itself), a certified check (a check accepted by the bank on which it has been drawn), or other bank check or obligation [UCC 4–211(1)(d)] [UCC 4–211, now 4–213, has been completely revised]. Should the buyer tender his personal check on another bank, the presenting bank may hold the documents while it gets the check certified. Should it release the documents against his personal check, it will be liable to the seller for any loss caused by the dishonor of the check. The proceeds received from the buyer are then remitted by the presenting bank through banking channels.

"When the buyer honors the draft, he receives the bill of lading. When the goods arrive, he is notified by the carrier and surrenders the bill of lading in return for the goods. At this point the buyer will be able to inspect the goods. Should he find them to be defective, his only recourse will ordinarily be to journey to the seller's jurisdiction and there litigate the issues of breach and damages. Other possible remedies will be discussed presently.

"If the buyer does not pay the draft as outlined earlier, the presenting bank must treat it as dishonored. In this event the presenting bank 'must use diligence and good faith to ascertain the reason for dishonor, must notify its transferor of the dishonor and of the results of its effort to ascertain the reasons therefor and must request instructions' (UCC 4–503(b)) [UCC 4–503(1)]. It need not, however, return the draft and documents unless so instructed (UCC 4–202(1)(b)) [UCC 4–202(a)(2)]. When the notice gets back to the depositary bank, which first took the draft for collection, it must 'seasonably notify its customer' of the dishonor (UCC 4–501). [The presenting bank] 'is under no obligation with respect to goods represented by the documents except to follow any reasonable instructions seasonably received; it has a right to reimbursement for any expense incurred in following instructions and to payment of or indemnity for such expenses' (UCC 4–503). If it has seasonably requested instructions after dishonor but has not received them in a reasonable time, it may 'store, sell or otherwise deal with the goods in any reasonable manner' (UCC 4–504(1)) [UCC 4–504(a)], and has a lien * * * on the goods or their proceeds for reasonable expenses incurred in doing so (UCC 4–504(2)) [UCC 4–504(b)]. If, for example, it was commercially reasonable to put the goods in storage pending receipt of requested instructions, the presenting bank would be protected if it did so even though the requested instructions were later received (Comment to UCC 4–504). The Code seems, however, to make a request for instructions and a failure to receive them within a reasonable time prerequisites to the exercise of initiative by the presenting bank in dealing with the goods.

"In addition to the requirement that notice be given of the dishonor, there may be in some cases the additional requirement of protest. Protest, a formal statement of dishonor executed by a public functionary, such as a notary, is generally required in Continental countries in the case of any dishonor of a negotiable instrument. * * * (See UCC 3–501(3), 3–509 and 4–202(1)(d).) [UCC 3–505 and 4–202(a)]

"This, then, is the standard pattern followed in the documentary exchange where payment is to be made against a sight draft with bill of lading attached. How adequate a substitute for the face-to-face transaction has been achieved can be seen by a comparison with the five consequences noted earlier. First, the seller is still assured of payment when he gives up control of the goods, through surrender of the bill of lading. Second, the buyer is assured of control of the goods when he pays, through possession of the bill of lading. Third, the seller must now finance the transaction *after* the goods leave his hands and until the documentary draft has been paid and the proceeds remitted. Fourth, the buyer must now finance the transaction *before* the goods reach his hands, from the time that he pays the documentary draft until they have arrived. And fifth, the buyer can *not* inspect the goods before he pays. Thus while the first two consequences are unchanged, the third, fourth and fifth are different.

PART II. SOME VARIATIONS

"*Discount of the Draft.* As to the third consequence, the seller must now finance the transaction for an additional period of time between his delivery of the goods to the carrier and the remission to him of the proceeds after the buyer has paid the draft. The seller may shift this burden of financing to his bank by having that bank discount the draft rather than merely take it for collection. The seller can then receive the face value of the draft, less a discount to cover interest charges, before collection, as soon as he has obtained the bill of lading, and the bank will finance the sale from that point until it receives payment. The bank that does this has a 'security interest' in the draft and in the accompanying documents, and this holds true even if the credit which it gives the seller is not withdrawn, as long as he has the right to withdraw it (UCC 4–208) [UCC 4–210]. The bank, however, has the same obligations to the seller with respect to presentment and notification on dishonor as if it were an ordinary collecting bank (UCC 4–501). In case of dishonor of course, the bank can hold the seller ultimately liable on the draft even though it has been discounted. By purchasing the draft it acquires not only its own rights under the draft and bill of lading, but also 'any rights of the seller in the goods including the right to stop delivery and the shipper's right to have the draft honored by the buyer'

(UCC 2–506(1), 2–707). The right to stop delivery is a right to order the carrier not to deliver to the buyer goods in the possession of the carrier when the buyer has been discovered to be insolvent (UCC 2–705). If the goods are carload, truckload, planeload or larger shipments, delivery may be stopped in the event of buyer's breach regardless of his solvency. Since the bill of lading is a negotiable document of title, however, the carrier is not obliged to obey a notification to stop until surrender of the document (UCC 2–705(3)(c)).

"Where the depositary bank discounts the draft for the seller, it succeeds to his rights under the sales contract as would an assignee. This suggests the possibility that the discounting bank might also assume the obligations of the seller under the sales contract, and more particularly that it might be liable under the seller's warranties of quality in the event that the goods are defective. The Code makes it clear that this is not the case and that a collecting bank 'known to be entrusted with documents on behalf of another or with collection of a draft or other claim against delivery of documents warrants by such delivery of documents only its own good faith and authority,' and this is true 'even though the intermediary has purchased or made advances against the claim or draft to be collected' (UCC 7–508; compare UCC 7–507).

"This sets the stage for an analysis of the position of the buyer in the rare but not impossible event that he has discovered a breach by the seller after he has paid the draft but before the collecting bank has remitted the proceeds. In the event of the seller's breach, it may be possible for the buyer to get personal jurisdiction over the seller in the buyer's own state. The chances of this have increased with the enactment of 'long arm' statutes. But where personal jurisdiction over the seller cannot be had in the buyer's state, he will ordinarily have to journey to the seller's state and there litigate the issues of breach and damages. He would, of course, prefer to bring his action at home—and may be able to do so if he can attach the proceeds as the basis of jurisdiction in his action. Usually the proceeds will have been remitted well before the arrival of the goods. But in the unusual case where this is not so, the buyer may attach the proceeds as the basis of quasi in rem jurisdiction in an action against the seller, and if successful in the action, have judgment in an amount up to the amount of the proceeds. This, however, assumes that the proceeds are indeed the *seller's* proceeds. Should the draft have been discounted by the depositary bank, then it and not the seller would be entitled to the proceeds, and attachment of the proceeds would not give jurisdiction in an action against the seller. Since the depositary bank, even though it discounts the draft, makes no warranties, there is no possibility of using the proceeds as the jurisdictional basis of an action against the bank. In sum, the buyer's advantage through attachment of the proceeds is not only limited to the rare case where the breach is discovered before the proceeds are remitted, but even then is available only when the draft has not been discounted." [Footnotes omitted.]

Notes

1. What factors motivate some sellers to use the device called the "documentary sale?"

2. What are the functions of the bill of lading and the sight draft in this transaction?

3. The so-called "documentary sale" for cash is not the only type of transaction in which documents of title and/or drafts figure. See White and Summers, Chapter 19.

4. For an interesting argument that the technology of electronic data interchange should be utilized in transactions involving bills of lading, see Williams, *Something Old, Something New: The Bill of Lading in the Days of EDI,* 1 Transnat'l L. & Contemp.Prob. 555 (1991). See generally, Report, *The Commercial Use of Electronic Data Interchange—A Report and Model Trading Partner Agreement,* 45 Bus.Law. 1645 (1990).

SECTION 3. POSSIBLE BREAKDOWNS IN DEALS INVOLVING THE USE OF DOCUMENTS; APPLICABLE LAW

Here we will provide an inventory of the basic ways documentary and similar sales in which bailees hold the goods can break down, and we will identify the relevant sources of law governing these breakdowns. In subsequent sections of this chapter, we will focus on several of these types of breakdowns in more detail.

Below is a list of most of the important types of breakdowns:

(1) The goods may be lost, destroyed or damaged while in the hands of the issuer of the document of title. We have already treated this breakdown earlier in Chapter Sixteen. For additional discussion, see Grewal, *Risk of Loss in Goods Sold During Transit: A Comparative Study of the U.N. Convention on Contracts for the International Sale of Goods, the U.C.C. and the British Sale of Goods Act,* 14 Loy. L.A. Int'l & Comp. L.J. 93 (1991); Berman & Ladd, *Risk of Loss or Damage in Documentary Transactions Under the Convention On the International Sale of Goods,* 21 Cornell Int'l L.J. 423 (1988).

(2) The carrier or other bailee may misdeliver the goods to a party other than a party authorized in the document of title. We will take up this breakdown in section 4 below.

(3) Third parties may intervene and claim goods and/or the documents. This will be treated in section 5 below.

(4) One of the parties to the underlying sales transaction may repudiate or become insolvent while the goods are en route. This will be the subject of section 6 below.

(5) The carrier or other bailee may fail, because of non-receipt, misdescription or the like, to deliver what the documents call for. See section 7 below.

(6) The carrier or other bailee may make late delivery. See Chapter Sixteen supra.

(7) The goods on arrival may fail to conform to warranties and either be rejectable or afford a basis for a breach of warranty action. Breakdowns of this nature will be treated in Chapters Nineteen–Twenty-two.

In the event of breakdowns such as the above, what law governs? As the Farnsworth extract indicates, most of the strictly sales aspects and commercial paper aspects are governed by Articles 2, 3 and 4 of the Uniform

Commercial Code. But what of the rights and liabilities arising specifically from use of bills of lading and warehouse receipts as such?

A. *Law Governing Bills of Lading*

Of course, the language of the bill of lading itself will have important bearing. Otherwise, the rights and liabilities of parties to bills of lading (and related documents) are found principally in three places: Article Seven of the Uniform Commercial Code, the Federal Bills of Lading Act—also called the "Pomerene Act" (Federal Bills of Lading Act of 1916, ch. 415, §§ 1–44, 39 Stat. 538, 49 U.S.C.A. §§ 81–124 (1970)), and the Carmack Amendment to the Interstate Commerce Act (Interstate Commerce Act of 1887, ch. 104, Part I, § 20, 24 Stat. 386, as added, June 29, 1906, ch. 3591, § 7, 34 Stat. 593, as amended, 49 U.S.C.A. § 20(11), (1970)), and reenacted without substantial change in 1980, 49 U.S.C.A. § 11707. Article Seven of the Code displaced, in relevant part, the Uniform Bills of Lading Act which had been law in all states. Article Seven also applies to warehouse receipts.

In 1916, Congress enacted the Federal Bills of Lading Act (FBLA) which is substantially identical to the old Uniform Bills of Lading Act. The FBLA includes 44 sections. (We will refer to it as the "FBLA" and will cite it by reference to its United States Code section numbers (49 U.S.C.A. §§ 81–124)). Courts have decided hundreds of cases under the FBLA. Its presence and the presence of the Carmack Amendment on the federal statute books, and the vast case law under both, greatly diminish the significance of Article Seven's provisions on bills of lading. Whenever the FBLA is applicable, it rather than Article Seven controls. The FBLA is applicable to:

> Bills of lading issued by any common carrier for the transportation of goods in any Territory of the United States, or the District of Columbia, or from a place in a State to a place in a foreign country, or from a place in one State to a place in another State, or from a place in one State to a place in the same State through another State or foreign country * * *.
>
> 49 U.S.C.A. § 81.

Given the broad scope of the FBLA, what is left for Article Seven to govern? That Article applies mainly to (1) bills of lading issued for the transportation of goods from a place within one state to another place in the same state, provided the goods are not to pass through another state or foreign country *en route,* and (2) bills of lading issued for the transportation of goods from a foreign country into the United States. (A useful general discussion of the latter role of Article Seven is McCune, *Delivery of Cargo Carried Under Straight Bills of Lading,* 17 U.C.C.L.J. 344 (1985)). Even then the scope of Article Seven is cut down to the extent that other federal statutes besides the FBLA apply. Of other federal statutory law in this field the "Carmack Amendment" to the Interstate Commerce Act, 49 U.S.C.A. § 20(11) & (12), is of greatest importance. That amendment codifies the common law liability of interstate carriers for loss, destruction, or damage to goods, imposes this liability on the first of two or more connecting carriers for loss, destruction, or damage caused by any carrier in the chain of carriers transporting an interstate shipment, and proscribes carriers from using certain contract clauses limiting their liability. The Amendment applies to interstate shipments and to export shipments to adjoining countries. The Carmack Amendment covers two full pages in the statute book. The courts have interpreted and applied it in hundreds of cases. There are also various special federal statutes more limited in scope. In 1938, for instance, Congress enacted the Perishable Agricultural Commodities Act. 7 U.S.C.A. §§ 499a–499r. In 1893 and 1936, Congress passed the Harter Act, 46 U.S.C.A. §§ 190–196, and the Carriage of Goods by Sea Act, 46 U.S.C.A. §§ 1300–1315, respectively; both apply to ocean bills of lading.

Besides federal statutes, Article Seven, and relevant case law, the lawyer must often consult regulations and rulings of regulatory bodies, including those of the Interstate Commerce Commission. The I.C.C. has prescribed mandatory forms for bills of lading and has prescribed that "order" bills, which are negotiable because they state "deliver to order or bearer," must be printed on yellow paper and "straight" bills, which are nonnegotiable, on white paper. The I.C.C. has also promulgated numerous rules and regulations that affect the liabilities of interstate carriers.

B. *Law Governing Warehouse Receipts*

Again, the language of the receipt itself will have important bearing. Generally, Article Seven of the Code will govern, but even though a given state's version of Article Seven applies under relevant conflict of laws principles, some other law may control in the end. This law might be local non-Code state law, or it might be federal law, depending on the facts. Many states have enacted essentially regulatory statutes applicable to the dealings of warehousemen. As to these, UCC 7–103 is quite explicit: "To the extent that any * * * regulatory statute of this state or tariff, classification, or regulation filed or issued pursuant thereto is applicable, the provisions of this article are subject thereto." An illustrative example of a *state* regulatory provision is this California law:

> No warehousemen shall begin to operate any business of a warehouseman, as defined in subdivisions (b) or (c) of Section 239, without first having obtained from the commission a certificate declaring that public convenience and necessity require or will require the transaction of business by such warehouseman.

In addition to state regulatory law, federal law (statute, treaty, judicial decision) may also supersede or supplement Article Seven. The effect of federal law on warehouse receipts is confined mainly to the impact of the United States Warehouse Act, which applies to receipts covering agricultural products stored for interstate or foreign commerce. Most sections of this Act are regulatory, but those sections that specify the content of warehouse receipts and define delivery obligations override Article Seven.

The Code draftsmen intended originally to consolidate the old Uniform Warehouse Receipts Act and Uniform Bills of Lading Act into one unified statute, but the plan could not be fully executed. The result is that the lawyer must usually look in two places. He must look first in the relevant "special provisions" on warehouse receipts and second in the more general provisions covering *both* warehouse receipts and bills of lading. Sometimes the lawyer must search outside of Article Seven in other Articles of the Code, such as Article Nine, which applies to pledges of warehouse receipts.

SECTION 4. MISDELIVERY BY CARRIER OR OTHER BAILEE

As the cases in this section will indicate, "misdelivery" can take a variety of forms. In a misdelivery case, the lawyer must first determine the nature of the transaction involved. Was it a true documentary sale? Or what? Then the lawyer must determine how the case should be decided under *applicable law.* This law is to be found (1) in the terms of the document issued by the carrier or other bailee and (2) in relevant statutory and case law. Be sure to review the terms of any bill of lading. Also, review not only relevant Code provisions (especially UCC 7–403) but also sections 88 and 89 of the Federal Bill of Lading Act below:

§ 88. Duty to Deliver Goods on Demand; Refusal

A carrier, in the absence of some lawful excuse, is bound to deliver goods upon a demand made either by the consignee named in the bill for the goods or, if the bill is an order bill, by the holder thereof, if such a demand is accompanied by—

(a) An offer in good faith to satisfy the carrier's lawful lien upon the goods;

(b) Possession of the bill of lading and an offer in good faith to surrender, properly indorsed, the bill which was issued for the goods, if the bill is an order bill; and

(c) A readiness and willingness to sign, when the goods are delivered, an acknowledgment that they have been delivered, if such signature is requested by the carrier.

In case the carrier refuses or fails to deliver the goods, in compliance with a demand by the consignee or holder so accompanied, the burden shall be upon the carrier to establish the existence of a lawful excuse for such refusal or failure.

§ 89. Delivery; When Justified

A carrier is justified, subject to the provisions of sections 90–92 of this title, in delivering goods to one who is—

(a) A person lawfully entitled to the possession of the goods, or

(b) The consignee named in a straight bill for the goods, or

(c) A person in possession of an order bill for the goods, by the terms of which the goods are deliverable to his order; or which has been indorsed to him, or in blank by the consignee, or by the mediate or immediate indorsee of the consignee.

REFRIGERATED TRANSPORT CO. v. HERNANDO PACKING CO.

Supreme Court of Tennessee, 1976.
544 S.W.2d 613.

HENRY, JUSTICE.

This controversy between a consignor and a common carrier of property involves the carrier's liability for misdelivery of cargo transported under a straight bill of lading. The trial court found the issues against the carrier and we conclude that he reached the correct conclusion.

I.

On January 3, 1975, Hernando Packing Company, Inc., of Memphis, shipped via Refrigerated Transport Company, Inc., a truck load of frozen meat consigned as follows:

> [T]o BROWARD COLD STORAGE (acct. of J & A Trading Co.) 3220 S.W. 2nd Avenue * * * Fort Lauderdale, Florida.
>
> Broward is a public warehouse.

Prior to making this shipment Hernando had received a call from an individual who identified himself as *Al Hark* and held himself out to be a representative of J & A Trading Company. In point of fact he had no connection with J & A Trading Company and that company had gone out of business. Hernando had never done business with Al Hark, but on one prior occasion, had shipped to J & A Trading Company pursuant to a transaction with *Joseph Hark,* its then representative and owner, and father of Al Hark.

It is fairly inferable from the record that this unfamiliarity with Al Hark prompted the precaution of making the shipment to Broward, a public warehouse, for the account of J & A. However, the record is not specific in this regard and the shipment may have been made thusly as a matter of custom in the business or trade.

On January 6, 1975, upon the arrival of Refrigerated's truck in Fort Lauderdale, it was met *across the street from Broward* by Al Hark, but within sight of Broward's manager. Without the knowledge of Hernando or reconsignment or assent of Broward, and after representing himself to Refrigerated's driver as being a representative of J & A, Al Hark caused 84 boxes, or 5,040 pounds of boneless beef to be delivered to another address. Refrigerated's driver did not contact Broward and, insofar as the record shows, delivery was made solely on the basis of the verbal representations of Al Hark.

The next morning Refrigerated's truck came to Broward's dock and was again met by Al Hark. In the sight and presence of the Broward manager, Hark directed that a part of the remaining meat be reloaded on another truck and that the balance be stored with Broward to the account of J & A. Al Hark again represented himself to be a representative of J & A. The record does not show when, to whom, or if the driver surrendered the bill of lading.

By these maneuvers, Al Hark acquired possession of 246 boxes, or 9,520 pounds of meat ranging from ribeyes to oxtails and having a stipulated value of $5,880.86.

On January 7, 1976, Joseph Hark was informed of the arrival of the meat, whereupon he called Hernando and advised that J & A was out of business; that it had placed no order; and that this was not the first time his son, Al Hark, had placed such orders in the name of J & A. Hernando called Broward to direct that the meat not be delivered to Al Hark but was informed that delivery had already been made and without any reconsignment from Broward.

The trial judge, on this set of facts found and decreed:

That the consignee on the Straight Bill of Lading herein was Broward Cold Storage at 3220 S.W. Second Avenue, Ft. Lauderdale, Florida, and that the Defendant had an absolute duty to deliver the frozen meat involved herein to said consignee and to no other.

II.

This controversy pivots upon the precise provisions of the bill of lading, viz: the consignment to "Broward Cold Storage (account of J & A Trading Co.)." Refrigerated earnestly insists that this, in effect, was a consignment to "J & A Trading Co., care of Broward Cold Storage." While this position is plausible, when consideration is given to the nature and purpose of bills of lading, the duties and obligations arising thereunder, and to the plain terms of the consignment, we cannot embrace this theory of the case.

At the very outset we point out that we are dealing with a "straight" bill of lading which is "[a] bill in which it is stated that the goods are consigned or destined to a specified person", 49 U.S.C. Sec. 82, which is not negotiable and must be so marked (it was in this case), 49 U.S.C. Sec. 86, as opposed to an "order" bill, 49 U.S.C. Sec. 83.[1]

Delivery under a straight bill of lading may only be made to "[a] person lawfully entitled to the possession of the goods, or (b) the consignee named" therein. 49 U.S.C. Sec. 89.

While there are various areas of potential disagreement inherent in this controversy they all boil down to a single question: Who was the consignee under the bill of lading?

In our view, there is no ambiguity. The consignment was to Broward. The parenthetical matter inserted simply advised the warehouse as to the identity of the ultimate receiver of the goods upon Broward's reconsignment. The only address inserted was that of Broward. Al Hark's name does not appear on the bill. It is fairly inferable that the consignment was to Broward as a precautionary measure against an unknown purchaser. Such would have been reasonable and prudent. But we need not speculate since the language was clear. There is no way that this delivery could have been properly made except to Broward and at Broward's address. Most assuredly a street corner delivery to a stranger not named in the bill and not shown by the record to have presented any credentials or authority cannot constitute valid delivery. All the driver ever had to do was to present his bill of lading to an authorized representative of Broward. The failure to do so was a breach of the contract of carriage.

To constitute a valid delivery, absent special circumstances, it is imperative that delivery be made to the right person, at the proper time and place and in a proper manner. This is implicit in the Contract of Carriage.[2]

1. "Bills of lading issued by any common carrier for the transportation of goods. * * * from a place in one State to a place in another State", among others, are governed by the Federal Bills of Lading Act 49 U.S.C. Sections 81–124.

2. See Vol. 13 Am.Jur.2d, Carriers, Sec. 405 et seq., and particularly Sections 405, 406, 411 and 415.

It is stated in Volume 13, American Jurisprudence, 2nd, Carriers § 416 that "a carrier who delivers to an alleged agent of the consignee does so at its own peril with respect to his status as such." Cited in support of this assertion is our own case of *Dean v. Vaccaro & Co.,* 39 Tenn. 488 (1859), which is fully supportive.

Pertinent to the issue is the North Carolina case of *Griggs v. Stoker Service Co.,* 229 N.C. 572, 50 S.E.2d 914 (1948), wherein the Court said:

> The duty of a common carrier is not merely to carry safely the goods entrusted to him, but also to deliver them to the party designated by the terms of the shipment, or to his order, at the place of destination. 50 S.E.2d at 919.

Another case involving misdelivery of cargo, is *Dickman v. Daniels Motor Freight,* 185 Pa.Super. 374, 138 A.2d 165 (1958), wherein the delivery was made to a business establishment having a similar name and under circumstances suggestive of fraudulent conduct by a "swindler" who placed the order. The bill of lading was directed to a definite company at a definite address. The Court said:

> A common carrier is under an absolute duty to deliver goods to the person designated in the instructions of the shipper. If it fails to follow the express instructions of the shipper in making delivery, it acts at its peril and assumes the risk of wrong delivery. 138 A.2d at 167.

In *Richardson v. Railway Express Agency, Inc.,* 258 Or. 170, 482 P.2d 176 (1971), the Court held that a carrier making a delivery to one other than the named consignee "has the burden of proof to establish the ownership and right of possession of the goods at the time of such delivery." 482 P.2d at 178. The Court indicated the settled rule to be that carriers

> * * * are held strictly to the performance of their duty to make delivery of goods at the place of destination to the person designated to receive them if he presents himself or can be found with reasonable diligence. 482 P.2d at 179.

Refrigerated makes the urgent insistence that delivery to an imposter will discharge the common carrier "if it is to the imposter that the consignor actually intends to ship." We do not fault this as a general rule of law; but, as already pointed out, the shipment, for reasons we think self-evident, was to Broward.

Refrigerated relies upon *Chicago, M., St. P. & P.R. Co. v. Flanders,* 56 F.2d 114 (8th Cir.1932); however, there the imposter held all documentary indicia of ownership and the cattle were consigned to him.

Also relied upon is *Malvern Cold Storage Co. v. American Ry. Exp. Co.,* 206 Iowa 292, 220 N.W. 322 (1938); however, according to Refrigerated's brief filed in this Court, "[t]he circumstances were such that the consignor's actual *intention* was to deliver to [the imposter]." (Emphasis supplied).

Next we are cited to *Fulton Bag & Cotton Mills v. Hudson Navigation Co.,* 157 F. 987 (S.D.N.Y.1907). There no public warehouse was involved; identity of names was involved; due inquiry was made by the carrier prior to delivery; and proper notification was given pursuant to the bill of lading.

Other cases cited by appellee are also distinguishable.

In 54 A.L.R. at 1330, in an annotation relating to delivery to an imposter, it is stated that "the general rule places liability on a carrier for a misdelivery to an imposter of goods placed in the hands of the carrier for shipment". Among the cases cited in support of this proposition is our case of *Sword v. Young,* 89 Tenn. 126, 14 S.W. 481 (1890).

Sword is analogous to the instant case. One Gillenwaters ordered a brick machine under the assumed name of Magrauder, representing Magrauder to be a firm name. Upon arrival of the machine in Knoxville, Gillenwaters presented the bill of lading made in the name of Charles G. Magrauder, paid the freight and took possession of the machine.

The Court recognized the "well settled general rule that the carrier must deliver to the consignee at the place appointed", and thereafter stated:

> It can make no difference that the defendant carrier thought, because Gillenwaters had the bill of lading, that he was Charles G. Magrauder. If he was a stranger, as the proof shows him to be, it was the duty of the carrier to have required him to identify himself as the consignee or his rightfully constituted agent.
>
> * * *
>
> The consignment was to Charles G. Magrauder. That name was fixed on the machine, and it was a duty to deliver to him only, or, if he could not be discovered, to notify the consignor.
>
> There is no difference between this case and one in which a consignment has been made to an actual person, and the goods delivered by accident, mistake, or carelessness to a cheat who represents himself as the real consignee. It is necessary in both to have proof of identity or authority to receive. 89 Tenn. at 128–29, 14 S.W. at 481.

We hold that Refrigerated breached its duty to deliver the cargo to Broward, the party designated in the bill of lading; that delivery to Al Hark was at Refrigerated's peril; that the burden of validating this delivery by establishing Al Hark's ownership and right to possession was upon Refrigerated and that it failed to carry that burden.

While we make this holding within the context of our view that Broward was the consignee, had we adopted Refrigerated's view that J & A Trading Company was the consignee, with the goods being shipped "in care of" Broward, the result would be the same. This necessarily follows from the facts that J & A was not in existence; that Al Hark had no connection with J & A; and that delivery was made to him without proper inquiry and without notice to Broward, or J & A. Had such inquiry been made and such notice given the driver would have discovered that he was dealing with an imposter.

III.

Refrigerated counter-claimed for the unpaid freight bill in the sum of $675.00 together with interest thereon. The trial court dismissed the counter-claim, without assigning any reason therefor.

We note that the bill of lading contains the entry "FREIGHT TO BE PAID BY: J & A TRADING CO." in Miami. This may have prompted the trial judge.

The record before us is not sufficient to pass upon this portion of the controversy. The bill of lading shows that 498 boxes of meat, weighing 31,068¾ pounds were shipped. The stipulation shows that Al Hark diverted 246 boxes weighing 9,520 pounds. The remaining 252 boxes, containing 21,548 pounds were delivered to Broward.

We have no hesitancy in declaring that Refrigerated, by misdelivery of the diverted meat, breached its contract of carriage and forfeited its right to receive compensation to that extent. Superficially it would appear that Refrigerated would be entitled to recover for the carriage of that portion of the meat ultimately delivered to Broward. However, we make no holding in the latter regard; we merely recognize the considerations involved.

On remand, the trial judge will reconsider the counter-claim and enter such judgment as the facts may indicate and justice may require.

Affirmed in part and remanded.

COOPER, C.J., and FONES, BROCK and HARBISON, JJ., concur.

Notes

1. Why did the court apply section 89 of the FBLA rather than section 7–403 of the UCC? Does it make any difference?

2. Does the result really depend in part on the statute or would it have been enough merely for the court to have invoked the language of the straight bill of lading?

3. In Rountree v. Lydick-Barmann, 150 S.W.2d 173 (Tex.Civ.App.1941), the seller was Lydick-Barmann, the buyer Crone Co., and the carrier Rountree. The carrier issued to Lydick-Barmann a bill which was captioned: "Uniform Motor Carrier Straight Bill of Lading—Original—Not Negotiable—Domestic." The bill also acknowledged receipt of the goods from seller (Lydick-Barmann) at its address in Fort Worth, Texas "Consigned to Lydick-Barmann Company, destination 616 Street, Louisiana City, Little Rock, Ark. State. Notify Crone Company." Seller had no office or agent at the street address in Little Rock given in the bill of lading. The carrier delivered to Crone Company and seller was never paid. Held, for seller, Lydick-Barmann. "Notify Crone Co. was not equivalent to 'Consigned to Crone Co.' When the carrier learned that it could not deliver to Lydick-Barmann at the address given, it should have sought instructions from Lydick-Barmann."

4. In *Refrigerated Transport Co.,* the bill of lading was non-negotiable which is by far the most common case. But a not uncommon transaction is one in which a seller in a foreign country ships goods to the U.S. pursuant to an agreement whereby the carrier issues a negotiable bill of lading to the seller who then sends it and a draft to a bank in the U.S. who acts as collecting agent on behalf of the seller by taking payment from the buyer and endorsing the bill to the buyer who then presents it to the carrier and receives the goods. Such an arrangement breaks down if the carrier delivers the goods to the buyer without insisting on the bill of lading. This is what happened in Koreska v. United Cargo Corp., 23 A.D.2d 37, 258 N.Y.S.2d 432 (1965) and the carrier was held liable to the seller (who did not receive payment from the buyer). The carrier

may have a defense in such a case, however, as when the carrier can show that the buyer already had acquired the bill of lading from the collecting agent (without payment) so that the carrier's wrong was not the cause of the loss. Such a defense prevailed in The Pere Marquette Ry. v. J.F. French & Co., 254 U.S. 538, 41 S.Ct. 195, 65 L.Ed. 391 (1921). Still other defenses may be available in such cases. The carrier may be able to show that the seller or the seller's agent waived the requirement of picking up the bill of lading from the buyer. Or the carrier may be able to show that the seller ratified the misdelivery by accepting a partial payment from the buyer subsequently.

5. Sometimes the unpaid seller will find that the collecting agency (often a bank) will be liable. Such a case is Bunge v. First Nat'l Bank, 118 F.2d 427 (3d Cir.1941) where the bank became liable to the seller for accepting a bad check and handing over the bill of lading duly endorsed to the buyer. The court said the bank became liable "when it received something other than money in payment."

Note: Terminology

The carrier's so-called "absolute liability" for misdelivery can be extracted from the text of sections 88 and 89 of the FBLA, 7–403 of the Code, and the contract of carriage of the parties. But it does not clarify analysis to say that the liability is absolute. After all, the contract between shipper and carrier calls on the carrier to deliver to a given party, and when the carrier fails to do this, a breach of contract occurs. The liability of a carrier for misdelivery is no more and no less absolute than the liability of any party for breach of contract. Ordinarily, it is no defense for the party who breaks his contract to respond that what he did under the circumstances was reasonable, or even that it was his very best effort.

Note: Substitutes for Surrender of "Order" Bills

When one uses a negotiable bill of lading he expects that the carrier will not surrender the goods until the original copy of the bill is presented to him. As we saw, the fine print at the top of such bill provides: "The surrender of this original ORDER BILL OF LADING properly indorsed shall be required before delivery of the property." UCC 7–502 makes plain the idea that this bill of lading embodies the rights to the goods; it specifies that one to whom a document of title has been duly negotiated acquires thereby "title to the document, title to the goods and the direct obligation of the issuer to hold or deliver the goods according to the terms of the document. * * *"

What happens when in the humdrum of real life the mailman fails to get the original of the order bill of lading to the bank and instead returns it with a stamp, "undeliverable," or when the bank loses the bill, or takes two or three days to process the bill and the goods have arrived in the meantime? Of course somebody is going to have to pay a charge to the railroad for holding the goods. And if the goods are melons or peaches or other perishable commodities, it would be intolerable and in no one's interest to have them rot on the siding while everyone hunted for the bill of lading. Shippers and carriers have worked out certain substitutes for surrender of the original bill. These provisions are described in § 3 of Rule 7 of the Uniform Freight Classification and they read as follows:

> **Substitute 1:** cash or its equivalent to the carrier equal to 125% of the invoice value of the property.

Substitute 2: a specific bond of indemnity equal to double the invoice value.

Substitute 3: a blanket bond of indemnity. This bond can be used repeatedly so long as the bill-of-lading is surrendered within five days of delivery of the freight. If the bill-of-lading does not become available within that time, Substitutes 1 or 2 must be substituted.

Substitute 4: an open-end bond. (If an order-notify bill is lost the surety automatically assumes liability for the lading in perpetuity. The open-bond becomes an individual bond, without limit, on each car released.)

If the one for whom delivery is intended under the order bill of lading has not been able to procure the original of the order bill, he can offer any one of the four substitutes and thereby procure the goods. Of course the effect of the substitute is to provide the carrier with a fund out of which he can satisfy his liability for breaching his contract with the shipper.

One way to avoid the problem is this: The shipper can retain control of the goods by using a straight bill of lading if he names himself as the consignee. The following excerpt taken from a letter of the late Mr. J.L. Shissler, Jr., former General Traffic Manager of the Pillsbury Company, explains the Pillsbury Company's use of this method:

"Under Section 4 of Rule 7 of the Uniform Freight Classification the rail carriers provide for shipments under straight bills-of-lading consigned to one party with provision for notification to a second party with surrender of a written order prior to delivery. Under this system we would simply bill a car to ourselves with the carrier to advise the customer. The bill-of-lading carries the notation 'Do not surrender except upon receipt of written order from The Pillsbury Company.' A delivery order is prepared and accompanies the draft to the bank. When the customer accepts the draft, he receives the delivery order. This in turn he presents to the carrier's destination agent for release of the car.

"In the event the delivery order is lost or delayed the consignee can secure release of the car on the same four substitutes available under the order-notify bill.

"Perhaps, at this point I should point out the difference in the two methods. Under the order bill, once the shipment moves neither the shipper nor the receiver can release the car without surrender of the bill or use of one of the four substitutes. Under the straight-notify bill the receiver must either surrender the delivery order or use one of the four substitutes. The consignor, however, can release cars by simply notifying the carrier in writing that delivery can be made without surrender of the delivery order."

Observe that in the type of transaction Mr. Shissler describes, the buyer does not pay a sight draft; rather, he "accepts" a time draft as a condition of getting the goods. See UCC 3–410. This device affords seller less protection than does use of a sight draft, yet more protection than sale on open account. Do you see why?

SECTION 5. ASSERTION OF CLAIMS AGAINST SELLER, BUYER OR OWNER BY THIRD PARTIES (Herein of "negotiability")

Third parties (parties other than the seller, the buyer, and the bailee) sometimes assert claims to the goods at some stage of the transaction, and this can cause a breakdown. These parties include: (1) persons who claim to be creditors of the seller or buyer, (2) persons who claim to be purchasers from the seller or buyer, and (3) other persons claiming paramount title (e.g. an alleged prior owner).

Generally, the buyer will be best off in these cases if he has acquired title to the goods by taking (through due negotiation) negotiable documents covering them. Both Article Seven of the Code (UCC 7–104) and the Federal Bill of Lading Act distinguish between negotiable and non-negotiable documents. The relevant sections of the FBLA provide as follows:

82. Straight bill of lading

A bill in which it is stated that the goods are consigned or destined to a specified person is a straight bill. Aug. 29, 1916, c. 415, § 2, 39 Stat. 539.

83. Order bill of lading; negotiability

A bill in which it is stated that the goods are consigned or destined to the order of any person named in such bill is an order bill. Any provision in such a bill or in any notice, contract, rule, regulation, or tariff that it is nonnegotiable shall be null and void and shall not affect its negotiability within the meaning of this chapter unless upon its face and in writing agreed to by the shipper. Aug. 29, 1916, c. 415, § 3, 39 Stat. 539.

The most common type of transaction in which a buyer purchases a *negotiable* bill occurs when a contract between him and his seller calls for him to pay "cash against documents." (See section 2 of this chapter.) Today this type of transaction is not nearly as common in domestic trade as in import-export transactions. As we saw earlier, when a buyer agrees to pay "cash against documents," this ordinarily calls for him to pay a sight draft presented by the seller's agent in exchange for a negotiable bill of lading which entitles the buyer to procure the goods from the carrier and without which the carrier will not deliver them. The seller is not obligated to hand over the bill (and thus control over the goods) until the buyer pays the draft, and the buyer does not have to pay in advance but only simultaneously with acquiring the bill (the means to procure the goods from the carrier when they arrive).

What rights does a good faith purchaser of a negotiable document acquire? First, he generally gets the same rights against the bailee as the bailor had, including the right to have the bailee care for the goods and the right to have the bailee deliver in accordance with the purchaser's instructions. Thus, section 112 of the FBLA provides that the transferee gets "the direct obligation of the carrier to hold possession of the goods for him according to the terms of the bill as fully as if the carrier had contracted directly with him." Section 7–502(1) of Article Seven includes a similar provision. Second, a good faith purchaser of a negotiable bill of lading gets (under section 111 of the FBLA) "such title to the goods as the person negotiating the bill to him had or had ability to convey to a purchaser in good faith for value. * * *" Under section 7–502 of Article Seven, the purchaser gets (subject to UCC 7–503), "title to the document" and "title to the goods." Third, once the bailee issues a negotiable document covering the goods, whatever title to the goods that the document covers can generally be transferred only by appropriate transfer of the document. That is, appropriate transfer of the document is generally the exclusive method of moving title to the goods. Under Article Seven for a purchaser of a negotiable document to acquire rights under UCC 7–502, he must take by "due negotiation." The Article Seven requirements for due negotiation are set forth in UCC 7–501. Under the FBLA, for the purchaser to acquire the rights set forth in section 111, he must "give value therefor in good faith, without notice," and take by indorsement or delivery (as provided in sections 107 and 108).

Problem 17–1

Seller and buyer entered a contract for the purchase of 500 wooden rails. Seller got a negotiable bill of lading from the carrier while the rails were still in seller's yard to be loaded on nearby boxcars. Two days later buyer bought and paid for the bill and took the same by due negotiation. A day later, Ajax, a creditor of seller, levied on the rails while still in seller's yard. As between Ajax and buyer, who prevails? Cf., UCC 7–602, 7–501 and 7–502. See also FBLA section 103.

Problem 17–2

Construct an example in which the holder of a negotiable document received from the seller prevails under the Code over another purchaser of the same goods covered by the bill. Also be sure to note the exception in UCC 7–205.

Problem 17–3

Joe held a negotiable warehouse receipt in "order" form. Art stole the receipt and artfully forged it to John, a good faith purchaser. Joe claims the goods. John claims the goods. To whom must the bailee deliver under the Code? (And where does UCC 7–404 come into play?)

LINEBURGER BROS. v. HODGE

Supreme Court of Mississippi, 1951.
212 Miss. 204, 54 So.2d 268.

ALEXANDER, JUSTICE.

Separate bills were filed against the Federal Compress & Warehouse Company, a corporation, by E.S. Vancleve, J.R. Hodge, and E.A. Bates & Company, a partnership, each praying for a mandatory injunction against the defendant to compel delivery of cotton held by the defendant to them as purchasers and holders of the warehouse receipts covering the number of bales of cotton held respectively by each of the complainants, or in the alternative for the value of the cotton thereby represented. The total number of bales is twenty-four, Vancleve claiming nine, Hodge six, and E.A. Bates & Company nine.

It is adequately shown that all of the cotton was grown and ginned by Lineburger Brothers, B.C. Lineburger, J.G. Outlaw and F.A. Little, and stolen by one J.V. Carr from a gin where the cotton had been processed and tagged. This asportation occurred at night and was conducted with the aid of a truck driver who was not a regular employee of Carr. Early the next morning Carr carried the cotton to the defendant warehouse, and, after weighing, had the receipts issued in three fictitious names and delivered to him. Carr took the receipts to nearby towns and sold the cotton, so identified, to the three complainants in separate lots. The purchasers gave their separate checks to Carr who procured payment by endorsing them respectively in the names of the three fictitious persons. He then disappeared and has not since been located.

As stated, the three buyers filed their separate bills against the warehouse. The gin company was not made a party. Upon application of the planters or owners, they were allowed to intervene and claim the cotton. From a decree dismissing the petition of the intervenors, absolving the warehouse of negligence in the issuance of the receipts, and awarding title to the respective warehouse receipts to the purchasers with full rights to claim the cotton thereby represented, after paying storage charges to the warehouse, the planters, or owners, appeal. A cross-appeal is filed by the complainants which urges that in event of a reversal of the decree, they be awarded a decree against the warehouse for the value of the cotton.

We deal first with the cross-appeal. It is grounded chiefly upon the alleged negligence of the warehouse in issuing the receipts to Carr in the names given by him.

* * *

Regardless of the plausibility of the contention of the appellees, there was an issue of fact in the matter of negligence of the warehouse, and we find no basis for overturning the finding of the chancellor, whose acquittance of the warehouse must of necessity have been upon such absence of negligence.

We approach, then, the rights of the appellants, the planters and owners. As heretofore stated, they had given Carr no authority to take and haul away any of this cotton. Specific instructions, including the time and identity of cotton to be so hauled, were always given, and Carr knew this. It is immaterial whether the warehouse knew of this limitation upon Carr's authority. It is sufficient that this limitation was understood between Carr and appellants. Here there was no dispute, and it is without question that the taking by Carr, under all the circumstances, was larceny, and that the receipts were fraudulently obtained. The next morning Carr was seen and made two different and untrue statements as to where the receipts were. One of these reports was to one of the owners who had discovered that the cotton was missing and was seeking to locate the receipts. There was no one at the gin when the cotton was abstracted, except Carr, his driver, and Mrs. Carr and her small son. The manager of the gin was not present, and he later testified that he had instructions that Carr was not to haul the Lineburger cotton except upon specific instructions. We repeat that the gin is not a party here and the test of the right of the owners must depend on whether this cotton was under any circumstances entrusted to Carr by permission and knowledge of the owners.

We find that the cotton was not so entrusted to Carr, and since the cotton was in fact stolen and the receipts fraudulently obtained, the defense of apparent authority, although available to the warehouse, does not aid the claim of the purchasers of the receipts.

It was held in Unger v. Abbott, 92 Miss. 563, 46 So. 68, that the rule caveat emptor applies against the claim of an innocent purchaser of warehouse receipts who purchased them from the owner's servant who had been sent with cotton to a compress company with instructions to have it weighed and to bring the receipts back to the owner, but who, contrary to his authority and instructions, took the receipts in his own name and sold them.

If it be observed that this case was decided prior to our statutes upon Warehouse Receipts, Chap. 16, Vol. 4, Code 1942, attention is directed to Section 5051, which is as follows: "A negotiable receipt may be negotiated: * * *

"(b) By any person to whom the possession or custody of the receipt has been entrusted by the owner, if, by the terms of the receipt, the warehouseman undertakes to deliver the goods to the order of the person to whom the possession or custody of the receipt has been entrusted, or if at the time of such entrusting the receipt is in such form that it may be negotiated by delivery."

We look next at Section 5052: "A person to whom a negotiable receipt has been duly negotiated acquires thereby:

"(a) Such title to the goods as the person negotiating the receipt to him had or had ability to convey to a purchaser in good faith for value, and also such title to the goods as the depositor or person to whose order the goods were to be delivered by the terms of the receipt had or had ability to convey to a purchaser in good faith for value, and * * *."

Section 5058 is also in point. It is as follows: "The validity of the negotiation of a receipt is not impaired by the fact that such negotiation was a breach of duty on the part of the person making the negotiation, or by the fact that the owner of the receipt was induced by fraud, mistake, or duress to entrust the possession or custody of the receipt to such person, if the person to whom the receipt was negotiated, paid or a person to whom the receipt was subsequently negotiated, paid value therefor, without notice of the breach of duty, or fraud, or mistake or duress."

Appellees cite for support Weil Bros., Inc. v. Keenan, 180 Miss. 697, 178 So. 90. Here there was an interpleader suit filed by the warehouse. The testimony disclosed that the receipts had been entrusted to one Spencer by the owner, and were misappropriated by the former. After recognizing that one, especially a trespasser, can not convey a better title than he has, the Court found that the receipts had been entrusted to the thief and an innocent purchaser was protected. To the same effect is Lundy v. Greenville Bank & Tr. Co., 179 Miss. 282, 174 So. 802, and other cases cited by appellees. See also 56 Am.Jur.Warehouses, Sec. 62.

Our statutes do not go so far as those of some other states in protecting a bona fide purchaser of negotiable receipts in cases where the receipts had been stolen. See 56 Am.Jur., Warehouses, Sec. 53. Since such receipts were not negotiable at common law, their negotiability is to be measured by our statutes.

We hold, therefore, that neither the cotton nor the receipts had been entrusted to Carr by the owners and that the latter are not estopped to set up their claim to the cotton as against the several appellees who purchased the receipts.

* * *

The assertion wants no support that the statutes referred to were designed to insure the negotiability of warehouse receipts and to facilitate commerce in the market places where cotton is bought and sold. The innocent purchaser of a negotiable receipt is guaranteed an assurance without which the traffic could not be conducted. Yet, such assurance must take into account the older principle that an owner of cotton may not be divested of title by a trespasser or a thief. In order to strike a just balance between these two concepts the statutes were enacted. The buyer must still beware lest he is buying receipts which have been fraudulently obtained or cotton which has been stolen. We need not analyze the statutes to divine whether the owner, who has voluntarily clothed another with indicia of ownership or entrusted him with possession of receipts, is barred of recovery from an innocent purchaser by principles of estoppel or pursuant to the rule that where two innocent persons must suffer from a fraud, he who reposes confidence in the fraudulent agent must suffer. It is enough that the statute recognizes title in the innocent purchaser who has bought receipts from one to whom they have been entrusted by the owner.

Here, as in all such cases, one of two innocent persons must suffer the loss. The thief has stolen or fraudulently obtained property from someone. We hold that the unlawful act was committed against the owners and that the title to the cotton remains in them. As stated in Unger v. Abbott, supra, "(The appellees) are to be condoled with for their loss by this swindle; but their misfortune can not affect the right of (the appellants) to have (their) cotton. * * * 'Caveat emptor' applies." [92 Miss. 563, 46 So. 68.]

The cause will be reversed and decree awarded to the appellants for the cotton, and the Federal Compress & Warehouse Company is directed to hold the same to the order of appellants, but without storage charges thereon. The cross-appeal is thereby decided adversely.

Reversed and decree here for appellants.

Notes

1. Would this case have been decided the same way under UCC 7–501, 7–502, and 7–503? Explain. What if Carr had been the manager of the gin with power to store?

2. In re Jamestown Farmers Elevator Inc., 49 B.R. 661, 41 UCC Rep. Serv. 578 (Bkrtcy.N.D.1985) posed a parallel problem. There, the goods were not stolen and then warehoused and passed to buyers. Rather, Bank had a security interest in the goods, yet allowed debtor to warehouse them and procure a further loan from third party, giving the receipts as security. Held: third party prevails over bank under UCC 7–503.

3. Suppose that Secured Party creates and perfects a security interest in commercial goods owned by Bailor. With SP's permission, B stores the goods in Walter's Warehouse. WW issues a non-negotiable warehouse receipt in proper

form naming B as the person entitled. B does not pay storage and other charges and WW properly asserts a statutory lien under UCC 7–209(1) and claims priority over SP under UCC 9–310, dealing with the priority of liens arising by operation of law. UCC 9–310 states that WW takes priority "over a perfected security interest unless the lien is statutory and the statute expressly provides otherwise." Thus, WW has priority over SP unless UCC 7–209 "provides otherwise."

UCC 7–209(3) "provides otherwise" in two situations. First, WW's lien is "effective against any person who so entrusted the bailor with possession of the goods that a pledge by him to a good faith purchaser for value would have been valid." SP is not such a person, since a pledge by B to a good faith purchaser would be subject to a perfected security interest. Comment 3. For a case so holding, see Curry Grain Storage, Inc. v. Hesston Corp., 120 Idaho 328, 815 P.2d 1068 (1991). Second, WW's lien is "not effective against a person as to whom the document confers no right in the goods covered by it under Section 7–503." This language deals with the owner's interest against a depositor who is a thief and does not apply to our hypothetical. See Comment 3.

SECTION 6. A PARTY TO THE SALE REPUDIATES, BECOMES INSOLVENT, OR THE LIKE

A party to the sale may repudiate or become insolvent while the goods (1) are in the hands of a carrier or other bailee and (2) a document of title covering the goods is outstanding. Suppose, for example, that while the goods are en route, the buyer repudiates or becomes insolvent. What may the seller do? May he "stop in transit" under UCC 2–705? May he divert? This depends on (1) the terms of the outstanding document and (2) the applicable statutory and case law. In any event, any new carriage or delivery instructions of the seller will be addressed to the carrier (or other bailee).

It is important to distinguish between the carrier's *right* (without fear of suit) to follow the instructions of a consignor or consignee and its *duty* to do so. In some cases a carrier must follow instructions; in others it may but need not. Likewise one should distinguish a shipper-seller's rights and powers vis-a-vis the carrier from those vis-a-vis his buyer-consignee. The shipper may have the power to halt shipment, but his act may constitute a breach of his sales contract. UCC 2–705(1) gives the seller a right to stop delivery in a case in which "he discovers the buyer to be insolvent" or in the case of the "delivery of carload, truckload, planeload or larger shipments of express or freight when the buyer repudiates or fails to make a payment due before delivery, or if for any other reason the seller has a right to withhold or reclaim the goods." Subsection (3) of UCC 2–705 specifies certain limits on this right to stop. For example, the carrier is not obliged to obey any order to stop a shipment under an order bill until the document has been surrendered.

UCC 7–303(1) gives the carrier the authority but not the obligation to divert a shipment on instructions from:

(a) the holder of a negotiable bill; or

(b) the consignor on a non-negotiable bill notwithstanding contrary instructions from the consignee; or

(c) the consignee on a non-negotiable bill in the absence of contrary instructions from the consignor, if the goods have arrived at the billed destination or if the consignee is in possession of the bill; or

(d) the consignee on a non-negotiable bill if he is entitled as against the consignor to dispose of them.

Note well that the quoted section of the UCC states the law of *intra-state* shipment. Unless the courts adopt it as the federal common law, one must still search for that common law in the federal cases interpreting the Federal Bills of Lading Act in interstate shipments. Because case law is scarce and because the Code represents the current thinking of people who deal with bills of lading, one can hope that the federal courts will adopt the Code rules as the federal common law under the Bills of Lading Act where that Act does not speak explicitly.

CLOCK v. MISSOURI–KANSAS–TEXAS RAILROAD CO. v. CRAWFORD

United States District Court, Eastern District of Missouri, 1976.
407 F.Supp. 448.

Opinion

NANGLE, DISTRICT JUDGE.

Plaintiff Gerald Clock brought this action to recover the cost of goods which were allegedly converted by defendant Missouri-Kansas-Texas Railroad Company. By amended complaint, plaintiff added Stanley L. Crawford as defendant. Plaintiff also alleges that defendant Railroad breached its obligation to deliver the goods. Prior to the filing of plaintiff's amended complaint, defendant Railroad filed a third-party complaint against Crawford, alleging that if the Railroad should be liable to plaintiff, third-party defendant would be liable to the Railroad to the extent of the liability to plaintiff. Crawford now being a defendant in this action, defendant Railroad's complaint is in fact a cross-claim and will be treated as such.

This case was tried before the Court without a jury. The Court having considered the pleadings, the testimony of the witnesses, the documents in evidence, and being otherwise fully advised in the premises, hereby makes the following findings of fact and conclusions of law as required by Rule 52, Federal Rules of Civil Procedure:

Findings of Fact

1. Plaintiff, Gerald Clock, is, and was at all times relevant herein, a citizen of the State of Indiana. Defendant, Missouri-Kansas-Texas Railroad Company ("Railroad") is a corporation incorporated under the laws of the State of Delaware, having its principal place of business in Texas. Defendant Stanley L. Crawford, is, and was at all times relevant herein, a citizen of the State of Oklahoma.

2. On January 14, 1975, Crawford sold two carloads of bulk ammonium nitrate fertilizer to Buford Cunningham and received two checks in payment therefor. On the same date, the goods were placed in the care and custody of defendant Railroad for shipment from Oklahoma to Eaton Agricultural

Center in Indiana. Defendant Railroad issued bills of lading to cover the goods. The bills of lading were signed by Crawford. Both bills of lading specify on the top of each that they are

UNIFORM STRAIGHT BILL OF LADING

ORIGINAL—NOT NEGOTIABLE

3. At the time of sale, Crawford knew that Cunningham was going to sell the goods to a third party. Soon after the sale to Cunningham, Cunningham did sell the goods to plaintiff for $30,195.12. At the time of this sale, plaintiff had no knowledge of any infirmities in title, or right to possession, by Cunningham.

4. On January 23, 1975, the bank notified Crawford that there were insufficient funds in Cunningham's account to cover the checks. Accordingly, they were returned to Crawford.

5. The goods were still in transit at this point. Crawford instructed the Railroad to hold the railroad cars containing the goods until further instructions from him. Defendant Railroad complied.

6. On February 3, 1975, Crawford certified to defendant Railroad that he was the true owner of the goods and he issued a reconsignment order on the goods, instructing that they be sent to Farmers Union Coop, instead of Eaton Agricultural Center. Defendant Railroad complied with these instructions.

7. Plaintiff furnished replacement goods to Eaton Agricultural Center of a like quantity and value, and acquired the right, title and interest of Eaton Agricultural Center to the goods, by reason of an assignment by Eaton Agricultural Center executed on February 10, 1975.

CONCLUSIONS OF LAW

This Court has jurisdiction over the subject matter and of the parties. 28 U.S.C. § 1332.

The bills of lading involved herein are straight bills of lading. 49 U.S.C. §§ 82, 86. It is clear that "[a] straight bill can not be negotiated free from existing equities * * *". 49 U.S.C. § 109. While not negotiable, straight bills are transferable. The transferee stands in the shoes of the transferor, acquiring no additional rights over those held by the transferor. See *Arizona Feed v. Southern Pacific Transportation Co.*, 21 Ariz.App. 346, 519 P.2d 199 (1974); *Southern Pacific Co. v. Agencia Joffroy, S.A.*, 65 Ariz. 65, 174 P.2d 278 (1946); *Quality Shingle Co. v. Old Oregon Lumber & Shingle Co.*, 110 Wash. 60, 187 P. 705 (1920); § 400.7–104, R.S.Mo. (1969).

A carrier may deliver goods to "[a] person lawfully entitled to the possession of the goods" or to the consignee. 49 U.S.C. § 89. The question for determination therefore is whether Crawford was lawfully entitled to possession of the goods. While it is true that title passes to a buyer when the seller completes his performance under the contract, § 400.2–401, R.S.Mo. (1969), it is equally true that

> where the buyer * * * fails to make a payment due * * * the aggrieved seller may

(a) withhold delivery of such goods;

(b) stop delivery by any bailee * * *;

* * *

(d) resell and recover damages * * *

* * *

(f) cancel. § 400.2–703, R.S.Mo. (1969).

It is the Court's conclusion, therefore, that upon the failure of the checks presented by Cunningham to Crawford, Crawford was "lawfully entitled to the possession of the goods". Plaintiff, as transferee of a straight bill of lading, can not have any greater rights than did Cunningham, and can not have the status of a bona fide purchaser for value. Since Crawford was entitled to possession of the goods, defendant Railroad can not be liable for delivering the goods in accordance with Crawford's instructions. 49 U.S.C. § 89, *Turner Lumber & Investment Co. v. Chicago, R.I. & P. Ry. Co.*, 223 Mo.App. 564, 16 S.W.2d 705 (1929).

The applicable provisions of the Commercial Code provide that

(1) Unless the bill of lading otherwise provides, the carrier may deliver the goods to a person or destination other than that stated in the bill or may otherwise dispose of the goods on instructions from

(b) the consignor on a nonnegotiable bill notwithstanding contrary instructions from the consignee * * * § 400.7–303, R.S.Mo. (1969).

Under the facts established herein, Crawford was the consignor, as Crawford was "the person from whom the goods have been received for shipment". § 400.7–102(c), R.S.Mo. (1969). Since the bills of lading were nonnegotiable, and defendant Railroad delivered the goods pursuant to the instructions of the consignor, there can be no liability. See Comments, § 400.7–303 and § 400.7–504(3), R.S.Mo. (1969).

Under 49 U.S.C. § 112, the authority of the shipper to stop shipment in transit and redirect it is well established. See *Weyerhaeuser Timber Co. v. First National Bank of Portland,* 150 Or. 172, 38 P.2d 48 (1934); *Cashmere Fruit Growers' Union v. Great Northern Railway Co.,* 149 Wash. 319, 270 P. 1038 (1928), *cert. denied,* 279 U.S. 851, 49 S.Ct. 347, 73 L.Ed. 994; *Quality Shingle Co. v. Old Oregon Lumber & Shingle Co., supra.* The same right is recognized in the Commercial Code. See §§ 400.2–703 and 400.2–705. Accordingly there can be no recovery by plaintiff against Crawford.

Plaintiff has claimed that both the Railroad and Crawford converted the shipments in question to their own use. Conversion has been defined as "* * * an *unauthorized* assumption and exercise of the right of ownership over the personal property of another to the exclusion of the owners' right". *Carson Union May Stern Co. v. Pennsylvania Railroad Co.,* 421 S.W.2d 540 (Mo.App.1967) [emphasis in the original]. Having concluded that Crawford was lawfully entitled to possession of the goods, it is clear that recovery for conversion will not lie.

The cases cited by plaintiff are inapposite as they involve a bona fide purchaser for value. Under the authority of 49 U.S.C. § 81 *et seq.,* there can not be such status where one is a transferee under a straight bill of lading.

North American Van Lines, Inc. v. Heller, 371 F.2d 629 (5th Cir.1967) is equally unavailing since the Court concludes that Crawford was lawfully entitled to possession.

Accordingly, judgment will be for defendants Railroad and Crawford. Since plaintiff will not recover any damages from defendant Railroad, judgment will be for defendant Crawford on the Railroad's cross-claim.

Problem 17–4

Seller ships under a straight bill of lading and names buyer (in the same state) as consignee. The shipment is a full truckload of leather. On the day the shipment leaves the seller's city, seller receives a "Dun & Bradstreet" on buyer which shows that buyer's fortunes have gone into precipitous decline and that he may have become insolvent.

1. If he instructs truck company not to deliver goods to buyer, will it comply? If it refuses, does he have a cause of action against it? (UCC 7–303, 2–705)

2. If carrier does stop shipment, will seller be in breach of his contract with buyer? (UCC 2–705, 2–609)

3. Would it change your answer if buyer had already received his copy of the bill of lading and had transferred his interest in it and the goods to a third party by an assignment of that bill and had given notice of such transfer to the carrier? (UCC 7–504)

4. Would it make any difference that the shipment was under a negotiable bill of lading and the bill had been negotiated to the third party? (UCC 7–502, 2–705)

5. In this problem does UCC 2–705 enlarge seller's rights against buyer, his control of the goods, neither, or both?

6. If the buyer had not become insolvent and was not otherwise in breach of the contract and if seller ordered the truck company to return the shipment to him, do you think the company would have complied? Would it have had any liability to buyer for doing so?

SECTION 7. BAILEE'S NON-RECEIPT, MISDESCRIPTION OR THE LIKE—EFFECTS ON BUYERS, SELLERS AND FINANCERS

For a variety of reasons the carrier or other bailee may issue documents covering goods that it did not receive, or misdescribe the goods it did receive. As a result buyers or *financers* of buyers (or of sellers for that matter) may rely on the documents to their detriment. The relevant Code sections are UCC 7–203 & 7–301. Relevant sections of the Federal Bill of Lading Act (49 U.S.C.A.) provide:

§ 100. Loading by carrier; counting packages, etc.; contents of bill

When goods are loaded by a carrier, such carrier shall count the packages of goods if package freight, and ascertain the kind and quantity if bulk freight, and such carrier shall not, in such cases, insert in the bill of lading or in any notice, receipt, contract, rule, regulation, or tariff, "Shipper's weight, load, and count," or other words of like purport, indicating that the goods were loaded by the shipper and the description of them made by him, or in case of bulk freight and freight not concealed by packages the description made by him. If so inserted contrary to the provisions of this section, said words shall be treated as null and void and as if not inserted therein.

§ 101. Loading by shipper; contents of bill; ascertainment of kind and quantity on request

When package freight or bulk freight is loaded by a shipper and the goods are described in a bill of lading merely by a statement of marks or labels upon them or upon packages containing them, or by a statement that the goods are said to be goods of a certain kind or quantity or in a certain condition, or it is stated in the bill of lading that packages are said to contain goods of a certain kind or quantity or in a certain condition, or that the contents or condition of the contents of packages are unknown, or words of like purport are contained in the bill of lading, such statements, if true, shall not make liable the carrier issuing the bill of lading, although the goods are not of the kind or quantity or in the condition which the marks or labels upon them indicate, or of the kind or quantity or in the condition they were said to be by the consignor. The carrier may also by inserting in the bill of lading the words "Shipper's weight, load, and count," or other words of like purport, indicate that the goods were loaded by the shipper and the description of them made by him; and if such statement be true, the carrier shall not be liable for damages caused by the improper loading or by the nonreceipt or by the misdescription of the goods described in the bill of lading: *Provided, however,* Where the shipper of bulk freight installs and maintains adequate facilities for weighing such freight, and the same are available to the carrier, then the carrier, upon written request of such shipper and when given a reasonable opportunity so to do, shall ascertain the kind and quantity of bulk freight within a reasonable time after such written request, and the carriers shall not in such cases insert in the bill of lading the words "Shipper's weight," or other words of like purport, and if so inserted contrary to the provisions of this section, said words shall be treated as null and void and as if not inserted therein.

§ 102. Liability for nonreceipt or misdescription of goods

If a bill of lading has been issued by a carrier or on his behalf by an agent or employee the scope of whose actual or apparent authority includes the receiving of goods and issuing bills of lading therefor for transportation in commerce among the several States and with foreign nations, the carrier shall be liable to (a) the owner of goods covered by a straight bill subject to existing right of stoppage in transitu or (b) the holder of an order bill, who has given value in good faith, relying upon the description therein of the goods, or upon the shipment being made upon the date therein shown, for damages caused by the nonreceipt by the carrier of all or part of the goods upon or prior to the date therein shown, or their failure to correspond with the description thereof in the bill at the time of its issue.

G.A.C. COMMERCIAL CORP. v. WILSON

United States District Court, Southern District of New York, 1967.
271 F.Supp. 242.

BRYAN, DISTRICT JUDGE.

Plaintiff G.A.C. Commercial Corporation (G.A.C.), a Delaware corporation, brings this action sounding in fraud against the five individual defendants and in negligence against a New York corporation, Norwood & St. Lawrence Railroad Co. (Norwood), a rail carrier in interstate commerce. Defendant Norwood now moves, pursuant to Rule 12(c), F.R.Civ.P., for judgment on the pleadings dismissing the fourth count of the complaint. Since matters outside the pleadings have been presented and considered the motion will be treated as one for summary judgment under Rule 56, F.R.Civ.P.

The gravamen of the action is spelled out in the first three counts of the complaint, laid solely against the individual defendants. It is alleged that on October 17, 1963, plaintiff G.A.C. entered into an accounts receivable financing agreement with St. Lawrence Pulp & Paper Corp. (St. Lawrence), a New York corporation. Under the terms of the agreement G.A.C. was to make advances to St. Lawrence, which agreed to "pledge, assign and transfer to G.A.C. all the [b]orrower's right, title and interest in and to accounts receivable * * * then owing" to St. Lawrence.

Pursuant to the agreement St. Lawrence forwarded copies of its invoices together with copies of bills of lading to G.A.C., which, upon receipt, advanced the monies to St. Lawrence at the agreed discount. Repayment of the debts due was guaranteed in writing by the defendant Wilson who was a corporate officer of St. Lawrence. G.A.C. ultimately advanced $356,883.57 under the financing agreement, no part of which has been repaid. St. Lawrence is now a bankrupt.

The first claim for relief seeks recovery of the entire amount from the individual guarantor Wilson. The second claim alleges that certain of the accounts receivable forwarded to plaintiff were false and fraudulent, and that in reliance upon these accounts G.A.C. advanced the sum of $254,173.42 which has not been repaid. The individual defendants, who, with the exception of Lalvani, are described as officers and/or directors of St. Lawrence, are charged with knowledge that these accounts were false and fraudulent. The third claim simply adds a conspiracy allegation against the individual defendants describing a scheme to "defraud and deceive the plaintiff" by forwarding false and fraudulent accounts receivable.

This motion is addressed to the fourth claim for relief laid solely against Norwood. That claim alleges that the fraudulent accounts receivable described were "upon the form of bill of lading" of defendant Norwood "and were countersigned by its agent." Norwood is charged with negligence in failing to require any inspection of the quantity of goods shipped before verifying the bills of lading and in permitting a situation to occur in which the fraudulent and nonexistent accounts could be forwarded to G.A.C.

Norwood's answer alleges failure to state a claim on which relief can be granted and contributory negligence. By way of separate defense it denies any knowledge or information as to the falsity of the bills of lading or with respect to the financing agreement between St. Lawrence and G.A.C. The answer also alleges that the bills of lading involved are "uniform straight bill[s] of lading—not negotiable," as in fact they are, under Section 2 of the Federal Bills of Lading Act. 49 U.S.C.A. § 82.

The controversy here concerns 62 invoices and accompanying straight bills of lading forwarded to G.A.C. by St. Lawrence during 1964. Sixty of these bills concern interstate shipments of paper from St. Lawrence in Norfolk, New York, to Mohegan Converters in Hillside, New Jersey, and involve advances of $245,811.19. Each of the sixty interstate bills was on Norwood's bill of lading, and it is conceded for purposes of this motion, though denied in the answer, that the bills were signed by one of Norwood's agents.

The other two bills involve advances of $8,362.23 on two intrastate shipments from St. Lawrence to Norwood Converting, Inc. in Norfolk, New York, and to Board of Education Depository, Long Island City, New York, respectively. The bills of lading on these shipments were not on Norwood forms and were not signed by Norwood's agents. In fact there is no evidence that Norwood issued these bills or had anything to do with them.

The method by which the alleged fraudulent scheme was carried out appears for purposes of this motion to be as follows: the bankrupt St. Lawrence, as part of its facilities in Norfolk, New York, maintained a railroad siding connected with the lines of defendant carrier which had a freight office approximately ⅛th of a mile from the siding. St. Lawrence was permitted to load freight at its spur track in preparation for shipments on defendant's line. The railroad cars were sealed by St. Lawrence with seals provided by the railroad. St. Lawrence also prepared the bills of lading on blanks furnished in quadruplicate by defendant Norwood. The bills thus prepared were then presented to Norwood's agent who signed the original and one copy without inspecting the contents of the cars. No notation such as "contents of packages unknown" or "shipper's weight, load and count" was written on the bills. The signed copies were returned to St. Lawrence and forwarded with the invoices to G.A.C. which made advances on the goods described, which, as it turned out, had not been shipped.

Since sixty of the bills of lading were issued by a common carrier for the transportation of goods in interstate commerce, the issues as to these bills are controlled by the provisions of the Federal Bills of Lading Act. 49 U.S.C.A. § 81. This statute stands as "a clear expression of the determination of Congress to take the whole subject matter of such bills of lading within its control." 2 Williston, Sales § 406a, at 535 (rev. ed. 1948); see Adams Express Co. v. Croninger, 226 U.S. 491, 33 S.Ct. 148, 57 L.Ed. 314 (1913). As such, it squarely bars the fourth claim asserted against defendant Norwood on the sixty bills representing interstate shipments.

Prior to the passage of the Federal Bills of Lading Act "the United States courts held that a carrier was not liable for the act of its agent in issuing a bill of lading for goods where no goods had in fact been received." Josephy v. Panhandle & S.F. Ry., 235 N.Y. 306, 310, 139 N.E. 277, 278 (1923);

see, e.g., Clark v. Clyde S.S. Co., 148 F. 243 (S.D.N.Y.1906). The liability of carriers for acts of their agents was expanded, but not drastically, by the passage of the federal legislation which draws a sharp distinction between order bills of lading and straight bills where in fact the goods are never received for shipment by the carrier. Under § 22 of the Act, 49 U.S.C. § 102, "[i]f a bill of lading has been issued by a carrier or on his behalf by an agent or employee * * *, the carrier shall be liable to * * * the holder of an order bill, who has given value in good faith, relying upon the description therein of the goods, * * * for damages caused by the nonreceipt by the carrier of all or part of the goods upon or prior to the date therein shown." However, the liability of the carrier for nonreceipt extends only to "the owner of goods covered by a straight bill,"[1] provided, of course, he also gives value in good faith in reliance upon the description of goods contained in the bill. See Strohmeyer & Arpe Co. v. American Line S.S. Corp., 97 F.2d 360, 362 (2d Cir.1938).

It is clear that a party in the position of Norwood is not included within the narrow category of those liable on a straight bill under the federal legislation. In the first place there is no question that the straight bills of lading here involved are nonnegotiable. * * * As a consequence plaintiff G.A.C., as apparent transferee of these bills and invoices representing accounts receivable under the agreement with St. Lawrence, upon notification to the carrier of the transfer,[2] could only "become the direct obligee of whatever obligations the carrier owed to the transferor of the bill immediately before the notification." 49 U.S.C.A. § 112; see id. § 109. Norwood obviously owed St. Lawrence nothing because no goods in fact were received. There was therefore no outstanding obligation to G.A.C. * * *

By no stretch of the imagination does G.A.C. qualify as an "owner of goods covered by a straight bill" who can sue the carrier under § 22 of the Federal Bills of Lading Act, 49 U.S.C.A. § 102, for representing that goods in fact had been received. The reason for this is that it is completely illusory to attempt to assign an "owner" to non-existent goods. R. Braucher, Documents of Title 23 (1958); 2 S. Williston, Sales § 419a, at 576–77 (rev. ed. 1948). While the consignee is generally deemed to have title to goods shipped under a straight bill of lading, see George F. Hinrichs, Inc. v. Standard Trust & Sav. Bank, 279 F. 382, 386 (2d Cir.1922), even he cannot sue the carrier for representing in a straight bill that non-existent goods had in fact been received. Martin Jessee Motors v. Reading Co., 87 F.Supp. 318 (E.D.Pa.), aff'd, 181 F.2d 766 (3d Cir.1950). The rationale applied in Martin

1. Section 22 of the Act, 49 U.S.C. § 102, in its complete form, reads as follows:

§ 102. Liability for nonreceipt or misdescription of goods

"If a bill of lading has been issued by a carrier or on his behalf by an agent or employee the scope of whose actual or apparent authority includes the receiving of goods and issuing bills of lading therefor for transportation in commerce among the several States and with foreign nations, the carrier shall be liable to (a) the owner of goods covered by a straight bill subject to existing right of stoppage in transitu or (b) the holder of an order bill, who has given value in good faith, relying upon the description therein of the goods, or upon the shipment being made upon the date therein shown, for damages caused by the nonreceipt by the carrier of all or part of the goods upon or prior to the date therein shown, or their failure to correspond with the description thereof in the bill at the time of its issue."

2. The defendant Norwood apparently first received notice from G.A.C. by letter dated February 16, 1965. See Def.Ex.B.

Jessee Motors—that the consignee can prevail against the carrier "only by proving its title to specific property," 181 F.2d at 767—applies a fortiori to bar the claim of G.A.C. Plaintiff's interest in the "aggregate face value of the accounts receivable pledged as security" [3] under no conceivable reading of the statute can be deemed an "[ownership] of goods covered by a straight bill." G.A.C. is not one of the favored few who can recover under the Federal Bills of Lading Act. * * *

Plaintiff G.A.C. fares no better with respect to the two bills of lading representing intrastate shipments in New York. Of decisive importance, of course, are the facts that these shipments were not on Norwood forms and were not signed by Norwood's agents. Even if they were, the carrier would escape liability. Although the awkward term "owner" in 49 U.S.C.A. § 102 has been replaced by the word "consignee" in the Uniform Commercial Code § 7–301 and the Uniform Bills of Lading Act § 23, each of which would govern the issues of liability on one of the bills of lading representing an intrastate shipment,[4] the change is immaterial for purposes of this case. Plaintiff, perhaps an assignee, transferee or pledgee of the non-negotiable bills, though it claims not to be, is certainly not a "consignee," which is the only party protected. 2 Anderson, Uniform Commercial Code 261 n. 9 (1961); see R. Braucher, Documents of Title 23–24 (1958). Contrast U.C.C. § 7–203. Thus, as with the sixty interstate bills, G.A.C. cannot successfully sue on the two intrastate bills.

G.A.C. cannot avoid the results dictated by the statute by casting its claim for relief in terms of common law negligence. G.A.C. was sent sixty straight interstate bills of lading by St. Lawrence. The alleged negligence consists of Norwood's permitting a situation to develop in which St. Lawrence could make untrue representations that goods had in fact been shipped under the straight bills. G.A.C. claims that it relied to its detriment upon certain statements contained in the bills. The action is based on the bills not on Norwood's negligence. * * * A holding to the contrary would permit any party to circumvent the restrictions of the Federal Bills of Lading Act through the insertion of a talismanic characterization of its claim as one for "negligence." It is quite plain, however, that the declaration in 49 U.S.C.A. § 81—"bills of lading issued by any common carrier for the transportation of goods" between the states "shall be governed by this chapter"—must be taken to preclude alternative and supplementary liability under state law. * * * The substance of the rule cannot be avoided by the form of the complaint.

* * *

It is true that the result dictated by the federal legislation may lead to some inequities. A straight bill under the Federal Bills of Lading Act is obviously not a good security risk. Casenote, 63 Harv.L.Rev. 1439, 1440 (1950). The fraud of the shipper by failing to deliver goods to the carrier can result, as it did here, in misleading statements on the bills of lading, which

3. Accounts Receivable Agreement Between St. Lawrence and G.A.C., Oct. 17, 1963, ¶ 3.

4. One of the bills is dated September 24, 1964; the other is dated September 28, 1964. In New York the Uniform Commercial Code superseded the Uniform Bills of Lading Act on September 27, 1964.

operate to the detriment of banks and other commercial financers making advances on the basis of the bills. See Olivier Straw Goods Corp. v. Osaka Shosen Kaisha, 27 F.2d 129, 134 (2d Cir.1928) (A. Hand, J.). Moreover, the carrier can readily prevent such a situation from arising by inserting "in the bill of lading the words, 'Shipper's weight, load, and count,' or other words of like purport" to "indicate that the goods were loaded by the shipper and the description of them made by him." 49 U.S.C.A. § 101.

But the overriding policy considerations in the Act look the other way on the issue of liability. First, "[t]here is nothing in the statute to indicate that the mere omission of the words 'Shipper's weight, load, and count' in and of itself makes the carrier liable for damages to goods improperly loaded. The omission of the statutory words merely serves to shift upon the carrier the burden of proving that the goods were improperly loaded by the shipper, and that the damage ensued from that cause." Modern Tool Corp. v. Pennsylvania R. Co., 100 F.Supp. 595, 596–597 (D.N.J.1951); see U.C.C. § 7–301(4). According to the allegations the true culprits in this case were the shipper and its agents; there is no reason to saddle defendant Norwood with liability simply because it did not insert the "Shipper's weight, load, and count" language in the bills. In addition, practicality demands loading arrangements such as those here, where the shipper places his goods aboard and seals the railroad car which the carrier has provided. Section 21 of the Act, 49 U.S.C.A. § 101, anticipates that shippers are expected to do much of the counting and loading on their own sidings or spur tracks. The rapid flow of commerce might well be hindered if the carrier in every instance were charged with ascertaining whether in fact there were goods behind every one of its straight bills.

Moreover, denying security value to a straight bill of lading does not work a hardship upon banks and other commercial institutions. G.A.C., as a knowledgeable lender, is fully aware of the risks inherent in straight bills, and could well have required order bills to protect itself. See Chicago & Northwestern Ry. v. Stevens Nat'l Bank, 75 F.2d 398 (8th Cir.1935). It nevertheless chose to rely upon straight bills to lend money to the now bankrupt St. Lawrence at a profitable rate of interest. Wiser now, G.A.C. seeks to shift its loss to Norwood, an undoubtedly solvent defendant. The Federal Bills of Lading Act protects against this type of hindsight by requiring the lender to accept this kind of security subject to the defenses between the carrier and the shipper.

The motion of defendant Norwood for judgment on the pleadings treated as a motion for summary judgment is granted.

It is so ordered.

Notes

Seller delivered 61 bales of an inferior cotton known as "grabbots" to Carrier for shipment to Buyer. Carriers agent, knowing it to be false, issued a negotiable bill of lading to the Seller's order which described the goods as "61 bales of cotton." In the trade, this description meant "merchantable lint cotton," not "grabbots," an inferior grade. As was customary, Seller indorsed the bill of lading to Buyer, drew a draft on buyer for the purchase price, $3,965, and sent the documents through banking channels to the Buyer. Buyer paid the draft before the goods arrived. After delivery, the goods were stored in a warehouse and, later, destroyed by fire. Buyer sued Carrier for the difference between the amount of the draft paid and the value of the "grabbots", some $2,953, on the theory that the Carrier failed to use ordinary care in issuing the bill of lading. *Held,* for Buyer. The goods were misdescribed and Carrier's agent had notice of this and that the buyer might rely in good faith on that description in paying the sight draft. It was negligence for Carrier to issue the bill of lading without an appropriate qualification under these circumstances. Chicago, R.I. & P.R. Co. v. Cleveland, 61 Okl. 64, 160 P. 328 (1916).

SECTION 8. SALE OF GOODS LOCATED IN A WAREHOUSE—AN ADDENDUM

Sellers not uncommonly sell goods already stored in a warehouse. Since goods in a warehouse are not in motion and are not necessarily the subject of an executory sale transaction, the problems of control over goods in the hands of warehousemen are not as severe as those encountered with goods in the hands of the carrier. UCC 7–403(1) tells us that unless the bailee establishes one of the several defenses there described, the warehouseman is obliged to deliver the goods to "a person entitled under the document." A "person entitled" is defined by subsection (4) as follows: "[The] holder in the case of a negotiable document, or the person to whom delivery is to be made by the terms of or pursuant to written instructions under a non-negotiable document." Moreover UCC 7–403(3) instructs "the bailee [to] cancel the document or conspicuously note the partial delivery thereon or be liable to any person to whom the document is duly negotiated."

Thus the holder of a negotiable document and at least the first possessor-bailor on a non-negotiable document control the goods. The upshot of these rules is that the warehouseman with any sense will demand to see a negotiable warehouse receipt and make a notation on it before he will make any delivery under that warehouse receipt. However he will honor delivery orders signed by the person whom he believes to be the owner of a non-negotiable document without demanding the production of that document. One can easily see the potential for fraud if the owner of a non-negotiable warehouse receipt transfers it to one party and thereafter issues a delivery order to a second party. Presumably each of these acts constitutes "written instructions under a non-negotiable document." In this connection consider the following problem:

Problem 17–5

Repeunzel has 10,000 cans of beans. He puts them in a warehouse and receives a non-negotiable warehouse receipt. On December 1 he transfers his interest in the non-negotiable warehouse receipt together with possession of that receipt to Cicero. On December 3 he signs a non-negotiable delivery order instructing the warehouseman to deliver all of the beans to Leroy. On December 5 Leroy presents his delivery order and takes the beans. On December 10 Cicero comes to you for advice about his rights against the warehouseman. What are his rights? You may assume that everyone except for Repeunzel gave value and acted in good faith. See UCC 7–403, 7–503, 7–504, 7–402, 7–404.

PART FIVE

THE RECEIPT–INSPECTION STAGE

CHAPTER EIGHTEEN

THE BUYER'S RIGHTS TO INSPECT, TO REJECT, OR TO REVOKE ACCEPTANCE OF THE GOODS

SECTION 1. IMPORTANCE TO BUYER OF DISCOVERING NON-CONFORMITY PRIOR TO ACCEPTANCE OR PAYMENT

It is at the "receipt-inspection" stage that the buyer typically has his first opportunity to determine whether the seller's performance conforms to the contract. The seller's failure to perform may take a variety of forms, including breach of delivery obligations (UCC 2–301, 2–307, 2–308, 2–507(1), 2–503, 2–504 & 2–505), failure to perform on time (UCC 2–309), delivery of less than the contract quantity, and, perhaps most important in the usual transaction, non-compliance with contract requirements as to quality of goods sold (UCC 2–313, 314 & 315). Many non-conformities will be readily discoverable ("patent"); others will be harder to discover ("latent"). For non-conformity discovered at the receipt-inspection stage, the buyer *may*, depending upon the circumstances, have a choice between (1) such "goods-oriented" remedies as "rejection" (UCC 2–601) and revocation of acceptance (UCC 2–608), and (2) "damages-oriented" remedies (UCC 2–713 and 2–714). And the buyer may be able, in the circumstances, to combine these remedies, e.g., throw the goods back at the seller and also seek damages. See UCC 2–711(1).

Why might it be important for the buyer to discover non-conformity and reject the goods prior to accepting or paying for them? We will consider sales on credit first, for they are more usual. Although such a buyer need not worry about being out the price before he finds a defect, he may wish to avoid costly unloading and storage of bulky goods. And he should be concerned to identify any non-conformity at least in advance of "acceptance" (UCC 2–606). Absent this, acceptance imposes a duty on the buyer to pay, UCC 2–607(1), and buyers do not want to pay for significantly non-conforming goods. Moreover, acceptance precludes *rejection* of the goods. UCC 2–607(2) and 2–601. But it is true that this does necessarily mean the buyer will be unable rightfully to throw the goods back at the seller. Even after acceptance, should the non-conformity then be discovered, the buyer may be able to revoke his acceptance under UCC 2–608. But we will see that it is harder to throw goods back at a seller under UCC 2–608 than it is under

UCC 2–601. Finally, the burden of establishing breach with regard to accepted goods is on the buyer. UCC 2–607(4). Thus it remains true that so far as goods-oriented remedies are concerned the buyer will be best off if he discovers non-conformity prior to acceptance and rejects. But if the buyer either discovers a defect and rejects or later revokes acceptance, the buyer will in both instances escape the bargain (which may in itself be highly advantageous), and also shift any resulting loss due to depreciation back on the seller.

SECTION 2. BUYER'S RIGHT TO "INSPECT" BEFORE ACCEPTANCE OR PAYMENT—GENERAL RULES AND EXCEPTIONS

The general rule is that the buyer has a right to inspect the goods before payment or acceptance, and this is true even in deals in which the seller discharges his delivery obligations at the point of shipment, e.g. "F.O.B. point of origin." UCC 2–513 and 2–310. Note, too, that this rule applies to cash on the barrelhead deals.

What of exceptions? First of all, the buyer can, of course, by contract, agree in so many words to give up the right to inspect prior to acceptance or payment. Second (and this frequently confuses students) the buyer can give up the right of prior inspection before payment by agreeing to a *mode* of payment inconsistent with such a right. For examples see UCC 2–513(3)(a) and (b). For exceptions to this exception, see the "except" clause in UCC 2–513(3)(b) and 2–512(1)(a). Note, too, that payment in a deal calling for payment before inspection does not constitute acceptance. UCC 2–512(2).

A. The General Right to Inspect

Although the right to inspect has important practical consequences, there are few cases interpreting UCC 2–513. For a rare example, see HCI Chemicals (USA), Inc. v. Henkel KGaA, 966 F.2d 1018 (5th Cir.1992), holding that the place for inspection specified in UCC 2–513(1) was not displaced by agreement. See also, D.C. Leathers, Inc. v. Gelmart Indus., Inc., 125 A.D.2d 738, 509 N.Y.S.2d 161 (1986) (trade usage and prior course of dealing help determine reasonable place for inspection).

Analytically, one should ask and answer at least four questions under UCC 2–513: (1) Does Buyer have a right to inspect at all (in most cases the answer is yes) and, if so, is the right exercisable before or after payment and acceptance (in most cases the answer is before); (2) Where is the place and time of inspection, see UCC 2–513(1); (3) What is the proper method of inspection; and (4) How are the expenses of inspection allocated between the parties?

Problem 18–1

Suppose that student A, who was on the law review and actually attended class, agreed to sell his notes from the course on Commercial Transactions to student B for $100. The agreement was made on January 20 and A was to deliver the notes on February 1 at the law school. On February 1, A and B met to complete the exchange. A had placed the notes in a green canvas bag. Displaying the bag, A said to B: "Here are the notes. May I please have the $100." B refused to pay until he had a chance to inspect the contents of the bag.

A refused either to untie the string around or relinquish possession of the bag. When the impasse could not be broken, A stated to B that the "deal was off." Later that afternoon A sold the notes to student C for $150. What is the legal position of A and B under the UCC?

Do you agree with the following analysis?

The basic question is whether B had a duty to accept and pay for the notes at the time when A cancelled the contract. UCC 2–301. At first blush, this seems to turn on whether A has tendered delivery of the goods. If tender has been made, A is entitled to "acceptance of the goods and to payment according to the contract" under UCC 2–507(1) and a tender of payment by B is a condition to A's "duty to tender and complete any delivery." UCC 2–511(1). If the contract requires A to tender delivery at a particular place, i.e., the law school, the tender must meet the standards of UCC 2–503(1). Has it done so here? The answer is that no matter how closely A's conduct matches the language of UCC 2–503(1), B's duty to tender payment or be in breach of the contract has not yet arisen. On the facts of this case, B "has a right before payment or acceptance to inspect" the goods. UCC 2–513(1). By refusing to grant this "right," A has "impaired" his tender of delivery. UCC 2–503, comment 2. Cf. UCC 2–311(3). At the very least, B is excused from any contractual duty to pay the price. See Consolidated Boiler Corp. v. Bogue Electric Co., 141 N.J. Equity 550, 561–64, 58 A.2d 759, 766–68 (1948). In addition, A's unjustified cancellation is a repudiation which entitles B to the appropriate remedies specified in UCC 2–711.

B. *Inspection in Documentary Deals*

Documentary sales were studied in Chapter Seventeen. Here we *focus* on their possible impact on the buyer's inspection rights.

Problem 18–2

Maple Woods, Inc., a manufacturer, agreed to sell 10 dining room sets to Rosen's Furniture, a retail business located 1,000 miles away in the city of Baker.

(1) If the contract said nothing of mode of payment or inspection, but Maple Woods, worried about Rosen's credit, shipped the goods "under reservation" by procuring a non-negotiable bill of lading naming itself as consignee, UCC 2–505(1)(b), would this be a breach of contract? Would it "alter" Rosen's right to inspect? UCC 2–310(b) and 2–513(1) and (3). What if Maple Woods shipped C.O.D.? Would the carrier allow inspection before payment? Are there two contracts here: one between Maple Woods and the carrier, and one between Maple Woods and Rosen's?

(2) If the contract called for Rosen's to pay against a sight draft with bill of lading (negotiable) attached, would Rosen's be entitled to inspect before payment? Would it make any difference that the goods happened to arrive in Baker ahead of the documents? UCC 2–513 and Comment 5.

(3) If the documents were in due form but the goods had been destroyed by fire while in the carrier's possession and Rosen's knew this, could it dishonor the sight draft without breaching the contract?

In Chapter Seventeen we saw that the seller realizes several advantages via use of the "sight draft with negotiable bill of lading" technique. Can he retain any of these and still allow inspection before payment? Buyers can bargain to have seller stamp the bill of lading, even a negotiable one "inspection allowed."

Here the carrier would still retain control on behalf of the shipper-seller. Another way the buyer might try to protect himself is via so-called "third-party inspection", which is the subject of the next case.

BARTLETT & CO., GRAIN v. MERCHANTS CO.

United States Court of Appeals, Fifth Circuit, 1963.
323 F.2d 501, 7 A.L.R.3d 541.

WISDOM, CIRCUIT JUDGE.

This action is for breach of contract. The subject of the contract is a barge load of corn which, according to official inspection certificates, was one grade when shipped and two very different grades when it reached its destination. As we see it, the case turns on the construction of a contract which contains two apparently inconsistent provisions. The overall issue is whether the loss should fall on the purchaser or the seller. The district court decided in favor of the buyer. We reverse and remand.

The Merchants Company, and buyer and appellee, is a Mississippi corporation. As the Vicksburg Terminal Division, it is in the business of buying and selling grains. As the Valley Mills Division it manufactures feeds. Bartlett and Company, the seller and appellant, is a Missouri Corporation which maintains grain storage facilities in six mid-western states, including terminal elevators on the Missouri River at Nebraska City, Nebraska. Its general offices are in Kansas City, Missouri.

Merchants contracted through a broker to purchase from Bartlett four barge loads of No. 2 yellow corn. The terms and conditions of sale are found in three documents: (1) a confirmation order from Bartlett to Valley Mills (Merchants); (2) a confirmation order from the broker to both parties; and (3) a confirmation of purchase from Valley Mills (Merchants), signed "accepted" by B.O. Cottier, Bartlett's official secretary in charge of merchandising. The contract called for four barges of No. 2 yellow corn at 5¼ cents under the Chicago July option, F.O.B. the buyer's barges, "*If seller elects to load at Nebraska City 'In Barge' Official Weights & Grades to Govern.*" Merchant's confirmation order, accepted by Bartlett's representative, contained the following clause: "Mark bills of lading 'inspection allowed'. If draft is paid at sight, *we do not waive our right to reject shipment in event quality proves to be below contract grade.*"

Bartlett loaded four double-skin barges, furnished by the buyer, at Nebraska City, Nebraska, on June 19, 1959. The grain in only one of these barges, ABL–2519, is involved in this dispute. That barge was examined at Nebraska City by a federally licensed grain inspector, who, on the date the loading was completed, certified that the barge contained No. 2 yellow corn. Meanwhile, since Merchants had sold four barges of No. 2 yellow corn to O.J. Walls in Guntersville, Alabama, Merchants routed the barges to Guntersville and applied the grain in barge ABL–2519 on the Walls contract. While the barge was in transit from Nebraska City to Guntersville, Merchants paid Bartlett for the grain by draft with the bill of lading attached.

The grain arrived in Guntersville on July 7, Walls first discovered it to be partly "overheating and musty" on July 13. He refused to accept it, since it was below contract grade, and he called for a federal appeal grade inspection. At this inspection, on July 16, 1959, it was certified that approximately 17,000 bushels of the corn in barge ABL–2519 were No. 1 yellow corn and approximately 15,000 bushels were sample grade yellow corn. Walls agreed to handle the barge for Merchants's account and accordingly unloaded, trucked, dried, turned, stored, and again trucked the grain. For these services he charged $7,164.61 and deducted that amount from Merchants's invoice. Both parties to this action agree that these charges were excessive, but Merchants contends that no one else was available to perform the services.

Merchants then sued Bartlett, seeking $7,164.61 for breach of contract and $5,000 in punitive damages. The suit was originally brought in a Mississippi state court as an attachment in chancery (a quasi-in rem action) by attaching Bartlett's deposits in a Mississippi bank. The suit was removed to the United States District Court for the Southern District of Mississippi where it was tried before the court without a jury. The district court found that the grain inspection certificate of June 19, 1959, at Nebraska City "was erroneous and inaccurate"; that it was "not fair * * * and failed to reveal the true condition in this barge on the date of shipment."

The district court found that an inescapable inference from the evidence * * * [is] that barge was loaded in Nebraska City with an excessive amount of molded wheat which contaminated the cargo and accounted for the unsalable condition at Guntersville." The court held that Merchants was not bound by the certificate's recitals, because of the clause in Merchants's purchase confirmation, accepted by Bartlett, giving the buyer the right to reject shipment in the event that the quality proved to be below contract grade. The court awarded damages in the amount of $6,500 with six per cent interest from July 3, 1959, against the funds in the hands of the resident bank. The suit was dismissed as to Bartlett personally for lack of in personam jurisdiction. The court declined to award punitive damages, since the court found no evidence of gross negligence, willfulness, or oppressiveness on the part of the seller.

On appeal, Bartlett makes two major contentions. First, Bartlett contends that there is no evidence the grain in barge ABL–2519 was other than No. 2 yellow corn when it left Nebraska City in the buyer's barge. Second, the official grade certificate at origin should have been conclusive under the terms of the sale agreement, in the absence of gross neglect or willful wrongdoing.

[The Court determined that the law of Missouri governed.]

* * *

I. The Buyer's Right to Inspect

A buyer dealing with a distant vendor and purchasing goods of a specified quality without first seeing them has a right to inspect them upon receipt. * * * And, in the absence of any contractual provision to the contrary, the buyer may reject an F.O.B. shipment at destination. * * * But the parties may agree instead to abide by the judgment of another, and that judgment, if honestly exercised, is binding on the buyer. * * * The buyer cannot thereafter substitute his own inspection for that conducted by the third party.

* * *

Such an inspection is held to have a conclusive effect even if there is no express provision in the contract that it shall be final. * * *

The contract in question here provides that " 'in barge' official weights & grades" are to govern—if the shipment is made from Nebraska City. But—if the shipment is made from Omaha, although "official in 'in barge' grades" still govern, "*destination official weights*" are to govern. Thus, the contract is drawn to distinguish between an inspection where the grain is loaded and an inspection at its destination. An inspection at the destination is to determine the *weight,* if the grain is loaded at Omaha. That is the only circumstance in which a destination inspection is to control. The terms of the contract therefore required that the transaction be governed by the origin *grades and weights,* since the grain was shipped from Nebraska City.

As we noted, where an inspection by a third party is stipulated, it supersedes the buyer's right to inspect. Merchants, however, seeks to avoid this result by urging that the clause in its printed form contract, which was accepted by Bartlett's agent, gave it the right to inspect at destination and to reject the shipment if the *quality* proved to be below the specified grade at the destination. This interpretation of the contract would nullify the provision for inspection at origin. The obvious purpose of that inspection at origin was to establish a certain, reliable, and objective standard at a fixed place and time to give the transaction certainty. It would serve little use to have this inspection if the buyer were free to accept or reject the shipment after its arrival on the basis of its own inspection at destination. To the extent then that the *printed* clause in the contract may be interpreted to allow Merchants the right, for which it contends, to reject on the basis of its own destination inspection, it is inconsistent with the *typewritten* clause providing for one official inspection at origin. In such case the typed portions prevail. * * *

The contract before us, however, may be construed so as to reconcile the two clauses and thus satisfy the very sensible canon of construction requiring that effect be given to all terms of the contract. The typed clause provides that official grades are to govern, whereas the printed clause, upon which Merchants relies, reserves to it the "right to reject shipment *in event* quality proves to be below contract grade." (Emphasis supplied.) This gives Merchants the right to reject, *if* the quality does not satisfy the contractual requirements; it does not give Merchants the right to determine *whether* the quality measures up to the standard specified. Thus Merchants could reject the grain, if the grade given it by the Nebraska City inspector proved to be lower than that specified in the contract, but the reservation clause does not give it the power to ascertain the grade independently of the origin inspection. Furthermore, this reserved right to reject is expressly conditioned on the draft being paid at sight. Since it is possible that the draft would be paid before receipt of the inspection certificate, this is a reasonable provision. It simply avoids any question that payment of the sight draft might be deemed a waiver of the right to reject the shipment. See Ryder & Brown Co. v. E. Lissberger Co., 1938, 300 Mass. 438, 15 N.E.2d 441, 118 A.L.R. 521, 525–

526, in which the court assumed that the right to reject is lost when the title passes to the buyer on payment of a sight draft.

The testimony of Merchants's agent shows that in the customary dealings in the trade lower prices are fixed on condition that there is no right to reject on the basis of a destination inspection when the grain is inspected at origin. Mr. Harriss, Merchants's manager, agreed that Mr. Walls, who received the shipment in Alabama and bought on the same terms as Merchants, had no right to inspect the shipment at Guntersville. Moreover, the broker testified that his confirmation order showed the entire arrangement between the two parties; that it contained no right to reject. We hold, therefore, that Merchants did not have any right to reject the shipment destination on the basis of inspection at destination.

* * *

[The Court reversed the Judgment of the district court and remanded the case for the trial court to ascertain whether there existed fraud, bad faith, or gross mistake amounting to fraud which would warrant setting the inspection certificate aside.]

Notes

1. Considering the legal effect of third-party inspection, what commercial interests of either seller or buyer are protected by establishing such procedures and insuring their finality? Is UCC 2–515 relevant to this problem? Note that in *Bartlett* the parties agreed in advance to allow a third-party inspection and certification with finality. This agreed procedure resembles arbitration, see Comment 3, par. 3, except that the certification is made before a dispute arises and without a hearing. Such an agreement was invalidated in one of the few remaining states that refuse to enforce agreements to arbitrate future disputes. See Warren v. Jim Skinner Ford, Inc., 565 So.2d 210 (Ala.1990). In other states and under the Federal Arbitration Act, 9 U.S.C.A. § 2, such an agreement is clearly enforceable.

2. If the buyer has paid before inspecting the goods and, after discovering a non-conformity when the goods arrive, brings suit to recover the price and damages for breach of warranty, who has the burden of proving the condition of the goods at the time loaded on the barges, the buyer-plaintiff or the seller-defendant? Suppose the goods have been totally destroyed in transit without the fault of the buyer, who thereafter claims that they did not conform at the time of tender by the seller. Under the UCC, the critical time is at "tender of delivery." UCC 2–725(2), 2–503(2), 2–504, 2–509(1), and UCC 2–510(1). While UCC 2–607(4) provides that the "burden is on the buyer to establish any breach with respect to the goods accepted," there is no specific allocation for other situations. Under the Uniform Sales Act, the principal antecedent of Article Two, the burden was placed upon the party seeking affirmative relief here, the buyer. Glanzer v. J.K. Armsby Co., 100 Misc. 476, 165 N.Y.S. 1006 (S.Ct.1917). This result has been criticized in cases where the goods have been lost in transit: "In the situation where the goods are completely destroyed while in transit, the seller alone will know the facts about conformity. Where the seller delivers the goods which do not conform to the contract and the buyer has not impliedly approved them by acceptance, the seller by virtue of experience in fulfilling the terms of the contract will be better able to sustain the burden of proof in an action for non-delivery. But where the buyer has refused to accept the goods and has sold them

justifiably on behalf of the seller, the facts on conformity are then peculiarly within the knowledge of the buyer." Note, 20 U.Chi.L.Rev. 125, 130 (1952). Do you agree? Should the concern over proper burden of proof allocation be influenced by the feasibility and availability of third-party inspection at the point of shipment as with many agricultural commodities? See S–Creek Ranch, Inc. v. Monier & Co., 509 P.2d 777 (Wyo.1973) (buyer must prove goods defective at time risk of loss was to pass).

C. Inspection in Overseas Transactions

This chapter has focused upon the relationship between the buyer's "right" of inspection and his "duty" to accept the goods and pay the contract price. In non-credit domestic transactions under the UCC where a shipment is under an f.o.b. term, the buyer has no right to inspect before payment unless otherwise agreed where the contract calls for payment against documents of title. UCC 2–513(3). The reverse is true in overseas sales where greater shipping distances delay even more the seller's ability to receive payment. Accordingly, the usual practice, reflected in the cases and the Revised American Foreign Trade Definitions of 1941, is that unless otherwise agreed the buyer must pay against documents of title even though the goods are still in the middle of the ocean. See E. Clemens Horst Co. v. Biddel Bros., (1912) A.C. 18. While the buyer must wait until the goods arrive to inspect, he can discount the documents of title or use them as collateral to obtain a loan if the delay puts him under a financial strain. This approach is reflected in the UCC when shipment, whether domestic or overseas, is on a C.I.F. or C & F basis. The UCC seems to rely upon use of the shipping term C.I.F. or C & F to establish the seller's right to payment and does not clearly state whether the usual practice would apply in an overseas sale under a different shipping term. See UCC 2–320(4) and 2–321(3). The Final Act of the United Nations Conference on Contracts for the International Sale of Goods, approved in Vienna in 1980, provides that the buyer is "not bound to pay the price until he has had an opportunity to examine the goods, unless procedures for delivery or payment agreed upon by the parties are inconsistent with his having such an opportunity." Article 58(3). But Article 58(2) states that if the contract involves "carriage of the goods, the seller may dispatch the goods on terms whereby the goods, or documents controlling their disposition, will not be handed over to the buyer except against payment of the price." These and other issues are well treated in J. Honnold, Uniform Law for International Sales, Chapter III, § 1 (2d ed. 1990). The United States Senate ratified the United Nations Convention on Contracts for the International Sale of Goods on December 11, 1986. The treaty became effective on January 1, 1988.

A common practice in international sales, however, is for the seller to obtain payment contemporaneously with shipment of the goods. This is accomplished through a letter of credit. In essence, the buyer (customer) obtains from a bank (issuer) a promise for the benefit of the seller (beneficiary) that it will honor a draft drawn on it upon presentation of required documents and compliance with other terms in the letter of credit, which has been sent to the seller. See UCC 5–102(1)(a) and 5–103(1). This is a "documentary" credit which is normally irrevocable. See UCC 5–106(2). Thus, the issuing bank on behalf of the buyer agrees to pay the price against documents presented by the seller shortly after those documents have been issued by the carrier, and usually at the place where the goods have been shipped. While this device does not preclude the buyer's right of inspection when the goods arrive, UCC 5–114(1) provides that the issuing bank cannot dishonor the seller's demand which complies with the credit even though the goods or the documents do not conform with the underlying contract for sale. Compare UCC 2–512. An important case testing the scope of inspection in a transaction using a letter of credit is Banco Espanol De Credito v. State Street Bank & Trust Co., 385 F.2d 230 (1st Cir.1967).

SECTION 3. BUYER'S RIGHT TO REJECT THE GOODS

A. Introduction: Rejection Under Pre-Code Law

If a promisor's tendered performance conforms in every way to the contract, the buyer must accept and pay for it or break the contract. UCC 2–507(1). Conversely, if the promisor repudiates the contract or fails to tender any performance at all, the promisee is excused from rendering any return performance and, since the promisor's breach is material, may cancel the contract and pursue appropriate remedies. But suppose that the promisor tenders some but not all of the promised performance and then fails to complete the job. Under what circumstances can the promisee seize upon the defective performance as a ground for avoiding any contractual duty to pay for work actually done?

In construction and personal service contracts where, in the absence of agreement to the contrary, the duty to pay is "constructively" conditioned upon completion of all or part of the work, it is usually said that the constructive condition is satisfied by "substantial" performance. See Patterson, *Constructive Conditions in Contracts,* 42 Colum.L.Rev. 903 (1942). Stated another way, if the promisor's defective performance is not material, the promisee must pay for the work at the contract price, adjusted for any damages caused by the breach. Who can forget Judge Cardozo's "sermon" in the classic case of Jacob & Youngs v. Kent, 230 N.Y. 239, 129 N.E. 889 (1921): "The transgressor whose default is unintentional and trivial may hope for mercy if he will offer atonement for his wrong." Since the promisor has rendered an expensive performance which, in many cases, has conferred benefits upon the promisee and is extremely difficult to return, the substantial performance doctrine blunts the rigors of constructive conditions by limiting the promisee's ability to avoid liability under the contract. According to Restatement, Contracts § 275 (1932) and Restatement (Second) of Contracts § 241, whether the promisee can treat the non-performance as material will depend upon several factors: the extent to which the injured party will obtain the substantial benefits which he could reasonably have anticipated; the extent to which the injured party may be adequately compensated in damages for lack of complete performance; the greater or less hardship on the party failing to perform in terminating the contract; the willful, negligent, or innocent behavior of the party failing to perform, and the greater or less uncertainty that the party failing to perform will perform the remainder of the contract. In short, the question is whether the non-performance substantially impairs the value of the bargain to the promisee. If more than substantial performance is desired, the services of an architect or third party expert can be employed. His refusal to issue a certificate or give approval until the specifications are met expressly conditions the promisee's duty to pay and is final and conclusive unless fraudulent or made in bad faith. See Restatement (Second) of Contracts § 227, Ill. No. 5.

In contracts for the sale of goods, however, pre-code law generally held that the doctrine of "substantial" performance is not applicable. See J.W. Anderson & Co., Inc. v. Tomlinson Chair Mfg. Co., Inc., 206 N.C. 42, 172 S.E. 538 (1934); Note, 33 Colum.L.Rev. 1021 (1933). This position can be justified on the following grounds. When a buyer rejects a defective tender by a seller, he does not retain any of the goods without payment. Even though the seller has invested time and expense in obtaining the goods and preparing the tender, upon rejection he still has the goods and may dispose of them elsewhere. Since the element of unjust enrichment present in construction and various other contracts is absent in such a sale of goods case, it makes some sense to put the responsibility for making a perfect tender upon the seller rather than getting involved in a complicated evaluation of objective and subjective factors which underlie the substantial performance doctrine. At the very least if the seller has in fact made a defective tender and the buyer's dissatisfaction is honest and genuine, there seems to be less reason for invoking the doctrine of substantial performance to limit the power to reject.

This justification was reflected, to a large degree, in the Uniform Sales Act, especially where the seller had breached a warranty of quality, USA §§ 12 & 69(1), or had tendered less than the quantity called for by the contract, USA § 44. See Prescott & Co. v. J.B. Powles & Co., 113 Wash. 177, 193 P. 680 (1920) (general rule is that the delivery of goods under an executory contract must be of the exact quantity ordered). However, more concern for the interests of the seller was expressed where the non-conformity merely involved delay or the manner of shipment or delivery. See 2 Williston, Sales §§ 452a–453e (rev. ed. 1948). Cf. Continental Grain Co. v. Simpson Feed Co., Inc., 102 F.Supp. 354 (E.D.Ark.1951), affirmed, 199 F.2d 284 (8th Cir.1952). This concern was heightened when the delay or defect caused no measurable damage and the facts strongly suggested that the buyer had seized upon the non-conformity as a reason to avoid an unprofitable bargain or to take advantage of a price break. See LeRoy Dyal Co. v. Allen, 161 F.2d 152, 153–56 (4th Cir.1947) (rejection improper under both the common law and the Perishable Agricultural Commodities Act). As a result, there was some criticism of the so-called "perfect tender" rule under pre-Code law. Honnold, *Buyer's Right of Rejection,* 97 U.Pa.L.Rev. 457 (1949). See also, Peters, *Remedies for Breach of Contracts Relating to the Sale of Goods Under the Uniform Commercial Code: A Roadmap for Article Two,* 73 Yale L.J. 199, 206–209 (1963). We will now see that the Code cuts back the perfect tender rule rather dramatically.

B. Scope of Rejection Right Under the Code

Suppose a buyer, in the exercise of his inspection right, discovers some defect in the seller's tender of delivery—a defect in quality or quantity, delay, an improper tender or documents not in due form. Assume further that this defect is relatively insignificant. May the buyer reject the goods, thus avoiding the contract, or must he accept them with an appropriate adjustment in the contract price? As we have seen, this is an important question. If rejection is effective the goods remain at the seller's risk, UCC 2–510(1), and the buyer may pursue appropriate remedies under UCC 2–711 as if no tender had been made. If rejection would be ineffective and acceptance required, title and risk of loss would upon acceptance pass to the buyer who must pay for the goods at the contract rate, subject to any adjustment for the nonconformity. UCC 2–607(1), 2–714, 2–717. If the buyer improperly rejects, the seller may pursue appropriate remedies under UCC 2–703. See UCC 2–301, 2–602(3).

UCC 2–601 provides that unless the breach is of an installment contract or there is agreement to the contrary, "if the goods or the tender of delivery fail in any respect to conform to the contract, the buyer may (a) reject the whole; or (b) accept the whole; or (c) accept any commercial unit or units and reject the rest." Thus the Code in 2–601 appears to adopt a "perfect tender" rule regardless of the nature of the defect or its impact upon the buyer, subject only to agreement, special rules for installment contracts, UCC 2–612(3) and the buyer's option to accept part or all of the goods. See Moulton Cavity & Mold, Inc. v. Lyn-Flex Indus., Inc., 396 A.2d 1024 (Me. 1979) (trial court erred in charge that UCC 2–601 was satisfied by "substantial performance"). And it is true that the Permanent Editorial Board of the UCC declined to follow a recommendation that the buyer's right to reject be limited to cases of material breach. The Board's reasons were that the buyer should not be required to guess at his peril whether a breach is material and that proof of materiality would sometimes require disclosure of the buyer's private affairs, such as trade secrets and processes. Without more, it might seem that the only other limit upon the rejection remedy is the possibility that a buyer will not discover the non-conformity until after acceptance. In that event, the buyer can revoke his acceptance only if the non-conformity of the lot or unit "substantially impairs its value to him." See Wiseman, *The Limits of Vision: Karl Llewellyn and the Merchant Rules,* 100 Harv.L.Rev. 465, 510–521 (1987) (discussing legislative history). UCC 2–608(1). But we will now introduce other important limits.

Problem 18–3
The Case of the Lady Dove Tomatoes

Sodfill, Inc., is a grower of vegetables and Blurtaste Co. is a manufacturer of catsup. On April 1, the parties entered into a written contract for the sale of 1,000 bushels of Lady Dove tomatoes at $4.50 per bushel, to be shipped f.o.b. point of shipment on or before July 15 and delivered to Blurtaste in "green" condition, a term having definite meaning in the trade. The goods were to be delivered in a single lot and payment was to be made 30 days after the goods were received. Nothing was said in the agreement about rejection. Assuming that there is no evidence regarding the impact upon the value of the bargain, could Blurtaste properly reject all of the goods in the following circumstances:

1. a timely tender of 990 bushels of "green" Lady Doves;

2. a timely tender of 1,000 bushels of tomatoes, 10 of which did not contain "green" Lady Doves;

3. a tender of 1,000 bushels of "green" Lady Doves which were shipped on July 16;

4. a tender of 1,000 bushels of "green" Lady Doves which were shipped on July 14 but, because of an erroneous delivery instruction by Sodfill, did not arrive until 3 days after the normal time for shipment had expired (see UCC 2–504 & 2–614).

5. Could Blurtaste accept 500 bushels of good tomatoes and reject 500 bushels of bad without incurring liability for the whole? See UCC 2–601, 2–105(6).

6. Suppose Sodfill agreed to ship 500 bushels by July 15 and the balance by August 1, payment to be made by September 1. Could the buyer reject if the first tender was: 10 bushels short; 1% off on quality; shipped 1 day late? See UCC 2–612.

7. If you represented Sodfill, what sort of clause would you draft to limit or eliminate the buyer's rejection right under UCC 2–601? How could you insure that it became part of the contract?

1. Good Faith as a Limit on the Right to Reject

Suppose in the case of Sodfill v. Blurtaste the seller is able to establish that the real reason for the buyer's rejection is a drop in the market price of tomatoes to $3.00 per bushel. If the buyer assigns as a reason for rejection an insubstantial breach by the seller, has he violated the obligation of good faith imposed by UCC 1–203 on the "performance or enforcement" of "every contract or duty within this Act?" It has been suggested that a buyer will "often try to escape from a performance quite within the business understanding of the contract, though not quite the legal, if he finds either that he can purchase the very same goods at a cheaper price on the open market or that his resale market has all but disappeared." The desire to avoid losses or to make greater profits "overcomes the possible desire to be a 'square-shooter' and to shoulder his part of that risk of price fluctuation which any present contract for future delivery carries, both for the seller and for the buyer." Eno, *Price Movement and Unstated Objections to the Defective Performance of Sales Contracts,* 44 Yale L.J. 782, 801 (1935). According to Judge Learned Hand, in this setting "such words as * * * 'good faith' appear to us to obscure the issue. The promisor may in fact be satisfied with the performance, but not with the bargain, in which case, of course, he must pay. * * *" Thompson-Starrett Co. v. La Belle Iron Works, 17 F.2d 536, 541 (2d Cir.1927). But is the conclusion one which a court should reach under the UCC? If so, does this cut down the Code's "perfect tender" rule in 2–601?

NEUMILLER FARMS, INC. v. CORNETT

Supreme Court of Alabama, 1979.
368 So.2d 272.

SHORES, JUSTICE.

Jonah D. Cornett and Ralph Moore, Sellers, were potato farmers in DeKalb County, Alabama. Neumiller Farms, Inc., Buyer, was a corporation engaged in brokering potatoes from the growers to the makers of potato chips. The controversy concerns Buyer's rejection of nine loads of potatoes out of a contract calling for twelve loads. A jury returned a verdict of $17,500 for Sellers based on a breach of contract. Buyer appealed. We affirm.

From the evidence, the jury could have found the following:

On March 3, 1976, the parties signed a written contract whereby Sellers agreed to deliver twelve loads of chipping potatoes to Buyer during July and August, 1976, and Buyer agreed to pay $4.25 per hundredweight. The contract required that the potatoes be United States Grade No. 1 and "chipt [sic] to buyer satisfaction." As the term was used in this contract, a load of potatoes contains 430 hundredweight and is valued at $1,827.50.

Sellers' potato crop yielded twenty to twenty-four loads of potatoes and Buyer accepted three of these loads without objection. At that time, the market price of chipping potatoes was $4.25 per hundredweight. Shortly thereafter, the market price declined to $2.00 per hundredweight.

When Sellers tendered additional loads of potatoes, Buyer refused acceptance, saying the potatoes would not "chip" satisfactorily. Sellers responded by having samples of their crop tested by an expert from the Cooperative Extension Service of Jackson County, Alabama, who reported that the potatoes were suitable in all respects. After receiving a letter demanding performance of the contract, Buyer agreed to "try one more load." Sellers then tendered a load of potatoes which had been purchased from another grower, Roy Hartline. Although Buyer's agent had recently purchased potatoes from Hartline at $2.00 per hundredweight, he claimed dissatisfaction with potatoes from the same fields when tendered by Sellers at $4.25 per hundredweight. Apparently the jury believed this testimony outweighed statements by Buyer's agents that Sellers' potatoes were diseased and unfit for "chipping."

Subsequently, Sellers offered to purchase the remaining nine loads of potatoes from other growers in order to fulfill their contract. Buyer's agent refused this offer, saying "* * * 'I'm not going to accept any more of your potatoes. If you load any more I'll see that they're turned down.' * * * 'I can buy potatoes all day for $2.00.'" No further efforts were made by Sellers to perform the contract.

At the time of Buyer's final refusal, Sellers had between seventeen and twenty-one loads of potatoes unharvested in their fields. Approximately four loads were sold in Chattanooga, Tennessee; Atlanta, Georgia; and local markets in DeKalb County. Sellers' efforts to sell their potato crop to other buyers were hampered by poor market conditions. Considering all of the evidence, the jury could properly have found that Sellers' efforts to sell the potatoes, after Buyer's final refusal to accept delivery, were reasonable and made in good faith.

This case presents three questions: 1) Was Buyer's refusal to accept delivery of Sellers' potatoes a breach of contract? 2) If so, what was the proper measure of Sellers' damages? and 3) Was the $17,500 jury verdict within the amount recoverable by Sellers under the proper measure of damages?

§ 7–2–703, Code of Alabama 1975 (UCC), specifies an aggrieved seller may recover for a breach of contract "Where the buyer *wrongfully* rejects * * * goods * * *" (Emphasis added.) We must determine whether there was evidence from which the jury could find that the Buyer acted wrongfully in rejecting delivery of Sellers' potatoes.

A buyer may reject delivery of goods if either the goods or the tender of delivery fails to conform to the contract. § 7–2–601, Code of Alabama 1975. In the instant case, Buyer did not claim the tender was inadequate. Rather, Buyer asserted the potatoes failed to conform to the requirements of the contract; i.e., the potatoes would not chip to buyer satisfaction.

The law requires such a claim of dissatisfaction to be made in good faith, rather than in an effort to escape a bad bargain. Shelton v. Shelton, 238 Ala. 489, 192 So. 55 (1939); Jones v. Lanier, 198 Ala. 363, 73 So. 535 (1916); Electric Lighting Co. v. Elder Bros., 115 Ala. 138, 21 So. 983 (1896).

Buyer, in the instant case, is a broker who deals in farm products as part of its occupation and, therefore, is a "merchant" with respect to its dealings in such goods. § 7–2–104, Code of Alabama 1975. In testing the good faith of a merchant, § 7–2–103, Code of Alabama 1975, requires " * * * honesty in fact and the observance of reasonable commercial standards of fair dealing in the trade." A claim of dissatisfaction by a merchant-buyer of fungible goods must be evaluated using an objective standard to determine whether the claim is made in good faith. Because there was evidence that the potatoes would "chip" satisfactorily, the jury was not required to accept Buyer's subjective claim to the contrary. A rejection of goods based on a claim of dissatisfaction, which is not made in good faith, is ineffectual and constitutes a breach of contract for which damages are recoverable.

We next consider the proper measure of damages under the UCC. * * * [The court held that the jury verdict on damages was compatible with UCC 2–708(2) and that the judgment should be affirmed.]

* * *

Questions

1. Did the court need to invoke an obligation of good faith or could the court simply have relied on UCC 2–601 and UCC 2–313? What was the relevant contract language?

2. How does the Code define and delineate obligations of good faith?

3. *The Seller's Right to Cure as a Limit on the Right to Reject and Cancel.* UCC 2–508, in two circumstances, permits the seller to cure a defective tender and thus avoid the buyer's rejection remedy under 2–601. The first circumstance, stated in UCC 2–508(1), is fairly straightforward. If "the time for performance has not yet expired" and the buyer has rejected a non-conforming tender, the seller, "may seasonably notify the buyer of his intention to cure and may then within the contract time make a conforming delivery." Note that if the conditions of UCC 2–508(1) are met, the seller has the right to cure whether the buyer likes it or not. However, the buyer may not compel the seller to cure under any circumstances. If the buyer wants a defect corrected by the seller, his basic recourse is a negotiated agreement. Otherwise, he must reject and cover under UCC 2–712. One scholar has argued that UCC 2–508 should be repealed because it imposes inefficient legal restraints upon post-breach bargaining. Schwartz, *Cure and Revocation for Quality Defects: The Utility of Bargains,* 16 Bost.Coll.Indus. & Com.L.Rev. 543 (1975).

There are some notable variations on this theme. Many manufacturers of complex, expensive goods seek, with the help of retailers, to make a single warranty that the goods are "free from defects in material and workmanship" and to limit the remedy for breach of that warranty to "repair or replacement" of defects. If these efforts are successful, the buyer must permit the seller to cure and may not reject the goods under UCC 2-601 or revoke acceptance under UCC 2-608. See UCC 2-719.

The second circumstance, found in UCC 2-508(2), is undoubtedly explained by the fact that many defective tenders are quite within the business understanding of the contract though not quite the legal. Here, the seller ought to have a chance to cure even though the time for performance has expired. But when does a seller have "reasonable grounds" to believe that his non-conforming tender will be acceptable to the seller?

T.W. OIL, INC. v. CONSOLIDATED EDISON CO. OF NEW YORK, INC.

Court of Appeals of New York, 1982.
57 N.Y.2d 574, 457 N.Y.S.2d 458, 443 N.E.2d 932.

OPINION OF THE COURT

FUCHSBERG, JUDGE.

In the first case to wend its way through our appellate courts on this question, we are asked, in the main, to decide whether a seller who, acting in good faith and without knowledge of any defect, tenders nonconforming goods to a buyer who properly rejects them, may avail itself of the cure provision of subdivision (2) of section 2-508 of the Uniform Commercial Code. We hold that, if seasonable notice be given, such a seller may offer to cure the defect within a reasonable period beyond the time when the contract was to be performed so long as it has acted in good faith and with a reasonable expectation that the original goods would be acceptable to the buyer.

The factual background against which we decide this appeal is based on either undisputed proof or express findings at Trial Term. In January, 1974, midst the fuel shortage produced by the oil embargo, the plaintiff (then known as Joc Oil USA, Inc.) purchased a cargo of fuel oil whose sulfur content was represented to it as no greater than 1%. While the oil was still at sea en route to the United States in the tanker *M T Khamsin*, plaintiff received a certificate from the foreign refinery at which it had been processed informing it that the sulfur content in fact was .52%. Thereafter, on January 24, the plaintiff entered into a written contract with the defendant (Con Ed) for the sale of this oil. The agreement was for delivery to take place between January 24 and January 30, payment being subject to a named independent testing agency's confirmation of quality and quantity. The contract, following a trade custom to round off specifications of sulfur content at, for instance, 1%, .5% or .3%, described that of the *Khamsin* oil as .5%.[1] In the course of the negotiations, the plaintiff learned that Con Ed was then authorized to buy and burn oil with a sulfur content of up to 1% and would even mix oils containing more and less to maintain that figure.

When the vessel arrived, on January 25, its cargo was discharged into Con Ed storage tanks in Bayonne, New Jersey.[2] In due course, the indepen-

1. Confirmatorily, Con Ed's brief describes .92% oil as "nominally" 1% oil.

2. The tanks already contained some other oil, but Con Ed appears to have had no

dent testing people reported a sulfur content of .92%. On this basis, acting within a time frame whose reasonableness is not in question, on February 14 Con Ed rejected the shipment. Prompt negotiations to adjust the price failed; by February 20, plaintiff had offered a price reduction roughly responsive to the difference in sulfur reading, but Con Ed, though it could use the oil, rejected this proposition out of hand. It was insistent on paying no more than the latest prevailing price, which, in the volatile market that then existed, was some 25% below the level which prevailed when it agreed to buy the oil.

The very next day, February 21, plaintiff offered to cure the defect with a substitute shipment of conforming oil scheduled to arrive on the *S.S. Appollonian Victory* on February 28. Nevertheless, on February 22, the very day after the cure was proffered, Con Ed, adamant in its intention to avail itself of the intervening drop in prices, summarily rejected this proposal too. The two cargos were subsequently sold to third parties at the best price obtainable, first that of the *Appollonian* and, sometime later, after extraction from the tanks had been accomplished, that of the *Khamsin.*[3]

There ensued this action for breach of contract,[4] which, after a somewhat unconventional trial course, resulted in a nonjury decision for the plaintiff in the sum of $1,385,512.83, essentially the difference between the original contract price of $3,360,667.14 and the amount received by the plaintiff by way of resale of the *Khamsin* oil at what the court found as a matter of fact was a negotiated price which, under all the circumstances,[5] was reasonably procured in the open market. To arrive at this result, the Trial Judge, while ruling against other liability theories advanced by the plaintiff, which, in particular, included one charging the defendant with having failed to act in good faith in the negotiations for a price adjustment on the *Khamsin* oil (Uniform Commercial Code, § 1–203), decided as a matter of law that subdivision (2) of section 2–508 of the Uniform Commercial Code was available to the plaintiff even if it had no prior knowledge of the nonconformity. Finding that in fact plaintiff had no such belief at the time of the delivery, that what turned out to be a .92% sulfur content was "within the range of contemplation of reasonable acceptability" to Con. Ed., and that seasonable notice of an intention to cure was given, the court went on to hold that plaintiff's "reasonable and timely offer to cure" was improperly rejected (*sub nom. Joc Oil USA v. Consolidated Edison Co. of N.Y.*, 107 Misc.2d 376, 390, 434 N.Y.S.2d 623 [Shanley N. Egeth, J.]). The Appellate Division, 84 A.D.2d 970, 447 N.Y.S.2d 572, having unanimously affirmed the

concern over the admixture of the differing sulfur contents. In any event, the efficacy of the independent testing required by the contract was not impaired by the commingling.

3. Most of the *Khamsin* oil was drained from the tanks and sold at $10.75 per barrel. The balance was retained by Con Ed in its mixed form at $10.45 per barrel. The original price in January had been $17.875 per barrel.

4. The plaintiff originally also sought an affirmative injunction to compel Con Ed to accept the *Khamsin* shipment or, alternatively, the *Appollonian* substitute. However, when a preliminary injunction was denied on the ground that the plaintiff had an adequate remedy at law, it amended its complaint to pursue the latter remedy alone.

5. These circumstances included the fact that the preliminary injunction was not denied until April so that, by the time the *Khamsin* oil was sold in May, almost three months had gone by since its rejection.

judgment entered on this decision, the case is now here by our leave (CPLR 5602, subd. [a], par. 1, cl. [i]).

In support of its quest for reversal, the defendant now asserts that the trial court erred (a) in ruling that the verdict on a special question submitted for determination by a jury was irrelevant to the decision of this case, (b) in failing to interpret subdivision (2) of section 2–508 of the Uniform Commercial Code to limit the availability of the right to cure after date of performance to cases in which the seller knowingly made a nonconforming tender and (c) in calculating damages on the basis of the resale of the nonconforming cargo rather than of the substitute offered to replace it. For the reasons which follow, we find all three unacceptable.

* * *

II

We turn then to the central issue on this appeal: Fairly interpreted, did subdivision (2) of section 2–508 of the Uniform Commercial Code require Con Ed to accept the substitute shipment plaintiff tendered? In approaching this question, we, of course, must remember that a seller's right to cure a defective tender, as allowed by both subdivisions of section 2–508, was intended to act as a meaningful limitation on the absolutism of the old perfect tender rule, under which, no leeway being allowed for any imperfections, there was, as one court put it, just "no room * * * for the doctrine of substantial performance" of commercial obligations (*Mitsubishi Goshi Kaisha v. Aron & Co.,* 16 F.2d 185, 186 [Learned Hand, J.]; see Note, Uniform Commercial Code, § 2–508; Seller's Right to Cure Non-Conforming Goods, 6 Rutgers—Camden L.J. 387–388).

In contrast, to meet the realities of the more impersonal business world of our day, the code, to avoid sharp dealing, expressly provides for the liberal construction of its remedial provisions (§ 1–102) so that "good faith" and the "observance of reasonable commercial standards of fair dealing" be the rule rather than the exception in trade (see § 2–103, subd. [1], par. [b]), "good faith" being defined as "honesty in fact in the conduct or transaction concerned" (Uniform Commercial Code, § 1–201, subd. [19]). As to section 2–508 in particular, the code's Official Comment advises that its mission is to safeguard the seller "against surprise as a result of sudden technicality on the buyer's part" (Uniform Commercial Code, § 2–106, Comment 2; see, also, Peters, Remedies for Breach of Contracts Relating to the Sale of Goods under the Uniform Commercial Code: A Roadmap for Article Two, 73 Yale L.J. 199, 210; 51 N.Y.Jur., Sales, § 101, p. 41).

Section 2–508 may be conveniently divided between provisions for cure offered when "the time for performance has not yet expired" (subd. [1]), a precode concept in this State (*Lowinson v. Newman,* 201 App.Div. 266, 194 N.Y.S. 253), and ones which, by newly introducing the possibility of a seller obtaining "a further reasonable time to substitute a conforming tender" (subd. [2]), also permit cure beyond the date set for performance. In its entirety the section reads as follows:

"(1) Where any tender or delivery by the seller is rejected because non-conforming and the time for performance has not yet expired, the seller may seasonably notify the buyer of his intention to cure and may then within the contract time make a conforming delivery.

"(2) Where the buyer rejects a non-conforming tender which the seller had reasonable grounds to believe would be acceptable with or without money allowance the seller may if he seasonably notifies the buyer have a further reasonable time to substitute a conforming tender."

Since we here confront circumstances in which the conforming tender came after the time of performance, we focus on subdivision (2). On its face, taking its conditions in the order in which they appear, for the statute to apply (1) a buyer must have rejected a nonconforming tender, (2) the seller must have had reasonable grounds to believe this tender would be acceptable (with or without money allowance), and (3) the seller must have "seasonably" notified the buyer of the intention to substitute a conforming tender within a reasonable time.[7]

In the present case, none of these presented a problem. The first one was easily met for it is unquestioned that, at .92%, the sulfur content of the *Khamsin* oil did not conform to the .5% specified in the contract and that it was rejected by Con Ed. The second, the reasonableness of the seller's belief that the original tender would be acceptable, was supported not only by unimpeached proof that the contract's .5% and the refinery certificate's .52% were trade equivalents, but by testimony that, by the time the contract was made, the plaintiff knew Con Ed burned fuel with a content of up to 1%, so that, with appropriate price adjustment, the *Khamsin* oil would have suited its needs even if, at delivery, it was, to the plaintiff's surprise, to test out at .92%. Further, the matter seems to have been put beyond dispute by the defendant's readiness to take the oil at the reduced market price on February 20. Surely, on such a record, the trial court cannot be faulted for having found as a fact that the second condition too had been established.

As to the third, the conforming state of the *Appollonian* oil is undisputed, the offer to tender it took place on February 21, only a day after Con Ed finally had rejected the *Khamsin* delivery and the *Appollonian* substitute then already was en route to the United States, where it was expected in a week and did arrive on March 4, only four days later than expected. Especially since Con Ed pleaded no prejudice (unless the drop in prices could be so regarded), it is almost impossible, given the flexibility of the Uniform Commercial Code definitions of "seasonable" and "reasonable" (n. 7, *supra*), to quarrel with the finding that the remaining requirements of the statute also had been met.

Thus lacking the support of the statute's literal language, the defendant nonetheless would have us limit its application to cases in which a seller *knowingly* makes a nonconforming tender which it has reason to believe the buyer will accept. For this proposition, it relies almost entirely on a critique in Nordstrom, Law of Sales (§ 105), which rationalizes that, since a seller who believes its tender is conforming would have no reason to think in terms

7. Essentially a factual matter, "seasonable" is defined in subdivision (3) of section 1–204 of the Uniform Commercial Code as "at or within the time agreed or if no time is agreed at or within a reasonable time". At least equally factual in character, a "reasonable time" is left to depend on the "nature, purpose and circumstances" of any action which is to be taken (Uniform Commercial Code, § 1–204, subd. [2]).

of a reduction in the price of the goods, to allow such a seller to cure after the time for performance had passed would make the statutory reference to a money allowance redundant.[8] Nordstrom, interestingly enough, finds it useful to buttress this position by the somewhat dire prediction, though backed by no empirical or other confirmation, that, unless the right to cure is confined to those whose nonconforming tenders are knowing ones, the incentive of sellers to timely deliver will be undermined. To this it also adds the somewhat moralistic note that a seller who is mistaken as to the quality of its goods does not merit additional time (Nordstrom, *loc. cit.*). Curiously, recognizing that the few decisions extant on this subject have adopted a position opposed to the one for which it contends, Con Ed seeks to treat these as exceptions rather than exemplars of the rule (e.g., *Wilson v. Scampoli,* 228 A.2d 848 (D.C.App.) [goods obtained by seller from their manufacturer in original carton resold unopened to purchaser; seller held within statute though it had no reason to believe the goods defective]; *Appleton State Bank v. Lee,* 33 Wis.2d 690, 148 N.W.2d 1 [seller mistakenly delivered sewing machine of wrong brand but otherwise identical to one sold; held that seller, though it did not know of its mistake, had a right to cure by substitution]).[9]

That the principle for which these cases stand goes far beyond their particular facts cannot be gainsaid. These holdings demonstrate that, in dealing with the application of subdivision (2) of section 2–508, courts have been concerned with the reasonableness of the seller's belief that the goods would be acceptable rather than with the seller's pretender knowledge or lack of knowledge of the defect (*Wilson v. Scampoli, supra;* compare *Zabriskie Chevrolet v. Smith,* 99 N.J.Super. 441, 240 A.2d 195).

It also is no surprise then that the aforementioned decisional history is a reflection of the mainstream of scholarly commentary on the subject (e.g., 1955 Report of N.Y.Law Rev.Comm., p. 484; White & Summers, Uniform Commercial Code [2d ed.], § 8–4, p. 322; 2 Anderson, Uniform Commercial code [2d ed.], § 2–508:7; Hogan, The Highways and Some of the Byways in the Sales and Bulk Sales Articles of the Uniform Commercial Code, 48 Cornell L.Q. 1, 12–13; Note, Uniform Commercial Code, § 2–508: Seller's Right to Cure Non-Conforming Goods, 6 Rutgers—Camden L.J. 387, 399; Note, Commercial Law—The Effect of the Seller's Right to Cure on the Buyer's Remedy of Rescission, 28 Ark.L.Rev. 297, 302–303).

White and Summers, for instance, put it well, and bluntly. Stressing that the code intended cure to be "a remedy which should be carefully

8. The premise for such an argument, which ignores the policy of the code to prevent buyers from using insubstantial remediable or price adjustable defects to free themselves from unprofitable bargains (Hawkland, Sales and Bulk Sales Under the Uniform Commercial Code, pp. 120–122), is that the words "with or without money allowance" apply only to sellers who believe their goods will be acceptable with such an allowance and not to sellers who believe their goods will be acceptable without such an allowance. But, since the words are part of a phrase which speaks of an otherwise unqualified belief that the goods will be acceptable, unless one strains for an opposite interpretation, we find insufficient reason to doubt that it intends to include both those who find a need to offer an allowance and those who do not.

9. The only New York case to deal with this section involved a seller who knowingly tendered a "newer and improved version of the model that was actually ordered" on the contract delivery date. The court held he had reasonable grounds to believe the buyer would accept the newer model (*Bartus v. Riccardi,* 55 Misc.2d 3, 284 N.Y.S.2d 222 [Utica City Ct., Hymes, J.]).

cultivated and developed by the courts" because it "offers the possibility of conforming the law to reasonable expectations and of thwarting the chiseler who seeks to escape from a bad bargain" (*op. cit.,* at pp. 322–324), the authors conclude, as do we, that a seller should have recourse to the relief afforded by subdivision (2) of section 2–508 of the Uniform Commercial Code as long as it can establish that it had reasonable grounds, tested objectively, for its belief that the goods would be accepted (*ibid.,* at p. 321). It goes without saying that the test of reasonableness, in this context, must encompass the concepts of "good faith" and "commercial standards of fair dealing" which permeate the code (Uniform Commercial Code, § 1–201, subd. [19]; §§ 1–203, 2–103, subd. [1], par. [b]).[10]

As to the damages issue raised by the defendant, we affirm without reaching the merits. At no stage of the proceedings before the trial court did the defendant object to the plaintiff's proposed method for their calculation, and this though the plaintiff gave ample notice of that proposal by means of a preliminary statement and pretrial memorandum filed with the court. So complete was defendant's acquiescence in the theory thus advanced that the plaintiff was permitted to introduce its proof of the *Khamsin* resale alone, and without opposition. Furthermore, in consensually submitting the four jointly framed advisory questions that went to the jury, the language of one of them, which was damages-related, indicates that both parties were acting on the assumption that the *Khamsin* oil was the one with which the court was to be concerned. And, even after the decision at nisi prius revealed that the Judge had acted on such an assumption, so far as the record shows, no motion was ever made to correct it.

It has long been the law that agreement on a theory of damages at trial, even if only implied, must control on appeal (see *Martin v. City of Cohoes,* 37 N.Y.2d 162, 165–166, 371 N.Y.S.2d 687, 332 N.E.2d 867, *supra; Hartshorn v. Chaddock,* 135 N.Y. 116, 123, 31 N.E. 997; 10 Carmody-Wait 2d, N.Y.Prac., § 70:419, p. 690).

For all these reasons, the order of the Appellate Division should be affirmed, with costs.

COOKE, C.J., and JASEN, GABRIELLI, JONES, WACHTLER and MEYER, JJ., concur.

Order affirmed.

Notes

1. In cases like *T.W. Oil, Inc.,* where the market price has moved against the buyer, the probable objective of rejection is to cancel the contract rather than to give the seller an opportunity to cure under UCC 2–508. Read UCC 2–711(1) carefully. Except where installment contracts are involved, a buyer who "rightfully rejects" may "with respect to any goods involved * * * cancel" the

10. Except indirectly, on this appeal we do not deal with the equally important protections the code affords buyers. It is as to buyers as well as sellers that the code, to the extent that it displaces traditional principles of law and equity (§ 1–103), seeks to discourage unfair or hypertechnical business conduct bespeaking a dog-eat-dog rather than a live-and-let-live approach to the marketplace (e.g., §§ 2–314, 2–315, 2–513, 2–601, 2–608). Overall, the aim is to encourage parties to amicably resolve their own problems (*Ramirez v. Autosport,* 88 N.J. 277, 285, 440 A.2d 1345; compare Restatement, Contracts 2d, Introductory Note to chapter 10, p. 194 ["the wisest course is ordinarily for the parties to attempt to resolve their differences by negotiations, including clarification of expectations [and] cure of past defaults"]).

contract. There is no separate cancellation requirement that the breach "substantially impair" the value of the contract. Compare UCC 2–612(3). Nevertheless, if Buyer has rightfully rejected and Seller has "seasonably" notified Buyer of its intention to make a cure permitted by UCC 2–508, Buyer's power to cancel should be suspended until Seller has a reasonable time to cure. See Leitchfield Development Corp. v. Clark, 757 S.W.2d 207 (Ky.App.1988). If, however, the proffered cure exceeds the scope of UCC 2–508, then Buyer is free to pursue the remedial option granted in UCC 2–711(1). See Travelers Indemnity Co. v. Maho Machine Tool Corp., 952 F.2d 26 (2d Cir.1991) (seller improperly conditioned cure offer on buyer's payment of cost to return rejected goods).

2. *Cure of nonconforming consumer goods.* Assuming a rightful rejection and a "seasonable" notice by Seller of an intention to cure, the question remains: What is a "conforming" delivery, UCC 2–508(1), or tender, UCC 2–508(2). Is it a tender of repaired goods, or new conforming goods or a money allowance? Put differently, should Buyer be permitted to cancel and cover if Seller tenders repaired rather than new goods? The question has arisen with some frequency in cases involving consumer goods.

Two early cases staked out the territory. In Wilson v. Scampoli, 228 A.2d 848 (D.C.App.1967), the goods were a new color T.V. with a defective picture tube. Seller offered to replace the tube and Buyer, insisting on a new T.V., refused. The court held that the right to cure under UCC 2–508 included the making of "minor repairs or reasonable adjustments" and that Buyer had deprived Seller of an adequate opportunity to determine whether repair or replacement was proper. In Zabriskie Chevrolet, Inc. v. Smith, 99 N.J.Super. 441, 240 A.2d 195 (1968), the goods were a new car with a defective transmission. The court, conceding that UCC 2–508 was unclear and influenced by recent consumer law developments in New Jersey, concluded that Seller's offer to cure by replacing the transmission was inadequate. The court stated that it "was not the intention of the Legislature that the right to 'cure' is a limitless one to be controlled only by the will of the seller." Rather, the limits of "cure" are defined by the "agreement or contemplation of the parties" and for a "majority of people the purchase of a new car is a major investment, rationalized by the peace of mind that flows from its dependability and safety."

UCC 2–508 is, of course, the "default" rule on cure. It can be varied by agreement. In most consumer cases involving complicated, expensive goods, there is an agreement that the seller shall have the right for a stated period of time to "repair or replace" defective parts. There is no agreement to provide substitute goods. The legal effect of these agreed methods of cure is treated in Chapter Twenty-one, section 5.

McKENZIE v. ALLA-OHIO COALS, INC.

United States District Court, District of Columbia, 1979.
29 UCC Rep.Serv. 852, affirmed 610 F.2d 1000.

GASCH, DISTRICT JUDGE. This diversity action for breach of contract is before the court on cross-motions for summary judgment. Plaintiff contends that he is entitled to judgment in his favor because defendant wrongfully rejected coal shipped to it by plaintiff pursuant to their agreement. Plaintiff argues that the only remedy available to defendant was a reduction in the price of the coal, as set forth in a penalty clause contained in the purchase order. Defendant replies that the penalty clause was not the exclusive remedy, and that its timely rejection of the coal was fully justified. Plaintiff brought this action seeking recovery of approximately $7,000 as the difference between what defendant should have paid and what plaintiff received on resale. Plaintiff also seeks approximately $40,000 for the cost of demurrage and transporting the coal. Defendant counterclaimed for $800 in costs for inspecting the coal, and for compensatory and punitive damages for plaintiff's alleged misrepresentations made by plaintiff about delay and the quality of the coal.

Background

Defendant Alla-Ohio is a coal broker who agreed to buy coal from plaintiff to resell to certain of its customers. The agreement resulted from oral negotiations over the telephone in June, 1977. During these negotiations, there was no discussion of possible penalties to be applied against deviations in the quality of the coal. On July 5, 1977, defendant sent to plaintiff a purchase order confirming the prior agreement, and specifying the order of 3,000 net tons of coal at an agreed price of $34.00 per net ton F.O.B. car. The letter-purchase order included the specification that the ash content of the coal not exceed 7.5%. The letter also stated: "Should the ash content exceed 7.5% dry, a penalty of $.80 per 1% of ash in excess of 7.5% shall be assessed, fractions in proportion." The letter also stipulated other specifications, including a Free Swelling Index (FSI) of "7 Min."

On or about July 21, 1977, plaintiff shipped 43 railroad cars containing approximately 3,000 tons of coal to Hampton Roads, Virginia for defendant. Plaintiff received defendant's July 5 letter-purchase order on July 25, 1977. The next day, plaintiff sent a reply to defendant, informing defendant that the purchase order did not conform to the oral understanding. Plaintiff also objected to the ash and FSI specifications, claiming 8% and 6, respectively, to be the correct standards. Plaintiff further objected to the penalty provisions, saying, "I consider this order to be incorrect and that all specifications on the coal should be on an as received basis." On July 28, 1977, defendant responded by asserting that the purchase order of July 5 was an accurate embodiment of the oral agreement. Defendant also noted that preliminary test results showed that the ash content of the coal was at least 13.5% and ranged upward. Plaintiff did not respond to the July 28 letter.

On August 15, 1977, defendant rejected the 43 railroad cars of coal, after completing tests of 42 of the cars. Plaintiff demanded that delivery be accepted but defendant refused. Subsequently, plaintiff found a buyer for the coal at a price of $26.74 per ton. The price defendant would have paid pursuant to the penalty clause in the purchase order would have been $29.20 per ton, according to plaintiff's calculation.

This case turns primarily on the issue of whether the penalty clause set out in the purchase order of July 5 was the exclusive remedy for defendant, or whether defendant was entitled to reject coal that did not conform to the specifications. There are, however, other matters which also must be untangled before resolution of the case may be achieved. Therefore, the court will undertake to examine the contentions of the parties roughly in chronological order.

I. The Contract and Its Terms

* * *

Under these circumstances, the court concludes that the contract between the parties contained penalty terms for excess ash content.

II. Limitation of Remedies

Plaintiff argues that the penalty clause was defendant's exclusive remedy in the event that the coal did not conform to the requirements of the contract, and that the parties did not intend to permit the "radical" remedy of rejection. * * * In the absence of an express indication in the writings of the parties, or a course of conduct clearly establishing use of only one kind of remedy, the court cannot conclude that the presumption that remedies be cumulative is overcome.

In addition, the UCC has codified the "perfect tender" rule of the common law,[2] and provides that goods not sold in installments may be rejected if they "fail in any respect to conform to the contract." UCC § 2–601. There is substantial authority, however, that the perfect tender rule has been greatly diminished, and that, where a buyer has suffered no damage, he should not be allowed to reject goods because of an insubstantial nonconformity. See J. White and R. Summers, supra § 8–3 at 256–57, and cases cited therein. Assuming this approach to be the correct one, in this case the nonconformity was substantial. The July 5 purchase order specified that the ash content of the coal was not to exceed 7.5%. The coal delivered to defendant had ash content of at least 13.5% and up to 16%.[3] Moreover, the UCC provides that if the nonconformity will impair the value of the goods to the buyer because of the buyer's particular circumstances, he is entitled to reject the goods even though the seller had no advance knowledge of the circumstances. UCC § 2–608.[4] The coal ordered by defendant here was intended for use as metallugical coal. Metallurgical coal must be high quality coal and may have ash content no greater than 8%, or, for marginal grade metallurgical coal, no greater than 12%. See Defendant's Supplemental Memorandum at 9 n. 4. On the basis of the foregoing facts, the court concludes that the coal tendered by plaintiff did not conform substantially to the requirements of the contract. On that basis, defendant was entitled to reject the nonconforming coal.[5]

A troublesome question, however, is the potential capacity for the seller to cure a nonconforming performance. Under UCC § 2–508, a seller may cure after the time for performance has passed if (1) he had reasonable

2. See Priest, Breach and Remedy for the Tender of Nonconforming Goods under the Uniform Commercial Code: An Economic Approach, 91 Harv.L.Rev. 960 (1978). Although plaintiff has suggested a novel economic analysis in conformance with the scholarly article cited above, the court declines plaintiff's invitation to undertake that approach on the facts presented.

3. See Letter from Ms. Ursula Mosby to Eugene McKenzie, July 28, 1977.

4. Although UCC § 2–608 governs revocations after acceptance of goods, and not rejection before acceptance, the analysis applicable to both §§ 2–608 and 2–601 is the same. See J. White and R. Summers, supra § 8–3, at 260.

5. A buyer is permitted a reasonable opportunity to inspect goods tendered under a contract, see UCC § 2–606, and may reject nonconforming goods within a reasonable time after inspection reveals the nonconformity, and the buyer must seasonably notify the seller of rejection. UCC § 2–602. Defendant in this case has complied with the above requirements.

grounds to believe that a nonconforming tender would be acceptable, (2) he seasonably notifies the buyer of his intention to cure, and (3) he cures within a further reasonable time. Addressing these considerations, the court notes that it is unlikely that a reasonable seller in plaintiff's position would be ignorant of such drastic variances in the quality of the coal. Similarly, no evidence of trade custom in the record indicates that coal with such high ash content would be suitable for use as metallurgical coal, the purpose for which it was purchased. Therefore, the court finds that plaintiff did not have reasonable grounds for believing that a nonconforming tender would be acceptable. Furthermore, although there is evidence that plaintiff offered to take a reduced price for the coal, such attempted cure by price allowance is not one of the methods of cure approved by the UCC. See UCC § 2–508, Comment 4. Under all of these circumstances, then, plaintiff could make no effective cure short of tendering conforming coal. There was never any offer to do so, and defendant was justified in rejecting the high ash coal.

In sum, the contract between plaintiff and defendant did not limit the parties to accepting a price reduction for coal that did not meet the specifications for ash content that were imposed. The coal actually tendered deviated so substantially from the coal promised that defendant was entitled, after inspection, to reject the whole. UCC § 2–601. Furthermore, defendant is entitled to recover damages incurred in inspecting the coal. UCC § 2–715(1) provides in part that, "Incidental damages resulting from the seller's breach include expenses reasonably incurred in inspection * * * of goods rightfully rejected * * *" Defendant has by affidavit established that its inspection costs amount to $495.70.

* * *

Accordingly, in view of the foregoing, the court will deny plaintiff's motion for summary judgment, grant defendant's motion for summary judgment on plaintiff's claim, grant defendant's motion for summary judgment on the first count of its counterclaim, and will dismiss without prejudice the second count of defendant's counterclaim.

[Some footnotes omitted.]

C. Procedural Requirements of Effective Rejection

Suppose, upon inspection, the buyer finds a non-conformity which would justify rejection of the goods under UCC 2–601. What conditions must be met before the buyer can make an effective rejection? Section 2–602(1) provides that "rejection of goods must be within a reasonable time after their delivery and tender" and that the rejection is "ineffective unless the buyer seasonably notifies the seller." Compare UCC 2–607(3)(a). If the buyer has had a reasonable option under UCC 2–602(1), and fails to act, he has accepted the goods. Section 2–606(1)(b). A second set of problems concerns the content of the notice the buyer is to give the seller. Need it state all, part or none of the defects ascertainable by reasonable inspection as a condition to relying upon them to justify rejection? The UCC answer is provided in UCC 2–605(1). The pre-Code cases are collected and analyzed in Eno, *Price Movement and Unstated Objections to the Defective Performance of Sales Contracts,* 44 Yale L.J. 782 (1935).

Problem 18–4

1. Suppose that the seller tenders goods at the time specified in the contract. Upon inspection, the buyer finds what he considers to be two defects. Accordingly, he promptly notifies the seller that he is rejecting the goods, thus satisfying UCC 2–602(1). However, his notice of rejection specified only one defect and this later turns out to be an insufficient ground for rejection. The unstated objection, while present in fact, could have been cured by the seller under UCC 2–508(2). Shortly after the notice is received by the seller, the goods are destroyed while in the possession of the buyer but without his fault or negligence. May the seller recover the price of the destroyed goods from the buyer? See UCC 2–602, 2–605, 2–606, and 2–607(1).

2. In Bead Chain Manufacturing Co. v. Saxton Products, Inc., 183 Conn. 266, 439 A.2d 314 (1981) the Supreme Court of Connecticut, Ellen Peters J, remarked that the "consequence of an ineffective rejection is that the buyer is held to have accepted the goods, and thereafter becomes liable for their purchase price." 439 A.2d at 318, n. 2. On the other hand, in Integrated Circuits Unlimited v. E.F. Johnson Co., 875 F.2d 1040 (2d Cir.1989), the court held that a rejection which was "wrongful" under UCC 2–601 but "rightful" under UCC 2–602(1) and 2–605 was not an acceptance under 2–606. The Seller could recover damages for wrongful rejection but not the price. Do these distinctions find any support in the statute? Do they make sense as a matter of good commercial policy?

D. Buyer's Duties Regarding Rejected Goods

BORGES v. MAGIC VALLEY FOODS, INC.

Supreme Court of Idaho, 1980.
101 Idaho 494, 616 P.2d 273.

SHEPARD, J. This is an appeal from a judgment following a jury verdict which awarded plaintiffs-respondents Borges and G & B Land and Cattle Company $12,832.00 for potatoes received by defendant-appellant Magic West pursuant to a contract with respondents. We affirm.

In 1975, respondents grew and harvested approximately 45,000 c.w.t. of potatoes, which were stored in a cellar near Buhl, Idaho. Magic West inspected those potatoes and, although their inspection indicated that some contained a "hollow heart" defect, Magic West agreed to purchase them for $3.80 per c.w.t. "Hollow heart" indicates a vacant space in the middle of the potato. The purchase contract provided that "if internal problems develop making these potatoes unfit for fresh pack shipping, this contract becomes null and void." It was agreed that the cost of transporting the potatoes from the storage cellar to the processing plant would be borne by Magic West. Examination of the potatoes by State inspectors would occur at the plant to determine that the number of potatoes affected by the hollow heart defect did not exceed the limit prescribed for shipping under the fresh pack grade.

The potatoes were transported to the processing plant, where more than 30,000 c.w.t. were processed and shipped under the fresh pack grade. In March, 1976, State inspectors declared the remaining 4,838.77 c.w.t. of potatoes unfit for the fresh pack grade because of the increased incidence of hollow heart condition.[1] On March 31, 1976, the parties met to discuss the

1. There were also potatoes still in storage which Magic West never paid for due to the hollow heart problems. There is no dispute with regard to those potatoes. Respon-

problem of the remaining potatoes and it was apparently agreed that Magic West should attempt to blend them with other potatoes of a higher grade in the hope that such a blend would meet fresh pack grade standards. That experiment failed and Magic West, without notifying the respondents, processed the remaining 4,838.77 c.w.t. of potatoes into flakes and sold them for $1.25 per c.w.t. The evidence in the record disclosed that the remaining potatoes could not be removed from the processing plant without destroying at least one-third of the potatoes.

Respondents demanded the contract price of $3.80 per c.w.t. for the potatoes sold as flakes. Magic West refused, and instead offered to pay $1.25 per c.w.t. This action resulted. The jury returned a general verdict to the respondents of $12,832.00 and the trial court also awarded $6,975.00 as and for attorney fees and costs to the respondents.[2]

Magic West's basic contention is that the 4,838.77 c.w.t. of potatoes were clearly defective and that they were never accepted. It is claimed that when Magic West processed the potatoes into flakes and sold them for $1.25 per c.w.t., they were only following respondents' instructions.

The potatoes in the instant case were clearly movable at the time they were identified in the contract, I.C. § 28–2–105, and, hence, were "goods" within the purview of the Idaho Uniform Commercial Code, I.C. §§ 28–2–101 to –2–725, and the dispute is governed by the provisions of the Uniform Commercial Code.

It is clear and undisputed that Magic West had the responsibility of transporting the potatoes from the storage cellar to the processing plant and that State inspection would occur at the plant. It is also clear that the 4,838.77 c.w.t. of potatoes, unable to make the fresh pack grade, did not conform to the contract and gave Magic West the right of rejection. IC § 28–2–601(a). Also, it is not disputed that when Magic West determined that the potatoes would not meet fresh pack grade, Magic West so notified the respondents and met with them to determine what disposition should be made of the potatoes. The record is unclear as to precisely what was decided at that March 31, 1976 meeting, but respondents apparently approved of Magic West's proposal to blend the defective potatoes with those with higher quality in an attempt to meet the fresh pack grade. However, it is clear that no agreement on price was reached at that meeting.

A buyer must pay the contract rate for any goods accepted. I.C. § 28–2–607(1). Generally, a buyer is deemed to have accepted defective goods when, knowing of the defect, he resells the goods without notifying the seller. See White & Summers, Uniform Commercial Code, § 8–2 (2d ed. 1980); 67 Am Jur2d Sales (1973). A buyer accepts goods whenever he does any act

dents eventually sold them for $3.00 per c.w.t. to be used as french fries. There were also 702 c.w.t. of defective potatoes in transit to the plant on March 31, 1977. The respondents agreed to accept $1.25 per c.w.t. for those potatoes from Magic West.

2. Both parties agreed that the jury had apparently awarded respondents the full contract price of $3.80 per c.w.t. for the potatoes in dispute. If no deductions were made, a jury award of $3.80 per c.w.t. would have resulted in a jury verdict of $18,387.32 [$3.80 × 4838.77]. Obviously, some deductions were made although they are not apparent from the record and were not explained or challenged by counsel. For purposes of this appeal, we assume, as counsel do, that the jury awarded $3.80 per c.w.t. for the potatoes in dispute.

inconsistent with the seller's ownership. I.C. § 28–2–606(1)(c). Respondents assert that Magic West's processing of the remaining potatoes into flakes and the subsequent sale constituted acts inconsistent with the respondents' ownership.

Magic West argues, however, that their processing of the potatoes into flakes and their subsequent sale did not constitute an acceptance, but rather was a permissible resale under the provisions of either I.C. § 28–2–603(1) or I.C. § 28–2–604. I.C. § 28–2–603(1) provides:

> "Subject to any security interest in the buyer * * *, when the seller has no agent or place of business at the market of rejection a merchant buyer is under a duty after rejection of goods in his possession or control to follow any reasonable instructions received from the seller with respect to the goods and in the absence of such instructions to make reasonable efforts to sell them for the seller's account if they are perishable or threaten to decline in value speedily."

I.C. § 28–2–604 provides:

> "Subject to the provisions of the immediately preceding section on perishables if the seller gives no instructions within a reasonable time after notification of rejection the buyer may store the rejected goods for the seller's account or reship them to him or resell them for the seller's account with reimbursement as provided in the preceding section. Such action is not acceptance or conversion."

We note that both I.C. § 28–2–603(1) and I.C. § 28–2–604 were given in their entirety as instructions to the jury. We find it unclear from the record whether the respondents had agents or a place of business at the "market of rejection." Also, the duty to resell under I.C. § 28–2–603(1) is triggered by an absence of instructions from a seller. Here, given the state of the record and its lack of clarity and the conflicting evidence, the jury could have reasonably found that the respondents did instruct Magic West to attempt to blend the potatoes, but did not instruct them to process the potatoes into flakes. While I.C. § 28–2–604 allows a buyer an option to resell rejected goods if the seller gives no instructions within a reasonable time after the notification of rejection, the jury could have reasonably found that respondents' instructions were only to blend the potatoes in hope of accomplishing fresh pack grade and that Magic West's processing of the potatoes into flakes and subsequent resale thereof was a precipitate action taken before the lapse of a reasonable time within which respondents could give further instructions.

In addition, even if a reasonable time had elapsed, thus permitting Magic West to resell the potatoes, the jury properly could have concluded that processing of the potatoes by Magic West was an acceptance rather than a resale. There was no evidence presented either of an attempt to resell the potatoes in the bins to an independent third party, or of the value of the potatoes in the bins, less damage caused by removal, should it have been effected. Absent any evidence that the $1.25 per c.w.t. offered by Magic West was the highest value obtainable for the potatoes, Magic West's use of the potatoes in the ordinary course of its own business (presumably for profit) was an act inconsistent with the seller's ownership, and constituted an acceptance of the goods. I.C. § 28–2–606(1)(c).

The jury was adequately and correctly instructed regarding the provisions of I.C. § 28–2–603(1) and I.C. § 28–2–604, which constituted Magic West's theory of its duty or option of resale because of an absence of instructions from respondents. The jury was at liberty to reject Magic West's theory of defense based on substantial, albeit conflicting, evidence that Magic West's resale of the potatoes after processing them into flakes constituted an acceptance and Magic West was hence liable for the full contract price.

We have examined appellants' remaining assignments of error and find them to be without merit.

Affirmed. Costs to respondents.

DONALDSON, C.J., BAKES, MCFADDEN and BISTLINE, JJ., concur.

Problem 18–5

Suppose in the Sodfill-Blurtaste problem, above, that the bill of lading had permitted inspection and that Blurtaste had discovered the defect in 1, above, while inspecting goods still in the possession of the carrier. Blurtaste did not take possession and promptly notified Sodfill of his decision to reject as required by UCC 2–602. Assume, further, that (1) the weather was quite hot, putting a strain on the refrigeration unit in the railroad car, (2) the tomato market had started a steady decline due to a bumper crop and (3) Sodfill had no local agent at the place of destination. Does Blurtaste have any obligation to Sodfill with regard to the rejected goods? If so, what would you advise Blurtaste to do? See UCC 2–602(2), 2–603 and 2–604.

Note: Perishable Agricultural Commodities

Under section 2(2) of the Perishable Agricultural Commodities Act, 7 U.S.C.A. § 499b, as amended, it is unlawful in interstate transactions "for any dealer to reject or fail to deliver in accordance with the terms of the contract without reasonable cause any perishable agricultural commodity bought or sold or contracted to be bought or sold in interstate * * * commerce by such dealer." The Act was "intended to prevent produce from becoming distress merchandise and to protect sellers who often were at great distance from the buyer." L. Gillarde & Co. v. Joseph Martinelli & Co., 168 F.2d 276, amended, 169 F.2d 60, 61 (1st Cir.1948), cert. denied, 335 U.S. 885, 69 S.Ct. 237, 93 L.Ed. 424 (1948). Remedies include reparation orders for aggrieved shippers and suspension or revocation of licenses. See Chidsey v. Guerin, 443 F.2d 584 (6th Cir.1971). The Secretary has defined "reject without reasonable cause" to include "refusing or failing without legal justification to accept produce within a reasonable time" and "advising the seller, shipper, or his agent that produce, complying with the contract, will not be accepted." 7 C.F.R. § 46.2(bb). Reasonable time for rejection is defined with reference to the type of produce and the method of shipment. 7 C.F.R. § 46.2(cc). A number of commonly used trade terms are crisply defined and, to the extent used by the parties, both preempt state law definitions, e.g., UCC 2–319, and define rights and duties. For example, "rolling acceptance final" means that the buyer "has no recourse against the seller because of any change in condition of the produce in transit" but if the shipment is not rejected the buyer has recourse in damages against the seller for any material breach. 7 C.F.R. § 46.43(t). The thrust of the definitions is to restrict or prohibit the rejection remedy, especially where the reason for rejection affects the condition or quality of the goods. See Schuman Co. v. Nelson, 219 F.2d 627

(3d Cir.1955) (under earlier regulations, "rolling acceptance final" does not preclude rejection for breach not relating to quality or condition of goods). Since buyers subject to the Act often pay against documents or under a letter of credit arrangement, the need for adequate inspection of the produce at the point of shipment is acute. Federal inspection is available and, in some cases, required under the Act. See 7 U.S.C.A. § 499n; 7 C.F.R. §§ 46.39 & 46.40; Cove Valley Packers, Inc. v. Pilgrim Fruit Co., 297 F.Supp. 200 (D.Mass.1969).

Note: "Avoidance" of the Contract in International Sales

Professor John Honnold has observed that one of the "thorniest problems" in the law of sales is "when will the breach by one party free the other party of his obligation to perform?" J. Honnold, Uniform Law for International Sales 27–28 (2d ed. 1990). This problem has special significance in international sales "because of the cost of transporting goods to a distant buyer and the difficulty of disposing of rejected goods." Ibid.

The 1980 United Nations Convention on Contracts for the International Sale of Goods, which the United States Senate ratified on Dec. 11, 1986 and which became effective on Jan. 1, 1988, deals with problems created by the seller's delay in performance or delivery of non-conforming documents or goods in the following manner.

Let us consider only the case of non-conforming goods or documents. Suppose the seller has tendered goods or documents which fail to conform to the contract. The buyer discovers the non-conformity after "examination" of the goods or documents, Article 38, and preserves his rights by giving "notice to the seller specifying the nature of the lack of conformity within a reasonable time after he has discovered it or ought to have discovered it." Article 39(1). What are these "rights"?

First, the buyer may recover damages for breach of contract. Article 74.

Second, the buyer may, in carefully defined situations, compel the seller either to deliver "substitute goods," if the breach is "fundamental," or to "remedy the lack of conformity by repair" if reasonable under all of the circumstances. Article 46. If this remedy is successful, the buyer will owe the price, subject to adjustment for any losses caused by the breach.

Third, the buyer may attempt to "avoid" the contract ("cancel" in UCC parlance)—a remedy that substitutes for "rejection" of the goods. "Avoidance" of the contract requires the buyer to: (a) establish that the non-conformity amounted to a "fundamental" breach, Article 49(1), and (b) give notice to the buyer of the attempt to avoid within a reasonable time after he "knew or ought to have known of the breach." Article 49(2)(b). A breach is "fundamental if it results in such detriment to the other party as substantially to deprive him of what he is entitled to expect under the contract, unless the party in breach did not foresee and a reasonable person of the same kind in the same circumstances would not have foreseen such a result." Article 25.

Fourth, the "right" to avoid the contract for a fundamental breach, however, is limited by the seller's right to "cure" the defect by replacing or repairing the defective goods, Articles 37 (cure until date of delivery) and 48 (cure after delivery) or conforming the documents. Article 34. See Honnold at 368–372. Thus, if the buyer discovered a "fundamental" breach after delivery, the seller could prevent an "avoidance" of the contract by remedying "at his own expense any failure to perform his obligations, if he can do so without unreasonable delay and without causing the buyer unreasonable inconvenience. * * *" Article 48(1).

Enough has been said to indicate that the 1980 Convention has rejected a "perfect tender" rule for rules that require "fundamental" breach and maximize the seller's opportunity to cure. In short, the 1980 Convention seeks to preserve the contract and to foster adjustments, while protecting the buyer's right to damages for losses caused during the "cure" period. At the same time, one can see that the Convention's solution will not be simple to understand and administer and this problem is complicated by a sometimes murky drafting history. See Speidel, Book Review, 5 Nw.J.Int'l.Law & Bus. 432 (1983). Nevertheless, we believe Professor Honnold's book sheds considerable light on the 1980 Convention and recommend it as the perfect place to start. If your interest is piqued, go next to Rosett, *Critical Reflections on the United Nations Convention on Contracts for the International Sale of Goods,* 45 Ohio S.L.J. 305 (1984).

For now, you may wish to review the UCC's approach to the problem of "rejection" and "cancellation" and compare it with the 1980 Convention.

Note: Should the "Perfect Tender" Rule be "Rejected" in Revised Article 2?

The "perfect tender" rule in UCC 2–601 has been criticized in the courts, see D.P. Technology Corp. v. Sherwood Tool, Inc., 751 F.Supp. 1038 (D.Conn.1990) (unfair where breach is delay in delivery with no serious harm to buyer) and by the commentators, see, e.g., Sebert, *Rejection, Revocation and Cure Under Article 2 of the UCC: Some Modest Proposals,* 84 Nw.U.L.Rev. 375 (1990). A Study Group appointed to consider the possible revision of Article, however, concluded that the "perfect tender" rule should be retained, with an effort made to collect citations to the various limitations on its exercise all in one place. Since the strict performance rule does not apply in installment contracts and, in *de facto* operation, results in a substantial impairment test, no revision is required. See Preliminary Report, Uniform Commercial Code Article 2 Study Group, reprinted under the title *An Appraisal of the March 1, 1990, Preliminary Report of the Uniform Commercial Code Article 2 Study Group,* 16 Del.J. of Corp.Law 981, 1157–1162 (1991). See also, *PEB Study Group: Uniform Commercial Code, Article 2 Executive Summary,* 46 Bus.Law. 1869, 1881 (1991).

Suppose that you are a state Commissioner on Uniform State Laws and a member of the Drafting Committee appointed to revise Article 2. The following arguments for "rejecting" the perfect tender rule and substituting a "substantial impairment" test have been made. How would you vote?

1. The strict performance rule has been criticized by most commentators and ignored by the courts.

2. In most cases, a substantial impairment test will be applied anyway. The contract will either be an installment contract, UCC 2–612(3), or the buyer will accept the goods before discovering the nonconformity, see UCC 2–608. In either case, a substantial impairment test is involved.

3. There is no justification for having a difference between international and domestic sales law on this point.

4. Most parties, if they had considered it, would probably prefer to have a complex rather than a simple test for rejection. Moreover, the "perfect tender" rule as a "default" rule creates questionable bargaining incentives. The buyer has no incentive to communicate information about particular needs and prefer-

ences to the seller at the time of contracting. A "substantial impairment" test would encourage disclosure and promote informed bargaining over the standard for rejection. More importantly, it would not penalize the seller when there are no particular needs and the buyer rejects for a minor nonconformity under UCC 2–601.

5. A "substantial impairment" test would work equally well for commercial and consumer buyers. If doubts exist, however, an exception for consumers should be made.

SECTION 4. NATURE AND CONSEQUENCES OF ACCEPTANCE

So far, we have focused upon the buyer's right to inspect and the remedy of rejection when defects in the seller's tender of delivery are actually discovered. Through both inspection and rejection the buyer seeks to avoid accepting defective goods. Now we will be concerned with three additional but related questions. First, exactly when does a buyer accept tendered goods? The critical section here is UCC 2–606. Second, what is the legal effect of an acceptance? This is particularly important when the goods accepted are actually non-conforming. See UCC 2–510(1) and UCC 2–607. Third, when may the buyer "revoke" his acceptance under UCC 2–608 and what is the effect of a proper revocation of acceptance? Regardless of how the acceptance occurs, a buyer with defective goods on his hands will be in a different and, perhaps, more difficult remedial posture than if the remedy of rejection had properly been invoked. Because the complexity of many goods and the casualness of most inspections naturally contribute to a high incidence of acceptance, a thorough appreciation of this "posture" by the commercial lawyer is required.

PLATEQ CORP. OF NORTH HAVEN v. MACHLETT LABORATORIES, INC.

Supreme Court of Connecticut, 1983.
189 Conn. 433, 456 A.2d 786.

Before SPEZIALE, C.J., and PETERS, ARTHUR H. HEALEY, PARSKEY and GRILLO, JJ.

PETERS, JUDGE.

In this action by a seller of specially manufactured goods to recover their purchase price from a commercial buyer, the principal issue is whether the buyer accepted the goods before it attempted to cancel the contract of sale. The plaintiff, Plateq Corporation of North Haven, sued the defendant, The Machlett Laboratories, Inc., to recover damages, measured by the contract price and incidental damages, arising out of the defendant's allegedly wrongful cancellation of a written contract for the manufacture and sale of two leadcovered steel tanks and appurtenant stands. The defendant denied liability and counterclaimed for damages. After a full hearing, the trial court found for the plaintiff both on its complaint and on the defendant's counterclaim. The defendant has appealed.

The trial court, in its memorandum of decision, found the following facts. On July 9, 1976, the defendant ordered from the plaintiff two leadcovered steel tanks to be constructed by the plaintiff according to specifications supplied by the defendant. The parties understood that the tanks were designed for the special purpose of testing x-ray tubes and were required to be radiation-proof within certain federal standards. Accordingly, the contract provided that the tanks would be tested for radiation leaks after their installation on the defendant's premises. The plaintiff undertook to correct, at its own cost, any deficiencies that this post-installation test might uncover.[1] The plaintiff had not previously constructed such tanks, nor had the defendant previously designed tanks for this purpose. The contract was amended on August 9, 1976, to add construction of two metal stands to hold the tanks. All the goods were to be delivered to the defendant at the plaintiff's place of business.[2]

Although the plaintiff encountered difficulties both in performing according to the contract specifications and in completing performance within the time required, the defendant did no more than call these deficiencies to the plaintiff's attention during various inspections in September and early October, 1976. By October 11, 1976, performance was belatedly but substantially completed. On that date, Albert Yannello, the defendant's engineer, noted some remaining deficiencies which the plaintiff promised to remedy by the next day, so that the goods would then be ready for delivery. Yannello gave no indication to the plaintiff that this arrangement was in any way unsatisfactory to the defendant. Not only did Yannello communicate general acquiescence in the plaintiff's proposed tender but he specifically led the plaintiff to believe that the defendant's truck would pick up the tanks and the stands within a day or two. Instead of sending its truck, the defendant sent a notice of total cancellation which the plaintiff received on October 14, 1976. That notice failed to particularize the grounds upon which cancellation was based.[3]

On this factual basis, the trial court, having concluded that the transaction was a contract for the sale of goods falling within the Uniform Commercial Code, General Statutes §§ 42a–2–101 et seq., considered whether the defendant had accepted the goods. The court determined that the defendant had accepted the tanks, primarily by signifying its willingness to take them despite their nonconformities, in accordance with General Statutes § 42a–2–606(1)(a), and secondarily by failing to make an effective rejection, in accordance with General Statutes § 42a–2–606(1)(b). Once the tanks had been accepted, the defendant could rightfully revoke its acceptance under General Statutes § 42a–2–608 only by showing substantial impairment of their value to the defendant. In part because the defendant's conduct had foreclosed any post-installation inspection, the court concluded that such impairment had not been proved. Since the tanks were not readily resaleable on the open market, the plaintiff was entitled, upon the

1. The contract incorporated precise specifications in the form of detailed drawings. The drawings for the tank and the tank cover contained specific manufacturing instructions as well as provision 6: "Tank with cover will be tested for radiation leaks after installation. Any deficiencies must be corrected by the vendor."

2. The purchase order sent by the defendant to the plaintiff stipulated that the goods were to be shipped "F.O.B. Origin."

3. The defendant sent the plaintiff a telegram stating: "This order is hereby terminated for your breach, in that you have continuously failed to perform according to your commitment in spite of additional time given you to cure your delinquency. We will hold you liable for all damages incured [sic] by Machlett including excess cost of reprocurement."

defendant's wrongful revocation of acceptance, to recover their contract price, minus salvage value, plus interest. General Statutes §§ 42a–2–703; 42a–2–709(1)(b). Accordingly, the trial court awarded the plaintiff damages in the amount of $14,837.92.

In its appeal, the defendant raises four principal claims of error. It maintains that the trial court erred: (1) in invoking the "cure" section, General Statutes § 42a–2–508, when there had been no tender by the plaintiff seller; (2) in concluding, in accordance with the acceptance section, General Statutes § 42a–2–606(1), that the defendant had "signified" to the plaintiff its willingness to take the contract goods; (3) in misconstruing the defendant's statutory and contractual rights of inspection; and (4) in refusing to find that the defendant's letter of cancellation was occasioned by the plaintiff's breach. We find no error.

Upon analysis, all of the defendant's claims of error are variations upon one central theme. The defendant claims that on October 11, when its engineer Yannello conducted the last examination on the plaintiff's premises, the tanks were so incomplete and unsatisfactory that the defendant was rightfully entitled to conclude that the plaintiff would never make a conforming tender. From this scenario, the defendant argues that it was justified in cancelling the contract of sale. It denies that the seller's conduct was sufficient to warrant a finding of tender, or its own conduct sufficient to warrant a finding of acceptance. The difficulty with this argument is that it is inconsistent with the underlying facts found by the trial court. Although the testimony was in dispute, there was evidence of record to support the trial court's findings to the contrary. The defendant cannot sustain its burden of establishing that a trial court's findings of fact are clearly erroneous; Practice Book § 3060D; *Pandolphe's Auto Parts, Inc. v. Manchester,* 181 Conn. 217, 221–22, 435 A.2d 24 (1980); by the mere recitation in its brief of conflicting testimony entirely unsupported by reference to pages of the transcript. Practice Book § 3060F(b). There is simply no fit between the defendant's claims and the trial court's finding that, by October 11, 1976, performance was in substantial compliance with the terms of the contract. The trial court further found that on that day the defendant was notified that the goods would be ready for tender the following day and that the defendant responded to this notification by promising to send its truck to pick up the tanks in accordance with the contract.

On the trial court's finding of facts, it was warranted in concluding, on two independent grounds, that the defendant had accepted the goods it had ordered from the plaintiff. Under the provisions of the Uniform Commercial Code, General Statutes § 42a–2–606(1) "[a]cceptance of goods occurs when the buyer (a) after a reasonable opportunity to inspect the goods signifies to the seller * * * that he will take * * * them in spite of their nonconformity; or (b) fails to make an effective rejection." [10]

In concluding that the defendant had "signified" to the plaintiff its willingness to "take" the tanks despite possible remaining minor defects, the

10. General Statutes § 42a–2–606(1)(c) provides a third ground, the exercise of dominion, for finding acceptance but that ground was not considered by the trial court, presumably because it has no apparent factual relevance to the circumstances of this case. * * *

trial court necessarily found that the defendant had had a reasonable opportunity to inspect the goods. The defendant does not maintain that its engineer, or the other inspectors on previous visits, had inadequate access to the tanks, or inadequate experience to conduct a reasonable examination. It recognizes that inspection of goods when the buyer undertakes to pick up the goods is ordinarily at the seller's place of tender. See General Statutes §§ 42a–2–503, 42a–2–507, 42a–2–513; see also White & Summers, Uniform Commercial Code § 3–5 (2d Ed.1980). The defendant argues, however, that its contract, in providing for inspection for radiation leaks after installation of the tanks at its premises, necessarily postponed its inspection rights to that time. The trial court considered this argument and rejected it, and so do we. It was reasonable, in the context of this contract for the special manufacture of goods with which neither party had had prior experience, to limit this clause to adjustments to take place after tender and acceptance. After acceptance, a buyer may still, in appropriate cases, revoke its acceptance, General Statutes § 42a–2–608, or recover damages for breach of warranty, General Statutes § 42a–2–714. The trial court reasonably concluded that a post-installation test was intended to safeguard these rights of the defendant as well as to afford the plaintiff a final opportunity to make needed adjustments. The court was therefore justified in concluding that there had been an acceptance within § 42a–2–606(1)(a). A buyer may be found to have accepted goods despite their known nonconformity and despite the absence of actual delivery to the buyer * * *.

The trial court's alternate ground for concluding that the tanks had been accepted was the defendant's failure to make an effective rejection. Pursuant to General Statutes § 42a–2–606(1)(b), an acceptance occurs when, after a reasonable opportunity to inspect, a buyer has failed to make "an effective rejection as provided by subsection (1) of section 42a–2–602." The latter subsection, in turn, makes a rejection "ineffective unless the buyer seasonably notifies the seller." General Statutes § 42a–2–605(1)(a) goes on to provide that a buyer is precluded from relying, as a basis for rejection, upon unparticularized defects in his notice of rejection, if the defects were such that, with seasonable notice, the seller could have cured by making a substituted, conforming tender. The defendant does not question the trial court's determination that its telegram of cancellation failed to comply with the requirement of particularization contained in § 42a–2–605(1). Instead, the defendant argues that the plaintiff was not entitled to an opportunity to cure, under General Statutes § 42a–2–508, because the plaintiff had never made a tender of the tanks. That argument founders, however, on the trial court's finding that the seller was ready to make a tender on the day following the last inspection by the defendant's engineer and would have done so but for its receipt of the defendant's telegram of cancellation. The trial court furthermore found that the defendant's unparticularized telegram of cancellation wrongfully interfered with the plaintiff's contractual right to cure any remaining post-installation defects. In these circumstances, the telegram of cancellation constituted both a wrongful and an ineffective rejection on the part of the defendant. See *Uchitel v. F.R. Tripler & Co.*, 107 Misc.2d 310, 434 N.Y.S.2d 77, 81–82 (Supreme Court 1980); White & Summers, supra, § 8–3, p. 315.

Once the conclusion is reached that the defendant accepted the tanks, its further rights of cancellation under the contract are limited by the governing provisions of the Uniform Commercial Code. "The buyer's acceptance of goods, despite their alleged nonconformity, is a watershed. After acceptance, the buyer must pay for the goods at the contract rate; General Statutes § 42a–2–607(1); and bears the burden of establishing their nonconformity. General Statutes § 42a–2–607(4)." *Stelco Industries, Inc. v. Cohen,* 182 Conn. 561, 563–64, 438 A.2d 759 (1980). After acceptance, the buyer may only avoid liability for the contract price by invoking the provision which permits revocation of acceptance. That provision, General Statutes § 42a–2–608(1), requires proof that the "nonconformity [of the goods] substantially impairs [their] value to him." * * * On this question which is an issue of fact; * * * the trial court again found against the defendant. Since the defendant has provided no basis for any argument that the trial court was clearly erroneous in finding that the defendant had not met its burden of proof to show that the goods were substantially nonconforming, we can find no error in the conclusion that the defendant's cancellation constituted an unauthorized and hence wrongful revocation of acceptance.

Finally, the defendant in its brief, although not in its statement of the issues presented, challenges the trial court's conclusion about the remedial consequences of its earlier determinations. Although the trial court might have found the plaintiff entitled to recover the contract price because of the defendant's acceptance of the goods; General Statutes §§ 42a–2–703(e) and 42a–2–709(1)(a); the court chose instead to rely on General Statutes § 42a–2–709(1)(b), which permits a price action for contract goods that cannot, after reasonable effort, be resold at a reasonable price.[19] Since the contract goods in this case were concededly specially manufactured for the defendant, the defendant cannot and does not contest the trial court's finding that any effort to resell them on the open market would have been unavailing. In the light of this finding, the defendant can only reiterate its argument, which we have already rejected, that the primary default was that of the plaintiff rather than that of the defendant. The trial court's conclusion to the contrary supports both its award to the plaintiff and its denial of the defendant's counterclaim.

There is no error.

In this opinion the other Judges concurred.

[Footnotes in which court quoted from statute omitted.]

Notes

1. In Zabriskie Chevrolet, Inc. v. Smith, cited supra at p. 810, the court had this to say about whether the defendant accepted a new car with a defective transmission:

19. * * * It should be noted that § 42a–2–709(1)(b) is not premised on a buyer's acceptance. Instead, it requires a showing that the goods were, before the buyer's cancellation, "identified to the contract." In the circumstances of this case, that precondition was presumably met by their special manufacture and by the defendant's acquiescence in their imminent tender. See White & Summers, Uniform Commercial Code, § 7–5 (2d Ed.1980). The defendant has not, on this appeal, argued the absence of identification.

It should further be noted that § 42a–2–709(1)(b), because it is not premised on acceptance, would have afforded the seller the right to recover the contract price even if the trial court had found the conduct of the buyer to be a wrongful rejection (because of the failure to give the seller an opportunity to cure) rather than a wrongful revocation of acceptance.

"It is clear that a buyer does not accept goods until he has had a 'reasonable opportunity to inspect.' Defendant sought to purchase a new car. He assumed what every new car buyer has a right to assume and, indeed, has been led to assume by the high powered advertising techniques of the auto industry—that his new car, with the exception of very minor adjustments, would be mechanically new and factory-furnished, operate perfectly, and be free of substantial defects. The vehicle delivered to defendant did not measure up to these representations. Plaintiff contends that defendant had 'reasonable opportunity to inspect' by the privilege to take the car for a typical 'spin around the block' before signing the purchase order. If by this contention plaintiff equates a spin around the block with 'reasonable opportunity to inspect,' the contention is illusory and unrealistic. To the layman, the complicated mechanisms of today's automobiles are a complete mystery. To have the automobile inspected by someone with sufficient expertise to disassemble the vehicle in order to discover latent defects before the contract is signed, is assuredly impossible and highly impractical. Cf. Massari v. Accurate Bushing Co., 8 N.J. 299, 313, 85 A.2d 260. Consequently, the first few miles of driving become even more significant to the excited new car buyer. This is the buyer's first reasonable opportunity to enjoy his new vehicle to see if it conforms to what it was represented to be and whether he is getting what he bargained for. How long the buyer may drive the new car under the guise of inspection of new goods is not an issue in the present case. It is clear that defendant discovered the nonconformity within 7/10 of a mile and minutes after leaving plaintiff's showroom. Certainly this was well within the ambit of 'reasonable opportunity to inspect.' That the vehicle was grievously defective when it left plaintiff's possession is a compelling conclusion, as is the conclusion that in a legal sense defendant never accepted the vehicle.

"Nor could the dealer under such circumstances require acceptance. Cf. Code Comment 2 (subsection 2) to N.J.S. 12A:2–106, N.J.S.A.:

> 'It is in general intended to continue the policy of requiring exact performance by the seller of his obligations as a condition to his right to require acceptance. * * * ' "

2. Of the many cases involving UCC 2–606, the bulk involve the question whether the buyer, after having a reasonable opportunity to inspect the goods, has failed to "make an effective rejection," UCC 2–606(1)(b), that is, has failed to reject the goods within "a reasonable time after their delivery of tender." UCC 2–602(1). Like words or conduct indicating that the buyer will take the goods, silence for an unreasonable time induces the seller to believe that there is no problem with the tender of delivery. Whether an acceptance by failing to reject has occurred may turn on several factors, e.g., the nature of the defect (latent or patent), agreement on the time in which notice must be given, express warranties or assurances that problems will be corrected by the buyer, effort or lack of it by the buyer to test or inspect the goods, use of the goods by the buyer after the defect was or should have been discovered, special conditions indicating that prompt action is required, and so forth. For an excellent example, see Intervale Steel Corp. v. Borg & Beck Div., Borg-Warner, 578 F.Supp. 1081 (E.D.Mich.1984). In most cases, the difficulty will be in applying the legal principles to complicated or controverted facts. More may be at stake than simply losing the right to reject. At some point an unreasonable delay in rejecting may foreclose either a subsequent revocation of acceptance, UCC 2–608(2), or any remedy for the nonconformity, UCC 2–607(3)(a).

3. Under UCC 2–607(2), as well as its predecessor, Uniform Sales Act § 49, the fact of acceptance does not automatically preclude further remedies even though the buyer had a reasonable opportunity to inspect and the defect was "patent." This is an apparent concession to the assumption that the normal buyer's inspection will be less than adequate to deal with the complexities of defective tenders or products. In short, the buyer will not be deprived of any remedy simply because he should have discovered the particular defect complained of. But if acceptance "precludes rejection of the goods accepted," UCC 2–607(2), and the "buyer must pay at the contract rate for any goods accepted," UCC 2–607(1), what remedies remain for the buyer? The choice is between "revoking" the acceptance under UCC 2–608 or seeking damages "for breach in regard to accepted goods" under UCC 2–714. If revocation of acceptance is available and pursued, the buyer "has the same rights and duties with regard to the goods involved as if he had rejected them." UCC 2–608(3). He may, if the breach goes to the entire contract, cancel, recover so much of the price as has been paid and "cover" under UCC 2–712 or recover damages under UCC 2–713. UCC 2–711(1). If UCC 2–608 is not invoked or unavailable, the buyer must pay the contract price reduced by the amount of damages caused by the breach, UCC 2–717, and measured under UCC 2–714 and UCC 2–715.

The distinction between "latent" and "patent" defects, however, does appear in the UCC. UCC 2–607(3)(a) provides that where a tender has been accepted "the buyer must within a reasonable time after he discovers or should have discovered any breach notify the seller of breach or be barred from any remedy." As we shall see, this provision has generated controversy where defects in accepted goods cause damage to person or property. In commercial cases, however, the purpose of notification would seem to be to inform the seller "that the transaction is claimed to involve a breach, and thus [open] the way for normal settlement through negotiation." UCC 2–607, comment 4. Unlike the detail required by UCC 2–605 when goods are rejected, the content of notification under UCC 2–607(3) "need merely be sufficient to let the seller know that the transaction is still troublesome and must be watched." Comment 4. Consider the following problem.

Problem 18–6
The "Red Carpet" Treatment

On October 19, Dr. Miron, a physician who owned some race horses, attended an auction without his trainer. He observed a race horse named "Red Carpet" as he was led into the ring for sale. During a lull in the bidding, the auctioneer recited Red Carpet's "track record" and warranted him to be "sound." Thereafter, bidding picked up and Dr. Miron was the high bidder at $32,000. He took immediate possession and transported Red Carpet by van to his barn at a racetrack some 50 miles away. The next morning, Dr. Miron's trainer inspected Red Carpet and found him to be lame. The left hind leg was swollen and sensitive. X-rays later revealed a broken splint bone. Before noon on October 20, Dr. Miron notified the seller that the horse was not sound as warranted and demanded that the horse be taken back. Seller refused and insisted that the full price be paid.

1. You have been retained to represent Dr. Miron. After some probing, you have accumulated the following evidence:

(a) X-rays showing a broken splint bone in the left hind leg;

(b) Expert testimony that a broken splint bone renders a race horse unsound and, because the symptoms appear quickly, can be discovered by an inspection;

(c) Dr. Miron's affidavit that he was an inexperienced horse buyer, that he attended the auction without a trainer, that he did not examine the horse before the sale and that he did not inspect the horse's legs before transporting him to the barn;

(d) The testimony of other persons who attended the sale that they had examined Red Carpet before the auction and found no symptoms of a broken splint bone;

(e) Testimony of Dr. Miron's trainer that the problem was found and notice given within 24 hours of the sale. However, no blood tests were taken to determine whether the horse had been drugged at the time of sale.

The Seller has agreed to take the horse back if Dr. Miron will pay $20,000. Otherwise, he will sue for the full price under UCC 2–709(1). What would you advise the good doctor to do?

2. Suppose that Dr. Miron could establish that Red Carpet was not sound when the hammer fell. The seller, however, argued that Dr. Miron had accepted the horse and that either revocation of acceptance was barred under UCC 2–608(2) or that the buyer was barred from any remedy under UCC 2–607(3). How would you respond?

3. Suppose that Dr. Miron conceded that he had accepted a lame horse and attempted to revoke that acceptance under UCC 2–608(2). Who has the burden of proof in this situation? Compare UCC 2–607(4). See also, Keck v. Wacker, 413 F.Supp. 1377 (E.D.Ky.1976), another horse case, holding that where an acceptance was revoked the burden was on the seller to show that the horse conformed to the contract. Does this make sense? See UCC 2–515.

[For horse lovers, the case upon which this problem is based is Miron v. Yonkers Raceway, Inc., 400 F.2d 112 (2d Cir.1968).]

SECTION 5. SCOPE OF BUYER'S RIGHT TO REVOKE ACCEPTANCE

One of the consequences of accepting goods is that the buyer loses the rejection remedy provided in UCC 2–601. UCC 2–607(2). He is not necessarily "stuck" with the goods, however, since UCC 2–608 provides a controlled opportunity to "revoke" the acceptance and states that a "buyer who so revokes has the same rights and duties with regard to the goods involved as if he had rejected them." UCC 2–608(3). There is a temptation to equate "revocation of acceptance" with the remedy of rescission given by section 69 of the Uniform Sales Act for breach of warranty with regard to accepted goods. This temptation should be resisted. An effective revocation of acceptance neutralizes the effect of acceptance and enables the buyer to cancel the contract and pursue other available remedies under UCC 2–711. See Welken v. Conley, 252 N.W.2d 311 (N.D.1977). The buyer, however, may wish to keep the contract intact and negotiate for the repair or replacement of the goods involved. In any event, if an effective revocation occurs the remedies available to the buyer are broader and more flexible than under the USA. This is not to say that UCC 2–608 is easy to work with—it is loaded with "weasel" words which must be particularized in each case. Yet the commercial lawyer should spend some time with this section since the frustrated buyer who is unable to get satisfaction from the seller will be likely to seek advice about what to do with non-conforming goods which have been accepted, are still in his possession and may have been paid for in whole or in part.

Note, for example, the conditions attached to the "revocation of acceptance" remedy.

First, what is the effect of accepting the goods under UCC 2–606 without discovering the non-conformity? Or, suppose the buyer knew of the non-conformity and still accepted the goods? In either case, the buyer is protected if the seller made assurances that known defects would be cured or that there were no defects. UCC 2–608(1)(a) & (b). In the former case, the ancient distinction between latent and patent defects seems to be preserved: a buyer is not foreclosed from revocation where the acceptance of non-conforming goods "was reasonably induced * * * by the difficulty of discovery before acceptance. * * * " UCC 2–608(1)(b).

Second, the non-conformity, to justify revocation, must "substantially impair" the value "to him" of the goods accepted. UCC 2–608(1). What does this mean? An emerging view is that the court must make an objective determination that the value of the goods has been substantially impaired but that the determination must be made from the perspective of the particular buyer. Thus, even though leaks and dry rot in a sloop could have been repaired, the defect occurred in a vital part of the boat and "severely undermined" the buyer's confidence in its integrity as a sailing vessel. Its value was "substantially impaired."

Third, revocation of acceptance "must occur within a reasonable time after the buyer discovers or should have discovered the ground for it * * * " UCC 2–608(2). What is prompt action and what is an unreasonable delay are questions of fact.

Fourth, the revocation of acceptance, even if otherwise proper, must occur "before any substantial change in condition of the goods which is not caused by their own defects." This puts a premium on quick action where perishable commodities are involved. It also limits the scope of revocation where the goods were components or other items to be used or consumed in a manufacturing process.

Finally, the revocation is "not effective until the buyer notifies the seller of it." UCC 2–608(2). Is it enough for the buyer to pick up the telephone and say to the seller: "That last delivery was a disaster. We're getting out of this deal?" Apparently not. In Solar Kinetics Corp. v. Joseph T. Ryerson & Son, Inc., 488 F.Supp. 1237 (D.Conn.1980), the court held that the notice, to be adequate, must inform the seller that the buyer has revoked, which goods are involved and the nature of the defect. Cf. UCC 2–607(3).

ATLAN INDUSTRIES, INC. v. O.E.M., INC.

United States District Court, Western District of Oklahoma, 1983.
555 F.Supp. 184.

MEMORANDUM AND ORDER

SAFFELS, DISTRICT JUDGE, Sitting by Designation.

This case involves a complaint for the price of goods sold by plaintiff to defendant. Defendant denies liability for the price of the goods, and contends that the goods contained a latent defect which caused them to be unacceptable and out of conformity with the specifications in the sales contract between plaintiff and defendant.

Plaintiff is a prime supplier of reground plastic and wide specification machinery in the plastics industry. The goods in dispute between defendant and plaintiff are nine hundred thirty-five pounds (935 lbs.) of "Noryl-R-Beige FN 215" at eighty-five cents (85¢) per pound, as described in plaintiff's invoice No. 16886; nine thousand nine hundred fifty pounds (9,950 lbs.) of "Noryl-R-Grey FN 215" at eighty-five cents (85¢) per pound, as described on plaintiff's invoice No. 17114; and seventeen thousand two hundred ninety-five pounds (17,295 lbs.) of "Noryl-R-Grey FN 215" at eighty-five cents (85¢) per pound, as described on plaintiff's invoice No. 17449.

FN 215 is a high density, very hard plastic used primarily in the computer industry for making computer cabinets. There are two types of FN 215 on the market. "Virgin" FN 215 is plastic material which has never been molded and is manufactured only by General Electric. FN 215 "regrind" is plastic which has been molded once or more in its life, has been scrapped and has been ground for use again in a molding process. Defendant is a company which molds plastic into various parts and sells them to the computer industry. Defendant was under contract to a computer company, Magnetic Peripherals, Inc. (hereinafter MPI), to mold a number of computer cabinet parts from FN 215. Plaintiff agreed to supply defendant with raw FN 215 for this molding job. Plaintiff did not know the end use of the FN 215 it was supplying to defendant, and the name of the user was kept secret.

After agreeing to supply defendant with FN 215, plaintiff contacted a supplier about a supply of reground FN 215. Plaintiff tested the FN 215 for contamination and foreign matter, and forwarded a 935–pound sample of the FN 215 to defendant for testing.

In the plastics industry, it is a common practice for a supplier of raw plastic to forward a sample to the molder for testing. The purpose of the test is to see if the plastic material will mold well. No injection molder has facilities to do any other test. The reason for testing regrind material is that some regrind is badly contaminated with metal, which clogs the injection molding equipment and requires the molding machine to be shut down and cleaned. "Regrind" is plastic which has been molded once, and then is ground into pellets to be re-used. The regrinding process sometimes leaves small pieces of metal and metal chips in the plastic.

FN 215 is an expensive plastic which is specially compounded for use in office machines and computers. FN 215 is heat sensitive, but is able to withstand temperatures of at least two hundred five degrees (205°). Because the material is generally used in office machines and computers, it is almost always painted after molding to improve its cosmetic appearance. Defendant does not paint the parts it molds; they forward them to the ultimate user, who paints them.

The particular shipments involved in this lawsuit were molded by defendant and forwarded to their ultimate user, MPI. MPI painted the parts and heated them in an infrared oven to dry the paint. The parts molded from FN 215 "regrind" supplied by plaintiff warped when exposed to the temperature of the infrared heat ovens. The computer parts were warping when exposed to temperatures of between one hundred thirty degrees (130°) and one hundred seventy degrees (170°). Noryl FN 215 will not warp at this temperature range. Defendant molded the entire shipment of Noryl FN 215 into computer parts and tendered them to MPI before the problem surfaced. MPI immediately rejected the goods as defective and non-conforming because of the warping problem. Defendant immediately notified plaintiff that MPI had rejected the goods because of warpage, and that the material supplied by plaintiff was defective and non-conforming.

Defendant was instructed by plaintiff sometime in March, 1982, to return the material to plaintiff. Subsequently, all but four thousand pounds (4,000 lbs.) of the material supplied by plaintiff was returned to plaintiff by defendant in substantially the same condition. Plaintiff was unable to furnish Noryl FN 215 from another source. Due to plaintiff's inability to furnish conforming FN 215, defendant purchased forty thousand pounds (40,000 lbs.) of FN 215 from General Electric at forty-two cents (42¢) per pound higher than plaintiff's price. Defendant invested eighty (80) hours of labor at Ten Dollars ($10) per hour to inspect and regrind the non-conforming FN 215 back to its original state to return to plaintiff. The material was reground because it would therefore be cheaper to ship and easier for plaintiff to resell. In addition, plaintiff agreed that it would be better to regrind the material.

This lawsuit is governed by Article 2 of the Uniform Commercial Code. The court finds that there was a contract for sale of goods between plaintiff and defendant. Plaintiff agreed to sell to defendant a known quantity of Noryl FN 215. It is undisputed that Noryl FN 215 does not warp at one hundred fifty degrees (150°), and it is undisputed that parts made from the Noryl FN 215 supplied by plaintiff did warp when exposed to temperatures of one hundred fifty degrees (150°). Therefore, we find that the goods tendered by plaintiff failed to conform to the contract. Pursuant to Okla. Stat. 12A, § 2–601, if goods fail in any respect to conform to a contract, the buyer may reject all of them or accept all of them.

Acceptance of goods occurs when the buyer, after a reasonable opportunity to inspect them, signifies to the seller that the goods are conforming or that he will take them despite their non-conformity, or where the buyer fails to make an effective rejection, or does any act inconsistent with the seller's ownership. Okla.Stat. 12A, § 2–606(1). A buyer is deemed to have accepted goods when, without making any effort to reject them, he receives the goods, processes them, and sells the finished product to a third-person. *A & G Construction Co., Inc. v. Reid Brothers Logging Co., Inc.,* 547 P.2d 1207 (Alaska 1976). Such actions on the part of the buyer are clearly inconsistent with ownership by the seller. Anderson, *Uniform Commercial Code,* § 2–606:31 (1971). The court finds defendant accepted the goods.

A buyer must pay at the contract rate for any goods he has accepted. Okla.Stat. 12A, § 2–607(1). However, a buyer may revoke his acceptance of goods whose non-conformity substantially impairs their value to him if he has accepted those goods without discovery of the non-conformity where his acceptance was reasonably induced by the difficulty of discovery before acceptance. Okla.Stat. 12A, § 2–608(1)(b). As a condition precedent to revoking acceptance, the buyer must show that the goods are both non-conforming and that the non-conformance substantially impairs the value of the goods to the buyer.

Goods are "conforming" when they are in accordance with the obligations under the contract. Okla.Stat. 12A, § 2–106(2). The Noryl FN 215 in issue in this case was not conforming because it would not tolerate the temperature that Noryl FN 215 is specifically able to tolerate.

The test for whether the non-conformity substantially impairs the value of the goods to the buyer is whether the non-conformity is such as will in fact cause a substantial impairment of the value to the buyer even though the seller had no advance knowledge as to the buyer's particular circumstances. Okla.Stat. 12A, § 2–608, Official Code Comment 2. The court finds that the non-conformity substantially impaired the value of the Noryl FN 215 to the buyer, plaintiff Atlan. FN 215 is primarily used to make computer cabinets and to house office machines. The plastic, when molded, is a dull, off-white or a dull, grey color. It is virtually always painted a more pleasant color before it is sold to its ultimate user. Noryl FN 215 does not have any other reasonable use. The Noryl FN 215 in question, when painted, could not withstand the temperatures in a drying oven. Therefore, the parts could not be painted and dried in the ordinary manner. If the parts could not be painted, they could not be used in the computer and office machinery industry. They were, therefore, substantially without value to the ultimate user and to the molder who had manufactured them. Therefore, the value of this particular Noryl FN 215 was substantially impaired because it did not conform to the characteristics inherent in normal Noryl FN 215.

If the buyer did not know of the non-conformity when he accepted the goods, he must show his acceptance was reasonably induced by the difficulty of discovering the non-conformity before acceptance. The undisputed testimony revealed that in the plastics industry it is common for a molder to test samples only to see whether or not they will mold well. The Noryl FN 215 in question was so tested and did mold well. Plaintiff contends that the defendant was under an additional duty to forward samples he had molded to his customer, MPI, to see whether or not the molded samples would conform to MPI's specifications. While this might be a reasonable provision to place in a contract for sale between plaintiff and defendant, the court finds that the law does not require the buyer to perform any more tests than are common in the industry. Okla.Stat. 12A, § 1–205(2).

Revocation of acceptance must occur within a reasonable time after the buyer discovers the non-conformity. There is no claim in this case that defendant unreasonably delayed notifying plaintiff of the non-conformity, and the court finds that plaintiff was notified within a reasonable time after defendant discovered the warping problem.

A buyer who revokes acceptance has the same rights with regard to the goods involved as if he had rejected them. Okla.Stat. 12A, § 2–608(3). "Rights" includes remedies. Okla.Stat. 12A, § 1–201(36). A buyer who has rightfully rejected goods has no further obligation in regard to those goods, including an obligation to pay their purchase price. Okla.Stat. 12A, § 2–

602(2)(c). Therefore, the court finds against plaintiff on his complaint for the purchase price of the Noryl FN 215 involved in this lawsuit, and now turns to the question of defendant's remedies for rejection of non-conforming goods.

* * *

It is by the court therefore ordered that plaintiff take nothing of defendant on plaintiff's complaint. It is further ordered that judgment be entered in favor of defendant and against plaintiff on defendant's counterclaim in the sum of Sixty-Four Thousand Fourteen and 47/100 Dollars ($64,014.47). It is further ordered that costs are assessed against plaintiff.

JOHANNSEN v. MINNESOTA VALLEY FORD TRACTOR CO.

Supreme Court of Minnesota, 1981.
304 N.W.2d 654.

Considered and decided by the court en banc without oral argument.

OPINION

PETERSON, JUSTICE.

The defendants, Ford Motor Co. and Minnesota Valley Ford (dealer), appeal from the judgment entered in favor of the plaintiff, Harvey Johannsen, the buyer of a defective tractor manufactured by Ford and sold to him by the dealer. After a trial in which the jury found that Johannsen had effectively revoked his acceptance of a Ford Model 9700 tractor (9700), the district court entered judgment for the plaintiff in the amount of the purchase price of the tractor less an offset for use and depreciation. Defendants appeal from the order denying post-trial motions for judgment notwithstanding the verdict or a new trial and also appeal from the judgment. We affirm.

The plaintiff revoked his acceptance of the 9700 tractor pursuant to Minn.Stat. § 336.2–608(1)(b) (1980) after he experienced mechanical problems that substantially interfered with its intended use on his 330–acre farm. On July 13, 1977, plaintiff, together with his wife, went to the premises of the dealer to pick up his 1974 Ford Model 9600 tractor (9600), which had been taken to the dealer for repairs. Johannsen had experienced a number of problems with the fourth gear and hydraulic system of his 9600. The tractor had jumped out of fourth gear on a number of occasions while Johannsen was plowing. Johannsen expressed his concern to Brian Gaard, one of the dealer's employees, that the 9600 would again jump out of gear.

Gaard told Johannsen that the transmission of the new 1977 Ford Model 9700 had been redesigned to avoid the transmission defects of the 9600 and that he could solve his tractor transmission problems by purchasing a new 9700 for $26,000. Gaard did not tell Johannsen that Ford had sent a letter to its tractor dealers in May of that year detailing transmission defects in the 9700. Dealers were informed that some 9700's jumped out of fourth and/or eighth gear. They were instructed to check all 9700's in stock for the defect and to sell defective tractors only if they would lose a sale. Johannsen purchased a 9700 from the dealer and traded in his 9600.

The dealer delivered the tractor to Johannsen's farm in late July. The tractor jumped out of fourth gear upon its first use, and at about the same time the frost plugs blew out of the engine, causing a loss of all of the coolant. The dealer sent a repairman to plaintiff's farm on that day who told Johannsen to see the dealer about the transmission defect. On August 3, 1977, the tractor developed a fuel restriction problem and a hydraulic leak, which made it difficult to lower the implements into the soil. The dealer informed Johannsen that it could not fix the hydraulic defect until replacement parts became available in April, 1978. Johannsen told every serviceman who called at his farm that he wanted to return the tractor.

On September 19, 1977, Johannsen, by his attorney, formally notified the dealer in writing of his revocation of acceptance due to transmission, hydraulic and fuel line defects, and he directed the dealer to pick up the tractor immediately.

Johannsen continued to use the tractor after the written revocation and called the dealer on September 28 because the tractor continued to exhibit the same problems. The dealer made service calls on September 28, October 2, and October 9 in response to Johannsen's complaints. Ray Chaik, an employee of the dealer, told Johannsen that he could finish his fall work and bring the tractor in for winter servicing. Johannsen used the tractor for a total of 120 hours but was able to plow or disk only 150 acres of his farm with it. Approximately 90 of those hours were put on the tractor after the revocation letter of September 19. Johannsen put the tractor in storage in late October, 1977.

The defendants contend that the plaintiff did not effectively revoke his acceptance of the 9700 tractor because (1) he did not allow the defendants to attempt to cure the defects, (2) the defects did not substantially impair the value of the tractor, (3) the plaintiff did not revoke his acceptance of the tractor seasonably, and (4) the plaintiff continued to use the tractor after revocation of acceptance.

1. The defendants, although acknowledging that the seller's right to cure pursuant to Minn.Stat. § 336.2–508(2) (1980) is expressly limited by the language of the statute to cases in which the buyer rejects a non-conforming tender, argue that the right to cure should be incorporated into Minn.Stat. § 336.2–608(3) (1980) governing revocation of acceptance.[4] It is our view that any right to cure should be limited to cases in which the defects are minor, and we hold that the seller has no right to cure defects which substantially impair the good's value.

2. We reject defendants' contention that the jury's finding that the defects substantially impaired the value of the tractor to plaintiff is not supported by the evidence. In *Durfee v. Rod Baxter Imports, Inc.,* 262 N.W.2d 349, 353–54 (Minn.1977), we set forth guidelines to establish the substantial impairment requirement of Minn.Stat. § 336.2–608(1):

4. Commentators are divided on the issue of whether the seller has a right to cure after the buyer revokes his acceptance. *See e.g.,* J. White & R. Summers, *Uniform Commercial Code,* 293 (1980) (no right to cure); *contra* 3 S. Williston, Williston on Sales 119 (Supp.1980).

[T]wo respected commentators suggest that the test ultimately rests on a commonsense perception of substantial impairment, akin to the determination of a material breach under traditional contract law. White & Summers, Uniform Commercial Code, § 8–3, p. 257. The cases that involve revocation of acceptance of defective new automobiles are amenable to classification by this practical criterion. Minor defects not substantially interfering with the automobile's operation or with the comfort and security it affords passengers do not constitute grounds for revocation. On the other hand, if the defect substantially interferes with operation of the vehicle or a purpose for which it was purchased, a court may find grounds for revocation. Indeed, substantial impairment has been found even where the defect is curable, if it shakes the faith of the purchaser in the automobile.

Substantial evidence supports the jury's finding that the transmission and hydraulic defects substantially impaired the value of the tractor to plaintiff. He specifically purchased the 9700 to avoid problems with the essential fourth gear which he had experienced with the 9600. As a result of the defects, he was only able to use the tractor on 150 acres of his 330–acre farm. Plaintiff testified that due to the defect it took him two weeks to plow 50 acres of sweet corn ground, a task that should have taken less than 4 hours to complete. Under these circumstances, the jury's finding is supported by the evidence.

3. We likewise reject defendants' contention that plaintiff did not revoke his acceptance within a reasonable time after discovering the defect. The issue of what constitutes a reasonable time within the context of revocation of acceptance is a jury question that depends on the facts and circumstances of the case. We hold that the jury's finding that plaintiff's revocation was timely is supported by the evidence because it could have reasonably concluded that plaintiff gave notice within a reasonable time after discovering through his use of the tractor that it would not adequately perform the tasks for which it was purchased.

4. Defendants additionally contend that plaintiff's use of the tractor after he gave written notice of revocation of acceptance constitutes a second acceptance. Although the revoking buyer's continued use of defective goods may be wrongful under some circumstances,[5] we think that there can be no blanket rule which prohibits such a buyer from continuing to use the goods. A blanket rule prohibiting a revoking buyer from continuing to use the goods would contravene the code's rule of reasonableness and its underlying purpose of modernizing commercial transactions. We agree with those jurisdictions that have so held. *See Minsel v. El Rancho Mobile Home Center, Inc.,* 32 Mich.App. 10, 188 N.W.2d 9 (1971). *Fablok Mills, Inc. v. Cocker Machinery & Foundry Co.,* 125 N.J.Super. 251, 310 A.2d 491 (Super.Ct.App.Div.1973), *cert. denied,* 64 N.J. 317; 315 A.2d 405 (1973).

The reasonableness of the buyer's use of a defective good after revocation is a question of fact for the jury that is to be based on the facts and

5. Minn.Stat. § 336.2–602(2)(a) (1980) provides that any exercise of ownership by a rejecting buyer is wrongful as against the seller. Defendants contend that because section 336–2–608(3) imposes upon revoking buyers the same rights and duties as if they had rejected the goods, that a revoking buyer's continued use of goods is always wrongful.

circumstances of each case. Several factors that the jury may consider include the seller's instructions to the buyer after revocation of acceptance; the degree of economic and other hardship that the buyer would suffer if he discontinued using the defective good; the reasonableness of the buyer's use after revocation as a method of mitigating damages; the degree of prejudice to the seller; and whether the seller acted in bad faith.

We hold, limited to the facts and circumstances of this case, that the jury could find that plaintiff's continued use of the 9700 tractor was reasonable and did not constitute a waiver of his revocation of acceptance. The defects in the 9700 tractor were major. Employees of the dealer knew that Johannsen specifically purchased the 9700 to avoid the transmission defect in the 9600, knew of the possibility of the identical defect in the 9700, and yet they led Johannsen to believe that buying the 9700 would solve all of his tractor transmission problems. In addition, evidence in the record tends to show that Johannsen used the tractor only to perform necessary tasks.

We note that the trial court, based upon expert testimony, allowed the defendants a setoff for use and depreciation of the tractor. Allowing the seller to recover for the revoking buyer's use of the tractor best serves the equitable principle incorporated into the code through Minn.Stat. § 336.1–103 (1980)[6] that a party seeking rescission of a contract must return or offer to return that which he had received under it in order to restore the parties to the positions that they occupied prior to the transaction. *See Village of Wells v. Layne-Minnesota Co.,* 240 Minn. 132, 138, 60 N.W.2d 621, 625 (1953).

5. Defendants contend that the trial court improperly excluded for lack of foundation a warranty which limited a buyer's remedies to repair or replacement. Defendants asserted that plaintiff had been given a copy of Ford's standard warranty, but they were unable to produce an executed copy of the warranty. Plaintiff denied that he had executed any such warranty. We conclude that the trial court did not err in the exclusion of the alleged warranty.

The instructions given to the jury by the trial court are in conformity with the law as we have stated it. Defendants' other claims of error on evidentiary matters do not require discussion.

Affirmed.

Note: Effect of Use After Revocation of Acceptance

Clearly, the buyer may need to use tendered goods to determine whether they conform to the contract. In short, use is necessary to have a "reasonable opportunity" to inspect them. UCC 2–606(1)(b). The buyer, however, must avoid doing "any act inconsistent with the seller's ownership." UCC 2–606(1)(c). Suppose, for example, that the seller tenders coiled steel and the buyer processes it before discovering the nonconformity. The use and fabrication may both accept the goods, UCC 2–606(1)(c), and preclude revocation because of "substantial change in the condition of the goods." UCC 2–608(2). See Intervale Steel

6. Minn.Stat. § 336.1–103 (1978) provides: "Unless displaced by the particular provisions of this Act, the principles of law and equity, including the law merchant and the law relative to capacity to contract, principal and agent, estoppel, fraud, misrepresentation, duress, coercion, mistake, bankruptcy, or other validating or invalidating cause shall supplement its provisions."

Corp. v. Borg & Beck Div., Borg–Warner, 578 F.Supp. 1081 (E.D.Mich.1984). But see Alimenta (U.S.A.), Inc. v. Anheuser–Busch Companies, Inc., 803 F.2d 1160 (11th Cir.1986), finding that a use (blanching peanuts) that constituted acceptance did not preclude revocation of acceptance because the value of the goods was not diminished.

Suppose, however, that the buyer continues to use the goods after a rightful rejection or revocation of acceptance. UCC 2–602(2)(a) provides that "after rejection any exercise of ownership by the buyer with respect to any commercial unit is wrongful as against the seller." Presumably, a "wrongful" exercise of ownership can be treated by the seller as either an acceptance or a tort. See UCC 2–606(2)(c). If so, the continued use neutralizes the rejection, constitutes a reacceptance and obligates the buyer to pay the price.

Article 2 is silent on the effect of continued use after a justified revocation of acceptance. Note that *Johannsen v. Minnesota Valley Ford Tractor* rejected the blanket rule of UCC 2–606(2)(a) in favor of the principle of reasonable use and held that a reasonable use did not constitute an acceptance. Rather, the buyer was entitled to return the goods to and obtain damages from the seller, subject to an offset for the reasonable value of their use or depreciation. Accord: Romy v. Picker International, Inc., 1992 WL 70403 (E.D.Pa.1992), affirmed, 986 F.2d 1409 (3d Cir.1993), (use of MRI machine by doctor after revocation was reasonable and part of the duty to mitigate damages); North River Homes, Inc. v. Bosarge, 594 So.2d 1153 (Miss.1992) (use of mobile home for 12 months after revocation justified by seller's assurances of cure and buyer's financial inability to move); Braden v. Stem, 571 So.2d 1112 (Ala.1990) (buyer's use of used car for seven months after revocation justified because buyer needed the car to transport a child).

Is there any justification for the different treatment of continued use after rejection and revocation of acceptance?

Problem 18–7

On April 19, 1976, defendant Clarence Miller ordered a 1976 Dodge Royal Monaco station wagon from plaintiff Colonial Dodge which included a heavy-duty trailer package with extra wide tires.

On May 28, 1976, defendant picked up the wagon, drove it a short distance where he met his wife, and exchanged it for her car. Defendant drove that car to work while his wife returned home with the new station wagon. Shortly after arriving home, Mrs. Miller noticed that their new wagon did not have a spare tire. The following morning defendant notified plaintiff that he insisted on having the tire he ordered immediately, but when told there was no spare tire then available, he informed the salesman for plaintiff that he would stop payment on the two checks that were tendered as the purchase price, and that the vehicle could be picked up from in front of his home. Defendant parked the car in front of his home where it remained until the temporary ten-day registration sticker had expired, whereupon the car was towed by the St. Clair police to a St. Clair dealership. Plaintiff had applied for license plates, registration, and title in defendant's name. Defendant refused the license plates when they were delivered to him.

According to plaintiff's witness, the spare tire was not included in the delivery of the vehicle due to a nation-wide shortage caused by a labor strike. Some months later, defendant was notified his tire was available.

Plaintiff sued defendant for the purchase price of the car. On January 13, 1981, the trial court entered a judgment for plaintiff finding that defendant wrongfully revoked acceptance of the vehicle. The Court of Appeals decided that defendant never accepted the vehicle. On rehearing, the Court of Appeals, noting the trial court found the parties had agreed that there was a valid acceptance, affirmed the trial court's holding there was not a substantial impairment in value sufficient to authorize defendant to revoke acceptance of the automobile.

1. How should this case be resolved on appeal to the Supreme Court?

2. Suppose after Buyer rightfully revoked acceptance Seller promptly tendered a conforming tire. Buyer, citing UCC 2–508, argued that seller had no right to cure after a revocation of acceptance and canceled the contract. Is Buyer correct?

CHAPTER NINETEEN

SELLER'S BREACH OF WARRANTY AS TO THE QUALITY OF GOODS SOLD

SECTION 1. INTRODUCTION

A. Warranty Theory: Some History

Disputes over the quality of goods sold frequently end up in court. The buyer's claim is that the goods, because of a condition existing at the time of tender, failed to conform to his expectations regarding basic attributes or suitability. The seller's response may be that the buyer assumed the risk. More particularly, the argument is that since neither party knew of the condition at the time of delivery, i.e., both were equally ignorant, and the buyer could have discovered the condition by inspection or otherwise, there is no sound reason, absent fraud, deceit or mutual mistake, why the seller should bear the risk. Thus, the stage is set, the seller will contend, for application of the doctrine of caveat emptor, the "universal structural characteristic of the law of sales." Rabel, *The Nature of Warranty of Quality,* 24 Tulane L.Rev. 273 (1970). See Hamilton, *The Ancient Maxim of Caveat Emptor,* 49 Yale L.J. 1133 (1931).

One "sound" reason for protecting the buyer's expectations is found in the law of warranty. Warranty is a representational theory of liability. It depends upon the answers to two key questions: (1) What did the seller affirm, represent or promise, expressly or impliedly, about the quality of the goods sold to the buyer; and (2) Was the buyer justified in incorporating the representations into its expectations of quality? The first question poses primarily a question of fact. The second question is primarily a question of law. Clearly, not everything a seller says about the goods will become part of the contract for sale. To the extent that representations of quality become part of the agreement, however, they constitute a standard of quality—a warranty—to which the goods must conform at the time of delivery.

The Anglo-American history of warranty reveals, in commercial transactions at least,* a slow but steady erosion of the doctrine of caveat emptor.

* There are, in fact, three legal worlds of product liability. The first, with which these Chapters are concerned, concerns disputes over quality between commercial parties where only economic loss is involved. These disputes are governed, in the main, by Article 2. The second involves disputes between individuals and commercial sellers over "defective" products which have caused personal injuries. These disputes are governed by the law of torts, primarily the law of strict products liability. See Section 402A of the Restatement, Second, of Torts. The third involves disputes between individual consumers and commercial sellers over quality where economic loss and, perhaps, property damage has occurred. These are governed in part by Article 2 and in part by a patchwork of federal and supplemental state consumer protection laws. See Rice, *Product Quality Laws and the Economics of Federalism,* 65 B.U.L.Rev. 1 (1985).

The following account, taken from the sources cited below, touches the doctrinal tip of a much larger social iceberg. Speidel, Warranty Theory, Economic Loss, and the Privity Requirement: Once More Into the Void, 67 B.U.L. Rev. 9, 14–27 (1987); Hillinger, *The Merchant of Section 2–314: Who Needs Him?,* 34 Hastings L.Rev. 747, 788–807 (1983); Titus, *Restatement (Second) of Torts Section 402A and the Uniform Commercial Code,* 22 Stan.L.Rev. 713, 728–344 (1970); Prosser, *The Implied Warranty of Merchantable Quality,* 27 Minn.L.Rev. 117 (1943); Llewellyn, *On Warranty of Quality and Society, I,* 36 Colum.L.Rev. 699, 716–31 (1936); Hamilton, *The Ancient Maxim Caveat Emptor,* 40 Yale L.J. 1133, 1163–78 (1931); Williston, *Representation and Warranty in Sales,* 27 Harv.L.Rev. 1 (1913); McClain, *Implied Warranties in Sales,* 7 Harv.L.Rev. 213 (1903).

Warranty disputes involving claims for economic loss first arose between sellers and buyers of goods who were in privity of contract. In the early 17th Century, however, they were asserted in tort as an action on the Case. The buyer had to establish the elements of deceit, i.e., that the seller made an express representation about the nature of the goods knowing it to be false.

By 1790, the action of Deceit, with its requirements of scienter by the representor and reliance by the representee, had developed into a separate writ or action. At about the same time, the English courts first permitted an express warranty claim to be brought in assumpsit, the action in which most contract claims were pursued.

By 1802, it was decided that scienter was not a requirement in Assumpsit for breach of an express warranty, but other limiting formalities, i.e., the representation must be an express term of the contract and intended by the seller to be a warranty, still remained. This early interaction between representations of quality made in exchange transactions and the tort forms of action led Dean Prosser to conclude that warranty was a "freak hybrid born of the illicit intercourse of tort and contract." Prosser, *The Assault Upon the Citadel (Strict Liability to the Consumer),* 69 Yale L.J. 1099, 1126–27 (1960). The New York Court of Appeals, in a personal injury case, concluded: "Accordingly, for some 400 years the action rested not on an enforcible (sic) promise but on a wrong or tort. In the historical development of the law of warranty, however, as so often happens in law and life in general, accident was evidently confused with essence: from the fact that the cases which arose involved contractual relationships and represented enforcible (sic) promises, the courts seem to have concluded that the contract was the essence of the action. * * * The occasion for the warranty was constituted a necessary condition of it." Randy Knitwear, Inc. v. American Cyanamid Co., 11 N.Y.2d 5, 226 N.Y.S.2d 363, 366 n. 2, 181 N.E.2d 399, 401 n. 2 (1962).

During the 19th Century, warranty theory developed into the tripartite form which we know today, an express warranty, an implied warranty of fitness for particular purpose and an implied warranty of merchantability (fitness for "ordinary" purposes). The implied warranties emerged, inferentially, at the point where the seller's express representations about or description of the goods failed to cover the exact issue in dispute. All three

were captured, in the late 19th Century, by the British Sale of Goods Act and, later, in the American Uniform Sales Act. They appear as Sections 2–313, 2–314 and 2–315 of the Uniform Commercial Code. We will return to examine each and all in more detail.

Before looking at warranty theory under the UCC, a few general questions should be kept in mind.

First, warranties, arising as they do from contracts for sale, have been treated as terms of the contract. Two consequences flow from this treatment: (1) A breach of warranty is a breach of contract, entitling the seller to recover direct and consequential economic loss measured by the expectation interest; (2) Privity of contract has usually been required between the seller and buyer, especially where the buyer claims only economic loss. Are these consequences inevitable? For example, should a plaintiff injured in person by a defective product be permitted to recover under a warranty theory? Or, should a buyer who suffers only economic loss caused by an unmerchantable product manufactured by a remote seller be permitted to recover on a warranty theory without privity of contract?

Second, the tort of misrepresentation has developed apart from warranty theory. In general, the misrepresentation must be material and negligently made. In addition, the plaintiff must justifiably rely upon it and is limited, in many cases, to the recovery of out-of-pocket economic loss. But when the misrepresentation concerns goods sold, there is an obvious overlap with the theory of express warranty. Which should prevail in these cases, express warranties under the UCC or tort theory?

Third, in the last 25 years a special body of law has developed to protect individual consumers who purchase goods for personal, family or household purposes and suffer economic loss. Uneven though this development has been, it reflects a conclusion that there is usually an imbalance of capacity between the individual and the enterprise and that this imbalance creates a risk of exploitation in bargaining or unprovable fraud by the enterprise. The legal response includes the federal Magnuson-Moss Warranty Act and state legislation, such as the "lemon" laws. Is this development justified? If so, how much government regulation is necessary to correct the imbalance, whether it be in bargaining power, information or capacity for choice, and should that regulation be included in the UCC?

Fourth, defective and dangerous products manufactured by sellers frequently cause damage to the person or property of purchasers and other foreseeable users or consumers. Since the great case of *McPherson v. Buick Motor Company,* decided in 1920, injured parties have been able, privity or not, to sue the manufacturer in negligence. Since the 1960s, with the promulgation of Section 402A of the Restatement, Second, Torts, injured parties have been permitted to sue under the theory of strict products liability. Although negligence theory has not been preempted, it has been eclipsed by strict liability.

Given these developments in the law of products liability, to what extent does the UCC preempt tort law where the seller has breached a warranty and the buyer has suffered personal injuries or property loss? Should the buyer with both a claim in warranty and a claim in strict tort be able to choose which to pursue? And what about products that cause only economic loss or cause damage only to the goods sold? Should these claims be limited to warranty theory under the UCC or may they also be pursued under negligence or strict tort theory? What difference does it make? In the materials to follow, we will try to provide some answers to these questions.

B. *Warranties Under the Code: An Introduction*

According to Comment 4 to UCC 2–313, the basic purpose of warranty law is to determine "what it is that the seller has in essence agreed to sell." As you are now fully aware, agreement means the "bargain in fact as found in their language or by implication from other circumstances." UCC 1–201(3). Thus, whether the buyer's understanding of quality is consistent with the agreement may depend, among other things, upon the description, what the seller has said, common uses in the trade, the price paid and the extent to which the buyer has communicated particular needs to the seller. Interestingly enough, the more detailed the agreement on quality and the allocation of risks, the less room there is for legitimate dispute over conformity of the goods to the contract and the less likely it is that the warranty label will be applied to the controversy.

The UCC draftsmen, however, have selected an approach which yields warranties of different kinds, including express warranties, UCC 2–313, implied warranties of merchantability, UCC 2–314, and implied warranties of fitness for particular purpose, UCC 2–315—a tripartite approach. (The implied warranty of title, UCC 2–312, will be treated later.) In so doing, the draftsmen rejected the unitary approach suggested by the theory of contract and, at the same time, preserved the close tie between warranty and the contract. The initial question, therefore, will be whether the Code's tripartite approach to the problem supports any breach of warranty claim at all. The answer to this question will also be affected by the possible application of exclusionary rules, i.e., disclaimers or rules of interpretation, which neutralize facts which otherwise would support a warranty claim. See UCC 2–316, 2–317 & 2–202. These rules proceed on the assumption that what is rooted in contract can, under controlled circumstances, be taken away or altered by contract.

A second question is when did the buyer discover the alleged breach of warranty? This has immense practical importance. If the defect is discovered before acceptance, the remedy of rejection, UCC 2–601 through 2–605, and the remedial options in UCC 2–711(1) are available. The remedial problems become more complicated after acceptance, and the degree of complication is closely related to how soon thereafter the defect was discovered. The risks of delay are pinpointed in UCC 2–725(2), 2–608(2) and 2–607(3)(a). Other problems flowing from acceptance have to do with revoking acceptance, UCC 2–608(1), burden of proof, UCC 2–607(4), uncertainty in the measure of "direct" damage, UCC 2–714(2), and the increased risk that consequential damages will be involved. UCC 2–715(2). As a general rule, the earlier the breach is discovered and the quicker remedial options are exercised, the better off the buyer will be.

Another question is the extent to which the seller has validly altered by contract the normal remedies available to the buyer upon breach of warranty. Relevant Code sections include UCC 2–316, 2–718, 2–719 & 2–302. A final question is, of course, whether a warranty made by the seller has in fact been breached.

The problem and case that follow introduce the relevant Code warranty sections.

Problem 19–1
The Case of the Hot Casserole

Sam Sweeney owns and operates a supermarket which specializes in produce from many lands. The produce is displayed in open bins at one end of the store under a large sign which reads "Foods from Many Lands." Above each bin is space for a written description of the produce and a price. On the morning of March 5, Sam received a shipment of pepper beans from Africa. The dried beans, which closely resembled lima beans, were extremely hot to the taste. The beans were displayed in an empty bin but, because of the press of other matters, Sam did not describe the goods or fix a price at that time. Sam did not sell dried lima beans at this store, but they could be purchased at other stores for between \$.20 and \$.25 per pound. On the morning of March 6, Mrs. Banks, a new resident in the area, entered Sam's store for the first time. She wanted to purchase lima beans for a special casserole to be served that evening at a dinner party for her husband's new boss. Mrs. Banks did not notice the "Foods from Many Lands" sign. After walking around the produce bins, she found what seemed to be plain old garden variety lima beans. She asked a salesman the price and was told "\$.23 a pound." Pointing to the unmarked bin, she stated, "I will take two pounds of those." The beans were weighed, put into a sack and paid for. Later that afternoon, Mrs. Banks prepared her special casserole which was served to her guests without the true nature of the beans being discovered. The casserole, of course, was somewhat difficult to eat and the dinner party, while interesting, was something less than a success. The next morning, a furious Mrs. Banks consults her attorney.

1. Does she have any legal recourse against Sam? What advice would you give?

2. Suppose that one of Mrs. Banks' guests had become violently ill after eating the beans. Would the guest have a warranty claim against Sam? See UCC 2–318.

3. At what point would Sam, who had knowledge superior to Mrs. Banks, be impressed with a duty to caution or warn about the special nature of the beans? See Addis v. Bernardin, Inc., 226 Kan. 241, 597 P.2d 250 (1979) (seller knew goods sold would not suit buyer's purposes).

4. In many cases, the buyer will lose despite claims that the seller made and breached all three UCC warranties. See, e.g., Jay Dee Contractors, Inc. v. Tews Co., Inc., 787 F.Supp. 160 (E.D.Wis.1992); Hobson Const. Co., Inc. v. Hajoca Corp., 28 N.C.App. 684, 222 S.E.2d 709 (1976). Is this the correct result in the Case of the Hot Casserole?

SECTION 2. NON-COMPLIANCE WITH EXPRESS WARRANTIES

A. Liability for Statements Constituting "Core" Descriptions or as to Basic Attributes

Exactly what is an express warranty? Let us first consider what it was (or seemed to have been) before the Code.

CHANDELOR v. LOPUS

Exch. Chamber, 1625.
79 Eng.Rep. 3, Cro.Jac. 4.

Action upon the case. Whereas the defendant being a goldsmith, and having skill in jewels and precious stones, had a stone which he affirmed to Lopus to be a bezar-stone, and sold it to him for one hundred pounds; ubi revera it was not a bezar-stone: the defendant pleaded not guilty, and verdict was given and judgment entered for the plaintiff in the King's Bench.

But error was thereof brought in the Exchequer Chamber; because the declaration contains not matter sufficient to charge the defendant, viz. that he warranted it to be a bezar-stone, or that he knew that it was not a bezar-stone; for it may be, he himself was ignorant whether it were a bezar-stone or not.

And all the Justices and Barons (except Anderson) held, that for this cause it was error: for the bare affirmation that it was a bezar-stone, without warranting it to be so, is no cause of action: and although he knew it to be no bezar-stone it is not material; for every one in selling his wares will affirm that his wares are good, or the horse which he sells is sound; yet if he does not warrant them to be so, it is no cause of action, and the warranty ought to be made at the same time of the sale; as F.N.B. 94, c and 98, b; 5 Hen. 7, pl. 41; 9 Hen. 6, pl. 53; 12 Hen. 4, pl. 1, 42 Ass. 8; 7 Hen. 4, pl. 15. Wherefore, forasmuch as no warranty is alleged, they held the declaration to be ill.

ANDERSON to the contrary; for the deceit in selling it for a bezar, whereas it was not so, is cause of action.

But, notwithstanding, it was adjudged to be no cause, and the judgment reversed.

GILMORE, PRODUCTS LIABILITY: A COMMENTARY, 38 U.Chi. L.Rev. 103, 107–08 (1970).

"In connection with the point that most cases—perhaps all cases—are sensibly, or even 'correctly,' decided as of their own time and place, I will indulge myself in a brief digression on a landmark of the common law * * *—a case called Chandelor v. Lopus, which was decided by the Exchequer Chamber in 1625. A goldsmith had sold for £100 a stone which he affirmed to be a bezoar. The stone turned out not to be a bezoar. The disappointed buyer, who had presumably paid the price for a true bezoar, brought an action to recover damages for, as we should say, breach of warranty. Judgment for the goldsmith-seller: he had merely 'affirmed' that the stone was a bezoar without 'warranting' it to be one—wherefore the buyer's action did not lie. For several hundred years the case has been cited, with approval or with scorn, as illustrative of the extremely narrow scope of liability which seventeenth century law placed on sellers for the quality of the goods they sold.

"The report of the case does not bother to explain what a bezoar was—presumably everybody knew what a bezoar was, just as we all know what a diamond is. It occurred to me one day, in thinking about the case, that I for one had no idea what a bezoar might be. The new Oxford Dictionary proved to be illuminating. A bezoar (or 'bezar') was, descriptively, 'a calculus or concretion found in the stomachs of some animals, chiefly ruminants, formed of concentric layers of animal matter deposited round some foreign substance, which serves as a nucleus.' That explains everything except why a bezoar would have been worth £100 in the early 17th century. The true value of a bezoar, it appears, lay in its magic or, as we should say, medicinal properties: application of the bezoar to a diseased part of the body cured the disease. 'Everything that frees the body of any ailment,' it was said, 'is called the Bezoar of that ailment.' And the East India Company had reported in 1618 that: 'On the island of Borneo, diamonds, bezoar stones and gold might be obtained.'

"Now that we know more about bezoars than we did, we may begin to wonder whether our initial reaction to the holding in Chandelor v. Lopus was, historically, correct—or even relevant to the case. It was generally known that there were true, or magic, bezoars. It must also have been a matter of common knowledge that it was extremely difficult, if not impossible, to tell a true bezoar from a false one. And no doubt the attitude of the user counted for something: if I believed in my bezoar it might indeed preserve me from the plague while the same stone in the hands of a skeptical rationalist would be worthless. Under such circumstances a court might hesitate to impose liability on a seller who had merely said that, to the best of his knowledge, he believed (or affirmed) the stone to be a bezoar, but did not warrant it. It may be that the 17th century concept of liability was not as narrow as we have supposed it to be. This digression, at all events, goes to the point that law cases—and rules of law—are really not abstract propositions, although we like to phrase them, and talk about them, as if they were. The cases and the rules—and indeed the codifying statutes—are merely particular responses to particular states of fact (assumed to be true whether or not they are). The law is, and I dare say always will be, *ad hoc* and *ad hominem* to a fault."

[Footnotes omitted.]

SEIXAS v. WOODS

Supreme Court of New York, 1804.
2 Caines 48, 2 Am.Dec. 215.

Action on the case for selling peachum wood for brazilletto; the former being almost worthless, the latter of considerable value. The defendant received the wood from a house in New Providence, whose agent he was, and the invoice described it as brazilletto. He advertised it as such, had shown the invoice to the plaintiff, and had the bill made out for brazilletto. But it was not pretended that he knew that it was peachum, nor did the plaintiff suspect it to be such, as it was delivered from the vessel, and picked out from other wood by a person on behalf of the plaintiff. In fact, either party was ignorant that the wood was other than brazilletto, nor was any fraud imputed. On discovery of the real quality of the wood, it was tendered back to the defendant, and a return of the purchase money demanded. On his refusal, he having remitted the proceeds to his principal, the present action was brought, and a verdict was given for the plaintiffs, subject to the opinion of the court.

KENT, J.

* * *

In the case of Chandelor v. Lopus, Cro.Jac. 4, it was determined in the exchequer by all the judges except one, that for selling a jewel which as affirmed to be a bezoar stone when it was not, no action lay, unless the defendant knew it was not a bezoar stone or had warranted it to be one. This appears to be a case in point and decisive. * * * The mentioning the wood as brazilletto wood in the bill of parcels and in the advertisement some days previous to the sale, did not amount to a warranty to the plaintiffs. To make an affirmation at the time of the sale a warranty, it must appear by evidence to be so intended; Buller, J., 3 T.R. 57; Carth. 90; Salk. 210; and not to have been a mere matter of judgment and opinion, and of which the defendant had no particular knowledge. Here it is admitted the defendant was equally ignorant with the plaintiffs, and could have had no such intention. * * *

* * *

Notes

1. Did the New York court appropriately rely on *Chandelor v. Lopus?* Or, did the court "confuse accident with essence in an earlier court's decision and thereby stunt the law's growth?"

2. Suppose the seller and buyer are of relatively equal capacity and are equally ignorant about the nature of the goods sold. If the seller affirms or describes the goods (things) as a "bezoar stone" or as "brazilleto," how does one determine whether the seller has made a warranty or merely a statement purporting to be an opinion? For what they are worth, here are a few alternative tests. Which do you prefer?

A. The affirmation must be in writing and use the word "warrant" or "guarantee." This test was rejected in UCC 2–313(2).

B. The seller must intend the affirmation to be a warranty, i.e., state a "fact which is or should be within his own knowledge * * *, intending that the buyer should act on it. * * * " Denning, L.J. in Oscar Chess, Ltd. v. Williams, 1 All Eng.Rep. 325, 328–29 (C.A.1957). See Stoljar, *Conditions, Warranties and Descriptions of Quality in Sale of Goods,* Part I, 15 Mod.L.Rev. 425, 428–29 (1952).

The intention requirement was part of the pre-Code American law of warranty: "Though to constitute a warranty requires no particular form of words, the naked averment of a fact is neither a warranty itself nor evidence of it. In connection with other circumstances, it certainly may be taken into consideration; but the jury must be satisfied, from the whole that the vendor actually, and not constructively, consented to be bound for the truth of his representation." Gibson, C.J. in McFarland v. Newman, 9 Watts 55, 34 Am.Dec. 497 (Pa.1839). Accord: *Seixas v. Woods,* supra (warranty must appear from evidence to be intended); McNeir v. Greer-Hale Chinchilla Ranch, 194 Va. 623, 74 S.E.2d 165 (1953) (representations constituted warranty if seller intended that they should be relied upon and they were in fact relied upon by buyer as an inducement to purchase). But under UCC 2–313(2), the buyer need not have a "specific intention to make a warranty."

C. Regardless of the seller's actual intention, did the affirmation lead a reasonable buyer to believe that such statements had been made to induce the bargain and to make the purchase in reliance on them? See Section 12, Uniform Sales Act; Hansen v. Firestone Tire & Rubber Co., 276 F.2d 254, 257 (6th Cir.1960); Williston, Sales 206 (rev. ed. 1948). But see UCC 2–313(1)(a), where the affirmation or promise must become "part of the basis of the bargain."

D. None of the foregoing tests are appropriate. The question is whether the buyer is entitled to believe what the seller says about the goods. The answer will depend, in each case, upon the presence of certain factors which, in a proper combination, will induce the court to allow the case to reach the jury. These factors include but are not limited to:

a. The seller's statement was plain and unambiguous.

b. The seller's statement concerned a matter of objective importance to the buyer.

c. The attribute or quality involved was not something the buyer could easily ascertain on his own.

d. The seller was more of an expert in the matter than the buyer.

e. The buyer was not making up his own mind to buy entirely without regard to the seller's statements.

f. Nothing in the facts indicated that the seller should not be taken seriously.

g. The seller did not himself say things to the buyer that should have put him "on his guard" so to speak.

h. The remedy that the buyer sought was especially appropriate and would not be unduly harsh on the seller.

i. The price tends to support the buyer's claim.

Problem 19–2
The Case of the Unmarked Vitriol

Saldo is a dealer in dry chemicals, selling at wholesale to a variety of buyers. Saldo purchased 2,000 pounds of a copper sulphate described as "blue vitriol" from the Copco Mfgr. Co. The goods arrived in 20 barrels. The barrels were unmarked but the invoice described the goods as "vitriol." The barrels were offered for sale at a quarterly wholesale auction. One of the barrels was opened for prospective buyers to examine. It contained a bluish crystalline substance which one of the prospective buyers thought "looked strange." The purchasing agent of Barston Chemicals, Inc., a dealer which frequently sold at retail, also inspected the barrel. He stated to the auctioneer that while the substance looked like blue vitriol, it could be "green" vitriol, a less valuable chemical. Upon consultation with Saldo, the auctioneer announced that "the next sale will be a 20–barrel lot of blue vitriol in sound order." After spirited bidding, Barston Chemicals was high bidder at $.15 per pound. The price was paid and the goods were removed to the Barston warehouse, where they were immediately resold to a third party at $.18 per pound. The next day, however, it was discovered that the substance in the open barrel had turned green. Chemical analysis revealed that the substance was in fact "green" vitriol in sound order, worth about $.10 per pound at wholesale and $.13 per pound at retail. All of the other barrels contained "green" vitriol. In order to distinguish "green" from "blue" vitriol, either a chemical analysis must be done or the "green" vitriol allowed to stand in the open air for 10 or more hours. Barston promptly notified Saldo of the situation, revoked its acceptance, and demanded the return of the purchase price paid and damages for breach of warranty. The Barston purchasing agent stated that he was "not sure" what was in the barrel when he first examined it but after the auctioneer announced the sale, bid on the assumption that it was blue vitriol. Saldo claims that its officers honestly believed that the barrels contained blue vitriol, but that no warranty was intended and that Barston, as a professional chemical dealer, assumed the risk that the substance was green vitriol.

1. Did the seller make an express warranty in this case? If so, was it by affirmation or promise, description or sample? See UCC 2–313(1).

2. Suppose that the seller had stated that the goods were "vitriol" yet the buyer had assumed they were "blue" vitriol. What result? Compare UCC 2–313(1)(b) with UCC 2–314(2)(a). Does the description "vitriol" simply identify the goods or does it reveal basic attributes or quality? See Ziegel, *The Seller's Liability for Defective Goods at Common Law,* 12 McGill L.J. 183, 186–87 (1966).

SESSA v. RIEGLE

United States District Court, Eastern District of Pennsylvania, 1977.
427 F.Supp. 760, affirmed without opinion, 568 F.2d 770 (3d Cir.1978).

[Sessa purchased from Riegle a standard bred race horse named Tarport Conaway for $25,000. Before the sale, Sessa's friend Maloney examined the horse and reported that he "liked him." Also, Riegle, in a telephone conversation with Sessa, stated among other things that Sessa would like the horse and that he was a "good one" and "sound." The sale was then completed and, after problems in transportation were resolved, the horse was delivered some days later. Shortly thereafter the horse went lame in his hind legs due to a thrombosis which stopped the flow of blood through the arteries. The experts were unable to identify the cause of the thrombosis and the testimony did not establish that the condition was present before Riegle shipped the horse by carrier. Although the condition improved and Tarport Conaway was able to race, Sessa sued for damages under UCC 2–714(2) to be measured in part by the costs incurred in treating the condition.

The case was tried without a jury and the court, after making findings of fact, issued the following opinion.]

HANNUM, DISTRICT JUDGE.

* * *

II. EXPRESS WARRANTIES

On March 10, 1973, the day of the sale of Tarport Conaway, Sessa and Riegle had a telephone conversation during which the horse was discussed in general terms. Arrangements were made for transportation, and Riegle gave Sessa some instructions for driving Tarport Conaway based on Riegle's experience with him. Sessa contends that certain statements made by Riegle during that conversation constitute express warranties on which

Riegle is liable in this action. The most important of these is Riegle's alleged statement that, "the horse is sound," or words to that effect.

In deciding whether statements by a seller constitute express warranties, the court must look to UCC § 2–313 which presents three fundamental issues. First, the court must determine whether the seller's statement constitutes an "affirmation of fact or promise" or "description of the goods" under § 2–313(1)(a) or (b) or whether it is rather "merely the seller's opinion or commendation of the goods" under § 2–313(2). Second, assuming the court finds the language used susceptible to creation of a warranty, it must then be determined whether the statement was "part of the basis of the bargain." If it was, an express warranty exists and, as the third issue, the court must determine whether the warranty was breached.

With respect to the first issue, the court finds that in the circumstances of this case, words to the effect that "The horse is sound" spoken during the telephone conversation between Sessa and Riegle constitute an opinion or commendation rather than express warranty. This determination is a question for the trier of fact. Gillette Dairy, Inc. v. Hydrotex Industries, Inc., 440 F.2d 969 (8th Cir.1971); Brunner v. Jensen, 215 Kan. 416, 524 P.2d 1175 (1974). There is nothing talismanic or thaumaturgic about the use of the word "sound." Whether use of that language constitutes warranty, or mere opinion or commendation depends on the circumstances of the sale and the type of goods sold. While § 2–313 makes it clear that no specific words need be used and no specific intent need be present, not every statement by a seller is an express warranty.

Several older Pennsylvania cases dealing with horse sales show that similar statements as to soundness are not always similarly treated under warranty law. In Wilkinson v. Stettler, 46 Pa.Super. 407 (1911), the statement that a horse "was solid and sound and would work any place" was held not to constitute an express warranty. This result was followed in Walker v. Kirk, 72 Pa.Super. 534 (1919) which considered the statement, "This mare is sound and all right and a good worker double." Walker was decided after the passage of § 12 of the Uniform Sales Act, the precursor of U.C.C. § 2–313 and thus presumably rests on the standard there established. The Official Comments to U.C.C. § 2–313 indicate that no changes in the law of warranties under Uniform Sales Act § 12 were intended.

However, in Flood v. Yeager, 52 Pa.Super. 637 (1912) an express warranty was found where the plaintiff informed the defendant that, "he did not know anything at all about a horse and that he did not want * * * the defendant to make a mean deal with him; whereupon the defendant said that the horse was solid and sound; that he would guarantee him to be solid and sound" 52 Pa.Super. at 638. While all three of these cases are premised partly on the now displaced rule that specific intent to warrant is a necessary concomitant of an express warranty, they do show that statements of the same tenor receive varying treatment depending on the surrounding circumstances.

The results in these cases are all consistent with custom among horse traders as alluded to by Gene Riegle. He testified that it is "not a common thing" to guarantee a horse, that he has never guaranteed a horse unless he had an "understanding" with the buyer and that he did not guarantee

Tarport Conaway. In other words, because horses are fragile creatures, susceptible to myriad maladies, detectable and undetectable, only where there is an "understanding" that an ignorant buyer, is relying totally on a knowledgeable seller not "to make a mean deal," are statements as to soundness taken to be anything more than the seller's opinion or commendation.

The facts suggest no special "understanding" between Sessa and Riegle. Sessa was a knowledgeable buyer, having been involved with standardbreds for some years. Also, Sessa sent Maloney, an even more knowledgeable horseman, as his agent to inspect the horse.

Also mitigating against the finding of express warranty is the nature of the conversation between Sessa and Riegle. It seemed largely collateral to the sale rather than an essential part of it. Although Sessa testified that Riegle's "personal guarantee" given during the conversation was the quintessence of the sale, the credible evidence suggests otherwise. While on the telephone, Riegle made statements to the effect that "the horse is a good one" and "you will like him." These bland statements are obviously opinion or commendation, and the statement, "The horse is sound," falling within their penumbra takes on their character as such.

Under all the facts and circumstances of this case, it is clear to the court that Riegle's statements were not of such a character as to give rise to express warranties under § 2–313(1) but were opinion or commendation under § 2–313(2).

Even assuming that Riegle's statements could be express warranties, it is not at all clear that they were "part of the basis of the bargain," the second requisite of § 2–313. This is essentially a reliance requirement and is inextricably intertwined with the initial determination as to whether given language may constitute an express warranty since affirmations, promises and descriptions tend to become part of the basis of the bargain. It was the intention of the drafters of the U.C.C. not to require a strong showing of reliance. In fact, they envisioned that all statements of the seller became part of the basis of the bargain unless clear affirmative proof is shown to the contrary. See Official Comments 3 and 8 to U.C.C. § 2–313, 12A P.S. § 2–313.

It is Sessa's contention that his conversation with Riegle was the principal factor inducing him to enter the bargain. He would have the court believe that Maloney was merely a messenger to deliver the check. The evidence shows, however, that Sessa was relying primarily on Maloney to advise him in connection with the sale. Maloney testified that he had talked to Sessa about the horse on several occasions and expressed the opinion that he was convinced "beyond the shadow of a doubt" that he was a good buy. With respect to his authority to buy the horse he testified:

> "Well, Mr. Sessa said he had enough confidence and faith in me and my integrity and honesty that I, what I did say about the horse, I was representing the horse as he is or as he was, and that if the horse, in my estimation, was that type of a horse and at that given price, the fixed price of $25,000 he would buy the horse."

When, at the airport, Maloney protested that he did not want to accept full responsibility to go to Ohio alone, Sessa told him "* * * I take your word. I—I trust your judgment and I trust your—your honesty, that if this horse is right, everything will be all right." In Ohio, Maloney examined the horse, jogged him and reported to Sessa over the telephone that he "liked him."

The court believes that Maloney's opinion was the principal, if not the only, factor which motivated Sessa to purchase the horse. The conversation with Riegle played a negligible role in his decision.

* * *

[The court concluded that even if an express warranty had been made, Sessa had accepted the horse and had failed to prove by a preponderance of the evidence that the horse was not sound at the time of tender.]

[Footnotes omitted.]

KEITH v. BUCHANAN

Court of Appeals of California, Second District, 1985.
173 Cal.App.3d 13, 220 Cal.Rptr. 392.

OCHOA, ASSOCIATE JUSTICE.

This breach of warranty case is before this court after the trial court granted defendants' motion for judgment at the close of plaintiff's case during the trial proceedings. We hold that an express warranty under section 2313 of the California Uniform Commercial Code was created in this matter, and that actual reliance on the seller's factual representation need not be shown by the buyer. The representation is presumed to be part of the basis of the bargain, and the burden is on the seller to prove that the representation was not a consideration inducing the bargain. We affirm all other aspects of the trial court's judgment but reverse in regard to its finding that no express warranty was created and remand for further proceedings consistent with this opinion.

STATEMENT OF FACTS

Plaintiff, Brian Keith, purchased a sailboat from defendants in November 1978 for a total purchase price of $75,610. Even though plaintiff belonged to the Waikiki Yacht Club, had attended a sailing school, had joined the Coast Guard Auxiliary, and had sailed on many yachts in order to ascertain his preferences, he had not previously owned a yacht. He attended a boat show in Long Beach during October 1978 and looked at a number of boats, speaking to sales representatives and obtaining advertising literature. In the literature, the sailboat which is the subject of this action, called an "Island Trader 41," was described as a seaworthy vessel. In one sales brochure, this vessel is described as "a picture of sure-footed seaworthiness." In another, it is called "a carefully well-equipped, and very seaworthy live-aboard vessel." Plaintiff testified he relied on representations in the sales brochures in regard to the purchase. Plaintiff and a sales representative also discussed plaintiff's desire for a boat which was ocean-going and would cruise long distances.

Plaintiff asked his friend, Buddy Ebsen, who was involved in a boat building enterprise, to inspect the boat. Mr. Ebsen and one of his associates, both of whom had extensive experience with sailboats, observed the boat and advised plaintiff that the vessel would suit his stated needs. A deposit was paid on the boat, a purchase contract was entered into, and optional accessories for the boat were ordered. After delivery of the vessel, a dispute arose in regard to its seaworthiness.

Plaintiff filed the instant lawsuit alleging causes of action in breach of express warranty and breach of implied warranty. The trial court granted defendants' Code of Civil Procedure section 631.8 motion for judgment at the close of plaintiff's case. The court found that no express warranty was established by the evidence because none of the defendants had undertaken in writing to preserve or maintain the utility or performance of the vessel, nor to provide compensation for any failure in utility or performance. It found that the written statements produced at trial were opinions or commendations of the vessel. The court further found that no implied warranty of fitness was created because the plaintiff did not rely on the skill and judgment of defendants to select and furnish a suitable vessel, but had rather relied on his own experts in selecting the vessel.

Discussion

I. Express Warranty

California Uniform Commercial Code section 2313 provides, inter alia, that express warranties are created by (1) any affirmation of fact or promise made by the seller to the buyer which relates to the goods and becomes part of the basis of the bargain, and (2) any description of the goods which is made part of the basis of the bargain. Formal words such as "warranty" or "guarantee" are not required to make a warranty, but the seller's affirmation of the value of the goods or an expression of opinion or commendation of the goods does not create an express warranty.

* * *

California Uniform Commercial Code section 2313, regarding express warranties, was enacted in 1963 and consists of the official text of Uniform Commercial Code section 2–313 without change. In deciding whether a statement made by a seller constitutes an express warranty under this provision, the court must deal with three fundamental issues. First, the court must determine whether the seller's statement constitutes an "affirmation of fact or promise" or "description of the goods" under California Uniform Commercial Code section 2313, subdivision (1)(a) or (b) or whether it is rather "merely the seller's opinion or commendation of the goods" under section 2313, subdivision (2). Second, assuming the court finds the language used susceptible to creation of a warranty, it must then be determined whether the statement was "part of the basis of the bargain." Third, the court must determine whether the warranty was breached. (See *Sessa v. Riegle* (E.D.Pa.1977) 427 F.Supp. 760, 765.)

A warranty relates to the title, character, quality, identity, or condition of the goods. The purpose of the law of warranty is to determine what it is that the seller has in essence agreed to sell. (*A.A. Baxter Corp. v. Colt*

Industries, Inc. (1970) 10 Cal.App.3d 144, 153, 88 Cal.Rptr. 842.) "Express warranties are chisels in the hands of buyers and sellers. With these tools, the parties to a sale sculpt a monument representing the goods. Having selected a stone, the buyer and seller may leave it almost bare, allowing considerable play in the qualities that fit its contours. Or the parties may chisel away inexactitudes until a well-defined shape emerges. The seller is bound to deliver, and the buyer to accept, goods that match the sculpted form. [Fn. omitted.]" (*Special Project: Article Two Warranties in Commercial Transactions, Express Warranties—Section 2–313* (1978–79) 64 Cornell L.Rev. 30 (hereafter cited as *Warranties in Commercial Transactions*) at pp. 43–44.)

A. *Affirmation of Fact, Promise or Description Versus Statement of Opinion, Commendation or Value*

"The determination as to whether a particular statement is an expression of opinion or an affirmation of fact is often difficult, and frequently is dependent upon the facts and circumstances existing at the time the statement is made." (*Willson v. Municipal Bond Co.* (1936) 7 Cal.2d 144, 150, 59 P.2d 974.) Recent decisions have evidenced a trend toward narrowing the scope of representations which are considered opinion, sometimes referred to as "puffing" or "sales talk," resulting in an expansion of the liability that flows from broad statements of manufacturers or retailers as to the quality of their products. Courts have liberally construed affirmations of quality made by sellers in favor of injured consumers. (*Hauter v. Zogarts* (1975) 14 Cal.3d 104, 112, 120 Cal.Rptr. 681, 534 P.2d 377; see also 55 Cal.Jur.3d, Sales, § 74, p. 580.) It has even been suggested "that in an age of consumerism all seller's statements, except the most blatant sales pitch, may give rise to an express warranty." (1 Alderman and Dole, A Transactional Guide to the Uniform Commercial Code (2d ed. 1983) p. 89.)

Courts in other states have struggled in efforts to create a formula for distinguishing between affirmations of fact, promises, or descriptions of goods on the one hand, and value, opinion, or commendation statements on the other. The code comment indicates that the basic question is: "What statements of the seller have in the circumstances and in objective judgment become part of the basis of the bargain?" The commentators indicated that the language of subsection (2) of the code section was included because "common experience discloses that some statements or predictions cannot fairly be viewed as entering into the bargain." (See U.Com.Code com. 8 to Cal.U.Com.Code, § 2313, West's Ann.Com.Code (1964) p. 250.)

Statements made by a seller during the course of negotiation over a contract are presumptively affirmations of fact unless it can be demonstrated that the buyer could only have reasonably considered the statement as a statement of the seller's opinion. Commentators have noted several factors which tend to indicate an opinion statement. These are (1) a lack of specificity in the statement made, (2) a statement that is made in an equivocal manner, or (3) a statement which reveals that the goods are experimental in nature. (See *Warranties in Commercial Transactions, supra,* at pp. 61–65.)

It is clear that statements made by a manufacturer or retailer in an advertising brochure which is disseminated to the consuming public in order to induce sales can create express warranties. * * * In the instant case, the vessel purchased was described in sales brochures as "a picture of sure-footed seaworthiness" and "a carefully well-equipped and very seaworthy vessel." The seller's representative was aware that appellant was looking for a vessel sufficient for long distance ocean-going cruises. The statements in the brochure are specific and unequivocal in asserting that the vessel is seaworthy. Nothing in the negotiation indicates that the vessel is experimental in nature. In fact, one sales brochure assures prospective buyers that production of the vessel was commenced "after years of careful testing." The representations regarding seaworthiness made in sales brochures regarding the Island Trader 41 were affirmations of fact relating to the quality or condition of the vessel.

B. "Part of the Basis of the Bargain" Test

Under former provisions of law, a purchaser was required to prove that he or she acted in reliance upon representations made by the seller. (*Grinnell v. Charles Pfizer & Co.* (1969) 274 Cal.App.2d 424, 440, 79 Cal.Rptr. 369.) California Uniform Commercial Code section 2313 indicates only that the seller's statements must become "part of the basis of the bargain." According to official comment 3 to this Uniform Commercial Code provision, "no particular reliance * * * need be shown in order to weave [the seller's affirmations of fact] into the fabric of the agreement. Rather, any fact which is to take such affirmations, once made, out of the agreement requires clear affirmative proof." (See U.Com.Code com. 3 to Cal.U.Com.Code, § 2313, West's Ann.Com.Code (1964) p. 249.)

The California Supreme Court, in discussing the continued viability of the reliance factor, noted that commentators have disagreed in regard to the impact of this development. Some have indicated that it shifts the burden of proving non-reliance to the seller, and others have indicated that the code eliminates the concept of reliance altogether. (*Hauter v. Zogarts, supra,* 14 Cal.3d at pp. 115–116, 120 Cal.Rptr. 681, 534 P.2d 377.) The court did not resolve this issue, but noted that decisions of other states prior to that time had "ignored the significance of the new standard and have held that consumer reliance still is a vital ingredient for recovery based on express warranty." (*Id.,* at p. 116, fn. 13, 120 Cal.Rptr. 681, 534 P.2d 377; see also *Fogo v. Cutter Laboratories, Inc.* (1977) 68 Cal.App.3d 744, 760, 137 Cal.Rptr. 417.)

The shift in language clearly changes the degree to which it must be shown that the seller's representation affected the buyer's decision to enter into the agreement. A buyer need not show that he would not have entered into the agreement absent the warranty or even that it was a dominant factor inducing the agreement. A warranty statement is deemed to be part of the basis of the bargain and to have been relied upon as one of the inducements for the purchase of the product. In other words, the buyer's demonstration of reliance on an express warranty is "not a prerequisite for breach of warranty, as long as the express warranty involved became part of the bargain. See White & Summers, Uniform Commercial Code (2d ed. 1980) § 9–4. If, however, the resulting bargain does not rest at all on the representations of the seller, those representations cannot be considered as becoming any part of the 'basis of the bargain.' * * * " (*Allied Fidelity Ins. Co. v. Pico* (Nev.S.Ct.1983) 656 P.2d 849, 850.)

The official Uniform Commercial Code comment in regard to section 2–313 "indicates that in actual practice affirmations of fact made by the seller about the goods during a bargain are regarded as part of the description of those goods; hence no particular reliance on such statements need be shown in order to weave them into the fabric of the agreement." (*Young & Cooper, Inc. v. Vestring* (1974) 214 Kan. 311, 521 P.2d 281, 291; *Brunner v. Jensen* (1974) 215 Kan. 416, 524 P.2d 1175, 1185.) It is clear from the new language of this code section that the concept of reliance has been purposefully abandoned. * * *

The change of the language in section 2313 of the California Uniform Commercial Code modifies both the degree of reliance and the burden of proof in express warranties under the code. The representation need only be part of the basis of the bargain, or merely a factor or consideration inducing the buyer to enter into the bargain. A warranty statement made by a seller is presumptively part of the basis of the bargain, and the burden is on the seller to prove that the resulting bargain does not rest at all on the representation.

The buyer's actual knowledge of the true condition of the goods prior to the making of the contract may make it plain that the seller's statement was not relied upon as one of the inducements for the purchase, but the burden is on the seller to demonstrate such knowledge on the part of the buyer. Where the buyer inspects the goods before purchase, he may be deemed to have waived the seller's express warranties. But, an examination or inspection by the buyer of the goods does not necessarily discharge the seller from an express warranty if the defect was not actually discovered and waived. * * *

Appellant's inspection of the boat by his own experts does not constitute a waiver of the express warranty of seaworthiness. Prior to the making of the contract, appellant had experienced boat builders observe the boat, but there was no testing of the vessel in the water.[3] Such a warranty (seaworthiness) necessarily relates to the time when the vessel has been put to sea (*Werner v. Montana* (1977) 117 N.H. 721, 378 A.2d 1130, 1134–35) and has been shown to be reasonably fit and adequate in materials, construction, and equipment for its intended purposes (*Daly v. General Motors Corp.* (1978) 20 Cal.3d 725, 739, 144 Cal.Rptr. 380, 575 P.2d 1162; *Vittone v. American President Lines* (1964) 228 Cal.App.2d 689, 693–694, 39 Cal.Rptr. 758).

3. Evidence was presented of examination or inspection of the boat after the making of the contract of sale and prior to delivery and acceptance of the vessel. Such an inspection would be irrelevant to any issue of express warranty. Although it deals with implied warranties as opposed to express warranties, the Uniform Commercial Code comment 8 to section 2–316 (Cal.U.Com. Code, § 2316) is instructive: "Under paragraph (b) of subdivision (3) warranties may be excluded or modified by the circumstances where the buyer examines the goods or a sample or model of them *before entering into the contract. 'Examination' as used in this paragraph is not synonymous with inspection before acceptance or at any other time after the contract has been made. It goes rather to the nature of the responsibility assumed by the seller at the time of the making of the contract.*" (See U.Com.Code com. 8 to Cal.U.Com.Code, § 2316, West's Ann.Com.Code (1964) p. 308, emphasis added.)

In this case, appellant was aware of the representations regarding seaworthiness by the seller prior to contracting. He also had expressed to the seller's representative his desire for a long distance ocean-going vessel. Although he had other experts inspect the vessel, the inspection was limited and would not have indicated whether or not the vessel was seaworthy. It is clear that the seller has not overcome the presumption that the representations regarding seaworthiness were part of the basis of this bargain.

* * *

[The court upheld the trial court's conclusion that the seller did not make and breach an implied warranty of fitness for particular purpose under UCC 2–315: The buyer did not rely on the seller's skill and judgment in selecting a suitable boat.]

[Some footnotes omitted.]

Notes

1. The court in *Keith* cites with approval the three step "basis of the bargain" test employed in *Sessa* but then reaches the opposite result. Can the cases be reconciled? Should Buddy Ebsen be fired as an expert on seaworthiness?

2. How do we know initially whether a statement is an affirmation of fact or an opinion? In Royal Business Machines, Inc. v. Lorraine Corp., 633 F.2d 34, 41 (7th Cir.1980), the court stated: "(T)he decisive test for whether a given representation is a warranty or merely an expression of the seller's opinion is whether the seller asserts a fact of which the buyer is ignorant or merely states an opinion or judgment on a matter of which the seller has no special knowledge and on which the buyer may be expected also to have an opinion and to exercise his judgment." Accord: Royal Typewriter Co. v. Xerographic Supplies Corp., 719 F.2d 1092 (11th Cir.1983).

Note: "Basis of the Bargain" and the Cipollone Cigarette Litigation

The extent to which the "basis of the bargain" requirement in UCC 2–313(1) requires reliance by the buyer was tested in the litigation styled as *Cipollone v. Liggett Group, Inc.*

The plaintiff, a heavy smoker from 1942 until 1983, died of lung cancer in 1984. Her estate and her husband sued claiming, inter alia, that smoking defendant's cigarettes caused her cancer and that despite growing evidence of health risk she was induced to continue smoking by defendant's advertisements from 1945 to 1966, the date when the Federal Cigarette Labeling and Advertising Act, 15 U.S.C.A. §§ 1331–1340, became effective. At the conclusion of plaintiff's evidence, defendant moved for a directed verdict, which the trial court denied. 683 F.Supp. 1487 (D.N.J.1988). The trial court concluded that the jury could find that the plaintiff's smoking prior to 1966 was the proximate cause of her death. Moreover, the court concluded that a jury could find that (1) defendant's advertisements were affirmations of fact concerning safety and health, (2) Plaintiff "saw" those advertisements during the relevant period, and (3) the advertisements became "part of the basis" of Plaintiff's bargain when she purchased cigarettes, without the need to show any particular reliance on them. Judge Sarokin, the trial judge, discussed UCC 2–313(1), relevant comments and cases, and noted that defendants could attempt to "rebut the presumption that plaintiff relied" in their evidence. 683 F.Supp. at 1497.

After the defendant's case was presented, the court charged the jury that the "law does not require plaintiff to show that Rose Cipollone specifically relied on Liggett's warranties." The question is whether the advertisement "would naturally induce the purchase of the product." If so, it becomes part of the basis of the bargain. 693 F.Supp. 208, 212 (D.N.J.1988). The jury returned a $400,000 verdict for the plaintiff and awarded nothing to the estate. The defendants moved for a judgment notwithstanding the verdict and, inter alia, attacked the court's charge on "basis of the bargain." The defendants argued that specific reliance by the buyer was required and the jury's finding that Mrs. Cipollone had voluntarily and unreasonably encountered a known risk meant that there was no reliance. Judge Sarokin rejected this argument and denied the NOV motion. 693 F.Supp. 208 (D.N.J.1988).

> The comments indicate that [UCC 2–313(1)(a)] centers on whether the agreement or bargain between the warrantor and buyer, objectively viewed, contains the affirmations or promises—not on whether a buyer's purchasing decision, subjectively viewed, depends on the statements. In the court's view, a statement in an advertisement becomes part of the basis of the bargain if, objectively viewed, the statement would tend to induce the purchase of the advertised product. Whether or not the statement actually induced a particular purchase is not relevant to a determination of whether the statement may constitute an express warranty. 693 F.Supp. at 214.

On appeal to the Third Circuit, the court reversed the judgment and ordered a new trial. 893 F.2d 541 (3d Cir.1990). Judge Sarokin's charge on express warranty was flawed "to the extent that it prevented Liggett from proving, by a preponderance of the evidence, that Mrs. Cipollone did not *believe* the advertisements." [Emphasis added.] The court also stated that the advertisements became part of the basis of the bargain "as long as Mr. Cippollone can prove that Mrs. Cipollone was aware of the advertisements and as long as Liggett does not prove that she disbelieved them."

The Court's detailed analysis of UCC 2-313(1) will not be reprinted here. See 893 F.2d at 563–70. In sum, the court confirmed that the advertisements were "affirmations of fact" and that Mrs. Cippolone was aware of them, even though the trial court did not charge, as it should have, that the plaintiff must prove awareness. This was sufficient to "weave" the affirmations "into the fabric of the agreement" and thus make it part of the basis of the bargain. [Citing Comment 3.] The critical error was that the trial court's charge did not give the defendants an opportunity to exclude the affirmations by "clear and convincing proof" that the buyer knew that the affirmation of fact was untrue. If the defendants could prove that Mrs. Cipollone did not believe the advertisements, then the express warranty claim would fail.

Whether Mrs. Cipollone believed that the advertisements were false was also relevant to whether a comparative fault defense was available in express warranty cases. Assuming that she did not misuse or abuse the product, a basis for comparative fault would be proper use after learning that the warranty was false. According to the court, however, such use would mean that the advertisements did not become part of the basis of the bargain, i.e., she did not believe them to be true, and, if so, there was no need for a comparative fault defense. 893 F.2d at 574. Ironically this interpretation of the reliance requirement means that the extent of the warranty given by the seller of a potentially dangerous product is inversely related to the knowledge of the plaintiff. One of the briefs filed in Cipollone made the point as follows concerning Rose's knowledge:

> Before Rose Cipollone smoked her first cigarette in 1942 she was warned by her mother that her father's cigarette smoking caused his death. Her mother told her that her father had been advised by his doctor to quit, but did not do so. Rose Cipollone's own physician advised her to quit smoking during her first pregnancy in 1947. From the very beginning of their relationship in 1946, Antonio Cipollone warned his wife that smoking was bad for her health, repeatedly telling her of the health risks of cigarettes, including the risk that smoking would kill her. Beginning in the 1950s, Mr. Cipollone brought to his wife's attention information appearing in the print media and on radio and television news programs concerning the health risks of smoking, including the risks of lung cancer, heart disease and a reduced life expectancy. Rose Cipollone read the articles her husband showed her.
>
> Rose Cipollone was aware of the 1964 Surgeon General's Advisory Committee Report on cigarette smoking and health, which she understood to mean smoking could cause heart disease and cancer. She became aware of the warnings on cigarette packages as soon as they appeared in 1966, and understood the warnings to mean that smoking posed serious health risks. (Trial transcript references are omitted.)

A final note on the effect of the Federal Cigarette Labeling and Advertising Act, enacted in 1965 and reenacted in 1969 as the Public Health Cigarette Smoking Act. 15 U.S.C.A. § 1531. This act requires a warning label that cigarette smoking is "dangerous" and bans cigarette advertising in "any medium of electronic communication subject to [FCC] jurisdiction." It also provides that "no requirement or prohibition based on smoking and health shall be imposed under State law with respect to the advertising or promotion of any cigarettes the packages of which are labeled in conformity with the provisions of this act." Early in the Cipollone litigation, it was ruled that this statute preempted state warranty law after the date of its effect, and thus required the exclusion of most of the evidence relevant to basis of the bargain or comparative issues fault after 1966. The Supreme Court granted certiorari and, in a 7–2 decision, reversed the preemption decision. In essence, preemption in this setting meant limitations imposed by state law rather than limitations imposed by the contract itself. Express warranties fell into the latter category and were not preempted. Cipollone v. Liggett Group, Inc., 505 U.S. ___, 112 S.Ct. 2608, 120 L.Ed.2d 407 (1992).

A fair conclusion is that the plaintiffs lost on the "basis of the bargain" issue and won on the preemption issue. The $400,000 judgment was reversed and a new trial ordered, where 40 years of evidence relevant to the warranty claim and comparative fault would now be relevant. It is reported that the plaintiff's attorneys have withdrawn, and the case probably will not proceed to trial.

Note: History of Basis of the Bargain

As we have indicated above, the basis of the bargain language came from the reliance requirement in section 12 of the Uniform Sales Act that required the buyer to purchase goods "relying thereon". That language first turned into the basis of the bargain language in section 37 in the 1943 draft of the Uniform Revised Sales Act. What is now section 2–313(1)(a) read as follows in the 1943 act:

Express warranties by the seller are created as follows:

(a) Any affirmation of fact or promise which relates to the goods and is made by the seller to the buyer as a part of the bargain creates an express warranty that the goods shall conform to the affirmation or promise.

The quoted language was later changed to its current form apparently to make section 2–313(1)(a) correspond with (1)(b) and (1)(c).

In the 1943 meeting of the National Commissioners in Chicago, Professor Mentschikoff, the associate reporter, described the relevant changes as follows: "Major changes in this section over the old act [Uniform Sales Act] are simply verbal." It is possible, therefore, that all the commentators and courts (including White and Summers) who have read so much into the omission of any form of the verb "rely" and into its replacement with the "basis of the bargain" language have been barking up the wrong tree. Conceivably Llewellyn, Mentschikoff and the Commissioners did not mean to dilute the reliance requirement at all, but only to expand it—ever so slightly—the acts that might be regarded as reliance.

In fact, the comment published in 1944 with section 37, almost certainly written by Professor Llewellyn, suggests that he would not have intended to include events remote from the deal to be part of the basis of the bargain.

> *Unified contract basis of warranty:* Under this Act warranties are an essential part of the contract for sale. Fundamentally, all warranties are summed up in "description" under the present section; it requires the whole net effect of the bargain to effectively describe what kind and quality of thing the seller has assumed obligation to sell and deliver. It does serve convenience to particularize rules on warranty which deal with some familiar and recurrent sets of fact, but the object remains single: it is to arrive at the net description which defines the seller's obligation. *The present section therefore deals with affirmations of fact by the seller exactly as it deals with any other part of a negotiation which ends in a contract.* No specific intention to make a warranty is needed, to make the affirmation a part of the net description of the goods. No agreement that the affirmation shall constitute a warranty is needed. *In life, affirmations of fact which relate to the goods and which are made by a seller in connection with a bargain about goods are taken as part of the description of the goods contracted about; in life, no particular reliance needs to be shown in order to weave such affirmations into the fabric of the agreement. Instead, what needs an affirmative showing is that there has been any fact which gives clear objective justification for the unusual result of taking such affirmations out of what has been agreed upon.* Under some circumstances, an examination by a buyer before he closes the bargain may go very far in this direction; see Section 41(2)(b) and Comment thereon. Under some circumstances, words may do the same, either in regard to an "affirmation" or in regard to the content of what looks on the surface as a "description"; see Comment to Section 53 on sale by auction.

2 E. Kelly, *Drafts of the Uniform Commercial Code* at 155–56 (1984) (emphasis added).

The quoted comment suggests that Llewellyn was not abandoning the idea of reliance and that mostly he had in mind face-to-face dealings where the affirmations might be made orally or in writing by the seller to the buyer. The comment discusses disclosures as a "part of negotiation." The comment also recognizes the possibility that some affirmations, even those made in face-to-face settings, might not constitute warranties because there was no reliance. This is consistent with the position of the Third Circuit in Cipollone. The comment also contemplates cases where the buyer's examination or the fact that there was an auction sale might exclude reliance.

If one chooses to expand the "bargain" beyond things actually seen and perceived, the buyer is on a slippery slope. In the *Cipollone* case, Judge Sarokin was fond of challenging the defense lawyer by posing in a hypothetical case of the purchaser of packaged products such as an electric razor and asking whether the assertions contained on the document inside the package—unseen at the time of purchase—constituted express warranties. It is hard to deny that such statements could and should give rise to liability; indeed, cases hold that assertions in operating manuals for automobiles and the like that are never read by the buyer prior to the purchase may constitute express warranties. Yet if one acknowledges that such terms can become the basis of the bargain, where does one stop on the slope that leads to advertisements published by the defendants but never seen by the plaintiff. Perhaps never seen by any resident of the particular plaintiff's state? For example, would an assertion by Liggett that its cigarettes were healthy made in the interior of China, only in Chinese, and seen only by Chinese citizens constitute an express warranty that is part of the basis of Rose Cipollone's bargain when she buys Camels in New Jersey? If reliance means anything, that case is hard to swallow, but where then does one draw the line between the case of the electric razor and the case of the advertising published in a distant land and never seen? Of course, one can say that the purchaser of an electric razor expects to get some instructions and statements within the box and that the buyer of a GM pickup truck expects the same. In that sense there might possibly be "reliance." Is that a satisfactory distinction?

B. Liability for Statements as to "Special Suitability"

Suppose the buyer wants to buy a racehorse that runs well on a slow track, or an office copier with low maintenance costs or a computer system that will process some rather complicated financial data. In short, the buyer has particular or special needs to be satisfied. Compare UCC 2–315.

It is, of course, quite possible that a properly informed seller will make an express warranty that the goods are fit or suitable for the buyer's particular purposes. Northern States Power Co. v. ITT Meyer Industries, 777 F.2d 405 (8th Cir.1985) (seller's technical specifications became part of basis of buyer's bargain). But, as the next case indicates, establishing such an express warranty may be more difficult than when the seller's statements go to core description or basic attributes.

AXION CORP. v. G.D.C. LEASING CORP.

Supreme Judicial Court of Massachusetts, 1971.
359 Mass. 474, 269 N.E.2d 664.

BRAUCHER, JUSTICE.

These cases arise out of the sale of three valve testing machines. The three machines were delivered and two of them were paid for. The seller brings two actions of contract for failure to pay for the third machine, and the buyer brings an action of contract or tort against the seller for damages for breach of express and implied warranties. The cases were consolidated for trial by jury. At the close of the evidence the judge denied the buyer's motions for directed verdicts in the two cases brought by the seller, and allowed the seller's motions for directed verdicts in all three cases. The cases are here on the buyer's exceptions to these actions.

The following facts are substantially undisputed except as indicated. Negotiations began in late 1963, and included a good deal of correspondence. The buyer's purchase order, "To Design and build" the first machine for $7,500, is dated January 9, 1964. The machine was delivered the following May and was paid for in June, 1964. There were many problems with it, and the parties and the buyer's parent company, Watts Regulator Company (Watts), worked together to solve them. In August, 1964, the seller by letter to the buyer listed twenty-eight "revisions in the next two valve setters to be built." The buyer ordered the second and third machines in October, 1964, for a total price of $14,950; they were delivered in December, 1964, and one of them was paid for in March, 1965. At the time of the second order, the first machine was sent back, modified to conform to the new design, then shipped back to the buyer and put into service.

Development and testing continued. In July, 1965, the buyer by letter told the seller it "would like to negotiate a price [for the third machine] which would take into account the amount of money and time that we have had to expend trying to perfect these devices." In August, 1965, the buyer told the seller that the third machine was useless and that the buyer would not pay for it unless it would meet a "plus or minus five per cent" specification. The seller then agreed to take back the third machine at the buyer's expense and to work on it. In January, 1966, representatives of the buyer went to the seller's plant to conduct a series of tests. The parties do not agree on the meaning of the specification or on what the tests showed. In February, 1966, the buyer notified the seller that it was reserving its rights for recovery of its losses and expenses, and that the third machine was unacceptable and would not be paid for.

* * *

Express warranties. Since the buyer has accepted the goods and has not revoked the acceptance, the seller may recover the unpaid portion of the price. UCC § 2–709(1)(a). But if the goods were nonconforming, the buyer may have an offsetting claim for damages. § 2–714. The buyer claims that there were breaches of express warranties, of an implied warranty of merchantability, and of an implied warranty of fitness for a particular purpose. The burden is on the buyer to establish such breaches. § 2–607(4).

The buyer claims express warranties made in the seller's preliminary correspondence. On October 12, 1963, the seller wrote: "About the valve adjustment, we would shoot for a mean of 125 psi [pounds per square inch] and hit it more closely than an operator can. * * * With the air pressure sensing there is bound to be a gain in accuracy * * *. Probably a better statement is that the tolerance will be better than it is by the present method." Again, on October 19, 1963, the seller wrote: "With few reservations the automatic valve setter would be a turnkey operation. * * * We would set up the unit at your plant, check it out, train the people stated, and make whatever changes are then indicated to meet the specifications. * * *

Failing to meet performance specifications under these guidelines you could ship back the unit with no charge other than freight to New Fairfield."

The buyer now asserts that these letters created express warranties by "affirmation of fact" and "promise," UCC § 2–313(1)(a), that the machine would be a turnkey device and would be more accurate than the hand method. We think they savor more of prediction than of promise. The former general manager of the buyer understood a "turn-key device" to be "one which operates 100 per cent from the day you receive it," as distinguished from a prototype needing further development; he considered the first machine a "semi-experimental" prototype. The order for the first machine, dated January 9, 1964, was to design and build the machine "substantially as per" an attached inter-office letter of the buyer; that letter described the "automatic pressure setting procedure," referred to items which were "suggested," and closed with the following: "It is probable that some tolerances on this will have to be established but deviations from our basic specification can be determined when the machine is checked out." There was no "turnkey" warranty, and no warranty that the machine would be more accurate than the hand method.

The buyer also claims a breach of a warranty that the machine would set valves "entirely within the ± 5% range," quoting from the seller's letter of January 6, 1966. There was testimony that the buyer followed such a standard and that it was one of the specifications discussed between the parties and referred to in the letter of October 19, 1963. But the standard was not referred to in either of the purchase orders and was never written down with any precision until after the meeting in August, 1965.

At that meeting the parties seem to have thought they had reached an oral agreement on the five per cent specification, to be used in reëvaluating the third machine after the seller had reworked it, but their subsequent correspondence disclosed two conflicting versions: the seller's version called for the machine "to set within the prescribed 5% range 90% of the valves presented for setting"; the buyer's version allowed the machine to reject no more than ten per cent of the valves capable of being set, but required *all* of the valves set to be within the five per cent range. The seller's letter of January 6, 1966, pointed out the discrepancy, said it believed "that our equipment will satisfy also the new criterion, but subject to these conditions." One of the conditions was that the buyer "define the quantity of valves which may be incorrectly set and passed. * * * We are confident that * * * the machine will set valves entirely within the ± 5% range. Recognizing, however, the possibilities of mechanical aberration and therefore of 'strays,' we recommend as the standard that no more than 2% of the valves set by our machine as being within the ± 5% range may be rejected on the water test."

The buyer's representatives reported on January 12, 1966, that in tests made on January 10, 1966, the machine rejected twenty-four out of 452 valves (5.3%), set twenty-four more than five per cent too high (5.3%), and set eighteen more than five per cent too low (3.98%), a total of forty-two set out of tolerance range (9.3%). There was other testimony that all the valves in the test were set within the five per cent tolerance, and if the seller had agreed to the buyer's version of the five per cent specification, there would have been a question of fact whether the machine met the test. But there was no evidence that the seller agreed to the buyer's version, or that the buyer agreed either to the seller's original version or to its January 6, 1966, recommendation. In these circumstances, it cannot be said that the buyer carried its burden of establishing that its version of the five per cent specification became "part of the basis of the bargain" within UCC § 2-313(1)(a).

* * *

Exceptions overruled. [Footnotes omitted.]

Notes

1. In *Axion,* is it fair to say that the buyer tried and failed to establish that the seller made an express warranty that the goods were fit for buyer's particular purposes? Compare UCC 2–315. In Uganski v. Little Giant Crane & Shovel, Inc., 35 Mich.App. 88, 192 N.W.2d 580 (1971), the court concluded that the manufacturer of a crane—the only one of its kind—especially designed to meet a particular need of the buyer made and breached an express warranty that the crane would be suitable for that need.

2. S, a manufacturer, sold a number of office copying machines to B. The machines were to be leased to B's customers. S represented to B that the machines had a useful life of 10 years and that the "maintenance factor" was ½ cent per copy produced. B sued for damages, claiming, inter alia, that the machines did not conform to the representations. Held, even though the machines were fit for "ordinary" purposes, i.e., they were merchantable, see UCC 2–314(1), the seller may have made and breached an express warranty of special suitability. Royal Typewriter Co. v. Xerographic Supplies Corp., 719 F.2d 1092, 1101–02 (11th Cir.1983). The court stated: "Such an express warranty regarding maintenance costs would be tantamount to a guarantee by Royal that no matter what XSC's wage costs and other expenses might reach during the life of the machine, XSC would spend ½ cent per copy for maintenance. To state the nature of such a statement illustrates the difficulty of its proof. Nevertheless, a guarantee is actionable under (UCC 2–313). * * * As unrealistic as such a guarantee may appear, Royal may have made such an express warranty regarding maintenance costs."

In an earlier case between the same seller and a different buyer, the transaction involved a series of copier sales "between the same parties over approximately an 18–month period and concerned two different machines." The court noted that the knowledge and reliance of the parties "may be expected to change in light of their experience during that time." The court concluded: "Therefore, as to each purchase, Booher's expanding knowledge of the capacities of the copying machines would have to be considered in deciding whether Royal's representations were part of the basis of the bargain. The same representations that could have constituted an express warranty early in the series of transactions might not have qualified as an express warranty in a later transaction if the buyer had acquired independent knowledge as to the fact asserted." Royal Business Machines, Inc. v. Lorraine Corp., 633 F.2d 34, 44 (7th Cir.1980).

DOWNIE v. ABEX CORP.

United States Court of Appeals, Tenth Circuit, 1984.
741 F.2d 1235.

[Plaintiffs, the Downies, sued for personal injuries suffered when an airplane passenger loading bridge (Jetway) manufactured by defendant, Abex, collapsed. The defendant filed a third-party complaint against General Motors, the manufacturer of ball-screw assembly which, allegedly, caused the Jetway to fail. The jury found that GM had made and breached a post-sale express warranty that the ball-screw assembly would not fail. The trial court, however, granted GM's motion for judgment n.o.v. on the express warranty claim. Upon appeal, the ruling of the trial court was reversed and the case remanded.]

* * *

II

A

Abex contends that the trial court erred in granting GM's motion for judgment n.o.v. on the express warranty issue. A trial judge may grant a motion for judgment notwithstanding the verdict only if "the facts and inferences point so strongly and overwhelmingly in favor of one party that the Court believes that reasonable men could not arrive at a contrary verdict." *Boeing Co. v. Shipman,* 411 F.2d 365, 374 (5th Cir.1969). Further, in considering a motion for judgment n.o.v. the trial judge must consider all the evidence and reasonable inferences therefrom in the light most favorable to the party against whom the motion is directed. *Wilkins v. Hogan,* 425 F.2d 1022, 1024 (10th Cir.1970). Section 2–313 of the Uniform Commercial Code governs express warranties. It provides:

"(1) Express warranties by the seller are created as follows:

(a) Any affirmation of fact or promise made by the seller to the buyer which relates to the goods and becomes part of the basis of the bargain creates an express warranty that the goods shall conform to the affirmation or promise.

(b) Any description of the goods which is made part of the basis of the bargain creates an express warranty that the goods shall conform to the description."

Thus, we must determine whether a rational jury could have concluded that GM made an affirmation of fact or promise concerning the failed ball-screw assembly, and, if so, whether it could find that affirmation of fact or promise became part of the basis of the bargain.

B

The original GM warranty was limited to defects in materials and workmanship and specifically excluded all other express or implied warranties. However, the evidence would permit a reasonable jury to find that on at least three occasions GM represented to Abex that its ball-screw assembly was fail-safe and would prevent a free-fall of the Jetway even if the bearings fell out of the assembly.

First, there was the following testimony concerning an exchange that took place on March 30, 1977, when GM employees John Martuch and Lowell Smith made a sales maintenance call on the Jetway manufacturing facilities in Ogden, Utah:

> "Q. (by Abex's counsel) And at that time did either you or Mr. Smith state to Russ Williams and Bob Saunders that if the balls were lost and the deflectors were in place, that there would be interference and there would be no free-fall?
>
> A. (by Mr. Martuch) That is correct.
>
> Q. And there was discussion about that being a fail-safe feature; isn't that correct?
>
> A. That is correct.
>
> Q. And in that discussion neither you nor Mr. Smith limited that statement to the 3–inch ball screw?
>
> A. We were talking about specifically a 3–inch ball screw.
>
> Q. But no one said 3–inch, did they?
>
> A. They didn't have to. There was a print on the table that we were using as a reference that was a 3–inch ball screw.
>
> Q. But no one said, 'We want to make perfectly certain that we're only talking about that drawing'?
>
> A. We were talking about that assembly.
>
> Q. But you never pointed that out, did you?
>
> The Court: Gentlemen, Let's not talk two at one time. She's got to take everything here.
>
> Q. (by Abex's counsel): You never specifically said that, though, did you?
>
> A. Not that I remember."

R. X, 106–07.

Second, Martuch sent a letter to Abex dated April 7, 1977, which referred specifically to life/load charts for "the 3 inch and 4 inch BCD units you use." Pl.Ex. 8. The letter included ten copies of a document describing the design and operation of the patented yolk deflector system. The document stated, "If all balls should be lost from a ball nut equipped with deflectors, these yolk-type units will then cause the ball not to function as a threaded nut. This is a true fail safe feature." Pl.Ex. 7.

Third, GM invited Kenneth Noall and Russell Williams of Abex's Jetway division to Saginaw, Michigan, in May 1977 to observe a test of the fail-safe features of the ball-screw assembly. The test impressed Williams and he asked for and received the test sample. Noall remarked that the fail-safe feature was "worth its weight in gold to our customers." R. IX, 109.

GM argues that all discussions and representations regarding the safety of the ball-screw assemblies were limited to the three-inch assembly, and that the evidence unequivocally establishes that no one from Abex specifically recalled the use of the words "fail-safe" either during the conversations in Ogden or the testing in Saginaw. However, regardless of whether anyone specifically used the words "fail-safe," the literature on the ball-screw assemblies described the yolk deflector mechanism as a "fail safe feature" and did not distinguish between three- and four-inch assemblies. Pl.Ex. 7.[2] In 1977 the three- and four-inch ball-screw assemblies were the only assemblies with yolk deflectors that Abex used in its passenger loading bridges. GM knew that Abex used three- and four-inch assemblies to elevate the bridge. More important, GM, in an internal memorandum, acknowledged Abex's keen interest in the safety features of both the three- and four-inch assemblies. Lowell Smith, in a consumer contact report, stated, "I was requested by Bob Saunders of Jetway to supply a written communication to verify the deflectors in the 3″ or 4″ BCD ball screws will support the 10 [6]″ load rating with the balls removed from the ball nut." Pl.Ex. 13. Kenneth Noall testified that he understood that the load compression test in Saginaw applied to all ball-screw assemblies equipped with yolk deflectors, R. IX, 105–06, and Russell Williams declared that GM never stated that its tests or representations were limited only to the three-inch assemblies. *Id.* at 230–31.

GM contends that even if GM salesmen and Abex engineers used the word "fail-safe," the use constituted mere puffing rather than any affirmation of fact or promise giving rise to an express warranty. The line between puffing and warranting is often difficult to draw, but the more specific the statement the more likely it constitutes a warranty. J. White & R. Summers, *Uniform Commercial Code* 329 (1980). On the basis of the evidence in the record and resolving all facts and inferences in the light most favorable to Abex, we conclude that a rational jury could have found that GM made affirmations of fact or promises that both the three- and four-inch ball-screw assemblies equipped with yolk deflectors were fail-safe.

C

We next must determine whether a rational jury could have found that GM's affirmations of fact or promises became part of the basis of the bargain for the sale of the ball-screw assemblies. UCC § 2–313 clearly contemplates that warranties made after the sale may become a basis of the bargain. Official Comment 7 to § 2–313 provides:

> "The precise time when words of description or affirmation are made * * * is not material. The sole question is whether the language

2. The full text of Plaintiff's Exhibit 7 is as follows:

"*Design Considerations for Maximum Reliability* (con't)

Deflection Yokes vs Pickup Fingers—There are currently two generally used methods of deflecting the bearing balls from the active circuit to the return tube—yoke deflectors and pickup fingers. The yoke deflectors are a patented innovation of Saginaw designed to provide the utmost reliability. Pickup fingers are simple extensions of the return tube guide and normally provide long trouble free service. However, obstructions in the ball groove, such as ice, and the force of skidding balls can break the finger off. If the outer finger of any circuit is broken, the balls in that circuit could be lost. Breakage of inner fingers result in balls being trapped between circuits and the failure of adjacent circuits can occur. The deflection yoke is a solid insert between circuits and outboard of the outer circuits. They are rugged enough to chip away ice in the ball groove. They also fill the space between circuits, thus eliminating the possibility of balls being trapped between circuits. If all balls should be lost from a ball nut equipped with deflectors, these yoke-type units will then cause the ball nut to function as a threaded nut. This is a true fail safe feature."

> * * * [is] fairly to be regarded as a part of the contract. If language is used after the closing of the deal (as when the buyer when taking delivery asks and receives an additional assurance), the warranty becomes a modification, and need not be supported by consideration if it is otherwise reasonable and in order."

In *Bigelow v. Agway, Inc.,* 506 F.2d 551 (2d Cir.1974), the court considered whether a salesman's oral statements constituted a valid post-sale warranty modification. In *Bigelow* a farmer sued the manufacturer and distributor of a chemical used to treat hay before baling. Although most farmers will not bale hay with a moisture level higher than twenty to twenty-five percent, apparently the plaintiff was told that the chemical would safely permit the baling of hay with a higher moisture level. Two months after the sale and use of the chemical, defendant's salesman guaranteed that hay treated with the chemical was safe to bale even though it contained a moisture level of thirty-two to thirty-four percent. The farmer baled the hay, and the level of moisture resulted in a fire that destroyed his entire crop. Rejecting defendant's argument that the salesman's representation was not a basis of the bargain, the Second Circuit noted,

> "Although defendants might conceivably contend that since [the salesman's] representations postdated the delivery of the [treatment] * * * and therefore could not be the 'basis of the bargain' as required for recovery * * *, it is undisputed that the [salesman's] visit * * * was to promote the sale of the product. Thus, they might constitute an actionable modification of the warranty."

Id. at 555 n. 6. Similarly, in the case at bar a rational jury could have found that GM's post-sale representations about the safety of ball-screw assemblies with yolk deflectors were designed to promote future sales. This is especially true since GM sent Abex brochures discussing the safety features for distribution to Abex's customers.

GM argues, citing *Durbano Metals, Inc. v. A & K Railroad Materials, Inc.,* 574 P.2d 1159 (Utah 1978); *Terry v. Moore,* 448 P.2d 601 (Wyo.1968); and *Speed Fastners Inc. v. Newsom,* 382 F.2d 395 (10th Cir.1967), that Abex must prove reliance on the express warranty in order to establish that the warranty was part of the basis of the bargain. Official Comment 3 to UCC § 2–313 states, "in actual practice affirmations of fact made by the seller * * * are regarded as part of the description of those goods; hence no particular reliance on such statements need be shown in order to weave them into the fabric of the agreement * * *." We need not decide whether an express warranty may exist without reliance, *see* J. White & R. Summers, *Uniform Commercial Code* 333 (1980) ("Possibly for lack of any other meaningful standard, courts must employ the test of whether buyer relied on the affirmation of fact or promise * * * "), because Abex presented sufficient evidence for a rational jury to find that Abex did rely on GM's express warranty. Robert Saunders, Director of Research and Development and Technical Marketing for Abex, testified that he was not concerned about making safety modifications on Abex's existing stock of ball-screw assemblies because of GM's representations:

"Q. (by Abex's counsel) Did you feel it was necessary to either alter your existing stock or the ball screws out in the field with runout threads?

A. (by Mr. Saunders) No.

Q. Why not?

A. Because the design that we had, either the thread runout or— the washer was somewhat less critical because of the existence of the deflector yokes.

Q. All right. In other words, you weren't so concerned about the safety features because of the representations about the yoke deflectors?

A. That's correct."

R. IX, 42.

GM contends that Abex cannot recover for breach of express warranty because there was no mutual agreement to modify the limited written warranty as required by § 2–313. In *Cargill, Inc. v. Stafford,* 553 F.2d 1222, 1225 (10th Cir.1977), we noted that the UCC contains an objective test of mutuality of assent as "manifested by the conduct of the parties." On the basis of the evidence presented in this case, we hold that after resolving all factual inferences in favor of Abex, a rational jury could have found that both parties recognized and assented to a warranty on the absolute safety of ball-screw assemblies equipped with yolk deflectors.

III

GM contends that its breach of the express warranty did not proximately cause Abex damage because the collapse of the Jetway had nothing to do with the failure of the yolk [sic] deflectors. However, since Abex presented evidence that the screw free-fell through the nut and that GM warranted that the yolk [sic] deflectors would engage the nut, we must resolve any doubts in favor of Abex.

Reversed and remanded for further proceedings consistent with this opinion.

[Some footnotes omitted.]

SECTION 3. NON-COMPLIANCE WITH IMPLIED WARRANTIES

A. Introduction

The line between an express warranty and the implied warranties of merchantability, UCC 2–314, and fitness for particular purpose, UCC 2–315, can be very fine. The common ground, of course, is the contract description of the goods. Depending on the facts, the description can create an express warranty, UCC 2–313(1)(b), provide a standard to measure merchantability, UCC 2–314(1)(a), and describe goods which meet the buyer's particular purposes. See UCC 2–315. In fact, the "sale by description" is thought to be the transaction from which implied warranty theory evolved. See, e.g., Gardiner v. Gray, 4 Camb. 144, 171 Eng.Rep. 46 (1815); Prosser, *The Implied Warranty of Merchantable Quality,* 27 Minn.L.Rev. 117, 139–45 (1943); Williston, *Representation and Warranty in Sales—Heilbut v. Buckleton,* 27 Harv. L.Rev. 1, 13 (1913).

But if neither the description of the goods nor the seller's other affirmations or promises cover the buyer's particular expectations of quality, how, if at all, is the gap in the agreement to be filled? See UCC 2–314 & 2–315? Implied warranties are clearly terms of the agreement. Are they implied in fact or imposed by law? If the latter, what justifications support the imposition?

We will consider these questions in this Section.

Problem 19–3

Read UCC 2–314 and 2–315. Make up an abstract list of the basic types of facts a plaintiff would *not* have to prove to show breach of an implied warranty of merchantability but would have to prove to show breach of an implied warranty of fitness for a particular purpose.

B. *Merchantability*

UCC 2–314(1) provides that "a warranty that the goods shall be merchantable is implied in a contract for their sale if the seller is a merchant with respect to goods of that kind." Subsection (2) provides standards to measure merchantability and Subsection (3) provides that "other implied warranties may arise from course of dealing or usage of trade." But the implied warranty of merchantability may be "excluded or modified" by agreement, the content of which is regulated by UCC 2–316(2).

AGOOS KID CO., INC. v. BLUMENTHAL IMPORT CORP.

Supreme Judicial Court of Massachusetts, 1933.
282 Mass. 1, 184 N.E. 279.

[Blumenthal Import Corporation contracted to sell to Agoos Kid Company four thousand dozen "Bagdad goat skins dry salted." Payment was to be: "Net cash or domestic letter of credit against documents"; Agoos paid without inspecting the skins. Serious defects in the skins showed up for which Agoos sued Blumenthal. Plaintiff got judgment and Blumenthal appealed.]

CROSBY, J.

* * *

Upon the question whether there was an implied warranty of merchantable quality under [Uniform Sales Act 15(2)] the following facts were found: The goods described in the contracts known in the trade as "Bagdad goat skins dry salted" are a well known article of commerce. The defendant maintains an organization in various places in Asia Minor and India for the purpose of collecting dry salted skins for shipment to the United States and at the time of the collection of the skins in question it had a representative in Bagdad. At times such representatives buy from local collectors and butchers skins which have been cured by the dry salting process. This process is efficient in preserving the texture of the skins only when an attempt is not made to dry them too quickly by the hot rays of the sun, which is likely to result in a rotting of the inside of the skin, where it cannot be detected by ocular or manual inspection or in any other practicable way until the skins are put into the process of being made into leather. With reasonable precaution in the care and selection of the skins in the Orient, a certain number of improperly cured and rotted skins is likely to be found in a large lot. Both parties were aware of this fact. In the trade it is considered that a lot is normal if it does not appear that more than one and one half per cent, or at the most three per cent, are improperly cured and therefore worthless. "Certainly a lot containing more than three per cent of rotted skins is abnormal." It was found that so far as defects appeared the defendant was ignorant of their condition, and the same was true of the plaintiff until the defects were shown in the plaintiff's tannery. Beginning with the first pack of skins of the first shipment the plaintiff, on January 14, 1931, began the process of manufacturing them into leather, and at different times thereafter all the other packs were put through the process, and many of them showed that more than three per cent were rotten. The entire first shipment was finally put through the process, and it was found that "the defects in the first shipment were very material and important and extended to nearly half the skins contained in it." Upon the foregoing findings which were warranted by the evidence, the further finding was warranted that the goods delivered by the first shipment were not of merchantable quality.

The contracts in question were for a sale of goods by description and there was an implied warranty that they would correspond with the description. G.L. c. 106, § 16. "The goods are merchantable when they are of the general kind which they are described or supposed to be when bought." Williston on Sales (2d Ed.) § 243. "Where goods of a character commonly known in trade are ordered by description, and there is no inspection, there is an implied warranty that those furnished will be such as are merchantable under the descriptive term used by the parties. The purchaser is entitled to get what he ordered." Leavitt v. Fiberloid Co., 196 Mass. 440, 451, 82 N.E. 682, 687, 15 L.R.A., N.S., 855, and cases cited. See, also, Randall v. Newson, 2 Q.B.D. 102; Bristol Tramways, &c. Carriage Co., Ltd. v. Fiat Motors, Ltd., [1910] 2 K.B. 831, 841; Nichol v. Godts, 10 Ex. 191. The plaintiff did not contract to buy seven thousand dozen goat skins, one half of which were to be rotten and worthless. It agreed to buy that number of skins dry salted, and there was an implied warranty that, with the exception of not more than three per cent thereof, they should be of merchantable quality. Keown & McEvoy, Inc. v. Verlin, 253 Mass. 374, 377, 149 N.E. 115, 41 A.L.R. 1319, Whitty Manuf. Co. v. Clark, 278 Mass. 370, 180 N.E. 315. Although it was found that a lot of dry salted goat skins is deemed of merchantable quality and reasonably fit for the purpose of making it into leather if the defect here existing is limited to not more than three per cent of the lot, it was found that the first shipment was not merchantable throughout "within this definition, and was not reasonably fit throughout within this definition for the purpose of being made into leather." * * * [The court reversed because the trial court had excluded defendant's evidence of a custom in the trade to notify the seller of defective skins before starting to process them.]

Notes

1. In a seminal article, written in 1943, William Prosser, later a principal architect of strict tort liability, suggested three overlapping justifications for the implied warranty of merchantability. The first was that the seller had made a

"misrepresentation of fact" upon which the buyer had relied. For Prosser, this was "obviously" a tort theory. The second was that the warranty "has in fact been agreed upon by the parties as an unexpressed term of the contract for sale." The warranty was inferred from language, conduct, circumstances and was "pure" contract. The third was that the warranty was "imposed by law" as a matter of policy. The loss from "defective" goods should be placed upon the seller "because he is best able to bear it and distribute it to the public, and because it is considered that the buyer is entitled to protection at the seller's expense." For the third justification, Prosser had in mind cases where defective food caused personal injuries to buyers and consumers. See Prosser, The Implied Warranty of Merchantable Quality, 27 Minn.L.Rev. 117, 122 (1943). Do you agree with Prosser's classifications?

2. Which justification(s) supports the result in *Agoos Kid Co.*? Can you add to the list?

VALLEY IRON & STEEL CO. v. THORIN

Supreme Court of Oregon, 1977.
278 Or. 103, 562 P.2d 1212.

LENT, J.

Plaintiff brought an action in assumpsit for the reasonable value of goods sold and delivered to the defendant. Defendant pleaded affirmative defenses, alleging breaches of the implied warranties of merchantability and fitness for particular purpose. ORS 72.3140; 72.3150. Following a trial to the court, judgment was entered in favor of plaintiff. Defendant appeals, claiming that the court erred in failing to find breaches of the implied warranties and improperly fixed the amount of damages.

Because of the trial court's general finding in favor of plaintiff, we review the evidence in the light most favorable to its contentions.

Plaintiff is a corporation engaged in the manufacture of cast iron products. In 1974 defendant was establishing a retail store to sell equipment and supplies for tree-planting contractors and workers. In September of that year, defendant's agent, Steven Gibbs, met with Roger Herring, Manager of Valley Iron & Steel. Mr. Gibbs inquired if plaintiff could manufacture castings of hoedad collars. A hoedad is a forestry tool used for planting seedling trees. The collar of a hoedad secures the metal blade to a wooden handle.

Mr. Gibbs showed plaintiff a sample collar casting made by Western Fire Equipment and asked if plaintiff could duplicate the casting. The sample collar was shown with a handle, and Mr. Gibbs explained that the tool was an impact tool used for planting trees and that occasionally rocks are struck during the planting process. Plaintiff's witness, Mr. Herring, testified:

> "* * * Mr. Gibbs came in, spoke to me, told me that he needed this particular type of casting, briefly described its intended use, asked me if we could make them.
>
> "I indicated we could. It was a very brief discussion in regards to the type of material we were going to use, and I indicated that because

there was potential chance of hitting rock in this * * * operation * * * that it would have to be made out of somewhat of a durable material."

Mr. Herring suggested that the castings be made of durable iron. The parties agreed upon a price, and after defendant obtained a core box and pattern from the model collar, manufacturing commenced. The collars were delivered to defendant in early October, 1974.

Problems developed with the finished product. Defendant's customers complained that the castings were breaking. Eventually defendant returned up to 80% of the castings to the plaintiff. Another foundry later made satisfactory castings from the same core box and pattern but from mild steel instead of cast iron.

At the conclusion of the trial, the court made the following findings:

"I am not going to make any specific findings—just some general findings—but I will say that my general findings are based upon two findings, I suppose. One is that Mr. Gibbs' directions to Mr. Herring in this case were not sufficient in the sense that the court believes that he knew enough about what he was doing when he went out there to give directions, and the court does not feel that Mr. Herring did anything that was legally wrong and then didn't comply with what he said he was going to do.

"In other words, the court believes that the one at fault was Mr. Gibbs in this particular case. 'Fault' may not be exactly the correct word, but that it was the legal duty of Mr. Gibbs to do more than he did, rather than Mr. Herring doing more than he did.

"So, the court—then, the general finding is that I am finding for the plaintiff."

Defendant contends on appeal that the court erred in failing to find the existence of an implied warranty of merchantability under ORS 72.3140 and an implied warranty of fitness for a particular purpose under ORS 72.3150. ORS 72.3140 provides that:

"72.3140. Implied warranty: merchantability; usage of trade. (1) Unless excluded or modified as provided in ORS 72.3160, a warranty that the goods shall be merchantable is implied in a contract for their sale if the seller is a merchant with respect to goods of that kind * * *

"(2) Goods to be merchantable must be at least such as:

* * *

"(c) Are fit for the ordinary purposes for which such goods are used; * * *"

In denying defendant any recovery under this theory, the trial court must have concluded either that plaintiff was not a "merchant with respect to goods of that kind" or that the goods were "fit for the ordinary purposes for which such goods are used." It is undisputed that the products were "goods" [1] and that there was a "contract for their sale." Any implied

1. "Specially manufactured goods" are included within the definition of "goods" in ORS 72.1050.

warranty which existed was not excluded or modified under ORS 72.3160.[2]

"Merchant" is defined by ORS 72.1040 as "a person who deals in goods of the kind or otherwise by his occupation holds himself out as having knowledge or skill peculiar to the practices or goods involved in the transaction * * *." While the evidence shows that plaintiff was unfamiliar with hoedads and had not previously manufactured hoedad collars, plaintiff did hold itself out, by operating a foundry, as having skill in the "practice" of casting iron and presumably in the selection of materials to be used in manufacturing castings. Inasmuch as this transaction involved the selection of the type of metal appropriate for hoedad collars, plaintiff was a merchant.[3]

Likewise, plaintiff, for purposes of ORS 72.3140, was a merchant "with respect to goods of that kind"; i.e., castings. Whether this provision is interpreted broadly (in this case to mean castings) or narrowly (to mean hoedad collars) would depend upon the facts of the case. Only merchants, under the Code, warrant merchantability; and this is so because of their expertise or familiarity with the processes or products involved in the transaction. This skill or knowledge is presumed from previous similar transactions. Plaintiff has in the past assisted buyers in choosing particular types of metals to fulfill various tasks in its manufacture of castings.[4] Where the alleged unfitness under ORS 72.3140 arises from this type of choice, plaintiff should be held to the stricter standard imposed on merchants.[5]

The remaining issue is whether the collars were "fit for the ordinary purposes for which such goods are used." The ordinary purpose of custom-made castings depends upon their designated use. Without such a tag the uses would vary so much that any function could be isolated as "ordinary."

The trial court felt that plaintiff was unaware of the intended use. However, the testimony of Mr. Herring shows the contrary. Plaintiff knew that the castings were to join the handle and blade in tree-planting impact tools which occasionally would strike rock. Since the castings were not fit for this purpose, the warranty was breached.

2. We do not conclude that plaintiff, by promising to make the castings out of "durable iron" or saying that it was not performing engineering services, effectively modified or excluded any implied warranties as to the ingredients used in manufacturing the castings under ORS 72.3160. Such language does not "in common understanding call the buyer's attention to the exclusion of warranties and make plain that there is no implied warranty." ORS 72.3160(3)(a).

3. In Blockhead, Inc. v. Plastic Forming Company, Inc., 402 F.Supp. at 1017 (D.Conn. 1975) the court held that: "The term 'practices' indicates that one may be a merchant of goods by virtue of his involvement in the process by which those goods are produced as well as by sale of the finished goods from inventory." (402 F.Supp. at 1025.)

4. Mr. Herring testified that he tried to imply to buyers that no guarantee was made as to the selection of the appropriate material for casting but that any lack of guarantee was not discussed with Mr. Gibbs. In special order situations like the present case, it was customary with plaintiff to use the "best efforts at foundry" as to the choice of the proper alloy.

5. Thus in cases where the seller possesses no degree of discretion so as to warrant his or her expertise; e.g., where the product is manufactured strictly in accordance with buyer specifications, there may be no implied warranties. See Official Comments to the U.C.C., § 2–316, Comment 9; School Supply Service Co. v. J.H. Keeney & Co., 410 F.2d 481, 483 (5th Cir.1969); Rust Engineering Co. v. Lawrence Pumps, Inc., 401 F.Supp. 328, 333 (D.Mass.1975).

Similarly, plaintiff breached the warranty of fitness for a particular purpose. ORS 72.3150 provides:

> "Implied warranty: fitness for particular purpose. Where the seller at the time of contracting has reason to know any particular purpose for which the goods are required and that the buyer is relying on the seller's skill or judgment to select or furnish suitable goods, there is unless excluded or modified under ORS 72.3160 an implied warranty that the goods shall be fit for such purpose."

Official Comment 1 to this section states that:

> "Under this section the buyer need not bring home to the seller actual knowledge of the particular purpose for which the goods are intended or of his reliance on the seller's skill and judgment, if the circumstances are such that the seller has reason to realize the purpose intended or that the reliance exists. The buyer, of course, must actually be relying on the seller."

In this case, the undisputed evidence shows that the buyer made known the intended purpose and that the choice of metal to be used was left to the discretion of the seller. From this the seller had "reason to know" that buyer was relying on its judgment. It is also plain that the buyer did so rely. It follows that the warranty existed and evidence existed that it was breached.[6]

The trial court rested its decision upon the "fault" of the defendant in failing to provide additional information on the intended use of the castings. "Fault," as such, is irrelevant when dealing with implied warranties. State ex rel. Western Seed v. Campbell, 250 Or. 262, 266, 442 P.2d 215 (1967). It is true that the existence of a warranty of fitness for a particular purpose depends in part upon the comparative knowledge and skill of the parties. Blockhead, Inc. v. Plastic Forming Company, Inc., 402 F.Supp. 1017, 1024 (D.Conn.1975). Here, however, defendant made known his general requirements and the purpose for which the goods were to be used. We fail to see what more the defendant could have disclosed. Where, as here, the needs of a buyer are disclosed and the seller has reason to know of the buyer's reliance, it is incumbent upon the seller to further inquire as to the buyer's wants before representing that the goods can be provided. Lewis v. Mobil Oil Corp., 438 F.2d 500 (8th Cir.1971). See also, Northern Plumbing Supply, Inc. v. Gates, 196 N.W.2d 70 (N.D.1972).

In this case the trial court found that the reasonable value of each casting was $3.75. She estimated the value of the goods returned to be $27.42. Implicit in this finding is the conclusion that 457 of the 571 pieces were returned to the seller.[7] Because we conclude that defendant rightfully

6. Where goods are specially manufactured goods the ordinary purpose of such goods may be equivalent to their particular purpose for purposes of the warranty enumerated in ORS 72.3150. See, generally, Filler v. Rayex Corp., 435 F.2d 336 (7th Cir.1970); Tennessee Carolina Transp., Inc. v. Strick Corp., 283 N.C. 423, 196 S.E.2d 711 (1973). Contra, Blockhead, Inc. v. Plastic Forming Company, Inc., supra n. 3.

Official Comment 2 to the Code states: "A contract may of course include both a warranty of merchantability and one of fitness for a particular purpose."

7. Testimony at the trial by Mr. Herring was that the individual castings weighed around two pounds apiece and that the scrap value was three cents per pound. If each piece was worth six cents as scrap, an offset of $27.42 equates to 457 returned castings.

revoked acceptance under ORS 72.6080(1)(b), inasmuch as the goods were unfit, defendant has no further obligation as to the returned goods. ORS 72.6020(2)(c). The defendant, however, is obligated to pay for the remaining 114 castings which it accepted. Accordingly, under our powers as enumerated in the Oregon Constitution, Am Art VII § 3, plaintiff's judgment is reduced to $427.50 (the value of 114 pieces at $3.75 per unit).

Affirmed as modified.

Notes

1. Why should the implied warranty of merchantability be limited to sellers who are merchants "with respect to goods of that kind?" UCC 2–314(1). As the court in *Thorin* recognizes, the merchant requirement for UCC 2–314(1) is narrower than the definition of "merchant" in UCC 2–104(1). Compare UCC 2–201(2) & 2–207(2). How can a seller who had never made or sold a hoedad collar be a merchant "with respect to goods of that kind?" See Fred J. Moore, Inc. v. Schinmann, 40 Wash.App. 705, 700 P.2d 754 (1985) (farmer who made "isolated" sale not a dealer in goods of that kind); Smith v. Stewart, 233 Kan. 904, 667 P.2d 358 (1983) (seller of used yacht does not make an implied warranty of merchantability).

2. Who is a merchant for purposes of UCC 2–314(1) is a mixed question of law and fact that depends upon the circumstances of each case. Ferragamo v. Massachusetts Bay Transportation Authority, 395 Mass. 581, 481 N.E.2d 477 (1985) (upheld jury verdict that MBTA is merchant with respect to sporadic sale of old trolley cars). The question whether a farmer who sells livestock or raises crops grown on his own land is a merchant is frequently litigated with diverse results. In Dotts v. Bennett, 382 N.W.2d 85 (Iowa 1986), however, the court rejected the argument that a farmer who sells only a crop grown annually (hay) was not, as a matter of law, a merchant. The jury verdict that the farmer was a merchant with respect to hay was supported by the following factors: "He had been a lifetime farmer; he had 100 to 150 acres in hay in 1981; he has sold about twenty percent of his hay for fifteen years; he has advertised hay for sale; at one time he sold a large quantity of hay to parties in southern Missouri; he has done some custom hay farming; he considers himself a knowledgeable hay farmer; and he has had continuing education in farming. * * *" 382 N.W.2d at 89. A related case is Vince v. Broome, 443 So.2d 23 (Miss.1983) (farmer held to be merchant with regard to cattle sold, four judges dissenting).

3. Cattle and other livestock are frequently sold at auction. Suppose the farmer-owner is not a merchant under UCC 2–314(1) but the auctioneer clearly is: He regularly deals in goods of that kind. Does the auctioneer make an implied warranty of merchantability? In Powers v. Coffeyville Livestock Sales Co., Inc., 665 F.2d 311 (10th Cir.1981), the answer was no if the auctioneer had revealed the identity of its principal. Disclosure prevented the auctioneer from being a seller at common law and the court incorporated the common law rule through UCC 1–103 to supplement the definition of seller in UCC 2–103(1)(d), which was ambiguous on the point.

This is consistent with Mr. Herring's testimony that 60–8 of the castings were returned, as 457 is 80% of the 571 units sold.

DELANO GROWERS' COOPERATIVE WINERY v. SUPREME WINE CO., INC.

Supreme Judicial Court of Massachusetts, 1985.
393 Mass. 666, 473 N.E.2d 1066.

Before HENNESSEY, C.J., and LIACOS, NOLAN, LYNCH and O'CONNOR, JJ.

NOLAN, JUSTICE.

The plaintiff, Delano Growers' Cooperative Winery (Delano), appeals from a final judgment dismissing its complaint and awarding $160,634, with interest, to the defendant, Supreme Wine Co., Inc. (Supreme), on its counterclaim. Supreme appeals from that portion of the judgment which granted Delano an "offset" of $25,823.25 to Supreme's damages under the counterclaim. For the reasons stated below, we affirm the judgment.

Delano filed a complaint in Suffolk County Superior Court seeking $25,823.25 for wine sold and delivered. Supreme admitted receipt of the wine and filed a counterclaim for breach of contract alleging that earlier shipments of wine for which payment had been made and all of the wine for which no payment had been made had spoiled due to the presence of lactobacillus trichodes (Fresno mold). As a defense, Supreme asserted that it did not owe Delano $25,823.25 because the wine was not merchantable. Supreme also sought incidental and consequential damages alleging that the "sick wine" destroyed its reputation and market thereby forcing the company into liquidation.[1]

* * *

The facts as found by the master and accepted by the judge may be summarized as follows. Supreme operated a wine bottling plant in Boston from 1935 to November, 1978. It purchased finished wine, ready for bottling and consumption, from California, selling it to retailers after bottling under Supreme's label.

In 1968, Supreme began buying sweet wine from Delano, a California winery. By the spring of 1973, Supreme was purchasing all its sweet wine from Delano. Delano shipped this wine to Supreme's bottling plant in

1. Supreme purchased all of its sweet wine and some of its nonsweet wine from Delano. Fresno mold only damaged the sweet wine. Supreme's customers began returning defective Delano wine prior to the shipment for which Delano claims in its complaint that it is owed $25,823.25 (the unpaid shipment). Supreme paid for all prior shipments. Supreme's customers continued to return defective Delano wine after Supreme received and bottled the wine in the unpaid shipment. One-half of the unpaid shipment consisted of sweet wine. The record does not indicate what portion of the unpaid shipment or total shipments consisted of damaged wine. However, we need not resolve this question to affirm the judgment in this case. Supreme proved that 8,000 cases of wine were defective. Supreme normally sold this wine to its retail customers for $13 per case. This per case price included the amount Supreme paid Delano for the wine, Supreme's other costs, and its profits. The judge calculated damages by multiplying the number of cases proved as damaged (8,000) by the per case price ($13). The resultant amount includes all of Supreme's cost for wine including the amount remaining unpaid on the last shipment. The judge then deducted the amount that Supreme had not paid for wine ($25,823.25) and made other adjustments as discussed below. This prevents overcompensating Supreme because the per case price ($13) included Supreme's cost for the wine as if it were actually paid. The $25,823.25 represents a portion of this cost that was not paid. This calculation also factors out any need to determine the amount of undamaged wine Supreme received as damages are based solely on the actual amount of defective wine.

Boston in tank cars. When the wine arrived, Supreme took samples from each compartment of the tank cars. The samples were labeled, dated, sealed, and kept in Supreme's safe. Supreme then pumped the wine into redwood vats in its building. The wine was pumped through a filter into storage tanks from which it was later filtered into bottles for delivery.

Until April or May, 1973, Supreme did not experience any difficulty with Delano wine. Supreme then began receiving widespread returns of certain sweet wine from its customers. The wine was producing sediment, was cloudy, and contained a cottony or hairy substance. Supreme could identify the defective sweet wine as Delano wine because it purchased all its sweet wine from Delano. Supreme also matched the returned defective wine with the samples taken from the Delano wine on delivery. This identification was corroborated somewhat by shipment records, the dates of bottling and the color to which the Delano wine was blended.

Supreme made oral reports and complaints about the problem to Delano. It also sent Delano samples from the Delano shipment. When the help promised by Harold Roland, Delano's manager, did not materialize, Supreme purchased wine from another California grower in June, July, and August, 1973. Supreme bottled and sold that wine and received no complaints or returns on it. Roland, with renewed promises of assistance, induced Supreme to recommence purchasing from Delano in September, 1973.

Delano made four shipments of sweet wine to Supreme between September 28 and December 20, 1973. Each shipment invoice stated that payment was due forty-five days from the invoice date. Supreme paid all but the last invoice, which was in the amount of $25,823.25. It withheld payment for that amount as customers continued to return defective wine which was identified as Delano wine. When oral reports and complaints evoked no tangible help, Vito Bracciale, assistant to Supreme's president, wrote to Roland on April 9, 1974. This letter requested assistance and explained Supreme's crisis caused by the defective wine. The letter also indicated the high number of returns caused by this defective wine.

In response to this letter, Delano sent James Lunt, an assistant winemaker, to Supreme's bottling plant. His microscopic examination of the defective wine and a microscopic examination by Delano's chemist in California showed that the wine contained Fresno mold. Lunt had earlier observed the mold in the samples returned to Delano by Supreme. These were samples from the tank cars taken on arrival at Supreme and samples from wine returned by Supreme's customers.

While Lunt was at Supreme, customers returned a number of cases of Delano wine containing Fresno mold. After examining these returns, Lunt told Supreme to pasteurize, refilter, rebottle, and resell the defective wine. Supreme followed Lunt's directions and reprocessed 8,000 cases of spoiled wine (5,000 cases returned from customers and 3,000 cases still on hand). During this process, 1,000 cases were lost through breakage, spillage, and shrinkage. Supreme sold the remaining cases of reprocessed wine at a reduced rate.

* * *

2. *Delano's breach of the implied warranty of merchantability.* This sale of wine by Delano is governed by the Uniform Commercial Code, G.L. c. 106. Delano impliedly warranted that the goods were of merchantable quality. G.L. c. 106, § 2–314. See *Regina Grape Prods. Co. v. Supreme Wine Co.,* 357 Mass. 631, 635, 260 N.E.2d 219 (1970). This warranty required the wine to "pass without objection in the trade under the contract description" and be reasonably suited for ordinary uses for which goods of that kind are sold. G.L. c. 106, § 2–314(2)(*a*). See *Vincent v. Nicholas E. Tsiknas Co.,* 337 Mass. 726, 729, 151 N.E.2d 263 (1958); *Gilbert & Bennett Mfg. Co. v. Westinghouse Elec. Corp.,* 445 F.Supp. 537, 548 (D.Mass.1977).

The contract in this case required Delano to deliver "finished wine" to Supreme. Delano contends that, when it delivered wine that appeared good and which could be bottled, its obligation was satisfied. In support, Delano argues that all California sweet wine contained Fresno mold. Therefore, the presence of Fresno mold could not cause a wine to be unmerchantable. Furthermore, Delano states that an alleged trade usage required Supreme to add sulfur dioxide to the wine to inhibit further growth of these bacteria. Delano's arguments fail to persuade us.

Delano argues that uncontroverted testimony indicated that all California sweet wine contained Fresno mold. The judge acknowledged this testimony. However, the judge found that Supreme never experienced any trouble with bacteria until the 1973 problem with Delano wine. The sweet wine which Supreme bought from other California growers in 1973 did not present any bacterial problems. None of this wine was returned with Fresno mold. Furthermore, the judge found that the bacterial problem could have been prevented and controlled by Delano. Although Fresno mold may have been present in all California sweet wine, there is no indication that it was allowed to go unchecked and thereby destroy the merchantability of finished wine. Supreme's prior experience with Delano and its experience with other California sweet wine in 1973 indicate that the mold could be controlled. The presence of Fresno mold, as it was in the Delano wines, caused those wines to be unmarketable.

Delano argues that Supreme's failure to follow minimum industry standards prevents it from recovering for the unmerchantable wine. The judge specifically ruled that Delano had failed to meet its burden of establishing such standards as a usage of trade applicable to Supreme. Even if Delano had met its burden, its argument would fail. A course of dealing between parties controls the interpretation of usage of trade. G.L. c. 106, § 1–205(4). In this case, Supreme consistently followed the same procedure in processing Delano wine since 1968. This clearly established a course of dealing between Delano and Supreme. Any usage of trade followed in areas outside of Massachusetts cannot control this long-standing course of dealing between the parties.

Once Supreme initially accepted Delano wine it had the burden of establishing that there was a breach of the warranty of merchantability. *Axion Corp. v. G.D.C. Leasing Corp.,* 359 Mass. 474, 479, 269 N.E.2d 664 (1971). Supreme has met that burden. Supreme identified all the returned wine as Delano wine. Delano's chemist also found traces of Fresno mold in the samples "from the compartments of the tank cars in which Delano wine arrived in Boston and wine from the bottles returned by customers." The wine in its returned state was neither merchantable nor fit for bottling or consumption. Only through extensive reprocessing could Supreme mitigate the loss from this wine. The course of dealing between the parties supports the conclusion that the finished wine shipped by Delano normally was ready for bottling and drinking. Although the Delano sweet wine could be bottled shortly thereafter, it could not be drunk.

Delano was required to anticipate the environment in which it was reasonable for its product to be used. *Back v. Wickes Corp.*, 375 Mass. 633, 640–641, 378 N.E.2d 964 (1978). It was reasonably foreseeable that the unchecked presence of Fresno mold would substantially impair the value of the wine. That result occurred. The Delano wine could not pass in the trade as finished wine without objection, was not fit for the ordinary purposes for which finished wine was used, and therefore, was unmerchantable. See G.L. c. 106, § 2–314.

* * *

Notes

1. The buyer, to prevail, must establish that the goods were unmerchantable at the time the seller tendered delivery. See UCC 2–725(2). In *Delano Growers',* to which standards of merchantability in UCC 2–314(2) did the wine fail to conform? How did the buyer avoid the possible conclusion that there was a normal amount of Fresno mold in the wine at delivery but that it got "out of hand" while the wine was being processed by the buyer?

2. In most disputes over merchantability, the key factual question is whether goods sold under a contract description were "fit for the ordinary purposes for which such goods are used." UCC 2–314(2)(c). The trier of fact must know whether the product "conformed to the standard performance of like products used in the trade * * * (and this determination) depends upon testimony of persons familiar with industry standards and local practices and is a question of fact." Pisano v. American Leasing Co., 146 Cal.App.3d 194, 194 Cal.Rptr. 77, 80 (1983). Without any evidence of relevant trade standards or uses, the merchantability claim may fail. Royal Business Machines, Inc. v. Lorraine Corp., 633 F.2d 34 (7th Cir.1980). Similarly, if, because of the newness or complexity of the product, no average or usual standards for determining performance or quality can be determined, the "ordinary purposes" standard will not help the buyer. See, e.g., Price Brothers Co. v. Philadelphia Gear Corp., 649 F.2d 416 (6th Cir.1981). See also, Comark Merchandising, Inc. v. Highland Group, Inc., 932 F.2d 1196 (7th Cir. 1991) (no warranty liability where ordinary use not established and buyer refused to inform seller of its particular intended use).

3. *Food.* The *Delano Growers* case involved wine sold by the producer to a dealer for resale to individuals for consumption. Although Fresno mold was arguably a natural ingredient in the wine, the course of dealing between the parties and the seller's failure to treat the wine before delivery persuaded the court that the particular wine was unmerchantable. The buyer suffered only economic loss. No personal injuries were involved.

Suppose, however, that a restaurant serves an oyster stew containing ground glass, causing personal injury to a customer. This is an easy case, right? Under UCC 2–314(1), the seller is a "merchant with respect to goods of that kind" and the "serving for value of food or drink to be consumed either on the premises or elsewhere is a sale." Moreover, the glass, a "foreign" ingredient, makes the stew unmerchantable under UCC 2–714(2)(a) and (c). Thus, in most states Customer can sue Restaurant for breach of the implied warranty and recover for "injury to person ... proximately resulting from any breach of warranty." UCC 2–715(2)(b).

The issue is more complicated if personal injury results from, say, an oyster shell in the stew or from a virus contained in the tissue of the oyster. Is this stew, like cigarettes made from good tobacco and not contaminated by pesticides, "fit for the ordinary purposes for which such goods are used?" Traditionally, the answer turned on whether the ingredient was classified as foreign or natural to the goods. If the former, the seller is liable. If the latter, the responsibility to take precautions is on the buyer. See Mix v. Ingersoll Candy Co., 6 Cal.2d 674, 59 P.2d 144 (1936) (chicken bone in chicken pie is a substance "natural" to that type of food).

More recently, many states have adopted some variation of a "reasonable expectations" test. Under this test, the seller will not prevail simply because the ingredient is "natural" to the product. Thus, in Illinois the question is whether a "reasonable consumer" would expect that the product might contain the substance which caused the injury. See Jackson v. Nestle–Beich, Inc., 147 Ill.2d 408, 168 Ill.Dec. 147, 589 N.E.2d 547 (1992) (presence of pecan shell in chocolate covered pecan caramel candy a "factor" in analysis). On the other hand, Massachusetts has rejected a test based on what a hypothetical reasonable consumer would expect in favor of a more particularized inquiry. The question is what a consumer of the buyer's age and experience might reasonably expect. Phillips v. Town of West Springfield, 405 Mass. 411, 540 N.E.2d 1331 (1989) (turkey bone in processed turkey served in a school cafeteria). See also, Mexicali Rose v. Superior Court, 1 Cal.4th 617, 4 Cal.Rptr.2d 145, 822 P.2d 1292 (1992), where the court stated that if the ingredient (a chicken bone) was natural to the preparation of the food served (a chicken enchilada) it is reasonably expected by its very nature and the food is not unfit for human consumption.

What about a virus or bacteria in a raw oyster under the reasonable expectation test? What about that highly toxic Fugu fish served at a very high price in some Japanese restaurants? If properly prepared, the customer is left with minor numbness in the extremities. If improperly prepared, the customer, so to speak, "joins the fishes." What about cigarettes made from "good" tobacco that still cause cancer?

Problem 19–4

Fisher's, a retail book store, has an extensive inventory in specialized categories, such as law, business, psychology and investments. A new investment book by Barry Greene, entitled "How to go Short in A Bear Market," was published by Big Red Company and heavily advertised in the trade journals as the "key" to success in selling short in the stock market and selling "Puts" in the option markets. Fisher's purchased 300 copies for resale and the books sold well. Mr. N.O. Vice, an inexperienced investor, purchased a copy of the book for $20 and, following Greene's advice, committed $25,000 of his funds over a three month period. He lost $15,000 of that investment before covering his shorts. About the same time, a scathing review of Greene's book by Malcolm P. Barron appeared in the Wall Street Journal. Barron stated that the advice was seriously flawed and should not be taken seriously. Other experts agreed and sales of the book dropped precipitously. Angered, N.O. Vice retains you as counsel to consider whether a law suit against either Fisher's or Big Red could be maintained on a warranty theory. Greene, who went long while others were going short, is now "long gone." What is your advice? Cf. Cardozo v. True, 342 So.2d 1053 (Fla.App.1977).

DOE v. TRAVENOL LABORATORIES, INC.

United States District Court, Minnesota, 1988.
698 F.Supp. 780.

MEMORANDUM AND ORDER

MACLAUGHLIN, District Judge.

This case is a products liability action in which the plaintiff, who appears under the pseudonym J.D. Doe, alleges that he contracted AIDS–Related Complex (ARC) from an antihemophilic factor which he received prior to surgery. Defendant Baxter Healthcare Corporation (Baxter) brings a motion to dismiss Doe's strict liability and breach of warranty claims on the ground that Minnesota law insulates the suppliers of blood products from such claims. The motion will be granted.

FACTS

On a motion to dismiss, the Court takes the facts as pled in the complaint. *Hishon v. King & Spalding,* 467 U.S. 69, 73, 104 S.Ct. 2229, 2232, 81 L.Ed.2d 59 (1984).

Doe is a hemophiliac. His body does not produce human antihemophilic Factor VIII, a protein necessary for the effective clotting of blood. As a result, Doe must take Factor VIII Concentrate whenever he suffers injury causing bleeding or undergoes surgery. Factor VIII Concentrate is manufactured by pooling the blood plasma of thousands of donors and extracting the desired protein.

In August 1984, Doe underwent an operation to remove a kidney stone at the University of Minnesota Hospital and Clinic. Because of his hemophilia, Doe received prophylactic quantities of Factor VIII Concentrate from a lot manufactured by Baxter.

On or about October 10, 1984, the University of Minnesota Comprehensive Hemophilia Center notified Doe that the lot from which he had received Factor VIII was being recalled; a donor who had contributed plasma to that lot had subsequently died of Acquired Immune Deficiency Syndrome (AIDS).

In June 1986, almost two years after receiving the Factor VIII Concentrate processed by Baxter, Doe had his blood tested for the presence of antibodies to the AIDS virus, HIV. The test results indicated that Doe had been infected with HIV. Doe has since developed ARC and stands a great likelihood of contracting AIDS.

Doe sued Baxter in state court on June 24, 1988 for breach of warranty, strict liability and negligence. Baxter removed the case to federal court on July 22, 1988. Pursuant to Fed.R.Civ.P. 12(b)(6), Baxter now moves to dismiss Doe's breach of warranty and strict liability claims as failing to state a claim upon which relief can be granted.

DISCUSSION

This case is the most recent in a series of cases nationwide in which individuals infected with HIV have advanced breach of warranty and strict liability claims against processors of blood products. Every case but one has found that either a state blood shield statute or state common law barred recovery without a showing of fault.

The statutory and common law protection of the suppliers of blood and blood products from strict liability and breach of warranty claims developed during the mid 60's through early 70's in response to the transmission of the hepatitis virus by blood and blood products. At that time, no means existed for ensuring that blood and its components were not infected with the hepatitis virus. States feared that the threat of liability without fault would drive the suppliers out of the very necessary business of providing blood. *See* Comment, *Hospital and Blood Banks Liability to Patients Who Contract AIDS through Blood Transfusion,* 23 San Diego L.Rev. 875, 883 (1986).

In Minnesota, this issue was first addressed in *Balkowitsch v. Minneapolis War Memorial Blood Bank,* 270 Minn. 151, 132 N.W.2d 805 (1965). The plaintiff in *Balkowitsch* brought breach of warranty claims against a non-profit blood bank to recover damages after she contracted hepatitis through a transfusion of impure blood that had been collected, processed and sold by the blood bank. 132 N.W.2d at 806. The court, adopting the reasoning of *Perlmutter v. Beth David Hospital,* 308 N.Y. 100, 123 N.E.2d 792 (1954), held that furnishing blood did not constitute a sale of goods, but a service. Because warranty claims must be based on a sale of goods, the holding functioned to protect the defendant from causes of action which impose liability "on the theory of implied warranty." 132 N.W.2d at 810. The breach of warranty claims were dismissed. Although the doctrine of strict liability for defective products was not adopted in Minnesota until 1967 and therefore *Balkowitsch* cannot itself be read as protecting the suppliers of blood from strict liability in tort, there is no question that the reasoning in *Balkowitsch* has the effect of barring such claims because, like claims for breach of warranty, strict liability claims must be based on a sale of goods. *See,* Restatement (Second) of Torts § 402A; *Hudson v. Snyder Body, Inc.,* 326 N.W.2d 149 (Minn.1982).

Four years after *Balkowitsch* was decided, the Minnesota Legislature adopted the Uniform Anatomical Gift Act, now codified as amended at Minn.Stat. § 525.921 *et seq.* The Legislature added a "blood shield" provision which was not part of the Uniform Act. That provision states:

> The use of any part of a body for the purpose of transplantation in the human body shall be construed, for all purposes whatsoever, as a rendition of a service by each and every person participating therein and shall not be construed as a sale of such part for any purpose whatsoever.

Minn.Stat. § 525.928. "Part" is defined as "organs, tissues, eyes, bones, arteries, blood, other fluids and any other portions of a human body." Minn.Stat. § 525.921, subd. 6. The statute follows the reasoning of *Balkowitsch* and protects any person participating in the transplantation of a body part from claims for breach of warranty or strict liability by defining the activity as a rendition of a service, not a sale.

The furnishing of Factor VIII Concentrate is squarely within the meaning of section 525.928. First, Factor VIII is a portion of human blood and "part," as defined in the statute, includes blood or any other portion of the human body.[5] Second, the University of Minnesota Hospital used Factor VIII Concentrate to transfuse into plaintiff's body during an operation for the purpose of ensuring that his blood would clot. Third, Baxter, a "person" within the meaning of the statute, prepared the Concentrate which was furnished to the hospital. In preparing the Concentrate, Baxter participated in the use of the blood derivative. By including every person participating in the use of a body part, and defining person to include corporations, the Minnesota Legislature ensured that entities like Baxter would fall within the statute's protection.

Plaintiff argues that section 525.928 is designed only to provide the donor of an anatomical gift or his estate with "certain protections and immunities," relying principally on the fact that the section is located with those provisions of Minnesota law concerning probate proceedings. Plaintiff's argument is untenable. The implications drawn from the statute's location in the Code cannot be so great as to contradict the plain meaning of the statute's language. In light of the *Balkowitsch* holding, the statute is clearly an effort to protect entities like Baxter from liability without fault. The statute provides that the use of any part of a body "shall be construed, for all purposes whatsoever, as a rendition of a service by each and every person participating therein and *shall not be construed as a sale of such part for any purpose whatsoever.*" Minn.Stat. § 525.928 (emphasis added). Moreover, the fact that this section is codified amongst the probate laws is not inconsistent with the statute's plain meaning. In fact, statutory provisions shielding the processors of blood from strict liability and breach of warranty claims are located within the Anatomical Gift Acts in other states. *See, e.g.,* Iowa Code § 142A.8 (1988 Supp.); N.C.Gen.Stat. § 130A–410 (1987); Va.Code § 32.1–297 (1985); Wyo.Stat. § 35–5–110 (1988).

The public policy considerations relevant to the transmission of the AIDS virus through distribution of Factor VIII Concentrate are identical to those raised by the transmission of the hepatitis virus through whole blood. The first cases of the syndrome that has since been named AIDS were diagnosed in June and July of 1981. *Kozup v. Georgetown University,* 663 F.Supp. 1048, 1051 (D.D.C.1987), *aff'd in relevant part,* 851 F.2d 437 (D.C.Cir. 1988). In July 1982, three cases of *pneumocystis carinii* pneumonia, one of the infections that characterizes AIDS, were diagnosed in hemophiliacs. 663 F.Supp. at 1051. By January 1983 some health care professionals and public health organizations had come to believe that the still unidentified virus was blood-borne. 663 F.Supp. at 1051–52. However, it was not until early 1984 that the medical community reached a consensus that AIDS was transmitted through blood and soon afterwards, in April 1984, scientists identified a virus, initially called HTLV–III, as the cause of AIDS. 663 F.Supp. at 1052.

5. The Texas Blood Shield Statute, Tex. Civ.Prac. & Rem.Code Ann. § 77.003, like the Minnesota statute, employs the term "body part." That term is defined as "any tissue, organ, blood or components thereof from a human." *Id.* § 77.001. In *Doe v. Cutter Laboratories,* — F.Supp. — No. CA–2–87–0013, slip op. (N.D.Tex. Feb. 5, 1988), the court held that a supplier of blood derivative products, including lyophilized plasma products (like Factor VIII), was immune under the blood shield statute from strict liability and breach of warranty claims.

The virus was later renamed HIV. By May 1985, an enzyme-linked immunosorbent assay (ELISA) test that could detect antibodies to the AIDS virus in the blood became available. 663 F.Supp. at 1052. Despite use of the ELISA test, suppliers of blood and blood products have been unable to insure that the blood supply is 100 percent free from HIV. This is because a person infected with HIV may not develop antibodies detectable by the ELISA test until several weeks or even months after the infection began. *Transmission of Human Immunodeficiency Virus (HIV) by Blood Transfusions Screened as Negative for HIV Antibody,* 318 New.Eng.J.Med. 473, 476 (Feb. 25, 1988).

Thus, just as was the case with the hepatitis virus, blood processors are not able through the exercise of due care to insure that the blood supply is free from HIV. Yet, their various products must remain available. Hemophiliacs, like Doe, depend on the availability of Factor VIII Concentrate which has lengthened and improved the quality of their lives. Because the market for these products is small,[8] their availability would be threatened if the cost of the inherent risk of HIV infection were imposed on the manufacturer. Therefore, despite the devastating consequences resulting from the transmission of HIV through products like Factor VIII Concentrate, virtually every court that has considered the question has interpreted blood shield statutes to apply to the commercial processors of antihemophilic factors.

This decision does not, of course, foreclose recovery upon a showing of negligence.

Accordingly, based on the foregoing, and upon review of all the files, records and proceedings herein,

It is ordered that Baxter's motion to dismiss Doe's claims for breach of warranty and strict liability be granted.

[Some footnotes omitted.]

Note

Almost every state has some type of "blood shield" statute. At a minimum, the legislature attempts to immunize suppliers of blood and other body parts from implied warranty liability under Article 2 and, in some cases, from strict liability in tort. See, e.g., Gibson v. Methodist Hospital, 822 S.W.2d 95 (Tex.App. 1991) (since blood not a "product" under statute, no liability in warranty or strict tort). In general, liability for negligence in testing or failing to test the blood is preserved. See Note, *Blood Bank and Blood Products Manufacturer Liability in Transfusion–Related AIDS Cases,* 26 U.Rich.L.Rev. 519 (1992). Obviously, the "blood shield" legislation is far from uniform, so care must be taken to determine the scope of immunity in each state.

Note: Merchantability and Used Goods

Used or "pre-owned" goods are frequently sold at auctions or directly by their owners. These goods include such "big ticket" items as automobiles, trucks, farm and construction equipment and computers. In the absence of an

8. Baxter states that the entire patient population for Factor VIII Concentrate is between 10,000 and 20,000 people. Fewer than 10,000 of these are severe A hemophiliacs. Baxter also states that more than seventy-five percent of severe A hemophiliacs were infected with HIV by the end of 1982. Defendant's Reply to Plaintiff's Memorandum in Opposition to Its Motion to Dismiss Pursuant to Rule 12(b)(6) at 10.

express warranty, to what standard of merchantability must a merchant seller conform under UCC 2–314?

Some help is provided by a leading case, International Petroleum Services, Inc. v. S & N Well Service, Inc., 230 Kan. 452, 639 P.2d 29 (1982).

First, assuming that the seller is a merchant, most courts and commentators recognize that an implied warranty of merchantability arises, unless disclaimed, in contracts for the sale of new and used goods.

Second, UCC 2–314(2) provides a minimum standard of merchantability. This standard can be augmented by agreement, including course of dealing and relevant trade usages. UCC 2–314(3). Otherwise, the goods must conform to "normal commercial expectations." The "ordinary buyer in a commercial transaction has a right to expect that the goods * * * will not turn out to be completely worthless."

> The purchaser cannot be expected to purchase goods offered by a merchant for sale and use and then find the goods are suitable only for the junk pile. On the other hand, a buyer who has purchased goods without obtaining an express warranty as to their quality and condition cannot reasonably expect that those goods will be the finest of all possible goods of that kind. Protection of the buyer under the Uniform Commercial Code lies between these two extremes. If an item is used or is second hand, surely less can be expected in the way of quality than if the item is purchased new.

Third, what standard is appropriate to determine the merchantability of used goods of a particular description? This depends upon the circumstances of the transaction. The type and complexity of the goods is one factor. In addition: "The buyer's knowledge that the goods are used, the extent of their prior use, and whether the goods are significantly discounted may help determine what standards of quality should apply to the transaction." For example, if there is a functioning market for goods of that type and description and a competitive price can be determined, the price paid in the particular sale may be an excellent index of the nature and scope of the seller's obligation. See UCC 2–314, Comment 7. Although a "sound price" does not always warrant a "sound product," the price charged can provide some assistance in determining the level of quality the buyer can reasonably expect.

Problem 19–5

B, a farmer, purchased a used 1980 Dodge Rambler from S, a dealer, for $5,000. The four-wheel drive vehicle had been driven 80,000 "tough" miles without any serious mechanical problems. Although refusing to make any express warranties, the seller made no attempt to disclaim or exclude warranties at the time of sale.

Thirty days and 10,000 miles later, the engine failed due to a condition existing at the time of sale. B had the engine replaced for $2,500 and sued S for breach of the implied warranty of merchantability. At the trial, B established that the $5,000 purchase price was at the low end of the "blue book" range for 1980 Dodge Ramblers. B's expert testified that a 1980 Dodge Rambler with the particular condition of B's would have a fair market value of $750. On cross-examination, the expert conceded that the particular vehicle would "pass without objection in the trade under the contract description." B introduced no additional evidence. S moved for a directed verdict. What result?

C. *Fitness for Particular Purpose*

VAN WYK v. NORDEN LABORATORIES, INC.

Supreme Court of Iowa, 1984.
345 N.W.2d 81.

LARSON, JUSTICE.

A large number of cattle owned by the plaintiffs became sick shortly after injection of a vaccine produced by the defendant Norden Laboratories, Inc. and this suit followed. While several theories of liability were asserted by the plaintiffs, the court submitted only one: the implied warranty of fitness for a particular purpose (Iowa Code section 554.2315). The defendant appeals from a judgment for the plaintiffs, arguing that the court erred in submitting this theory under the facts of the case. It contends the implied warranty of fitness did not fit, so to speak. The plaintiffs cross-appeal, complaining that it was error to exclude certain expert evidence and to refuse submission of their alternative theories of strict liability and implied warranty of merchantability. We reverse on both appeals and remand.

In the fall of 1978, three groups of the plaintiffs' cattle, totaling about 750, were treated with a live-virus vaccine, manufactured by the defendant and called Resbo–3, serial 54. Some of the cattle had been raised by the plaintiffs, and some had been shipped in. Some were treated on the farm and some in a sale barn. The cattle were given other treatments such as worming, castration, and dehorning, simultaneously with the series 54 vaccine, but not all of them received the same combination of treatments. Yet, the incidence of bovine viral diarrhea (BVD) appeared, to a large extent, in all three herds. (BVD is one of the illnesses which the series 54 vaccine was designed to prevent.) Within a week of their injection, most of the cattle were sick. Almost 50 died. Plaintiffs' veterinarian witnesses testified that the sickness had been caused by the vaccine. They testified that before and after this incident they had used serial 54 vaccine without similar problems and that while it is reasonable to expect a few cattle to have an adverse reaction, they had never seen anything like the extent of sickness in this case. In view of this common denominator among the separate herds of cattle—their treatment with series 54 vaccine—a strong circumstantial case is claimed by the plaintiffs that the illness was in fact caused, or at least exacerbated by, the vaccine. No direct evidence of a defect was produced, however.

I. THE IMPLIED WARRANTY OF FITNESS

The only theory of liability submitted by the court was breach of implied warranty of fitness for a particular purpose, Iowa Code § 554.2315 (Uniform Commercial Code § 2–315). That section provides:

> Where the seller at the time of contracting has reason to know any particular purpose for which the goods are required and that the buyer is relying on the seller's skill or judgment to select or furnish suitable goods, there is unless excluded or modified under the next section an implied warranty that the goods shall be fit for such purpose.

The implied warranty of fitness for a particular purpose under section 554.2315 is perhaps better understood when viewed with the implied warranty of merchantability, or fitness for ordinary purposes. Iowa Code section 554.2314 sets out the latter:

* * *

The official comment to the Uniform Commercial Code illustrates the difference between "ordinary" and "particular" purposes under the respective warranties:

> A "particular purpose" differs from the ordinary purpose for which the goods are used in that it envisages a specific use by the buyer which is peculiar to the nature of his business whereas the ordinary purposes for which goods are used are those envisaged in the concept of merchantability and go to uses which are customarily made of the goods in question. For example, shoes are generally used for the purpose of walking upon ordinary ground, but a seller may know that a particular pair was selected to be used for climbing mountains.

U.C.C. § 2–315, Comment 2, 1 U.L.A. 483 (1976).

The warranty of merchantability, Iowa Code § 554.2314, is based on a purchaser's reasonable expectation that goods purchased from a "merchant with respect to goods of that kind" will be free of significant defects and will perform in the way goods of that kind should perform. It presupposes no special relationship of trust or reliance between the seller and buyer. In contrast, the warranty of fitness for a particular purpose, Iowa Code § 554.2315, is based on a special reliance by the buyer on the seller to provide goods that will perform a specific use envisaged and communicated by the buyer. Thus, any recovery under warranty for a specific purpose is predicated on a showing that (1) the seller had reason to know of the buyer's particular purpose; (2) the seller had reason to know the buyer was relying on the seller's skill or judgment to furnish suitable goods; and (3) the buyer in fact relied on the seller's skill or judgment to furnish suitable goods. *Semler v. Knowling,* 325 N.W.2d 395, 399 (Iowa 1982); J. White and R. Summers, *Handbook of the Law Under the Uniform Commercial Code* § 9–9 at 358 (2d Ed.1980). *See also Farm Bureau Mutual Insurance Co. v. Sandbulte,* 302 N.W.2d 104, 111 (Iowa 1981).

The warranty of fitness under section 554.2315 is said to turn on the "bargain-related" facts as to what the seller had reason to know about the buyer's purpose for the goods and about his reliance on the seller's skill or judgment in selecting them. *Jacobson v. Benson Motors, Inc.,* 216 N.W.2d 396, 404 (Iowa 1974). In this case the vaccine was not purchased by the veterinarians to treat these particular cattle but to keep in stock for their general veterinary practice. The plaintiffs, as owners of the cattle, and the defendant, had no direct dealing with regard to the vaccine. The decision as to what vaccine to use was made by the buyers' veterinarians, not by the defendant. There was no evidence that the seller had reason to know of any purpose for the plaintiffs' use of the vaccine, other than its ordinary use, or that the buyer was relying on the seller's skill and judgment in providing it. The implied warranty of fitness for a particular purpose would appear, therefore, to be inapplicable by its terms. *See* Iowa Code § 554.2315; *Semler v. Knowling,* 325 N.W.2d at 399; *Jacobson v. Benson Motors, Inc.,* 216 N.W.2d at 404.

The plaintiffs argue, however, that if the buyer's particular purpose is the same as its general use, a warranty of fitness arises, especially when the product has a specific and limited use. In that case, the other elements of the fitness warranty, i.e., the knowledge of the buyer's purpose, knowledge of the buyer's reliance, and the buyer's actual reliance, are apparently to be presumed. The plaintiffs cite only one case, *Tennessee Carolina Transportation Inc. v. Strick Corp.,* 283 N.C. 423, 196 S.E.2d 711 (1973), in support of this theory. That case involved the sale of truck trailers which proved to be faulty. There the court held that because the buyer's "specific use" was the same as the "general use" to which trailers are usually put, hauling cargo, the warranty of fitness would apply. It rejected the general rule that a "particular" use must be a use not normally expected to be made of the goods, a rule recognized by our cases, e.g., *Madison Silos v. Wassom,* 215 N.W.2d 494, 499–500 (Iowa 1974); *Peters v. Lyons,* 168 N.W.2d 759, 763 (Iowa 1969), and by the Uniform Commercial Code. *See* U.C.C. § 2–315, Comment 2, 1 U.L.A. 483 (1976).

Cases such as *Tennessee Carolina,* moreover, have been criticized as enlarging the fitness warranty beyond the intent of the drafters of the Uniform Commercial Code. *See* J. White and R. Summers, *supra,* § 9–9 at 357, n. 122.

In this case, written material furnished with the vaccine stated that "[f]or reducing the economic loss associated with these viruses, vaccination of healthy animals is recommended before or upon entering the feedlot or dairy herd. Vaccination of stressed animals should be delayed." Use of the vaccine on healthy, unstressed cattle, in accordance with these instructions, is the "ordinary" use for warranty purposes, according to the defendant, and the plaintiffs' evidence was aimed at showing a use in compliance with the instructions, in other words, an "ordinary" use. While there was contradicting evidence presented by the defendant that the cattle were stressed and perhaps not healthy at the time they were vaccinated, there is no claim by the plaintiffs that this deviation from ordinary use is itself a "particular" use. They merely claim that their use here is an ordinary use which we should consider as a particular use for warranty purposes. For the reasons to be discussed, we decline to do so.

Obviously, in some cases a buyer's particular purpose will be the same as the ordinary purpose for which a product is furnished. In that case, both types of implied warranty may arise. *See Jacobson v. Benson Motors, Inc.,* 216 N.W.2d 396, 404 (Iowa 1974) (sale of motor vehicle); *Madison Silos v. Wassom,* 215 N.W.2d 494, 499–500 (Iowa 1974) (stave silo); 1 R. Anderson, *Uniform Commercial Code,* § 2–314:60 (1970); Iowa Code § 554.2315, official comment 2. It is quite another matter, however, to impose an implied warranty of fitness solely on the basis of this identity of purpose. A particular purpose of the buyer is only one of the elements of that warranty; it still turns on what the seller had reason to know—both as to the buyer's particular purpose and as to the buyer's reliance on the seller's skill and judgment. *Jacobson,* 216 N.W.2d at 404. There are no bargain-related facts in this case to support a finding of these elements and we will not assume their existence merely on the basis of the limited-use nature of cattle vaccine. We will not assume, as the plaintiffs suggest, that the seller had reason to know of the buyers' particular purpose, and their reliance on the skill and judgment of the seller, merely because cattle vaccine is only usable for one purpose. As the record shows in this case, the vaccine may still be used in different ways, some anticipated by the seller and some not. (The defendant claims it was used in a manner proscribed by the written material accompanying the vaccine.)

The plaintiffs have an alternative theory: They claim that the seller had actual reason to know of the particular purpose for the vaccine and to know of the buyers' reliance on the skill and judgment of the seller so as to come within the literal requirements of the implied warranty of fitness. They rely on evidence that sales representatives of the defendant made regular calls on Dr. Hauser, that they discussed the vaccine, and that "[i]t is reasonable to infer from this fact that the representative was familiar with the vaccination procedures of Dr. Hauser and with the use he made of the vaccine." There is no evidence that the representative had reason to know the proposed use of the vaccine on these specific cattle, or even that it was to be used in circumstances similar to these, that is when other treatments such as worming, castration, and dehorning would accompany the vaccination, or that there would be a possibility the cattle could already be incubating the disease. Any conclusion that the defendant was put on notice of the plaintiffs' particular use is simply too speculative.

It was error to submit the theory of warranty of fitness for a particular purpose.

* * *

COMMENT, MANUFACTURER'S RESPONSIBILITY FOR DEFECTIVE PRODUCTS, 54 Calif.L.Rev. 1681, 1691, n. 48 (1966).

"Communication between buyer, seller, and manufacturer play no small role in determining whether or not a product is being supplied which will meet the particular economic needs of the commercial consumer. For example, in a typical * * * situation of the purchase of a heavy-duty diesel truck, most manufacturers offer dozens of different combinations of vehicle wheelbase, engines, transmissions, axles, suspension systems, air brakes, fifth wheel devices, and other component parts, all of which play a vital role in determining the capacity of a truck to meet various hauling requirements of the purchaser. Normally, the experienced trucker comes to the dealer with a good idea of the purpose for which he will use the truck, and often, based on his previous experience with similar vehicles in similar applications, with a fairly specific notion of the type of major component parts he will require. Dealer and customer go over in detail these needs, correlating them with the particular options which the manufacturer offers, and in effect arrive at some preliminary conclusions about the 'design' of the particular vehicle. Even at this stage the manufacturer may be involved, since a phone call to the factory by the dealer may answer a question like: 'Will an *X* diesel engine, coupled with a *Y* transmission and a *Z* rear axle enable our customer to achieve a road speed of *S* miles per hour under normal conditions?' Beyond this, the manufacturer becomes involved in the selection process when he receives the sales order from the dealer and submits it for review to his engineering department; the engineers may suggest several changes to be incorporated. Ultimately, the customer receives a heavy-duty truck which is reasonably tailored to his specific needs.

"Another method of merchandising commonly used in the trucking industry is for a manufacturer to build a certain number of what are called 'stock' trucks, which are then sold or consigned to the dealer. These are built with no particular customer in mind, or perhaps it should be said with the average customer in mind; these are analogous to an automobile dealer's 'showroom' models in that they incorporate most of the standard, *i.e.*, most popular, combinations of running gear. While not tailored to the specific needs of the customer, they of course do have the advantage of being available for immediate delivery. Normally, when a dealer recognizes that a customer's needs can be reasonably satisfied with a 'stock' truck, he will attempt to locate one within the dealer network which will serve the purpose, perhaps with a modification of a few component parts. Here, too, the manufacturer may become involved in the selling process through conferences concerning the ability of a particular 'stock' truck to meet the customer's needs.

"Thus the customer plays an important role in the selection process which is altogether different than that of the average new-car buyer who 'selects' such items as whitewall tires, radio, and heater. The component parts of a truck chosen by buyer, dealer, and/or manufacturer play an important role in determining whether or not the vehicle will be 'fit for a particular purpose,' * * * and the customer's communication of these economic needs is vital. While no spectacular case can be made out for the use of sales law where a manufacturer sells a truck which is so defective as to be virtually unsuited for any purpose, the requirement that the buyer's needs be communicated to the manufacturer before an implied warranty of fitness for a particular purpose would arise * * * would certainly tend to serve the useful purpose of enabling a court to determine whether or not the product was 'defective' in relation to the reasonable expectations of the buyer."

LEWIS v. MOBIL OIL CORP.

United States Court of Appeals, Eighth Circuit, 1971.
438 F.2d 500.

GIBSON, CIRCUIT JUDGE.

In this diversity case the defendant appeals from a judgment entered on a jury verdict in favor of the plaintiff in the amount of $89,250 for damages alleged to be caused by use of defendant's oil.

Plaintiff Lewis has been doing business as a sawmill operator in Cove, Arkansas, since 1956. In 1963, in order to meet competition, Lewis decided to convert his power equipment to hydraulic equipment. He purchased a hydraulic system in May 1963, from a competitor who was installing a new system. The used system was in good operating condition at the time Lewis purchased it. It was stored at his plant until November 1964, while a new mill building was being built, at which time it was installed. Following the installation, Lewis requested from Frank Rowe, a local Mobil oil dealer, the proper hydraulic fluid to operate his machinery. The prior owner of the hydraulic system had used Pacemaker oil supplied by Cities Service, but plaintiff had been a customer of Mobil's for many years and desired to continue with Mobil. Rowe said he didn't know what the proper lubricant for Lewis' machinery was, but would find out. The only information given to Rowe by Lewis was that the machinery was operated by a gear-type pump; Rowe did not request any further information. He apparently contacted a Mobil representative for a recommendation, though this is not entirely clear, and sold plaintiff a product known as Ambrex 810. This is a straight mineral oil with no chemical additives.

Within a few days after operation of the new equipment commenced, plaintiff began experiencing difficulty with its operation. The oil changed color, foamed over, and got hot. The oil was changed a number of times, with no improvement. By late April 1965, approximately six months after operations with the equipment had begun, the system broke down, and a complete new system was installed. The cause of the breakdown was undetermined, but apparently by this time there was some suspicion of the oil being used. Plaintiff Lewis requested Rowe to be sure he was supplying the right kind of oil. Ambrex 810 continued to be supplied.

From April 1965 until April 1967, plaintiff continued to have trouble with the system, principally with the pumps which supplied the pressure. Six new pumps were required during this period, as they continually broke down. During this period, the kind of pump used was a Commercial pump which was specified by the designer of the hydraulic system. The filtration of oil for this pump was by means of a metal strainer, which was cleaned daily by the plaintiff in accordance with the instruction given with the equipment.

In April 1967, the plaintiff changed the brand of pump from a Commercial to a Tyrone pump. The Tyrone pump, instead of using the metal strainer filtration alone, used a disposable filter element in addition. Ambrex 810 oil was also recommended by Mobil and used with this pump, which completely broke down three weeks later. At this point, plaintiff was visited for the first time by a representative of Mobil Oil Corporation, as well as a representative of the Tyrone pump manufacturer.

On the occasion of this visit, May 9, 1967, plaintiff's system was completely flushed and cleaned, a new Tyrone pump installed, and on the pump manufacturer's and Mobil's representative's recommendation, a new oil was used which contained certain chemical additives, principally a "defoamant." Following these changes, plaintiff's system worked satisfactorily up until the time of trial, some two and one-half years later.

Briefly stated, plaintiff's theory of his case is that Mobil supplied him with an oil which was warranted fit for use in his hydraulic system, that the oil was not suitable for such use because it did not contain certain additives, and that it was the improper oil which caused the mechanical breakdowns, with consequent loss to his business. The defendant contends that there was no warranty of fitness, that the breakdowns were caused not by the oil but by improper filtration, and that in any event there can be no recovery of loss of profits in this case.

I. The Existence of Warranties

Defendant maintains that there was no warranty of fitness in this case, that at most there was only a warranty of merchantability and that there was no proof of breach of this warranty, since there was no proof that Ambrex 810 is unfit for use in hydraulic systems generally. We find it unnecessary to consider whether the warranty of merchantability was breached, although there is some proof in the record to that effect, since we conclude that there was a warranty of fitness.

Plaintiff Lewis testified that he had been a longtime customer of Mobil Oil, and that his only source of contact with the company was through Frank Rowe, Mobil's local dealer, with whom he did almost all his business. It was common knowledge in the community that Lewis was converting his sawmill operation into a hydraulic system. Rowe knew this, and in fact had visited his mill on business matters several times during the course of the changeover. When operations with the new machinery were about to commence, Lewis asked Rowe to get him the proper hydraulic fluid. Rowe asked him what kind of a system he had, and Lewis replied it was a Commercial-pump type. This was all the information asked or given. Neither Lewis nor Rowe knew what the oil requirements for the system were, and Rowe, knew that Lewis knew nothing more specific about his requirements. Lewis also testified that after he began having trouble with his operations, while there were several possible sources of the difficulty the oil was one suspected source, and he several times asked Rowe to be sure he was furnishing him with the right kind.

Rowe's testimony for the most part confirmed Lewis'. It may be noted here that Mobil does not contest Rowe's authority to represent it in this transaction, and therefore whatever warranties may be implied because of the dealings between Rowe and Lewis are attributable to Mobil. Rowe admitted knowing Lewis was converting to a hydraulic system and that Lewis asked him to supply the fluid. He testified that he did not know what should be used and relayed the request to a superior in the Mobil organization, who recommended Ambrex 810. This is what was supplied.

When the first Tyrone pump was installed in April 1967, Rowe referred the request for a proper oil recommendation to Ted Klock, a Mobil engineer. Klock recommended Ambrex 810. When this pump failed a few weeks later, Klock visited the Lewis plant to inspect the equipment. The system was flushed out completely and the oil was changed to DTE–23 and Del Vac Special containing several additives. After this, no further trouble was experienced.

This evidence adequately establishes an implied warranty of fitness. Arkansas has adopted the Uniform Commercial Code's provision for an implied warranty of fitness:

> "Where the seller at the time of contracting has reason to know any particular purpose for which the goods are required and that the buyer is relying on the seller's skill or judgment to select or furnish suitable goods, there is unless excluded or modified under the next section an implied warranty that the goods shall be fit for such purpose." 7C Ark.Stat.Ann. § 85–2–315 (1961).

Under this provision of the Code, there are two requirements for an implied warranty of fitness: (1) that the seller have "reason to know" of the use for which the goods are purchased, and (2) that the buyer relies on the seller's expertise in supplying the proper product. Both of these requirements are amply met by the proof in this case. Lewis' testimony, as confirmed by that of Rowe and Klock, shows that the oil was purchased specifically for his hydraulic system, not for just a hydraulic system in general, and that Mobil certainly knew of this specific purpose. It is also clear that Lewis was relying on Mobil to supply him with the proper oil for the system, since at the time of his purchases, he made clear that he didn't know what kind was necessary.

Mobil contends that there was no warranty of fitness for use in his particular system because he didn't specify that he needed an oil with additives, and alternatively that he didn't give them enough information for them to determine that an additive oil was required. However, it seems that the circumstances of this case come directly within that situation described in the first comment to this provision of the Uniform Commercial Code:

> "1. Whether or not this warranty arises in any individual case is basically a question of fact to be determined by the circumstances of the contracting. Under this section the buyer need not bring home to the seller *actual knowledge of the particular purpose* for which the goods are intended or of his reliance on the seller's skill and judgment, if the circumstances are such that the seller has reason to realize the purpose intended or that the reliance exists." 7C Ark.Stat.Ann. § 85–2–315, Comment 1 (1961) (emphasis added).

Here Lewis made it clear that the oil was purchased for his system, that he didn't know what oil should be used, and that he was relying on Mobil to supply the proper product. If any further information was needed, it was incumbent upon Mobil to get it before making its recommendation. That it could have easily gotten the necessary information is evidenced by the fact that after plaintiff's continuing complaints, Mobil's engineer visited the plant, and, upon inspection, changed the recommendation that had previously been made.

Additionally, Mobil contends that even if there were an implied warranty of fitness, it does not cover the circumstances of this case because of the abnormal features which the plaintiff's system contained, namely an inadequate filtration system and a capacity to entrain excessive air. There are several answers to this contention. First of all, the contention goes essentially to the question of causation—i.e., whether the damage was caused by a breach of warranty or by some other cause—and not to the existence of a warranty of fitness in the first place. Secondly, assuming that certain peculiarities in the plaintiff's system did exist, the whole point of an implied warranty of fitness is that a product be suitable for a specific purpose, and that a seller should not supply a product which is not so suited. Thirdly, there is no evidence in the record that the plaintiff's system was unique or abnormal in these respects. It operated satisfactorily under the prior owner, and the new system has operated satisfactorily after it was adequately cleaned and an additive type oil used.

* * * Thus, Mobil's defense that there was no warranty of fitness because of an "abnormal use" of the oil is not appropriate here.

[The court next held that there was adequate evidence to sustain the jury's verdict that the plaintiff's damage was caused by the breach of warranty and not by variations in the plaintiff's system or inadequate maintenance.]

* * *

Notes

1. Was UCC 2–315 the proper warranty provision for application in *Lewis?* Put another way, could the court have reached the same result under an express warranty or an implied warranty of merchantability?

2. Suppose Mr. Lewis had asked Mr. Rowe to provide him with literature describing "oil that I might use in my new commercial hydraulic equipment." If Rowe had furnished literature describing oil with and oil without chemical additives and Mr. Rowe had thereafter ordered Ambrex 810, would the subsequent sale be with an implied warranty of fitness for particular purpose? To test your judgment, see Axion Corp. v. G.D.C. Leasing Corp., 359 Mass. 474, 269 N.E.2d 664 (1971) (reprinted at p. 859, supra).

3. Assuming that Mr. Lewis relied upon Mobil's skill and judgment, suppose Mobil had established that Ambrex 810 would work satisfactorily in some "commercial pump" hydraulic systems but not work in the particular system owned by Mr. Lewis. Assume further that Mr. Lewis was using his system for ordinary purposes. Should this affect the result in the case?

CHAPTER TWENTY

WARRANTY LITIGATION: BUYER'S PROOF, SELLER'S DEFENSES

SECTION 1. INTRODUCTION

To recover damages for a claimed breach of warranty, the buyer must plead and prove that: (1) the seller made some warranty, express or implied, (2) the warranty was breached, see UCC 2–607(4), and (3) the breach "caused" the damages sought. Compare UCC 2–715(2)(b). Since failure to satisfy any of these three requirements is fatal to the claim, it is important for the buyer's attorney to master the strategies for proof.

In addition, the buyer has a number of possible defenses to the claim.

First, a buyer who has accepted the goods may fail to give the notice required by UCC 2–607(3)(a). If so, the claim is barred.

Second, the seller may claim, by way of an affirmative defense, that the buyer misused the goods or failed to follow directions for use. Similarly, the seller may argue that the buyer should have discovered the non-conformity before use or assumed the risk by using goods with a known non-conformity. If so, the buyer's claim may be barred or, at the very least, the damages reduced.

Third, the seller may assert that the suit is time barred under the statute of limitations, UCC 2–725. This defense has posed some complicated questions for the courts.

Fourth, the seller may argue that the warranty claim is inappropriate and should be dismissed. Suppose there is no privity of contract and the buyer, bypassing the retailer, sues the product manufacturer for breach of warranty. Is lack of privity a defense? Or suppose that there is privity of contract between the parties but the UCC statute of limitations has run on the warranty claim. Can the buyer "escape" the UCC statute of limitations by invoking a tort theory, such as strict liability or negligence?

Note: Warranty as a Theory of Strict but Limited Liability

Why is a seller strictly liable for breach of warranty? According to Professor William Bishop, in Bishop, *The Contract-Tort Boundary and the Economics of Insurance,* 12 J.Legal Stud. 241 (1983), the reason is that warranties, when regarded as information provided by the seller to the buyer, are a form of insurance in a setting where there is imperfect information. At the time of contracting, the seller is in the best position, cost considered, to determine the true condition of the goods or to assess their suitability for use. To use the jargon, the seller is the "least-cost-information-provider." When the seller, without a disclaimer, provides information about the goods to the seller in the form of representations, including the price charged, the buyer should be able to hold the seller strictly liable for accuracy, provided that the scope of liability is limited. The warranty, therefore, is guaranteed but limited information for which the buyer has paid. (Bishop argues that "strict duties with known, limited liabilities are the preferred, albeit second best alternative to perfect information." Id. at 246.

What limitations should be imposed upon this form of strict liability? Two such limitations, derived from insurance, are the need to avoid adverse selection and moral hazard.

Adverse selection refers to the probability that the worst risks in a given population will be the most likely to obtain insurance. The insurer, here the seller, must obtain information about the riskiness of the insured. Otherwise, the insurer may insure a "selection of the population whose average risk is adversely different from the general population." Id. at 245. According to Bishop, this limitation provides the buyer with an incentive to convey information to the seller when the value of the information to the seller is greater than the cost to the buyer of transmitting it.

This limitation works in at least two ways under the Code: (1) the seller's warranty does not reach a buyer's particular purposes for the goods unless "at the time of contracting" the seller "has reason to know of any particular purpose for which the goods are required," UCC 2–315, a limitation which we covered in Chapter 19, Section 3(B), and (2) the seller is not liable for any consequential "loss resulting from general or particular requirements and needs" of which, at the time of contracting, he had no "reason to know." UCC 2–715(2)(a). This problem is treated in Chapter 21.

Moral hazard involves the risk that a buyer will fail, either before or after the loss occurred, to take reasonable action to avoid or to minimize the loss. Even though the risk is "average" or communicated to the seller, the buyer may fail to take precautions whose cost to him is less than their value to the insurer. Economic theory and contract law in general suggest that the buyer should bear those losses which he could have avoided by a reasonable expenditure of time and effort.

As you read the materials in this Chapter and Chapter 21, make a list of the limitations upon warranty liability associated with either adverse selection or moral hazard. Do these limitations favor the seller or the buyer? See Speidel, *Warranty Disputes in the Seventh Circuit Under Article 2, Sales: Advantage Seller?,* 65 Chi.-Kent L.Rev. 813 (1991).

Does Bishop's analysis offer a persuasive explanation of the nature of warranty? Is it a useful analogy to insurance?

SECTION 2. THE EFFECT OF PLAINTIFF'S FAILURE TO GIVE NOTICE REQUIRED BY UCC 2–607(3)

Access to various buyer's remedies is hedged by notice requirements. Thus, an attempt at rejection is "ineffective unless the buyer seasonably notifies the seller," UCC 2–602(1), and a revocation of acceptance is "not effective until the buyer notifies the seller of it." UCC 2–608(2). Similarly, where a tender has been accepted and acceptance has not been revoked under UCC 2–608, the "buyer must within a reasonable time after he discovers or should have discovered any breach notify the seller of breach or be barred from any remedy; * * *" UCC 2–607(3)(a). Note that UCC 2–

607(3)(a) says "barred" from any remedy, not that the buyer is simply shunted to a less desirable remedy. Also, the buyer may be "barred" even though the nonconformity was not actually discovered.

A number of continuing questions surround the judicial interpretation of UCC 2–607(3)(a):

(1) What purposes are served by notice in commercial cases?

(2) When "should" the buyer have discovered the breach?

(3) When does a "reasonable time" expire?

(4) At what point does the buyer "notify" the seller?

(5) What should the form and content of the notice be?

Regardless of how these questions are answered from case to case, two things are clear: (1) The buyer must, at the very least, plead and prove that adequate notice was given to state a cause of action for breach of warranty, and (2) The notice condition does not apply to actions grounded in strict products liability, i.e., where a defective product has caused damage to person or property. See Restatement, Torts 402A, Comment m.

Problem 20–1

Bristow, the holder of a McDonalds franchise, contracted with Stiko, Inc. a manufacturer, for 17 dozen pans expressly designed for the preparation of Big Mac sandwiches. A December 1 shipment date was agreed. On November 28, Stiko telephoned Bristow to say that they were having "a bit of trouble" and that the pans "could not be delivered until late January." Bristow replied that timely delivery was important and if the pans were not shipped by December 1, "we will consider that you have breached the contract." The pans were shipped on January 17. Bristow accepted the pans and there was no further communication until Stiko sued for the contract price in May. Bristow claimed an offset from the contract price based upon damages for late delivery. The trial court, relying on UCC 2 607(3), denied the offset and entered judgment for the contract price. In his memorandum opinion, the trial judge held that UCC 2–607(3) required notice after acceptance. Here none was given. Further, even if the answer were treated as a notice, "the delay was unreasonable as a matter of law."

What arguments will you make on appeal?

STANDARD ALLIANCE IND. v. BLACK CLAWSON CO.

United States Court of Appeals, Sixth Circuit, 1978.
587 F.2d 813.

[Defendant sold Plaintiff a 175 ton "horizontal automatic radial forging facility", known as the "green monster." After extensive negotiations where Plaintiff persuaded Defendant to manufacture the machine to meet Plaintiff's special needs, Defendant made a series of express performance warranties and agreed to repair or replace defective parts for one year after acceptance. Implied warranties were disclaimed and consequential damages were excluded in the agreement. There were problems with the machine from the start. For five months, Defendant, with Plaintiff's assistance, attempted to remedy the difficulties. Defendant then ceased working on the machine. Thereafter, efforts by Plaintiff, under new ownership, to resolve the problems were unsuccessful and the machine was dismantled and sold for scrap. Just over eleven months after Defendant ceased efforts to repair the machine, Plaintiff brought suit on various warranty theories, claiming damages in excess of $525,000. After trial, the trial court submitted two questions to the jury: 1) did Defendant breach the negotiated performance warranties; and 2) did Defendant breach the express warranty to repair and replace defective parts? The jury found for Plaintiff on both questions. On appeal, Defendant argued that the claim based upon breach of performance warranties was barred by the statute of limitations. Defendant also argued that the claim based upon breach of the warranty to repair and replace was barred because Plaintiff failed to give notice as required by UCC 2–607(3).]

KEITH, CIRCUIT JUDGE.

* * *

B. NOTICE AND COUNT II

Standard Alliance's claim against Black Clawson is not ended by our decision on Count I. In Count II, Standard Alliance alleges a cause of action for breach of the express warranty to repair or replace defective parts. This cause of action, which is virtually identical to Count I, was not barred by the statute of limitations. Thus, even if Standard Alliance sued too late on its claim that the machine was defective, it did sue on time on its claim that Black Clawson failed to repair the machine.

Black Clawson concedes that suit on Count II was timely filed, but strongly argues that it had no knowledge that anything was wrong with the machine after it quit work on it and that plaintiff's failure to report the machine's defects barred the suit.

To recapitulate: The machine was installed in October of 1967, and plaintiff's employees attempted to make it operable. A letter was sent to Black Clawson on December 27, 1967, fully outlining the machine's defects. Black Clawson responded by sending a team of employees to try to fix the machine. These employees were at Standard Alliance's plant for over five months. On June 21, 1968, Black Clawson's repairmen left Standard Alliance's plant, never to return. Plaintiff claims that this action constituted knowing abandonment of the unrepaired machine. Black Clawson claims that it thought that the machine was satisfactorily repaired and that it knew nothing about any further problems.

The controlling statute is UCC § 2–607(3)(a) which provides:

"The buyer must within a reasonable time after he discovers or should have discovered any breach notify the seller of breach or be barred from any remedy."

Whether proper notice was given is a question of fact. * * *

Moreover, inasmuch as § 2–607 operates as a condition precedent to any recovery, the burden of proof is on the plaintiff to show that notice was given within a reasonable time. * * *

The district judge submitted the notice issue to the jury, which found for the plaintiff. The question presented here is whether the district judge erred when he refused to overrule the jury's decision and enter judgment N.O.V. for the defendant.

The standard which defendant must meet is a stiff one. To grant a directed verdict or J.N.O.V., the evidence must be "such that there can be but one reasonable conclusion as to the proper verdict." Wolfel v. Sanborn, 555 F.2d 583, 593 (6th Cir.1977). Ohio's standard is the same. Ohio R.Civ.Pro. 50(A). See O'Day v. Webb, 29 Ohio St.2d 215, 280 N.E.2d 896 (1972). If the evidence is clear, however, a court can rule as a matter of law that a party failed to give proper notice. * * *

The notice requirement of § 2–607 is explained by Official Comment 4:

> "The time of notification is to be determined by applying commercial standards to a merchant buyer. 'A reasonable time' for notification from a retail consumer is to be judged by different standards so that in his case it will be extended, for the rule of requiring notification is designated to defeat commercial bad faith, not to deprive a good faith consumer of his remedy.
>
> "The content of the notification need merely be sufficient to let the seller know that the transaction is still troublesome and must be watched. There is no reason to require that the notification which saves the buyer's rights under this section must include a clear statement of all the objections that will be relied on by the buyer, as under the section covering statements of defect upon rejection (Section 2–605). Nor is there reason for requiring the notification to be a claim for damages or of any threatened litigation or other resort to a remedy. The notification which saves the buyer's rights under this Article need only be such as informs the seller that the transaction is claimed to involve a breach, and thus opens the way for normal settlement through negotiation."

Some courts and commentators have taken the liberal view that almost any kind of notice of dissatisfaction is sufficient. "Quite clearly the drafters [of the UCC] intended a loose test; a scribbled note on a bit of toilet paper will do." J. White & R. Summers Uniform Commercial Code 347 (1972). See e.g., Lewis v. Mobil Oil Corp., 438 F.2d 500, 509 (8th Cir.1971); Metro Investment Corp. v. Portland Rd. Lumber Yard, Inc., 263 Or. 76, 501 P.2d 312 (1972). Other courts have required more than minimal notice where both parties were merchants engaged in on-going transactions. Eastern Air Lines, Inc. v. McDonnell Douglas Corp., 532 F.2d 957, 970–980 (1976); Kopper Glo Fuel, Inc. v. Island Lake Coal Co., 436 F.Supp. 91, 95–97 (E.D.Tenn.1977). * * *

There is no dispute that Standard Alliance gave timely notice that the machine was not in compliance with the performance warranties and that Black Clawson then spent over five months trying to fix the machine. The dispute concerns whether defendant was properly notified that the repairs were inadequate.

Black Clawson's argument can be conveniently subdivided into two subparts. First, it contends that it understood the machine to be operating properly on June 21, 1968, and that it had no knowledge that the machine was defective after that date. Second, it contends that it had no notice that

Standard Alliance considered it to be in breach of the warranty to repair or replace defective parts.

The jury's implicit finding that Black Clawson had knowledge that the machine was defective and improperly repaired is supportable by the evidence. Black Clawson Vice-President Romagano did testify that he thought that the machine was repaired on July 21, 1968, and that he had no idea anything was wrong afterward. The jury, however, could have disbelieved this testimony, relying on a June 24, 1968, memo written by Mr. Romagano which reveals that the machine suffered repeated failures on both June 20, 1968, and June 21, 1968. In addition, the jury could have credited letters written in June, July and August of 1968 from Mr. Romagano to a Black Clawson subcontractor, Reliance Electric Co., complaining about the failings of the machine's electric drive, a critical component. Finally, the jury could have believed expert testimony that the machine was so poorly designed that it could not be made to operate in synchronization nor be repaired to meet any of the express warranties. If so, the jury could have reasonably inferred that defendant was aware that its attempts to repair were an utter failure. Thus, there exists evidence to support a jury finding that Black Clawson had knowledge that it was in breach of the repair or replace warranty.[1]

The critical issue is whether Black Clawson had notice that it was considered to be in breach. Black Clawson emphatically argues that there is no evidence at all that it received notice of breach after it quit repair work on June 21, 1968. Standard Alliance directs us to none, and our independent examination of the record reveals none. Incredible as it may seem, Black Clawson quit repair work on June 21, 1968 and was never told anything was wrong until May 29, 1969, when suit was filed.[2]

1. The evidence is not one-sided, however. The record indicates that the machine would operate, but was subject to breakdowns and produced a poor product. Repair efforts at times achieved temporary success or offered the hope of success. For example, in a July 15, 1968 internal memorandum, Standard Alliance's Harold Challman indicated that with two weeks of certain indicated repairs, the machine would be ready to make a production run. There thus exists some basis for Black Clawson's subjective belief that the machine was in compliance with the page twelve warranties. Internal Black Clawson memoranda, notably an October 3, 1968 memo from Vice-President Romagano to President Landegger support this belief.

This confusion further underscores the need to give clear notice; especially in a commercial setting where two companies have interacted at different levels, from President to maintenance worker.

2. Black Clawson pressed this issue at trial. Standard Alliance's President Erwin Schulze admitted that no written notice was sent; he did not know whether oral notice was given. Executive Vice-President William G. Shaw, who at the time was head of Standard Alliance's forging division, knew of no communication between the parties concerning the machine's defects after June 21, 1968. Roy W. Clansky, a Standard Alliance Vice-Chairman of the Board intimately involved in the machine's purchase, testified that Black Clawson never failed to respond when called. He did not recall ever getting in touch with his counterpart at Black Clawson to complain about the machine after January 4, 1968. Russell E. Reum, Standard Alliance's purchasing agent, knew of no notice to Black Clawson indicating dissatisfaction with repair efforts after January of 1968. Black Clawson Executive Alfred Romagano testified that Black Clawson never heard a complaint about the machine after June of 1968.

The evidence in the record concerning the circumstances of Black Clawson's termination of repair efforts on June 21, 1968, shows an amicable parting after months of mutual cooperation. Contacts between the parties after June 21, 1968, were minimal and most had nothing to do with the machine's defects. Standard Alliance invited Black Clawson to a trade association tour of its plant in September, 1968, and discussed settling "backcharge" claims for repairs. In addition, two brief service calls were made.

Standard Alliance argues that it fully informed Black Clawson of the machine's defects at the beginning and that Black Clawson abandoned the machine knowing that it was defective and unrepaired. Under these circumstances, the question presented is whether it was necessary to give additional notice of the failure of repair efforts.

We think that notice should have been given. Section 2–607 expressly requires notice of "any" breach. Comment 4 says that notice "need only be such as informs the seller that the transaction is claimed to involve a breach." The express language of the statute and the official comment mandate notice regardless whether either or both parties had actual knowledge of breach. * * *

We also note that this same result would take place under § 2–607's predecessor, section 49 of the Uniform Sales Act.[3] Judge Learned Hand's oft-quoted words applying section 49 are equally applicable here:

> "The plaintiff replies that the buyer is not required to give notice of what the seller already knows, but this confuses two quite different things. The notice 'of the breach' required is not of the facts, which the seller presumably knows quite as well as, if not better than, the buyer, but of buyer's claim that they constitute a breach. The purpose of the notice is to advise the seller that he must meet a claim for damages, as to which, rightly or wrongly, the law requires that he shall have early warning."

American Mfg. Co. v. United States Shipping Board E.F. Corp., 7 F.2d 565, 566 (2d Cir.1925), cited with approval in Columbia Axle Co. v. American Automobile Ins. Co., 63 F.2d 206 (6th Cir.1933).

An examination of the policy reasons which underlie 2–607 further support our view. Notice of breach serves two distinct purposes. First, express notice opens the way for settlement through negotiation between the parties. Comment Four, supra; Eckstein v. Cummins, 41 Ohio App.2d 1, 321 N.E.2d 897, 901 (1974). Second, proper notice minimizes the possibility of prejudice to the seller by giving him "ample opportunity to cure the defect, inspect the goods, investigate the claim or do whatever may be necessary to properly defend himself or minimize his damages while the facts are fresh in the minds of the parties." Note, Notice of Breach and the Uniform Commercial Code, 25 U.Fla.L.Rev. 520, 522 (1973). * * * Compare 3 Williston on Sales (4th Ed.), § 22–11 and White & Summers, supra at 344 which identify three policy reasons behind the notice requirement: 1) To enable the seller to make adjustments or replacement or to suggest opportunities for cure; 2) To enable the seller to prepare for negotiation or litigation; and 3) To give the seller peace of mind from stale claims. See Steel & Wire Corp. v. Thyssen, Inc., 20 U.C.C.Rep. 892 (E.D.Mich.1976). See also Mattos, Inc. v.

Although the record as to the service calls and backcharge negotiations is sketchy, * * * there is no evidence that the issue of breach of warranty was ever raised directly, and Standard Alliance does not argue that it was.

3. Section 49 provided:

"In the absence of express or implied agreement of the parties, acceptance of the goods by the buyer shall not discharge the seller from liability in damages or other legal remedy for breach of any promise or warranty in the contract to sell or the sale. But, if, after acceptance of the goods, the buyer fails to give notice to the seller of the breach of any promise or warranty within a reasonable time after the buyer knows, or ought to know of such breach, the seller shall not be liable therefor."

Hash, 279 Md. 371, 368 A.2d 993, 996 (1977) (protection against stale claims is the purpose of the statute of limitations, not the purpose of section 2–607(3)).

We do not know whether this lengthy, acrimonious lawsuit could have been settled beforehand. We do know that Standard Alliance's failure to give notice precluded the possibility of compromise.

More important, the record contains evidence suggesting the kind of prejudice which § 2–607's notice requirement seeks to avoid. After Standard Alliance sold its Forgings Division to "the Wiener Group" on September 30, 1968, Wiener attempted to put the machine into operation. When that failed, the machine lay dormant. On May 28, 1969, the day before suit was filed, Standard Alliance, in cooperation with Wiener, started the machine and filmed its malfunctions. On July 14, 1969, a scant six weeks after suit was filed, Wiener began to dismantle the machine. Although Black Clawson was informed of the machine's sale, it never inspected the machine after terminating repair efforts on June 21, 1968, nor was it aware that the machine was to be destroyed.

Standard Alliance contends that the destruction of the machine by a third party was proper and that Black Clawson was remiss in not seeking to inspect the machine during the six-week period after suit was filed, but before the machine was destroyed. This ignores the realities of the litigation process. Six weeks is an insignificant period of time in a case such as this which has dragged on for over nine years. In addition, it was pure chance that the machine was destroyed when it was; Wiener could have taken the machine apart whenever it wanted. Had Black Clawson gotten even minimal notice that it was being held in breach, it might very well have sought inspection and perhaps even made its own film of the machine.

Measuring the impact of potential prejudice here is, of course, difficult since Black Clawson was unable to have its own experts examine the machine. Standard Alliance emphasizes that Black Clawson designed and built the machine and worked on it for over five months. As the machine's creator, it arguably did not need to inspect it. Also, the evidence that the machine was defective was overwhelming. On the other hand, preparing for litigation is a sui generis task. Black Clawson may have been able to put on a spirited defense, especially as to damages, had it gotten early notice and followed up by inspecting the machine. Whatever the degree of prejudice to Black Clawson, UCC § 2–607's notice requirement is designed to forestall the very difficulties which developed here. While we see no justification for the strong language in defendant's brief charging a conspiracy to hide the facts and destroy the machine, we think that this case demonstrates the wisdom of section 2–607's requirement of prompt notice.

Black Clawson also raises independent objections to the film and the circumstances of the machine's destruction, arguing that it should have had specific advance notice of both the film's production and of the machine's demolition. We need not decide these issues. We do note, however, that this court has never sanctioned the sporting theory of justice. Adherents of the theory among the bar are reminded that a law suit is a serious matter; there is no room for games of hide and seek. Neither the federal rules nor statutory law can anticipate every twist and turn which can take place in litigation. "Legal" moves by ingenious litigants will not be countenanced where injustice would result.

These events further demonstrate the merit in those cases which hold merchants to higher standards of good faith than consumers. * * * Black Clawson and Standard Alliance worked together at all times. Black Clawson responded promptly when informed that the machine was not working properly; commercial good faith mandated that it be told that repair efforts had failed and that it was being held in breach. A new car buyer can be excused for failing, in ignorance and exasperation, to notify a car dealer of an obvious breach after persistent repair efforts have ended in failure. A merchant like Standard Alliance cannot be so excused, it should have met section 2–607's non-rigorous notice requirements.

Standard Alliance points to two cases, Ernst v. General Motors Corp., 482 F.2d 1047 (5th Cir.1973), appeal following remand, 537 F.2d 105 (5th Cir.1976), and Metro Invest. Corp. v. Portland Rd. Lumber Yard, Inc., 263 Or. 76, 501 P.2d 312 (1972), for the proposition that proper notice, once given, is sufficient for all related breaches. Standard Alliance's position is that since it concededly gave proper notice that the machine was defective on December 27, 1967, it did not have to give notice later on that repair efforts to cure the defects had failed.

We reject this argument. In Ernst, supra, the court merely concluded that a letter complaining of delays in the start-up of a construction project could be reasonably construed to encompass problems caused by severe winter working conditions which would not have occurred but for the delay. Also, the court did not think that once initial complaint about delay was made, that additional notice of delay had to be given on a regular basis. In Metro Invest. Corp., supra, the buyer gave prompt notice of a defect. The parties met and agreed to wait and see if the defect improved. The Oregon Supreme Court found that the initial notice was sufficient, even though no complaint was made for two years thereafter.

In the instant case, the two warranties are distinct and notice serves different functions for each. When the machine was found to be in breach of the page twelve performance warranties, notice was necessary so that Black Clawson could come in and try to fix the machine. When repair efforts failed, and Black Clawson was allegedly in breach of its warranty to repair or replace defective parts, notice would alert Black Clawson that Standard Alliance thought that repairs were defective and that perhaps litigation was contemplated. At this point, the parties could have discussed settlement, and Black Clawson could have sought evidentiary support for its position that the machine was indeed repaired. Black Clawson was alerted that the machine was defective, but not alerted that its repair efforts were defective. We cannot allow notice of one breach to be carried over to create notice of a subsequent related, but distinct, breach.

We realize that our holding bars what is apparently a meritorious claim. Standard Alliance's inexplicable failure to give any notice whatsoever that Black Clawson was in breach of its repair/replace warranty is fatal; underlying standards of commercial good faith, codified in UCC § 2–607, mandate this result.

Our ruling makes it unnecessary to consider the numerous other issues raised concerning the liability or the damages trial.

* * *

[Some footnotes omitted. Others renumbered.]

Notes

1. UCC 2–607(3)(a) states that the buyer must "notify the seller of breach or be barred from any remedy." In Comment 4, however, there is an apparent conflict: Is the notice sufficient if it "merely" lets the seller know that the "transaction is still troublesome and must be watched" or must the notice inform the seller that the "transaction is claimed to involve a breach * * * ?" The latter interpretation, embraced by *Standard Alliance,* would require notice of the buyer's conclusion both that the goods failed to conform to the warranties and that the non-conformity was considered to be a breach.

If, as White and Summers suggest at p. 481, the principal reason for requiring notice "is to enable the seller to make adjustments or replacements or to suggest opportunities for cure to the end of minimizing the buyer's loss and reducing the seller's own liability to the buyer," is such a strict notice requirement necessary? In Paulson v. Olson Implement Co., Inc., 107 Wis.2d 510, 319 N.W.2d 855 (1982), the court held that a seller who had received a timely notice of nonconformity and was unable to effect a cure was not entitled to a further notice from the buyer before the law suit was filed. Compare K & M Joint Venture v. Smith International, Inc., 669 F.2d 1106 (6th Cir.1982), in which the court held that the buyer's claims was barred because of its failure to give the seller any indication that it was claiming a breach of warranty or that it considered the seller to be liable to it.

2. What amendment to UCC 2–607(3)(a) would you recommend to resolve this issue? Would it be sufficient simply to substitute the word "nonconformity" for breach?

Problem 20–2

Your client entered into a contract to purchase a specified quantity of yarn. The expected quality was spelled out in some detail. As part of the contract, client agreed to the following clauses in the sales contract:

> "2. No claims relating to excessive moisture content, short weight, count variations, twist, quality or shade shall be allowed *if made after weaving, knitting, or processing,* or more than 10 days after receipt of shipment. * * * The buyer shall within 10 days of the receipt of the merchandise by himself or agent examine the merchandise for any and all defects."
>
> "4. This instrument constitutes the entire agreement between the parties, superseding all previous communications, oral or written, and no changes, amendments or additions hereto will be recognized unless in writing signed by both seller and buyer or buyer's agent. It is expressly agreed that no representations or warranties, express or implied, have been or are made by the seller except as stated herein, and the seller makes no warranty, express or implied, as to the fitness for buyer's purposes of yarn purchased hereunder, seller's obligations, except as expressly stated herein, being limited to the *delivery of good merchantable yarn of the description stated herein.*"

The yarn was tendered on March 1 and, after an inspection, accepted by client on March 2. Thereafter the yarn was cut and knitted into sweaters and the finished product was washed. During the washing, which took place on March 15 and 16, it was discovered that the color of the yarn had "shaded," that is, there was a variation in color from piece to piece and within the pieces. This was clearly a defect that made the yarn unmerchantable and could not have been discovered by a reasonable inspection. Client promptly gave notice to the seller of the defect. Since revocation of acceptance was not possible (do you see why?), client asserted a claim for damages under UCC 2–714(2) and 2–715(2). Seller, pointing to the contract, denied any liability.

Client comes to you for advice. Is the clause enforceable? See UCC 1–204, 2–302 & 2–719. After you have completed your analysis, you may wish to compare it with Wilson Trading Corp. v. David Ferguson, Ltd., 23 N.Y.2d 398, 297 N.Y.S.2d 108, 244 N.E.2d 685 (1968).

SECTION 3. PROOF OF BREACH: EFFECT OF LACK OF CAUSATION AND PLAINTIFF'S CONTRIBUTORY BEHAVIOR

In Chapter 19, the primary issue was whether the seller had made a warranty, express or implied, to the buyer. Here we are concerned about what the buyer must prove to establish a breach of that warranty and that the breach caused the loss complained of. The answers turn, in part, upon the type of warranty made and the quantum and quality of proof required to get the case to the jury. In addition, the seller must be alert to possible misuse of the goods by the buyer and other conduct suggesting contributory "fault" or assumption of risk. These issues frequently arise in commercial litigation. See, e.g., Phelan and Falhof, *Proving a Defect in a Commercial Products Liability Case,* 24 Trial Law.Guide 10 (1980).

According to Mr. Phelan, an experienced Chicago trial attorney, the plaintiff maximizes the chances of proving both breach and causation when the facts and inferences from the following sources are cumulated:

1. The allegedly non-conforming product;
2. The circumstances surrounding the "accident;"
3. The life history of the product;
4. Relevant trade usages and practices with regard to products of the same description; and
5. Conduct by the buyer in inspecting, maintaining and using the product, both before and after the "accident."

CHATFIELD v. SHERWIN–WILLIAMS CO.

Supreme Court of Minnesota, 1978.
266 N.W.2d 171.

PER CURIAM.

In this action to recover damages allegedly resulting from breaches of warranty in the sale of red barn paint, the jury found by a special verdict that defendant paint manufacturer breached an express warranty that the paint was "good barn paint" and the implied warranties of merchantability and fitness for a particular purpose. It also found that the breaches were a direct cause of plaintiff's damages; that plaintiff was negligent and his negligence was a direct cause of his consequential damages; that 85 percent of the fault causing such consequential damages was attributable to defendant and 15 percent to plaintiff; and that plaintiff sustained general damages of $1,116 and consequential damages of $13,357. The court ordered judgment for plaintiff for $14,473, the total amount assessed by the jury. Defendant appeals, challenging the sufficiency of the evidence to establish breaches of the warranties and that such breaches were a proximate cause of plaintiff's damages. Defendant also contends that plaintiff is precluded from recovery of damages because he did not follow defendant's directions in using its product. Our review satisfies us that the issues raised were properly submitted to the jury and that the judgment appealed from should be affirmed.

In the winter of 1974, plaintiff, an experienced professional painter of farm buildings, purchased 330 gallons of "Commonwealth Ranch Red" paint from defendant for $4.65 per gallon. Before making the purchase plaintiff asked Wendell Swenson, manager of defendant's Wilmar store, if it would be good paint and if he would have any trouble with it. Swenson told plaintiff that people had used this paint on barns for many years and that it was "tried and true." He added, "Besides, this is Sherwin-Williams, you know. It couldn't have a bad name and be that big." Plaintiff then purchased the paint, used 240 gallons on barns and other buildings at 11 farms, and sold the rest to his father who is also a professional painter.

The label on the paint cans plaintiff purchased contained the following directions:

> "New Wood and Extremely Weathered Surfaces:
>
> Add 1 to 2 quarts of raw linseed oil per gallon to the *first coat.* Brush it well into surface. When spraying follow immediately with thorough brushing to work paint into pores. Second coat should be brushed on at package consistency or thinned with up to a pint of S–W exolvent or turpentine per gallon for spraying."

Plaintiff admitted that he never added as much as 1 to 2 quarts of linseed oil and said that when he used that much the paint wrinkled. He said that when painting dry areas, he added as much linseed oil as he thought necessary, depending on the condition of the wood. He thought a ratio of 20 percent was usually correct. He said that under the eaves and along the upper two-thirds of the buildings the wood is often in better condition than the wood below, the lower 5 or 6 feet of a barn usually requiring linseed oil. Plaintiff did not apply the paint with a brush, claiming that his spraying equipment made the paint penetrate into the surfaces far more thoroughly than brushing could.

Several customers testified that plaintiff spray-painted their buildings with Commonwealth Ranch Red during the summer of 1975. The buildings varied in age (from a barn built in 1906 to one built in 1965) and in their need for paint. The customers said they were well satisfied with plaintiff's work in preparing the surfaces and painting the buildings. Within 1 to 4 months after the jobs were completed, however, the owners noticed that the color was fading on their buildings. Witnesses said the surfaces looked chalky, the color continued to bleach, and the paint was chipping and could be rubbed off. Plaintiff testified that the buildings which his father had painted with the 90 gallons he had obtained from plaintiff also faded. After receiving complaints from his customers, plaintiff in turn made complaints to defendant which were ignored for several months. Finally, in April 1975, defendant sent George Linmark, a chemist employed by defendant, to investigate the matter. Linmark looked at the buildings plaintiff had painted on two farms and told him, plaintiff testified, that the wood had been well prepared and the paint well applied. Plaintiff testified that Linmark could not explain why the fading had occurred. Subsequently, plaintiff received a letter saying that defendant had decided to do nothing about the paint because the fading "was to be expected with that quality of paint."

Plaintiff admitted on cross-examination that he had read the instructions on the paint cans and had not added as much linseed oil as they directed. When plaintiff rested, defendant moved for a directed verdict on the ground that plaintiff's evidence showed no negligence on its part and showed that plaintiff had been negligent in using his judgment instead of the manufacturer's. The court denied the motion.

Defendant then called Linmark, a chemist with experience in formulating Sherwin-Williams paint, as an expert witness. He said that the 330 gallons of paint which plaintiff had bought was from a 3,000–gallon batch and that defendant had received no complaints about the rest of the batch. Although defendant stores a sample from each batch it manufactures, it did not test any sample from the batch which was the source of plaintiff's paint to see if it would fade, apparently because it was not clear at first which batch had been the source of plaintiff's purchase.

Linmark testified that paint has two essential ingredients, pigments and vehicles or binders. In Commonwealth Ranch Red, the pigment which gives the color is iron oxide, comprising 14 percent of the pigment, and most of the rest of the pigment is calcium carbonate, which by itself is a white powder but is colorless when added to the paint. The vehicle or binder holds the pigment and causes the paint to adhere to the surface of a building. The binder in defendant's paint consisted of tall oil alkyd resin, blown fish oil, mineral spirits, and raw linseed oil. In Linmark's opinion the fading was caused by insufficient reinforcement of the paint with more linseed oil. He said that on weathered surfaces some of the binder in the paint soaks into the wood or old paint if the new paint being applied is not reinforced with linseed oil, and that when the remaining binder is eroded by the ultraviolet rays of the sun, the pigment stands loose. Thus, he said, the calcium carbonate in Commonwealth Ranch Red became visible, giving the paint the appearance of fading.

Linmark also testified that paint wrinkles if applied too thickly and that linseed oil in any quantity does not cause wrinkling. He admitted telling plaintiff in April 1975 that he had done a good job and that in Linmark's opinion there was "a fade problem." He looked at only two of the sets of buildings plaintiff had painted and admitted that he did not know whether plaintiff had added enough linseed oil in the various jobs. He also said that the paint plaintiff purchased was "the bottom of the line."

In rebuttal, plaintiff's father, Robert Chatfield, testified that he used some of the 90 gallons he had acquired from plaintiff and that he too received complaints of fading. He added 1 quart of linseed oil to 5 gallons of paint while painting a barn for a customer and found that the paint became too thin and would run. He said he applied some of the paint to part of his own buildings without using any linseed oil and they also faded. He purchased other Commonwealth Ranch Red from defendant's Wilmar store himself and applied it to his buildings without adding linseed oil. He said the areas to which he had applied this paint did not fade.

In submitting the case to the jury, the trial court refused to charge that defendant was not liable if plaintiff's use of the product was abnormal or not in accordance with adequate instructions. He instructed the jury that in determining whether plaintiff was negligent they could consider whether he used the paint in accordance with defendant's directions and submitted questions in response to which, as stated, the jury found plaintiff negligent and attributed 15 percent of the fault causing his consequential damage to that negligence.

1. Although apparently not contesting the existence of the warranties on which plaintiff brought suit, defendant argues that its motions for a directed verdict and for judgment notwithstanding the verdict should have been granted because plaintiff did not adduce sufficient proof that the paint faded prematurely because of an inherent defect and thus did not establish any breach of the warranties. It also argues that plaintiff did not prove that any breach of warranty proximately caused his damages, as is essential to recovery. Heil v. Standard Chemical Mfg. Co., 301 Minn. 315, 323, 223 N.W.2d 37, 41 (1974). Defendant's contentions require an examination of plaintiff's evidence in the light most favorable to the verdict.

At the time defendant moved for a directed verdict, plaintiff had presented testimony that he had done a good workmanlike job, testimony which permitted the jury to infer that poor workmanship did not cause the fading. Plaintiff's proof also showed that some areas he had painted did not need linseed oil and that the paint had faded quite uniformly within 1 to 4 months after application, both in areas where he had used linseed oil and in areas where he had not. He admitted that he never added as much linseed oil as defendant's directions advised he should use with "extremely weathered" surfaces but said he added it in a ratio of 20 percent when he thought it was needed. He further testified that defendant informed him that fading was to be expected with a paint of the quality of Commonwealth Ranch Red. This evidence, although it does not directly establish the cause of the fading, furnishes substantial support for the inference that the paint faded because of an inherent defect.

Defendant urges, however, that plaintiff was required to have the paint analyzed and to present expert testimony about the existence and nature of any alleged defect. Although the importance of expert testimony in products liability actions has been emphasized in several cases, this court has said that there is no hard-and-fast rule requiring plaintiff to introduce such testimony. Peterson v. Crown Zellerbach Corp., 296 Minn. 438, 209 N.W.2d

922 (1973). In several earlier breach-of-warranty cases, chemical analysis of the product was not required to establish the breach of warranty. * * *

In Nelson v. Wilkins Dodge, Inc., Minn., 256 N.W.2d 472, 476 (1977), an action for breach of implied warranties in the sale of a pickup, the court held that a defective condition can be proved by circumstantial evidence, saying:

> "Plaintiffs assert that there can be no question that proximate cause has been demonstrated with respect to the paint bubbles, the inverted taillight covers, and the loosened windshield-wiper blade and arm and shift lever. Defendant suggests that the paint bubbles and the loosened windshield wiper, horn bracket, and shift lever just as probably resulted from the continuous and hard use to which plaintiffs put the pickup as from any defect inherent in the vehicle when plaintiffs purchased it. Although liability for breach of warranty attaches only when a defect existing in the goods causes a breakdown in quality, * * * generally no specific defect need be alleged, and a defective condition can be proved by circumstantial evidence * * * No direct evidence was introduced as to the causes of the conditions in question. It is reasonable to suppose, however, that vehicles that are fit for ordinary purposes probably do not display these defects this early, even if they are driven a great deal within a short period of time. Thus, the causes of the faulty paint, windshield wiper, horn bracket, and shift lever were questions that should have been decided by the jury. A fortiori, the cause of the inverted taillight covers was a jury question."

Other courts have also held that circumstantial evidence may be sufficient to show the causal relation between the use of a warranted product and the injury which followed its use. See, 77 C.J.S. Sales, § 367. Thus, in Yormack v. Farmers Co-op. Assn. of N.J., 11 N.J.Super. 416, 78 A.2d 421 (1950), in an action for breach of a statutory implied warranty of quality and fitness in the sale of an insecticide (carbolineum) for use about chicken roosts, the court said (11 N.J.Super. 423, 78 A.2d 424):

> "We recognize the absence of any evidence which definitely informed the jury of the particular ingredient or constituent of the carbolineum which would in reasonable probability gravely injure and kill the chickens. Proof of unfitness does not necessarily require that degree of exactness and precision. * * *
>
> "Furthermore it was not necessary for the plaintiff to prove by direct evidence the causal relation between the use of the carbolineum and the injurious result; it could be established by circumstantial evidence."

We conclude that although plaintiff's proof of causation was not direct, if his evidence is viewed in the light most favorable to the verdict, the jury could infer from the fact that the fading was quite uniform that the presence or absence of linseed oil had no effect on the fading. Defendant admitted that there was a "fade problem" and fading within so short a time was to be expected with Commonwealth Ranch Red. From this it could be inferred that it was not "good barn paint," not of merchantable quality, and not suitable for the purpose for which plaintiff bought it. Thus, defendant's motions for a directed verdict and for judgment notwithstanding the verdict were properly denied.

2. Defendant also argues that, assuming the warranties involved here were breached, plaintiff is precluded from recovery of damages because he used the paint contrary to the directions and such "misuse" was beyond the scope of the warranties. Although defendant cites several cases in support of this claim—Chisholm v. J.R. Simplot Co., 94 Idaho 682, 495 P.2d 1113 (1972); Elanco Products Co. v. Akin-Tunnell, 516 S.W.2d 726 (Tex.Civ.App. 1974); Iverson Paints, Inc. v. Wirth Corp., 94 Idaho 43, 480 P.2d 889 (1971); Brown v. General Motors Corp., 355 F.2d 814 (4 Cir.1966)—all are distinguishable from this case. In the Chisholm case, watering the fields within a specified time was essential to activate the weed killer which was alleged to have been defective, and the importance of following that direction should have been obvious to plaintiffs. In Iverson also, the directions for using the machine were very precise, and they were almost completely ignored—neither of which is the fact here. In the Elanco case the manufacturer had stressed the necessity of following directions and had disclaimed any affirmations made about the product unless the directions were followed. The court accordingly treated compliance with the directions as a condition precedent to the existence of the express warranty sued on. Here no comparable stress was laid on the importance of the directions, and they certainly were not specific and precise as to quantity. In Brown, plaintiff did not establish that there had been a breach of warranty, and that his use of a tractor by starting it when it was in gear was abnormal and unpredictable. Plaintiff used the paint here for its intended purpose.

We conclude that the trial court correctly instructed the jury that it could consider whether plaintiff complied with defendant's directions in determining whether he was negligent and whether his negligence was a cause of his consequential damages.

We also find little merit in defendant's argument that, if there was a defect in the paint, plaintiff failed to mitigate his damages by continuing to use the paint after he found it wrinkled when combined with the prescribed amount of linseed oil. Plaintiff did not know the paint would fade because, as he thought, defendant's directions called for too much linseed oil. Defendant's argument also assumes that plaintiff was at all times required to add linseed oil, a conclusion not compelled by the evidence. In any event, the court properly instructed the jury on plaintiff's duty to mitigate damages after learning of the breaches of warranty.

Defendant urges, finally, that the trial court improperly awarded plaintiff all of the consequential damages assessed by the jury and argues that these damages should have been reduced by 15 percent to reflect the proportion of fault which the jury attributed to plaintiff's negligence. Whether a comparative-fault principle should be applied in breach-of-warranty actions has not been determined in this state. Wenner v. Gulf Oil Corp., Minn., 264 N.W.2d 374, filed February 17, 1978. Although reducing a party's consequential damages by an amount reflecting the extent to which his own conduct caused them appears to be equitable, appropriate under Minn.St. 336.2–715(2)(b), and compatible with our approach in a recent products liability action based on strict liability, Busch v. Busch Const. Co., Minn., 262 N.W.2d 377 (1977), we decline to consider this issue since it was not presented to the trial court and has been raised for the first time on appeal. International Union of Operating Eng. v. City of Mpls., 305 Minn. 364, 233 N.W.2d 748 (1975).

Affirmed.

Notes

1. No sample was offered from the batch of paint purchased and applied to the barns. How did the buyer survive the seller's motion for directed verdict? In American Fertilizer Specialists v. Wood, 635 P.2d 592, 595–96 (Okl.1981), the court, in affirming the trial court's decision for the buyer, stated: "Facts may be proved by circumstantial, as well as by positive or direct evidence, and it is not necessary that the proof rise to that degree of certainty which will exclude every other reasonable conclusion than the one arrived at by the trier of facts. It is only required that it appear more probable that the defendant's poor grass crop was the result of the failure of the fertilizer sold by plaintiff to defendant to nourish and enrich defendant's grass lands than any other possible cause." For cases in accord, see Davidson Oil Country Supply Co. v. Klockner, Inc., 908 F.2d 1238 (5th Cir. 1990) (court erred in excluding evidence that similar goods had failed under similar circumstances); Plas–Tex, Inc. v. U.S. Steel Corp., 772 S.W.2d 442 (Tex.1989) (proof of defect in product and proper use by plaintiff gets case to jury); McLaughlin v. Michelin Tire Corp., 778 P.2d 59 (Wyo. 1989) (test for circumstantial evidence differs for merchantability and fitness warranties). As one court put, the buyer must present circumstantial proof "which if believed by the trier of fact, makes the plaintiff's theory of the case more probable than the theory of the defendant." Hollingsworth v. Queen Carpet, Inc., 827 S.W.2d 306, 309 (Tenn.App. 1991).

2. The buyer, in *Chatfield,* concededly failed to follow the seller's printed directions for use. Why didn't the buyer's failure constitute either a use of the product that was not ordinary, thereby undercutting the claim that an implied warranty of merchantability was breached, or a misuse of a product otherwise fit for ordinary purposes, thereby establishing that breach of warranty did not cause the loss? In Hutchinson Utilities Commission v. Curtiss-Wright Corp., 775 F.2d 231 (8th Cir.1985), the Eighth Circuit, relying on *Chatfield,* held that an agreed inspection schedule was not a condition precedent to the buyer's claim and that a defect in the goods rather than the failure to inspect was the "proximate" cause of the loss.)

3. Assuming that the plaintiff in *Chatfield* was, to some degree, at "fault" in mixing the paint, what effect should that have on the issues of liability and remedy? Consider these possibilities:

(a) The warranty, although made, was not breached;

(b) Although the warranty was made and breached, the plaintiff's "fault" barred it from recovery;

(c) The plaintiff's "fault", whether misuse or failure to discover, is no per se bar, but it may be considered in determining whether the breach caused the loss complained of; and

(d) The plaintiff's "fault" may be used to reduce damages otherwise proximately caused by the breach.

Which, if any, of these possibilities did *Chatfield* employ?

4. The Minnesota Comparative Negligence Statute, Minn.Stat.Ann. § 604.-01(1) (Supp.1987), provides that contributory fault is no bar in an action to

"recover damages for fault resulting in death or injury to person or property, if the contributory fault was not greater than the fault of the person against whom recovery is sought, but any damages allowed shall be diminished in proportion to the amount of fault attributable to the person recovering." In 1978, the statute was amended to define "fault" to include "breach of warranty, unreasonable assumption of risk not constituting an express consent, misuse of a product and unreasonable failure to avoid an injury or to mitigate damages." § 604.01(1a). The Supreme Court of Minnesota has since held that, in an action to recover for personal injuries and economic loss allegedly caused by a breach of warranty, it was proper to use the plaintiff's "fault" to reduce consequential damages but not direct damages caused by the breach. Peterson v. Bendix Home Systems, Inc., 318 N.W.2d 50 (Minn.1982). Should these later developments change the outcome in *Chatfield?*

Problem 20–3

The courts and legislatures, in applying concepts of comparative fault to product liability suits, have stopped short of cases where only economic loss is involved: The plaintiff, when suing on a warranty theory, must claim damages to person or property before any "fault" comparison will be made. An example is Fiske v. MacGregor, Div. of Brunswick, 464 A.2d 719 (R.I.1983). See also the Cipollone "cigarette" litigation, supra at p. 855. The issues are discussed in Leff & Pinto, *Comparative Negligence in Strict Products Liability: The Courts Render the Final Judgment,* 89 Dick.L.Rev. 915 (1985); Sobelsohn, *Comparing Fault,* 60 Ind.L.J. 413 (1985); Note, *Use of the Comparative Negligence Doctrine in Warranty Actions,* 45 Ohio St. U.L.J. 763 (1984).

As we shall see in Section 5, infra, Article 2 of the UCC is the exclusive source of law in warranty disputes where only economic loss is involved. How does Article 2 deal with problems of the buyer's fault? With this question in mind, re-read Article 2, Parts Six and Seven. Make a list of the "penalties," if any, that the buyer must pay for failure to take reasonable steps to discover the non-conformity or otherwise to avoid the loss.

SECTION 4. THE STATUTE OF LIMITATIONS

Read UCC 2–725 and work the following problem.

Problem 20–4

On May 1, 1982, Seller and Buyer, a grain dealer, entered a written contract for the sale of three prefabricated metal grain bins, each 30 feet tall, for a total price of $50,000. The bins were to be shipped to Buyer FOB Point of Destination and Seller agreed to erect and install them at Buyer's place of business. The contract provided, inter alia, that "the above described bins will, if properly installed, withstand winds up to 90 MPH."

The bins were shipped on June 1, 1982 and arrived on June 5, 1982. The buyer removed the disassembled parts from the carrier and notified the Seller, who completed the installation by July 1, 1982. On June 15, 1986, a severe storm with winds up to 80 MPH hit the area where Buyer did business. Two of the bins were toppled by the wind, resulting in damage to the bins and the stored grain. An expert will testify that the internal support seams had gradually and imperceptibly deteriorated since installation.

Buyer's attorney has asked you, his associate, whether the statute of limitations has run.

STANDARD ALLIANCE INDUS., INC. v. BLACK CLAWSON CO.

United States Court of Appeals, Sixth Circuit, 1978.
587 F.2d 813.

[The facts and the court's opinion on the notice issue are reprinted, supra at p. 896.]

* * *

A. The Statute of Limitations and Count I

Chronology is important to a precise understanding of the issues. The machine was delivered and assembled at Standard Alliance's plant in the fall of 1967. The machine proved defective, and Standard Alliance wrote Black Clawson on December 27, 1967, delineating exactly what was wrong with the machine and requesting that Black Clawson fix it. Black Clawson worked on the machine until June 21, 1968, when it abandoned repair efforts. This suit was filed on May 29, 1969.

The original contract contained a one-year limitations period;[*] the minimum allowable under UCC § 2–725(1). UCC § 2–725(1) also provides that the limitations period begins to run when the cause of action accrues. UCC § 2–725(2) explains that a cause of action accrues when a breach occurs. A breach of warranty is deemed to occur upon tender of delivery "except that where a warranty explicitly extends to future performance of the goods and discovery of the breach must await the time of such performance the cause of action accrues when the breach is or should have been discovered." UCC § 2–725(2). Black Clawson argues that the machine was tendered in the fall of 1967 and that, even granting that the warranty extends to future performance, the cause of action under Count I accrued no later than December 27, 1967, when Standard Alliance wrote its letter claiming that the machine was defective. Standard Alliance makes numerous arguments in reply. Primarily, we must consider the question of when breach occurred. This involves analysis of two separate issues: when tender of delivery was made; whether the warranty extended to future performance. In addition, we must consider various estoppel and policy arguments.

Standard Alliance first contends, with some support in the record, that novel machines like the one here often have long "shakedown" periods before they can be made to function properly. The import of its argument is that "tender" of a defective machine should not be deemed to take place until the machine is made to run properly. Since the machine in the instant case did not function properly when initially installed in October of 1967, Standard Alliance argues, tender of delivery was never really made until June 21, 1968, when Black Clawson halted its efforts to get the machine going. Thus, even assuming that the warranty did not extend to future

[*] Based upon information provided by counsel, the editors of the Callaghan Uniform Commercial Code Reporting Service state that the exact language of the "limitation" clause was as follows: "Any action or arbitration proceeding for breach of this agreement must be brought within one year after the cause of action has accrued."

performance, the earliest a breach could have occurred and a cause of action accrued, on Standard Alliance's theory, was June 21, 1968.

This argument is plausible, but withers upon proper examination of the Uniform Commercial Code. UCC § 2–503(1) defines "tender of delivery" as requiring "* * * that the seller put and hold conforming goods at the buyer's disposition * * *" Comment 1 to UCC § 2–503 explains that at times "tender" means "due tender" meaning "* * * an offer coupled with a present ability to fulfill all the conditions resting on the tendering party [which must be] followed by actual performance if the other party shows himself ready to proceed." "At other times [tender] is used to refer to an offer of goods or documents under a contract as if in fulfillment of its conditions even though there is a defect when measured against the contract obligation." Id. We think that "tender" as used in UCC § 2–725(2) is the latter and not the former. A contrary interpretation would extend the statute of limitations indefinitely into the future since a defect at the time of delivery would prevent proper "due tender" from taking place until it was corrected. Under section 2–725, a cause of action accrues upon initial installation of the product regardless whether it functions properly or not so long as the warranty does not extend to future performance. See Val Decker Packing Co. v. Corn Products Sales Co., 411 F.2d 850 (6th Cir.1969).

Secondly, Standard Alliance argues that the page twelve warranties ** did extend to future performance under section 2–725(2), and that the statute of limitations thus ran from the date of discovery of the defect. It particularly points to the phrase, "Black Clawson warrants that the subject machinery *will* perform the following mechanical functions." Plaintiff's argument proves too much. Since all contracts contain future promises, words of futurity such as "will" are common. When the contract at issue here was signed, the machine was not yet built; the word "will" was necessarily used. The proper question is whether the statute of limitations is meant to run from the day of delivery or from the day when a defect is found sometime in the future.

** The negotiated performance or "page twelve warranties" provided:

"The following express warranties, which relate to mechanical function only become an adjunct to our contract clause # 1 page 11 and supersede all references to warranties that may be contained in the description of the machine pages 2–7, either expressed or implied.

"Black Clawson warrants that the subject machinery will perform the following mechanical functions:

"1. Press will deliver 1000 ton ram capacity at 150 strokes per minute @ 1/4″ from bottom dead center.

"2. Press will have a maximum speed of 250 strokes per minute—with a range of 10 to 250 SPM.

"3. Rams at bottom of stroke will have a parallelism of within .005″.

"4. Peel and press will trace template within plus or minus .015″.

"5. Feed adjustments will have a range up to 0.375″ per second.

"6. Peel rotation will have a range of 5 to 100 RPM and will be designed to lock at the 90° positions.

"7. Peel traverse speed will have a range of 1 ft/minute to 45 ft/minute, and will be designed to lock in position.

"8. The mechanical functions can be programmed to operate in automatic sequence in the specified capacities and accuracies or may be operator interrupted and/or commanded as required.

"The quality and quantity of production is not the responsibility of the seller."

Most courts have been very harsh in determining whether a warranty explicitly extends to future performance. Emphasizing the word "explicitly," they have ruled that there must be specific reference to a future time in the warranty. As a result of this harsh construction, most express warranties cannot meet the test and no implied warranties can since, by their very nature, they never "explicitly extend to future performance." * * *

Two rare examples where express warranties were found to explicitly extend to future performance are Rempe v. General Electric Co., 28 Conn.Super. 160, 254 A.2d 577 (1969) (product was to "work properly for a lifetime") and Mittasch v. Seal Lock Burial Vault, Inc., 42 A.D.2d 573, 344 N.Y.S.2d 101 (1973) (warranty that vault "will give satisfactory service at all times").

It is clear that a buyer and a seller can freely negotiate to extend liability into the future; that is why specific allowance was made for warranties "explicitly" extending to future performance. * * * In the absence of explicit agreement, however, UCC § 2–725(2) reflecting the drafters' intention to establish a reasonable period of time, four years,[16] beyond which business persons need not worry about stale warranty claims is applicable. This policy consideration underlying § 2–725 makes it acceptable to bar implied warranty claims brought more than a specified number of years after the sale; otherwise merchants could be forever liable for breach of warranty on any goods which they sold. * * * Similarly, an express warranty which makes no reference at all to any future date should not be allowed to extend past the limitations period. Thus, where a manufacturer warrants that a welder will meet certain performance warranties, but makes no mention of how long the warranties are meant to last; the statute of limitations begins to run at delivery. * * *

Where, however, an express warranty is made which extends for a specific period of time, i.e. one year, the policy reasons behind strict application of the limitations period do not apply. If a seller expressly warrants a product for a specified number of years, it is clear that, by this action alone, he is explicitly warranting the future performance of the goods for that period of time. As J. White & R. Summers Uniform Commercial Code 342 (1972), points out, if an automobile is warranted to last for twenty-four thousand miles or four years, the warranty should extend to future performance. If the car fails within the warranty period, the limitations period should begin to run from the day the defect is or should have been discovered.

In the case at bar, Black Clawson expressly warranted the machine for a period of one year. Thus, we hold that the warranties explicitly extended to future performance for a period of one year. Therefore, under § 2–725(2) the cause of action accrued when Standard Alliance discovered or should have discovered that the machine was defective, so long as the defect arose within the warranty period.[17]

16. We are aware that some states have adopted a limitations period greater than four years, e.g. Wis.Stat. § 402.725 (6 years); Okla.Stat. tit. 12A § 2–725 (5 years). Ohio, however, follows the majority of the states in establishing a four year period. Ohio Rev. Code § 1302.98 [UCC § 2–725]. The parties agree that Ohio law governs this diversity action.

17. Centennial Ins. Co. v. General Electric Co., [253 N.W.2d 696] and Voth v. Chrysler Motor Corp., [545 P.2d 371], indicated that contractual provisions to repair or re-

Unfortunately, this holding does not assist the plaintiff. Under the contractual limitations period, Standard Alliance had one year from the date of discovery of defect to bring suit. Standard Alliance reported the machine's problems to Black Clawson by letter on December 27, 1967. At least as of this date, Standard Alliance had discovered the breach. Since suit was not brought until over a year later, on May 29, 1969, this action is barred by section 2–725(2). See Gemini Typographers v. Mergenthaler Lino Co., 48 A.D.2d 637, 368 N.Y.S.2d 210 (1975).

Plaintiff thirdly argues that Black Clawson should be estopped from asserting the statute of limitations as a defense because it promised to repair the defects and spent over five months attempting to do so. In effect, plaintiff contends that it reasonably relied on the repair efforts, to its detriment. Decisions in other jurisdictions are split. * * *

We must determine what the Ohio courts would do if confronted with this issue. Although we have been unable to find direct case authority, an examination of the statute is illuminative. UCC § 2–725(4), as promulgated by the drafters of the Uniform Commercial Code, states:

> "This section does not alter *the law* on tolling of the statute of limitations nor does it apply to causes of action which have accrued before this Act becomes effective." (Emphasis added)

Ohio's version of UCC § 2–725(4) is codified at Ohio Rev.Code § 1302.98(d). That section provides:

> "This section does not alter *sections 2305.15 and 2305.16 of the [Ohio] Revised Code* on tolling of the statute of limitations nor does it apply to causes of action which have accrued before this Act becomes effective." (Emphasis added)

Thus, when the Ohio legislature adopted the Uniform Commercial Code, it substituted "sections 2305.15 and 2305.16 of the [Ohio] Revised Code" for "the law" in the text of UCC § 2–725(4). This significant change in the UCC's wording requires that we limit our analysis to the two Ohio statutes cited.

An examination of these statutes reveals that the limitation period is tolled if a defendant has removed himself from the state, Ohio Rev.Code § 2305.15, or if a plaintiff has suffered from some type of disability. Ohio Rev.Code § 2305.16. Neither is applicable here.

It is, of course, quite possible that the Ohio courts would apply the doctrine of equitable estoppel in a case where an innocent purchaser has relied to his detriment on a seller's promises to repair. "The principle that '* * * no man may take advantage of his own wrong' prevents a defendant whose actions have induced a plaintiff to delay filing a suit until after the running of the limitation period from asserting the statute of limitations as

place defective parts for a period of one year were not warranties extending into the future for one year, but remedies to be invoked should something go wrong. We see no conceptual distinction between saying that a product is warranted for one year against defects, the remedy limited to repair or replacement and saying that should a breach be discovered within one year, the seller will repair or replace defective parts. Both are warranties explicitly extending to future performance. We recognize that there may be differences between remedies and warranties, * * * but we do not believe that these distinctions make a difference here.

a defense to the action." Ott v. Midland-Ross Corp., 523 F.2d 1367, 1370 (6th Cir.1975). See Markese v. Ellis, 11 Ohio App.2d 160, 229 N.E.2d 70 (1967). Here, however, we have two corporate behemoths, well able to look out for themselves, and no evidence that one lulled the other into not suing on time. * * *

Standard Alliance's two remaining arguments, unsupported by any authority, merit only brief mention. Standard Alliance argues that this court should toll the running of the limitations period or otherwise find timely filing because the limitations period was contractually reduced from four years to one year. It would also find significant that approximately one-half the one-year limitations period was spent in attempted repairs.

The one-year limitations period is specifically allowed by UCC § 2–725(1). We see nothing unfair about this provision in a negotiated contract between two parties of equal bargaining power. Similarly, we find no prejudice to plaintiff resulted from the lengthy repair time. Standard Alliance still had time to file suit on the original breach of warranty claim even after termination of the repair efforts; it also had a cause of action under Count II for failure to fulfill the repair or replacement warranty.[20]

* * *

[Some footnotes omitted.]

Notes

1. In Dowling v. Southwestern Porcelain, Inc., 237 Kan. 536, 701 P.2d 954 (1985), the court held that where the buyer contracted to purchase a completed silo to be installed by the seller, the statute of limitations began to run when the installation was completed, not when the component parts were delivered.

2. Seller, in furnishing spandrel and visions panels for a building, represented that the goods would be free from defects in material and workmanship for a "period of twenty years." The exclusive remedy for breach was limited to replacement of defective panels. The panels, which were delivered between 1974 and 1976, were defective. The buyer sued for damages in 1981 and the district court granted the seller's motion to dismiss based upon the statute of limitations: The court held that seller had only made replacement commitments, not warranties explicitly extending to future performance. *Held,* reversed. The warranties, by explicitly stating a time beyond delivery when the condition would exist, extended the warranty to "future" performance of the goods, with a limitation of the remedy to replacement in the event of a breach. The buyer filed suit within 4 years of the time the breach was or "should have been discovered." R.W. Murray Co. v. Shatterproof Glass Corp., 697 F.2d 818 (8th Cir.1983).

Despite the *Shatterproof Glass* decision, there is still some unease in the cases about when a "warranty explicitly extends to future performance of the goods." UCC 2–725(2). For example, suppose there is an express warranty that goods are "free from defects in material and workmanship" and that seller will repair any such defects discovered during the first twelve months after delivery.

20. Our disposition of Count I on limitations grounds makes it unnecessary to consider the interesting question whether notice of breach had to be given a second time, after repairs failed. Since the repair or replacement warranty is also a remedy to be invoked if the machine did not meet its performance warranties, there is certainly room to argue that UCC § 2–607(3) requires notice that the repair or replacement remedy has failed "of its essential purpose" under UCC § 2–719(2).

Is this simply a limited agreement to "cure" defects existing at the time of delivery or an affirmation that the goods will function properly for 12 months after delivery? Unless there is some clear language stating, in effect, that these goods will conform to the warranty for a stated post-delivery period, the probability is that an explicit extension will not be found. *Compare* Tittle v. Steel City Oldsmobile, Inc., 544 So.2d 883 (Ala.1989) (no explicit extension) *with* Krieger v. Nick Alexander Imports, Inc., 234 Cal.App.3d 205, 285 Cal.Rptr. 717 (1991) (extension). See also, Rosen v. Spanierman, 894 F.2d 28 (2d Cir.1990) (warranty of title did not extended to future performance).

For a holding that an art dealer's express warranty that a painting was a "genuine" Dali did "explicitly" extend the warranty to future performance, see Balog v. Center Art Gallery–Hawaii, Inc., 745 F.Supp. 1556 (D.Haw.1990).

3. Suppose that S, upon delivery on November 1, 1980, explicitly stated that "this warranty shall last for three years." B "should have" discovered a nonconformity on November 1, 1986 and actually discovered the defect on July 1, 1987. B sued S on October 30, 1987. S moved to dismiss on grounds that B failed to give notice under UCC 2–607(3)(a) before filing suit. What result?

4. For samples of literature highly critical of UCC 2–725, see Williams, *The Statute of Limitations, Prospective Warranties, and Problems of Interpretation in Article 2 of the UCC,* 52 G.W.L.Rev. 67 (1983); Note, *UCC Section 2–725: A Statute Uncertain in Application and Effect,* 46 Ohio St. U.L.Rev. 755 (1985).

Problem 20–5

B contracted to purchase factory equipment from S on June 1, 1984. S warranted that the goods were free from defects in material and workmanship for the period of one year after installation and agreed to repair or replace defective parts or work. The equipment was delivered and installed on July 1, 1984. On June 1, 1985, B notified S that the machine had stopped working. S, on June 5, arrived at B's plant and attempted to "cure" the problem. After three weeks of effort, the equipment still did not work. S left the premises on June 26, 1985 insisting that he would repair the machine. "Don't worry," he said. In August, 1985, B notified S that the cure had not worked and that he considered S in breach. Again, S assured B that a cure would be forthcoming. S never returned to the plant and B removed the equipment from the floor and put it in storage. In July, 1989, B consults you, his attorney, about the matter. Has the statute of limitations run on B's claim for breach of warranty?

SECTION 5. THE LIMITATIONS OF WARRANTY THEORY

To summarize, warranty is a theory of strict but limited liability. Warranties arise when the seller makes representations, express or implied, about the quality of goods sold upon which a buyer is entitled to depend. Disputes involving warranties are resolved within Article 2 of the UCC, which has a set of limitations and policies associated primarily with exchange transactions, i.e., contracts for the sale of goods. In addition to limitations associated with concerns about adverse selection and moral hazard, which have been noted, Article 2 also permits the parties by agreement to disclaim or limit warranties and limit remedies for breach, issues which will be treated in Chapter Twenty-one.

A number of recurring problems, however, have tested the nature of warranty theory and, perforce, the limitations of Article 2. We will identify some of them here, and follow with a decision where the issues are put to the test.

First, should warranty theory be extended to transactions where personal or professional services predominate and the transfer of goods is incidental? The usual answer is no, unless the defendant has expressly promised or represented that the services, when performed, will achieve a specific result. Without an express commitment to achieve a particular result, the performance of the services is judged under tort standards—negligence—rather than implied warranty. See, e.g., Milau Associates v. North Ave. Development, 42 N.Y.2d 482, 398 N.Y.S.2d 882, 368 N.E.2d 1247 (1977); Greenfield, *Consumer Protection in Service Transactions—Implied Warranties and Strict Liability in Tort,* 1974 Utah L.Rev. 661. (Query whether there is much difference between a tort duty to perform services with reasonable care and an implied warranty that the services will be "reasonably fit" for ordinary purposes.)

Second, suppose a seller sells unmerchantable goods which cause damage to the person or property of a buyer. Suppose, further, that the buyer would be foreclosed from recovery by one or more limitations upon warranty liability found in the Code, e.g., failure to give notice of the breach, lack of contractual privity, an enforceable disclaimer or expiration of the statute of limitations. Does Article 2 preempt the dispute or may the buyer also pursue the claim in strict products liability or negligence, where tort rather than contract limitations apply?

Despite the fact that Article 2 explicitly covers personal injury and property damage claims, see UCC 2–715(2)(b), 2–719(3) and 2–318, Alternatives A and B, the usual answer to the question is no: Neither the drafters of Article 2 nor the state legislatures which enacted it intended to preempt the developing theory of strict liability under Section 402A of the Restatement, Second of Torts. See Phipps v. General Motors Corp., 278 Md. 337, 363 A.2d 955 (1976); Murray, *Products Liability vs. Warranty Claims: Untangling the Web,* 3 J.Law & Commerce 269 (1983); Wade, *Tort Liability for Products Causing Physical Injury and Article 2 of the U.C.C.,* 48 Mo.L.Rev. 1 (1983). For contrary opinions, see Cline v. Prowler Industries of Maryland, 418 A.2d 968 (Del.1980); Shanker, *A Reexamination of Prosser's Products Liability Cross Word Game: The Strict or Stricter Liability of Commercial Code Sales Warranty,* 29 Case Wes.Res.L.Rev. 550 (1979) (Article 2 applies to physical damage claims). The upshot is that a plaintiff who is injured in person or property by a defective product may escape Article 2 for the more favorable law of Tort, if he so elects. In Florida, a warranty theory is not available to a buyer who is injured in person by "defective" goods. Kramer v. Piper Aircraft Corp., 520 So.2d 37 (Fla.1988).

Third, suppose a commercial buyer in privity with the seller suffers damage to property or pure economic loss from a breach of warranty. No personal injuries are involved. May the buyer "escape" from Article 2 into tort by invoking either strict products or negligence theory? To put the matter concretely, suppose that the statute of limitations has run under UCC 2–725(1) but has not run in tort. As *Spring Motors,* infra, reveals, the judicial answer is clear where pure economic loss is involved—UCC 2–725 controls—but is uncertain where damage to personal property has occurred.

Fourth, suppose a commercial buyer has suffered pure economic loss caused by an unmerchantable product but is not in privity of contract with the manufacturer. If the buyer cannot escape the UCC into tort, lack of privity is no defense and warranty theory must be pursued. May the manufacturer, who is a seller, defend on the ground that there was no privity of contract? See the next case.

Finally, suppose the buyer is a consumer, i.e., a person who purchased the goods for personal, family or household purposes, who has suffered only economic loss. How, if at all, should the answers to the third and fourth questions, above, differ? Should the "ordinary" consumer with less overall capacity than the professional seller be entitled to greater protection than a commercial buyer and, if so, what and why? See, e.g., Rice, *Product Quality Laws and the Economics of Federalism,* 65 B.U.L.Rev. 1 (1985); Vogel, *Squeezing Consumers: Lemon Laws, Consumer Warranties, and a Proposal for Reform,* 1985 Ariz.St.L.Rev. 589, and Chapter Twenty-one, Section 5.

SPRING MOTORS DISTRIBUTORS, INC. v. FORD MOTOR COMPANY

Supreme Court of New Jersey, 1985.
98 N.J. 555, 489 A.2d 660.

The opinion of the Court was delivered by

POLLOCK, J.

The fundamental issue on this appeal concerns the rights of a commercial buyer to recover for economic loss caused by the purchase of defective goods. More specifically, the question is whether the buyer should be restricted to its cause of action under the Uniform Commercial Code (hereinafter U.C.C. or the Code) or should be allowed to pursue a cause of action predicated on principles of negligence and strict liability. The difference is important because the buyer in the present case instituted its action beyond the four-year period provided by the U.C.C., *N.J.S.A.* 12A:2–725, but within the six-year period applicable to tort actions, *N.J.S.A.* 2A:14–1.

The defendants are a motor vehicle manufacturer, its dealer, and a supplier of transmissions. The gravamen of the complaint is that defects in the transmissions, which were installed in commercial trucks, caused the buyer to sustain a loss in the benefit of its bargain and consequential damages. Specifically, the buyer sought recovery for repair, towing, and replacement parts, as well as for lost profits and a decrease in the value of the trucks.

The trial court perceived the matter as sounding in contract and found that the plaintiff had not instituted its action within the four-year period provided by the U.C.C. *N.J.S.A.* 12A:2–725. In an unreported decision, the court granted summary judgment for defendants. The Appellate Division reversed on the ground that the action was more appropriately characterized as one in strict liability in tort, not contract, and that the six-year period of limitations applicable for tort actions had not expired. 191 *N.J.Super.* 22, 465 *A.*2d 530 (1983). We granted defendants' petition for certification. 95 *N.J.* 208, 470 *A.*2d 427 (1983).

We hold that a commercial buyer seeking damages for economic loss resulting from the purchase of defective goods may recover from an immediate seller and a remote supplier in a distributive chain for breach of warranty under the U.C.C., but not in strict liability or negligence. We hold also that the buyer need not establish privity with the remote supplier to maintain an action for breach of express or implied warranties. Accordingly, the four-year period of limitations provided by the Code, *N.J.S.A.* 12A:2–275, not the six-year general statute of limitations, *N.J.S.A.* 2A:14–1, determines the time within which an action must be commenced against the immediate seller and remote supplier.

I

Because this matter is presented on defendants' motion for summary judgment, we accept as true plaintiff's version of the facts, according that version the benefit of all favorable inferences. *Pierce v. Ortho Pharmaceutical Corp.*, 84 *N.J.* 58, 61, 417 *A.*2d 505 (1980). Plaintiff, Spring Motors Distributors, Inc. (Spring Motors), which is in the business of selling and leasing trucks, operates a fleet of 300 vehicles. Spring Motors agreed to purchase from defendant Turnpike Ford Truck Sales, Inc. (Turnpike) 14 model LN8000 trucks made by defendant Ford Motor Company (Ford) at a purchase price of $265,029.80. Turnpike is a Ford dealer, and throughout these proceedings the two defendants have been treated as a single entity.

In the agreement, Spring Motors specified that the trucks should be equipped with model 390V transmissions made by Clark Equipment Company (Clark), a supplier to Ford. Spring Motors specified Clark transmissions because of "excellent service and parts availability on past models" and because of Clark's advertisements and brochures.

At the time of the sale to Spring Motors, Ford issued a form warranty with each truck to

> repair or replace any of the following parts that are found to be defective in factory material or workmanship under normal use in the United States or Canada on the following basis: * * * any part during the first 12 months or 12,000 miles of operations, whichever is earlier * * * transmission case and all internal transmission parts (including auxiliary transmission) * * * after 12,000 miles and during the first 12 months or 50,000 miles of operation, whichever is earlier, for a charge of 50% of the dealer's regular warranty charge to Ford for parts and labor. * * * For series 850 and higher trucks, any part of the * * * transmission * * * for the first 12 months or 100,000 miles of operation, whichever is earlier * * *.

The warranty also stated: "To the extent allowed by law, this WARRANTY IS IN PLACE OF all other warranties, express or implied, including ANY IMPLIED WARRANTY OF MERCHANTABILITY OR FITNESS." Furthermore, the Ford warranty expressly stated: "Under this warranty, repair or replacement of parts is the only remedy, and loss of use of the vehicle, loss of time, inconvenience, commercial loss or consequential damages are not covered."

The warranty that Clark extended to Ford provided: "WARRANTY. Clark Equipment Company ('Clark') warrants to Buyer that each new Clark axle, transmission, torque converter and drive train product, and components thereof, shall be free from defects and material and workmanship under normal use and maintenance" for 12 months or 12,000 miles for on-highway vehicles used on highways or 2,000 miles for off-highway equipment. At Clark's option, the warranty could be limited to repairs or replacements. The warranty also stated: "THIS WARRANTY IS IN LIEU OF ALL OTHER WARRANTIES (EXCEPT OF TITLE), EXPRESSED OR IMPLIED, AND THERE IS NO IMPLIED WARRANTY OF MERCHANTABILITY OR OF FITNESS FOR A PARTICULAR PURPOSE. IN NO EVENT SHALL CLARK BE LIABLE FOR INCIDENTAL, CONSEQUENTIAL OR SPECIAL DAMAGES."

Spring Motors took delivery of the trucks in November 1976, and leased them to Economic Laboratories, Inc. (Economic), which used the trucks in cities and on highways for their intended purpose of hauling. Spring Motors, which serviced the trucks during the period of the lease, began experiencing problems with the performance of the Clark transmissions as early as February 1977. The problems persisted, and Spring Motors communicated directly with Clark, writing in October 1977 that it had "had nothing but trouble" with the transmissions. Later correspondence, dated January 26, 1978, confirmed that Clark analyzed the transmissions and found that "the failure in these gear boxes was a result of improper angle degree in the way certain gears were cut," resulting "in additional strain on the actual gear and the mating gear and related shafts." Still later, Spring Motors pointed out that the transmission failures had cost it "several thousand dollars in out of pocket expenses plus many additional thousands of dollars in lost revenues, customer ill will, replacement equipment, etc."

Clark provided Spring Motors with replacement parts, but the transmission failures continued. On July 11, 1978, Spring Motors wrote to Clark that in the absence of a satisfactory response by August 1, it would remove and replace the Clark transmissions and "take whatever action is necessary to hold you financially responsible." Thereafter, on November 1, 1979, Spring Motors and Economic terminated the truck lease and, as part of a settlement, Economic purchased the trucks for $247,580.97. Four years and one month after the delivery of the trucks, on December 23, 1980, Spring Motors instituted this action.

In the complaint, which contained three counts, Spring Motors sought judgment against all defendants for consequential damages: the expenses of towing, repairs, and replacement of parts; lost profits; and decrease in market value of the trucks. The first count asserted that the defendants breached certain express and implied warranties; the second count claimed a violation of the Magnuson-Moss Act, 15 *U.S.C.* § 2301 to -2312, a claim that Spring Motors no longer pursues; and the third count sought recovery in strict liability and negligence.

The trial court found that a lack of privity barred the action between Spring Motors and Clark and that the four-year period of limitations under the U.C.C., *N.J.S.A.* 12A:2-725, barred any action against Ford and Turnpike. The Court further found the six-year statute of limitations, *N.J.S.A.* 2A:14-1, pertaining to tort actions for property damage, inapplicable. Consequently, the trial court dismissed the complaint as to all defendants.

The Appellate Division affirmed the dismissal of the breach of warranty claim in the first count, but reversed the dismissal of the tort claims, without discussing the negligence aspect of the third count. That court concluded that Spring Motors, as a commercial buyer, could maintain its strict-liability claim against all defendants. 191 *N.J.Super.* at 41, 465 *A.*2d 530. The court also determined that the six-year limitation period provided by *N.J.S.A.* 2A:14–1 applied and that plaintiff's action was, therefore, timely. *Id.* at 44, 465 *A.*2d 530.

We granted petitions for certification by Ford, Turnpike, and Clark to review that part of the Appellate Division judgment that reversed the dismissal of the tort claims. Spring Motors did not file a cross-petition seeking review of the dismissal of the warranty claims, and that issue is not before us.

II

If the legal relationships among the parties are governed by the U.C.C., then plaintiff's action, which was instituted more than four years after the delivery of the trucks, is time-barred. Hence, one question is whether the Code provides the exclusive remedies available to Spring Motors. In answering that question, we turn to the structure and purpose of the Code, which constitutes a comprehensive system for determining the rights and duties of buyers and sellers with respect to contracts for the sale of goods. *Ramirez v. Autosport,* 88 *N.J.* 277, 285–90, 440 *A.*2d 1345 (1982). Its underlying purpose is to clarify and make uniform throughout the United States the law governing commercial transactions. *N.J.S.A.* 12A:1–102.

The Code provides for express warranties regarding the quality of goods, *N.J.S.A.* 12A:2–313, as well as implied warranties of merchantability, *N.J.S.A.* 12A:2–314, and of fitness for a particular purpose, *N.J.S.A.* 12A:2–315. As is subsequently discussed in greater detail, a seller's warranty, whether express or implied, extends to members of the buyer's family or his household guests, who are viewed as third-party beneficiaries, and a seller may not exclude or limit the extension of those warranties to such persons. *N.J.S.A.* 12A:2–318.

Subject to requirements of good faith, diligence, and reasonableness, parties may vary the terms of the Code. *N.J.S.A.* 12A:1–102. A seller may exclude or modify its liability on warranties, and if in writing, the exclusion or modification must be "conspicuous." *N.J.S.A.* 12A:2–316. Furthermore, a buyer and seller may agree to limit the buyer's remedy to the repair and replacement of parts. *N.J.S.A.* 12A:2–719(1)(a). Similarly, the parties may agree to limit or exclude consequential damages, "unless the limitation or exclusion is unconscionable." *N.J.S.A.* 12A:2–719(3). Although a limitation of consequential damages for personal injuries in the case of consumer goods is *prima facie* unconscionable, a limitation of damages for a commercial loss is not. *Id.*

When a seller delivers goods that are not as warranted, the buyer's measure of damage is the difference between the value of the defective goods and the value they would have had if they had been as warranted. *N.J.S.A.* 12A:2–714. In a proper case, a buyer may also recover incidental damages, which include reasonable expenses incidental to the breach, *N.J.S.A.* 12A:2–

715; consequential damages, including losses resulting from the buyer's particular needs of which the seller had knowledge, *id.* at (2)(a); and property damage, *id.* at (2)(b).

Economic loss can take the form of either direct or consequential damages. A direct economic loss includes the loss of the benefit of the bargain, *i.e.,* the difference between the value of the product as represented and its value in its defective condition. Consequential economic loss includes such indirect losses as lost profits. J. White & R. Summers, *Handbook of the Law Under the Uniform Commercial Code* §§ 11–4 to 11–6 at 405–10 (2d ed. 1980) [hereinafter cited as White & Summers]; Note, "Economic Loss in Products Liability Jurisprudence," 66 *Colum.L.Rev.* 917, 918 (1966); Note, "Manufacturer's Liability to Remote Purchasers for 'Economic Loss' Damages—Tort or Contract?," 114 *U.Pa.L.Rev.* 539, 542 (1966). Because it presents a claim for economic loss, which is not normally recoverable in a tort action, rather than a claim for physical harm, this case probes the boundary between strict liability and the U.C.C. The delineation of that boundary requires a brief summary of the history and nature of strict liability.

One year before the adoption of the U.C.C. in New Jersey, this Court delivered its landmark opinion in *Henningsen v. Bloomfield Motors, Inc.,* 32 *N.J.* 358, 161 *A.*2d 69 (1960). *Henningsen* involved a defective automobile that crashed and caused property damage to the car and personal injuries to the driver, who was the owner's wife. The Court affirmed a judgment in favor of the plaintiffs on the theory of breach of implied warranty of fitness. Justice Francis wrote in now familiar language: "[U]nder modern marketing conditions, when a manufacturer puts a new automobile in the stream of trade and promotes its purchase by the public, an implied warranty that it is reasonably suitable for use as such accompanies it into the hands of the ultimate purchaser." 32 *N.J.* at 384, 161 *A.*2d 69. By extending a warranty of safety to consumers of all products, not just those intended for human consumption, *Henningsen* removed the notion of privity of contract from all cases involving the sale of defective goods that cause physical injury.

Prosser describes the effect of the *Henningsen* holding as "the most rapid and altogether spectacular overturn of an established rule in the entire history of the law of torts." W. Prosser & W. Page Keeton, *Handbook of the Law of Torts* § 97 at 690 (5th ed. 1984) [hereinafter cited as Prosser & Keeton]. Courts throughout the country followed the lead of New Jersey, *id.,* and the American Law Institute (ALI) included a new section, 402A, captioned "Special Liability of Seller of Product for Physical Harm to User or Consumer," in the *Restatement (Second) of Torts.* The comment to section 402A disavows that the section is governed by the warranty provisions of the U.C.C. or by U.C.C. limitations on the scope and content of the warranties.

Underlying the *Henningsen* decision was the Court's recognition that consumers were in an unequal bargaining position with respect to automobile manufacturers and dealers, who required them to sign standard contracts. *Henningsen, supra,* 32 *N.J.* at 389–404, 161 *A.*2d 69. One of the main purposes of strict liability, as declared in *Henningsen,* is the allocation of the risk and distribution of the loss to the better risk-bearer. *Id.* at 379, 161 *A.*2d 69; *Suter v. San Angelo Foundry & Mach. Co.,* 81 *N.J.* 150, 173, 406

*A.*2d 140 (1979). Generally, the manufacturer, who is better able to eliminate defects from its product and who can spread the cost of the risk among all of its customers, is the better risk-bearer. *Restatement, supra,* § 402A comment c. By contrast, the individual consumer is poorly situated to bear the entire risk of loss from injuries caused by a defective product. Through allocation of the risk of loss to the manufacturer, strict liability achieves its objective of protecting the consumer who, because of unequal bargaining power, cannot protect him or herself.

The year after the *Henningsen* decision, 1961, the Legislature adopted the U.C.C., effective January 1, 1963. *L.*1961, *c.* 120. Then in 1965 this Court decided *Santor v. A. & M. Karagheusian, Inc.,* 44 *N.J.* 52, 207 *A.*2d 305, which, like *Henningsen,* involved facts that occurred before the adoption of the U.C.C. In *Santor,* a carpet manufacturer sold a defective carpet to a consumer through its wholly-owned distributor. The Court found that the consumer could recover against the manufacturer, although there was no privity between the parties and the action was for an economic loss.

The action was couched in terms of a breach of implied warranty of merchantability, *id.* at 63, 207 *A.*2d 305, but the Court acknowledged that the action could be described better as one in strict liability. *Id.* at 63–67, 207 *A.*2d 305. In *Santor,* Justice Francis made clear that neither mass advertising by the manufacturer nor personal injuries to the consumer was essential to the invocation of strict liability. *Id.* at 65, 207 *A.*2d 305. Echoing his words in *Henningsen,* he stated that the purpose of a strict-liability action was to shift the risk of loss so that it was borne by "the makers of the products who put them in the channels of trade, rather than by the injured or damaged persons who ordinarily are powerless to protect themselves." *Id.* Like the plaintiff in *Henningsen,* the plaintiff in *Santor* was an individual consumer. Furthermore, the action was for a direct economic loss, and the Court limited recovery to the lost benefit of the bargain, *i.e.,* "the difference between the price paid by the plaintiff and the actual market value of the defective carpeting at the time when plaintiff knew or should have known it was defective * * *." *Id.* at 68–69, 207 *A.*2d 305.

* * *

[The court discussed other New Jersey decisions which held that the tort rather than the UCC statute of limitations governed where a defective product caused damage to person or property.]

As the preceding cases demonstrate, the U.C.C. rules pertaining to the sale of goods overlap the doctrine of strict liability for placing a defective product in the stream of commerce. One reason for the overlap is that strict liability, in this regard, evolved from implied warranties of fitness and merchantability under the U.C.C. and its predecessor, the Uniform Sales Act. Those warranties originated as a matter of social policy to compensate consumers who sustained personal injuries from defective food. Prosser & Keeton, *supra,* § 97 at 690. Neither the ALI, which published the *Restatement (Second) of Torts,* nor the permanent editorial board of the U.C.C., which operates as a joint project of the ALI * * * and the Commissioners on Uniform State Laws, has undertaken to resolve the overlap between strict liability as declared in section 402A and the breach of warranty provisions under the U.C.C. 112 *N.J.L.J.* 700 (1983).

From the perspective of the injured party, strict liability generally provides a more congenial environment than contract principles, which may prevent recovery because of a lack of privity with the manufacturer. In addition to privity, the Code retains two other requirements that may pose considerable obstacles to a buyer. The first requirement is that of notice to a seller of a breach of warranty, *N.J.S.A.* 12A:2–607(3); the second arises from the seller's ability to limit or disclaim liability to an innocent purchaser. *N.J.S.A.* 12A:2–316. A buyer who does not deal directly with a manufacturer cannot negotiate over the terms of a disclaimer and might find it impossible to give the manufacturer notice of the breach of warranty following an injury. Prosser & Keeton, *supra,* § 97 at 691–92. Strict liability, on the other hand, circumvents the technical requirements of the U.C.C. with respect to privity, notice, and limitation of damages. Avoiding those requirements is particularly important for persons outside the distributive chain who sustain physical damage caused by a defective product.

By comparison, the U.C.C. emphasizes the simplification of the law governing commercial transactions and the expansion of commercial practices through agreement. *N.J.S.A.* 12A:1–102. Underlying the U.C.C. policy is the principle that parties should be free to make contracts of their choice, including contracts disclaiming liability for breach of warranty. Once they reach such an agreement, society has an interest in seeing that the agreement is fulfilled. Consequently, the U.C.C. is the more appropriate vehicle for resolving commercial disputes arising out of business transactions between persons in a distributive chain.

The problem is ascertaining where on the spectrum to place a cause of action brought by a commercial entity, or even a consumer, for purely economic loss. One gains perspective by reviewing the decisions of this Court and those of the Supreme Court of California.

As explained earlier, this Court's decision in *Henningsen* was couched in warranty terms. In *Greenman v. Yuba Power Prods., Inc.,* 59 *Cal.*2d 57, 27 *Cal.Rptr.* 697, 701, 377 *P.*2d 897, 901 (1962), which involved personal injuries sustained by a husband from a defective power saw purchased by his wife, the California court drew on *Henningsen,* but declared that the cause of action could be more appropriately denominated as strict liability in tort.

The cross-pollination between the two jurisdictions continued through our *Santor* decision, which relied on *Greenman.* Five months later, however, when the California court was confronted with an individual's claim for economic loss resulting from the purchase of a defective truck, that court rejected *Santor* and held that the consumer could not recover in strict liability for economic loss. *Seely v. White Motor Co.,* 63 *Cal.*2d 9, 45 *Cal.Rptr.* 17, 403 *P.*2d 145 (1965).

In *Seely,* an individual owner-driver purchased a truck for use in his heavy duty hauling business. From the time the purchaser took possession, the truck bounced violently, but the dealer was unable to correct the defect. Thereafter, a brake failure caused the truck to overturn. The truck sustained property damage, and Seely, who stopped making payments after the accident, sued the dealer and the manufacturer for lost profits and the money paid on the purchase price of the truck.

Chief Justice Traynor, writing for the majority of the court, affirmed a judgment for Seely. The absence of privity did not preclude judgment against the manufacturer for the breach of an express warranty that the truck was "free from defects in material and workmanship under normal use and service * * *." *Seely, supra,* 63 *Cal.*2d at 13, 45 *Cal.Rptr.* at 20, 403 *P.*2d at 148. After reaching that result, the court rejected plaintiff's alternative contention of strict liability. The court ruled that in the absence of personal injuries or property damage strict liability was inapplicable. Although the truck had been damaged, the court sustained a finding of the trial court that defendant had not created the defect that caused the damage.

While rejecting plaintiff's right to recover in strict liability, Chief Justice Traynor observed that the law of sales has been carefully articulated to govern economic relationships between suppliers and consumers. He stated further that strict liability was not intended to undermine the warranty provisions of the U.C.C., but "to govern the distinct problem of physical injuries." *Seely, supra,* 63 *Cal.*2d at 15, 45 *Cal.Rptr.* at 21, 403 *P.*2d at 149.

In a concurring and dissenting opinion, Justice Peters embraced *Santor,* and stated that an individual consumer should be allowed to recover in strict liability for economic damages such as those sustained by Seely. *Seely, supra,* 63 *Cal.*2d at 20–22, 45 *Cal.Rptr.* at 25–27, 403 *P.*2d at 153–55. According to Justice Peters, the roles played by the parties and the nature of the transaction, not the nature of the damage, were important. *Id.* He also distinguished transactions involving consumers from those "*within* the world of commerce, where parties generally bargain on a somewhat equal plane and may be presumed to be familiar with the legal problems involved when defective goods are purchased." *Seely, supra,* 63 *Cal.*2d at 27, 45 *Cal.Rptr.* at 29, 403 *P.*2d at 157 (emphasis in original).

* * *

[The court reviewed decisions from other states and the views of commentators, the substantial majority of which favored the result in *Seely* rather than that in *Santor.*]

In the present case, which involves an action between commercial parties, we need not reconsider the *Santor* rule that an ultimate consumer may recover in strict liability for direct economic loss. To determine whether a commercial buyer may recover economic loss, however, we must reconsider the policies underlying the doctrine of strict liability and those underlying the U.C.C. Those policy considerations include, among others, the relative bargaining power of the parties and the allocation of the loss to the better risk-bearer in a modern marketing system. As a general rule, the rights and duties of a buyer and seller are determined by the law of sales, which throughout this century has been expressed first in the Uniform Sales Act and more recently in the U.C.C. As indicated, however, strict liability evolved as a judicial response to inadequacies in sales law with respect to consumers who sustained physical injuries from defective goods made or distributed by remote parties in the marketing chain.

The considerations that give rise to strict liability do not obtain between commercial parties with comparable bargaining power. *Iowa Elec. Light & Power Co. v. Allis-Chalmers Mfg. Co., supra,* 360 *F.Supp.* at 32 (stating doctrine of strict liability loses all meaning when plaintiff is a large company suing for commercial loss). Furthermore, perfect parity is not necessary to a determination that parties have substantially equal bargaining positions. *Cf. Moreira Constr. Co., Inc. v. Moretrench Corp.,* 97 *N.J.Super.* 391, 394–95, 235 *A.*2d 211 (App.Div.1967), *aff'd o.b.,* 51 *N.J.* 405, 241 *A.*2d 236 (1968) (refusing to apply rule of *Santor* to suit between corporations even though plaintiff was a small company and defendant was the world's largest well point company). Suffice it to state that Spring Motors had sufficient bargaining power to persuade Ford to install Clark transmissions in the trucks that were the subject of the contract.

Insofar as risk allocation and distribution are concerned, Spring Motors is at least as well situated as the defendants to assess the impact of economic loss. Indeed, a commercial buyer, such as Spring Motors, may be better situated than the manufacturer to factor into its price the risk of economic loss caused by the purchase of a defective product. *See* Note, "Economic Loss in Products Liability Jurisprudence," *supra,* 66 *Colum.L.Rev.* at 952–58.

Presumably the price paid by Spring Motors for the trucks reflected the fact that Ford was liable for repair or replacement of parts only. By seeking to impose the risk of loss on Ford, Spring Motors seeks, in effect, to obtain a better bargain than it made. In such a context, the imposition of the risk of loss on the manufacturer might lead to price increases for all of its customers, including individual consumers. *Id.* at 956–57. As between commercial parties, then, the allocation of risks in accordance with their agreement better serves the public interest than an allocation achieved as a matter of policy without reference to that agreement.

Delineation of the boundary between strict liability and the U.C.C. requires appreciation not only of the policy considerations underlying both sets of principles, but also of the role of the Legislature as a coordinate branch of government. By enacting the U.C.C., the Legislature adopted a carefully-conceived system of rights and remedies to govern commercial transactions. Allowing Spring Motors to recover from Ford under tort principles would dislocate major provisions of the Code. For example, application of tort principles would obviate the statutory requirement that a buyer give notice of a breach of warranty, *N.J.S.A.* 12A:2–607, and would deprive the seller of the ability to exclude or limit its liability, *N.J.S.A.* 12A:2–316. In sum, the U.C.C. represents a comprehensive statutory scheme that satisfies the needs of the world of commerce, and courts should pause before extending judicial doctrines that might dislocate the legislative structure.

By allowing this case to proceed under strict liability principles, the Appellate Division erred, * * * it relied too heavily on *Santor,* which did not consider the effect of the U.C.C. on a commercial transaction.

* * *

For the preceding reasons, we hold that a commercial buyer seeking damages for economic loss only should proceed under the U.C.C. against parties in the chain of distribution. Hence, we reverse that part of the judgment of the Appellate Division that permitted Spring Motors to maintain against the defendants an action in strict liability for economic loss.

III

What we have said about Spring Motors' strict liability claim applies substantially to its negligence claim. Underlying that conclusion is the principle that a seller's duty of care generally stops short of creating a right in a commercial buyer to recover a purely economic loss. Thus viewed, the definition of the seller's duty reflects a policy choice that economic losses inflicted by a seller of goods are better resolved under principles of contract law. In that context, economic interests traditionally have not been entitled to protection against mere negligence.

* * *

Although the nature of the damage may be a useful point of distinction, it also signals more subtle differences in the roles that tort and contract play in our legal system. The differences include judicial evaluation of the status, relationship, and expectations of the parties; the ability of the parties to protect themselves against the risk of loss either by contractual provision or by insurance, and the manner in which the loss occurred. *See Pennsylvania Glass Sand Corp. v. Caterpillar Tractor Co.,* 652 *F.*2d 1165, 1173 (3rd Cir.1981) (allowing recovery for damage to defective machinery resulting from fire caused by defect). This evaluation reflects, among other things, policy choices about the relative roles of contracts and tort law as sources of legal obligations. As among commercial parties in a direct chain of distribution, contract law, expressed here through the U.C.C., provides the more appropriate system for adjudicating disputes arising from frustrated economic expectations.

* * *

It follows from our determination that Spring Motors should be restricted to its U.C.C. remedies as against Ford and Turnpike Ford that the appropriate statute of limitations is the four-year time bar contained in *N.J.S.A.* 12A:2–725. More than four years elapsed between the date of the delivery of the trucks and the institution of this action against Ford and Turnpike Ford. Consequently, Spring Motors' suit against them is time-barred.

We also conclude that Spring Motors should be restricted to its U.C.C. remedies against Clark, which are time-barred because of the expiration of the four-year period of limitations provided by the Code. The trial court dismissed Spring Motors' warranty claim against Clark not because of late filing, but because of lack of privity, and the Appellate Division affirmed the dismissal of the warranty claim. 191 *N.J.Super.* at 48, 465 *A.*2d 530. Spring Motors did not cross-petition for certification on that issue and has not pursued it before us. Nonetheless, as we subsequently explain, we conclude that the better rule is to restrict parties that are part of a single distributive chain to the U.C.C. in a suit for economic loss arising out of a commercial transaction. Prosser & Keeton, *supra,* § 101 at 708.

We conclude that the absence of privity between a remote supplier and an ultimate purchaser should not preclude the extension to the purchaser of the supplier's warranties made to the manufacturer. We reach that conclusion notwithstanding our recognition that the Code generally applies to parties in privity, *Herbstman v. Eastman Kodak Co.,* 68 *N.J.* 1, 9–10, 342 *A.*2d 181 (1975); *Heavner v. Uniroyal, Inc., supra,* 63 *N.J.* at 150, 305 *A.*2d 412, and that no privity exists between Spring Motors and Clark.

Privity, the relationship between two contracting parties, developed as a means of limiting relief on warranties. At this late date, little purpose would be served by a lengthy discussion of the erosion of privity as a defense in modern products liability law. * * *

More recently, strict liability in New Jersey has evolved as a means of permitting a consumer to recover for physical damage and direct economic loss against a remote seller, notwithstanding the absence of privity. Insofar as indirect economic losses arising out of a commercial transaction between business entities are concerned, we believe that the U.C.C., not tort law, provides the more appropriate analytical framework. By recognizing the supervening role of the U.C.C. in that context, we come closer to fulfilling the expectations of the parties and the intent of the Legislature. The intended effect of our decision is to satisfy the combined, if occasionally contending, goals of simplifying the law pertaining to business transactions and providing a system of compensation that responds to the needs of the commercial world.

Fundamental to our decision is the role of privity in modern business law, a role that is often described in terms of vertical and horizontal relationships. A vertical relationship describes one that exists between parties in a distributive chain, *i.e.,* between a manufacturer, wholesaler, retailer, and ultimate buyer. A buyer within this chain that did not buy goods directly from the named defendant would be a "vertical non-privity plaintiff" as to that defendant. 2 Hawkland, *supra,* § 2–318:01 at 419; White & Summers, *supra,* § 11–2 at 399. Here, Spring Motors, which purchased the trucks from Ford, is in vertical privity with the Ford defendants, but not with Clark. Thus, Spring Motors is a vertical non-privity plaintiff as to Clark.

"Horizontal non-privity," on the other hand, describes the relationship between the retailer and someone, other than the buyer, who has used or consumed the goods. For example, in an action against a retailer, a "horizontal non-privity plaintiff" would refer to the buyer's spouse or child, but not to the buyer. White & Summers, *supra,* § 11–2 at 399.

In drafting the U.C.C., the Commissioners on Uniform State Laws acknowledged the decline of horizontal privity as a defense to an action for personal injuries caused by the purchase of defective goods. Consequently, section 318, adopted in New Jersey as *N.J.S.A.* 12A:2–318 and now identified as "Alternative A," extends warranties horizontally to "any natural person who is in the family or household of [the] buyer or who is a guest in his home if it is reasonable to expect that such person may use, consume, or be affected by the goods and who is injured in person by breach of the warranty." With respect to vertical privity, the drafters specifically state that the section is "neutral and is not intended to enlarge or restrict the developing case law on whether the seller's warranties, given to his buyer who resells, extend to other persons in the distributive chain." Official Comment 3, § 2–318.

Courts in some states that have adopted Alternative A, however, have abolished the requirement of horizontal privity and allowed "any person," natural or legal, to sue a party in the distributive chain for breach of warranty. *See, e.g., Salvador v. Atlantic Steel Boiler Co.,* 457 *Pa.* 24, 26, 319 *A.*2d 903, 904 (1974) (lack of horizontal privity may no longer bar the plaintiff from recovering for personal injuries under breach of warranty); *JKT Co., Inc. v. Hardwick,* 274 *S.C.* 413, 416, 265 *S.E.*2d 510, 512 (1980) (no valid reason exists for distinguishing between consumer plaintiffs and corporate plaintiffs on the issue of horizontal privity).

In other states, legislatures have refused to adopt Alternative A. California was the first to criticize the section as "a step backward" and to omit the section from its version of the Code. Permanent Editorial Board note, following Official Comment to section 2–318. Still other states developed variants of section 318. In 1966, to stem the proliferation of non-uniform provisions, the members of the Permanent Editorial Board of the U.C.C. recommended Alternatives B and C. *Id.;* 3 Anderson, *Uniform Commercial Code UCC,* § 2–318:2 at 400 (3rd ed.1983) [hereinafter cited as Anderson]. Respectively, these alternatives provide that:

ALTERNATIVE B

> A seller's warranty whether express or implied extends to any natural person who may reasonably be expected to use, consume or be affected by the goods and who is injured in person by breach of the warranty. A seller may not exclude or limit the operation of this section.

ALTERNATIVE C

> A seller's warranty whether express or implied extends to any person who may reasonably be expected to use, consume or be affected by the goods and who is injured by breach of the warranty. A seller may not exclude or limit the operation of this section with respect to injury of the person of an individual to whom the warranty extends.

Alternatives B and C go beyond Alternative A in eroding the privity defense. Alternative C, for example, allows "any person" on the horizontal level, including a corporation, to sue for breach of warranty. *Cf. N.J.S.A.* 12A:1–201(30) (defining person as an individual or an organization) and *N.J.S.A.* 12A:1–201(28) (defining organization as including a corporation). Some treatises declare that Alternative C eliminates the requirement of vertical privity, 2 Hawkland, *supra,* § 2–318:04 at 430; Anderson, *supra,* § 2–318:31 at 417, but another text disagrees, White & Summers, *supra,* §§ 11–5 to –6 at 406–10.

The Permanent Editorial Board's comment on Alternative C states that the section reflects "the trend of more recent decisions as indicated by Restatement of Torts 2d § 402A * * *, extending the rule beyond personal injuries." As previously indicated, in most jurisdictions section 402A precludes claims for economic loss. In New Jersey, however, a consumer may recover direct economic loss in a strict liability action against a remote supplier. *Santor v. A & M Karagheusian, Inc., supra,* 44 *N.J.* 52, 207 *A.*2d 305. Because the Code provides the more appropriate framework for resolving disputes between commercial entities, we eschew permitting recovery by a business entity for economic loss under principles of strict liability. Nonetheless, it is consistent with the principles underlying *Santor* and with the intent of the Code's drafters to recognize a claim under the U.C.C. for economic loss in a breach of warranty action without regard to vertical privity.

Furthermore, a plaintiff in a suit for breach of warranty against a remote seller, like a plaintiff in a strict liability action, need not establish privity with or negligence by the defendant. To this extent, our recognition of a warranty action for economic loss by a commercial buyer parallels our recognition in *Santor* of a similar claim by a consumer. One significant difference, of course, is that the plaintiff in a warranty action need not establish the existence of a defect; the failure of the goods to perform as warranted is sufficient. By bringing the action within the ambit of the Code, we believe we come closer to fulfilling the expectations of the parties and the intention of the Legislature that the Code should govern commercial transactions.

* * *

Eliminating the requirement of vertical privity is particularly appropriate in the present action where Spring Motors read advertisements published by Clark, specifically requested Clark transmissions, expected the transmissions to be incorporated into trucks to be manufactured by Ford, contracted with Ford only, and now seeks to recover its economic loss. Given the nature of the transaction and the expectations of the parties, the absence of a direct contractual relationship should not preclude Spring Motors from asserting a cause of action for breach of express warranty against Clark. Because the Code, not principles of tort law, governs the relationship between Spring Motors and Clark, the appropriate period of limitations is that provided by the Code. As previously indicated, the expiration of this period bars Spring Motors' claim against Clark.

Because any action by Spring Motors against Clark is time-barred, we need not determine the outer limits of a suit by an ultimate purchaser against a remote supplier for economic loss. Therefore, we reserve determination on the effectiveness of a remote manufacturer's disclaimer or limitation on express and implied warranties to an ultimate purchaser that did not have the opportunity to negotiate over the terms of the agreement. *N.J.S.A.* 12A:2–316: *N.J.S.A.* 12A:2–719. White & Summers, *supra,* § 11–6 at 409 (the extent to which a remote seller may disclaim warranties is an unresolved issue). We note, however, that in certain circumstances a buyer may recover incidental and consequential damages. *N.J.S.A.* 12A:2–715. We also leave unreviewed the Code requirement that a purchaser notify the seller about the defective condition of the product. *N.J.S.A.* 12A:2–607(3). Similarly, we do not resolve whether a warranty of fitness for a particular purpose, unlike an implied warranty of merchantability, extends only to parties in privity with the seller. *See Pawelec v. Digitcom, Inc.,* 192 *N.J.Super.* 474, 477–78, 471 *A.*2d 60 (App.Div.1984) (holding that implied warranty of fitness for a particular purpose, unlike implied warranty of merchantability, requires privity). For our purposes, it is sufficient to acknowledge that a commercial buyer in a distributive chain may maintain an action under the U.C.C. for purely economic loss arising out of a breach of warranty by a remote supplier.

Accordingly, we reverse the judgment of the Appellate Division and reinstate the dismissal of the complaint as to all defendants.

* * *

[Justice Handler concurred in the result. He concluded that the Court's ruling on privity was, in essence, dictum because of the interaction between Clark and Spring Motors, both before and after the purchase. In short, the privity ruling was attenuated. In addition, he expressed reservations about whether Spring Motors, a commercial buyer, needed the extra protection, when it was capable of bargaining with the dealer or Ford. Although an imbalance in capacity between even commercial parties might justify a direct suit against the manufacturer, no such imbalance was evident in this case.]

Problem 20–6

Suppose, in *Spring Motors,* that the transmissions manufactured by Clark were unmerchantable, UCC 2–314(2). Furthermore, assume that Spring Motors had purchased the trucks from Ford without knowing whose transmissions would be used and, after the problems arose, Ford not Clark made all efforts to "cure." Finally, assume that Spring Motors suffered substantial direct and consequential economic loss caused by the transmissions.

1. Under the reasoning in Spring Motors, can Spring Motors sue Clark under a warranty theory for economic losses caused by the unmerchantable transmissions? Why?

2. If the privity defense is no bar, which if any of Article 2's limitations upon warranty claims should apply to Spring Motors?

Problem 20–7

B, a commercial fisherman, owns a fishing vessel powered by two diesel engines. B needs extra power to reach distant fishing grounds and to operate gear designed for dragging the bottom. S, a dealer, recently sold and installed a new diesel engine in the boat. The engine was manufactured by M but B dealt only with S, who knew B's particular needs, and relied upon S to obtain a suitable engine. In the contract for sale, however, S limited its liability for any breach of warranty to repair and replacement of defective parts and excluded any liability for consequential damages. Assume that this limitation is effective between S and B. M, in turn, had limited its liability to S in a similar manner.

Shortly thereafter, when B was on the fishing grounds some 60 miles from port, a loud "crack" was heard and smoke poured from the new engine. The engine was quickly shut down and, although the smoke stopped, the engine would not start. When B returned to port, limping under one engine, S discovered that a defective part, manufactured by C, had disintegrated within, and had caused substantial damage to, the engine. Furthermore, B learned that he had missed a "truly remarkable" run on King Crabs at the spot where the engine malfunctioned.

S informed B that the entire engine should be replaced and that this form of "cure" was beyond the scope of the limited warranty.

1. Assess the strength of B's warranty claims, if any, against M and C.

2. Would B have a tort claim against either or both? What difference would it make?

Note: Scope and Effect of the "Economic Loss" Doctrine.

In drawing the line between contract and tort, *Spring Motors* applied the so-called "economic loss" doctrine. If the nonconforming goods, no matter how dangerous, cause only economic loss to the buyer, i.e., loss of bargain damages, whether direct or consequential, then Article 2 with its contract limitations rather than the law of torts applies. In commercial cases at least, the courts have enthusiastically endorsed this method of line drawing.

Suppose, however, that the nonconforming goods cause damage to other property of the buyer. If the "other" property is the goods in which a nonconforming component is installed (the *Spring Motors* facts), most courts, influenced by the Supreme Court's *East River Steamship* decision, East River Steamship Corp. v. Transamerica Delaval, Inc., 476 U.S. 858, 106 S.Ct. 2295, 90 L.Ed.2d 865 (1986), have still applied the "economic loss" doctrine. See, e.g., Midwhey Powder Co., Inc. v. Clayton Industries, 157 Wis.2d 585, 460 N.W.2d 426 (App. 1990) ("other" property does not include property so integrally connected to the product as to be a component part). Thus, if a defective blade in a turbine tears loose during operation and seriously damages the turbine, buyer is limited to a warranty theory. On the other hand, if the turbine, shaken by the accident, collapses and damages other property, a tort theory is available. Why this is so tends to defy rational explanation. In short, the line drawn is clear but somewhat arbitrary.

The effect of this somewhat arbitrary line is that a commercial buyer, in "economic loss" cases, is stuck with warranty theory under Article 2, including the "tolling" statute of limitations in UCC 2–725 and the requirement of privity of contract, unless UCC 2–318 or a court dispenses with the need for privity. To date, the *Spring Motors* decision goes as far as any in dispensing with the privity requirement in "economic loss" cases where commercial buyers are involved.

Here are some questions.

1. If, in an economic loss case, tort law is not available and privity is required, are the buyer's expectations adequately protected if its remedies are limited to the immediate seller? Is there a dubious gap in protection if the buyer cannot sue the manufacturer, who is arguably in the best position cost considered either to prevent the nonconformity or insure against the loss or to allocate the risk by agreement? One of your co-authors would argue "yes."

2. Under what circumstances should advertising by a manufacturer about a product become part of the basis of the bargain between a remote buyer and a retailer? Is it sufficient that the advertising would be an "affirmation of fact" under UCC 2–313(1) and that buyer purchased the product? Or, must the buyer also be aware of the advertising? Rely on it? Review the Note on the Cigarette litigation, supra at p. 855.

3. What are the strongest arguments for abolishing the privity requirement in cases where a manufacturer distributes unmerchantable goods and they are purchased by a remote buyer from a dealer? Does the manufacturer, by the

product description and the price charge, represent that the goods are fit for ordinary purposes?

4. If privity is not required and a remote buyer sues a manufacturer for breach of warranty, what complications arise in applying Article 2? For example, must the buyer give notice to the manufacturer under UCC 2–607(3)(a)? When does the statute of limitations begin to run? Can the buyer revoke acceptance against the manufacturer? What price is appropriate for measuring damages, the price at which the manufacturer sold the goods to the dealer or the price the dealer charged to the buyer? Obviously, there is some confusion here that a revision of Article 2 will have to clarify.

CHAPTER TWENTY-ONE

BUYER'S REMEDIES FOR BREACH OF WARRANTY FOR ACCEPTED GOODS UNDER THE CODE AND PER AGREEMENT (HEREIN, TOO, OF DISCLAIMERS)

SECTION 1. INTRODUCTION

First, some words in summary. If the commercial buyer can establish that a warranty was made and breached, the timing of that discovery will be critical to the available remedy choices. If the breach was discovered before acceptance, then rejection may be a proper remedy. UCC 2–601. If the breach was discovered after acceptance and the buyer acts fast, a revocation of acceptance may be proper under UCC 2–608. In both cases, the goods are "thrown back" at the seller. Unless the seller has a right to cure under UCC 2–508 or under the contract, the seller is basically responsible for disposing of the goods and the buyer may shoot for the remedies contained in UCC 2–711.

But our buyer may never reach this position, either because it wants to accept the goods despite their defects, or because it is unable to reject or revoke acceptance, or because the breach may have rendered the goods worthless. What then? Again, if the buyer has given proper notice under UCC 2–607(3), initiated suit before the statute of limitations expires, UCC 2–725, and established that a warranty was made to him and breached, the remedies for breach with regard to accepted goods are available. See UCC 2–714 & 2–715.

In this Chapter, we will, first, explore the scope of protection under these sections. Next we will consider the extent to which the seller can, by agreement with the buyer, disclaim warranties under UCC 2–316 and alter remedies and exclude consequential damages under UCC 2–719.

SECTION 2. THE DIRECT DAMAGE FORMULA: UCC 2–714

UCC 2–714, entitled "Buyer's Damages for Breach in Regard to Accepted Goods," is a functional counterpart of UCC 2–712 and UCC 2–713. All three sections attempt to preserve the benefit of the buyer's bargain with the seller. See UCC 1–106(1). Under UCC 2–714, however, the buyer still has the goods and is liable for their price, UCC 2–607(1), & 2–719(1)(a), subject to the power, upon notice to the seller, to "deduct all or any part of the damages resulting from any breach of the contract from any part of the price still due under the same contract." UCC 2–717. Furthermore, UCC 2–714 is somewhat open-ended and difficult to apply with precision. For example:

1. UCC 2–714(2) provides the measure of damages for breach of warranty. To what disputes does UCC 2–714(1) apply? How does one determine what losses resulted "in the ordinary course of events from the seller's breach as determined by any manner which is reasonable?"

2. In UCC 2–714(2), how does the buyer prove the "difference at the time and place of acceptance between the value of goods accepted and the value they would have had if they had been as warranted?"

3. In UCC 2–714(2), what "special circumstances" show proximate damages of a different amount?

4. How is the line between "direct" damages under UCC 2–714(2) and "incidental and consequential damages" under UCC 2–715 to be drawn?

Problem 21–1

1. Sunshine Cannery contracted on May 1 to purchase 10,000 bushels of # 1 grade tomatoes for $10 a bushel from Seller, a grower. The market price at that time was $8 a bushel. On August 10, the time for delivery, Seller tendered 10,000 bushels of # 2 grade tomatoes. Caught at the end of the canning season, Sunshine accepted the goods. The market value of the tomatoes accepted was $7 per bushel. The market value of # 1 grade tomatoes was $9 per bushel. Seller claims the contract price of $100,000. What damages may Sunshine deduct under UCC 2–714(2)?

2. Assume, above, that at the time of acceptance # 1 tomatoes had risen in value to $12 per bushel and # 2 tomatoes were worth $9 per bushel. What damages?

3. Suppose, in (1) above, the Seller tendered and Sunshine accepted what passed in the trade as # 1 tomatoes. Upon unpacking, however, the entire lot was found to be decayed and suffering from the notorious Law School Rot. Sunshine salvaged the lot for $1,000 and replaced it from another grower for $13 per bushel. What damages? Should Sunshine recover the difference between the replacement cost and the salvage value?

SOO LINE RAILROAD CO. v. FRUEHAUF CORP.

United States Court of Appeals, Eighth Circuit, 1977.
547 F.2d 1365.

[Fruehauf agreed to manufacture, sell and deliver 500 railroad hopper cars to Soo Line for the approximate price of $9,750,000. After delivery, Soo Line discovered cracks in the structure and weld of many cars. Fruehauf refused to repair, claiming it had no responsibility for the alleged defects, and Soo implemented its own program of repair at a total cost of $506,-862.78. Soo Line brought suit on the theories of breach of warranty and negligence. The jury found for Soo Line on the warranty theory and the trial court ruled as a matter of law that certain contract provisions were ineffective to limit Fruehauf's liability. The jury, in a special verdict, awarded Soo Line $975,970 "for the difference between the value of the cars as accepted and their value if built to conform to the contract specifications" and additional amounts for consequential and incidental damages. The verdict on the "difference in value" issue reflected that Soo Line's repairs "did not fully restore the cars to totally acceptable operating condition." Fruehauf appealed. The trial court's judgment was affirmed.]

STEPHENSON, CIRCUIT JUDGE.

* * *

III.

The third issue in this appeal is whether the district court erred in allowing the testimony of T.R. Klingel, an expert witness who testified with respect to the diminution in value of the railroad cars resulting from their structural collapse. In general, Klingel expressed the opinion that the market value of the railcars as actually constructed was approximately $1,000,000 or $2,000 per car less than the value of the cars had they been built in accordance with the contract.

Klingel, who is executive vice president of Soo Line, testified initially that the market value of the railcars had they been constructed according to the contract would have approximated their purchase price of $19,500 per car. He further expressed the opinion, over Magor's objection, that the fair market value of the cars as actually constructed was at the most $17,500 per car. Klingel's opinion, as to the diminution in fair market value of the railcars, basically derived from his viewpoint that a hypothetical buyer of the cars would be confronted with immediate and substantial expenditures for repair and continuation of financing costs without any concomitant receipt of revenue while the railcars were out of service being repaired, and even after the repairs the buyer would possess rebuilt and patched cars worth less than those properly constructed.

Appellant contends that the trial court erred in allowing Klingel's testimony on damages. In Magor's view, Klingel was not qualified to provide expert opinion on the necessity and cost of repair because he allegedly did not possess sufficient practical or technical knowledge. Magor asserts additionally that Klingel's prediction of future maintenance costs was speculatively improper without proof that such damages are reasonably certain to occur. Finally, Magor claims that Klingel's reliance on financing costs as a basis for damages erroneously resulted in a duplicate consequential damage award for revenue lost while the railcars were being repaired.

The trial court's determination that Klingel possessed adequate qualifications, pursuant to Fed.R.Evid. 702, to testify with respect to the diminished market value of the railcars was not an abuse of discretion or clear error of law. * * * Fed.R.Evid. 702 is not limited to experts in the strictest sense of the word but also encompasses a large group called "skilled" witnesses, such as owners, bankers, and landowners testifying on the value of property. * * *

Klingel's responsibilities as Soo Line's executive vice president included overseeing the operations of all trains and the maintenance of all rolling stock and fixed property. He also was charged with determination of the market value of the railroad's rolling stock. Klingel was directly familiar with the railcars manufactured by Magor, and he collaborated closely with Soo Line's mechanical department and H.D. Hollis concerning the problematic conditions in the Magor-constructed railcars. In some instances, Klingel conducted personal inspections of the railcars. Klingel's knowledge was such that his opinion on valuation most likely assisted the trier of fact in arriving at the truth. * * *

In reviewing the substance of Klingel's testimony on valuation, the measure of damages and the limits of relevancy are set by the substantive law of Minnesota. See Johnson v. Serra, 521 F.2d 1289, 1294 (8th Cir.1975). Under Minnesota law, the measure of damages applicable to breach of contract is the difference between the actual value of the cars at the time of acceptance and the value they would have had if they had been as warranted. Minn.Stat.Ann. § 336.2–714(2). * * * The buyer is not limited to repair costs when repair does not completely restore the goods to the value which they would have had if built in conformity with the contract; remaining diminution in value may also be recovered. * * *

Taking into consideration the structural and welding defects existing in the cars manufactured for Soo Line by Magor, Klingel expressed the opinion that the reasonable market value per car was $17,500 at the most. Klingel further opined that he would probably discount the purchase price of the cars by an additional $1,000 or $2,000, which would result in a fair market value of approximately $15,500 per car.

In formulating the diminution in fair market value of the cars, Klingel properly placed reliance on the necessity for present and future repairs and the fact that even a rebuilt patched railcar would be worth less than a correctly constructed one. * * * The record reflects that approximately $1,000 per car in immediate repair costs was expended by Soo Line and that, even after implementation of the repairs, Soo Line had experienced continued maintenance costs beyond those expended for cars other than those manufactured by Magor.

Klingel also stated that a hypothetical buyer of the railcars would discount the purchase price because the buyer's financing costs would continue while the cars were out of service being repaired with no ability to generate revenue. Klingel testified that approximately $200,000 and $400 per car in interest payments would be lost without concomitant benefit during repairs. This statement, of course, may not be considered as evidence of diminution in value of the Soo Line railcars. Cost of financing is not an element of reduced market value pursuant to Minn.Stat.Ann. § 336.2–714. Nonetheless, we reject appellant's contention that this aspect of Klingel's testimony rendered inadmissible his overall opinion on the diminution in market value of the railcars. An objection that an expert's opinion is based on elements of damage not lawfully recoverable generally relates to the weight rather than the admissibility of the testimony. * * *

In addition, the trial court carefully instructed the jury with respect to this element of damages. It stated in part as follows:

> "The measure of damages is, generally speaking, the difference between the fair market value of the cars as accepted by Soo Line, and the fair market value they would have had if they had not been deficient in the particulars in which you found them deficient. This is called the difference or diminution in value approach.
>
> * * *
>
> "If you find that the repair of the cars restored the cars to substantially the same condition as they would have been in if properly

manufactured, the difference or diminution value is the same as the reasonable cost of repairing the cars.

"So, if the repair costs actually restored them then the repair cost would equal the diminution in value. However, if you find that the repair of the cars did not restore them to substantially the same condition as they would have been if properly manufactured, then the difference or diminution in value is the reasonable cost of repair, plus the difference between the fair market value of the covered hopper cars if they had been manufactured without faults or defects, and the fair market value of the repairs.

"The total figure, however, cannot exceed the difference between the fair market value as accepted, and the fair market value in the defective condition you find.

"* * * [The court then gave an illustration.]

"Therefore, if you find that the repairs of the cars placed the cars in a better condition than they would have been at the time of acceptance if they had been properly manufactured, then the difference or diminution in value recoverable by plaintiffs is the difference between the fair market value of the covered hopper cars as accepted by Soo Line and the fair market value they would have had if Magor had manufactured them properly. So, Soo Line in this situation would not be able to recover the full amount spent for repairs.

"In the course of the charge and the special verdict you will find use of the word value. Value is described as the highest price in terms of money for which a product would have sold on the open market, the seller having a reasonable time within which to sell and being willing to sell but not forced to do so; the buyer being ready, willing and able to buy, but not forced to do so, and a full opportunity to inspect the property in question and to determine its condition, suitability for use, and all things about the property that would naturally and reasonably affect its market value."

Moreover, there is sufficient evidence in the record upon which the jury could have relied in awarding $975,970 or $1,951.94 per car, approximately 10% of their original cost, for diminution in market value of the cars. It cannot be said that the verdict constituted a shocking result. * * *

For similar reasons, we reject appellant's assertion that Klingel's reference to "future maintenance costs" was unduly speculative and erroneous. Klingel merely expressed an opinion on the present value of the railcars at the time of acceptance in light of known risks associated with existing defects. Soo Line had already experienced increased maintenance costs with Magor cars previously repaired. Klingel's testimony overall had sufficient probative value to outweigh the danger that it would lead the jury to assess damages on an improper basis. * * * Magor had adequate opportunity to cross-examine and refute Klingel's testimony on valuation. * * * Under these circumstances, we conclude that the trial court did not commit an abuse of discretion in the admission of Klingel's testimony concerning the diminution in market value of the railroad cars resulting from their structural failure.

* * *

[Footnotes omitted]

Note

The buyer's cost to repair accepted, non-conforming goods is a common method to measure damages under UCC 2–714(2). See Schroeder v. Barth, Inc., 969 F.2d 421 (7th Cir.1992) (cost to repair is the preferred method). This is the functional substitute for "cover" under UCC 2–712, which is not available. But how much can the buyer spend? Assuming that the repair costs are otherwise reasonable, suppose that when combined with the value of the goods actually delivered they exceed the contract price? Would compensating the buyer in that situation put it in a better position than full performance? UCC 1–106(1). In Perth Amboy Iron Works, Inc. v. American Home Assur. Co., 226 N.J.Super. 200, 543 A.2d 1020 (1988) the court found "special circumstances" from latent defects which the buyer found piecemeal over time and rejected the contract price as a limitation on recovery.

Problem 21–2

In July, 1993, CRN Corporation sold Burgess Industries a computer system for $85,000, including a three year service contract. The system, called a CRN 400, consisted of computer hardware valued at $50,000 and six computer software programs, valued at $20,000. The sale followed an extensive analysis of Burgess's computer needs and was induced by CRN's written representation that the CRN 400 would meet all of Burgess's needs.

By December, 1993, it was clear that the CRN 400 met only 40% of those needs and that CRN would be unable to improve its performance. Frustrated, Burgess consulted a computer expert who concluded that the CRN 400 was not capable of meeting those computer needs. In her opinion, the only system with that capability was a CRN 1500 or a comparable system made by others for a price of $250,000. Burgess, after consulting with counsel, offered to settle the dispute by exchanging the CRN 400, which had hardly been used, for a CRN 1500. CRN refused. Next, Burgess presented a claim for damages under UCC 2–714(2), measured by the difference in value between the CRN 400 and a CRN 1500 or equal. Burgess claimed that this amount was $210,000, since the value of a CRN 1500 was $250,000 and the value of the CRN 400, which could only meet 40% of Burgess's needs, was $40,000.

CRN rejected this claim for the following reasons:

(1) The value of the CRN as warranted cannot exceed the contract price;

(2) Burgess must value the "goods as accepted" under UCC 2–714(2), not another or a hypothetical computer system. See also, UCC 2–712(1); and

(3) The award of $210,000 in damages would put Burgess in a better position than if CRN had fully performed and, therefore, constitute improper punitive damages. See UCC 1–106(1).

What arguments should Burgess make in reply? How should the court decide?

HILL v. BASF WYANDOTTE CORP.

Supreme Court of South Carolina, 1984.
280 S.C. 174, 311 S.E.2d 734.

LITTLEJOHN, JUSTICE:

This case comes before us as a certified question from the United States District Court, District of South Carolina, pursuant to Supreme Court Rule 46.

The question presented is as follows:

> Given the distinction between (1) actual or direct and (2) consequential damages as set forth in §§ 36–2–714 and 36–2–715 of the South Carolina Code of Laws, 1976, as amended, what is the measure of actual damages in a herbicide failure case where there is a valid limitation of consequential, special or indirect damages?

This is a breach of warranty case involving an alleged herbicide failure which caused crop damage.

Plaintiff Hill (Farmer) purchased a quantity of the herbicide, Basalin, from a retail distributor. Basalin is manufactured by defendant BASF Wyandotte Corporation (BWC).

Among other things, to each can of Basalin there were attached the following statements:

1) "BWC" warrants that this product conforms to the chemical description on the label and is reasonably fit for the purpose referred to in the Directions for Use subject to the inherent risks referred to above,
2) In no case shall "BWC" or the Seller be liable for consequential, special or indirect damages resulting from the use or handling of this product, and
3) Read "CONDITIONS OF SALE AND WARRANTY" before buying or using. If terms are not acceptable, return product at once, unopened.

Farmer alleges that he used Basalin on approximately 1,450 acres of soybeans and another herbicide, Treflan, on approximately 200 acres. He further alleges that although there was a severe drought that year, the Treflan treated crops were significantly better than the Basalin crops both in quality and yield per acre.

Farmer initially brought suit in United States District Court on oral and written warranties for damages. A jury awarded him $207,725.00. BWC appealed and the Fourth Circuit Court of Appeals reversed and remanded the case, holding that only the written warranties on the labels of the product apply and that the limitation of remedies quoted above is valid. *Hill v. BASF Wyandotte Corp.*, 696 F.2d 287 (4th Cir.1982).

In footnote 6 the court stated:

> We express no opinion as to whether under subsections (1) and (2) of § 36–2–714 and on the evidence that may be adduced on retrial the appropriate measure of damages would be the purchase price of the herbicide or some other measure.

This question was certified to us by the trial court after remand.

Ordinarily, *S.C.Code Ann.* § 36–2–714(2) (1976) is controlling as the measure of damages in a breach of warranty case. This section provides:

> (2) The measure of damages for breach of warranty is the difference at the time and place of acceptance between the value of the goods accepted and the value they would have had if they had been as warranted, *unless special circumstances show proximate damages of a different amount.* (Emphasis added.)

We find that the formula in this subsection is inapplicable to a herbicide failure case. This formula is most appropriate where the nonconforming good can be repaired or replaced and value (both as warranted and as accepted) can be defined with certainty.

A herbicide failure is a latent defect in the product. There is no reasonable way a farmer can determine in advance whether a herbicide will perform as warranted. Discovery of the problem must await the development of the crop at which time it is usually too late to correct.

The value of a herbicide as warranted is difficult to define. Price and value are not equivalents. From the farmer's perspective, the value of the herbicide is a healthy crop at maturity. In the manufacturer's viewpoint, the value is its selling price.

The value as accepted is equally uncertain and difficult to define. There is no market for such goods and thus no market price. If anything, it has a negative value.

In our view, the inability of a court to ascertain with certainty the value of goods both as warranted and as accepted creates a special circumstance within the meaning of § 36–2–714(2). It is this special circumstance which removes cases of this type from the § 36–2–714(2) measure of damages into subsection (1).

Subsection (1) provides:

> (1) Where the buyer has accepted goods and given notification (subsection (3) of § 36–2–607) he may recover as damages for any nonconformity of tender the loss resulting in the ordinary course of events from the seller's breach as determined in any manner which is reasonable.

Official Comment 2 to § 36–2–714 indicates that subsection (1) is applicable in breach of warranty cases.

It has consistently been held by this Court that the measure of actual damages, in cases similar to this, is the value the crop would have had if the product had conformed to the warranty less the value of the crop actually produced, less the expense of preparing for market the portion of the probable crop prevented from maturing. *See, McCown Clark Co. v. Muldrow,* 116 S.C. 54, 106 S.E. 771 (1929); *Amerson v. F.C.X. Co-Op Service,* 227 S.C. 520, 88 S.E.2d 605 (1955); *W.R. Grace and Co. v. LaMunion,* 245 S.C. 1, 138 S.E.2d 337 (1964) and *Simmons v. Ciba-Geigy Corp.,* 279 S.C. 26, 302 S.E.2d 17 (1983). *See also, Klein v. Asgrow Seed Co.,* 246 Cal.App.2d 87, 54 Cal.Rptr. 609, 620 (1966). We hold this formula to be appropriate in the present case.

BWC has argued that this formula includes lost profits and that lost profits are a consequential damage barred by the limitation of remedies on the cans of Basalin. We disagree.

In *W.R. Grace and Co., supra,* it was noted that the "... destruction or loss of a mature crop, which has a realizable value in excess of the cost of harvesting, processing and marketing, results in a monetary loss to the owner, regardless of whether the farming operation would, otherwise, have been profitable."

If the measure of damages we have adopted includes an element of lost profits, such inclusion is merely coincidental as the measure covers the direct loss resulting in the ordinary course of events from the alleged breach of the warranty. *See,* § 36–2–714(1).

The foregoing is the order of this Court.

LEWIS, C.J., and NESS, GREGORY and HARWELL, JJ., concur.

Notes

1. In Martin v. Joseph Harris Co., Inc., 767 F.2d 296 (6th Cir.1985), the plaintiffs purchased and planted cabbage seed infected with "black leg" fungus from the defendant. When the condition was discovered, plaintiffs took action to minimize the damage but still lost a "large portion" of their cabbage crop. Because of the high demand for cabbage, caused by the "black leg" epidemic, plaintiffs were able to sell the smaller cabbage crop at a profit equal to or higher than in previous years. Defendant argued that there is "no breach of the implied warranty of merchantability where there is no economic loss." Although "black leg" was damaging the plaintiffs' cabbage, the "law of supply and demand was making them * * * whole."

The court of appeals affirmed the district court's conclusion that the defendant's attempt to disclaim warranties and exclude liability for consequential damages was unconscionable. The court also affirmed the district court's decision to uphold a jury verdict of $52,000 for the plaintiffs.

> "(W)e are persuaded by the district court's finding that the defendant's sale of diseased seed to these two plaintiffs did not create the increased market price. Similarly, we note that [they] purchased some healthy seed from other companies and some other farmers produced completely healthy crops. To further complicate the problem, there was evidence to the effect that the black leg epidemic was partially caused by the sale of diseased seed by other merchants and, thus, the rise in the market price of cabbage did not result entirely from Harris Seed's breach. Therefore, following the dictates of U.C.C. 1–106(1). * * * in order to put Martin and Rick in the same position as many of their neighboring farmers who purchased healthy seed, we hold that the proper measure of damages as applied by the district court is the difference in value between the cabbage crops actually raised by these plaintiffs and the cabbage crops that they would have raised if their seed had not been diseased." [767 F.2d at 302–03.]

2. In *Hill,* the court enforced the clause excluding liability for consequential damages and awarded the buyer the net value of the lost crop as "direct" damages under UCC 2–714(1). In *Martin,* the court invalidated the clause excluding liability for consequential damages and awarded damages for the net value of the lost crop, citing UCC 1–106(1) but not UCC 2–714 or 2–715.

Assuming that the excluder clauses were not enforceable, how should the damages claimed be classified, as "direct" or "consequential?"

SECTION 3. INCIDENTAL AND CONSEQUENTIAL DAMAGES: UCC 2–715

Commercial buyers purchase goods for use, perhaps to resell to customers or to consume in the business. If accepted goods fail to conform to warranties made, the buyer's planned use of the goods may be impaired. Put differently, a result of the breach may be that the buyer is deprived of the use of the goods during the time when they are being repaired or replaced.

Damages resulting from loss of use are called consequential damages and are recoverable under UCC 2–714(3) & 2–715(2). They may be recovered without proof of either "special circumstances" or a "tacit agreement" of the seller to assume them, see R.I. Lampus Co. v. Neville Cement Products Corp., 474 Pa. 199, 378 A.2d 288 (1977), if four conditions are satisfied:

(1) The loss results "from general or particular requirements and needs of which the seller at the time of contracting had reason to know," UCC 2–715(2)(a). Compare UCC 2–315.

(2) The buyer has mitigated damages, i.e., the loss "could not reasonably be prevented by cover or otherwise," UCC 2–715(2)(a). The burden is on the seller to prove that the buyer failed to mitigate. Cates v. Morgan Portable Building Corp., 780 F.2d 683 (7th Cir.1985). But see International Petrol. Serv., Inc. v. S & N Well Serv., 230 Kan. 452, 639 P.2d 29, 38 (1982) (burden of proving mitigation on buyer).

(3) The breach was the substantial cause in fact of the loss. Compare UCC 2–715(2)(b). Overstreet v. Norden Laboratories, Inc., 669 F.2d 1286 (6th Cir.1982) (no proof that allegedly defective vaccine caused mares to abort foals).

(4) The type and amount of loss is proved by the buyer with reasonable certainty. Horizons, Inc. v. Avco Corp., 714 F.2d 862 (8th Cir.1983).

The conditions are easy to state. Applying them is another matter.

NEZPERCE STORAGE CO. v. ZENNER

Supreme Court of Idaho, 1983.
105 Idaho 464, 670 P.2d 871.

[In March, 1976, Zenner, a wheat farmer, sold Nezperce 2,000 bushels of "spring" wheat. Nezperce resold a portion of the wheat to eight farmers. Six weeks after planting, it became obvious that some of the wheat was not maturing and that the seed had been a mixture of spring and winter wheat. Since winter wheat requires several weeks of freezing weather to mature, the farmers suffered a crop failure. Nezperce settled the farmer's claims for $84,000 and brought suit against Zenner for indemnification.

Zenner, who grew both winter and spring wheat, had harvested his crop in August, 1975 and, according to his testimony, stored it in different bins over the winter. The Winter of 1975–76 was severe and much of the winter wheat planted in the previous fall was killed. A shortage of spring wheat developed, of which Zenner was aware at the time of the sale to Nezperce. Zenner also knew that Nezperce was purchasing his wheat to meet the shortage of spring wheat in the Camas Prairie area.

Nezperce cleaned and bagged the wheat without mixing it with another variety. Nezperce performed a successful "germination" to determine if the seed would grow but did not conduct other tests, i.e., a "grow out" test or an electrofloresis test, to determine if the seed was in fact spring wheat. The evidence was conflicting as to whether either test was available or practical.

The jury returned a verdict that Zenner had made and breached an express warranty and that Nezperce should recover the amount of the settlement made with the farmers.]

* * *

Although many of the allegations of the Nezperce complaint and the Zenners' counterclaim were disputed at trial, the essential arguments upon this appeal are the Zenners' assertions of error relating to the findings of the jury that Joseph Zenner was aware of the shortage of spring wheat seed in the Camas Prairie area and that he knew or had reason to know that Nezperce was purchasing his wheat for processing into spring wheat seed for resale to its customers; that the award of consequential damages was improper and that Nezperce did not reasonably mitigate its damages by testing the seed.

The propriety of awarding consequential damages in the instant case is governed by I.C. § 28–2–715(2)(a), which provides in pertinent part:

> "(2) Consequential damages resulting from the seller's breach include
>
> (a) Any loss resulting from general or particular requirements and needs of which the seller at the time of contracting had reason to know and which could not reasonably be prevented by cover or otherwise. * * *"

Clearly, Nezperce sustained a "loss" in reimbursing its customers for the damages they suffered by purchasing and planting seed which was not spring wheat. In a breach of warranty action, indemnification for this kind of a loss is proper when a seller such as Nezperce receives a warranty from a supplier such as Zenner and passes that warranty on to customers. * * *

As stated in *Clark v. International Harvester Co.*, 99 Idaho 326, 346, 581 P.2d 784, 804 (1978), "there are certain limitations on the right to recover consequential damages under § 28–2–715(2)(a). First, the losses must have resulted from needs which the seller knew or had reason to know at the time of contracting." Here the special interrogatories returned by the jury indicate that Zenner was aware of the shortage of spring wheat seed in the Camas Prairie area and that Zenner had reason to realize that "Nezperce Storage Company's purpose in purchasing MP–1 wheat was to meet an apparent shortage of spring wheat seed on the Camas Prairie," and that Zenner had reason to know that Nezperce was buying the wheat from Zenner to process it into spring wheat seed for resale. Those findings are supported by substantial, albeit conflicting, evidence, and therefore they will not be disturbed on appeal. I.R.C.P. 52(a); *Ellis v. Northwest Fruit &*

Produce, 103 Idaho 821, 654 P.2d 914 (1982); *Jolley v. Clay,* 103 Idaho 171, 646 P.2d 413 (1982); *Rueth v. State,* 103 Idaho 74, 644 P.2d 1333 (1982). Hence, the foreseeability requirement of I.C. § 28–2–715(2)(a) has been satisfied.

The propriety of an award of consequential damages must also satisfy the second condition of I.C. § 28–2–715(2)(a), *i.e.,* that they could not have been *reasonably* prevented by cover or otherwise. As to this condition, the Court in *Clark v. International Harvester Co.,* 99 Idaho 326, 347, 581 P.2d 784, 805 (1978), held that "the plaintiffs were only required to take reasonable efforts to mitigate their damages, [citation] and the burden of proving that the damages could have been minimized was on the defendants". In *S.J. Groves & Sons Co. v. Warner Co.,* 576 F.2d 524, 528 (3rd Cir.1978), it was held that, in an action to recover consequential damages under the same UCC provision, "[t]he requirement of * * * mitigation of damages is not an absolute, unyielding one, but is subject to the circumstances," and "[t]he test for plaintiff's efforts [to mitigate damages] is reasonableness * * *." *Id.,* at n. 5. In the instant case the Zenners presented testimony attempting to convince the jury that Nezperce could have mitigated or avoided its consequential damages by subjecting the seed to tests to determine seed variety prior to the time it resold the seed to its customers. As indicated in *West v. Whitney-Fidalgo Seafoods, Inc.,* 628 P.2d 10 (Alaska 1981), and *AES Technology Systems, Inc. v. Coherent Radiation,* 583 F.2d 933 (7th Cir.1978), the question of whether Nezperce acted properly to mitigate its damages is a factual matter to be determined by the trier of the fact. Here the jury specifically found:

> "it [was] reasonable for plaintiff Nezperce Storage to sell the seed it manufactured from the Zenner wheat to its customers without doing any more than the facts show it did do to determine whether or not such seed was actually of a spring wheat variety."

That finding is supported by substantial, albeit conflicting, testimony and will not be disturbed on appeal. I.R.C.P. 52(a); *Ellis v. Northwest Fruit & Produce, supra; Jolley v. Clay, supra; Rueth v. State, supra.*

The Zenners argue that the finding of the jury should be disregarded because the jury was not properly instructed as to what a "reasonable man" would have done in that the court failed to give Zenners' submitted instructions regarding negligence per se. We disagree and find no error in the refusal of the trial court to give Zenners' requested instructions. In the instant case we need not decide whether negligence per se can ever be used to limit a party's consequential damages under I.C. § 28–2–715(2)(a). While a court may adopt the requirements of a legislative enactment as the standard of conduct of a reasonable man, *Brizendine v. Nampa Meridian Irrigation Dist.,* 97 Idaho 580, 548 P.2d 80 (1976), that doctrine is ordinarily applied in negligence actions where a plaintiff has suffered injury by a defendant who was in violation of a statute or ordinance. However,

> "In order for the violation of a statute to be pertinent in a particular case, the statute must be * * * designed to protect (1) the class of persons in which the plaintiff is included (2) against the type of harm which has in fact occurred as a result of its violation." *Kinney v. Smith,* 95 Idaho 328, 331, 508 P.2d 1234, 1237 (1973); *Anderson v. Blackfoot*

Livestock Commission Co., 85 Idaho 64, 375 P.2d 704 (1962); *Curoe v. Spokane Etc. R.R. Co.,* 32 Idaho 643, 186 P. 1101 (1920); *W. PROSSER, LAW OF TORTS* § 36 (4th ed. 1971).

The statute at issue, I.C. § 22–417(3), imposes penalties upon one who sells seeds which are incorrectly labeled when the person selling the seed "has failed to obtain an invoice or growers declaration giving kind, or kind and variety * * * and to take such other precautions as may be necessary to insure the identity to be that stated." We deem it clear and obvious that, in the instant case, the statute was designed to protect the following class of persons: those customers who purchased the seed from Nezperce. Cases construing similar seed laws, *e.g., Agr. Services Ass'n, Inc. v. Ferry-Morse Seed Co., Inc.,* 551 F.2d 1057 (6th Cir.1977), and *Klein v. Asgrow Seed Co.,* 246 Cal.App.2d 87, 54 Cal.Rptr. 609 (1966), have so held. Equally clearly, the statute was not designed to provide protection to the Zenners, who can best be described as suppliers of mislabeled seed. Hence, we deem the statute and the doctrine of negligence per se in the instant case irrelevant. *See also S.J. Groves & Sons Co. v. Warner, supra,* which states:

> "Where both the plaintiff and the defendant have had equal opportunity to reduce the damages by the same act and it is equally reasonable to expect the defendant to minimize damages, the defendant is in no position to contend that the plaintiff failed to mitigate. Nor will the award be reduced on account of damages the defendant could have avoided as easily as the plaintiff." At page 530; *See also Shea—S & M Ball v. Massman—Kiewit—Early,* 606 F.2d 1245 (D.C.Cir.1979).

* * *

The judgment of the district court is affirmed. Costs to respondents. No attorney fees allowed.

Notes

1. Suppose Zenner warranted the wheat to be spring wheat, knew that Nezperce intended to resell it to his customers but was unaware of the shortage of spring wheat seed in the Camas Prairie area. Should that alter the result in this case?

2. Suppose that Zenner sold and delivered grain described as "spring wheat" to Nezperce in the Fall of 1975 at $5.00 per bushel. Nezperce immediately resold 50% to customers for April, 1976 delivery at $6.00 per bushel. All of the Zenner wheat was stored together. In March, after the big chill, the price of spring wheat had risen to $20. Nezperce resold the balance to customers for $22 per bushel. Nezperce then had an electrofloresis test performed on a sample of Zenner wheat and discovered that it was mixed substantially with winter wheat. Nezperce promptly purchased replacement spring wheat in the open market for $22 per bushel, which was delivered to customers, and sold the Zenner wheat for $5 per bushel. What damages should Nezperce recover for Zenner's breach of warranty?

3. How does the Code treat expenditures made by the buyer after the breach is discovered? If they are made to repair or replace the non-conforming goods, they may be recoverable as "direct" damages under UCC 2–714(2): Repair or replacement costs are frequently used to measure the value of the goods as warranted. In addition to *Soo Line,* see Vista St. Clair, Inc. v. Landry's

Commercial Furnishings, Inc., 57 Or.App. 254, 643 P.2d 1378 (1982). If they are made to avoid losses or to pursue permissible remedies, they may be "incidental" damages under UCC 2–715(1). Or, they may be "consequential" damages under UCC 2–715(2)(a). How is the line to be drawn between incidental and consequential damages? The question is important, for incidental damages need not satisfy all the conditions for the recovery of consequential damages and will not be covered by clauses in the contract purporting to exclude the seller's liability for consequential damages. See, e.g., Carbontek Trading Co., Ltd. v. Philbro Energy, Inc., 910 F.2d 302 (5th Cir. 1990); Reynolds Metals Co. v. Westinghouse Elec. Corp., 758 F.2d 1073 (5th Cir.1985).

4. The buyer's claim for consequential damages caused by the seller's delay or nondelivery is treated in Chapter Fifteen, Section 6.

LEWIS v. MOBIL OIL CORP.

United States Court of Appeals, Eighth Circuit, 1971.
438 F.2d 500.

[The facts and the decision on the warranty issue in this case are reprinted in Section 3(c) of Chapter 19. We now turn to the damages issues.]

* * *

III. Damages

The question with which we are here confronted is what damages are recoverable by the plaintiff for the defendant's breach of warranty. The applicable statutes are §§ 2–714(2), (3) and 2–715 of the Uniform Commercial Code, 7C Ark.Stats.Ann. §§ 85–2–714(2), (3), 85–2–715 (1961), which provide in pertinent part: [The court quoted UCC 2–714(2) and (3) and UCC 2–715.]

* * *

In the instant case the ordinary measure of damages for breach of warranty is not applicable, since the plaintiff-buyer did not pay a price exceeding the value of the goods delivered. Rather, since the breach was of an implied warranty of fitness for a particular purpose, the "special circumstances" exception is applicable here. The proximate damages in this case consisted of the plaintiff's incidental and consequential damages which may be recoverable. The incidental damages consist of the excessive amounts of oil used in the system and the costs incurred in the repair and replacement of mechanical parts damaged by the oil's failing to function properly. There is no controversy between the parties as to the allowability of these damages. There are two major points of controversy on damages: (1) for what period of time are damages recoverable and (2) whether loss of profits during the time plaintiff was unable to operate at full capacity are recoverable.

[The court first rejected plaintiff's "unique" theory that damages should be recoverable for the period of time after the correct oil was used and the system was operating satisfactorily. Plaintiff had argued that the drain on his financial resources during the period of difficulty had restricted his ability to operate at 100% capacity later on. In the view of the court, the cause of this condition was inadequate capitalization not breach of warranty and the proper remedy was a bank loan at the time not damages in subsequent litigation.]

* * *

A more troublesome question is whether the plaintiff should be allowed to recover damages for the full two and one-half year period during which he was using Ambrex 810. Under § 2–715(2)(a) of the Uniform Commercial Code, only those losses are recoverable "which could not reasonably be prevented by cover or otherwise." 7C Ark.Stat.Ann. § 85–2–715 (1961). The "cover" provision of the Uniform Commercial Code, § 2–712, is not applicable here, since that section applies to the buyer's remedies upon failure of the seller to deliver goods or upon the rightful rejection of goods known to be defective. Hence the question here is whether the plaintiff's damage could otherwise have been reasonably prevented. The applicable doctrine is stated by Professor Williston:

> "* * * [D]amages which the plaintiff might have avoided with reasonable effort without undue risk, expense, or humiliation are either not caused by the defendant's wrong or need not have been, and, therefore, are not to be charged against him.
>
> "The principle has wide application and frequently involves the establishment of a standard of reasonable conduct.
>
> * * *
>
> "Where inferior goods have been furnished under a contract, the buyer cannot recover greater consequential damages caused by using them when he knew of their unfitness, than would have been caused by another possible course, although the seller had sold the goods for that purpose. And the principle is general that there can be no recovery for consequences that reasonably could have been avoided." 11 S. Williston, Contracts § 1353 (Jaeger, 3d ed. 1968) (footnotes omitted). * * *

Defendant's argument on this issue is not precise, but the gist of its complaint is that the plaintiff used Ambrex 810 for a period of two and one-half years, during which time there was at least some suspicion that the oil was not functioning properly, and that plaintiff should have taken steps to solve his problems sooner than he did. It is unclear to us whether or not the defendant is contending that the plaintiff used Ambrex 810 with actual knowledge of its unfitness, so as to preclude at least in part his recovery of damages caused by its use. If such is the claim, it is clearly refuted by the evidence. Neither plaintiff nor the Mobil dealer who sold him Ambrex 810 knew the chemical composition of the oil nor what the exact requirements of plaintiff's equipment were. Plaintiff was relying on Mobil to provide him with the proper oil and it was not discovered during that time that the oil was improper. Indeed, plaintiff changed the brand of pump he was using because of the possibility that the problem was mechanical. It was not until a Mobil engineer visited the mill and changed the type of oil recommended that it was discovered that an improper oil had been supplied.

Neither does the defendant precisely phrase its argument in terms of a failure to give timely notice under Ark.Stat.Ann. § 85–2–607, although it relies on an Arkansas case under this section, Ingle v. Marked Tree Equipment Co., 244 Ark. 1166, 428 S.W.2d 286 (1968). However, it seems that under the circumstances of this case, the reasonable notice required by this section was given by the plaintiff. * * *

* * *

Here there is not the slightest suggestion of bad faith on the part of the plaintiff. Furthermore the evidence shows that soon after using Ambrex 810, plaintiff notified the Mobil dealer, Rowe, that he wasn't sure if a proper oil was being supplied, and was constantly in touch with Rowe about his problems thereafter. Mobil certainly had notice that the "transaction [was] still troublesome and must be watched." Defendant continued to supply Ambrex 810. Therefore we cannot conclude that any damages must be barred under this section. See Boeing Airplane Co. v. O'Malley, 329 F.2d 585, 593–596 (8th Cir.1964). The trial judge properly instructed the jury that the plaintiff must have notified the defendant within a reasonable time after he should have discovered the breach, and we cannot say that the jury's verdict was erroneous in this respect.

The only way in which it would have been possible for plaintiff's damages to have been minimized in this case would have been for him to have brought in an independent expert to assess the cause of his trouble. While such a course might have been desirable, and would probably have saved both plaintiff and defendant considerable expense, we cannot say that failure to do so requires a reduction of damages allowable under § 2–715 of the Uniform Commercial Code as a matter of law. This is essentially a question of the plaintiff's duty to use diligence to minimize his damages, which is ordinarily a question of fact for the jury. The trial judge properly instructed the jury that plaintiff had the duty to use diligence to minimize his damages, that defendant was not liable for any damages which resulted from plaintiff's failure to minimize his damages, and that diligence meant the care of a reasonably careful person under the circumstances of the case. The jury's verdict reflects its finding that the plaintiff had acted reasonably in these circumstances, and again we cannot say that it lacks evidentiary support.

Plaintiff was in continuous contact with both the manufacturer of his equipment and with the defendant in an effort to ascertain the cause of his problems. Various remedies were tried and failed until the oil problem was ultimately identified. Throughout this period, defendant continued to supply plaintiff with Ambrex 810, knowing both of his reliance on it to supply the proper oil and his difficulties in operation. Thus we do not think that defendant can rely on plaintiff's failure to obtain an independent opinion to absolve it of liability for its breach of warranty. "The duty to mitigate damages is not an unlimited one * * *." Steele v. J.I. Case Company, 197 Kan. 554, 419 P.2d 902, 911 (1966). We conclude that defendant should be liable for all of plaintiff's damages during the period he was using Ambrex 810.

The final question to be determined is whether under Arkansas law, loss of profits may be recovered as consequential damages for breach of warranty. Defendant relies on a series of Arkansas cases which stand for the proposition that loss of profits cannot be recovered unless the circumstances of the transaction are such as to make it reasonable to assume that the defendant knew he was to be held responsible for such damages and agreed to such liability. See Hawkins v. Delta Spindle of Blytheville, Inc., 245 Ark. 830, 434 S.W.2d 825 (1968); Lamkins v. International Harvester Co., 207 Ark. 637, 182 S.W.2d 203 (1944); Hooks Smelting Co. v. Planters' Compress Co., 72 Ark. 275, 79 S.W. 1052 (1904). The problem with this argument is that all of these cases are non-Code cases which rely on a rule which is expressly rejected by the Uniform Commercial Code Official Commentary to § 2–715:

> "2. * * * The 'tacit agreement' test for the recovery of consequential damages is rejected. * * *
>
> "3. * * * It is not necessary that there be a conscious acceptance of an insurer's liability on the seller's part, nor is his obligation for consequential damages limited to cases in which he fails to use due effort in good faith.
>
> "Particular needs of the buyer must generally be made known to the seller while general needs must rarely be made known to charge the seller with knowledge.
>
> "Any seller who does not wish to take the risk of consequential damages has available the section on contractual limitation of remedy." 7C Ark.Stat.Ann. § 85–2–715, Comments 2 and 3 (1961).

The question essentially is whether lost profits are damages which the seller had reason to know of at the time the contract was made. With respect to breach of warranty, lost profits are held to be foreseeable if they are proximately caused by and are the natural result of the breach. 5 A. Corbin, Contracts § 1012 (1964); Seely v. White Motor Co., 63 Cal.2d 9, 45 Cal.Rptr. 17, 403 P.2d 145, 148–149 (1965). Cf. Superwood Corp. v. Larson-Stang, Inc., 311 F.2d 735 (8th Cir.1963). Where a seller provides goods to a manufacturing enterprise with knowledge that they are to be used in the manufacturing process, it is reasonable to assume that he should know that defective goods will cause a disruption of production, and loss of profits is a natural consequence of such disruption. Hence, loss of profits should be recoverable under those circumstances. Here, the defendant seller knew that the oil it was supplying to plaintiff was to be used in the operation of the sawmill. It also knew that a defective oil would cause the sawmill equipment to operate improperly. It is a natural consequence of the failure of the equipment to function that production would be curtailed and loss of profits would follow. See 5 A. Corbin, Contracts § 1013, p. 92 (1964). We think these damages are the proximate result of the breach and should be recoverable.

Most jurisdictions which have considered the question of the recoverability of lost profits under the Uniform Commercial Code for a breach of warranty in circumstances similar to those in the instant case seem to have allowed them. * * *

We think Arkansas would follow this rule. * * *

* * *

Defendant also contends there was no proper proof of lost profits in this case, and that the damages were purely speculative. We do not agree.

While it is true that the damages were excessive in this case because they were allowed for an improper time period, we do not think that the method utilized was unreasonable under the circumstances of this case. First of all, the plaintiff offered considerable evidence that there was a substantial market for his lumber which he was not able to supply. Evidence was offered of a number of customers who testified they would have bought more of his lumber had it been available. A substantial part of plaintiff's business was done as an exclusive supplier of timbers to a bridge building company. Plaintiff was the only sawmill operator who would furnish these timbers with the close tolerances demanded; he was unable to supply all of that customer's needs.

In addition to this market evidence, there is evidence of the profits made by his business both before and after using Ambrex 810. These were substantial, even in the later period when he was unable to operate at full capacity. During the period he was using Ambrex 810 they were significantly less, due to the lost production and added expenses. Past profits of an established business may be utilized to prove loss of profits as an element of damages. 5 A. Corbin, Contracts § 1023 (1964); 11 S. Williston, Contracts § 1346A (Jaeger, 3d ed. 1968). And under the circumstances of this case, we think the jury was entitled to take account of the profits earned by plaintiff once the business was operating successfully after the breach of warranty. While the lost profits could not be proved with absolute certainty of course, we think a reasonable approximation can be made from the evidence in this case.

To summarize our decision in this case, having reviewed the evidence as a whole and the instructions of the able trial judge, we conclude that there was a warranty of fitness for a particular purpose in this case, that the warranty was breached, and that the defendant was liable for the damages caused by this breach, including loss of profits during the time plaintiff was using Ambrex 810. Defendant is not liable for any loss of profits which may have occurred after plaintiff quit using Ambrex 810. The jury's verdict was in the single amount of $89,250. We are unable to determine from the record what would be a proper amount to award for direct damages plus loss of profits for the appropriate time period. Therefore, the judgment must be reversed and remanded for a new trial on the issue of damages.

On Petitions for Rehearing

The petitions for rehearing of both the appellant and the appellee raise questions as to the issue of damages for loss of profits which merit some further comment. At the outset, we would note that the record and the arguments are not entirely clear as to how this element of damages was submitted in this particular case. While we adhere to our opinion that loss of profits is a proper element of damages in a case of this sort, these damages must of course be proved with a certain degree of specificity. For the purposes of this memorandum we will discuss the damages in this case in round figures approximating those in the record.

Plaintiff's profit records show that for the four years prior to his shift to new equipment and using Ambrex 810, he made a total profit of $32,000. In 1961, his profit was $19,000, in 1962, $7,000, in 1963, $8,000, and in 1964, the year in which he was converting his equipment, he had a loss of $2,000.

This works out to an annual rate of profits in the pre-Ambrex period of $8,000, and we are not saying that any particular period of time prior to the period the damage was sustained should be used as the basis for calculation. It appears obvious that the immediate prior year's profit has more relevancy to the issue of what profits might be anticipated in the following years than do the more remote years' profits. Likewise, on the other end of the calculation the immediate succeeding year's profit after the use of Ambrex was discontinued would be of greater relevancy than the succeeding years. But even eliminating the year of conversion, this is an annual rate of $11,000. During the period he was using Ambrex 810, approximately 30 months, he made a total of $12,000, for an annual rate of $4,800. In the post-Ambrex period, a period of 24 months, he made a total of $41,000, for an annual rate of approximately $20,500.

The jury verdict in this case was for $89,250, of which approximately $9250 may be attributed to direct damages, leaving $80,000 as the recovery for loss of profits. As we will shortly demonstrate, such a recovery, if it is interpreted as being limited to loss of profits for only the period in which Ambrex 810 was being used, bears no reasonable relationship to the proof in the record of plaintiff's capacity for making profits, with or without Ambrex 810. We were thus confronted with the problem of determining what the basis of this recovery was. We were led by certain arguments made in plaintiff's brief to the conclusion that this recovery represented a loss of profits during the period Ambrex 810 was used, plus a loss of profits for the period of time after Ambrex 810 was used because of his inability to operate at full capacity. We held that such later profits could not be recovered. Plaintiff now contends that the loss of profits recovery did not extend to the later period and was confined to the period in which he was using Ambrex 810. We accept this interpretation of the damage award and find this award is excessive.

If the $80,000 loss of profits is confined to the 30–month period during which Ambrex 810 was used, to this figure must be added the $12,000 in profits which he actually made. This works out to an annual rate of profits of approximately $37,000. There simply is no proof in the record that plaintiff has ever approached such a profit record. Plaintiff argues that his post-Ambrex profit rate, during which he was operating at 50–60 per cent capacity must be inflated to a 100 per cent capacity rate in order to determine his profit rate during the time he was using Ambrex 810. We cannot agree that such a method of determining loss of profits is acceptable, for this accomplishes much the same result as that we disapproved in our original interpretation of the damage award—i.e., it penalizes the defendant Mobil Oil Company for the plaintiff's capital structure and bears no reasonable relationship to actual damages caused by the use of Ambrex 810.

We further wish to emphasize the fact that nothing said in our prior opinion should be taken to mean that the profit rate made in the post-Ambrex period is the sole measure of damages in the period of the use of Ambrex 810. In view of the immediate proximity in time of these two periods, the significant increase in profits in the post-Ambrex period is highly suggestive of the fact that additional profits could have been made in the period Ambrex was used, and may be used as a guide as to what those profits should have been, at least as to their outer limit. However, there is also proof in the record that the market conditions of the plaintiff's business were not entirely similar, particularly in the fact that the selling price for lumber was fluctuating.

Plaintiff's recovery for a loss of profits must take into account these different market conditions, his actual production capacity, his type of operation, its efficiency and any and all other relevant factors that would have a bearing upon and that would influence the amount of profits during the period that profits are recoverable as well as the years used for comparative purposes. See Frank Sullivan Company v. Midwest Sheet Metal Works, 335 F.2d 33, 41 (8th Cir.1964).

Other questions raised in the petitions for rehearing have been considered and rejected as being without merit. The judgment must still be reversed and remanded for a new trial on the issue of damages.

Both petitions for rehearing are denied.

DELANO GROWER'S CO–OP. WINERY v. SUPREME WINE CO.

Supreme Judicial Court of Massachusetts, 1985.
393 Mass. 666, 473 N.E.2d 1066.

[The court's decision on the liability issue is printed supra in Chapter Nineteen, Section 3.]

* * *

6. *Calculation of damages for lost good will.* Delano argues that there is no basis in the record for the conclusion that it caused injury to Supreme's business reputation. The master found that the primary reason for Supreme's decline in sales after 1973 was the defective Delano wine. This finding was prima facie evidence of the causal connection between Delano's acts and the damage to Supreme's business reputation. At trial, Delano presented the testimony of several former Supreme customers to rebut the evidence of a causal connection. Supreme presented testimony of its former officers to support the evidence that Delano caused the injury to Supreme's business reputation. This record is hardly one, as Delano argues, that is totally devoid of any basis for finding a causal connection between Delano's acts and Supreme's damages. Rather, it exhibits an instance where the judge was required to weigh the credibility of the evidence before him and to determine whether a causal connection existed. The judge's finding that Supreme had proved a causal connection between its loss of business reputation and Delano's breach is not clearly erroneous.

Delano contends that the record contains scant evidence supporting a valuation of Supreme's good will. However, it did not produce any direct evidence at trial before the judge which rebutted Supreme's evidence of the good will value. At trial, Supreme presented the testimony of an expert in business appraising. This expert had over eight years' experience as a business broker engaged in buying and selling businesses in and around Boston. In this connection he was required to appraise a business's value, including the value of its good will. The judge's acceptance of the expert testimony implies that he found this expert sufficiently qualified to render an opinion. *Commonwealth v. Boyd,* 367 Mass. 169, 183, 326 N.E.2d 320 (1975). A finding that this expert possessed sufficient knowledge, skill, and experience to render an opinion was neither an abuse of discretion nor erroneous as matter of law. *Id.* See P.J. Liacos, Massachusetts Evidence 112 (5th ed. 1981).

The expert valued the business at $593,700, including assets and good will. The assets were valued at $237,092. This valuation was based on the business records introduced in evidence and certain other facts. This was a sufficient basis for his opinion. *Uberto v. Kaufman,* 348 Mass. 171, 173, 202 N.E.2d 822 (1964). Supreme's president and its treasurer testified that Supreme's value was $500,000.

The judge found that Supreme's loss of good will attributable to Delano's breach was $100,000. He based this on the evidence in the record and an examination of valuation methods. He rejected Supreme's theories supporting its valuation as lacking factual grounding. In determining the value of Supreme's good will, the judge was not bound by the expert testimony. P.J. Liacos, *supra* at 117, citing *Dodge v. Sawyer,* 288 Mass. 402, 408, 193 N.E. 15 (1934).

Delano argues that the trial judge relied on extraneous materials, not admitted at trial, in determining good will. Specifically, he discussed certain statistics from Business Week, indicating an increased consumption of wine and a growth in the wine industry. This reference occurred in a lengthy discussion of various methods used in valuing good will. This same discussion specifically refers to evidence introduced at trial which sufficiently supported a valuation of the lost good will. There is no clear indication to what degree, if any, the discussion of the extraneous material influenced the good will valuation. The judge found sufficient grounds to reduce the value from that given by Supreme. Where there was sufficient evidence to warrant a valuation of lost good will and the causal connection of that loss, we will not upset this finding. It was not clearly erroneous and was based on the judge's weighing the credibility of the evidence before him. The weight given this evidence was then used in accepted formulations of good will to determine the damage. We do not require that such damages be proved with mathematical certainty. *Productora e Importadora de Papel, S.A. de C.V. v. Fleming,* 376 Mass. 826, 840, 383 N.E.2d 1129 (1978). The judge did not err in calculating the damages for good will.

Neither party has addressed the issue whether lost good will is a proper consequential damage under G.L. c. 106, § 2–715. This court has stated that prospective profits are recoverable in the appropriate case. *Matsushita Elec. Corp. of America v. Sonus Corp.,* 362 Mass. 246, 264, 284 N.E.2d 880 (1972). In examining whether good will is also recoverable, we note that Pennsylvania, in disallowing such recovery, based its decision on the interpretation of its prior law, which did not allow recovery for good will. *Harry Rubin & Sons v. Consolidated Pipe Co. of America,* 396 Pa. 506, 153 A.2d 472 (1959). Other cases in which recovery for good will has been denied are based on the speculative nature of damages in the particular case or on a failure of proof. 96 A.L.R.3d § 18[b], at 396 (1979). Cf. 96 A.L.R.3d § 18[a], at 395 (1979) (loss of good will held recoverable). Under our law as it was before the enactment of the Uniform Commercial Code, "[l]oss of good will [was] recognized as an element of damages flowing from the use of unfit material received from one who warranted it to be fit." *Royal Paper Box Co. v. Munro & Church Co.*, 284 Mass. 446, 452, 188 N.E. 223 (1933) (interpreting G.L. [Ter.Ed.] c. 106, § 17[1]). Where a seller of goods reasonably knows that substantially impaired goods provided for resale could affect continued operations and established good will, the buyer's loss of good will caused by the seller's breach is properly recoverable as consequential damages unless the loss could have been prevented by cover or otherwise. G.L. c. 106, § 2–715(2)(a). This is not a harsh result as the seller may contractually limit this remedy. Uniform Commercial Code § 2–715, comment 3 1A U.L.A. 446 (1976). In this case, Supreme's loss of good will was found to be a direct consequence of Delano's breach. Once sufficiently ascertained, the award of damages for lost good will was properly allowed.

* * *

[Footnotes omitted.]

Notes

1. The scope of lost profits recovery under UCC 2–715(2)(a) is influenced by the use to which the buyer put the goods.

In *Lewis v. Mobil Oil Corp.*, for example, the oil was used to lubricate equipment needed to operate a sawmill. The breach diminished the capacity of the sawmill to produce lumber. Assuming a strong demand for lumber, the buyer lost the profits that would have been made during the relevant period. There was not enough lumber to sell. See Merritt Logan, Inc. v. Fleming Companies, Inc., 901 F.2d 349 (3d Cir.1990) (defective refrigeration unit in a supermarket).

In other cases, the goods purchased are intended for resale. If the breach is discovered before the resale, the buyer may be able to cure the nonconformity or find substitutes without disappointing its customers. Even so, the buyer may lose profits on the goods involved or on ancillary sales. In Migerobe, Inc. v. Certina USA, Inc., 924 F.2d 1330 (5th Cir.1991), the buyer proved that the seller's failure to deliver watches purchased as a "loss leader" caused lost profits on more expensive items that customers probably would have purchased if they had been induced to enter the store.

If the nonconformity is discovered after the goods have been resold by the buyer, the consequences may be more dramatic. In addition to loss of value under UCC 2–714(2), the resale buyer may have a greater loss because the crop was planted or the wine had been delivered to customers. These losses, including good will, are recoverable as consequential damages, so long as the limitations of foreseeability, causation, reasonable proof and mitigation are satisfied. See Hendricks & Assoc., Inc. v. Daewoo Corp., 923 F.2d 209 (1st Cir.1991) (lost profits from contract terminated by disappointed resale buyer); AM/PM Franchise Assn. v. Atlantic Richfield Co., 526 Pa. 110, 584 A.2d 915 (1990) (loss of good will when defective gas supplied to a franchise caused damage to customer's cars).

2. *Consequential Damages From a Product Recall.* S is a manufacturer of heart valves. In 1992, S manufactured 10,000,000 valves and sold them to five medical supply corporations for an average price of $15 each. In June, 1993, it was discovered that 5% of the heart valves were not fit for ordinary purposes.

After insertion in a patient, they would fail within 18 months. A merchantable heart valve would last for at least 10 years. It was estimated that 500,000 of the valves had already been inserted in patients. The others were in the possession of either the medical supply corporations (the original buyers) or resale buyers, such as hospitals and clinics. With the approval of the Food and Drug Administration, all of the heart valves were recalled by the original buyers and doctors who had inserted heart valves in patients were warned of the problem. When the news hit the press, S's other customers canceled or refused to make orders for the product, and business dropped 85% from 1992 levels.

A. What is the scope of S's potential liability on these facts?

B. In your judgment, does Article 2 adequately protect a buyer under these circumstances?

C. What contractual provisions should S consider to deal with this problem? See the next Section.

SECTION 4. SELLER'S DISCLAIMER OF WARRANTY AND CONTRACTUAL MODIFICATION OF REMEDIES FOR BREACH

MARTIN v. JOSEPH HARRIS CO., INC.

United States Court of Appeals, Sixth Circuit, 1985.
767 F.2d 296.

MILBURN, CIRCUIT JUDGE.

The defendant, Joseph Harris Co., Inc., brings this appeal following the district court's granting the plaintiffs' motion for a judgment not withstanding the verdict and a second trial in plaintiffs' action for damages as a result of defective seeds. Because we hold that the district court was correct in holding that, under the facts of this case, the disclaimer of warranty and limitation of remedy clause used by the defendant was unconscionable under Michigan law, and because we further hold that the district court properly held that the implied warranty of merchantability was breached as a matter of law, we affirm.

I.

Plaintiffs Duane Martin and Robert Rick ("Martin and Rick") were commercial farmers in Michigan. In August of 1972, Martin and Rick placed independent orders for cabbage seed with the defendant, Joseph Harris Co., Inc. ("Harris Seed"), a national producer and distributor of seed. Plaintiffs had been customers of Harris Seed for several years and, as in earlier transactions, the order form supplied by Harris Seed included a clause disclaiming the implied warranty of merchantability and limiting buyers' remedies to the purchase price of the seed.[1] A similar clause was

1. The disclaimer of warranties and exclusion of remedies clause, which was printed in the order form, seed catalogs and on the seed packages, appeared as follows:

NOTICE TO BUYER: Joseph Harris Company, Inc. warrants that seeds and plants it sells conform to the label descriptions as required by Federal and State seed laws. IT MAKES NO OTHER WARRANTIES, EXPRESS OR IMPLIED, OF MERCHANTABILITY, FITNESS FOR PURPOSE, OR OTHERWISE, AND IN ANY EVENT ITS LIABILITY FOR BREACH OF ANY WARRANTY OR CONTRACT WITH RESPECT TO SUCH SEEDS OR PLANTS IS LIMITED TO THE PURCHASE PRICE OF SUCH SEEDS OR PLANTS.

also used by Harris Seed's competitors for the same purpose. Neither of the plaintiffs read the clause nor did the salesman make any attempt either to point it out or to explain its purpose.

Three to four months after placing their orders, plaintiffs received Harris Seed's 1973 Commercial Vegetable Growers Catalog. Included in the lower right-hand corner of one page of the catalog was a notification that Harris Seed would no longer "hot water" treat cabbage seed. Hot water treatment had successfully been used since 1947 to eradicate a fungus known as *phoma lingam* or "black leg," a seed borne disease that causes affected plants to rot before maturing.[2]

Plaintiffs planted their cabbage crop in April and May of 1973, using, among other seed, that supplied by Harris Seed. In mid-July, Harris Seed notified plaintiffs that the seed lot used to fill plaintiffs' order was infected with black leg. Although plaintiffs attempted to minimize the effect of the disease, large portions of their cabbage crops were destroyed. However, in marketing their smaller than usual crop, both plaintiffs made a profit equal to or higher than previous years. This unusual profit margin was due to the rise in market price for cabbage in 1973, which in turn was affected in part by the fact that the 1973 black leg epidemic reduced the amount of available cabbage.

On August 5, 1975, plaintiffs brought this action. After a hearing on the enforceability of the disclaimer of warranty and limitation of liability clause, the district court ruled that the clause was unconscionable and, therefore, unenforceable. A jury was impaneled to try plaintiffs' legal liability theories of negligence and breach of implied warranty. Following a six-day trial the jury returned a verdict against plaintiffs on both theories; however, the district court granted the plaintiffs' motion for a j.n.o.v. on the implied warranty issue. A second jury impaneled to hear the issue of damages returned verdicts in favor of Martin in the amount of Thirty-six Thousand ($36,000.00) Dollars and in favor of Rick in the amount of Sixteen Thousand ($16,000.00) Dollars.

II.

Our review of the district court's rulings in this diversity case is controlled by the State of Michigan's version of the Uniform Commercial Code, Mich.Comp.Laws Ann. § 440.1101 *et seq.* As we have often stated, "[w]hen this court is reviewing a district judge's interpretation of state law, we give 'considerable weight' to the interpretation of the judge." *Bagwell v. Canal Insurance Co.,* 663 F.2d 710, 712 (6th Cir.1981). Accordingly, "if a federal district judge has reached a permissible conclusion upon a question of local law, the Court of Appeals should not reverse even though it may think the law should be otherwise." *Insurance Co. of North America v. Federated Mutual Insurance Co.,* 518 F.2d 101, 106 n. 3 (6th Cir.1975) (quoting *Rudd-Melikian, Inc. v. Merritt,* 282 F.2d 924, 929 (6th Cir.1960)).

No question has been raised as to whether this clause complies with the requirements of Mich.Comp.Laws Ann. § 440.2316 (U.C.C. § 2–316).

2. According to testimony at trial, the only black leg epidemic between 1947 and 1973 was in 1966, and was traced to cabbage seed imported from Australia. The 1947 and the 1973 black leg was traced to State of Washington produced cabbage seed.

A.

The first issue raised by Harris Seed is whether the district court erred in holding the disclaimer and limitation clause unconscionable under U.C.C. § 2–302. The question of the unconscionability of a contract clause is one of law for the court to decide in light of "its commercial setting, purpose and effect." U.C.C. § 2–302. Since the Code does not define unconscionability, the district court reviewed case law to aid it in its resolution of this question.

A threshold problem in this context is whether under Michigan law warranty disclaimers which comply with U.C.C. § 2–316 are limited by U.C.C. § 2–302. In holding Harris Seed's disclaimer clause unconscionable under the facts of this case, the district court implicitly held that U.C.C. § 2–302 is a limitation on U.C.C. § 2–316. Harris Seed argues that by enacting § 2–316 the Michigan Legislature "unequivocally [authorized the] exclusion or modification of the implied warranty of merchantability by disclaimer." We have been presented with no Michigan cases resolving this issue; however, a number of arguments support the district court's conclusion that § 2–316 is not insulated from review under § 2–302. First, § 2–302 provides that "any clause" of a contract may be found unconscionable. Similarly, "section 2–316 does not state expressly that all disclaimers meeting its requirements are immune from general policing provisions like section 2–302. * * *" J. White & R. Summers, *Handbook of the Law Under the Uniform Commercial Code,* § 12–11, at 476 (2d Ed.1980). Had the drafters of the Uniform Commercial Code or the Michigan Legislature chosen to limit the application of § 2–302, language expressly so stating could easily have been included. Furthermore, as pointed out by Professors White and Summers:

> Comment 1 [to § 2–302] lists and describes ten cases which are presumably intended to illustrate the underlying basis of the section: In seven of those cases disclaimers of warranty were denied full effect. It is difficult to reconcile the intent on the part of the draftsman to immunize disclaimers from the effect of 2–302 with the fact that they used cases in which courts struck down disclaimers to illustrate the concept of unconscionability.

Id. (footnotes omitted). Therefore, because this issue is unsettled under Michigan law and according the district court's conclusion "considerable weight," we hold that the district court correctly relied upon § 2–302 as a limitation on § 2–316.

We next turn to a more troublesome subissue; viz., whether within the special facts of this case the disclaimer and exclusionary clause was unconscionable under Michigan law. As has often been stated, commercial contracts will rarely be found unconscionable, *see, e.g., A & M Produce Co. v. FMC Corp.,* 135 Cal.App.3d 473, 186 Cal.Rptr. 114 (1982), *Stanley A. Klopp, Inc. v. John Deere Co.,* 510 F.Supp. 807, 810 (E.D.Pa.1981), *aff'd,* 676 F.2d 688 (3rd Cir.1982),[4] because in the commercial setting the relationship is between

4. It is unclear whether the contract at issue is a commercial contract. As noted by the district court, some courts have held farmers and ranchers are not merchants. *See, e.g., Fear Ranches, Inc. v. Berry,* 470 F.2d 905 (10th Cir.1972); *Cook Grains, Inc. v. Fallis,* 239 Ark. 962, 395 S.W.2d 555 (1965). Other courts have taken the opposite position and held farmers are merchants. *See, e.g., Campbell v. Yokel,* 20 Ill.App.2d 702, 313 N.E.2d 628 (1974); *Nelson v. Union Equity Co-Operative Exchange,* 548 S.W.2d 352

business parties and is not so one-sided as to give one party the bargaining power to impose unconscionable terms on the other party.

In making its determination of unconscionability, the district court relied upon *Allen v. Michigan Bell Telephone,* 18 Mich.App. 632, 171 N.W.2d 689 (1969).[5] In *Allen* an insurance agent contracted with Michigan Bell Telephone Company to place advertisements in the classified telephone directory. When the advertisements were not included, he brought an action for damages. To defend the action, Michigan Bell Telephone Company relied on a limitation of remedies clause which, if upheld, would have limited the plaintiff's recovery to the contract price. In refusing to uphold the limitation, the Michigan court stated "the principle of freedom to contract does not carry a license to insert any provision in an agreement which a party deems advantageous." *Id.* at 691–92. Rather, the court stated that:

> [i]mplicit in the principle of freedom of contract is the concept that at the time of contracting each party has a realistic alternative to acceptance of the terms offered. Where goods and services can only be obtained from one source (or several sources on non-competitive terms) the choices of one who desires to purchase are limited to acceptance of the terms offered or doing without. Depending on the nature of the goods or services and the purchaser's needs, doing without may or may not be a realistic alternative. Where it is not, one who successfully exacts agreement to an unreasonable term cannot insist on the court's enforcing it on the ground that it was "freely" entered into, when it was not. * * *
>
> There are then two inquiries in a case such as this: (1) what is the relative bargaining power of the parties, their relative economic strength, the alternative sources of supply, in a word, what are their options?; (2) is the challenged term substantively reasonable?

Id. at 692.

With reference to the test announced in *Allen,* Harris Seed argues that the relative bargaining power of the parties is not a proper consideration under § 2–302. This is an issue on which courts and commentators have taken varying approaches. *Compare, e.g., Phillips Machinery Co. v. LeBlond, Inc.,* 494 F.Supp. 318 (N.D.Okla.1980) (no requirement of equality of bargaining power, but rather must be some element of deception or substantive

(Tex.1977). Although these cases deal with the definition of "merchant" in § 2–104 for purposes of application to § 2–201(2) (the "between merchants" exception to the statute of frauds), the inquiry is relevant here for purposes of determining whether the transaction at issue occurred in a true "commercial setting," where unconscionability is rarely found. However, since we hold that, even if considered a "commercial setting," the clause at issue was unconscionable under the facts of this case, we do not reach the issue.

5. Although it may be, as Harris Seed argues, that the criticisms of *Allen* by courts, *see, e.g., Robinson Insurance & Real Estate, Inc. v. Southwestern Bell,* 366 F.Supp. 307 (W.D.Ark.1973), and commentators, *see* J. White & R. Summers, *Handbook of the Law Under the Uniform Commercial Code,* § 4–9, at 172 (2d Ed.1980) are well founded, the Michigan Appellate Court's holding is nevertheless an appropriate guide to our inquiry in the present case. *Cf. Simpson v. Jefferson Standard Life Insurance Co.,* 465 F.2d 1320, 1323 (6th Cir.1972) ("[d]ecisions of intermediate state courts must be followed by the federal courts unless there is reason to believe they would not be followed by the state's highest court.").

unfairness) *and Majors v. Kalo Laboratories, Inc.,* 407 F.Supp. 20, 23 (M.D.Ala.1975) ("[T]he Official Comment to § 2–302 suggests that [consideration of bargaining power] would be inappropriate.") *with Kerr-McGee Corp. v. Northern Utilities, Inc.,* 673 F.2d 323, 329 (10th Cir.1982) (relative considerations include whether "there was a gross inequality of bargaining power.") *and* J. White & R. Summers, *supra,* § 12–11, at 477 ("[o]ne can argue that when a seller has such a strong bargaining position that he can impose a perfectly drafted disclaimer, which operates to deprive the buyer of virtually all protection that a law would otherwise provide, and he refuses to bargain at all concerning its scope, then that clause has become 'oppressive' and so 'one-sided' as to be unconscionable."). We agree with the district court that relative bargaining power is an appropriate consideration in determining unconscionability under the Michigan Uniform Commercial Code.

Other closely related factors suggested by the Michigan court in *Allen* for determining the presence of procedural unconscionability are the relative economic strength of the parties and the alternative sources of supply. With reference to the relative economic strength of the parties, we note that Harris Seed is a large national producer and distributor of seed, dealing here with independent, relatively small farmers. As to alternative sources of supply, the farmers were faced with a situation where all seed distributors placed disclaimers and exclusionary clauses in their contracts. Thus, this presents a situation where "goods [could] only be obtained from * * * several sources on non-competitive terms * * * and doing without [was] not a realistic alternative." *Allen, supra,* 171 N.W.2d at 692.

Another pertinent factor considered by the district court in its unconscionability finding was that Harris Seed's salesman did not make Martin and Rick, who were uncounseled laymen, aware of the fact that the clauses in question altered significant statutory rights. Such a disclosure is an important consideration under Michigan law. *Mallory v. Conida Warehouses, Inc.,* 134 Mich.App. 28, 350 N.W.2d 825, 827 (1984); *cf. Johnson v. Mobil Oil Corp.,* 415 F.Supp. 264, 269 (E.D.Mich.1976) ("[b]efore a contracting party with * * * immense bargaining power * * * may limit its liability vis-a-vis an uncounseled layman * * * it has an affirmative duty to obtain the voluntary knowing assent of the other party.").

Furthermore, although the terms of the 1972 sale appeared to be the same as in previous years (unknown to Martin and Rick), Harris Seed decided to discontinue the hot water treatment of its cabbage seed, a standard practice for the previous twenty-six years. This decision by Harris Seed was one which had far-reaching consequences to the purchasers of its cabbage seed. As noted above, hot water treatment had been successful in preventing black leg in Washington State produced cabbage seed since 1947, and although Martin and Rick were unaware of the potential effects of black leg, or indeed even what black leg was, Harris Seed had considerable expertise in such matters.

Another important consideration is the fact that the presence of black leg in cabbage seed creates a *latent* defect. Although in many cases the fact that a latent defect is present seems to be dispositive, see *Majors v. Kalo Laboratories, Inc.,* 407 F.Supp. 20 (M.D.Ala.1975); *Corneli Seed Company v.*

Ferguson, 64 So.2d 162 (Fla.1953), we note only that it is important to the disposition of this case.

Significantly, in the present case not only was the defect latent, but it was also one which was within the control of Harris Seed to prevent. Even if Martin and Rick had been apprised of and understood the significance of Harris Seed's decision to discontinue hot water treatment, they would have been unable to detect the presence of the disease in the seed until their crop had developed into young plants. If Harris Seed were permitted to rely on the disclaimer and limitation clause to avoid liability under the facts of this case, the farmers who had no notice of, ability to detect, or control over the presence of the black leg could lose their livelihood. On the other hand, Harris Seed which had the knowledge, expertise and means to prevent the disease would only lose a few hundred dollars. Given the unique facts of this case, and giving "considerable weight" to the district court's decision that Michigan law would not permit the disclaimer and limitation clause to be enforced under such circumstances, we affirm the district court's finding of unconscionability.

* * *

[Some footnotes omitted.]

Notes

1. Did the seller's disclaimer satisfy the requirements of UCC 2–316(2)? How would you describe those requirements? For a highly critical analysis, see Cate v. Dover Corp., 790 S.W.2d 559 (Tex.1990).

2. How could the seller have avoided the result in this case?

3. Note that the disclaimer was printed on the order form supplied by the seller. In seed cases, the courts have been even more hostile to disclaimers printed on the package or bag of seeds and not seen by the buyer until after the contract is formed, if at all. See, e.g., Gold Kist, Inc. v. Citizens & Southern National Bank of South Carolina, 286 S.C. 272, 333 S.E.2d 67 (1985) (disclaimer not part of agreement). See also, Step-Saver Data Systems, Inc. v. Wyse Technology, 939 F.2d 91 (3d Cir.1991) (disclaimer on box containing computer software not conspicuous).

4. The United States and many states have enacted laws to protect the purchasers of seeds from falsely labeled products. The laws are backed by criminal sanctions. See 7 U.S.C.A. § 1551 (1985). These seed statutes, however, do not preempt Article 2 of the UCC. Thus, even if the seller complies with the statutory labeling requirements, it may still be liable for breach of warranty under the UCC. See, e.g., Hanson v. Funk Seeds International, 373 N.W.2d 30 (S.D.1985).

5. In Herrick v. Monsanto Co., 874 F.2d 594 (8th Cir.1989), the plaintiff's crop failed due to an allegedly defective herbicide. The court, relying upon UCC 2–719(3) and UCC 2–302, held that a clause excluding seller's liability for consequential damages was unconscionable because it left the buyer without an adequate remedy. In Lindemann v. Eli Lilly & Co., 816 F.2d 199 (5th Cir.1987), however, the court upheld a clause excluding consequential damages resulting from an allegedly defective weed control chemical. The clause was present during a 20 year course of dealing, and the parties dealt at arms length and

intended to allocate unknown or undeterminable risks. The *Martin* case was distinguished by the court in *Lindemann* but was not discussed in *Herrick.*

Problem 21–3

B, an experienced commercial fisherman, purchased a new diesel engine for his fishing boat from S. The engine was installed by S. Over the next 4 months, however, a number of mechanical problems arose, including the emission of excessive quantities of heavy black smoke. S was unable to correct them and the engine was removed from the boat. Experts will testify that it was unmerchantable.

At the time of contracting, B had signed a purchase order prepared by S. The face of the purchase order contained a number of terms and conditions. In the center of the face, this statement appeared: BOTH THIS ORDER AND ITS ACCEPTANCE ARE SUBJECT TO TERMS AND CONDITIONS STATED IN THIS ORDER. On the reverse side of the order at the top of the page, the following words appeared: TERMS AND CONDITIONS. Under that caption were eleven numbered paragraphs, one of which contained a disclaimer in the following form: THE SELLER HEREBY DISCLAIMS AND EXCLUDES ALL IMPLIED WARRANTIES, INCLUDING THE IMPLIED WARRANTY OF MERCHANTABILITY. B did not nor was he asked to read anything on the back of the purchase order. B received a fully executed copy of the order by mail before the engine was installed.

B sued S for damages resulting from breach of an implied warranty of merchantability. S defended on the ground that the warranty had been effectively disclaimed under UCC 2–316(2). What result?

Problem 21–4

S, a boat dealer, advertised a 42 foot Pearson sailing sloop for sale. The boat was manufactured in 1960 and had a wooden hull. B, an experienced sailor, had never owned a sloop with a wooden hull. Without the assistance of a third party, B examined the boat carefully and could find nothing wrong. She questioned S who, at various times stated: "This beauty was her owner's pride and joy. It's in great shape;" "The boat is sound. It rides the waves like a dream;" "The wood is solid throughout. We will replace any dry rot free of charge."

B agreed to purchase the sloop for $50,000. At the time of contracting, B signed a writing prepared by S which on the front provided, in part, as follows: "WARRANTIES. Buyer is buying the goods AS IS WHERE IS and no representations or statements have been made by seller except as herein stated, so that no warranty, express or implied, arises apart from this writing."

B took delivery of the boat, paid the price and went for a long, wet sail. The boat appeared to leak at the stern. An expert was hired to inspect the area and found extensive dry rot, which had clearly been there at the time of the sale. The estimated cost to repair the boat was $15,000.

B claimed damages for breach of warranty, measured by the cost to repair. S argued that all warranties, express or implied, had been disclaimed, citing UCC 2–316(1) & 2–202, UCC 2–316(3)(a) and UCC 2–316(3)(b). Is S correct? How is UCC 2–317 relevant to this case?

Problem 21–5

B, a baker, planned to expand its capacity by 30%. Accordingly, on March 1, it ordered a custom made oven from S, a manufacturer, to be delivered not later than September 1. B informed S of its planned expansion and stated that "time was of the essence:" B had developed a new bread for hotels and restaurants and wanted to be in production for the Fall convention season. S and B negotiated over how to deal with the risk of delay in delivery.

1. After discussing B's current profit margin and the probabilities that an expansion would be profitable, S agreed, in a clause labeled LIQUIDATED DAMAGES, to pay B $1,000 for every day of a non-excusable delay in delivery. S did not deliver the oven until October 1. B claimed liquidated damages in the amount of $15,000. S, however, can establish that the convention business during September was very slow and that, at best, B would have made only $2,500 in net profits if the oven had been delivered on time. Is the agreed damage clause enforceable under UCC 2–718?

2. Suppose that the clause was labeled LIMITATION OF DAMAGES and S agreed to pay "no more than $500 for each day of unexcused delay." The oven was delivered on October 1. B is prepared to establish that the convention market boomed during September and that the delay in delivery deprived it of at least $2,500 in net profits per day. B claims that the limitation clause was unreasonable. Is B correct? See UCC 2–718 & 2–719.

CAYUGA HARVESTER, INC. v. ALLIS–CHALMERS CORP.

Supreme Court of New York, Appellate Division, 1983.
95 A.D.2d 5, 465 N.Y.S.2d 606.

HANCOCK, JUSTICE:

Under the Uniform Commercial Code, the parties to a sale may, within certain limitations, allocate the risks of their bargain by limiting the remedy of the buyer (Uniform Commercial Code, § 2–719, subd. 1, par. a). When, however, a limited remedy such as an exclusive repair and replacement warranty fails of its essential purpose, the buyer is relieved of its restrictions and may resort to other remedies as provided in section 2–719 (subd. 2). The Code also permits the parties to agree to exclude consequential damages unless the exclusion is unconscionable (Uniform Commercial Code, § 2–719, subd. 3). Here the contract in issue contains both an exclusive repair and replacement warranty and an exclusion of consequential damages; plaintiff claiming that the limited remedy failed of its essential purpose seeks to recover consequential as well as other damages for breach of warranty. A major question arises from plaintiff's contention that proof of the failure of the limited repair and replacement warranty would free it not only from the restrictions of that clause but also from the clause excluding consequential damages.

The action arises out of the sale of an N–7 harvesting machine manufactured by defendant Allis-Chalmers Corporation ("Allis"). Plaintiff, the operator of an extensive corn-growing business in Cato, New York, purchased the machine for $142,213 from defendant R.C. Church & Sons, Inc. ("Church"), a farm machinery dealer, under a written purchase order containing a limited repair and replacement warranty and an exclusion of consequential damages. The balance of the purchase price, after a down payment of $36,-989.80, was financed through defendant Allis-Chalmers Credit Corporation ("Allis Credit"). Plaintiff alleges that the machine did not operate or function properly and that it suffered numerous failures and breakdowns preventing it from making a timely and effective harvest of its 1981 corn crop.

The issues considered concerning various sections of the Uniform Commercial Code are as follows:

I. A. whether the limited repair and replacement warranty failed of its essential purpose (§ 2–719, subd. 2);

B. if so, whether, despite the failure, the consequential damages exclusion remains in effect; and

C. whether the clause excluding consequential damages is unconscionable (§§ 2–719, subd. 3; 2–302, subds. 1, 2).

* * *

I

We consider first the grant of summary judgment dismissing the first two causes of action against Allis alleging breaches of express warranties. In the purchase order under the "Allis-Chalmers New Farm Equipment Warranty", Allis gave an express warranty limited to the repair or replacement of defective parts in the following provisions which we quote in part:

> WHAT IS WARRANTED
>
> Allis-Chalmers Corporation ("Company") warrants new farm equipment sold by it to be merchantable and free of defects in workmanship and material at the time of shipment from the Company's factory. THERE ARE NO WARRANTIES WHICH EXTEND BEYOND THOSE EXPRESSLY STATED HEREIN. The warranty is made to the original purchaser or lessee from an authorized Allis-Chalmers Dealer of each item of new Allis-Chalmers farm equipment.
>
> 1. *Equipment Warranty.* Parts which are defective in workmanship and material as delivered will be repaired or replaced as follows:
>
> * * *

(There follow several paragraphs detailing the terms and conditions of Allis' obligation to make repairs and replacements and the periods during which the warranty is effective.)

> I. Remedies Exclusive
>
> THE COMPANY'S LIABILITY, WHETHER IN CONTRACT OR IN TORT, ARISING OUT OF WARRANTIES, REPRESENTATIONS, INSTRUCTIONS, OR DEFECTS FROM ANY CAUSE SHALL BE LIMITED EXCLUSIVELY TO REPAIRING OR REPLACING PARTS UNDER THE CONDITIONS AS AFORESAID, AND IN NO EVENT WILL THE COMPANY BE LIABLE FOR CONSEQUENTIAL DAMAGES, INCLUDING BUT NOT LIMITED TO LOSS OF CROPS, LOSS OF PROFITS,

RENTAL OR SUBSTITUTE EQUIPMENT, OR OTHER COMMERCIAL LOSS.

In granting Allis' motions Special Term held that the provision excluding consequential damages in Paragraph "I", above, was, as a matter of law, not unconscionable under Uniform Commercial Code (§§ 2–719, subd. 3; 2–302, subd. 1) and that it acted as a total bar to plaintiff's express warranty claims. The court did not find it necessary to reach the issues before us concerning the alleged failure of the essential purpose of the repair and replacement warranty under the Uniform Commercial Code (§ 2–719, subd. 2) and the effect of that failure on the exclusion of consequential damages.

A

Ordinarily, whether circumstances have caused a "limited remedy to fail of its essential purpose" (Uniform Commercial Code, § 2–719, subd. 2) is a question of fact for the jury and one necessarily to be resolved upon proof of the circumstances occurring after the contract is formed (see *Johnson v. John Deere Co.,* 306 N.W.2d 231, 237, 238 [S.D.1981]). It should be noted that in order to establish a failure of a limited remedy under section 2–719 (subd. 2) it is not necessary to show that the warrantor's conduct in failing to effect repairs was wilfully dilatory or even negligent. Rather, the section is to apply "whenever an exclusive remedy, which may have appeared fair and reasonable at the inception of the contract, as a result of later circumstances operates to deprive a party of a substantial benefit of the bargain" (*Clark v. International Harvester Co.,* 99 Idaho 326, 340, 581 P.2d 784; see Uniform Commercial Code, § 2–719, Official Comment 1; White & Summers, Handbook of the Law under the Uniform Commercial Code, [2d ed.], § 12–10). The damage to the buyer is the same whether the seller diligently but unsuccessfully attempts to honor his promise or acts negligently or in bad faith (see *Beal v. General Motors Corp.,* 354 F.Supp. 423, 427 [D.C. Del., 1973]). Moreover, a "delay in supplying the remedy can just as effectively deny the purchaser the product he expected as can the total inability to repair. In both instances the buyer loses the substantial benefit of his purchase" (*Chatlos Systems, Inc. v. National Cash Register Corp.,* 635 F.2d 1081, 1085 [CCA 3d, 1980]). Thus, if it is found at trial that plaintiff, because of defendant Allis' failure to repair or replace parts within a reasonable time, has been deprived of a substantial benefit of its bargain, it may prevail even though, as is the case here, there is no claim of bad faith or wilfully dilatory conduct and the record demonstrates that defendant made extensive efforts to comply.

The precise question here is whether plaintiff has made a prima facie showing that the limited remedy failed of its essential purpose. On our review of the record we hold that plaintiff has made such a showing and that Special Term was in error in granting summary judgment dismissing the first two causes of action against Allis in their entirety (C.P.L.R. 3212, subd. b). Mr. Sheckler, plaintiff's president, states in an affidavit "that the N–7 combine purchased by plaintiff suffered over 100 mechanical failures and over 100 parts replacements resulting in over 640 actual hours of machine down-time. Because of the inoperability of the N–7 combine a full eight months were required for plaintiff to complete the process of driving the combine over all the acres of corn." Annexed to plaintiff's affidavits are a detailed log of the numerous machine failures and a lengthy list of warranty claims totaling many thousands of dollars submitted by Church to Allis covering work performed and parts supplied from the delivery of the machine in July of 1981 through February, 1982.

It is settled that a finding that a limited warranty has failed of its essential purpose frees the buyer to pursue his remedies under other provisions of the Uniform Commercial Code as if the clause did not exist (see *S.M. Wilson & Co. v. Smith Intern., Inc.*, 587 F.2d 1363 [CCA 9th, 1978]; *County Asphalt, Inc. v. Lewis Welding & Engineering Corp.*, 323 F.Supp. 1300, 1309 [S.D.N.Y.1970], affd. 444 F.2d 372 [CCA 2d, 1971], cert. den. 404 U.S. 939, 92 S.Ct. 272, 30 L.Ed.2d 252; *Johnson v. John Deere Co.*, 306 N.W.2d 231, 236 [S.D.1981], supra). Plaintiff would, therefore, not be precluded by the exclusive remedy clause from recovering under the usual measure of damages in warranty cases; i.e., "the difference at the time and place of acceptance between the value of the goods accepted and the value they would have had if they had been as warranted" (Uniform Commercial Code, § 2–714, subd. 2) (see *American Elec. Power Co., Inc. v. Westinghouse Elec. Corp.*, 418 F.Supp. 435, 457, 458 [S.D.N.Y.1976]; *County Asphalt, Inc. v. Lewis Welding & Engineering Corp.*, supra, p. 1309; *Johnson v. John Deere Co.*, supra, p. 236).

The order granting summary judgment to defendant Allis should be reversed to the extent that it dismisses the first and second causes of action in their entirety.

B

We come next to the legal question whether the consequential damage exclusion in Paragraph "I" would survive a finding that the limited repair and replacement warranty in that paragraph had failed of its essential purpose. We have found no controlling authority on the point in this state, and the numerous decisions in federal courts and the courts of other states are in conflict.

As we view it, the problem requires a two-step analysis: first, construing Paragraph "I" in its context as one clause in a contract concerning a substantial commercial transaction in order to ascertain the allocation of the risks as intended by the parties; and, second, determining whether that agreed-upon allocation of the risks leaves "at least a fair quantum of remedy for breach of the obligations or duties outlined in the contract" (McKinney's Cons.Laws of N.Y., Book 62½, Part 1, Uniform Commercial Code, § 2–719, Official Comment 1, p. 691). Paragraph "I" states:

> THE COMPANY'S LIABILITY, WHETHER IN CONTRACT OR IN TORT, ARISING OUT OF WARRANTIES, REPRESENTATIONS, INSTRUCTIONS, OR DEFECTS FROM ANY CAUSE SHALL BE LIMITED EXCLUSIVELY TO REPAIRING OR REPLACING PARTS UNDER THE CONDITIONS AS AFORESAID, AND IN NO EVENT WILL THE COMPANY BE LIABLE FOR CONSEQUENTIAL DAMAGES, INCLUDING BUT NOT LIMITED TO LOSS OF CROPS, LOSS OF PROFITS, RENTAL OR SUBSTITUTE EQUIPMENT, OR OTHER COMMERCIAL LOSS.

Preliminarily, it may be helpful to set forth two factors which are material to our analysis and, we think, significant: (1) this is not a case involving bad faith or wilfully dilatory conduct on the part of the defendant (compare, e.g., *Jones & McKnight Corp. v. Birdsboro Corp.*, 320 F.Supp. 39, 43 [D.C. Ill., 1970]; *Adams v. J.I. Case Co.*, 125 Ill.App.2d 388, 402, 261 N.E.2d 1: and (2) plaintiff, if it should succeed in proving that the limited warranty has failed, would, regardless of a contrary ruling on the survivability of the consequential damages exclusion, be permitted to recover damages allowed by Uniform Commercial Code (§ 2–714, subd. 2) (see subpart A, supra).

Plaintiff argues that the promise of defendant to repair and replace defective parts in the first part of Paragraph "I" and the clause exempting defendant from the assessment of consequential damages in the second part are mutually dependent, i.e., that a failure on the part of defendant to perform its obligations under the first, as a matter of law, deprives it of its exemption under the second part and frees plaintiff from its limitations. Defendant, on the other hand, maintains that the two provisions are unrelated and independent.

In our view defendant has the better of the argument. Certainly, no wording in Paragraph "I", itself, indicates that the provisions are interrelated or that the failure of defendant to perform under the repair and replacement warranty deprives it of the protection of the consequential damages exclusion. The purposes of the two clauses are totally discrete: that of the first is to restrict defendant's obligations under the transaction to repairing or replacing defective parts while that of the second is to rule out a specific type of damage. Each clause stands on its own and may be given effect without regard to the other. Thus, the plain meaning of Paragraph "I" appears to favor defendant.

Nor, given the larger context of Paragraph "I" as one term in a transaction involving the sale of an expensive piece of farm machinery to a large commercial grower, would it be reasonable to give it a different construction. Adopting plaintiff's interpretation, defendant's failure to repair and replace defective parts would, despite its good-faith efforts to fulfill its obligations, subject it to a lawsuit for consequential damages and loss of profits which, in view of the size of plaintiff's operation, could result in a recovery many times the value of the N–7 combine. It defies reason to suppose that defendant could have intended to assume such risks. The contrary construction urged by defendant entails a more plausible allocation of the risks and one that the parties could reasonably have had in mind: i.e., that a failure of the repair and replacement warranty, despite defendant's good faith efforts to comply, would permit plaintiff to recover the ordinary breach of warranty damages (Uniform Commercial Code, § 2–714, subd. 2) but not loss of profits or other consequential damages.

We find nothing in the Uniform Commercial Code that rules out defendant's construction. On the contrary, under Uniform Commercial Code (§ 2–719) the "parties are left free to shape their remedies to their particular requirements and reasonable agreements limiting or modifying remedies are to be given effect" (McKinney's Cons.Laws of N.Y., Book 62½, Part 1, Uniform Commercial Code, § 2–719, Official Comment 1, p. 691), provided that the remedy limitations are not unconscionable and that "there be at least a fair quantum of remedy for breach of the obligations or duties outlined in the contract" (McKinney's Cons. Laws of N.Y., Book 62½, Part 1, Uniform Commercial Code, § 2–719, Official Comment 1, p. 691). Moreover, Uniform Commercial Code (§ 2–719, subd. 3) provides specifically that consequential damages "may be limited or excluded unless the limitation or exclusion is unconscionable." In a similar vein, the Official Comment 3 to section 2–719 states: "Subsection (3) recognizes the validity of clauses limiting or excluding consequential damages but makes it clear that they may not operate in an unconscionable manner. Actually such terms are merely an allocation of unknown or undeterminable risks. The seller in all cases is free to disclaim warranties in the manner provided in Section 2–316" (McKinney's Cons.Laws of N.Y., Book 62½, Part 1, Uniform Commercial Code, § 2–719, Official Comment 3, p. 691). In sum, plaintiff has offered no good reason why the consequential damage exclusion clause should not be given effect in these circumstances, where the failure of the repair and replacement warranty is not due to bad faith or willfully dilatory conduct. That the clause be given effect here would be an allocation of the risks which leaves the buyer a fair quantum of remedy as required by the Code and one that the parties to this commercial contract could reasonably have intended. We conclude, therefore, that if plaintiff succeeds in establishing that the repair and replacement warranty failed of its essential purpose (Uniform Commercial Code, § 2–719, subd. 2), the exclusion of consequential damages provided by Paragraph "I" remains in effect.

As stated, the decisions are in conflict but the proper rule, we think, is that set forth in *Chatlos Systems, Inc. v. National Cash Register Corp.*, 635 F.2d 1081, 1086 [CCA 3d, 1980], supra: "The limited remedy of repair and a consequential damages exclusion are two discrete ways of attempting to limit recovery for breach of warranty. (Citations omitted.) The Code, moreover, tests each by a different standard. The former survives unless it fails of its essential purpose, while the latter is valid unless it is unconscionable. We therefore see no reason to hold, as a general proposition, that the failure of the limited remedy provided in the contract, without more, invalidates a wholly distinct term in the agreement excluding consequential damages."

* * *

The leading cases cited as supporting the opposite view are *Jones & McKnight Corp. v. Birdsboro Corp.*, 320 F.Supp. 39 [DC Ill., 1970], supra, and *Adams v. J.I. Case Co.*, 125 Ill.App.2d 388, 261 N.E.2d 1, supra (see also *Koehring Co. v. A.P.I., Inc.*, 369 F.Supp. 882 [DC Mich., 1974]; *Beal v. General Motors Corp.*, 354 F.Supp. 423 [DC Del., 1973], supra; *Clark v. International Harvester Co.*, 99 Idaho 326, 581 P.2d 784, supra; *Ehlers v. Chrysler Motor Corp.*, 88 S.D. 612, 226 N.W.2d 157; *Goddard v. General Motors Corp.*, 60 Ohio St.2d 41, 396 N.E.2d 761; *Murray v. Holiday Rambler, Inc.*, 83 Wis.2d 406, 265 N.W.2d 513).

On analysis, however, neither *Jones & McKnight* nor *Adams* is inconsistent with our holding. Each case involves outright repudiation of the repair and replacement warranty or conduct by the seller that was wilfully dilatory. Thus, in *Jones & McKnight* the court held that the buyer was entitled to assume that the seller "would not be unreasonable or wilfully dilatory in making good their warranty in the event of defects in the machinery and equipment" and refused to allow the defendant "to shelter itself behind one segment of the warranty when it has allegedly repudiated and ignored its very limited obligations under another segment of the same warranty" (*Jones & McKnight Corp. v. Birdsboro Corp.*, supra, p. 43). Similarly, in *Adams* the court, in holding that the repair and replacement warranty and the consequential damages exclusion were "not separable" held that "plaintiff could not have made [its] bargain and purchase with knowledge that defendant [ ] would be unreasonable, or, * * * wilfully dilatory or careless and negligent in making good [its] warranty in the event of its breach" (*Adams v. J.I. Case Co.*, supra, 125 Ill.App.2d at p. 402, 261 N.E.2d 1).

We need not decide whether we would follow *Jones & McKnight* and *Adams* if plaintiff could contend, as did the buyers in those cases, that in agreeing to the consequential damages exclusion it never contemplated that defendant would not make good-faith efforts to effect repairs. That issue is not before us.

While not all of the cases following the *Jones & McKnight* and *Adams* rule involve bad faith or wilful repudiation of the repair and replacement warranty, several arise from non-commercial sales where the purchaser was an individual consumer (see, e.g., *Clark v. International Harvester Co.*, supra; *Ehlers v. Chrysler Motor Corp.*, supra; *Goddard v. General Motors Corp.*, supra; *Murray v. Holiday Rambler, Inc.*, supra). Moreover, in *Clark v. International Harvester Co.* (supra), which entailed a purchase of a tractor by an individual custom farmer, the court points to a factor not present in the case at bar, i.e., that there "was a significant disparity in bargaining power between the parties in this case" (*Clark v. International Harvester Co.*, supra, 99 Idaho at p. 343, 581 P.2d 784).

Although we hold that plaintiff may not recover consequential damages, it will, if successful at trial, be entitled to other damages (Uniform Commercial Code, § 2–714, subd. 2). The order granting summary judgment should, therefore, be modified to a grant of partial summary judgment dismissing only those elements of the first two causes of action against Allis which seek consequential damages.

* * *

Finally, we analyze plaintiff's contentions that Paragraph "I" is unconscionable under sections 2–719 (subd. 3) and 2–302 (subds. 1, 2) of the Code. A determination as to the conscionability of a contract relates to the circumstances existing at the time of its formation (Uniform Commercial Code, § 2–302, subd. 1). As a practical matter, however, the determination is inevitably made after a dispute has arisen. Thus, the agreement must be tested as to conscionability as it is applied to the particular breach which has occurred. Here, there is no claim of bad faith or that the failure to repair was wilfully dilatory, and we have held that the parties did not intend in Paragraph "I" that defendant's good faith but unsuccessful efforts to repair would negate the consequential damages exclusion. We have also held that such an agreed upon allocation of the risks does not offend the Code requirement that there be at least a fair quantum of remedy for breach of defendant's obligations. We must now decide whether this agreed upon allocation of the risks is unconscionable.

* * *

On this record, in view of the nature of plaintiff's business as a large commercial grower, the size of the transaction involved, the fact that plaintiff had available other sources for purchasing similar equipment, the experience of its president and his familiarity with similar damage exclusion clauses, we agree with Special Term that plaintiff was not put in a bargaining position where it lacked a meaningful choice; nor was the agreement allocating the risk of crop loss and other consequential damages to the plaintiff, provided that good faith efforts be made to fulfill the repair warranty, unreasonably favorable to the defendant (see *Matter of State of New York v. Avco Fin. Serv. of N.Y.*, 50 N.Y.2d 383, 429 N.Y.S.2d 181, 406 N.E.2d 1075, supra).

The significant facts germane to the conscionability issue were essentially undisputed and we hold that Special Term correctly determined, as a legal question, that Paragraph "I" was not unconscionable and properly did so on the affidavits and other documents before it without the aid of a hearing (see Uniform Commercial Code, § 2–302).

* * *

[Footnotes omitted.]

Notes

1. *Cayuga Harvester* involved a fairly typical risk allocation package with four parts: (1) A limited warranty, i.e., that the goods were "merchantable and free of defects in material and workmanship at the time of shipment. * * *; (2) A disclaimer of all other warranties, express or implied plus a "merger" clause; (3) An agreed, exclusive limited remedy for breach, i.e., the "repair or replacement" of parts which are "defective in workmanship and material as delivered" within a stated period of time; and (4) An exclusion in any event of liability for consequential damages for liability, "whether in contract or tort, arising out of any warranties made." These packages vary from industry to industry, but the thrust is essentially the same. See Transamerica Oil Corp. v. Lynes, Inc., 723 F.2d 758 (10th Cir.1983), where the court concluded that a similar limitation was so "pervasive" in the trade that the parties must have contracted with reference to it.

The problem arises when, after a defect is discovered, the seller is unable or unwilling to repair it within the stated time.

> This rosy picture of the limited repair warranty, however, rests upon at least three assumptions: that the warrantor will diligently make repairs, that such repairs will indeed 'cure' the defects, and that consequential loss in the interim will be negligible. So long as these assumptions hold true, the limited remedy appears to operate fairly and * * * will usually withstand contentions of 'unconscionability.' But when one of these assumptions proves false in a particular case, the purchaser may find that the substantial benefit of the bargain has been lost.

Eddy, *On the "Essential" Purposes of Limited Remedies: The Metaphysics of U.C.C. Section 2–719(2)*, 65 Calif.L.Rev. 28, 63 (1977).

When a disappointed buyer attacks the limited remedy, the cases tend to agree on the questions which must be answered and that the answers may vary from case to case. Here is a brief sample.

1. Was the limited remedy "expressly agreed to be exclusive"? UCC 2–719(1)(b). If not, resort to it by the buyer is optional. See, e.g., Leininger v. Sola, 314 N.W.2d 39 (N.D.1981). If so, it is "the sole remedy."

2. Did the "circumstances cause an exclusive or limited remedy to fail of its essential purpose. * * *?" UCC 2–719(2). If not, it is enforceable. If so, "remedy may be had as provided in this Act." The most common "circumstances" are the seller's failure to "cure" the defect within the time stated or a reasonable time. As Judge Aspen put it: A limited remedy of repair and replacement fails of its essential purposes when it is inadequate to provide the buyer with goods which conform to the contract within a reasonable time. * * * It is irrelevant to this standard whether the seller's failure to correct the defect is willful or not." Custom Automated Machinery v. Penda Corp., 537 F.Supp. 77 (N.D.Ill.1982). See also, Employers Ins. of Wausau v. Suwanee River SPA Lines, Inc., 866 F.2d 752 (5th Cir. 1989) (good faith failure to repair). Rudd Construction Equipment Co., Inc. v. Clark Equipment Co., 735 F.2d 974 (6th Cir.1984) (limited remedy fails essential purpose when defect causes fire which destroyed goods before seller had opportunity to cure).

3. If the limited remedy of repair or replacement failed its essential purpose, what is the effect on the total risk allocation package? More particularly, if the failure enables the buyer to pursue normal remedies for "direct" damages under UCC 2–714, what about the clause excluding consequential damages?

There are several closely related subquestions.

First, did the parties intend the exclusion clause to be an integral part of the risk allocation package? If so, the failure of one part dooms the entire package, with the result that the buyer can pursue consequential damages under UCC 2–715(2). See Waters v. Massey-Ferguson, Inc., 775 F.2d 587 (4th Cir.1985); Milgard Tempering, Inc. v. Selas Corp. of America, 761 F.2d 553 (9th Cir.1985) (whether clause separate is question of intent). See also, Hawaiian Telephone Co. v. Microfilm Data Systems, Inc., 829 F.2d 919 (9th Cir.1987) (operation of exclusion clause dependent upon delivery of goods).

Second, if the parties did not so intend, does the separate exclusion clause drop out because UCC 2–719(2) provides that "remedy may be had as provided in this Act" and "this Act" permits consequential damages? Some courts have answered "yes", e.g., Fidelity & Deposit Co. v. Maryland v. Krebs Engineers, 859 F.2d 501 (7th Cir.1988) (Wisconsin), but the majority have answered "no", e.g. Smith v. Navistar Intern. Transp. Corp., 957 F.2d 1439 (7th Cir.1992) (Illinois). Under the majority interpretation, the separate exclusion clause must be evaluated under UCC 2–719(3).

Third, was the exclusion clause unconscionable at the time it was made? As the seed cases indicate, see supra p. 957, there is no certain answer, even in commercial cases. A number of factors are relevant to the inquiry: Was there a prior course of dealing between the parties; was the exclusion clause conspicuous or brought to the buyer's attention; did the parties bargain in good faith; did the buyer have any realistic choices other than to deal with the seller; did the parties intend to allocate unknown or indeterminate risks? In most cases, however, the exclusion clause is upheld against an unconscionability attack.

See, e.g., Lindemann v. Eli Lilly & Co., 816 F.2d 199 (5th Cir.1987); Island Creek Coal Co. v. Lake Shore, Inc., 832 F.2d 274 (4th Cir.1987); American Nursery Products, Inc. v. Indian Wells Orchards, 115 Wash.2d 217, 797 P.2d 477 (1990).

Fourth, are there any equitable considerations that should prompt a court to invalidate the entire package, including the exclusion clause? For example, suppose the seller suspected that the goods were defective and knew that the limited remedy would not correct them. Or, suppose that the seller made no effort to cure or engaged in a careless or unprofessional effort. Or, suppose that the agreed remedy limited the buyer to less than the contract price if a cure was not forthcoming. In any of these cases, should the court conclude that the operation of the failed remedy package was unconscionable and the buyer should have the full remedies provided by Article 2?

Where does *Cayuga Harvester* fit in this range of possibilities?

Note: Contracting Out of Tort Liability

In *Cayuga Harvester,* the seller attempted to exclude or "contract out" of "liability * * * in tort, arising out of warranties, representations, instructions, or defects from any cause," at least to the extent consequential damages were involved. What is the effect of these provisions?

If a defect in the product caused personal injuries, strict products liability would apply and the clause would be unenforceable (against public policy) against the plaintiff. See Note, *Enforcing Waivers in Products Liability,* 69 Va.L.Rev. 1111 (1983).

Between commercial parties ("extraordinary" consumers) where only economic loss is involved, the seller is, in most states, not liable in either strict products liability or negligence. In short, the buyer can pursue a warranty but not a tort theory. Review *Spring Motors,* supra at 828. Thus, the disclaimer would be tested under the Code, not in tort.

But suppose a defect in the product caused both economic loss and damage to the property sold, e.g., a defective part caused extensive damage to a turbine sold to the buyer but to no other property. Does warranty or tort theory apply and, if the latter, is the exclusion clause enforceable outside of the Code?

In this borderland between contract and tort where commercial parties are involved and property damage is confined to the goods sold, many courts have concluded that strict tort liability applies if the nature of the defect, the risk created and the manner in which the accident occurred raised an issue of product safety. The emphasis is upon the nature of the risk created to person and property, not upon the type of damage actually caused.

On the tort side of the line, the UCC does not apply. Nevertheless, commercial parties can agree to exculpate the seller from tort liability or from consequential damages if high standards insuring the quality of bargaining have been met. Thus, in Salt River Project Agr. v. Westinghouse Electric Co., 143 Ariz. 368, 694 P.2d 198 (1984), a turbine case, the court upheld an exculpation clause where the parties dealt in a commercial setting from positions of relatively equal bargaining strength, bargained over the specifications of the product and negotiated concerning the risk of loss from defects in the product. See McNichols, *Who Says That Strict Tort Disclaimers Can Never Be Effective? The Courts Disagree,* 28 Okl.L.Rev. 494 (1975).

SECTION 5. CONSUMER BUYERS, PRODUCT WARRANTIES AND ECONOMIC LOSS

An individual purchases a car, or a stereo or furniture or even a mobile home from a dealer for personal, family or household purposes. In short, they are consumer goods. See UCC 9–109(1). A common assumption is that consumer buyers, as a class, have less capacity than the professional seller to protect themselves in the bargain. They are at a disadvantage in assessing risk, evaluating quality, obtaining adequate information, bargaining over contract provisions and pursuing remedies if problems arise. They are "ordinary" consumers who are more susceptible to exploitation or unprovable fraud by the seller than a commercial or "extraordinary" buyer. (The distinction between "ordinary" and "extraordinary" consumers was advanced by Justice Peters, dissenting in Seely v. White Motor Co., 69 Cal.2d 9, 45 Cal.Rptr. 17, 403 P.2d 145 (1965), to draw the line between warranty and tort in products liability cases. According to Peters, the test should depend upon the "relative roles played by the parties to the purchase contract and the nature of the transaction" rather than the type of loss caused and ask whether, at the time of contracting, the goods were sold to a commercial party or to an "ordinary consumer who is usually unable to protect himself * * *" or a commercial buyer who possessed "more bargaining power than does the usual individual who purchases * * * on the retail level." (403 P.2d at 152–58.)

The conclusion from this, sometimes disputed, see, e.g., Schwartz & Wilde, *Imperfect Information in Markets for Contract Terms: The Examples of Warranties and Security Interests,* 69 Va.L.Rev. 1387 (1983); compare Kronman, *Paternalism and the Law of Contracts,* 92 Yale L.J. 763, 766–74 (1983) (assessing risk of unprovable fraud by seller), is that consumers need more legal protection than commercial buyers.

When the losses are solely economic, the consumer buyer's legal protection from breach of warranty by the seller is, without more, governed by the UCC. Additional, albeit uneven, protection is provided by the Magnuson-Moss Warranty Act on the federal level and, in some states, consumer protection legislation, including the so-called "lemon" laws. See C. Reitz, Consumer Product Warranties Under Federal and State Laws (2d Ed. 1987).

In this Section, we will see how the consumer buyer of a "big ticket" item, a new car, might fare under this mix of federal and state law against the risk allocation package discussed in Section 4, supra. For general background and more detail, we recommend, Rice, *Product Quality Laws and the Economics of Federalism,* 65 B.U.L.Rev. 1 (1985). See also, Braucher, *An Informal Resolution Model of Consumer Product Warranty Law,* 1985 Wis. L.Rev. 1405; Vogel, *Squeezing Consumers: Lemon Laws, Consumer Warranties, and a Proposal for Reform,* 1985 Ariz.St.L.J. 589; Coffinberger & Samuels, *Legislative Responses to the Plight of New Car Purchasers,* 18 U.C.C.L.J. 168 (1985); Miller & Kanter, *Litigation under Magnuson-Moss,* 13 U.C.C.L.J. 10 (1980).

VENTURA v. FORD MOTOR CORP.

Superior Court of New Jersey, Appellate Division, 1981.
180 N.J.Super. 45, 433 A.2d 801.

[Marino Auto sold Ventura a new 1978 Ford. The car was substantially impaired due to persistent and continual stalling and hesitation. Ventura sued both Marino Auto and Ford, the manufacturer, for damages and Marino Auto cross-claimed against Ford for indemnification. At the conclusion of the non-jury trial, the trial judge concluded that Ford had breached a warranty to Ventura, made through Marino Auto, but that Ventura had not proven damages against Ford. Ventura, however, could recover attorney's fees in the amount of $5,165 from Ford under the Magnuson-Moss Warranty Act, 15 U.S.C.A. § 2310(d)(2). In addition, despite an attempt by the dealer to disclaim all warranties, express or implied, Ventura could revoke its acceptance against and recover the purchase price less an allowance for use, a total of $6,745.59, from Marino Auto. Finally, the trial court entered a judgment in favor of Marino Auto against Ford for $2,910.59 and rejected Ventura's claims for interest, punitive damages and treble damages.

On appeal, the judgment was affirmed. The court assumed that Marino Auto's disclaimer of the implied warranty of merchantability was valid under the UCC, and concluded that the judgment was supported by the Magnuson-Moss Warranty Act.]

* * *

The Magnuson-Moss Warranty-Federal Trade Commission Improvement Act, *supra,* was adopted on January 4, 1975, 88 *Stat.* 2183. Its purpose was to make "warranties on consumer products more readily understandable and enforceable." Note, 7 *Rutgers-Camden L.J.* 379 (1976). The act enhances the consumer's position by allowing recovery under a warranty without regard to privity of contract between the consumer and warrantor, by prohibiting the disclaimer of implied warranties in a written warranty, and by enlarging the remedies available to a consumer for breach of warranty, including the award of attorneys' fees. *Id.* The requirement of privity of contract between the consumer and the warrantor has been removed by assuring consumers a remedy against all warrantors of the product.[3] A consumer is defined in 15 *U.S.C.A.* § 2301(3) as follows:

> (3) The term 'consumer' means a buyer (other than for purposes of resale) of any consumer product, any person to whom such product is transferred during the duration of an implied or written warranty (or service contract) applicable to the product, and any other person who is entitled by the terms of such warranty (or service contract) or under applicable State law to enforce against the warrantor (or service contract) the obligations of the warranty (or service contract).

A "supplier" is defined as any person engaged in the business of making a consumer product directly or indirectly available to consumers, § 2301(4), and a "warrantor" includes any supplier or other person who gives or offers

3. In Miller and Kanter, "Litigation Under Magnuson-Moss: New Opportunities in Private Actions," 13 *U.C.C.L.J.* 10, 21–22 (1980), the authors discuss the broad definition of a consumer and state that "an assumption is now created that no privity restriction exists."

to give a written warranty or who is obligated under an implied warranty. § 2301(5). The term "written warranty" is defined in § 2301(6) to include:

> (A) any written affirmation of fact or written promise made in connection with the sale of a consumer product by a supplier to a buyer which relates to the nature of the material or workmanship and affirms or promises that such material or workmanship is defect free or will meet a specified level of performance over a specified period of time, or
>
> (B) any undertaking in writing in connection with the sale by a supplier of a consumer product to refund, repair, replace or take other remedial action with respect to such product in the event that such product fails to meet the specifications set forth in the undertaking.

The Magnuson-Moss Warranty Act provides for two types of written warranties on consumer products, those described as "full" warranties and those described as "limited" warranties. 15 *U.S.C.A.* § 2303. The nature of the "full" warranty is prescribed by § 2304. It expressly provides in subsection (a)(4) that a consumer must be given the election to receive a refund or replacement without charge of a product or part which is defective or malfunctions after a reasonable number of attempts by the warrantor to correct such condition. For the breach of any warranty, express or implied, or of a service contract (defined in 15 *U.S.C.A.* § 2301(8)), consumers are given the right to sue for damages and "other legal and equitable relief" afforded under state or federal law, 15 *U.S.C.A.* § 2310(d); 15 *U.S.C.A.* § 2311(b)(1).

Appellant Ford contends that the trial judge improperly invoked § 2304 of the act as a basis for allowing "rescission" in the case since the warranty given by Ford was a limited warranty and not a full warranty. 15 *U.S.C.A.* § 2303(a)(2) provides that all warranties that do not meet federal minimum standards for warranty contained in § 2304 shall be conspicuously designated a "limited warranty." "Limited" warranties protect consumers by prohibiting disclaimers of implied warranties, § 2308, but are otherwise not described in the act. Note, *supra,* 7 *Rutgers-Camden L.J.* at 381. Clearly, Ford's warranty, which is quoted later in this opinion, was a limited warranty.

15 *U.S.C.A.* § 2308 provides as follows:

> (a) No supplier may disclaim or modify (except as provided in subsection (b) of this section) any implied warranty to a consumer with respect to such consumer product if (1) such supplier makes any written warranty to the consumer with respect to such consumer product, or (2) at the time of sale, or within 90 days thereafter, such supplier enters into a service contract with the consumer which applies to such consumer product.
>
> (b) For purposes of this chapter (other than section 2304(a)(2) of this title), implied warranties may be limited in duration to the duration of a written warranty of reasonable duration, if such limitation is conscionable and is set forth in clear and unmistakable language and prominently displayed on the face of the warranty.
>
> (c) A disclaimer, modification, or limitation made in violation of this section shall be ineffective for purposes of this chapter and State law.

We will first consider the application of this act to the dealer, Marino Auto. As quoted above, paragraph 7 of the purchase order-contract provides that there are no warranties, express or implied, made by the selling dealer or manufacturer except, in the case of a new motor vehicle, "the warranty expressly given to the purchaser upon delivery of such motor vehicle. * * *" This section also provides: "The selling dealer also agrees to promptly perform and fulfill all terms and conditions of the owner service policy." Ford contended in the trial court that Marino Auto had "a duty" to properly diagnose and make repairs, that such duty was "fixed both by the express warranty * * * which they passed on * * * and by the terms of [paragraph 7 of the contract with plaintiff]" by which Marino Auto expressly undertook "to perform its obligations under the owner service policy." See 15 *U.S.C.A.* § 2310(f); 16 *C.F.R.* § 700.4 (1980). The provision in paragraph 7 in these circumstances is a "written warranty" within the meaning of § 2301(6)(B) since it constitutes an undertaking in connection with the sale to take "remedial action with respect to such product in the event that such product fails to meet the specifications set forth in the undertaking. * * *" In our view the specifications of the undertaking include, at the least, the provisions of the limited warranty furnished by Ford, namely:

> *LIMITED WARRANTY (12 MONTHS OR 12,000 MILES/19,312 KILOMETRES) 1978 NEW CAR AND LIGHT TRUCK*
>
> Ford warrants for its 1978 model cars and light trucks that the Selling Dealer will repair or replace free any parts, except tires, found under normal use in the U.S. or Canada to be defective in factory materials or workmanship within the earlier of 12 months or 12,000 miles/19,312 km from either first use or retail delivery. All we require is that you properly operate and maintain your vehicle and that you return for warranty service to your Selling Dealer or any Ford or Lincoln-Mercury Dealer if you are traveling, have moved a long distance or need emergency repairs. Warranty repairs will be made with Ford Authorized Service or Remanufactured Parts.
>
> THERE IS NO OTHER EXPRESS WARRANTY ON THIS VEHICLE.[4]

The record does not contain a written description of the "owner service policy" which the dealer agreed to perform. Nevertheless, since Ford is the appellant here, we take its contentions at trial and documents in the record to establish the dealer's obligation to Ford and to plaintiff to make the warranty repairs on behalf of Ford (subject to the right of reimbursement or other terms that may be contained in their agreement). For the purpose of this appeal we are satisfied that the dealer's undertaking in paragraph 7 constitutes a written warranty within the meaning of 15 *U.S.C.A.*

4. The warranty also provided:

TO THE EXTENT ALLOWED BY LAW:

1. ANY IMPLIED WARRANTY OF MERCHANTABILITY OR FITNESS IS LIMITED TO THE 12 MONTH OR 12,000-MILE/19,312-KM DURATION OF THIS WRITTEN WARRANTY.

2. NEITHER FORD NOR THE SELLING DEALER SHALL HAVE ANY RESPONSIBILITY FOR LOSS OF USE OF THE VEHICLE, LOSS OF TIME, INCONVENIENCE, COMMERCIAL LOSS OR CONSEQUENTIAL DAMAGES.

Some states do not allow limitations on how long an implied warranty lasts or the exclusion or limitation of incidental or consequential damages, so the above limitations may not apply to you.

This warranty gives you specific legal rights, and you also may have other rights which vary from state to state.

§ 2301(6)(B). Accordingly, having furnished a written warranty to the consumer, the dealer as a supplier may not "disclaim or modify [except to limit in duration] any implied warranty to a consumer. * * *" The result of this analysis is to invalidate the attempted disclaimer by the dealer of the implied warranties of merchantability and fitness.[5] Being bound by those implied warranties arising under state law, *N.J.S.A.* 12A:2–314 and 315, Marino Auto was liable to plaintiff for the breach thereof as found by the trial judge, and plaintiff could timely revoke his acceptance of the automobile and claim a refund of his purchase price. *N.J.S.A.* 12A:2–608 and *N.J.S.A.* 12A:2–711. *Zabriskie Chevrolet, Inc. v. Smith,* 99 *N.J.Super.* 441, 240 *A.*2d 195 (Law Div.1968). In this connection we note that the trial judge found that plaintiff's attempted revocation of acceptance was made in timely fashion, and that finding has adequate support in the evidence.

As the trial judge noted, 15 *U.S.C.A.* § 2310(d)(1) provides that a consumer who is damaged by the failure of a warrantor to comply with any obligation under the act, or under a written warranty or implied warranty or service contract, may bring suit "for damages and other legal and equitable relief. * * *" Although the remedy of refund of the purchase price is expressly provided by the Magnuson-Moss Warranty Act for breach of a full warranty, granting this remedy under state law for breach of a limited warranty is not barred by or inconsistent with the act. 15 *U.S.C.A.* § 2311(b)(1) provides that nothing in the act restricts "any right or remedy of any consumer under State law or other Federal law." See also 15 *U.S.C.A.* § 2311(c)(2). Thus, for breach of the implied warranty of merchantability, plaintiff was entitled to revoke acceptance against Marino Auto, and a judgment for the purchase price less an allowance for the use of the vehicle was properly entered against Marino Auto. *N.J.S.A.* 12A:2–608 and 711. *Cf.* 15 *U.S.C.A.* § 2301(12) which defines "refund" as the return of the purchase price "less reasonable depreciation based on actual use where permitted" by regulations.

Plaintiff also could have recovered damages against Ford for Ford's breach of its written limited warranty. Marino Auto was Ford's representative for the purpose of making repairs to plaintiff's vehicle under the warranty. *See Henningsen v. Bloomfield Motors, Inc., supra,* 32 *N.J.* at 374, 161 *A.*2d 69; *cf. Conte v. Dwan Lincoln-Mercury, Inc.,* 172 *Conn.* 112, 122–126, 374 *A.*2d 144, 149–150 (Sup.Ct.Err.1976). The limited warranty expressly required the purchaser to return the vehicle "for warranty service" to the dealer or to any Ford or Lincoln-Mercury dealer if the purchaser is traveling or has moved a long distance or needs emergency repairs. Ford contends that it put purchasers on notice that they should advise Ford's district office if they have problems with their cars that a dealer is unable to fix. The record contains a document listing "frequently asked warranty questions" which states:

> The Dealership where you purchased your vehicle has the responsibility for performing warranty repairs; therefore, take your vehicle to that Dealership. * * * If you encounter a service problem, refer to the service assistance section of your Owner's Guide for suggested action.

5. The same holding would apply if the undertaking by Marino Auto to perform the "owner service policy" is construed as a "service contract." 15 *U.S.C.A.* § 2308(a), *supra.*

We do not read these provisions as requiring notice to Ford as a condition of relief against Ford when Ford's dealer has failed after numerous attempts to correct defects under warranty.

Normally, the measure of damages for a breach of warranty is the difference between the price paid by the purchaser and the market value of the defective product. *Santor v. A & M Karagheusian, Inc., supra,* 44 *N.J.* at 63, 68–69, 207 *A.*2d 305; *see Herbstman v. Eastman Kodak Co., supra,* 68 *N.J.* at 11, 342 *A.*2d 181. However, as Judge Conford said in his concurring opinion in *Herbstman, supra,* 68 *N.J.* at 15–16, 342 *A.*2d 181, under principles of strict liability in tort a purchaser may be entitled to rescind the transaction and receive the return of the purchase price from the manufacturer without privity if the defect causes substantial impairment of value of the product. The strict liability in tort doctrine as developed in this state in the *Santor case, supra,* eliminated the need for privity of contract between the purchaser and the manufacturer as a condition for the purchaser's claim for his loss of bargain caused by a defect in the product. As noted above, the Magnuson-Moss Warranty Act accomplished the same result.

One question posed by this case is whether recovery of the purchase price from the manufacturer was available to plaintiff for breach of the manufacturer's warranty. If the warranty were a full warranty plaintiff would have been entitled to a refund of the purchase price under the Magnuson-Moss Warranty Act. Since Ford's warranty was a limited warranty we must look to state law to determine plaintiff's right to damages or other legal and equitable relief. 15 *U.S.C.A.* § 2310(d)(1). Once privity is removed as an obstacle to relief we see no reason why a purchaser cannot also elect the equitable remedy of returning the goods to the manufacturer who is a warrantor and claiming a refund of the purchase price less an allowance for use of the product. *See Seely v. White Motor Co.,* 63 *Cal.*2d 9, 45 *Cal.Rptr.* 17, 20, 403 *P.*2d 145, 148 (Sup.Ct.1965); *Durfee v. Rod Baxter Imports, Inc., supra,* 262 *N.W.*2d at 357–358, where the Minnesota Supreme Court held as a matter of state law that lack of privity does not bar a purchaser of a foreign car from revoking acceptance and recovering the purchase price from the distributor of such cars as distinguished from the local dealer. The decision was made without regard to the Magnuson-Moss Warranty Act.

We are dealing with the breach of an express contractual obligation. Nothing prevents us from granting an adequate remedy under state law for that breach of contract, including rescission when appropriate. Under state law the right to revoke acceptance for defects substantially impairing the value of the product (*N.J.S.A.* 12A:2–608) and to receive a refund of the purchase price (*N.J.S.A.* 12A:2–711) are rights available to a buyer against a seller in privity. Where the manufacturer gives a warranty to induce the sale it is consistent to allow the same type of remedy as against that manufacturer. *See Durfee v. Rod Baxter Imports, Inc., supra; cf. Seely v. White Motor Co., supra.* Only the privity concept, which is frequently viewed as a relic these days, *Koperski v. Husker Dodge, Inc.,* 208 *Neb.* 29, 45, 302 *N.W.*2d 655, 664 (Sup.Ct.1981); *see Kinlaw v. Long Mfg. N.C., Inc.,* 298 *N.C.* 494, 259 *S.E.*2d 552 (Sup.Ct.1979), has interfered with a rescission-type remedy against the manufacturer of goods not purchased directly from the manufacturer. If we focus on the fact that the warranty creates a direct contractual obligation to the buyer, the reason for allowing the same remedy that is available against a direct seller becomes clear. Although the manufacturer intended to limit the remedy to the repair and replacement of defective parts, the failure of that remedy, *see N.J.S.A.* 12A:2–719(2); *Goddard v. General Motors Corp.,* 60 *Ohio St.*2d 41, 396 *N.E.*2d 761 (Sup.Ct.1979); *Seely v. White Motor Co., supra,* and the consequent breach of the implied warranty of merchantability which accompanied the limited warranty by virtue of the Magnuson-Moss Warranty Act, make a rescission-type remedy appropriate when revocation of acceptance is justified. *Durfee v. Rod Baxter Imports, Inc., supra,* 262 *N.W.*2d at 357.

Lastly, we consider Ford's contention that a counsel fee was improperly granted to plaintiff since no judgment was entered in favor of plaintiff against Ford and Ford contends it was not given adequate notice of the defects in the car. 15 *U.S.C.A.* § 2310(d)(2) provides that a consumer who "prevails in any action brought [in any court] under paragraph (1) of this subsection * * * may be allowed by the court to recover as part of the judgment * * * expenses (including attorney's fees based on the actual time expended). * * *" This section is subject to the provisions contained in § 2310(e). Subsection (e) provides that, with certain exceptions, no action based upon breach of a written or implied warranty or service contract may be prosecuted unless a person obligated under the warranty or service contract "is afforded a reasonable opportunity to cure such failure to comply." Here that opportunity was given to Ford's designated representative to whom the purchaser was required to bring the car. A direct employee of Ford, Bednarz, also met with plaintiff or his wife and was made aware of some difficulty with the car. We are not certain of the extent of Ford's knowledge of those difficulties. However, in our view the opportunities given to Marino Auto to repair the vehicle satisfied the requirements of 15 *U.S.C.A.* § 2310(e) in this case.

As noted, Ford also contends that a counsel fee could not be awarded against Ford because plaintiff did not recover a judgment against Ford. The Magnuson-Moss Warranty Act permits a prevailing consumer to recover attorney's fees "as part of the judgment." The trial judge found that Ford had breached its warranty and that the car's value was substantially impaired. He entered no damage judgment against Ford. However, in the absence of proof of actual damages, plaintiff was entitled to a judgment against Ford for nominal damages. *Ruane Dev. Corp. v. Cullere,* 134 *N.J.Super.* 245, 252, 339 *A.*2d 229 (App.Div.1975); *Ench v. Bluestein,* 52 *N.J.Super.* 169, 173–174, 145 *A.*2d 44 (App.Div.1958); *Winkler v. Hartford Accident and Indem. Co.,* 66 *N.J.Super.* 22, 29, 168 *A.*2d 418 (App.Div.), certif. den. 34 *N.J.* 581, 170 *A.*2d 544 (1961); *Packard Englewood Motors, Inc. v. Packard Motor Car Co.,* 215 *F.*2d 503, 510 (3 Cir.1954). Ford was not prejudiced by the failure of the trial judge to enter a judgment for nominal damages to which the award of attorney's fees could be attached. *See Nobility Homes, Inc. v. Ballentine,* 386 *So.*2d 727, 730–731 (Sup.Ct.Ala.1980). The award of counsel fees fulfills the intent of the Magnuson-Moss Warranty Act. Without such an award consumers frequently would be unable to vindicate warranty rights accorded by law.

As to the amount of counsel fees allowed by the trial judge, we find no abuse of discretion. The allowance was for actual time spent at an hourly rate of $75. Consideration could properly be given to the fact that plaintiff's attorney undertook this claim on a contingency basis with a relatively small retainer. *DR* 2–106(A)(8). The normal breach of warranty case ought not require four separate appearances before the trial court. To some extent this was not in the control of plaintiff's attorney, and plaintiff might have obtained all the relief required against Ford on the first day of trial. But it did not work out that way. In other cases it may be possible to stipulate damages and simplify the issues, thus limiting the cost of this type of litigation for consumers and suppliers alike. But the issues raised in this case were novel in this State, and no one can be faulted for the difficulty and time consumed in this litigation.

We have stated that in an appropriate case a consumer could recover the purchase price from a manufacturer for breach of a limited warranty causing a substantial impairment of the value of the product. The application of the Magnuson-Moss Warranty Act is one distinction between this case and *Herbstman v. Eastman Kodak Co., supra,* 68 *N.J.* at 9–12, n. 1, 342 *A.*2d 181. However, we need not determine whether plaintiff had the right to such relief in this case. Ordinarily, a purchaser seeking such relief after unsuccessful repairs should be required to give timely notice to the manufacturer of revocation of acceptance of defective goods and of his demand for a refund of the purchase price. *See Durfee v. Rod Baxter Imports, Inc., supra,* 262 *N.W.*2d at 353. Plaintiff's complaint alleges that such notice and demand were given to Ford in this case, but no finding was made by the trial judge on plaintiff's claim against Ford. Having determined that plaintiff was entitled to a judgment for nominal damages and counsel fees against Ford, and that judgments against Marino Auto and for indemnification by Ford were properly entered, it makes no difference in this case whether plaintiff was also entitled to a refund of his purchase price from Ford.

The result in this case differs from that reached in *Edelstein v. Toyota Motors Distributors, supra.* However, the differences in the cases, the absence there of proof of any warranty from defendants, and the apparent failure of the purchaser to rely on the Magnuson-Moss Warranty Act make it unnecessary for us to comment on that holding.

Affirmed.

Notes

Here are some questions about the *Ventura* case.

1. The court assumes that the Dealer had effectively disclaimed all warranties under the Code. How does the Magnuson-Moss Warranty Act support the court's conclusion that, nevertheless, the dealer breached an implied warranty of merchantability?

Note that the dealer failed to "cure" the problem and that the buyer's remedy included revocation of acceptance, UCC 2–608(1), and a refund of the price, UCC 2–711(1), adjusted for the value of buyer's use after the revocation. Consequential damages were not claimed. Compare Bogner v. General Motors Corp., 117 Misc.2d 929, 459 N.Y.S.2d 679 (N.Y.Civ.Ct.1982) (although consequential damages excluded, court awards damages for emotional distress). See also, Ramirez v. Autosport, 88 N.J. 277, 440 A.2d 1345 (1982) (buyer properly rejects camper-van for defects, cancels contract and recovers price); Jacobs v. Rosemount Dodge-Winnebago South, 310 N.W.2d 71 (Minn.1981) (limited remedy fails essential purpose, buyer permitted to revoke acceptance and recover consequential damages).

2. Suppose that the dealer made no "written warranty," see 15 U.S.C.A. § 2301(6), and effectively disclaimed all warranties under UCC 2–316. Would the buyer have any claims against the dealer under either the Magnuson-Moss Act or the UCC?

A few states have passed special consumer legislation to deal with perceived shortcomings in the Code. See, for example, Section 2–316A of the Massachusetts UCC, enacted in 1973:

2–316A. Limitation of Exclusion or Modification of Warranties

> The provisions of section 2–316 shall not apply to sales of consumer goods, services or both. Any language, oral or written, used by a seller or manufacturer of consumer goods and services, which attempts to exclude or modify any implied warranties of merchantability and fitness for a particular purpose or to exclude or modify the consumer's remedies for breach of those warranties, shall be unenforceable.
>
> Any language, oral or written, used by a manufacturer of consumer goods, which attempts to limit or modify a consumer's remedies for breach of such manufacturer's express warranties, shall be unenforceable, unless such manufacturer maintains facilities within the commonwealth sufficient to provide reasonable and expeditious performance of the warranty obligations.
>
> The provisions of this section may not be disclaimed or waived by agreement.

3. The manufacturer, Ford Motor Company, made a written, "limited" warranty to Ventura. The express warranty was breached and the dealer failed to "cure." What was the maximum protection, liability and remedy, to which Ventura was entitled against Ford under the Magnuson-Moss Act? Read the entire statute, please. Why was Ventura's recovery limited to the recovery of attorney's fees?

4. Suppose that Ford (or the Dealer) had made a written, "full" warranty to Ventura. To what additional protection would Ventura be entitled? See, particularly, 15 U.S.C.A. § 2304(a). How does this differ from protection available under the UCC when a limited remedy "fails" its essential purpose?

As a matter of practice, few manufacturers or sellers are willing to make "full" written warranties, and there is no penalty imposed for that omission under *Magnuson-Moss*.

5. *Privity Revisited.* Suppose a manufacturer makes a "limited" express warranty on a product and this warranty is passed on by the dealer to the consumer. The product has several substantial defects which neither the manufacturer nor the dealer are able to cure. Clearly, the consumer is not entitled under a "limited" warranty to either a refund or a new product under Magnuson–Moss. In Gochey v. Bomardier, Inc., 153 Vt. 607, 572 A.2d 921 (1990), however, the court permitted the consumer to invoke UCC 2–608, revoke his acceptance against the manufacturer and recover the purchase price under UCC 2–711(1). The court stated:

> We agree with the rationale expressed in *Ventura* that when a manufacturer expressly warrants its goods, it, in effect, creates a direct contract with

> the ultimate buyer. Accordingly, in an action pursuant to the Magnuson–Moss Warranty Act, the consumer may collect reasonable attorneys' fees, 15 U.S.C. § 2310(d)(2), and secure any available state remedies, including a refund of the purchase price along with incidental and consequential damages and interest, directly from the manufacturer when the manufacturer's defect substantially impairs the product. * * * When the manufacturer's defect results in revocation by the consumer, the manufacturer must assume the liability it incurred when it warranted the product to the ultimate user. 572 A.2d at 924.

Suppose the manufacturer made a "limited" express warranty to the consumer but did not breach it. The goods, however, were unmerchantable under UCC 2–314. In Rothe v. Maloney Cadillac, Inc., 119 Ill.2d 288, 116 Ill.Dec. 207, 518 N.E.2d 1028 (1988), the Illinois Supreme Court, elaborating on its earlier decision in Szajna v. General Motors Corp., 115 Ill.2d 294, 104 Ill.Dec. 898, 503 N.E.2d 760 (1986), held that the consumer could sue the manufacturer for breach of implied warranty under the Magnuson–Moss Act even though lack of privity would bar the suit under state law. The court concluded that Magnuson–Moss imposed the same implied warranties on the manufacturer that would be imposed under state law, with the differences that they could not be disclaimed and lack of privity was no defense.

Problem 21–6

Assume the same facts as in Ventura v. Ford Motor Company. Assume, also, that the state where the dispute arose had enacted a "New-Car Buyer Protection Act," based upon that enacted in Illinois. 815 ILCS 380/1 et seq.

What protection does this "Lemon Law" add to that available under the Magnuson-Moss Warranty Act?

How does the "Lemon Law" mesh with the applicable provisions of the UCC?

NEW–CAR BUYER PROTECTION ACT

1201. Short title

§ 1. This Act shall be known and may be cited as the New-Car Buyer Protection Act.

1202. Definitions

§ 2. For the purposes of this Act, the following words have the meanings ascribed to them in this Section.

(a) "Consumer" means an individual who purchases a new car from the seller for the purposes of transporting himself and others, as well as their personal property, for primarily personal, household or family purposes.

(b) "Express warranty" has the same meaning, for the purposes of this Act, as it has for the purposes of the Uniform Commercial Code.

(c) "New car" means a passenger car, as defined in Section 1–157 of The Illinois Vehicle Code, which does not qualify under the definition of a used motor vehicle, as set forth in Section 1–216 of that Code. The term does not include motor homes, mini motor homes or van campers, as defined in Section 1–145.01 of The Illinois Vehicle Code.

(d) "Nonconformity" refers to a new car's failure to conform to all express warranties applicable to such car, which failure substantially impairs the use, market value or safety of that car.

(e) "Seller" means the manufacturer of a new car, that manufacturer's agent or distributor or that manufacturer's authorized dealer.

(f) "Statutory warranty period" means the period of one year or 12,000 miles, whichever occurs first after the date of the delivery of a new car to the consumer who purchased it.

1203. Failure of new car to conform to express warranties—Remedies—Presumption—Allowance for consumer use—Suspension of warranty period

§ 3. (a) If after a reasonable number of attempts the seller is unable to conform the new car to any of its applicable express warranties, the manufacturer shall either provide the consumer with a new car of like model line, if available, or otherwise a comparable motor vehicle as a replacement, or accept the return of the car from the consumer and refund to the consumer the full purchase price of the new car, including all collateral charges, less a reasonable allowance for consumer use of the car.

(b) A presumption that a reasonable number of attempts have been undertaken to conform a new car to its express warranties shall arise where, within the statutory warranty period,

(1) the same nonconformity has been subject to repair by the seller, its agents or authorized dealers during the statutory warranty period, 4 or more times, and such nonconformity continues to exist; or

(2) the car has been out of service by reason of repair of nonconformities for a total of 30 or more business days during the statutory warranty period.

(c) A reasonable allowance for consumer use of a car is that amount directly attributable to the wear and tear incurred by the new car as a result of its having been used prior to the first report of a nonconformity to the seller, and during any subsequent period in which it is not out of service by reason of repair.

(d) The fact that a new car's failure to conform to an express warranty is the result of abuse, neglect or unauthorized modifications or alterations is an affirmative defense to claims brought under this Act.

(e) The statutory warranty period of a new car shall be suspended for any period of time during which repair services are not available to the consumer because of a war, invasion or strike, or a fire, flood or other natural disaster.

(f) Refunds made pursuant to this Act shall be made to the consumer, and lien holder if any exists, as their respective interests appear.

(g) For the purposes of this Act, a manufacturer sells a new car to a consumer when he provides that consumer with a replacement car pursuant to subsection (a).

(h) In no event shall the presumption herein provided apply against a manufacturer, his agent, distributor or dealer unless the manufacturer has received prior direct written notification from or on behalf of the consumer, and has an opportunity to correct the alleged defect.

1204. Informal settlement procedure—Notice

§ 4. (a) The provisions of subsection (a) of Section 3 shall not apply unless the consumer has first resorted to an informal settlement procedure applicable to disputes to which that subsection would apply where

(1) The manufacturer of the new car has established such a procedure;

(2) The procedure conforms:

(i) substantially with the provisions of Title 16, Code of Federal Regulation, Part 703, as from time to time amended, and

(ii) to the requirements of subsection (c); and

(3) The consumer has received from the seller adequate written notice of the existence of the procedure.

Adequate written notice includes but is not limited to the incorporation of the informal dispute settlement procedure into the terms of the written warranty to which the car does not conform.

(b) If the consumer is dissatisfied with the decision reached in an informal dispute settlement procedure or the results of such a decision, he may bring a civil action to enforce his rights under subsection (a) of Section 3. The decision reached in the informal dispute settlement procedure is admissible in such a civil action. The period of limitations for a civil action to enforce a consumer's rights or remedies under subsection (a) of Section 3 shall be extended for a period equal to the number of days the subject matter of the civil action was pending in the informal dispute settlement procedure.

(c) A disclosure of the decision in an informal dispute settlement procedure shall include notice to the consumer of the provisions of subsection (b).

1205. Application of Uniform Commercial Code

§ 5. Persons electing to proceed and settle under this Act shall be barred from a separate cause of action under Chapter 26.

1206. Limitations

§ 6. Any action brought under this Act shall be commenced within eighteen months following the date of original delivery of the motor vehicle to the consumer.

1207. Seller to provide statement of consumer's rights

§ 7. The seller who sells a new car to a consumer, shall, upon delivery of that car to the consumer, provide the consumer with a written statement clearly and conspicuously setting forth in full detail the consumer's rights under subsection (a) of Section 3, and the presumptions created by subsection (b) of that Section.

VOGEL, SQUEEZING CONSUMERS: LEMON LAWS, CONSUMER WARRANTIES, AND A PROPOSAL FOR REFORM, 1985 Ariz.St.L.J. 589, 615, 644–47.

* * *

Acting on consumer complaints, legislatures in 37 states have passed lemon laws to help car owners. Although the laws vary in many important respects, they still have a number of features in common. First, the lemon laws apply only to new cars and generally only to cars purchased for noncommercial purposes. Second, the laws require the manufacturer to conform the vehicle to the terms of the warranty upon receiving notice of the problem from the consumer. If the manufacturer is unable to correct the defect within a stated period of time or after a certain number of attempts, the lemon laws allow purchasers to return defective cars and to receive either a refund of the purchase price or a replacement vehicle. However, the refund or replacement remedy may not be available to a consumer unless he or she gives the manufacturer notice that efforts to repair the car have failed. Finally, a number of lemon laws also restrict the resale of returned vehicles to other purchasers.

* * *

As has been seen, the lemon laws by themselves do not provide consumers with an effective remedy. In many respects, they simply restate the present law. In other respects they are more restrictive than alternative legal remedies. Consequently, if a consumer has a warranty problem, it may be necessary to bring an action under the UCC, the Magnuson-Moss Warranty Act, and the lemon law. Generally, the lemon laws allow for this. With the exception of Arizona, Florida, Illinois, New Mexico, North Dakota, and Tennessee,* all the lemon laws contain a provision which states that the lemon law does not limit rights or remedies under other law.**

If lawmakers wish to provide increased protection to purchasers of automobiles, there are certain modifications which would make the lemon laws more effective: (1) clear rules or standards; (2) presumptions which ease the burden of proof, (3) a minimum of technicalities; and (4) a choice between a refund and other damages or a replacement vehicle. They could also publicize consumers' rights under the improved laws.

* Ariz.Rev.Stat.Ann. § 44–1261 to –1265 (Supp. 1984–85); Fla.Stat.Ann. § 681.10–.108 (West Supp.1985); 1985 N.D.Sess.Laws 1378, § (6); Tenn.Code Ann. § 55–24–108 (Supp. 1984). The Tennessee lemon law specifically forecloses any action under another law if the consumer chooses to sue under the lemon law. Given the deficiencies of the lemon law, this provision is highly undesirable. In Tennessee, a consumer might fare better ignoring the lemon law and suing under the U.C.C. The Illinois and New Mexico lemon laws specifically bar any action under the U.C.C. if the consumer sues under the lemon law. Ill.Ann.Stat. ch. 121, ¶ 1205 § 5 (Smith-Hurd 1984–85); 1985 N.M.Laws 126, § 5.

** Alaska Stat. ch. 101, § 45.45.340 (Supp. 1984); Colo.Rev.Stat. § 42–12–105 (1984); Conn.Gen.Stat.Ann. § 42–179(h) (West Supp. 1985); Del.Code Ann. tit. 6 § 5008 (Supp. 1984); 1985 Kan.Sess.Laws 118, § 2; La.Rev. Stat.Ann. § 51:1946 (West Supp.1985); Me. Rev.Stat.Ann. tit. 10, § 1162(1) (Supp.1984–85); Md.Com.Law Code Ann. § 14–1501(b) (Supp.1984); Mass.Gen.Laws Ann. ch. 90, § 7N½(5) (West Supp.1985); Minn.Stat.Ann. § 325F.655(8) (West Supp.1985); Mo.Ann. Stat. § 407.579 (Vernon Supp.1985); Mont. Code Ann. § 61–4–506 (1983) and 1985 Mont. Laws 295; Neb.Rev.Stat. § 60–2708 (1984); Nev.Rev.Stat. § 598.786 (1983); N.H.Rev. Stat.Ann. § 357–D:7 (1984); N.J.Stat.Ann. § 56:12–27 (West Supp.1985); N.Y.Gen.Bus. Law § 198–a(f) (Consol.Supp. 1984–85); Or. Rev.Stat. § 646.375 (1983); Pa.Stat.Ann. tit. 73, § 1962 (Purdon 1985); R.I.Gen.Laws § 31–5.2–6 (Supp.1984); Tex.Rev.Civ.Stat. Ann. art. 4413(36), § 6.07(f) (Vernon Supp. 1985); 1985 Utah Laws 29, §§ 13–21–6(3); Vt.Stat.Ann. tit. 9, § 4178 (Supp.1984); Va. Code § 59.1–207.13(F) (Supp.1984); Wash. Rev.Code Ann. § 19.118.070 (Supp.1984); W.Va.Code § 46A–6A–9 (Supp.1984); Wis. Stat.Ann. § 218.015(5) (West 1984–85); Wyo. Stat. § 40–17–101(e) (Supp.1985). The Mississippi law does not specifically state whether other remedies are allowed. 1985 Miss. Laws 224, §§ 1–9.

For consumers and manufacturers to know their rights under the lemon laws, the laws must contain clear rules or standards specifying when the consumer may return the defective car and seek a refund or a replacement vehicle. The lemon laws make strides in this direction by spelling out the number of repair attempts and the number of days a car must be in the shop for repair before the consumer can invoke the refund and replacement provision. However, the standard is often stricter than that governing failure of essential purpose under the UCC. Consumers need a clear rule that does not grant an unreasonable amount of time to repair the car. There is little reason to require that the consumer give the manufacturer more than one repair attempt or one week in the shop. The consumer should not have to suffer through numerous trips to the dealer or long delays in repair.

Specification of a time for repair can significantly ease the burden of the consumer. The easier it is for the consumer to prove that he or she is entitled to the remedies under the lemon laws, the more likely that the consumer will seek redress and reach an equitable agreement with the manufacturer. A short, but reasonable, statutory period should suffice. If the consumer is able to show that the defect was not repaired within the period (perhaps a week), the presumption would apply. The manufacturer would then have the burden of establishing that more time was necessary and reasonable under the circumstances.

The typical lemon law contains other provisions which are unclear. For example, the laws do not define what constitutes substantial impairment of value, safety, or use. As a result, consumers will often not know what they are entitled to, even if the lemon law applies. These terms can be defined and clarified, as has been done in some cases interpreting UCC section 2–608. Specific provision should be made for taking account of the consumer's individual circumstances, as well as of clusters or groups of defects that substantially impair the value of the car.

Having clear rules and presumptions that ease the burden of proof will not mean much if other technical requirements deprive a consumer of the ability to use the lemon law. The notice requirements are especially troublesome. Consumers rarely know about notice requirements and often fail to comply with them. The only notice requirement the lemon laws should contain is the requirement that the consumer notify the dealer of the problem with the car. As was mentioned, the manufacturer will find out about the problem when the dealer seeks reimbursement for the warranty work. The manufacturer should have the responsibility of seeing to it that the dealer supplies it with this information promptly.

Once the consumer establishes that the car was not or could not be fixed, the lemon laws should provide that the consumer can choose between a refund or a replacement vehicle. If the consumer opts for a replacement vehicle, the manufacturer should be required to supply one of equal value. If the consumer chooses a refund, the lemon law should allow the recovery of the purchase price, collateral charges, and incidental and consequential damages when appropriate. If the manufacturer is allowed an offset for use, it should only cover use before the defects occurred and the manufacturer should have the burden of establishing its right to any offset and its amount.

All such changes will have little effect, however, if consumers do not fully understand them. The usual approach to informing consumers is to require the dealers and the manufacturers to supply a written statement which explains consumers' rights under the lemon law. The experience with the Magnuson-Moss Warranty Act indicates that this approach is ineffective. Consequently, legislators should consider using the broadcast media and newspapers to present information concerning consumer remedies. Public service ads on radio and television could greatly increase awareness of consumer warranty rights. Certainly, there is enough talent and knowledge available to structure such a campaign and the expense of conducting it is not likely to be much more than that of printing forms. A number of state and federal consumer protection agencies already conduct such campaigns, and there is no reason why similar efforts cannot be mounted to inform consumers of their rights under automobile lemon laws.

PART SIX

DISPUTES AMONG CREDITORS OVER POSSESSION OF GOODS SOLD

CHAPTER TWENTY-TWO

RIGHTS OF OWNERS, SELLERS OR BUYERS TO GOODS NOT IN THEIR POSSESSION: CLAIMS OF THIRD PARTIES

SECTION 1. INTRODUCTION

When a person has good title to chattels, our legal system affords him extensive protection against a wide range of claims by third persons to the goods. A sale is a transaction whereby title is passed "from the seller to the buyer for a price * * *." UCC 2–106(1). In an effort to clarify when title passes in a contract for sale, Article 2 prescribes the conditions which must exist before any interest in goods can pass, UCC 2–105(1), makes a careful distinction between present and future sales, UCC 2–106(1), and provides an intricate set of rules to assist in transactions where the parties have not otherwise explicitly agreed. UCC 2–401. To this extent, Article 2 closely follows the Uniform Sales Act.

Here, however, the resemblance ends. UCC 2–401 provides that "each provision of this Article with regard to the rights, obligations and remedies of the seller, the buyer, purchasers or other third parties applies irrespective of title to the goods except where the provision refers to such title." See also UCC 9–202 and 2A–303, where the same policy is announced for secured transactions and leases of goods. As stated in the comment to UCC 2–101, the "purpose is to avoid making practical issues between practical men turn on the location of an intangible something, the passing of which no man can prove by evidence and to substitute for such abstractions proof of words and actions of a tangible character." Two such practical issues are risk of loss and the seller's action for the price. Under the USA they turned on which party had title to the goods. Under the UCC they are determined by such considerations as whether the seller has completed his tender of delivery, UCC 2–509, or whether the buyer has accepted the goods, UCC 2–709(1).

It is clear that the rules about title contained in UCC 2–401 may be relevant in resolving controversies beyond the scope of Article 2, e.g., the right of the buyer's creditors to levy on goods still in the seller's possession, the coverage of an insurance policy, the applicability of a state sales tax or the criminal responsibility of a person accused of larceny. However, when the transaction is within the scope of Article 2, title becomes relevant only when the applicable provisions specifically refer to title. Such specific reference is made in UCC 2–403 and UCC 2–312. The range of problems emanating from these sections and their frequent overlap with Article 9 and the special difficulties posed by "bulk" sales will be the subject of this Chapter. See, generally, Tabac, *The Unbearable Lightness of Title Under the Uniform Commercial Code,* 50 Md.L.Rev. 408 (1991).

SECTION 2. RIGHTS OF BUYERS IN GOODS SOLD

A. Claims of "True" Owners

Problem 22–1

Abbie, a widow, owned a 10–carat diamond valued at $60,000. Boscoe, a thief, stole the diamond from Abbie's wall safe and sold it to Casper, a diamond merchant, for $55,000. Casper honestly believed that Boscoe was the true owner. Casper then sold the diamond to Dimwit, a buyer in the ordinary course of business, for $60,000. May Abbie replevy the diamond from Dimwit? See UCC 2–403. Assume that the common law gives Casper only "void title," not "voidable title." Justice v. Fabey, 541 F.Supp. 1019 (E.D.Pa.1982) (yes).

Problem 22–2

Suppose that Abbie delivered the diamond to Casper for the purpose of having the clasp on the necklace in which the stone was set repaired. Casper, with intent to defraud, removed the stone from the necklace and sold it to Dimwit, a buyer in the ordinary course of business. May Abbie replevy the diamond from Dimwit? See UCC 2–403(2), (3), and UCC 1–201(9). Cf. Carlsen v. Rivera, 382 So.2d 825 (Fla.App.1980) (no).

Problem 22–3

Suppose that Abbie owned several diamonds and was in the habit of lending the stones to her society friends for use on important occasions. She charged a good fee for this service and was, of course, fully insured against loss. Abbie leased the stone worth $60,000 to Bessie to be worn at the Muckraker's Ball. Bessie, who was short of cash, sold the diamond to Casper for $55,000. Casper, who had purchased in good faith, sold the stone to Dimwit, a buyer in the ordinary course of business, for $65,000. May Abbie (or her insurance company claiming by subrogation) replevy the necklace from Dimwit? See UCC 2–403(1), (2). Assume that the common law only gives Bessie, as a lessee, void title.

How should the court deal with the argument made by Dimwit that Bessie in fact had a voidable title under UCC 2–403 because she took in a transaction of "purchase" as that term is defined in UCC 2–403 and 1–201? (Dimwit's argument was rejected in similar circumstances by the Indiana Court of Appeals in McDonald's Chevrolet, Inc. v. Johnson, 176 Ind.App. 399, 376 N.E.2d 106 (1978)).

Problem 22–4

While vacationing in Miami Beach, Abbie was approached by a middle-aged man who asked if the lovely diamond necklace was for sale. He said that his name was Boscoe and offered to pay $90,000. Abbie, who was a bit short of cash, agreed to sell but then balked when Boscoe started to write a check. She wanted cash. Boscoe assured her that he was solvent and stated that he was Mr. Fred C. Boscoe of Grosse Pointe. Abbie excused herself from the room and confirmed by a telephone call to a friend in Detroit that Mr. Fred C. Boscoe owned a large home in Grosse Pointe and was a vice-president of a well-known automobile manufacturer. Abbie returned to the room and informed the man that she would accept a check for the stone. Boscoe then drew a counter check on a Detroit bank and delivered it to Abbie in exchange for the necklace. The check, of course, bounced and Abbie then discovered that her purchaser had no account at that bank and was not Mr. Fred C. Boscoe of Grosse Pointe. Further, before disappearing, the "rogue" had sold the diamond for $91,000 to Dimwit, who purchased the stone in good faith. May Abbie replevy the stone from Dimwit? See UCC 2–403(1)(a).

Problem 22–5

In Problem 22–4 would it make any difference if the transaction and the exchange of check for necklace had been completed by mail?

Problem 22–6

Suppose, in Problem 22–2, above, that Casper and Dimwit had entered into a contract for the sale of the stone, delivery and payment to take place in 10 days. Is Abbie's interest cut off at this point or must payment and delivery first take place? Suppose there has been payment but not delivery? Delivery but no payment? Part payment? See UCC 2–403. Compare UCC 1–201(44).

INMI-ETTI v. ALUISI

Court of Appeals of Maryland, 1985.
63 Md.App. 293, 492 A.2d 917.

[Appellant, a resident of Nigeria, ordered a new Honda Prelude while visiting her sister in the United States. Butler, an acquaintance of her family, offered to assist. Appellant returned to Nigeria, leaving cash with the sister to complete the purchase. The sale was completed and a certificate of title was issued in appellant's name. The car, however, was delivered to Butler, who removed it from the sister without permission. The sister had an arrest warrant issued, but it was later quashed. Butler, claiming that appellant was an absconding debtor, then brought suit against her and filed an application for an attachment on the Honda. When appellant did not answer, Butler was granted a summary judgment. Thereafter, appellee, a deputy sheriff, executed the writ of attachment on the Honda but left it in Butler's possession.

Butler, representing that he was the owner, then contracted to sell the Honda to Pohanka, a dealer, for $7,200. Pohanka paid Butler $2,000 and agreed to pay the balance when Butler obtained a certificate of title. After executing a false affidavit in his application for a certificate of title, Butler was issued a certificate in his own name by the Motor Vehicle Administration. Butler then returned to Pohanka and exchanged the certificate for the balance of the contract price.

Appellant, upon returning to the United States, had Butler's summary judgment set aside. In addition, she sued Butler and Pohanka for conversion and appellee for negligent attachment. In the lower court, appellant obtained a default judgment against Butler. The court, however, granted a summary judgment to Pohanka and appellee. On appeal, the summary judgment in favor of appellee was sustained but the summary judgment in favor of Pohanka was reversed.]

* * *

I.

In order for the appellant to establish her right to summary judgment against Pohanka, we must be convinced that the record before the lower court contained undisputed facts and inferences properly deducible therefrom, demonstrating that Pohanka committed a conversion of the appellant's vehicle as a matter of law. Former Md.Rule 610 (new Md.Rule 2–501). In *Interstate Ins. Co. v. Logan,* 205 Md. 583, 588–89, 109 A.2d 904 (1959), the Court of Appeals summarized the law of conversion:

> [F]orcible dispossession of personal property is not essential to constitute a conversion. A "conversion" is any distinct act of ownership or dominion exerted by one person over the personal property of another in denial of his right or inconsistent with it. *Merchants' National Bank of Baltimore v. Williams,* 110 Md. 334, 72 A. 1114 [(1909)]; Martin v. W.W. Lanahan & Co., 133 Md. 525, 105 A. 777 [(1919)].

* * * In the instant case it is undisputed that Pohanka exerted acts of use or ownership over the automobile in question by selling it on February 1, 1982. Nevertheless, our analysis cannot end here. We explain.

At common law the maxim was: "He who hath not cannot give (nemo dat qui non habet)." Black's Law Dictionary 935 (5th ed. 1979). Although at times the Uniform Commercial Code may seem to the reader as unintelligible as the Latin phrases which preceded it, we find in § 2–403 of the Code a definite modification of the above maxim. That section states: * * *. Md.Code (1975), § 2–403 of the Commercial Law Article. *See generally* Hawkland UCC Series § 2–403:01 *et seq.* for an enlightening history of the origins of § 2–403.

In short, the answer to the appellant's claim against Pohanka depends on whether Butler had "void" or "voidable" title at the time of the purported sale to Pohanka. If Butler had voidable title, then he had the power to vest good title in Pohanka.[1] If, on the other hand, Butler possessed void title (i.e., no title at all), then Pohanka received no title and is liable in trover for the conversion of the appellant's automobile. Preliminarily, we note that there was no evidence that Butler was a "merchant who deals in goods of that kind" (i.e. automobiles). Md.Code, *supra,* §§ 2–403(2) and 2–104(1). Therefore the entrustment provisions of § 2–403(2)–(3) do not apply.

It has been observed that:

> Under 2–403, voidable title is to be distinguished from void title. A thief, for example, "gets" only void title and without more cannot pass any title to a good faith purchaser. "Voidable title" is a murky concept. The Code does not define the phrase. The comments do not even discuss

1. Inasmuch as we decide this case on the basis of a motion for summary judgment, and the evidence regarding Pohanka's good faith purchaser for value status is disputed, we must assume here that Pohanka was entitled to that status.

> it. Subsections (1)(a)-(d) of 2-403 clarify the law as to particular transactions which were "troublesome under prior law." Beyond these, we must look to non-Code state law.

J. White & R. Summers, Handbook of the Law Under the Uniform Commercial Code § 3-11 (2d ed. 1980) (footnote omitted). White and Summers further explain that: subsection (a) of § 2-403(1) deals with cases where the purchaser *impersonates* someone else; subsection (b) deals with "rubber checks"; subsection (c) deals with "*cash sales* ";[2] and subsection (d) deals with cases of *forged checks* and other acts fraudulent to the seller. *Id.* None of these subsections apply to the facts of the present case and we, therefore, must turn to "non-Code state law" to determine whether Butler had voidable title.

Hawkland, *supra,* § 403:04, suggests that "voidable title" may only be obtained when the owner of the goods makes a voluntary transfer of the goods. He reaches that conclusion from the Code definitions of the words "delivery" and "purchase" and summarizes:

> Section 2-403(1)(d) does not create a voidable title in the situation where the goods are wrongfully taken, as contrasted with delivered voluntarily because of the concepts of "delivery" and "purchaser" which are necessary preconditions. "Delivery" is defined by section 1-201(14) "with respect to instruments, documents of title, chattel paper or securities" to mean "voluntary transfer of possession." By analogy, it should be held that goods are not delivered for purposes of section 2-403 unless they are voluntarily transferred. Additionally, section 2-403(1)(d) is limited by the requirement that the goods "have been delivered under a transaction of purchase." "Purchase" is defined by section 1-201(32) to include only voluntary transactions. A thief who wrongfully takes goods is not a purchaser within the meaning of this definition, but a swindler who fraudulently induces the victim to voluntarily deliver them is a purchaser for this purpose. This distinction, reminiscent of the distinction between larceny and larceny by trick made by the common law, is a basic one for the understanding of the meaning of section 2-403(1)(d).

Hawkland later states that the above language applies generally to § 2-403(1) and not merely to subsection (1)(d). *See* Hawkland, *supra,* § 2-403:05. The following cases and, indeed, (a) through (d) of § 2-403(1) seem to support Hawkland's theory that only a voluntary transfer by the owner can vest "voidable title" in a "person."

* * *

Without attempting to specify all the situations which could give rise to a voidable title under § 2-403 of the Uniform Commercial Code, we refer to the above authorities to support our conclusion that voidable title under the Code can only arise from a voluntary transfer or delivery of the goods by the owner. If the goods are stolen or otherwise obtained against the will of the owner, only void title can result.

2. See *First National Bank of Ariz. v. Carbajal,* 132 Ariz. 263, 645 P.2d 778, 781-82 (1982).

Under the undisputed facts of the present case Butler possessed void title when Pohanka dealt with him. Although the record simply is not sufficient for us to decide whether Butler actually stole the appellant's vehicle, it is undisputed that the appellant at no time made a voluntary transfer to Butler. Thus, Pohanka obtained no title, and its sale of the vehicle constituted a conversion of the appellant's property. We believe the above analysis sufficient to impose liability upon Pohanka. We will nevertheless answer certain of Pohanka's collateral arguments.

We reject any notion that Butler obtained voidable title to the vehicle as a result of the attachment on original process carried out pursuant to former Maryland District Rules G40–60.

* * *

The only way Butler could have obtained title in the vehicle through those attachment proceedings was if he had purchased it at a judicial sale. That clearly never occurred.

Implicit in all that we have said so far is the fact that Butler did not obtain title (voidable or otherwise) merely from the fact that he was able to convince the Motor Vehicle Administration to issue a certificate of title for the automobile to him. Although "[a] certificate of title issued by the Administration is prima facie evidence of the facts appearing on it," Md. Code (1977, 1984 Repl.Vol.), § 13–107 of the Transportation Article, the erroneous issuance of such a certificate cannot divest the title of the true owner of the automobile. *Metropolitan Auto Sales v. Koneski,* 252 Md. 145, 249 A.2d 141 (1969); *Huettner v. Sav. Bank of Balto.,* 242 Md. 477, 219 A.2d 559 (1966); *Lawrence v. Graham,* 29 Md.App. 422, 349 A.2d 271 (1975).

Likewise, we find unpersuasive Pohanka's argument that since Butler had possession of the automobile and a duly issued certificate of title in his name, Pohanka should be protected as a "good faith purchaser for value" under § 2–403 of the Commercial Law Article, *supra.* Such status under that section of the Uniform Commercial Code is relevant in situations where the seller (transferor) is possessed of voidable title. It does not apply to the situation presented by the instant case where the seller had no title at all. * * *

Finally, whether Pohanka converted the vehicle with innocent intent is immaterial. The Restatement (Second) of Torts § 229 (1979) provides:

> One who receives possession of a chattel from another with the intent to acquire for himself or for a third person a proprietary interest in the chattel which the other has not the power to transfer is subject to liability for conversion to a third person then entitled to the immediate possession of the chattel.

Comment e. to § 299 explains:

> Under the rule stated in this Section, one receiving a chattel from a third person with intent to acquire a proprietary interest in it is liable without a demand for its return by the person entitled to possession, *although he takes possession of the chattel without knowledge or reason to know that the third person has no power to transfer the proprietary*

interest. The mere receipt of the possession of the goods under such circumstances is a conversion.

(Emphasis added).

Accordingly, we shall reverse the summary judgment in favor of Pohanka and enter judgment in favor of the appellant against Pohanka for $8,200, an amount representing the agreed fair market value of the appellant's automobile at the time of its conversion, plus interest at 10 percent per annum from February 1, 1982, the date when Pohanka sold the automobile. Md.Rule 1075. * * *

Note: Certificates of Title and the BFP of Motor Vehicles

Almost all states have statutes which require motor vehicles to be "titled." Suppose that Owner, whose certificate of title is in the possession of a secured party, entrusts the motor vehicle to a car dealer for repairs. Suppose, further, that the dealer, without Owner's or secured party's consent, puts the car on the lot and sells it to Cal in the ordinary course of business. Cal pays cash and takes delivery of the car only, without knowledge of Owner's title or the outstanding security interest. Assume owner pays off secured party and seeks return of the car from Cal, certificate of title in hand. May owner replevy the car from Cal, or is Cal entitled to a duly endorsed certificate?

Under the Code the answer would appear to be no: UCC 2–402(3) does not apply. UCC 2–403(2) protects Cal and title has passed under UCC 2–401. But the critical question, then, is whether the particular certificate of title act involved preempts 2–403(2) and, in effect, conditions passage of title upon delivery of the certificate. In some states it does, e.g., Messer v. Averill, 28 Mich.App. 62, 183 N.W.2d 802 (1970) but in most states it doesn't, e.g., Godfrey v. Gilsdorf, 86 Nev. 714, 476 P.2d 3 (1970); Martin v. Nager, 192 N.J.Super. 189, 469 A.2d 519 (1983). Even where the Code controls, however, a buyer may have some responsibility for inquiring after the required certificate. See Mattek v. Malofsky, 42 Wis.2d 16, 165 N.W.2d 406 (1969) (merchant buyer from dealer to whom titled car had been entrusted is "unreasonable as a matter of law" in not obtaining the required certificate); Reliance Insurance Co. v. Market Motors, Inc., 498 A.2d 571 (D.C.App.1985); Ellsworth v. Worthey, 612 S.W.2d 396 (Mo. App.1981). See also, Dartmouth Motor Sales, Inc. v. Wilcox, 128 N.H. 526, 517 A.2d 804 (1986) (certificate of title, even though not authorized, must be "facially valid").

Assume Owner does not pay off secured party and it is secured party who seeks return of the car from Cal. Similarly, while UCC 9–307(1) may protect the buyer against the perfected security interest, this result is subject to any specific rule of priority contained in a preemptive certificate of title act. Compare Williams v. Western Surety Co., 6 Wash.App. 300, 492 P.2d 596 (1972) (buyer wins under Code) with Security Pacific Nat'l Bank v. Goodman, 24 Cal.App.3d 131, 100 Cal.Rptr. 763 (1972) (buyer loses under California statute.)

These issues are well treated in Kunz, *Motor Vehicle Ownership Disputes Involving Certificate of Title Acts and Article Two of the U.C.C.,* 39 Bus.Law. 1599 (1984).

JOHNSON & JOHNSON PROD. v. DAL INTERN. TRADING

United States Court of Appeals, Third Circuit, 1986.
798 F.2d 100.

OPINION OF THE COURT

STAPLETON, CIRCUIT JUDGE.

This is an appeal from a preliminary injunction restraining appellants from selling, distributing, or otherwise disposing of certain products manufactured by appellees and in appellants' possession. Because we conclude that the district court committed an error of law and that the present record will not support a resolution of the legally relevant issue in appellees' favor, we will vacate the preliminary injunction.

I.

Appellants are Quality King Manufacturing, Inc. and Quality King Distributors, Inc., both New York corporations ("Quality King"). Quality King is an independent distributor of national brand health and beauty aids. Its customers include large wholesalers and retail chains. Quality King participates in the so-called "gray market," where imported products are sold in the United States outside the manufacturer's distribution system, often contrary to the wishes of the manufacturer.

Appellees are Johnson & Johnson Products, Inc. ("J & J"), a New Jersey corporation, Johnson & Johnson, Ltd. ("J & J Ltd."), a corporation organized under the laws of Great Britain, and Johnson & Johnson Baby Products Company, a New Jersey corporation. Appellees are all operating subsidiaries of Johnson & Johnson, Inc., a New Jersey corporation.

Appellees claimed in the district court that J & J Ltd., which has its place of business in Great Britain, was fraudulently induced to sell 80,000 dozen toothbrushes and certain baby products to Dal International Trading Company, an instrumentality of the Polish People's Republic (hereinafter "Dal"). The alleged fraud consisted of an oral misrepresentation by Dal in February of 1985 that it intended to distribute the products in Poland only. But for this fraudulent assurance, say appellees, J & J Ltd. would not have entered the transaction.

In March of 1985, Dal ordered the products from J & J Ltd. No written contract was entered. However, J & J Ltd. did execute, in April of 1985, a written contract related to the Dal transaction with Wendexim Trading Company, Ltd., a British firm. The reason for the inclusion of Wendexim in the Dal transaction was the weakness of Polish currency, which necessitated an intermediate barter trade. This intermediate step involved an agreement under which Dal shipped a quantity of wood to Wendexim in return for Wendexim's transmittal of the payment for the wood to J & J Ltd., in satisfaction of Dal's obligation to pay J & J Ltd. for the toothbrushes and baby products.

At the end of June, 1985, J & J Ltd. delivered the toothbrushes to Dal at a J & J Ltd. factory in West Germany. The baby products were shipped from Great Britain at the beginning of June, 1985. Subsequently, J & J Ltd.

learned that some or all of these goods had been diverted from their intended destination of Poland and were en route to the United States.

J & J Ltd. investigators followed the goods to the United States, where they came into the possession of Quality King. The goods were packaged in cartons, some of which bore J & J Ltd. shipping labels. The production codes on these labels corresponded to those of the products designated for Dal.

The route by which the J & J Ltd. products came into Quality King's hands was not fully documented below. In early 1985, a British firm called Cubro Trading Company, Ltd. somehow learned of the availability of the J & J Ltd. products and passed this information to Morris Greenfield, the proprietor of Tereza Merchandise Corporation in New York. Greenfield was not interested in the products but advised Glenn Nussdorf, the vice president of Quality King, of the availability of the goods. Nussdorf prepared a purchase order for 75,000 dozen toothbrushes in February of 1985, about the time when Dal and J & J Ltd. were negotiating the sale of 80,000 dozen toothbrushes. Later, Nussdorf added baby products to this purchase order.

Nussdorf had never done business with Cubro before this transaction, so he used Greenfield as an intermediary. The details of the transaction are unclear due to discrepancies in the record as to the disbursements made by Quality King. What is clear is that Quality King purchased and received the goods.

Before the goods arrived at Quality King's warehouse, the J & J Ltd. shipping labels had been stripped from most of the shipping cartons. Greenfield and Nussdorf testified that this was a common gray market practice designed to obscure the identity of supply sources. The protection of these sources is important to gray market middlemen, Nussdorf and Greenfield testified, because if the sources became known, the middlemen would be bypassed in subsequent transactions.

The J & J Ltd. products were priced by it for the Polish market at a level lower than the wholesale price in the United States for Johnson & Johnson products, and even lower than the wholesale price normally offered in Great Britain by J & J Ltd. By purchasing these products in Europe, Quality King was thus in a position to distribute them in the United States at prices below those being charged by J & J.

II.

The district court granted the preliminary injunction after concluding that appellees were likely to prevail on the merits, that appellees would suffer irreparable harm if the injunction were not granted, that an injunction would not harm any other interested person, and that an injunction would not be contrary to the public interest. * * *

The court predicted that appellees would prevail on the merits because it found that Quality King was not a good faith purchaser under Section 2–403(1) of the Uniform Commercial Code (UCC). Under this provision of the UCC, a seller with voidable title, such as that acquired by common law fraud, can transfer good title to a subsequent good faith purchaser. For merchants like Quality King, the UCC defines good faith as "honesty in fact and the observance of reasonable commercial standards of fair dealing in the trade." UCC § 2–103(1)(b). If the subsequent purchaser lacks good faith, however, he acquires only the seller's voidable title and may be required to surrender the goods to the defrauded party.

While the district court concluded that Quality King had no actual knowledge of the alleged fraud, it found that the gray market transaction was conducted under "suspicious circumstances" that "cried out for inquiry." District Court Opinion at 23–24. In the district court's view, Quality King, as a result, should have made inquiries that would have uncovered the voidable title. In the absence of such inquiries, the court concluded, Quality King could not be said to have been "honest in fact."

The most suspicious circumstance noted by the court was the fact that "the entire trade in which Quality King is engaged is conducted in a manner designed to insulate a purchaser of goods from knowledge of potential illegality." District Court Opinion at 22. That is, the gray market trade practice of purposely obscuring the chain of title suggested to the court a silent conspiracy to avoid the consequences of bad faith purchase by preventing the transmission of actual knowledge of fraud in prior transactions. This practice was illustrated by the fact that the J & J Ltd. shipping labels had been stripped prior to arrival at Quality King's warehouse.

An additional suspicious circumstance, in the district court's view, was the fact that Nussdorf used Greenfield as an intermediary, thereby indicating Nussdorf's mistrust of Cubro. Finally, the price of the goods was so low that "Quality King must have known that * * * [J & J Ltd. would not have knowingly sold] * * * its products in Europe for resale in the United States." District Court Opinion at 24.

III.

The district court was undoubtedly justified in concluding that Quality King had reason to suspect that appellees would not approve of a sale of the toothbrushes and baby products to a U.S. distributor. Further, we believe the district court, having reached this conclusion, could appropriately infer that Quality King, in the minds of its officers and agents, subjectively suspected that appellees would not approve of its purchase of these goods. We believe the legally relevant question, however, is whether Quality King knew that the goods had been obtained from J & J Ltd. by fraud, or suspected as much and closed its eyes to the truth. This is a far different question involving an inquiry as to whether Quality King knew or had some reason to know that Dal orally represented to J & J Ltd. that it would distribute only in Poland and that this representation was made at a time when Dal had an affirmative intent to do otherwise.[2] The district court did not address this legally relevant question, and we believe the present record will not support an affirmative answer to it.

2. It is important to note that the title of a purchaser from Dal would not have been voidable if all Dal had done was resell the goods in violation of a contract clause prohibiting resale outside Poland. If, at the time of contracting with J & J Ltd., Dal had intended to restrict the distribution of goods to Poland and only later decided to distribute the goods elsewhere, no fraudulent inducement to contract would have existed. J & J Ltd. would then have had a cause of action against Dal for breach of contract but subsequent purchasers from Dal would obtain good title. UCC § 2–403(1).

While the district court relied heavily on what it understood to be the nature of the gray goods market, there was very little evidence before it concerning that market and *no* evidence before it on the legitimacy of the means by which goods normally get into the gray goods market. The only substantial testimony concerning the workings of that market was the testimony given by Messrs. Nussbaum and Greenfield. Their testimony indicated only that the gray market exists because prices are often lower overseas than in the United States, and that gray market sellers are reluctant to reveal their supply sources for fear of being bypassed in subsequent transactions. This testimony provided a plausible explanation about why there is a gray goods market and why merchants in that market do not generally inquire about the intermediate sources in the distribution chain. However, it does not provide a basis for an inference that all those involved in importing less expensive gray goods know or suspect that there is a defect in the title of the goods which they purchase. Nor does the fact that Quality King was cautious in its dealings with Cubro, its immediate supplier, add enough to win the day for appellees.

Rather than address the legally relevant question of whether Quality King subjectively knew or suspected that there was a flaw in the title of one of its predecessors, the district court found that the circumstances called for inquiry and that, if Quality King had investigated, it would have learned that it was acquiring a voidable title. It is not as clear to us as to the district court that inquiry in this case would have uncovered the fraud. We consider that unimportant, however, because we believe the court committed an error of law when it held that Quality King had a duty to inquire and charged it with the knowledge that an investigation would have arguably disclosed.

The purpose of the good faith purchaser doctrine, codified in Sections 2–403 and 2–102 of the UCC, is to promote commerce by reducing transaction costs; it allows people safely to engage in the purchase and sale of goods without conducting a costly investigation of the conduct and rights of all previous possessors in the chain of distribution. Gilmore, The Commercial Doctrine of Good Faith Purchase, 63 YALE L.J. 1057, 1057 (1954) (The good faith purchaser "* * * is protected * * * to the end that commercial transactions may be engaged in without elaborate investigation of property rights and in reliance on the possession of property by one who offers it for sale * * * "; Farnsworth, Good Faith Performance and Commercial Reasonableness under the Uniform Commercial Code, 30 U.CHI.L.REV. 666, 671 (1963) ("Authority happens to favor the subjective test [of good faith purchase] in order to promote the circulation of goods and commercial paper."); Hawkland, Curing an Improper Tender of Title to Chattels: Past, Present and Commercial Code, 46 MINN.L.REV. 697, 721 (1962); 3 ANDERSON ON THE UNIFORM COMMERCIAL CODE 569–570 (3d ed. 1983). The imposition on a purchaser of a duty to investigate is thus fundamentally at odds with the rationale underlying these two sections of the UCC. Accordingly, in the absence of clear and controlling precedent so requiring, we are unwilling to sanction the imposition of such a duty on one in the position of Quality King.

As the district court recognized, we are required to apply the law of New Jersey, the forum state. *Erie R.R. Co. v. Tompkins,* 304 U.S. 64, 58 S.Ct. 817,

82 L.Ed. 1188 (1938). Neither the district court nor the appellees have referred us to any New Jersey case which suggests that its Supreme Court would impose a duty of inquiry upon a purchaser of goods under the circumstances of this case and we believe the New Jersey case law suggests the contrary.

The only case relied on by the appellees is a New York case, *Porter v. Wertz,* 68 A.D.2d 141, 416 N.Y.S.2d 254, 259 (1979), *aff'd on other grounds,* 53 N.Y.2d 696, 439 N.Y.S.2d 105, 421 N.E.2d 500 (1981). In *Porter,* a painting was entrusted to an art merchant who asked Peter Wertz, a delicatessen employee, to find a buyer for the painting. Wertz sold it to an art gallery that was unaware of the circumstances by which Wertz had come into possession of the painting. The lower court ruled that the gallery was not protected by UCC Section 2–403 because Wertz was not an art merchant selling the painting in the ordinary course of business. In addition, the court held that even if Wertz had been an art merchant, the gallery would not have been protected by the good faith purchaser provision of Section 2–403 because of its failure to inquire as to Wertz' source. The New York Court of Appeals affirmed on the first ground and withheld opinion on the second. *Porter,* 439 N.Y.S.2d at 107, 421 N.E.2d at 502. Whether or not a duty of inquiry exists in New York in these circumstances is accordingly unclear.

* * *

[The Court, based upon *Breslin v. New Jersey Investors, Inc.,* 70 N.J. 466, 361 A.2d 1 (1976), predicted that New Jersey would "not impose on Quality King a duty to inquire." Rather, "whether Quality King was honest in fact is to be 'determined by looking to the mind of [Quality King]' and not to 'what the state of mind of a prudent man should have been' as a result of inquiry."]

We also note that by adopting the subjective, "pure heart and * * * empty head" standard of *Lawson v. Weston,* 170 Eng.Rep. 640 (K.B.1801), the New Jersey Supreme Court would be aligning itself with the prevailing view of the good faith purchaser concept. *See Goodman v. Simonds,* 61 U.S. (20 How.) 343, 15 L.Ed. 934 (1857) (adopting subjective standard of *Lawson*); Braucher, The Legislative History of the Uniform Commercial Code, 58 COLUM.L.REV. 798, 812 (1958) ("honesty in fact" standard is subjective); Farnsworth, 30 U.CHI.L.REV. at 671.

As we have previously noted, the district court did not make, and the record will not support, a finding that Quality King suspected that fraud had been committed by a predecessor in interest. Accordingly, we may assume for present purposes that New Jersey would exclude from the good faith purchase category one who, though without actual knowledge, subjectively suspects that the title is flawed and proceeds with the purchase despite his or her suspicions. A purchaser may not be certain of the existence of a flaw and still have knowledge of sufficient facts to keep him from being fairly characterized as having been "honest in fact." Excluding such a person from the good faith purchaser category is not the same, however, as judging a purchaser by the facts he or she might have obtained through an investigation of all prior transfers of the goods. By adopting the latter approach, the district court in this case imposed a burden on commerce which we believe the UCC did not intend that it should bear.

We hold, therefore, that the district court erred in concluding on this record that Quality King had a duty to inquire into the chain of title of the gray market goods.[4] Since the only inference supported by the record is that Quality King had neither knowledge nor suspicion of a fraud by Dal, appellees did not demonstrate a likelihood of ultimate success and Quality King was improperly enjoined *pendente lite.*

IV.

For the foregoing reasons, we will vacate the preliminary injunction.

[Some footnotes omitted.]

B. Claims of Secured Parties and Other Lien Holders

Assume that the buyer obtained good title from the seller. No claims against the goods will be asserted by an earlier owner. The goods, however, may be subject to a security interest created under Article 9, or a judicial lien, or, perhaps, a claim that the sale of "gray" goods infringed a trade mark. See, e.g., Ferrero USA, Inc. v. Ozak Trading, 952 F.2d 44 (3d Cir.1992). The first question is whether the buyer takes free of that interest or lien. If not, the second question, to be considered in the next subsection, is whether the seller has breached a warranty under UCC 2–312(1)(b).

Consider when a buyer of goods takes free of an Article 9 security interest created by a secured party before the sale. Under 9–201, that security interest is "effective * * * against purchasers of the collateral" unless otherwise provided in other sections of Article 9. Our buyer is clearly a purchaser (buyer) of the collateral (goods). See UCC 1–201(33) and 9–109. The buyer's status depends initially upon whether the security interest is perfected by filing or otherwise.

Under UCC 9–301(1)(c), an unperfected security interest is "subordinate" to the rights of a buyer of goods "not in the ordinary course of business * * * to the extent that he gives value and receives delivery of the collateral without knowledge of the security interest and before it is perfected." Thus, a qualifying buyer in this case has priority over but does not take free from the unperfected security interest.

The more common dispute is between the holder of a perfected security interest and the buyer. The applicable section is UCC 9–307. Assume that neither consumer goods nor farm products are involved, because there are different rules for them. See UCC 9–307(1) and (2). In ordinary commercial sales, then, UCC 9–307(1) provides that a "buyer in the ordinary course of business (subsection (9) of Section 1–201) * * * takes free of a security interest created by his seller even though the security interest is perfected and even though the buyer knows of its existence." To be a BIOCB under

4. At oral argument, appellees suggested that the district court's decision may have rested in part on that portion of the definition of good faith that refers to an objective standard: "the observance of reasonable commercial standards of fair dealing in the trade." UCC § 2–103(1)(b). While the court spoke at length about practices in the gray goods market, it did not find that it was the practice in that market to investigate the chain of title. Indeed, the evidence suggested that this was not normally done. When a party relies upon trade practice in a situation of this kind, it bears the burden of producing admissible evidence of that practice. *Brattleboro Auto Sales v. Subaru,* 633 F.2d 649, 651 (2d Cir.1980). Since appellees tendered no evidence of trade practice, this portion of the definition of good faith does not aid them.

UCC 1–201(9), a person must buy (1) "in good faith" and (2) "without knowledge that the sale to him is in violation of the ownership rights or security interest of a third party in the goods" and (3) in the "ordinary course from a person in the business of selling goods of that kind * * *"

Why protect the buyer in this situation? Reread UCC 2–403. The secured party has entrusted goods subject to a perfected security interest to a debtor (a merchant?) who sells goods of that kind in the ordinary course of business. In most cases, the debtor will be authorized to sell the goods and the security interest will continue in the proceeds of sale. See UCC 9–306(1). The secured party is benefited from the sale, since the proceeds are available to pay off the debt. Also, the secured party is in the "best position" to monitor the conduct of the debtor under the security agreement. Thus, UCC 9–307(1) permits a good faith buyer to assume that there is authority to sell in every case unless it knows that there is no such authority (because of a restriction in the security agreement) or the sale is not in the ordinary course of business.

Another limitation in UCC 9–307(1) is that the security interest must be "created by his seller." Suppose, for example, that the security interest was created in favor of the secured party by Seller # 1 who sold the goods to Seller # 2 who sold them to a buyer in the ordinary course of business. Under UCC 9–307(1), the BIOCB takes subject to the security interest. But what about UCC 2–403(2)? Can the BIOCB use UCC 2–403(2) as grounds to take free from an Article 9 perfected security interest? See the next case.

EXECUTIVE FINANCIAL SERVICES, INC. v. PAGEL

Supreme Court of Kansas, 1986.
238 Kan. 809, 715 P.2d 381.

[Executive Financial Services (EFS) purchased three tractors from Tri-County Farm Equipment Company (Tri-County), a John Deere dealership. EFS then leased the tractors to Mohr-Loyd Leasing, a partnership between the owners of Tri-County. The "lease" was a financing transaction, subject to Article 9, and EFS perfected its security interest in the tractors by filing. EFS neither took possession of the tractors nor segregated them from other tractors held for sale by Tri-County.

Tri-County sold tractor # 1 to Thompson Implement Company, a merchant engaged in the business of selling farm equipment. Thompson, in turn, sold the tractor to Pagel, a buyer in the ordinary course of business. Pagel granted John Deere a purchase money security interest in the tractor, which Deere perfected by filing a financing statement. Tractor # 2 was sold by Thompson to Allen, who also granted Deere a purchase money security interest which Deere perfected by filing. Tractor # 3 was sold by Thompson to Morse. Deere took a purchase money security interest in the tractor but, because it was not perfected on time, it was subject to a preexisting security interest of PCA on Morse's equipment and machinery.

When Mohr-Loyd defaulted on the leases, EFS brought suit, inter alia, to recover the tractors from Pagel, Allen and Morse. The lower courts granted the defendants a summary judgment on the ground that they took free of EFS's security interest under UCC 2–403(2). The cases were consolidated on appeal and the judgments were affirmed. The Supreme Court first held that the transaction between EFS and Mohr-Loyd Leasing was "essentially a financing transaction whereby EFS acquired a security interest in the three tractors.]

* * *

Having so determined, we turn to the issue of whether the buyers of the tractors took free of EFS's security interest pursuant to K.S.A. 84–9–307(1), which provides:

> "A buyer in ordinary course of business * * * other than a person buying farm products from a person engaged in farming operations takes free of a security interest *created by his seller* even though the security interest is perfected and even though the buyer knows of its existence." (Emphasis added.)

Under this section, if Allen, Riverview Farms, Thompson and Pagel were "buyers in ordinary course of business" they would take free of any security interest created "by the seller," which is Tri-County. However, K.S.A. 84–9–307(1) is inapplicable to the facts in this case because Mohr-Loyd created the security interest in question—not Tri-County. A buyer in ordinary course can only take free of a security interest created "by his seller." Since the seller of the tractors, Tri-County, did not create the security interest, the buyers cannot take free of that interest under 84–9–307(1).

We next consider whether, as a matter of law, EFS entrusted the three tractors to Tri-County and, under K.S.A. 84–2–403(2), thereby lost any interest it had in them.

The entrustment doctrine is codified at K.S.A. 84–2–403(2):

> "Any entrusting of possession of goods to a merchant who deals in goods of that kind gives him power to transfer all rights of the entruster to a buyer in ordinary course of business."

"Entrusting" is defined in K.S.A. 84–2–403(3):

> " 'Entrusting' includes any delivery and any acquiescence in retention of possession regardless of any condition expressed between the parties to the delivery or acquiescence and regardless of whether the procurement of the entrusting or the possessor's disposition of the goods have been such as to be larcenous under the criminal law."

Since this statute has not been considered by the court in an analogous fact situation, some general background regarding its purpose and effect is helpful.

The Kansas Comment 1983 to K.S.A. 84–2–403 briefly describes the purpose of the provisions in question:

> "Subsections (2) and (3) extend prior law in protecting buyers in ordinary course of business from hidden entrusting arrangements with merchant-sellers who deal in goods of the kind. Under these subsections, an owner who entrusts goods to a merchant who deals in goods of the kind may lose his rights as against a buyer in ordinary course of

business. Under prior law, such good faith purchasers were protected only under the doctrines of estoppel and the like."

At common law, the mere entrustment of goods to a merchant who dealt in goods of a kind did not estop the owner from recovering them from a bona fide purchaser for value. This common law rule has been reversed by UCC § 2–403(2), which provides that any entrusting of possession of goods to a merchant who deals in goods of that kind accords the merchant power to transfer all the entruster's rights to a buyer in ordinary course of business. Hawkland, UCC Series § 2–403:07, p. 611 (1984).

The entrustment doctrine operates on the assumption that both the entruster and the buyer have been equally harmed by the dishonesty of the merchant-dealer, and resolves the issue in favor of the buyer. This result is explained in Hawkland, UCC Series § 2–403:07, as follows:

"In a broad sense, § 2–402(2) exemplifies one effort to 'modernize the law governing commercial transactions' in keeping with the underlying philosophy of the UCC. Accordingly, when a housewife takes her vacuum cleaner for repairs to a merchant who also is in the business of selling vacuum cleaners new and old, the sale by him to a buyer in the ordinary course of business passes a good title to the latter. In this case, the equities of the housewife and the buyer may be said to be equal. The housewife may not have been prudent in entrusting her goods to the dishonest dealer, but, by the same token, the buyer may not have been prudent in buying from him. On the assumption that both the entruster and buyer have been equally victimized by the dishonesty of the merchant-dealer, § 2–403(2) resolves the issue so as to free the marketplace, rather than protect the original owner's property rights. The rule, however, is an absolute one and does not depend in its operation on any balancing of equities or notions of comparative negligence." p. 612.

Entrusting typically falls into one of four fact patterns. These patterns are illustrated in White and Summers, Uniform Commercial Code § 3–11, p. 143 (2d ed. 1980):

"First, Ernie Entruster turns his car over to Dave Dealer so that Dave can sell it for Ernie. A buyer in ordinary course takes free of Ernie's ownership rights. Second, a wholesaler gives Dealer the goods 'on consignment' or under a 'floor planning' agreement. A buyer in ordinary course from Dealer is not bound by any 'title retention' agreement between Dealer and the wholesaler as to passage of title. Third, George leaves goods to be repaired with Dealer who resells them to a buyer in ordinary course. Finally, Edgar buys goods from Dealer but leaves the goods in Dealer's hands. A buyer in ordinary course cuts off Edgar's interest."

The last example is similar to the fact pattern in the present case. EFS purchased three tractors from Tri-County, but left the tractors on Tri-County's lot. Tri-County later resold the tractors to third parties in ordinary course of business. The situation is made more complicated, however, by the fact that prior to the resale by Tri-County, EFS leased the tractors to Mohr-Loyd Leasing, which operated from the same business premises as Tri-County. Furthermore, EFS obtained a security interest in the tractors from Mohr-Loyd Leasing.

Prior to applying K.S.A. 84–2–403(2) to the facts of the instant case, we must consider its potential conflict with our previous application of 84–9–307(1).

Appellant contends that if a buyer does not qualify for the preferred treatment of K.S.A. 84–9–307(1) because the competing security interest is not created by the seller, the buyer cannot then argue it took free of the security interest under the entrustment theory of 84–2–403(2). This argument has received support among some courts and commentators.

White and Summers argue that priority disputes between secured creditors and subsequent purchasers must be governed exclusively by Article 9 and that a subsequent purchaser who is disappointed under 84–9–307 cannot fall back on 84–2–403 and argue that it renders him superior to a prior security interest. They point to the language of 84–9–306(2) which states:

> "Except where *this article* otherwise provides, a security interest continues in collateral notwithstanding sale, exchange or other disposition thereof unless the disposition was authorized by the secured party in the security agreement or otherwise. * * * " (Emphasis added.)

See White and Summers, Uniform Commercial Code § 25–15, pp. 1073–74 (2d ed. 1980).

There is also authority, however, for applying the entrustment theory where a buyer is unable to prevail under 84–9–307(1). In his treatise, The Law of Secured Transactions Under the Uniform Commercial Code ¶ 3.4[3] (1985 Cum.Supp. No. 3), Professor Barkley Clark recognizes that an entrustment theory may be applicable, even when 84–9–307(1) is not applicable:

> "But even if the buyer in ordinary course loses his protection under § 9–307(1) because the security interest was created further up the line, he may be able to prevail on a different theory. This is what happened in In re Woods, where the buyer discovered that a bank had a perfected security interest in the collateral created by a previous owner. The court determined that the ultimate buyer could prevail on an *entrustment* theory under §§ 2–403(2) and 2–403(3). Those subsections provide that a person who 'entrusts' the possession of goods to a dealer loses title to a buyer in ordinary course from the dealer. In the usual case, the outright owner entrusts the goods to the dealer for repair. In this case, it was the bank with its prior perfected security interest which did the entrusting. Certainly there is nothing in the language of § 2–403 that would limit that provision to outright owners as entrusters. The Woods case makes the important point that a prior secured party may do sufficient 'entrusting' so that its security interest is lost, even though the security interest was not created by the dealer to which the goods were entrusted. The court in Woods suggested yet another theory to protect the ordinary course buyer: Insofar as the prior secured party permitted the collateral to be delivered to the dealer, it authorized the sale free of its security interest under § 9–306(2). Finally, under either alternative theory, the ultimate buyer was protected even though it knew of the bank's prior perfected security interest; the court correctly concluded that, in order for the secured party to prevail, it would have to show that the ordinary course buyer knew that the sale was in violation of the prior security interest."

The facts here, as in In re Woods, 25 B.R. 924 (Bkrtcy.Tenn.1982), are distinguishable from the usual case. Typically, the entruster and the holder of the security interest are separate entities with the security holder not involved in the entrustment. In such a case the security interest would continue in the goods because under K.S.A. 84–2–403(2) only the "rights of the entruster" would be transferred. Here, however, the security holder is the entruster and its rights as such are transferred to the buyer.

For K.S.A. 84–2–403(2) to be applicable, three steps are required: (1) An entrustment of goods to (2) a merchant who deals in goods of that kind followed by a sale by such merchant to (3) a buyer in ordinary course of business.

Neither party argues Tri-County is not a "merchant who deals in goods of that kind," but they disagree as to whether EFS entrusted the tractors to Tri-County and whether one of the transferees was a buyer in the ordinary course of business.

The first question for our consideration is whether EFS entrusted the goods to Tri-County. As noted earlier, "entrusting" is defined at K.S.A. 84–2–403(3) and includes "any delivery and any acquiescence in retention of possession."

In support of their theory of entrustment, appellees point out that although EFS purchased the tractors from Tri-County, it did not take possession of them. Nor did EFS segregate the tractors from Tri-County's other inventory, identify the tractors in any way as EFS's property, or otherwise manifest any sign of ownership which would be evidence to a subsequent purchaser. Appellees contend that by its lack of action, EFS acquiesced in Tri-County's retention of possession of the tractors.

On the other hand, EFS argues that the mere fact that EFS did not take possession of the tractors does not justify the conclusion that EFS acquiesced in the retention of possession of the tractors by Tri-County. EFS contends that once it leased the tractors to Mohr-Loyd Leasing with the understanding and representation by Mohr-Loyd that the tractors would be leased out to farmers, it became impossible for EFS to acquiesce in the retention of possession of the tractors by Tri-County.

The reason possession was left with the merchant-seller is immaterial under the Code. 3 Anderson, Uniform Commercial Code § 2–403:42, pp. 592–93. The entrustment definition specifically provides that an entrustment can occur "regardless of any condition expressed between the parties to the delivery or acquiescence...." K.S.A. 84–2–403(3).

Thus, the key factor here is EFS's knowledge that the tractors would remain in the Tri-County lot. The fact that EFS expected Mohr-Loyd to eventually lease the tractors to farmers is immaterial. We conclude the tractors were entrusted to Tri-County by EFS.

EFS next contends that even if an entrustment occurred, the Johnson County District Court improperly applied K.S.A. 84–2–403(2) to the transaction involving Riverview Farms because Riverview Farms was not a buyer in ordinary course of business. There is no dispute that Allen and Thompson Implement were buyers in ordinary course of business.

K.S.A. 84–1–201(9) defines "buyer in ordinary course of business":

" 'Buyer in ordinary course of business' means a person who in good faith and without knowledge that the sale to him is in violation of the ownership rights or security interest of a third party in the goods buys in ordinary course from a person in the business of selling goods of that kind. * * * 'Buying' may be for cash or by exchange of other property or on secured or unsecured credit and includes receiving goods or documents of title under a preexisting contract for sale but does not include a transfer in bulk or as security [for] or in total or partial satisfaction of a money debt."

"Good faith" is defined at K.S.A. 84–1–201(19); " 'Good faith' means honesty in fact in the conduct or transaction concerned."

First, EFS argues the model No. 8640 tractor was not acquired by Riverview Farms for cash or other valid consideration. Rather, EFS contends the tractor was acquired by utilizing $30,000 of credit owed to Riverview Farms by Tri-County. This contention is based on the fact that in March of 1982, Riverview Farms received two checks from Tri-County totalling nearly $30,000. Ted Morse, one of the partners in Riverview Farms, was unable to explain why the checks were given to Riverview Farms. A few months later in August 1982, Riverview Farms delivered a model No. 8630 tractor to Tri-County to be sold by Tri-County.

Appellees argue Riverview Farms acquired the model No. 8640 tractor in an even exchange for the No. 8630 tractor. They concede Tri-County initially offered to sell the No. 8640 tractor to Riverview Farms for a trade-in of the No. 8630 tractor plus $10,000. Later, however, Tri-County agreed to accept the No. 8630 tractor in an even exchange for the No. 8640 tractor. Appellees explained the $30,000 payment to Riverview Farms as credit received when Tri-County sold a No. 7020 tractor and disc which Riverview Farms had traded to Tri-County.

K.S.A. 84–1–201(9) specifically provides that a transfer in total or partial satisfaction of a money debt does not give the purchaser the status of a "buyer in ordinary course." Thus, if Riverview Farms acquired the No. 8640 tractor as the result of a credit obtained initially for the model No. 8630 tractor and the extinguishment of a money debt, it did not have "buyer in ordinary course" status. However, if Riverview Farms acquired the No. 8640 tractor in an even exchange for the No. 8630, it did have buyer in ordinary course status since 84–1–201(9) includes an exchange within the definition of "buying."

The Johnson County District Court made specific findings that Riverview Farms had no actual notice that Mohr-Loyd Leasing existed, that Mohr-Loyd leased the No. 8640 tractor from EFS, or that EFS claimed any interest in the tractor. We conclude the facts justify the district court's ruling that Riverview Farms, like Thompson, Pagel and Allen, was a buyer in ordinary course of business.

We hold all three tractors were entrusted to Tri-County, a merchant who deals in tractors, by EFS and then sold to Allen, Thompson Implement and Riverview Farms in ordinary course of business.

A final issue presented by this appeal is whether EFS may be estopped from claiming any interest in the tractors. We need not discuss this issue since the case is resolved by our application of the entrustment provisions of K.S.A. 84–2–403(2) and (3).

The judgments of the trial courts are affirmed.

Notes

The *Pagel* case, by using UCC 2–403(2), expands the protection of a buyer in ordinary course of business beyond that granted by UCC 9–307(1). Is this result sound? How does the court deal with UCC 2–403(4), which states that the "rights of other purchasers of goods * * * are governed by the Articles on Secured Transactions (Article 9) * * * "?

Note: Rights of Buyer When Goods in Seller's Possession

In a contest with a secured party with a perfected security interest, at what point does a buyer become a "buyer in the ordinary course of business?" Assuming that the conditions in UCC 1–201(37) are satisfied, including the giving of value, there are three possibilities.

First, the status is not achieved until the goods are delivered by the seller. This was a requirement under the Uniform Trust Receipts Act and it has some support in UCC 9–301(1)(c), where the buyer is other than in the ordinary course, and in the case law. See, e.g., Chrysler Corp. v. Adamatic, Inc., 59 Wis.2d 219, 208 N.W.2d 97 (1973), where the court stated that the "status" of a buyer in ordinary course must be determined "as of the time he actually took possession of the goods." Section 9–307(1), however, does not require that possession be transferred.

Second, the status is achieved when the buyer obtains title to the goods even though possession has not been transferred. Obtaining title before delivery requires that the goods be both existing and identified to the contract, see UCC 2–105(2) & 2–501(1), and that the parties agree that title shall pass before delivery. See UCC 2–401(1). Thus, where a buyer made progress payments to a seller who was manufacturing goods for the buyer and the parties agreed that title to all parts and components and to the goods in process should pass to the buyer when the seller acquired them, Kinetics Technology International Corp. v. Fourth National Bank of Tulsa, 705 F.2d 396 (10th Cir.1983), held that the status was achieved when title passed to the buyer under the agreement. Accord: Fischer v. Bar Harbor Banking & Trust Co., 857 F.2d 4 (1st Cir. 1988); Puget Sound Nat. Bank v. Honeywell, Inc., 40 Wash.App. 313, 698 P.2d 584, 587 (1985).

Third, the status is achieved when the goods are identified to the contract under UCC 2–501(1), even though neither title nor possession have passed. Support for this position can be found in Martin Marietta Corp. v. New Jersey National Bank, 612 F.2d 745 (3d Cir.1979), and Big Knob Vol. Fire Co. v. Lowe & Moyer Garage, 338 Pa.Super. 257, 487 A.2d 953, 956–58 (1985). See also, Daniel v. Bank of Hayward, 144 Wis.2d 931, 425 N.W.2d 416 (1988) (adopting the identification test and purporting to overrule, *Chrysler Corp. v. Adamatic,* supra). Thus, the "special property interest" obtained by identification is sufficient to confirm the status of BIOCB and to support an action by the buyer to replevy the goods or to obtain specific performance. See UCC 2–716. See also Tanbro Fabrics Corp. v. Deering Milliken, Inc., 39 N.Y.2d 632, 385 N.Y.S.2d 260, 350 N.E.2d 590 (1976), where the court apparently held that a buyer with at least as "special property" interest became a BIOCB even though the secured party of its seller had possession of the goods.

If, in each of these cases, the buyer has advanced all or part of the contract price to the seller, which approach makes the most sense? Clearly, if the status of BIOCB depends upon the transfer of possession to the buyer, the presumed problems associated with "ostensible ownership" are resolved. The buyer will not be asserting a property interest of which no public notice has been given to reclaim goods in the seller's possession. Compare Note, *"Bailment for Processing:" Article Nine Security Interest or Title Retention Contract,* 61 Ore.L.Rev. 441 (1982), written by the son of one of your co-authors. But will the buyer's interest be adequately protected before delivery?

The answer is yes if the buyer could create and perfect an Article 9 purchase money security interest in the goods being manufactured by the seller and obtain priority over any existing perfected security interests in the collateral. See UCC 9–107 & 9–312(3). This step, however, is easier to recommend than to implement. In short, there are several practical pitfalls in the path of the "financing buyer" which interfere with the use of Article 9. A full exploration of this step should be postponed until you study the materials on Secured Transactions and, more particularly, Chapter 7. See, generally, Jackson & Kronman, *A Plea for the Financing Buyer,* 85 Yale L.J. 1 (1975) (buyer may be unable to insure that funds advanced to seller are used in fact to obtain materials and components for completed goods).

SECTION 3. SELLER'S WARRANTY OF TITLE

In Section 2, a primary question was when does the buyer of goods get "good" title from a seller whose title is defective or nonexistent? Another was when does the buyer "take free" from a perfected security interest? These questions are often litigated when the "true" owner or secured party asserts claims to goods in the possession of the buyer. If "true" owner wins, the buyer will be deprived of the goods and, of course, the benefit of his bargain. Does the buyer have any recourse against his seller? If so, what remedies are available? If "true" owner loses, the buyer may keep the goods. However, he has been put through the stress and expense of a law suit and may have been temporarily deprived of possession. Does he have any recourse against his seller? In short, we are here concerned with whether the seller has made and breached a warranty of title under UCC 2–312 and what the buyer must and may do to achieve adequate redress.

SUMNER v. FEL–AIR, INC.

Supreme Court of Alaska, 1984.
680 P.2d 1109.

OPINION

RABINOWITZ, JUSTICE.

This appeal arises from a dispute over the sale of a Piper Navajo airplane by William Sumner, an Anchorage commercial aircraft dealer, to Fel-Air, Inc., a Barrow air taxi operator. In March 1976, Sumner and Fel-Air orally agreed to the basic terms of the sale, including the purchase price of $105,000.00. Sumner was to receive a Piper Aztec aircraft valued at $30,000 as a downpayment on the Navajo. Fel-Air was to remit the $75,000 balance of the purchase price in monthly installments of $2,000. Interest on the unpaid balance was to accrue at a rate of 12%. These terms were confirmed in a March 31, 1976, letter from Fel-Air's general manager to Sumner.

The Navajo was delivered to Fel-Air in April 1976. Sumner received the Aztec as a downpayment in accordance with the parties' agreement. The Navajo began to experience mechanical difficulties and was taken to Seattle Flight Service for repairs in the early summer of 1976. Two months later, after paying a repair bill of $20,000, Fel-Air regained use of the airplane.

Fel-Air sent the Navajo back to Seattle for repairs in October 1976. Two months later, while the plane was still in the custody of Seattle Flight Service, the president of Century Aircraft, Inc. informed Fel-Air that title to the Navajo was held by Century rather than by Sumner. Century's president had also told Seattle Flight Service that Century owned the aircraft. Sumner's interest in the Navajo was that of a lessee with an option to purchase. After the discovery that Century was the record owner of the Navajo, Seattle Flight Service filed a mechanic's lien against the Navajo for unpaid repair bills.

Fel-Air asserted that it telephoned Sumner in December 1976 and requested either a conditional sales contract or bill of sale which would provide the Federal Aviation Administration with a record of Fel-Air's authority to operate the Navajo, or a full refund of payments made to date on the Navajo, including return of the Aztec. Fel-Air contended that Sumner assured it that the contract would be prepared within three days. Sumner testified that he did not remember such a conversation.

In May of 1977, Fel-Air ceased making monthly payments on the Navajo. On May 10, 1978, Sumner sent a telegram to Fel-Air demanding satisfaction of the lien Seattle Flight Service had filed and payment of monthly installments then due. Fel-Air did not respond. Sumner discharged the $8,000 lien himself and had the plane flown back to Anchorage.

Sumner arranged to have the Navajo's documents of title held in escrow to assure Fel-Air that it would receive title upon payment of the balance of the purchase price and upon compensation of Sumner for payments made to satisfy the Seattle Flight Service lien. On August 3, 1977, the escrow arrangement was completed. The balance then due on the aircraft, including the payment made to discharge the mechanic's lien, was $64,936.47.

Fel-Air subsequently filed suit against Sumner, alleging Sumner had breached implied warranties of merchantability and title and that he was liable to Fel-Air for fraud and misrepresentation. Sumner denied these claims and alleged that Fel-Air had abandoned the Navajo, requested that consideration paid by Fel-Air be deemed an offset for rent owed to Sumner for use of the Navajo, and filed a counterclaim for the $8,000 he had paid to discharge the lien.

The case was tried to the superior court sitting without a jury. The court rejected Fel-Air's claims for breach of the warranty of merchantability and negligent and intentional misrepresentation. However, it concluded that Sumner had breached a warranty of title to the aircraft and awarded Fel-Air $51,166.82 in damages. This sum represented the value of the Aztec used as a downpayment ($30,000), and $21,700 in monthly payments made by Fel-Air to Sumner, less the $533.18 expense of transporting the plane back to Alaska saved by Fel-Air as a result of the breach. Pre-judgment interest accruing at 8% per annum from February 1, 1977, to May 1, 1980, was also awarded, and totaled $13,300.16. Judgment against Sumner was entered for $64,466.98. Fel-Air was also awarded costs and attorney's fees. This appeal followed.

Breach of Warranty of Title

Title 45 of the Alaska Statutes adopts Article 2 of the Uniform Commercial Code as the applicable law of sales in Alaska. Under A.S. 45.02.312, an implied warranty of title accompanies the sale of goods in Alaska. It may expressly be disclaimed. A focal point of the parties' dispute is whether Sumner excluded or modified by specific language the warranty of title. Sumner does not claim that he had good title to the Navajo, but rather alleges that he informed Fel-Air that he leased, but did not own, the Navajo. Fel-Air denies that it was so informed.

The superior court specifically found that Sumner did not inform Fel-Air prior to the sale that he had neither title to the Navajo nor the right to sell it, and that the circumstances surrounding the transaction did not give Fel-Air any reason to know that Sumner did not claim title to the plane in himself. The court concluded that Sumner had therefore breached the warranty of title imposed by A.S. 45.02.312.

Sumner concedes that the superior court's conclusion that there was no express or implied disclaimer of the A.S. 45.02.312 warranty was a finding of fact which may be reversed only if clearly erroneous. Alaska R.Civ.P. 52(a); *Uchitel Co. v. Telephone Co.,* 646 P.2d 229, 233 (Alaska 1982); *Strack v. Miller,* 645 P.2d 184, 186 (Alaska 1982). In the case at bar, the superior court's factual finding was based upon an assessment of the credibility of conflicting testimonial evidence. We have observed that "[i]t is the trial court's function, and not that of a reviewing court, to judge the credibility of the witnesses and to weigh conflicting evidence. This is especially true where the trial court's decision depends largely upon oral testimony." *Penn v. Ivey,* 615 P.2d 1, 3 (Alaska 1980) (citations omitted). Thus, particular deference must be accorded to the superior court's finding that Sumner did not disclaim the A.S. 45.02.312 warranty of title. After review of the entire record before us, and guided by these principles of appellate review, we conclude that the superior court's finding that an implied warranty of title accompanied the sale of the Navajo must be upheld. The question now becomes whether or not Sumner breached that warranty.[8]

Since Sumner did not have good title to the plane when he purported to convey it to Fel-Air, the answer to this question may seem obvious. Yet both parties agree that Century "entrusted" the plane to Sumner within the

8. Sumner argues that Fel-Air should be held to have had "constructive notice" of Century's interest prior to consummation of the sale, since pertinent documents of title to the Navajo were on file at the Federal Aviation Administration (FAA) at that time. This argument is without merit. It is clear from the wording of A.S. 45.02.312 that only actual knowledge on the part of the buyer of the seller's lack of title, or of circumstances which would reasonably lead the buyer to reach such a conclusion, can defeat the statutory warranty. The official commentary to § 2–312 of the U.C.C. specifically states that "[t]he 'knowledge' referred to in subsection 1(b) is actual knowledge as distinct from notice." § 2–312 comment 1, 1 U.L.A. 303 (1976).

meaning of A.S. 45.02.403. Under the UCC a merchant to whom goods have been entrusted may give a buyer a better title than the merchant himself possessed. To quote A.S. 45.02.403(b):

> An entrusting of possession of goods to a merchant who deals in goods of that kind gives him power to transfer all rights of the entruster to a buyer in ordinary course of business.

Because Sumner had possession of the Navajo and was a dealer in airplanes, he had the power to transfer all of Century's rights, including its good title to the airplane. Given the facts as the parties have presented them, Fel-Air could have defeated any attempt by Century to regain possession of the Navajo.

It does not follow from the fact that the parties now agree that Fel-Air's title was good that Sumner did not breach the implied warranty of title. This question has divided the commentators. *Compare* 1 Anderson, Uniform Commercial Code § 2–312:36 (3d ed. 1982) (warranty not breached) with 1 Alderman, A Transactional Guide to the Uniform Commercial Code § 1.53–52 (2d ed. 1983) (warranty breached, seller should have chance to cure). Alderman emphasizes the full text of UCC 2–312(a)(1), which provides:

> (a) Subject to (b) of this section there is in a contract for sale a warranty by the seller that
>
> (1) the title conveyed shall be good, *and its transfer rightful.*

A.S. 45.02.312(a) and (a)(1) (emphasis added). As Alderman states, the entrustee's "wrongfulness (lack of right) in making the conveyance * * * is unquestionable, for the transfer of title [is] not made pursuant to any 'right' ". Alderman, *supra,* at 266–67. Here Sumner's lease-purchase arrangement with Century did not authorize him to transfer title to Fel-Air. The transfer he made to Fel-Air was wrongful, and thus we conclude that the warranty UCC 2–312(a)(1) establishes was breached.

Wright v. Vickaryous, 611 P.2d 20 (Alaska 1980), supports this conclusion. *Wright* suggests that a court attempting to determine whether or not a warranty of title was breached must consider the facts as they appeared to the buyer at the time title was called into question. If a reasonable buyer would conclude that "marketable title" had not been conveyed to him, the seller—assuming that he does not save the transaction by showing that the facts are not what the buyer believes them to be—has breached the warranty of title. A "substantial shadow" on title is enough to justify the buyer's refusal to proceed with his contractual performance.[10] Similarly in the instant case the revelation of Century's interest in the Piper Navajo cast such a shadow on the transaction between Sumner and Fel-Air.

10. In *Wright* various third parties had taken security interests in the seller's cattle. All of them orally consented to the sale, thus releasing their security interests pursuant to UCC 9–306(2). However, the liens remained on the books, the buyer discovered them, and delivery of the cattle was refused, the seller all this time failing to point out that the security interests had been released. We held that this circumstance put a "substantial shadow" on the title and justified refusing to proceed with the sales contract. *Wright* explicitly recognized that the buyer could successfully have defended himself against any former lienholder's lawsuit, but reasoned that the risk of such a lawsuit was enough to excuse the buyer's refusal to accept delivery.

To dispel a similar shadow, the buyer in *Wright* would have had to call all the people he believed to be lienholders; had he done so, he would have discovered that their liens had been released. To dispel the shadow of Century Aircraft, Fel-Air would have had to become an expert on the UCC and would then have had to determine that Sumner had not stolen or borrowed the Navajo from Century, that Sumner was indeed a "merchant who deals in [airplanes]" as the UCC defines "merchant," and that Fel-Air itself qualified as a "buyer in ordinary course of business." The parties' present agreement on these matters does not mean that these things were obvious at the time the transaction between Sumner and Fel-Air began to break down. Even if we decided to ignore A.S. 45.02.312's intimation that a "wrongful" transfer of title breaches the warranty which that section contains, we would be loath to conclude that a breach did not occur in this case. The superior court correctly decided that Sumner breached the implied warranty of title.

* * *

For the foregoing reasons, the judgment of the superior court is affirmed.

[Some footnotes omitted.]

Note: Fifty Ways to Breach the 2–312 Warranty of Title

Paradoxically, the warranty of title was broken in Sumner v. Fel-Air, although the buyer actually got good title. Is the result supported by any specific language in UCC 2–312? Is such a result justified?

A breach of warranty of title has been held to occur when the seller of a motor vehicle fails to provide his purchaser with adequate proof of ownership because of the reasonable doubts which faulty documentation (number on title certificate did not correspond with number on frame of vehicle) raises as to the validity of the title the buyer acquires. Jefferson v. Jones, 286 Md. 544, 408 A.2d 1036 (1979). Here, because of the faulty documentation, the vehicle was seized by the police and the buyer had to incur legal expenses to resolve the matter favorably, expenses he then successfully sought from the seller.

Beyond full adverse ownership claims, various "clouds" have been held to breach the title warranty. Frank Arnold Contractors, Inc. v. Vilsmeier Auction Co., Inc., 806 F.2d 462 (3d Cir.1986) (possible security interest); Elias v. Dobrowolski, 120 N.H. 212, 412 A.2d 1035 (1980) (valid filed security interest of which buyer had no actual knowledge); Wright v. Vickaryous, 611 P.2d 20 (Alaska 1980) (security interests the prior discharge of which had not been communicated to buyer who then rejected the cattle); National Crane Corp. v. Ohio Steel Tube Co., 213 Neb. 782, 332 N.W.2d 39 (1983) (tax liens); Catlin Aviation Co. v. Equilease Corp., 626 P.2d 857 (Okl.1981) (repairman's lien); Jeanneret v. Vichey, 693 F.2d 259 (2d Cir.1982) (regulations of foreign country applicable to export of paintings could constitute cloud if not complied with).

Not just any assertion of a claim by a third party will breach the warranty of title. Unfounded claims that are also not colorable will not. C.F. Sales, Inc. v. Amfert, Inc., 344 N.W.2d 543 (Iowa 1983).

Also, whenever the buyer has reason to know that the seller does not claim title to himself or that he is purporting to sell only such right or title as he or a third person may have, there is no warranty of title. UCC 2–312(2). For example, where a buyer of a used car received from the seller a certificate of title listing another person as the seller, the jury could have found that the buyer had such "reason to know." Spoon v. Herndon, 167 Ga.App. 794, 307 S.E.2d 693 (1983). But under 2–312(2), a warranty of title or the like can be "excluded or modified only by specific language." Rockdale Cable T.V. Co. v. Spadora, 97 Ill.App.3d 754, 53 Ill.Dec. 171, 423 N.E.2d 555 (1981) (language in bill of sale purporting to transfer "all Seller's right, title, and interest, of every kind and nature, in and to" held insufficiently specific).

JONES v. BALLARD

Supreme Court of Mississippi, 1990.
573 So.2d 783.

ON PETITION FOR REHEARING

ROBERTSON, JUSTICE, for the Court:

I.

This case requires that we articulate an auctioneer's liability where the title he conveys at public auction contains a fatal defect. The facts reflect that the auctioneer sold stolen goods, and the buyer at auction has sued to get his money back. The Circuit Court entered judgment against the auctioneer summarily. We affirm.

II.

Bill Jones is an adult resident citizen of Scott County who does business as Sunbelt Auctions in Forest, Mississippi. On January 9, 1988, Jones offered for sale at public auction a used John Deere 410–D backhoe. Several days earlier, Robert Luckey of Clinton, Mississippi, had delivered the backhoe to Jones under a consignment agreement which authorized Jones to sell it for an eight percent commission. These facts, however, were not disclosed, and in due course, Dwayne D. Ballard of Clinton, Mississippi, purchased the backhoe at public auction for the sum of $10,500.00. Immediately thereafter, Ballard delivered his check to Jones and took possession of the backhoe.

Ballard improved the backhoe, making certain repairs at an expense of in excess of $1,000.00. Ballard then sold the backhoe to a third party, Stan Black, for the sum of $15,000.00.

On April 22, 1988, Officer Thomas Ward of the Mississippi Department of Public Safety, Criminal Investigation Division, contacted Black and asked to examine the backhoe. After investigation, Officer Ward determined that the backhoe was one that had been stolen from one Sam Thomas in Shelby County, Tennessee, on January 5, 1988—four days before Jones sold it to Ballard at auction. Officer Ward then took possession of the backhoe and returned it to its lawful owner in Tennessee. Understandably miffed, Black contacted Ballard, told him of what had happened, and demanded return of his $15,000.00 purchase price. Under the circumstances, Ballard had no alternative but to accede to the demand and, in fact, refunded what Black had paid him.

Ballard, plaintiff below and appellee here, then looked to Jones, his auctioneer, and demanded that Jones reimburse him for his purchase price and the money he was out due to the work he had done on the backhoe. Jones refused the demand, and, on May 28, 1988, Ballard commenced the present civil action by filing his complaint in the Circuit Court of Scott County, Mississippi, naming Bill Jones, d/b/a Sunbelt Auctions and Associates, as defendant. Ballard charged that under the circumstances, Jones had impliedly warranted that he had title to the backhoe at the time of the auction sale and that the title had proved defective, in consequence of which Ballard was out the $10,500.00 purchase price and the sums he had expended improving the backhoe.

Jones answered and denied the essential allegations of the complaint and thereafter filed a third party complaint against Robert Luckey, demanding indemnity of and from Luckey in the event Jones should be held liable to Ballard. *See* Rule 14(a), Miss.R.Civ.P. Ballard then moved for summary judgment on his complaint against Jones and supported his motion with his own affidavit and that of Barney Barefield, who also attended the January 9 auction in Forest, Mississippi. The record reflects no formal opposition to the motion and, particularly, no counter affidavits or other materials filed on Jones' behalf. On September 5, 1989, the Circuit Court granted the motion and entered judgment in favor of Ballard and against Jones in the principal sum of $11,500.00 together with interest and costs. The Circuit Court granted Jones' motion for an immediate appeal, his third party complaint against Luckey remaining active on the docket. *See* Rule 54(b), Miss. R.Civ.P.

III.

What quality of title an auctioneer conveys a purchaser may, of course, be the subject of contract. Insofar as we are aware, this state has never addressed the question of the quality of title the auctioneer is held to convey absent contract. The record before us reflects a conventional public sale held at Jones' auction house in Forest, Mississippi. Nothing before us suggests any special contract or agreement between Jones and Ballard beyond the simple fact that Ballard was the successful bidder for the John Deere 410 backhoe for the sum of $10,500.00 and that Ballard did, in fact, pay Jones that amount.

Years ago, the United States Court of Appeals for the Fifth Circuit made an *Erie*-guess that we would follow the general rule and hold that an auctioneer impliedly warrants that he has title to that which he sells. *McElroy v. Long,* 170 F.2d 345, 347 (5th Cir.1948) recognized that an auctioneer who sells property without divulging his principal is considered to be a vendor responsible to the buyer for any deficiency in the title in the goods conveyed. The *McElroy* court explained that

> The fact that [a person] is known to a bidder to be an auctioneer, by profession selling as an agent for others, is of no import and is no notice that he may not be selling his own property.

McElroy, 170 F.2d at 347. More than four decades later, we declare *McElroy's Erie* prophesy fulfilled.

This rule—that an auctioneer who fails to disclose his principal—is deemed to warrant title to goods he sells—is widely accepted in other states. These courts have replied to the intuitive thought that surely an auctioneer is not acting for himself but selling the property for someone else in language such as this:

> That argument proceeds on a mistaken view of the law. * * * [T]he mere fact that a defendant is acting as an auctioneer is not in itself sufficient notice to provide immunity from liability. The requirement is that auctioneer disclose the name of its principal, and the record in this case is abundantly clear that this was not done. * * * [Moreover, * * * the] bidder was not advised and could not ascertain the name of the selling dealer until after the sale had already been consummated. Under these admitted facts, Auction Company must be held to the obligation of an implied warranty to Banning. * * *

Universal C.I.T., 493 S.W.2d at 391.

The theory of the rule is that an auctioneer is in a better position than buyers at an auction to ascertain the title to property being sold which would indicate the true owners. Under the rule the auctioneer may protect himself by the simple act of disclosing his principal.

The facts before the Circuit Court consist of the affidavit of Dwayne D. Ballard that

> * * * the name of the owner and seller of the backhoe was not disclosed to me or any other persons present and I did not know the name of the owner but relied on the reputation of Bill Jones in purchasing the backhoe.

Barney Barefield furnished a supporting affidavit stating that he also was present at the auction, naming a number of other persons who were present, and stating unequivocally

> * * * the name of the owner and seller of that backhoe and other equipment sold at the auction on that date was not disclosed by Bill Jones or anyone else involved in conducting the auction.

In the face of our well established summary judgment rule that the party opposing the motion must be diligent in countering the movant's affidavits, *see Bourn v. Tomlinson Interest, Inc.*, 456 So.2d 747, 749 (Miss.1984); Jones offered nothing which contradicted Ballard and Barefield on this critical issue.

* * *

VI.

We find the appeal of Bill Jones, d/b/a Sunbelt Auctions and Associates without merit and affirm the judgment of the Circuit Court. All of this, of course, is without prejudice to Jones' rights on his third party complaint against Robert Luckey.

Petition for rehearing denied; affirmed.

[Footnotes omitted.]

UNIVERSAL C.I.T. CREDIT CORP. v. STATE FARM MUT. AUTO. INS. CO.

Court of Appeals of Missouri, 1973.
493 S.W.2d 385.

[Auction Company, in business to conduct auctions on behalf of automobile dealers with surplus cars, sold a Dodge at auction to Banning, a dealer. Banning resold the car to Mr. Sensenich, the sale being financed by a credit corporation. The car was destroyed in an accident. Thereafter it was discovered that the car had been stolen before the auction and that good title was not passed to Banning. Banning, after litigation in which Auction Company had been impleaded, settled with Sensenich and the credit corporation and claimed damages from Auction Company for breach of warranty of title. The trial court ruled that since Auction Company did not reveal the name of its principal, it made and breached a warranty of title under UCC 2–312(1). This ruling was affirmed on appeal. The trial court awarded Banning $3,523.50 in damages plus an allowance of $525 as an attorney fee to Banning in defending the claim of Sensenich for breach of warranty of title. Auction Company also appealed this award.]

III

Auction Company's alternative argument is that if liable at all, its liability cannot exceed the value of the automobile, measured by the amount received by it from Banning. In making this argument, Auction Company is relying basically on the general measure of damages for breach of warranty as set forth in § 400.2–714 V.A.M.S.; and it denies that this case comes within the concept of "consequential damages" which is recognized by § 400.2–714(3).

The extent to which consequential damages will be allowed is provided in § 400.2–715(2)(a), where that term is defined as including "any loss resulting from general or particular requirements and needs of which the seller at the time of contracting had reason to know * * * " This statutory definition of allowable consequential damages is essentially the same as the rule at common law. Under the common law, the courts of this State prior to the Uniform Commercial Code in an unbroken line of cases have held that a buyer may collect as consequential damages his expenses including attorney's fees in defending title after having given notice to his seller that a third party is claiming adversely. * * *

This result is especially compelled under the circumstances of this case. Under the evidence here, Auction Company should have known and must have realized that Banning would have loss beyond the wholesale value of the car paid by him, should it turn out that the title to the car was defective. By Auction Company's own argument, it knows that all bidders who attend its auction sales are automobile dealers. Obviously, those dealers are buying automobiles for resale; and also obviously, those dealers will be warranting title in turn to their vendees. Thus, if the title received by the auction bidder, in this case Banning, turned out to be bad, then the bidder-purchaser would stand to lose a good deal more than the bare original auction purchase price. For this reason, it must be concluded that the potential loss within the contemplation of the parties included costs which might be incurred in defending suits by subvendees, as well as lost profit of the resale and incidental expense.

In support of its contention that judgment will not lie against it for the attorney's fees paid by Banning in defense of the Sensenich claim, Auction Company cites 46 Am.Jur., Sales, § 755, p. 884, where it is stated: "* * * it has been held that the measure of damages against the original seller cannot be increased by reason of liability subsequently incurred by the buyer on account of independent warranties of the same property to later purchasers." In support of that statement, the text cites Smith v. Williams, 117 Ga. 782, 45 S.E. 394. An opposite result was reached in Thurston v. Spratt, 52 Me. 202. The Smith case is also out of harmony with the philosophy of the Missouri decisions on this point cited above. No significant distinction can be perceived for present purposes whether the claim made against the buyer is by a subvendee or someone completely outside the chain of transactions initiated by Auction Company. Moreover, the Smith case is readily distinguishable from the present case on the ground that the case at bar involves a sale to a dealer who the seller was bound to know would make a resale of the goods in the ordinary course of his business, whereas there is nothing in the Smith opinion to indicate that this was true in that case.

It follows that there was no error in including in Banning's judgment an allowance for attorney's fee incurred in defense of the Sensenich claim.

* * *

MENZEL v. LIST

New York Court of Appeals, 1969.
24 N.Y.2d 91, 298 N.Y.S.2d 979, 246 N.E.2d 742.

BURKE, JUDGE.

In 1932 Mrs. Erna Menzel and her husband purchased a painting by Marc Chagall at an auction in Brussels, Belgium, for 3,800 Belgian francs (then equivalent to about $150). When the Germans invaded Belgium in 1940, the Menzels fled and left their possessions, including the Chagall painting, in their apartment. They returned six years later and found that the painting had been removed by the German authorities and that a receipt for the painting had been left. The location of the painting between the time of its removal by the Germans in 1941 and 1955 is unknown. In 1955 Klaus Perls and his wife, the proprietors of a New York art gallery, purchased the Chagall from a Parisian art gallery for $2,800. The Perls knew nothing of the painting's previous history and made no inquiry concerning it, being content to rely on the reputability of the Paris gallery as to authenticity and title. In October, 1955 the Perls sold the painting to Albert List for $4,000. However, in 1962, Mrs. Menzel noticed a reproduction of the Chagall in an art book accompanied by a statement that the painting was in Albert List's possession. She thereupon demanded the painting from him but he refused to surrender it to her.

Mrs. Menzel then instituted a replevin action against Mr. List and he, in turn, impleaded the Perls, alleging in his third-party complaint that they were liable to him for breach of an implied warranty of title. At the trial, expert testimony was introduced to establish the painting's fair market value at the time of trial. The only evidence of its value at the time it was purchased by List was the price which he paid to the Perls. The trial court charged the jury that, if it found for Mrs. Menzel against List, it was also to "assess the value of said painting at such an amount as you believe from the testimony represents its present value." The jury returned a verdict for Mrs. Menzel and she entered a judgment directing the return of the painting to her or, in the alternative, that List pay to her the value of the painting, which the jury found to be $22,500. (List has, in fact, returned the painting to Mrs. Menzel.) In addition, the jury found for List as against the Perls, on his third-party complaint, in the amount of $22,500, the painting's present value, plus the costs of the Menzel action incurred by List. 49 Misc.2d 300, 267 N.Y.S.2d 804.

The Perls appealed to the Appellate Division, First Department, from that judgment and the judgment was unanimously modified, on the law, by reducing the amount awarded to List to $4,000 (the purchase price he had paid for the painting), with interest from the date of the purchase. In a memorandum, the Appellate Division held that the third-party action was for breach of an implied warranty of *quiet* possession and, accordingly, held that the Statute of Limitations had not run on List's claim since his possession was not disturbed until the judgment for Mrs. Menzel. 28 A.D.2d 516, 279 N.Y.S.2d 608. In addition, the court held that the "applicable measure of damages was the price List paid for the painting at the time of purchase, together with interest", citing three New York cases (Staats v. Executors of Ten Eyck, 3 Caines 111, 113; Armstrong v. Percy, 5 Wend. 535; Case v. Hall & Van Elten, 24 Wend. 102).

List filed a notice of appeal as of right from the unanimous modification insofar as it reduced the amount of his judgment to $4,000, with interest from the date of purchase. The Perls filed a notice of cross appeal from so much of the Appellate Division's order as failed to dismiss the third-party complaint, denied costs and disbursements and fixed the date from which interest was to run on List's judgment. The Perls have now abandoned the cross appeal as to the failure to dismiss the third-party complaint and the denial of costs and disbursements, leaving only the issue as to the date from which interest should run.

List's appeal and the Perls' cross appeal present only questions of law for resolution, the facts having been found by the jury and affirmed by the Appellate Division (its modification was on the law as to the proper measure of damages and the running of interest). The issue on the main appeal is simply what is or should be the proper measure of damages for the breach of an implied warranty of title (or quiet possession) in the sale of personal property. The cases cited by the Appellate Division do not hold that the measure of damages is the purchase price plus interest. The *Staats* case (*supra*) was an action for breach of a real property covenant in which there was dicta to the effect that the rule was the same for personal property. The dicta was compromised one year later by the same jurist (Chief Justice KENT who wrote the opinion in *Staats* in Blasdale v. Babcock, 1 Johns. 517 [1806], where it was held that the buyer was entitled to recover in damages the amount which he had been compelled to pay to the true owner, the actual value of the chattel. In Armstrong v. Percy, 5 Wend. 535, *supra* the buyer recovered the purchase price but only because the chattel, a horse, was found to have depreciated in value below the price paid. In Case v. Hall & Van Elten, 24 Wend. 102, *supra,* there is contained a statement which is pure dicta to the effect that warranty damages are the purchase price (the action was in contract for goods sold and delivered). The parties have cited no New York case which squarely meets the issue and it is, therefore, concluded that, contrary to the counter assertions of the parties, neither "purchase plus interest" (Perls) nor "value at date of dispossession" (List) is presently the law of this State. In fact, there is a marked absence of case law on the issue. One legislative source has described this paucity of case law with the understatement that "[t]he implied warranty of title under the Uniform Sales Act [N.Y. Personal Property Law, Consol.Laws, c. 41, § 94] has seldom been invoked." (1955 Report of N.Y.Law Rev.Comm., Vol. 1, p. 387, n. 68, citing Pinney v. Geraghty, 209 App.Div. 630, 205 N.Y.S. 645, a case dealing with the effect of the vendor's ignoring a vouching-in notice.) Furthermore, the case law in other jurisdictions in this country provides no consistent approach, much less "rule", on this issue and it is difficult even to add up jurisdictions to pinpoint a "majority" and a "minority". One attempt to collect and organize the law in this country on this issue concludes that there are at least four distinct "rules" for measuring the damages flowing from the breach of a personal property warranty of title: purchase price plus interest; "value", without specification as to the time at which value is to be determined; value at the time of dispossession; and value at the time of the sale (Ann., Breach of Warranty of Title—Damages, 13 A.L.R.2d 1369). Interestingly enough, the annotator was able to find New York cases each of which used language which would apparently suggest that a different one of these four "rules" was *the* rule. (Ann., *supra,* p. 1380.) In the face of such unsettled and unconvincing "precedent", the issue is one which is open to resolution as a question which is actually one of first impression.

At the time of the sale to List and at the commencement of the *Menzel* replevin action, there was in effect the New York counterpart to section 13 of the Uniform Sales Act (N.Y.Personal Property Law, § 94 [PPL]) which provided that "In a contract to sell or a sale, unless contrary intention appears, there is

1. An implied warranty on the part of the seller that * * * he has a right to sell the goods * * *

2. An implied warranty that the buyer shall have and enjoy quiet possession of the goods as against any lawful claims existing at the time of the sale".

In addition, section 150 of the PPL provided for remedies for breach of warranty and subdivision 6 provided: "The measure of damages for breach of warranty is the loss directly and naturally resulting, in the ordinary course of events, from the breach of warranty". Subdivision 7 applies, by its terms, only to a breach of warranty of quality and is, therefore, not controlling on the question of damages for breach of warranty of title and quiet enjoyment. (3 Williston, Sales [rev.ed.], § 615, n. 9.) Thus, the Perls' reliance on this subdivision is misplaced. The Perls contend that the only loss directly and naturally resulting, in the ordinary course of events, from their breach was List's loss of the purchase price. List, however, contends that that loss is the present market value of the painting, the value which he would have been able to obtain if the Perls had conveyed good title. The Perls support their position by reference to the damages recoverable for breach of warranty of quiet possession as to real property. However, this analogy has been severely criticized by a leading authority in these terms: "This rule [limiting damages to the purchase price plus interest] virtually confines the buyer to rescission and restitution, a remedy to which the injured buyer is undoubtedly entitled if he so elects, but it is a violation of general principles of contracts to deny him in an action on the contract such damages *as will put him in as good a position as he would have occupied had the contract been kept.*" (11 Williston, Contracts [3d ed.], § 1395A, p. 484 [emphasis added].) Clearly, List can only be put in the same position he would have occupied if the contract had been kept by the Perls if he recovers the value of the painting at the time when, by the judgment in the main action, he was required to surrender the painting to Mrs. Menzel or pay her the present value of the painting. Had the warranty been fulfilled, i.e., had title been as warranted by the Perls, List would still have possession of a painting currently worth $22,500 and he could have realized that price at an auction or private sale. If List recovers only the purchase price plus interest, the effect is to *put* him in the same position he would have occupied *if the sale had never been made.* Manifestly, an injured buyer is not compensated when he recovers only so much as placed him in *status quo ante* since such a recovery implicitly denies that he had suffered any damage. This rationale has been applied in Massachusetts in a case construing a statute identical in language to section 150 (subd. 6) of the PPL where the buyer was held entitled to the value "which [he] lost by not receiving a title to it as warranted. * * * His loss cannot be measured by the [price] that he paid for the machine. He is entitled to the benefit of his bargain" (Spillane v. Corey, 323 Mass. 673, 675, 84 N.E.2d 5 [1949]; see, also, Pillgrene v. James J. Paulman, Inc., 6 Terry 225, 226, 45 Del. 225–226, 71 A.2d 59 [1950] ["The purpose of compensatory damages is to place the buyer in as good condition as he would have occupied had the title been good."]). This measure of damages reflects what the buyer has actually lost and it awards to him only the loss which has directly and naturally resulted, in the ordinary course of events, from the seller's breach of warranty.

An objection raised by the Perls to this measure of damages is that it exposes the innocent seller to potentially ruinous liability where the article sold has substantially appreciated in value. However, this "potential ruin" is not beyond the control of the seller since he can take steps to ascertain the status of title so as to satisfy himself that he himself is getting good title. (Mr. Perls testified that to question a reputable dealer as to his title would be an "insult." Perhaps, but the sensitivity of the art dealer cannot serve to deprive the injured buyer of compensation for a breach which could have been avoided had the insult been risked.) Should such an inquiry produce no reasonably reliable information as to the status of title, it is not requiring too much to expect that, as a reasonable businessman, the dealer would himself either refuse to buy or, having bought, inform his vendee of the uncertain status of title. Furthermore, under section 94 of the PPL, the seller could modify or exclude the warranties since they arise only "unless contrary intention appears". Had the Perls taken the trouble to inquire as to title, they could have sold to List subject to any existing lawful claims unknown to them at the time of the sale. Accordingly, the "prospects of ruin" forecast as flowing from the rule are not quite as ominous as the argument would indicate. Accordingly, the order of the Appellate Division should be reversed as to the measure of damages and the judgment awarding List the value of the painting at the time of trial of the *Menzel* action should be reinstated.

On the cross appeal by the Perls, the issue is as to the time from which interest should run on the judgment in favor of List against the Perls. The Appellate Division indicated that interest should be recovered from the date of purchase in October, 1955, but it did so only in conjunction with its determination that the measure of damages should be the purchase price paid by List on that date. Manifestly, the present-value measure of damages has no necessary connection with the date of purchase and is, in fact, inconsistent with the running of interest from the date of purchase since List's possession was not disturbed until the judgment directing delivery of the painting to Mrs. Menzel, or, in the alternative, paying her the present value of the painting. Accordingly, List was not damaged until that time and there is no basis upon which to predicate the inclusion of interest from the date of purchase. Accordingly, on the cross appeal, the order of the Appellate Division, insofar as it directed that interest should run from the date of purchase, should be reversed and interest directed to be included from the date on which Mrs. Menzel's judgment was entered, May 10, 1966.

SCILEPPI, BERGAN, BREITEL and JASEN, JJ., concur.

FULD, C.J., and KEATING, J., taking no part.

Order reversed, with costs to third-party plaintiff-appellant-respondent, and case remitted to Supreme Court, New York County, for further proceedings in accordance with the opinion herein.

Notes

1. Would the court reach the same result under UCC 2–312? Is this result sound? See UCC 2–714.

2. The thrill of damages in *Menzel v. List* under the Uniform Sales Act is tempered by the agony of the statute of limitations under the Uniform Commercial Code. Review *Menzel's* treatment of the pre-code statute of limitations. When did that statute start to run and why? Compare UCC 2–725. In a case like *Menzel,* when will the Code statute begin to run and why?

An antidote to the four year limitation period in UCC 2–725(1) may be to obtain an express warranty that "explicitly extends to future performance of the goods." In this case, "the cause of action accrues when the breach is or should have been discovered." UCC 2–725(2). In Balog v. Center Art Gallery–Hawaii, Inc., 745 F.Supp. 1556 (D.Hawaii 1990), the court held that a dealer certification that art work was a "Dali original" was such an explicit extension and that the cause of action accrued upon discovery that the work was counterfeit. Should the court treat a representation by a seller or an auctioneer that "title is good" or that "the goods are free from liens" in the same manner?

Problem 22–7

1. On October 1, Domino Truck Sales, Inc. sold and delivered to Paul's Lines, Inc., a second-hand diesel tractor for $5,000. Paul made a down payment

consisting of $1,500 cash and a truck valued at $1,000 and agreed to pay the balance in equal monthly installments commencing on December 1. Domino created and perfected by filing a security interest in the tractor. Paul operated two tractor-trailer rigs (the new purchase was a replacement) out of the town where Domino did business. Over the past five years, Paul's Lines has averaged an annual net profit of $75,000 doing 45% of its business in the State of New York.

On October 15, Paul discovered that there was an unpaid fuel tax lien in the amount of $2,000 against the tractor in the State of New York. A New York permit for operation could not be obtained until the lien was paid. He promptly advised the president of Domino who expressed surprise and promised to have it removed. By November 25, nothing had been done. Paul again visited Domino and stated that the truck could not be profitably operated without access to New York and that he would not make any monthly payments until the lien was removed. Domino's president repeated his promise to remove the lien but, on December 10, after Paul had failed to make his first payment, repossessed the tractor. It is now December 15. The New York lien has not been removed and Paul has already lost more than two months of profits that could have been earned by operating in that state. Domino still has the tractor but, in an effort to resell, has received a $4,500 offer from a trucker which does no business in New York.

Assuming that Paul could block the resale and recover the tractor if Domino's repossession was improper, what are the rights of the parties under the UCC? Consider both the questions posed by UCC 2–312 and the remedies available to Paul.

2. Suppose that Domino Truck Sales was unable to pass good title to Paul and that one year after the truck had been delivered the "true" owner had it replevied. The evidence will show that the value of the truck at the time of delivery was $7,500, Paul had spent $2,000 in repairs, the value of the use to Paul over the year was $4,800 and that the truck was worth $5,000 on the date of replevin. Paul claims damages in the amount of $7,500, the difference in value between the truck received and the truck as warranted. UCC 2–714(2). Is this correct? How much should Paul recover against Domino for breach of warranty?

SECTION 4. RIGHTS OF SELLER VERSUS CLAIMS OF THIRD PARTIES TO GOODS

A. *Introduction*

In Section 2, we considered the extent to which a good faith buyer of goods for value can obtain better title than his seller or take free from a perfected security interest in the goods created by his seller or another secured party. In Section 5, infra, we will examine how the Bulk Sales Law, Article 6, gives unsecured creditors of the seller power to avoid certain presumptively fraudulent transfers to a buyer. These problems can implicate Articles 2, 6 and 9 of the UCC. In addition, the possibility of a breach of the warranty of title, treated in Section 3, hangs over the entire proceedings.

In this Section, we will treat a more focused variation of the same problem. Suppose a seller has delivered possession of goods sold to the buyer. Suppose, further, that credit has been extended in both transactions.

To what extent can the seller recover possession of the goods from the buyer without perfecting a security interest under Article 9? In what circumstances can possession be reclaimed without the conclusion that the parties intended to create a security interest which should have been perfected under Article 9? See UCC 9–102(1).

These problems extend beyond the parties to the transaction. They involve third parties as well—secured parties who have perfected a security interest under Article 9, purchasers from the party in possession, and lien creditors. They also raise issues similar to those posed when possession is sought by bailors, lessors under a "true" lease, and consignors—parties who are not sellers and buyers but whose property interest in the goods frequently resembles a security interest. These problems have been treated extensively in Chapter Seven. See, generally, Baird & Jackson, *Possession and Ownership: An Examination of the Scope of Article 9,* 35 Stan.L.Rev. 175 (1983).

Transactional hair splitting aside, there is a common theme: Whenever a seller asserts a property interest to recover possession of goods who has defaulted in payment, someone, frequently a trustee in bankruptcy, will contend that the interest is, in fact, a security interest that should have been perfected under Article 9. The questions, therefore, involve a proper characterization of the interest, the scope of Article 9, see UCC 1–201(37), 9–102(1), and the extent to which the party seeking possession should, in planning the transaction, create and perfect a security interest under Article 9.

B. *Possession Retained*

In a contract for sale, it is clear that if the goods are existing and identified, the buyer will obtain, at least, a special property interest and, at most, title. In short, the buyer could be the owner of the goods before they are delivered.

It is also clear that, as between the parties, the seller may withhold delivery of the goods if the buyer has become insolvent, UCC 2–702(1), or otherwise breached the contract, UCC 2–703, even though the time for delivery has arrived. By retaining possession, the seller has, in effect, a security interest arising under Article 2. See UCC 9–113. If the dispute cannot be resolved by agreement, the seller can resort to remedies for breach of contract under UCC 2–703, including resale of the goods under UCC 2–706. Resale is a method of enforcing this possessory security interest arising under Article 2, but, unlike the enforcement of security interests arising under Article 9, the seller has no obligation to account to the buyer for any surplus. Compare UCC 9–504(2) with UCC 2–706(6).

Assuming that possession is retained, the seller's rights in the goods should also be effective against creditors of and purchasers from the buyer. Or should they? Consider the following problems.

Problem 22–8

S agreed to manufacture factory equipment according to B's specifications for $100,000. Under the agreement, title was to pass to B when conforming goods were identified to the contract. In addition, B agreed to pay $50,000 upon delivery and to give S a promissory note, due six months after delivery, for the balance. S completed and identified conforming goods to the contract on July 1. On August 1, the date for delivery, S tendered delivery but B failed to pay the $50,000 due. Shortly thereafter, S was beset with the following claims by third parties who had dealt with B:

1. Bank, who had a perfected security interest in B's equipment, existing and after-acquired. Bank argued that B had "rights in the collateral" on July 1, the security interest attached on that date, see UCC 9-203(1), and that it was perfected with priority over S, citing UCC 9-312(5).

2. Lien creditor, whose judgment against B was executed by levy on July 15.

3. Buyer, who paid B $90,000 for the goods, to be delivered later, on July 20.

Which, if any, of these parties should prevail over S, the party in possession of the goods? See UCC 2-403, 2-702, 2-703, 9-113, 9-301(1) & 9-312(5).

Problem 22-9

In Problem 22-8, above, suppose that S had shipped a carload of goods to B "FOB the point of shipment." This meant that both title, UCC 2-401(1), and risk of loss, UCC 2-509(1)(a), passed to B even though the goods were still in the possession of the carrier. Suppose, further, that the carrier issued a non-negotiable bill of lading, naming B as the person entitled to the goods. Suppose, finally, that B repudiated the contract while the goods were in transit. If S were able to stop delivery of the goods against the carrier under UCC 2-705, would this be effective against the third parties asserting claims to the goods? See In re Hillcrest Foods, Inc., 40 B.R. 360 (Bkrtcy.Me.1984), where the court held that UCC 9-113 was effective until the buyer obtained lawful possession of the goods from the carrier. The seller had shipped FOB point of shipment and obtained a negotiable bill of lading. When the carrier delivered the goods to the buyer without surrender of the indorsed bill, the buyer did not obtain lawful possession. Accord: In re Brio Petroleum, Inc., 800 F.2d 469 (5th Cir.1976) (bailee did not acknowledge, seller did not negotiate bill of lading, buyer did not receive goods).

Note: When Is Retention of Possession After a Sale or Identification of Goods Fraud Against Creditors of the Seller?

A final potential problem area involves UCC 2-402. Suppose that Seller and Buyer have concluded a contract for the sale of factory equipment. Buyer pays 50% of the agreed price. The goods are identified to the contract, see UCC 2-501(1), and, by agreement of the parties, left in Seller's possession until Buyer can take delivery in 30 days. As noted previously, the rights of Buyer against a secured creditor of Seller are determined under Article 9. Buyer *may* be a buyer in the ordinary course of business under UCC 9-307(1).

What about unsecured creditors of Seller? UCC 2-402(1) provides that "rights of unsecured creditors of the seller with respect to goods which have been identified to a contract for sale are subject to the buyer's rights to recover goods under this Article," subject to subsections (2) and (3). The buyer's rights are defined in UCC 2-502 and UCC 2-716. Read those sections again, please. Note that rights in the former are sharply limited and rights in the latter depend upon the scope of specific performance or replevin. Note also, that Article 2 does nothing special for the buyer who is also an unsecured creditor. See UCC 2-402(3)(a). Thus, a buyer who has advanced money to the seller and wants more protection than that provided in UCC 2–502 or UCC 2–716, should create and perfect a purchase money security interest under Article 9.

What about subsections (2) and (3) to UCC 2–402? To recap, assume that Buyer has paid Seller 50% of the price, Seller has retained identified goods and Buyer would be entitled to specific performance under UCC 2–716(1). UCC 2–402(2) imposes limitations on Buyer's right to the goods against unsecured creditors under UCC 2–402(1).

First, the retention of possession is immunized against a "creditor of the seller" if the retention is "in good faith and current course of trade by a merchant-seller for a commercially reasonable time after a sale or identification." If so (and that would seem to be the case here), the retention is not fraudulent. This gives Buyer a safe harbor against claims of fraud by Seller's creditors.

Second, if the retention is not within the safe harbor, a "creditor of the seller may treat a sale or an identification of goods to a contract for sale as void if as against him a retention of possession by the seller is fraudulent under any rule of law of the state where the goods are situated." Obviously, this requires a search for and evaluation of any such rule of law. For an excellent example of this effort, see In re Black & White Cattle Co., 783 F.2d 1454 (9th Cir.1986) (California law).

Finally, if the retention is outside of the safe harbor but is not fraudulent under "rule of law of the state where the goods are situated," the retention is protected unless the limitations of UCC 2–402(3) apply. Read that subsection, please. Article 9 still protects the secured creditors of Seller, UCC 2–402(3)(a), and the identification may still be a fraudulent transfer or a voidable preference. UCC 2–402(3)(b).

Despite all of this complexity, there has been little litigation under UCC 2–402.

C. *Possession Delivered to Buyer*

1. *Credit Sales*

A seller who delivers possession of goods sold to the buyer on credit may create and perfect a security interest in those goods under Article 9. This would be a "purchase money" security interest, see UCC 9–107, which might have priority over pre-existing security interests if the conditions of UCC 9–312(3) & (4) were met. If the buyer defaulted, i.e., failed to pay the price when due, the seller, as a secured party, could enforce the security interest by repossessing the goods, UCC 9–501(1) & 9–503, selling them in a commercially reasonable manner, UCC 9–504(3), and applying the proceeds to the obligation, UCC 9–504(1).

What about claims of third parties to the goods? Our secured party-seller: (1) would clearly have priority over a subsequent lien creditor, UCC 9–301(1)(b); (2) could have priority over an existing secured party with a perfected security interest in after-acquired property, UCC 9–312(3) & (4); and (3) might lose the security interest to a buyer in the ordinary course of business from B, UCC 9–307(1), but would retain a security interest in the proceeds of the sale. In short, playing the Article 9 game is the route to maximum protection in this situation.

If, however, the seller delivers the goods and retains title until the price is paid, the effect is to create a security interest in the goods which is subject to Article 9. See UCC 9–102(1) & 1–201(37). Unless that security interest is perfected under Article 9 by filing or otherwise, it is vulnerable to creditors of and purchasers from the buyer. The reasons for this become clear when you read UCC 9–301(1).

What happens if the seller delivers the goods in a credit transaction without playing the Article 9 game? Consider the following problem, drawn from In re Samuels & Co., 526 F.2d 1238 (5th Cir.1976), cert. denied *sub nom.,* 429 U.S. 834, 97 S.Ct. 99, 50 L.Ed.2d 99 (1976).

Problem 22–10

Farmer raises cattle for beef. When the cattle are ready, Farmer sells them to Bravo, a meat processor. Bravo agrees to pay the price within 30 days after delivery. On March 1, Farmer delivered 50 head of cattle to Bravo for $35,000. Unknown to Farmer, Bravo was insolvent at that time. UCC 1–201(33).

1. Assume that no third parties are involved. If Farmer discovers the insolvency on March 8, what can he do to reclaim the cattle from Bravo. See UCC 2–702(2). Suppose the cattle have been processed and sold but the proceeds of that sale can be identified. Can Farmer reclaim the proceeds under UCC 2–702(2). Compare UCC 9–306. (The cases disagree. An affirmative answer was given in United States v. Westside Bank, 732 F.2d 1258, 1263 (5th Cir.1984), reprinted at p. 382, supra, where the court stated that to "hold otherwise would in many instances render the statutory remedy a nullity.") But see In re Diversified Food Service Distributors, Inc., 130 B.R. 427 (Bkrtcy.D.C.N.Y.1991) (reclamation limited to goods).

2. Suppose that Farmer, on March 8, made an oral demand on Bravo for the cattle, which had not yet been slaughtered. On March 6, however, Eric, a creditor, had obtained a judicial lien on all of Bravo's personal property. Can Farmer reclaim the cattle from Bravo free from Eric's lien? See UCC 2–702(3). Note that the '72 version of UCC 2–702(3) does not mention lien creditors. What does one do next? See UCC 1–103.

3. Suppose that Farmer made an oral demand on March 8. On March 6, however, Bravo had filed a voluntary case in bankruptcy. Could Farmer reclaim the cattle against the trustee? The answer is no. Do you see why? Read UCC 9–301(3) and Sections 544(a) and 546 of the Bankruptcy Code.

4. How would Farmer, who made an oral demand on March 8, fare against a buyer from Bravo who, on March 6, had paid the price and satisfied the conditions of ordinary course of business, UCC 1–201(9), but had not taken possession from Bravo on March 8? See UCC 2–702(3).

5. The last (but not least) variation. Suppose that First Bank had created and perfected an Article 9 security interest in Bravo's "inventory, existing and after-acquired," on February 1. The effect of this is that when Bravo obtains "rights" in the cattle (upon delivery by Farmer), First Bank's security interest attaches to and becomes perfected in the cattle. Assuming that First Bank is unaware of Farmer's claim but has made no new advances between March 1 and March 8, could Farmer effectively reclaim against First Bank? Most courts have held no. Do you see why? See UCC 1–201(32).

Note: The Reclaiming Credit Seller in Bankruptcy

Section 546(c) of the Bankruptcy Code provides that the avoidance powers of the trustee in Sections 544(a), 545, 547 and 549 are "subject to any statutory or common law right of a seller of goods that has sold goods to the debtor, in the ordinary course of such seller's business, to reclaim such goods if the debtor has received such goods while insolvent, but—(1) such a seller may not reclaim any such goods unless such seller demands in writing reclamation of such goods before ten days after receipt of such goods by the debtor * * *." This provision has been criticized as unduly restrictive, in that it (1) narrows the scope of reclamation available under UCC 2–702(2) and (2) is the exclusive avenue of relief for the reclaiming seller under the Bankruptcy Code. See Mann & Phillips, *Section 546(c) of the Bankruptcy Reform Act: An Imperfect Resolution of the Conflict Between the Reclaiming Seller and the Bankruptcy Trustee,* 54 Am.Bankr.L.J. 239 (1980). In short, unless the reclaiming seller satisfies both UCC 2–702(2) and Section 546(c), the reclamation claim will fail against the trustee. Even then, it may still be subject to the claim of a "floating lienor" who qualifies as a good faith "purchaser" under UCC 2–403. See, In re Pester Refining Co., 964 F.2d 842 (8th Cir.1992), holding that the seller was "subject to" the rights of the qualifying secured party). See also, McDonnell, *The Floating Lienor as Good Faith Purchaser,* 50 S.Cal.L.Rev. 429 (1977), who explores the equities of that result.

2. *Cash Sales*

Reclamation under UCC 2–702(2) depends upon delivery of the goods by the seller to an insolvent buyer in a credit transaction. The buyer agrees to pay at a later date.

What about reclamation in a so-called cash sale? No credit is extended. The goods are delivered in exchange for what purports to be payment, usually but not always a check. [It could be a counterfeit $10,000 bill or paper stuffed into a sealed envelope.] Later, the check is dishonored [or the phony money discovered] and the seller demands that the buyer return the goods.

Under UCC 2–511(3), "payment by check is conditional and is defeated as between the parties by dishonor of the check on due presentment." UCC 2–507(2) provides that where "payment is due and demanded on the delivery to the buyer of goods or documents of title, his right as against the seller to retain or dispose of them is conditional upon his making the payment due." Revised Comment 3 in the 1990 Official Text states that UCC 2–507(2) "codifies the cash seller's right of reclamation which is in the nature of a lien." Further, there is "no specific time limit for a cash seller to exercise the right of reclamation." Finally, the right to reclaim may be "defeated by delay causing prejudice to the buyer, waiver, estoppel, or ratification of the buyer's right to retain possession," see Holiday Rambler Corp. v. First National Bank & Trust Co. of Great Bend, Kansas, 723 F.2d 1449 (10th Cir.1983) (seller waived reclamation right by delay) or cut off by the rights of a good faith purchaser under UCC 2–403(1). The revision in Comment 3 to the 1990 Official Text was recommended by the Permanent Editorial Board of the Uniform Commercial Code in PEB Commentary No. 1, Section 2–507(2).

What about this reclamation right in bankruptcy? Consider the following argument.

MANN & PHILLIPS, THE RECLAIMING CASH SELLER AND THE BANKRUPTCY CODE 39 S.W.L.J. 603, 651–53 (1985).

A. Summary of Our Position

Although the textual discussion of the matter was equivocal, we believe that UCC section 2–507(2) should apply solely to those cash sales not involving payment by check or draft, and UCC section 2–511(3) should be the lone provision governing check or draft cases. Regardless of which section is applicable, the right to reclaim when payment is not made or the check or draft is dishonored should be regarded as inherent to the section in question and as in no way dependent on UCC section 2–702(2). Moreover, UCC section 2–702(2)'s ten-day demand requirement should have no application to cash sale cases in general, and to bad check cases in particular. Due presentment of the check and a demand for reclamation, however, must be made within a reasonable time after notice of dishonor.

UCC section 2–403 should govern all priority questions involving the competing rights of the UCC cash seller and third parties. UCC section 2–403(1) resolves the previous uncertainty surrounding the conflict between the cash seller and the good faith purchaser by subordinating the former to the latter. Since most article 9 secured parties qualify as good faith purchasers for value, UCC section 2–403(1) also enables these parties to defeat the reclaiming cash seller. Section 2–403, however, enables the cash seller to defeat the lien creditor circuitously by compelling reference to UCC section 1–103, which authorizes the use of pre-UCC state law. Under pre-UCC priority rules the cash seller triumphed over the lien creditor.

When the buyer goes into bankruptcy, the reclaiming cash seller should usually be able to prevail in a clash with the trustee. Section 546(c) of the Bankruptcy Code should have no application in such situations. Although judicial interpretations of the section and the section's legislative history provide some support for a contrary position, they are decidedly outweighed by the section's express language, which clearly and unambiguously excludes the cash seller. As a result, a trustee wishing to defeat the cash seller's reclamation petition must utilize other bankruptcy provisions. The two weapons in the trustee's arsenal best suited for this task, sections 544(a) and 547 of the Bankruptcy Code, are unlikely to prove sufficient. The trustee's success under Bankruptcy Code section 544(a) depends upon whether a hypothetical ideal lien creditor assuming that status on the date of bankruptcy can defeat a reclaiming cash seller. Since the reclaiming cash seller will defeat a lien creditor, the cash seller will also defeat a trustee utilizing Bankruptcy Code section 544(a). For a number of reasons articulated above, the reclaiming cash seller should also overcome a trustee asserting that the reclamation is preferential under Bankruptcy Code section 547. To summarize, a seller who complies with either UCC section 2–507(2) or section 2–511(3) should be able to reclaim from the buyer, lien creditors of the buyer, and the buyer's trustee. Good faith purchasers from the buyer and article 9 secured parties, however, generally have rights in the goods superior to those of the reclaiming cash seller.

This interpretation of the cash seller's reclamation rights is in marked contrast to the results that should obtain when a credit seller attempts to reclaim goods sold to the buyer. Unlike the unpaid cash seller, an unsecured credit seller is ordinarily unable to reclaim the goods upon the buyer's failure to pay. Instead, such a seller is limited to such damages as the UCC makes available. Only when the specific conditions of UCC section 2–702(2) are met can the credit seller reclaim. These conditions impose procedural limitations on the exercise of the credit sale reclamation right that are more restrictive than those we believe should apply to the cash seller. The credit seller may reclaim only if the buyer is insolvent and, in most cases, only if demand has been made within ten days after the receipt of the goods. The cash sale reclamation right, on the other hand, is clearly not premised on the buyer's insolvency, and the ten-day demand limitation should not apply in the cash sale context. In addition, the UCC seems to give the reclaiming cash seller more remedial options than the reclaiming credit seller. UCC section 2–702(3) provides that the seller's reclamation of the goods excludes all other remedies. In contrast, neither UCC section 2–507(2) nor section 2–511(3) contains such a limitation. In a proper case, accordingly, the cash seller may be able to reclaim and still recover various types of damages from the buyer. Recovery of such damages is foreclosed to the credit seller who successfully reclaims the goods under UCC section 2–702.

The reclaiming cash seller should also fare better against third parties than his credit sale counterpart. Here the main difference between the two sellers occurs in the bankruptcy context. Under UCC sections 2–403(1) and 2–702(3) both the cash and credit sellers will be subordinate to a good faith purchaser for value. For that reason, both sellers should also lose to a party with a security interest in the goods. Despite the tremendous confusion on this question, however, both the cash and credit sellers should defeat a lien creditor's competing interest in the goods. In bankruptcy the UCC section 2–702 seller's fate is exclusively controlled by Bankruptcy Code section 546(c), while the cash seller's prospects are determined under other Bankruptcy Code provisions. Because Bankruptcy Code section 546(c)'s ten-day written demand limitation will often pose a major obstacle to reclamation and because no ten-day limitation should apply in most cash sale cases, the credit seller should fare less well in bankruptcy than his cash sale counterpart.

[Footnotes omitted]

3. Consignments

From the foregoing, it is clear that a seller who delivers goods to a buyer on credit will encounter resistance from creditors of and purchasers from the buyer when it seeks, upon non-payment, to regain possession. Unless the seller has perfected a security interest in the goods, the resistance may escalate to a victory for those third parties. The lesson here is plain: When ownership interests, however described, are separated from possession or control of the goods, the need to give public notice to neutralize the perils of ostensible ownership, i.e., the "secret lien," increases.

Another transaction where this need for public notice is evident is the consignment. Here an owner of goods delivers them to an agent or "factor," who is usually a merchant with regard to goods of that kind, with power to sell them to third parties. The owner retains title and fixes the price and conditions of sale. If the goods are sold, the factor delivers possession to the buyer and the title passes directly from the owner. The factor, after taking a commission, accounts to the owner for the price. If the goods are not sold, they are returned by the factor to the owner, usually without obligation. In the interim between delivery and sale, most consignment agreements permit the owner to recover the goods and obligate the factor to return them on request.

A number of questions shroud this transaction with uncertainty.

1. When is the transaction a "true" consignment and when is it a "consignment intended for security?" See UCC 1–201(37)? A leading case stated that the "easiest way to determine the intention of the parties is to concentrate on the function of the consignment." The court continued:

> (C)onsignments are used in two ways: (1) As a security consignment where the goods go to the merchant who is unwilling to risk finding a market for the goods so the "title" remains in the consignor; and (2) as a price-fixing device. Number (1) is clearly a secured transaction with the reservation of title to goods acting as collateral. Number (2) is designed only to insure resale maintenance and has nothing to do with security.

Columbia International Corp. v. Kempler, 46 Wis.2d 550, 562–63, 175 N.W.2d 465, 470–71 (1970). But see Hawkland, *The Proposed Amendments to Article 9 of the UCC: Consignments and Equipment Leases,* 77 Com.L.J. 108, 109 (1972), who suggests that the distinction between true and false consignments was "never clearly articulated or defined by the common law courts" and this "led to uncertain results and made consignment planning hazardous." (For example, suppose that the function of the transaction was to control resale prices and to require the consignee to pay for all or part of the price, even though there was no sale of the goods.) See also Harrington, *The Law of Consignments: Anti-Trust and Commercial Pitfalls,* 34 Bus.Law. 431, 446 (1979), who claims that "any widespread consignment program aimed at resale price maintenance must be viewed as suspect, particularly if there are any elements of coercion of distributors." In short, the characterization process is uncertain and the anti-trust problem lurks in the background. For identification and application of the factors in the determination, see In re Ide Jewelry Co., 75 B.R. 969 (Bkrtcy.D.C. 1987).

2. Even if the transaction is a "true" consignment and not within the scope of Article 9, UCC 1–201(37) provides that "a consignment is in any event subject to the provisions on consignment sales (Section 2–326)." At a minimum, UCC 2–326(3) appears to deal with a transaction that is a "true" consignment and not a "sale or return." See UCC 2–326(2) & 2–327(2). See also, General Electric Co. v. Pettingell Supply Co., 347 Mass. 631, 199 N.E.2d 326 (1964), holding that UCC 2–326(3) applies to a transaction which establishes only a principal-agent relationship.

Read UCC 2–326(3) carefully. Note that if three conditions are satisfied, i.e., (1) the goods are "delivered to a person for sale," (2) the person "maintains a place of business at which he deals in goods of the kind involved"; and (3) the person does business "under a name other than the name of the person making delivery," then with respect to the creditors of the person doing business, the "goods are deemed to be on sale or return." In short, the goods are subject to the claims of the consignee's creditors while in the consignee's possession. See UCC 2–326(2).

How is the consignor to deal with this problem of ostensible ownership? Work the following problems. See also, In re Flo–Lizer, Inc., 946 F.2d 1237

(6th Cir.1991) (creditor of consignment entitled to rely on inference from consignee possession unless UCC 2–326(3) notice given).

Problem 22–11

1. Under a "true" consignment, Consignor intends to deliver goods (textbooks) to a Consignee who operates a university bookstore under its own name. Consignor discovers that a secured party has perfected a security interest in Consignee's "inventory, existing and after-acquired." There is no applicable law "providing for a consignor's interest * * * to be evidenced by a sign," UCC 2–326(3)(a), and there is no certain basis for establishing that Consignee is "generally known by his creditors to be substantially engaged in selling the goods of others." UCC 2–326(3)(b). How can Consignor avoid Secured Party's security interest? See UCC 9–408, & 9–114. Compare UCC 9–312(3). If Consignor files under UCC 9–408 and complies with UCC 9–114, what is the effect against Secured Party? What about a lien creditor? What about a purchaser of the goods from Consignee? See UCC 2–403.

2. Suppose that Consignee did not maintain a place of business where he dealt with textbooks. Rather, Consignee entered into contracts with retail outlets under which Consignee would insure that textbooks were delivered in exchange for a commission on sales. Under the contract with Consignor, the books were delivered directly to the retail outlets: Consignee never had possession or control. Consignee, however, would remit the price for books sold and insure that unsold books were returned. Is this transaction subject to UCC 2–326(3)? In re Mincow Bag Co., 29 A.D.2d 400, 401, 288 N.Y.S.2d 364, 366 (1968), affirmed mem. 24 N.Y.2d 776, 300 N.Y.S.2d 115, 248 N.E.2d 26 (1969) held, over a dissent, that it was not: "The unwary could not have been led into becoming creditors * * * based on any ostensible ownership of the merchandise." But this transaction is neither fish (a consignment covered by UCC 2–326(3)) nor fowl (a sale or return covered by UCC 2–326(2)). Can (should) Consignor make a UCC 9–408, 9–114 filing anyway?

3. Suppose the transaction was a "sale or return" rather than a consignment. How does the seller protect itself against the buyer's creditors? Should it create and perfect a security interest under Article 9 or can it simply comply with UCC 2–326(3)? See American National Bank of Denver v. First National Bank of Glenwood Springs, 28 Colo.App. 486, 476 P.2d 304 (1970), holding that the exceptions in UCC 2–326(3) did not apply to a "sale or return" and the goods were subject to the buyer's creditors. But see Simmons First National Bank v. Wells, 279 Ark. 204, 650 S.W.2d 236 (1983), holding that UCC 2–326(3) may apply to a bailment as well as a consignment.

SECTION 5. ARTICLE 6, THE BULK SALE: ANOTHER LIMITATION ON THE DOCTRINE OF BONA FIDE PURCHASE

Article 6, Bulk Sales, has increasingly come under attack. The 1989 Official Text of the UCC responded to that attack by recommending that either Article 6 be repealed altogether or that it be replaced by a revised Article 6. As of July 1992, fifteen states had repealed Article 6 without enacting the revision and five states, including California, had enacted the revision. Action was pending in several other states.

In this section, we will briefly examine the strengths and weaknesses of the original Article 6 and then consider the major changes in the revised Article 6.

A. Transactions Under the Original Article 6.

Suppose that Sam owns and uses various types of personal property in his business—equipment, fixtures, inventory and intangibles. Sam is in reasonably good financial health. There are no judgment liens outstanding. Sam, however, owes Cal, an unsecured creditor, $50,000, and owes $75,000 to Bank, who has perfected a security interest under Article 9 in Sam's "inventory, existing and after-acquired."

From Cal's perspective, there is a continuing risk that Sam might sell some or all of the assets that would, in the case of a financial disaster, be marshalled to pay the claims of Cal and other unsecured creditors. Where inventory is concerned, Cal is subject to Bank's security interest in any event, whether Bank claims the security interest in inventory or the identifiable proceeds of sales in the ordinary course of business. Where other assets are involved, Cal has no interest in either the assets or the proceeds from any sale unless Sam has practiced some form of fraud. Thus, if Sam made a fraudulent transfer, i.e., a sale while insolvent where no "fair consideration" was received, Cal could avoid the transfer and recover the assets for the estate.

But suppose that Sam received "fair" consideration for a sale of inventory or equipment and did not inform Cal or other unsecured creditors before or after the sale. If financial disaster then strikes or Sam dissipates the proceeds, does Cal have any legal grounds to complain? If so, when and against whom?

Article 6, the Bulk Sales Law, provides some protection to Cal when Sam makes a "bulk" transfer of inventory or a transfer of a "substantial part" of the equipment if made "in connection with a bulk transfer of inventory." UCC 6–102. The operative provision is UCC 6–105 which reads, in part, as follows: "* * * Any bulk transfer subject to this article * * * is ineffective against any creditor of the transferor unless at least ten days before he takes possession of the goods or pays for them, whichever happens first, the transferee gives notice of the transfer in the manner and to the persons hereafter provided." Put differently, unless the notice conditions are satisfied, Cal would have a claim, established by a judicial lien, to the assets in the hands of B, even though the transaction between Sam and B was enforceable between them and otherwise passed good title.

Cal, therefore, is given protection against what the drafter's concluded was "two common forms of commercial fraud, namely: (a) The merchant, owing debts, who sells out his stock in trade to a friend for less than it is worth, pays his creditors less than he owes them, and hopes to come back into the business through the back door some time in the future," and (b) The merchant, owing debts, who sells out his stock in trade to any one for any price, pockets the proceeds, and disappears leaving his creditors unpaid." Comment 2, UCC 6–101.

But what, exactly, is a bulk sale? What enterprises are subject to Article 6? What transfers are "excepted" from the Act? Read UCC 6–102 & 103 and the following case.

OUACHITA ELECTRIC COOPERATIVE CORP. v. EVANS–ST. CLAIR

Court of Appeals of Arkansas, 1984.
12 Ark.App. 171, 672 S.W.2d 660.

CORBIN, JUDGE.

Appellant, Ouachita Electric Cooperative Corporation, sued for the collection of past due electric bills in the amount of $37,676.80 for electricity furnished to St. Clair Rubber Company of Arkansas. Appellant sought to charge appellee, Evans-St. Clair, Inc., the purchaser of certain assets of St. Clair Rubber Company of Arkansas, with this responsibility. Appellant alleged below and here on appeal that the transfer of assets violated the Bulk Sales Act of Arkansas, Ark.Stat.Ann. §§ 85–6–101–109 (Add.1961), and that the transfer was a fraudulent conveyance. The chancellor found to the contrary on both issues, but awarded judgment to appellant in the amount of $37,676.80 against St. Clair Rubber Company of Arkansas. We affirm.

On August 3, 1982, St. Clair Rubber Company of Arkansas ("St. Clair"), St. Clair Rubber Company located in Michigan ("St. Clair-Michigan"), National Acceptance Company of America ("NAC") and Evans-St. Clair, Inc. ("Evans-St. Clair") entered into an agreement whereby St. Clair and St. Clair-Michigan would transfer certain machinery, equipment, tools and other property they owned to Evans-St. Clair. In return for the transfer, Evans-St. Clair paid NAC $200,000.00 in cash and signed a promissory note to NAC in the sum of $500,000.00. NAC had previously made loans to St. Clair and St. Clair-Michigan totaling $2,244,524.21 and had a blanket perfected security interest in all the assets transferred to Evans-St. Clair which was cross-collateralized so that the assets of both St. Clair companies secured the full indebtedness. NAC agreed not to sue St. Clair, St. Clair-Michigan, or Mr. S.S. Livingstone, the prior owner and seller of St. Clair, if Evans-St. Clair defaulted on the $500,000.00 promissory note, and further agreed to release any and all security interest which it had in the remaining assets of St. Clair, St. Clair-Michigan and Mr. Livingstone upon payment of $1,544,524.21, a net reduction of indebtedness by $700,000.00.

No inventory was transferred as part of the asset purchase. Evans-St. Clair did receive an option to purchase the inventory at a price equal to 50% of the St. Clair companies' book value, subject to the right of these companies to sell the inventory to anyone else at any time as part of the transaction. If Evans-St. Clair had not purchased the inventory at the end of one year, the St. Clair companies had the right to demand that Evans-St. Clair purchase the inventory still on hand at its wholesale fair market value. At the date of trial, approximately ⅓ of the inventory had been used on an as-needed basis by Evans-St. Clair. The remaining ⅔'s of the inventory was still located at the Evans-St. Clair plant in East Camden and was identifiable as the St. Clair companies' property. The value paid for the assets purchased was arrived at by Evans-St. Clair in reliance upon appraisals furnished by an appraisal company which had a good reputation and had been relied upon in the past by Evans Industries, the parent company of Evans-St. Clair. The representations of the St. Clair companies' owner, Mr. S.S. Livingstone, were also relied upon in arriving at the amount of consideration to be paid. The machinery and equipment located in Michigan were appraised at a forced liquidation value of $167,787.00; the machinery and equipment in Arkansas were appraised at a forced liquidation value of $497,731.00, with $56,925.00 to be subtracted for the toxological boot equipment which was deleted from the transfer; and the real estate in Michigan conveyed was valued at approximately $100,000.00, based upon a three-year old appraisal. Evans-St. Clair negotiated for these assets as a whole package, and not as separate purchases. The allocation of purchase prices set forth in the Bills of Sale was made at the request of NAC, for its own internal accounting purposes.

Appellant contends that the transfer was in violation of the Bulk Sales Act. Ark.Stat.Ann. § 85–6–102 (Add.1961), defines bulk transfers as follows:

> (1) A 'bulk transfer' is any transfer in bulk and not in the ordinary course of the transferor's business of a major part of the materials, supplies, merchandise or other inventory (Section 9–109 [§ 85–9–109]) of an enterprise subject to this Article [chapter].
>
> (2) A transfer of a substantial part of the equipment (Section 9–109 [§ 85–9–109]) of such an enterprise is a bulk transfer if it is made in connection with a bulk transfer of inventory, but not otherwise.
>
> (3) The enterprises subject to this Article [chapter] are all those whose principal business is the sale of merchandise from stock, including those who manufacture what they sell.
>
> (4) Except as limited by the following section all bulk transfers of goods located within this state are subject to this Article [chapter].

Appellant Ouachita Electric Cooperative Corporation argues that a bulk transfer between appellees took place since a major part of the materials, supplies, merchandise and other inventory was sold as well as a substantial part of the equipment as evidenced by the Bill of Sale. Appellant also contends that the fact that title to the inventory did not pass immediately should not be decisive in a determination of a bulk transfer. Finally, appellant argues that although a transfer to a lien creditor in lieu of foreclosure would be within the provisions set out above, the facts in the instant case do not establish a transfer to NAC. We do not agree.

The provisions of the Bulk Sales Act are primarily for the protection of creditors of the seller and compliance with the Act is not compulsory, insofar as the seller is concerned, unless compliance is required by the buyer. *Herrick v. Robinson,* 267 Ark. 576, 595 S.W.2d 637 (1980). We believe the evidence clearly supports the chancellor's finding that the transaction between appellees was not in violation of the Act. The trial court in the case at bar based its finding on the following evidence: (1) no inventory was transferred by the August 3, 1982, agreement; (2) on the day of trial, approximately ⅖'s of all the inventory on hand as of the August 3, 1982, agreement to transfer had not been purchased by appellee; (3) the ⅓ of the inventory which had been used was purchased by appellee on a daily basis, when needed in its industrial process, but not in bulk; and (4) the transfer was in settlement of a valid security interest, and did not harm the position of any unsecured creditors.

Ark.Stat.Ann. § 85–6–103(3) (Supp.1983), provides in part: "The following transfers are not subject to this Article [chapter]: transfers in settlement of realization of a lien or other security interest." NAC had a perfected security interest in all the assets purchased from St. Clair and St. Clair-Michigan, and the assets of both of the companies stood as collateral for an indebtedness which was undisputedly far in excess of their value. Evans-St. Clair paid $700,000.00 to NAC, and the St. Clair companies transferred the assets to Evans-St. Clair. NAC reduced these companies' obligation to it by $700,000.00, and agreed not to sue or look to the St. Clair companies for payment in the event that Evans-St. Clair defaulted on the $500,000.00 note. The transfer was clearly in satisfaction of NAC's security interest. Appellant in its brief cites *Starman v. John Wolfe, Inc.*, 490 S.W.2d 377 (Mo.App. 1973), for the proposition that in order to come within the § 85–6–103(3) exception, the transfer should be made to the holder of the security interest and not to a transferee for the benefit of the security interest holder. We agree with appellee that *Starman, supra,* cannot be properly interpreted for such a broad proposition, since in that case the consideration paid for the transfer was not used entirely to pay the superior lien held by the secured creditor, but rather was used to pay in part other parties for the benefit of the transferor, resulting in a preference to some creditors. Furthermore, in *Starman, supra,* there was no evidence in the record to support the proposition that the alleged secured creditor even had a security interest in the property transferred.

In *American Metal Finishers, Inc. v. Palleschi,* 55 App.Div.2d 499, 391 N.Y.S.2d 170, 20 U.C.C.Rept.Ser. 1283 (1977), the plaintiff complained that the transfer would not qualify under U.C.C. § 6–103(3) because the property transfer was made to a third person who assumed the indebtedness of the transferor with a secured creditor who held a security interest in the property transferred. The New York court disagreed, stating as follows:

> The chief rationale of the Bulk Transfers article is the avoidance of the "major bulk sales risk" of "[t]he merchant, owing debts, who sells out his stock in trade * * *, pockets the proceeds, and disappears leaving his creditors unpaid" (citations omitted). But where the transfer is in settlement of a lien or security interest, there are no cash proceeds with which the seller could abscond. Thus, where the consideration is settlement of an indebtedness with no receipt of cash proceeds, the protective purposes of the Bulk Transfers article do not apply.
>
> We see no reason to read subdivision (3) of § 6–103 of the Uniform Commercial Code so restrictively as to add a requirement that the transferee must be the holder of the security interest, thus ruling out transfer to one who in good faith takes over the position of the security holder. The interposition of such new party is not that of an officious volunteer; it serves a socially beneficial purpose of avoidance of foreclosure with its concomitant hardships to creditors, employees and the commercial community.

Similarly, we cannot say appellant in the instant case was prejudiced by the transaction. If St. Clair had closed its doors, NAC could have replevied the collateral and sold it in satisfaction of its security interest. If appellant had levied upon the collateral, any proceeds from a sale would have been subject to the prior security interest of NAC, which secured an indebtedness of $2,244,524.21. St. Clair could have transferred the property directly to NAC without any conceivable violation of the Bulk Sales Act.

The Bulk Sales Act of Arkansas does not purport to regulate agreements to sell inventory in the future. Here we have an option to purchase agreement for the sale of inventory in the future which is not a transfer of inventory and, therefore, is not subject to the Bulk Sales Act, since Ark.Stat. Ann. § 85–6–102(1) (Add.1961), by its terms applies only to "transfers in bulk." The Bulk Sales Act does not purport to regulate agreements for the sale of inventory as opposed to actual transfers of inventory because until the inventory is actually sold, title to it remains in the seller and is at all times subject to being levied upon by the seller's creditor. An agreement to sell the inventory gives the purchaser no property interest in the inventory, but is merely an executory contractual right. Accordingly, we find no merit to this contention.

Appellant also contends that the trial court erred in finding that the transfer was not a fraudulent conveyance pursuant to Ark.Stat.Ann. § 68–1302 (Repl.1979). This statute provides as follows:

> Every conveyance or assignment, in writing or otherwise, of any estate or interest in lands, or in goods and chattels, or things in action, or of any rents issuing therefrom, and every charge upon lands, goods or things in action, or upon the rents and profits thereof, and every bond, suit, judgment, decree or execution, made or contrived with the intent to hinder, delay or defraud creditors or other persons of their lawful actions, damages, forfeitures, debts or demands, as against creditors and purchasers prior and subsequent, shall be void.

Fraud is never presumed, but must be affirmatively proved, and the burden of proving fraud is upon the party who alleges it and relies on it. *Rees v. Craighead Inv. Co., Inc.,* 251 Ark. 336, 472 S.W.2d 92 (1971). In a suit to set aside a fraudulent conveyance, the allegation of fraud must be shown by a preponderance of the evidence. *Killian v. Hayes,* 251 Ark. 121, 470 S.W.2d 939 (1971). It has also been held that while fraud may be established by circumstantial evidence, the circumstances must be so strong and well connected as to clearly show fraud. *Stringer v. Georgia State Savings Assoc. of Savannah,* 218 Ark. 683, 238 S.W.2d 629 (1951). Badges or indicia of fraudulent conveyances include insolvency or indebtedness of the transferor, inadequate or fictitious consideration, retention by the debtor of property, the pendency or threat of litigation, secrecy or concealment, and the fact that disputed transactions were conducted in a manner differing from usual business practices. *Harris v. Shaw,* 224 Ark. 150, 272 S.W.2d 53 (1954).

In the case at bar we cannot say that the finding of the chancellor that the transfer was not fraudulent is against the preponderance of the evidence. The assets transferred were the subject of a perfected security interest in favor of NAC which secured an indebtedness of $2,244,524.21 of St. Clair and St. Clair-Michigan. The assets purchased were negotiated as an entire package and not as separate parcels. While the Bill of Sale for the Arkansas assets showed approximately $440,000.00 of assets being transferred at a stated purchase price of $225,000.00, the Michigan Bill of Sale showed assets having a liquidation value of only $167,787.00 and real property having a value of only $100,000.00 which was purchased from St. Clair-Michigan at a price of $475,000.00. All of the assets of both St. Clair companies were pledged to secure the $2,244,524.21 indebtedness to NAC. The allocation of the monies as reflected on the Bills of Sale was at the suggestion of and for the internal accounting purposes of NAC. Furthermore, appellant offered no evidence at trial which would contradict the appraised values of the property transferred.

The $700,000.00 was paid to the lienholder, NAC, in the form of $200,000.00 cash and a $500,000.00 promissory note. It was not paid to St. Clair. Consideration flowed to St. Clair in that NAC agreed not to look to St. Clair for payment in the event that Evans-St. Clair defaulted under the terms of the $500,000.00 promissory note, and further agreed to release the assets of St. Clair upon payment of $1,544,524.21, which constituted a reduction in St. Clair's liability to NAC by $700,000.00. A conveyance by a debtor to a third party of mortgaged property is supported by adequate consideration if the third party grantee agrees to pay the debts owed by the grantor and which are secured by the property. *First State Bank of Corning v. Gilchrist,* 190 Ark. 356, 79 S.W.2d 281 (1935).

In *Sieb's Hatcheries v. Lindley,* 111 F.Supp. 705 (W.D.Ark.1953), the district court quoted from a prior Arkansas decision as follows:

> The creditor who seeks to set aside a conveyance as fraudulent must show that his debtor has disposed of property that might otherwise have been subjected to the satisfaction of his debt.

Here, the record is barren of any evidence which would demonstrate that the lien of NAC was not perfected, or that the value of the assets transferred exceeded the amount secured by the assets.

The transfer would not have been fraudulent unless an inadequate consideration was established. The preference of one creditor over another does not in itself make the transfer to the preferred creditor void or voidable as a fraudulent conveyance. *Nicklaus v. Peoples Bank & Trust Co., Russellville, Ark.,* 258 F.Supp. 482 (E.D.Ark.1965), *aff'd,* 369 F.2d 683 (8th Cir.1966). The consideration in this case was clearly adequate. Appellant presented no evidence which would indicate that a greater price could have been obtained. In determining fraudulent intent on the part of the parties to a transaction, mere inadequacy of price for consideration is insufficient; it is only when the inadequacy of price is so gross that it shocks the conscience, and furnishes satisfactory and decisive evidence of fraud, that it will be sufficient proof that the purchase is not *bona fide. Fluke v. Sharum,* 118 Ark. 229, 176 S.W. 684 (1915). We find no merit to this point. In conclusion, we cannot say that the chancellor's findings were clearly erroneous (clearly against the preponderance of the evidence), A.R.C.P. Rule 52(a), and we affirm.

Affirmed.

CRACRAFT and GLAZE, JJ., agree.

Notes (with answers!)

1. Was the seller, St. Clair Rubber Company, an "enterprise" subject to Article 6? UCC 6–103(3). (Yes.) Suppose S was a lessor rather than a seller of inventory? (No, if "sale" is read literally.) Suppose the total value of the assets sold was $1,000? (There is no *de minimis* limitation.)

2. If St. Clair Rubber sold "a substantial part" of its equipment not in the ordinary course of business, why wasn't the sale a bulk transfer? (Because no inventory was transferred.) Is Article 6 clear enough about when a transfer occurs in a contract to sell inventory? (No.) When a transfer is "not in the ordinary course of the transferor's business?" When a transfer is a "major part" or a "substantial part" of the assets involved?

3. S, a restaurant, owned equipment valued at $200,000. S also owed unsecured creditors $300,000. Without notice to the creditors, S sold the equipment to B for $190,000, closed the restaurant, gave what was left of its food inventory to charity and left with the cash for the Bahamas. Is this a bulk transfer? (Not under 6–102 in the uniform text, but yes in at least 16 states which have amended the statute).

4. Suppose S, an enterprise within UCC 6–103(3) and heavily laden with unsecured creditors, was advised that the Bulk Sales Act would not apply if it sold all or substantially all of its corporate stock to B, rather than inventory or equipment. Is that advice correct? (Yes.) Should it be? (Not according to Rapson, U.C.C. Article 6: Should it Be Revised or "Deep-Sixed"?, 38 Bus.Law. 1753 (1983) infra p. 1040.)

5. True or False: If a present transfer of inventory was "in settlement or realization of a lien or other security interests," 6–103(3), it is unnecessary to consider whether either the seller or the transfer were within the scope of Article 6. (True.)

Problem 22–12

S, a sole proprietorship, owned and operated a used book store in leased premises. The average monthly value of the inventory was $100,000 and the equipment was valued at $15,000. S had several unsecured creditors with claims totalling $20,000. There were no secured creditors or judgment lien creditors. The book store grossed around $200,000 per year.

S, who was ready to retire, reached an agreement to sell all of the inventory and equipment and to assign the lease to B for $125,000 cash. B, who intended to operate the bookstore under a new name, did not wish to assume S's business debts. The agreed price, therefore, was reached on the assumption that S would pay all business creditors.

Assume that the transfer of inventory and equipment is a "bulk" sale under UCC 6–102 by an "enterprise" subject to Article 6. B needs advice on the following questions.

A. Could the transfer be excepted from Article 6 under UCC 6–103? (Subsections 6 and 7 are obvious possibilities.)

B. Assuming that UCC 6–106 has not been enacted in our jurisdiction and the sale is not at auction, UCC 6–108, what must B do to comply with Article 6? See UCC 6–104, 6–105, 6–107 & 6–109. Suppose there are creditors of which B is unaware at the time of transfer?

C. Still assuming that UCC 6–106 does not apply, what happens in the following situation: Notice is not given in time to one creditor with a $1,000 claim who was entitled to it. Other unsecured creditors, with claims totalling $14,000, were given notice. Within 6 months of the transfer, see UCC 6–111, the entire inventory "turned over." Assuming that the creditor brings a timely action, which of the following assertions are correct:

1. All of the unsecured creditors may pursue claims even though only one did not receive notice;

2. Claims may be asserted against books sold by B to its customers;

3. B is liable as a converter of assets in which creditors had an enforceable claim;

4. B is personally liable for the amount of the debt;

5. The creditors entitled to notice may pursue claims against the identifiable proceeds of sale, including books purchased with those proceeds.

D. Suppose the state has enacted UCC 6–106. (16 states have). How, if at all, would UCC 6–106 change the scope of B's obligation and the answers to C, above?

RAPSON, U.C.C. ARTICLE 6: SHOULD IT BE REVISED OR "DEEP-SIXED"? 38 The Business Lawyer 1753, 1762–66 (1983).

This leads us to the next question: If the special classification of coverage of Article 6 is no longer justifiable, should the statute be expanded to cover all businesses, or would it make commercial sense to scrap the entire statute? Article 6, in its present form and under the proposed revision, imposes substantial burdens on bulk purchasers in order to protect sellers' creditors. On balance, does the imposition of that burden serve a commercially useful purpose?

WHAT ARE THE CREDITORS' REMEDIES IF THE PARTIES COMPLY WITH ARTICLE 6?

Assume that seller and buyer have contracted for an all-cash sale (with no down payment) of a business that is clearly covered by Article 6; that the jurisdiction has not enacted section 6–106; that the seller has the secret undisclosed intention of pocketing the proceeds and disappearing without paying his creditors; that seller and buyer fully comply with all the requirements of the present Article 6, with seller furnishing a complete and accurate sworn list of all his creditors; and that, pursuant to section 6–105, "at least 10 days before" the buyer either "takes possession of the goods or pays for them" he "gives notice of the transfer in the manner" provided by section 6–107.[48] Assume further that absent extraordinary circumstances, a creditor cannot acquire a lien against the business assets until he obtains a judgment against the seller; and that (as is usually the case) the jurisdiction's rules of civil procedure require that the creditor first institute a

48. UCC 6–107(3) 1978 requires that the notice "be delivered personally or sent by registered or certified mail. * * * "

lawsuit and that the seller has twenty days to answer following service of process.[49]

What are the rights and remedies of an unsecured creditor who receives notice of that bulk transfer? Specifically, (1) Does the buyer have any further duties to that creditor? and (2) Does the fact that a bulk sale is about to take place entitle the creditor to any kind of extraordinary relief against the closing of the sale or the assets themselves, such as an injunction, attachment, or the like?

The answer clearly seems to be no to both questions. As stated by the Maryland Court of Appeals: "The sanction for noncompliance, established by the Bulk Transfer Act, is that the transfer is ineffective against the seller's creditors who may levy, attach or garnish the goods transferred to a buyer. § 6–104 and § 6–105; see § 6–111, Official Comment 2. Where there is compliance, however, that sanction is unavailable." [50] According to Chancellor Hawkland: "It is generally held that the liquidation of one's inventory is not, of itself, proof of an intent to defraud creditors. * * * " [51] The conclusion is inescapable. In a jurisdiction that has not enacted section 6–106, if the parties comply with Article 6, the notice given to the creditor affords him little or no practical remedies, absent grounds for extraordinary relief.

If the jurisdiction has enacted section 6–106, the conclusion is quite different. The creditor has significant protection. The buyer must apply the purchase price to the debts owed to the creditors, and, if there is not enough money to go around, then the sales proceeds must be applied pro rata. If the buyer breaches this duty he may end up having to pay twice.[52] Clearly, section 6–106 gives very meaningful protection to the creditors, but only by imposing very substantial burdens upon the purchaser.[53]

Is this logical? The avowed purpose of a bulk sale statute is to protect creditors of businesses against the risk that sellers of those businesses will pocket the proceeds and disappear, leaving the creditors unpaid.[54] Yet, the majority of jurisdictions, by rejecting section 6–106, have a toothless statute that does not effectively serve that purpose when the parties comply.

Why have most jurisdictions rejected section 6–106 [55] and the opportunity to put teeth into the statute? The answer may well lie in a sense of

49. If the closing of the sale was scheduled for a Monday, a notice mailed by certified mail on the second preceding Thursday would be "ten days before" and timely. Thus, a creditor receiving notice on the following Monday would have no more than five business (or court) days to take action. *See* Hawkland, *Remedies of Bulk Transfer Creditors Where There Has Been Compliance with Article 6,* 74 Com.L.J. 257, 258 (1969).

50. FICOR, Inc. v. Ghingher, 287 Md. 150, 411 A.2d 430 (1980) (emphasis added).

51. Hawkland, *supra* note 49, at 258.

52. If noncompliance with UCC 6–106 results in the buyer becoming personally liable for the debt * * * and the debt is not otherwise satisfied, that would be the result. If the seller goes into bankruptcy, that is also the result. * * *.

53. Suppose the seller takes back a purchase money negotiable note as part of the payment of the purchase price and then discounts it with a party qualifying as a holder in due course (UCC 3–302)? Whom does the bulk purchaser pay when the note becomes due? The holder in due course or the seller's creditors? The answer may be that he has to pay both. The solution is to make the note nonnegotiable.

54. Official Comment 2(b) to UCC 6–101 (1978).

55. Section 6–106 is presented in the Official Text as an optional provision "bracketed to indicate division of opinion as to whether

discomfort with the means by which Article 6 attempts to protect the seller's creditors, especially section 6–106.

The rationale of Article 6 is that the creditors should be protected by imposing substantial burdens and sanctions upon *buyers* of businesses, even though they may have acted in good faith and paid top dollar for the purchase. Is that really fair? Does it make sense to place burdens upon a *buyer* in order to protect creditors of the seller who have taken the risk of extending unsecured credit? Can we support a value judgment that the purchaser should bear the risk that a seller will not pay his creditors? If not, as has happened in most jurisdictions,[56] section 6–106 will be rejected and the purchaser will have no duty to apply the purchase proceeds to the payment of the seller's debts. Compliance with Article 6 will be achieved by notifying the creditors, but the purpose of Article 6 will be frustrated because the creditors will not have practical remedies.

Do the Consequences of Noncompliance With Article 6 Make Commercial Sense?

By contrast, if the bulk purchaser fails to notify the creditors the sanctions for noncompliance are drastic. The sale is "ineffective" as to the seller's creditors,[57] which means that the creditors can enforce their claims by resorting to the purchased assets, even though the purchaser has paid the purchase price in full.[58]

The consequences of failing to comply with Article 6 *may* be more severe in a jurisdiction which has section 6–106. The authorities are divided whether noncompliance with section 6–106 merely furnishes an additional ground for rendering the transaction ineffective against the seller's creditors, or whether it also results in the buyer being personally liable for the seller's debts.[59]

The proposed revision deals directly with the question. First, it wisely introduces the concept of "omitted" creditor[60] and makes it clear that noncompliance makes the sale ineffective only as to an omitted creditor, and not as to all the creditors including those who receive notice—a theoretical possibility under present Article 6. Second, it would add new sections 6–104(4) and 6–106(5) to provide that the bulk purchaser is not personally liable unless he thereafter

or not it is a wise provision. * * *" Section 6–106 reflects the pre-U.C.C. minority "Pennsylvania rule." It may be that such bracketing deterred adoption. If section 6–106 (or any other provision) is the better rule, brackets should not be used.

56. * * *.

57. UCC 6–104(1) and 6–105 (1978).

58. As stated in Official Comment 2 to UCC 6–104 (1978): "Any such creditor or creditors may therefore disregard the transfer and levy on the goods as still belonging to the transferor, or a receiver representing them can take them by whatever procedure the local law provides."

59. * * *.

60. U.C.C. section 6–104(1) would be amended to define an "omitted" creditor as follows:

An "omitted" creditor is a creditor (Section 6–109) who has not been notified of the bulk transfer as provided by sections 6–105 and 6–107 or who has not had the protection provided by this section [or section 6–106], but a creditor is not omitted after the full payment of his claim has been tendered to him by the transferor or transferee.

> transfers the property to a purchaser for value in good faith and without notice of any noncompliance * * * in which case the transferee shall be personally liable to the creditors (Section 6–109) in an amount measured by the fair market value of the property at the time it was subsequently transferred to the said purchaser.[61]

Thus, the sanction for noncompliance would be identical in all jurisdictions whether or not they had enacted section 6–106. This proposal is questionable. It would remove the compulsion of immediate personal liability for noncompliance with section 6–106. Consequently, it would make the alternative of complete noncompliance with Article 6 more attractive because the parties incur no additional risk by not paying the creditors pursuant to section 6–106. If the buyer is not going to apply the purchase price to the creditors' claims, there is no point in notifying them and stirring them up—and the sanction is no worse.

Logically, if we are to retain Article 6, there is little point in doing so without requiring compliance with section 6–106 and making the bulk purchasers personally liable for noncompliance. Otherwise, the statute is a time-consuming, expensive burden having minimal practical benefits.

The proposed revision would significantly increase the burdens and risks of bulk purchasers. Section 6–104(3) would be amended to place an objective duty of care on the bulk purchaser to make reasonable inquiries concerning the completeness and accuracy of the creditors' list:

> (3) Responsibility for the completeness and accuracy of the list of creditors rests on the transferor, and the transfer is not rendered ineffective by errors or omissions therein unless the fact of such errors or omissions is known or disclosed to or reasonably discoverable by the transferee. Such fact is known to or disclosed to or reasonably discoverable by the transferee if, prior to the giving of notice provided in Section 6–105, it is revealed by the transferor's regular bookkeeping records, its existence is known or in any way made known to the transferee, or it would be discovered by his reasonable inquiry concerning the transferor's creditors.

This revision is designed to reject the controversial decision of the New York Court of Appeals in *Adrian Tabin Corp. v. Climax Boutique, Inc.*[62] permitting the bulk purchaser to rely upon an "affidavit of no creditors" furnished by the seller of an ongoing business. Under the revision, the purchaser would be required to "make reasonable inquiries concerning the transferor's creditors and examine the books of the transferor."[63]

The change would adopt the pre-Code New York rule[64] and apply to any creditor's list, not just affidavits of no creditors. If one believes that the substantial burdens imposed on purchasers by Article 6 are a justifiable means of protecting sellers' creditors, the revision makes sense because it is

61. In essence, the buyer would become "liable for damages as a converter when he conveys the property to a bona fide purchaser and cuts off the creditors' rights to reach that property." Final Report, *Justifications for Changes in § 6–106,* par. 2. Inasmuch as the property is usually inventory held for sale, that is a likely result.

62. 34 N.Y.2d 210, 356 N.Y.S.2d 606, 313 N.E.2d 66 (1974).

63. Final Report, *Justifications for Changes in § 6–104,* par. 2.

64. *See* Adrian Tabin Corp. v. Climax Boutique, Inc., 34 N.Y.2d at ___, 356 N.Y.S.2d at ___, 313 N.E.2d at ___ (1974).

consistent with the objective of furnishing meaningful protection to the creditors. However, the added burden and risk may be highly objectionable to purchasers of businesses. One of the motivations for a buyer to enter into an asset sale, as distinguished from a stock sale, is that the buyer does not want to be concerned with the seller's creditors.[65] This would no longer be the case under revised section 6–104(3).

The decision to retain Article 6 requires a value judgment that a commercially useful purpose is served by allocating to the bulk purchaser the risk that the seller will not pay his creditors. *If* such a judgment is sound, the protection afforded creditors should be made meaningful by adopting this revision to section 6–104(3) and by requiring enactment of section 6–106.

B. Transactions Under Revised Article 6.

Revised Article 6 appears in the 1990 Official Text of the UCC. Read the Comment to UCC 6–101, entitled "Rationale for Revision of the Article," review Mr. Rapson's criticisms of the original Article 6 and then work the following problem.

Problem 22–13

1. Some of you have been retained by the Commercial Law League of America to give an opinion on whether the original Article 6 should be replaced by the revised Article 6. The League is primarily involved with secured and unsecured creditors, so the evaluation should be from the standpoint of creditors of the seller who has made a bulk sale. How are they protected in the revision? Is that protection adequate?

2. Some of you have been retained by the Association of Commercial Purchasers. The Association is primarily composed of purchasers, so the evaluation should be made from the standpoint of a buyer in bulk who has no actual or constructive knowledge of claims by creditors of the seller. How are they protected in the revision? Is that protection adequate?

3. Would you vote to repeal the original Article 6? If so, would you vote to enact revised Article 6? What are the risks of having no bulk sales law?

65. This is no longer possible in acquisitions of manufacturing businesses in jurisdictions adopting the "product line" approach to successor corporation liability for injuries caused by defective products. As enunciated by the New Jersey Supreme Court in Ramirez v. Amsted Indus., Inc., 86 N.J. 332, 431 A.2d 811 (1981):

> [W]e hold that where one corporation acquires all or substantially all the manufacturing assets of another corporation, even if exclusively for cash, and undertakes essentially the same manufacturing operation as the selling corporation, the purchasing corporation is strictly liable for injuries caused by defects in units of the same product line, even if previously manufactured and distributed by the selling corporation or its predecessor. The social policies underlying strict products liability in New Jersey are best served by extending strict liability to a successor corporation that acquires the business assets and continues to manufacture essentially the same line of products as its predecessor, particularly where the successor corporation benefits from trading its product line on the name of the predecessor and takes advantage from its accumulated good will, business reputation and established customers.

Id. at 358, 431 A.2d at 825. *Accord* Cyr v. B. Offen & Co., Inc., 501 F.2d 1145 (1st Cir. 1974); Turner v. Bituminous Casualty Co., 397 Mich. 406, 244 N.W.2d 873 (1976); Ray v. Alad Corp., 19 Cal.3d 22, 136 Cal.Rptr. 574, 560 P.2d 3 (1977); Dawejko v. Jorgensen Steel Co., 290 Pa.Super. 15, 434 A.2d 106 (1981).

CHAPTER TWENTY–THREE

ARTICLE 2A, LEASES OF GOODS

SECTION 1. INTRODUCTION

This chapter surveys the new Article 2A on leases of goods. The leasing of goods has for a long while been big business. In 1987 alone, the U.S. Dept. of Commerce reported that the approximate volume of lease payments owed for the year was more than 310 billion dollars. There are two main explanations for the growth of leasing. First, the lessee can have a better looking financial statement. This is largely because a lessee's duty to pay rent often need not be listed as a debt. Second, the lessee's rental payments are unquestionably a tax deduction.

In 1987, the first Official Text of Article 2A on leases of goods was promulgated, and several states adopted it. In 1990, a revised Official Text of Article 2A was promulgated. Either the 1990 revised text, or the 1987 text plus the 1990 amendments had been adopted in 31 states as of December 1, 1992. All but a tiny handful of these states adopted the 1990 amendments. Here we focus on the amended version, i.e. the 1990 Official Text.

Many of the legal problems that arise in regard to leases of goods are substantially the same as, or highly similar to, problems arising under Article 2 on sales of goods and Article 9 on secured transactions. However, some problems are special to leases of goods. Article 2A was drafted mainly to cope with these special problems, but it includes as well many provisions that have counterparts elsewhere in the UCC, especially in Article 2 on sales.

The basic structure of Article 2A is revealed in its main parts:

Part 1. General Provisions
Part 2. Formation and Construction of Lease Contract
Part 3. Effect of Lease Contract
Part 4. Performance of Lease Contract: Repudiated, Substituted and Excused
Part 5. Default
- A. In general
- B. Default by lessor
- C. Default by lessee

The materials in this chapter will focus on general aspects of the leasing of goods that are relatively distinctive. The special problems arising with regard to the so called "finance lease" are treated in the final section of this chapter. The student should begin by consulting the definitional section, 2A–103.

SECTION 2. SCOPE OF ARTICLE 2A ON LEASES

There are two definitions in the Code that the student should now read at least for the purpose of initial familiarity. The first is the definition of "lease" in Article 2A–103(1)(j). The second is long and tedious but very important. It is the definition of "security interest" in UCC 1–201(37). The student should focus on the lengthy part of the definition beginning with the words "whether a transaction creates a lease or a security interest. * * *" which goes on to provide rules and criteria for drawing the distinction between a lease and a security interest.

Prior to the promulgation of Article 2A by the Code sponsors, the distinction between a lease and a security interest was the most litigated distinction in the entire Uniform Commercial Code. Much was and is at stake. For example, if the transfer creates a security interest rather than a true lease, and if the transferor has failed to file an Article Nine financing statement, the transferor's interest is generally vulnerable to various third party creditors and to the transferee's trustee in bankruptcy. With the promulgation of Article 2A, UCC 1–201(37) was thoroughly revised to do a better job of excluding the true lease from the definition of a security interest.

The new definition in UCC 1–201(37) does do a better job of drawing a bright line between leases and security interests. At least the new line in revised UCC 1–201(37) is brighter than the old line in UCC 1–201(37). The major advances are two. First, the overall emphasis of the new definition is on whether the transferor retained a reversionary interest. As one commentator has put it,

> "[T]he central feature of a true lease is the reservation of an economically meaningful interest to the lessor at the end of the lease term. Ordinarily this means two things: (1) at the outset of the lease the parties expect the goods to retain some significant residual value at the end of the lease term; and (2) the lessor retains some entrepreneurial stake (either the possibility of gain or the risk of loss) in the value of the goods at the end of the lease term." (Huddleson, "Old Wine in New Bottles: UCC Article 2A—Leases", 39 Ala.L.Rev. 615, 625 (1988)).

Second, unlike the definition in the pre-Article 2A section 1–201(37) version of the Code, the new one largely abandons the "laundry list" approach ("indicia" of security vs. "indicia" of lease interest), and seeks to substitute two broad rules. The first rule is one of *inclusion* and provides in the second paragraph of 1–201(37) that the transfer creates a security interest where:

(1) the lessee pays the lessor for the right to use and possess the goods and,
(2) the lessee's obligation is for the term of the lease not subject to termination by the lessee, and
(3) the immediately following language of 1–201(37)(a)–(d) is satisfied:
"(a) the original term of the lease is equal to or greater than the remaining economic life of the goods,
(b) the lessee is bound to renew the lease for the remaining economic life of the goods or is bound to become the owner of the goods,
(c) the lessee has an option to renew the lease for the remaining economic life of the goods for no additional consideration or

nominal additional consideration upon compliance with the lease agreement, or

(d) the lessee has an option to become the owner of the goods for no additional consideration or nominal additional consideration upon compliance with the lease agreement."

In such a case, the "lessor" has no reversionary interest, and the transaction is not a lease but a secured sale. A simple example illustrating the inclusionary operation of UCC 1–201(37) here to create a security interest is as follows: In return for periodic payments, T transfers heavy duty truck tires with an estimated life of 200,000 miles to U for three years during which time the truck on which they are placed is expected to be driven more than 200,000 miles. It seems most unlikely that T expects to have any significant reversionary interest after the three year term is up. Hence, the transaction is a secured sale, not a true lease, and is included within the security interest definition of new UCC 1–201(37).

We may further illustrate the operation of the rule of inclusion in 1–201(37) as follows. Assume a case in which T transfers a new truck for three years under a contract that grants the transferee the right to become the owner at the end of the period by exercising a purchase option and paying a $1.00 sum to the transferor. Unless the present value of the monthly payments the transferee is to make to the transferor equals the value of the new truck, the transferor has made a foolish bargain, for surely the transferee will exercise the option at the end of the three years. Thus, the parties have really entered into a three year secured sale agreement, not a lease.

Now, we turn to the second basic general rule in the new section 1–201(37). This is a rule of exclusion. It is a less firm rule, and provides that a transaction "does not create a security interest," and thus may remain a true lease, "merely because it provides that. * * * " and the language goes on to specify five circumstances or conditions that are not alone enough to make the transaction one for security. These circumstances or conditions are as follows:

"(a) the present value of the consideration the lessee is obligated to pay the lessor for the right to possession and use of the goods is substantially equal to or is greater than the fair market value of the goods at the time the lease is entered into,

(b) the lessee assumes risk of loss of the goods, or agrees to pay taxes, insurance, filing, recording, or registration fees, or service or maintenance costs with respect to the goods,

(c) the lessee has an option to renew the lease or to become the owner of the goods,

(d) the lessee has an option to renew the lease for a fixed rent that is equal to or greater than the reasonably predictable fair market rent for the use of the goods for the term of the renewal at the time the option is to be performed, or

(e) the lessee has an option to become the owner of the goods for a fixed price that is equal to or greater than the reasonably predictable fair market value of the goods at the time the option is to be performed."

We suspect that the drafters specified (a) through (e) not just because they believed those factors are not alone enough to make the transaction a security interest, but because they believed most of those factors have no real bearing and should not, therefore, be used even as one among several factors in determining whether a transfer involves a security agreement or a lease. Except perhaps for (a) we regard these factors, even in combination, not only "not enough", but as generally not relevant.

Subpart (a) in the exclusionary set of factors tells us that something is not a security agreement merely because the present value of the projected payments is substantially equal to or greater than the fair market value of the goods at the time the lease is entered into. One might have thought that when that test is met, the parties have signed a secured sale arrangement, not a lease agreement, and many courts have fallen into this error. Actually, there are various explanations for why this feature of a transaction should not be alone enough to make the deal a secured sale. The case of Rushton v. Shea, 419 F.Supp. 1349 (D.Del.1976) explores this issue under the pre-Article 2A version of 1–201(37) and yet comes out consistently with the new 1–201(37), second subpart (a). The court found that over a 15 year lease period the lessor would have received payments with a real value equal to the entire fair market value of the leased tank cars at the beginning plus about one percent per month interest, yet because the tank cars were expected to have significant residual value at the end of the 15 year lease which would revert to the lessor, the court found a true lease.

Problem 23–1

ABC Rent-to-Own offers furniture and electronic devices of various sorts for rent and at the same time for purchase if that is what the "lessee" so desires. While such a choice is in the offering the "lessee" may be thought of as "renting to own".

Under the terms of the standard ABC contract, one "leases" the item for 16 months, making an identical payment each month. At the end of this period the "lessee" has the right to purchase the goods and get full title by paying an additional two months of such payments as the "option price". Also, at any time, the "lessee" has the right to return the goods and cease making payments. Typically, however, those who enter into such contracts do so with the hope of buying. The "prices" are substantially higher than the prices that would be charged if the goods were sold on a cash basis or if financed in a more conventional way. The reason those who wish to purchase do so by the "rent-to-own" means and not by more conventional borrowing from a bank or finance company are several. First, the "rent-to-own" clientele are typically less credit-worthy, have more defaults and weaker credit than those who borrow from banks or finance companies. Second, the "rent-to-own" clientele are often unable to make a significant down-payment and thus for this reason, too, frequently do not qualify for loans from banks or finance companies.

Assume that Edgar wanted a large TV set to be located in a small business office in a room attached to his house. He signed the standard "lease" agreement with ABC where he was to make 18 monthly payments of $50 each. Edgar has made 16 payments. At this point, the wholesale value of the TV set is $45 to $70 and the used retail value is $90 to $110.

(1) Assume Edgar takes bankruptcy. ABC Rent-to-Own seeks as "lessor" to take back the TV. Assume Edgar's trustee contends that Edgar was not a lessee but a borrower pursuant to a secured installment sale with ABC as lender in effect retaining a security interest in the TV. Who prevails on this issue under 1–201(37)?

(2) Assume that ABC Rent-to-Own is sued in a class action suit in Oregon. The suit alleges that ABC "rent-to-own" deals are not leases but installment sales under 1–201(37), and that properly analyzed these sales are at a usurious rate of interest and therefore unenforceable under the law of Oregon. Again, are such transactions sales or leases under 1–201(37)? Assume that a search for further data reveals that less than 30 percent of the people who commence "rent-to-own" arrangements complete them by purchase. Approximately 70% return the goods and stop paying somewhere along the way. But almost all renters who reach the 16th month go on to exercise the option to purchase. Be sure to consider whether the option is a sham—not really an option price at all. Also consider whether if the option price is a genuine option price, it is still for nominal consideration under 1–201(37).

SECTION 3. FORMATION AND CONSTRUCTION OF LEASE CONTRACT; ENFORCEABILITY AND FREEDOM OF CONTRACT

Article 2A includes a statute of frauds requirement (2A–201) and various provisions from 2A–202 through 2A–220 on formation and construction of the lease contract, warranties of the lessor, risk of loss, and casualty to identified goods. All these provisions have familiar counterparts in Article Two on sales.

Section 2A–301 is modeled on section 9–201 of Article Nine, and provides:

> Except as otherwise provided in this Article, a lease contract is effective and enforceable according to its terms between the parties, against purchasers of the goods and against creditors of the parties.

Moreover, section 2A–103(4) provides that "In addition, Article 1 contains general definitions and principles of construction and interpretation applicable throughout this Article." Section 1–102(3), among other things, states that: "The effect of provisions of this Act may be varied by agreement, except as otherwise provided in this Act. * * * "

As in Article 2, in Article 2A freedom of contract and enforceability of the agreement of the parties, is the rule rather than the exception. Some provisions elaborate on this freedom in some detail. See, e.g., 2A–214 on exclusion or modification of warranties by the lessor, 2A–503 on contract modification of Article 2A remedies, and 2A–504 on liquidation of damages.

But there are also major exceptions to freedom of contract, and thus to enforceability of the agreement of the parties. Some of these are familiar. Thus Article 2A–108 is a counterpart to 2–302, on unconscionability. In addition, Article 2A includes various provisions specifically protecting a consumer party to a "consumer lease" which is defined in 2A–103(1)(e) as follows:

> (e) "Consumer lease" means a lease that a lessor regularly engaged in the business of leasing or selling makes to a lessee who is an

individual and who takes under the lease primarily for a personal, family, or household purpose [, if the total payments to be made under the lease contract, excluding payments for options to renew or buy, do not exceed $______].

Among the special provisions that in effect or in terms protect consumers and thus restrict freedom of contract, see 2A–214 on exclusion and modification of warranties, 2A–109 on option to accelerate payments, 2A–106 on choice of law and forum, and 2A–407 (on finance leases, treated in section eight below). Moreover, 2A–104(1)(d) and (2) make a consumer lease subject to and subordinate to any rule of law found in a consumer protection statute.

Section 2A–303 is a complex provision that also generally preserves freedom of contract, but with exceptions. Thus, in general, the parties may effectively agree to prohibit various transfers at least by making them events of default under the lease which trigger the remedies in 2A–501(2). Thus under 2A–303(2) the lease can in this way effectively prohibit the "sale, sublease, creation or enforcement of a security interest, or attachment, levy or judicial process, of an interest of a party under the lease contract or of the lessor's residual interest in the goods." Even if the transfer is not made an event of default but is only "prohibited", or the transfer "materially impairs the prospect of return performance * * * by the other party" (or the like), the transferor generally becomes liable in damages and the court may even cancel the lease or enjoin the transfer.

Exceptions to this general principle of freedom of contract are set forth in subsections (3) and (4) of 2A–303. For example, subsection (3) states that a provision prohibiting the "creation or enforcement of a security interest in an interest of a party under the lease contract or in the lessor's residual interest in the goods," or a provision that "makes such a transfer an event of default, is not enforceable unless, and then only to the extent that, there is an actual transfer by the lessee of the lessee's right to possession or use of the goods in violation of the provision or an actual delegation of a material performance of either party to the lease contract in violation of the provision." Section 2A–303(1) makes it clear that this exception applies to prohibitions of (or events of default with respect to) the transfer of the lessor's leasehold interest, i.e., chattel paper, and thus validates those transfers except insofar as the "unless" clause applies.

Subsection 2A–303(4) sets forth a further exception to the principle of free contract. It renders unenforceable certain provisions prohibiting transfer of a right to damages for default or of a right to payment arising out of the transferor's due performance of the transferor's entire obligation.

Freedom of contract generally prevails with respect to remedies. The parties may even provide for a power to cancel the lease for non-material breach. See 2A–503(1). But again, there are exceptions. See, e.g., 2A–503(2), and (3) and 2A–504 (on liquidated damages clauses).

SECTION 4. PRIORITY CONFLICTS BETWEEN LESSOR (AND LESSOR'S SECURED CREDITOR) AND PARTIES CLAIMING THROUGH THE LESSEE

Numerous priority conflicts over who has rights to the goods or interests in the goods may arise between the lessor (and the lessor's secured creditors) on the one hand and parties claiming through the lessee on the other.

A lessor of goods ordinarily retains a valuable residual interest as well as creates a leasehold interest in the lessee, and the lessor acquires a right to rents in accord with the lease contract. In general, these and other of lessor's interests are protected against the lessee, against creditors of the lessee, and against buyers and sublessees of the lessee.

Section 2A–301 provides: that "Except as otherwise provided in this Article, a lease contract is effective and enforceable according to its terms between the parties, against purchasers of the goods and against creditors of the parties." Section 2A–305 adds that a "buyer or sublessee" generally takes "subject to the existing lease contract."

The general priority in interest of the lessor against creditors of the lessee, buyers from the lessee, and sublessees from the lessee is by operation of law and by contract, and thus does not require the lessor to file the lease contract or any financing statement or the like as under Article Nine. Comment 2 to 2A–301 identifies an exception. It says that "the priority of the interest of a lessor of fixtures with respect to the interests of certain third parties in such fixtures is subject to the provisions of the Article on Secured Transactions (Article 9). Section 2A–309." Furthermore, any lessor who is concerned about whether the transaction might be construed to create a security interest rather than merely a lease should file a protective financing statement as permitted under section 9–408 of Article Nine.

We will now consider the main types of priority conflicts under Article 2A, with special emphasis on any exceptions where the lessor loses to parties claiming through or under the lessee. First, there is the category of creditors of the lessee. An Article Nine secured creditor with a duly perfected interest in the lessee's leasehold interest takes subject to the lease and so loses to the lessor. And, of course, so do general creditors with or without liens. The basic rule is set forth in section 2A–307(1): "Except as otherwise provided in Section 2A–306, a creditor of a lessee takes subject to the lease contract." Section 1–201(12) defines "creditor" widely to include "a general creditor, a secured creditor, a lien creditor" etc. The exception provided for in section 2A–306 is a narrow and familiar one in favor of certain creditors who "furnish services or materials with respect to the goods" where those goods are in the possession of the creditor.

Second and third, a buyer from, and also any sublessee of the lessee generally take "subject to the existing lease contract" between lessor and lessee under section 2A–305. That is, under section 2A–305(1), the buyer and the sublessee only obtain, "to the extent of the interest transferred" by the lessee, "the leasehold interest in the goods that the lessee had." Thus, it follows that a buyer or a sublessee generally acquires only the rights of the lessee and no more. There are two exceptions. The first exception is set forth in 2A–305(1) and provides that a lessee with a leasehold interest that the lessor could void, as where the lessee paid the rent with a bad check, can nevertheless pass a good leasehold interest to a good faith buyer for value or a good faith sublessee for value, still subject to the existing lease, however. The second exception is set forth in 2A–305(2) which provides:

> (2) A buyer in the ordinary course of business or a sublessee in the ordinary course of business from a lessee who is a merchant dealing in goods of that kind to whom the goods were entrusted by the lessor

> obtains, to the extent of the interest transferred, all of the lessor's and lessee's rights to the goods, and takes free of the existing lease contract.

Observe that this second exception comes into play only where the lessor himself has put the goods in the hands of a lessee who is also in the business of leasing or selling such goods.

So far we have only posed conflicts between the lessor and subsequent parties. What if the conflict is between a party with an Article Nine security interest in the goods perfected before the lease contract became enforceable and parties subsequent to the lessee? Section 2A–307(2)(c) accords general priority to such a secured creditor. One exception arises where a subsequent creditor "furnishes services or materials" with respect to the goods in possession of that person, under 2A–306.

Where the competition is between a prior secured party of the lessor and the lessee, 2A–307(2)(b) accords priority even to an unperfected secured creditor of the lessor over the subsequent lessee who did not take in ordinary course, i.e., "did not give value and receive delivery of the goods without knowledge of the security interest." But under 2A–307(3), a "lessee in the ordinary course of business takes the leasehold interest free of a security interest in the goods created by the lessor even though the security interest is perfected (9–303) and the lessee knows of its existence."

SECTION 5. PRIORITY CONFLICTS BETWEEN LESSEE AND THIRD PARTIES

The general rule of priority as to clashes between the lessee and creditors of the lessor is that such creditors "take subject to the lease contract" and so lose to the lessee to the extent of the lessee's interest. See 2A–301 and 2A–307. However, there are several exceptions to this in 2A–307(2). One is that a "creditor [who] holds a lien" that attached to the goods before the lease contract became enforceable prevails over the lessee. As already noted, another exception is set forth in 2A–307(2)(c) to the effect that the lessee also loses to a creditor who "holds a security interest in the goods which was perfected (Section 9–303) before the lease contract became enforceable", unless the lessee falls in 2A–307(3) which provides:

> (3) A lessee in the ordinary course of business takes the leasehold interest free of a security interest in the goods created by the lessor even though the security interest is perfected (Section 9–303) and the lessee knows of its existence.

Moreover, the lessee loses under 2A–306 to certain creditors who furnish "services or materials with respect to goods subject to a lease contract" where those are in the possession of the creditor.

Section 2A–304(1) generally provides that where a lessor wrongfully leases the same goods to a subsequent lessee, the latter takes "subject to the existing lease contract." An exception for a rather special and unusual type of case is provided for in section 2A–304(2). Assume Ajax is in the business of leasing forklifts, and Ajax leases one to A for a 6 month term. A returns the forklift after one month to Ajax for repairs. Ajax wrongfully releases the same forklift to B for one year. A and B claim the forklift. B prevails under section 2A–304(2), which provides:

(2) A subsequent lessee in the ordinary course of business from a lessor who is a merchant dealing in goods of that kind to whom the goods were entrusted by the existing lessee before the interest of the subsequent lessee became enforceable against the lessor obtains, to the extent of the leasehold interest transferred, all of the lessor's and the existing lessee's rights to the goods, and takes free of the existing lease contract.

SECTION 6. LESSOR'S REMEDIES

The existence of a default is determined by 2A–501 and the lease contract. Many lease agreements include elaborate default clauses. Students who have studied the remedies of an aggrieved seller of goods against a defaulting buyer under Article Two on sales will find the basic outlines of the remedies of an aggrieved lessor against a defaulting lessee entirely familiar. Nearly all of the lessor's possible remedies under Article 2A have their parallel counterparts in the remedies of a seller under Article 2 (or, in some cases under Article 9).

Just as section 2–703 of Article Two provides a basic index to the various remedies of a seller of goods, 2A–523 likewise provides an index to the various remedies of a lessor of goods. The lessor remedies appear in sections 2A–524 through 2A–531. Comment 4 to 2A–523 says that the purpose of the remedy provisions is to put the lessor "in as good a position as if the lessee had fully performed the lease contract". Official Comments 5 through 18 present extended variations on a single detailed example illustrating all the basic remedial possibilities. The student should study this set of comments carefully.

On appropriate lessee default, the lessor may repossess the leased goods under 2A–523(1)(c) and 2A–525. (Compare, 2–703, 2–702(1) and 9–503). Under 2A–527, the aggrieved lessor may then release the goods and, among other things, recover from the defaulting lessee essentially "the present value" as of the date of "the commencement of the term of the new lease agreement" of the "total rent for the then remaining lease term of the original lease agreement minus the present value, as of the same date, of the rent under the new lease agreement applicable to that period of the new lease term which is comparable to the then remaining term of the original lease agreement", provided that the new re-lease agreement is "substantially similar" to the original lease agreement and provided that the new re-lease agreement is made "in good faith and in a commercially reasonable manner." (Note that the projected income stream from the original lease is discounted to present value separately from the income stream under the new lease agreement.) This "re-lease plus damages" remedy of the lessor is, of course, the Article 2A counterpart of the aggrieved seller's remedy under Section 2–706 of Article Two on sales which enables a seller to resell the goods and recover the difference between the contract price and the amount the seller received on resale.

Many re-lease agreements arranged by an aggrieved lessor will not commence to run until sometime after the lessee's default on the original lease agreement. UCC 2A–537(2) also gives the lessor the "accrued and unpaid rent" as of the date of the commencement of the term of the new lease agreement.

It is possible to have a substantially similar re-lease agreement which extends well beyond the date of termination of the original lease. However, the difference money damages allowed in such a case under 2A–527(2) are only for "that period of the new lease term which is comparable to the then remaining term of the original lease agreement."

Various facts may support a finding that a lessor's re-lease agreement is not substantially similar to the original lease agreement. For example, the original agreement may have included a valuable option to purchase but the new re-lease agreement not have included such an option. The original agreement may have included valuable warranties but the new re-lease agreement, not. The original agreement may have imposed a significant maintenance obligation on the lessor but the new not. Yet Comment 5 to 2A–527 includes this key sentence: "If the differences between the original lease and the new lease can be easily valued, it would be appropriate for a court to find that the new lease is substantially similar to the old lease, adjust the difference in the rent between the two leases to take account of the differences, and award damages under this section."

If the new lease agreement is not "substantially similar" to the old, or if the new lease agreement is not made in good faith and in a commercially reasonable manner, then, according to 2A–527(3) "the lessor may recover from the lessee as if the lessor had elected not to dispose of the goods and Section 2A–528 governs." Under this section, the lessor is relegated to the difference between the rental in the original agreement and market rent, if any. Thus, subsection (1) of 2A–528 allows the aggrieved lessor here "the present value" as of the date of the lessor's repossession of the goods "of the total rent for the then remaining lease term of the original lease agreement minus the present value as of the same date of the market rent at the place where the goods are located computed for the same lease term." Market rent is computed pursuant to 2A–507. This remedy is comparable to the aggrieved seller's 2–708(1) contract-market differential under Article Two on sale of goods. The aggrieved lessor also gets "the accrued and unpaid rent" as of the date the lessor repossesses the goods. See 2A–528(1).

Subsection (2) of 2A–528 parallels the seller's remedy under 2–708(2) of Article Two on the sale of goods and thus allows an expected net profit recovery whenever the contract-market differential under subsection (1) "is inadequate to put a lessor in as good a position as performance would have." For example, a lessor may simply lose volume from a lessee's breach even though there is no contract-market differential on a new transaction. Here, as under Article Two, the aggrieved party gets the lost profit attributable to the lost volume, upon proper proof. See the apt example in Comment 2 to 2A–529.

It will be recalled that under restricted circumstances, an aggrieved seller of goods under section 2–709 of Article Two is entitled to recover the price. Is an aggrieved lessor ever entitled to recover the present value of expected rentals from a defaulting lessee under Article 2A? Section 2A–529 grants that right under circumstances far more limited than under Article Two. First, the lessor so recovers for goods "accepted by the lessee and not repossessed by or tendered to the lessor." See section 2A–529(1)(a). Second, the lessor so recovers for "conforming goods lost or damaged within a commercially reasonable time after risk of loss passes to the lessee (Section 2A–219)." See section 2A–529(1)(a). Third, the lessee so recovers "for goods identified to the lease contract if the lessor is unable after reasonable effort to dispose of them at a reasonable price or the circumstances reasonably indicate that effort will be unavailing." See section 2A–529(1)(b). It is under the first of the above that the lessor's right to recover the rent is far more limited than the parallel right of a seller of goods under 2–709 who is entitled to the price simply for "goods accepted." If the goods are in the possession of or available to the lessor, and if they have some reasonable lease potential, the lessor must exploit that potential and thus mitigate the lessor's losses. Thus, Article 2A in effect rejects a flat rule parallel to that of Article 2 allowing recovery of the price of accepted goods. Article 2A requires the lessor to take back accepted goods (if tendered) and pursue other remedies. Comment 1 to Section 2A–529 explains the rationale for this in terms of basic differences between a sale and a lease. A lessor already has a residual interest and it is no imposition on the lessor to require that the goods be taken back on lessee's tender to the lessor for redisposition. Indeed, precisely because the lessee has only a partial interest, redisposition by the lessee is not so viable an option anyway.

Throughout this discussion, we have said nothing about what happens remedially when a lessee defaults and the lessor simply retakes the goods and resells them rather than releases them. Here 2A–527(3) says that 2A–528 governs in such a case. The general measure under 2A–528(1) is "the present value * * * of the total rent for the then remaining lease term of the original lease agreement minus the present value as of the same date of the market rent at the place where the goods are located computed for the same lease term. * * *"

Problem 23–2

Assume that Lessor leases a truck to Lessee for 5 years, with an option to buy for $1.00 at the end of that period. The agreed rent is $1,000 a month. After one year has elapsed and $12,000 in rent is paid, Lessee repudiates. At this time, the projected market rent for the remaining four years of the lease is $900 a month. However, Lessor is able to sell the truck a few days after the repudiation for $60,000. Lessee argues that Lessor is entitled to recover nothing under 2A–528(1), for Lessor has sustained no damages. Lessee also cites 1–106. What result?

The foregoing discussion of the lessor's remedies only treats the main contingencies and the basic remedies. It also assumes that the Article 2A remedies govern. They may not. The parties may insert special clauses in their agreement that will validly control remedies. Section 2A–523(1)(f) so provides. See also 2A–503 and 2A–504. Section 2A–504(1) says that a liquidated damage clause is valid if liquidation is "at an amount or by a formula that is reasonable in light of the then anticipated harm caused by the default or other act or omission." Many leases include such clauses. Subsection (2) of 2A–504 provides that if a clause fails if its essential purpose, "remedy may be had as provided in this Article."

The case below was decided prior to the promulgation of Article 2A. Consider how the case would be decided under the relevant lessor remedy provisions of Article 2A.

HONEYWELL, INC. v. LITHONIA LIGHTING, INC.

United States District Court, Northern District of Georgia, 1970.
317 F.Supp. 406.

[Plaintiff Honeywell leased computer equipment to defendant Lithonia, prior to January 1966. Disputes arose over performance and lessee Lithonia terminated. Lessor Honeywell sued Lithonia for breach of the lease contract and Lithonia counterclaimed for alleged breach by Honeywell. After trial, the court found that Honeywell had performed its contract and therefore that Lithonia was in breach of the lease contract for terminating it. The portion of the opinion relating to damages appears below.]

Damages

With respect to damages, Lithonia concedes that "The measure of recovery by Honeywell as lessor would be the equivalent of the specified rentals for the remainder of the lease term, less the expense of performance by Honeywell during the remainder of the term as respects the hardware leased and other Honeywell responsibilities under the contract." (Lithonia's Post–Trial Brief, p. 81.)

Lithonia contends further, however, that any net damage to Honeywell—as computed above—must be reduced by the amount of rentals that might have been obtained from a leasing by Honeywell to someone else. Lithonia recognizes that the burden of showing potential reduction in rentals by such a releasing is upon Lithonia but apparently contends that it has done so since Honeywell disassembled the equipment after its return instead of keeping it intact for sale or lease. If Lithonia had shown that Honeywell had more customers than it could supply from inventory this contention would have merit. However, the evidence shows that Honeywell had more equipment than customers. Furthermore, Lithonia's own witness (who unhesitatingly gave a figure as to what the equipment would have sold for) testified to the effect that there was little or no market for used equipment of this kind.

Lithonia also makes much of the fact that a few components from the Lithonia equipment have been used in equipment supplied to other customers, but there was no evidence to show that Honeywell would not have had an adequate supply of those parts if the Lithonia equipment had not been returned.

Honeywell contends, and the court agrees, it should recover from Lithonia the net profit which Honeywell would have realized on the remainder of the contract, computed by deducting from the gross rental due for the balance of the contract period both the direct costs [1] (maintenance, deprecia-

1. Under "Direct Costs" Honeywell includes:

(1) Maintenance costs of $40,100, computed by figuring the ratio of M200 maintenance expense to H200 revenue income [Lithonia says historical maintenance cost of the Lithonia equipment itself should be used here, but since these costs vary with

tion, amortization, taxes and insurance) and the indirect costs [2] (marketing support and operating expenses) which Honeywell would have incurred in performing its part of the agreement if no breach had occurred.

Stated in equation form this comes out in dollar amounts as follows: Gross rental due, $315,750—Direct costs, $121,435—Indirect costs $44,393—Profit (damages), $159,922.

Counsel for the plaintiff may present a judgment in accordance herewith.

It is so ordered. [footnotes renumbered]

Note: "Present Value" Under Article 2A

Most of the key damages formulae of Article 2A both for aggrieved lessors and for aggrieved lessees require that projected streams of rental payments be discounted to "present value." See, e.g., 2A–528 on lessor's "contract-market" damages, and 2A–519 on lessee's "market-contract" damages.

The concept of present value is defined in 2A–103(1)(u) as follows:

> "(u) "Present value" means the amount as of a date certain of one or more sums payable in the future, discounted to the date certain. The discount is determined by the interest rate specified by the parties if the rate was not manifestly unreasonable at the time the transaction was entered into; otherwise, the discount is determined by a commercially reasonable rate that takes into account the facts and circumstances of each case at the time the transaction was entered into.

Consider this example: Assume a ten year lease with payments of $1,000. per month. Assume that the lessee repudiates the lease after the first month and the lessor immediately enters a re-lease arrangement at $900. per month Assume the lease itself provides a discount rate of three percent per year. Here, the present value of each stream of payments would be as follows: (1) 1000 × 119 × 3% discount, for the projected payments under the original lease agreement, and (2) 900 × 119 × 3% discount, for the projected payments under the release contract. Under 2A–528(1), the lessor's damages would be the difference between these two "present value" figures.

the age of the equipment, Honeywell's method appears to be more accurate].

(2) Depreciation of the production cost of the Lithonia configuration for remaining life of contract, amounting to $60,625.

(3) Amortization of research and development costs over the remaining life of contract, amounting to $13,132.

(4) Taxes and insurance in the amount of $7,578, computed as the ratio of property taxes and insurance expenses to revenue [Annese, T. p. 521].

2. Under "Indirect Costs" Honeywell includes:

(1) Marketing support costs in the amount of $2,818. This figure represents the cost of manpower support to be furnished during the remainder of the contract life and is based on figures from their marketing personnel section showing that such support requires eight manpower months during the first year after installation of the equipment, 1½ man months the second year, and one-half man months per year after that.

(2) Operating expenses of $31,575, representing the ratio of total operating expenses (excluding marketing expenses, which are incurred prior to, and in early days of, the contract and are written off then) to total revenue of computer division. [Lithonia says no deduction has been made for software expenses saved, but this is included in operating expenses. Annese, T. 572.]

SECTION 7. LESSEE'S REMEDIES

The existence of a default is determined by 2A–501 and by the contract, and many agreements have elaborate default clauses. Again, students who have already studied the remedies of an aggrieved buyer against a defaulting seller under Article Two on sales will find the broad outlines of the lessee's remedies against the lessor highly familiar. Nearly all of the lessee's remedies under Article 2A have their parallel counterparts in the remedies of a buyer under Article Two.

Just as section 2–711 of Article Two provides a basic index to the various remedies of a buyer of goods, so too, section 2A–508 provides a basic index to the lessee's remedies against the lessor. These remedies are set forth in sections 2A–509 through 2A–522. Again, the basic purpose of the Code's lessee remedies is to put the lessee in the position that performance would have. The main contingencies and the main remedies are as follows.

The lessee is accorded the goods-oriented remedies of rejection and revocation of acceptance under sections 2A–509 and 2A–517. Indeed, the lessee may revoke for defects that do not go to the accepted goods yet impair their value, as in the case of the lessor's failure to maintain leased equipment as agreed.

On appropriate lessor default under 2A–508, as where the lessor refuses to deliver the goods, or delivers nonconforming goods, or wrongfully repudiates or the like, the lessee will often seek a substitute, i.e., "cover" lease, and, then under 2A–518(2), recover from the defaulting lessor essentially the present value, as of the date of the commencement of the term of the new lease agreement, of the rent under the new lease agreement applicable to that period of the new lease term which is comparable to the then remaining term of the original lease agreement minus the present value as of the same date of the total rent for the then remaining lease term of the original lease agreement", provided that the new lease agreement is "substantially similar to the original lease agreement and the new lease agreement is made in good faith and in a commercially reasonable manner." (The projected income stream from the original lease is discounted to present value separately from the income stream under the cover lease.) This lessee remedy is, of course, the Article 2A counterpart of the aggrieved buyer's "cover" remedy under section 2–712 of Article Two which enables a buyer to buy substitute goods and charge the seller any increase in their cost over the contract price. Most cover leases will not start to run until sometime after the lessor's default on the original lease agreement. Section 2A–518 also gives the lessee any "incidental or consequential damages" sustained as a result of the lessor's nonperformance in this "gap" period.

It is possible to have a substantially similar cover lease which extends beyond the date of termination of the original lease. However, as the above formula indicates, the cover damages are allowed under 2A–518(2) only for "that period of the new lease term which is comparable to the then remaining term of the original lease agreement."

Again, various facts may indicate that a lessee's cover lease is not substantially similar to the original lease agreement with the defaulting lessor. For example, the goods acquired under the alleged cover lease might be of a significantly higher quality or fulfill other functions and so cost rather more. Or the cover lease might include a valuable option to purchase not included in the original lease. Or the cover lease might include valuable warranties. However, Official Comment 5 to section 2A–518 says: "If the differences between the original lease and the new lease can be easily valued, it would be appropriate for a court to adjust the difference in rental to take account of the difference between the two leases, find that the new lease is substantially similar to the old lease, and award cover damages under this section".

If the cover lease is not substantially similar to the original lease or the cover lease is not made in good faith and in a commercially reasonable manner, then 2A–518(3) provides that "the lessee may recover from the lessor * * * [under] Section 2A–519 * * * " Under Section 2A–519(1), which also applies if the lessee simply elects not to cover, the aggrieved lessee's measure of damages for non-delivery or repudiation by the lessor or for rejection or revocation of acceptance by the lessee is the excess, if any, of the market rent over the rental contracted for in the broken lease. More precisely, the lessee gets "the present value, as of the date of the default, of the then market rent minus the present value as of the same date of the original rent, computed for the remaining lease term of the original lease agreement". The aggrieved lessee also gets any "incidental and consequential damages" under 2A–519(1) and 2A–520. The student familiar with Article Two will immediately perceive that the foregoing remedy is comparable to the aggrieved buyer's market-contract differential under sections 2–713 and 2–714 of Article Two.

In some cases, the aggrieved lessee will accept goods despite lessor default, give the lessor due notice of default under 2A–516(3), and seek damages. Where the default is for other than breach of warranty, the lessee's measure of recovery is spelled out in 2A–519(3) as "the loss resulting in the ordinary course of events from the lessor's default as determined in any manner that is reasonable together with incidental and consequential damages, less expenses saved in consequence of the lessor's default."

Where the lessee seeks damages for breach of warranty, the measure is spelled out in 2A–519(4) as "the present value at the time and place of acceptance of the difference between the value of the use of the goods accepted and the value if they had been as warranted for the lease term, unless special circumstances show proximate damages of a different amount, together with incidental and consequential damages, less expenses saved in consequence of the lessor's default or breach of warranty."

Section 2A–521(1) gives the lessee the right to specific performance "if the goods are unique or in other proper circumstances." Subsection 2A–521(3) adds further similar rights where the lessee is unable to cover.

In the foregoing discussion, we have said nothing about what happens remedially when a lessor defaults and the aggrieved lessor then simply buys "cover" goods outright rather than seeks a cover lease. Section 2A–518(3) says that 2A–519 governs in such a case. This general measure under 2A–519(1) is "the present value, as of the date of default, of the then market rent minus the present value as of the same date of the original rent, computed for the remaining lease term of the original lease agreement. * * * "

SECTION 8. FINANCE LEASES UNDER ARTICLE 2A

So far in this chapter we have been concerned largely with the garden-variety lease of goods. We now turn to a special kind of transaction under Article 2A, namely the "finance lease." This kind of lease is written almost entirely by financing institutions, and although it is a true lease and not a security agreement, it does not normally carry with it certain of the responsibilities that the typical lessor bears under Article 2A such as liability for breach of warranty.

The provisions of Article 2A generally apply to finance leases except as they indicate otherwise or except as they make special exceptions or other provision for such leases. There are twelve sections that should be specially consulted (apart from the definitional provisions): 2A–209, 2A–211(2), 2A–212(1), 2A–213, 2A–219(1), 2A–221, 2A–405(c), 2A–406(1)(b), 2A–407, 2A–516(2) and 2A–517(1)(a).

Section 2A–103(1)(g) includes a complex definition of "finance lease" and reads as follows:

(g) "Finance lease" means a lease with respect to which:

(i) the lessor does not select, manufacture, or supply the goods;

(ii) the lessor acquires the goods or the right to possession and use of the goods in connection with the lease; and

(iii) one of the following occurs:

(A) the lessee receives a copy of the contract by which the lessor acquired the goods or the right to possession and use of the goods before signing the lease contract;

(B) the lessee's approval of the contract by which the lessor acquired the goods or the right to possession and use of the goods is a condition to effectiveness of the lease contract;

(C) the lessee, before signing the lease contract, receives an accurate and complete statement designating the promises and warranties, and any disclaimers of warranties, limitations or modifications of remedies, or liquidated damages, including those of a third party, such as the manufacturer of the goods, provided to the lessor by the person supplying the goods in connection with or as part of the contract by which the lessor acquired the goods or the right to possession and use of the goods; or

(D) if the lease is not a consumer lease, the lessor, before the lessee signs the lease contract, informs the lessee in writing (a) of the identity of the person supplying the goods to the lessor, unless the lessee has selected that person and directed the lessor to acquire the goods or the right to possession and use of the goods from that person, (b) that the lessee is entitled under this Article to the promises and warranties, including those of any third party, provided to the lessor by the person supplying the goods in connection with or as part of the contract by which the lessor acquired the goods or the right to possession and use of the goods, and (c) that the lessee may communicate with the person supplying the goods to the lessor and receive an accurate and complete statement of those promises and warranties, including any disclaimers and limitations of them or of remedies.

The foregoing definition does not fully reveal what is distinctive about a finance lease, however. Consider this example. Airline, as prospective lessee, selects a Boeing 747 and negotiates over its particular configuration with Boeing, the supplier. But instead of purchasing the 747 outright, the airline then arranges for Bank to purchase it from Boeing and lease it to Airline. The agreement between Bank as lessor and Airline as lessee is a true lease under Article 2A and not a secured transaction under Article 9. Yet Bank is buying the plane from Boeing so to lease it to Airline, and is thus providing the financial backing for lessee Airline so that Airline can have the plane made and can put it into use. And Bank is not like an ordinary buyer. Bank is not providing the specifications for the plane, is not selecting the type of seating, interior, engines, or anything else concerning the aircraft. Rather, Airline is doing these things. Moreover, in substance, most promises and warranties made by Boeing during negotiations are directed not to Bank but to Airline as prospective lessee. This is so even though "in law" the promises and warranties run immediately to the buyer, lessor.

Now, return to the Code definition of a finance lease set forth above. First, note that 2A–103(1)(g)(i) says "the lessor does not select, manufacture, or supply the goods." In our example, the lessor Bank did not do these things. Rather, the prospective lessee, Airline, did. Second, note that subsection 2A–103(1)(g)(ii) says that Airline as "lessor acquires the goods or the right to possession and use of the goods in connection with the lease", a provision which requires interconnectedness between the sale and the lease, and thus is to "insure the lessee's reliance on the supplier, and not on the lessor." Third, note that subsection 2A–103(1)(g)(iii) requires one of four procedures. Each one of these is designed to assure that the lessee—Airline—will be informed of the promises, warranties, disclaimers of warranties, limitation or modifications of remedies, or liquidated damages agreed to by the supplier, Boeing, with the lessor, Bank, under which lessee, Airline, may claim not against the lessor Bank, but against the *supplier*, Boeing, if something goes wrong with the goods.

On what basis may the lessee Airline claim against the supplier for breach of promise or breach of warranty? There are three possibilities. First, the agreement between the supplier (Boeing) and the lessor (Bank) may include an express provision to the effect that the promises and warranties in that agreement run to the benefit of the lessee (Airline). This is called a "consensual" finance lease, and it makes the finance lessee a third party beneficiary by contract. Second, the lessee (Airline) may claim under Article 2A as a statutory finance lessee. See section 2A–209 which makes the lessee a statutory third party beneficiary of the supply contract between the manufacturer (or other supplier) and the lessor, to the extent that the supply contract includes express or implied warranties or other promises to the lessor (Bank). Third, the finance lessee (Airline) may have also entered into some kind of contract directly with the supplier (Boeing) on the basis of which the lessee might claim. See 2A–209(4).

The Official Comments to 2A–209 make it clear that the finance lessee is a third party beneficiary of the supply contract between the manufacturer (or other supplier) and the lessor, to the extent that the supply contract includes express and implied warranties or other promises to the lessor. Article Two on the sale of goods, not Article 2A, generally defines the nature of the warranty rights in the contract between the supplier and the lessor (who are, as between themselves, buyer and seller). Official Comment 1 to 2–209 makes it clear that this third party beneficiary feature of the contract between supplier and lessor must in effect extend warranties that the supplier made to the lessor also to the lessee. Of course, the supplier can disclaim and modify the relevant warranties and promises, but as we have seen, above, 2A–103(1)(g)(iii) requires that the lessee know what these terms are to be or have access to them, and the lessee is hardly without bargaining power here. Indeed, the lessee is normally the "prime mover", as in our airplane lease example.

The emphasis in the preceding analysis has been on what rights the finance lessee might have against the supplier either as a consensual third party beneficiary or as a statutory third party beneficiary under Section 2A–209 in the event something goes wrong with the goods. Does the lessee have no rights against the lessor? The answer is very few, and this is a major difference between the rights of a finance lessee and the rights of an ordinary lessee. The finance lessor is a financing institution and deals in paper, not in goods, and thus it makes sense that the finance lessor makes no implied warranties of quality or against infringement of patent, copyright or the like. See Comment 1 to 2A–209. See also 2A–211(2), 2A–212, 2A–213. Of course, the finance lessor is bound by any express warranties it happens to make. It also warrants under 2A–211(1) against interference with the lessee's enjoyment of its leasehold interest. But the finance lessor commonly disclaims all warranties to the lessee.

Suppose the goods are defective—the airplane has wing faults. Apart from suing as a third party beneficiary of promises and warranties under 2A–209 and Article Two, can the lessee Airline withhold payment of rent to lessor Bank? Normally, a lessee facing a defaulting lessor can withhold rent payments as a self-help remedy. But as to business finance leases, section 2A–407(1) and (2) provide:

> (1) In the case of a finance lease that is not a consumer lease the lessee's promises under the lease contract become irrevocable and independent upon the lessee's acceptance of the goods.
>
> (2) A promise that has become irrevocable and independent under subsection (1):
>
> (a) is effective and enforceable between the parties, and by or against third parties including assignees of the parties; and
>
> (b) is not subject to cancellation, termination, modification, repudiation, excuse, or substitution without the consent of the party to whom the promise runs.

One effect of this provision is generally to require that the lessee pay the finance lessor the agreed rent regardless of any deficiencies in the goods or any breach of promises or warranties made to lessee as a third party beneficiary of the contract between the supplier and the lessor. Section 2A–407(1) and (2), above, is called a statutory "hell or high water" clause. Under it, the lessee must pay the lessor "come hell or high water." After all, the lessor deals in paper, not goods, and the lessee and lessor have, as between themselves, entered into a financing transaction in which the lessor is, in effect, financing the lessee's access to the goods, not supplying them as such. Thus, in our example, if the Boeing 747 explodes into small pieces in flight and is completely uninsured, lessee Airline's obligation to pay rent to the lessor Bank continues. Indeed, a contractual "hell or high water" clause that is broader than the 2A–407 provision may even be enforceable.

Of course, that the lessee becomes a third party beneficiary of the supplier's promises and warranties in the supplier's agreement with the lessor under section 2A–209, can itself be viewed as a kind of quid pro quo to the lessee for generally forfeiting warranty and related claims against the lessor. Section 2A–209 allows the lessee to recover against the supplier directly, and as we have seen, the liability of the supplier to the lessor cannot be reduced by agreement merely to cut out the lessee, though it can be modified by agreement as provided in Article 2A.

In sum, there are at least two agreements: one between the supplier and the finance lessor—the supply contract, and one between the finance lessor and the lessee—the finance lease. The finance lessee has few rights against the finance lessor but is a third party beneficiary of the supply contract and can sue the supplier directly. But the finance lessee must pay rent to the finance lessor, come hell or high water, unless otherwise agreed.

We have said little of the rights of the supplier against the lessor where the lessor is a finance lessor. The supplier-finance lessor relation is largely a buyer-seller relation governed by Article Two.

The two cases below were decided prior to the promulgation of Article 2A. The first involves an attempt to enforce a version of a hell or high water clause against a finance lessee. The second involves the rights of the supplier against the finance lessor. Among other things, consider whether these cases would come out differently under Article 2A.

ANGELLE v. ENERGY BUILDERS CO., INC.

Court of Appeal of Louisiana, First Circuit, 1986.
496 So.2d 509.

SHORTESS, JUDGE.

This suit arose from a dispute over a lease agreement. Late in 1981, Lennie Angelle (plaintiff), a contractor, became interested in obtaining a Low Ground Pressure (LGP) tractor for clearing swamp land. An LGP tractor is designed to do work in unstable and muddy terrain. The machine plaintiff wanted had to be equipped with a KG blade, which is used for shearing and cutting purposes. He had an opportunity to do some swamp work for Supreme Contractors, but before he could realistically bid on the work, he needed equipment that he did not have, namely, an LGP tractor with a KG blade. He discovered that Energy Builders Company, Inc., (EBCO) had such a tractor which it wanted to sell. Plaintiff and an EBCO official flew to North Carolina and examined the machine. Plaintiff concluded that if it were equipped with a KG blade it would suit his needs.

Plaintiff had on other occasions rented heavy equipment from General Leasing Services, Inc. (GLS). He contacted GLS which agreed to purchase the equipment from EBCO and lease it to plaintiff. On November 10, 1981, GLS purchased the LGP tractor, a winch, an original angle blade, and KG blade from EBCO for $65,000.00. On November 16, 1981, Angelle Backhoe Rentals and GLS executed a contract by which plaintiff leased the equipment from GLS for a three-year term at $2,988.00 per month. The lease absolved GLS of any warranty obligations and of any liability for EBCO's failure to deliver the described merchandise.[1]

GLS then assigned its rights under the lease to one of its creditors, Walter E. Heller & Company Southeast, Inc. (Heller); that assignment, dated November 24, 1981, contains the following germane language:

> BORROWER [GLS] does hereby sell, assign, transfer and set over unto HELLER all of its right, title and interest in and to the above described lease contract, together with all the rents, issues and profits due and to become due under said lease contract, subject to the following:
>
> SO LONG as the BORROWER is not in default under the terms of the LOAN AGREEMENT, NOTE and MORTGAGE referred to above, or under any other notes or mortgages held by HELLER, BORROWER shall continue to collect the rents and profits from the lease contract for the benefit of HELLER and as provided in the LOAN AGREEMENT.

EBCO delivered the equipment to plaintiff in late January, 1982. The KG blade was not included in this initial shipment, but, according to his testimony, plaintiff allowed the haulers to leave the LGP tractor with him because they promised that the blade was on another truck and would arrive later. Eventually, a KG blade was sent to plaintiff, but he refused to accept it because it did not fit the LGP tractor. Plaintiff notified GLS that he had not received the blade he needed, and it in turn contacted EBCO, which began attempts to locate an appropriate blade. Although plaintiff never took delivery of a satisfactory KG blade, he made sporadic payments to GLS totaling, he contends, $21,253.00.

1. The following are portions of the contract pertinent here:

> 2. SELECTION OF EQUIPMENT. Lessee has requested equipment of the type and quantity specified above and has selected the supplier named on the reverse side. Lessor agrees to order the equipment from the supplier, but shall not be liable for specific performance of this lease or for damages if for any reason the supplier delays or fails to fill the order. Lessee shall accept such equipment if delivered in good repair, and authorizes Lessor to add to this lease the serial number of each item of equipment so delivered. Any delay in such delivery shall not affect the validity of this lease.
>
> * * *
>
> 4. WARRANTIES. Lessor will request the supplier to authorize Lessee to enforce in its own name all warranties, agreements or representations, if any, which may be made by the supplier to Lessee or Lessor, but Lessor itself makes no express or implied warranties as to any matter whatsoever, including, without limitation, the condition of equipment, its merchantability or its fitness for any particular purpose. No defect or unfitness of the equipment shall relieve Lessee of the obligation to pay rent or of any other obligation under this lease.
>
> * * *
>
> 18. INDEMNITY. Lessee shall indemnify Lessor against, and hold Lessor harmless from, any and all claims, actions, expenses, damages and liabilities, including attorney's fees, arising in connection with the equipment, including, without limitation, its manufacture, selection, purchase, delivery, possession, use, operation or return and the recovery of claims under insurance policies thereon, even though caused, occasioned or attributed to by the negligence, either sole or concurrent, of Lessor, its agents, servants, and employees.

In February, 1983, plaintiff filed suit for damages against GLS, EBCO, and the EBCO official, alleging that the failure to deliver the correct KG blade was a breach of contract. Apparently only GLS was served, and by the summer of 1982 it was involved in reorganization under the jurisdiction of the bankruptcy court. A plan submitted by GLS allowed Heller to enforce the lease and assignment agreements. Heller intervened in plaintiff's suit, praying for cancellation of the lease contract and damages for nonpayment. Plaintiff then amended his petition to make Heller a defendant and asked that the $21,253.00 in payments be refunded. Thus, plaintiff and Heller were the only parties before the trial court.

The trial court rendered judgment denying both Heller's claims in intervention and plaintiff's claims against Heller. It found that the warranty waiver did not relieve GLS of its obligation to deliver the equipment plaintiff had ordered and that there had never been a binding contract of lease between plaintiff and GLS because the appropriate KG blade was never delivered. Plaintiff's demand against Heller for the payments made to GLS was also dismissed. Both parties have appealed.

The trial court reasoned that no contract of lease was perfected between GLS and plaintiff because the KG blade, an integral and essential part of the thing leased, was never delivered. "*Lease* or *hire* is a synallagmatic contract, to which consent alone is sufficient." LSA–C.C. art. 2669. "[T]hree things are necessary to the perfection of a lease: the thing, the price, and the consent." S. Litvinoff, Smith's Materials on the Louisiana Law of Sales and Leases 468 (1978); LSA–C.C. art. 2670. Delivery of the thing is not essential to the perfection of the contract, although delivery is among the obligations of the lessor. LSA–C.C. art. 2692. The November 16, 1981, agreement between plaintiff and GLS contained all the elements required, and we find that it was a perfected contract of lease. Our remaining inquiry must determine the rights of the parties and their assigns under this lease.

To determine Heller's right to receive rental payments under the lease we must determine GLS's rights thereunder. The crux of Heller's position is that GLS validly waived all lessor warranties; if GLS made no warranties, the fact that plaintiff never received the KG blade does not relieve plaintiff of his obligation as lessee to make rental payments. Heller cites *Louisiana National Leasing Corporation v. ADF Service, Inc.*, 377 So.2d 92 (La.1979), as support for its argument. In that case, the lessor of a defective photocopying machine sued its lessee for nonpayment of rent. The lease provided that lessor made no warranties and that no defect in the equipment would relieve lessee of the obligation to pay rent. The Supreme Court, at p. 95, ruled that the implied warranty of fitness could be renounced and that "since it is not expressly or impliedly prohibited by law to waive implied warranties by disclaiming liability for vices and defects in the leased object while retaining the right to collect rentals for the entire term of the lease, it is not against public policy."

In *Louisiana National Leasing* the lessee had taken possession of the photocopying machine and used it without trouble for three months before it began to malfunction. In the instant case, plaintiff never received a very essential part of the equipment that the lessor agreed to provide. Without the KG blade, plaintiff had no need for this type of tractor. The trial court found that the KG blade was never delivered. We cannot say that this finding was clearly wrong. This failure of delivery meant that plaintiff never acquired peaceable possession of the thing leased. LSA–C.C. art. 2692. It is one thing to permit a lessee and lessor by convention to renounce the lessor's implied warranties against defects and unfitness; it is quite another to permit them to waive the lessor's obligation to deliver and thus avoid his duty to cause the lessee to be in peaceable possession.

* * *

To allow the parties to waive fundamental obligations, such as delivery of the thing leased and peaceable possession, would be to allow them to destroy "the character or effect of the contract." *Louisiana National Leasing,* 377 So.2d at 94. In a discussion of leases such as the one in question here, a doctrinal writer makes the following observations:

> It is also common for personal property leases to contain so-called "hell or high water" covenants under which the lessee unconditionally agrees to make lease payments to the lessor notwithstanding any foreseeable or unforeseeable circumstances. While such "hell or high water" covenants are generally enforceable in Louisiana, arguably they may not be enforced in situations in which a lessee lawfully withholds rental payments as a result of the lessor's failure to provide the lessee with peaceable possession of the leased equipment over the lease term. The right of peaceable possession guaranteed by Civil Code article 2692(3) as a matter of public policy may not be waived.

Willenzik, *Personal Property Leases in Louisiana,* 44 La.L.Rev. 755, 780 (1984), footnotes omitted.

* * *

We must now determine whether the failure of delivery relieves plaintiff of the obligation to make rental payments. Heller asks that we compare the plaintiff's nonpayment to nonpayment by a lessee whose lessor refuses to make necessary repairs. It is true that cases have held that a lessee may not withhold rental payments because of the lessor's failure to make repairs. *Commercial Equipment Distributors, Inc. v. Anderson,* 431 So.2d 29 (La.App. 1st Cir.1983). But the courts have also ruled that when a lessee is prevented from making repairs which the lessor should have made, the lessee will be absolved of making the lease payments. *Bowers Electronic Enterprises v. Tiffin Inn Pancake House of Baton Rouge, Inc.,* 444 So.2d 222 (La.App. 1st Cir.1983). Plaintiff attempted to obtain the KG blade he required, but his considerable efforts were unsuccessful. As the obligations to deliver and assure peaceable possession are not waivable and are deemed part of the contract, GLS breached the law between parties. Under those circumstances, the lessee is not required to make rental payments. *See Honeywell, Inc. v. Courtesy Discount House, Inc.,* 413 So.2d 222 (La.App. 4th Cir.1982).

* * *

Having determined that GLS had no right to lease payments, we hold that Heller, GLS's assignee, has no right to those payments.

Plaintiff contends that Heller is liable for the $21,253.00 in payments he made under the lease agreement. These payments were made by checks payable to GLS. Nothing in the record indicates that these payments went to Heller. The agreement by which GLS assigned its rights under the lease to Heller provided that Heller did "not assume any of the obligations of Borrower [GLS] under the lease contract." The trial court was correct in describing Heller as "an assignee of the lease for security purposes." As such, Heller is not liable to plaintiff for payments he made to GLS.

For the foregoing reasons, the judgment of the trial court denying the claims of Heller against plaintiff and of plaintiff against Heller is affirmed. Costs of this appeal are to be divided equally between the parties.

Affirmed.

MIDWEST PRECISION SERVICES v. PTM INDUSTRIES CORP.

United States Court of Appeals, First Circuit, 1989.
887 F.2d 1128.

LEVIN H. CAMPBELL, CHIEF JUDGE.

A federal district court jury found that Shawmut Bank of Boston, N.A. (Shawmut), the lessor in a tripartite leasing transaction, broke its contract with a supplier when Shawmut's lessee wrongfully rejected the supplier's goods. Shawmut appeals, arguing that its minimal role in the three-party transaction, as well as the express language of its contract with the supplier, absolves it of any liability. Midwest Precision Services, Inc. (Midwest), the supplier, also appeals, claiming that the district court erroneously instructed the jury against duplicating damages and requesting, among other things, that this court quadruple the damages awarded below against Shawmut. Midwest further contests the district court's dismissal of its claims under Mass.Gen.Laws Ann. ch. 93A. We affirm in part, reverse in part, and order a new trial on the issue of breach of contract damages only.

I.

In October of 1982, a salesman representing Midwest, an industrial machinery distributor based in Illinois, met with employees of PTM Industries Corporation (PTM), a machine shop business located in Westfield, Massachusetts. They discussed PTM's possible purchase of Midwest's crush and creep feed grinder (the machine), a computer-driven industrial grinder utilized for sophisticated metal grinding tasks. During these early discussions, Midwest tentatively offered to customize the machine to suit PTM's needs in exchange for $345,500.

PTM then turned to Shawmut for assistance. Shawmut and PTM discussed four financing options: (1) a short term loan; (2) a long term loan; (3) a fair market value lease; or (4) a dollar option lease. On November 8, 1982, PTM and Shawmut entered into a dollar option lease (the lease), in which Shawmut agreed to lease the machine to PTM for a period of 60 months, at the end of which PTM could buy the machine from Shawmut for one dollar.

On the next day Shawmut issued Midwest a purchase order for the machine. Shawmut's purchase order, the complete text of which is reproduced in the Appendix, included the following terms. First, the purchase order constituted the "complete and exclusive statement of the agreement" between Shawmut and Midwest. Second, Shawmut promised to pay Midwest $345,500 for the machine. Third, Midwest agreed to ship the machine directly to PTM. Fourth, Midwest expressly warranted the machine, providing both Shawmut and PTM with the right to enforce all applicable warranties. Finally, Shawmut indicated that it would have no liability and could cancel the purchase order unless within 90 days Midwest had delivered the machine and Shawmut had received from PTM a "signed acceptance certificate" acknowledging receipt of the machine in good condition and requesting payment of Midwest's invoice.

Midwest received and read Shawmut's purchase order, but it never received nor was it ever aware of the terms of the lease between Shawmut and PTM. After modifying the machine to meet PTM's requirements, Midwest shipped the machine to PTM. On January 25, 1983, the machine arrived at PTM's Westfield plant. Upon inspection, however, PTM immediately complained to Midwest that the machine was damaged and declared that it would not accept delivery. Midwest made repeated offers to cure any damage, irrespective of its nature or cause, but PTM steadfastly rejected Midwest's proposals.

During this time, Midwest kept Shawmut informed of the situation. On February 17, 1983, 101 days after Shawmut's issuance of the purchase order, Shawmut notified Midwest that it was cancelling their agreement.

On May 23, 1983, Midwest brought suit against PTM in the United States District for the Northern District of Illinois, alleging claims in contract and tort. PTM filed a motion to dismiss, or in the alternative, to transfer the case to Massachusetts, asserting that Shawmut, not PTM, was the "real party in interest" because Shawmut had issued the purchase order. On November 30, 1983, the case was transferred to the District of Massachusetts pursuant to 28 U.S.C. § 1404(a).

On February 22, 1984, Midwest amended its complaint to include Shawmut as a defendant. The amended complaint included the following claims: (1) breach of contract against PTM; (2) breach of contract against Shawmut; (3) tortious interference in Midwest's contractual relations with Shawmut against PTM; and (4) unfair and deceptive conduct under Mass.Gen.Laws Ann. ch. 93A against both defendants. PTM brought counterclaims against Midwest for (5) breach of contract and (6) misrepresentation.

At the end of the eight day jury trial, the district court dismissed Midwest's claims under 93A and instructed the jury on claims (1), (2), (3), (5) and (6). With regard to Midwest's breach of contract claim against Shawmut (claim two), the court told the jury that Shawmut's purchase order constituted a contract between Shawmut and Midwest, and that in that contract Shawmut had delegated to PTM its duty to accept the machine or permit cure. The court further told the jury that if it found that PTM acted unlawfully or unreasonably in rejecting the machine or refusing to permit cure, it could find that Shawmut breached its contract with Midwest.

On Midwest's breach of contract claim against PTM (claim one), and the latter's counterclaim (claim five), the court instructed the jury first to decide whether a separate contract existed between PTM and Midwest. If one existed, then the jury could find PTM liable for any unlawful or unreasonable rejection of the machine or, conversely, it could find Midwest liable for supplying defective goods and failing to make legally adequate offers to cure.

After also instructing the jury on Midwest's tortious interference claim against PTM (claim three), and PTM's counterclaim for misrepresentation against Midwest (claim six), the court turned to damages. The court cautioned the jury "to be sure not to duplicate any damages you feel should be awarded" to either party. The court then presented the jury with a special verdict form comprising fourteen questions.

The jury's responses were favorable to Midwest and adverse to Shawmut and PTM on every claim and counterclaim. On claim one, the jury found that Shawmut caused Midwest $52,339.50 in damages when it breached its purchase order contract. On claim two, it found that PTM caused Midwest $157,018.50 in damages (three times the amount awarded against Shawmut) when it breached its separate contract. The special verdict form further stated that each defendant's contract violation occurred on January 25, 1983, the day PTM rejected the machine. On claim three, the jury found that PTM caused Midwest $2,807.55 in damages when it tortiously interfered with Midwest's contractual relations with Shawmut.

The district court denied the parties' post-trial motions and entered judgment, from which both Midwest and Shawmut appeal. PTM, which is apparently insolvent, has not appealed. The appeals raise a number of issues, which we now address.

II.

The district court found that Shawmut was a "buyer" under Massachusetts law. *See* Mass.Gen.Laws Ann. ch. 106, § 2–103(1)(a) (defining "buyer" as "a person who buys or contracts to buy goods."). Shawmut maintains that its role in the three-party transaction was that of a mere financing agent, not a buyer, and that therefore the district court erred in entering judgment against Shawmut for breach of contract. We reject Shawmut's argument.

The tripartite structure of the present transaction is not uncommon. Commercial leasing arrangements often involve three parties: (1) the supplier of the goods (Midwest); (2) the lessee (PTM), who chooses the supplier and selects the goods; and (3) the lessor (Shawmut), who supplies the money necessary to purchase the equipment. *See* Boss, *Panacea or Nightmare? Leases in Article 2,* 64 B.U.L.Rev. 39, 57–58 (1984); Mooney, *True Lease or Lease "Intended as Security"—Treatment by the Courts,* in 1C P. Coogan, W. Hogan, D. Vaghts & J. McDonnel, *Secured Transactions Under the Uniform Commercial Code* § 29A.03. As in this case, the lessor is often a bank which performs a limited role in the transaction:

> The bank performs no procurement functions. The [lessee] chooses the property he wishes to lease, selects a vendor and negotiates with him the terms of the purchase. Assuming the bank finds the [lessee] an acceptable credit risk, it then purchases the property and leases it to the consumer. Delivery by the seller is made directly to the customer-lessee who makes the lease payments to the bank.

M & M Leasing Corp. v. Seattle First Nat'l Bank, 563 F.2d 1377, 1380–81 (9th Cir.1977), *cert. denied,* 436 U.S. 956, 98 S.Ct. 3069, 57 L.Ed.2d 1121 (1978).

Thus the standard tripartite transaction comprises two related exchanges. First, the bank purchases the equipment from the supplier. Second, the bank leases that equipment to the lessee, often through some form of "dollar option lease," in which the bank retains title to the equipment for the duration of the lease term but then transfers title to the lessee for nominal consideration at the end of the term.

The presence of three parties and two related exchanges complicates the analysis of the rights and duties between any two parties in the transaction. For example, if PTM (the lessee) sued Shawmut (the lessor) for breach of warranty, a court would have to examine carefully the terms of Shawmut's lease with PTM to determine, among other things, whether Shawmut should be characterized as a "merchant lessor" or a "finance lessor." *See, e.g., Patriot General Life Ins. v. CFC Inv. Co.,* 11 Mass.App.Ct. 857, 420 N.E.2d 918, 921 (1981). *See generally* Boss, 64 B.U.L.Rev. at 67–72 (discussing lessor/lessee warranty issue). Although Shawmut persuasively argues that it was a "finance lessor" in relation to PTM, this issue is immaterial in the present case because no claim by PTM against Shawmut is before us.

The issue, rather, is Shawmut's status vis-a-vis Midwest. That status is defined by the purchase order issued by Shawmut to Midwest, which purports to be the "complete and exclusive statement" of the agreement between Shawmut and Midwest. It has all the makings of a bilateral contract: there are promises on both sides (Shawmut's promise to pay and Midwest's promise to deliver); duties on both sides (Shawmut's duty to pay and Midwest's duty to deliver); and rights on both sides (Midwest's right to payment and Shawmut's right to delivery). *See* E. Farnsworth, *Contracts* 109–10 (1982). Nothing in the agreement expressly states that Shawmut and Midwest have no rights under the contract as against each other. All indications are to the contrary, including language stating that the supplier's express warranties in the purchase order shall be valid and enforceable directly by PTM or Shawmut.

* * *

We are satisfied that the district court did not err in finding that Shawmut was a buyer in the transaction at issue.

III.

The second issue involves the effect of paragraph five of the purchase order contract between Shawmut and Midwest, which states:

> Shawmut shall have no liability hereunder and may terminate this Purchase Order unless within 90 days after the date shown below (a) you shall have delivered all of the Equipment as above provided and we shall have received your invoice, (b) we shall have received Lessee's signed acceptance certificate acknowledging receipt of the Equipment in good condition and repair, accepting the Equipment as satisfactory in all respects, approving your invoice for the Equipment and requesting us to pay you the amount of such invoice.

The district court held that the interpretation of this paragraph was a matter of law, and instructed the jury that by this provision Shawmut delegated to PTM the task of performing Shawmut's duties with regard to accepting the machine, including the duty to accept or permit cure. Under this interpretation of paragraph five, the jury was free to find Shawmut liable for PTM's wrongful rejection of the machine. *See* Mass.Gen.Laws Ann. 106, § 2–210 ("No delegation of performance relieves the party delegating of any duty to perform or any liability for breach.").

On appeal, Shawmut does not dispute that PTM wrongfully rejected the machine. Rather, Shawmut contends that paragraph five insulates it from any liability for PTM's wrongful rejection. We disagree.

Two general propositions of contract construction inform our analysis of paragraph five. First, "[c]ontracts, where possible, are to be construed to reach a sensible result." *Garbincius v. Boston Edison Co.,* 621 F.2d 1171, 1177 (1st Cir.1980). Second, in a case of doubt, a contract provision is to be construed against the party that drew it (in this case Shawmut). *See Chelsea Industries, Inc. v. Accuray Leasing Corp.,* 699 F.2d 58, 61 (1st Cir.1983). *See generally* A. Farnsworth, *Contracts* at 498–99 (the "against the profferer" rule "may be invoked even if the parties bargained as equals.").

Here, we recognize that the language of paragraph five, read literally, supports Shawmut's construction: Shawmut never received a "signed acceptance certificate" from PTM and, therefore, it can be said, had no "liability thereunder." However, we think that paragraph five's requirement of a "signed acceptance certificate" was intended to protect Shawmut against the seller's non-performance, not to erect a technical barrier to Midwest's right to payment upon delivery either of conforming goods or else of nonconforming goods with a timely offer to cure made in conformity with Massachusetts law. *See* Mass.Gen.Laws Ann. ch. 106, § 2–508 (granting seller right to cure).

We think the primary thrust of paragraph five in circumstances such as the present cannot be that Shawmut receive a signed certificate from its lessee but rather that the lessee receive the performance to which the certificate must attest: namely, that Midwest deliver the equipment "in good condition and repair, * * * satisfactory in all respects * * * ". Paragraph five, reasonably construed, does not absolve Shawmut of its payment obligation when the seller has fully performed and the lessee has unlawfully rejected the goods. At trial, Midwest introduced evidence that the goods were conforming when delivered or, in the alternative, that it had made legally adequate offers to cure. Midwest promptly informed Shawmut of its delivery and of its position. The jury found that PTM and Shawmut had broken the contract on the day of delivery, when PTM first rejected the machinery. Midwest thus met all of its substantive obligations under the contract, and Shawmut must meet its obligation to pay for the delivered equipment.

Shawmut's interpretation of paragraph five would contradict the well-recognized commercial practice of relying on section 2–508 of the Uniform Commercial Code in transactions involving the sale of goods. *See* U.C.C. § 2–508, Comment 2 (stating that the goal of § 2–508 is "to avoid injustice to the seller by reason of a surprise rejection by the buyer"); J. White and R. Summers, *Uniform Commercial Code* § 8–5 at 425 (3d ed. 1988) (commenting that "2–508 simply recognizes a general pattern of business behavior and adds a legal sanction to those economic and nonlegal sanctions which parties had and still have."); * * * Before we would accept Shawmut's interpretation (and thus reach the public policy question) we would expect explicit language showing that the parties meant to excuse Shawmut from a buyer's normal duty to accept and pay for conforming goods and to permit cure when appropriate.

* * * Paragraph five simply delegated to PTM Shawmut's duty to accept or permit cure, a duty which PTM breached.

IV.

Because Midwest contests the jury instructions as they relate to both its breach of contract claim and its intentional interference with contractual relations claim, we separately review the instructions as they apply to each claim.

* * *

[The court then found error in the damage instructions and remanded for a new trial on that issue.]

Problem 23–3. Ernst Goes Trucking

Rudy, Inc. either sells or leases heavy duty trucks which are manufactured by and obtained from Flord Motors. If Rudy acquires the standard truck model for resale, the price to Flord is $35,000. If Rudy acquires the truck for lease, the price to Flord is $40,000, since Flord wants a piece of Rudy's leasing action. In either case, the truck has a resale or lease market value of $48,000, and has an estimated useful life of 10 years.

After first discussing models with Flord, Ernst, a trucker, approached Rudy and requested that Rudy acquire a standard model truck from Flord for use in its business. Rudy agreed and after negotiations Rudy and Ernst agreed in writing that, among other things, Ernst could use the truck in its business for 4 years and pay $500 per month. At the end of four years, Ernst had an option to return the truck to Rudy or to use it again for four years at $450 per month. At the end of 8 years, Ernst was to return the truck to Rudy. The agreement stated that the estimated market value of the truck at the end of 8 years was $2,500. But if the actual fair market value was more than $2,500, Rudy agreed to pay Ernst the excess and if the actual fair market value was less than $2,500, Ernst agreed to pay Rudy the deficiency.

Ernst signed the written agreement with Rudy on March 1. Thereafter, Rudy obtained delivery of the truck from Flord under a "sale or return" agreement. [See UCC 2–326 and 2–327.] In essence, if Rudy sold the truck it agreed to pay Flord the $35,000 price but if the truck was not sold it was to be returned. Rudy delivered possession of the truck to Ernst on April 1 and mailed Flord a certified check for $35,000.

After 4 years of use, Earnst renewed the agreement with Rudy. Early in the second year of the renewal, Rudy got into a violent dispute with Flord over business practices. Soon a Flord representative appeared with a sheriff at Ernst's place of business, claimed to be the true owner, and replevied the truck from Ernst. The agreement with Rudy then had 30 months to go and it is apparent that due to ordinary wear and tear and a weak market for used trucks, the actual fair market value of the truck at the end of the agreement will be less than $100.

Question. Ernst comes to you for advice. What rights and remedies, if any, does Ernst have against either Flord or Rudy? In resolving this problem, consider the following:

1. Is the transaction a "true" lease under UCC 1–201(37)? If not, what law governs, Article 9 or Article 2?

2. Is the transaction a finance lease under 2A–103(1)(g)? If so, what difference does it make on these facts?

3. Flord claims that Rudy, because of the "sale or return" term in their contract, had no authority to lease the goods to Ernst. Flord, then, claims the goods from Ernst as a true owner rather than a secured party. Does Ernst take a protected leasehold interest from Rudy under Article 2A, Part 3. Which section(s) are relevant to the question?

4. What claims does Rudy have against Ernst? See 2A–211. If the claims are valid and Rudy cannot recover the goods from Flord, what remedies does Rudy have against Ernst?

5. Has the statute of limitations run in Rudy's claim against Ernst? See 2A–506.

6. How would this case come out under Article 2?

CHAPTER TWENTY-FOUR
LETTER OF CREDIT

SECTION 1. INTRODUCTION

To most students the letter of credit will be completely foreign. In the United States the use of such letters originated in foreign trade, and they still find their most frequent use there. In the last two decades they have been used much more frequently in domestic transactions, both trade and non-trade.

A. Traditional Letters of Credit

To understand the names of the players in this drama and their general responsibilities consider a case in which a Danish seller is going to sell goods to a Newark, New Jersey buyer. If the parties have dealt with one another over a long period of time, the seller might be willing to ship to the buyer on open credit and to rely upon the buyer's willingness and ability to make payment upon receipt of the goods. If the seller has not dealt with the buyer, he would be foolish to make such an arrangement without doing extensive investigation about the buyer's creditworthiness and reliability. Conversely, the buyer could prepay for the goods, but then he would be taking the entire risk of default. He would be forced to pay without any assurance that the goods had been manufactured, much less manufactured correctly. The letter of credit represents an intermediate position between the two suggested. In such a setting the Newark buyer might procure a letter of credit from his bank; that letter would promise (i.e., put the bank's credit behind the agreement) to pay the purchase price to the seller upon presentation of certain documents. Usually these documents would consist at least of an invoice and bills of lading that showed shipment. They may also include an inspection certificate or a certificate of insurance or other documents.

Note that the American bank officer will make payment at his or her desk. The officer will look at the documents presented and only at those documents. The condition of the goods—that they are marred and scarred, defective or out of style—will be not just irrelevant, but unknown, to the bank officer. In this setting the bank is labeled the "issuer," the American buyer is the "customer," and the Danish seller is the "beneficiary." The bank should look at the transaction as though it were a loan to its "customer," i.e., the person with whom it deals in Newark. If it is unwilling to make that loan, it probably should not write the letter of credit. The bank is essentially relying upon its customer in this transaction, and it will likely have no knowledge of the seller or of the seller's capabilities. The seller, on the other hand, is relying upon the bank. It assumes, correctly, that the bank is less likely to go bankrupt than is a random buyer, that the bank is less likely to withhold some or all of the payment on a trumped up ground and, if the bank is a large international bank, the bank's reputation may itself be known to the Danish seller.

By entering into a letter of credit transaction, how have the parties altered the risks and responsibilities that would otherwise be present in a conventional sales transaction? First, and most obvious, the transaction has, in effect, substituted the credit of the American bank for the credit of its customer. If the customer goes into bankruptcy, that will be no defense to the bank's payment. The risk of the customer's bankruptcy has thus been shifted from the seller (in a credit transaction) to the buyer's bank. Secondly, the debt obligation of the buyer has likely become more liquid. Assume, for example, that shipment is to occur 90 days after the agreement is signed. If the obligation to pay is backed by a letter of credit by a well-known American bank, it is likely that the Danish seller will be able to borrow against that obligation much more readily than if it were simply peddling the obligation of the Newark buyer.

Third, the transaction has shifted the litigation cost and probably shifted the forum in any subsequent dispute. If the buyer later claims that the goods were defective, the buyer will now be made into a plaintiff instead of a defendant because of the letter of credit transaction. This is because the bank will have paid the Danish seller and the burden will be upon the American buyer to find the seller and bring suit against him. If the buyer had not paid, he could simply set off and thus force the seller to come to him. Usually this means not only that the American buyer will be the plaintiff, but also that he will have to go to Denmark to sue. With the expansion of the long-arm statutes and such, and with the more expansive view of doing business, it will now be more likely than formerly that the American buyer could get jurisdiction in the American court over the Danish seller, but that will not invariably be true. So the third and fourth functions of the letter of credit are to shift the burden of bringing suit and in many cases to shift the forum from the hometown of one party to the hometown of the other.

Finally, the letter of credit reduces costs by comparison with other insurance and security devices such as bonds and surety agreements. That is so because the bank presumably already knows its "customer" and need not do an extensive credit search to determine whether to issue the letter of credit. It can call upon its pre-existing knowledge to decide that it will issue a letter and that knowledge, gained from other transactions, will enable it to make an accurate estimation of the credit risk.

Problem 24–1

Examine the document set out below. It is a letter of credit. By referring to it answer the questions that follow.

No. G.C. 58954 irrevocable $97,460.00

THE FIRST NATIONAL BANK OF CHICAGO
CHICAGO 90, ILLINOIS

November 29, 1979

Associated Steel Corporation,
176 West Adams Street

Chicago, Illinois
or Assigns

This letter of credit is Assignable and divisible

GENTLEMEN:

WE HEREBY AUTHORIZE YOU TO DRAW AT ______ SIGHT ON ______ FOR ANY SUM OR SUMS NOT EXCEEDING IN ALL Ninety Seven Thousand Four Hundred Sixty U.S. Dollars FOR ACCOUNT OF Decker Steel Co., Grand Rapids, Michigan.

Drafts are to be accompanied by the following documents:

Commercial invoices showing approximately 500 tons prime Thomas quality 36 inch by coil hot rolled steel.

Railroad or truck clean bill of lading issued to order of shipper blank endorsed notify Decker Steel Company, 1620 Turner Avenue, N.W., Grand Rapids 4, Michigan, and showing shipment from New York, New York to Grand Rapids, Michigan.

This credit will remain in force until February 29, 1980 and drafts must be negotiated on or before that date.

WE HEREBY AGREE WITH DRAWERS, ENDORSERS AND BONA FIDE HOLDERS OF DRAFTS NEGOTIATED UNDER AND IN COMPLIANCE WITH THE TERMS OF THIS CREDIT THAT THE SAME SHALL BE DULY HONORED UPON PRESENTATION AT THE COUNTER OF The First National Bank of Chicago. EACH AMOUNT DRAWN MUST BE ENDORSED ON THE REVERSE HEREOF BY THE NEGOTIATING BANK.

INSURANCE ______

DRAFTS UNDER THIS CREDIT MUST BEAR UPON THEIR FACE THE WORDS:

"DRAWN UNDER THE FIRST NATIONAL BANK OF CHICAGO"

CREDIT NO. G.C. 58954 DATED November 19, 1979

RESPECTFULLY YOURS,

THE FIRST NATIONAL BANK OF CHICAGO
Assistant Vice President
Assistant Cashier

Questions

1. Who is the customer, who the beneficiary, and who the issuer?

2. Assume that Decker and First National Bank of Chicago decided to cancel the letter of credit:

a. After it had been mailed but before it had been delivered to Associated Steel.

b. After it had been delivered to Associated Steel but before Associated had taken any action in reliance upon it.

Could they do so?

3. The letter specifically states that it is assignable. In view of the statement in UCC 5–116(3), how does the fact that this document is "assignable" give the beneficiary greater rights that he would have even if it were not assignable?

B. *Standby Letter of Credit*

In the past twenty years a pattern of transactions quite unrelated to international trade or, indeed, to the sale of goods of any sort, has grown up in the United States. This is the issuance of "standby" letters of credit. To the dismay of federal regulators and to the concern of accountants, much of this growth has occurred off the balance sheet, and sometimes, one suspects, without careful consideration of the exposure that a large body of standby letters of credit presents to the issuer of those credits. First, what is a standby letter of credit? Basically, it is one in which the issuer promises to make payment to a beneficiary on the occurrence of a default by the customer other than a default in the shipment of goods. For example, a bank might issue a letter of credit to an owner that promises to make payment to the owner in the event that a builder defaults in constructing a home or a building. A bank might grant a letter of credit to a football player (beneficiary) to secure the payment of a multi-year salary by a shaky football team in a new league. It is even conceivable that a letter of credit could be issued on behalf of a seller, as customer, to a buyer to agree to pay the buyer a certain amount of money in case the seller did not deliver goods.

In general the same rules of law apply to the liabilities under standby letters of credit as under those for the sale of goods. One might wish to distinguish the two, first, because standbys present somewhat different risks to the issuer than do traditional letters of credit and, secondly, because they present somewhat different practical issues in connection with the obligations of payment and responsibilities for performance by the beneficiary and the issuer.

If the buyer fails to pay for the goods in our Denmark/Newark transaction, the bank at least will have a security interest (assuming it has executed the proper documents; see UCC 9–304) in the goods and will be able to recoup some of its loss by resale of those goods. In a traditional case, therefore, its exposure is somewhat limited. Compare that with the traditional standby case in which it promises to pay a city $500,000 upon certification that the curb and gutter contractor has defaulted. If the curb and gutter contractor is now in bankruptcy, the payment of the $500,000 to the municipality may be a dead loss for the bank. Thus, the bank's exposure tends to be larger because of the absence of any obvious security growing out of the transaction in the standby case.

Even more significant, in your editor's view, is a distinction in the obligation which the bank secures between the two different kinds of letters. In the traditional letter of credit the bank is making a bet upon its customer's ability to pay money. That is grist for a banker's mill: determining whether a customer can pay money. In a standby case, a bank is making a bet on its customer's ability and willingness to do something that may be much more complex—to build gutters, to drill a well, to construct a development of houses, etc. Here one suspects some bankers are over their heads and are less likely to make an accurate prediction than in the former case. For all of those reasons the federal bank regulators cluck nervously, but ineffectually, as they watch their chicks write a larger and larger volume of standby letters of credits.

C. Documents

What then are the documents that compose the usual letter of credit transaction and what are the basic legal liabilities? In the usual transaction there will be at least three separate documents. First there will be the underlying contract between the beneficiary and the customer. This is the contract of sale between the Danish seller and the Newark buyer; in a standby case it is the contract for the construction of the curbs and gutters by the local contractor and the municipality. Second is the letter of credit itself. As one will see from the letter quoted below, it is addressed to the beneficiary and signed by the issuer. A wise lawyer will call it a letter of credit, not a contract, not a guarantee, not a bond. The third contract is between the issuer and the customer. Examination of this contract shows the guts of the letter of credit transaction, namely, a potential loan to the customer. In it the customer will promise to pay the bank (usually before the bank has to pay the beneficiary), it will grant the bank a security interest to secure any payments that must be made under the letter, and it will make still other promises to the bank. Many bank officers and their lawyers have rued the day when they issued a letter of credit without first having secured the customer's signature on the contract, or having secured that signature on a contract without all of the proper terms.

How does one characterize the legal relation established by the execution of these various documents? The characterizations that come to mind and the analogies that one most easily draws are all flawed in important ways. The bank is not really a guarantor. Nor is its obligation on the letter of credit exclusively a contractual one. Moreover, strictly speaking, the "beneficiary" is not really a beneficiary of the underlying agreement between the bank and the customer. Finally, the bank's issuance of the money to the beneficiary might be regarded as a loan to the customer, but most would not so characterize it. Perhaps the writing of the letter itself should be regarded as a commitment to make a loan to the customer, not so?

Advice for the beneficiary - Avis pour le bénéficiaire

NOM DE LA BANQUE ÉMETTRICE - NAME OF ISSUING BANK
Issuing Bank Limited International Division
23, High Street
London S.W. 25

Lieu et date d'émission - Place and date of issue
London
13 October 1984

Irrevocable documentary credit
Crédit documentaire irrévocable

Number - Numero: 16358

Date and place of expiry - Date et lieu de validite: 30 November 1984 at counters of advising bank

Applicant - Donneur d'ordre:
Joan's Boutique
14 Charlotte Street
London W.C.36

Beneficiary - Beneficiaire:
The Eastern Trading Company
29, London Road
Hong Kong

Advising Bank - Banque notificatrice — Ref. nr. - No. Ref.:
Bank "X"
35 Kings Road North
Hong Kong

Amount - Montant: HK$ 10,000 (Hong Kong Dollars ten thousand)

Credit available with - Credit utilisable chez

- [ ] by sight payment / par paiement a vue
- [X] by acceptance / par acceptation
- [ ] by negotiation / par negociation
- [ ] by deferred payment at / par paiement differe a

against the documents detailed herein / contre les documents precises ci-apres

[X] and beneficiary's draft at / et la traite du beneficiaire au: 90 days sight

on / sur: Bank "X", 35 Kings Road North, Hong Kong

Partial shipments / Expeditions partielles: [ ] allowed / autorisees [X] not allowed / non autorisees

Transhipment / Transbordement: [ ] allowed / autorisees [X] not allowed / non autorisees

Shipment/dispatch/taking in charge from/at / Embarquement/expedition/prise en charge de/a: Hong Kong

for transportation to / a destination de: Heathrow Airport, London

SIGNED INVOICE IN THREE COPIES certifying that the goods are in accordance with Joan's Boutique Order Number 35 dated 14.8.1984.

AIR CONSIGNMENT NOTE evidencing goods dispatched to Joan's Boutique, 14 Charlotte Street, London W.C. 36 marked "Freight Paid".

PACKING LIST IN TRIPLICATE

We are informed that insurance is being arranged by our principals.

covering Ladies Dresses
C and F Heathrow Airport, London

Documents to be presented within 7 days after the date of issuance of the transport document(s) but within the validity of the credit
Documents a presenter dans les 7 jours apres la date d'emission du des document(s) de transport mais dans la periode de validite du credit

We hereby issue the Documentary Credit in your favour. It is subject to the Uniform Customs and Practice for Documentary Credits (1983 Revision, International Chamber of Commerce, Paris, France, Publication No. 400) and engages us in accordance with the terms thereof. The number and the date of the credit and the name of our bank must be quoted on all drafts required. If the credit is available by negotiation, each presentation must be noted on the reverse of this advice by the bank where the credit is available.

Nous emettons par la presente ce credit documentaire en votre faveur. Il est soumis aux Regles et Usances Uniformes relatives aux Credits Documentaire (Revision 1983, Publication No. 400 de la Chambre de Commerce Internationale, Paris, France) et nous engage selon leurs termes. Le numero et la date du credit ainsi que le nom de notre banque devront être mentionnes sur toute traite requise. Si le credit est utilisable par negociation chaque presentation devra être inscrite au verso de cet avis par la banque ou le credit est utilisable.

Issuing Bank Limited International Division
23, High Street
London S.W. 25

This document consists of 1 signed page(s)
Ce document consiste en 1 page(s) signee(s)

Notes

1. Would the bank pay on the following draft?

Pay to the order of Eastern Trading Company $1,000 H.K.
–One thousand dollars Hong Kong–

To: Issuing Bank Ltd.
25 High Street
London S.W. 25.......... A.R. Rogers
Eastern Trading Co.

2. What if the invoices presented appeared to have a stamp on the signature line or a printed inscription? Should the bank pay against those?

3. If the letter of credit set out above were changed to a standby letter of credit, what would the conditions of performance say?

INVOICE FACTURE FACTURA RECHARGING FACTURA

Seller (Name, Address, VAT Reg. No.)
Clearchem PLC
Riverside Works, Warren Road
Banbury
Oxfordshire
United Kingdom

Shrine No.
1

Invoice No. & Date (Tax Point)
RT 67244 8 Nov 84

Seller's Reference
SPEX/548/789/DEM

Buyer's Reference
Order ARB–548771

Other Reference

Consignee
General Trading Company Limited
Suite 18/88, Eastern House
3487 Soleiman Jamshid Mojdeh
Riyadh
Saudi Arabia

Buyer (if not consignee)

Country of Origin of Goods
UK (EEC)

Country of Destination
Saudi Arabia

Import licence 892E–44319

Terms of Delivery and Payment
CIF Jeddah
Confirmed Irrevocable Letter of
Credit payable at sight
Payment should be made through:
British Bank Limited
88 Waterloo Place, London SW1
Account no. 120 7532 68

Vessel/Aircraft etc.
Orient Adventurer

Port of Loading
Liverpool

Port of Discharge
Jeddah

Marks and Numbers and Container No.	Number and Kind of Packages Description of Goods	IT Code No.	Total Gross Wt (Kg)	Total Cube (??)
G.T.C. ARB–548771 Riyadh via Jeddah 1–80	1 × 20ft Container Chemical products in drums		kg 2141.1	20.620
			Total Net Wt(Kg) 2000.0	

Item/pkges	Gross Net Cube	Description	Quantity	Unit Price	Selling Price
1)	816.8 750.0 7.620	Product D101/5877 Hydrofluoric Acid Solution 50% w/w	30 drums	17.26 /25kg	517.80
2)	1325.0 1250.0 13.000	Product D100/6755 Antimony Trichloride	50 drums	20.47 /25kg	1023.50
					1541.30
		Freight			180.55
		Insurance			39.70

We hereby guarantee that this is a true and correct invoice and that the goods referred to are of the origin, manufacture and production of the United Kingdom.	Invoice Total GBP £ 1761.55 Name of Signatory AC Smith, Director Place and Date of Issue Banbury 8 NOV 1984 Signature AC. Smith

Notes

Assume that the letter of credit described the commodity as 816.8 Product D101/5857; 750.0 Hydrofluoric Acid; 7.620 Solution 50% w/w.

1. Under which of the following descriptions would you reject the invoice as improper if you were an employee of the issuing bank?

a. "816.8 Product D101/5877."

b. Description as set out in the invoice printed above, but listing 29 or alternatively 32 drums.

c. "750.0 Hydrofluoric Acid."

2. What if the invoice was not that of Clearchem, but an invoice with a proper description of Ambercamp, a related company also located in Banbury?

3. Assume that the invoice contained the precise description, but that an insurance certification was included that described the product merely as "Approximately 30 drums, more or less, hydrofluoric acid."

4. What if the invoice or bill of lading came to the bank not through the mail but by a computer connection from the carrier or shipper, between the sender's computer and bank, which when properly stimulated printed out the above invoice? Would such a document be acceptable? How would you authenticate a document in such case?

D. Sources of Law

In addition to the cases there are two significant sources of law. First is Article 5 of the Uniform Commercial Code. As this is written, Article 5 is nearing the conclusion of the amendment process. The references in all of the cases and most of the notes will be to Article 5 of the Code as it existed prior to 1993. Students should beware because the new version of Article 5 will be somewhat expanded and the new section numbers will not correlate with the old.

The second important source of non-case law is the Uniform Customs and Practices for Documentary Credit. This is a document issued by the International Chamber of Commerce and, by agreement, it covers a large share of all letters of credit written in international and in domestic transactions. It has recently undergone a revision; the current version of the "UCP" is titled I.C.C. Publication No. 500—Uniform Customs and Practice for Documentary Credits. It was adopted by the I.C.C. in 1993.

A comparison of Article 5 with the rules in the Uniform Customs and Practices shows that they are by no means identical, but it would be mistake to believe that they contain significantly different rules of law; they do not. The basic rules are the same under either. Because of long experience and because it is devoted particularly to the international trade arena, the Uniform Customs and Practices have many detailed provisions that deal explicitly with the sale of goods. For example, Article 25 contains a series of specific rules on the kinds of documents that are appropriate, the kinds of descriptions that are necessary, etc. These rules can be determinative in a case governed by the UCP; they can be persuasive in one governed by the Uniform Commercial Code. At the behest of its banks, New York added the following non-uniform amendment to 5–102. In New York 5–102(4) reads as follows:

> Unless otherwise agreed, this Article 5 does not apply to a letter of credit or a credit if by its terms or by agreement, course of dealing or usage of trade such letter of credit or credit is subject in whole or in part to the Uniform Customs and Practice for Commercial Documentary Credits fixed by the 13th or by any subsequent Congress of the International Chamber of Commerce.

In an earlier version of this book we accused Henry Harfield, then a partner in Sherman and Sterling, and America's preeminent expert on letters of credit, of leading the New York lawyers in an attack on the UCC out of a neurotic attachment to the Uniform Customs and Practices. Mr. Harfield responded to that charge as follows:

"Dear Professor White:

"* * * As regards the matter discussed and the material referred to in the second paragraph of your letter, I gladly waive any rights I may have and am content that this letter constitutes my release of any liability you may have to me for defamation. On the other hand, you will understand that I cannot and do not undertake to indemnify you against liability to others arising out of the inaccuracy of your statements. The New York Bar was far from uniform in its reaction to the Uniform Commercial Code in general and to Article 5 in particular. I can well imagine that those outstanding members of the Bar who supported the Code with apostolic zeal (and there are many of them) might feel justifiably aggrieved at their unwarranted inclusion with a group of intellectual muckers. At the other end of the spectrum, there is good ground for umbrage by those outstanding members of the New York Bar (and there are many of them) who then were and still are persuaded that the Code is the most mischievous piece of contrivance since the Communist Manifesto. Each of these groups may regard as actionable, your proposed assertion that I was their leader.

"That statement is simply not supported by the record. The facts are that the New York Bar was divided, perhaps even fragmented, and the proceedings before the Law Revision Commission resembled a Donnybrook rather than a knightly tournament. There was a significant group who supported Article 5 in all its aspects and they had their leaders who were devout and dedicated men. There was a group which regarded Article 5, in every aspect, as anathema and they had their leaders who were devout and dedicated men; but I was not a leader of either group. My recollection is that my approach was singular, objective, statesmanlike, and always reasonable. For this I deserve no credit; it is just my nature. * * * "

"Faithfully yours,

"Henry Harfield."

The preference of the UCP over the UCC is not limited to the New York bankers. Most letters of credit arising out of international sale of goods transactions and many arising in domestic transactions incorporate the UCP. It is important, therefore, that the student know the UCP not just as a basis for analogy in Code cases, but as the governing rules in many transactions.

In rare cases the relationship between the UCP and the UCC may be quite complicated. The incorporation of the UCP by any letter of credit means that the UCP govern in most circumstances where there is conflict between the UCP and the UCC. This would not be true where the UCC rule was mandatory (e.g., a rule that prohibited a bank from disclaiming its liability for lack of good faith).

In some circumstances there will be disagreement between the parties on the question whether the UCC or UCP governs even when the letter adopts the UCP. This could arise, for example, where one party argues that a Code provision governed because it was not "in conflict with the UCP". Here the other party might argue that even though there was no UCP provision directly in conflict, the silence of the UCP directs the outcome not specifically authorized and thus that the UCC should not apply to the transaction. Such a dispute might arise, for example, where one party asserted a right in warranty under the UCC and the other party claimed there was no warranty because the UCP, that say nothing about warranties, had been adopted. The question where is "conflict" between the two is not always easy.

Almost all of the cases, an incredibly complex array, arise out of a single problem. Nearly all ask the question: Was the bank which was presented with certain documents required to pay? The basic rule is that if there is compliance with the documentary requirements of the letter, the bank must pay, even though there is a breach of the underlying contract, even though its own customer has gone bankrupt, even though the world is about to come to an end. However, beginning with the *Sztejn* case, infra p. 1122, the courts and now the Uniform Commercial Code have recognized at least one exception to the bank's obligation to pay on presentation of complying documents, the so-called fraud exception. Many of the cases that now come to the court call upon it to draw the line between fraud on the one hand (where payment is excused) and cases of mere breach of the underlying contract (where payment is not excused).

Many other cases deal in tedious detail with the form of documents that are necessary to comply with the credits. When the bank wishes not to pay, it will of course examine the documents microscopically and may seize on any small detail as a basis for its refusal to pay and as an excuse. Often the defect in the documents is not the true reason the bank has chosen not to pay. It may choose not to pay because its customer has asked it not to pay, because its customer has gone bankrupt, or because, for some other reason, it believes it or its customer will not be reimbursed. Each time the bank is freed from payment by a court, a little chip is taken out of the solid rock of letter of credit law and practice. Each time the courts grant an injunction against payment, in the words of Henry Harfield: "I fear that the sacred cow of equity may trample the tender vines of letter of credit law." Harfield, *Code, Custom, and Conscience in Letter of Credit Law,* 4 UCC L.J. 7, 11 (1971). Thus, many of the cases are bitterly fought wars over words with nary a mention of the true motivation of the bank and of the other party.

A final set of cases involves the right of a bank who has paid to be repaid out of the assets of its customer, to be subrogated to its customer's or beneficiary's rights or otherwise to protect itself by taking and selling the underlying assets.

SECTION 2. THE ISSUER'S DUTY TO PAY

The issuer's duty to its customer is to examine the documents presented and to refuse to pay if the documents are not correct. The revised version of Article 5 will explicitly incorporate a rule of "strict compliance". It will not be enough that documents almost comply or comply more or less, they will have to be in strict compliance with the letter of credit. That said, there will still be disputes. Even under a doctrine of strict compliance, documents need not slavishly conform with the letter of credit to be "strictly complying". For example, a Texas court correctly held that a draft requesting payment on a "letter of credit No. 86–122–5" strictly complied with a letter specifying drafts on "letter of credit No. 86–122–S." By the same token, an invoice that identified the seller as "Jeneral Motors" under a letter of "General Motors" would strictly comply even though the same invoice with a modest deviation in the quantity or description of the goods might not comply. Particularly where there are multiple documents, some to be prepared by persons not involved in the underlying transaction (such as carriers), the demands of strict compliance do not mean exact conformity to the description on the letter of credit. What is and what is not strict compliance is an irrepressible issue.

To understand the relevant sections of the UCP and the UCC and the cases in this section, one needs to imagine a letter of credit department in a large bank. Here are many clerical workers, sophisticated clerical workers, but clerical workers nevertheless. On the one hand they have a stack of letters of credit that call for certain kinds of bills of lading, invoices, insurance certificates, certificates of inspection, certifications of default, etc. The letters have dates of expiration and call for specific kinds of drafts signed by particular persons. The bank officers sitting with these documents look from one to the other and ultimately decide whether the conditions have been met.

The job is the same on the bitterest winter day as it is at the height of summer. It is uninfluenced by the destruction of the goods in the most violent storm of the century, by the bankruptcy of the buyer or the seller, or, theoretically, by any other set of events going on outside the room where our hypothetical bank officers are sitting. The issue is plain and simple in every instance: do these documents meet the conditions of this letter?

As the examples illustrate, even after one has decided the standard, reasonable document checkers may have disagreements about the compliance of a particular document. In many cases the true party in interest, the customer, will be happy to waive certain conditions of the letter because it wants the goods and is willing to take the chance that the goods conform to the contract even though the documents do not conform to the letter of credit. Waivers are commonplace; some have estimated that as many as 50 percent of all presentments are defective.

The issuing bank may lose its opportunity to dishonor by failing to give the proper and timely notice to the beneficiary of the basis for its dishonor. An explicit requirement to give such notice has long been in the UCP; with the adoption of the new version of Article 5, a similar explicit requirement comes to Article 5. Cases decided under the old version of Article 5 sometimes imposed an obligation on the bank—at least where the beneficiary had acted in reliance on the bank's silence. Sometimes the beneficiary can make out a case for reliance and sometimes not. Where substitute documents could have been procured in response to an early notice of defect, presumably the beneficiary relies on the issuer's silence. Where no such documents could have been procured, it is hard to make out a case for reliance. The cases below deal with these questions.

Finally, there are the mysterious warranty provisions in section 5–111 of the old Article. These lay dormant for many years; they never produced more than a handful of cases. With the new Article 5 the section is replaced by a more expansive and quite different warranty rule. Whether the new warranty rule will be a source of litigation remains to be seen.

As students read the cases below, they should understand that the presentment and payment process is much more than a cut and dried determination of the kind that might be made upon presentment of a check for payment. First is the question whether the documents comply. Even after one has decided the standard, compliance remains a complicated and subtle question in many cases. When non-conforming documents are presented, there will often be discussion by the issuer with the customer or in some cases with the beneficiary. Under the new law the issuer will have a duty to institute these discussions with the beneficiary; its dishonor must be prompt and must be accompanied by an explanation.

In the cases that follow the students should ask how the current UCP and the new Article 5 would influence the outcome. In addition, one should ask how to advise a bank to avoid the problems the banks here confront or to advise a customer or beneficiary.

BANCO ESPANOL de CREDITO v. STATE STREET BANK AND TRUST CO.

United States Circuit Court, First Circuit, 1967.
385 F.2d 230, cert. denied, 390 U.S. 1013, 88 S.Ct. 1263, 20 L.Ed.2d 163 (1968), appeal after remand 409 F.2d 711 (1st Cir.1969).

Before ALDRICH, CHIEF JUDGE, MCENTEE and COFFIN, CIRCUIT JUDGES.

COFFIN, CIRCUIT JUDGE. This suit began as a claim by appellant, a Spanish bank (Banco Espanol), against appellee, a domestic bank (State Street), for the latter's allegedly wrongful refusal to accept and pay two drafts drawn upon it pursuant to two irrevocable commercial letters of credit. Each letter was issued by State Street at the behest of its customer, Robert Lawrence, Inc. (Lawrence), a Boston clothing concern. Banco Espanol was designated the advising bank and two Spanish suppliers (Alcides and Longuer) were named as beneficiaries. The cases were consolidated for trial in the district court sitting without a jury and, following judgment for State Street, appellant took these appeals.

The issue is whether State Street, whose letters of credit, as amended, called for the presentation of an inspection certificate by a named firm stipulating "that the goods are in conformity with the order", was justified in refusing to honor the drafts of Banco Espanol on the ground that the inspection certificate did not meet the terms of the letters of credit.

The transaction was initiated by Lawrence to finance the purchase of raincoats, beach jackets, knit shirts, and cardigans from Alcides and Longuer. Based upon preliminary arrangements apparently worked out by an intermediary, of which more later, Lawrence obtained two irrevocable letters of credit from State Street. One letter covered Lawrence orders Nos. 101, 102, and 103 for beach jackets, outer coats and cotton garments in the revised final amount of $105,630, and the other covered Lawrence order No. 100 for wool knit shirts and cardigans in the revised final amount of $13,320. Both letters constituted Banco Espanol the correspondent bank, and required signed invoices, customs invoices, inspection certificates, and full sets of clean on board ocean bills of lading dated not later than March 31, 1963.

At the time of issuance of the letters of credit, State Street called to the attention of its customer, Lawrence, that the requirement of an inspection certificate without a named inspector left a hazardous gap in the documents. Lawrence replied that the letters would be later amended to include the name of an inspection agent.

The next three and one half months were significantly devoted to continuing efforts to resolve this problem. On November 22, 1962 one of the Spanish manufacturers (Alcides) wrote Lawrence's representative that it agreed with the idea of naming an inspection agent and suggested that Lawrence put forward a name. Lawrence's man replied shortly that since he would be in Barcelona near the time of delivery, he would be the inspector. Accordingly, State Street sought to amend the letters in January. Foreseeably, this was not acceptable to the beneficiary as Lawrence learned in early February. Lawrence then wrote State Street (notwithstanding the hiatus in the letters of credit which State Street had noted) that it should not make payment unless inspection certificates were signed by a party acceptable to it. It further agreed to indemnify State Street for any damages resulting from carrying out these instructions, coupling this with a threat to refuse reimbursement if payment were made.

After a meeting between Lawrence and State Street, the object of which was to decide what to do about the inspection issue, a representative of Lawrence went to Spain. This trip resulted in an amendment to the letters of credit, cabled to Alcides on March 1, 1963, which required the inspection certificate to be issued by Supervigilancia Sociedad General de Control S.A. (Supervigilancia) certifying that "the goods are in conformity with the order". While it is not clear on whose initiative this firm was selected, it was apparently well regarded by the State Street official who had been closely associated with this transaction.

Identification of the underlying orders to which the letters of credit referred is not an easy task. In the first place, the record before us contains no document purporting to be an order for the shirts and cardigans (No. 100—the Longuer order). As to the Alcides order, we face two sets of somewhat inconsistent documents, both of which Lawrence sent to the manufacturer: two unnumbered papers dated November 5 and 6, 1962, labelled "order placed by Cavendish Co."—apparently an intermediary for Lawrence; and three papers dated November 13, 1962, labelled "stock sheet", and bearing numbers 101, 102, and 103. Though the earlier set is the only one bearing the label "order" there is evidence both external and internal that it was superseded by the latter: a reference in a letter from Lawrence's representative that he had to create orders to match the numbers in the letter of credit; a reference in another letter to asterisks in the orders—which are found only in the "stock sheets", not in the "orders"; additional documentary requirements in the "stock sheets", not found in the "orders"; and a major change in half the sizes specified in one "order", from "small" to "medium". We cite such minutiae because of the difficulty of interpretation created by Lawrence and because of the assertion of appellee's counsel at trial that the inspecting agency could not determine what the orders were. Leaving aside consideration of what might be the legal effect of a buyer-created impossibility of clear identification of orders where a letter of credit required a certificate of conformity to order, we simply observe here that close scrutiny of the two sets of papers reveals that the "stock sheets" supplanted the earlier "orders".

In any event the most important notation found on the "stock sheets"—and not on the "orders"—was "Coats [and jackets] to be as sample inspected in Spain. Letter of credit to be cashed by presentation of bill of lading and signature of superintendent or local inspection (buyers preference) (will confirm)."

The amendment to the letters of credit—appointing Supervigilancia the inspecting agent—was accepted by the major manufacturer involved—Alcides (and presumably Longuer)—on March 12, 1963 on which date both manufacturers requested Supervigilancia to begin inspection. State Street notified Lawrence on March 13.

Then began a barrage of cabled messages from Lawrence to both Supervigilancia and the manufacturers, which was to endure for two weeks. On March 13 Supervigilancia was asked, without explanation, to delay inspection until further instructions from Lawrence. On March 14, it was told that Lawrence had cabled the manufacturers to postpone shipment to permit Supervigilancia to inspect according to samples "they air mailing you directly". On the same day another cable was sent to Supervigilancia saying that Lawrence was airmailing "our approved samples per order and instructions". On the next day Supervigilancia was told to obtain three complete sets of samples properly marked from each concern, send two to Lawrence, and await instructions. On March 18 this message was repeated.

After these two conflicting sets of instructions, Supervigilancia, on March 23, cabled Lawrence, saying in effect that it was going ahead, acting "according your own indications on credits and orders". To this Lawrence replied on March 25 that Supervigilancia should "withhold certificate until after arrival and inspection of goods by your New York correspondent * * *." This, if we read it aright, is a third position taken by Lawrence. At this point in time the latest date for completion of the bills of lading was five days away, March 31, with no alternative shipping date available within that period.

Supervigilancia, on March 26, executed its two certificates of inspection. It divided each certificate into two parts. The first part tended to the matter at hand saying that (1) it had carried out its inspection

> "* * * basing ourselves on the details shown in the orders or Stocksheets Nos. [100], 101, 102 and 103 * * * and in the samples that were handed to us by the Requirer [Alcides and Longuer], that corresponded, according to his sayings ratified in presence of a Public Notary, to the samples seen and approved by the Delegate of Firm ROBERT LAWRENCE INC., during his stay in Barcelona, and with [sic] are mentioned in the notes appearing in orders Stocksheets Nos. [100], 101, 102 and 103, where there is a note reading:
>
> 'COATS or JACKETS [Germents (sic)] TO BE AS SAMPLE INSPECTED IN SPAIN' ";

that (2) the letters of credit required it to certify "THAT THE GOODS ARE IN CONFORMITY WITH THE ORDER"; that (3) a ten per cent random sample had been taken; and that (4) the "whole * * * [was] found conforming to the conditions estipulated [sic] on the Order–Stock–sheets."

The second part of each certificate contained a chronological account of the cabled messages we have summarized, followed by this language: "Requirer * * * is formally requiring us for delivering this certificate what we are doing today under reserves, not as far as the goods are concerned, which correspond to the samples seen and produced referred to at the beginning of this certificate, but to the existing difference between both interested parties as per the quoted cables."

All documents were presented to Banco Espanol, which honored them and made payment or the equivalent on March 28 and 29. On April 3 State Street cabled its refusal to accept the drafts on it "because accompanying inspection certificates nonconforming with terms of credits which require certificates certifying goods are in conformity with the orders". A later letter amplified its position by specifying that the certificates merely indicated conformity to samples alleged by the seller to "correspond" to other samples allegedly approved by the buyer and that the certificates were issued "under reserves".

The district court sustained this position, referring to the requirement that documents strictly conform to letter of credit provisions, and pointing out that each certificate failed in three respects: (1) that it merely certified that the goods conformed to "conditions"—which left it unclear if the conformity was to the whole of the order or only part; (2) that there was a doubt whether the "order-stock-sheet" was different from the order; and (3) that the certificate was confined to samples handed to the inspecting agency by a representative of the manufacturer. The court concluded that "* * * this was not the unqualified certificate required by the letter of credit and defendant bank was justified in its refusal to accept it."

We do not agree. Since, in our view, the third alleged defect noted by the court presents the most difficult problem, we shall deal with it first.

We note, at the outset, that an issuing bank's duty to honor a demand for payment is, to some extent, determined by statute. The Uniform Commercial Code, M.G.L.A. (Mass.) c. 106 § 5–114(1) (1958), provides, in relevant part, that "An issuer must honor a draft or demand for payment which complies with the terms of the relevant credit regardless of whether the goods or documents conform to the underlying contract for sale or other contract between the customer and the beneficiary." [1] This Code provision, however, simply codifies long-standing decisional law and does not assist us here in determining whether the inspection certificate submitted by Supervigilancia complied with the terms of the credit.

We take as a starting point the substantial body of case law which establishes and supports the general rule that documents submitted incident to a letter of credit are to be strictly construed. This is because international financial transactions rest upon the accuracy of documents rather than on the condition of the goods they represent. But we note some leaven in the loaf of strict construction. Not only does *haec verba* not control absolutely, see, e.g., O'Meara v. National Park Bank, 239 N.Y. 386, 146 N.E. 636, 39 A.L.R. 747 (1925), but some courts now cast their eyes on a wider scene than a single document. We are mindful, also, of the admonition of several legal scholars that the integrity of international transactions (i.e., rigid adherence to material matters) must somehow strike a balance with the requirement of their fluidity (i.e., a reasonable flexibility as to ancillary matters) if the objective of increased dealings to the mutual satisfaction of all interested parties is to be enhanced. See, e.g., Mentschicoff, How to Handle Letters of Credit, 19 Bus.Lawyer 107, 111 (1963). Finally, we recognize that this is not a litigation about the nomenclature of goods. Consequently, we are not measurably helped by such cases as those cited in the margin which turn on discrepancies between the actual terms of invoices or bills of lading and requirements of a letter of credit.

1. The district court noted that

"Both parties appear to agree that the case is governed by the Uniform Commercial Code as enacted in Massachusetts. Plaintiff [appellant] also relies upon the Uniform Customs and Practice for Documentary Credits issued by the International Chamber of Commerce, particularly Article 8 thereof. This, however, in substance states only what is contained in the Uniform Commercial Code."

What we face here is a matter of procedure which can, in the first instance, be structured by the purchasing party. How may a buyer in the international market place be assured before payment that his purchase as delivered is of the quality agreed upon by the parties? As buyers become more concerned about quality, this issue is likely to become more important. That there are so few cases or comments addressed to the issue of reasonable precautions to assure quality is indicative of the relatively novel status of the problem, at least so far as courts have dealt with it. We are mindful of the testimony in this case that an official of appellee, a busy bank, engaged in passing upon the issuance of 1,500 to 2,000 letters of credit a year for several decades, has encountered in this case his first experience with a letter of credit calling for a certificate of conformity to the order.

What are the realities of such a requirement on the part of the buyer? It is not enough that he receive the quantity of goods he ordered, nor that he receive goods capable of standard measure or grade. He must also, in such a case as this, receive them cut, tailored, sewn according to a style he has in mind. He must therefore rely on a sample he has seen and liked. Being in a distant part of the globe, the buyer must usually elect one of two alternatives. He may be present during the inspection process to verify the sample or he may select, with his seller's acquiescence, a person or firm in whom he has confidence to represent him. Unless he elects to be present, he is acting on faith—faith that the representative is capable and honest, and faith that the representative has the right samples or criteria to serve as a standard. Even if he mails an approved sample direct to the representative, he must rely on the integrity of the mails.

This act of faith—or its converse, the risk that merchandise will not turn out as hoped—is that of the buyer. As one contemporary student has written,

> "* * * there is one risk against which protection is required and which is less easy to guard against. That is the risk that the goods shipped may not comply with the terms of the sales contract as to quality. This is a risk which normally the buyer will have to bear * * * but * * * [he] can guard against the risk by requiring in his letter of request to the bankers that, in addition to the usual shipping documents, the vendor shall deliver a certificate of quality showing the goods to be as specified in the contract, signed by some responsible person at the place of shipment. The only risk then left to the buyer is that the person nominated to give the certificate may fail in his duty. But an entire absence of risk would mean an absence of business." A.G. Davis, The Law Relating to Commercial Letters of Credit, 3d ed., London, Sir Isaac Pitman & Sons Ltd., 1963, p. 19.
>
> Or, in the words of other scholars,
>
> "The requirement of such other documents, and particularly certificates of analysis, quality, weight, and the like, is a reasonable precaution for a prudent buyer to take, since he may in this way obtain some measure of assurance that the merchandise is as ordered * * *. The bank is under no obligation and bears no responsibility for the accuracy of any such representations and certificates. Nevertheless, through selection of a reputable third party, the buyer does have a degree of

assurance that the merchandise is as represented." Ward and Harfield, Bank Credits and Acceptances, 4th ed., Ronald Press, 1958, p. 45.

These observations go to the heart of this case. For the buyer here—Lawrence—was striving to assure the delivery of quality goods. To be sure, it deliberately postponed the problem when it caused the letters of credit to be issued without resolving the question of the inspecting agent. Then it naively sought to have the sellers accept one of its own representatives. It had long since sewn the seeds of dispute by sending to the sellers both "stock sheets" which were really orders and "orders" which were merely preliminary papers. When it finally reached agreement with the seller as to an inspecting agency, it neglected to specify precisely how it would conduct the inspection operation, leaving only the bland instruction that the goods must conform to orders. And, so far as the inspecting agency was concerned, the orders merely referred to samples that might very well have been inspected in Spain at some past time.

Consequently when faced on the eve of the shipping deadline both with a barrage of contradictory telegrams from the buyer and with samples which the sellers under oath stated "corresponded" with samples approved earlier by the buyer's representative in Barcelona, Supervigilancia had to act to the dissatisfaction of one of the parties to the basic contract. That it took the word, under oath, of the seller as to the appropriateness of the sample is no more than any inspector must ordinarily do. Unless the buyer is physically present (and Lawrence presumably could have arranged this during the frenetic two week period of cable traffic), the inspector must take someone's word that he is judging by the proper samples.

Even in the well known case of O'Meara v. National Park Bank, 239 N.Y. 386, 146 N.E. 636, 39 A.L.R. 747, (1925), a letter of credit calling for newsprint to "test 11/12–32 pounds" was held to be satisfied by an affidavit that annexed samples "stated [by the affiant] to be representative of the shipment" met the prescribed test. We fail to see how this is any more reliable than the affidavit of "correspondence" in the instant case.

In Basse & Selve v. Bank of Australasia, 90 L.T.R. (n.s.) 618 (K.B.1904), the letter of credit covering a purchase of cobalt ore called for a certificate of analysis of a local chemist showing at least five per cent protoxide. The shipper (bent on delivering worthless ore) gave the chemist a packet of ore for analysis. The chemist furnished a certificate that the ore he examined contained the requisite amount of protoxide. But the negotiating bank refused to pay since there was nothing to indicate that the ore examined was that described in the bill of lading. The unscrupulous shipper then gave the chemist a packet of ore marked as was the bill of lading, "P.M. 2680 bags representing 100 tons". The chemist then referred in his certificate to "The sample of cobalt ore marked 'P.M. 2680 bags representing 100 tons' received from you * * *." The bank paid the shipper and prevailed in a suit against it by its customer to recover the sum so paid. The court said:

> "It is said that [the certificate] professes to show merely the test of the contents of a sample packet with a mark upon it, and does not purport to show a test of the bill of lading of 100 tons of ore. This, I think, is a fanciful objection. Large quantities of produce are necessarily tested by means of samples. Such samples are drawn either by the

servants of the owner of the goods or (as it seems) by the servants of the analyst, and if the samples are carefully and skilfully drawn they generally fairly represent the bulk. But in this case it would be no part of the bank's duty to see to the sampling or to ascertain that it was fairly done." 90 L.T.R. (n.s.) at 620.

So we say in this case that, while the sample may be just as misleading as the ore sample in Basse & Selve, the advising bank was equally justified in paying on the strength of the documents.

We see no significant difference in Supervigilancia being told by the manufacturers that the samples were those approved by the buyer and being told that they "corresponded" to such samples. Webster's Dictionary (3d Int'l ed.) gives such meanings of "correspond" as "in agreement", "conformity", "equivalent", "match", "equal". In the context and considering the language difficulty, we think these meanings apply more than the looser ones like "analogous", "parallel", or "similar". In effect, Lawrence in this case, by providing as a referent to the letter of credit requirement of conformity to orders merely the early cryptic description on the stock sheets ("Coats * * * to be as samples inspected in Spain"), procured no more reliable assurance of authenticity than the credit termination clause in Fair Pavilions, Inc. v. First Nat. City Bank, 24 A.D.2d 109, 264 N.Y.S.2d 255 (1965), which was to be triggered "* * * if our Travelers Letter of Credit Department receives * * * from an officer (or one describing himself therein as an officer) of [bank's customer] an affidavit that one or more * * * events * * * has occurred." 264 N.Y.S.2d at 256.

Moreover, if there be ambiguity surrounding the words "correspond" or "sample approved in Spain" we would, like the court in *Fair Pavilions,* "* * * take the words as strongly against the issuer as a reasonable reading will justify. * * *." Supra at 258.

To hold otherwise—that a buyer could frustrate an international transaction on the eve of fulfillment by a challenge to authenticity of sample—would make vulnerable many such arrangements where third parties are vested by buyers with inspection responsibilities but where, apart from their own competence and integrity, there is no iron-clad guarantee of the sample itself.

As for the argument that Supervigilancia's finding that the goods conform "to the conditions estipulated [sic] on the Order–Stock–sheets" is a meaningful variance from the terms of the letters of credit, we confess to semantic myopia. "The conditions" mean, as we read the certificates, all the conditions, hence the order itself. As for the dual use by the agency of the words "Order–Stock–sheets", we have already indicated both the nature and cause of the confusion and conclude that Supervigilancia acted solomonically in borrowing the substance of the stock sheets and the label of the "orders". We do not see how it could have done otherwise.

The remaining contention that "under reserves" has some mysterious meaning which infects the entire certificate is not borne out by the inapposite cases cited to us and is directly refuted by the limiting language immediately following—"not as far as the goods are concerned". Further reading of the document indicates clearly that the phrase was directed to the underlying dispute between buyer and seller, which could not be the concern of the advising bank.

We hold, therefore, that the inspection certificate in this case conformed in all significant respects to the requirements of the letter of credit.

Appellee has urged that, in the event we might reverse the district court's judgment, the case should be remanded for a new trial or at least further findings, since the district court did not find it necessary to reach additional defenses. Appellant urges otherwise. It is not clear to us which is correct. We reverse the judgment of the District Court and remand for such further proceedings, consistent with this opinion, as the court feels appropriate. We do say that these additional defenses were not argued before us, nor directly passed upon, but whether this is chargeable to appellee, so that judgment should be entered for appellant forthwith, we leave to the district judge before whom this case was originally heard. [Footnotes omitted.]

COURTAULDS NORTH AMERICA, INC. v. NORTH CAROLINA NATIONAL BANK

United States Court of Appeals, Fourth Circuit, 1975.
528 F.2d 802.

BRYAN, SENIOR CIRCUIT JUDGE. A letter of credit with the date of March 21, 1973 was issued by the North Carolina National Bank at the request of and for the account of its customer, Adastra Knitting Mills, Inc. It made available upon the drafts of Courtaulds North America, Inc. "up to" $135,000.00 (later increased by $135,000.00) at "60 days date" to cover Adastra's purchases of acrylic yarn from Courtaulds. The life of the credit was extended in June to allow the drafts to be "drawn and negotiated on or before August 15, 1973." Bank refused to honor a draft for $67,346.77 dated August 13, 1973 for yarn sold and delivered to Adastra. Courtaulds brought this action to recover this sum from Bank.

The defendant denied liability chiefly on the assertion that the draft did not agree with the letter's conditions, viz., that the draft be accompanied by a "Commercial invoice in triplicate stating [inter alia] that it covers * * * 100% acrylic yarn"; instead, the accompanying invoices stated that the goods were "Imported Acrylic Yarn."

Upon cross motions for summary judgment on affidavits and a stipulation of facts, the District Court held defendant Bank liable to Courtaulds for the amount of the draft, interest and costs. It concluded that the draft complied with the letter of credit when each invoice is read together with the packing lists stapled to it, for the lists stated on their faces: "Cartons marked:—100% Acrylic." After considering the insistent rigidity of the law and usage of bank credits and acceptances, we must differ with the District Judge and uphold Bank's position.

The letter of credit prescribed the terms of the drafts as follows:

> "Drafts to be dated same as Bills of Lading. Draft(s) to be accompanied by:

"1. Commercial invoice in triplicate stating that it covers 100,000 lbs. 100% Acrylic Yarn, Package Dyed at $1.35 per lb., FOB Buyers Plant, Greensboro, North Carolina Land Duty Paid.

"2. Certificate stating goods will be delivered to buyers plant land duty paid.

"3. Inland Bill of Lading consigned to Adastra Knitting Mills, Inc. evidencing shipment from East Coast Port to Adastra Knitting Mills, Inc., Greensboro, North Carolina."

The shipment (the last) with which this case is concerned was made on or about August 8, 1973. On direction of Courtaulds bills of lading of that date were prepared for the consignment to Adastra from a bonded warehouse by motor carrier. The yarn was packaged in cartons and a packing list referring to its bill of lading accompanied each carton. After the yarn was delivered to the carrier, each bill of lading with the packing list was sent to Courtaulds. There invoices for the sales were made out, and the invoices and packing lists stapled together. At the same time, Courtaulds wrote up the certificate, credit memorandum and draft called for in the letter of credit. The draft was dated August 13, 1973 and drawn on Bank by Courtaulds payable to itself.

All of these documents—the draft, the invoices and the packing lists—were sent by Courtaulds to its correspondent in Mobile for presentation to Bank and collection of the draft which for the purpose had been endorsed to the correspondent.

This was the procedure pursued on each of the prior drafts and always the draft had been honored by Bank save in the present instance. Here the draft, endorsed to Bank, and the other papers were sent to Bank on August 14. Bank received them on Thursday, August 16. Upon processing, Bank found these discrepancies between the drafts with accompanying documents and the letter of credit: (1) that the invoice did not state "100% Acrylic Yarn" but described it as "Imported Acrylic Yarn," and (2) "Draft not drawn as per terms of [letter of credit], Date [August 13] not same as Bill of Lading [August 8] and not drawn 60 days after date" [but 60 days from Bill of Lading date 8/8/73]. Finding of fact 24. Since decision of this controversy is put on the first discrepancy we do not discuss the others.

On Monday, August 20, Bank called Adastra and asked if it would waive the discrepancies and thus allow Bank to honor the draft. In response, the president of Adastra informed Bank that it could not waive any discrepancies because a trustee in bankruptcy had been appointed for Adastra and Adastra could not do so alone. Upon word of these circumstances, Courtaulds on August 27 sent amended invoices to Bank which were received by Bank on August 27. They referred to the consignment as "100% Acrylic Yarn", and thus would have conformed to the letter of credit had it not expired. On August 29 Bank wired Courtaulds that the draft remained unaccepted because of the expiration of the letter of credit on August 15. Consequently the draft with all the original documents was returned by Bank.

During the life of the letter of credit some drafts had not been of even dates with the bills of lading, and among the large number of invoices transmitted during this period, several did not describe the goods as "100% Acrylic Yarn." As to all of these deficiencies Bank called Adastra for and received approval before paying the drafts. Every draft save the one in suit was accepted.

Conclusion of Law

The factual outline related is not in dispute, and the issue becomes one of law. It is well phrased by the District Judge in his "Discussion" in this way:

> "The only issue presented by the facts of this case is whether the documents tendered by the beneficiary to the issuer were in conformity with the terms of the letter of credit."

The letter of credit provided:

> "Except as otherwise expressly stated herein, this credit is subject to the 'Uniform Customs and Practice for Documentary Credits (1962 revision), the International Chamber of Commerce, Brochure No. 222'." Finding of fact 6.

Of particular pertinence, with accents added, are these injunctions of the Uniform Customs:

> "Article 7.—Banks must examine all documents with reasonable care to ascertain that they *appear on their face* to be in accordance with the terms and conditions of the credit."
>
> "Article 8.—In documentary credit operations all parties concerned deal in documents and not in goods.
>
> * * *
>
> "If, upon receipt of the documents, the issuing bank considers that they *appear on their face* not to be in accordance with the terms and conditions of the credit, that bank must determine, on the basis of the documents alone, whether to claim that payment, acceptance or negotiation was not effected in accordance with the terms and conditions of the credit."
>
> * * *
>
> "Article 9.—Banks * * * do [not] assume any liability or responsibility *for the description,* * * * quality, * * * of the goods represented thereby * * *"
>
> * * *
>
> "The description of the goods in the commercial *invoice* must correspond with the description in the credit. *In the remaining documents the goods may be described in general terms.*"

Also to be looked to are the North Carolina statutes, because in a diversity action, the Federal courts apply the same law as would the courts of the State of adjudication. Here applied would be the Uniform Commercial Code—Letters of Credit, Chap. 25 G.S.N.C. Especially to be noticed are these sections:

"§ 25-5-109. Issuer's obligation to its customer.—

"(1) An issuer's obligation to its customer includes good faith and observance of any general banking usage but unless otherwise agreed does not include liability or responsibility

"(a) for performance of the underlying contract for sale or other transaction between the customer and the beneficiary; or

* * *

"(c) based on knowledge or lack of knowledge of any usage of any particular trade.

"(2) An issuer must examine documents with care so as to ascertain that on their face they appear to comply with the terms of the credit but unless otherwise agreed assumes no liability or responsibility for the genuineness, falsification or effect of any document which appears on such examination to be regular on its face."

In utilizing the rules of construction embodied in the letter of credit—the Uniform Customs and state statute—one must constantly recall that the drawee bank is not to be embroiled in disputes between the buyer and the seller, the beneficiary of the credit. The drawee is involved only with documents, not with merchandise. Its involvement is altogether separate and apart from the transaction between the buyer and seller; its duties and liability are governed exclusively by the terms of the letter, not the terms of the parties' contract with each other. Moreover, as the predominant authorities unequivocally declare, the beneficiary must meet the terms of the credit—and precisely—if it is to exact performance of the issuer. Failing such compliance there can be no recovery from the drawee. That is the specific failure of Courtaulds here.

Free of ineptness in wording the letter of credit dictated that each invoice express on its face that it covered 100% acrylic yarn. Nothing less is shown to be tolerated in the trade. No substitution and no equivalent, through interpretation or logic, will serve. Harfield, Bank Credits and Acceptances (5th Ed.1974), at p. 73, commends and quotes aptly from an English case: "There is no room for documents which are almost the same, or which will do just as well." Equitable Trust Co. of N.Y. v. Dawson Partners, Ltd., 27 Lloyd's List Law Rpts. 49, 52 (1926). Although no pertinent North Carolina decision has been laid before us, in many cases elsewhere, especially in New York, we find the tenet of Harfield to be unshaken.

At trial Courtaulds prevailed on the contention that the invoices in actuality met the specifications of the letter of credit in that the packing lists attached to the invoices disclosed on their faces that the packages contained "cartons marked:—100% acrylic". On this premise it was urged that the lists were a part of the invoice since they were appended to it, and the invoices should be read as one with the lists, allowing the lists to detail the invoices. But this argument cannot be accepted. In this connection it is well to revert to the distinction made in Uniform Customs, supra, between the "invoice" and the "remaining documents", emphasizing that in the latter the description may be in general terms while in the invoice the goods must be described in conformity with the credit letter.

The District Judge's pat statement adeptly puts an end to this contention of Courtaulds:

> "In dealing with letters of credit, it is a custom and practice of the banking trade for a bank to only treat a document as an invoice which clearly is marked on its face as 'invoice' ". Finding of fact 46.

This is not a pharisaical or doctrinaire persistence in the principle, but is altogether realistic in the environs of this case; it is plainly the fair and equitable measure. (The defect in description was not superficial but occurred in the statement of the *quality* of the yarn, not a frivolous concern.) The obligation of the drawee bank was graven in the credit. Indeed, there could be no departure from its words. Bank was not expected to scrutinize the collateral papers, such as the packing lists. Nor was it permitted to read into the instrument the contemplation or intention of the seller and buyer. Adherence to this rule was not only legally commanded, but it was factually ordered also, as will immediately appear.

Had Bank deviated from the stipulation of the letter and honored the draft, then at once it might have been confronted with the not improbable risk of the bankruptcy trustee's charge of liability for unwarrantably paying the draft moneys to the seller, Courtaulds, and refusal to reimburse Bank for the outlay. Contrarily, it might face a Courtaulds claim that since it had depended upon Bank's assurance of credit in shipping yarn to Adastra, Bank was responsible for the loss. In this situation Bank cannot be condemned for sticking to the letter of the letter.

Nor is this conclusion affected by the amended or substituted invoices which Courtaulds sent to Bank after the refusal of the draft. No precedent is cited to justify retroactive amendment of the invoices or extension of the credit beyond the August 15 expiry of the letter.

Finally, the trial court found that although in its prior practices Bank had pursued a strict-constructionist attitude, it had nevertheless on occasion honored drafts not within the verbatim terms of the credit letter. But it also found that in each of these instances Bank had first procured the authorization of Adastra to overlook the deficiencies. This truth is verified by the District Court in its Findings of Fact:

> "42. It is a standard practice and procedure of the banking industry and trade for a bank to attempt to obtain a waiver of discrepancies from its customer in a letter of credit transaction. This custom and practice was followed by NCNB in connection with the draft and documents received from Courtaulds.
>
> "43. Following this practice, NCNB had checked all previous discrepancies it discovered in Courtaulds' documents with its customer Adastra to see if Adastra would waive those discrepancies noted by NCNB. Except for the transaction in question, Adastra waived all discrepancies noted by NCNB.
>
> "44. It is not normal or customary for NCNB, nor is it the custom and practice in the banking trade, for a bank to notify a beneficiary or the presenter of the documents that there were any deficiencies in the draft or documents if they are waived by the customer."

This endeavor had been fruitless on the last draft because of the inability of Adastra to give its consent. Obviously, the previous acceptances of truant invoices cannot be construed as a waiver in the present incident.

For these reasons, we must vacate the decision of the trial court, despite the evident close reasoning and research of the District Judge, Courtaulds North America, Inc. v. North Carolina N.B., 387 F.Supp. 92 (M.D.N.C.1975). Entry of judgment in favor of the appellant Bank on its summary motion is necessary.

Reversed and remanded for final judgment.

Notes

1. The two cases set out above are commonly claimed to be in conflict. Applying the Uniform Customs and Practices to the two of them, can their holdings be read as consistent?

2. Assuming that their holdings are inconsistent and that Judge Coffin is truly espousing a less strict standard of interpretation, who is right and what policies are at issue?

The doctrines of estoppel and waiver found in the common law and those of indemnity and warranties set out in Article 5 offer, in the words of Judge Coffin, some "leaven" for the loaf. On the one hand they accommodate the practical necessity of paying in certain circumstances against documents that are not adequate. On the other hand they give some room for a court's requiring or approving deviation from the strict standards.

MARINO INDUSTRIES CORP. v. CHASE MANHATTAN BANK, N.A.

United States Court of Appeals, Second Circuit, 1982.
686 F.2d 112.

FRIEDMAN, CHIEF JUDGE, UNITED STATES COURT OF CLAIMS. This is an appeal from a judgment of the United States District Court for the Eastern District of New York entered upon the opinion of United States Magistrate John L. Caden dismissing, after trial, a suit seeking recovery under two letters of credit that the defendant, Chase Manhattan Bank ("Chase"), issued to the plaintiff, Marino Industries Corp. ("Marino"). The magistrate held that Chase justifiably refused to pay under the letters because Marino had not complied with the requirements in the letters for obtaining payment. We affirm in part, reverse in part, and remand for further proceedings.

I.

The dispute grew out of a contract under which Marino, a manufacturer of construction materials, agreed with Bautechnik GmbH, a German company, to ship material to a job site in Kassim, Saudi Arabia. At Bautechnik's request, the Berliner Bank in West Germany issued two similar irrevocable letters of credit in favor of Marino. Chase confirmed the letters. One letter was for $212,456.48, and the other was for $489,956.41. Both letters explicitly were subject to the Uniform Customs and Practice for Documentary Credits (1974 Revision), International Chamber of Commerce Publication No. 290, which, under New York laws, supersedes the Uniform Commercial Code. N.Y.U.C.C.L. § 5–102(4) (McKinney 1964).

Each letter was to be paid in two installments: 40 percent when the goods were shipped and 60 percent when they were received. The letters contained detailed requirements that Marino was required to follow to obtain payment. Marino shipped all the goods to Saudi Arabia. After Bautechnik went bankrupt in late November or early December 1980, Chase refused to pay three of Marino's drafts under the letters, on the ground that Marino had not complied with the requirements for payment.

The complaint, filed in the district court after the suit had been transferred from the New York State Supreme Court where it originally had been filed, contains two counts. Count I seeks recovery of $99,083.80 for Chase's refusal to pay the plaintiff's draft for that amount under the first letter of credit. Count II seeks $270,779.84 for Chase's refusal to make payments of $46,388.00 and $224,391.84 under the second letter. Both parties agreed to a trial before a United States Magistrate.

After trial, the magistrate dismissed the complaint. He held that with respect to each of the three payments Chase refused to make, Marino had not complied with the requirements for payment in the letter. The magistrate rendered a comprehensive opinion discussing in detail the various respects in which he found that Marino had not complied, and made findings of fact and conclusions of law. Marino has appealed from the judgment dismissing the complaint, and Chase has cross-appealed from the magistrate's resolution of one subsidiary issue against Chase.

* * *

III.

Chase refused to pay three different drafts on the two letters that Marino presented. Since each refusal was made for different reasons, we discuss each claim separately. In determining whether Chase's refusal to pay was justified, we are guided by and apply the general principles governing letters of credit just summarized.

A. The $99,000 Claim

The first claim was for $99,083.80. It was made under the 60 percent portion of the first letter of credit, i.e., Marino sought payment from Chase after the goods had been received in Saudi Arabia.

To obtain payment Marino was required to submit a certificate that the goods had been inspected prior to shipment and a certificate that the goods had been received. The letters specified precisely what these certificates were required to state. As extended, the letter of credit expired on Monday, December 1, 1980. This meant that to obtain payment Marino was required to submit by that date certificates that conformed to the requirements in the letter.

1. Marino submitted the inspection certificates on October 15, 1980. On October 17, a Chase employee prepared a discrepancy sheet covering the

certificates, which noted various respects in which they did not comply with the requirements in the letter. One of the defects noted was that the certificates did not include copies of the invoices for the shipped goods. The discrepancy sheet contains handwritten comments based upon phone conversations with Marino. The record does not show when these comments were written or which of the deficiencies Chase called to Marino's attention.

On December 2, 1980, the day after the letter had expired, Chase returned the inspection certificates to Marino because the bank was "not able to utilize" them. An accompanying memorandum stated that Chase had "contacted Miss Cinthya [apparently a Marino employee] on the phone several times." It requested Marino: "Please complete requirement of L/C and send documents to us complete." On December 8, Marino resubmitted the inspection certificates to Chase.

2. The letter of credit required the certificates of receipt to be "signed by [a] Midica [sic] [Mdica was the joint venture in Saudi Arabia] representative confirming the arrival of the material on job site Kassim." An amendment to the letter of credit provided that in lieu of a Mdica signature, the notarized signature of the freight forwarder, Zuest & Bachmeier Ag., would be accepted. Berliner Bank had sent to Chase three signature samples of Mdica representatives acceptable to it. Chase never told Marino that only those three signatures would be acceptable or that other signatures would be acceptable if they identified the signer as a Mdica representative (as a Chase representative testified at trial).

On Wednesday, November 26, 1980, a Marino representative, Mr. DeWeil, delivered the certificates of receipt to Pacifico Bautista in Chase's Letter of Credit Department. According to the magistrate, "Mr. Bautista refused to accept the certificates of receipt because they did not contain an authorized signature. * * * In order to rectify the absence of an authorized signature, Mr. Bautista told Mr. DeWeil to have the certificates of receipt countersigned by an officer of the international freight forwarding company, Zuat Bachmeier." Mr. DeWeil had the certificates countersigned about 5 p.m., that day, but because it was then too late to return them to the bank, he took the certificates to Marino's office on Long Island.

Mr. Pagano, Marino's vice president in charge of exporting, testified that on Monday, December 1 (the date on which the letter expired), he told Mr. Bautista on the telephone that he had six countersigned certificates of receipt and asked Mr. Bautista when he should bring them in. According to Mr. Pagano, Mr. Bautista "decided that I could send them the following day and hopefully that we would get paid as soon as possible." On cross-examination Mr. Pagano stated that the expiration date of the letter had not been mentioned. Mr. Pagano mailed the certificates of receipt the following day (December 2).

On December 8, Chase informed Marino that it would not make payment because proper certificates had not been timely presented. On December 10 and 12, Chase, with Marino's approval, cabled the Berliner Bank, stated that payment had not been made "due to late presentation" and asked, "May we pay[?]" Berliner Bank cabled back "Do not pay * * * as presented too late." Berliner Bank also rejected a third cabled request from Chase for permission to pay.

3. The magistrate held that Marino had not made a timely presentation of the necessary documents and that Chase had not waived the requirement of timely presentation. He apparently accepted Chase's evidence that bringing documents to the bank and taking them back to have them countersigned, as happened on November 26, "is not a presentation of documents." The magistrate stated that documentary evidence showed that "a full set of documents was not received by Chase until December 8, 1980—eight days after the expiration of the letter of credit on November 30, 1980" and that "[i]n the face of such documentary proof, it is unrealistic to give credence to plaintiff's assertion that there was a timely presentation of conforming documents."

In holding that Chase had not waived the timely presentation requirement, the magistrate pointed to Pagano's admission that neither in his telephone conversation of December 1, 1980, with Mr. Bautista nor in a subsequent meeting with Ms. Soula Stephanides of Chase, at which Marino contended Chase also had waived timely presentation, was it mentioned that the letter had expired. The magistrate further ruled that Chase's cabled requests to the Berliner Bank to make late payment were not waivers but merely were "a courtesy to plaintiff."

4. As we have noted, an important corollary of the strict compliance rule is that the letter of credit must specify precisely and clearly the requirements for payment and that ambiguities in the letter are to be resolved against the bank. Nothing in the letter in this case indicated that the requirement that the certificates of receipt be "signed by [a] Mdica representative" could be satisfied only if one of the three acceptable signatures that Berliner Bank had submitted to Chase was affixed. If that was a condition of payment, Chase was required so to inform Marino. Sun Bank, 609 F.2d at 833; 34 N.Y.Jur. Letters of Credit § 13 at 431 (1964). Similarly, if Chase would accept signatures of other Mdica representatives provided they were expressly identified as such, as Chase's representative testified at trial, Chase also was required to inform Marino of that condition of payment.

The magistrate did not determine whether the signature on the certificates was that of a Mdica representative. On the remand that we order, the magistrate should determine that fact. If the answer is affirmative, Marino made a timely presentation of the certificates of receipt (on November 26) that complied with the requirements in the letter.

Even if Marino had not made a timely presentation on November 26, there is the question whether Chase waived the time limit when, according to Mr. Pagano, Mr. Bautista, on December 1, 1980, authorized Mr. Pagano to submit the documents after that date. The fact that neither Pagano nor Bautista referred to the expiration date of the bill in that conversation is not necessarily dispositive of the question, although it is significant. The magistrate did not determine whether Mr. Bautista had authority to make such a commitment. It would seem, however, that Mr. Bautista had at least apparent authority to do so, upon which Marino's representative was justified in relying.

5. If Marino made a timely presentation of proper certificates of receipt or if Chase waived the time limit, Marino still was not entitled to payment unless it also timely presented certificates of inspection. As noted, Marino

supplied those certificates to Chase on October 15, well in advance of the expiration date of the letter.

Chase's initial inspection of those certificates revealed what Chase believed to be various defects, including the failure to include with the certificates copies of the invoices for the goods. The record does not show, however, whether at that time Chase called these alleged deficiencies to Marino's attention. When Chase finally returned the invoices to Marino for correction on December 2, 1980, the letter had expired.

The letter of credit required Marino to submit

"[c]lean inspection certificate, 4 copies, issued by superintendent-company acting in conformity with the regulations of S.G.S. (Societe Generale de Surveillance) stating the full compliance of the quantities and qualities of the goods with the specifications, the commercial invoice and the instructions given by Dietrich Garski Bautechnik KG, Berlin."

This is somewhat ambiguous. It is unclear whether Marino was required to submit a single inspection certificate stating that the goods complied with the three conditions, or to submit separately the certificates, the invoices and the instructions. In light of the obvious purpose of the requirement to insure that the goods shipped were as ordered, the most reasonable reading of the provision is that Marino was required to submit a single certificate stating that the "quantities and qualities of the goods" complied with "[i] the specifications, [ii] the commercial invoices, and [iii] the instructions given by" Bautechnik (the purchaser). The magistrate did not determine whether the certificates Marino submitted complied with this requirement.

A further problem with respect to the certificates of inspection is presented by the fact that Chase waited a month-and-a-half before returning them to Marino for correction. Under article 8(d) of the Uniform Customs & Practice for Documentary Credits, Chase had "a reasonable time" within which to examine the documentation. See N.Y.U.C.C. § 5–112(1)(a) (giving banks three banking days). If Chase had returned the certificates promptly, Marino would have had ample time to correct any deficiencies. By not returning the certificates until after the letter had expired, Chase made it impossible for Marino to correct any deficiencies and still make timely presentation. Cf. Barclays Bank D.C.O. v. Mercantile National Bank, 481 F.2d 1224, 1236 (5th Cir.1973), cert. dismissed, 414 U.S. 1139 (1974) (when bank says documents conform, it cannot then deny conformity after expiration). There is a question, therefore, whether Chase is estopped from relying upon defects in the certificates of inspection as a justification for refusing payment.

6. We therefore conclude that we cannot affirm the magistrate's dismissal of the $99,000 claim. The portion of the judgment that dismissed that claim is reversed, and this portion of the case is remanded to the magistrate for further proceedings in accordance with this opinion.

* * *

Conclusion

The judgment of the United States District Court for the Eastern District of New York is affirmed in part and reversed in part, and the case is remanded to it for further proceedings before the magistrate on the $99,000 claim in accordance with this opinion.

Problem 24–2

Chase was the beneficiary of a letter of credit issued by Equibank in Pittsburgh. The letter provided that Chase (the "take out" lender on a construction contract) had a right to draw upon Equibank if the underlying debtor failed to complete the loan transaction. Equibank was the interim lender to the developer. The developer failed to carry out the construction on time and on April 30 Chase sent (1) a certification "that [developer] has defaulted and the default has not been cured" and (2) a demand for payment of $108,000.

The letter of credit expired on April 30, 1973. In the afternoon of April 30 a representative of Chase had a phone conversation with a representative of Equibank. The Chase employee stated that the Equibank employee agreed that the document could be forwarded through "domestic collections." Because such collections take several days, the demand did not arrive in Pittsburgh until late in the first week of May when it was rejected on the ground the letter of credit had expired on April 30.

1. Can Chase win on the ground of estoppel?

2. Can it win on the ground of waiver?

3. Would it matter that only three hours intervened between the expiration of the letter on April 30 and the phone conversation?

4. On behalf of Chase can you use UCC 2–209?

Problem 24–3

Assume that Citicorp has issued a letter of credit that will expire December 21, 1995. Assume in all of the following cases alternatively that a statute of the kind quoted below or the quoted UCP provision applies.

1. On November 26 beneficiary presents its documents. The documents are defective and that fact is discovered by inspection by the bank on November 26. The bank returns the documents and dishonors on December 2.

   a. Would it matter that the defect was on an invoice (where the defect could have been cured by the beneficiary's preparation of a new invoice), or in a bill of lading (where the beneficiary would not have been able to get a new bill of lading because the goods had already been shipped).

   b. Would the case be any different if the presentment had been made on December 21 and the dishonor had occurred on December 27 after the expiration date? (Assume in both cases that the issuer gave no statement for the basis of dishonor.)

2. What if the beneficiary had omitted one of the five documents required when it made its presentment on December 20. Could the bank simply return the documents after the expiration date without an explanation?

3. Assume now that the documents were submitted not to Citicorp, but to First Chicago. Assume alternatively (a) that First Chicago was a confirmer or (b) a bank identified in Citicorp's letter as a "negotiating bank." Would First Chicago have the same obligations to give notice of defects as Citicorp would have? If First Chicago paid over defective documents where it was (a) a confirmer or (b) a negotiating bank, would it have a right to payment from Citicorp?

SECTION 5–109. EXAMINATION, NOTICE, AND PRECLUSION.

(a) Unless a different period is specified by a letter of credit or by agreement between the beneficiary and the issuer and except as otherwise provided in Section 5–113, an issuer has a reasonable time, but not beyond the close of the seventh banking day after receipt of documents submitted under the letter of credit, to determine whether to honor. Unless the issuer has either paid, accepted, or made an unconditional commitment to pay within the time permitted by this section, it has dishonored.

(b) If an issuer decides to dishonor, it shall give notice to the presenter without delay and by expeditious means. The notice must state all discrepancies in the documents or tender on which the dishonor is based. The issuer is precluded from asserting as a basis for dishonor any discrepancy not stated in the notice. Except as otherwise provided in subsection (c), failure to give timely notice precludes the issuer from asserting a discrepancy in the tender or the documents.

(c) Failure to comply with the requirements of subsection (b) does not preclude the issuer from asserting as a basis for dishonor that the beneficiary has presented documents that it knows to be forged or materially fraudulent or that the letter of credit expired before presentment.

(d) Upon dishonor, unless otherwise instructed, the issuer shall either return the documents to the presenter or hold them at the disposal of the presenter and send the presenter an advice to that effect.

(e) Neither the issuer's duties in subsection (b) nor the issuer's preclusion in subsection (b) may be varied by agreement.

Article 14 of UCP 500

Article 14. Discrepant Documents and Notice

a. Where the Issuing Bank authorizes another bank to pay, incur a deferred payment undertaking, accept Draft(s), or negotiate against documents which appear on their face to be in compliance with the terms and conditions of the Credit, *the Issuing Bank and the Confirming Bank, if any, are bound:*
   i. to reimburse the bank which has paid, incurred a deferred payment undertaking, accepted Drafts, or negotiated,
   ii. to take up the documents.
b. Upon receipt of the documents the Issuing Bank or Confirming Bank, if any, [or a Nominated Bank acting on their behalf,] must determine on the basis of the documents alone whether they appear on their face to be in compliance with the terms and conditions of the Credit. If the documents appear on their face not to be in compliance with the terms and conditions of the Credit such banks may refuse to take up the documents.
c. If the Issuing Bank determines that the documents on their face are not in compliance with the terms and conditions of the Credit it may in its sole judgment approach the Applicant for a waiver of the discrepancies. This does not, however, extend the period mentioned in Article 13(b).
d. i. If the Issuing Bank or Confirming Bank, if any, [or a Nominated Bank acting on their behalf,] decides to refuse the documents, it must give notice to that effect by telecommunication or, if that is

not possible, by other expeditious means, no later than the close of the seventh banking day following the day of receipt of the documents. Notice shall be given to the bank from which it received the documents (the "Remitting Bank"), or to the Beneficiary, if it received the documents directly from him.

ii. Such notice must state all discrepancies in respect of which the bank refuses the documents and must also state whether it is holding the documents at the disposal of, or is returning them to, the presenter.

iii. The Issuing Bank or Confirming Bank, if any, shall then be entitled to claim from the Remitting Bank a refund, with interest, or any reimbursement which has been made to that bank.

e. If the Issuing Bank and/or Confirming Bank, if any, fail to act in accordance with the provisions of this article and/or fail to hold the documents at the disposal of, or return them to the presenter, the Issuing Bank and/or the Confirming Bank, if any, shall be precluded from claiming that the documents are not in compliance with the terms and conditions of the Credit;

f. If the Remitting Bank draws the attention of the Issuing or Confirming Bank, if any, to any discrepancies in the documents or advises such banks that it has paid, incurred a deferred payment undertaking, accepted Draft(s) or negotiated under reserve or against an indemnity in respect of such discrepancies, the Issuing or Confirming Bank, if any, shall not be thereby relieved from any of their obligations under any provision of this article. Such reserve or indemnity concerns only the relations between the Remitting Bank and the party towards whom the reserve was made, or from whom, or on whose behalf, the indemnity was obtained.

MANUFACTURERS HANOVER INTERNATIONAL BANKING CORP. v. SPRING TREE CORPORATION

United States District Court, District of Massachusetts, 1990.
752 F.Supp. 522.

McNaught, District Judge.

This matter comes before the Court on plaintiff's and defendant's cross motions for summary judgment on Counts I and II of the Complaint in accordance with Fed.R.Civ.P., Rule 56(c).

The underlying lawsuit involves a dispute regarding an international letter of credit transaction. In May, 1988, the defendant, a Vermont corporation, contracted to sell cocoa to Summer Commodities Trading Limited, a Hong Kong organization. The Hua Chiao Commercial Bank Ltd. of Hong Kong ("HCCB") issued the letter of credit in dispute which provides that Citibank will be the advising bank. At defendant's request, plaintiff agreed to act as negotiating bank.

After final shipment, defendant delivered a draft to plaintiff for the full amount of the letter of credit, along with the required supporting documents. Subsequently plaintiff transmitted the documents to HCCB, allegedly disclaiming any responsibility for their validity or accuracy. Upon receipt of reimbursement from Citibank, plaintiff issued a check for $81,886.69 to defendant. HCCB, the issuing bank, refused to accept the documents claiming that they did not conform exactly to the terms of the letter of credit and declined to reimburse plaintiff. In turn, plaintiff so notified defendant and requested return of the advanced proceeds.

The issue before the Court is whether plaintiff negotiating bank or defendant beneficiary should bear the financial cost of a Letter of Credit dispute. Pursuant to U.C.C. § 5–111, plaintiff had the right to rely on defendant's warranty that the documents defendant submitted were in compliance with the requirements stated in the Letter of Credit. As negotiating bank, plaintiff has recourse against defendant beneficiary for proceeds advanced to the beneficiary, where the issuing bank dishonored the draft because of defects in the supporting documents. Defendant must reimburse the proceeds advanced by plaintiff, notwithstanding any dispute between the issuing bank and defendant as to whether issuing bank's dishonor was proper. *Delta Brands Inc. v. Mbank Dallas N.A.,* 3 U.C.C.Rep.Serv.2d 1099, 1101–02, 719 S.W.2d 355 (Tex.App.1986); *First Nat'l City Bank v. Klatzer,* 28 U.C.C.Rep.Serv. 497, 498 (N.Y.Sup.Ct.1979).

For the foregoing reasons the plaintiff's motion for summary judgment on Counts I and II of the Complaint is granted and, the defendant's motions, are hereby denied.

PHILADELPHIA GEAR CORPORATION v. CENTRAL BANK

United States Circuit Court, Fifth Circuit, 1983.
717 F.2d 230.

GEE, CIRCUIT JUDGE:

The terrain of the present appeal is a failed business transaction, one that culminated in several and mutual allegations of failure to honor contractual obligations. The contract at issue is a documentary letter of credit.[1] The district court determined that the issuing bank wrongfully dishonored drafts presented pursuant to the letter of credit. In consequence, it ordered the issuer to pay the face value of all drafts presented. Because we conclude that the district court did not strike the correct balance between the parties' competing duties and obligations, we reverse its judgment.

BACKGROUND

On April 23, 1981, Central Bank, appellant, issued a document entitled "Irrevocable Commercial Letter of Credit No. 02408" in the amount of 4.5 million dollars (hereinafter "credit" or "letter of credit"). The credit was issued on behalf of Central's customer United Machinery Services, Inc. ("United") in favor of Philadelphia Gear Corporation ("Philadelphia") as beneficiary. The record reflects that the credit was issued to support Central's obligations to Philadelphia under a sale of goods contract. By its

1. "A 'documentary draft' or a 'documentary demand for payment' is one honor of which is conditioned upon the presentation of a document or documents. 'Document' means any paper including document of title, security, invoice, certificate, notice of default and the like." La.R.S. 10:5–103(1)(b).

terms, the credit could accommodate individual drafts in maximum amounts of 75 thousand dollars; thereafter to be automatically reinstated to a limit of 4.5 million dollars. Each draft presented pursuant to the credit was required to bear the notation: "DRAWN UNDER LETTER OF CREDIT OF CENTRAL BANK." The record also reveals that each draft was to be accompanied by a copy of the credit. In addition, payment was conditioned upon presentation by Philadelphia's intermediary, Provident National Bank of Philadelphia ("Provident"), of an "inland bill of lading evidencing shipment of any of the above described units to United Machinery, Inc." Contrary to this provision, the credit did not specify the exact nature of the goods to be delivered. More, the credit was expressly subject to the Uniform Customs and Practices for Commercial Documentary Credits fixed by the Thirteenth Congress of the International Chamber of Commerce (1974 Revision Publication 290) (hereinafter "I.C.C. Pub. 290").

Sometime during the latter half of 1981 relations between United and Philadelphia soured. United refused to pay for goods which it claimed were not ordered; and Philadelphia, in contradiction, demanded payment—maintaining that the goods were delivered pursuant to contractual agreement. As a result of this dispute Philadelphia, through Provident, tendered six drafts on the letter of credit in late December of 1981. Several days later Central decided that it would not pay the drafts and returned them to Provident with notice to that effect. The notice stated that the drafts were being returned "due to their non-compliance with the terms of the relevant credit." In early January of 1982 Philadelphia tendered three additional drafts on the credit. Again Central refused to pay, in each case citing as its reason general noncompliance with the credit's terms. Undeterred, Philadelphia wired Central requesting a more definite statement of Central's reasons. Central responded that "[t]he reasons for dishonor are as previously stated."

Oblivious to the manifest logic of Central's position, on February 10, 1982, Philadelphia instituted this diversity action for breach of contract in the Western District of Louisiana. Specifically, Philadelphia sought a declaratory judgment that the drafts were payable under the credit, damages for wrongful dishonor, and—because the credit remained a valid contractual obligation—a preliminary and permanent injunction ordering that future drafts be timely paid. Without result the district court attempted to reconcile the parties' differences at pretrial conference. By this time Philadelphia had been made aware of the exact defect in each of the drafts previously tendered. On the eve of trial Philadelphia presented to Central eleven additional drafts with supporting documentation. These were placed in the registry of the court. The record also reflects that throughout trial Philadelphia presented additional drafts; each was placed in the registry.

At the conclusion of all the evidence the district court found: (1) Each of Philadelphia's tendered drafts failed in some respect to conform to the letter of credit; (2) all the defects were curable; (3) some of the deficiencies were known to agents of Philadelphia and Provident; and (4) Central neither returned the supporting documentation to Philadelphia's drafts (submitted before institution of suit) nor informed Philadelphia that it would hold the documentation on file for its inspection. Applying to these findings what it perceived to be the relevant statutory and case law, the district court determined that Central was liable for the face value of all drafts presented and entered judgment in a corresponding amount. Central now appeals that judgment.

RELEVANT STANDARD

Because the resolution of all other issues flows from its determination, the crucial issue of this appeal is whether the district court struck the proper balance between the parties' competing duties and obligations under the credit. We conclude that it did not. The district court characterized the present case as an action for wrongful dishonor. So doing, it relied extensively on the following provisions of the Louisiana Uniform Commercial Code (hereinafter the "Code") and I.C.C. Pub. 290:

Time allowed for honor or rejection; withholding honor or rejection by consent; presenter

(1) A bank to which a documentary draft or demand for payment is presented under a credit may without dishonor of the draft of credit

(a) defer honor until the close of the third banking day following receipt of the document; and

(b) further defer honor if the presenter has expressly or impliedly consented thereto.

Failure to honor within the time here specified constitutes dishonor of the draft or demand and of the credit.

(2) Upon dishonor the bank may unless otherwise instructed fulfill its duty to return the draft or demand and the documents by holding them at the disposal of the presenter and sending him an advice to that effect.

(3) "Presenter" means any person presenting a draft or demand for payment for honor under a credit even though that person is a confirming bank or other correspondent which is acting under an issuer's authorization.

La.R.S. 10:5–112.

(c) If, upon receipt of the documents, the issuing bank considers that they appear on their face not to be in accordance with the terms and conditions of the credit, that bank must determine, on the basis of the documents alone, whether to claim that payment, acceptance or negotiation was not effected in accordance with the terms and conditions of the credit.

(d) The issuing bank shall have a reasonable time to examine the documents and to determine as above whether to make such a claim.

(e) If such claim is to be made, notice to that effect, stating the reasons therefor, must, without delay, be given by cable or other expeditious means to the bank from which the documents have been received (the remitting bank) and such notice must state that the documents are being held at the disposal of such bank or are being returned thereto.

(f) If the issuing bank fails to hold the documents at the disposal of the remitting bank, or fails to return the documents to such bank, the issuing bank shall be precluded from claiming that the relative payment, acceptance or negotiation was not effected in accordance with the terms and conditions of the credit.

I.C.C. Pub. 290 art. 8(c)–(f).

Against the background of these provisions, the district court first reasoned that at all times pertinent to the present case Provident was a presenter as defined by La.R.S. 10:5–112 and a remitting bank as defined by article 8(e) of I.C.C. Pub. 290. In consequence, Central was obliged to inform Provident of the precise reasons it considered the tendered documents to be non-conforming. *See* I.C.C. Pub. 290, arts. 8(c), (e). Concluding in each instance that Central failed to meet this obligation, the district court determined that Central was estopped to raise the documents' deficiencies as a defense, the requirement of strict compliance with the terms of letters of credit notwithstanding. *Cf. Flagship Cruises, Ltd. v. New England Merchants Nat'l Bank,* 569 F.2d 699 (1st Cir.1978). More, the district court reasoned that estoppel was proper because Central's failure either to return the drafts' supporting documentation or to give notice that it was being held at Provident's disposal violated article 8(f) of I.C.C. Pub. 290, thwarting any attempt to cure the drafts' defects.

While the above analysis is plausible, it is incomplete. The primary flaw in this analysis is its approach to the concept of dishonor in credit transactions. The district court focused upon the duty of the issuer to pay, finding Central's performance wanting in this respect. It appears to us, however, that in the first instance dishonor puts at issue the adequacy of the *beneficiary's* performance under the letter of credit. While the adequacy of that performance must be examined in light of the issuer's corresponding duties, it must always remain the primary focus of analysis. We reach this conclusion by tracing the contours of a credit transaction.

* * *

This doctrine of strict compliance is firmly grounded in commercial reality. In the event payment is made upon presentations that do not conform to the credit, the issuer loses its right to reimbursement from its customer. *See* J. White & R. Summers, Uniform Commercial Code § 18.7 at pp. 742–43 (1972) (hereinafter cited as "J. White & R. Summers"). In this event the beneficiary's debt is satisfied and the customer escapes liability on both the underlying and letter of credit contracts while the issuer incurs a corresponding liability—without defense or recourse. More, the rejection of strict compliance as a doctrine would vitiate the economic value of a credit transaction; for not only would the issuer be compelled to assume the risks of the underlying contract's nonperformance, it would also be required to assume the additional risks of judicial realignment of its obligations under the credit:

> [T]he peculiar values of the letter of credit are (1) that they provide the assurance of payment, (2) that they can provide that assurance in respect to any transaction, and (3) that they are inexpensive. These values will be lost if performance of the letter of credit is to be infected by the nonperformance of the underlying transaction because *when* that happens the letter of credit is not an assurance of payment and because *if* that happens the cost of a letter of credit must include the issuer's problematic litigation expense.

Harfield, The Increasing Domestic Use of the Letter of Credit, 4 Uniform Commercial Code L.J. 251, 257 (1972) (emphasis in original). There can be no wrongful dishonor where the drafts presented are nonconforming and the issuer gives timely and sufficient notice to that effect. *See* La.R.S. 10:5–112, 114. Because it is undisputed that Philadelphia received timely notice of nonpayment, accompanied in each instance by a statement that payment was refused because of Philadelphia's noncompliance with the terms of the credit, our inquiry must focus upon the sufficiency of Central's notice.

Central contends and the district court found that there were substantial irregularities in Philadelphia's first ten presentations. *See supra* note 2. The record reflects that six were accompanied by photocopies of "shipping evidences" or "shipping notices" rather than the required inland bills of lading. In addition, the shipping documents accompanying the first ten presentations were stale. Article 41 of I.C.C. Pub. 290, incorporated by reference into the credit, provides that "[i]f no ... period of time is stipulated in the credit, banks will refuse documents presented to them more than 21 days after the issuance of the Bills of Lading or other shipping documents." The district court found that Philadelphia was aware of "some" of these defects at the time of presentation. With respect to the drafts that Philadelphia knew to be defective, we hold that Central's notice was not deficient and that the district court erred in concluding that it wrongfully dishonored these drafts.

Philadelphia does not seriously dispute the facts we have stated. Instead, it presents a three-tiered argument designed to vitiate their impact. First, it urges that because the shipping documents were stale by virtue of an agreement between it and United, Central was required to seek United's approval prior to dishonor. Next, it contends that the defects were curable because it could have reshipped the goods, generating fresh bills of lading, had Central permitted United to return the shipped merchandise. Finally, Philadelphia urges that Central possessed an unqualified duty to notify it of the precise defects within its drafts and that absent such notice liability must attach. We believe this argument to be without merit.

As noted above, a letter of credit and the underlying contract are completely separate agreements, and the issuer may not use the terms of the underlying transaction as a defense unless the credit expressly incorporates its terms. It follows that an underlying contract may not be used to amplify the terms of a credit not expressly incorporating them. It further follows that because the underlying transaction does not affect the credit, any proof concerning a particular custom or course of dealing between the issuer's customer and the beneficiary within the underlying transaction cannot cure the apparent nonconformity of a required document. *See* La.R.S. 10:5–109. Nor are we persuaded that custom requires an issuer, in every instance, to notify its customer before rejecting nonconforming drafts. We find nothing in the Code or I.C.C. Pub. 290 that warrants such a result.

Louisiana law provides that: "[a] course of dealing between parties and any usage of trade in the vocation or trade in which they are engaged or of which they are or should be aware give particular meaning to and supplement or qualify terms of an agreement." La.R.S. 10:1–205(3). Concomitantly, that law imposes an obligation of good faith in the performance of every contract. *Id.*, 10:1–203. Here it is undisputed that I.C.C. Pub. 290 reflects a codification of accepted banking practice. Article 3(c) of that publication provides that "[an irrevocable letter of credit] can neither be amended nor cancelled without the agreement of all parties thereto." This language is precise in its meaning and requires no interpretation. Because Central has obviously chosen to decline Philadelphia's invitation to modify the credit, the only inquiry is whether good faith—required by the law of Louisiana—imposes a duty beyond both custom and the credit's terms. We believe not. Good faith "means honesty in fact in the conduct or transaction concerned." La.R.S. 10:1–201(9). Nothing in the record suggests that Central acted dishonestly in any aspect of the present transaction. We are not prepared to hold that the timely rejection of a facially nonconforming draft constitutes an act of bad faith. *See Corporacion de Mercadeo Agricola v. Mellon Bank International,* 608 F.2d 43, 49 (2d Cir.1979). Nor are we prepared to lay it down that good faith imposes a duty to rewrite a contract where there is no hint of unconscionability or fraud. We recognize that issuers often consult their customers before rejecting nonconforming drafts submitted under a credit:

> It must not be thought that every instance of alleged noncompliance generates a dispute leading to wrongful dishonor. When doubts arise in the issuer's mind as to whether or not a presentment complies, it is not at all uncommon for the issuer to reach an agreement whereby the customer in effect waives the alleged noncompliance or makes some other adjustment so that the occasion for the beneficiary to assert wrongful dishonor does not arise.

J. White & R. Summers, *supra* § 18.6 at p. 623. Doubtless such a course of action is good commercial etiquette; we cannot, however, require it where the terms of the credit do not.

Appellee's second and third points we treat together, since even assuming that the defects in the documentation submitted to Central were curable, we are unable to conclude that the district court's judgment was correct. To answer these compounded issues we must determine the legal consequences where a beneficiary knowingly submits nonconforming documents. The credit clearly permits the issuer to refuse payment on drafts accompanied by bills of lading more than 21 days old. *See* I.C.C. Pub. 290, article 41. Central refused payment on the ground that each draft failed to comply with the credit and declined to furnish Philadelphia with any amplifying information. At oral argument, Central asserted that the drafts were rejected because the bills of lading were stale. *See supra* note 2. By the district court's analysis, however, although Philadelphia knew at least some of the drafts to be nonconforming when tendered, Central was required to specify its reasons for refusing payment irrespective of Philadelphia's knowledge.

Our reading of the relevant case law and commentaries confirms that at its essence a credit is a peculiar form of executory contract, one whereby the issuer makes a continuing offer to pay upon the beneficiary's performance of the terms and conditions stipulated in the credit. *See* J. White & R. Summers, *supra,* § 18.2 at p. 711–715 (and cases cited there). In consequence, an issuer's obligation to pay is wholly conditioned upon the beneficiary's performance, here, the delivery of specified documents. Further, nonpayment by the issuer gives rise to an action by the beneficiary for breach of contract in which the beneficiary must plead and prove due performance on its part. *Id.* As stated above, due performance may be demonstrated only by a showing of compliance with the credit's terms.

As we have noted above, the Code incorporates a standard of good faith in every contract made pursuant to its injunctions. La.R.S. 10:1–203. That standard requires honesty in fact in the conduct or transaction concerned. *Id.,* 10:1–201(9). Section 10:5–111 of the Code provides that a beneficiary warrants, in presentation, that its drafts conform to the conditions of the credit.[6] By knowingly tendering nonconforming drafts, Philadelphia breached both of these provisions. It would be a strange rule indeed under which a party could tender drafts containing defects of which it knew and yet attain recovery on the ground that it was not advised of them. *See District of Columbia v. Moulton,* 182 U.S. 576, 21 S.Ct. 840, 45 L.Ed. 1237 (1901). For these reasons, we conclude that the district court's judgment was in error regarding those drafts in which the deficiencies were known. We do not hold today that a beneficiary may never prevail where its supporting documentation fails to meet the credit's requirements but only that, upon the present facts, the beneficiary has failed so abysmally in meeting its contractual obligations that no inquiry beyond that failure is required.

We also find little substance in Philadelphia's contention that the present case is best treated as one for injunctive relief. Because a letter of credit transaction deals solely with the payment of monies there can be no argument that no adequate remedy exists at law. *See Productos Carnic S.A. v. Cent. Am. Beef, Etc.,* 621 F.2d 683 (5th Cir.1980). Next, to our reading the Code contemplates judicial intervention only in narrowly proscribed circumstances: (1) where the issuer's customer seeks to enjoin payment, La.R.S. 10:5–114(2)(b), or (2) where the issuer wrongfully cancels or repudiates a credit prior to presentment or a demand for payment, *id.,* 10:5–115(2).[7] In

6. **Warranties on transfer and presentment**

(1) Unless otherwise agreed the beneficiary by transferring or presenting a documentary draft or demand for payment warrants to all interested parties that the necessary conditions of the credit have been complied with. This is in addition to any warranties existing under the law.

(2) Unless otherwise agreed a negotiating, advising, confirming, collecting or issuing bank presenting or transferring a draft or demand for payment under a credit warrants only the matters warranted by a collecting bank under Chapter 4.

La.R.S. 10:5–111.

7. As one commentator has characterized it: '[t]he idiosyncratic character of the letter of credit transaction necessarily minimizes the number of cases in which judicial intervention is appropriate.' Harfield, Letters of Credit at 73 (1979). Our research has revealed no instances of judicial intervention in these transactions absent allegations of fraud. By our reasoning this is in deference to the peculiar inflexibility of a credit transaction and the inability of courts to function as effective referees prior to dishonor or some egregious circumstance in light of the Code's mandate to honor facially complying drafts:

The Code's *general principle* is that the 'issuer must honor a draft or demand for payment that complies with the terms of the relevant credit.' The issuer who refuses payment wrongfully dishonors unless it can show either (1) that the documents presented for payment do not comply with the terms of the relevant credit or (2) that the case falls into an exception to the foregoing general principle.

When does a presentment comply with the terms of the relevant credit? This question is crucial, for the issuer's refusal to pay a complying presentment generally constitutes wrongful dishonor entitling the beneficiary to some remedy. Most of the letter of credit court cases have arisen over whether a particular presentment complied with the terms of the relevant letter of credit. When Article Five was

the former, judicial intervention is predicated upon allegations of fraud and a corresponding fiction. *See Sztejn v. J. Henry Schroder Banking Corp.*, 177 Misc. 719, 31 N.Y.S.2d 631 (Sup.Ct.1941). The fiction provides that although the documents are facially complying, they are in fact noncomplying as a result of the fraud, thus preserving the doctrine that the issuer's duties are defined exclusively by the credit. *See Old Colony Trust Co. v. Lawyers Title and Trust Co.*, 297 F. 152, 158 (5th Cir.1923); *see also* Harfield, Enjoining Credit Transactions, *supra* at 602.

As to the latter circumstance, because the Louisiana court has yet to make its views known, our analysis relies upon the language of the Code:

> When an issuer wrongfully cancels or otherwise repudiates a credit before presentment of a draft or demand for payment drawn under it the beneficiary has the rights of a seller after repudiation by the buyer if he learns of the repudiation in time reasonably to avoid procurement of the required documents. Otherwise the beneficiary has an immediate right of action for wrongful dishonor.

La.R.S. 10:5–115(2). It appears to us that the above language contemplates a factual pattern where a beneficiary is either prevented from performing because of the issuer's wrongful repudiation of a credit or because presentment would be a needless exercise in view of the issuer's past conduct. It follows that a beneficiary must establish a case of wrongful repudiation. And even in so doing, a court could go no further than to compel the issuer to honor the terms of its agreement. Here appellee has submitted no evidence to that end. An issuer is not compelled to rewrite the terms of a credit so as to acquiesce to substantial compliance, if in fact that is our case. The short of the matter is that every one of appellee's drafts was nonconforming. To the extent that appellee had knowledge of this, there can be no argument of wrongful repudiation.

As noted above, the district court found only that Philadelphia knew of "some" of the defects in the presented drafts:

> All drafts submitted to Central by Philadelphia failed to conform to the requirements of the letter of credit in various respects. Some of the deficiencies were known to agents of Philadelphia and Provident. All of these defects were curable.

Our review of the record indicates that the court did not clearly focus on this aspect of the case. In Philadelphia's brief to us, it twice speaks of the "fact" that it knew that the documents accompanying the earlier drafts were stale, and the district court's opinion observes that Philadelphia did not seriously dispute that it knew of defects in all the drafts. Since knowledge of the defects is crucial under our holding, we think the best course is to remand.

being drafted, various individuals urged that it include specific rules on what constitutes compliance with the terms of a letter of credit. Wisely the drafters ignored these urgings. Section 5–114(1) merely requires that issuer honor a draft or demand for payment 'which complies with the terms of the relevant [letter of] credit. . . .' Whether there is compliance in a particular case cannot be soundly dictated in advance by general rules of law, at least if the parties are to have broad freedom of contract to prescribe the particular terms of the letter of credit. But as an alternative, the Code should have specified whether strict compliance is necessary or whether 'substantial performance' will do.

J. White & R. Summers, *supra* § 18–6 at 729 (footnotes omitted).

We do so, directing the district court to determine *which,* rather than *some,* of the presentations contained deficiencies known to the presenter at the time of presentation, and to enter judgment accordingly.

For the reasons stated above, the judgment of the district court is reversed and remanded for further proceedings. In consequence, we do not reach the parties' arguments concerning the proper allocation of damages in credit transactions.

REVERSED and REMANDED.

GOLDBERG, CIRCUIT JUDGE, dissenting:

Ever mindful of the persuasive force of the majority opinion, I must, nonetheless, dissent. The majority faults the district court for being unduly attentive to the issuing bank's duty to pay a draft under a letter of credit rather than the beneficiary's duty to comply strictly to the terms of the letter of credit. I fear that the majority has similarly been unduly attentive to the facts of this case and has uttered a rule insufficiently sensitive to the day-to-day use of letters of credit.

Briefly stated, the case's present posture is as follows: Central Bank issued a letter of credit of which Philadelphia Gear was the beneficiary. The letter of credit incorporated by reference two important terms:

> (e) If [the issuing bank claims a draft is not in compliance with the terms of the letter], notice to that effect, stating the reasons therefore, must, without delay, be given by cable or other expeditious means to the bank from which the documents have been received (the remitting bank) and such notice must state that the documents are being held at the disposal of such bank or are being returned thereto.
>
> (f) If the issuing bank fails to hold the documents at the disposal of the remitting bank, or fails to return the documents to such bank, the issuing bank shall be precluded from claiming that the relative payment acceptance or negotiation was not effected in accordance with the terms and conditions of the credit.

International Chamber of Commerce Pub. 290 art. 8(e), (f). Philadelphia Gear submitted defective drafts to Central Bank under this letter of credit, knowing that "some" of the drafts were defective. Central Bank dishonored the drafts, offering no explanation other than noting that the drafts were not in compliance with the letter of credit; Central Bank also failed to return promptly the drafts with supporting documentation or to hold them at the disposal of the remitting bank.

Philadelphia Gear sued Central Bank for wrongful dishonorment [sic]. The district court held that Central Bank was estopped from asserting defects in the drafts as a defense for two separate reasons. First, Central Bank failed to give notice to Philadelphia Gear of the specific defects; second, Central Bank did not return or hold at the disposal of the remitting bank the drafts and supporting documentation. The panel today holds that a knowing tender of defective drafts absolves the issuing bank of its duty to give notice of the defects and of its duty to return the drafts and supporting documentation; the panel remands for a determination of which drafts were knowingly defectively submitted. I believe this rule to be inadvisable for two reasons.

First, although the majority's rule might be an equitable treatment of the present litigants, it introduces a factor treading on the toes of principles basic to letters of credit. Letters of credit are near-mechanical forms of payment designed to facilitate commercial exchange. The terms of letters of credit and applicable laws choreograph an elaborate dance. As long as the steps are followed, payment also follows. There is no need to make inquiries into the underlying transaction; the parties need merely pirouette down the path prescribed by the letter and applicable statutes. Facial compliance is the watchword.

The procedures relating to dishonoring a draft are equally choreographed. One of the important turns in that dance is providing the beneficiary an opportunity to correct a defective draft. I.C.C. Pub. 290 arts. 8(e), (f) delineates two steps in this turn: an issuing bank must return the defective draft and give specific notice of the defects. These two steps are crucial to allowing an innocent beneficiary an opportunity to cure an inadvertent error in a draft. Though this motivation is less compelling when the beneficiary knew beforehand of the defects, the steps are still part of the dance.

An inherent advantage of letters of credit is that questions regarding dishonorment are easily answered—a court or potential litigant need merely look to the choreography and see if the dancers took the proper steps. This usually poses an objective question, with the answer obvious from the face of the documents and the terms of the letter of credit. The rule the majority has chosen to apply to this case injects into the otherwise mechanical and simple inquiry that most subjective issue of the knowledge of the beneficiary.

The result of the majority's rule does not clearly offend me in the case in which the beneficiary in fact knowingly presented defective drafts—as I mentioned earlier, the opportunity-to-cure rationale is not overly compelling in such cases. What deeply disturbs me is that the majority has encouraged dishonoring banks to remain silent as to their reasons, stonewalling and injecting a complex, subjective, litigable issue into *every* wrongful dishonorment. Henceforth defendant issuing banks will include in their responsive pleadings the boilerplate *Philadelphia Gear* defense: "Furthermore, the beneficiary knew of the defects at the time of submission." What was once a rigidly choreographed dance now contains a *grand jeté* to the psychoanalyst's couch to look inside the beneficiary's head.

My second major objection to the majority opinion is that it judicially alters the terms of the agreement between the parties before us. I.C.C. Pub. 290 art. 8(e) specifically requires a dishonoring issuing bank to give notice of the reasons for dishonorment and to return the draft and documentation. Article 8(f) even prescribes a sanction for failure to return the draft and documentation (upon which the trial court understandably based its decision). Nowhere is the issuing bank excused from its obligations by the state of mind of the beneficiary. The majority rule has simply engrafted a new term into the parties' agreements. This judicially imposed condition renders somewhat suspect the majority's nominal obeisance to the principle of free contracting.

Though the instant case is a diversity case and "writing in diversity we write on the wind," *Thompson v. Johns–Manville Sales Corp.*, 714 F.2d 581 at

583 (5th Cir.1983) (Gee, J.), the precedential force of the majority opinion is likely to be great considering the field of law and the stature of the author. It distresses me to think that the once useful device of letters of credit may be a less reliable device now. The previously impossible possibility of contentious litigation of a subjective element can now arise in every suit for wrongful dishonorment. Accordingly, I must leave the majority to their *pas de deux* and *glissade* offstage, dissenting.

Questions

1. The Devil quoteth scripture, not so?

2. Look particularly at the court's assertion about beneficiary's warranty and compare its interpretation of 5–111 in the old Article 5 to the proposed revision that is quoted below. This is a threatening precedent.

3. What if the relevant warranties now contained in 5–111 were changed to read as follows:

> (a) If its presentment is honored, the beneficiary under a letter of credit warrants to the issuer, any other person to whom presentment is made, and the applicant, that there is no fraud, the documents are what they purport to be, and the statements and representations in the documents are true in all material respects. These warranties are in addition to any warranties arising under [Articles] 3, 4, 7, and 8 because of the presentment of documents covered by any of those [articles]. Notwithstanding any term in the letter of credit or agreement to the contrary, the beneficiary does not give a warranty of the kind described in the first sentence of this subsection if the beneficiary's presentment is dishonored.

4. If the two foregoing cases were decided in a jurisdiction that did not have the UCC (and so no warranty of the kind in section 5–111), what outcome?

Problem 24–4

Assume the Bank has asked you whether it must pay in each of the following cases:

1. Letter of credit calls for "clean bill of lading." The bills presented contain the notation "Shippers load and count." Does that make them not clean?

2. What of a bill of lading that says "Carrier not responsible for rust." See Articles 17 and 18 of the UCP.

3. A letter of credit issued to the beneficiary "Danish Furniture Company" calls for invoices specifying certain items. Ultimately a draft is presented together with invoices that correctly describe the goods, but the invoices are those of "Copenhagen Manufacturers," not of "Danish Furniture Company." Beneficiary asserts that the two companies are one and the same. Must Bank pay? (See UCC 5–116.)

Problem 24–5

National Builders agreed to sell two prefabricated houses to Mohammud Sofan, a resident of Yemen. Sofan procured a letter of credit issued by the Yemen Bank for Reconstruction in favor of National Builders. Irving Bank in New York was the confirming bank and National Builders designated National Bank of Washington as its collecting bank. National Bank of Washington sent

Irving all of the documents required, but there were several discrepancies, among them the fact that the bill of lading listing the party to be notified by the shipping company as "Mohammud Soran." Irving agreed to request authorization from the Yemen Bank to pay the letter of credit despite the discrepancy. No authorization was forthcoming, and Irving refused to pay. National Builders now sues Irving and argues among other things the following:

1. A mistake as to a single letter in a name is insignificant and forms no basis for dishonor.

2. National Bank's promise to indemnify if the name in fact caused confusion on delivery to Yemen and to hold it harmless for any damages suffered because of the presence of the letter "r" instead of "f" required it to honor.

3. Irving was estopped from claiming the discrepancy because it held the documents for several days before it notified National Bank of Washington of the deficiency.

4. In any event the case should not have been decided on summary judgment because there was a legitimate issue of fact on the question whether "Soran" properly identifies "Sofan."

Problem 24–6

1. Bank calls you in with the following problem. It appears that Bank issued a letter of credit on behalf of its customer, a football team in a newly formed professional league to the beneficiary, who was their star quarterback, Lance Bugalowski. At the time the bank issued a letter of credit, it believed that the football team would make a go of it, and it issued the credit despite the fact that the team had no security. The team is now teetering on the verge of bankruptcy. It appears unlikely that the league will operate in the next year. Unfortunately the letter of credit obligation to Bugalowski is for $500,000 each of the next three years. The letter has an expiration date three years hence. It says neither that it is revocable or irrevocable. Is the letter revocable and, if so, can the bank revoke it and thus avoid its obligation to Bugalowski? Assume alternatively that the letter is governed by the Uniform Customs and Practices or by the Uniform Commercial Code.

2. Assume that one year has passed and that the football team has gone into bankruptcy and that Bugalowski is about to make a demand on the letter. From reading the local press you understand that Bugalowski has now signed a contract as the principal quarterback for a west coast NFL team and, according to the papers, will be earning in excess of $750,000 a year. Presumably that gain would be set off as mitigation against any damages that he could claim against the customer. Can the bank use that fact to escape any obligation to pay?

A youngster in your office has suggested the following: Any demand now would breach the UCC warranties because Bugalowski does not meet the conditions, namely, having a good claim against the club. Secondly, the youngster has suggested that the Bank simply refuse to pay, take an assignment of the club's rights against Bugalowski and assert them in a counterclaim when he sues the Bank. Will the trustee in bankruptcy of the Club agree to such an assignment, and if so, will it work? Finally, your colleague has suggested that the automatic stay under 362 as applied in the Club's bankruptcy will bar any suit against the Bank by Bugalowski. What do you suggest?

SECTION 3. ISSUER'S RIGHT TO DISHONOR BECAUSE OF FRAUD

Section 5–114(2) recognizes the bank's right to refuse to honor where a document is "forged or fraudulent or there is fraud in the transaction * * *". Note, however that UCC 5–114(2) permits an issuer acting in good faith to honor despite allegations of fraud, but the last clause in UCC 5–114(2)(b) suggests that "a court of appropriate jurisdiction may enjoin such honor." The extent to which UCC 5–114(2) and the cases decided under that rule cut back on the independence principle and authorize a bank to refuse payment has been a topic of continuing debate in the courts and in the scholarly literature.

First, how does one distinguish between "fraud" and mere breach of contract? As we will see, the case which spawned the subsection, Sztejn v. J. Henry Schroder Banking Corp., infra page 1122, might have been characterized merely as a case of gross and intentional breach of contract.

The second issue present in UCC 5–114(2) is what standard the court is to apply in determining whether to enjoin payment—the question whether the bank that has not been enjoined may use UCC 5–114(2) to justify a refusal of payment.

Professor Dolan has argued persuasively for a narrow interpretation of UCC 5–114(2). Surely he is right in cautioning the courts against broad interpretation of that subsection. An expansive view of it could undermine the utility of the letter of credit and give every bank under pressure from a powerful customer a colorable excuse for refusal to pay. Also lurking in the subsection is the question, what kind of fraud and by whom? Must the fraud be committed by the beneficiary or is it enough that there be fraud in some transaction one step remote from the beneficiary? What, for example, of the case in which a general partner of an oil well drilling partnership defrauds the bank's customer but causes the letter of credit to be drawn with the general partner's bank as the beneficiary? In such case, the beneficiary bank might be completely innocent of the fraud.

In an attempt to limit the broad exception, the redraft of Article 5 has changed the language. At this writing the redraft of 5–110(e) and (f) read as follows:

> (e) If a presentment is made that appears on its face strictly to comply with the terms of the letter of credit, but the beneficiary has presented documents that the beneficiary knows to be forged or materially fraudulent:
>
> > (1) the issuer shall honor a draft or demand if the honor is demanded by a nominated person that has honored in good faith without notice of a defense;
> >
> > (2) if the conditions in paragraph (e)(1) are not met, the issuer may honor or dishonor.
>
> (f) If the applicant claims that the beneficiary has presented documents that the beneficiary knows to be forged or materially fraudulent, a court of competent jurisdiction may enjoin the issuer from honoring, or grant similar relief, only if the court finds the following:

(1) that the beneficiary and issuer are adequately protected, by bond or otherwise, against loss that may be suffered by the beneficiary or issuer if honor is enjoined or otherwise forestalled, but the beneficiary is later found to be entitled to honor;

(2) that all of the conditions to entitle one to an injunction under the law of [the forum State] have been met; and

(3) that, on the basis of information presented, (i) the beneficiary is not entitled to honor under subsection (e)(1), (ii) the applicant will suffer irreparable harm if the draft or demand is honored, and (iii) the applicant is more likely than not to succeed under its claim of forgery or material fraud against the beneficiary.

* * *

Note the "fraud exception" has been limited in several ways. First it is now clear that not just any fraud will do; fraud must somehow appear in the documents. Moreover the restrictions upon acquiring an injunction further limit the power of an unhappy customer in getting an injunction.

One of the by-products of the rise of Islamic fundamentalism in Iran was a considerable pressure on American banks and on the obligation of American banks to pay their letters of credit on proper presentment of documents. During the heyday of American sale of goods to the Iranians under the Shah, American banks had written many standby letters of credit that assured Iranian buyers (and guarantors or lenders to Iranian buyers), the performance of American companies.

After the overthrow of the Shah and the rupture of relations between Iran and the United States, the various Iranian beneficiaries of the letters of credit called or threatened to call them. Of course the American customers feared that if payment were made and the money transmitted to Iran, the American customers would never have an opportunity to get a fair trial on their rights on the underlying contract. A customer might concede, for example, that the documents presented met the terms of the credit, but maintain that it had failed to perform the contract because of force majeure or because it was actively prevented from doing so by the Iranian officials who were now seeking payment under the letter. In such cases it is not easy to prove fraud, yet there was enormous political and economic pressure not to pay such letters. Not all of the American courts covered themselves with glory.

J. DOLAN, THE LAW OF LETTERS OF CREDIT: COMMERCIAL AND STANDBY CREDITS 7–45 TO 7–50.

[E] Iranian Cases

[i] Strict cases. The analysis of the *Intraworld* and *Dynamics* cases is helpful in explaining several decisions involving standby credit disputes that arose out of the U.S./Iranian political problems of 1979. It is the practice of economically strong buyers, especially government buyers dealing with economically weaker sellers, to insist on performance guaranties when they enter into supply contracts. In the Iranian cases, the American sellers induced Iranian banks to issue those guaranties by having a domestic bank issue a standby credit in favor of the Iranian bank. Generally, the standby credit would call for the Iranian bank's draft and a certificate to the effect that it had been required to honor its guaranty. When the Iranian revolution interrupted commerce between the United States and Iran, sellers became anxious about the standby credits. Political and diplomatic turmoil prevented performance of the underlying agreements, and the Iranian political and financial structure appeared to be in the hands of persons who did not inspire the confidence that their counterparts in Amsterdam or London inspire. The sellers resorted to the courts.

Some of the cases lent themselves to resolution on the grounds that the account parties had not satisfied the equity prerequisites for injunctive relief. In *KMW International v. Chase Manhattan Bank, N.A.*, for example, the account party sought an injunction alleging that the Iranian buyer had breached the contract of sale and that any draw on the credit would be fraudulent. There had been no draw, however, and the court held that no injunction against payment should issue. The plaintiff's claim for damages was too speculative and conjectural to satisfy the rules of equity. The court did, however, order the issuer to give the account party three days' notice before honoring any demand. In *United Technologies Corp. v. Citibank, N.A.*, the account party alleged that it had performed the contract of sale and that any demand under the credit would be wrongful. The court denied the injunction, holding that the account party had an adequate remedy at law in the event a draft was fraudulent. In *American Bell International Inc. v. Islamic Republic of Iran,* the account party claimed that the Iranian buyer had breached the contract of sale, and alleged further that the beneficiary's demand, which the issuer had received, was not timely. The court refused to grant the injunction. In response to the account party's argument that the demand was not timely, the court noted that if, in fact, the issuer honored a late demand, the account party would have an adequate remedy at law—a suit for money damages against the issuer. In *Werner Lehara International, Inc. v. Harris Trust & Savings Bank,* the court held that the plaintiff, who was seeking injunctive relief before the beneficiary made any demand, did not satisfy the equity prerequisites and had not made out a case of fraud.

It is perhaps also significant that in the *Werner Lehara, KMW,* and *American Bell* cases the courts weighed against the account party the fact that an injunction might affect the banking relationships of the issuer adversely. It is clear that the issuers in these cases were nervous about the effect the injunctions would have in general on the reputation of credits issued by American banks and by the implicit threat of retaliation from the Iranian government or Iranian banks. In *United Technologies,* the court explicitly found such eventualities too speculative to be considered.

The *Werner Lehara, KMW,* and *American Bell* cases reject firmly the account party's argument that the demands of the Iranian beneficiaries were or would be fraudulent. Those courts viewed the contests as contract disputes, the risks of which the account parties should have foreseen when they entered into the sales contract. The courts refused to let the account parties shift to the banks or to the letter-of-credit industry in general a contract risk that inheres in international sales, a risk of political upheaval. In *United Technologies,* the court did not consider it necessary to decide that issue.

The conclusion of these cases that there was no fraud in the transaction sufficient to invoke the rule of Section 5–114(2) is consistent with the general rule. It may be that the beneficiaries of the guaranties issued by the Iranian banks were guilty of fraud when those beneficiaries required the Iranian banks to pay under the guaranties. The plaintiff's allegations suggest as much. Fraud in that guaranty transaction is not fraud in the letter-of-credit transaction as the *Sztejn* rule requires. The certificates required in the *KMW* and the *American Bell* cases, moreover, did not invite the courts to look into that related contract as the *NMC* and *O'Grady* cases did. The Iranian certificates recited only that the beneficiary was called upon to pay under the letter of guaranty. These carefully drawn credits do not pierce the barrier that insulates the credit from the underlying transaction and do not force the court to look at that underlying transaction.

While a significant number of courts dealing with standby credits issued to Iranian beneficiaries granted notice injunctions requiring the issuer to delay honoring a credit for a short period of time, the more significant cases are those such as *KMW, American Bell,* and *United Technologies.* The latter demonstrate the obstacles facing an account party once the demand arrives. These cases show a marked willingness to enforce the equity prerequisites and a marked unwillingness to relax the strict fraud rule of *Sztejn* or to reallocate the commercial and political risks that these merchant sellers must now shoulder under letter-of-credit law.

[ii] Less strict cases. The adherence to the strict *Sztejn* rule was not unanimous. In *Itek Corp. v. First National Bank,* the defendant bank issued a standby credit to an Iranian bank which, in turn, issued a guarantee to the Iranian Ministry of War. The account party had agreed to sell optical equipment to the Iranian government, and the sales contract contained a force majeure clause permitting either party to cancel the contract before performance under it was complete. The U.S. Department of State revoked the account party's export license, and the account party notified Iran of its election to terminate the contract under the force majeure clause. Subsequently, the account party obtained a temporary restraining order against the issuer; and when the beneficiary presented a conforming demand under the credit, the court enjoined payment. The *Itek* court held that because the account party's suit against the Iranian government would be futile, irreparable injury was evident. With respect to the fraud question, the court held that Section 5–114(2) establishes an exception to the independence principle, but the court also held that it was not necessary to probe the question of whether the fraud would be in the credit transaction or in the underlying transaction. The *Itek* court found the fraud so "blatant" and "undisputed" that it issued the restraining order.

A similar disposition to find fraud was evident in *Touche Ross & Co. v. Manufacturers Hanover Trust Co.,* where the credit ran to the benefit of an Iranian bank that had issued a letter of guaranty to the Iranian Ministry of War. The underlying contract contained a force majeure clause and stipulated that upon invocation of the clause all letters of guaranty would terminate. The account party invoked the force majeure clause, and the court concluded, therefore, that there could be no legitimate call on the letter of credit. In short, the *Touche Ross* court resolved the underlying contract questions, concluded that the equities were with the account party, and issued the injunction.

The unlikelihood of recovery under the Iranian court system influenced the court in *Harris Corp. v. National Iranian Radio & Television.* In that case, the court rejected the argument that the account party was attempting to reallocate the risks. The court acknowledged that the purpose of the credit was to permit the Iranian buyer to recover its down payment, but the court refused to accept the view that the account party should bear the risk of a fraudulent demand. To the issuer's argument that the account party could have protected itself by negotiating different terms, the court responded vaguely that such an argument ignores "the realities of the drafting of commercial documents." The *Harris Corp.* case rejects the view that the letter of credit used in Middle Eastern transactions reflects the increased bargaining strength of the Middle Eastern buyer and is a device with a purpose of permitting the buyer to recover its down payment automatically. If the *Harris Corp.* case were accepted as the majority rule, such buyers could avoid its effect in a number of ways. They could refuse to accept credits issued by American banks (as Iranian buyers have apparently done), could refuse to make a down payment, or could insist that the down payment be held by the Middle Eastern bank that issues the guaranty letter. Although the account party in the *Harris Corp.* case might find solace in the result, it is doubtful that American sellers in general will be pleased by these attempts by strong buyers to avoid the *Harris Corp.* rule. [Footnotes omitted.]

SZTEJN v. J. HENRY SCHRODER BANKING CORP.

Supreme Court of New York, Special Term, 1941.
177 Misc. 719, 31 N.Y.S.2d 631.

SHIENTAG, JUSTICE.

This is a motion by the defendant, the Chartered Bank of India, Australia and China, (hereafter referred to as the Chartered Bank), made pursuant to Rule 106(5) of the Rules of Civil Practice to dismiss the supplemental complaint on the ground that it fails to state facts sufficient to constitute a cause of action against the moving defendant. The plaintiff brings this action to restrain the payment or presentment for payment of drafts under a letter of credit issued to secure the purchase price of certain merchandise, bought by the plaintiff and his coadventurer, one Schwarz, who is a party defendant in this action. The plaintiff also seeks a judgment declaring the letter of credit and drafts thereunder null and void. The complaint alleges that the documents accompanying the drafts are fraudulent in that they do not represent actual merchandise but instead cover boxes fraudulently filled with worthless material by the seller of the goods. The moving defendant urges that the complaint fails to state a cause of action against it because the Chartered Bank is only concerned with the documents and on their face these conform to the requirements of the letter of credit.

On January 7, 1941, the plaintiff and his coadventurer contracted to purchase a quantity of bristles from the defendant Transea Traders, Ltd.

(hereafter referred to as Transea) a corporation having its place of business in Lucknow, India. In order to pay for the bristles, the plaintiff and Schwarz contracted with the defendant J. Henry Schroder Banking Corporation (hereafter referred to as Schroder), a domestic corporation, for the issuance of an irrevocable letter of credit to Transea which provided that drafts by the latter for a specified portion of the purchase price of the bristles would be paid by Schroder upon shipment of the described merchandise and presentation of an invoice and a bill of lading covering the shipment, made out to the order of Schroder.

The letter of credit was delivered to Transea by Schroder's correspondent bank in India, Transea placed fifty cases of material on board a steamship, procured a bill of lading from the steamship company and obtained the customary invoices. These documents describe the bristles called for by the letter of credit. However, the complaint alleges that in fact Transea filled the fifty crates with cowhair, other worthless material and rubbish with intent to simulate genuine merchandise and defraud the plaintiff and Schwarz. The complaint then alleges that Transea drew a draft under the letter of credit to the order of the Chartered Bank and delivered the draft and the fraudulent documents to the "Chartered Bank at Cawnpore, India, for collection for the account of said defendant Transea". The Chartered Bank has presented the draft along with the documents to Schroder for payment. The plaintiff prays for a judgment declaring the letter of credit and draft thereunder void and for injunctive relief to prevent the payment of the draft.

For the purposes of this motion, the allegations of the complaint must be deemed established and "every intendment and fair inference is in favor of the pleading" Madole v. Gavin, 215 App.Div. 299, at page 300, 213 N.Y.S. 529, at page 530; McClare v. Massachusetts Bonding & Ins. Co., 266 N.Y. 371, 373, 195 N.E. 15. Therefore, it must be assumed that Transea was engaged in a scheme to defraud the plaintiff and Schwarz, that the merchandise shipped by Transea is worthless rubbish and that the Chartered Bank is not an innocent holder of the draft for value but is merely attempting to procure payment of the draft for Transea's account.

It is well established that a letter of credit is independent of the primary contract of sale between the buyer and the seller. The issuing bank agrees to pay upon presentation of documents, not goods. This rule is necessary to preserve the efficiency of the letter of credit as an instrument for the financing of trade. One of the chief purposes of the letter of credit is to furnish the seller with a ready means of obtaining prompt payment for his merchandise. It would be a most unfortunate interference with business transactions if a bank before honoring drafts drawn upon it was obliged or even allowed to go behind the documents, at the request of the buyer and enter into controversies between the buyer and the seller regarding the quality of the merchandise shipped. If the buyer and the seller intended the bank to do this they could have so provided in the letter of credit itself, and in the absence of such a provision, the court will not demand or even permit the bank to delay paying drafts which are proper in form. O'Meara Co. v. National Park Bank of New York, 239 N.Y. 386, 146 N.E. 636, 39 A.L.R. 747. * * * Of course, the application of this doctrine presupposes that the documents accompanying the draft are genuine and conform in terms to the requirements of the letter of credit. Lamborn v. Lake Shore Banking & Trust Co., 196 App.Div. 504, 188 N.Y.S. 162; affirmed 231 N.Y. 616, 132 N.E. 911; Bank of Montreal v. Recknagel, 109 N.Y. 482, 17 N.E. 217; 38 Y.L.J. 111, 112.

However, I believe that a different situation is presented in the instant action. This is not a controversy between the buyer and seller concerning a mere breach of warranty regarding the quality of the merchandise; on the present motion, it must be assumed that the seller has intentionally failed to ship any goods ordered by the buyer. In such a situation, where the seller's fraud has been called to the bank's attention before the drafts and documents have been presented for payment, the principle of the independence of the bank's obligation under the letter of credit should not be extended to protect the unscrupulous seller. It is true that even though the documents are forged or fraudulent, if the issuing bank has already paid the draft before receiving notice of the seller's fraud, it will be protected if it exercised reasonable diligence before making such payment. * * * However, in the instant action Schroder has received notice of Transea's active fraud before it accepted or paid the draft. The Chartered Bank, which under the allegations of the complaint stands in no better position than Transea, should not be heard to complain because Schroder is not forced to pay the draft accompanied by documents covering a transaction which it has reason to believe is fraudulent.

Although our courts have used broad language to the effect that a letter of credit is independent of the primary contract between the buyer and seller, that language was used in cases concerning alleged breaches of warranty; no case has been brought to my attention on this point involving an intentional fraud on the part of the seller which was brought to the bank's notice with the request that it withhold payment of the draft on this account. The distinction between a breach of warranty and active fraud on the part of the seller is supported by authority and reason. As one court has stated: "Obviously, when the issuer of a letter of credit knows that a document, although correct in form, is, in point of fact, false or illegal, he cannot be called upon to recognize such a document as complying with the terms of a letter of credit." Old Colony Trust Co. v. Lawyers' Title & Trust Co., 2 Cir., 297 F. 152 at page 158, certiorari denied 265 U.S. 585, 44 S.Ct. 459, 68 L.Ed. 1192. * * *

No hardship will be caused by permitting the bank to refuse payment where fraud is claimed, where the merchandise is not merely inferior in quality but consists of worthless rubbish, where the draft and the accompanying documents are in the hands of one who stands in the same position as the fraudulent seller, where the bank has been given notice of the fraud before being presented with the drafts and documents for payment, and where the bank itself does not wish to pay pending an adjudication of the rights and obligations of the other parties. While the primary factor in the issuance of the letter of credit is the credit standing of the buyer, the security afforded by the merchandise is also taken into account. In fact, the letter of credit requires a bill of lading made out to the order of the bank and not the buyer. Although the bank is not interested in the exact detailed performance of the sales contract, it is vitally interested in assuring itself that there are some goods represented by the documents. * * *

On this motion only the complaint is before me and I am bound by its allegation that the Chartered Bank is not a holder in due course but is a mere agent for collection for the account of the seller charged with fraud. Therefore, the Chartered Bank's motion to dismiss the complaint must be denied. If it had appeared from the face of the complaint that the bank presenting the draft for payment was a holder in due course, its claim against the bank issuing the letter of credit would not be defeated even though the primary transaction was tainted with fraud. This I believe to be the better rule despite some authority to the contrary. See Old Colony Trust Co. v. Lawyers' Title & Trust Co., 2 Cir., 297 F. 152, certiorari denied 265 U.S. 585, 44 S.Ct. 459, 68 L.Ed. 1192; Thayer, Irrevocable Credits in International Commerce, 37 C.L.R. 1326, 1344; Campbell, Guaranties & The Suretyship Phases of Letters of Credit, 85 U. of Pa.L.R. 261, 272; but see Finkelstein, Legal Aspects of Commercial Letters of Credit, p. 248; O'Meara Co. v. National Park Bank of New York, 239 N.Y. 386, 401, 146 N.E. 636, 39 A.L.R. 747.

The plaintiff's further claim that the terms of the documents presented with the draft are at substantial variance with the requirements of the letter of credit does not seem to be supported by the documents themselves.

Accordingly, the defendant's motion to dismiss the supplemental complaint is denied.

Note

How would the *Sztejn* case come out if the applicable law was as set out at page 1122.

Problem 24–7

At 1:00 on a lazy Friday afternoon as you are having your second martini at your favorite eating club, you are called to the phone and receive the following frantic message from your best client: He tells you that he has procured the issuance of a letter of credit naming his seller as the beneficiary, that he has it on excellent authority that his seller has sealed several freight cars and procured bills of lading stating that the goods are enclosed in those cars, when in fact they are not. He informs you that these documents are now in the hands of seller's bank in a distant city and will probably be presented for payment on Monday morning to the issuing bank in your city. The letter of credit calls for payment of $100,000 and your client is certain that he will have a difficult if not impossible time getting the money back from the seller once it gets into his hands. If the case is governed by the Uniform Commercial Code, what action will you take?

COLORADO NATIONAL BANK OF DENVER v. BOARD OF COUNTY COMMISSIONERS OF ROUTT COUNTY, COLO.

Supreme Court of Colorado, 1981.
634 P.2d 32.

HODGES, CHIEF JUSTICE.

We granted certiorari to review the court of appeals' decision affirming a district court's judgment holding the petitioner, the Colorado National

Bank of Denver (the Bank), liable for the face amounts of three letters of credit it issued to secure the completion of road improvements by its customer, the Woodmoor Corporation (Woodmoor). * * * We reverse the judgment as to letters of credit No. 1156 and No. 1157, and affirm the judgment as to letter of credit No. 1168.

Woodmoor planned to develop a mountain recreation community in Routt County, Colorado (the County), to be known as Stagecoach. Early in 1973, Woodmoor obtained plat approval from the Routt County Board of County Commissioners (the Commissioners) for several Stagecoach subdivisions. Pursuant to section 30–28–137, C.R.S.1973 (1977 Repl. Vol. 12), and county subdivision regulations, approval of three of these subdivision plats was conditioned upon Woodmoor's agreement to provide a bond or other undertaking to ensure the completion of roads in accordance with the subdivision design specifications. Accordingly, subdivision improvements agreements were executed between Woodmoor and the county.

At Woodmoor's request, the Bank issued three letters of credit to secure Woodmoor's obligations under the agreements. The first two letters of credit, No. 1156 and No. 1157, were issued January 23, 1973 in the respective amounts of $158,773 and $77,330 bearing expiry dates of December 31, 1975. The third letter of credit No. 1168 was issued March 7, 1973 in the amount of $113,732 bearing an expiry date of December 31, 1976. The face amounts of the letters of credit were identical to the estimated costs of the road and related improvements in the respective subdivision improvements agreements. The County was authorized by each letter of credit to draw directly on the Bank, for the account of Woodmoor, up to the face amount of each letter of credit. Each letter of credit required the County, in order to draw on the letters of credit, to submit fifteen-day sight drafts accompanied by:

> "A duly-signed statement by the Routt County Board of Commissioners that improvements have not been made in compliance with a Subdivision Improvements Agreement between Routt County and the Woodmoor Corporation dated [either January 9, 1973 or March 7, 1973] and covering the [respective subdivisions] at Stagecoach and that payment is therefore demanded hereunder."

Woodmoor never commenced construction of the roads and related improvements. On December 31, 1975, the expiry date of letters of credit No. 1156 and No. 1157, the County presented two demand drafts to the Bank for the face amounts of $158,773 and $77,330. The demand drafts were accompanied by a resolution of the Commissioners stating that Woodmoor had failed to comply with the terms of the subdivision improvements agreements and demanded payment of the face amounts of the letters of credit. On January 5, 1976, within three banking days of the demand,[1] the Bank dishonored the drafts. The Bank did not specifically object to the County's presentation of demand drafts rather than fifteen-day sight drafts as required by the letters of credit.

On December 22, 1976, the County presented the Bank with a demand draft on letter of credit No. 1168 which was accompanied by the required

1. Under § 4–5–112(1)(a), C.R.S.1973, a bank called upon to honor drafts under a letter of credit may defer until the close of the third banking day following receipt of the documents.

resolution of the Commissioners. The Bank dishonored this draft because of the County's nonconforming demand, viz., that a demand draft was submitted rather than a fifteen-day sight draft. On December 29, 1976, the County presented a fifteen-day sight draft to the Bank. This draft was not accompanied by the resolution of the Commissioners. On December 31, 1976, the Bank dishonored this draft.

The County sued to recover the face amounts of the three letters of credit plus interest from the dates of the demands. The Bank answered the County's complaints alleging several affirmative defenses. The fundamental premise of the Bank's defenses was the assertion that the County would receive a windfall since it had not expended or committed to spend any funds to complete the road improvements specified in the subdivision improvements agreements.

The County filed a motion in limine seeking a determination by the trial court to exclude evidence concerning matters beyond the four corners of the letters of credit and the demands made on the letters of credit. The Bank replied by filing a cross-motion in limine seeking a ruling that it would not be precluded at trial from offering evidence outside the four corners of the letters of credit. The trial court, after extensive briefing by the parties and a hearing, granted the County's motion to limit the admissibility of evidence to the letters of credit, documents and drafts presented thereunder, the demands on the letters of credit, and the Bank's refusals to honor the County's demands for payment.

The remaining issues were whether the County's demands conformed to the letters of credit or, if not, whether the Bank had waived nonconforming demands, and whether interest ought to be awarded. The parties agreed on a stipulated set of facts concerning these remaining issues. The Bank did, however, make an offer of proof as to the rejected affirmative defenses. The Bank would have attempted to prove that the subdivisions in question remained raw, undeveloped mountain property for which there was no viable market and that the County had neither constructed, made commitments to construct, nor planned to construct the roads or other improvements described in the subdivision improvements agreements secured by the letters of credit. These allegations were disputed by the County.

The trial court entered judgment against the Bank for the face amounts of the letters of credit plus accrued interest at the statutory rate from the date of the County's demands. Costs were awarded in favor of the County. The Bank's motion for new trial was denied, and the Bank appealed.

The court of appeals affirmed the judgment of the trial court ruling that standby letters of credit are governed by article 5 of the Uniform Commercial Code, section 4–5–101 et seq. C.R.S.1973, and that an issuer must honor a draft or demand for payment which complies with the terms of the relevant credit regardless of whether the goods or documents conform to the underlying contract. The court of appeals affirmed the trial court's refusal to consider any evidence regarding the County's alleged windfall. The court of appeals also held that any defects in the form of the County's demands were waived by the Bank.

I.

We first address the question whether the trial court properly limited the evidence to be presented at trial to the letters of credit, the demands by the County, and the Bank's replies to the demands. The Bank has continually asserted during each stage of this action that it ought to be permitted to show that the County will receive a windfall if the County is permitted to recover against the letters of credit. The Bank requested an opportunity to prove that the County will utilize the funds it would receive in a manner other than that specified in the road improvements agreements. Fundamentally, the Bank seeks to litigate the question of the completion of the purpose of the underlying performance agreements between Woodmoor and the County. This the Bank cannot do.

An overview of the history and law concerning letters of credit is useful in the consideration of this issue. The letter of credit arose to facilitate international commercial transactions involving the sale of goods. * * * Today the commercial utility of the letter of credit in both international and domestic sale of goods transactions is unquestioned and closely guarded. * * * Harfield, The Increasing Domestic Use of the Letter of Credit, 4 U.C.C.L.J. 251 (1972); Verkuil, Bank Solvency and Guaranty Letters of Credit, 25 Stan.L.Rev. 716 (1973). In recent years, the use of the letter of credit has expanded to include guaranteeing or securing a bank's customer's promised performance to a third party in a variety of situations. * * * This use is referred to as a standby letter of credit. Article five of the Uniform Commercial Code governs both traditional commercial letters of credit and standby letters of credit. * * *

Three contractual relationships exist in a letter of credit transaction. * * * Justice, Letters of Credit: Expectations and Frustrations, 94 Banking L.J. 424 (1977); Verkuil, Bank Solvency and Guaranty Letters of Credit, supra. Underlying the letter of credit transaction is the contract between the bank's customer and the beneficiary of the letter of credit, which consists of the business agreement between these parties. Then there is the contractual arrangement between the bank and its customer whereby the bank agrees to issue the letter of credit, and the customer agrees to repay the bank for the amounts paid under the letter of credit. See also § 4–5–114(3), C.R.S.1973. Finally, there is the contractual relationship between the bank and the beneficiary of the letter of credit created by the letter of credit itself. The bank agrees to honor the beneficiary's drafts or demands for payment which conform to the terms of the letter of credit. See generally §§ 4–5–103(1)(a) and 4–5–114(1), C.R.S.1973; White and Summers, Uniform Commercial Code § 18–6 (2d ed. 1980).

It is fundamental that the letter of credit is separate and independent from the underlying business transaction between the bank's customer and the beneficiary of the letter of credit. * * * Arnold & Bransilver, The Standby Letter of Credit—The Controversy Continues, 10 U.C.C.L.J. 272 (1978); * * * "The letter of credit is essentially a contract between the issuer and the beneficiary and is recognized by [article 5 of the Uniform Commercial Code] as independent of the underlying contract between the customer and the beneficiary. * * * In view of this independent nature of the letter of credit engagement the issuer is under a duty to honor the drafts for payment which in fact conform with the terms of the credit without reference to their compliance with the terms of the underlying contract." Section 4–5–114, Official Comment 1, C.R.S.1973.

The independence of the letter of credit from the underlying contract has been called the key to the commercial vitality of the letter of credit. * * * The bank must honor drafts or demands for payment under the letter of credit when the documents required by the letter of credit appear on their face to comply with the terms of the credit. Section 4–5–114(2), C.R.S.1973. An exception to the bank's obligation to honor an apparently conforming draft or demand for payment, see Foreign Venture Ltd. Partnership v. Chemical Bank, 59 App.Div.2d 352, 399 N.Y.S.2d 114 (1977), is when a required document is, inter alia, forged or fraudulent, or there is fraud in the transaction. Section 4–5–114(2). The application of this narrow exception is discussed in detail later in this opinion.

As mentioned above, letters of credit have recently come to be used to secure a bank's customer's performance to a third party. When a letter of credit is used to secure a bank's customer's promised performance to a third party, in whatever capacity that might be, the letter of credit is referred to as a "guaranty letter of credit," see East Bank of Colorado Springs v. Dovenmuehle, supra; Verkuil, Bank Solvency and Guaranty Letters of Credit, supra, or a "standby letter of credit," Arnold & Bransilver, The Standby Letter of Credit—The Controversy Continues, supra, 12 CFR § 7.1160 (1980). Standby letters of credit are closely akin to a suretyship or guaranty contract. The bank promises to pay when there is a default on an obligation by the bank's customer. "If for any reason performance is not made, or is made defectively, the bank is liable without regard to the underlying rights of the contracting parties." Verkuil, Bank Solvency and Guaranty Letters of Credit, supra at 723.

While banks cannot, as a general rule, act as a surety or guarantor of another party's agreed performance, see generally Lord, The No–Guaranty Rule and the Standby Letter of Credit Controversy, 96 Banking L.J. 46 (1979), the legality of standby letters of credit has been uniformly recognized. * * * What distinguishes a standby letter of credit from a suretyship or guaranty contract is that the bank's liability rests upon the letter of credit contract rather than upon the underlying performance contract between the bank customer and the beneficiary of the letter of credit. * * *

The utilization by banks of standby letters of credit is now widespread, although some commentators suggest that bankers may not appreciate the legal obligations imposed by the standby letter of credit. Where the bank issues a standby letter of credit, the bank naturally expects that the credit will not be drawn on in the normal course of events, i.e., if the customer of the bank fulfills its agreed-upon performance, then the credit will not be drawn upon. This expectation of the bank must be compared to the bank's expectation with respect to a traditional letter of credit issued as a means of financing a sale of goods. In the latter situation, the bank expects that the credit will always be drawn upon. * * * It has been suggested that bankers may be lax in considering the credit of a customer with respect to issuing a standby letter of credit to secure the integrity of its customer to complete an agreed-upon performance since it could be easily assumed by the bank that demand for payment would never be made. * * * One solution suggested by many commentators is that the issuing bank treat a standby letter of credit like an unsecured loan. National Banks issuing standby letters of credit are subject to the lending limits of 12 U.S.C. § 84 (1976).

We now turn to a discussion of the present case, and why the Bank cannot introduce evidence beyond that directly relating to its contract with the County. As discussed above, the letters of credit, and the Bank's obligations thereunder, are separate and independent from the underlying subdivision improvements agreements between Woodmoor and the County. The fact that the letters of credit issued by the Bank are standby letters of credit does not alter this general rule. The Bank is bound by its own contracts with the County.

Each of the letters of credit prepared and issued by the Bank in this case sets forth specifically the condition for payment, i.e., that Woodmoor failed to make the improvements in conformance with the respective subdivision improvements agreements. Had the Bank desired additional conditions for payment, such as the actual completion of the road improvements prior to payment under the letters of credit, it could have incorporated such a condition in the letters of credit. * * * To demand payment under the letters of credit, the County was only required to submit a "duly-signed statement by the [Commissioners] that improvements have not been made in compliance with [the] Subdivision Improvements Agreement[s]. * * * "

The Bank cannot litigate the performance of the underlying performance contracts. "[P]erformance of the underlying contract is irrelevant to the Bank's obligations under the letter of credit." West Virginia Housing Development Fund v. Sroka, supra at 1114 (W.D.Pa.1976). * * * Likewise, the question of whether the beneficiary of the letter of credit has suffered any damage by the failure of the bank's customer to perform as agreed is of no concern. Mid–States Mortgage Corp. v. National Bank of Southfield, 77 Mich.App. 651, 259 N.W.2d 175 (1977). Further, a bank cannot challenge the utilization of funds paid under a letter of credit. * * *

The Bank argues that it is entitled to dishonor the County's drafts under § 4–5–114(2), C.R.S.1973. This section provides: [quoting]

Under this section, the issuer of a letter of credit may in good faith honor a draft or demand for payment notwithstanding notice from its customer that documents are forged, or fraudulent, or there is fraud in the transaction. The issuer may, however, be enjoined from honoring such drafts or demands for payment. Impliedly, the issuer may also refuse to honor such drafts or demands for payment when it has been notified by its customer of these defects. Section 4–5–114, Official Comment 2, C.R.S.1973. * * *

In this case, the Bank has not argued, nor can it reasonably assert, that the documents presented by the County are forged or fraudulent. The Bank has not challenged the authenticity of the drafts and demands for payment by the County or the truthfulness of the statements that the requirements of the underlying subdivision improvements agreements have not been fulfilled. The Bank does assert, however, that there has been fraud in the transaction on the basis that the funds the County would receive would be utilized by the County other than to pay for the completion of the road improvements.

Fundamentally, "fraud in the transaction," as referred to in § 4–5–114(2), must stem from conduct by the beneficiary of the letter of credit as against the customer of the bank. See generally White and Summers, Uniform Commercial Code § 18–6 (2d ed. 1980). It must be of such an egregious nature as to vitiate the entire underlying transaction so that the legitimate purposes of the independence of the bank's obligation would no longer be served. * * * "[I]t is generally thought to include an element of intentional misrepresentation in order to profit from another. * * *" West Virginia Housing Development Fund v. Sroka, supra. This fraud is manifested in the documents themselves, and the statements therein, presented under the letter of credit. * * * One court has gone so far as to say that only some defect in these documents would justify a bank's dishonor. O'Grady v. First Union National Bank of North Carolina, 296 N.C. 212, 250 S.E.2d 587 (1978).

In this case, the Bank has not asserted that there is fraud in the transaction between Woodmoor and the County, nor can it reasonably make such an argument. No facts have been pled to establish fraud which vitiated the entire agreement between the County and Woodmoor. No fraud has been asserted by the Bank's offer of proof which would entitle it to dishonor the County's drafts and demands for payment. * * *

Thus, the trial court properly granted the County's motion in limine excluding all evidence beyond the four corners of the letters of credit, the demands thereunder, and the Bank's replies.

* * *

[Some footnotes omitted.]

Notes

1. If the allegations of the bank are correct, the risk against which the letters of credit were issued, namely that there would be a subdivision built, but that the subdividers would not provide the roads, will never arise. If, in such a case, the bank must pay the money and the county can keep the money, the law is "a ass," not so?

2. Had you advised the bank, how would you have drafted the letter to avoid the problem? (One of your editors is advised that the president of the bank typed out the letter on his very own typewriter without assistance of counsel.)

3. If the promise behind the developer's agreement to provide roads had been a conventional surety bond, how would that have changed the legal obligations?

CROMWELL v. COMMERCE & ENERGY BANK

Supreme Court of Louisiana, 1985.
464 So.2d 721.

DIXON, CHIEF JUSTICE. The plaintiffs in these consolidated cases seek reversal of the Court of Appeal decision in which the court found that plaintiffs were not entitled to enjoin the defendant banks from paying on standby letters of credit issued by the banks. We affirm the court of appeal decision insofar as it denies injunctive relief.

Facts

The plaintiffs in these five consolidated actions consist of the twenty-eight investors who purchased limited partnership interests in Combined Investments, Limited (C.I., Ltd.), a Louisiana limited partnership. C.I., Ltd. was formed by Combined Equities, Incorporated (C.E., Inc.), a company engaged in the syndication and management of investment partnerships. C.E., Inc. was the general partner of C.I., Ltd.

As security for their capital contribution in C.I., Ltd., the limited partners were required to execute letters of credit in favor of C.I., Ltd. The letters of credit were issued by fourteen Louisiana banks. The issuing banks were sued by the plaintiffs in order to prevent the beneficiary from drawing on the letters of credit. The primary basis of plaintiffs' claim was alleged fraudulent activities on the part of C.E., Inc. and C.I., Ltd.

The final beneficiary of the letters of credit was European American Bank (EAB). EAB became the beneficiary under the letters of credit as security for a ten million dollar line of credit established in favor of C.I., Ltd. EAB intervened in these cases in order to assert its right to draw on the letters of credit.

In addition to EAB, several other parties intervened in these cases to assert their interests. C.E., Inc. and C.I., Ltd. intervened in order to refute the plaintiffs' claim that they defrauded the plaintiff-investors. * * *

The formation of C.I., Ltd. began on June 1, 1981, when C.E., Inc. commenced offering partnership units in C.I., Ltd. C.E., Inc. had been in the business of syndicating partnerships since its formation in 1976. C.E., Inc. and its affiliated companies derived their income from fees charged for a variety of managerial and financial services provided to limited partnerships.

Prior to the creation of C.I., Ltd., the C.E., Inc. staff prepared a Private Placement Memorandum (PPM), a two hundred twenty page document which detailed the proposed structure of C.I., Ltd. and listed the terms of the partnership offering. All of the limited partners received a copy of the PPM prior to their investment in C.I., Ltd. The PPM included financial information and historical data concerning the general partner (C.E., Inc.) as well as a series of closing documents which were to be completed by each investor.

The closing documents were comprised of a series of forms to be completed by the investors. One of the purposes of the closing documents of the PPM was to require each investor to appoint an experienced investment advisor ("offeree representative") to review the PPM and advise him concerning the risks of the offering. The investors were each required to provide detailed information regarding their personal finances. Each investor was required to warrant that he was financially able to bear the risks of an investment in C.I., Ltd.

According to the PPM, the partnership's primary objectives were to acquire, transfer and invest in real estate in order to generate cash flow and to obtain long term capital gains. It was also the intention of C.I., Ltd. to secure significant tax advantages for the limited partners. These tax savings were to be obtained by passing through many of C.I., Ltd.'s losses onto the limited partners.

The PPM also indicated that C.I., Ltd. was a "blind pool" offering, since at the time of the offering the partnership did not own any property nor did it intend to acquire any specific property. The risks of such an offering were described in the PPM:

"RISK OF UNSPECIFIED INVESTMENTS

"The proceeds of this Offering are intended to be invested in Properties which have not yet been selected. There can be no assurance as to if or when the proceeds from the Offering will be fully invested. Pending investment of Limited Partners' capital contributions, the General Partner is not required to invest Partnership funds in any particular manner and during such period investors will not have the opportunity to earn any return on such contributions. Persons who purchase Units will not have an opportunity to evaluate for themselves the specific Properties in which funds of the Partnership will be invested or the terms of any such investments and, accordingly, the Limited Partners must depend solely upon the General Partner with respect to the selection of investments. * * *" PPM, p. 27.

Originally the syndication of C.I., Ltd. was intended solely to be accomplished through the sale of up to one hundred limited partnership interests. The purchase price of each unit was $250,000. In order to pay this sum, each limited partner was required to contribute $20,000 in cash, a two year, non-interest bearing demand note for $30,000, and a demand note for $200,000. Each investor was also required to obtain a $200,000 standby letter of credit, securing the $200,000 note.

The highly leveraged terms of the capital contribution allowed the limited partners to obtain significant tax advantages. The federal tax laws allow limited partnerships to pass through losses to their limited partners, based on the amount of the partner's money "at risk." Under the C.I., Ltd. proposal, each partner had $250,000 at risk in spite of the fact that his initial cash investment was only $20,000. During 1981 the partnership passed along a $76,000 tax loss to each investment unit.

Thirty-nine units in C.I., Ltd. were sold and the partnership officially came into existence on September 23, 1981. By the end of November, 1981 all plaintiffs except one had purchased interests; the last purchase was April 13, 1982.

In accordance with the terms of the capital contribution, each plaintiff secured a $200,000 letter of credit from his bank. The letters of credit were all issued in accordance with a form included in the closing package of the PPM. That form provided:

''(LETTERHEAD OF BANK)

ADDRESS

(Date)

Irrevocable Letter of Credit

Combined Investments, Ltd., a
Louisiana Limited Partnership

5551 Corporate Boulevard

Suite 3-A

Baton Rouge, Louisiana

Dear Sirs:

We hereby open our Irrevocable Letter of Credit in your favor for the account of (Name of Investor) (Address of Investor), for a sum or sums not exceeding in the aggregate the sum of Two Hundred Thousand and No/100 ($200,-000.00) Dollars, available by your drafts drawn on (Bank), (Address of Bank), at sight to be accompanied by:

An Affidavit signed by an officer of the holder of this Letter of Credit certifying that a default exists under

(i) any loan of Combined Investments, Ltd., a Louisiana Limited Partnership, due such holder, or

(ii) any indebtedness of (Name of Investor) due such holder,

which this Letter of Credit may secure.

Drafts must be drawn and negotiated on or before July 1, 1982, on which date this Letter of Credit expires. This Letter may be drafted against in full without being accompanied by the Affidavit referred to above from June 1, 1982 until July 1, 1982 if this Letter of Credit is not renewed by June 1, 1982 for a period of one year expiring July 1, 1983 in the face amount of $200,000 and in a form acceptable to the Beneficiary, its transferees or assigns.

The right to draw under this Letter of Credit is, by the holder hereof, absolutely irrevocable and unconditional (except as set forth herein) and is transferable and/or assignable in whole or in part.

Each draft must be marked 'Drawn under (Bank), (Address of Bank), Letter of Credit Number _____, Dated _____, 19__, and the amount of each draft so drawn endorsed by the negotiating bank. The final draft drawn under this Letter of Credit must be accompanied by this Letter of Credit. This credit is subject to the Uniform Customs and Practice for Documentary Credits, 1974 Revision, fixed by the International Chamber of Commerce Brochure No. 290.

We hereby agree with Drawers, Endorsers and Bona Fide Holders of Drafts drawn under and in compliance with the Credit that the same shall be duly honored upon presentation to the Drawee Bank as specified above.

Sincerely,
(NAME OF BANK)
By: ____________________
By: ____________________

(NOTE: NEED SIGNATURES OF

TWO (2) BANK OFFICERS)'' PPM Closing Documents,

Form 3-A.

The limited partners' letters of credit were intended to be used to secure bank financing for C.I., Ltd. The original letter of credit named C.I., Ltd. as beneficiary. In order to secure financing, the letters of credit were to be transferred to lending banks.

After its formation in September, 1981, C.I., Ltd., acting through its general partner, negotiated loans from Mercantile National Bank of Dallas and First National Bank of Lafayette. The Mercantile loan was for 5.4 million dollars and the First National loan was for 2.4 million dollars. In order to secure the loans, the letters of credit were transferred to the banks along with security interests in the demand notes. As further security for the financing, C.E., Inc. and two of its principal officers, Robert Jackson and E. Hardy Swyers, guaranteed payment of the loans.

The proceeds of the Mercantile and First National loans were used primarily to invest in other limited partnerships which were related to C.E., Inc. These affiliated partnerships generally owned real estate interests such as condominiums, hotels and apartments. Some of these investments were in the form of loans to the other limited partnerships.

C.I., Ltd.'s first contact with EAB took place in September, 1981. Representatives of EAB and C.E., Inc. met to discuss the establishment of a line of credit which would replace the Mercantile and First National loans. Through the consolidation of the prior loans with EAB, C.E., Inc. hoped to obtain a lower interest rate on its outstanding debt.

Subsequent meetings and discussions led to EAB's approval of a 10 million dollar line of credit for C.I., Ltd. The loan agreement was signed on March 15, 1982. Prior to the approval of the line of credit, EAB conducted an investigation into the credit worthiness of C.I., Ltd. and lengthy negotiations took place between EAB and C.I., Ltd.

EAB's primary representative throughout the negotiation process was Dennis Devito, the assistant vice president in charge of partnership lending. Devito first learned of C.E., Inc. on September 2, 1981 when he was contacted by Alan Jacobs, a New York attorney who was representing C.E., Inc. As a result of his discussions with Jacobs, Devito requested that C.E., Inc. forward the PPM of C.I., Ltd. to the bank.

On September 16, 1981 a meeting took place between representatives of EAB and C.I., Ltd. at the offices of EAB in New York. Devito, Jerold Frier, EAB's vice president, and Harvey Horowitz, a member of the partnership lending division, represented EAB at the meeting. C.E., Inc. was represented at the meeting by Alan Jacobs, E. Hardy Swyers, vice chairman of the board, and Gil Guidry, bank financing manager. The structure of C.I., Ltd. and the possibility of a 20 million dollar credit facility were discussed at the meeting. Subsequent to that meeting, Devito prepared a preliminary loan memorandum and went ahead with the loan approval process.

On September 22, 1981 Devito and Alan Churchill, EAB's vice president of real estate advisory services, made a day long trip to C.E., Inc. headquarters in Baton Rouge. The purpose of the meeting was for Devito and Churchill to familiarize themselves with the operation of C.E., Inc. and to meet its officers. Churchill went along on the trip because of his experience with real estate loans. A file memo written by Devito, which was introduced at trial, indicates that Churchill was satisfied with the operation of C.E., Inc.

Subsequent to the initial meetings, C.I., Ltd. sent a variety of financial data and other information concerning C.I., Ltd. and C.E., Inc. to EAB. One of the documents received by EAB was a portfolio of C.E., Inc., dated September, 1981, which gave specific details concerning the management of C.E., Inc. and its investments. Audited financial statements of C.E., Inc. for the fiscal year ending March 31, 1981 were also sent to EAB.

The bank conducted a credit reference check of C.E., Inc. by contacting five banks and three certified public accountants that had done business with C.E., Inc. The banks, except for Capital Bank & Trust Company, Baton Rouge, indicated that their relationship with C.E., Inc. was very satisfactory. Capital Bank indicated that it had increased its line of credit with C.E., Inc. due to cash flow problems. The accountants contacted by EAB recommended C.E., Inc. as a client.

After reviewing the information furnished by C.I., Ltd. and the credit references, an "internal offering memorandum" was prepared by Devito. This memorandum consisted of a loan proposal for a 10 million dollar credit facility to be secured by letters of credit of the limited partners of C.I., Ltd. The memorandum also included an inhouse appraisal of C.I., Ltd. and its general partner. The final paragraph of the memo set forth a recommendation in favor of approval of the C.I., Ltd. loan. This recommendation was primarily based upon the fact that the loan was to be secured by irrevocable letters of credit naming the bank as beneficiary.

The inter-office memo was approved by the bank on October 30, 1981. The bank's approval of the loan on that date was followed by several months of delay before the actual signing of the loan agreement on March 15, 1982. During that interval, EAB and C.I., Ltd. negotiated with regard to the language of the final loan agreement.

On December 10, 1981 EAB sent a proposed loan agreement to C.E., Inc. for review. On December 11, Robert Jackson, the chairman of C.E., Inc. and Glenn Bodin, the senior vice president of C.E., Inc., had dinner with Churchill and Devito to discuss the terms of the loan agreement.

On December 17, 1981 Churchill sent out an internal memo to Devito which stated that: "As of 2:30 today, no commitment of any kind should be made to Combined Equities prior to my review and approval." Churchill circulated the memo after hearing from a confidential source that C.E., Inc. was slow in its payment of a loan. Devito subsequently met with Churchill and on December 18 Churchill released his hold on the commitment to C.I., Ltd.

In response to Churchill's concerns, Devito contacted Capital Bank in Baton Rouge on December 19 to inquire about the credit worthiness of C.E., Inc. Keith Miller, the vice president of Capital Bank, indicated to Devito that the bank's overall relationship with C.E., Inc. was satisfactory but that C.E., Inc. was experiencing some cash flow difficulties. Miller indicated that these problems were the result of the fast growth of C.E., Inc., the delayed closing of real estate syndications and the fact that the cash of C.E., Inc. was not consolidated at a single bank. He also stated that C.E., Inc. was attempting to address these problems.

On January 25, 1982 EAB received a set of financial statements for C.E., Inc. and its subsidiaries. The most recent statements were for the year ending March 31, 1981. Those statements revealed that C.E., Inc. owned assets of $5,904,708 and that it sustained a net loss of $990,913. Devito attributed this loss to the seasonal nature of the real estate syndication business. He also testified that the March 31, 1981 statements of C.E., Inc. were just one set of many financial statements relied on in approving the credit facility.

EAB sent an amended draft of the loan agreement to C.E., Inc. on February 26, 1982. This amended version incorporated several changes which had been requested by C.E., Inc.

The loan agreement was finally signed on March 15, 1982 in New Orleans. Dwayne Broussard, C.E., Inc.'s legal counsel, and Gil Guidry were present at the signing on behalf of C.I., Ltd. Devito signed on behalf of EAB. Immediately prior to the signing of the agreement, four changes to the loan agreement were "penciled" in at the request of the C.E., Inc. representatives. The plaintiffs attach significance to a change made with regard to the guarantees of Robert Jackson and C.E., Inc. Prior to the change, the last sentence of § 2.06 provided: "The bank will only call on the Guarantees after having drawn under the Letters of Credit." The following phrase was added to that sentence at the time of the signing: "and only upon the failure or inability of the issuing bank to make payment under the terms of the Letters of Credit."

Following the consummation of the loan, the limited partners were contacted by C.I., Ltd. and advised to have new letters of credit issued naming EAB as beneficiary. This reissuance was accomplished by having new letters of credit issued in favor of C.I. Ltd. and then transferring those letters of credit to EAB. EAB contacted Mercantile National Bank of Dallas and First National Bank of Lafayette regarding payment of the prior loans. Those banks were instructed to cancel the letters of credit which they held. Upon the receipt of the new letters of credit, EAB paid off the Mercantile and First National loans with the proceeds of the new credit facility.

EAB placed C.I., Ltd. in default in September, 1982. On November 24, EAB drew drafts on the issuing banks for payment under the letters of credit. The plaintiffs sought and obtained a temporary restraining order which enjoined the issuing banks from honoring the drafts by EAB. A hearing was subsequently held after which the trial judge granted a preliminary injunction preventing honor of the drafts. The court held that the plaintiffs were entitled to injunctive relief under R.S. 10:5–114(2) since there was "fraud in the transaction."

The trial court based its holding of fraud on the acts of C.E., Inc. while acting as the general partner of C.I., Ltd. The court found that C.E., Inc. had disregarded the provisions of the PPM in making investments for C.I., Ltd. Also, the court found that C.E., Inc. did not fulfill its representation in the PPM that it would provide up to 5 million dollars in the event of negative cash flow for C.I., Ltd.

The court found that EAB had knowledge of these facts constituting fraud and therefore knew or should have known of the fraud being perpetrated on the investors. Therefore, the court found that EAB made the loan in bad faith. For these reasons, EAB was prohibited from drafting under the letters of credit.

The Court of Appeal reversed, holding that no fraud occurred within the intendment of R.S. 10:5–114(2). Therefore, injunctive relief was denied. The court found that the trial court erroneously concluded that EAB committed a fraud. The court did not decide whether C.E., Inc. had acted fraudulently since under its interpretation of R.S. 10:5–114, such fraud would not have been grounds for an injunction against the issuing banks.

The plaintiffs sought writs from this court to have the trial court judgment reinstated. They claim that the Court of Appeal erroneously overturned the factual findings of the trial court, misconstrued the meaning of "fraud in the transaction" and erroneously accorded EAB rights greater than those of C.I., Ltd.

ISSUES

In order to determine whether the issuing banks may be enjoined from paying under the letters of credit, the following issues must be decided:

1. What is the meaning of "fraud in the transaction," in R.S. 10:5–114(2), as applied to standby letters of credit which are used to secure bank financing?

2. Whether such fraud occurred in this case, entitling plaintiffs to the injunctive relief provided for in R.S. 10:5–114(2)(b)?

The right to enforce payment of drafts issued under a letter of credit is governed by R.S. 10:5–114, which provides: [quoting]

* * *

FRAUD IN THE TRANSACTION

The primary issue in this case is the interpretation of "fraud in the transaction" in R.S. 10:5–114. Under that provision, the issuing banks must honor EAB's drafts unless the documents presented by EAB were "* * * forged or fraudulent or there is fraud in the transaction." R.S. 10:5–114(2). The plaintiffs do not dispute the validity of the documents submitted by EAB. Therefore, the only issue is whether there was "fraud in the transaction." If such fraud is found to exist, a court is empowered, under R.S. 10:5–114(2)(b), to enjoin the issuing banks from honoring drafts under the credit.

There is more than one "transaction" involved when letters of credit are issued. The first is the contract between the customer and the issuing bank, present in all cases; the conventional case involves a sale and delivery of goods; the standby case involves a contract or performance, or a loan by the beneficiary bank to a borrower, secured by the customer's letter of credit. If the credit secures a loan by the beneficiary bank, that loan is the underlying transaction.

The plaintiffs maintain that "transaction" should be interpreted in its broadest sense. It is their position that by not qualifying "transaction," the drafters intended it to be given by a very general and expansive interpretation. More specifically, they claim that "if a fraud is practiced that would ultimately cause a loss to the customer, injunction will lie against honor regardless of who perpetrated the fraud."

Furthermore, they contend that "transaction" must be understood to include the underlying transaction between the limited partners and C.I., Ltd. Plaintiffs maintain that by not giving transaction a general meaning, lending banks would be permitted to "launder fraud," thereby damaging the integrity of the judicial system.

The intervenors advocate a restrictive interpretation of "transaction." They claim that an injunction may be properly issued only when fraudulent documents are issued, or when the beneficiary commits active fraud against the investors who obtained the letters of credit.

The UCC was adopted in Louisiana in an effort to harmonize the commercial law of Louisiana with that of the other states.[4] We should, therefore, examine the jurisprudence of other states interpreting R.S. 10:5–114(2).[5]

The most frequently cited case on the "fraud in the transaction" exception to UCC § 5–114(2) is Sztejn v. Henry Schroder Banking Corp., 177 Misc. 719, 31 N.Y.S.2d 631 (Sup.Ct.N.Y.1941). Although Sztejn arose before the drafting of the UCC, most commentators and courts agree that Sztejn was the impetus for the fraud exception.

* * *

In spite of its decision in favor of the plaintiff, the court was careful to leave the independence principle intact:

> "It is well established that a letter of credit is independent of the primary contract of sale between the buyer and the seller. The issuing bank agrees to pay upon presentation of documents, not goods. This rule is necessary to preserve the efficiency of the letter of credit as an instrument for the financing of trade. One of the chief purposes of the letter of credit is to furnish the seller with a ready means of obtaining prompt payment for his merchandise. It would be a most unfortunate interference with business transactions if a bank before honoring drafts drawn upon it was obliged or even allowed to go behind the documents, at the request of the buyer and enter into controversies between the buyer and the seller regarding the quality of the merchandise shipped. If the buyer and the seller intended the bank to do this they could have so provided in the letter of credit itself, and in the absence of such a provision, the court will not demand or even permit the bank to delay paying drafts which are proper in form. * * * Of course, the application of this doctrine presupposes that the documents accompanying the draft are genuine and conform in terms to the requirements of the letter of credit. * * *" (Citations omitted). 31 N.Y.S.2d at 633–34.

4. R.S. 10:1–102(2)(c).

5. R.S. 10:5–114 varies in two respects from the uniform version of 5–114. However, the differences are minor and have no bearing on the issues in this case.

In R.S. 10:5–114(1), "for sale or other contract" was omitted as being unnecessary. In R.S. 10:5–114(2), a reference to UCC Articles 7 and 8 was omitted.

The Sztejn court, in determining whether the customer could stop the issuing bank from honoring the draft, determined that the underlying transaction was fraudulent and that the Chartered Bank (presenting the draft for payment on behalf of Transea) was in no better position than the fraudulent Transea.

Sztejn was a commercial letter of credit case which involved active fraud on the part of the beneficiary. The bank (Chartered) that presented the draft for payment was merely the correspondent for the issuing bank, not a holder in due course, but an agent of the seller-beneficiary charged with fraud. The court refused to allow a seller-beneficiary to profit from its own fraudulent conduct.

The Sztejn holding was applied to standby letters of credit in Shaffer v. Brooklyn Park Garden Apartments, 311 Minn. 452, 250 N.W.2d 172 (1977). In Shaffer, two purchasers of units in a limited partnership had letters of credit issued in favor of the limited partnership as part of their capital contribution. The letters of credit provided they could be drawn on only after presentment of a promissory note and a certification by the partnership that the investors had failed "to meet payment of authorized loans which are payable." 250 N.W.2d at 175. The letters of credit were subsequently transferred to Wayzata Bank & Trust Company as security for loans to the partnership.

The partnership experienced financial difficulty and Wayzata Bank & Trust Company attempted to draw on the letters of credit. In compliance with the letter of credit, Wayzata presented notes and certifications by the partnership that the investors had failed "to meet payment of authorized loans which are payable."

The investors sued to enjoin Wayzata from drawing on the letters of credit, claiming that the certifications were false. The court found that an injunction was proper because *plaintiffs sought the injunction on the basis of fraud in the documentation.* The court reasoned that:

> "* * * [W]here injunctive relief is sought, the fraud alleged must be in respect to the documents presented and not as to the underlying transaction. The allegations of fraud made by [the plaintiff-investors] is appropriate for injunctive relief since it concerns the certifications by [the partnership] presented by Wayzata." 250 N.W.2d at 180.

Another standby letter of credit situation was faced in O'Grady v. First Union National Bank, 250 S.E.2d 587 (N.C.1978). In that case, the attachment of a letter of credit to a note it purported to secure, but which had been substituted for the original note and which omitted the signature of one endorser was interpreted by the court as a case involving "fraudulent documentation" which would give rise to injunctive relief. Plaintiffs before us interpret the case as involving fraud "in the underlying transaction."

* * *

Finally, in Cappaert Enterprises v. Citizens and Southern International Bank of New Orleans, 486 F.Supp. 819 (E.D.La.1980), plaintiff, Cappaert Enterprises, sued to enjoin a Kuwait bank from collecting under a letter of credit which was issued to secure a loan. The letter of credit was obtained by a joint venture comprised of Cappaert and United Fisheries of Kuwait. A dispute developed between Cappaert and United concerning performance of the joint venture agreement. Cappaert sued to enjoin the Kuwait bank from drawing on the letter of credit, claiming that United had committed a fraud against it.

The district court concluded that Cappaert's claim of "fraud in the transaction" was without merit. The court relied heavily on the principle of independence between the letter of credit and the underlying transaction. According to the court:

> "The accuracy of Cappaert's allegation that United Fisheries acted fraudulently in its role as a joint venturer is immaterial to the resolution of this issue, for impropriety in the underlying agreement is irrelevant to an interpretation of the letter of credit. * * *" 486 F.Supp. at 826.

As illustrated in the foregoing cases the independence principle is a strong influence in the decision of cases throughout the country. Adherence to that basic principle is necessary in order to protect the commercial utility of letters of credit.

Nevertheless, the jurisprudence and literature recognize and illustrate the need to extend the meaning of "fraud in the transaction" at least a step beyond fraudulent documentation. The strongest reason for such an extended interpretation is to deny rewarding fraudulent conduct by letter of credit beneficiaries. One author writes:

> "Notwithstanding dictum to the contrary in some of the cases, *the holding of the court in NMC Enterprises, Inc. v. Columbia Broadcasting System, Inc. that fraud in the underlying transaction is sufficient to justify relief is the better rule.* Since the issuer's obligation on a letter of credit is generally completely independent of the underlying transaction, the customer who obtains a letter of credit assumes the risk that payment may be made when the beneficiary has not properly performed the underlying contract. Moreover, the beneficiary may have required the letter of credit in part to assure that a dispute regarding performance of the underlying contract would not delay payment. By obtaining a letter of credit, however, the customer should not be required to assume the risk of making payment to a beneficiary who has engaged in fraudulent conduct in the underlying transaction. Furthermore, a rule that precludes injunctive relief where the fraud is in the underlying transaction will compensate the beneficiary for wrongful acts in situations where the customer will not have an effective legal remedy for the fraudulent conduct and thus tend to encourage fraud, a policy that should be avoided. As the court said in Dynamics Corp. of America v. Citizens & Southern Nat. Bank, there is as much public interest in discouraging fraud as in encouraging the use of letters of credit.
>
> "*While fraud in the underlying transaction should be sufficient to justify injunctive relief, mere failure to properly perform the underlying contract does not constitute fraud.* * * *" (Emphasis added). Hawkland & Holland, UCC Series § 5–114.09 (Art 5).

In the case before us, the "underlying transaction" is the loan transaction between EAB and C.I., Ltd. If the beneficiary EAB was guilty of fraud with respect to the plaintiffs (investors/customers), it should not be permitted to profit from that fraud.

If the banks want an instrument which will be paid without question upon demand, with no recourse by parties upon whom responsibility lies, other means are available.

Our holding is consistent with the cases cited by the parties as well as those found by our research. In all of the cases where letters of credit have been enjoined, the courts have found that either the documents were defective or the beneficiary was guilty of fraud. For example, in Sztejn, the customer sought to enjoin the payment of a draft, presented by the agent of the fraudulent beneficiary, at a time after the issuing bank had notice of the fraudulent shipment by the beneficiary.

Under the foregoing interpretation of "fraud in the transaction," it must now be decided whether such fraud occurred in this case. In accordance with our interpretation of R.S. 10:5–114(2), our analysis will be limited to the loan transaction and the conduct and knowledge of the beneficiary, EAB.

There is more than one measure of "fraud" in the various jurisdictions in the United States.

Cases and writers have called Sztejn an example of "egregious" fraud, and some have required "egregious" fraud in the transaction before according relief to the customer. (KMW International v. Chase Manhattan Bank, 27 UCC Rep. 203, 606 F.2d 10 (C.A.2 1979); Colorado National Bank of Denver v. Board of County Commissioners of Routt County, supra).

Cases and authorities have distinguished "egregious" fraud from "intentional" fraud, and have advocated "intentional" fraud as the better standard to afford injunctive relief to the customer. Hawkland & Holland UCC Series § 5–114:09 (Art. 5).

Civil Code provisions defining fraud and the rights of the fraud victim establish standards for commercial transactions in Louisiana and would seem to require the same results reached in most of the fraud cases involving letters of credit.

> "Fraud is a misrepresentation or a suppression of the truth made with the intention either to obtain an unjust advantage for one party or to cause a loss or inconvenience to the other. Fraud may also result from silence or inaction." C.C.1953.
>
> "Fraud does not vitiate consent when the party against whom the fraud was directed could have ascertained the truth without difficulty, inconvenience, or special skill.
>
> "The exception does not apply when a relation of confidence has reasonably induced a party to rely on the other's assertions or representations." C.C.1954.
>
> "Error induced by fraud need not concern the cause of the obligation to vitiate consent, but it must concern a circumstance that has substantially influenced that consent." C.C.1955.
>
> "Fraud committed by a third person vitiates the consent of a contracting party if the other party knew or should have known of the fraud." C.C.1956.

"Fraud need only be proved by a preponderance of the evidence and may be established by circumstantial evidence." C.C.1957.

"The party against whom rescission is granted because of fraud is liable for damages and attorney fees." C.C.1958.

Plaintiffs maintain that EAB obtained knowledge of fraudulent practices in its investigation of C.E., Inc. and C.I., Ltd. The trial court agreed with plaintiffs and found that the entire letter of credit transaction was permeated with fraud; the court also found that EAB had notice of the fraud. Such findings, if supported by the evidence, would warrant injunctive relief under our interpretation of R.S. 10:5–114.

The trial court relied on several factual findings in reaching its determination that "fraud in the transaction" occurred. The first finding relied on by the trial court was that the principals of C.E., Inc. made oral representations to the plaintiffs that C.I., Ltd. was going to invest directly in real estate. Contrary to these representations, C.I., Ltd. invested primarily in other partnerships. These representations have no relevance to the conduct of EAB since they were not written and it was not shown that EAB knew about them.

Secondly, the trial court found that EAB had knowledge of cash flow problems at C.E., Inc. This finding is supported by the testimony of Devito and the December 17, 1981 memo which placed the loan on hold. In spite of this knowledge, it is undisputed that EAB had received a significant number of positive recommendations concerning C.E., Inc.'s ability to pay its debts. It cannot be said that EAB's knowledge that a cash flow problem had existed constitutes fraud.

According to the trial court, the PPM misrepresented that C.E., Inc. could fund five million dollars of capital to C.I., Ltd. The PPM stated that C.E., Inc. would "* * * fund no more than $5,000,000 of working capital and/or negative cash flow * * *" (PPM, p 24). The plaintiffs argue that the trial court found that EAB knew that C.E., Inc. could not fulfill its funding commitment. They claim that this knowledge constituted fraud.

In addition to the above statement in the PPM regarding a capital commitment, the PPM also specifically described the risk of C.E., Inc. becoming unable to make funds available to C.I., Ltd. This risk is described on page 33 of the PPM as follows:

> "There can be no assurance that the General Partner [C.E., Inc.] shall have funds available to it or shall be able to make funds available to the Partnership [C.I., Ltd.] in either case sufficient in amount to satisfy the obligations of the Partnership."

At best, C.E., Inc.'s funding commitment was equivocal. Therefore, EAB did not obtain knowledge of fraud as a result of its review of the funding provisions in the PPM.

According to the trial court, EAB learned from the first supplement to the PPM that C.I., Ltd. had made investments which did not fall within the primary investment objectives stated in the PPM. The PPM stated that C.I., Ltd. intended to invest "primarily" in "existing Properties, such as apartment buildings and complexes, hotels, motels, office buildings and complexes and similar income producing properties." (PPM, p 18). The PPM qualified the above representation in the following terms:

> "It should be noted that although the Partnership currently intends to invest primarily in real property, the Partnership Agreement does not restrict the Partnership in any way from acquiring or investing in any other type of property or investment." (PPM, p 18).

The supplement to the PPM stated that C.I., Ltd. had made eight investments. The largest investment was the purchase of the Bourbon Orleans Hotel in New Orleans for $12,867,300. The majority of the remaining investments consisted of interests purchased in other partnerships. Contrary to the findings of the trial court, EAB cannot be held to have known that these investments were inconsistent with the representations stated in the PPM. The largest of these investments, the Bourbon Orleans Hotel, fell squarely within the primary investment objectives of the PPM. With regard to the other investments, the PPM clearly stated that no guarantees could be given regarding the types of investments to be made by C.I., Ltd.

The trial court attached significance to the fact that the March, 1981 audit of C.E., Inc. was "qualified" due to the existence of outstanding payables and receivables with its affiliated partnerships. The audit report contained the qualification since the scope of the audit did not extend to the affiliated partnerships. Such a qualification, standing alone, is not evidence of fraud on the part of EAB. Devito testified at trial that most syndicators would not have even provided audited financial statements.

The trial court found that since EAB knew that the proceeds of the EAB loan were to be used to pay off prior partnership loans, EAB had notice of an impropriety. The acknowledged reason for obtaining the EAB financing was to replace the Mercantile and FNB loans with lower interest financing. This purpose was legitimate and it was disclosed to the investors.[7] Therefore, EAB's knowledge of the proposed use of the proceeds was perfectly consistent with the interests of the plaintiff-investors.

* * *

Based on our foregoing analysis of the facts relied on by the trial court, we find that there was no evidence of fraud or knowledge of fraud on the part of EAB. Therefore, the "fraud in the transaction" exception of R.S. 10:5–114(2)(b) is not applicable to this case. The trial court's contrary holding was erroneous. Therefore, the Court of Appeal decision reversing the trial court in this respect must be affirmed.

7. The investors received letters from C.E., Inc. which stated that:

"In order to obtain substantial savings for Combined Investments, Ltd., the general partner has decided to take advantage of an opportunity to transfer to another bank the loan to which your Letter of Credit is now pledged as collateral. Transfer of this loan (now held by Mercantile National Bank at Dallas) to European American Bank and Trust of New York will enable the partnership to decrease the interest rate on this loan by one and one-half (1½%) percent, and therefore to acquire an annual savings of interest in the approximate amount of $115,692." (Letter to the Anderson and Savoy Partnership).

OTHER DEFENSES

We now address plaintiffs' contention that EAB is subject to all of the defenses which could be asserted against C.I., Ltd., since EAB was a mere assignee of the letters of credit from C.I., Ltd. The trial court rejected this argument and found that EAB was entitled to the protected status accorded by the independence principle. We find that EAB was a beneficiary under the letters of credit in its own right and therefore it was not subject to defenses assertable against prior beneficiaries under different letters of credit.

At the time of the EAB loan, the investors were asked to have new letters of credit issued. The investors knew that the letters of credit were to be used to secure bank financing and that EAB would have the right to draw on the credit in case of default. As the new letters of credit were issued, the issuing banks simultaneously wrote EAB acknowledging that "* * * European American Bank & Trust shall be deemed for all purposes to be the beneficiary of the Letter of Credit."

* * *

[Some footnotes omitted.]

Notes

1. Three cheers for the Louisiana Supreme Court. The customers will ultimately get exactly what they deserve in this case, not so? The moral of the story might be as follows: when a sophisticated investor spends a lot of money to buy a tax deduction, even a hometown court won't bend the law to protect his interests.

2. This case shows a quintessential standby letter of credit. The letter has nothing to do with goods; it serves purely as a guarantee of the investors' promises to pay. With the decline in oil and gas prices and with the failure of a number of banks that had made substantial loans to drillers and others in the oil field (Penn Square in Oklahoma City is the best example) many such letters of credit have been called and many courts have faced the question how to define "fraud in the transaction" in such cases. Invariably in such cases the investors have argued that they (the limited partners) were defrauded by the general partner and that this in turn is enough to upset the letter of credit under UCC 5–114. The Louisiana court rejects that argument and is correct in doing so, not so?

What form of interaction by the beneficiary bank with the underlying partnership would be necessary for a court to find the bank involved in the fraud and thus subject to the defense? For example, in the Penn Square case investors alleged that Penn Square (the beneficiary of the letters from other banks) was itself deeply involved with many of the general partners and had first-hand knowledge that the value of their oil and gas prospects were overstated. Based on such allegations, some courts enjoined payment on those letters.

3. If the court had concluded that there was fraud in the underlying transaction, could EAB have argued successfully under UCC 5–114(2)(a) that it was the "holder of the draft or demand which has taken the draft or demand under the credit and under circumstances which would make it a holder in due course"? If not, could the transaction have been arranged to give it that protection? It is unclear whether the court is addressing that issue at the end of

the opinion, but it seems to be talking more generally about the independence issue.

SECTION 4. RIGHTS AGAINST THE GOODS, THE CUSTOMER, AND OTHERS

At the outset we suggested that the bank should regard a letter of credit as tantamount to a loan to its customer and should realize at minimum that it is extending a line of credit to the customer that may be drawn upon. Recognizing that fact, the bank typically will require the customer to execute a document of the kind set out below. Note that the security agreement gives the bank the right to demand payment before it has to pay the money itself. It gives the bank a security interest in the assets that are subject to the credit and in some cases in other assets. Note that UCC 5–114(3) gives the bank a statutory right of "immediate reimbursement," and to be put "in available funds" no later than the day before maturity. Note that UCC 9–304(5) is specifically designed to give a bank a 21 day perfected security interest in goods or documents that are the subject of a letter of credit transaction.

COMMERCIAL LETTER OF CREDIT APPLICATION AND SECURITY AGREEMENT

(*APPLICANT: RETAIN INSIDE COPY FOR YOUR FILES.*)

To: NATIONAL BANK OF DETROIT
International Division
Detroit, Michigan 48232

L/C No.

Date

Please issue an irrevocable Letter of Credit as set forth below and forward to Beneficiary or your correspondent by
☐ Airmail ☐ Airmail, with short preliminary cable advice ☐ Full Cable, for delivery to the beneficiary.

For Bank use ONLY unless you designate advising bank	FOR ACCOUNT OF (APPLICANT)
IN FAVOR OF (BENEFICIARY)	AMOUNT
	Drafts must be presented for negotiation or presented to drawee on or before (Expiry Date)
☐TRANSFERRABLE AND THIRD PARTY SHIPPER ALLOWED	

Available by drafts at ☐ Sight ☐ ______ Days' After ______ drawn, at your option, on you or your correspondent for ______% of the Invoice value.

When accompanied by the following documents as checked:

☐ COMMERCIAL INVOICE in ______ copies covering: (Specify Commodity, omitting details as to Grade, Quality, and the like)

Terms ☐C & F) ☐CIF) ☐FOB) Port/Country ______ ☐ Other ______ (*Please specify*)

☐ SPECIAL U.S. CUSTOMS INVOICE

☐ CERTIFICATE OF ORIGIN

☐ PACKING LIST

☐ INSURANCE POLICY OR CERTIFICATE covering: (*State risks required*)

☐ Insurance effected by ourselves. We agree to keep insured until transaction completed.

☐ SHIPPING DOCUMENTS (Full set required if more than one original has been issued)

☐ On Board Ocean Bills of Lading consigned to the order of National Bank of Detroit
☐ Original signed Air Waybill)
☐ Original signed Truck Blading)
☐ Other: ______)

CONSIGNED TO:

"Notify" Party:

Shipment From:	Latest Shipping Date	Partial Shipments	☐ Permitted	☐ Prohibited
To:		Transshipments	☐ Permitted	☐ Prohibited
		Freight	☐ Collect	☐ Prepaid

☐ OTHER DOCUMENTS: ______________________________

____

☐ SPECIAL INSTRUCTIONS
☑ You may instruct negotiating bank to forward all documents in a single airmailing.
☐ All banking charges outside of the U.S. are for the beneficiaries account.
☐ Other ______________________________

____

ALL DOCUMENTS MUST BE PRESENTED TO NEGOTIATING OR PAYING BANK WITHIN _____ DAYS AFTER THE DATE OF ISSUANCE OF SHIPPING DOCUMENTS BUT WITHIN VALIDITY OF LETTER OF CREDIT.

Any questions concerning this application should be referred to:

____

Phone: (___)______________________

ALL PAYMENTS HEREUNDER TO BE CHARGED TO OUR NBD ACCOUNT NO.

____

This Application is made pursuant to Letter of Credit Security Agreement Terms and Conditions which appear as part of this form and apply to this Application and the credit issued pursuant hereto, receipt of which Terms and Conditions is hereby acknowledged.

____

Applicant Signature/Title

NBD 7329 9/80

COMMERCIAL LETTER OF CREDIT—REIMBURSEMENT AND SECURITY AGREEMENT TERMS AND CONDITIONS

To: National Bank of Detroit
International Division
Detroit, Michigan 48232

1. OBLIGATION OF BANK TO ISSUE CREDITS

Except for a contrary provision in the application for Letter of Credit ("Credit"), the terms and conditions herein set forth shall apply to issuance of the Credit, provided, until issuance of said Credit, you shall be under no obligation to issue the same.

2. OBLIGATION TO PAY

(a) DRAFTS OR ACCEPTANCES

As to drafts or acceptances drawn or purporting to be drawn under the Credit, we agree: (i) in the case of each sight draft, to reimburse you at your office, on demand, the amount paid on such drafts, or, if so demanded by you, to pay to you at your office in advance the amount required to pay such draft; and (ii) in case of each acceptance, to pay to you, at your office, the amount thereof, on demand, but in no event later than maturity, or, in case the acceptance is not payable at your office, then in time to reach the place of payment at maturity. As to drafts or acceptances which are payable in other than U.S. Currency to pay or reimburse you, on demand, in U.S. Currency the equivalent of the amount paid, or estimated by you to be paid, at your current rate of exchange as of the date of payment or at the date of transmission by you for cable transfers to the place of payment where and in the currency in which draft or acceptance is payable, or if there is no such rate at said time, then at such rate as you may fix.

(b) As to documents presented for payment at sight pursuant to the credit, without drafts, we agree our obligation thereunder shall be the same as though sight drafts had been presented or accompanied such documents.

(c) COMMISSIONS, CHARGES, EXPENSES, FEES AND INTEREST

We agree to pay you on demand such commission based on the amount of the credit as is your then current scheduled charges for the particular credit and all charges and expenses paid or incurred by you including, without limitation, FDIC Assessments and the cost of maintenance of required reserves, if any (including expenses of collection or of exercise of your rights hereunder as to security or otherwise and legal fees) and interest on the amount of any payment made by you under the credit and not reimbursed by us as herein provided (plus interest on commissions, charges and expenses not so reimbursed) at the rate of 3% per annum more than the prime rate announced by you as the prime rate for your commercial loans then in effect (which prime rate may not necessarily be the lowest rate charged by you to any of your customers), but not an amount greater than is allowable under the laws of the State of Michigan.

(d) ADVICE FROM CORRESPONDENTS

Telegraphic or other notice from your correspondent or agents of payment, acceptance, or other action under the Credit shall be presumptive evidence of our liability hereunder to reimburse you.

3. ADMINISTRATION OF CREDIT

(a) "UNIFORM CUSTOMS AND PRACTICES FOR DOCUMENTARY CREDITS"

The "Uniform Customs and Practices for Documentary Credits, 1983 revision, ICC Publication N° 400" of the International Chamber of Commerce (copy of which is available from you at our request) shall govern the rights and liabilities of you and us hereunder to the same effect as if stated word for word herein, and the Credit issued hereunder shall be subject to, and be governed by, the provisions of said uniform customs and practices unless the context of this agreement shall be contrary thereto, or in addition thereto, in which event any contrary or additional obligation or liability of us hereunder shall be as stated herein and your rights, obligation or liability as stated herein shall each govern notwithstanding the provisions of said uniform customs and practices which shall be thereby deemed to be superseded and not applicable to the extent of such contrary or additional provisions of this agreement, but not otherwise.

(b) REGULATIONS AND FOREIGN LAW * * *

(c) RELEASE OF PROPERTY OR DOCUMENTS

If you deliver to us, or upon our order, any of the property, documents or instruments relative to the Credit, or held by you as security hereunder, prior to payment in full of all our obligations secured hereby, we will deliver to you trust receipts thereof, or other security agreements and statements of trust receipt financing, or other financing statements, complying with applicable law and in such form as you may request, and pay all necessary filing fees, it being understood that any such delivery is made in reliance upon this Agreement and that your rights specified herein shall be an addition to your rights under any such applicable law, trust receipt or security agreement. Upon any transfer, sale, delivery or surrender or endorsement of any document or instrument at any time held by you, or for your account by any of your correspondents, relative to the Credit, on trust receipt or otherwise, we will indemnify and hold you and any such correspondents harmless from and against each and every claim, demand, action or suit asserted by reason thereof.

(d) STEAMSHIP GUARANTY—AIR RELEASE * * *

(e) LICENSES—INSURANCE * * *

(f) RESPONSIBILITIES OF YOU AND AGENTS

The users of the Credit shall be deemed our agents and we assume all risks of their acts and omissions. Neither you nor your correspondents shall be responsible: for the description, quantity, weight, quality, condition, packing, delivery, value or existence of the property purporting to be represented by documents; for any difference in character, quality, quantity, condition or value of the property from that expressed in documents; for the form, sufficiency, accuracy, genuineness, falsification or legal effect of any documents, even if such documents should in fact prove to be in any or all respects invalid, insufficient, fraudulent or forged; for the time, place, manner or order in which shipment is made; for partial or incomplete shipment, or failure or omissions to ship any or all of the property referred to in the Credit; for the character, adequacy, validity, or genuineness of any insurance; for the solvency or responsibility of any insurer, or for any other risk connected with insurance; for any deviation from instructions, delay, default or fraud by the shipper or anyone else in connection with the property or the shipping thereof; for the solvency, responsibility or relationship to the property of any party issuing any documents in connection with the property; for delay in arrival or failure to arrive of either the property or any of the documents relating thereto; for delay in giving or failure to give notice of arrival or any other notice; for any breach of contract between the shippers or vendors and ourselves or any of us; for failure of any draft to bear any reference or adequate reference to the Credit, or failure of documents to accompany any draft at negotiation, or failure of any person to note the amount of any draft on the reverse of the Credit, or to surrender or take up the Credit or to send forward documents apart from drafts as required by the terms of the Credit, each of which provisions, if contained in the Credit itself, it is agreed may be waived by you; or for errors, omissions, interruptions or delays in transmission or delivery of any messages, by mail, cable, telegraph, wireless, or otherwise, whether or not they be in cipher; nor shall you be responsible for any errors, neglect, or default of any of your correspondents; and none of the above shall affect, impair, or prevent the vesting of any of your rights or powers hereunder. In furtherance and extension, and not in limitation of, the specific provisions hereinbefore set forth, we agree that any action taken by you or by any correspondent of yours under or in connection with the Credit or the relative drafts, documents or property, if taken in good faith, shall be binding on us and shall not put you or your correspondents under any resulting liability to us; and we make like agreement as to any inaction or omission, unless in breach of good faith. We agree that any objection to action taken by you or any correspondent shall be deemed ratified by us unless within 10 days after receipt of such documents or acquisitions of knowledge thereof objection and notice to you is made by us.

(g) COPIES OF DOCUMENTS * * *

(h) DRAFT LESS THAN CREDIT AMOUNT * * *

4. SECURITY INTERESTS

As security for the prompt payment of all our obligations and liabilities hereunder, and in addition to any other security given to you by separate agreement, you are hereby granted a continuing security interest in and, the right to possession and disposition of, all property shipped, stored or dealt with in connection with the Credit, or the drafts drawn thereunder, and to all drafts, documents or instruments or contracts (including shipping documents or warehouse receipts or policies or certificates of insurance) or inventory or accounts or chattel paper or contract rights or general intangibles, arising from or in connection with this Credit, regardless of whether such property or documents or instruments, or other security herein described, are in your actual or constructive possession, or in transit to you, your agents, or correspondents, and the proceeds thereof, and we hereby further grant you a right of set-off upon all deposits and credits with you until our obligations or liabilities to you have been paid and discharged. We agree that this Agreement may be filed as a financing statement or that we will execute such financing statements or other documents or writings as shall be necessary, in your judgment, to perfect or maintain your security interest, as aforesaid, and to pay all costs of filing. We also agree you may execute on our behalf such financing statement and we do irrevocably appoint you as our attorney in fact for such purpose. You shall have all rights and remedies of a secured party under the Uniform Commercial Code of Michigan and you shall give us five (5) days prior written notice to the time and place of any sale upon exercise of your right to sale, public or private, before or after maturity, unless such security is perishable or threatens to decline speedily in value or is of a type customarily sold on a recognized market. You may discount, settle, compromise or extend any obligation, constituting such security, and sue thereon in your name. You shall not be liable for failure to collect or demand payment of, or protest or give notice of, or nonpayment of, any obligations, included in such security or part thereof, or for any delay, nor shall you be under any obligation to take any action in respect of such security, including any obligation to file, record or maintain or establish the validity, priority, or enforceability of your rights in or to the security. Any property or documents representing security hereunder may be held by you in your name or your nominee's name, all without notice and whether a Default exists, or not. Proceeds of sale or transfer of the security shall be applied, in order, to expenses of retaking, holding, preparing for sale, and the reasonable attorney fees and legal expenses incurred or paid by you, and then, to our obligation hereunder until paid in full.

5. DEFAULT

We shall be in Default under this agreement upon occurrence of any one of the following:

(a) Failure to perform or observe any of the terms and conditions hereof; or

(b) Failure to pay, when due, whether upon your demand or otherwise, any amounts due hereunder; or

(c) Any warranty, representation or statement made to or furnished you is untrue in any material respect; or

(d) The loss, theft, destruction, sale or encumbrance of any part or all of the security for this agreement; or

(e) The death, incapacity, insolvency, dissolution, termination of existence, suspension of business or if a receiver is appointed for any part of our property, or if we make an assignment for the benefit of creditors, or upon the commencement of bankruptcy or insolvency proceedings by or against us, or upon the issuance or service of any levy, lien, writ of attachment or garnishment or execution or similar process against us, or any of our property; or

(f) Failure to pay, when due, any tax; or

(g) If, in your sole opinion, our financial responsibility is impaired; or

(h) Any event occurs which results or could result in the acceleration of the maturity of any of our indebtedness to you or to others under any note, agreement or undertaking, in which event you shall have the right to take possession of the security given herein, set-off against same, or the rights of a secured creditor, with or without process of law, and foreclose, sell or otherwise liquidate the security both as herein provided and as provided in the Uniform Commercial Code of the State of Michigan.

6. MODIFICATION OF CREDIT

All extensions, including extensions of maturity or time for presentation of drafts, acceptances or documents, or renewals of the credit or increase or other modification of the terms hereof, or a temporary advance or acceptance or loan in connection with the credit, with or without further documentation or notice or agreement, shall continue to be governed by this agreement.

7. WAIVER

No delay on your part in the exercise of any of your rights or remedies shall operate as a waiver, nor shall any single or partial waiver, or any right or remedy preclude any other further exercise thereof, or the exercise of any other right or remedy, and no waiver or indulgence by you of any default shall be effective unless in writing and signed by you, nor shall a waiver on any one occasion be construed as a bar, or waiver of, any such right on any future occasion.

8. GOVERNING LAW * * *

9. BINDING EFFECT * * *

10. CONSTRUCTION * * *

11. PARTICIPANT * * *

12. DAMAGES

Your liability, if any, for your negligence, acts of omission or otherwise shall be limited to direct actual damages, but without liability for general, punitive or special damages or other consequential damages resulting therefrom.

Revised 1/8/86 (Commercial)

Problem 24–8

Answer the following questions with respect to the Reimbursement and Security Agreement set out above.

1. Assume that Bank knew that drafts for $500,000 would be presented under the letter on Tuesday. Would it have a right to demand payment by the customer of $500,000 on Monday? If the customer refused to pay, what rights would the Bank have under the Reimbursement and Security Agreement?

2. Assume that Bank made payment and now seeks reimbursement under the $500,000 letter of credit and that customer argues that the invoices were not in proper form because the description was not exactly the same as the description on the letter of credit. How will the Agreement affect that dispute between the Bank and its customer? (See (3)(f).)

3. If the customer fails to pay, the Bank has possession of the invoices and bills of lading. Does it have a perfected security interest? If it cannot liquidate the security within a short period of time, how can it maintain perfection of that security interest if the customer refuses to sign a financing statement? (See (4).)

4. What if the Bank extended the time for the beneficiary to present drafts under the letter by one day and the customer then complained that the Bank had violated their agreement? Does the agreement give the Bank the right to issue such waivers and extensions on behalf of customer?

To what extent can the Bank be subrogated to, and otherwise enjoy, rights of Beneficiary? The case that follows deals with that question.

TUDOR DEVELOPMENT GROUP, INC. v. UNITED STATES FIDELITY AND GUARANTY CO.

United States Circuit Court, Third Circuit, 1992.
968 F.2d 357.

Before: BECKER, COWEN and GARTH, CIRCUIT JUDGES.

OPINION OF THE COURT

COWEN, CIRCUIT JUDGE.

At issue in this case is which party is entitled to a fund of $594,000 paid into the district court. To settle this dispute we must determine whether a bank which has honored a letter of credit may be equitably subrogated to the rights of its customer vis-a-vis funds paid to the customer by a party unrelated to the original letter of credit. We conclude that because the issuing bank was satisfying its own primary liability rather than the liability of another when it made payment under the letter of credit, it may not avail itself of the common-law remedy of equitable subrogation. We will affirm the order of the district court granting summary judgment in favor of Green Hill Investors.

I.

The $594,000 fund which is the subject of this diversity dispute was paid into the district court by United States Fidelity and Guaranty Company ("USF & G"). This lawsuit began when Green Hill Associates ("Associates") sued USF & G for the proceeds of performance bonds issued by USF & G. York Excavating Co. ("York"), Dauphin Deposit Bank and Trust Company ("Dauphin Deposit") and Green Hill Project Investors ("Investors") subsequently intervened in the action, claiming an interest in the bond proceeds. The action itself arises from the construction of a multi-family residential development in Susquehanna Township ("the Township"), Dauphin County, Pennsylvania. Dauphin Deposit appeals the district court's order granting summary judgment in favor of Investors.

Associates was the owner and developer of a subdivision construction project, known as the Green Hill Project ("the Project"). Susquehanna Construction Corporation ("SCC") was a general manager of the Project under a written agreement entered into with Associate and as such undertook to construct certain buildings and complete certain other improvements on the site. USF & G issued two performance bonds guaranteeing the faithful and timely performance of all of SCC's duties under the contract with Associates ("the USF & G bonds"). The aggregate amount of these bonds totalled $2,965,873.

Eastern Consolidated Utilities, Inc. ("ECU") also entered into a contract with Associates for certain work on the Project. Under that contract, ECU agreed to construct such improvements as internal roadways, parking areas and storm drainage systems. ECU's responsibilities under this contract were guaranteed by performance bonds issued by Employers Insurance of Wausau ("the Wausau bonds").

In order to begin work on the Project, Associates needed the approval of the Township. Therefore, Associates entered into an agreement with the Township ("the Subdivision Agreement") to complete various improvements on the site of the proposed subdivision. These improvements included the construction of grading, roads, driveways, and parking and recreation areas. The Subdivision Agreement required Associates to provide either a bond or a standby letter of credit guaranteeing the completion of the specified improvements.

Associates applied for an irrevocable standby letter of credit from Dauphin Deposit in order to satisfy the Subdivision Agreement. Dauphin Deposit accepted Associates' application and issued a letter of credit in favor of the Township for the account of Associates. The face amount of the letter was $1,088,646. The letter provided that it would be payable upon the Township's certification that the required site improvements had not been completed as required by the Subdivision Agreement. Dauphin Deposit received a fee of $75 plus 1.5% per annum of the face amount of the letter of credit. Associates also agreed to reimburse Dauphin Deposit if Dauphin honored the letter of credit ("the reimbursement agreement"). The reimbursement agreement did not include an assignment of Associates' rights in the USF & G bonds in the event of honor.

As security in the event of honor, Dauphin Deposit received a collateral note executed by the Tudor Development Group ("Tudor"), Associates' general partner on the project, and an assignment of the proceeds of the Wausau performance bonds. As noted, Dauphin Deposit did not obtain an assignment of the USF & G bonds nor did it file financing statements perfecting its security interest in any of the collateral it did obtain in connection with the issuance of the letter of credit.

Sometime in May, 1987, SCC defaulted under its contract with Associates. Subsequently, Associates was declared in default of its obligations to build the site improvements under the subdivision agreement with the Township. As a result, on April 6, 1988, the Township issued its draft in the amount of $800,202 against the Dauphin Deposit letter of credit. Dauphin Deposit paid on the Township's draft. To date, Dauphin Deposit has not been reimbursed by Associates for its payment under the letter of credit.

Following SCC's default, Associates submitted a claim to USF & G for payment under the USF & G performance bonds. On September 14, 1989, Associates' bond claims against USF & G were settled, with USF & G agreeing to make a payment totalling $609,000. In exchange for this payment, Associates executed a release and assignment under which USF & G was freed from any and all claims arising from the Project. Of this settlement, $594,000 was paid into the district court to be held pending resolution of the various parties' claims to the fund.

Associates presently asserts a claim against the fund as obligee under the USF & G bonds. As a part of its settlement with USF & G, Associates assigned a portion of its rights in the bonds to Investors. Thus Investors now claims the proceeds of the fund based on Associates' partial assignment of the bond proceeds. Dauphin Deposit contends that it is equitably subrogated to Associates' interest in the fund by reason of its payment to the Township under the letter of credit, for which it has not been reimbursed. Furthermore, Dauphin Deposit claims that the partial assignment by Associates to Investors could not divest Dauphin Deposit of its rights to the fund because its right to be equitably subrogated attached at the time it honored the letter, which was prior to the time of Associates' partial assignment to Investors.

Dauphin Deposit obtained a judgment against Tudor under the collateral note which it obtained as security but has not executed that judgment. Dauphin Deposit has neither sought nor obtained a judgment against Associates.

The district court, on cross-motions for summary judgment by Investors and Dauphin Deposit, concluded that there were no disputed issues of material fact and granted summary judgment in favor of Investors.[1] The

1. The district court granted judgment on the pleadings against York. 768 F.Supp. 493. York did not appeal from that determination and thus is not a party to this appeal.

district court concluded that a bank which issues a standby letter of credit cannot accede to the rights of its customer on a theory of equitable subrogation and that even if such relief were available, the undisputed facts did not support granting Dauphin Deposit an equitable interest in the USF & G bond proceeds. This appeal followed.

Our review of the district court's determination of a question of law is plenary. *Carter v. Rafferty,* 826 F.2d 1299, 1304 (3d Cir.1987), *cert. denied,* 484 U.S. 1011, 108 S.Ct. 711, 98 L.Ed.2d 661 (1988). The clearly erroneous standard of review is applied to findings of fact. *Id.* When an action is decided on motion for summary judgment, this court must apply the same test that the district court was required to apply pursuant to Federal Rule of Civil Procedure 56(c): summary judgment is properly granted only if there is no genuine issue of material fact and the moving party is entitled to judgment as a matter of law. *Id.*

II.

* * *

Standby letters of credit differ from commercial letters in some respects. The beneficiary of a commercial letter of credit may draw upon the letter simply by presenting the requisite documents showing that the beneficiary has performed and is entitled to the funds. A standby letter requires the production of documents showing that the customer has defaulted on its obligation to the beneficiary, which triggers the beneficiary's right to draw down on the letter. *Id.* Standby letters are usually used in non-sales contracts such as contracts for the construction of a building, the provision of services, or some other contract where the performance of one party is executory. *See* John F. Dolan, *The Law of Letters of Credit: Commercial and Standby Credits* ¶ 1.06 (2nd ed. 1991). No distinction is made in the UCC between commercial and standby letters of credit.

* * *

In this case, the customer in the letter of credit transaction was Associates. The contract underlying the letter of credit was the subdivision agreement entered into by Associates and the Township, and the Township was the beneficiary of the letter of credit. Dauphin Deposit, the issuer, was obligated under the terms of the letter to honor the Township's demand for payment when the Township certified that the agreed upon improvements had not been made by Associates. *Id.* at § 5114(a). Once Dauphin Deposit honored the letter, Associates, as its customer, had an immediate statutory obligation to reimburse Dauphin, the issuer, *id.* at § 5114(c), and was also obligated to do so under the terms of the reimbursement agreement.

While section 5114(c) states that the issuer shall be reimbursed, there are no comparable statutory provisions indicating the manner in which such reimbursement shall occur. The method of reimbursement is a matter left to negotiations between the parties. In this case, the reimbursement obligation was memorialized contractually in the reimbursement agreement entered into by Associates and Dauphin Deposit. In addition, Dauphin Deposit negotiated for assignment rights in certain collateral held by Associates, namely its rights under the Wausau performance bonds and also looked to the Tudor promissory note as collateral in its dealings with Associates.

III.

The classic explanation of the doctrine of equitable subrogation is as follows:

> Where property of one person is used in discharging an obligation owed by another or a lien upon property of another, under such circumstances that the other would be unjustly enriched by the retention of the benefit thus conferred, the former is entitled to be subrogated to the position of the obligee or lien-holder.

Gladowski v. Felczak, 346 Pa. 660, 31 A.2d 718, 720 (1943) (quoting Restatement of Restitution § 162 (1937)). Generally, the following five prerequisites must be satisfied before a claimant may avail itself of the remedy of equitable subrogation: (1) the claimant paid the creditor to protect his own interests; (2) the claimant did not act as a volunteer; (3) the claimant was not primarily liable for the debt; i.e., secondary liability; (4) the entire debt has been satisfied; and (5) allowing subrogation will not cause injustice to the rights of others.

Pennsylvania law offers little guidance, however, on the question of whether the doctrine is applicable in the context of letters of credit. This dearth of state case law is best explained by the simple fact that the question of subrogation usually arises in the bankruptcy setting. The issuer which has honored a demand for payment under a letter of credit has an immediate and unconditional statutory right to reimbursement from its customer and has usually secured adequate collateral to make itself whole in the event of honor. If the customer becomes bankrupt, however, the issuer's only practical recourse is asserting a claim in the bankruptcy proceeding. Therefore, most of the law related to the issue presented in this appeal comes from the bankruptcy courts rather than state courts. We look, then, to those cases for guidance.

Those courts which have considered the question presently before us have disagreed as to whether the remedy of equitable subrogation is available. The minority view advocates the availability of equitable subrogation, whereas the majority of courts to consider the issue, as well as the district court in this case, have refused to grant the issuing bank equitable subrogation rights following honor under a letter of credit. We agree with the majority view that a bank which issues a letter of credit may not accede to the rights of its customer on a theory of equitable subrogation.

Courts grappling with this issue have generally concluded that while there are some superficial similarities between guarantees and letters of credit, their "legal" characteristics remain quite distinct and thus the remedies available should remain distinct as well. *See In re Carley Capital,* 119 B.R. 646; *In re Agrownautics,* 125 B.R. 350; *In re East Texas Steel,* 117 B.R. 235. As noted by the district court, the key distinction between letters of credit and guarantees is that the issuer's obligation under a letter of credit is primary whereas a guarantor's obligation is secondary—the guarantor is *only* obligated to pay if the principal defaults on the debt the principal owes. In contrast, while the issuing bank in the letter of credit situation may be secondarily liable in a temporal sense, since its obligation to pay does not arise until after its customer fails to satisfy some obligation, it is satisfying its own absolute and primary obligation to make payment rather than satisfying an obligation of its customer. Having paid its own debt, as it has contractually undertaken to do, the issuer "cannot then step into the shoes of the creditor to seek subrogation, reimbursement or contribution from the [customer]. The only exception would be where the parties reach an agreement to the contrary." *In re Kaiser Steel,* 89 B.R. at 153.

The distinct nature of the obligations which arise with respect to letters of credit and guarantees is also reflected in a number of provisions of the UCC itself. *See* 13 Pa.Cons.Stat.Ann. § 5103 cmt. ("[t]he issuer is not a guarantor of the performance of these underlying transactions"); 13 Pa. Cons.Stat.Ann. § 5101 cmt. ("[t]he other source of law respecting letters of credit is the law of contracts with occasional unfortunate excursions into the law of guaranty"); 13 Pa.Cons.Stat.Ann. § 5109 cmt. ("issuer receives compensation for a payment service rather than for a guaranty of performance"). While we recognize that arguments may be made and have been made in support of allowing subrogation, we believe that Article 5 of the UCC, when viewed in its entirety, evinces an intent to keep the law of guarantee and the law of letters of credit separate. In our view, the Uniform Commercial Code Committee, rather than the federal courts, is best equipped to address this problem. *See* The Task Force on the Study of U.C.C. Article 5, *An Examination of U.C.C. Article 5 (Letters of Credit),* 45 Bus.Law. 1527 (1990) (Task Force, while reaching no conclusion as to whether subrogation is appropriate, suggests it would be useful to resolve issue by statute); Michael E. Avidon, *U.C.C. Article 5 Symposium: Subrogation in the Letter of Credit Context,* 56 Brook.L.Rev. 128, 138 (1990) ("[i]n addition to providing needed guidance as to rights and obligations in what has been a murky area of the law, wellcrafted legislation will curb the excesses of courts ... in their zeal to do equity in particular cases").

The UCC does contain one direct reference to the possibility of subrogation in the letter of credit context: "[t]he customer will normally have direct recourse against the beneficiary if performance fails, whereas the issuer will have such recourse only by assignment of or in a proper case subrogation to the rights of the customer." 13 Pa.Cons.Stat.Ann. § 5109 cmt. This comment, however, is clearly limited to the possibility of the issuer being subrogated to the customer's rights against the beneficiary. In the present case, rather than seeking subrogation rights against the *beneficiary* of the letter, Dauphin Deposit seeks subrogation rights against a *stranger* to the letter of credit issued in favor of the Township. In any event, this comment merely suggests rather than mandates the availability of subrogation in certain cases.

Finally, we note that some courts have determined that equitable subrogation is not available to a bank which has honored a letter of credit, but has not been reimbursed. These courts have rejected the remedy of equitable subrogation in the belief that allowing subrogation would abrogate the independence principle which is the cornerstone of letter of credit law. *See In re Carley Capital,* 119 B.R. at 651; *In re East Texas Steel,* 117 B.R. at 241; *In re Economic Enterprises,* 44 B.R. at 232. The district court in this case disagreed with that assessment and concluded that "the independence principle is technically not violated by allowing Dauphin Deposit to proceed against its customer." App. at 1144. We agree with the district court that the vitality of the independence principle is unlikely to be substantially diminished were we to allow subrogation in this situation. However, as noted, one of the principal requirements of equitable subrogation has not been satisfied here—that the party seeking subrogation have satisfied the debt of another—and therefore we conclude that the district court correctly determined that the remedy cannot be invoked in this case. Moreover, as will be discussed, the equities do not favor granting subrogation rights in this case.

IV.

Even if we were to ignore the fact that Dauphin Deposit has failed to meet the technical requirements to avail itself of the remedy of subrogation since it was satisfying its own primary obligation in paying under the letter of credit, we would nevertheless be compelled to reject its claimed right to the remedy of equitable subrogation on these facts. As the district court concluded, the equities do not favor subrogation in this case.

When Dauphin Deposit agreed to issue a letter of credit on behalf of its customer, Associates, it was in a position to bargain for whatever security it thought appropriate. It chose to contract for an assignment of rights in the Wausau bonds and received a promissory note from Tudor. In addition, Dauphin Deposit received a large annual fee for the service of issuing the credit based upon the face amount of the letter. It could have contracted for an assignment of rights in the USF & G bonds but did not do so.

Presumably, at the time these arrangements were made Dauphin was satisfied with the collateral it received and the creditworthiness of its customer. However, now that Dauphin has discovered that it made a poor business decision in not contracting for an assignment of rights in the USF & G bonds, it seeks our help in gaining additional rights. As the district court properly concluded, there is no apparent reason why the court should exercise its equitable powers to rewrite the contract between the parties to give Dauphin Deposit more security than it bargained to receive. *See In re Carley Capital,* 119 B.R. at 650 (no equitable reason to grant subrogation where "the plaintiffs had the ability by virtue of the contracts with the parties with whom they dealt to protect themselves in exactly the same way that they seek to protect themselves by subrogation"); *In re Munzenrieder,* 58 B.R. at 231 (fact that security received turned out to be useless "means nothing more or less than that the Bank entered into a transaction which . . . turned out to be a total loss, a fact legally meaningless and insufficient to invoke the doctrine of equitable subrogation").[4]

4. Judge Garth would add to the majority's analysis:

Moreover, when Dauphin paid the letter of credit covering *site* improvements, it could not, and did not, acquire subrogation rights against the USF & G bonds, which contrary to Dauphin's claims, covered the construction of the buildings and not the *site* improvements.

The Supreme Court has stated that "it is elementary that one cannot acquire by subrogation what another whose rights he claims, did not have." *United States v. Munsey Trust Co.,* 332 U.S. 234, 242, 67 S.Ct. 1599, 1603, 91 L.Ed. 2022 (1947). Dauphin acknowledged in *Dauphin Deposit Bank & Trust v. Employers Insurance of Wausau,* Consolidated Cases Nos. 4099 S 1988 and 5062 S 1988 (C.P. Dauphin County, Pa.) that

In assessing the equities of the situation, we must also look to the other parties who could or would be affected by a decision to allow subrogation in this case. Those parties who engaged in business dealings with Associates subsequent to the issuance of the letter of credit, including Investors, to whom Associates assigned its rights in the USF & G bonds, assumed they would be free from any future claims by Dauphin Deposit with respect to the letter of credit. We do not believe the equities favor treating Dauphin Deposit in a manner which would be detrimental to those parties who had subsequent dealings with Associates.

Finally, we note that as a general matter, equitable relief is not appropriate where a party has an adequate legal or statutory remedy. *Clark v. Pennsylvania State Police,* 496 Pa. 310, 436 A.2d 1383, 1385 (1981). Here, Dauphin Deposit appears to have two legal remedies and one statutory remedy: (1) seek judgment against Tudor on the promissory note; (2) sue Associates directly under the Reimbursement Agreement; and (3) seek reimbursement under 13 Pa.Cons.Stat.Ann. § 5114(c) which provides that an issuer is entitled to immediate reimbursement from its customer in the event of honor. In determining whether a remedy is "adequate," we must look to its availability and not to the likelihood of its success. *Willing v. Mazzocone,* 482 Pa. 377, 393 A.2d 1155, 1158 (1978); *Chartiers Valley School Dist. v. Virginia Mansions Apts., Inc.,* 340 Pa.Super. 285, 489 A.2d 1381, 1386 (1985). Thus the fact that the remedies set forth above might not make Dauphin Deposit whole does not mandate a finding that such remedies are inadequate, thereby requiring this court to grant equitable relief.

V.

In sum, we conclude that equitable subrogation is not an appropriate remedy in this situation, both because an issuing bank which honors a letter of credit makes good its own primary obligation, rather than fulfilling the obligation of another, and because the equities of the case before us do not warrant it. We will affirm the judgment of the district court granting summary judgment in favor of Investors.

BECKER, CIRCUIT JUDGE, dissenting.

This appeal presents a close, difficult, and important question that has divided both courts and scholars. The majority concludes that, under Article 5 of the Uniform Commercial Code and the common law, a bank that has issued a standby letter of credit may never qualify for equitable subrogation to the rights of its defaulting customer in the underlying commercial transaction. The majority opinion is a fine piece of advocacy for a respectable position, one that has been adopted by a majority of the courts to face the issue (although rejected by the only federal appellate court that has reached the question). Nevertheless, I believe that the majority has backed the

the Wausau bonds issued in connection with ECU's contract responsibilities covered only the *site* improvements (A367).

Because Dauphin's letter of credit covered *site* improvements only while the USF & G bonds covered only specific *buildings,* Dauphin, even if otherwise eligible for equitable subrogation in the context of a letter of credit (which we hold it was not), cannot be subrogated to Associates' interest in the fund created by the proceeds of bonds issued by USF & G. This result must follow because Dauphin's letter of credit did not relate to the work covered by the USF & G bonds which, as stated, pertained solely to building improvements. *See* App. at 76 and 79.

wrong horse. I would hold that an issuer of a standby letter of credit may, in proper circumstances, obtain equitable subrogation to the rights of its customer.

The majority also concludes that, even assuming that equitable subrogation is available in some cases, the equities in this case do not warrant it. Because I believe that genuine issues of material fact remain on this issue, I would not decide it on summary judgment. I would instead remand the case to the district court for further proceedings to determine whether the facts and equities here weigh in favor of or against Dauphin Deposit's claim. I therefore respectfully dissent.

I. The General Availability of Subrogation to an Issuer of a Letter of Credit

Investors offers three reasons why issuers of standby letters of credit should not be entitled to subrogation. First, Investors argues that an issuer does not qualify for subrogation as a matter of common law because the issuer is primarily liable on its obligation to the beneficiary, not secondarily liable for the debt of another, as the common law requires. Second, Investors contends that the principles undergirding Article 5 of the U.C.C. bar subrogation by issuers of letters of credit. Finally, Investors suggests that an issuer can (and Dauphin Deposit did) protect itself adequately by insisting on security before agreeing to issue a letter of credit. In Investors' view, subrogation should be denied because it would only protect the imprudent issuer. Because each issue is close, difficult, and important, and because Article 5 of the U.C.C. is under study for possible major revision, I will discuss all three.

A. Common Law Bar: Primariness of the Issuer's Obligation

The centerpiece of the majority's position is that Dauphin Deposit was primarily liable on its own obligation to the township under the letter of credit. In its view, Dauphin Deposit, as a primary obligor paying its own debt rather than the debt of another, cannot seek subrogation. In my view, the majority takes undue advantage of the ambiguity of the terms "primary" and "secondary" liability.

Certainly, Dauphin Deposit was "primarily" liable in one temporal sense, in that, pursuant to the letter of credit arrangement, it had to pay the township immediately on the township's proper demand, with (unlike a guarantor or surety) no right to assert any defenses that Associates may have had. On the other hand, even the majority concedes that Dauphin Deposit was temporally "secondarily" liable in the sense that its obligation arose only after Associates failed to satisfy its obligation. [Majority op. at 362.] I agree with the majority that Dauphin Deposit was "primarily" liable in the sense that (like a surety) it was directly liable, under its own contractual agreement, to make a payment to the township. But that is not the relevant meaning of "primary" liability in the subrogation context, for if it were, then no guarantor or surety would ever qualify for equitable subrogation.

In my view, the relevant question is whether Dauphin Deposit was "secondarily" liable in the sense that it paid the debt of another, Associates. Investors, and the majority, have

> failed to distinguish the primary liability of a debtor to its creditor to repay a loan and the primary obligation of the issuer to its beneficiary to honor a letter of credit. When a standby credit supporting a loan is honored, the issuer admittedly is satisfying its obligation as a primary obligor to honor the standby credit, but at the same time it is in fact satisfying a debt for which a person other than the issuer is primarily liable....
>
> [T]he notion that an issuer's obligation to honor the letter of credit is a "primary obligation" should be interpreted to mean that, under the independence principle, the issuer may not avoid its obligation to honor the credit by identifying deficiencies in underlying contracts or by otherwise asserting defenses that are typically available to parties who are generally considered to be "secondarily liable" such as guarantors and sureties. Thus ... the "primary obligation" language in the letter of credit context concerns itself with the issuer's ability to avoid honoring its letter of credit, whereas the "primary liability" language in the subrogation context concerns itself with whether the entity, after reducing a claim of a creditor, received the consideration from the creditor.

In re Valley Vue Joint Venture, 123 B.R. 199, 204, 206 (Bankr.E.D.Va.1991).

In this case, Dauphin Deposit paid the debt of another when it satisfied Associates' obligation. Associates was liable to the township to make site improvements. Dauphin Deposit's letter of credit served as the township's backup in case Associates defaulted. Associates did default, and Dauphin Deposit, pursuant to its obligation under the letter of credit, satisfied Associates' obligation to the township.

As the issuer of a letter of credit, Dauphin Deposit had fewer defenses than would the issuer of a guaranty or performance bond, but the substance of Dauphin Deposit's obligation was nevertheless essentially similar to that of a guarantor or surety. There can be no doubt that all three parties considered Dauphin Deposit as a de facto surety and the letter of credit as a substitute for a performance bond. Paragraph 5 of the subdivision agreement provides:

> As a further condition to approval of said Plan, Subdivider shall furnish a ~~bond~~ * in the amount of One Million Eighty-eight Thousand Six Hundred Forty Six ($1,088,646.00) Dollars to guarantee the proper completion of the improvements required by the Ordinance. *Irrevocable Straight Letter of Credit No: S–10181 from Dauphin Deposit Bank and Trust Company

The parties struck out the word "bond" and replaced it with a reference to the letter of credit. Quite clearly, the parties intended the letter to serve the same economic role as a performance bond would have: "to *guarantee* the proper completion of the improvements required by the Ordinance" (emphasis added).

Guarantors and sureties pay their own legal obligations, yet they are still entitled to seek equitable subrogation as well as contractual subrogation. That is because in meeting their own "primary" obligations, guarantors and sureties are also "secondarily" liable to pay others' debts. So far as the common law is concerned, the same logic should apply to issuers of letters of credit such as Dauphin Deposit.

Thus I conclude that the common law by itself poses no bar to the assertion of subrogation rights by issuers of letters of credit. I next turn to whether the U.C.C.'s statutory provisions on letters of credit require a different result.

B. The U.C.C. Statutory Bar

1. Prohibition by the Text of Article 5

As just mentioned, Dauphin Deposit's basic theory is that its role was as a quasi-guarantor, and thus, like a guarantor, it is entitled to equitable subrogation. As the majority notes, however, the text of and official commentary to Article 5 of the U.C.C. make clear that a letter of credit is not equivalent to a guaranty.

The "independence principle" is the cornerstone of Article 5 and the law of letters of credit. Under the independence principle, the issuer of a letter of credit (unlike a guarantor) generally may not look to the underlying transaction and assert the defenses of the party whose obligation is guaranteed. Instead, the issuer must look only at the documents presented by the beneficiary and determine if they, on their face, meet the conditions that invoke the issuer's obligation to pay on the letter of credit. See 13 Pa.Cons. Stat.Ann. § 5114(a) (Purdon 1984) (equivalent to U.C.C. § 5–114(1)) and comment 1 thereto. In short, the issuer must pay first and worry about its reimbursement and the merits of the dispute involving its customer later. Id.

Accordingly, the issuer's duty to its customer does not ordinarily include liability for performance of the underlying contract. See 13 Pa.Cons.Stat. Ann. § 5109(a) (Purdon 1984) (equivalent to U.C.C. § 5–109(1)). The commentary explicitly notes that "the issuer receives compensation for a payment service rather than for a guaranty of performance." Id. comment 1. Correlatively, the customer must, upon request, immediately reimburse the issuer if the issuer honored the letter according to its terms, again without regard to the merits of any dispute over the underlying transaction. See 13 Pa.Cons.Stat.Ann. § 5114(c) (Purdon 1984) (equivalent to U.C.C. § 5–114(3)). Moreover, the commentary to Article 5 suggests that the law of letters of credit has been marred by "occasional unfortunate excursions into the law of guaranty." 13 Pa.Cons.Stat.Ann. § 5101 comment (Purdon 1984) (official comment to U.C.C. § 5–101). The U.C.C. undeniably declares its intention "to set an independent theoretical framework for the further development of letters of credit." Id.

From these snippets, Investors argues and the majority apparently concludes that subrogation would be contrary to the spirit, if not the letter, of the Code. I am not persuaded. The drafters' concern about importing the law of guaranty was not about subrogation, but about eroding the independence principle (which, as I shall explain in the next section, is *not* compromised by allowing subrogation). The drafters of Article 5 took great pains to establish the independence principle in order to promote smooth commercial relations, but it does not follow that they intended to do away with subrogation simply because guarantors are eligible for subrogation. As one court has observed,

> [w]hile a letter of credit may require conformity with certain obligations and formalities which are not required of a guarantee, where there is no contrary policy reason for treating them dissimilarly for other purposes, precluding the assertion of subrogation rights to issuers of standby letters of credit while allowing guarantors to assert them would be no more than an exercise in honoring form over substance.

In re Minnesota Kicks, Inc., 48 B.R. 93, 104–05 (Bankr.D.Minn.1985) (citation omitted).

Indeed, the U.C.C. commentary explicitly anticipates that issuers will have recourse against beneficiaries by way of subrogation to the rights of their customers, at least in appropriate cases:

> The customer will normally have direct recourse against the beneficiary if performance fails, whereas the issuer will have such recourse only by assignment of or in a proper case subrogation to the rights of the customer.

13 Pa.Cons.Stat.Ann. § 5109 comment 1 (official comment to U.C.C. § 5–109).

This official commentary disproves any suggestion that the drafters of Article 5 considered subrogation antithetical to the law of letters of credit. On the other hand, this comment does not prove that subrogation should apply in this case as a matter of course. First, the comment speaks of subrogation to the customer's right against the beneficiary, and Dauphin Deposit seeks subrogation to Associates' rights against USF & G, not the township. More basically, the question remains what classes of cases are "proper" cases. On that score, there is little legislative history behind Article 5 to turn to, for the case law on subrogation in letter of credit contexts was extremely sparse before the adoption of the Code. See Michael Evan Avidon, *Subrogation in the Letter of Credit Context,* 56 Brook.L.Rev. 129, 133–34 (1990); Peter R. Jarvis, *Standby Letters of Credit—Issuers' Subrogation and Assignment Rights—Part I,* 9 U.C.C.L.J. 356, 375–77 (1976).

In sum, the text and commentary of the U.C.C. itself do not rule in or rule out subrogation in the letter of credit context. I therefore look to policy reasons (including policies embedded in the Code, such as the independence principle) to determine what is a "proper" case for subrogation.

2. Interference with the Independence Principle

The recent American Bar Association/U.S. Council on International Banking Task Force on the Study of U.C.C. Article 5 reached no definitive conclusion on when and whether subrogation is available in the letter of credit context, although it agreed that statutory resolution of the question would be useful. See its report, *An Examination of U.C.C. Article 5 (Letters of Credit)* 21 (Sept. 29, 1989), reprinted in 45 Bus.Law. 1527 (1990). The task force did agree, however, that "the question of the availability of subrogation is one which must be regarded as being essentially outside of credit law and the letter of credit transaction," and that "the primary factor in determining [subrogation's] availability should be whether it would affect the integrity of principles vital to letter of credit law." Id.

As noted above, the cornerstone of the law of letters of credit is the independence principle, and thus if granting subrogation to issuers of letters of credit would undermine the independence principle, then such subrogation must not be permitted. In my view, allowing the issuer of a letter of credit to subrogate to the rights of its customer would not undermine the independence principle.

The independence principle ensures the beneficiary of prompt payment and basically determines that the beneficiary will have the dollars in its pocket if there is a dispute between it and the customer over the underlying transaction. See, for example, *Itek Corp. v. First National Bank of Boston,* 730 F.2d 19, 24 (1st Cir.1984). As discussed above, this distinguishes a letter of credit from an ordinary guaranty: a guaranty is not independent in this sense, and guarantors may generally assert defenses available to the party whose obligation is guaranteed.

Investors suggests that the independence principle must be viewed as a wall between the letter of credit side and the underlying transaction side. Some courts have similarly argued that allowing subrogation would permit an issuer to interfere with the underlying contract. See, for example, *In re Economic Enterprises,* 44 B.R. 230, 232 (Bankr.D.Conn.1984). But the point of the independence principle is not to set up a wall for the sake of a wall, but to serve certain purposes. The independence principle undoubtedly requires the issuer to pay first, without looking through to the underlying transaction. Subrogation should therefore be unavailable before the issuer has paid the beneficiary. Once the issuer has done so, however, as Dauphin Deposit has here, the purpose of the independence principle has been served: the beneficiary has the money.

Insistence on perpetual separation is thus pointless formalism. On a more pragmatic level, I would agree that if the possibility of subsequent subrogation would discourage issuers from honoring already-issued letters of credit, then subrogation should not be permitted, because that would undercut the purposes of Article 5. But I cannot see why that would be so. If anything, the *un*availability of subsequent subrogation might discourage issuers from honoring the letters because they would have one less means of obtaining reimbursement.

In sum, the policies underlying Article 5 of the U.C.C. do not require courts to deny subrogation to all issuers of standby letters of credit. The remaining question is whether other policy considerations commend the per se rule argued by Investors and adopted by the majority.

C. Other Policy Considerations

1. The Issuer's Ability to Protect Itself Contractually

In my view, Investors' (and the majority's) best argument is that the issuer of a letter of credit is perfectly able to protect itself contractually. That is, the issuer receives a payment for its services and may also demand assignment rights to collateral in the event that it is forced to pay on the letter. Investors argues that Dauphin Deposit made a deal with Associates and received certain collateral rights, including assignment rights to the other bonds involved in the Green Hill Project (the "Wausau bonds"). It is certainly fair to ask why Dauphin Deposit should receive the additional right of subrogation, simply because it made a bad gamble or wasn't wary enough when negotiating its reimbursement agreement with Associates. Many courts have voiced similar concerns. See, for example, *In re Agrownautics, Inc.*, 125 B.R. 350, 353 (Bankr.D.Conn.1991); *In re Carley Capital Group,* 119 B.R. 646, 650 (W.D.Wis.1990).

Nevertheless, this argument, although powerful, proves too much. Generally applied, the same argument would virtually eliminate equitable subrogation altogether, for it would apply to every guaranty or suretyship contract. Moreover, in many cases this may lead to the customer receiving an undeserved windfall. A customer may default on both its obligation on the underlying transaction and its obligation to reimburse the issuer of the letter of credit, yet retain any income deriving from the original transaction. In short, the issuer's ability to protect itself may be a strong equity against it, as is the fact that it receives a fee for its services, but countervailing equities may outweigh these considerations in certain cases. See *In re Glade Springs, Inc.*, 826 F.2d 440, 442 (6th Cir.1987) (reinstating the subrogation remedy that had been ordered by the bankruptcy court, 47 B.R. 780 (Bankr. E.D.Tenn.1985)).

2. *Efficiency*

At bottom, what concerns me most is how the rule that courts adopt will affect incentives to issue letters of credit in the first place. It is possible that if no equitable subrogation were permitted, fewer banks would issue such letters, which would be commercially undesirable. Given the vagaries of commerce, it may be difficult for the issuer to forecast precisely which security will have value years down the road. If courts allow traditional equitable subrogation, the transaction costs in negotiating letters of credit may be lower than under a rule where the parties must specify subrogation rights contractually.

On the other hand, with the law as unsettled as it now is, prudent would-be issuers may already have reacted by demanding greater fees or security, and the system appears to be functioning well. Parties may even be willing to incorporate the entire body of equity jurisprudence by contractual reference. Perhaps in the long run, the rule that the majority adopts will not make much of a difference, as good lawyers and prudent issuers will react accordingly. I concede too that a bright-line no-subrogation rule would promote legal certainty and thereby reduce litigation costs.

The issue is very close, but on balance I think that the better rule is to retain subrogation on a case-by-case basis and apply it sparingly. When the unexpected happens, as it so often does, it is desirable to leave courts with equitable powers to avoid windfalls and to achieve a result fair to all parties. Certainly that was the solution of the common law, and I have found nothing in the U.C.C. as adopted in Pennsylvania that justifies my predicting that the Pennsylvania Supreme Court would vote to oust the common law in this field. See also 13 Pa.Cons.Stat.Ann. § 1103 (equivalent to U.C.C. § 1–103) (supplemental common law principles continue to apply unless explicitly displaced by the U.C.C.).

As noted above, Article 5 of the U.C.C. has been under study by a task force. That study recommended that the question of subrogation rights be resolved statutorily. I agree that that is the best solution. Perhaps further policy study will show that the equitable subrogation game isn't worth the candle, and the U.C.C. will be amended so to provide. Under the law as it stands, however, I cannot agree with the majority that equitable subrogation should be completely unavailable in the letter of credit context.

II. Subrogation in This Case

A. Adequacy of a Remedy at Law

After Dauphin Deposit paid on the township's draft upon the letter of credit, it was statutorily and contractually entitled to immediate reimbursement from Associates. See 13 Pa.Cons.Stat.Ann. § 5114(c) (equivalent to U.C.C. § 5–114(c)). Dauphin Deposit was also, however, contractually entitled not only to a substantial annual fee for its services, which included taking some risk of nonreimbursement, but also to an assignment of a security interest in the Wausau bonds. Dauphin Deposit also received a collateral note from Tudor, Associates' general partner. The only apparent reason for this suit is that those legal remedies may not suffice to make Dauphin Deposit whole.

The majority suggests that Dauphin Deposit's legal remedies against possibly assetless Tudor and Associates are "adequate," precluding equitable relief. It cites *Willing v. Mazzocone,* 482 Pa. 377, 393 A.2d 1155, 1158 (1978), and *Chartiers Valley School District v. Virginia Mansions Apartments,* 340 Pa.Super. 285, 489 A.2d 1381, 1386–87 (1985), which hold *in nonsubrogation contexts* that the adequacy of a legal remedy is measured by its availability, not its likelihood of success, and, concomitantly, that a defendant's insolvency does not justify equitable intervention.

I find those cases distinguishable. Notably, Investors and the majority cite no case nor have I found any case from Pennsylvania or any other state that denies equitable subrogation (as opposed to injunctive or other equitable relief) on the ground of adequate remedies at law. The majority's conclusion also produces an anomaly. It denies equitable subrogation when the owing party is judgment-proof, yet that is precisely when subrogation is most likely to be necessary. Consider, too, a contract between a principal and its surety. If the principal has assets, its creditor is unlikely to have to call upon the surety for payment. Moreover, under Pennsylvania law a surety always has a contract action (express or implied) against its principal for indemnity, yet it is ordinarily entitled to subrogation as well. See generally 35 Pennsylvania Law Encyclopedia, *Suretyship* §§ 131–134 (West, 1961 & 1991 Supp.).

Thus, the nominal availability of legal action against Tudor and Associates should not bar Dauphin Deposit from seeking subrogation to the rights of Associates. At most, the availability of superior remedies should be a subject for the district court on remand as part of the equitable balance.

B. The Balance of Equities

The relevant equities are those between Dauphin Deposit and the remaining claimant to the USF & G bonds, Investors. I have already discussed the mixed equities in favor of Dauphin Deposit. The parties also dispute the equities as to Investors. Investors claims that it is an innocent assignee with no reason to expect that its assignment rights would be subject to the subrogation claim of Dauphin Deposit. Dauphin Deposit counters that Investors was not a good faith assignee for value, but the successor and affiliate of a foreclosing creditor, Summit. According to Dauphin Deposit, Investors knew of Dauphin Deposit's role from its participation at meetings with the township and is benefiting from the windfall of improvements financed by the draft on Dauphin Deposit's letter of credit.

I have no idea which version is the more accurate or whose story is more compelling. Because this balancing of the equities is quintessentially a matter for a trial court, and the district court has not undertaken this task, I would remand the issue.

C. Scope of the USF & G Bonds

Finally, the parties dispute whether the USF & G Bonds even covered the work that led to the default that required Dauphine Deposit to pay on the letter of credit. Investors argues that the USF & G bonds covered construction of buildings, not the site improvements that were the subject of Dauphin Deposit's letter of credit. Dauphin Deposit contends that the USF & G bonds covered the entire project, both buildings and site improvements. The district court and the majority never reached this issue, although Judge Garth, in concurring footnote 4 to the majority opinion, agrees with Investors.

This question involves contractual construction that is not simple: the Susquehanna Construction agreement is complex and probably ambiguous, and hearing parol evidence and evidence of the parties' course of conduct may prove necessary. Simply because the Wausau bonds covered only site improvements, it does not necessarily follow that the USF & G bonds were entirely complementary and covered only buildings. Moreover, Dauphin Deposit argues that Associates is estopped to deny that the USF & G bonds covered the site improvements. Because the district court did not reach these issues, I would remand them, too.

III. Conclusion

For the foregoing reasons, I would reverse the judgment of the district court and remand for further proceedings.

Questions

1. Do you think the drafters of the new version of Article 5 agreed with the majority or the dissent?

2. What should they have done?

In re VALLEY VUE JOINT VENTURE

United States Bankruptcy Court, Eastern District of Virginia, 1991.
123 B.R. 199.

MEMORANDUM OPINION

MARTIN V.B. BOSTETTER, JR., CHIEF JUDGE.

This matter is before the Court upon the objection by Valley Vue Joint Venture, a Virginia general partnership (the "Debtor"), to a proof of claim filed by S.W. Rodgers Co., Inc., a Virginia corporation ("Rodgers"), in the amount of $1,000,000. Rodgers' claim results from its reimbursement of a bank which honored a standby letter of credit issued for the account of Rodgers. The letter of credit was drawn upon by the Bank of Baltimore, a secured creditor of the Debtor, following the Debtor's pre-petition default on a loan made to the Debtor by the Bank of Baltimore. Rodgers asserts that it is entitled to be subrogated to the rights of the Bank of Baltimore pursuant to 11 U.S.C. § 509(a) and general principles of equity. For the reasons stated herein, this Court denies the Debtor's objection and holds that Rodgers is entitled to be subrogated to the rights of the Bank of Baltimore with respect to the bank's lien on certain property owned by the Debtor.

In February 1989, the Debtor, a real estate development partnership comprised of VSE Capital Corporation and John E. Alvey, III, obtained a short term $4,493,000 loan from Ameribanc Savings Bank to enable the Debtor to acquire land in Northern Virginia on which the Debtor intended to build single family homes. Ameribanc required that its loan be guaranteed and that the guaranty be secured by a $1,000,000 standby letter of credit. The Debtor asked Rodgers, one of its contractors, to furnish the guaranty and letter of credit to Ameribanc. Rodgers agreed to do so and entered into a Guaranty Agreement with the Debtor dated February 10, 1989 (the "Original Agreement"). Paragraph 3 of the Original Agreement states that:

> Rodgers agrees that it *waives subrogation and contribution* with respect to its guaranty *and acknowledges that it will have no recourse* against [the Debtor] or its partners, VSE Capital Corporation and John E. Alvey, III, or any guarantors including David K. Vitalis or John E. Alvey, III or their respective spouses, if any, or any other indorsers or guarantors of the loans issued by the Mortgagees for the Project in the event that a Mortgagee draws upon the Letter of Credit in the event [the Debtor] defaults in its obligations to such mortgagee.

(emphasis added).

Rodgers never delivered a guaranty to Ameribanc but did cause a $1,000,000 standby letter of credit to be issued for the benefit of Ameribanc.

In March 1989, the Debtor refinanced the Ameribanc loan with the Bank of Baltimore which required that its loan be secured by a deed of trust on the property that the Debtor acquired with the proceeds of the Ameribanc loan. The Bank of Baltimore required that its loan be guaranteed by VSE Capital Corporation, John E. Alvey, III, David K. Vitalis (the majority shareholder of VSE Capital Corporation) and Vitalis' wife (collectively, the "Guarantors"). The Bank of Baltimore also required the delivery of an additional guaranty to be secured by a $1,000,000 standby letter of credit. Rodgers agreed to furnish such guaranty and letter of credit. In addition, Rodgers, at the request of the Debtor, agreed to lend the Debtor $500,000 to enable the Debtor to satisfy all of the conditions to closing the Bank of Baltimore loan. The $500,000 loan was guaranteed by John E. Alvey, III, David K. Vitalis and Vitalis' wife. To evidence their agreement, Rodgers and the Debtor entered into an Amendment to Guaranty dated March 31, 1989 (the "Amendment"). Paragraph 3 of the Amendment states that "Paragraph 3 of the Guaranty Agreement is *replaced* by the following language: ..." (emphasis added). The language that followed did not contain the language in Paragraph 3 of the Original Agreement regarding waiver of subrogation and recourse. The Amendment was executed only by the Debtor and Rodgers. No formal consents to the execution of the Amendment were obtained from the Guarantors.

The Bank of Baltimore never received a guaranty from Rodgers but did receive an irrevocable standby letter of credit in the amount of $1,000,000 (the "Letter of Credit") issued by Security Bank Corporation and confirmed by Sovran Bank, N.A. (the "Confirming Bank") for the account of Rodgers. The Letter of Credit provided that it could be drawn by a written instrument stating that "[a] default or Event of Default has occurred as defined under the terms of a certain deed of trust from Valley Vue Joint Venture, as grantor, in favor of The Bank of Baltimore as beneficiary...."

The loan agreement between the Debtor and the Bank of Baltimore provided that "[i]n the event the [Bank of Baltimore] draws down the [L]etter of [C]redit, such proceeds will be applied to the outstanding principal balance under the Note" evidencing the Bank of Baltimore's loan to the Debtor.

On February 13, 1990, following a default by the Debtor on its loan from the Bank of Baltimore, the Bank of Baltimore drew the full amount of the Letter of Credit. Pursuant to its obligations to the Confirming Bank, Rodgers promptly reimbursed the Confirming Bank for the $1,000,000 that the Confirming Bank had paid to the Bank of Baltimore. On March 9, 1990, the Debtor filed its voluntary petition under Chapter 11 of the Bankruptcy Code.[5] Thereafter, Rodgers filed its proof of claim asserting that it is entitled to be subrogated to the rights of the Bank of Baltimore because it caused the Debtor's loan to be reduced by $1,000,000 pursuant to the Letter of Credit.

In objecting to Rodgers' proof of claim, the Debtor first contends that Rodgers, as the account party who arranged for the issuance of the Letter of Credit, is not entitled under either 11 U.S.C. § 509(a)[6] or general principles of equity to be subrogated to the rights of the Bank of Baltimore. The Debtor argues that the Confirming Bank's obligation to pay the Bank of Baltimore pursuant to the Letter of Credit was a primary obligation and not in the nature of a guaranty or suretyship agreement. Therefore, according to the Debtor, the Confirming Bank was not "liable with the debtor on, ... a claim of a creditor against the debtor" and Rodgers could not acquire any rights greater than those that the Confirming Bank possessed. The Debtor relies principally on *Bank of America Nat'l Trust & Sav. Assoc. v. Kaiser Steel Corp. (In re Kaiser Steel Corp.),* 89 B.R. 150 (Bankr.D.Colo.1988), which held that an issuer who pays a standby letter of credit is not entitled under 11 U.S.C. § 509(a) to be subrogated to the rights of the beneficiary.

The *Kaiser* court stated that because subrogation is an equitable principle, an entity seeking to be subrogated to the rights of a creditor under 11 U.S.C. § 509(a) must satisfy a five-part test derived from general equitable principles of subrogation. *Kaiser,* 89 B.R. at 152. The opinion of the court

5. On December 5, 1990, the Court entered an order converting this case from Chapter 11 to Chapter 7.

6. 11 U.S.C. § 509(a) provides that "... an entity that is liable with the debtor on, or that has secured, a claim of a creditor against the debtor, and that pays such claim, is subrogated to the rights of such creditor to the extent of such payment."

indicated that one element of such test is that any payment made by such entity to such creditor must have satisfied a debt for which the entity was "not primarily liable." *Id.* The court held that the issuer of a standby letter of credit "assumes an independent obligation to pay the creditor upon presentation of demand. When the issuer pays its own debt it cannot then step into the shoes of the creditor to seek subrogation, reimbursement or contribution from the debtor." *Kaiser,* 89 B.R. at 153.[7]

In *Kaiser,* the debtor obtained a standby letter of credit from a bank for the benefit of a leasing company that extended credit to the debtor through a sale/leaseback transaction. The debtor's obligations to the leasing company under their lease agreement were secured by a lien on all of the debtor's assets. After the debtor defaulted on its obligations to the leasing company, the leasing company drew against its letter of credit. The debtor failed to reimburse the issuer after the issuer honored the letter of credit. The issuer claimed that it was entitled, after the leasing company's claim was paid in full, to be subrogated to the leasing company's security interest in the debtor's assets. The court found that the payment under the letter of credit satisfied a debt for which the issuer was primarily liable and therefore rejected the issuer's claim. *Kaiser,* 89 B.R. at 152.

The *Kaiser* court correctly observed that an issuer's obligation to honor a standby letter of credit is considered a "primary" obligation. *See, e.g., Republic Nat'l Bank v. Northwest Nat'l Bank,* 578 S.W.2d 109, 114 (Tex.1978) ("[The issuer] assumes a primary obligation independent of the underlying contract and engages that it will pay upon the presentation of documents required by the instrument."). However, the *Kaiser* court failed to distinguish between the primary liability of a debtor to its creditor to repay a loan and the primary obligation of the issuer to its beneficiary to honor a letter of credit. When a standby credit supporting a loan is honored, the issuer[8] admittedly is satisfying its obligation as a primary obligor to honor the standby credit, but at the same time it is in fact satisfying a debt for which a person other than the issuer is primary liable. This distinction, although

7. *Kaiser's* rigid five-part test apparently is derived from a 1954 California case that consolidated various principles relating to subrogation discussed in American Jurisprudence. *See In re Kaiser Steel Corp.,* 89 B.R. 150, 152, *citing In re Flick,* 75 B.R. 204, 206 (Bankr.S.D.Cal.1987), *citing Simon v. United States,* 756 F.2d 696, 699 (9th Cir.1985), *citing Caito v. United California Bank,* 20 Cal.3d 694, 704, 576 P.2d 466, 471, 144 Cal. Rptr. 751, 756 (1978), *citing Grant v. de Otte,* 122 Cal.App.2d 724, 728, 265 P.2d 952, 955 (1954), *citing* 50 Am.Jur. *Subrogation* §§ 10 and 97. The *Kaiser* test requires that (1) the codebtor must have made payment to protect its own interests, (2) the codebtor must not have been a volunteer, (3) the payment must have satisfied a debt for which the codebtor was not primarily liable, (4) the entire debt must have been paid, and (5) subrogation must not cause injustice to the rights of others. *Kaiser,* 89 B.R. at 152. However, subrogation is an equitable principle to be applied not in a mechanical fashion but rather as necessary to accomplish equitable results. *See Federal Land Bank v. Joynes,* 179 Va. 394, 402, 18 S.E.2d 917, 920 (1942) ("[N]o general rule can be laid down which will afford a test in all cases for [the] application [of equitable subrogation].") (citation omitted). Because our holding does not depend upon using a different test but rather upon applying a different interpretation to part three of the test, we do not need to take exception to the five elements *Kaiser* uses in its analysis.

8. Because a confirming bank is obligated on the letter of credit to the same extent as the issuer, *see* U.C.C. § 5–107(2) (1987) [Va. Code Ann. § 8.5–107(2) (1965)], we use the term "issuer" throughout this opinion to include confirming banks, unless otherwise specified.

not recognized by the Debtor or the *Kaiser* court, is critical.[9] An issuer is not primarily liable on the debt supported by its standby credit.

We reject the *Kaiser* analysis and hold that where a standby letter of credit is used to support a loan from the beneficiary to the debtor, a confirming bank, by honoring the credit and thereby reducing the debtor's obligation to the beneficiary, is "an entity that is liable with the debtor on, . . . a claim of a creditor against the debtor" under 11 U.S.C. § 509(a)[10] and has satisfied a debt for which it is not primarily liable under general equitable principles of subrogation. We hold further that a nondebtor account party who reimburses such confirming bank is entitled under general equitable principles to be subrogated to the rights of such confirming bank.

As between the Debtor and the Confirming Bank here, the primary liability for repayment of the Debtor's loan rests with the Debtor. The Confirming Bank's liability was primary only with respect to its duty to the Bank of Baltimore to honor the Letter of Credit. The intent of the parties, as evidenced by the loan agreement between the Debtor and the Bank of Baltimore, was that the Confirming Bank would, by honoring the Letter of Credit, reduce a debt for which the Debtor, not the Confirming Bank, was primarily liable.

The Debtor seeks to have this Court rule, as did the *Kaiser* court, that because of the use of the phrase "primary obligation" in the letter of credit context, an issuer is disqualified from being awarded subrogation rights under both equitable principles of subrogation and 11 U.S.C. § 509(a). However, the Debtor confuses the notion that an issuer of a standby credit has a "primary obligation" to honor its letter of credit with the concept that an entity seeking subrogation must have satisfied a debt for which the entity was "not primarily liable." The latter principle appears to be founded upon the notion that a debtor, after paying a debt for which it is primarily liable, may not step into the shoes of his creditor and seek recourse against those who are secondarily liable, such as guarantors, or seek the benefit of collateral pledged by others to secure his debt. This principle has been codified in 11 U.S.C. § 509(b)(2) which provides that an entity may not be subrogated to the rights of a creditor if, "as between the debtor and such

9. When one considers the novel status the framers of Article 5 of the U.C.C. gave letters of credit, it is easy to understand why confusion exists regarding the availability of subrogation to issuers and nondebtor account parties. The intention of the framers of Article 5 was to give letters of credit a special status: "[I]t was one of the prime purposes of the drafters of Article Five to 'set an independent theoretical framework' for this device, a framework independent of contract, of guaranty, of third party beneficiary law, of the law of assignment, and of negotiable instruments." J. White & R. Summers, *Handbook of the Law Under the Uniform Commercial Code* § 19–2 at 812 (3d ed. 1988) [hereinafter "White & Summers"].

10. The Debtor also contends that Rodgers is not "an entity that . . . has secured . . . a claim of a creditor against the debtor" and that therefore it is not entitled to subrogation under that language contained in 11 U.S.C. § 509(a). We agree. Even though in general discourse it is commonly said that a standby credit "secures" a loan, such term, as used in Section 509(a), refers to the granting of a security interest in an asset. *See Beach v. First Union Nat'l Bank of North Carolina (In re Carley Capital Group),* 119 B.R. 646, 648 (W.D.Wisc.1990); 3 *Collier on Bankruptcy,* ¶ 509.02 at 509–4 (15th ed. 1988) ("[T]he subrogation provision of Section 509(a) applies when an entity has secured a creditor of the debtor by using his own property as collateral without incurring any personal obligation."). In the case at bar, neither the Confirming Bank nor Rodgers granted a security interest to the Bank of Baltimore.

entity, such entity received the consideration for the claim held by such creditor." We believe that Section 509(b)(2) correctly captures the purpose of the "primary liability" limitation under general equitable principles discussed in *Kaiser.* *See* 124 Cong.Rec. H11,095 (daily ed. Sept. 28, 1978) and 124 Cong.Rec. 17,411–12 (daily ed. Oct. 6, 1978), *reprinted in* 1978 U.S.Code Cong. & Admin.News 5787, 6452 and 6521 ("Section 509(b)(2) reiterates the well-known rule that prevents a debtor that is ultimately liable on the debt from recovering from a surety or a co-debtor."). We believe that the requirement in equity as well as under 11 U.S.C. § 509(b)(2) that a party seeking subrogation must not be "primarily liable" is designed to prevent a person who received the consideration (*e.g.,* the loan proceeds) from the creditor from being subrogated to the creditor's rights against a guarantor, surety, accommodation comaker or similar party after the debtor has satisfied his own obligations.[12]

In the letter of credit context, the statement that the issuer's obligation to honor a letter of credit is primary goes to the issue of whether the issuer can *avoid* its obligation by relying on underlying transaction defenses. The "primary obligation" language stems from the "independence principle" underlying letters of credit. It has been said that "[w]hen the bank issues an irrevocable letter of credit, it assumes an obligation to honor drafts which comply with that credit.... That obligation is fully independent of any underlying agreement." *Printing Dep't, Inc. v. Xerox Corp.,* 20 B.R. 677, 681 (Bankr.E.D.Va.1981). The independence principle is "the cornerstone of the commercial vitality of letters of credit." *Ward Petroleum Corp. v. F.D.I.C.,* 903 F.2d 1297, 1299 (10th Cir.1990). In *Ward Petroleum* the court stated that "[t]he independence of the letter of credit from the underlying commercial transaction facilitates payment under the credit upon a mere facial examination of documents; it thus makes the letter of credit a unique commercial device which assures prompt payment." *Ward Petroleum,* 903 F.2d at 1299; *see also In re Compton Corp.,* 831 F.2d 586, 590 (5th Cir.1987) ("Under the independence principle, an issuer's obligation to the letter of credit's beneficiary is independent from any obligation between the beneficiary and the issuer's customer.... Any disputes between the beneficiary and the customer do not affect the issuer's obligation to the beneficiary to pay under the letter of credit."); *Voest–Alpine Int'l Corp. v. Chase Manhattan Bank,* 707 F.2d 680, 682 (2d Cir.1983) ("[Attempts] to avoid payment premised on extrinsic considerations—contrary to the instruments' formal documentary nature—tend to compromise their chief virtue of predictable reliability as a payment mechanism."). According to *In re Originala Petroleum Corp.,* 39 B.R. 1003, 1008 (Bankr.N.D.Tex.1984), "[l]etter of credit financing will cease to be a viable component of finance world-wide unless the independence principle [is] preserved." *See also East Girard Sav. Ass'n v. Citizens Nat'l Bank and Trust Co.,* 593 F.2d 598, 602 (5th Cir.1979) ("This entitlement is independent of collateral obligations which may exist under the other underlying contracts.... Thus, even if the producer of the letter

12. The Debtor not only ignores the purpose behind the third element of *Kaiser's* five-part test, as embodied in 11 U.S.C. § 509(b)(2), but also the actual language of such element: "the payment [by the party seeking subrogation] must have satisfied a debt for which [such party] was not primarily liable." *Kaiser,* 89 B.R. at 152. The payment by the Confirming Bank here to the Bank of Baltimore certainly did satisfy a debt for which the Confirming Bank was not primarily liable (*i.e.,* the Debtor's).

has a valid defense on his contract with the recipient of the letter, the bank cannot assert it."); *Pringle–Associated Mortgage Corp. v. Southern Nat'l Bank,* 571 F.2d 871, 874 (5th Cir.1978) ("The key to the uniqueness of a letter of credit and to its commercial vitality is that the promise by the issuer is independent of any underlying contracts.").

In contrast to the rights of an issuer of a letter of credit, it is generally held that a guarantor may assert various defenses to his payment obligation under his guaranty and avoid such obligation entirely. *See, e.g., Bank of New Jersey v. Pulini,* 194 N.J.Super. 163, 476 A.2d 797, 799 (A.D.1984). For example, the extension of the due date of the debtor's loan or the impairment of the guarantor's recourse against the debtor or any collateral, without the guarantor's consent, or the illegality, invalidity or unenforceability of the debtor's obligations, will constitute valid defenses to the guarantor's obligation. *See* 10 Williston, *Law of Contracts* 714–786 (3d ed. 1967). By making it clear that issuers of letters of credit have an independent primary obligation to honor their letters of credit, Article 5 of the U.C.C. makes such defenses unavailable to issuers, thereby promoting the certainty feature of letters of credit. *See* White & Summers, *supra* note 8, § 19–2 at 814 ("Thus, the guarantor can often set up defenses that the principal debtor has against the creditor. An issuer of a letter of credit cannot do so. In that sense the issuer's obligation to the beneficiary (the creditor) is said to be primary, i.e., not subject to the defenses the debtor might have against the creditor."); *see also In re Carley Capital Group,* 119 B.R. 646, 649 (holding that because of the independence principle, nondebtor account parties may not avoid their obligations in a letter of credit transaction because substantial changes were agreed to by the beneficiary in the underlying loan documents without the consent of the account parties).

It would appear, therefore, that the notion that an issuer's obligation to honor the letter of credit is a "primary obligation" should be interpreted to mean that, under the independence principle, the issuer may not avoid its obligation to honor the credit by identifying deficiencies in underlying contracts or by otherwise asserting defenses that are typically available to parties who are generally considered to be "secondarily liable" such as guarantors and sureties. Thus, we believe that the "primary obligation" language in the letter of credit context concerns itself with the issuer's ability to avoid honoring its letter of credit, whereas the "primary liability" language in the subrogation context concerns itself with whether the entity, after reducing a claim of a creditor, received the consideration from the creditor.

Some of the confusion surrounding the application of subrogation in the standby letter of credit context may stem from the nature of letters of credit. The traditional letter of credit, also referred to as a commercial letter of credit, was developed as a means of facilitating international transactions involving sales of merchandise between distant buyers and sellers not commercially acquainted with each other. *See First Empire Bank v. F.D.I.C.,* 572 F.2d 1361, 1366 (9th Cir.1978). Typically, a seller of goods entering into a sales agreement with an unfamiliar buyer requires the buyer to deliver a commercial letter of credit issued by a creditworthy bank with whom the seller is familiar. Under the terms of the commercial credit, the bank agrees to honor the seller's draft following the seller's presentation of bills of lading, air freight receipts or other evidence of title to the goods. Following the honoring of the letter of credit, the buyer reimburses the issuer for the amount drawn. *See* White & Summers, *supra* note 8, § 19–1 at 807–809.

Standby letters of credit, on the other hand, evidence the obligation of the issuer to pay not in the ordinary course of business but in the event that a party defaults, and thereby accomplish results analogous to that of guaranties. *See Insurance Co. of North America v. Heritage Bank,* 595 F.2d 171, 173 (3d Cir.1979) ("In contrast to its traditional function, the letter of credit in its newer variations frequently serves as a guaranty, and the issuer anticipates that it will not be called upon to honor the credit."); *First Empire Bank,* 572 F.2d at 1367 ("[T]he standby letter of credit possesses more of the characteristics of a guarantee...."); *Bank of N.C. v. Rock Island Bank,* 570 F.2d 202, 206 n. 7 (7th Cir.1978) ("Indeed, the essential distinction between the letter of credit and the contract of guaranty is purely formal, not functional. Like the contract of guaranty, the letter of credit may be so designed as to secure the performance of another contractual obligation. Not surprisingly, such credits are called 'guaranty' letters of credit."); *Pastor v. Nat'l Republic Bank,* 76 Ill.2d 139, 147, 28 Ill.Dec. 535, 538, 390 N.E.2d 894, 897 (1979) ("Unlike the sales or traditional letter of credit, which obligates the issuer to pay in the ordinary course of a business transaction, the guaranty or standby letter of credit obligates the issuer to pay in the event of a default by one who procured its issuance."); *O'Grady v. First Union Nat'l Bank,* 296 N.C. 212, 231, 250 S.E.2d 587, 599 (1978) ("The term [guaranty letter of credit] is used to describe a transaction in which a letter of credit is used to accomplish the ends of a contract of guaranty or suretyship. In such transactions the letter functions to secure performance of an obligation. This differs from a more traditional use of a letter of credit in transactions for the sale of goods, ...").

Although both commercial and standby letters of credit are conditioned on the happening of some event, the difference lies in who is performing or failing to perform such event. The commercial letter of credit is conditioned on the beneficiary's performance while the standby letter of credit is conditioned on a party's failure to perform its obligations. *See* B. Wunnicke, *Standby Letters of Credit* § 2.8 at 23 (1989).

Despite ample dicta that a standby letter of credit is akin to a guaranty, virtually every court that has considered the device has emphasized that it is not a guaranty. In *Airline Reporting v. First Nat'l Bank,* 832 F.2d 823, 827 (4th Cir.1987), the court stated that

> [a]lthough the letter of credit is issued to guarantee the customer's obligation under an underlying contract between the customer and beneficiary, the letter of credit is a distinct transaction between the issuer and beneficiary, and the issuer's obligation under the letter of credit is independent of the underlying transaction....

Although a standby letter of credit issued to support a loan is not a guaranty, it accomplishes results analogous to that of a guaranty by ultimately reducing a debt for which another is liable. But the recognition that standby letters of credit are not guaranties does not preclude the application of subrogation principles to an issuer and nondebtor account party of a standby credit issued to support a loan. Neither equity nor 11 U.S.C. § 509(a) requires a party seeking subrogation to be a surety or guarantor.

Recognizing that issuers and nondebtor account parties of standby letters of credit have rights to subrogation does not impair the "independence principle" or any of the other features of letters of credit. Indeed, such recognition may indirectly promote the use of standby credits to support secured debt by protecting the issuers of such credits, especially where debtors have insufficient unencumbered assets to independently secure such credits. In addition, no rights of the beneficiary will be impaired by recognizing an issuer's or nondebtor account party's right to subrogation. Under principles of both equitable subrogation and 11 U.S.C. § 509(c), the right to subrogation is subordinate to the rights of the beneficiary until the entire amount of the beneficiary's claim has been satisfied. *See* 11 U.S.C. § 509(c); *see also Martin v. State Farm Mut. Auto. Ins. Co.,* 375 F.2d 720, 722 n. 2 (4th Cir.1967) ("[T]he insured party's insurer had no right of subrogation against the tortfeasor until the injured party received full satisfaction of his judgment."); *Obici v. Furcron,* 160 Va. 351, 362, 168 S.E. 340, 344 (1933) ("The right of subrogation cannot be enforced until the whole debt is paid, . . .") (citations omitted); *Combs v. Agee,* 148 Va. 471, 475, 139 S.E. 265, 266 (1927) ("There can be no subrogation to the rights of another unless the claim of that other is fully satisfied; and until the whole debt is paid, . . .") (citations omitted).

A recent case applying the *Kaiser* analysis observed that there are no strong equitable reasons to recognize an issuer's right to subrogation to a secured beneficiary's rights. *See In re Carley Capital Group,* 119 B.R. at 649. We disagree. After reviewing the goals of subrogation, we believe that the equities strongly favor allowing an issuer and a nondebtor account party of a standby letter of credit the right to stand in the shoes of a secured beneficiary.

The purpose of subrogation is to prevent the unearned enrichment of one party at the expense of another. *Compania Anonima Venezolana de Navegacion v. A.J. Perez Export Co.,* 303 F.2d 692, 697 (5th Cir.1962), *cert. den.* 371 U.S. 942, 83 S.Ct. 321, 9 L.Ed.2d 276 (1962). The rationale of subrogation is "bottomed on a sensitivity to the comparative equities involved. Where one is more fundamentally liable for a debt which another is obligated to pay, such person shall not enrich himself by escaping his obligation." *Federal Land Bank v. Joynes,* 179 Va. 394, 402, 18 S.E.2d 917, 920 (1942). Subrogation "is a device adopted or invented by equity to compel the ultimate discharge of a debt or obligation by him who in good conscience ought to pay it." *Moritz v. Redd,* 151 Va. 644, 652, 145 S.E. 245 (1928) (citations omitted). It is grounded on the notion that "one who has been compelled to pay a debt which ought to have been paid by another is entitled to exercise all the remedies which the creditor possessed against that other." *American Surety Co. v. Bethlehem Nat'l Bank,* 314 U.S. 314, 317, 62 S.Ct. 226, 228, 86 L.Ed. 241 (1941) (citations omitted).

The doctrine of subrogation was first applied only in favor of sureties, but through a process of liberalization its application has been enlarged. *Federal Land Bank v. Joynes,* 179 Va. 394, 402, 18 S.E.2d 917, 920 (1942). It is now "broad enough to cover all cases in which one person pays an obligation which in justice and good conscience should have been paid by another." *Morgan v. Gollehon,* 153 Va. 246, 249, 149 S.E. 485, 486 (1929); *see also Compania Anonima,* 303 F.2d at 697 ("[Subrogation] is now a mechanism so universally applied in new and unknown circumstances that it is easy to overlook that it originates in equity.... [I]t is broad enough to include every instance in which one person, not acting as a mere volunteer or intruder, pays a debt for which another is primarily liable, and which in equity and good conscience should have been discharged by the latter") (citations omitted); *Equity Mtg. Corp. v. Loftus,* 323 F.Supp. 144, 156 (E.D.Va.1970) ("Virginia is committed to a liberal application of the principle.") *rev'd* on other grounds, 504 F.2d 1071 (4th Cir.1974). "The doctrine is applicable wherever the *substance* of the relation of principal and surety exists without regard to the mere form." *Rosenbaum v. Goodman,* 78 Va. 121, 126 (1883) (emphasis in original). It is not essential that the party invoking the remedy [of subrogation] should technically occupy the position or relation of surety for the debt. *Colbert v. Priester,* 214 Va. 606, 608, 203 S.E.2d 134, 135 (1974) (citations omitted).

In the standby letter of credit context, subrogation requires that we focus on the comparative equities of two parties: the issuer and the debtor whose loan is supported by the standby credit. When the standby credit is drawn, the proceeds are applied to reduce the debt owed by a debtor to the beneficiary. Subrogation works to prevent a debtor from retaining the benefit of the reduction of his obligations at the expense of the issuer following the issuer's honoring of the standby credit. The debt supported by a standby credit is one, in the words of *Compania Anonima,* 303 F.2d at 697, "which in equity and good conscience should have been discharged by [another]." An issuer of a standby credit, in contrast to an issuer of a commercial credit, anticipates that the debtor will pay its own obligations and that the issuer will not be called upon to honor the credit. *See Consolidated Aluminum Corp. v. Bank of Virginia,* 544 F.Supp. 386, 399 (D.Md.1982) ("Rather, the bank issuing a standby letter of credit expects to pay only if its customer defaults on the underlying obligation."). In the words of *Federal Land Bank v. Joynes,* 179 Va. at 402, 18 S.E.2d at 920, the debtor is "more fundamentally liable" than is the issuer for the repayment of the debtor's loan.

* * *

We believe that *Kaiser, Carley Capital, Economic Enterprises* and *Texas Steel* are each a deviation from the sound trend of decisions holding that issuers, confirming banks and nondebtor account parties of standby credits issued to support secured debt are entitled to be subrogated to the rights of secured beneficiaries. *See Chemical Bank v. Craig (In re Glade Springs, Inc.),* 826 F.2d 440 (6th Cir.1987); *In re National Service Lines, Inc.,* 80 B.R. 144, 145 (Bankr.E.D.Mo.1987) ("A bank which pays a debtor's obligation pursuant to a letter of credit functions in substance like a guarantor or surety of the debtor's obligation.... Because [the beneficiary] would have been entitled to an administrative expense priority claim had it not been paid by [the issuer], it follows that [the issuer] is entitled to an administrative priority claim in this case."); *In re Sensor Systems, Inc.,* 79 B.R. 623, 626 (Bankr.E.D.Pa.1987) ("[A] party issuing a standby credit in favor of another is logically characterized as a 'guarantor' or a 'co-debtor'."); *In re Minnesota Kicks, Inc.*, 48 B.R. 93, 104 (Bankr.D.Minn.1985) ("[P]recluding the assertion of subrogation rights to issuers of standby letters of credit while allowing guarantors to assert them would be no more than an exercise in honoring form over substance."). Although we agree with the outcome in *Sensor Systems* and *National Service Lines,* we do not believe it is necessary or even helpful to characterize an issuer as a surety or guarantor. An issuer is clearly not a surety or guarantor and the right of an issuer of a standby credit to subrogation is not dependent upon such a characterization.

The United States Court of Appeals for the Sixth Circuit, in its *Glade Springs* holding, provided strong authority for the proposition that an entity should not be denied the remedy of subrogation merely because such entity is primarily liable under a standby letter of credit. In *Glade Springs,* a debtor's obligation to repay its note was supported by a standby letter of credit issued for the account of the debtor and for the benefit of the note holder. The debtor's obligation to reimburse the issuing bank was secured by a deed of trust covering certain real property owned by the debtor. The standby credit was confirmed by a confirming bank that ultimately honored the credit when the issuer failed and was taken over by the FDIC, which refused to honor the standby credit. The confirming bank sought to be subrogated to the rights of the issuing bank with respect to the deed of trust. The bankruptcy court concluded that the confirming bank was entitled to subrogation and observed that to deny the confirming bank the right to subrogation would result in a windfall to the debtor. *Glade Springs,* 826 F.2d at 441. On appeal, the district court reversed the decision of the bankruptcy court and, relying on the rationale of *Economic Enterprises,* determined that because the confirming bank's liability for honoring the standby credit constituted an independent and primary obligation and not a guaranty or suretyship, the confirming bank was not entitled to subrogation. *Id.* The United States Court of Appeals for the Sixth Circuit, reversing the district court, held that under equitable principles of subrogation, the confirming bank was entitled to be subrogated to the rights of the issuer. *Id.* at 442.

In *Glade Springs,* the Sixth Circuit implicitly rejected the rationale of *Kaiser, Carley Capital, Economic Enterprises* and *Texas Steel* in holding that an entity that is primarily liable under a standby letter of credit (*i.e.,* a confirming bank) is entitled to the remedy of subrogation. Under the U.C.C., a confirming bank's obligation to honor a letter of credit is, in accordance with the "independence principle," independent of the issuer's obligations. *See* U.C.C. § 5–107(2) (1987) [Va.Code Ann. § 8.5–107(2) (1965)] ("A confirming bank by confirming a credit becomes directly obligated on the credit to the extent of its confirmation as though it were its issuer and acquires the rights of an issuer."); U.C.C. § 5–107, Official Comment 2 (1987) [Va.Code Ann. § 8.5–107, Official Comment 2 (1965)] ("The most important aspect of this rule is that a beneficiary who has received a confirmed credit has the independent engagements of both the issuer and the confirming bank."). Notwithstanding the "primary obligation" of the confirming bank to honor the letter of credit, the *Glade Springs* court recognized that the confirming bank's payment of the letter of credit "extinguished the debtor's ... obligation to pay the debt to [the beneficiary]" and therefore held that the confirming bank was entitled to subrogation. *Glade Springs,* 826 F.2d at 442.

Having rejected the Debtor's argument that Rodgers, as a nondebtor account party under the Letter of Credit, is not entitled to subrogation, we turn next to the Debtor's contention that the Original Agreement created third party beneficiary rights in favor of the Guarantors. The Debtor argues that the Amendment subsequently entered into by Rodgers and the Debtor abrogated these third party beneficiary rights. Because the Guarantors did not consent to the Amendment, the Debtor contends that the Amendment is void leaving intact the waiver of subrogation language contained in Paragraph 3 of the Original Agreement.

A third party beneficiary is one who is intended by the parties to a contract to benefit from a promise contained in such contract. *See Professional Realty Corp. v. Bender,* 216 Va. 737, 739, 222 S.E.2d 810, 812 (1976) ("[T]he third party must show that the parties to the contract clearly and definitely intended it to confer a benefit upon him."). Furthermore, a third party beneficiary's rights vest when the party materially changes his position in justifiable reliance on the promise or brings suit or manifests assent to it in a manner invited by the promisor or promisee. *See* Restatement, Contracts 2d § 311(3), Comments f, g, and h. Here, a colorable argument could be made that the Guarantors are third party beneficiaries and their rights have vested. However, for the reasons stated herein, we do not so hold. For even if we were to assume that the Guarantors are third party beneficiaries whose rights have vested, the Debtor has not demonstrated that Rodgers has violated or intends to violate any promise made for the Guarantors' benefit.

The Guarantors were benefited by Rodgers' agreement to waive subrogation and its acknowledgment that it would have no recourse against the Guarantors only to the extent Rodgers precluded itself from seeking personal recoveries against the Guarantors under their guaranties delivered to the Bank of Baltimore. The Guarantors have acknowledged that the intent of the Original Agreement was for Rodgers to look to the real estate, and not to the Debtor or the Guarantors, to recoup any monies that it advanced. *See Transcript of Hearing on Rodgers' Proofs of Claim,* August 29, 1990, at 43 (Mr. Alvey testified that he told a representative of Rodgers that Rodgers "should look to the land and the [Debtor] to be made whole in this project, . . ."). The waiver of subrogation promise in the Original Agreement was not intended to benefit the Guarantors as it relates to the real property. It appears that if the waiver of subrogation language was to benefit the Guarantors at all it was only designed to limit their personal liability to Rodgers to the extent that Rodgers might seek subrogation with respect to their personal guaranties in favor of the Bank of Baltimore, an action not taken by Rodgers. There can be no action for breach of contract unless the plaintiff sets forth a breach by the defendant of the contract. *See Christopher v. Cavallo,* 662 F.2d 1082, 1083 (4th Cir.1981). Rodgers is seeking subrogation only with respect to the deed of trust held by the Bank of Baltimore. *See* Rodgers' *Response to Debtor's Memorandum of Law in Support of Debtor's Objection to Proof of Claim* at 3. If Rodgers were to seek recovery against the Guarantors under their guaranties through subrogation, only then might the Guarantors legitimately assert their rights as third party beneficiaries. We express no opinion on whether such assertions would have merit. Hence, even assuming that the Original Agreement created third party beneficiary rights in the Guarantors, the only promise contained in the Original Agreement that could survive would be the promise made by Rodgers not to seek recoveries against the Guarantors.

For the foregoing reasons, we hold that Rodgers shall be subrogated to the rights of the Bank of Baltimore in the collateral securing the bank's claim, but not in the guaranties, and that such rights of subrogation shall be subordinate to the rights of the bank until the entire amount of the bank's claim has been paid in full, in accordance with 11 U.S.C. § 509(c) and general equitable principles.

Accordingly, for the reasons stated herein, the Debtor's objection to Rodgers' proof of claim is denied. An appropriate order will be entered.

Notes and Questions

1. Students should read section 509 of the Bankruptcy Code and understand that subrogation in this case is inextricably entwined with the policies of that Code. Problem 8–9 is taken from *Glade Springs* that is discussed at length in the Valley Vue case. In that case the court allowed subrogation, but some have distinguished it on the ground that the one seeking subrogation was a confirmer going upstream against the issuer's customer when the issuer became insolvent. Most subrogation cases (like Valley Vue) have gone the other way, where upon payment to the beneficiary the issuer or applicant upstream seeks subrogation to the beneficiary's security.

2. By arguing that the bank's obligation under a letter of credit is "independent" and therefore not subject to the limitations on full payment of the debtor in section 509, potential subrogors may be making the independence principle bear weight it was never intended to carry.

3. What do you think? Do you side with Judges Becker and Bostetter or with Judges Cowan and Garth? If you cannot decide, do not lose any sleep; we doubt the judges are.

Problem 24–9

A Florida land development corporation, needing money for a new project, executes a promissory note in favor of Small Local Bank for $1.5 million. The bank, wanting assurance that the loan will be repaid, has the developer obtain a standby letter of credit from a larger Regional Bank. Regional Bank, upon issuing the letter of credit to developer signs its own promissory note with developer and takes a mortgage in land the developer owns in Texas. As further assurance, Large National Bank confirms Regional Bank's letter of credit (by promising it will honor upon proper presentment). Regional Bank fails and National Bank honors the letter of credit in favor of Local Bank when the developer files for bankruptcy. National Bank, as a confirming bank, seeks subrogation to Regional's mortgage on the Texas land. What do you think? Should a confirmer seeking subrogation to its issuer's claim be treated differently from an issuer seeking subrogation to its beneficiary's security?

*

Index

References are to Pages

References are to Pages

References are to Pages

References are to Pages

†